TIM RIDER

Days to mat.	.01% equiv.	Days to mat.	.01% equiv.	Days to mat.	.01% equiv.	Days to mat.	.01% equiv.	Days to mat.	.01% equiv.	Days to mat.	.01% equiv.
181	$50.28	212	$58.89	243	$67.50	274	$76.11	305	$84.72	336	$93.33
182	50.56	213	59.17	244	67.78	275	76.39	306	85.00	337	93.61
183	50.83	214	59.44	245	68.06	276	76.67	307	85.28	338	93.89
184	51.11	215	59.72	246	68.33	277	76.94	308	85.56	339	94.17
185	51.39	216	60.00	247	68.61	278	77.22	309	85.83	340	94.44
186	51.67	217	60.28	248	68.89	279	77.50	310	86.11	341	94.72
187	51.94	218	60.56	249	69.17	280	77.78	311	86.39	342	95.00
188	52.22	219	60.83	250	69.44	281	78.06	312	86.67	343	95.28
189	52.50	220	61.11	251	69.72	282	78.33	313	86.94	344	95.56
190	52.78	221	61.39	252	70.00	283	78.61	314	87.22	345	95.83
191	53.06	222	61.67	253	70.28	284	78.89	315	87.50	346	96.11
192	53.33	223	61.94	254	70.56	285	79.17	316	87.78	347	96.39
193	53.61	224	62.22	255	70.83	286	79.44	317	88.06	348	96.67
194	53.89	225	62.50	256	71.11	287	79.72	318	88.33	349	96.94
195	54.17	226	62.78	257	71.39	288	80.00	319	88.61	350	97.22
196	54.44	227	63.06	258	71.67	289	80.28	320	88.89	351	97.50
197	54.72	228	63.33	259	71.94	290	80.56	321	89.17	352	97.78
198	55.00	229	63.61	260	72.22	291	80.83	322	89.44	353	98.06
199	55.28	230	63.89	261	72.50	292	81.11	323	89.72	354	98.33
200	55.56	231	64.17	262	72.78	293	81.39	324	90.00	355	98.61
201	55.83	232	64.44	263	73.06	294	81.67	325	90.28	356	98.89
202	56.11	233	64.72	264	73.33	295	81.94	326	90.56	357	99.17
203	56.39	234	65.00	265	73.61	296	82.22	327	90.83	358	99.44
204	56.67	235	65.28	266	73.89	297	82.50	328	91.11	359	99.72
205	56.94	236	65.56	267	74.17	298	82.78	329	91.39	360	100.00
206	57.22	237	65.83	268	74.44	299	83.06	330	91.67	361	100.28
207	57.50	238	66.11	269	74.72	300	83.33	331	91.94	362	100.56
208	57.78	239	66.39	270	75.00	301	83.61	332	92.22	363	100.83
209	58.06	240	66.67	271	75.28	302	83.89	333	92.50	364	101.11
210	58.33	241	66.94	272	75.56	303	84.17	334	92.78	365	101.39
211	58.61	242	67.22	273	75.83	304	84.44	335	93.06	366	101.67

Value of an 01 per \$1 million = $\left(\dfrac{.01\% \times t}{360}\right)$ \$1 million

where t = days to maturity

THE MONEY MARKET

THE MONEY MARKET

Third Edition

Marcia Stigum

BUSINESS ONE IRWIN
Homewood, Illinois 60430

Project editor: Jean Roberts
Production manager: Bette K. Ittersagen
Compositor: Bi-Comp, Incorporated
Typeface: 11/13 Century Schoolbook
Printer: Arcata Graphics/Fairfield

Library of Congress Cataloging-in-Publication Data

Stigum, Marcia L.
    The money market/Marcia Stigum.—3rd ed.
      p.   cm.
    ISBN 1-55623-122-9
    1. Money market. I. Title.
HG226.S74 1990
332′.0412—dc20   89–16946
                                                  CIP

Printed in the United States of America

2 3 4 5 6 7 8 9 0 F 6 5 4 3 2 1

To the many market participants
who gave, with grace and enthusiasm, their time
that I might write this story.

PREFACE TO THE THIRD EDITION

This book is a comprehensive guide to the money market, U.S. and Eurodollar. It is intended for people working in banks, in dealerships, and in other financial institutions; for people running liquidity portfolios; and for accountants, lawyers, and others having an interest in the markets discussed.

The book begins with an introduction to what goes on in fixed-income financial markets—financial intermediation and money creation—plus an introduction to how fixed-income securities work—various concepts of yield, the meaning of the yield curve, and the concepts and calculation of duration and convexity.

Next, the book analyzes the operations (domestic and Euro) of money center banks, of money market dealers and brokers, of the Federal Reserve, and of managers of liquidity portfolios. Then, with this background, the book turns to the individual markets that comprise the money market. For each such market—Fed funds to interest-rate swaps—the book describes the instrument traded; its risks, liquidity, and return offered; its uses; and how the market for it is made by money market brokers, dealers, and investors.

Inevitably, the book presents an extensive description of the Euromarket; today, the Euromarket is always either an extension of or integrally related to the U.S. money market. Also, the interconnections between these two markets keep growing: for example, the U.S. commercial paper and U.S. medium-term note (MTN) markets spawned, respectively, in London, the Euro commercial paper and the Euro MTN markets. Moreover, the transatlantic traffic in ideas, products, and trading techniques isn't unidirectional: forward rate agreements (FRAs), first traded in London, are now actively traded in New York.

Hallmarks of the money market are growth, change, and innovation. The money market, which seemed large and sophisticated when the first edition of this book was published in 1978, seems, by 1989 standards, small and a touch primitive. For example, during the 1980s, a vast market in interest-rate swaps was created based on the simple idea of comparative advantage: Why didn't someone see the possibilities earlier? Also, trading in options and option-based products has mushroomed and matured. The commercial paper market, now bigger than the Treasury bill market, is today used for a multitude of purposes and in a multitude of ways undreamed of a decade ago. And then there's a huge MTN market, which, belying its name, is not only creating new product, but rapidly replacing a large chunk of the traditional bond market.

No small part of the changes that have occurred and are occurring in the money market reflects the growing trend toward the deregulation of national capital markets and the consequent globalization of these markets. Today, a portfolio manager who wants a government obligation has a choice of flavors: Treasuries, gilts, Bunds, OATS (French), or JGBs to name the most obvious. Today, a corporate treasurer, a sovereign, or a global bank who needs to borrow has an array of choices: the institution can pick an advantageous currency and an advantageous rate, fixed or floating, at which to borrow and then swap the debt thus created for debt, fixed-rate or floating-rate, in the currency of its choice. And, of course, once the institution has learned to swap liabilities, swapping assets is the logical next step. Finally, as noted throughout the book, the use of financial futures, especially bond and Euro futures, has exploded in recent years; futures are used to arbitrage, to hedge, to position, and to just plain trade.

Many readers of this book will be relatively new to the money market. Part 1 provides background such readers will require to follow the rest of the text; it answers such questions as: What are the principal instruments in which the market deals? How do the major players in the market operate?

Almost all of the material presented in this book is based on interviews with market participants. Rather little is written about the money market, and almost nothing is written about how instruments in it are traded. An obvious reason is that the people most involved in and most expert in the market are action-oriented: they do it, they don't write about it.

In every field, people develop special terms or give common terms special meanings in order to be able to communicate precisely and rapidly with each other; hence *jargon.* The money market is no exception, and this book uses money market jargon extensively. To aid the reader, each piece of jargon used is defined the first time it appears in the text; also, in the Glossary at the end of the book a wide range of money and bond market terms are defined.

I use the pronoun *he* thoughout this book. *He* has long been used in English to mean *person,* and any attempt to avoid this usage leads to nothing but bad and awkward English. Twelve years ago, when I wrote *he* to refer to a trader, broker, or portfolio manager, I was almost always literally correct: the money market was, at that time, very much a male world. Today, that's changed. In the market, women are everywhere doing everything; only a few women have reached the pinnacles of power, but then most of them got into the business no more than a decade or so ago. Occasionally, in quotes, *he* is used to refer to a bank or a dealer; the ubiquitous Brits talk that way.

The math of yield and payoff calculations has been kept to a minimum in this book. The reader who'd like to delve deeper into such topics is referred to Stigum's *Money Market Calculations*, also published by BUSINESS ONE IRWIN.

In conclusion, I'd like to thank the many people at various banks and dealerships who helped me put together charts and tables for this book. First and foremost, I want to thank Steve Magacs of the Morgan Bank who, with PC and plotter, produced with patience and enthusiasm so many of my charts. I also want to thank (1) David Boren and Seksom Suriyapa of Goldman Sachs, Philip Ginsberg of Cantor Fitzgerald, Robert Hegermiller of Merrill Lynch, and Franklin Robinson of Citibank for other charts; and (2) Christine Schneider of DLJ, Cynthia Andrade of the Donoghue Organization, and William Van Dyke of the Morgan Bank for the tables they created, respectively, on futures and options, on money funds, and on the size and composition of the Eurocurrency market. Thanks are also due to others at Merrill and Goldman who produced art for Chapters 22 and 24.

Also, I would like to extend a heartfelt thank you to Franklin Robinson, Philip Ginsberg, James Mehling, and Louis Crandall, each of whom collaborated with me on one of the chapters in this book.

Finally, I want to thank Ron Kipp of Bob Soto's Diving (Grand Cayman) for recharging, 150 feet down the Cayman Wall, the batteries of this tired author just as she entered the home stretch of this revision.

The now hundreds of people who, for this and previous editions, graciously took the time—often big chunks of it—to talk to me about what they do, how they do it, and why they do it— my standard questions—are thanked in the acknowledgments that follow.

Marcia Stigum
Quechee, Vermont

ACKNOWLEDGMENTS

There was only one way that research for this book could be conducted. That was by interviewing at length participants in *every* area of the market: in New York, Chicago, London, Tokyo, and elsewhere. During the months I spent originally studying the market and subsequently reviewing it, everywhere I went I received incredible cooperation. People freely gave me hours of time, discussed their operations frankly and articulately, and then sent me on to others elsewhere in the market.

To all of these people, I would like to express a very heartfelt thanks for the patient and thoughtful answers they proffered to my many questions. A particular thank you goes to those who volunteered to read and criticize those chapters that covered their area of speciality. Needless to say, the author bears full responsibility for any remaining errors of fact, of which I hope there are few.

I. Interviews U.S.

Fred A. Adams
Richard Adams
Robert P. Anczarki
J. Joseph Anderson
James T. Anderson
Timothy H. Anderson
John Astorina
Howard Atkins
Irving M. Auerbach
Edward G. Austin
Stephen Baker

Stanley E. Ball
Vernon R. Barback
David J. Barry
Kevin D. Barry
Robert Bartell
John F. Baumann
Sandra D. Beckner
Paul M. Belica
William Berkowitz
Robert H. Bethke
Paul J. Bielat

Jean Blin

John Blin

Irving V. Boberski

Vincent S. Bonaventura

David R. Boren

Frank Boswell

Chuck Bradburn

Thomas M. Brady

Milton Brafman

Rene O. Branch, Jr.

Donald G. Brodie

Joseph G. Brown

Ernst W. Brutsche

James Byrne

Donald C. Cacciapaglia

Neil J. Call

Francis X. Cavanaugh

Robert Toshiro Yamamoto Chan

Herman Charlip

Bronislaw Chrobok

Allen B. Clark

Mary Clarkin

Joel I. Cohen

Olivier Colas

Thomas Coleman

George E. Collins, Jr.

Wayne Cook

Michael J. Corey

Mark Corti

Louis v. B. Crandall

Leonard F. Crescenzo

John P. Curtin

Roy L. Dainty

Edward T. Daly

William D. Dawson

James J. DeCantillon

Nicholas J. De Leonardis

Paul de Rosa

Lawrence Deschere

John Desidero

Stanley Diller

Edward I. Dimon

Jay E. Dittus

Donald F. Donoghue

William Donoghue

Robert Dow

Barry Drayson

William J. Duffy

A. Fraser Dunnett

John F. Eckstein III

Burtt R. Ehrlich

Richard P. Eide, Jr.

Bruce A. English

Kenneth F. Entler

Charles J. Errichiello

Richard L. Falk

Emanuel J. Falzon

Hilliard Farber

Michael Farrell

Edward C. Fecht

Chester B. Feldberg

Robert G. Fice

Richard C. Fieldhouse

Maureen Finn

Alvin Flamenbaum

Dennis G. Flynn

David A. Forster

Allen B. Frankel

Peter E. Gall

Thomas E. Gardner

William P. Garry

Leonard Gay

Yoshiyasu Genma

Kenneth L. Gestal

Philip Ginsberg

Barry N. Goldenberg

Ronald B. Gray

Peter L. Greene

Eric A. Gronningsater
Albert A. Gross
Til M. Guldimann
Matthew Hale
P. Jordan Hamel
Alan Hanley
Gabriel Hauge
Ira Haupt III
Ralph T. Helfrich
John Helmer
Paul Henderson
N. John Hewitt
Bill Hick
Andrew Hieskel
Russel G. Hiller
George R. Hinman
Neil Hirsch
Linda M. Holland
Alan R. Holmes
Richard A. Hottinger
Donald Howard
Mary Joy Hudecz
Howard G. Hudson
Nancy Humphrey
James E. Jack
Richard G. Jackson
Dale H. Jenkins
Colin Johnson
Glen Johnson
David A. Jones
William J. Jordan
Arthur Kaley
Michael Kamins
Bernard P. Kane
Kerry A. Kaneda
Michael M. Karnes
S. Bruce Kauffman
George P. Kegler
James R. Kelly

Richard F. Kezer
Yukyo Kida
William M. Kidder
James R. Killeen
Dennis S. Kite
James Koster
Aline Krala
John Krause
Morton Lane
Curt J. Landtroop
Gerald Laurain
David N. Lawrence
Ronald Layard-Liesching
Ralph F. Leach
James F. Leary
John F. Lee
Maureen R. Lee
John Lee-Tin
Julia S. D. Leung
John J. Li Vecchi
Robert M. Lynch
Peter G. MacDonald
Richard MacWilliams
James G. McCormick
William H. McDavid
John D. McElhinney
Daniel M. Mc Evoy
James E. McKee
Margaret A. McKenna
Robert McKnew
Robert Mackin
Steven Magacs
William T. Maher, Jr.
John Mann
Daniel Markaity
Donald R. A. Marshall
Stephen Marshall
Michael F. Martin
Karin L. Maupin

Bruce B. Maxwell

Charles B. Mayer

Elizabeth Anne Mayer

Stan Meheffey

Roger Mehle

James Mehling

James W. Meighen

William Melton

Robert L. Meyers

Ellen Michelson

Michael Mickett

J. Allen Minteer

Joseph T. Monagle, Jr.

Angelo Monteverde

James C. Morton

Edward J. Murphy

John J. Murray

John E. Myers, Jr.

Tsunehiro Nakayama

Hans U. Neukomm

Lawrence Ng

Ann Noonan

Talat M. Othman

Jill Ousely

Bernard Pace

Michael J. Paciorek

Edward L. Palmer

Thomas Panosky

James Pauline

Oscar J. Pearl, Jr.

Frank Pedrick

John D. Perini

John H. Perkins

Ralph F. Peters

Joseph M. Petrie

William H. Pike

Joseph P. Porino

Howard Potter

Donald Reid

Gerald M. Reilly

Robert Rice

Christine A. Rich

Donald B. Riefler

Michael P. Rieger

Franklin L. Robinson

David L. Roscoe III

Paul J. Rozewicz

Alfred C. Ryan, Jr.

Lawrence J. Saffer

Richard Sandor

Irwin D. Sandberg

John Santulli

R. Duane Saunders

Hugo J. H. Schielke

Christina Seix

Charles O. Sethness

Howard Shallcross

Edward Shannon

Nancy F. Shaw

Donald P. Sheahan

Richard Sheldon

Patricia M. Shields

Robert L. Siebel

Vance W. Siler

Robert M. Simonson

Ronald S. Simpson

Stephen A. Sinacore

Richard Singer

Dennis Slattery

Frank P. Smeal

Anne Smith

Brian E. Smith

Lowell S. Smith

Philip Smith

Thomas H. Smith

Thomas S. Smith

Vaughn F. Smith

John S. Spencer

John A. Staley IV
Mark Stalnecker
John William Stanger
James Stanko
Peter D. Sternlight
Robert W. Stone
Werner A. Strange
Neil Stratford
Thomas Sullivan
David G. Taylor
Myron R. Taylor
Edward M. Thomas
John Tritz
Sheila Tschinkel
Stephan A. Tyler
George M. Van Cleave
John A. Vernazza
Edward M. Voelker

Gary R. Vura
Stephen B. Ward
Douglas A. Warner III
James R. Wartinbee
Henry S. Wattson
Dennis Weatherstone
Peter Werner
Jerry D. Wetterling
Gary F. Whitman
H. David Willey
Gary V. Williamson
Bryan Wilson
John R. Windeler
Richard H. Wrightson
Thomas R. York
C. Richard Youngdahl
Edward F. Zimmerman, Jr.
Gene R. Zmuda

II. Interviews U.K.

Michael J. Allen
A. T. Bell
William C. Bigelow
Ian Bond
John M. Bowcott
Brian G. Brown
Colin R. Brown
Trevor N. Cass
Peter Clayton
John E. Clinch
Brian J. Crowe
John A. Cummingham
David O. S. Dobell
Peter Edge
James E. Geiger
Paul Gilbert
James L. M. Gill
Walter A. Gubert
Kirk R. Hagan

Kenneth Haith
Ian Hall
David Hallums
John B. Helmers
Jay R. Helvey III
John G. Hill
E. G. Holloway
Clive Jackson
Maurice Jacques
David B. Johnson
Colin I. Jones
Peter Lee
R. C. Lewis
Anthony M. Liberatore
Ian McGaw
Allen C. Marple
Dante Montalbetti
Richard J. Moreland
Peter Nash

Peter V. Nash
Brian Norman
Alan D. Orsich
Geoffrey Osmint
Edward Pank
Francesco Redi
Kevin Regan
John Robertson
Kenneth G. Robinson
Fabian P. Samengo-Turner
Ivan Schum
John F. Sickles
Trevor K. Slade
Robert D. Sleeper

Isabel H. Sloane
T. R. Smeeton
Thomas Franklin Smith
Jakob T. Stott
Tim Summerfield
Harrison F. Tempest
Jaswinber Thind
Rodney M. Thomas
C. C. Tucker
John Thorne
Robert A. Utting
Lord Wakehurst
Michael Weeks
Jerald M. Wigdortz

III.   Interviews Tokyo
Joseph A. Kelly
Morihiro Matsumoto
Junsuke Motai

Douglas Skolnick
Noboru Takesaka

IV.   Interview Luxembourg
Roland Scharif

M. S.

CONTENTS

PART 3
THE MARKETS

ABBREVIATIONS

This book is replete with quotations, many of which contain Street abbreviations of the names of various institutions. The most common are:

Bankers Trust Co.	Bankers
Bank of America	B of A
Chase Manhattan Bank	Chase
Citibank	Citi
The Continental Bank	Contil
Goldman Sachs	Goldman
Merrill Lynch	Merrill
Manufacturers Hanover Trust Co.	Manny Hanny
Morgan Guaranty Trust Co.	Morgan
Salomon Brothers	Sali

Also, we·follow the common money market practice of using several abbreviations. These are:

100 million	100MM
10 basis points	10 bp

CHAPTER 1

INTRODUCTION

The U.S. money market is a huge and significant part of the nation's financial system in which banks and other participants trade hundreds of billions of dollars every working day. Where those billions go and the prices at which they are traded affect how the U.S. government finances its debt, how business finances its expansion, and how consumers choose to spend or save. Yet we read and hear little about this market. The conspiratorially minded might consider its existence intentionally obscured. The reason most people are unaware of the money market is that it is a market that few businessmen encounter in their daily activities and in which the general public rarely invests.

The money market is a wholesale market for low-risk, highly liquid, short-term IOUs. It is a market for various sorts of debt securities rather than equities. The stock in trade of the market includes a large chunk of the U.S. Treasury's debt and billions of dollars worth of federal agency securities, negotiable bank certificates of deposit, bank deposit notes, bankers' acceptances, short-term participations in bank loans, municipal notes, and commercial paper. Within the confines of the money market each day, banks—domestic and foreign—actively trade in multimillion-dollar blocks billions of dollars of Federal funds and Eurodollars, and banks and nonbank dealers are each day the recipients of billions of dollars of secured loans through what is called the "repo market." State and municipal governments also finance part of their activities in this market.

1

The heart of the activity in the money market occurs in the trading rooms of dealers and brokers of money market instruments. During the time the market is open, these rooms are characterized by a frenzy of activity. Each trader or broker sits in front of a battery of direct phone lines linking him to other dealers, brokers, and customers. The phones never ring, they just blink at a pace that makes, especially in the brokers' market, for some of the shortest phone calls ever recorded. Despite the lack of ringing phones, a dealing room is anything but quiet. Dealers and brokers know only one way to hang up on a direct-line phone; they BANG the off button. And the more hectic things get, the harder they bang. Banging phones like drums in a band beat the rhythm of the noise generated in a trading room. Almost drowning that banging out at times is the constant shouting of quotes and tidbits of information.

Unless one spends a lot of time in trading rooms, it's hard to get a feel for what is going on amid all this hectic activity. Even listening in on phones is not very enlightening. One learns quickly that dealers and brokers swear a lot (it's said to lessen the tension), but the rest of their conversation is unintelligible to the uninitiated. Money market people have their own jargon, and until one learns it, it is impossible to understand them.

Once adjusted to their jargon and the speed at which traders converse, one observes that they are making huge trades— $5MM, $50MM, $250MM—at the snap of a finger.[1] Moreover, nobody seems to be particularly awed or even impressed by the size of the figures. A Fed funds broker asked to obtain $100MM in overnight money for a bank might—nonchalant about the size of the trade—reply, "The buck's yours from the San Fran Home Loan," slam down the phone, and take another call. Fed funds brokers earn only $1 per $1MM on overnight funds, so it takes a lot of trades to pay the overhead and let everyone in the shop make some money.

---

[1] *MM* is a convenient money market abbreviation for *million*. Thus, $100MM means $100 million.

Despite its frenzied and incoherent appearance to the outsider, the money market efficiently accomplishes vital functions everyday. One is shifting vast sums of money between banks. This shifting is required because many large banks, domestic and foreign, with the exception of the Bank of America, all need more funds than they obtain in deposits, whereas many smaller banks have more money deposited with them than they can profitably use internally.

The money market also provides a means by which the surplus funds of cash-rich corporations and other institutions can be funneled to banks, corporations, and other institutions that need short-term money. In addition, in the money market, the U.S. Treasury can fund huge quantities of debt with ease. And the market provides the Fed with an arena in which to carry out open market operations destined to influence interest rates and the growth of the money supply. The varied activities of money market participants also determine the structure of short-term interest rates, for example, what the yields on Treasury bills of different maturities are and how much commercial paper issuers have to pay to borrow. The latter rate is an important cost to many corporations, and it influences in particular the interest rate that a consumer who buys a car on time will have to pay on his loan. Finally, one might mention that the U.S. money market is increasingly becoming an international short-term capital market. In it the oil imports of the nationalized French electric company, Electricité de France, as well as the oil imports of Japan and a lot of other non–U.S. trade are financed.

Anyone who observes the money market soon picks out a number of salient features. First and most obvious, it is not one market but a collection of markets for several distinct and different instruments. What makes it possible to talk about *the* money market is the close interrelationships that link all these markets. A second salient feature is the numerous and varied cast of participants. Borrowers in the market include foreign and domestic banks, the Treasury, corporations of all types, the Federal Home Loan Banks and other federal agencies, dealers in money market instruments, and many states and municipalities. The lenders include almost all of the above plus insurance companies, pension funds—public and private—and various other financial institutions. And, often, standing between borrower and lender is one or more of a varied collection of brokers and dealers.

Another key characteristic of the money market is that it is a wholesale market. Trades are big, and the people who make them are almost always dealing for the account of some substantial institution. Because of the sums involved, skill is of the utmost importance, and money market participants are skilled at what they do. In effect, the market is made by extremely talented specialists in very narrow professional areas. A bill trader extraordinaire may have only vague notions as to what the Euromarket is all about, and the Euro specialist may be equally vague on other sectors of the market.

Another principal characteristic of the money market is honor. Every day traders, brokers, investors, and borrowers do hundreds of billions of dollars of business over the phone, and however a trade may appear in retrospect, people do not renege. The motto of the money market is: *My word is my bond.* Of course, because of the pace of the market, mistakes do occur but no one ever assumes that they are intentional, and mistakes are always ironed out in what seems the fairest way for all concerned.

The most appealing characteristic of the money market is innovation. Compared with our other financial markets, the money market is lightly regulated. If someone wants to launch a new instrument or to try brokering or dealing in a new way in existing instruments, he does it. And when the idea is good, which it often is, a new facet of the market is born.

The focus of this book is threefold. First, attention is paid to the major players—who are they, why are they in the market, and what are they attempting to do? A second point of attention is on the individual markets—who is in each market, how and why do they participate in that market, what is the role of brokers and dealers in that market, and how are prices there determined? The final focus is on the relationships that exist among the different sectors of the market, for example, the relationship of Euro rates to U.S. rates, of Treasury bill rates to the Fed funds rate, of the repo rate to the Fed funds rate, and so on.

This book is organized in a manner to enable readers with different backgrounds to read about and understand the money market. Part 1 contains introductory material for readers who know relatively little about the market. It is preface and prologue to Parts 2 and 3, which are the heart of the book. Thus, readers may skim or skip Part 1 depending on their background and interests. They are, however, warned that they do so at their own peril, since an understanding of its contents is essential for grasping subtleties presented later in the book.

PART 1

SOME FUNDAMENTALS

CHAPTER 2

FUNDS FLOWS, BANKS, AND MONEY CREATION

As preface to a discussion of banking, a few words should be said about the U.S. capital market, how banks create money, and the Fed's role in controlling money creation.

Roughly defined, the U.S. capital market is composed of three major parts: *the stock market*, *the bond market*, and *the money market*. The money market, as opposed to the bond market, is a wholesale market for high-quality, *short-term debt instruments*, or IOUs.

FUNDS FLOWS IN THE U.S. CAPITAL MARKET

Every spending unit in the economy—business firm, household, or government body—is constantly receiving and using funds. In particular, a business firm receives funds from the sale of output and uses funds to cover its costs of production (excluding depreciation) and its current investment in plant, equipment, and inventory. For most firms, *gross saving* from current operations (i.e., *retained earnings plus depreciation allowances*) falls far short of covering current capital expenditures; that is, net funds obtained from current operations are inadequate to pay capital expenditures. As a result, each year most nonfinancial business firms and the nonfinancial business sector as a whole run a large *funds deficit*.

The actual figures rung up by nonfinancial business firms in 1988 are given in column (2) of Table 2–1. They show that

TABLE 2–1
Funds flows in the U.S. capital market by sector, 1988 annualized rate ($ billions)

Transaction Categories	(1) Households	(2) Nonfinancial Business	(3) State and Local Governments*	(4) U.S. Government*	(5) Financial Business†	(6) Rest of the World
1. Savings (net)	362.9	43.0‡	-9.3	-160.1	22.0§	135.9
2. Depreciation	412.1	290.6	0.0	0.0	—	0.0
3. Gross savings (1) + (2)	775.0	333.6	-9.3	-160.1	—	135.9
4. Capital expenditures	690.3	395.8	0.0	0.0	—	0.0
5. Funds surplus or deficit (3) − (4)	84.7	-62.2	-9.3	-160.1	—	135.9
6. Net financial assets acquired	400.6	40.9	21.5	-0.8	729.2	164.1
7. Net financial liabilities incurred	259.1	103.5	37.1	178.2	756.8	44.3
8. Net financial investment (6) − (7)	141.5	-62.6	-15.6	-178.2	-27.6	119.8
9. Sector discrepancy (5) − (8)	-56.8	0.4	6.3	18.1	3.0	16.1

*Capital expenditures are included with current expenditures in U.S. and state and local government spending accounts.
†The large size of the entries in lines 6 and 7 for this sector reflects the intersectoral and intrasectoral funds flows that are funneled through financial institutions.
‡Includes repatriated foreign earnings.
§Current surplus.

Source: Board of Governors, Federal Reserve System.

during this year business firms retained earnings of $43.0 billion and their capital consumption allowances totaled $290.6 billion, giving them a grand total of $333.6 billion of gross saving with which to finance capital expenditures. The latter, however, totaled $395.8 billion, so the business sector as a whole incurred a $62.2 billion-funds deficit.

Running a large funds deficit is a chronic condition for the business sector. It is, moreover, to be expected, since every year the business sector receives a relatively small portion (9 to 13%) of total national income but has to finance a major share of national capital expenditures. Established business firms obtain relatively little new financing from the sale of new shares. The bulk of the funds they obtain to cover their deficits comes through the sale of bonds and money market instruments.

In contrast to the business sector, the consumer sector presents a quite different picture. As Table 2–1 shows, households in 1988 had gross savings of $775.0 billion and made capital expenditures of only $690.3 billion, leaving the sector with a *funds surplus* of $84.7 billion. This funds surplus is, moreover, a persistent phenomenon. Every year consumers as a group save more than they invest in housing and other capital goods.

Most of the consumer sector's annual funds surplus is absorbed by making loans to and equity investments in business firms that must seek outside funds to cover their funds deficits. This flow of funds from the consumer to the business sector is no cause for surprise. In any developed economy in which the bulk of investing is carried on outside the government sector, a substantial amount of funds flow, year in and year out, from consumers, who are the major income recipients, to business firms, which are the major investors.

Consumers and nonfinancial business firms do not make up the whole economy. Two other sectors of major importance are the U.S. government and state and local governments. In neither of these sectors are capital expenditures separated from current expenditures. Thus, for each sector, the recorded funds deficit or funds surplus incurred over the year equals total revenue minus total expenditures, or *net saving*. Both sectors have run funds deficits in most recent years, with the result that they compete with the business sector for the surplus funds generated in the consumer sector. This is what possible "crowding out" of business borrowers by government borrowing is all about.

For completeness, still another domestic sector must be added to the picture, *financial* business firms—banks, savings and loan associations, life insurance companies, and others. Most of the funds that these firms lend out to funds-deficit units are not funds of which they are the *ultimate* source. Instead, they are funds that these institutions have "borrowed" from funds-surplus units. If financial institutions only funneled funds from surplus to deficit units, we could omit them from our summary table. However, such activity is profitable, and every year financial firms accumulate gross savings, which exceed their modest capital expenditures, so net, the sector tends to be a *small* supplier of funds.

The final sector in Table 2–1 is the rest of the world. Domestic firms cover some portion of the funds deficits they incur by borrowing abroad, and domestic funds-surplus units occasionally invest abroad. Thus, to get a complete picture of who supplies and demands funds, we must include the rest of the world in our summary table. Also, when the exchange value of the dollar is weak, the central banks of Germany, Japan, and other countries become big buyers of dollars; they typically invest these dollars in U.S. government securities, thereby becoming financers of the U.S. government debt. When the dollar is strong, the converse occurs. Finally, note that when the U.S. is experiencing a big trade deficit, that deficit must be matched by an equally big net inflow of foreign capital as shown by the numbers in column (6) of Table 2–1.

Every funds deficit has to be covered by the receipt of debt or equity capital from outside sources, and every funds surplus must be absorbed by supplying such capital. Thus, if the funds surpluses and deficits incurred by all sectors are totaled, their sum should be zero. Actually, the figures on line 5 of Table 2–1 don't sum horizontally to zero because of inevitable statistical errors. In 1988, recorded sector deficits exceeded recorded sector surpluses by $11.0 billion, indicating that some sectors' deficits had been overestimated and other sectors' surpluses underestimated. The net discrepancy, however, was small relative to various figures calculated for the major sectors, so the table presumably gives a good overall picture of the direction and magnitude of intersector funds flows within the economy.

Net Financial Investment by Sector

Funds flows between sectors leave a residue of *newly* created financial assets and liabilities. In particular, spending units that borrow incur claims against themselves which appear on their balance sheets as liabilities, while spending units that supply capital acquire financial assets in the form of stocks, bonds, and other securities.

This suggests that, since the consumer sector ran an $84.7 billion funds surplus in 1988, the sector's holdings of financial assets should have increased by a like amount over that year. Things, however, are not so simple. While the consumer sector as a whole ran a funds surplus, many spending units within the sector ran funds deficits. Thus, the appropriate figure to look at is the sector's *net financial investment*, that is, financial assets acquired minus liabilities incurred. For the household sector, this figure (line 8, Table 2–1) was $141.5 billion in 1988, a number of the right sign but much larger than the sector's funds surplus; the difference between the two figures is due to the statistical errors that inevitably creep into such estimates.

The big funds deficit that the nonfinancial business sector ran up during 1988 indicates that the net rise in its financial liabilities outstanding over the year must have been substantial. The estimated figure ($62.2 billion) confirms this, but again a discrepancy has crept into the picture.

Similar but smaller discrepancies exist between the funds surpluses or deficits run up by the other sectors in Table 2–1 and their net financial investments.

FINANCIAL INTERMEDIARIES

As noted, every year large numbers of business firms and other spending units in the economy incur funds deficits that they cover by obtaining funds from spending units running funds surpluses. Some of this *external financing* involves what's called *direct finance*. In the case of direct finance, the *ultimate funds-deficit unit* (business firm, government body, or other spending unit) either borrows directly from *ultimate funds-surplus units* or sells equity claims against itself directly to such spending units. An example of direct finance would be a corporation covering a funds deficit by issuing new bonds, some of which are sold directly to consumers or to nonfinancial business firms running funds surpluses.

While examples of direct finance are easy to find, external financing more typically involves *indirect finance*. In that case, the funds flow from the surplus to the deficit unit via a *financial intermediary*. Banks, savings and loan associations, life insurance companies, pension funds, and mutual funds are all examples of financial intermediaries. As this list makes clear, financial intermediaries differ widely in character. Nevertheless, they all perform basically the same function. Every financial intermediary solicits and obtains funds from funds-surplus units by offering in exchange for funds "deposited" with it, claims against itself. The latter, which take many forms, including demand deposits, time deposits, money market and other mutual fund shares, and the cash value of life insurance policies, are known as *indirect securities*. Financial intermediaries use the funds that they receive in exchange for the indirect securities that they issue to invest in stocks, bonds, and other securities issued by ultimate funds-deficit units, that is, in *primary securities*.

All this sounds a touch bloodless, so let's look at a simple example of financial intermediation. Jones, a consumer, runs a $20,000 funds surplus, which he receives in cash. He promptly deposits his cash in a demand deposit at a bank. Simultaneously, some other spending unit, say, the Alpha Company, runs a temporary funds deficit. Jones's bank trades the funds Jones has deposited with it for a loan note (IOU) issued by Alpha. In doing this—accepting Jones's deposit and acquiring the note—the bank is funneling funds from Jones, an ultimate funds-surplus unit, to Alpha, an ultimate funds-deficit unit; in other words, it is acting as a financial intermediary between Jones and this company.

Federal Reserve statistics on the assets and liabilities of different sectors in the economy show the importance of financial intermediation. In particular, at the beginning of 1989, households, personal trusts, and nonprofit organizations, who, as a group, are the major suppliers of external financing, held $11.1 trillion of financial assets. Of this total, $3.0 trillion represented deposits at commercial banks, other thrift institutions, and money market funds; $0.3 trillion, the cash value of their life insurance policies; $2.6 trillion the reserves backing pensions eventually due them; and $0.6 trillion mutual fund (other than money market) shares. The other $4.6 trillion represented consumers' holdings of primary securities: corporate stock, U.S. government bonds, state and local bonds, corporate and foreign bonds, and assorted other IOUs. Thus, in early 1989, about 61% of the funds that had flowed out of households running funds surpluses had been channeled to other spending units through financial intermediation.

Financial intermediaries are a varied group. To give some idea of the relative importance of different intermediaries, Table 2–2 lists the assets of all the major intermediaries at the beginning of 1989. As one might expect, commercial banks are by far the most important intermediaries. Following them are

TABLE 2–2

Total financial assets held by major financial institutions, beginning of 1989 ($ billions)

Institutions	Assets
Commercial banks	2,939.8
Savings and loans	1,349.5
Life insurance companies	1,117.3
Private pension funds	1,123.2
State and local government retirement funds	608.6
Finance companies	488.3
Federally sponsored credit agencies	423.1
Money market funds	338.0
Other insurance companies	448.9
Federal Reserve Banks	304.6
Mutual savings banks	262.9
Mutual funds	475.2
Credit unions	194.0
Securities brokers and dealers	153.0
Real estate investment trusts	12.3

Source: Board of Governors, Federal Reserve System.

savings and loan associations (S&Ls), life insurance companies, private pension funds, and state and local government retirement funds.

The Reasons for Intermediation

The main reason for all of the intermediation that occurs in our economy is that the mix of primary securities offered by funds-deficit units is unattractive to many funds-surplus units. With the exception of corporate stocks, the minimum denominations on many primary securities are high relative to the size of the funds surpluses that most spending units are likely to run during any short-term period. Also, the amount of debt securities that deficit units want to borrow long term far exceeds the amount that surplus units—consumers and corporations that often desire high liquidity—choose to lend long term. Finally, some risk is attached to many primary securities, more than most surplus units would like to bear.

The indirect securities offered to savers by financial intermediaries are quite attractive in contrast to primary securities. Many such instruments, for example, time deposits, have low to zero minimum denominations, are highly liquid, and expose the investor to negligible risk. Financial intermediaries are able to offer such attractive securities for several reasons. First, they pool the funds of many investors in a highly diversified portfolio, thereby reducing risk and overcoming the minimum denominations problem. Second, to the extent that one saver's withdrawal is likely to be met by another's deposit, intermediaries, such as banks and S&Ls, can with reasonable safety borrow short term from depositors and lend long term to borrowers. A final reason for intermediation is the tax advantages that some forms of intermediation, for example, participation in a pension plan, offer individuals.

BANKS, A SPECIAL INTERMEDIARY

Banks in our economy are an intermediary of special importance for several reasons. First, they are by far the largest intermediary; they receive huge quantities of *demand deposits* (i.e., checking account money) and time deposits, which they use to make loans to consumers, corporations, and others. Second, in the course of their lending activity, *banks create money*. The reason is that demand deposits, which are a bank liability, count as part of the money supply—no matter how one defines that supply. And today, thanks to the attention paid to monetarists who argue that the money supply is immensely important in determining economic activity, all eyes tend to focus on growth of the money supply.

Just how banks create money takes a little explaining. We have to introduce a simple device known as a *T-account,* which shows, as the account below illustrates, the changes that occur in the assets and liabilities of a spending unit—consumer, firm, or financial institution—as the result of a specific economic transaction.

**T-Account for a
Spending Unit**

Changes in assets	Changes in liabilities

Consider again Jones, who takes $20,000 in cash and deposits that money in the First National Bank. This transaction will result in the following changes in the balance sheets of Jones and his bank:

Jones			**First National Bank**		
Cash	−20,000		Reserves		Demand
Demand			(cash) +20,000		deposits
deposits	+20,000				to Jones +20,000

Clearly, Jones's deposit results in $20,000 of cash being *withdrawn from circulation* and put into bank (cash) reserves, but simultaneously $20,000 of new demand deposits are created. Since every definition of the money supply includes both demand deposits and currency *in circulation,* this deposit has no net effect on the size of the money supply; instead, it simply alters the composition of the money supply.

Now enters the Alpha Company, a funds-deficit unit, which borrows $15,000 from the First National Bank. If the bank makes the loan by crediting $15,000 to Alpha's account, changes will again occur in its balance sheet and in that of the borrower, too.

Alpha Company		First National Bank	
Demand deposits +15,000	Bank loan +15,000	Loan to Alpha Co. +15,000	Demand deposits to Alpha Co. +15,000

As the T-accounts show, the immediate effect of the loan is to *increase* total demand deposits by $15,000, but no offsetting decrease has occurred in the amount of currency in circulation. Thus, by making the loan, the First National Bank has *created* $15,000 of new money (Table 2–3).

The Alpha Company presumably borrows money to make a payment. That in no way alters the money-creation aspect of the bank loan. To illustrate, suppose Alpha makes a payment for $15,000 to Beta Company by drawing a check against its new balance and depositing it in another bank, the Second National Bank. Then the following changes will occur in the balance sheets of these two banks:

Second National Bank		First National Bank	
Reserves (cash) +15,000	Demand deposits to Beta Co. +15,000	Reserves (cash) −15,000	Demand deposits to Alpha Co. −15,000

TABLE 2–3
Money supply

Step 1:   Jones holds $20,000 in cash.
   Money supply equals:
      $20,000 in cash.

Step 2:   Jones deposits his $20,000 of cash at the First National Bank.
   Money supply equals:
      $20,000 of demand deposits held by Jones.

Step 3:   The First National Bank lends $15,000 to the Alpha Co.
   Money supply equals:
      $20,000 of demand deposits held by Jones.
      +15,000 of demand deposits held by Alpha Co.
      $35,000 total money supply.

The assumed payment merely switches $15,000 of demand deposits and reserves from one bank to another bank. The payment therefore does not alter the size of the money supply.

Bearing this in mind, let's now examine how the Fed regulates the volume of bank intermediation and what effect its actions have on the money supply and interest rates.

THE FEDERAL RESERVE'S ROLE

The Fed's life has been one of continuing evolution, first in determining what its goals should be and second in learning how to use the tools available to it to promote these goals. When Congress set up the Fed in 1913, it was intended to perform several functions of varying importance. First, the Fed was charged with creating an elastic supply of currency, that is, one that could be expanded and contracted in step with changes in the quantity of currency (as opposed to bank deposits) that the public desired to hold. Creating an elastic currency supply was viewed as important because, under the then existing banking system, when a prominent bank failed and nervous depositors at other banks began demanding currency for deposits, the banks were frequently unable to meet these demands. Consequently, on a number of occasions, the panic of 1907 being a case in point, currency runs on solvent banks forced these banks to temporarily suspend the conversion of deposits into cash. Such suspensions, during which currency traded at a premium relative to bank deposits, inconvenienced depositors and disrupted the economy.

The Fed was to solve this problem by standing ready during panics to extend to the banks at the discount window loans whose proceeds could be paid out in Federal Reserve notes. To the extent that the Fed fulfilled this function, it was acting as a lender of last resort, satiating the public's appetite for cash by monetizing bank assets. Today, acting as a lender of last resort remains an important Fed responsibility, but the Fed fulfills it in a different way.

Congress also intended that the Fed carry out a second and more important function, namely, regulating the overall supply of money and bank credit so that changes in them would promote rather than disrupt economic activity. This function, too, was to be accomplished at the discount window. According to the prevailing doctrine, changes in the money supply and bank credit would be beneficial if they matched the direction and magnitude of changes in the economy's level of productive activity. Such beneficial changes in money and bank credit would, it was envisioned, occur semiautomatically with the Fed in operation. When business activity expanded, so, too, would the demand for bank loans. As growth of the latter put pressure on bank reserves, banks would obtain additional reserves by rediscounting at the Fed (i.e., borrowing against) *eligible paper*— notes, drafts, and bills of exchange arising out of actual commercial transactions. Conversely, when economic activity slackened, bank borrowing at the discount window, bank loans, and the money supply would contract in step.

Events never quite followed this smooth pattern, which in retrospect is not to be regretted. As theorists now realize, expanding money and bank credit without limit during an upswing and permitting them to contract without limit during a downswing, far from encouraging stable growth, would amplify fluctuations in income and output. In particular, unlimited money creation during a boom would fuel any inflationary fires and other excesses that developed.

Today, the Fed sees its major policy job as pursuing a *countercyclical monetary policy*. Specifically, it attempts to promote full employment and price stability by limiting the growth of bank intermediation when the economy expands too vigorously and by encouraging it when the economy slips into recession.

Controlling the Level of Bank Intermediation

The Fed controls the level of bank intermediation—the amount of bank lending and money creating—through several tools. One is *reserve requirements*. Since the 1930s, the Fed has been responsible for setting the limits on the percentage of reserves that member banks are required to hold against deposits made with them. Under the Monetary Control Act of 1980, all depository institutions, including S&Ls, mutual saving banks, and foreign bank branches, are today subject to reserve requirements. Each bank must place all of its reserves, except vault cash, on deposit in a non–interest-bearing account at one of the 12 regional Federal Reserve Banks. Thus, each district Federal Reserve Bank acts in effect as a banker to commercial banks in its district, holding what amounts to checking accounts for them.

The existence at Federal Reserve Banks of member bank reserve accounts explains, by the way, how the Fed can clear checks drawn against one bank and deposited with another so easily. It does so simply by debiting the reserve account of the bank against which the check is drawn and crediting by an equal amount the reserve account of the bank at which the check is deposited.

The member banks' checking accounts also make it easy for the Fed to circulate currency in the form of Federal Reserve notes (a non–interest-bearing *indirect security* issued by the Fed). Currency runs on banks are a thing of the past, but the Fed must still constantly increase the amount of currency in circulation because, as the economy expands, more currency is needed by the public for ordinary transactions. Whenever people demand more currency, they demand it from their commercial banks, which in turn get it from the Fed by trading reserve deposits for currency. Since the Fed, as noted below, creates bank reserves by buying government securities, the currency component of our money supply is in effect created by the Fed through *monetization* of a portion of the federal debt. All of this correctly suggests that the Fed, despite its lofty position at the pinnacle of the financial system, is none other than one more type of financial intermediary.

The second key tool of the Fed is *open market operations*, that is, purchases and sales of government securities through which it creates and destroys member bank reserves. Whenever the Fed, operating through the trading desk of the New York district bank, buys government securities, its purchases inevitably increase bank reserves by an amount equal to the cost of the securities purchased. When the source of the securities purchased is a member bank, this result is obvious. Specifically, a purchase of $10MM of government securities would lead to the following changes in the balance sheets of the Fed and of a member bank:

The Fed			A Member Bank	
Government securities +10MM	Member bank reserves +10MM	Reserves +10MM Government securities −10MM		

Even if the source of the government securities purchased by the Fed is a nonbank spending unit, the result will be essentially the same, since the money received by the seller, say, a nonbank dealer, will inevitably be deposited in a commercial bank, leading to the following balance-sheet changes:

The Fed		A Member Bank	
Government securities +10MM	Member bank reserves +10MM	Reserves +10MM	Deposits to nonbank seller +10MM

A Nonbank Seller	
Government securities −10MM Demand deposits +10MM	

In the case of sales of government securities by the Fed, the process described above operates exactly in reverse, and member bank reserves are destroyed.

With the exception of loans extended by the Fed at the discount window (discussed below), the *only* way bank reserves can be created is through Fed purchases of government securities, and the only way they can be destroyed is through sales by the Fed of such securities.[1] Thus, the Fed is in a position to

---

[1]There are some minor exceptions: In particular, movements of Treasury deposit balances between commercial banks and Fed banks affect member bank reserves, but the Fed tracks these movements daily and offsets them through purchases and sales of government securities. Seasonal and long-term changes in the public's demand for currency also affect bank reserves, but these changes too can be and are offset by the Fed through appropriate open market operations. Finally, under the current system of "dirty" currency floats, cum outright intervention, U.S. and foreign central-bank operations in the foreign exchange market may have some effect on domestic bank deposits and reserves.

control directly and precisely the quantity of reserves available to the banking system.

The Lid on Bank Intermediation

Taken together, reserve requirements and the Fed's ability to control the level of bank reserves permit the Fed to limit the level of intermediation in which banks may engage. Let's use a simple illustration. Suppose the Fed were to require banks to hold reserves equal to 10% of total deposits. If the Fed were then to create, say, $90 billion of bank reserves, the maximum deposits banks could create through intermediation would be $900 billion (10% of $900 billion being $90 billion).

Naturally, if the Fed were to increase bank reserves through open market purchases of government securities, that would increase the quantity of deposits banks could create, whereas open market sales by the Fed would do the reverse. For example, with a 10% reserve ratio, every $1 billion of government security purchases by the Fed would permit a $10-billion increase in bank assets and liabilities, whereas $1 billion of sales would do the opposite.

Our example, which points up the potency of *open market operations* (purchases and sales by the Fed of government securities) as a tool for controlling the level of bank intermediation, is oversimplified. For one thing, the percentage of reserves that must be held by a bank against its deposits varies depending on the type of deposit and the size of the bank accepting the deposit. Currently, required reserve ratios range from a high of 12% on net transactions accounts to a low of 0% against certain classes of time deposits. Thus, the actual amount of deposits (demand plus time) that a given quantity of reserves will support depends partly on the mix of deposits demanded by the public and partly on which depository institutions receive those deposits.

This, together with the fact that banks may choose not to fully utilize the reserves available to them, means that slack exists in the Fed's control over deposit creation. Nevertheless, open market operations are a powerful tool for controlling the level of bank activity, and they are used daily by the Fed to do so.

The Discount Window

As noted earlier, the founders of the Fed viewed discounting as its *key* tool. In practice, things have worked out differently. The main reason is that over time the Fed switched from controlling bank reserves through discounting to controlling them through open market operations. This switch makes sense for several reasons. First, it puts the Fed in the position of being able to take the initiative. Second, the size and liquidity of the market for government securities are such that the Fed can make substantial purchases and sales there without disrupting the market or causing more than negligible price changes. The latter is important because the Fed, to fine-tune bank reserves, must constantly be in the market buying and selling such securities. Part of this activity results from what is called the Fed's *defensive* operations, open market purchases and sales designed to counter the effect on bank reserves of outside forces, such as changes in currency in circulation and movements of Treasury balances between member banks and the Fed. In addition, the Fed undertakes open market operations to effect whatever overall changes in bank reserves are called for by current monetary policy.

　　The discount window still exists and banks borrow there. This activity creates some slack in the Fed's control over bank reserves, so the Fed has to limit borrowing at the window. One way it could do this would be to charge a high penalty rate on discounts, one that would discourage banks from borrowing except in cases of real and temporary need. The Fed, however, has not followed this course.[2] Instead, it typically sets the discount rate at a level in step with other money market rates, with the result that banks can at times profit by borrowing at the discount window and relending elsewhere. To limit such arbitrage and maintain control over bank reserves, the Fed has made it a policy that borrowing at the discount window is a privilege that a bank may use only sparingly and on a temporary basis.

---

[2]Except for a brief experiment with a modest surcharge in 1980 to 1981.

Today, borrowing at the discount window represents a small but highly variable element in the total reserves available to member banks. In recent years, December monthly average figures on such borrowings have ranged from \$0.8 to \$1.7 billion, representing no more than 0.2 to 4.5% of total bank reserves.

EXTENDING THE FED'S REACH

Holding non–interest-bearing reserve deposits at the Fed imposes an opportunity cost on a member institution, namely, the interest income foregone by the institution because it cannot use these deposits productively. As interest rates rose secularly over time, so too did the opportunity cost to banks of meeting reserve requirements. As a result, the trend during the 1960s and '70s was for banks to leave the Federal Reserve System, since at that time only member banks were subject to reserve requirements.[3]

The Fed viewed this trend with alarm. It was prepared to live with a situation in which many small state banks were not members. However, the Fed feared that the exit from the system of increasingly more and increasingly larger banks would decrease the effectiveness of its policies and, in particular, limit its ability to control the money supply. As a result, the Fed from 1964 onward urged Congress to amend the Federal Reserve Act to make nonmember banks subject to the same reserve requirements as member banks. A second smaller but growing problem faced by the Fed was that thrift institutions outside its control began to issue *NOW* (*negotiable order of withdrawal*) *accounts*. Deposits in such accounts amount, in effect, to interest-bearing demand deposits and as such are *money* by any reasonable definition.

In 1980, Congress passed the landmark *Depository Institutions Deregulation and Monetary Control Act*. One objective of this wide-ranging act was to increase the Fed's control over

---

[3]At that time, nationally-chartered banks were required to become members of the Federal Reserve System, but state-chartered banks were not.

money creation. To this end, the act, dubbed the *Banking Act of 1980*, called for the Fed to impose, over a phase-in period, reserve requirements on nonmember banks and on thrift institutions offering checking accounts, as well. At the same time, reserve requirements on savings and time deposits held by individuals at all depository institutions were to be eliminated. (This act was to some extent amended and superseded by the Banking Act of 1982, which speeded up rate deregulation.)

As a quid pro quo for the new reserve requirements, the 1980 act empowered banks and all other depository institutions to issue NOW accounts. It also empowered thrift institutions to make a wider range of investments and granted them access to the discount window. Full implementation of the 1980 act further blurred the once clear line of demarcation between commercial banks and thrifts.

Money Supply and Fed Control over It

As will be explained in Chapter 3, banks borrow and lend excess reserves to each other in the *Federal funds market*. The rate at which such lending and borrowing occurs is called the *Fed funds rate*. When the Fed cuts back on the growth of bank reserves, this tightens the supply of reserves available to the banking system relative to its demand for them; that, in turn, drives up the Fed funds rate, which, in turn, drives up other short-term interest rates. Thus, any easing or tightening by the Fed necessarily alters not only money supply growth, but interest rates.

Because of this, the Fed cannot have two independent policies, one to control money supply growth, a second to influence interest rates. If the Fed focuses on pegging interest rates, money supply becomes a residual variable; it is what it is and falls outside the control of the Fed. Conversely, a Fed decision to strictly control money supply growth implies a loss by the Fed of its ability to independently influence the level of interest rates.

In implementing monetary policy, the Fed in the early 1970s focused primarily on interest rates and more particularly on the Fed funds rate. The Fed viewed money as tight if interest rates were high or rising, as easy if interest rates were low or falling. This policy stance was predicated on the view that high and rising interest rates would discourage spending and the expansion of economic activity, while low or falling rates would do the reverse.

The monetarists, with Milton Friedman at the fore, argued that this analysis was incorrect. According to their theory, giving people more money causes them to increase their spending on goods and services. Therefore, the key to achieving steady economic growth and to controlling inflation is a monetary policy that holds the rate of growth of the money supply strictly in line with the rate of growth of real output achievable by the economy. The clear implication of the monetarist position is that the Fed should seek to peg not the Fed rate, but the rate of growth of money.

Gradually, grudgingly, and with a prod from Congress in the form of the Humphrey-Hawkins bill passed in 1978, the Fed accepted (or said it did) the monetarist doctrine and shifted the focus of its policy from controlling interest rates to controlling money supply growth, the policy shift being implemented under Chairman Paul Volcker.

Pitfalls of Monetarism

For monetarists, particularly those residing in the ivory towers of academe, it appeared that the mandate to strictly control the growth of the money supply is one that the Fed could carry out with reasonable ease and a high degree of precision. In practice, however, the policy of controlling money supply growth—whether wise or foolish—posed serious problems for the Fed.

The first, and hardly trivial, problem facing the Fed was to determine just what money is. Clearly, the old definition of money, demand deposits plus currency in circulation, is too restrictive since the long-term upward trend in interest rates had spawned not only new types of deposit accounts—NOW accounts and ATS (automatic transfer from savings to demand deposit) accounts—that could be used for transactions purposes, but a host of other highly liquid investment options, including placements in *money market funds*. Since liquidity—unlike virginity—is measured in degrees, drawing a line between money and near monies necessarily involves *arbitrary* choices. This being the case, the Fed found itself struggling for some time simply to define what it was that it was supposed to control.

The Fed's difficulties in defining money are reflected in its decision to publish four different measures of money supply (Table 2–4). Obviously, the Fed cannot independently control the growth of each of these aggregates. It currently focuses its attention primarily on M2 and M3. The Fed has no target range for M1, but it does set one for the growth of total domestic nonfinancial debt.

In late 1982 and early 1983, the Fed found that the problem of defining money supply went from being difficult to nigh impossible. In the inelegant but apt words of one Street observer, "It's a can of worms." The immediate cause of the problems faced by the Fed, as 1982 became 1983, lay in the Banking Act of 1982. One of its provisions was a mandate to the Depository Institutions Deregulation Committee (DIDC) that this committee design within 60 days an interest-rate-lid-free account to be offered by banks and thrifts that would permit these institutions to compete on equal terms for deposits with money funds.

The DIDC came up, to the surprise of many observers, with not one but two new accounts. The first, called the *money market deposit account* (*MMDA*), required the depositor, private or corporate, to maintain a minimum balance of $2,500 (subsequently eliminated); in exchange the depositor obtained a federally insured account on which he could write three checks and make three preauthorized withdrawals per month and on which the deposit-accepting institution could pay any rate it wished. The Fed chose to view this account as more akin to a savings than a demand deposit account and included it in M2.

The introduction of MMDAs on December 14, 1982 was followed by the introduction of *Super-NOW accounts* on January 5, 1983. These accounts, which initially at least were available only to individuals, also required the depositor to maintain a minimum balance of $2,500 (later eliminated); in exchange, the depositor obtained a federally insured checking account on which he could make unlimited withdrawals and on which the deposit-accepting institution could pay any rate and impose any service charges it wished. Today, there is no real distinction

TABLE 2–4
The Fed's measures of money stock, liquid assets, and debt; June 1989

M1:   (1) Currency outside the Treasury, Federal Reserve Banks, and the vaults of depository institutions; (2) travelers checks of nonbank issuers; (3) demand deposits at all commercial banks other than those due to depository institutions, the U.S. government, and foreign banks and official institutions less cash items in the process of collection and Federal Reserve float; and (4) other checkable deposits (OCD) consisting of negotiable order of withdrawal (NOW) and automatic transfer service (ATS) accounts at depository institutions, credit union share draft accounts, and demand deposits at thrift institutions.

M2:   M1 plus overnight (and continuing contract) repurchase agreements (RPs) issued by all commercial banks and overnight Eurodollars issued to U.S. residents by foreign branches of U.S. banks worldwide, MMDAs, savings and small-denomination time deposits (time deposits—including retail RPs—in amounts of less than $100,000), and balances in both taxable and tax-exempt general purpose and broker/dealer money market mutual funds. Excludes individual retirement accounts (IRA) and Keogh balances at depository institutions and money market funds. Also excludes all balances held by U.S. commercial banks, money market funds (general purpose and broker/dealer), foreign governments and commercial banks, and the U.S. government.

M3:   M2 plus large-denomination time deposits and term RP liabilities (in amounts of $100,000 or more) issued by commercial banks and thrift institutions, term Eurodollars held by U.S. residents at foreign branches of U.S. banks worldwide and at all banking offices in the United Kingdom and Canada, and balances in both taxable and tax-exempt, institutions-only money market mutual funds. Excludes amounts held by depository institutions, the U.S. government, money market funds, and foreign banks and official institutions. Also subtracted is the estimated amount of overnight repos and Eurodollars held by institution-only money market mutual funds.

L: M3 plus the nonbank public holdings of U.S. savings bonds, short-term Treasury securities, commercial paper and bankers acceptances, net of money market mutual fund holdings of these assets.

Debt: Debt of domestic nonfinancial sectors consists of outstanding credit market debt of the U.S. government, state and local governments, and private nonfinancial sectors. Private debt consists of corporate bonds, mortgages, consumer credit (including bank loans), other bank loans, commercial paper, bankers acceptances, and other debt instruments. The source of data on domestic nonfinancial debt is the Federal Reserve Board's flow of funds accounts. Debt data are based on monthly averages.

between NOW and Super-NOW accounts. The Fed includes Super-NOW accounts in M1.

The introduction of MMDAs and Super-NOW accounts made measuring money supply more difficult than ever for the Fed because it blurred even further, if possible, the distinction between instruments in which people hold transactions balances and instruments in which they hold savings. MMDAs were an immediate success and in the early weeks of their existence were drawing several billions of dollars per week from money funds, whose deposits are counted in M2. The new MMDA accounts were also drawing billions of dollars of deposits out of old lower-yielding accounts at banks and thrifts. All this shifting of balances from place to place combined with the introduction of the new accounts made it impossible for the Fed—for a period at least—to interpret the meaning of the growth rates of M1 and M2. Responding to this, the Fed suspended its use of

FIGURE 2–1

The growth of M1, no longer targeted by the Fed, has turned sluggish

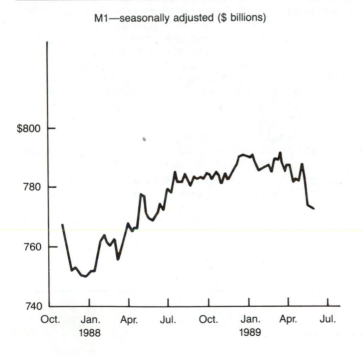

M1—seasonally adjusted ($ billions)

M1 as a guide in policy making and declared that henceforth it would be guided by M2; in fact, however, it permitted M2 to grow at out-of-bounds rates without responding by tightening. Whatever the Fed said it was doing, it appeared that the Fed by 1983 was backsliding from a monetarist policy of controlling money supply to its former policy of controlling interest rates.

Defining money, while a tough nut to crack, is only the beginning of the Fed's problems in controlling money supply. A second, equally intractable and, from a policy point of view, equally serious problem is that a large erratic element appears to be intrinsic in money supply behavior with the result that week-to-week money supply figures fluctuate sharply; the Fed also has difficulty in seasonally adjusting these figures. The up-

FIGURE 2–2
The growth of M2 began 1989 below the Fed's target band

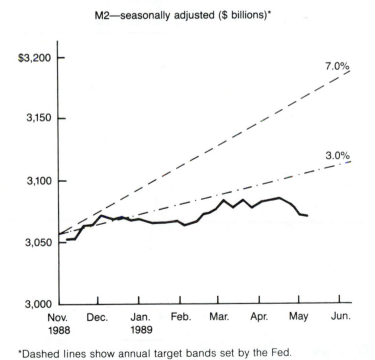

M2—seasonally adjusted ($ billions)*

*Dashed lines show annual target bands set by the Fed.

shot is that underlying trends in money supply growth are hard to perceive both for the Fed and for outside observers reacting to actual and potential Fed moves. In any case, the Bush administration began in a period of restrained monetary growth (Figures 2–1 (p. 30), 2–2 (p. 31), and 2–3).

In accepting and seeking to implement a strictly monetarist policy, the Fed—as had to be the case—lost control over interest rates (Figure 2–4). This permitted rates, beginning in 1979, to take off on a roller coaster ride. It also created a situation in which strong reactions by money and bond market traders to weekly money supply figures made interest rates highly volatile and unpredictable, even on a week-to-week basis.

The price of a monetarist policy in a highly inflationary economy was an extremely high degree of uncertainty with re-

FIGURE 2–3
The growth of M3 began 1989 at roughly the Fed's lower target band

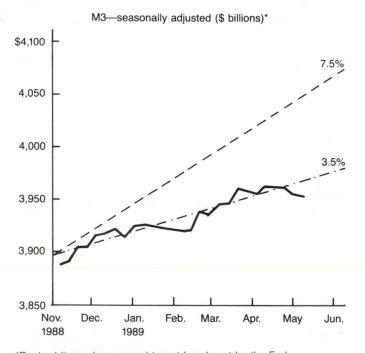

M3—seasonally adjusted ($ billions)*

*Dashed lines show annual target bands set by the Fed.

FIGURE 2–4

By temporarily becoming monetarist, the Fed temporarily lost control over the Fed fund rate

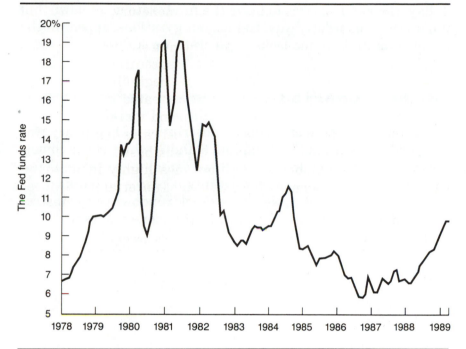

Source: J. P. Morgan Securities, Inc.

spect to rates in the capital market. This untoward consequence of monetarism could hardly be viewed as contributing to economic stability. The Fed knew this and wanted to feed to credit market participants money-supply numbers that delineated longer-term trends in monetary growth. Unfortunately, it could find no way to do so.

As the meaning of Fed numbers on money supply became increasingly unclear, the Fed used this as an excuse to retreat from outright monetarism—to disregard, "temporarily" it said, money-supply figures in making policy. Today, the Fed still sets monetary goals—Humphrey-Hawkins says that it must—but in actual fact, the Fed has gone back to its old game of pegging the funds rate and of nudging up that rate when it wants to tighten, as it did in the spring of 1989.

The Fed's shift in policy emphasis is clearly seen in Figure 2–4; it shows that the Fed funds rate, after a period of high volatility, from late 1979 through 1983, became far less volatile. Today, the Fed feels free to move the funds rate up or down, but it does so in an orderly way: trends, not gyrations, appear in the series, especially if one looks at week-to-week data.

THE NEXT CHAPTER

The primary purpose of this brief description of Fed policy was to provide background for Chapters 6 and 7, which cover domestic and Eurobanking. In Chapter 9, we examine in greater detail current Fed policy and the constraints it places on banks.

In the next chapter, we give a quick rundown of the instruments, domestic and Euro, traded in the money market.

CHAPTER 3

THE INSTRUMENTS IN BRIEF

Here's a quick rundown of the major money market instruments. Don't look for subtleties; just enough is said to lay the groundwork for later chapters.

DEALERS AND BROKERS

The markets for all money market instruments are made in part by brokers and dealers. *Brokers* bring buyers and sellers together for a commission. By definition, brokers never position securities. Their function is to provide a communications network that links market participants who are often numerous and geographically dispersed. Most brokering in the money market occurs between banks that are buying funds from or selling funds to each other and between dealers in money market instruments.

Dealers make markets in money market instruments by quoting—to each other, to issuers, and to investors—bid and asked prices at which they are prepared to buy and sell. Whenever a dealer trades securities, he is acting as *principal*, that is, he trades for his own account; thus, assuming positions—long and short—is an essential part of dealing. Naturally, when a dealer goes long or short, he hopes to profit: to later *sell* at a *higher* price securities he goes *long*, and to later *buy* at a *lower* price securities he *shorts*.

Dealers also act as *agent* in the issuance of commercial paper and medium-term notes (MTNs), including bank deposit notes. To say that a dealer acts as an agent in the issuance of new paper means that, through his distribution network, he sells to investors for a *fee* (or commission) new paper that an issuer wants distributed. In this case, the dealer is representing the issuer rather than dealing with him as principal. Like a broker, a dealer acting strictly as agent does not position. It is, however, not unusual for a dealer to act both as agent and principal in the same market. For example, a dealer will typically act as an agent in distributing MTNs, that is, in the *new issue market* for MTNs, but as principal when, to provide market liquidity, he makes bids for and offers of outstanding MTNs. A market in which outstanding issues are traded is referred to as a *secondary market*.

U.S. TREASURY SECURITIES

To finance the U.S. national debt, the Treasury issues several types of securities. Some are nonnegotiable, for example, savings bonds sold to consumers and special issues sold to government trust funds. The bulk of the securities sold by the U.S. Treasury are, however, negotiable.

What form these securities take depends on their maturity. Those with a maturity at issue of a year or less are known as *Treasury bills*, *T bills* for short or just plain *bills*. T bills bear no interest. An investor in bills earns a return because bills are issued at a discount from face value and redeemed by the Treasury at maturity for face value. The amount of the discount at which investors buy bills and the length of time bills have to be held before they mature together imply some specific yield that the bill will return if held to maturity.

T bills are currently issued in 3-month, 6-month, and 1-year maturities.[1] In issuing bills, the Treasury does not set the amount of the discount. Instead, the Federal Reserve auctions off each new bill issue to investors and dealers, with the bills going to those bidders offering the highest price, that is, the lowest interest cost to the Treasury. By auctioning new bill is-

---

[1]For tactical debt management purposes, the Treasury occasionally meets cash flow gaps by issuing very short-term "cash management bills."

sues, the Treasury lets currently prevailing market conditions establish the yield at which each new issue is sold.

The Treasury also issues interest-bearing *notes*. These securities are issued at or very near face value and redeemed at face value. Notes have an *original maturity* (maturity at issue) of 2 to 10 years.[2] Currently, the Treasury issues 2-, 3-, 4-, 5-, 7-, and 10-year notes on a regular cycle. Notes of other maturities are issued periodically depending on the Treasury's needs. Interest on Treasury notes is paid semiannually. Notes, like bills, are sold through auctions held by the Federal Reserve. In these auctions, participants bid yields, and the securities offered are sold to those dealers and investors who bid the lowest yields, that is, the lowest interest cost to the Treasury. Thus, the coupon rate on new Treasury notes, like the yield on bills, is determined by the market.

In addition to notes, the Treasury issues interest-bearing negotiable *bonds* that have a maturity at issue of 10 years or more. The only difference between Treasury notes and bonds is that bonds are issued in longer maturities. Over the years, the volume of bonds the Treasury could issue was limited because Congress imposed a 4.25% ceiling on the rate the Treasury might pay on bonds. Since this rate was for years far below prevailing market rates, the Treasury was able to sell bonds only to the extent that Congress authorized it to issue bonds exempt from the ceiling; the current exemption was successively raised and finally eliminated in 1988. Treasury bonds, like notes, are normally sold at yield auctions.

Banks, other financial institutions, insurance companies, pension funds, and corporations are all important investors in U.S. Treasury securities. So, too, are foreign central banks and other foreign institutions. The market for government securities is largely a wholesale market, and especially at the short end, multimillion-dollar transactions are common. However, when interest rates get extremely high, as they did in 1974 and again in 1978 to 1982, individuals with small amounts to invest are drawn into the market.

---

[2]A 5-year note has an *original maturity* at issue of five years. One year after issue, it has a *current maturity* of four years.

Because of the high volume of Treasury debt outstanding, the market for bills and short-term government securities is the most active and most carefully watched sector of the money market. At the heart of this market stands a varied collection of dealers who make the market for *governments* (market jargon for government securities) by standing ready to buy and sell huge volumes of these securities. These dealers trade actively not only with investors, but with each other. Most trades of the latter sort are carried out through brokers.

Governments offer investors several advantages. First, because they are constantly traded in the *secondary market* in large volume and at narrow spreads between the bid and asked prices, they are highly *liquid*. Second, governments are considered to be free from credit risk because it is inconceivable that the government would default on them in any situation short of destruction of the country. Third, interest income on governments is exempt from state taxation. Because of these advantages, bills and governments having a short current maturity normally trade at yields below those of other money market instruments.

Generally, yields on governments are higher the longer their *current maturity*, that is, time left to maturity. The reason, explained in Chapter 4, is that the longer the current maturity of a debt security, the more its price will fluctuate in response to changes in interest rates and therefore the greater the *price risk* to which it exposes the investor. There are times, however, when the yield curve *inverts*, that is, yields on short-term securities rise above those on long-term securities. This, for example, was the case during much of the period 1979 to 1981 and again in early 1989. The reason for an inverted yield curve is that market participants anticipate, correctly or incorrectly, that interest rates will fall. As a result, borrowers choose to borrow short-term while investors seek out long-term securities; the result is that supply and demand force short-term rates above long-term rates.

Thirty-Year Bills, Alias STRIPs

Recently, the Treasury has permitted the creation, out of standard T bonds, of what amount to T bills with distant maturities. Here's the story.

The Treasury once issued, upon request, notes and bonds in bearer form. Some dealers came up with the idea of *stripping*— clipping off coupons from—bearer bonds and selling, at discounted prices, the resulting pieces. Each such piece was a *non– interest-bearing security with a fixed maturity and a fixed value at maturity*. Such securities are known generically as *zero-coupon securities*, or simply as *zeros*.

Dealers could make money stripping bearer Treasuries because demand for the pieces was so great that the sum of the values of the pieces exceeded the value of the whole bond. Unfortunately, the Treasury and the Fed opposed, for various reasons (including possibilities for tax evasion), the stripping of bearer Treasuries.

To satisfy investors' desire for long-term zeros, Merrill got a bright idea: It bought Treasuries, placed them with a custodian in a special trust, and then sold to investors participations in its trust. Under the Merrill scheme, each such participation sold was a *zero-coupon security*, backed by unstripped Treasuries. Merrill named its product TIGRs. Soon, every other major dealer was offering its addition to the zoo. Sali sold CATs; Lehman, LIONs; and so on. Also, some dealers sold plain vanilla TRs (trust receipts).

The new "zoo" zeros sold extremely well to institutional investors and even to individuals. The Treasury, eyeing this success, said, "There's money to be made in stripping, let *us* earn it." So in 1985, the Treasury introduced, for certain new T-bond issues, an additional feature: Any owner of such a bond, Merrill, a small dealer, or even an individual, can ask the Treasury to cut that bond into pieces, provided it is in book-entry (electronic-recordkeeping) form. Each such piece corresponds to a different payment due on the bond, and each carries its own CUSIP (ID) number.[3] On a 30-year bond, there are 61 such payments: 60 semiannual interest payments and 1 payment of *corpus* (princi-

---

[3]*CUSIP* is an acronym for the *Committee on Uniform Securities Identification Procedures*. Treasury securities, most federal credit agency securities (including mortgage backs), municipal bonds, corporate stocks, and corporate bonds all have identifying CUSIP numbers. These numbers are assigned, for a fee, by Standard & Poor's.

pal) at maturity. Stripped Treasuries created in the manner we've just described were dubbed *STRIPs*.

Today on Wall Street, STRIPs are a popular item, actively traded by the same dealers who make markets in regular Treasury notes, bonds, and bills.

Internationalization of the Market for Treasuries

A decade ago, when one spoke of *the* market for Treasuries, one was referring to a market that was almost exclusively domestic. The borrower, of course, was domestic and so too were most of the investors, except for a few foreign central banks. Today, that situation has changed dramatically. Foreigners, and most importantly Japanese investors, have become big buyers of Treasury securities.

Not surprisingly, there are now active markets for Treasuries in Tokyo, in London, and, to a lesser extent, in certain other foreign financial centers. Today, reflecting in part the fact that foreigners currently own approximately 18.5% of all outstanding marketable Treasuries, the market for these securities has in truth become a 24-hour, international market.

The dealers who make this round-the-globe market are of two sorts: big American dealers, such as Merrill and Sali, who have opened offices in major financial centers around the globe, and foreign dealers, particularly Japanese dealers, who have opened offices in the U.S. and become a big factor in the domestic trading of Treasury securities.

Financial Futures

In discussing the market for governments, we have focused on the *cash market*, that is, the market in which existing securities are traded for same- or next-day delivery. In addition, there are markets in which Treasury bills, notes, and bonds are traded for *future* delivery. The futures contracts in Treasuries that are actively traded are for 3-month bills with a face value of $1MM at maturity and for notes and long bonds with a par value of $100,000.

Interest-rate futures markets offer institutions that know

they are going to borrow or lend in the future a way to *hedge* that future position, that is, to lock in a reasonably fixed borrowing or lending rate. They also provide speculators with a way to bet money on interest-rate movements that provides greater leverage—bang for the buck—than going short or long cash securities.

Since being introduced in 1976, futures markets for financial instruments have grown at an unforeseen and astonishing rate. In fact, futures contracts for Treasury bills and bonds have been among the most successful contracts ever launched on commodities exchanges. Their success has led to the introduction of trading of similar contracts on a number of futures exchanges in foreign financial centers.

The rapid growth and internationalization of markets for financial futures has, not surprisingly, created situations in which the relationship between the rates on different futures contracts or between the rates on a futures contract and the corresponding cash instrument get, as the Street would say, "out of sync," that is, out of synchronization or line. Thus, yet another major class of traders in financial futures has been arbitrageurs who seek to establish positions from which they will profit when a reasonable relationship between the out-of-line rates is inevitably reestablished.

FEDERAL AGENCY SECURITIES

From time to time Congress becomes concerned about the volume of credit that is available to various sectors of the economy and the terms on which that credit is available. Congress's usual response is to set up a federal agency to provide credit to that sector. Thus, there are the Federal Home Loan Bank System, which lends to the nation's savings and loan associations as well as regulates them; the Government National Mortgage Association, which funnels money into the mortgage market; Banks for Cooperatives, which make seasonal and term loans to farm cooperatives; Federal Land Banks, which give mortgages on farm properties; Federal Intermediate Credit Banks, which provide short-term financing for producers of crops and livestock; and a host of other agencies.

Initially, all the federal agencies financed their activities by selling their own securities in the open market. Today, all except the largest borrow from the Treasury through an institution called the Federal Financing Bank. Those agencies still borrowing in the open market do so primarily by issuing notes and bonds. These securities (known in the market as *agencies*) bear interest, and they are issued and redeemed at face value. Instead of using the auction technique for issuing their securities, federal agencies typically look to the market to determine the best yield at which they can sell a new issue, put that yield on the issue, and then sell it through a syndicate of dealers. Some agencies also sell short-term discount paper that resembles Treasury bills.

Normally, agencies yield slightly more than Treasury securities of the same maturity for several reasons. First, agency issues are smaller than Treasury issues and are therefore less liquid. Second, while all agency issues have *de facto* backing from the federal government (it's inconceivable that the government would let one of them default on its obligations), the securities of only a few agencies are explicitly backed by the full faith and credit of the U.S. government. Third, interest income on some federal agency issues is subject to state taxation.

The market for agencies, while smaller than that for governments, is an active and important sector of the money market. Agencies are traded by the same dealers that trade governments and in much the same way.

FEDERAL FUNDS

All banks and other *depository institutions* (savings and loan associations, savings banks, credit unions, and foreign bank branches) are required to keep reserves on deposit at their district Federal Reserve Bank.[4] The reserve account of a depository

---

[4]The Federal Reserve System, which comprises 12 district Federal Reserve Banks, is the U.S.'s central bank, and as such it is responsible for the implementation of domestic monetary policy. The Fed is described in Chapter 9 of the book. Prior to passage of the Monetary Control Act of 1980, only *member banks* in the Federal Reserve System were required to hold reserves at the Fed.

institution (*DI* for short) is much like an individual's checking account; the DI makes deposits into its reserve account and can transfer funds out of it. The main difference is that, while an individual can let the balance in his checking account run to zero and stay there, each DI is required by law to maintain some *minimum* average balance in its reserve account over the week—Wednesday to Wednesday. Under *contemporaneous reserve accounting*, introduced by the Fed in February 1984, that minimum average balance is based on the total deposits of various types held by the DI during the current settlement week.

The category of DIs that holds by far the largest chunk of the total reserves that all DIs together maintain at Federal Reserve Banks is commercial banks. Funds on deposit in a bank's reserve account are referred to as *Federal funds* or *Fed funds*. Any deposits a bank receives add to its supply of Fed funds, while loans made and securities purchased reduce that supply. Thus, the basic amount of money any bank can lend out and otherwise invest equals the amount of funds it has received from depositors minus the reserves it is required to maintain.

For some banks, this supply of available funds roughly equals the amount they choose to invest in securities plus that demanded from them by borrowers. But for most banks it does not. Specifically, because the nation's largest corporations tend to concentrate their borrowing in big money market banks in New York and other financial centers, the loans and investments these banks must fund exceed the deposits they receive. Many smaller banks, in contrast, receive more money from local depositors than they can lend locally or choose to invest otherwise. Because large banks have to meet their reserve requirements regardless of what loan demand they face and because excess reserves yield no return to smaller banks, it was natural for large banks to begin borrowing the excess funds held by smaller banks.

This borrowing is done in the *Federal funds market*. Most Fed funds loans are overnight transactions. One reason is that the amount of excess funds a given lending bank holds varies daily and unpredictably. Some transactions in Fed funds are made directly, others through New York brokers. Despite the fact that transactions of this sort are all loans, the lending of Fed funds is referred to as a *sale* and the borrowing of Fed funds as a *purchase*. While overnight transactions dominate the Fed funds market, transactions for longer periods also occur there. Fed funds traded for periods other than overnight are referred to as *term* Fed funds.

DIs other than domestic commercial banks also participate in the Fed Funds market. Foreign banks are particularly active buyers and sellers of funds.

The rate of interest paid on overnight loans of Federal funds, which is called the *Fed funds rate*, is a key interest rate in the money market; all other short-term rates relate to the funds rate. This rate used to be closely pegged by the Fed, but starting in October 1979, the Fed allowed the Fed funds rate to fluctuate over a wide band; in more recent years, the Fed has gone back to pegging the Fed funds rate.

REPOS AND REVERSES

A variety of bank and nonbank dealers act as market makers in governments, agencies, CDs, and BAs. Because dealers, by definition, buy and sell for their own accounts, active dealers inevitably end up holding some securities. They will, moreover, buy and hold substantial positions if they believe that interest rates are likely to fall and that the value of these securities is therefore likely to rise. Speculation and risk taking are an inherent and important part of being a dealer.

While dealers have large amounts of capital, the positions they take are often a large multiple of that amount. As a result, dealers have to borrow to finance their positions. Using the securities they own as collateral, they can and do borrow from banks at the dealer loan rate. For the bulk of their financing, however, they resort to a cheaper alternative, entering into *repurchase agreements* (*repos*, for short) with investors.

Much repo financing done by dealers is on an overnight basis. It works as follows: The dealer finds a corporation, money fund, or other investor who has funds to invest overnight. He sells this investor, say, $10MM of securities for roughly $10MM, which is paid in Federal funds to his bank by the investor's bank against delivery of the securities sold. At the same time, the dealer agrees to repurchase these securities the next day at a slightly higher price. Thus, the buyer of the securities is in effect making the dealer a one-day loan secured by the obligations sold to him. The difference between the purchase and sale prices on the repo transaction is the interest the investor earns on his loan. Alternatively, the purchase and sale prices in a repo transaction may be identical; in that case, the dealer pays the investor some explicit rate of interest.

Often a dealer will take a speculative position that he intends to hold for some time. He might then do a repo for 30 days or longer. Such agreements are known as *term* repos.

From the point of view of investors, overnight loans in the repo market offer several attractive features. First, by rolling overnight repos, investors can keep surplus funds invested without losing liquidity or incurring a price risk. Second, because repo transactions are secured by top-quality paper, investors expose themselves to little or no credit risk.

The overnight repo rate generally is less than the Fed funds rate. The reason is that the many nonbank investors who have funds to invest overnight or very short term and who do not want to incur any price risk, have nowhere to go but the repo market because (with the exception of S&Ls and other DIs) they cannot participate directly in the Fed funds market. Also, lending money through a repo transaction is safer than selling Fed funds because a sale of Fed funds is an unsecured loan.

On term, as opposed to overnight, repo transactions, investors still have the advantage of their loans being secured, but they do lose some liquidity. To compensate for that, the rate on a repo transaction is generally higher the longer the term for which funds are lent.

Banks that make dealer loans fund them by buying Fed funds, and the lending rate they charge—which is adjusted daily—is the prevailing Fed funds rate plus a one-eighth to one-quarter markup. Because the overnight repo rate is lower than the Fed funds rate, dealers can finance their positions more cheaply by doing repos than by borrowing from banks.

A dealer who is bullish on the market will position large amounts of securities. If he's bearish, he will *short* the market, that is, sell securities he does not own. Since the dealer has to deliver any securities he sells whether he owns them or not, a dealer who shorts has to borrow securities one way or another. The most common technique today for borrowing securities is to do what is called a *reverse repo*, or simply a *reverse*. To obtain securities through a reverse, a dealer finds an investor holding the required securities; he then buys these securities from the investor under an agreement that he will resell the same securities to the investor at a fixed price on some future date. In this transaction, the dealer, besides obtaining securities, is extending a loan to the investor for which he is paid some rate of interest.

A repo and a reverse are identical transactions. What a given transaction is called depends on who initiates it; typically, if a dealer hunting money does, it's a repo; if a dealer hunting securities does, it's a reverse.

A final note: The Fed uses reverses and repos with dealers in government securities to adjust the level of bank reserves.

EURODOLLARS

Many foreign banks will accept deposits of dollars and grant the depositor an account *denominated in dollars*. So, too, will the foreign branches of U.S. banks. The practice of accepting dollar-denominated deposits outside of the U.S. began in Europe, so such deposits came to be known as *Eurodollars*. The practice of accepting dollar-denominated deposits later spread to Hong Kong, Singapore, the Middle East, and other centers around the globe. Consequently, today, *a Eurodollar deposit is simply a deposit denominated in dollars in a bank or bank branch outside the U.S.*, and the term *Eurodollar* has become a misnomer. To make things even more confusing, in December 1981, domestic and foreign banks were permitted to open *international banking facilities (IBFs)* in the U.S. Dollars deposited in IBFs are also Eurodollars.

Most Eurodollar deposits are for large sums. They are made by corporations—foreign, multinational, and domestic; foreign central banks and other official institutions; U.S. domestic banks; and wealthy individuals. With the exception of *call money*,[5] all Eurodeposits have a fixed term, which can range from overnight to five years. The bulk of Euro transactions are in the range of six months and under. Banks receiving Eurodollar deposits use them to make loans denominated in dollars to foreign and domestic corporations, foreign governments and government agencies, domestic U.S. banks, and other large borrowers.

Banks that participate in the Eurodollar market actively borrow and lend Euros among themselves, just as domestic banks borrow and lend in the Fed funds market. The major difference between the two markets is that in the market for Fed funds, most transactions are on an overnight basis, whereas in the Euromarket, interbank placements (deposits) of funds for longer periods are common.

For a domestic U.S. bank with a reserve deficiency, borrowing Eurodollars is an alternative to purchasing Fed funds. Also, for a domestic bank with excess funds, a *Europlacement* (i.e., a deposit of dollars in the Euromarket) is an alternative to the sale of Fed funds. Consequently, the rate on overnight Euros tends to closely track the Fed funds rate. It is also true that, as one goes out on the maturity scale, Euro rates continue to track U.S. rates, though less closely than in the overnight market.

Currently, *futures* for 3-month Eurodollar deposits are actively traded in Chicago and abroad as well.

FRAs

In recent years, Eurodollar futures have been joined by an over-the-counter (OTC) product known as a *forward rate agreement* (FRA, pronounced like frog with no g). Under a FRA, two parties agree to trade a specific amount of Euros for specified period at a specified rate on a specified future date. For example, the parties might agree to trade $5MM of 3-month Euros two months hence

---

[5]Call money is money deposited in an interest-bearing account that can be called (withdrawn) by the depositor on a day's notice.

at a rate of 9.50. What distinguishes a FRA from a forward trade is that, when the future date specified in the FRA agreement arrives, no Eurodeposit changes hands. Instead, there is a cash settlement. A FRA thus turns out to be not a forward trade, but an OTC futures contract that permits cash settlement only, not delivery. We talk about trades in which FRAs are used in Chapter 18.

COMMERCIAL PAPER

While some cash-rich industrial firms participate in the bond and money markets only as lenders, many more must, at times, borrow to finance either current operations or expenditures on plant and equipment. One source of short-term funds available to a corporation is bank loans. Large firms with good credit ratings, however, have an alternative source of funds that is cheaper, namely, the sale of commercial paper.

Commercial paper is an unsecured promissory note issued for a specific amount and maturing on a specific day. All commercial paper is negotiable, but most paper sold to investors is held by them to maturity. Commercial paper is issued not only by industrial and manufacturing firms, but by finance companies. Finance companies normally sell their paper directly to investors. Industrial firms, in contrast, typically issue their paper through dealers. Over the years, bank holding companies, municipalities, and municipal authorities have joined the ranks of commercial paper issuers.

The maximum maturity for which commercial paper may be sold is 270 days, since paper with a longer maturity must be registered with the Securities and Exchange Commission (SEC), a time-consuming and costly procedure. In practice, very little 270-day paper is sold. Most paper sold is in the range of 30 days and under.

Since commercial paper has such short maturities, the issuer rarely will have sufficient funds coming in before the paper matures to pay off his borrowing. Instead, he expects to *roll* his paper, that is, sell new paper to obtain funds to pay off his maturing paper. Naturally, the possibility exists that some sudden change in market conditions, such as when the Penn Central went "belly up" (bankrupt), might make it difficult or impossible for him to sell paper for some time. To guard against this risk, commercial paper issuers back all or a large proportion of their outstanding paper with lines of credit from banks.

The rate offered on commercial paper depends on its maturity, on how much the issuer wants to borrow, on the general level of money market rates, and on the credit rating of the issuer. Almost all commercial paper is rated with respect to credit risk by one or more of several rating services: Moody's, Standard & Poor's, and Fitch. While only top-grade credits can get ratings good enough to sell paper these days, there is still a slight risk that an issuer might go bankrupt. Because of this, and because of illiquidity, yields on commercial paper are higher than those on Treasury obligations of similar maturity.

Over the years, one pronounced change that has occurred in the domestic commercial paper market is that an increasing number of foreign entities, sovereigns, government agencies, banks, and corporates have taken to selling commercial paper in the U.S. money market. Some do so to raise dollars; others swap the dollars they get into their native currency.

In recent years, the growth in commercial paper outstanding has outstripped that of any other money market security with the result that the commercial paper market is now bigger than the Treasury bill market.

So long as banks were regarded as top-quality credits and made loans at tight spreads off Euro interbank rates, there was little or no opportunity for the growth in London of a market in Euro commercial paper. However, in recent years, conditions have changed. Banks are out of favor with investors; sovereigns, corporates, and others are in favor. Consequently, the spread has gone out of a lot of Eurobank lending, and a viable market in *Euro commercial paper* finally seems to be developing. Borrowers in this market cover the lot: they include sovereigns, government agencies, top corporate credits, and lower-quality corporate credits; they are domiciled anywhere from Iceland to Amman, but principally in Europe and the U.S.

INTEREST-RATE SWAPS

The rate that a borrower must pay depends on his credit, whether he wants to borrow fixed- or floating-rate money, and on the term for which he wants to borrow. Generally, if a credit is a particularly good credit, he will find not only that he is able to borrow more cheaply than other borrowers can, but that the advantage he enjoys over other borrowers in the rate he gets will be greatest when he borrows at a *fixed rate* for three to five years or longer. To reap the maximum benefit from his privileged access to the capital market, that's how a good credit should borrow. In contrast, a lesser credit will find that, when he borrows medium- to longer-term funds, his poor rating will penalize him least if he borrows at a *variable rate*.

Often, a top credit, say a Morgan to pick a bank name, will find that its comparative advantage lies in borrowing medium-term, fixed-rate money, whereas what it really wants to borrow is variable-rate money. Meanwhile somewhere, some single B corporate will be saying, "The penalty I have to pay for borrowing medium term at a fixed rate is awfully high, but fixed-rate money is what I really need." This sets the stage, realized a few prescient dealers in the early 1980s, for a *liability swap*. The triple-A credit borrows medium term at a fixed rate; the single-B credit borrows medium term at a variable rate; and then in effect, they *swap liabilities*—more precisely they swap on negotiated terms the future interest-rate payments each contracts to pay. Surprisingly, such a swap is *not a zero-sum game*. Far from it, the situation is a perfect example of the gains that can be realized from specialization along lines of comparative advantage (recall that Ricardo based his famous argument for free trade on differences in national comparative advantage, and the argument for free trade still stands today on that same ground). Triple A and single B can together reduce their joint costs of borrowing by each borrowing in the market where they get the best terms; then, using a swap, they can divvy up the savings they have realized *and* each end up with the type of liability they wanted in the first place.

All this may sound a touch esoteric and theoretical, but it's the basis in a nutshell of a business that grew, during the 1980s, from a zero base into one where outstandings are now measured in the hundreds of billions.

The swap we've just described, fixed for floating, is known as a *coupon swap*. A natural variation of this swap is to a *cross-currency swap*. Depending on who a borrower is, what currency he wants to borrow, and whether he wants to pay fixed or floating, it may be cheaper for him to do one sort of borrowing in one currency and then, via a swap or swaps, end up with a different borrowing in a different currency. For example, a borrower wanting to borrow dollars at a floating rate might find that his cheapest alternative is to borrow fixed-rate Swissy, swap it into fixed-rate dollars, and then do a coupon swap fixed to floating. The possibilities are endless and exist thanks to all sorts of market anomalies: differences in the terms at which corporates may borrow in different markets (e.g., Spain lacks a corporate bond market), differences in the way credits are perceived in different markets (e.g., to a German lender, Lufthansa is *the* national flag carrier, not just another credit), national differences in accounting practices or in tax policies, and so on. When an entity borrows X and then does several swaps to get to Y, which is what he wants, he is said *to cocktail* swaps.

As the swap market grew, swap terms became standardized. Today, swaps are quoted at Treasuries plus, with the understanding that the Treasuries plus rate is the fixed rate for a swap against *LIBOR*, the *London Interbank Offered Rate* for Eurodollar deposits (there are many LIBORs—3-month LIBOR, 6-month LIBOR, and so on). Those terms would leave a borrower in the commercial paper market who wanted to pay fixed, as a number of paper issuers do, with a spread risk: the spread of the LIBOR to the commerical paper rate. To eliminate that risk, the commercial paper issuer would first swap floating to floating—the commercial paper rate to LIBOR—and then he'd swap floating to fixed—LIBOR to Treasuries plus.

A borrower, unless he happens to also be, say, a bank dealer in swaps, lacks the resources to follow all of the ins and outs of and the opportunities in the swap market. So swaps are a big business for dealers who concoct and often cocktail them. Every big swap dealer—both bank and nonbank dealers are big in the business—runs a hedged swap book. Banks also use unhedged swaps as a tool of gap management.

The swap business began with the swapping of liabilities. Then some entrepreneurial type recalled that what's good for the goose is good for the gander, and *asset swaps* were born. In the past, an investor who held a fixed-rate, Canadian dollar bond and who then said, "Hey, what I'd really like to be in at this moment is Aussi-dollar, floating-rate paper," would figure that to make the switch he'd have to sell his bonds, do a foreign exchange transaction, and buy new paper. His friendly corporate finance swap advisor—bank or nonbank—now tells him otherwise: With a swap or two, he can get from the asset he has to a *synthetic* version of the asset he desires; and when the play he wants to make has run its course, he can return to his initial position simply by reversing the swaps he's put on. Today, asset swaps are a rapidly expanding part of the swap business.

OPTIONS

Another recent innovation in the money market is the introduction of trading in *options*, rights to buy or to sell at a fixed price over a preset period, certain money market securities and futures contracts for such securities. Options, like futures, are actively traded by hedgers, speculators, and arbitrageurs.

The most actively exchange-traded options are options on futures contracts. There are also over-the-counter (OTC) options traded on cash governments. In particular, *government-plus* mutual funds like to sell to dealers covered calls against their holdings of cash governments, their objective being to enhance yield on the fund. The dealers have not found this to be attractive business, since they are asked to buy calls for which they can find no natural buyers to take the other side of the trade.

The area in which dealers stand to make the biggest profit is in selling proprietory products. A dealer might, for example, sell a borrower a *cap* on the rate he must pay over time on a variable-rate loan priced at a spread to LIBOR. Such a cap is simply a series of options: on each (rate) reset date, the cap gives the borrower the right to pay either the cap rate or the formula, loan-agreement rate, whichever is lower. A *floor* in contrast is a series of options that promises a receiver of a variable rate the right to receive either the floor rate or the formula variable rate, whichever is higher. A *collar* is a cap cum floor that holds a rate within a given range.

In selling an option product, a dealer assumes a risk for which he naturally charges a fee. Since the risk is often large, so too is the fee. One way a borrower might use a collar would be to reduce the fee for buying a cap by collecting a fee for selling a floor.

In pricing options, caps, collars, and floors, dealers rely heavily on the classic Black-Scholes model for options pricing. This model, which was developed for the pricing of options on equities, must be modified in order to be applied to fixed-income securities. Also, theoreticians—*rocket scientists* or *quants* to the Street—are constantly tinkering with this model to improve its accuracy and extend its reach.

Dealers trade option products in a *book* in which they generally seek to maintain a hedged position. Because of their peculiar nature, an option—except when a dealer is lucky enough to have one option position that's the mirror image of another—is far more difficult to hedge than is a straight security. A testimony to the difficulty of both pricing and hedging options, particularly options on complex products, is the fact that more than one big house has taken a major bath in its options book.

The most recent option product to become faddish is a *swaption*, which is an option on an interest-rate swap.

CERTIFICATES OF DEPOSIT AND DEPOSIT NOTES

The maximum rate banks may pay on savings deposits and time deposits (a time deposit is a deposit with a fixed maturity) used to be set by the Fed through *Regulation Q*. Essentially, what Reg Q did was to make it impossible for banks and other depository institutions (who were each subject to their own versions of

Reg Q) to compete with each other for small deposits by offering depositors higher interest rates.[6] One exception to Reg Q was that, on large deposits, $100,000 or more, banks used to be able to pay any rate they chose so long as the deposit had a minimum maturity of 14 days. This exception led, so to speak, to the invention in 1961 of negotiable certificates of deposit.

There are many corporations and other large investors that have hundreds of thousands, even millions, of dollars they could invest in bank time deposits. Few do so, however, because they would lose liquidity by making a deposit with a fixed maturity. The illiquidity of time deposits and their consequent lack of appeal to investors led banks, who were free to bid high rates for large deposits, to begin to offer big investors *negotiable certificates of deposit, CDs* for short.

CDs are normally sold in $1MM units. They are issued at face value and typically pay interest at maturity. CDs can have any maturity longer than 14 days, and some 5- and even 7-year CDs have been sold (these pay interest semiannually). Most CDs, however, have an *original maturity* of one to six months.

Less than a decade ago, CDs issued by money center banks were a top money market instrument; and well over 100 billion of them were issued by money center and other large banks. Today, thanks to a variety of factors, which include the weakening of bank credits, the rise of the interest-rate swap market, deregulation of the rates that banks may pay on deposits, changes in reserve requirements, and the creation of the deposit note market, money center banks issue so few wholesale CDs that the Fed has ceased tracking outstanding large-denomination CDs issued by large banks.

Today, when large banks want to buy term deposits wholesale, they turn typically to the *deposit note* market. In this mar-

---

[6]The rates banks and thrifts may pay depositors were gradually deregulated under the Monetary Control Act (MCA) of 1980. Also the Banking Act of 1982 permitted depository institutions to begin offering unregulated rates on Super-NOW and money-market deposit accounts.

ket, banks sell notes that are designed to resemble and to trade in the secondary market like a corporate note or bond, but which are in fact a bank deposit. Original maturities on deposit notes range from 18 months out to five years. The lower cutoff is 18 months because on a deposit of this length or longer, reserve requirements drop to zero. Deposit notes pay a fixed rate, but what banks want today is floating-rate money; so, when they sell deposit notes, they usually do an interest-rate swap, fixed for floating, and end up in the best of all possible worlds: with no reserve requirements and with floating-rate debt that does not have to be constantly rolled as did short-term CDs.

Bank notes are a variant on deposit notes. A bank selling a bank note claims that the money garnered is *not* a deposit and that it therefore does not have to pay FDIC insurance premiums on it, a point that the FDIC has disputed. The deposit and bank note markets are a part of the medium-term note market we described above.

The old standard variety of 1-, 3-, and 6-month wholesale CDs are still issued by some regional banks and thrifts that are good credits. Currently, however, the CD market is but a glimmer of its past glory. "Today," said one banker in jest, "CD is an acronym for Certificate of Death."

Banks used to sell a lot of their CDs directly to investors. Sometimes, however, banks paid dealers a small fee to sell their new CDs. These same dealers made an active secondary market in bank CDs. Today, banks issue deposit notes through dealers who, depending on the situation, may act as agent or principal. These dealers also make a secondary market in deposit notes.

Bank paper, whatever form it takes, always trades at a spread above Treasuries of the same maturity. Investors regard bank paper as carrying some credit risk, which Treasuries do not; also, investors regard bank paper as being significantly less liquid than Treasuries; hence, investors demand some extra yield for buying bank paper rather than Treasuries.

In the spring of 1982, a futures market for 3-month CDs was launched in Chicago. For various reasons, including differences in the credit ratings of the top banks whose paper could be delivered by sellers of the contract, the CD contract died.

Eurodollar CDs

A Eurodollar time deposit, like a domestic time deposit, is an illiquid asset. Since some investors in Eurodollars wanted liquidity, banks in London that accepted such deposits began to issue *Eurodollar CDs*. These resemble domestic CDs except that, instead of being the liability of a domestic bank, they are the liability of the London branch of a U.S. bank, of a British bank, or of some other foreign bank with a branch in London.

Many of the Eurodollar CDs issued in London are purchased by other banks operating in the Euromarket. A large proportion of the remainder are sold to U.S. corporations and other U.S. institutional investors. Many Euro CDs are issued through dealers and brokers who also make a secondary market in these securities.

For the investor, a key advantage of buying Euro CDs is that they offer a higher return than do domestic CDs. The offsetting disadvantages are that they are less liquid and expose the investor to some extra risk (perceived by some, not by others) because they are issued outside of the U.S.

The Eurodollar CD market is, today, more active than the market domestic wholesale CDs, but less active than it was in the past. One change from the past is that, whereas quality-conscious American investors used to want top 10 American names only, today they are more likely to be willing to buy foreign-name paper. It has finally dawned on U.S. investors that a number of foreign banks are top credits and don't, in particular, have LDC debt weighting down their balance sheets to the extent that a number of U.S. money center banks do.

Yankee CDs

Foreign banks issue dollar-denominated CDs not only in the Euromarket, but in the domestic market through branches established there. CDs of the latter sort are frequently referred to as *Yankee CDs;* the name is taken from Yankee bonds, which are bonds issued in the domestic market by foreign borrowers.

Yankee, as opposed to domestic, CDs expose the investor to the extra (if only in perception) risk of a foreign name; they are also less liquid than domestic CDs. Consequently, Yankees trade at yields close to those on Euro CDs. The major buyers of Yankee CDs are corporations that are yield buyers and that "fund to dates" (i.e., invest in short-term securities maturing on the date funds will be needed).

Today, the market in Yankee CDs is, like that in domestic CDs, far smaller than it once was. To the extent that Yankee banks need term deposits of dollars, they find, for many of the same reasons that domestic banks do, that the best place to buy them is in the deposit note market. Yankee banks, including the top Japanese banks, are big buyers of funds in the deposit note market.

BANKERS' ACCEPTANCES

Bankers' acceptances (BAs) are an unknown instrument outside the confines of the money market. Moreover, explaining them isn't easy because they arise in a variety of ways out of a variety of transactions. The best approach is to use an example.

Suppose a U.S. importer wants to buy shoes in Brazil and pay for them four months later after he has had time to sell them in the U.S. One approach would be for the importer to borrow from his bank; however, short-term rates may be lower in the open market. If they are, and if the importer is too small to go into the open market on his own, then he can go the bankers' acceptance route.

In that case, he has his bank write a letter of credit for the amount of the sale and sends this letter to the Brazilian exporter. Upon export of the shoes, the Brazilian firm, using this letter of credit, draws a time draft on the importer's U.S. bank and discounts this draft at its local bank, thereby obtaining immediate payment for its goods. The Brazilian bank, in turn, sends the time draft to the importer's U.S. bank, which then stamps "accepted" on the draft (i.e., the bank guarantees payment on the draft and thereby creates an *acceptance*). Once this is done, the draft becomes an irrevocable primary obligation of the accepting bank. At this point, if the Brazilian bank did not want cash immediately, the U.S. bank would return the draft to that bank, which would hold it as an investment and then present it to the U.S. bank for payment at maturity. If, on the other hand, the Brazilian bank wanted cash immediately, the U.S. bank would pay it and then either hold the acceptance itself or sell it to an investor. Regardless of who ends up holding the acceptance, it is the importer's responsibility to provide its U.S. bank with sufficient funds to pay off the acceptance at maturity. If the importer fails to do so, the bank is still responsible for making payment at maturity.

Our example illustrates how an acceptance can arise out of a U.S. import transaction. Acceptances also arise in connection with U.S. export sales, trade between third countries (e.g., Japanese imports of oil from the Middle East), the domestic shipment of goods, and domestic or foreign storage of readily marketable staples. Currently, most BAs arise out of foreign trade; they may be in manufactured goods but more typically are in bulk commodities, such as cocoa, cotton, coffee, and crude oil. Because of the complex nature of acceptance operations, only large banks with well-staffed foreign departments act as accepting banks.

Bankers' acceptances closely resemble commercial paper in form. They are short-term, non–interest-bearing notes sold at a discount and redeemed by the accepting bank at maturity for full face value. The major difference is that payment on commercial paper is guaranteed only by the issuing company. In contrast, bankers' acceptances, in addition to carrying the issuer's pledge to pay, are backed by the underlying goods being financed and also carry the guarantee of the accepting bank. Consequently, bankers' acceptances are less risky than commercial paper and thus sell at slightly lower yields.

The big banks through which bankers' acceptances are originated generally keep some portion of the acceptances they create as investments. The rest are sold to investors through dealers or directly by the bank itself. Major investors in BAs are other banks, foreign central banks, money market funds, corporations, and other domestic and foreign institutional investors. BAs have liquidity because dealers in these securities make an active secondary market in those that are eligible for purchase by the Fed. Today, Japanese banks are major issuers of BAs in the U.S. domestic money market.

LOAN PARTICIPATIONS

Because the natural spread that once existed in bank commercial and industrial lending has been vanishing, money center banks are trying more and more to get into the business of investment banking. One step in this direction has been the banks' efforts to get out of their old make-a-loan-and-hold-it business into a new make-a-loan-and-distribute-it business.

Today, banks are selling basically two kinds of loans. First, they sell high-quality, short-term loans that they make under a bid option built into backup lines of credit that they extend to issuers of commercial paper. Banks sell participations in such loans to traditional money market investors who view them as a substitute for commercial paper, since such loans, like commercial paper, are short-term, unsecured, corporate IOUs; also, such loan participations carry yields in line with those on commercial paper.

The second sort of loan participations that money center banks sell is participations in big, lower-credit-quality loans that banks make to folks doing leveraged buys-outs (LBOs). Loan participations of this second sort generally have maturities ranging out to seven years and could in no sense be considered money market paper. The principal buyers of participations in LBO loans are foreign and other domestic banks.

MEDIUM-TERM NOTES

Medium-term notes (MTNs) began really as an extension of the commercial paper market to longer maturities. Basically, the issuer files, if it's not a bank—bank securities are exempt—a shelf registration with the SEC; it then posts rates for different maturities and sells its paper off the shelf through a dealer or group of dealers. MTNs are interest-bearing, not discount, securities, and they pay on a corporate bond basis.

Initially, maturities of MTNs ranged from nine months out to several years; the paper really was medium term. Then, as both investors and issuers became comfortable with the MTN market, maturities of new MTNs sold began to lengthen; MTN maturities now run out, in a few instances, as far as 30, even 40 years. Also, over time, all sorts of bells and whistles have been added to MTNs: some are all callable, some have put features, some are collateralized, some are floating rate, and so on. Gradually, MTNs have encroached on the turf of the traditional bond market. That raises the question of what differences, if any, there are today between MTNs and corporate bonds.

The answer is the corporate bonds differ from MTNs in that they are underwritten. If an issuer wants a goodly chunk of money, at least 100MM in a single maturity, on a given date at a given rate, it makes sense and is cost effective for him to go to the expense and trouble of doing an underwritten deal. If, alternatively, the issuer wants to raise money continuously in different maturities, he's better off selling MTNs. Finance companies are big issuer of MTNs. Because of their large and varied financing needs, it suits finance companies to make a continuous offering of their paper in different maturities and to receive continuous inflows of monies in different maturities.

MTNs are the success story of the 1980s. During this period, outstandings of MTNs went from literally zero to over 70 billion, and they are still growing at an explosive pace.

In recent years, dealers have tried to transplant the MTN market in the Euromarket. Their efforts have succeeded, but in early 1989, the Euro MTN market, though rapidly growing, was still a small market.

MUNICIPAL NOTES

Debt securities issued by state and local governments and their authorities are referred to as *municipal securities*. Such securities can be divided into two broad categories: bonds issued to finance capital projects and short-term notes sold in anticipation of the receipt of other funds, such as taxes or proceeds from a bond issue.

Municipal notes, which are an important money market instrument, are issued with maturities ranging from a month to a year or more. They bear interest, and minimum denominations are highly variable ranging anywhere from $5,000 to $5MM.

Most muni notes are general obligation securities; that is, payment of principal and interest is secured by the issuer's pledge of its full faith, credit, and taxing power. This sounds impressive, but as the spectacle of New York City tottering on the brink of bankruptcy brought home to all, it is possible that a municipality might default on its securities. Thus, the investors in evaluating the credit risk associated with publicly offered muni notes rely on ratings provided principally by Moody's and by Standard & Poor's.

The major attraction of municipal notes to an investor is that interest income on them is exempt or at least partially exempt from federal taxation and usually also from any income taxes levied within the state in which they are issued. The value of this tax exemption is greater the higher the investor's tax bracket, and the muni market thus attracts highly taxed investors, such as cash-rich corporations and wealthy individuals, and tax-free mutual funds designed to appeal to high-tax-bracket investors.

Large muni-note issues are sold to investors by dealers who obtain the securities either through negotiation with the issuer or through competitive bidding. The same dealers also make a secondary market in muni notes.

The yield a municipality must pay to issue notes depends on its credit rating, the length of time for which it borrows, and the general level of short-term rates. It used to be that a good credit risk could normally borrow at a rate well below the yield on governments of equivalent maturity because of the value to the investor of the tax exemption on municipal securities. Over the years, numerous complex changes and proposed changes in the federal tax code have lessened the value of the tax exemption attached to municipal securities. As a result, muni securities have, at times, actually traded at rates above Treasuries, which is precisely where they would trade were it not for the tax advantages they offer. Because of the ever-changing federal tax code and the consequent changing nature of the spread of Treasury to muni yields, some municipal bodies have begun, in recent times, to issue fully taxable securities and even to tap the Euromarket for money. Today, the muni market is an innovative place, and some muni issuers have even experimented with issuing zero-coupon securities.

MORTGAGE-BACKED, PASS-THROUGH SECURITIES

Mortgage-backed, pass-through securities are a hybrid debt instrument, one that has correctly been called the most complex security ever traded on Wall Street. Strictly speaking, pass-throughs are *not* a money market instrument, since their average life, a variable number at best, exceeds by far that of true money market instruments. However, pass-throughs are traded so actively and in such volume that it is hard to write about the money market without mentioning them here and there.

The Securities

Total residential mortgage debt outstanding exceeds $1.5 trillion, a sum far greater than total Treasury and federal agency debt outstanding. About a fifth of total residential mortgage debt has been used to back various types of negotiable securities, which in turn have been sold to investors. Of the more than $300 billion of mortgage-backed securities outstanding, all but about $20 billion are pass-throughs.

Pass-through securities are formed when mortgages are pooled and undivided interests in the pool are sold. *Pass-through* means that the cash flow from the underlying mortgages is *passed through* to the holders of the securities via *monthly payments of interest and principal. Undivided* means that each security holder has a proportionate interest in each cash flow generated by the pool. Payments of principal on a pass-through include *prepayments;* the latter occur when a mortgage holder prepays the remaining principal on his mortgage because he moves, refinances his mortgage, or less commonly, dies.

Pass-throughs have existed for decades, but they first made sense on a broad scale when several federal credit agencies began to provide credit guarantees and standards of uniformity for pass-throughs issued through them. This made pools of mortgages underlying pass-throughs readily marketable; in particular, the standardization of mortgage characteristics within pools made the resulting securities easier to analyze and, thus, more suitable for nontraditional mortgage investors. Also, the credit guarantee by a federal agency lessened investor concerns about collection of amounts due.

Mortgage originators such as savings and loans, commercial banks, and mortgage companies are active in pooling mortgages to back pass-throughs. An originator can either issue a private pass-through or file the necessary documents with a guarantor to issue a pass-through backed by the latter. The sale of a pass-through security represents a sale of assets; thus a pass-through is not a debt obligation of the originator.

The Issuers

Pass-throughs come in four flavors: there are Ginnie Mae, Freddie Mac, and Fanny Mae pass-throughs issued by federal or quasi-federal credit agencies; also, there are private pass-throughs. All pass-throughs are structured similarly, but differences exist among the four types with respect to the nature of the credit guarantee, if any; the size of the pools used; and the nature of the underlying mortgages. Because of these, different types of pass-throughs trade at varying spreads to each other.

Ginnie Mae pass-throughs are guaranteed by the *Government National Mortgage Association (GNMA)*, known to the Street as Ginnie Mae. The mortgage pools underlying GNMA pass-throughs are made up of mortgages that are either insured by the Federal Housing Administration (FHA) or guaranteed by the Veterans Administration (VA). GNMA pass-throughs are backed by the full faith and credit of the U.S. government. Pass-throughs issued by GNMA are fully modified: regardless of whether mortgage payments are received, the holders of GNMAs receive full and timely payment of principal and interest due them.

The *Federal Home Loan Mortgage Corporation (FHLMC)*, created by the Federal Home Loan Banks, also issues pass-throughs. These pass-throughs, the second largest class of pass-throughs, have been dubbed *Freddie Macs*. Freddie Macs are based on *conventional mortgages:* single-family residential mortgages that are neither guaranteed by the VA nor insured by the FHA. Whereas GNMA and FNMA (discussed next) guarantee the timely payment of interest and principal, FHLMC guarantees only the timely payment of interest and the ultimate payment (within a year) of principal. Because of the difference in guarantee, Freddie Macs trade at a spread above Ginnie Maes.

A third type of pass-through, *Fannie Maes*, is issued by the *Federal National Mortgage Association (FNMA)*. Fannie Maes are similar to Freddie Macs except that they carry a guarantee like the one on GNMAs.

The fourth type of pass-through security is private pass-throughs. In terms of volume outstanding, this type pass-through is the least important of the four types discussed.

Pass-throughs are based on mortgages with a 30-year life, but due to prepayments, they have, in normal times, if such exist, an expected life of only 12 years. Prepayments rates on pass-throughs vary with the level of mortgage rates. In years when mortgage rates are high, people choose not to move or to refinance, which cuts prepayment rates sharply. In contrast, low mortgage rates in 1986 brought forth a flood of refinancings of existing high-rate mortgages. The resulting high rate of prepayment on some high-coupon Ginnies caused these securities to be viewed and traded as oddball, short-term (2-year in some cases) Treasuries.

Pass-throughs are attractive to investors; they carry little or no credit risk but yield more than Treasuries of approximately similar maturity. Pass-throughs are bought by banks, savings and loan associations, GNMA mutual funds, and a range of other investors.

THE NEXT CHAPTER

In the next chapter, we discuss, with a little simple math: first, non–interest-bearing IOUs, T bills, and other short-term paper, which the Street refers to as discount securities or *discount paper;* second, interest-bearing (*coupon*) securities.

CHAPTER 4

DISCOUNT AND
INTEREST-BEARING SECURITIES

Banks deal in essentially two types of securities, *interest-bear-ing securities* and *discount paper*. Yields on these two types of instruments are calculated and quoted in quite different ways. Thus, a discussion of banking should be prefaced by some simple math which shows how yields on these different instruments are calculated and how they can be made comparable. We start with discount securities.[1]

TREASURY BILLS

To illustrate how a discount security works, we assume that an investor who participates in an auction of new Treasury *year bills* picks up $1MM of them at 10%. What this means is that the Treasury sells the investor $1MM of bills maturing in one year at a price approximately 10% below their face value. The "ap-proximately" qualifier takes a little explaining. Offhand, one would expect the amount of the discount to be the face value of the securities purchased times the rate of discount times the *fraction of the year* the securities will be outstanding. In our example, the discount calculated this way would equal $1MM times 10% times one full year, which amounts to $100,000. That

---

[1]For a complete description, see Marcia Stigum in collaboration with John Mann, *Money Market Calculations: Yields, Break-Evens, and Arbitrage* (Homewood, Ill.: Dow Jones-Irwin, 1981).

figure, however, is incorrect for two reasons. First, the bill is outstanding not for a year but for 52 weeks, which is 364 days. Second, the Treasury calculates the discount as if a year had only 360 days. So the fraction of the year for which the security is outstanding is 364/360, and the true discount on the security is:

$$\binom{\text{Discount on \$1MM of}}{\text{year bills issued at 10\%}} = \$1,000,000 \times 0.10 \times \frac{364}{360}$$

$$= \$101,111.11$$

Because the Treasury calculates the discount as if the year had 360 days, our investor gets his bills at a discount that exceeds \$100,000 even though he invests for only 364 days. The price he pays for his bills equals *face value minus the discount*, that is,

$$\binom{\text{Price paid for \$1MM of}}{\text{year bills bought at 10\%}} = \$1,000,000 - \$101,111.11$$

$$= \$898,888.89$$

Generalizing from this example, we can construct formulas for calculating both the discount from face value and the price at which T bills will sell, depending on their current maturity and the discount at which they are quoted. Let

D = discount from value value
F = face value
d = rate of discount
t = days to maturity
P = price

Then

$$D = F\left(\frac{d \times t}{360}\right)$$

and

$$P = F - D = F\left(1 - \frac{d \times t}{360}\right)$$

EQUIVALENT BOND YIELD

If an investor lent $1MM for one 365-day year and received at the end of the year $100,000 of interest plus the $1MM of principal invested, we would—calculating yield on a *simple interest basis*—say that he had earned 10%.[2] Using the same approach—earned return divided by principal invested—to calculate the return earned by our investor who bought a year bill at a rate of 10%, we find that, on a simple interest basis, he earned significantly *more than* 10%. Specifically,

$$\left(\begin{array}{c}\text{Return on a simple interest basis on}\\ \text{\$1MM of 10\% year bills held to maturity}\end{array}\right) = \frac{\$101,111.11}{\$898,888.89} \div \frac{364}{365}$$

$$= 11.28\%$$

In this calculation, because the bill matures in 364 days, it is necessary to divide by the fraction of the year for which the bill is outstanding to annualize the rate earned.

Treasury notes and bonds, which—unlike bills—are *interest bearing,* pay the holder interest equal to the face value times the interest (i.e., *coupon*) rate at which they are issued. Thus, an investor who bought $1MM of Treasury notes carrying a 10% coupon would receive $100,000 of interest during each year the securities were outstanding.

The way yields on notes and bonds are quoted, 10% notes selling at *par* (i.e., face value) would be quoted as offering a 10% yield. An investor who bought these notes would, however, have the opportunity to earn more than 10% simple interest. The reason is that interest on notes and bonds is paid in semiannual installments, which means that the investor can invest, during the second six months of each year, the first semiannual interest installment.

To illustrate the effect of this on return, consider an investor who buys at issue $1MM of 10% Treasury notes. Six months later, he receives $50,000 of interest, which we assume he rein-

---

[2]By *simple interest* we mean interest paid once a year at the end of the year. There is no compounding as, for example, on a savings account.

vests at 10%. Then at the end of the year, he receives another $50,000 of interest plus interest on the interest he has invested; the latter amounts to $50,000 times 10% times the one-half year he earns that interest. Thus, his total dollar return over the year is:

$$\$50,000 + (0.10)(\$50,000)(0.5) + \$50,000 = \$102,500$$

and the percentage return that he earns, expressed in terms of simple interest, is:

$$\frac{\$102,500}{\$1,000,000} = 10.25\%$$

Note that what is at work here is *compound interest;* any quoted rate of interest yields more dollars of return, and is thus equivalent to a higher simple interest rate, the more frequently interest is paid and the more compounding that can thus occur.

Because return can mean different things depending on the way it is quoted and paid, an investor can meaningfully compare the returns offered by different securities only if these returns are stated on a comparable basis. With respect to *discount* and *coupon* securities, the way yields are made comparable in the money market is by restating yields quoted on a *discount basis*—the basis on which T bills are quoted—in terms of *equivalent bond yield*—the basis on which yields on notes and bonds are quoted.

We calculated above that an investor in a year bill would, on a simple interest basis, earn 11.28%. This is slightly higher than the rate he would earn measured on an equivalent bond yield basis. The reason is that equivalent bond yield understates, as noted, the true return on a simple interest basis that the investor in a coupon security would earn if he reinvested interest. When adjustment is made for this understatement, the equivalent bond yield offered by a 10% year bill turns out to be something less than 11.28%. Specifically, it is 10.98%.

The formula for converting yield on a bank discount basis to equivalent bond yield is complicated for discount securities that have a current maturity of longer than six months, but that is no problem for investors and other money market participants because bill yields are always restated on dealers' quote sheets in terms of equivalent bond yield at the *asked* (or *offered*) rate (Table 4–1).

On bills with a current maturity of six months or less, equivalent bond yield is the simple interest rate yielded by a bill. Let

$$d_b = \text{equivalent bond yield}$$

Then, on a security quoted at the discount rate d, equivalent bond yield is given by

$$d_b = \frac{365 \times d}{360 - (d \times t)}$$

For example, on a 3-month bill purchased at 8%, equivalent bond yield is:

$$d_b = \frac{365 \times 0.08}{360 - (0.08 \times 91)} = 8.28\%$$

From the examples we have considered, it is clear that the yield on a discount security is *significantly less* when measured on a discount basis than when measured in terms of equivalent bond yield. The absolute divergence between these two measures of yield is, moreover, not constant. As Table 4–2 shows,

TABLE 4–1
Selected quotes on U.S. Treasury bills, January 12, 1989

Billions Outstanding	Days to Maturity	Maturity	Discount (%) Bid	Discount (%) Asked	Dollar Price	Equivalent Bond Yield
22.6	2	1/19/89	7.62	7.58	99.958	7.689
13.4	16	2/02/89	7.92	7.88	99.650	8.018
13.8	44	3/02/89	8.00	7.96	99.027	8.150
14.2	65	3/23/89	8.19	8.15	98.528	8.387
14.0	91	4/20/89	8.36	8.32	97.851	8.621
15.7	114	5/11/89	8.34	8.30	97.372	8.642
15.9	142	6/08/89	8.39	8.35	96.706	8.754
8.7	170	7/06/89	8.43	8.38	96.038	8.857
9.0	226	8/31/89	8.42	8.38	94.739	8.892
9.2	282	10/26/89	8.44	8.40	93.420	8.974
9.0	338	12/21/89	8.42	8.38	92.132	9.034

Source: J. P. Morgan Securities, Inc.

TABLE 4–2
Comparisons, at different rates and maturities, of rates of discount and equivalent bond yields

Yields on a Discount Basis (%)	Equivalent Bond Yields (%)		
	30-Day Maturity	182-Day Maturity	364-Day Maturity
6	6.114	6.274	6.375
8	8.166	8.453	8.639
10	10.227	10.679	10.979
12	12.290	12.952	13.399
14	14.362	15.256	15.904

the greater the yield and the longer the maturity of the security, the greater the divergence.

MONEY MARKET YIELD

Equivalent bond yield on a bill is calculated on the basis of a 365-day year. Bill rates are—to make them directly comparable to rates on CDs and other interest-bearing, money market instruments—often converted to a simple interest rate on a 360-day-year basis. That number, dubbed *money market yield,* is obtained by substituting 360 for 365 in the above equation for equivalent bond yield; specifically,

$$\begin{pmatrix} \text{Money market yield} \\ \text{on a bill} \end{pmatrix} = \frac{360 \times d}{360 - (d \times t)}$$

FLUCTUATIONS IN A BILL'S PRICE

Normally, the price at which a bill sells will rise as the bill approaches maturity. For example, to yield 9% on a discount basis, a 6-month bill must be priced at $95.45 per $100 of face value. For the same bill three months later (three months closer to maturity) to yield 9%, it must have risen in price to $97.72.

The moral is clear: If a bill always sold at the same yield throughout its life, its price would rise steadily toward face value as it approached maturity.

A bill's yield, however, is unlikely to be constant over time. Instead, it will fluctuate for two reasons: (1) changes may occur in the general level of short-term interest rates and (2) the bill will move along *the yield curve*. Let's look at each of these factors.

Short-Term Interest Rates

T bills are issued through auctions in which discounted prices (yields) are bid. The rate of discount determined at auction on a new bill issue depends on the level of short-term interest rates prevailing at the moment of the auction. The reason is straightforward. Investors who want to buy bills at the time of a Treasury auction have two alternatives—to buy new bills or to buy existing bills from dealers. This being the case, investors will not bid for new bills a rate of discount lower than that available on existing bills. If they did, they would be offering to buy new bills at a price higher than that at which they could buy existing bills. Also, investors will not bid substantially higher rates of discount (lower prices) than those prevailing on existing bills. If they did, they would not obtain bills, since they would surely be underbid by others trying to get a slightly better return than that available on existing securities. Thus, the prevailing level of short-term rates determines, within a narrow range, the discount established on new bills at issue.

However, the going level of short-term rates is not constant over time. It rises and falls in response to changes in economic activity, the demand for credit, investors' expectations, and monetary policy as set by the Federal Reserve System. Figure 4–1, which plots rates on 6-month T bills for the period 1980 through early 1989, portrays vividly the volatility of short-term interest rates. It shows both the sharp ups and downs that occurred in these rates as the Fed successively eased and tightened and the myriad of smaller fluctuations over the period in

FIGURE 4–1
Average auction rate on 6-month T bills (monthly averages, date
through April 1989)

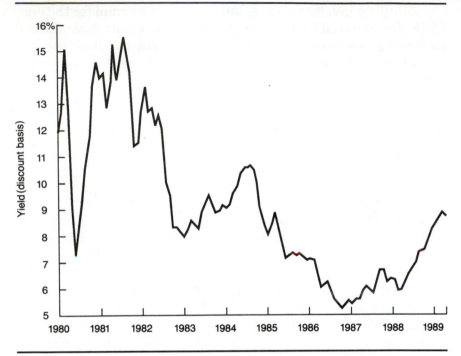

Source: Federal Reserve, J. P. Morgan Securities, Inc.

response to short-lived changes in other determinants of these
rates.

If the going level of short-term rates (which establishes the
rate at which a bill is initially sold) falls after a bill is issued,
then this bill—as long as its price doesn't change—will yield
more than new bills. Therefore, buyers will compete for this bill,
and in doing so, they will drive up its price and thereby force
down its yield until the bill sells at a rate of discount equal to
the new, lower going interest rate. Conversely, if short-term
rates rise after a bill is issued, the unwillingness of buyers to
purchase any bill at a discount less than that available on new
issues will drive down its price and thereby force up its yield.

The Yield Curve

Even if the going level of short-term interest rates does not change while investors hold bills, it would be normal for the rate at which they could sell their bills to change. The reason lies in the *yield curve*. How this works is a function of several factors, described below.

Price Risk

In choosing among alternative securities, an investor considers three things: risk, liquidity, and return. Purchase of a money market instrument exposes an investor to two sorts of risk: (1) *credit risk*—Will the issuer pay off at maturity? and (2) *price risk*—If the investor later sold the security, might he have to do so at a loss because interest rates had subsequently risen? Most money market investors are *risk averse:* they will accept lower yields to obtain lower risk.

The price risk to which bills and other money market instruments expose the investor is *larger* the *longer* their current maturity. To see why, suppose that short-term interest rates rise a full percentage point across the board; then the prices of all bill issues will drop, *but the price drop will be greater, the longer an issue's current maturity.* For example, a one percentage point rise in market rates would cause a 3-month bill to fall only $2,500 in price per $1MM of face value, whereas the corresponding price drop on a 9-month bill would be $7,600 per $1MM of face value.

The Slope of the Yield Curve

Because a 3-month bill exposes the investor to less price risk than a 9-month bill does, it will normally yield less than a 9-month bill. In other words, the bill-market yield curve, which shows the relationship between yield and current maturity, normally slopes upward, indicating that the longer the time to maturity, the higher the yield. We say "normally" because other factors, such as the expectation that interest rates are going to fall, may, as explained below, alter this relationship.

FIGURE 4–2
Yield curve for Treasury bills, January 12, 1989

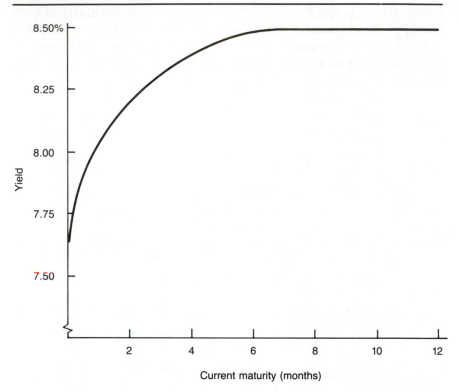

Current maturity (months)

To illustrate the concept of the yield curve, we have used the bid quotes in Table 4–1 to plot a *smoothed* yield curve in Figure 4–2. Our results show a normal upward-sloping yield curve. Lest you try doing the same and be disappointed, we should admit that we cheated a bit in putting together our demonstration yield curve. On January 12, 1989, there were many more bill issues outstanding than those quoted in Table 4–1. Had we plotted yields on all of these in Figure 4–2, we would have found that yield did not rise quite so consistently with maturity; the points plotted for some bill issues would have been somewhat off a smooth yield curve. Yields may be out of line for various reasons. For example, a bill issue maturing around a tax date might be highly desired by investors who had big tax payments to make and, for this reason, trade at a yield that was relatively low compared to yields on surrounding issues.

While the yield curve for short maturities normally slopes upward, its shape and slope vary over time. Thus, it is difficult to pinpoint a "normal" spread between, say, 1-month and 6-month bills. Yield spreads between different securities are always measured in terms of basis points. *A basis point is 1/100th of 1 percentage point.* Thus, if 5-month bills are quoted at 10.45 and 6-month bills at 10.56, the spread between the two is said to be 11 basis points (bp). A yield spread between two securities of 100 bp would indicate a full 1% (or *one point*) difference in their yields. A basis point is also frequently referred to as an 01 (pronounced *oh one*).

Yield Realized on Sales before Maturity

If an investor buys 1-year bills at 10% and holds them to maturity, he will earn, on a discount basis, precisely 10% over the holding period. If, alternatively, he sells the bills before maturity, he will earn 10% over the holding period only if he sells at 10%, a relatively unlikely outcome. If he sells at a lower rate, he will get a higher price for his bills than he would have if he had sold them at 10%, and he will therefore earn more than 10%. If, on the other hand, he sells at a rate higher than 10%, he will earn something less than 10%.

The holding-period yield, as a simple interest rate, that an investor earns on bills purchased at one rate and subsequently sold at another can be calculated using the formula

$$i = \frac{\text{Sales price} - \text{Purchase price}}{\text{Purchase price}} \div \frac{t}{365}$$

where t equals the number of days held. To illustrate, assume that an investor buys $1MM of 1-year bills at 10% and sells them three months later at 10.25%. His holding-period yield would be

$$i = \frac{\$924{,}166.67 - \$898{,}888.89}{\$898{,}888.89} \div \frac{91}{365} = 11.28\%$$

Bankers' Acceptances and Commercial Paper

In talking about discount securities, we have focused on bills since they are the most important discount security traded in the money market. All we have said about yields on bills is, however, equally applicable to yields on BAs and commercial paper, both of which are sold on a discount basis with the discount being calculated on a 360-day year.

INTEREST-BEARING SECURITIES

The stock-in-trade of the money market includes, besides discount securities, a variety of *interest-bearing* instruments: Treasury and federal agency notes and bonds, municipal notes and bonds, and bank certificates of deposit. Notes, bonds, and other interest-bearing debt securities are issued with a fixed *face value;* they mature at some specified date and carry a *coupon rate* which is the annual interest rate the issuer promises to pay the holder on the security's face value while the security is outstanding.

Some notes and bonds are issued in *registered* form; that is, the issuer keeps track of who owns its outstanding IOUs, just as a corporation keeps track of who owns its common stock. Other notes and bonds are issued in *bearer* form. To prove ownership of bearer security, the owner must produce or bear it. An issuer with $50MM of bearer bonds outstanding does not know where to send interest when a payment date comes along. Consequently, such securities carry *coupons,* one for each interest date. On the interest date, the investor or his bank clips the appropriate coupon from the security and sends it to the issuer's paying agent, who, in turn, makes the required payment.[3] Generally, interest payments are made semiannually on coupon se-

---

[3]The procedure is different on Treasury and agency securities, which are now being issued in *book-entry* form; computerized records of ownership maintained by the Fed and banks have been substituted for actual securities.

curities. Because notes and bonds carry coupons, the return paid on face value is called the *coupon rate,* or simply the *coupon.*

Notes and bonds with a short current maturity are referred to as *short coupons,* those with an intermediate current maturity (two to seven years) as *intermediate coupons,* and those with a still longer current maturity as *long coupons.*

Call and Refunding Provisions

Once a bond issue is sold, the issuer might choose to redeem it early. For example, if interest rates fell, the borrower could reduce his interest costs by refunding his loan; that is, by paying off outstanding high-coupon bonds and issuing new lower-coupon bonds.

For the investor, early repayment on a bond is almost always disadvantageous because a bond issuer will rarely be tempted to repay early when interest rates are rising, a time when it would be to the bondholder's advantage to move funds out of the issuer's bonds into new, higher-yielding bonds. On the other hand, early payment looks attractive to the issuer when interest rates are falling, a time when it is to the investor's advantage to keep funds invested in the issuer's high-coupon securities.

To protect investors making long-term commitments against frequent refundings by borrowers out to minimize interest costs, most bonds contain call and refunding provisions. A bond issue is said to be *callable* when the issuer has the option to repay part or all of the issue early by paying some specified redemption price to bondholders. Most bonds offer some call protection to the investor. Some are noncallable for life; others for some number of years after issue.

Besides call protection, many bonds offer refunding protection. Typically, long-term industrial bonds are immediately callable *but* offer 10 years of protection against calls for refunding. Such a bond is referred to as *callable except for refunding purposes.* If a bond offered refunding protection through 1995, that would be indicated on a dealer's quote sheet by the symbol NR95.

Call provisions usually specify that the issuer who calls a

bond must pay the bondholder a price above face value. The *call premium* frequently equals the coupon rate on early calls and then diminishes to zero as the bond approaches maturity.

Price Quotes

Note and bond prices are quoted in slightly different ways depending on whether they are selling in the new issue or the secondary market. When notes and bonds other than governments are issued, the price at which they are offered to investors is normally quoted as a *percentage* of face value. To illustrate, the corporate subordinated notes announced in Figure 4–3 were offered at a price of 97.994%, which means that the investor had to pay $97.994 for each $100 of face value. This percentage price is often called the bond's *dollar price*. The security described in Figure 4–3 was offered below par, so the actual yield it offered exceeded the coupon rate of 97⁄8%.

Once a note or bond issue is distributed and trading in it moves to the secondary market, prices are also quoted on a percentage basis but always, depending on the security, in 32ds, 8ths, 4ths, or halves. Table 4–3 reproduces, by way of illustration, a few quotes on Treasury notes and bonds posted by a dealer on January 12, 1989. The first bid 115–30, means that this dealer was willing to pay $115³⁰⁄₃₂, which equals $115.94

TABLE 4–3*
Selected quotes on U.S. Treasury notes and bonds, January 12, 1989

Publicly Held ($ billions)	Coupon	Maturity	Bid	Asked	Yield to Maturity	Yield Value (1/32)
5.23	13⅛	5/15/94	115–30	116– 0	9.245	0.0069
7.13	10½	8/15/89	105–31	106– 1	9.252	0.0062
1.48	11¾	2/15/01	118–29	119– 1	9.116	0.0038
1.91	10	5/15/10–05	107– 1	107– 1	9.145	0.0035
9.00	9	11/15/18	101– 8	101–10	8.872	0.0030

*The next-to-last issue quoted matures in 2010 but is callable in 2005. Its maturity, 5/15/10–05, indicates this.

Source: J. P. Morgan Securities, Inc.

FIGURE 4–3
Pricing announcement for subordinated notes

This announcement is under no circumstances to be construed as an offer to sell or as a solicitation of an offer to buy any of these securities. The offering is made only by the Prospectus.

New Issue   **March 2, 1989**

$200,000,000

BANK≡ONE.

BANC ONE CORPORATION

9⅞% Subordinated Notes due March 1, 2009

Price 97.994%

(Plus accrued interest, if any, from March 9, 1989 to the date of delivery.)

Copies of the Prospectus may be obtained in any State in which this announcement is circulated from only such of the undersigned or other dealers or brokers as may lawfully offer these securities in such State.

Merrill Lynch Capital Markets

Goldman, Sachs & Co.

Dean Witter Reynolds Inc.

per $100 of face value for that issue. The advantage of dollar pricing of notes and bonds is that it makes the prices of securities with different denominations directly comparable.

Treatment of Interest in Pricing

There's another wrinkle with respect to note and bond pricing. Typically, interest on notes and bonds is paid to the holder semi-annually on the coupon dates. This means that the value of a coupon security rises by the amount of interest accrued as a payment date approaches and falls thereafter by the amount of the payment made. Since notes and bonds are issued on every business day and consequently have coupon dates all over the calendar, the effect of accrued interest on the value of coupon securities would, if incorporated into the prices quoted by dealers, make meaningful price comparisons between different issues difficult. To get around this problem, the actual prices paid in the new issue and secondary markets are always the quoted dollar price *plus* any accrued interest. For example, if an investor—three months before a coupon date—bought $100,000 of 8% Treasury notes quoted at 100, he would pay $100,000 plus $2,000 of accrued interest:

$$\$100,000 + 0.5 \left[\frac{(0.08)(\$100,000)}{2} \right]$$

where $(0.08)(\$100,000)/2$ represents the $4,000 semiannual interest due on the notes.

Fluctuations in a Coupon Security's Price

When a new note or bond issue comes to market, the coupon rate on it is, with certain exceptions, set so that it equals the yield prevailing in the market on securities of comparable maturity and risk. This permits the new security to be sold at a price equal or nearly equal to par.

The price at which the security later trades in the secondary market will, like that of a discount security, fluctuate in response to changes in the general level of interest rates.

Yield to Maturity
To illustrate, let's work through a simple example. Suppose a new 6-year note with an 8% coupon is issued at par. Six months later, the Fed tightens, and the yield on comparable securities rises to 8.5%. Now what is this 8% security worth? Since the investor who pays a price equal to par for this "seasoned issue" is going to get only an 8% return, while 8.5% is available elsewhere, it is clear that the security must now sell at *less* than par.

To determine how much less, we have to introduce a new concept—*effective yield*. When an investor buys a coupon security at a *discount* and holds it to maturity, he receives a two-part return: the promised interest payment *plus* a capital gain. The capital gain arises because the security that the investor bought at less than par is redeemed at maturity for full face value. The investor who buys a coupon issue at a *premium* and holds it to maturity also receives a two-part return: interest payments due plus a capital *loss* equal to the premium paid.

For dollars invested in a coupon issue that sells at a discount or premium, it is possible to calculate the overall or effective rate of return received, which is the rate that the investor earns on his dollars when both interest received *and* capital gains (or losses) are taken into account. Naturally, an investor choosing between securities of similar risk and maturity will do so not on the basis of coupon rate, but on the basis of effective yield, referred to in the financial community as *yield to maturity*.

To get back to our example, it is clear that once rates rise to 8.5% in the open market, the security with an 8% coupon has to be priced at a discount sufficiently great so that its yield to maturity equals 8.5%. Figuring out how many dollars of discount this requires involves complicated calculations. Dealers used to use bond tables, but all have now switched to bond calculators or computers. A trader can thus determine in a few seconds that, with interest rates at 8.5%, a $1,000 note with an 8% coupon and a 3½-year current maturity must sell at $985.13 (a discount of $14.87) to yield 8.5% to maturity.

Current Maturity and Price Volatility

A capital gain of $14.87, which is what the investor in our discounted 8% note would realize if he held it to maturity, will raise effective yield more the faster this gain is realized (the shorter the current maturity of the security). Conversely, this capital gain will raise effective yield less the more slowly it is realized (the longer the current maturity of the security).[4]

---

[4]If you don't see this, just think—somewhat imprecisely—of the capital gain as a certain number of dollars of extra interest paid out in yearly installments to the investor as his security matures. Clearly, the shorter the security's current maturity, the higher these extra annual interest installments will be and, consequently, the higher the overall yield to the investor.

But if this is so, then a one-half percentage point rise in the yield on comparable securities will cause a larger fall in price for a security with a long current maturity than for one with a short current maturity. In other words, the discount required to raise a coupon security's yield to maturity by one-half percentage point is *greater* the *longer* the security's maturity.

By reversing the argument above, it is easy to see that if six months after the 6-year, 8% note in our example was issued, the yield on comparable securities *fell* to 7.5%, the value of this note would be driven to a *premium;* that is, it would sell at a price above par. Note also that a one-half percentage point *fall* in the yield on comparable securities would force an outstanding high-coupon security to a *greater* premium the *longer* its current maturity.

As these observations suggest, when prevailing interest rates change, prices of long coupons respond more dramatically than prices of short coupons. Figure 4–4 shows this sharp contrast. It pictures, for a $1,000 note carrying an 8% coupon, the relationship between *current* maturity and the discount that would prevail if the yield on comparable securities rose to 8.5% or to 10%. It also plots the premium to which a $1,000 note with an 8% coupon would, depending on its current maturity, be driven if the yield on comparable securities fell to 6%.

Coupon and Price Volatility

The volatility of a note or bond's price in the face of changing interest rates also depends on its coupon; the *lower* the coupon, the *greater* the percentage change in price that will occur when rates rise or fall. To illustrate, consider two notes with 4-year current maturities. Note A has an 8% coupon; note B a 6% coupon. Both are priced to yield 8%. Suppose now that interest rates on comparable securities rise to 10% (the Fed tightens). Note A will fall in price by $6.46; since it was initially priced at $100, that works out to a 6.46% fall in value. Note B's dollar price drops from $93.27 to $87.07—a $6.20 fall, which equals a 6.65% loss of value. The reason for the greater percentage fall in the price of the low-coupon note is that capital appreciation represents a greater proportion of promised income (capital appreciation plus coupon interest) on the low coupon than on the

FIGURE 4–4
Premiums and discounts at which a $1,000 note with an 8% coupon would sell, depending on current maturity, if market yields on comparable securities were 6%, 8.5%, and 10%

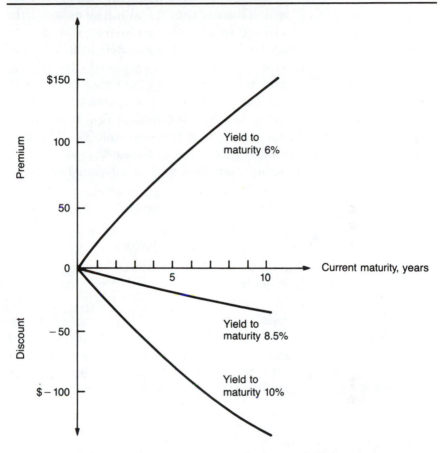

high coupon. Therefore, for the low-coupon note's yield to maturity to rise two percentage points, its price has to fall relatively *more* than that of the high-coupon note.

Yield Value of 1/32

Prices of government and federal agency securities are quoted in 32ds. The greater the change in yield to maturity that results from a price change of 1/32, the less volatile the issue's price will be in the face of changing interest rates. As a result, dealers include on their quote sheets for such securities a column titled *Yield Value of 1/32*. Looking back at Table 4–3, we see that the yield value of 1/32 on the 13⅛s Treasury notes maturing on May 15, 1994, was 0.0069, which means that a fall in the asked price on this security from 116– 0 to 115–29 (a 1/32 fall) would have raised yield to maturity by 0.0069%, from 9.245 to 9.252. The yield value of 1/32 drops sharply as current maturity lengthens. Thus, on the 9% Treasury bonds maturing on October 20, 2018 (the last line of the table), the yield value of 1/32 was only 0.0030, indicating that these notes would have had to fall in value by approximately 2.3/32 for their yield to rise 0.0069%. The contrast in yield values of 1/32 would have been far sharper had we compared a T bond nearing maturity with a 30-year bond.

Current Yield

So far we have focused on yield to maturity, which is the yield figure always quoted on coupon securities. When the investor buys a note or bond, he may also be interested in knowing what rate of return interest payments per se will give him on the principal he invests. That rate is called *current yield*.

To illustrate, consider our earlier example of a note with an 8% coupon selling at $985.13 to yield 8.5% to maturity. Current yield on this note would be: ($80/$985.13) × 100, or 8.12%. On a discount note or bond, current yield is always less than yield to maturity; on a premium bond, it exceeds yield to maturity.

THE YIELD CURVE

From the examples we have worked through, it is clear that investors in notes and bonds expose themselves, like buyers of discount securities, to a *price risk*. Moreover, even though longer-term rates fluctuate less violently than do short-term rates (Figure 4–5), the price risk associated with holding debt securities tends to be greater the longer the current maturity. Thus, one would expect the yield curve to slope upward over the full maturity spectrum. And *normally,* it does.

FIGURE 4–5

Short-term rates are more volatile than long-term rates: Rate comparison—3-month T bill, 5-year note, and 30-year bond (monthly averages through April 1989)*

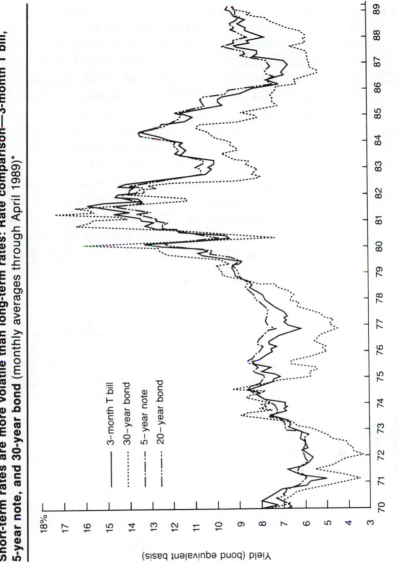

*The 20-year bond was discontinued in early 1977, and the 30-year bond was added.

Source: Federal Reserve, J. P. Morgan Securities, Inc.

Price risk, however, is not the only factor affecting the shape of the yield curve. Borrowers' and investors' *expectations* with respect to future interest rates are also an important—at times dominant—factor.

If the general expectation is that interest rates are going to rise, investors will seek to keep their money in short coupons to avoid getting locked into low-yield, long coupons. Borrowers, on the other hand, will try to lengthen the maturity of their out-standing debt to lock in prevailing low rates for as long as possi-ble. Both responses tend to force short-term rates down and long-term rates up, thereby accentuating the upward slope of the yield curve. The expectation that interest rates would rise is one reason that the December 11, 1987, yield curve sloped steeply upward (see Figure 4–6).

People, of course, may expect interest rates to fall. When

FIGURE 4–6
Three upward-sloping yield curves at different points in time

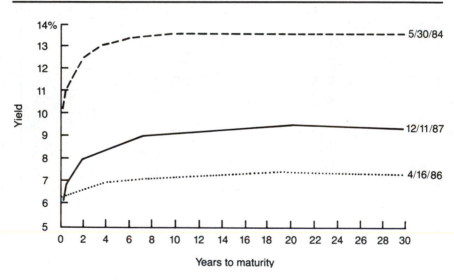

Curves plot yields on U.S. Treasury securities.

Source: J. P. Morgan Securities, Inc.

this is the case, investors respond by buying long coupons in the hope of locking in a high yield. In contrast, borrowers are willing to pay extremely high short-term rates while they wait for long rates to fall so that they can borrow more cheaply. The net result of both responses is that, when interest rates are expected to fall, the yield curve (or at least some part of it) may *invert,* with short-term rates above long-term rates. Figure 4–7 pictures the yield curves on March 28, 1989, and March 26, 1980, when people anticipated a fall in rates. Note that the slopes of both curves are negative except at very short current maturities.

If, inspired by our yield curves, you start pouring over dealer quote sheets on governments, you are bound to discover some out-of-line yields. The reasons are varied.[5] For one thing, sale of a large new issue may cause a temporary upward bulge in the yield curve in the maturity range of the new issue. Also, a security with an out-of-line yield may have some special characteristic. Some government bonds (*flower bonds* to the Street) are acceptable at par in payment of federal estate taxes when owned by the decedent at the time of death. These bonds, which all sell at substantial discounts, have yields to maturity much lower than those on straight government bonds.

In calculating the yield on discount securities, we found a considerable discrepancy between yield measured on a discount basis and equivalent bond yield. There are also many discrepancies—albeit smaller ones—between the ways that interest is measured and quoted on different interest-bearing securities. For example, interest on Treasury notes is calculated for actual days on the basis of a 365-day year, while interest on CDs is calculated for actual days on the basis of a 360-day year. Thus, a 1-year CD issued at 10% would yield a higher return than a 10% year note selling at par. Partially offsetting this advantage,

---

[5]One trivial reason may be a mistake in the quote sheet. These are typically compiled daily in great haste with the result that errors creep in. For this reason, such sheets often carry a footnote stating that the quotes are believed to be reliable but are not "guaranteed."

FIGURE 4–7
Two inverted yield curves at different points in time

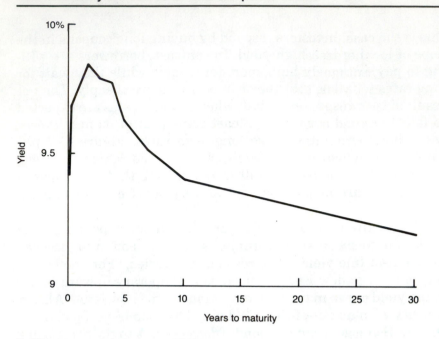

B. U.S. government yield curve on 3/26/80

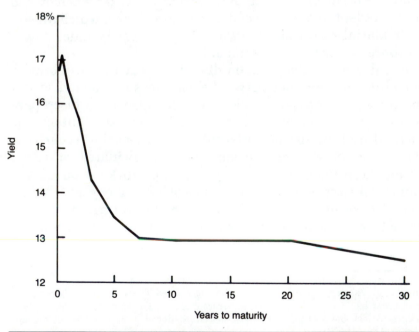

Source: J. P. Morgan Securities, Inc.

however, is the fact that a 1-year CD would pay interest only at maturity, whereas a 1-year note would pay it semiannually. This disadvantage disappears, however, on CDs with a maturity longer than 1 year, since such CDs pay interest semiannually.

Another discrepancy: When government notes and bonds are sold, accrued interest is calculated between coupon dates on the basis of actual days passed since a coupon date, whereas on agency securities, it accrues as if every month had 30 days. Thus, for example, agency securities accrue no interest on October 31, but they do accrue interest on February 30!

These and the many other minor discrepancies among yields on interest-bearing securities have little importance for understanding the workings of the money market, but they are important to the market participant out to maximize return.

The *Normal* Shape of the Yield Curve

Earlier, we said that the yield curve *normally* has a positive slope. Just how often is "normally"? Figure 4–8 plots for recent years the yield on the 30-bond *minus* the yield on the 3-month bill. A *negative* spread indicates that, over the range from 3 months to 30 years, the yield curve was *inverted*. A *positive spread,* by far more typical, indicates that over this range the yield curve was *positively sloped.*

ZERO-COUPON SECURITIES

Technically, a Treasury bill is a zero-coupon security, but no one ever calls it that. Streetfolk refer to bills, BAs, and commercial paper as discount securities. Such paper is all short in term: typically, it's 1-, 3-, or 6-month paper; in the case of the year bill, it's 364-day paper.

While most discount paper is short in term, there is no reason why the concept of no-payment-of-coupon-interest could not be applied to a note or bond with a 2-, or 20-, or even a 30-year current maturity. And, as noted in Chapter 2's discussion of STRIPs (stripped Treasuries), precisely this has been done. Longer-term securities that pay no interest are referred to as

FIGURE 4–8

The yield on the 30-year bond minus the yield on T bills (monthly averages, bond equivalent basis, through April 1989); during periods where the spread is *negative,* the yield is *inverted*

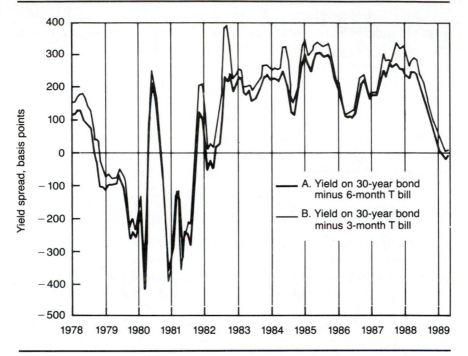

Source: J. P. Morgan Securities, Inc.

zero-coupon securities (*zeros* for short). Treasury zeros are always created by stripping interest-bearing Treasury bonds. An assortment of other issuers issue zeros directly to the market. Such securities are popular with investors such as pension funds that receive tax-sheltered income and want to avoid uncertainty with respect to the rate at which they will be able to reinvest coupon interest they receive in future years.

Naturally, a zero-coupon security sells at a discount from its value at maturity; also, the discount is bigger (1) the *longer the current maturity* of the zero and (2) the *greater the yield* at which interest-bearing securities of similar maturity trade. With respect to (2), note that, unless some tax or other advantage affects

TABLE 4–4
Price of a zero-coupon security at selected current maturities and yields (on a bond equivalent basis)*

Current Maturity (years)	Yield to Maturity (%)	Price of a Zero-Coupon Security (per $100 of face value)
2	8	85.4804
2	12	79.2093
10	8	45.6386
10	12	31.1804
20	8	20.8289
20	12	9.7222

*The formula for this calculation is

$$P = \frac{100}{\left(1 + \frac{y}{2}\right)^N}$$

where P equals price, y equals yield expressed as a decimal, and N equals the number of coupon periods corresponding to current maturity.

the value to investors of zeros versus coupon securities, one would expect a 10-year STRIP to trade at a discount sufficient to make its yield to maturity roughly equal to that of an interest-bearing, 10-year Treasury note.

Table 4–4 gives some numbers that illustrate how the price at which a zero trades is affected by its current maturity and the yield to maturity at which it trades.

CHAPTER 5

DURATION AND CONVEXITY

In this chapter, we treat two bond-market concepts that often appear in money market discussions: duration and convexity.[1]

DURATION

It's impossible to derive results concerning duration without using simple calculus. A nonmathematical reader, willing to accept such results on faith, can easily follow our discussion of duration with *no* loss of continuity. Proofs of all results presented in this chapter will be found in the forthcoming revision of Stigum's *Money Market Calculations* (Homewood, Ill.: Dow Jones-Irwin). For ease of reference, we present in the box on page 93 all of the notation used in this chapter. All math used is limited to *simple algebra.*

In recent years, especially as interest rates have become more volatile, the concept of duration has gained much attention among portfolio managers, traders, and other money market participants. In particular, duration calculations are widely used in immunizing portfolios, in hedging trading positions, in comparing investment alternatives, and in performing various other analyses. Duration has become a key measurement for

---

[1]The author would like to thank Lawrence Ng, founder of SpectraSoft, for his collaboration in writing this chapter.

List of Principal Symbols Used in Chapter 5*

---

c coupon rate (*as a decimal*)

D duration

D' modified duration

$\mathcal{P}_i$ payment received at the end of year i

P the price (per \$1 of face value) at which a coupon security trades

PV present value

t_i time, measured in years, to the receipt of payment $\mathcal{P}_i$

v_{32} yield value of $1/32$†

v_{01} price value of an 01†

w weighted average of time periods (of t_i)

y yield to maturity (*as a decimal*)

Δ change in a variable (e.g., ΔP denotes change in price)

---

*We use a few subscripts. There is nothing mathematical about them as they denote names, not operations. To illustrate, suppose we want to represent *in symbols* the Hanson family, comprised of Helen, Peter, and Marcia. A mathematician would observe that the important identifying characteristic of the group is that they are all Hansons; and, to identify the individuals in the group, he would use subscripts as follows: H_h for Helen Hanson, H_p for Peter Hanson, and H_m for Marcia Hanson. *Moral:* If you understand how surnames and given names are used, you understand all you need know about subscripts.

†The concepts, the yield value of $1/32$ and the price value of an 01, were introduced in Chapter 4.

---

fixed-income securities; and frequently, it is quoted between a buyer and a seller before a trade is executed.

The Concept

A bond's current maturity gives a notion of the *futurity* of the cash flows that it will throw off over time; clearly, the owner of a 20-year bond will have to wait 10 years longer for a payback of principal than will the owner of a 10-year bond. Nonetheless, current maturity is an *imperfect* measure of futurity.

     Table 5–1 illustrates this; it describes the cash flows (*per \$1 of face value*) thrown off by three different notes, all having a 3-

TABLE 5–1
Cash flows generated, *per $1 of face*
***value*, by three different 3-year notes**

	Year 1	Year 2	Year 3
Note A	0.00	0.00	1.00
Note B	0.10	0.10	1.10
Note C	0.20	0.20	1.20

year current maturity.[2] Note A is a zero-coupon security, and the futurity of its cash flow clearly coincides with its current maturity, three years. But if this is so, then, since note B pays significant amounts of coupon interest in years 1 and 2, the futurity of its cash flow must be something less than three years; and the futurity of note C's cash flow must be still less, since it pays yet more coupon interest.

Clearly, we need an alternative measure of futurity. One approach would be to calculate, for a note or bond, a *weighted average* of the *time periods* an investor must wait to receive all promised cash flows. Specifically, we could calculate a *weighted average* of the *time periods* in which cash flows occur, with the *weights* being *the cash flows* that actually occur in each time period. To illustrate, let

w = weighted average of time periods

t_i = time, measured in years to the receipt of payment $\mathcal{P}_i$

and

$\mathcal{P}_i$ = payment received at t_i

Then, for a 3-year note, such a weighted average is given by the following expression:

$$w = \frac{\mathcal{P}_1 t_1 + \mathcal{P}_2 t_2 + \mathcal{P}_3 t_3}{\mathcal{P}_1 + \mathcal{P}_2 + \mathcal{P}_3}$$

---

[2]Because bonds are priced as so many dollars per $100 of face value, it's standard practice, in deriving bond formulas, to express all variables per $100 of face value. Doing so, however, forces one to do a lot of confusing dividing through and multiplying by 100. It's far easier to work, as we do, with all variables expressed per $1 of face value and yields expressed as decimals.

TABLE 5–2

The weighted-average time to payment, w, of the cash flows generated by each of the notes described in Table 5–1

I. The formula:

$$w = \frac{\sum\limits_{i=1}^{3} \mathscr{P}_i t_i}{\sum\limits_{i=1}^{3} \mathscr{P}_i}$$

II. The calculations:

Note A: $w = \dfrac{0 + 0 + (1)(3)}{0 + 0 + 1} = \dfrac{3}{1} = 3$

Note B: $w = \dfrac{(0.1)(1) + (0.1)(2) + (1.1)3}{0.1 + 0.1 + 1.1} = \dfrac{3.6}{1.3} = 2.77$

Note C: $w = \dfrac{(0.2)(1) + (0.2)(2) + (1.2)3}{0.2 + 0.2 + 1.2} = \dfrac{4.2}{1.6} = 2.63$

which, if one uses a *sum sign,* reduces to:[3]

$$\underline{w} = \frac{\sum\limits_{i-1}^{3} \mathscr{P}_i t_i}{\sum\limits_{i-1}^{3} \mathscr{P}_i}$$

If we use this formula to calculate the average waiting time to payment for the notes described in Table 5–1, we get the results shown in Table 5–2. As we'd expect, the futurity—by this measure—of A's cash flow (3 years) exceeds the futurity of B's cash flow (2.77 years), which in turn exceeds the futurity of C's cash flow (2.63 years).

Present Value

In seeking to measure the futurity of a stream of payments, we have, however, neglected something important. *So long as interest rates differ from zero, dollars to be received in different peri-*

---

[3]Note, the *sum sign,* $\sum\limits_{i=1}^{3}$, is simply a convenient abbreviation that says, "Add these terms using appropriate values in each of *three* time periods."

ods differ in value. To allow for this, we must introduce the concept of *present value.*

Suppose that someone offered to "sell" you $1 for delivery today. Obviously, the dollar offered would be worth exactly $1. A more interesting question is: What would $1 to be delivered one year from now be worth? As a moment's thought suggests, it would be worth whatever *principal* you would have to invest today in order that principal *plus* accrued interest equal $1 in one year.

Let

I = principal invested

i = simple interest rate (as a decimal) available on a 1-year investment

Then, by solving the expression,

$$I + iI = \$1$$

for I, we can determine that the *present value* (PV), as it's called, of $1 to be received one year from now is given by

$$PV = \frac{\$1}{(1 + i)}$$

Note several things about present value. First, it is a *discounted* value of a future sum. Second, i is the rate at which this sum is discounted. Third, the higher i, the smaller is the present value of the future sum.

Naturally, *the more years one must wait to get $1, the less it will be worth today, that is, the smaller will be its present value.* By continuing the approach we used above, we could easily show that the present value of $1 to be received *two* years hence is given by the expression

$$PV = \frac{\$1}{(1 + i)^2}$$

Also, and more generally, the present value of $1 to be received some indefinite number of years, n, hence is given by the expression

$$PV = \frac{\$1}{(1 + i)^n}$$

MACAULAY'S DURATION

Once we think in terms of present value, it's clear that the mean waiting time to payment, w, that we calculated above is flawed because it averages apples and oranges—dollars to be received in different periods. To correct for this, we must use as weights not the dollars to be received in each period, but rather the present values of these dollars. This approach gives us a measure of futurity known as *duration* (or *Macaulay's duration* after its author).

In developing a formula for duration, we consider, for simplicity, a note or bond that pays coupon interest only *once a year*, at the end of the year. Also, in calculating the present values of the cash flows thrown off by the security, we follow the standard approach for pricing a bond, namely, we *discount all cash flows in all periods at the yield to maturity at which the security currently trades*. For an investor who wants to know how much money he'd have by the time a bond matured if he bought that bond today and reinvested all coupons paid before maturity, this approach is equivalent to the investor assuming that he'd be able to reinvest every coupon at a rate equal to the bond's current yield to maturity. For him to be able to do that, the yield curve would have to be *flat* and *constant over time*, a pretty strong assumption (but nonetheless one that the Street often makes in various calculations). Let

D = duration

c = coupon rate (as a decimal)

t_i = time in years to the receipt of payment $\mathcal{P}_i$

y = yield to maturity (as a decimal)

Then, the duration of a note—again we use a 3-year note—can be written in symbols as follows:[4]

$$D = \frac{\left(\dfrac{c}{(1+y)}\right) t_1 + \left(\dfrac{c}{(1+y)^2}\right) t_2 + \left(\dfrac{c+1}{(1+y)^3}\right) t_3}{\dfrac{c}{(1+y)} + \dfrac{c}{(1+y)^2} + \dfrac{c+1}{(1+y)^3}}$$

---

[4]Note a number or expression written next to another expression in parentheses, small or large, means multiply the one by the other.

In this expression, $(c + 1)$ represents the note's cash flow, per \$1 of face value, in year 3, the year in which principal is repaid. Also, since we're considering a 3-year note, $t_1 = 1$, $t_2 = 2$, and $t_3 = 3$.

Finally, an important observation: *The denominator in our expression for the duration of a note equals the sum of the present values of the note's cash flows in different periods; this sum in turn equals the price (P) that a rational investor would pay for the note.*[5] Thus, for a 3-year note that pays interest annually, duration can be rewritten as follows.

Let

P = the price (per \$1 of face value) at which a bond trades

Then,

$$D = \frac{1}{P}\left(\frac{1c}{(1 + y)} + \frac{2c}{(1 + y)^2} + \frac{3(c + 1)}{(1 + y)^3}\right)$$

Using the expression we've just obtained for duration, we can now calculate the duration of each of the 3-year notes described in Table 5–1. The results of these calculations are given in Table 5–3. A comparison of the numbers in Tables 5–2 and 5–3 shows that the addition of present value to our calculation of the futurity of the cash flows thrown off by a note *lowers* the number obtained. This makes sense, since *the present value of a future sum is always smaller than that sum.*

From our expression for duration, D, it's easy to generalize that, for a security yielding annual payments, $\mathcal{P}_i$, in any or all of n years, duration is given by the expression:

$$D = \frac{1}{P}\left(\sum_{i=1}^{n} \frac{t_i \mathcal{P}_i}{(1 + y)^i}\right)$$

where i denotes through the ith year.

This expression in turn can be modified to allow for a security that pays coupon interest *semiannually,* but we need no such general expression to continue our discussion. Because du-

---

[5]See the forthcoming revision of Stigum's *Money Market Calculations* (Homewood, Ill.: Dow Jones-Irwin).

TABLE 5–3

Calculating the duration of each of the three 3-year notes described in Table 5–1 (formula used is that given on p. 97; all three notes are assumed to be trading at a yield to maturity, y, of 8%)

Note A: $D = \dfrac{0 + 0 + 3\left(\dfrac{1}{(1 + 0.08)^3}\right)}{0 + 0 + \dfrac{1}{(1 + 0.08)^3}} = 3$

Note B: $D = \dfrac{1\left(\dfrac{0.1}{(1.08)^1}\right) + 2\left(\dfrac{0.1}{(1.08)^2}\right) + 3\left(\dfrac{1.1}{(1.08)^3}\right)}{\dfrac{0.1}{(1.08)^1} + \dfrac{0.1}{(1.08)^2} + \dfrac{1.1}{(1.08)^3}} = 2.74$

Note C: $D = \dfrac{1\left(\dfrac{0.2}{(1.08)^1}\right) + 2\left(\dfrac{0.2}{(1.08)^2}\right) + 3\left(\dfrac{1.2}{(1.08)^3}\right)}{\dfrac{0.2}{(1.08)^1} + \dfrac{0.2}{(1.08)^2} + \dfrac{1.2}{(1.08)^3}} = 2.59$

ration calculations become messy, no one does them manually; every trader has a programmed computer into which he plugs the issue, the price, and the settlement date.

Determinants of Duration

From our equation for duration, it's clear that the duration of a note or bond depends on *three* variables: (1) its current maturity; (2) its coupon, c; and (3) its yield to maturity, y, at which future cash flows from it are discounted.

As intuition and the numbers in Tables 5–2 and 5–3 suggest, the duration of a security will, *all else constant,* be *higher the longer its current maturity,* the *lower its coupon,* and the *lower the yield* at which it currently trades.[6]

---

[6]Duration is a function of three variables. Thus, our saying *all else constant* is equivalent in mathematical terms to our saying, "If we took the partial derivatives of duration with respect to each of these three variables, the signs of the expressions we'd get would be *positive* for the partial derivatives with respect to maturity and to yield to maturity, *negative* for the partial derivative with respect to coupon."

Since our topic is the money market, we pause to note that many money market securities are in effect *zero-coupon* securities. This is true of bills, BAs, short-term CDs, commercial paper, muni notes, Treasury notes and bonds in their last coupon period, and Treasury STRIPs. *The duration of every zero-coupon security equals its current maturity.*

Duration and Price Sensitivity

To understand how duration is used, we must examine its relationship to price and yield. This relationship is easily derived mathematically, but most Street people take it on faith.[7] Let

$$\Delta = \text{change in a variable,}$$

then, the relationship between duration and yield is as follows:

$$\frac{\Delta P}{\Delta y} = -D \frac{P}{(1 + y/2)}$$

The left side of the equation, $\Delta P/\Delta y$, is the rate of change of the security's price with respect to its yield. Specifically, it is the relationship between a change in a security's yield to maturity and the impact of that change on the security's price. This relationship is sometimes referred to as the *risk* of a security.

Rearranging terms in the above equation, we get

$$\frac{\Delta P}{P} = \left(\frac{-D}{(1 + y/2)} \right) \Delta y$$

Stating the equation for duration this way tells us something important: *The percentage change in a note's price, $\Delta P/P$, created by a change in its yield, Δy, is directly proportional to its duration.* In other words, duration is a measure of the *price sensitivity* of a note or bond to a change in the yield at which it trades; and it is for this reason that duration is so widely used in the financial community.

---

[7]For a derivation of this result, see the forthcoming revision of Stigum's *Money Market Calculations* (Homewood, Ill.: Dow Jones-Irwin).

MODIFIED DURATION

To simplify duration-based calculations, most Street people work not with duration, but with what's called *modified duration*. Let

D' = modified duration

Then, modified duration is defined as follows:

$$D' = \frac{D}{(1 + y/2)}$$

Substituting this expression for D' into the expression we earlier gave for $\Delta P/\Delta y$,

$$\frac{\Delta P}{\Delta y} = -D \frac{P}{(1 + y/2)}$$

we get

$$\frac{\Delta P}{\Delta y} = -D'P$$

By rearranging terms, we can restate this result as follows:

$$\frac{\Delta P}{P} = -D'\Delta y$$

Note modified duration, D', is simply an algebraic manipulation of duration, D; thus, D' implies nothing more or less profound than D does. The sole reason people work with D', instead of with D, is to save themselves the trouble of having to divide through by $(1 + y/2)$.

Using Modified Duration

Table 5–4 gives quotes on selected Treasury issues as of 5/22/89, a time when the yield curve happened to be exceptionally flat. Recalling the expression,

$$\frac{\Delta P}{P} = -D'\Delta y$$

we can, using the figures given in Table 5–4 for D', easily calculate how a 10-bp change in yield would affect the prices of sev-

TABLE 5–4
Quotes on selected Treasury notes and bonds for settlement 5/22/89

	Coupon	Maturity (-call)	Price	Yield	Modified Duration	Yield Value of 1/32
	8.00	5/31/89	99–31	8.927	0.02	1.2206
#	9¼	4/30/91	100–14	8.985	1.73	0.0178
#	8⅞	5/31/91	99–28	8.945	1.80	0.0174
wi	9.00	5/15/92	100–06	8.920	2.56	0.0122
#	9⅝	3/13/93	102–10	8.897	3.14	0.0096
#	9½	5/15/94	102–13	8.871	3.85	0.0075
#	9⅜	4/15/96	102–27	8.813	5.00	0.0060
#	9⅛	5/15/99	102–10	8.772	6.50	0.0047
	11¾	2/15/10–05	123–00	8.987	7.72	0.0032
#	8⅞	2/15/19	101–00	8.778	10.26	0.0029

Note: # in first column denotes an on-the-run (most recently auctioned) issue.
wi in the first column denotes an issue trading on a when issued basis.

Source: Citicorp Fixed Income Research.

eral of the issues quoted in this table. Specifically, our formula tells us that a 10-bp *rise* in the yield on the 8⅞s of 19 would cause its price to *fall* 1.026%:

$$\frac{\Delta P}{P} = -(10.26)(0.001)$$

$$= -0.01026$$

$$= -1.026\%$$

In contrast, a 10-bp *rise* in the yield on the 9¼s of 91 would cause its price to *fall* by only 0.173%:

$$\frac{\Delta P}{P} = -(1.73)(0.001)$$

$$= -0.00173$$

$$= -0.173\%$$

THE YIELD VALUE OF 1/32

Starting with either an issue's duration or its modified duration, we can easily compute two other frequently quoted bond statistics: (1) the yield value of 1/32 and (2) the price value of an 01 (i.e., the price value of a 1-bp change in yield).

Treasury coupons are quoted in points and 32nds of a point. *The yield value of 1/32 measures the amount by which the yield on such a security would change if its price changed by 1/32* (recall Chapter 4). Although the relationship between a change in an issue's price and the resulting change in its yield is *negative,* the yield value of 1/32 is always quoted as a *positive* number. Street people automatically know that, as yields *rise,* bond prices *fall.*

Let

$$v_{32} = \text{yield value of } 1/32$$

Then, substituting 1/32 for ΔP and v_{32} for Δy into the equation

$$\frac{\Delta P}{P} = -D'\Delta y$$

we get

$$\frac{1/32}{P} = -D'v_{32}$$

Next, we solve this expression for v_{32} and, following Street practice, we delete the minus sign.

Mathematically, the way we do the latter is to put *brackets* around the term $1/D'$; these brackets indicate that we are considering the *absolute value* of $1/D'$. A number's absolute value is always greater than or equal to zero: unless a number is zero, its absolute value is *positive.* The above steps give us:

$$v_{32} = \frac{1}{32P}\left[\frac{1}{D'}\right]$$

A Numerical Example

Consider again the 9¼s of 91. Substituting 100–14 for P and 1.73 for D' into our expression for v_{32}, we get

$$v_{32} = \frac{1}{32(100 + 14/32)}\left[\frac{1}{1.73}\right]$$

$$= 0.00018$$

$$= 0.018\%$$

$$= 1.80 \text{ bp}$$

The number we've calculated for the yield value of $\frac{1}{32}$ on the $9\frac{1}{4}$s of 91 differs by two hundredths of a basis point from the number given in Table 5–4, presumably due to the rounding in this table of the number given for modified duration.

In Chapter 4, we noted that the yield value of $\frac{1}{32}$ is—for intuitively obvious reasons—smaller, the longer is its current maturity. The figures quoted in the last column of Table 5–4 provide a dramatic illustration of this.

THE PRICE VALUE OF AN 01

Like the yield value of $\frac{1}{32}$, the price value of an 01 is a measure of an issue's price sensitivity. However, this measure gives the change in price, *measured in 32nds,* that will occur if an issue's yield changes by 1 bp. Let

$$v_{01} = \text{price value of } \tfrac{1}{32}$$

To obtain an expression for v_{01}, we begin with our expression for $\Delta P/P$,

$$\frac{\Delta P}{P} = [-D']\Delta y$$

If we substitute v_{01}, *measured in 32nds,* for ΔP, we get

$$\frac{v_{01}}{32P} = [-D'](1 \text{ bp})$$

Next, solving this expression for v_{01}, we get

$$v_{01} = (32P)[-D'](1 \text{ bp})$$
$$= (32P)[-D'](0.0001)$$
$$= 0.0032P[-D']$$

Finally, we note that if one knows the yield value of $\frac{1}{32}$ for a security, it's easy to calculate the price value of an 01 for that security. Simple manipulation of our expressions for v_{32} and v_{01} shows that, for any coupon security,

$$v_{01} = \frac{0.001}{v_{32}}$$

The Relationship of Duration to Current Maturity

The figures in Table 5–4 indicate that, as we'd expect, a security's modified duration is longer, the longer is its current maturity. What's surprising is that an issue's modified duration is so much shorter than its current maturity. To obtain, in the yield environment prevailing on 5/22/89, an issue with a modified duration of 10.26 years, a portfolio manager would have had to buy the most recently auctioned long (30-year) bond.

Later, we discuss the stripping of Treasury coupons into a series of zeros (Chapter 14). A big attraction of zeros to an investor is that if he buys, say, a zero that corresponds to the corpus of the *new* 30-year bond, he'll get a security with duration of 30 years. No coupon security he could buy would offer him duration of that length.

Uses of Duration by a Portfolio Manager

Consider a portfolio manager who holds various fixed-income securities. He'd like to be able to answer the question: "What will happen to the market value of my portfolio if interest rates rise or fall by X basis points?" He knows what amounts of different securities he owns, what coupons these securities pay, and what prices these securities currently command. Thus, he can easily calculate duration for each of his securities; and having done that, he can determine *approximately* what *total* capital gain (or loss) he would experience on his portfolio if market rates were to fall (or rise) by X basis points.

We say approximately because, when the market moves, yields on different securities never move, *pari passu,* precisely the same number of basis points. Yields on individual securities, with their individual characteristics, may, when the market moves, change more, less, or not at all. Also, if the slope of the yield curve changes—say, it inverts—while our investor owns securities having widely varying maturities, a duration-based estimate of how a change in yields would affect the value of his portfolio isn't likely to help him much. Like other useful analytic tools, duration has its *limitations*. Where duration is very helpful is to a portfolio manager who wants to immunize his portfolio.

IMMUNIZING A PORTFOLIO

Consider a portfolio manager who needs money to fund a specific, known, dollar liability on some specific future date or to fund some set of liabilities on some set of specific future dates. Lots of institutions—pension funds, insurance companies that sell guaranteed investment contracts, and state lotteries that make multiyear payouts to winners, to name but a few—all face this situation.

If a portfolio manager must fund a liability on a future date, that date is referred to in bond-market lingo as his *investment horizon.* In bygone days, a portfolio manager who had to fund a 10MM liability coming due 10 years, might have said, "Simple. I'll buy 10-year notes. Currently, they're selling at a yield of Y, so if I buy XMM of them [and reinvest coupon interest at Y], I'll have 10MM in 10 years."

Unfortunately, life isn't that simple. Our portfolio manager's problem is that if, over time, rates go down, the coupon interest that he reinvests won't grow at as high a compound rate as he thought it would. (Of course, if rates fall, that will cause his bonds to rise in price, but that won't do him any good if he's planning, as he is, to hold his bonds to maturity.) Net, rates falling will cause our portfolio manager to be underfunded. Conversely, rates rising will cause our portfolio manager to be overfunded—for him, an easier problem with which to deal.

What our portfolio manager wants is certainty: he wants to know that if he invests X today, he can count on having X' at the end of his investment horizon. Enter duration. There's a well-known theorem, which we won't attempt to prove here, that states basically this: If a portfolio manager buys, to fund a future liability, securities that have the same duration (as opposed to the same current maturity) as does the future liability he's funding, then it's safe for him to reason: "I need 10MM in 10 years. Securities with a duration of 10 years are currently selling at a yield of Y, so if I buy XMM of them [and reinvest coupon interest at Y], I'll have 10MM in 10 years."

Intuitively, this theorem identifies duration as a sort of fulcrum point on the maturity spectrum. The theorem tells the portfolio manager to buy, at this fulcrum point, securities with a current maturity that far exceeds his investment horizon. If he does this and interest rates then drop, he will lose some reinvestment income that he was counting on, but offsetting this loss, he'll have an equal capital gain: when he gets to his investment horizon, he'll be able to sell his bonds at a capital gain that he was not counting on. Net, if he matches the duration of his assets with that of his future liability, the interest-income loss he wasn't counting on will be precisely matched by the capital gain he also wasn't counting on; and he will have the 10MM or whatever he needs on the date he needs it. Alternatively, if rates rise rather than fall, our portfolio manager earns more interest income than he counted on, but he suffers a precisely offsetting capital loss when he sells his bonds. Either way—interest rates go up or down—our portfolio manager gets certainty by matching the duration of his assets with that of his liabilities.

In a nutshell, what we have been talking about is the use by the portfolio manager of duration as a tool to mitigate the uncertainty that surrounds his long-term investment results due to *reinvestment risk,* the portfolio manager's inability to predict the future rates at which he will be able to reinvest future coupon interest.

Put another way, a portfolio manager who, to fund a future liability due on a known future date, selects assets whose duration matches that of his liability is creating a portfolio in which *his reinvestment risk will precisely balance (offset) his market risk*.

Duration sounds like a dandy way out of uncertainty. However, a portfolio manager funding a 10-year liability can't just duration weight his assets in year 1 and play golf for the next nine. As time passes and as market conditions change, the duration of the assets he owns will change. To offset that and to thereby preclude the incursion of unwanted uncertainty in his investment results, our portfolio manager must periodically readjust, *rebalance* in financial jargon, his portfolio.

The one surefire way for a portfolio manager to match fund a future liability is to buy *zero-coupon securities*. A portfolio manager who invests XMM today in 10-year zeros to fund a liability due 10 years hence has total certainty, to the penny, about what funds will be available to him on his horizon date. (Of course, if our portfolio manager invests not in Treasuries, but in corporates, he'll have credit risk. However, that's a different issue from the one we're discussing. If a portfolio manager buys bonds that expose him to credit risk, no amount of duration analysis can help him neutralize the resulting credit risk.) One indication of how strongly portfolio managers today crave certainty when making long-term investments in fixed-income securities is the strong demand that currently exists among institutional investors for long-term zeros. Merrill, Sali, Goldman, and others aren't stripping long Treasuries for fun; they're doing it to meet widespread demand for zero-coupon securities.

It's important to note that zeros are no exception to the theorem we paraphrased above. The duration of a zero always equals its current maturity; thus, a portfolio manager who buys 10-year zeros to fund a liability 10 years hence has, whether he thinks of it that way or not, matched the duration of his assets with that of his liabilities.

This observation correctly suggests another way to interpret funding a liability with securities of matching duration. Buying a duration-matched portfolio is like buying zeros having the same term as the liability to be funded. What is unique about a zero-coupon security bought to fund a future liability of the same term is that it exposes the holder to neither market risk nor to reinvestment risk. But those are precisely the properties of a duration-matched portfolio acquired to fund a future liability having a term equal to the duration of the assets acquired.

Our comments on zeros may cause the inquisitive reader to ask: What would happen if the yield curve in the market for STRIPS, called the *term structure of interest rates,* were used instead of the yield curve in Treasury coupons to calculate duration? Some people do in fact calculate duration off of the term structure of interest rates, but they rarely publish just how they do so; such routines are usually highly proprietory because they are also used for other purposes such as pricing OTC options. In any case, it's possible to show that Macaulay's duration equals term-structure duration under the assumption that each of the term-structure discounts equals its equivalent yield-to-maturity discount. This assumption is equivalent to saying that all of the discount yields for different periods must be equal, which in turn implies that the term structure must be *flat*. If the term structure is flat, then the yields to maturity implied by it are precisely the yields to maturity one would use to calculate Macaulay's duration for a coupon security.

A final point. Duration matching of assets and liabilities does not constrain a portfolio manager to buy just issues with the precise duration of each future liability he must fund. To fund any future liability on a duration-weighted basis, a portfolio manager may acquire assets of varying maturities so long as the weighted-average duration of the assets he acquires equals the duration of the liability he's funding. In calculating the *weighted-average duration* of his assets, the *weights* that the portfolio manager must use are the *face amounts* of each security he acquires.[8]

CONVEXITY

Today, convexity is another buzzword in the fixed-income community. In Figure 5–1, we suggest intuitively why portfolio managers prefer more to less convexity. Suppose that there exists a security A, whose payout is structured such that there's the linear relationship, pictured in Figure 5–1, between its price and the yield at which it trades.[9] Suppose also that there exists a

---

[8]When we implicitly assumed, in calculating duration, that the yield curve was flat, we also ensured that the durations of different securities would be *additive*. This means that it is correct to say that the duration of a portfolio equals the weighted-average duration of that portfolio where the weights used are the amounts of the different securities held in the portfolio. For example, the fact that duration is additive, permits us to say that, if a portfolio comprises 500MM of securities having a 4-year duration and 500MM of securities having a 6-year duration, then that portfolio's duration is five years. All of the results mentioned here and above are proved in the forthcoming revision of Stigum's *Money Market Calculations* (Homewood, Ill.: Dow Jones-Irwin).

[9]Maybe the security contains some oddball options. We don't care as we just want two contrasting price-yield lines that *define to the eye* convexity.

FIGURE 5–1
Price-yield curves for two securities, A and B

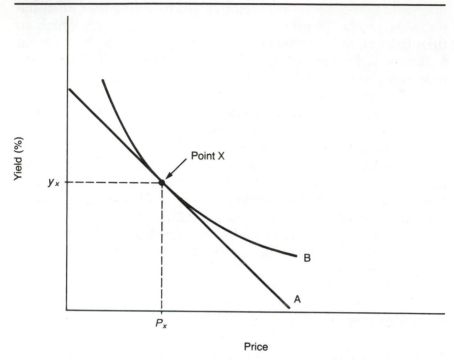

coupon security, B, whose payout is structured such that there's
the curvilinear (*convex* to the origin) relationship, pictured in
Figure 5–2, between its price and the yield at which it trades.
Finally, suppose that yields on both securities are at the level y_x,
prices on both securities at the level P_x.

Which security shall the investor, poised at X, buy? There's
no contest. If the investor buys security B over A and yield falls,
the price of B will rise faster than will that of A. Alternatively, if
the investor buys security B over security A and yields rise, the
price of B will fall more slowly than will that of A.

The price-yield line for security A is a straight line that
possesses *zero convexity*. The price-yield line for security B
curves upward and outward from the origin. It has *positive convexity*. Clearly, all else equal—the investor gets the same yield

FIGURE 5–2
Price-yield relationships for the 8⅞s of 19 and the 14s of 11

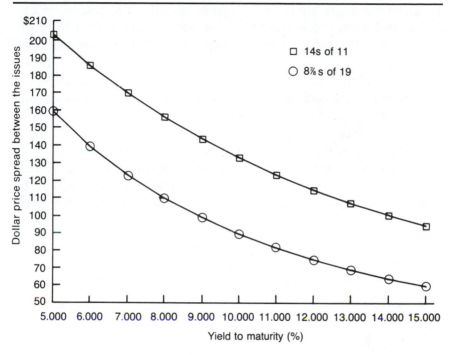

for the same price paid and the same duration too—he will always prefer, among all securities, the one that offers him the most convexity.[10]

Several comments are in order about convexity. First, if an issue's price-yield curve is convex, as those of most fixed-income securities are, then for that issue, $\Delta P/\Delta y$, the slope of the price-yield curve, can't be a constant; and if it isn't a constant, then neither duration nor modified duration can be constants. But we

---

[10]The mathematically inclined reader will note that the convexity of an issue's price-yield curve is the second derivative of yield with respect to price, that is, is the rate of change of the slope of the curve. Clearly, this rate of change is positive for issue B, because as its price increases, the slope of its price-yield relationship moves from highly negative toward zero.

already knew that: our formula for duration tells us that an issue's duration will change as its yield and price change; and if duration changes then so too must modified duration. What makes duration interesting to money managers is that they assume, correctly, that it won't change much unless yields change by a lot.

To illustrate the correctness of this assumption, we have plotted in Figure 5–2 the price-yield curve for the 8⅞s of 19 and for the 14s of 11. Note that over the wide price ranges we have used, the yields of both securities change a lot—1,000 bp—*but* the convexity of each issue's price-yield curve is small.

Figure 5–2 shows graphically why portfolio managers are on safe ground assuming that duration will be insensitive to *small* price-yield changes. However, as Figure 5–3 shows, over

FIGURE 5–3

The price spread between the 8⅞s of 19 and the 14s of 11 at different yield levels

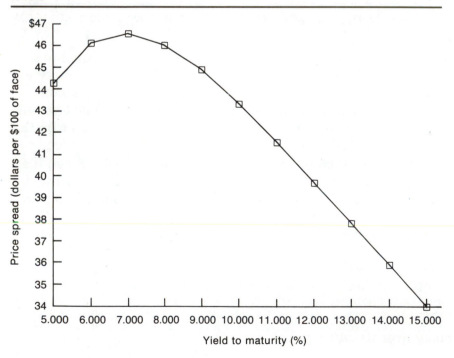

wide price-yield ranges, small differences in convexity can make a significant difference in how the prices of two issues will change in response to identical changes in yield.

Two other points are worth making. First, while it's true that an issue whose price-yield curve is more convex is preferable to one whose price-yield curve is less convex, the differences in convexity that in fact exist between different outstanding issues are smallish, second-order effects. Equally important, the markets have for some time recognized that, of two bonds with similar duration and yield, the higher-convexity bond will out-perform the lower-convexity bond from a risk/reward stand-point. Consequently, bonds of similar durations typically are priced such that those with higher convexity offer lower yields.

Nonetheless, portfolio managers who have a bogey—the Shearson or Sali bond index—try mightily to beat their bogey by constructing a portfolio of securities that, while it has *the same weighted-average duration* as the securities in the index portfolio, has *greater convexity*. Some might try to construct a portfolio with a sort of hockey-stick convexity: prices rise a lot if yields fall but won't fall much if yields rise. A portfolio manager attempting that ploy might look for securities with attached options that cause them to behave like a cushion bond: for exam-ple, securities that because of an imbedded option, failed to rise as much as they would have—absent the option—when yields fell, and consequently won't fall as far as they otherwise would if yields now rise. Over the price-yield range in question, such a security may actually display *negative convexity*. Mortgage-backs, like GNMAs, are an example of a class of securities that display in certain markets, due to imbedded prepayment op-tions, negative convexity.

A security that displays negative convexity, has, at least over some price-yield range, a price-yield curve that bows in toward, not out from, the origin. A mathematician would call such a price-yield curve *concave to the origin*. Only fixed-income folks, not mathematicians, have heard of negative convexity. In any case, it's obvious that negative convexity—or whatever one wants to call it—is, from a portfolio manager's viewpoint, a most undesirable property for an issue's price-yield curve to dis-play over its *entire* price-yield range.

THE NEXT CHAPTER

In the next chapter, we turn to the first of our portraits of the major players in the money market. We consider the money center banks whose activities impinge on every sector of the money market: in many sectors, these banks are buying and selling vast amounts of funds; in other sectors, they are busy acting as end users of various instruments, as dealers in those instruments, or as both.

PART 2

THE MAJOR PLAYERS

CHAPTER 6

THE BANKS: DOMESTIC OPERATIONS

There are various people, including bankers, who have an image problem. The first "crime" bankers are widely charged with is creating a situation in which interest rates range from high to damnably high. Their second alleged "crime" is that they periodically threaten the whole economy by acting so irresponsibly that some of them end up having problems or, worse still, failing.

Both charges reflect several serious misconceptions entertained by much of the public and more than a few politicians. First, low interest rates are always good for the economy. Second, it is bankers, not the Fed, that set the general level of short-term interest rates. Third, banking is riskless or, alternatively, riskless banking is what the country needs. Fourth, the Fed would permit or might not be able to avoid the failure of one or more major banks, which would indeed wreak economic havoc. None of these misconceptions is easy to correct; hence, bankers' rather intractable image problem. To be a banker is to be neither widely understood nor loved. It is not, however, to be unimportant. In the money market, in particular, bankers are players of such major importance that any serious discussion of the various markets that comprise the money market must be prefaced with a careful look at banking.

A MONEY MARKET BANK

The nation's largest banks, true giants, are often referred to as *money market* or *money center banks*. The term *money market bank* is apropos, since activity in every sector of the money market is strongly influenced and in some cases dominated by these institutions. Thus, to study the money market, one must first study the great banks.

To be a money market bank has always meant to be an important participant in many traditional markets: the Fed funds market; the repo market; the market for governments, agencies, and other domestic money market securities; the Euromarket; the foreign-exchange market; and at least some foreign domestic capital markets. Today, to be a money market bank also means to be an active participant in markets for sophisticated derivative products such as futures, swaps (coupon and cross currency), and various option products; also, the emphasis in such a bank on a global presence is becoming ever more pronounced.

While it's easy to talk about a money market bank, it's less easy to list just which banks fall in this category. The property of being a money market bank is, like liquidity, something measured in degrees. Also, as a glance at Table 6–1 shows, the top 20 U.S. banks are a mixed bag. Some are clearly global banks; others have a strong regional flavor. The figures on percentage of deposits derived from foreign (Euro and other) sources alone suffice to indicate that First Interstate Bancorp and Wells Fargo do not have the same ranking in the money market as do various traditional money center banks, such as Citicorp, Morgan, Chase, and Bankers Trust—to name but four.

The activities of a money center bank encompass several separate but related businesses. All money center banks engage in traditional banking operations: accepting deposits, lending, managing an investment portfolio, and running a trust department. In addition, they act as dealers in money market securities, in governments, in municipal securities, and in various synthetic and derivative products. Also, several have extensive operations for clearing money market trades for nonbank dealers. A final important activity for money center banks is foreign

TABLE 6–1
Top 20 U.S. banks, January 1, 1989

		Assets ($ billions)	Deposits ($ billions)	Interest Bearing (%)	Foreign (%)	Loans ($ billions)	Loan-Loss Prov. 1988 ($ millions)	Leverage 1988	Net Income 1988 ($ millions)	Net Income as % of Net Int. Income	Return on Assets 1988 (%)	Return on Equity 1988 (%)
1. Citicorp	New York	207.7	124.0	86	49	149.2	1,330.0	27.8	1,698.0	22.1	0.77	21.4
2. Chase Manhattan	New York	97.5	64.4	75	45	69.6	750.0	18.3	1,053.9	31.0	1.52	27.8
3. Bankamerica	San Francisco	94.7	77.2	77	23	69.0	645.0	33.1	547.0	14.8	0.51	16.8
4. Morgan (J. P.)	New York	83.9	42.4	86	70	28.3	200.0	16.0	1,001.8	49.1	1.20	19.1
5. Security Pacific	Los Angeles	77.8	47.7	75	13	55.5	413.5	23.1	639.9	23.5	0.82	18.9
6. Chemical Banking	New York	67.3	47.9	72	14	41.6	363.7	30.6	753.6	30.1	0.91	27.7
7. Manufacturers Hanover	New York	66.7	41.7	81	44	49.0	501.7	30.5	751.6	36.7	0.96	29.4
8. First Interstate Bancorp	Los Angeles	58.2	44.1	71	2	37.8	589.7	28.6	102.4	4.1	0.16	4.7
9. Bankers Trust New York	New York	57.9	32.5	76	59	24.1	50.0	18.0	647.7	63.5	1.12	20.3
10. Bank of New York	New York	47.4	32.7	75	35	33.1	168.5	20.0	213.0	26.4	0.78	15.6
11. Wells Fargo	San Francisco	46.6	35.1	80	4	37.7	300.0	22.1	512.5	25.7	1.09	24.0
12. First Chicago	Chicago	44.4	32.0	80	41	27.9	257.3	28.0	513.1	42.2	1.05	29.3
13. PNC Financial	Pittsburgh	40.8	27.5	83	5	24.0	162.1	16.4	442.7	35.1	1.18	19.3
14. Bank of Boston	Boston	36.1	23.6	81	24	26.5	144.0	20.1	322.3	27.5	0.91	18.3
15. Bank of New England	Boston	32.2	24.6	82	13	24.9	123.4	20.0	281.7	24.5	0.93	18.6
16. Mellon Bank	Pittsburgh	31.2	21.3	80	15	18.9	321.0	33.9	−65.0	−7.3	−0.34	−11.7
17. Continental Bank	Chicago	30.6	16.9	83	38	16.6	33.8	28.9	315.8	48.1	0.91	26.4
18. NCNB (i)	Charlotte, N.C.	29.8	20.7	81	4	18.9	121.5	18.1	252.5	25.8	0.86	15.5
19. Suntrust Banks	Atlanta	29.2	23.9	77	NA	20.1	186.1	15.4	308.7	24.8	1.13	17.4
20. Fleet/Norstar Financial Group	Providence	29.1	20.7	79	6	19.5	106.8	15.0	335.8	27.2	1.21	18.1

NA: not available

operations of two sorts: participating in the broad international capital market known as the *Euromarket* and operating within the confines of foreign capital markets (accepting deposits and making loans denominated in local currencies).

Of the various banking activities we have described, two—trust operations and clearing operations per se as opposed to granting dealer loans—could be described as largely off-balance-sheet profit centers. Both require capital in the form of space and equipment but do not require substantial funding from the bank.[1] The trust department invests other people's money, and the clearing operation provides a service. In contrast, the banks' three other primary domestic activities—lending, running a portfolio, and dealing in securities—must be funded, since each involves acquiring substantial assets.

In the U.S., unlike in most foreign countries, bank branching was traditionally severely restricted. Because bank charters were initially granted only by the states, banks were not permitted to branch interstate; and in most states—California being a notable exception—even intrastate branching was severely restricted or prohibited. As a result, there are in the U.S. 14,000-odd banks, a number unparalleled in any other developed country. Gradually, all this is changing; and bank branching, even interstate, is becoming common. In some geographic regions, states, seeing interstate banking on the horizon, formed exclusive regional pacts that permitted banks within the region to merge. The idea was to give regional banks time to build size and profitability before New York and other money center banks were permitted to bid for them. The result has been the creation of a number of large and highly successful superregional banks.

Comparing the largest and the smallest banks in the U.S., one might almost conclude that the most they have in common is the name *bank*. Actually, that's extreme: all institutions called banks accept deposits, make loans, and have at least a few government securities on their balance sheets. There, however,

---

[1]Clearing does impose large *intraday* funding needs on a clearing bank and thus contributes to daylight overdraft by such a bank at the Fed. When a bank incurs daylight overdraft, it goes *OD* (*overdrawn*) in its reserve account at the Fed (Chapter 8).

the similarity between the largest banks and their smallest sisters ends.

To finance its operations, a money market bank draws funds from various sources. It starts with a fairly stable base of money—bank capital and the demand, savings, and small-denomination time deposits it receives in the normal course of its commercial banking activities. The total of these is typically far below the value of the assets the bank wants to finance, so there is a funding gap that the bank fills by buying money in the Federal funds market, the repo market, the CD and deposit note markets, and the Euromarket.[2]

As the above suggests, managing a money market bank involves a host of decisions concerning what assets to hold and what liabilities to incur. Before we say more about these, two comments are in order. First, one cannot separate a bank's domestic operations from its foreign operations, but we are going to try—treating domestic operations in this chapter and Euro operations in the next; the Euromarket is a fascinating and complex story that deserves a full chapter. Second, big banks are a disparate collection of animals. Some of their differences reflect differences in circumstances: The Bank of America (B of A) with its hundreds of domestic branches is deposit rich; the Morgan with few domestic branches is, like most money market banks, deposit poor. Other differences reflect variations in historical patterns of development, areas of specialization, and management philosophy. More about that below.

Profit and Risk

However heterogeneous the nation's largest banks may be, there still are strong similarities in the way that top management in these banks view and attack the problem of managing a large bank. First, their objective is, like that of management in any industrial, manufacturing, or other business concern, to earn *profits*. Second, banks, like nonbank firms, operate under uncertainty and thus face *risk*. Risk in banking arises from sev-

---

[2]See Chapter 3 for an introduction to these markets and the instruments traded in them.

eral sources. On every loan a bank makes there is *credit risk:* the risk that the borrower won't pay back the money lent. Second, because of the mismatch, contrived or natural, that typically exists between the interest-rate maturities of the assets and liabilities on a bank's balance sheet (in banker's jargon, the *mismatch* or *gap* in the bank's book), a bank is exposed to *interest-rate risk*. This second risk arises not only in connection with a bank's loans, but as a result of its portfolio and dealer operations. A third risk is *liquidity risk,* which is really the risk of illiquidity. Every money market bank continually buys large quantities of short-dated (short-term) funds to finance its operations. Liquidity risk is the risk that the bank might at some point be unable to buy the monies it needs at a reasonable price or, worse still, at any price.

Because any attempt by a banker to make profits involves risks, his objective inevitably becomes to *maximize profits subject to the constraint that perceived risks be held to some acceptable level*. Also since bank analysts, investors, and bank depositors all focus strongly on current income, bankers have a strong predilection for an earnings pattern that displays steady growth over time.

MANAGING A MONEY MARKET BANK

In recent years, a number of dramatic changes have occurred in the environment in which money center banks operate. Taken together, these changes have decreased the profitability of certain of their traditional activities and have thus forced such banks to conclude that it's time for a change in strategy.

To highlight the changes that are occurring in big banks, we begin by describing how a money center bank was managed in the past. We then turn to the present.

The Way It Used to Be

Economists' favorite term, *decision variable,* denotes something having a value that is the result of a conscious decision. *Exogenous variables,* in contrast, are things having a value more or less thrust on the decision maker by the outside world. On a bank's balance sheet, in the short run at least, both sorts of variables are found. Let's start with the exogenous ones.

Every bank establishes standards to limit credit risk. Once it has done this, a bank will normally do everything possible to meet the legitimate loan demands of any customer who meets these standards. Loans are a source of bank profits, and loan customers normally provide a bank with deposits and other business as well. The quantity of loans demanded from a bank depends largely on the state of the economy and on what funds are available to would-be borrowers from other sources. These factors are beyond the control of the banks, so their loan volume is very much an exogenous variable. Bankers can wish they had more loans, but they can't decide to have them if loan demand is weak.

In the short run, bank capital is also an exogenous variable, having a value that depends on past decisions. A third variable that is largely exogenous in the short run is the sum of demand deposits, savings deposits, and small-denomination time deposits received by a bank. Over time a bank will have built up a customer base that supplies it with a quite stable amount of such deposits. To significantly enlarge that base would take time and effort. A final important exogenous variable is the reserves against deposits that a bank must keep with the Fed.

From a bank's viewpoint, the decision variables it faces in the short run are the size and composition of its investment portfolio, the dealer position it assumes, and the quantities and maturities of the monies it buys in the Fed funds market, the repo market, and various other markets.

In assigning values to these decision variables, the bank is determining in part what asset portfolio it will hold and how it will fund that portfolio. In other words, it is choosing a balance sheet that meets its goal of maximizing return subject to the constraint that perceived risks be held at an acceptable level.[3]

Several facts of life are of crucial importance for the bank in making these balance-sheet choices. One is that buying money is going to be a continuing way of life for a money market bank.

---

[3]See Marcia Stigum and Rene Branch, *Managing Bank Assets and Liabilities: Strategies for Risk Control and Profit* (Homewood, Ill.: Dow Jones-Irwin, 1982).

Capital plus what we called *exogenous deposits* minus whatever reserves have to be held against such deposits are available to a bank for funding loans. However, since money market banks as a group tend to be deposit poor, it's uncommon for these sources of funds to suffice to cover loans, not to speak of funding a securities portfolio and a dealer position.

Thus, a second crucial fact of life for a money market bank is that it must have the preservation of liquidity as a concern of overriding importance. By liquidity we mean the bank's ability to acquire money whenever it is needed in huge and highly variable sums. Since the principal, in fact almost the only, source of liquidity a money market bank has is its ability to buy money, maintaining access to its markets for bought money—Fed funds, repos, and other—becomes the *sine qua non* for the continued operation of such a bank.

A third fact of life facing a bank is the yield curve. As noted in Chapter 4, money market and bond yields are normally higher the longer the maturity of an instrument except when a downturn in interest rates is anticipated. This means, as any banker knows, that one path to profits and prosperity is often to acquire assets with maturities that are longer than those of the liabilities used to fund them—*borrowing short and lending long*. A domestic banker would refer to this as running a *gap* or *gapping*. A Euro banker would call this running a *mismatched* or *short book*. Gapping or mismatching contrasts with running a *matched book*—that is, funding every asset acquired with a liability of identical interest-rate maturity.

Asset and Funding Choices

The facts of life we have just discussed influence profoundly the asset and funding choices bankers make. Let's look first at loans. When loan demand increases, the shape of the yield curve often tempts bankers to fund those extra loans by buying the shortest-dated money they can. Yet bankers rarely do so except for short periods when they are waiting to see whether the increase in loans will be sustained. One reason is that regulators would frown on such a policy. A second and more important consideration is that funding loans with overnight money on a large scale would conflict with the bank's need for continued liquidity. As banker after banker will note: "If we tried to finance a big increase in loans by suddenly buying a lot more overnight money, that would be immediately visible in the market and later visible in our published statements. People, particularly suppliers of funds, would begin to question why we were getting out of line with 'safe practices' [roughly the average of what other banks are doing], and our ability to continue to buy money might be impaired. That is something we could not allow to happen." The upshot of all this concern is that bankers tend to fund loan increases largely through the purchase of funds having a maturity of 30 days or longer.

A bank's securities portfolio is a different breed of animal from its loan portfolio with respect to both acquisition and funding. On the funding side, the principal difference is that the Fed permits a bank to finance its holdings of governments and agencies in the repo market (by selling them under an agreement to repurchase on an overnight or longer basis) without incurring a reserve requirement.

Money market banks acquire portfolios of government securities for various reasons. First, there is a cosmetic motive. Traditionally, *all* banks held governments for liquidity; as a result, even today a money market bank that had no governments on its balance sheet might raise eyebrows. Second, and more important, money market banks hold governments, sometimes large amounts, for profit. Especially when economic growth slackens and interest rates are falling, money market banks increase their holdings of governments because at such times governments can normally be financed at an attractive positive spread in the repo market.[4] The trick, of course, in a hold-bonds-for-profit strategy is not to be holding too many when interest rates start their next cyclical upswing and bond prices begin to fall as financing costs rise. To the above, it should be added that in some years, characterized by an inverted yield curve and by volatile interest rates, the case for a bank to hold any governments was weak at best.

---

[4]The *financing spread* is said to be *positive* if the cost of the funds borrowed is less than the yield on the securities financed.

Bankers feel comfortable financing a large proportion of their government portfolios with overnight funds because government securities, unlike loans, are highly liquid and banks can and sometimes do sell large amounts of such securities over short periods. Consequently, long-term funding of the portfolio, besides being expensive, is neither needed nor appropriate.

To the extent possible, banks use the repo market rather than the Fed funds market for funding their portfolios. Generally, overnight repo money is cheaper than overnight Fed funds. Also the repo market, unlike the Fed funds market, is an anonymous market in the sense that no other banks or brokers are tracking how much a bank borrows there. Thus, a bank can make substantial use of the repo market without impairing its liquidity.

Many money market banks act as dealers in government and other exempt securities. Since a dealer by definition acts as a principal in all transactions, buying and selling for its own account, a bank running a dealer operation inevitably assumes both long and short securities positions. Bank dealerships also acquire securities holdings, at times quite large ones, because they are positioning for profit. Banks finance their dealer positions in the same way they finance their investment portfolios.

Mismatching the Book

Earlier, we said that banks must be concerned with interest-rate risk and liquidity risk. Matching asset and liability maturities to the extent possible would appear to be a way for a bank to limit both risks. However, it's impossible to find a banker who professes to follow this strategy. One reason is that it would be difficult if not impossible for a bank to do so. Few if any assets on a bank's balance sheet have a definite maturity. A 10-year bond or a 2-year note in the bank's portfolio might be sold tomorrow. Term loans are often prepaid, and 3-month loans are frequently rolled (renewed). On the liability side of a bank's balance sheet, many items have specific maturities—repos, Euro CDs, Fed funds purchased—but a question arises as to how to view demand deposits. Technically, demand deposits can be withdrawn at any time, but in practice demand deposits in the aggregate provide a bank with a quite stable source of funds. Besides being impractical, any attempt to match asset and liability maturities would be expensive to a bank because lending long and borrowing short is a potential source of bank profits.

All bankers profess to follow the *pool* concept of funding; instead of matching specific assets against specific liabilities, they think of all the funds raised by the bank as a pool that in the aggregate finances the bank's assets. In the next breath, the same bankers will say that they repo their governments and meet increases in loans with the sale of longer-term liabilities. What is really going on?

Typically, a bank sets up a high-level committee that, besides making general decisions about what sorts of assets the bank should acquire, attempts to measure in some way, however arbitrary, the average maturity of the bank's assets and liabilities and thereby the implicit mismatch in the bank's overall position. The committee's objective is to profit when possible from a maturity mismatch while also monitoring the size of that mismatch so that it never grows so large as to endanger the bank's liquidity or expose the bank to undue rate risk. Under this approach, big increases in loans inevitably end up calling for the bank to buy more term funds, while an increase in Treasury bill holdings can comfortably be accommodated by increased purchases of overnight money.

To this rough generalization, several comments should be added. First, banks don't just react to current conditions. Management is constantly attempting to predict the future and to position itself so as to maximize future earnings. In particular, banks are constantly forecasting loan demand, deposits, and interest rates. On the basis of such forecasts, a bank might, for example, decide to issue more term liabilities than normally because it expects interest rates and loan demand to rise sharply. Or it might decide to rely more heavily on purchases of Fed funds than normally because it expects loan demand and interest rates to fall. Interest-rate forecasts also strongly influence the bank's decision about the size and maturity distribution of its portfolio and dealer positions.

The brief picture we have presented of managing a big bank leaves much unsaid. The rest of the chapter attempts to update this picture and to fill in some of the missing subtleties. Also, banks are active in every market we describe, so they will be with us throughout the rest of the book.

TODAY'S CHANGED ENVIRONMENT

Our sketch of the issues involved in managing a money market bank and of how such a bank meets the resulting challenges remains correct in some, but not all, respects. In recent years, a number of major changes have occurred in the environment in which banks operate—changes that have forced big banks to make *strategic changes* in how they do run or would like to run, subject to regulatory changes, their businesses.

The Lending Business

Back in the 1970s, a money market bank could earn a natural *spread* between the rates at which it funded itself and the rates at which it could lend to good credits. Thus, banks looked to lending as a key source of profits, one that could be augmented by adroit funding and mismatching of maturities when appropriate.

The Third World Debt Crisis
As the 1980s dawned, things began to change. In 1982, Mexico stopped paying interest on its foreign debt, an event that ushered in the Third World debt crisis—the famous *ipse dixit* of Citi's Walter Wriston, "Sovereigns do not default," not withstanding. After much wringing of hands by bankers holding Third World debt and the granting of new bank loans to enable debtor countries to make interest payments due on previous loans, Citibank in early 1987 announced it was making a 150% increase in its loan loss reserve, to $5 billion. This move, which caused Citi to suffer a $1-billion loss in 1987, was taken by John Reed, Citi's chairman, in the hope of breaking the debt deadlock by allowing banks to swap debt or equity or to trade it on the secondary markets—something that increased reserves would give a bank the flexibility to do.

Banks that had the equity to do so followed in Citi's footsteps. However, the row proved tougher to hoe for some banks than others. Citi had the biggest chunk of loans to rescheduling countries ($15 billion at the end of 1982); but New York's Manny Hanny had the most such loans as a percentage of total assets, and it lacked the resources to write them off at the clip set by Citi. Other banks fell all over the lot in-between. As a result of additions to foreign-debt reserves made by U.S. banks in the second quarter of 1987, the U.S. banking industry posted for that quarter a loss of roughly $10 billion, its previous worst performance on record having been a $600MM loss for all of the Great Depression year of 1934.

Since they began adding to debt reserves, U.S. banks have done various deals to lighten their foreign debt loads, such as selling debt at big discounts from face value and trading debt for equity in debtor-country businesses. By buying bank debt at a discount and swapping it for equity investments, nonbank investors too have been able to make local-currency investments in debtor countries—including no less the purchase by a Dutch company on favorable terms of a Brazilian soccer star's contract.

As the spectre of banks, U.S. and foreign, rescheduling and otherwise dealing with hundreds of billions of Third World debt unfolded, investors began reappraising the relative credits of different classes of borrowers. Suddenly, good guy sovereigns—like the Kingdom of Sweden—who repaid their debts and top corporates who had no Third World debt on their balance sheets looked like attractive credits relative to big banks. Gradually, investors became willing to lend to such borrowers on the same or better terms than those at which they would lend to top banks (i.e., buy the paper of such banks); as this occurred, the natural spread in bank lending to good credits evaporated.

Banks found themselves in an unenviable position. "It used to be," noted one banker, "that we'd say: 'We need to make 25 bp on loans to compensate for the use of our balance sheet.' But 25 bp never paid for that use. Also, 25 bp is too much for a good credit who will probably repay in three months, and it's too little for a weak credit who will ask you to roll over. Consequently, we have less loans in the bank than in the past." In a few short years, wholesale lending by money center banks to better credits became a *bankrupt business*. That in itself was enough to call for strategic changes at banks, but other transformations in the banking environment were also occurring to stimulate such changes.

Capital Adequacy Requirements

In December 1987, the *Basel Supervisors' Committee* (*BSC*) of the Group of Ten (countries), which had been meeting in Basel under the auspices of the *Bank for International Settlements* (*BIS*), the central bankers' central bank, issued a memorandum that came to be called the Basel Accord or Agreement.[5] This memorandum contains proposals for *risk-based capital requirements* that were to be imposed on banks in the Group of Ten and certain other countries by their respective central banks. The objective of this move was twofold: (1) to strengthen the capital positions of major international banks and (2) to do so as uniformly as possible so that banks of no major country would in the future be advantaged by being able to operate with relatively low capital ratios. Banks were expected to meet interim capital targets by the end of 1990, final targets by the end of 1992.

Given all of the country-to-country differences that exist in bank regulation, accounting requirements, standards as to what counts as capital and how it counts, it took central banks some time to translate the BSC's guidelines into national guidelines and still more time for bankers to figure out what it all would mean both for them and for their international competitors.

By 1989, it appeared that imposition of Fed-interpreted BSC guidelines on U.S. banks would cause no hardship for the better capitalized U.S. banks. However, these guidelines foreclosed any opportunity for these banks to seek to make up for lost loan revenues by taking on new low-margin business, no matter how low the associated risks. Thanks both to the Third World debt on their balance sheets and to BSC guidelines, banks

---

[5]The BSC comprises representatives from the central banks and supervisory authorities of Belgium, Canada, France, Germany, Italy, Japan, the Netherlands, Sweden, Switzerland, the United Kingdom, the United States, and Luxembourg.

in general found themselves under pressure to improve their capital ratios, if necessary by paring their assets.

While BSC guidelines address the issue of creating a level playing field among global banks with respect to capital adequacy, U.S. money center banks still operate with one major disadvantage relative to foreign global banks: whereas foreign global banks operate from a nationwide domestic base, U.S. money center banks, thanks to restrictions on branching, do not and may not. Today, most of the global banks in the world who are doing well start with a successful, nationwide enterprise in their home country, one that is difficult, for example, to match for New York money center banks who are constrained to limit the bulk of their domestic banking activities to New York State.

Deregulation and Globalization of Debt Markets

The 1980s also saw another startling development: in the U.S. and worldwide, there was a breakdown of barriers of all kinds both around and within national capital markets; these included the lifting of restrictions on the issuance of securities, on who could borrow, and on who could lend; and the elimination of withholding taxes on interest paid to foreigners. These developments created for borrowers an explosion of opportunities in the open market.

"Europeans used," noted one U.S. banker, "to put great barriers around their domestic capital markets. Three years ago, our Paris branch was lending in France at a 100-bp spread—all the domestic francs we could lend. There were ceilings on the amount you could lend, and there were withholding taxes and other barriers to people coming from the outside in. Now, all the barriers are gone, and the spread is down to ⅛th. Once you allowed external markets to compete with the domestic French market, that market was no more interesting than any other to lend into. Just watch it happen. Everywhere in the world, it is going to happen."

The breaking down of the barriers in and around domestic capital markets has benefited not just native borrowers. It has also stimulated a rapid *globalization of financial markets;* specifically, borrowers who need ultimately to borrow their own local currency now consider borrowing opportunities—including the issuance of securities—not only in their own capital market, but in capital markets worldwide; similarly domestic investors who need ultimately to invest their own local currency now consider investment opportunities not only in their own capital market, but in capital markets worldwide.

Communications

Globalization of markets requires instantaneous global communications, something young traders take for granted. However, such communications did not exist 20 or 30 years ago. Thus, the globalization of markets that is occurring today could not have occurred then even if regulations worldwide had been congenial to the free exercise of capitalist finance and to free cross-border flows of capital.

A story told by a senior bank officer makes, tellingly, the point of how global communications have changed in a few short decades: "When I joined foreign exchange in 1957, there was in June–July a sterling crisis that had been going on since 1947. Everyone was focused on sterling. Unfortunately, on one trying day, sunspots disturbed the airwaves and thus cut out one of our lines of communication to London. Then, a Russian trawler dropped its anchor on *the* transatlantic cable putting it out of commission. Consequently, we spent a whole day trying to figure out whether we had or had not borrowed [a mere] 100,000 pounds in London. Today, in the trading room there are 10 arrays of screens. We have instantaneous information and instantaneous analysis; the computers crunch the numbers as they come in. Who is going to take the tubes away, say that we are not going to communicate any more?" The global linkage of financial markets—via communications—is irreversible.

Development of Sophisticated New Products

During the 1980s, globalization was thrust forward not just by the breaking down of various barriers to international capital flows, but by the introduction of new financial tools. The most important of these were swaps, cross currency and coupon. They too played a key role in the explosion of opportunities open to borrowers and lenders.

"All of this," noted one U.S. banker, "has created a menu for corporations that is much more efficient than just borrowing *your* currency from *your* bank. Thanks in part to the elimination of withholding taxes, U.S. and other corporations now have access to yen, Swissy, and other national capital markets; they can, for example, issue yen commercial paper hedged. The development of the swap market [interest rate and currency] was the piece that made the opening of these national barriers interesting—that made borrowing French francs interesting when you wanted dollars in the end. All this, together with currency hedging mechanisms, has created a global market."

Also, the big expansion, during the 1980s, in the menu of futures and options products—including caps, collars, and floors—available to borrowers and investors and in the volumes of such products traded expanded the horizon of possibilities open to borrowers and investors, both nationally and internationally.

Securitization

In discussing the trend toward deregularization, we mentioned the trend toward securitization of debt. The latter can't be overstressed. Thanks to the SEC's rule 415, which permits shelf registration of securities offerings, and to similar deregulation elsewhere, the whole procedure of issuing notes and bonds has become generally much less onerous and has resulted in a mushrooming of private debt securities everywhere. Worldwide, existing commercial paper markets are growing and new ones are being created; in the U.S., the original home of this market, commercial paper outstanding now exceeds T bills outstanding (Chapter 22). The 1980s also saw the explosion of the market for medium-term notes, domestic and Euro (Chapter 24). Yet another example of securitization is the packaging of receivables, such as car loans, into negotiable securities, dubbed CARS in the case of auto loans.

All of the above developments impacted the market for bank loans. Today, good credits need less and less to rely on a bank intermediary when they borrow; the world offers them a wide menu of direct borrowing opportunities, some of which are quite attractive viewed from the perspective of the terms and all-in cost that the borrower achieves.

Bank Funding

Bank lending has changed. So too has bank funding; it too has been affected by changes in the environment in which banks operate.

Rate Deregulation
In the early 1980s, the combination of high interest rates and ready availability of money funds proved a potent combination, one that finally forced Congress and the regulators to permit banks and other depository institutions to pay market rates of interest on deposits. That change had no effect on true-blue wholesale banks, such as Morgan and Bankers Trust, who had long been buying *all* the money they required to fund themselves. But it did raise funding costs at big banks that took substantial amounts of consumer deposits—Chase, Citi, and others. For them, no more cheap money from consumers.

Death of the Domestic CD Market
Back in the 1970s, the top 10 U.S. banks and a select few others had access to the national, wholesale CD market in which they sold tens of billions of $1MM-apiece, short-term (three to six months), fixed-rate CDs to institutional investors. Institutions were all happy to lend short term at market rates to these banks; and the wholesale CD market, ticking along, seemed to be as permanent a fixture of the U.S. money market as one might find.

Appearances, however, can be deceptive. The Third World debt crisis, the federal bailout of the Continental Bank, and a change in reserve requirements sufficed to sound the death knell of the CD market. Basically, investors got picky about whose paper they would buy; meanwhile, the banks discovered that they did not want to sell short-term, fixed-rate CDs any more anyway.

Today, banks have other more attractive funding opportunities. Mostly, banks lend at variable rates, so to reduce interest-rate risk they want variable-rate funding. Rolling short-term, fixed-rate CDs was an attractive way to get such funding so long as banks had to borrow for over 4 years, later for over 3½ years, to reduce significantly the reserve requirements with which they were hit when they borrowed. However, in September 1983, the Fed dropped to 0% reserves requirements on nonpersonal time deposits having a maturity at issue of 18 months or more. Under those circumstances, the cheapest way for banks to raise CD money was for them to sell 18-month, variable-rate CDs to money funds via a dealer who, by granting a *put* to the buyer, permitted such funds to buy what were long-term instruments relative to the investment parameters under which money funds are constrained to operate.

Issuing Deposit Notes Cum Swap

Also banks, eyeing the burgeoning MTN note market, concluded that, if nonfinancial institutions could sell MTNs, they could sell *deposit notes,* which amount to the same thing. Today, most MTNs have original maturities measured in years and pay a fixed rate, but that poses no problem for the banks. Interest-rate swaps too have arrived, so a bank that borrows by issuing fixed-rate debt can, using a swap, convert it to floating-rate debt. Also, if the bank is a top credit, say a Morgan, it can, by coupling its privileged access to medium-term, fixed-rate money to a swap, end up with variable-rate, sub-LIBOR funding—a very attractive deal for it.

And yet one more goody for banks who decided to borrow via the issuance of 18-month CDs and deposit notes. Since both yield medium-term, variable-rate funding, the classic trade-off faced by bankers between liquidity and interest-rate exposure vanishes presto. By issuing deposit notes and swapping the proceeds fixed to floating, a bank can have its cake and eat it— obtain liquidity without assuming undue interest-rate exposure. Specifically, a bank can lock up money for several years, and if rates subsequently fall, that's no problem for the bank— the rate it pays automatically adjusts down *pari passu* with market rates.

STRATEGIC CHOICES AVAILABLE

Of the changes in the banking environment we've described, some were definitely unfavorable to banks, while others were favorable. Together, these changes suggested that banks could go on being profitable, but to do so, they would have to make some tough and wise strategic choices.

High-Yield, High-Risk Loans

One possible strategy was to seek to earn higher profits by making riskier loans. With leveraged buy-outs (LBOs) going on galore, there was no dearth of opportunities for banks to make high-yield, high-risk loans. And banks have made some such loans, although they always claim that, in doing so, they have been choosy about credits and have "run the numbers" with great care; whether great care equals sufficient care is something only a bout of high interest rates and a subsequent recession will tell. In any case, bankers chastened by the albatross of "sovereigns-don't-default," Third World debt hanging around their necks, have in the main wisely decided that charging into the world of high-yield, high-risk loans was not the answer to their problems.

Investment Banking

Many bankers, with a thumb to the political winds and an eye to court decisions, fixed on the notion that Glass-Steagall was crumbling and sooner or later would be undone by Congress: that sooner or later banks and/or their affiliates would get powers to underwrite corporate debt and equity securities. Banks have long arranged private placements of such securities, but Glass-Steagall forbids them to do public offerings.

As noted below, such an evolution would be quite natural for banks at this point. With some retrofitting of existing personnel and the addition of a few new specialists, banks could with ease shift the focus of their wholesale activity from corporate lending to corporate finance. Also, in doing so, they would be making the appropriate response to their better customers who have by their actions made it clear that, more often than not, what they need today from their banks is expert advice, execution, and distribution, not loans.

Trading

Traditionally, banks, while they had big dealing rooms and trading staffs, did not compensate their traders as did nonbank dealers—the Salis and First Bostons. Bank trading rooms were thought of as a training ground, and it was no surprise to find that a bill trader who had made the grade at, say, Morgan moved on to First Boston. One strategy open to a money center bank is to put more resources, capital, and compensation into trading; be yet more professional; take bigger risks; and hopefully earn commensurate profits. The money center bank that has done this most successfully is Bankers Trust, a trading powerhouse. That, however, is not to say that Banker Trust is not pursuing simultaneously the let-us-become-an-investment-banker strategy and, for that matter, a merchant banker too.

A Strategy, Principally Domestic

A glance through Table 6–1 shows that a number of the largest U.S. banks, all to some extent regional, garner few of their deposits from foreigners and presumably have a minimal foreign presence. These banks, some of whom are—judged by profitability and growth—highly successful clearly must be pursuing a domestic as opposed to a global strategy.

It's hard to generalize about the strategies pursued by banks, such as First Interstate Bancorp, Wells Fargo, PNC Financial, NCNB, Fleet/Norstar, and others, other than to say that, in each, management has a defined strategy, a focus, and their results show it. To pick an example, Banc One, a big regional, has a very successful strategy based on innovation, technology, aggressive acquisitions, and a partnership approach toward management of acquired banks, one that is unique among banks that are trying to grow by acquisition. Judged by their results, they seem to have it right.

In identifying the source of success of a particular regional bank, one cannot point just to its retail base or to growth in its geographic area. More often, its success reflects a correct perception by its management of what things it's good at and a focus on doing those things.

Regionals, unlike money center banks, typically don't have a London branch and a bevy of sophisticated traders of swaps and options, but that doesn't mean that they do not understand the uses of these tools nor that they cannot provide them to their customers. A lot of regionals will call a money center bank, such as Morgan or Chase, when they have a client and say, "We want to offer our client X, Y, and Z. You give it to us wholesale, and we'll retail it." To the money center banks, regional banks are big clients for such products because a regional bank knows that money center banks won't compete directly with it for its customer business.

BANKING AS FOUR BUSINESSES

A senior officer of a money market bank, outlining his bank's current strategy for wholesale—corporate and institutional—banking said, "Today, we're in four distinct businesses—with certain things, such as trust business, at the periphery [Figure 6–1]."[6] While many bankers may not think in quite those terms, it's a useful approach for organizing the rest of our discussion of banking, which focuses principally on wholesale banking.

Business 1 might be called the *portfolio or Treasury business*. This is the business of asset (or position) accumulation and funding; otherwise own account; otherwise—and this is key—*what is best for the bank*. In business 1, the bank acquires assets, securities, or loans that it can fund at a spread over its cost of money; it also seeks to enhance that spread by mismatching its

---

[6]It's not uncommon, today, for a money center bank with a big retail base, e.g., a Chase, to think of its activities there—taking retail deposits, selling retail CDs, and making consumer loans—as a separate and distinct activity from its wholesale banking business.

FIGURE 6–1
The four businesses of banking

Portfolio Asset/position funding: "Own account" "What's best for the bank"	Corporate Finance Problem solving: "What's best for the client"
Distribution	**Trading**

book when rates and its rate view indicate that that's likely to be profitable.

Business 2 is corporate finance—the investment banking business that is emerging out of old-style lending. A client may come to a bank and say, "I want financing. How do I do it?" Business 2 calls for the banker to explore opportunities: a loan, a public offering with or without various bells and whistles. He might, for example, advise his client, "Do a public offering this and this way and you'll save 10 bp." Here the banker's focus is strictly on *what's best for the client,* and his reward is a *fee,* maybe 2 of the 10 bp he saves the client.

Business 3 is trading. Banks have always been in trading as part of us-first banking, but now they need to be in trading more for market making and liquidity than in the past. For example, a part of the strategy of money center banks today is to aggressively make loans with the notion that they will sell off, to investors at a slight markup, participations in those loans. That's a line of business with profit potential that does not impact a bank's balance sheet. Also, as banks and their affiliates get expanded powers to underwrite and trade corporate securities, they will need to expand their trading activities if they are to meet long-run success in business 2, corporate finance.

Business 4 is distribution. Banks have long had sales forces to sell their own paper and the *exempt* securities—governments, agencies, general obligation munis, BAs, Euro CDs, and other money market paper—that banks are permitted to trade. Today, those sales forces are augmented by new people selling participations in the bank's loans and also commercial paper, a security that banks have recently won the right to distribute. As banks and their affiliates are empowered to deal in yet other securities, banks' distribution will have to expand to cover these new securities. As noted below, all bank trading of securities is, for regulatory reasons, being shifted into an affiliate, which is a subsidiary of the bank's holding company.

THE BUSINESS OF TRADING

In discussing a money center bank's four businesses, we begin with trading because the expansion of bank and of bank affiliate powers to underwrite and trade a broad range of securities is crucial to the current strategy of many money center banks: to enter investment banking. Only if banks are permitted to trade in volume a wider range of securities than past and even present regulations permit will they be able to compete successfully with nonbank dealers in providing corporate finance services to their clients.

Just how important banks view an expansion of their powers to deal in securities is indicated by the fact that in 1987 Chase spent $4MM and a lot of executive time studying the pros and cons of giving up its banking charter. At that time, William Butcher, chairman and CEO of Chase, observed that, whereas big corporations used to come to banks for money 40 years ago, they don't do so any more. He also complained about regulatory rebuffs that Chase and other banks had experienced when they tried to follow their customers into the world of securitization. Butcher noted that Chase's businesses fall into three categories. One category is taking deposits, for which Chase needs a bank charter and on which Chase makes "zilch" profits. A second category is nontraditional banking activities, such as Chase's credit card operation, for which it, like American Express, needs no bank charter. A third category is activities, such as foreign exchange, that traditionally have been very bank oriented, but for which Chase again needs no bank charter. In the end, Chase was deterred from giving up its bank charter by the likelihood that the rating agencies would lower their ratings of Chase's bonds if Chase became a nonbank corporation. The rating agencies take comfort from their notion that, so long as Chase (which has a lot of Third World debt on its balance sheet) is a big bank, the Fed wouldn't allow it to fail.[7]

Most money market banks have long had extensive dealer operations. The biggest part of their dealing activity has been in Treasuries and agencies, but banks are also big dealers in and underwriters of state and local general obligation (GO) obligations. In addition, some banks deal in Euro CDs, deposit notes, and BAs.

Besides being a profit center, a bank's dealer department also provides it with useful, up-to-the-minute information on conditions in the money and bond markets. There's much to be said about how a dealer operation, bank or nonbank, runs. We turn to that in Chapter 10.

Glass-Steagall Act and the Bank Holding Company Act

Here, we focus on the slow progress banks have made, given the Glass-Steagall Act and the Bank Holding Act, in expanding the range of securities in which they may deal. This story is so crucial for the future of banking that we tell it in some detail.

The Rules of the Game

Just what banks are and are not permitted to do is a tangled question. There are two principal federal acts, the Glass-Steagall Act and the Bank Holding Company Act of 1956 as amended. Each U.S. money center bank is owned by a holding company, which also owns other companies; these other companies are *affiliates* of the bank.

There are four provisions of Glass-Steagall. Two provisions say what a bank may do; two provisions, what a bank affiliate

---

[7]"We Mean It, Says Butcher," *Euromoney,* November 1987, p. 187.

may do. Basically, a bank affiliate may engage in a wider range of activities than may a bank.

Section 16 of Glass-Steagall says that a bank may act as an *agent*—buy or sell securities with no recourse for the account of a customer. However, a bank may not *underwrite* securities (act as a *principal* in distribution and dealing activities) except for certain *exempt* securities.

Exempt securities that Glass-Steagall specifically permits a bank to *underwrite*—to position and to publicly offer—include U.S. Treasury securities, federally guaranteed securities, and municipal general obligations.

The Glass-Steagall exemption does not include CDs and BAs. However, by interpretations that have never been challenged, banks have been permitted to underwrite and deal in CDs and BAs. The grounds for these interpretations are two: (1) such paper is not securities for the purposes of Glass-Steagall and (2) underwriting such paper is not the sort of bank activity that Glass-Steagall intended to prohibit. Note there were no large-denomination, negotiable CDs until 1961, decades after Glass-Steagall was written. Recently, banks have also begun to trade bank deposit notes, which can be viewed as negotiable CDs having a long original maturity.

The agency provision of Glass-Steagall has enabled banks to do *private placements* in which they sell to a limited group of institutional investors in large minimum amounts corporate stocks, bonds, and other securities. These things may be and are done within the bank. In fact, in the U.S., the private placement market is huge and banks play a significant role in it.[8]

The Banks' Fight for Expanded Powers

In their long fight for expanded securities powers, the banks' principal adversary in the courts and before Congress has been

---

[8]It's estimated that in 1988 slightly over $250 billion was raised through the sale of publicly offered debt. In the same year, $150 billion was raised through the sale of privately placed debt, almost triple the amount five years earlier. The private placing of debt to finance leveraged buy-outs (LBOs) has fueled the rise in private placements. So too has the spectre of event risk (raised in particular by LBOs); thanks to event risk, prospective buyers of publicly offered bonds are today demanding restrictive covenants that no good credit wants to be the first to grant.

the *Securities Industry Association* (*SIA*), which is the nonbank dealers' trade group. Nonbank dealers naturally think that it would be dandy to have banks forever forbidden to tread on their turf.

The current skirmishing between banks and nonbank dealers goes back to at least 1978. In that year, Bankers Trust began to act as an advisor and *agent* to issuers of commercial paper, an activity that Bankers viewed as permissible under the Glass-Steagall Act. In 1979, the SIA asked the Fed to declare Bankers Trust's commercial paper activities unlawful; the Fed declined to do so. The SIA then turned to the courts, which in two rulings at the district court level determined (1) that commercial paper was a security and (2) that Bankers Trust's agency placements of commercial paper violated federal law. Bankers Trust, for its part, kept selling commercial paper while it appealed adverse court rulings. By the time its role as agent-advisor in the sale of commercial paper was upheld by a federal appeals court in Washington, Bankers Trust had 76 corporate clients with $6.8 billion of commercial paper outstanding; this made it the sixth-largest placement agent for such paper. Also, by that time, Morgan had entered the commercial paper business as agent-advisor, and it had 37 corporate clients.

Today, four bank holding companies, Bankers Trust, Citi, Morgan, and the B of A, rank among the nine firms that dominate the commercial paper market. That these particular bank holding companies do so is unsurprising, since only money center banks have securities subs with the sales staff, back office support, distribution capability, and trading apparatus in place to make an effective bid to enter the commercial paper market.

The tenacity with which banks have fought to gain a toehold in the commercial paper market is easily understood. "Things were getting to the point," observed one banker, "where a corporate treasurer needed a bank only for things such as a line of credit, money transfers, custodial services, and letters of credit, but not for financing. The focus of the banks in fighting for the right to do commercial paper was to get back commercial customers who had been walking out on the banks. Acting as an issuer's agent was an easy way for a bank to be able to talk finance with a corporate on a daily basis."

Banks Fight for the Right to Underwrite Ineligible Securities

Winning the battle described above gave the banks only the right to act as *agent* in the sale of commercial paper, *not* the right to *underwrite* it.

The banks' next step was to petition the Fed for the power to *underwrite* nonexempt securities *in a bank affiliate*. This fight has to do with what a bank affiliate may or may not do. Consequently, it is not only a Glass-Steagall issue, but also a matter for the Fed to decide under the Bank Holding Company Act.[9] Under the Bank Holding Company Act, the issue is: What activities are so closely related to banking so as to be appropriate for a bank affiliate? In April 1987, the Fed ruled that bank affiliates could *underwrite* certain types of securities, as opposed to just placing them as agent, provided that such activities amounted to no more than 5% of the gross revenues of the affiliate and that the latter was principally engaged in areas of trading and underwriting (or other activities) permitted by Glass-Steagall to a bank.[10] The *four* types of unexempt securities that bank affiliates were permitted to underwrite are *commercial paper, mortgage-backed securities, municipal revenue bonds, and securities backed by various debts*. Promptly, each major bank holding company formed a securities sub and put into that sub all trading done by its bank in exempt securities, such as Treasuries and agencies, and in nonexempt securities.[11]

The Fed's April 1987 ruling enraged nonbank securities dealers, who successfully lobbied Congress to impose in August 1987 a moratorium on the expansion of bank affiliate powers that expired the following March. In effect, Congress said: "It is our province, not the Fed's, to expand bank affiliates' powers, and we are going to do something here."

---

[9]Section 20 of Glass-Steagall prohibits a member bank from being affiliated with an entity engaged principally in underwriting securities.

[10]On June 22, 1989, the Fed proposed raising this 5% limit to 10%. It also proposed allowing bank securities affiliates to underwrite securities backed by assets of the bank holding company, such as credit card receivables. These proposals were sure to draw criticism from the SIA.

[11]For example, Morgan formed J. P. Morgan Securities, Inc.; Citi formed Citicorp Securities Markets, Inc.

In early 1988, the Senate passed a bill that would have permitted bank affiliates to underwrite anything but corporate equities and without the 5% restriction. The House, in contrast, got into a wrangle: St. Germain of the House Banking Committee declared that such a bill fell on his turf; Dingle of the House Energy and Commerce Committee said, "No, this is securities legislation, and as such, falls on my turf." The upshot was that the House did nothing; and Proxmire of the Senate said to the Fed, "It's up to you to act." Congress could yet act in a new session, but the cross fire on the issues involved is intense; one securities lobbyist likened legislating on the subject to Lebanon with factions within factions fighting each other.

In any case, in October 1988, Citi, Chase, Morgan, and Bankers Trust all petitioned the Fed for the right to underwrite all debt and equity securities (excluding mutual funds) in their respective affiliates. In response, the Fed ruled in January 1989 that the bank affiliates that had applied to it, including Security Pacific's, could underwrite corporate debt under the same restrictions that it had earlier applied in its April 1987 ruling. The Fed also indicated that it would consider increasing the ceiling on a bank affiliate's trading in nonexempt securities from 5% to 10% (later, in June 1989, it proposed doing so). Finally, the Fed said that it would defer for a year its decision on whether bank affiliates may underwrite corporate equities.

Predictably, the SIA (the Securities Industry Association— the nonbank dealers' trade association) threatened to challenge the Fed's new rulings in the courts. Note the issue here is not really a Glass-Steagall issue as the courts have already ruled that a bank affiliate may engage in underwriting activities that a bank may not so long as those activities aren't a substantial portion of the affiliate's total business. Thus, the thrust of the SIA case concerns the Bank Holding Company Act.

In entering the business of underwriting ineligible securities, the banks enjoy no advantage over nonbank dealers with respect to funding, since the Fed has created a firewall that prevents this. Specifically, under the Fed's 1989 ruling, a bank is prohibited from extending *any* credit to its securities affiliate, except intraday credit extended in connection with the clearing of U.S. government securities; also, under the Fed's 1987 ruling, a bank holding company is permitted to lend to its securities sub, but such loans must either be overcollateralized or deducted from the capital of the holding company. Where banks will have an advantage over most securities dealers is in international distribution. Generally, the biggest of the banks have operations in more foreign financial centers and have had them for longer than do the biggest of the U.S. nonbank dealers.

The Tide Is with the Banks

Generally, on the issue of what banks and their affiliates may do, the tide seems to be flowing in favor of the banks. The Fed is favorably disposed to expanding bank affiliate powers, and even Congress might amend Glass-Steagall to give the banks more freedom—that is, if Congress ever manages to act at all.[12] For some banks that aren't giants in the government securities market, such as Security Pacific, the 5% ceiling on bank affiliate activities poses serious problems to underwriting other securities. They and other banks will continue the fight to let banks themselves, as opposed to bank affiliates, underwrite those securities that the banks argue aren't securities for Glass-Steagall purposes, but rather a sale of bank assets in securitized form.

Meanwhile, 22 states have given banks chartered by them more freedom than federally chartered banks have to engage in insurance and real estate. So far, big banks have been slow to take advantage of this permissiveness, but if one does that may trigger a stampede.

The Foreign Front

On the foreign front, bank powers to underwrite securities vary from country to country, but the trend seems to be to let banks and nonbank dealers compete for the same business. The U.K. never had a Glass-Steagall–type act, and the London branches

---

[12]One cloud on the horizon in the spring of 1989 was that the Fed was considering limiting banks' overseas securities operations by extending "firewalls" imposed on banks' domestic securities affiliates to their foreign activities. Banks argue the Fed's doing so would cripple them competitively. The regulatory quagmire deepens when the Fed gets to the sticky issue of how to treat foreign banks, having no domestic firewalls, that want extended powers to trade securities in the U.S.

of U.S. banks have long been underwriting a wide range of securities there. In fact, U.S. banks point to their London record as evidence that they can responsibly underwrite and trade ineligible securities without threatening their financial stability.

Canada had a homegrown version of Glass-Steagall but abolished it in June 1987. Thanks to the American occupation, Japan has its version of Glass-Steagall (Article 65), but amid a flurry of deregulatory measures, Japan was, in the spring of 1989, considering just how to dismantle it.

Bad Timing?

Much of the time when U.S. banks were fighting for the right to underwrite an expanded menu of securities, U.S. nonbank dealers were running highly profitable operations in the areas banks wanted to get into. Ironically, that's no longer the case. Since 1984, corporate-bond underwriting in the U.S. has been consolidated among only six or seven big Wall Street securities firms, and by the spring of 1989, profit margins on corporate-bond underwriting appeared to be trending, due to intense competition, in one direction only—down.

While many bankers cheer each brick that falls as Glass-Steagall crumbles, not every banker shares their glee. "As a shareholder, I'd not be thrilled," noted one banker, "that my bank can now trade corporate bonds or underwrite equities. The securities business is an overcapitalized, overpeopled business that has, for the time, had its run."

CORPORATE FINANCE

The emphasis that a number of money center banks today want to place on corporate finance is a natural development out of their history as lenders. Thus, we begin this section by sketching the evolution of bank lending over recent decades.

Evolution of Bank Lending

A number of money market banks, like other banks, extend credit to consumers and make home mortgage and other real estate loans. However, a large proportion—the number varies considerably bank to bank—of their domestic lending is to commercial and industrial (C&I) customers.

Over the last 50 years, the environment in which banks operate has been subject to constant change. One result is that banks have had to continually alter their lending practices, searching for areas in which they have a profitable role to play in supplying credit.

Before World War II, much bank commercial lending was short term. Firms in wholesale trade and commodities needed financing, often on a seasonal basis, to fill their warehouses; and their bank supplied it. The normal arrangement was that the bank would look over the customer's books once a year and decide how large a line of credit it was willing to grant this firm. The firm could then borrow during the year any sum up to that amount, provided no material change occurred in its credit after the line was granted. The customer paid for its line with compensating balances, borrowed as necessary on the basis of 90-day notes, and was expected to give the bank a *cleanup* (pay off all its borrowings) at some time during the year.

When World War II came along, the situation changed. Defense contractors had to invest huge sums in new plant and equipment. They could have financed these investments by selling bonds, the traditional approach, but that seemed inappropriate. They didn't expect the war to continue forever. Also, they believed they could pay for their new plant and equipment rapidly because they had a customer, Uncle Sam, who was sure to pay and because they could depreciate their plant and equipment at an accelerated rate. So they asked the banks for term loans. The banks provided such credits with amortization built-in, and while criticized at the time for doing so, banks ended up successfully entering the area of medium-term commercial lending.

After the war, borrowers, who had become accustomed to 5-year credits, asked for more flexibility. On a term loan, they didn't always want to have to take down all the money right away; they also wanted the right to prepay some or all of their loan if their cash flow improved seasonally or permanently. So bankers said, "Alright, that's a revolving credit. You can have it, but at some point, you'll have to give us a cleanup." The final step in this evolution came when the customer said to his bank: "I'm not sure I will ever need to borrow from you, but I want to know that I can if I need to, not just now but for some number of years." In response, bankers developed a *revolving line of credit;* the customer paid balances *plus a commitment fee;* in exchange for the latter, the bank promised to honor the line for the life of the agreement. A customer could turn such a *revolver* into a term loan simply by borrowing.

Rate Risk
From the start of World War II until 1951, the Fed pegged yields on government bonds, and interest rates moved little. Then in 1951, after considerable infighting, the Treasury agreed that the Fed should be permitted to pursue an independent monetary policy.[13] This Treasury-Fed accord spelled the end of rate pegging, and interest rates began a secular climb punctuated with periodic ups and downs. The pace of this climb was, however, slow. As a result, bankers rarely changed the prime rate that they charged their best customers, and they felt safe lending at a fixed rate not only on 90-day notes, but on term loans; the rate risk in both sorts of lending seemed small. Then, as Figure 6–2 shows, things changed. Inflation became a problem, and to fight it, the Fed pushed up interest rates sharply and rapidly on a number of occasions starting in the mid-1960s.

The banks felt the impact of the initial credit crunch largely in terms of opportunity cost. At that point, they weren't buying huge amounts of money, so tight money didn't dramatically raise their funding costs. It did mean, however, that funds locked up in old low-interest, term loans could not be lent out at the higher current rates. Later, as banks began to rely more and more on bought money, tight money significantly increased their funding costs; and the rate risk implied in *fixed-rate* lending became pronounced.

To minimize this risk, banks changed their lending practices. They began changing the prime rate more frequently, and they started altering the rate on existing as well as on new

---

[13]See Chapter 9.

FIGURE 6–2

Over time the volatility of interest rates has increased: 3-month T bill, prime rate (monthly averages through April 1989)

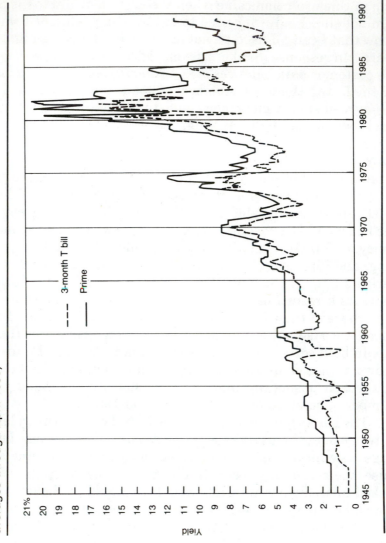

Source: Federal Reserve, J. P. Morgan Securities, Inc.

short-term loans whenever they changed prime. They also made it a rule to put term loans on a *floating*-rate basis. The rule, of course, wasn't always followed. As one executive noted at the time: "We bankers are not as smart as we could be. When rates get near the peak and we ought to be making fixed-rate term loans, we shy away from doing so. Then when loan demand and lending rates decline and we are out scrambling for loans, we are tempted to make fixed-rate term loans just when we shouldn't." Actually, even fixed-rate term loans made when interest rates are high are less advantageous to banks than one might suppose. Once rates decline, the borrower is likely to say to his banker, "You're my banker, and you know that the best thing for me would be to refinance this loan in the bond market or on other terms," and typically, the banker would let the borrower do so without penalty, regardless of whether the loan agreement called for one. On variable-rate term loans, the rate charged generally went to an increasing spread above the prime rate during the later years of the loan. This maturity spread was supposed to compensate the banker for his long-term commitment, but he rarely earned it because of prepayment or renegotiation.

To some extent, bankers used to think of their special niche in commercial and industrial lending today as that of providers of flexible medium-term financing. Also, the money they provided was "warm" money in the sense that the lending arrangement was not only open to negotiation initially, but subject to renegotiation should the borrower's position change. By moving to floating-rate loans, banks shifted much of the rate risk involved in lending from their shoulders to those of the borrower, which presumably made bank loans less attractive to borrowers.

The prime rate, although viewed by some as a collusive price-fixing device, has always been responsive to open market conditions. A fall in open market rates attracted bank customers to the open market and to other nonbank financing sources, and thus put pressure on banks to lower the prime, whereas a rise in open market rates increased the cost of bank funding and the demand for bank loans and so did the opposite.

When the Fed tightened credit, the resulting increases in the prime rate, particularly if they were frequent and sharp, made bankers unpopular with politicians and the public. So, gradually, bankers moved away from what appeared to be an arbitrarily set prime to one that was based on money market rates and fluctuated up and down with them. Citibank began the trend in 1971 by linking its prime to the 90-day commercial paper rate. Specifically, Citi said that henceforth it would set its prime at the 90-day paper rate plus a spread, which fluctuated from as little as ⅛ to as much as 1½ percentage points. Today, banks change their prime rate frequently and always in response to changes in money market conditions.

While pricing loans at a flexible prime was supposed to eliminate a bank's rate risk on loans by tying its lending rate to its cost of funds, banks still encountered difficulties during periods of tight money. In the U.S., as in many other countries, the prime rate was so politicized that at times it became impossible for the banks to raise it further. During several such periods, banks found themselves forced to make new loans at rates *below* their marginal cost of funds, that is, at rates below the cost of the extra money they had to buy to fund these loans.

The Passing of Prime

In the 1980s, the pace of change in bank lending practices has, if anything, accelerated. The world still keeps its eye glued on prime, but as one banker succinctly put it: "Prime is dead."

Bank lending terms used to be "10 plus 10." To get a line of credit, the customer had to put up 10% compensating balances; if he took down funds under the line—in addition to paying prime—he had to put up another 10% compensating balances on the amount of the loan. In those days, *prime was close to the banks' cost of funds, and what the banks really made money on was the free balances that granting lines and loans generated.* Then, competition began to whittle away at the balances. Instead of 10 plus 10, the terms became a straight 10% for the existence of the facility, and competition gradually cut that to 5%. By 1980, line and loan agreements for major loans were being written with no balance provisions.

As compensating balances vanished, banks found themselves earning on lines and loans just the rate charged on the funds taken down. Consequently, *banks had to administratively widen the spread between prime and their cost of funds so they could make some money.* Treasurers at major corporations, who push ever faster pens, reacted to a prime rate that floated at an increasing spread to banks' cost of funds by saying, "We won't borrow any more at prime except when it is to *our* advantage to do so. The spread between prime and other money market rates is so high that prime has become unrealistic. Worse still, we are being forced to accept the interest-rate risk our bank used to take. And to top things off, banks always raise prime in step with money market rates, but when they misjudge the direction of rates and mistakenly fund loans with high-cost, long-term funds, banks are slow to lower prime as money market rates drop."

Either/or Facilities

In bygone days, it was the practice that the terms on which major corporations could borrow from U.S. banks were as follows: they could get Eurodollar loans on Euro terms—LIBOR plus a small, fixed spread—to fund foreign operations, *but* they were supposed to borrow at prime to fund domestic operations.[14] The Euromarket is near perfect and consequently *very* efficient. Corporate treasurers, eyeing the terms they were getting from domestic banks on Euro loans booked outside the U.S. and on prime-rate loans booked at the bank's head office, were quick to conclude that a Euro loan was often the better deal. So on large loans—particularly large syndicated loans—they literally forced their banks to give them line agreements that provided an *either/or facility:* when the time came to take down funds, the corporate treasurer could choose—regardless of where the funds were to be spent—whether he wanted a Euro loan priced off LIBOR or a loan priced at prime. Since roughly 1980, every large-term loan negotiated by a major corporation with a money market bank has contained an either/or option.

The either/or option gives a borrower two advantages: (1) he can, at times, use it to lower his funding cost by getting money in the market where the bank's spread is lower; and

---

[14]See Chapter 7 for Euro lending terms.

(2) he can use it to place his own bet on rates. If rates are on a plateau, the borrower may find that a floating-note Euro loan at 3-month LIBOR plus a spread is cheaper than a prime-rate loan and opt for the former. Alternatively, the borrower may anticipate a rise in rates and decide that his cheapest option is to fix his borrowing rate by taking down 6-month money in the Euromarket even though the rate he pays, 6-month LIBOR plus a spread, exceeds prime. Finally, the borrower might ask for a loan at prime because he anticipates that money market rates will fall, and he wants to position himself so that his borrowing cost will fall with those rates.

Advances

After the advent of either/or facilities, the next change in bank lending practices was the introduction by major banks in the domestic market of short-term, fixed-rate loans priced off a bank's marginal cost of funds. On such loans, dubbed *advances,* a bank would price overnight funds at a spread over the Fed funds rate, 30-day money against 30-day CDs or 30-day term funds, and a 6-month advance against 6-month money. Advances in the domestic market are priced in much the same way as Euro loans are priced in the Euromarket, against money market rates.

It's a misconception that banks began making advances in the domestic market solely to compete with the commercial paper market. Another motive was to keep business that they would have lost had they insisted that borrowers pay prime at a time when borrowers felt that prime was unrealistically high. Big banks felt compelled to devise some pricing mechanism that would give the borrower a rate he'd view as realistic; that is what pushed banks into making loans at *subprime rates.*[15]

Eventually, the enthusiasm of banks for extending advances at subprime rates faded, because they found that doing

---

[15]Traditionally, prime-rate loans were considered, implicitly, to be 90-day working capital loans. As corporate treasurers' borrowing needs began to be identified with greater precision (because of major advances in cash-flow projection techniques), the underlying rationale for traditional prime-rate lending eroded.

so was unprofitable. "The good borrowers," noted one banker, "are doing commercial paper, so we have here the small guy who does not want to take any interest-rate risk. He comes in and takes money every day, every week, or every month. What he needs—the amounts are small—changes every day. It's a mess, and we are getting out of it. It isn't easy, of course, because some of our clients have long-term deals with us: they give us balances against an agreement that we will lend them money on a specific basis, which we call our daily advance rate or our fixed rate for advances. Still, these two programs are coming to an end."

Bank Competition with Commercial Paper

Back in the 1930s, banks basically financed the working capital of corporate America. Today, the commercial paper market does so. Once, bankers viewed the growing commercial paper market as threatening and unwanted competition, but eventually they realized that, if the billions of business done in the commercial paper market were added to the billions of C&I loans on their books, the impact on their capital ratios would be disastrous. Also, bankers began to perceive the commercial paper market as providing them with a tidy and steady flow of fee income for providing lines to paper issuers, lines that—because they were largely unused—had little or no impact on bank liquidity or interest-rate risk. In effect, the commercial paper market provided banks with fees for doing next to nothing.

To create the appearance of liquidity necessary to sell commercial paper, almost all issuers back a very high percentage of their outstanding paper with *committed* facilities. Specifically, the banks promise in exchange for balances and/or fees to provide commercial paper issuers with money should they encounter difficulties in rolling their paper.[16] This commitment gives the issuers the liquidity required to make their paper salable.

Initially, banks granting such lines would say to the issuer, "You can have the lines, but only if you commit to pay 1% over prime if you take down funds under it." The issuer would often

---

[16]To *roll* paper means to repay maturing paper by selling new paper.

respond, "We'll give you 2% over prime." That was rational since, as banks soon learned, most paper issuers made it a policy never to use their bank lines as a last-resort source of funds if they could avoid doing so. When money was tight, commercial paper issuers would pay up rather than come into their banks for funds. So bankers said, "OK, you can have the lines, but we want a fee," which they got and still get.

In the last few years, several things have occurred to change the relationships of banks to commercial paper issuers. First, some banks have begun, as noted, to sell commercial paper first as agent, more recently as underwriter. Second, banks have also begun to make short-term loans to issuers of commercial paper under bid options in their line agreements with issuers; such an option permits an issuer to bid a rate for short-term funds that its line bank may or may not accept. Banks making such loans often sell participations in them to managers of liquidity portfolios, who correctly view the latter as a close substitute for commercial paper (Chapter 23).

Bankers' Acceptances

The closest banks come to competing directly with the commercial paper market is by issuing loans in the form of bankers' acceptances. On certain types of transactions—financing exports, imports, and the storage and shipment of goods at home and abroad—the bank can take the borrower's note, accept it (guarantee payment at maturity), and then sell it in the open market without incurring a reserve requirement. The interest rate charged the borrower is determined by rates prevailing in the bankers' acceptance market. These are normally less than commercial paper rates, but the banks' standard acceptance fee adds additional cost, so the *all-in cost* to the BA borrower may exceed the rate on commercial paper. When loan demand is high, bankers normally sell the BAs they originate and take their spread, but when loan demand is slack, they may hold them as earning assets.

In recent years, BAs outstanding have declined somewhat. Also, Japanese banks have aggressively pursued BA business. Consequently, for domestic money market banks, originating BAs is today a declining and not very profitable business (Chapter 21).

Bank Lending Today: A Bankrupt Business

"Ten years ago," observed one banker, "we bankers lent money and sought to attract cheap deposits. We did a few other things—sold advice in an effort to get more loans and deposits or to charge a premium price for our loans. Now, the joy is almost completely out of this business insofar as our ability to get paid fairly for services provided. We can make money lending, but we can't do it with hundreds of bankers [loan officers] running around; it's too high cost. And the joy is out of it from the client's perspective because he can raise money much more cheaply than through us as an intermediary. So the traditional business of banking—bankers lending money and attracting deposits—is bankrupt from both perspectives."

Bankers: A Changing Mission

Old-style banking combined the bank's Treasury function—asset acquisition and funding on terms *best for the bank*—with its corporate finance function, where today the emphasis is increasingly on *what is best for the client*. In the old days, a client would come into a bank and say, "I want to finance this plant," and the banker [lending officer] would say, "Have I got a loan for you." What the banker was really doing was a combination of the above two functions—he was trying to position himself with his client so that his client thought the banker was doing him a favor, but what the banker was really trying to do was to acquire an asset suited to the bank. Thus, it was vague and unclear in the client's mind and indeed in the banker's mind exactly what solution loan negotiation was producing—best for the bank *or* best for the client. That was OK so long as there were not too many instruments out there. The client could clearly see what his options were: this, this, or this. He knew that when he came to his banker, he was getting a person who could deal in one or very few instruments and that he was going to get pitched to do what the bank did, loans. What has changed is that there are now hundreds of vehicles that a banker might use to solve his client's problem.

The explosion in the opportunities open to a borrower or for that matter to an asset manager reflects not just securitization encouraged by deregulation, but the breaking down of barriers that surrounded heretofore domestic capital markets plus the development of new financial tools—swaps, option products, and currency hedging mechanisms—that together have created a global market in financial assets and liabilities.

Today's banker no longer wants to be confined to a single-product capability or to a narrow product line. He has to have access to what can be done in Swissy, in yen, in sterling, and in dollars; to what can be done in short, medium, and long term; to what can be done swapped; to what can be done hedged and unhedged. Today's banker, if he's to do his job, must present all this to the client with a bank loan being but one option. That is fundamentally the difference in the role of a banker today from what it was a decade ago. The two businesses—(1) corporate finance, *what is best for the client,* and (2) asset acquisition, a Treasury function centered on *what is best for the bank*—have become two separate jobs.

The Evolution of Bankers

The trend in banking toward the provision of corporate finance has, not surprisingly, changed the banker's role. A bank now needs fewer bankers, and those it needs have to be more sophisticated and more senior than in the past. The new style banker is a *generalist* who has sufficient access to a lot of *specialists* (traders) so that, when a client comes in and says, "How do I finance it?", he can, getting his bank's traders' best advice, package and sell to the client a deal that meets the client's objectives. That today is a banker's job.

Delivery Choices

A banker, by definition a generalist, can never be an expert in all products—from cross-currency swaps to caps and floors. Therefore, a bank faces a choice as to how it will distribute expert advice, and banks are demonstrating that there's no one right solution to this. It depends on who a bank is and what it wants to do. A bank has to balance the amount of distribution it does through bankers, generalists who are supposed to know a lot about a lot of things, and the amount of distribution that it does though specialists such as its caps-and-floors trader. At one extreme is someone like a Merrill who does almost everything through specialists, and at the other extreme are commercial banks who still do everything mostly through bankers.

For a bank, it is crucial to give a client what he wants, so if a client wants to talk to a caps-and-floors trader and if that is the best way to get the client's business, a bank tries to get as close to that solution as possible. However, other bank clients are likely to be intimidated by a bank's caps-and-floors trader: they don't know enough to deal with him; they're afraid that they are going to get had; and they're more comfortable with a generalist. Whatever a bank does, it has to strike the balance that works for it organizationally.

Distribution via generalists and via specialists both have their own risks. If a bank tries to distribute purely via specialists, it's likely to find that its specialists talk their own game all the time; they are trying to make money; and although they won't admit to it, they talk their own book; they are very short term in outlook; and they don't really give a damn about how happy the client is at the end of the day. Also, overuse of specialists tends to create little fiefdoms where people do not cross sell. It can be done, but it is very tough to get someone who is focused narrowly on a product or a business to worry about what the client is going to do two weeks from now with another area of the bank. Thus, a risk in giving clients access to specialists is that a bank builds barriers to cross selling.

On the other hand, it is equally bad for a bank to have a sophisticated client—a Ford or a World Bank—talk to a generalist when the client wants serious and up-to-the-moment-please advice about opportunities in francs or DM, in swaps, or in caps and floors. A client can get general hand-holding wisdom from a generalist, but for a client who knows the game and what play he wants to make, a generalist is the wrong guy to talk to. At some senior level at a Ford, there's a guy who wants to talk to a senior generalist at a bank about strategy, but at another level there are, at a Ford, traders who want to talk to a bank's traders. Meshing who talks to whom and when calls for finesse. Specialists have to be channeled to specialists. More broadly, a bank has to organize its interface with a client to suit him, not it.

A senior banker noted, "I would talk to the Treasurer for global finance [of a firm with a sophisticated Treasury operation]. We would talk about trends, about how markets are evolving, about the soundness of various markets, about financial strategy, and at the level up from there. It would be very hard for us to talk down from there. Their traders are too specialized, too narrow, too good—and they're better informed than we are. For me to talk to the commercial paper trader of a big direct issuer, one who talks to the top 10 dealers every morning about their thinking on the market, would be nonsense; and we recognize that."

Another division of labor a bank faces is how to treat a client that does business worldwide. A reasonable solution is for a bank to have one officer looking after that client worldwide wherever he is, while the bank delivers product to the client from different places. According to this approach, a New York bank would look after Exxon, a U.S. company from New York, but if Exxon wanted something from London, the bank's London office, using its specialists, would deliver that product there. Conversely, London office would look after U.K. companies, but if a U.K. company needed a product from New York, the bank's head office would deliver that product in New York.

Corporate Finance: Assets and Liabilities

Once a bank focuses not just on lending and generating assets for the bank, but on the broader area of corporate finance, it becomes increasingly natural for the bank, in seeking what's best for the client, to work not just on the client's liabilities, but on his assets—his cash, his investment portfolio. "We have as a strategy," noted one senior banker, "taking every item on a client's balance sheet—both sides—and asking, 'Where can we bring value?' One place is in real estate. Twenty-five percent of corporate America's consolidated assets are real estate, so we are spending a lot of energy at the moment figuring out how we can solve real estate problems—how we take these great, immobile, illiquid investments clients have and realize shareholder value, create opportunities for the client." Corporate financial assets are also getting increasing attention from bankers; the same logic that has made liability swaps a huge business, can be and is being applied to asset swaps (Chapter 19).

"It's a whole different approach," continued the same banker. "Instead of being in business to lend money, I am in business to create value some way or another for the client—to do the best job I can for him. If I save the client a dollar—be it in his cash, his pension fund, his real estate, his inventories, his short-term debt, his medium-term debt, his equity, whatever—I will take 10 cents. That is our strategy. That is a different business; we are not just peddling loans. We need wholly different people who need to be trained differently, who have to interface with experts differently, who have to do everything differently."

The Glass-Steagall Imperative

If money center bankers have failed so far to implement their strategy of getting into investment banking as rapidly as they'd like to, it's not due to a lack of their thinking through this strategy. A binding constraint banks face whenever their advice to clients involves either the issuance or trading of securities is the constraints that Glass-Steagall cum the Bank Holding Company Act place on what securities banks may underwrite and trade. It's only half a loaf for a bank to advise a client, "Issue this and this security, but sorry we can't execute." That's why bankers are adamant that the substance of Glass-Steagall must go.

Mergers and Acquisitions

One area of investment banking that has consistently offered Wall Street investment bankers hefty fees and profits is *mergers and acquisitions* (*M&A*). This has not escaped the notice of money center banks whose strategy it is to shift from corporate lending to corporate finance. A number of banking titans— Bankers, Morgan, and Citi to name three—have been making a successful pitch to corporate America to do its M&A deals with them.

One veteran of this business observed that while it will take time, big banks will eventually become a serious competitive threat to traditional investment bankers in this area. Bankers Trust was one of the earlier banks to strike out into M&A. Morgan in 1987 got into the fray preaching its objectivity; also, it won't advise a deal that doesn't make sense, and it links its fees to the value added by a deal, not as other firms do, to the dollar value of the deal. Citi's pitch is that it wants to be known as the bank for lining up financing for deals, much as Drexel Burnham Lambert now is. One thing banks must be careful to avoid doing is to tie financing with advising; under the Bank Holding Company Act as amended, it's illegal for a bank to do "tie-in sales."

The attractions of M&A business to a bank are obvious. "I'd be happy," noted one banker, "to see our bank do more M&A. That's a nice business: you put up no capital and make a good fee without a lot of overhead. Unfortunately, that market is probably shrinking."

BUSINESS THREE: THE DOMESTIC TREASURY

The business we call domestic Treasury used to be twofold: to funds loans and whatever other assets the bank acquired and to contrive the bank's interest-rate gap based on the bank's view on interest rates.

Things have changed. "We have," noted one banker, "less loans in the bank than in the past. With securitization, our good and even our weaker clients can borrow elsewhere at less than the 25-bp spread [over funding costs] that we used to require on loans. So, our bankers said, 'Too bad, we are out of the lending business.' Then, my function as a funder had to be reconsidered. The significance of changing our name to Domestic Treasury is that we had to get conscious that if we did not generate assets on our own, they would not come to us on their own as they did in the past. In the past, my predecessor was just saying, 'My cost of funds plus reserves plus everything is X; and, banker, I need a spread.' That is how we priced transactions. Now if we do this, we have nothing."

Today, it is domestic Treasury's function to actively seek out assets and to fund them; to manage the interest-rate risk of the bank (no change from the past there); and depending on how the bank is organized, to trade foreign exchange, traditionally a money-making activity.

Reorganizing for Asset Acquisition

The idea of the bank's Treasury seeking assets to fund and manage is new, but fits nicely with the trend in banks to get into investment banking. "The general trend toward deregulation, our willingness to change from being a traditional lender to becoming more a securities firm, made us," noted one banker, "move toward this organization where corporate banking becomes corporate finance, and the Treasury becomes the part of the bank managing assets. In the current environment, bankers want more to be in the distribution of their liabilities, both loans and securities, and the Treasury wants more to be in the acquisition of assets to realize net interest earnings. That makes bankers and the Treasury complementary, but it calls for a change in organization.

"Instead of saying my marginal cost of funds is such and such, I have to be in an acquisition mode. We [the Treasury] have to think in terms of acquiring an asset that yields LIBID, not something that pays LIBOR plus everything because my alternative (my opportunity cost) is to go out and lend money to Chase at LIBID."

Loans

Over time, it's not so much the absolute amount of loans on the balance sheet of a money center bank that has shrunk; rather it is the bank's loans as a percentage of a growing balance sheet. Noted one banker, "Our capability to originate loans has grown, but that would not have happened if our capability to distribute them had not also been built. We now have a very large loan origination and distribution business."

Today, with bankers selling loans to investors—LBO loans to foreign banks, loans made under commercial paper lines to managers of conservative liquidity portfolios—the question arises, how does a bank determine which of the loans it originates it wants to keep? One bank's approach is that Domestic Treasury bids for the loans it wants, rejects those it does not.

"Because we did not want to hold loans on our balance sheet on very low terms, we have," noted one Treasury officer, "created a loan sales group that is selling loans to foreign banks in

New York as soon as we book them. Now, I have to say, 'I want an asset—why not a loan?' So I call the loan sales group and say, 'I want to take some of this business back to our balance sheet if I see the potential to realize a funding profit. Say, we are making a loan at LIBOR to a single A corporation for six months. Before our bank sells that loan to the Banco di Napoli, I want to be able to bid on it. If I want this loan at 7½ and Banco di Napoli is willing to bid 7.45, they get the loan. The guys in the loan sales group give me no privilege. If I bid the same rate, I get the loan—at least I get that. But for 5 bp, it will go elsewhere. However, now at least, I feel in charge of the acquisition of loans going on the balance sheet where in the past I was just passively waiting for my back office to tell me, 'These are the loans we have booked today.'"

Auctioning loans within the bank may not be the typical way that money center banks choose which loans to sell and which to keep, but clearly some rational criteria must be applied by every money center bank to make this choice. In that process, attention clearly must be paid to the relationship between rate and credit risk, because putting a loan on the bank's balance sheet exposes that bank to credit risk.

Our bid-for-loans banker is given a credit grid; depending on the rating of the borrower and the maturity of the loan, he is charged a loan loss reserve—maybe 20 bp on a triple-B loan, 5 bp on a triple-A loan. The idea of the loan loss reserve is to force the Treasury to differentiate between (1) getting paid to assume credit risk and (2) earning a funding profit. "I think that in the past," this banker observed, "we had an incorrect perception of how much was made on loans. If we can now say the lending business is generating so much funding profit, so much reserves to cover default risk, and so much to cover operating costs, then we have the three components of it—we know how much money we make on lending. Also, we can then rationally decide to lend because the ROE [return on equity] is good, or not to lend because the ROE is inadequate. Also, once we know how much we make on loans to a client, we can go on to figure out how much we make on doing other things for them—foreign exchange trading, the placing of securities. In the future, we could allocate credit lines depending on the profitability we get from a client.

We aren't there yet, but we're working on a system that will analyze total earnings on loans by client. That will be tremendously useful for our bankers in their allocation of credit lines among customers and among products."

Floating- versus Fixed-Rate Loans

The loans that a bank keeps on its balance sheet are almost all floating rate. "Our fixed-rate loan book is," noted one banker, "*de minimus*. Any fixed-rate loans we originate get sold away from the bank. We may have a commitment to extend cash for five years, but the basis is all floating rate." This asset structure explains why banks that sell 3- or 5-year, fixed-rate deposit notes immediately—in the interests of minimizing interest-rate exposure—swap the proceeds for floating-rate money.

Securities

Banks have always held portfolios of securities, governments, agencies, and munis. What is new is the trend toward holding what often amounts to securitized loans, such as corporate MTNs, car loans packaged as securities, and CMOs.

"Worldwide, we are heading," commented one banker, "towards a tremendous deregulation. The latter means the securitization of everything. What should we have in our assets? I am pushing for more securities because this is the reality—this is where the assets are. But it will be such a swing in the bank's balance sheet that it takes time."

Expanding on *this is where the assets are,* he added: "After the October 1987 crash, we called a lot of companies, all investment grade, and said, 'We are ready to make you a 2- or 3-year loan. How much do you need?' They all replied, 'For 2- or 3-year money, we issue medium-term notes for two reasons. It's cheaper; we get bids not only from banks, but from dealers. Second, it's standard documentation; we don't have to negotiate for days and nights with lawyers and banks over this or that covenant or provision.' Then, we started negotiating the price of such notes, and most of the medium-term assets we acquired were such notes."

Corporate MTNs

An obvious question a bank faces concerns how it earns a spread on corporate MTNs. It helps to have a privileged access to medium-term funds that can be swapped for sub-LIBOR funding. Several banks have also come up with the tactic of booking corporate, dollar-denominated securities in Nassau. One such banker noted: "I book corporate notes in Nassau where I do not have to pay any FDIC or reserve costs on my short-term funds." A bank that books in Nassau a loan to, as opposed to a note of, a U.S. corporation would incur under Reg D a 3% reserve requirement (Table 6–4, p. 187). More about a bank's Nassau book in Chapter 7.

A Bank's Taxable Bond Portfolio

It used to be standard practice for a bank to invest a part of the funds deposited with it in government securities that could be sold to meet increases in loan demand or depositor withdrawals. A bank's portfolio provided liquidity and some earnings.

For the nation's largest banks, with the exception of the deposit-rich B of A, this began to change in the early 1960s. At that time, many large banks, particularly those in New York, found that the secular uptrend in bank loans had eaten away most of the excess liquidity (bloated bond portfolios) with which they had emerged from World War II. At the same time, corporate treasurers began to manage their cash more actively, taking idle deposits out of the banks and investing them in commercial paper and other money market instruments. This too created liquidity problems. To solve them, the banks turned to the newly invented negotiable CD and other methods for buying money. Liability management was born, and the big banks' liquidity became in part their ability to *buy* money.

A second factor that discouraged banks from holding a bond portfolio primarily to provide liquidity was the ever-widening fluctuations that occurred in interest rates as a result of cyclical swings in economic activity and shifts in Fed policy. What the banks found was that, as loan demand slackened, interest rates would fall sharply; and as loan demand picked up, they would rise sharply. In this environment, using bonds as a source of liquidity meant buying bonds at high prices and selling them at low prices. Thus, a bank that viewed its bond portfolio as a source of liquidity found the latter to be an automatic money loser; over time, the portfolio provided some interest income and lots of capital losses.

Today, since a large bank's government portfolio is financed in the repo market, it is more a *use* than a *source* of liquidity. Also, if such a bank sells securities, the repo borrowings used to finance them have to be repaid, so portfolio sales produce *no* money to fund loans or to meet other cash needs.

Maturity Choice

Because the yield curve normally slopes upward, a bank will get a better spread between the yield on its portfolio and its financing cost the longer it extends along the maturity scale in buying governments. This tempts a bank building up its portfolio to buy at least some governments and agencies with 2-year, 4-year, or even much longer maturities, but doing so poses a risk.

An upturn in rates would cause not only a rise in financing costs, but a fall in the value of the securities held; and the longer the maturity of these securities, the more dramatic that fall would be. Thus, a bank with long governments might end up in a position where rising financing costs tell it to sell governments at a time when it can do so only at a substantial loss.

To avoid getting into such a bind, banks use several strategies. One is to minimize the damage that rising interest rates can do by holding securities with short current maturities. Another is to match the maturity of the securities purchased with the time span over which interest rates are expected to be down—a policy that will result in a runoff of the portfolio as rates start up again. A third strategy, more typical of money center banks, is to count on being smart enough to know when to buy and when to sell. Both of the latter strategies will be successful only to the extent that the bank succeeds in predicting interest-rate trends. That, however, is difficult. Strategy three in particular is tough because the best time for a bank to buy securities is when, thanks to Fed tightening, things look bleakest, and both the curve and carry are most negative; that's when long Treasuries are generally cheapest. Conversely, the best time to sell is when everything looks best. Thus, it's not surprising that many times a large bank's portfolio could have been managed better with hindsight than it was with foresight.

Portfolio Management. Active portfolio management by a bank—a willingness to make judgments about interest rates trends and adjust maturities accordingly—can significantly increase the return earned by the bank on its portfolio. Nevertheless, many banks, especially smaller ones, do not engage in such management.

Under federal tax laws, net capital gains earned by a bank on its portfolio used to be taxed at the capital gains rate, while net capital losses were deductible from ordinary income. This created an incentive for banks to bunch capital gains into one tax year and capital losses into another. Managing a bank's portfolio thus boiled down to deciding whether the current year was a gain or a loss year; this wasn't difficult. If the market was up, it was a gain year; if it was down, it was a loss year.

At the end of 1969, tax laws were changed: All bank capital gains on portfolio transactions are now treated as ordinary income and all capital losses as deductions from ordinary income. This tax change created for the first time a profit incentive for banks to actively manage their portfolios.

One reason many still don't has to do with bank accounting practices. Table 6–2 presents in bare-bones style the format of a bank income statement. Note that *two* profit figures are given,

TABLE 6–2
Typical format for a bank income statement

+Interest income
    (including interest income on securities held)
−Interest expenses
+Other operating income
    (including trading account profits)
−Noninterest operating expenses
    (including taxes other than those on capital gains)

Income before securities gains (losses)
+Securities gains (losses) net of tax effect

Net income

income before securities gains (losses) and *net income*. The first figure excludes capital gains and losses; the second reflects them as well as their effect on taxes due.

The special place given to securities gains and losses on a bank's income statement highlights them as an extraordinary item, and bank stockholders and stock analysts thus focus much attention on *income before securities gains or losses*. Since interest income on securities is included in this figure but capital gains and losses on securities trades are not, bankers prefer interest income from their portfolio to capital gains. Also, because stockholders and analysts like to see sustained earnings growth, bankers want this number to grow steadily from year to year.

That desire can at times discourage a bank from managing its portfolio. To illustrate, consider a bank that buys 3-year notes in a high-rate period. Two years later, interest rates have fallen, and the 3-year notes, which have moved down the yield curve, are trading at a yield to maturity well below their coupon. At this point, the bank might feel that, to maximize profits over time, it should sell these notes and buy new ones that have a longer current maturity and therefore sell at a higher yield. The logic of such an *extension swap* is that the capital gains earned immediately on the sale of the old notes plus the interest earned on the new notes would over time amount to more income than the interest that would have been earned by holding the old notes to maturity and then reinvesting. The swap, however, creates a capital gain in the current year and lowers interest income in the following year. To the banker who wants *income before securities gains or losses* to rise steadily, such a redistribution of income often seems too great a price to pay for maximizing profits over time; so he doesn't do the swap.

A concern with steady earnings may also lead a bank to hold more governments or governments of longer maturity than caution would dictate. Conditions may suggest that loan demand is about to pick up, that interest rates are about to rise, and that the bank should therefore reduce its holdings of governments or the maturity of those holdings. Doing so in anticipation of the event would, however, mean a temporary earnings dip, something a bank may be unwilling to accept.

A bank can put some of its portfolio into a *trading account*. The advantage in doing so is that capital gains realized in the trading account are included in the top-line income figure. The disadvantage is that securities in this account must be valued on the bank's balance sheet at the lower of market value or cost, whereas other securities in the bank's portfolio do not. At banks, one sometimes finds an anomalous situation: the bank works hard to earn profits on the 10 to 30% of its portfolio in a trading account, whereas it leaves the rest of its portfolio largely unmanaged.

The Current Environment.   Today, the B of A still has big core deposits that they must worry about investing, and some of these are matched up with investments in governments. Then, there are banks, like Citi and Chase, that get a lot of consumer deposits but that face as large or larger demands for funds to finance consumer loans, including mortgages, and their credit card businesses. Finally, there are classic wholesale banks, such as Bankers and Morgan, that are chronically deposit poor; Bankers' investment portfolio is zip, Morgan's is sizable.

The general comment to make about money center and other banks is that they all have some capital and are willing to take some risk. If they think that a good place to take a portion of that risk in an investment portfolio, they acquire one, all the while insisting to their accountants that they are acquiring the stuff to hold to maturity. (Otherwise the accountant would insist on marking the portfolio to market.) "Today," noted one banker, "what 90% of the big banks are doing in their taxable portfolios is just a crap shoot [an interest-rate play]. You go out and buy some securities and hope to hell that either you can finance them at a profit or that they are going to go up in price."

Despite the fact that banks are supposed to do their betting on rates in their trading accounts, occasionally a bank will make a big bet in its investment account, get it wrong, and suffer a dramatic loss. That happened to First Pennsy some years ago, more recently to First Minny. "In some regional banks," observed one banker, "You can get a chairman who is very aggressive, and he goes out and buys billions of governments [financed with repo]. Maybe, he thinks that's less risky than making loans because there's no credit risk. But in the meanwhile, he's taking on a lot of interest-rate risk."

Today, finding a lot of taxable securities on a money center bank's balance sheet needn't mean that the bank is making a big play in governments. "At our bank," said one banker, "U.S. Treasuries probably amount to 5% of our investment account, and they would be 0% were it not for the fact that we have some deposits that must be collateralized. Also, in some of our investment-agreement accounts—a pretty attractive source of funds—either we need Treasuries for collateral or we just need a good interest-rate match: a high-grade, dollar bullet security, and a Treasury meets that need." Another thing to bear in mind, is that today at a global bank, investment securities needn't be domestic securities. "We have today," noted the same banker, "more Belgian franc bonds than we have Treasuries, more French franc bonds than we have Treasuries, more German DM bonds than we have Treasuries, and more Aussi-dollar bonds than we have Treasuries."

The Case for Governments versus Corporates. At a bank where the norm is active management of its taxable portfolio, a question that's sometimes kicked around is this: If we're going to acquire dollar securities, why not acquire corporates instead of Treasuries, since corporates yield more? One bank portfolio manager's answer is: "I prefer by far to have Treasuries. I can repo them and earn half the corporate spread. Also, thanks to market liquidity, governments—even 10-year governments—are *all due in one day*. If I get into non-Treasury business, I go into agencies, the Ginnies or other mortgage-backed securities. In such securities, I am paid for market uncertainty that I can manage as opposed to credit uncertainty that I can't manage. The extra return we would get on corporates would not compensate us for the credit risk, the lack of liquidity, and the risk of downgrading. Look at what happened to Texaco—losing 10 billion because a judge in Texas said so and being downgraded from a triple A to a triple B; that really unsettled the corporate market; that, combined with raiders on corporates, have created fear." The market has a term for the risk of an unpredictable event, often a leveraged buy-out, turning a good credit's bonds into junk overnight: *event risk*. Governments expose a portfolio manager to market risk, but not to event risk.

"What's important in managing a government portfolio," continued the same manager, "is timing. You have enough volatility in the Treasury market to make huge money, provided that you pick the right time to acquire an asset and that you get rid of it ahead of a market downturn. That's how you can really make money, but you need flexibility to do this, and you don't have such flexibility with a portfolio of long corporates."

A Bank's Municipal Portfolio

In the past, a bank's municipal portfolio was a tax shelter. The bank paid no income taxes on the interest income it received from its munis, and it could deduct from its taxable income interest imputed to carrying this portfolio. All this changed with the Tax Reform Act of 1986, which eliminated the deductibility for banks of interest paid to carry municipals. This act, thus, guaranteed that carry on munis would be negative: if a bank were to acquire a muni that paid 7%, it would probably be paying 10% to finance it, and automatically lose 3%.

The act grandfathered muni bonds that a bank held as of June 1986. So banks today have at most a dying muni portfolio, one that is running off as securities in its mature.

The impact on the muni market of eliminating banks as investors in munis turned out to be limited. The tax act of 1986 also eliminated all sorts of tax shelters for individuals, from real estate to oil and gas. Now munis are just about the only tax shelter available to individuals, and thanks to sales of muni bonds to the latter, the muni market is in good shape.

Funding a Bank's Assets

With rate deregulation, banks have to "buy" all of the monies they require to fund their assets, either by paying an explicit rate of interest or by providing checking and other services at no cost. Today, banks get no free money.

Demand Deposits

Demand deposits have traditionally been a key source of bank funding, and as such, they are an important and valuable raw material to banks. Yet, in the U.S., unlike in many foreign countries, U.S. banks used not be to permitted to pay interest on demand deposits. So long as interest rates were low, forbidding the payment of interest on demand deposits caused bankers no problems; despite the fact that deposit balances offered a zero return, bank customers were willing to hold substantial demand deposits because the *opportunity cost* (forgone earnings opportunity) of doing so was negligible.

During the 1950s, however, things changed. Interest rates began a secular climb, which, coupled with the periodic forays the economy made into the world of tight money and high interest rates in the 1960s, drove home to corporate treasurers, state and local financial officials, and other holders of large short-term balances a new fact of life: The cost of holding idle balances was high and growing. In response, depositors trimmed their demand balances to the minimum level possible and invested excess short-term funds in interest-bearing instruments, including in particular money funds. In 1982, Congress permitted banks to offer MMDC and Super-NOW accounts specifically to compete with money funds.[17]

Because demand deposits are valuable to banks and because holders of such deposits incurred a substantial opportunity cost, an elaborate system of barter developed in which banks trade services to customers in exchange for deposits. On small accounts, the barter involves imprecise calculations. It

---

[17]The Depository Institutions Act was passed by Congress in September 1982. To help banks and thrifts compete with money funds, the act required the Depository Institutions Deregulatory Committee to establish, which it did in December 1982, a new account—dubbed the *money market deposit account (MMDA)*—that carries *no* interest rate lid and *no* withdrawal penalties. A depositor with such an account may each month make three preauthorized transfers from it and write three checks on it. The account, whether at a bank or thrift, resembles in many respects a money fund account but has the added attraction to depositors of carrying federal insurance from the FDIC or the FSLIC on deposits up to $100,000. In January 1983, the DIDC also permitted depository institutions to offer checking accounts paying unregulated rates. These accounts, quickly dubbed *Super-NOW accounts,* were initially available to consumers only.

The 1982 Banking Act also stipulated that all interest-rate controls on bank accounts as well as the ¼% advantage S&Ls enjoyed over banks on the rates they might pay on time deposits had to be phased out by January 1984, two years earlier than scheduled in the 1980 Banking Act.

amounts to the bank giving free checking services to all customers or to those with some minimum balance.

On large accounts, the barter is worked out more exactly; banks provide many services to corporate and other big customers: accepting deposits, clearing checks, wire transfers, safekeeping securities, and others. In providing these services, banks incur costs that they could recover by charging fees. Instead they ask customers to "pay" by holding demand deposits.

To determine the amount of deposit balances appropriate for each customer, the bank costs each type of service it provides. It then sets up an activity-analysis statement for each account, showing the types and volume of services provided and the costs incurred. Some of the demand deposits customers leave with a bank go to meet reserve requirements; the rest can be invested. Taking reserve requirements and current investment yields into account, the bank estimates the rate of return it earns on demand deposits. Finally, using that rate, it determines what balance each account must hold so that the bank's earnings on the account cover the costs incurred in servicing it.

A bank that requires compensating balances on lines and loans is getting at zero interest deposits on which it can earn a return. An alternative way it could earn the same return would be to charge a fee for lines and higher rates on loans. Some customers prefer the latter approach, and in recent years it has become more common for banks to grant fee lines and to quote two loan rates, a standard rate for loans with balances and a higher rate for loans without. For some public utilities this approach is mandatory since regulators will not permit utilities to hold large idle balances.

To the extent that banks obtain demand deposits either from retail customers by establishing expensive branch networks or from large depositors by exchanging services or reducing lending rates, they are paying some implicit rate of interest on such deposits even though the nominal rate is zero. Moreover, the *all-in* cost of demand deposits is still higher than this implicit rate because, as Table 6–3 shows, the reserve requirement on demand deposits for large banks is currently 12%. This means that such a bank can invest only $88 of every $100 it takes in. Also, a bank must pay the Federal Deposit Insurance

TABLE 6–3
Reserve requirements of depository institutions[1]

Type of Deposit, and Deposit Interval[2]	Depository Institution Requirements after Implementation of the Monetary Control Act of 1980	
	% of Deposits	Effective Date
Net transaction accounts[3,4]		
$0 million–$41.5 million	3	12/20/88
More than $41.5 million	12	12/20/88
Nonpersonal time deposits[5]		
By original maturity		
Less than 1½ years	3	10/6/83
1½ years or more	0	10/6/83
Eurocurrency liabilities		
All types	3	11/13/80

1. Reserve requirements in effect on December 31, 1988. Required reserves must be held in the form of deposits with Federal Reserve Banks or vault cash. Nonmembers may maintain reserve balances with a Federal Reserve Bank indirectly on a pass-through basis with certain approved institutions. For previous reserve requirements, see earlier editions of the *Annual Report* and of the *Federal Reserve Bulletin*. Under provisions of the Monetary Control Act, depository institutions include commercial banks, mutual savings banks, savings and loan associations, credit unions, agencies and branches of foreign banks, and Edge corporations.
2. The Garn–St Germain Depository Institutions Act of 1982 (Public Law 97–320) requires that $2MM of reservable liabilities (transaction accounts, nonpersonal time deposits, and Eurocurrency liabilities) of each depository institution be subject to a zero percent reserve requirement. The Board is to adjust the amount of reservable liabilities subject to this zero percent reserve requirement each year for the succeeding calendar year by 80% of the percentage increase in the total reservable liabilities of all depository institutions, measured on an annual basis as of June 30. No corresponding adjustment is to be made in the event of a decrease. On December 20, 1988, the exemption was raised from $3.2MM to $3.4MM. In determining the reserve requirements of depository institutions, the exemption shall apply in the following order: (1) net NOW accounts (NOW accounts less allowable deductions); (2) net other transaction accounts; and (3) nonpersonal time deposits or Eurocurrency liabilities starting with those with the highest reserve ratio. With respect to NOW accounts and other transaction accounts, the exemption applies only to such accounts that would be subject to a 3% reserve requirement.
3. Transaction accounts include all deposits on which the account holder is permitted to make withdrawals by negotiable or transferable instruments, payment orders of withdrawal, and telephone and preauthorized transfers in excess of three per month for the purpose of making payments to third persons or others. However, MMDAs and similar accounts subject to the rules that permit no more than six preauthorized, automatic, or other transfers per month, of which no more than three can be checks, are not transaction accounts (such accounts are savings deposits subject to time deposit reserve requirements).
4. The Monetary Control Act of 1980 requires that the amount of transaction accounts against which the 3% reserve requirement applies be modified annually by 80% of the percentage increase in transaction accounts held by all depository institutions, determined as of June 30 each year. Effective December 20, 1988, for institutions reporting quarterly and December 27, 1988, for institutions reporting weekly, the amount was increased from $40.5MM to $41.5MM.
5. In general, nonpersonal time deposits are time deposits, including savings deposits, that are not transaction accounts and in which a beneficial interest is held by a depositor that is not a natural person. Also included are certain transferable time deposits held by natural persons and certain obligations issued to depository institution offices located outside the United States. For details, see section 204.2 of Regulation D.

Source: Federal Reserve Bulletin.

Corporation (FDIC) a premium of $\frac{1}{12}$ of 1% (roughly 8 bp) on all deposits it accepts.

However high the all-in cost of demand deposits may be, banks are eager to obtain all the demand deposits they can. One reason is that the quantity of such funds supplied to a bank is quite stable over time, and a bank can thus count on these deposits being there regardless of what happens to economic conditions or interest rates. Banks also attach importance to demand and time deposits for other reasons: regulators like to see a lot of deposits as opposed to bought money on a bank's balance sheet; banks are typically ranked by deposit size rather than asset size; and bank analysts attach what is probably undue importance to the share of deposits in a bank's total liabilities.

While exchanging services for deposits has enabled banks to retain substantial amounts of demand deposits, banks, until introduction of MMDA and Super-NOW accounts, had no way to bid for additional funds from this source. The demand deposits they got were limited to the amounts consumers chose to leave with them plus the amounts needed to cover the services large customers chose to buy from them. This contrasted sharply and still does with the situation in the Euromarket where banks bid actively for deposits of all maturities, including call and overnight money (Chapter 7).

Time Deposits

The all-in cost of time-deposit money to a bank depends in part on the reserves the bank must hold against such deposits. As Table 6–3 shows, current reserve requirements are much lower on nonpersonal time deposits than on *transaction accounts* (governmentese for various personal deposit accounts that—unlike MMDA and similar accounts that carry a 0% reserve requirement—can be used to make numerous transactions but also pay interest). The reserve requirement on nonpersonal time deposits depends on the original maturity of the deposit: it's 3% if the original maturity is less than 18 months, 0% if the original maturity is 18 months or more. This requirement, effective 10/6/83, goes a long way toward explaining why money center banks became disenchanted with selling to institutional clients their old staple: large-denomination, 3- and 6-month CDs.[18]

Federal Funds

Smaller banks typically receive more deposits than they need to fund loans, whereas large banks are in the opposite position. The logical solution to this situation, in which small banks have excess reserves and large banks suffer reserve deficiencies, would be for large banks to accept the excess reserves of smaller correspondent banks as deposits and pay interest on them, a practice that used to be common before banks were forbidden in the 1930s to pay interest on demand deposits.

To get around this prohibition, the Federal funds market, somnolent since the 1920s, was revived during the 1950s. In this market, banks buy *Fed funds (reserve dollars)* from and sell Fed funds to each other. Since purchases of Fed funds are technically borrowings instead of deposits, banks buying Fed funds are permitted to pay interest on these funds. The all-in cost of Fed funds to the purchasing bank is the rate paid plus any brokerage incurred. Because Fed funds purchased are not deposits, there is no FDIC tax on them. They are also not subject to reserve requirements, since the reserve requirement has been met by the bank that accepted as a deposit the funds sold.

Most sales of Fed funds are made on an overnight basis, but some are for longer periods. Overnight transactions in Fed funds provide the purchasing bank with a cheap source of money and a convenient way to make sizable day-to-day adjustments in its reserves. For the selling bank, Fed funds sold provide a convenient form of liquidity. Small banks, unlike large money center banks, cannot count on being able to buy funds whenever they need them. Therefore they must keep their liquidity resident in their assets, and because overnight sales of Fed funds can be varied in amount from day to day, they give such banks flexibil-

---

[18]Initially, the Fed applied Req Q rate lids to deposits of all sizes, but in 1973, it exempted deposits of $100,000 or more. This freed banks to bid market rates for large time deposits and thus set the stage for the birth of the wholesale CD market (Chapter 20). S&Ls enjoyed a similar freedom to bid market rates for large-denomination CDs.

ity to adjust to the daily swings that occur in their reserve positions.

After the difficulties of the Franklin National were brought to light in 1974, banks became acutely aware that in selling Fed funds, they were making unsecured loans to other banks, and moreover they were doing so at one of the lowest rates prevailing in the money market. Consequently, banks began to monitor more closely the credit risks they assume by selling Fed funds. They will sell Fed funds only to banks to which they have established lines of credit, and they will sell to these banks only up the amount of the lines granted. In establishing a line to another bank, the selling bank will consider the other bank's reputation in the market, its size, its capital structure, and any other factors affecting its creditworthiness. The selling bank may also consider whether the buying bank is at times also a seller of funds. A bank that is always a buyer is viewed less favorably than one that operates both ways in the market. Selling funds is also important for a would-be buyer because the Fed funds market is one into which some banks have to buy their way. They do this by selling funds to a bank for a time and then saying to that bank, "We sell funds to you, why don't you extend a line to us?"

Repos

The reemergence of the Fed funds market gave banks a backdoor way to pay interest on demand deposits received from other banks. Corporations, state and local governments, and other big nonbank investors that have funds to invest for less than 30 days can't, however, sell that money directly in the Fed funds market because they are not banks. Partly to meet the needs of such investors, the repo market has developed into one of the largest and most active sectors of the money market. In it, banks and nonbank dealers create each day billions of dollars worth of what resembles interest-bearing demand deposits. In fact an investor that does a repo transaction with a bank is making a loan secured by U.S. Treasury or other securities; investing in repos thus exposes the investor to less credit risk than depositing funds directly in the bank would.

A large percentage of all repos done by banks are on an overnight basis, but term repos are also common. Since the yield curve typically slopes upward, the rate on term repos normally exceeds the overnight rate, with the spread being larger the longer the maturity of the term repo. Thus, from a cost point of view, an overnight repo tends to be more attractive. However, excessive reliance on overnight repos and purchases of Fed funds may create a shorter book (a greater mismatch between asset and liability maturities) than a bank wants to run. If so, the bank can use term repos to snug up its book.

Since the repo money a bank buys is not deposits, it pays no FDIC premiums on such funds. It also incurs no reserve requirements on money purchased in the repo market provided that the collateral used is government or federal agency securities. However, on repos done with other collateral, there is a reserve requirement if the repo is done by a bank but not if it is done by a bank affiliate, that is, by a bank holding company's securities-trading sub. Repo transactions always involve some paperwork, and if the buyer of the securities wants them safekept by another bank, there is a clearing charge. Banks doing a lot of repo carefully track these costs because they can raise significantly the all-in cost of repo money, especially if it is bought on an overnight basis. To avoid clearing charges, banks prefer to do repos with customers who will safekeep with them the securities "purchased."

The overnight repo rate is normally lower than the overnight Fed funds rate for two reasons. Lenders in this market lack direct access to the Fed funds market. Also, doing repo does not expose the lender to the same credit risk that selling Fed funds would. The banks' main alternative to buying funds in the term repo market is buying term Fed funds. The decision between the two is likely to be made strictly on the basis of which sells at the lower all-in cost. Normally this will be term repo, which tends to trade below term Fed funds for the same reasons that overnight repo money is normally cheaper than overnight Fed funds.

Because repo money is cheap and because a money market bank buys lots of it, such banks carefully search out and cultivate big investors in repo. They make it a point to know the needs of their big customers—whether they can buy commercial paper, repo, or what—and they call these customers every day to get a feel for what monies they have available. The banks also keep track of who is issuing bonds and who is therefore going to get big money. For example, if New York State floats a $2- or $3-billion bond issue to obtain funds that it intends to pay out to school districts two months hence, every money market bank will know that the state has money to invest in repo, and they will all be calling the state to get some of it.

Doing repo with customers is the way banks get most of the repo money they buy. However, banks that are primary dealers in government securities also frequently do repo transactions with the Fed and reverses as well. As explained in Chapter 9, the Fed relies heavily on repos and reverses with dealers in governments to make short-term adjustments in bank reserves.

Negotiable CDs and Deposit Notes

In the early 1960s, the demand for funds at New York money market banks began to outstrip their traditional sources of funds. Moreover, these banks had no way to bid for funds outside their own geographic area, for example, to pull time deposits in from the West Coast. To solve this problem, Citibank introduced the negotiable CD, an innovation that became an instant success and was widely copied.

The CD became important to top domestic banks not only because it allowed them to tap the national market for funds, but because it provided them with a means, really the only one available, to bid for longer-term funds in volume. In the domestic market, unlike the Euromarket, the supply of large-denomination time deposits offered by investors is thin at best. Large corporations don't want to hear about time deposits; they want liquidity. State and local governments used to give large time deposits to banks, but they too have become increasingly interested in liquidity. Also, time deposits held by state and local governments have the disadvantage from the point of view of the accepting bank that they must be collateralized by Treasury or municipal securities.

In buying longer-maturity funds, the only alternatives a bank had to issuing CDs was to do term repo or buy term Fed funds. Term repo is a limited alternative because if a bank repos any asset other than governments and agencies (banks have attempted to repo everything including loans), it incurs a re-serve requirement. Purchases of term Fed funds are a viable alternative, but they produce on a bank's balance sheet "other borrowings," not "deposits"; due to cosmetic considerations, banks regard the latter as more desirable.

The all-in cost to an issuing bank of CD money is the rate paid on the CD plus FDIC insurance plus the reserve cost plus the commission paid to the issuing dealer if one is used.

As late as the early 1980s, the sale of large-denomination, negotiable, short-term, fixed-rate CDs was an important source of funding to money center banks. The sale of 3-month CDs provided banks with a dependable source of variable-rate, short-term funds. The real depth in the wholesale CD market was in the 1- to 3-month range, but there was a thin market for 6-month paper, and a still thinner market for 1-year paper. When a bank took a strong view that rates were going to rise, it would often try to sell longer-term, fixed-rate CDs; if, at the time, the yield curve sloped upward, doing so increased not only a bank's liquidity, but its interest-rate exposure.

Since the 1983 change that eliminated reserve require-ments on bank deposits having an original maturity of 18 months or longer, banks have replaced the funds they once raised through the sale of wholesale, short-term CDs with funds raised though the sale of two new instruments: (1) 18-month, variable-rate CDs (coupled with a dealer put feature) that are sold to money funds;[19] and (2) 2- to 5-year, fixed-rate deposit notes, the proceeds of which the issuing bank swaps, fixed to floating (Chapter 24). The beauty, from the point of the issuing bank, of these new instruments is that, by using them, the bank eliminates a trying dilemma that it once faced in funding: to achieve greater liquidity, a bank had to take on more interest-rate risk; and to reduce interest-rate risk, it had to sacrifice liquidity. Today, that trade-off is dead.

---

[19]This is 18-month paper, but there is a put every month on the repricing date; this put is given by the dealer who intermediates the transaction. The issuing bank can't give the put, because if it did, it would have to pay reserves; instead it strikes a deal directly with the lender, who then says, "We want to transact through First Boston, Merrill, or whomever because we like their put best." The issuing bank then calls that dealer, tells them that the transaction has been done, and pays them 1 or 2 bp for their put.

"We have," noted one banker, "lengthened [using new liability tools] the average maturity of our funding. In the early 1980s, it used to go up to six months, maybe one year, rarely beyond one year. Now, we borrow very naturally 2-, 3-, even 5-year money. Also, since we borrow long, we need to go to the market less often. We still issue short-term domestic CDs, but only to retail clients—small insurance companies, small fund managers, clients of our private banking department—and when we do so, we issue at 50 bp below the [CD] index; it's not a market."

Issuing deposit notes is particularly attractive to a bank whose unquestioned credit rating gives it privileged access to funds. "We are," noted a funding officer of such a bank, "by far the number one issuer of deposit notes. I like them because they permit me to leverage on our better credit quality relative to other banks. If I raise 3-month money and I am against a good-to-average money center bank, the lender will not make a big difference—no more than 1/32, that is, 2 or 3 bp. However, if I go to a 2- or 3-year maturity, against the same name, I get a 3/8- to 40-bp yield differential. Then, I do a swap and I have the same price as the other bank on the swap, since the swap price is credit insensitive. So I have created LIBOR-minus funding: on 3-year money, where the swap spread is something like 80 bp, I pay 50 bp over Treasuries, and I thus create funding at 3-month LIBOR minus 30 bp. If, alternatively, I were to raise money for three months, I'd pay like another money center bank, probably LIBID to LIMEAN."[20]

Eurodollars

A final source of funding to which a bank may turn is the Euromarket, where it can bid for deposits (*take* money) of essentially any maturity from overnight on out. A bank can also invest (*place*) money it has raised in the domestic market in Euro time deposits. The reserve requirement on Euros is established under *Regulation D,* which currently requires a domestic bank to hold reserves equal to 3% of any *net* borrowings (borrowings minus

---

[20]LIMEAN is the average of LIBOR and LIBID.

placements) of Euros that it makes for its domestic book over a seven-day averaging period. Because of Reg *D*, a bank that takes Euros of one maturity will often place Euros of some other maturity during the averaging period so that its reserve cost on the money borrowed is zero.

The head offices of money market banks are very active in the Euromarket for several reasons. First, they are constantly alert to the opportunities for arbitrage between the domestic and the Euromarkets that arise because of transitory rate discrepancies.[21] For example, if 6-month Euros are selling at 10.50% and 6-month money can be purchased at 9% in the domestic market, a bank may take domestic 6-month money and place it in the Euromarket through its London branch. Doing so, besides locking in a spread, permits the bank to bring back short-dated Euros at no reserve cost. Such intrabank arbitrages play an important role in holding Euro and U.S. rates in line.

Gap Management

As noted, the Treasury business of a bank involves not only acquiring assets and funding them—building in an interest-rate spread—but gapping, betting on strongly held views on interest rates. "On the trading floor where I work," noted one banker, "we focus on interest income—probably 80% of our efforts on 20% of our income, which involves being right on the market day to day. We have a group that is continually monitoring the interest-rate gaps of the firm and trying to decide whether, in the context of the market, it wants to be long or short."

The Evolution of Swaps in Gap Management
It is probably typical of money market banks that they first began to use swaps to convert fixed-rate borrowings to floating-rate borrowings. Later, they saw the potential for using swaps

---

[21]Strictly defined to arbitrage means to buy something where it is cheap and to sell it where it is dear.

in gap management: by becoming a receiver of fixed, they could acquire a synthetic, medium-term, fixed-rate asset.

One banker recounted his bank's experience: "As our medium-term loans were contracting from the viewpoint of funding, there was a bull market in medium-term paper and our credit rating was improving; so a lot of customers were calling us wanting to buy fixed-rate, medium-term liabilities of the bank. We had no immediate need for such funding, since we had no equivalent loans to finance. So, we came into the swap market as an end user. We did this very much on a matched-book basis, turning medium-term, fixed-rate liabilities into medium-term, floating-rate liabilities. From there, we developed into an outright trader of interest-rate swaps. The next step was that we began to use interest-rate swaps in much the same way that a traditional asset-liability manager would use Treasuries. When we were constructive on the market, convinced that rates would come down, we would not only buy Treasuries, but start doing swaps in which we were receivers of fixed.

"That is where we started, and certainly the majority of the top 100 banks in the world are at that level of sophistication now. They use interest-rate swaps not only to match up assets and liabilities, but as a tool for gapping: instead of putting medium-term Treasuries on the balance sheet, they now use swaps as an off-balance-sheet way to acquire a fixed-rate, term asset."

In a bank, it's now typical to have a group of traders running a hedged swap book. If the bank's Treasury wants to received fixed as an asset play, it will often do the trade directly with its swap group, which will in turn hedge that position until it is able to lay it off (Chapter 19). To keep its swap group "honest," a bank's Treasury will, as an end user of swaps, probably reserve the right to get quotes from and also to transact swap business with other dealers.

Interest Rate Futures as a Tool of Gap Management

By regulation, banks are supposed to use futures only to hedge. But in point of fact, banks have so many assets and liabilities on their books that they can defend almost any position they might take in futures, from the 3-month Euros to the long bond contract, as a hedge. Consequently, bankers regard and use futures as one more tool of gap management. If a bank wants to be long, it may at times make more sense for it to buy futures than for it to buy cash instruments. Futures are off balance sheet, and at least Euro and bond futures possess the virtue of being highly liquid. A long in futures—like receiving fixed on a swap—can be an attractive alternative from the point of view of gapping; both will give a gap manager the approximate rate play of being long in Treasuries, provided he pays due attention to the factors affecting spread relationships and relative liquidity.

The Ball in Play

The following quote gives the flavor of how a gap manager at a big bank operates: "Within the context of a $60-billion balance sheet, we can generally find a way to describe a futures position as a hedge. That being the case, the issue becomes at the margin: Do I want to use a future, an interest-rate swap, an option, a Treasury, an interbank time deposit, a whole loan, or a mortgage? You couldn't do this with your entire portfolio, but you can do it with a chunk of the portfolio.

"You employ traders who are specialists and you allow them a degree of freedom which means that, if your swap trader likes the market, he will probably use swaps to express his view. That is fine as a way of training people, as a way of keeping the institution sharp, as a way of diversifying some of your risk, and as a way of being involved across markets. But there needs to be a management group within the institution that looks at relative value and that is prepared to shift the firm's capital so that you pursue relative value more efficiently. That group has several decisions to make: As an institution, should we be making a bet on interest rates? If so, on what part of the curve and in what product should we place our bet?

"You can look at matrices of relative yields, convexity, and the rest of it—as between options, mortgages, whole loans, futures, swaps, notes, and bonds—and make that decision. You can generally do good size in the swap market; you can generally do good size in the futures market, but there your maturities will be more limited; you can clearly do good size in the Treasury market; beyond that, all of the other markets have their problems. The options market falls on the far side of the dividing line. At times, buying options may be more efficient and more liquid than buying Marine's 3-year car loans or something. At other times, the reverse may be true. You have to look at both price and your confidence in your ability to unwind the transaction."

THE DISTRIBUTION BUSINESS

From what we've said about where banks are moving as Glass-Steagall walls crumble and about the increasing tendency of banks to originate loans to sell them, it's clear that for banks to get where their current strategies are leading them, they must continue to build distribution. That should be the least difficult of the tasks currently facing them, since money center banks have long had sizable and highly professional staffs selling Treasuries and other exempt securities. For them, the principal challenge is expanding product line.

BANK CAPITAL ADEQUACY

In talking about bank capital adequacy, the first thing to note is that the essence of banking is for a bank to raise the return on its equity capital through leverage.

Leverage

To illustrate *leverage* at work, here's a simple example. Suppose an investor has $1MM of capital to invest. He can borrow additional funds at 10% and he can invest at 15%. If he invests only his $1MM of capital, he will earn $150,000 for a return of 15% on that capital. If alternatively he borrows $5MM and invests a total of $6MM, he will have an investment income of $900,000, interest costs of $500,000, and profits of $400,000, which amount to a 40% return on his $1MM of capital (Table 6–4). By borrowing funds at a low rate and investing them along with his capital

TABLE 6–4
Leverage at work: Investor has $1MM of capital

Case I: No borrowed funds used; investment returns 15%:

$$\text{Investment income} = 15\% \times \$1\text{MM} = \$150,000$$
$$-\text{Interest cost} = 10\% \times 0 = \underline{\qquad 0}$$
$$\text{Profit} = \$150,000$$
$$\text{Rate of return on capital} = \frac{\$150,000}{\$1\text{MM}} = 15\%$$

Case II: $5MM of borrowed funds costing 10% used; investment returns 15%:

$$\text{Investment income} = 15\% \times \$6\text{MM} = \$900,000$$
$$-\text{Interest cost} = 10\% \times \$5\text{MM} = \underline{\quad 500,000}$$
$$\text{Profit} = \$400,000$$
$$\text{Rate of return on capital} = \frac{\$400,000}{\$1\text{MM}} = 40\%$$

Case III: $5MM of borrowed funds costing 10% used; investment returns 5%:

$$\text{Investment income} = 5\% \times \$6\text{MM} = \$300,000$$
$$-\text{Interest cost} = 10\% \times \$5\text{MM} = \underline{\quad 500,000}$$
$$\text{Profit} = -\$200,000$$
$$\text{Rate of return on capital} = \frac{-\$200,000}{\$1\text{MM}} = -20\%$$

at a higher rate, our investor has raised the return on his capital.

Unfortunately, there's "a terrible symmetry to leverage: it is as crushing on the way down as it is munificent on the way up."[22] If our investor, who anticipated earning 15% on his investment, earned only 5%, then his profit would be −$200,000 for a rate of return capital of −20% (Case III, Table 6–4).

Because bankers operate with borrowed funds that amount in total to a substantial multiple of their capital, they engage in leverage on a grand scale. Moreover, because assuming both a credit risk by lending and a rate risk by running a short book are fundamental elements of banking, the banker can never be sure either what average return he will earn on his assets or what his cost of funds will be. The purpose of bank capital is to cushion bank depositors and other suppliers of debt capital to

---

[22]Connie Bruck, "The World of Business," *The New Yorker,* May 8, 1989, p. 84.

banks against any losses the bank might incur due to unfavorable leverage—borrowing costs higher than return earned.

Past Views of Capital Adequacy

While it's easy to see that a bank needs capital, the question of how much is difficult, perhaps unanswerable. In attempting to measure bank capital adequacy, the yardstick used to be the ratio of a bank's deposits to its loans, its major risk assets. Then as banks became active buyers of money, focus shifted to the ratio of equity to total risk assets. However well or poorly this ratio may measure bank capital adequacy, it in no way solves the question of what minimum value the ratio should have. For every $1 of capital, should a bank borrow at most $10, $20, or what? Any intelligent answer to this question should probably be based on a bank's earning power as measured by certain historical indexes and modified to allow for the bank's bad-debt experience. Such numbers, however, vary from bank to bank, suggesting that no absolute industry-wide standard can or should be set.

As a practical matter, the capital ratios that prevailed in banking in the past in no way reflected reasoned decisions by either bankers or regulators as to what these ratios should be. To the contrary, what they were at any point reflected historical evolution and prevailing economic conditions. In particular, during the post–World War II period, as loan demand surged and banks strove for continued earnings growth, bank capital ratios declined substantially. Moreover, this downward trend continued until the 1980s.

The attitude that prevailed among bankers toward the capital adequacy question is well illustrated by the words of one bank president: "Back in the credit crunch of 1974, because of inflation and an insatiable demand for credit, we got to the point where equity was about 4% of assets, so we had leverage of 25 to 1. At the peak, we and a lot of bankers asked how far can this go, and we decided we had better slow down and tighten up. So we set a leverage maximum of 25 to 1." In the next breath, the same banker added: "We of course have to forget all about that standard when we deal with foreign banks. The leading Israeli banks have about 1% capital ratios, and in Japan the figure is 1 or 2%." In effect, this banker and other U.S. bankers measure capital adequacy in domestic and foreign banks by differing standards, a practice that suggests they have *no* absolute notion of what capital ratios should be.

Since the whole question of capital adequacy boils down to asking how much capital a bank needs to assure its survival under unknown future conditions, it is no surprise that neither bankers nor regulators have definitively answered this question. The typical U.S. banker's motto, in determining what minimum capital ratio his bank should maintain, used to be: *Stay with the herd.* Banking tends to be a homogeneous industry and as such is characterized by pattern thinking. A banker used to judge his leverage ratio to be high or low in terms of where he was vis-à-vis his peers. If the pack let their capital ratios fall, he was comfortable to follow, but he did not want to lead. This attitude made sense because the Fed tended to judge banks against the pattern of what their competitors were doing. Also, bank customers, who watch leverage carefully, were ever ready to penalize a bank that got out of line.

The Basel Accord

Implementation of the 1987 Basel Accord with respect to bank capital requirements will mark, in the U.S. at least, a sharp departure from past practices. Under these, all forms of bank capital were simply matched against all bank assets, whatever their risk might be; and off-balance-sheet items were largely ignored. Also, no specific minimum ratio of capital to assets was required, although the Fed did feel free to tell a bank that its capital was on the low side, especially if that bank were applying for permission to do this or that.

Under the Fed's interpretation of the Basel agreement, the above will change. First, banks will be required to hold 8% capital against their assets. Half of the capital must be *tier one* capital, largely equity capital. The other half, *tier two,* may comprise things such as preferred stock and long-term debt. Also, capital requirements are to be imposed according to *risk-based guidelines.* Under these, a bank loan carries a 100% risk rating and must thus be backed by the full 8% capital ratio. In contrast, U.S. governments with a current maturity of 91 days or less are assigned a zero risk rating; also, only 10% of governments having a current maturity exceeding 91 days need be backed by capital, and only 20% of paper issued by federal agencies and supranational institutions need be backed by capital. Finally, interbank deposits too enjoy favored status, a 20% risk rating.

The intent of this regulation is to protect the international financial system from the failure of a global bank and also to put global banks on a level playing field. Once banks ranked themselves by asset size. In the future, they will focus more on capital. For banks that will have to go to the capital market to bid for yet more capital, ROE is becoming an ever more important number. Concentration on profitability may in turn hasten the rationalization, in the U.S. at least, of the banking industry, where excessive regulation, particularly prohibitions on intrastate and interstate branching, has been preventing banks from exploiting economies of scale, particularly those permitted by new advances in technology.

While there seems to be general agreement that requiring banks to hold a goodly hunk of capital is a good idea, questions and quibbles about the Basel Accord and about the way various central banks are applying it have naturally arisen. One fair question concerns just how level the playing field will be when the Japanese stock market values domestic bank stocks at a much higher price-earnings ratio than that at which, say, the British and U.S. stock markets value their domestic banks.

Another fair question is whether risk-based capital guidelines, which are bound to change bank behavioral patterns, will result in unintended and undesirable forms of capital allocation. For example, the guidelines certainly create an incentive, for a bank that's concerned about meeting its capital constraint, to lend money to the World Bank or even to another bank rather than to a corporation, be the latter a bad or a good credit; specifically, they create a 5-to-1 hurdle between lending money to an IBM and lending money to Morgan or to the World Bank. How will such incentives affect capital allocation? In the future, will marginal dollars that many banks now invest in loan participations purchased from other banks be simply invested in the

Euromarket at LIBID? Will development projects be more often financed via World Bank loans rather than via investments by private corporations? These and related questions are important and worthy of thoughtful consideration.

A final point is that 1992 was in a sense already in place in 1989. At that time, several U.S. banks, including Morgan, Bankers, and Citi, met the Basel requirements and were quick to announce that to the world. That in turn forced 1992 standards to become, de facto, the industry norm in 1989. The requirements remained down the road, but banks were under pressure to get their balance sheets in order immediately.

BANK REGULATION

U.S. banks and foreign banks operating branches in the U.S. are highly regulated with respect to what they may do. As background, we present in an appendix to this chapter a short description of major U.S. banking acts.

Banking in America is often referred to as a "dual" system because some banks operate under federal charters obtained from the Comptroller of the Currency, while others are chartered by the states. U.S. bank regulation comes in layers. State banks are regulated by state banking authorities, national banks by the Comptroller; the Fed has its say; and the FDIC regulates insured banks.[23] The overlap in bank regulation has led to periodic calls for a single unified system of bank regulation. However, movement in this direction seems unlikely because state banks, which are numerous and have considerable clout in Congress, are anxious to preserve a system in which the primary responsibility for regulating them lies with the local state banking authority; these banks fear being forced into a single national banking system.

---

[23]Lest anyone think that layers of regulation preclude bank failures, we cite several numbers: in the U.S. in 1989, there were 200 bank failures and 21 federally assisted sales of failed banks.

Fortunately, the regulatory overlap is less than appears on paper. Often the state regulators will focus on checking the accuracy of the bank's audited statements, whereas examiners from the Fed will be more concerned with whether the bank is being properly run.

The regulations under which U.S. banks operate are numerous, detailed, and complex. Perhaps one reason is the checkered history of the U.S. banking system, which periodically experienced waves of failures and suspensions of payments right up into the 1930s. A second reason is that flexible regulation may be impractical in a country where there are 14,000 different banks, a situation unparalleled in any other major country.

Many people, particularly members of Congress, feel that, if the regulators were doing their job, no bank would have problems and that the existence of problem banks indicates the need for more or better regulation. Yet, as one regulator noted, the same member of Congress who says there should never be problem banks is also quick to complain, when wheat prices are low and there is a big overhang in the wheat market, that Nebraska farmers are having trouble getting bank credit.

The nature of banking is taking risks by lending and by doing some maturity arbitrage. Good regulators see their job as trying to keep these risks prudent. They also recognize that the regulatory structure should not be such that no bank ever fails. If it were, banking as a creative force would be stifled.

When a bank experiences such severe problems that it ceases to be a viable institution, the regulators will normally arrange some sort of merger between that bank and another strong bank. A big salvage operation may involve first substantial loans from the Fed to the ailing bank and later cash injections by the FDIC in exchange for some of the bank's less desirable assets.

The merger, if it occurs, is typically forced by events, not by the regulators. As one regulator noted: "When a bank has problems, we try to save it so long as it's a viable institution. We will make suggestions to management, but it's their responsibility to right the situation. A bank ceases to be viable when public confidence in the bank weakens, usually due to some easily identifiable event. Before that occurs, we may look in the wings for

potential marriage partners—act if you will as marriage brokers—but there is *no* shotgun for the marriage until public confidence is lost."

The fact that the Fed and the FDIC have not in recent
decades permitted a *major* bank to fail with losses to depositors
raises an interesting question: Would they ever? The answer,
most observers believe (including some inside the Fed), is no.
The reason is that the economic consequences of permitting a
major bank to fail with losses to depositors would be enormously
more costly than acting to protect depositors. Still, there is the
political risk, that is, the possibility that a large bank might
through its actions so arouse the public's ire that the Fed and
the FDIC would not be permitted to save it.

BANK HOLDING COMPANIES

Almost all large banks and many smaller banks in the U.S. are
owned by holding companies. Prior to the 1960s, bank holding
companies were used primarily to surmount restrictions on intrastate branching by bringing under a single organization a
number of separately chartered banks. Formation of multibank
holding companies was brought under regulation by the Bank
Holding Company Act in 1956. The purpose of this act, administered by the Federal Reserve Board, was twofold: to prevent the
creation of monopoly power in banks and to prevent banks from
entering via their holding company what were traditionally
nonbank lines of activity.

In the late 1960s, many of the nation's largest banks formed
one-bank holding companies, which were not subject to the provisions of the 1956 act. One objective in doing so was to create a
vehicle through which they could enter indirectly activities they
could not carry out directly. The banks' ability to achieve such
diversification was, however, severely limited by the Bank
Holding Company Act of 1970. This act brought one-bank holding companies under regulation by the Federal Reserve Board,
which is responsible for restricting their activities to those
"which are so closely related to banking as to be a proper incident thereto."

A second reason banks formed one-bank holding companies was to achieve greater flexibility in liability management. During the late 1960s, open market rates rose on several occasions above the Reg Q ceiling, and banks had difficulty selling CDs. To solve the resulting funding problem, the banks segregated certain loans on their books, put them in the holding company, and issued commercial paper, which was not subject to Regulation Q, to fund these loans. The Fed's response to this end run around Reg Q was to impose a reserve requirement on any paper sold to fund such loans. This reserve requirement does not apply to other assets sold by a bank to its holding company.

Today bank holding companies enter the story of the money market primarily as issuers of commercial paper. They use the proceeds to fund various assets on their own books and on those of their nonbank subsidiaries. These include bank credit card receivables purchased from the bank, assets leased, loans extended through finance companies and other nonbank subs of the holding company, and last but not least the bank affiliates that trade securities.

EDGE ACT CORPORATIONS

A 1919 amendment to the Federal Reserve Act permits national banks and state banks that are members of the Federal Reserve System to establish international banking corporations, known familiarly as Edge Act corporations.

The operations of *Edge Act corporations* within the U.S. are restricted to activities that are incidental to the parent bank's international business—holding demand and time deposits received from foreign sources, issuing letters of credit, financing foreign trade, and creating BAs. Edge Act corporations are also permitted to engage in overseas operations, to provide certain types of specialized financing, such as loan syndication, and to make equity investments in foreign financial institutions. As the origination of BAs by U.S. banks has diminished in importance, so too have their Edge Act subs.

APPENDIX TO CHAPTER 6
THE BANKING ACTS THAT MATTER*

Edge Act: 1919
Named after Senator Walter Edge of New Jersey, who played a prominent role in its passage, this act provided for federal chartering of
corporations formed to engage solely in international or foreign banking. The hope was that these Edge Act corporations would play a key
role in financing American exports.

McFadden Act: 1927
This prohibits interstate banking.

Glass-Steagall Act: 1933
This severed commercial from investment banking and forced banks to
divest themselves of any security-trading affiliates. The 1933 Banking
Act also created the Federal Deposit Insurance Corporation and
brought bank holding companies—except, as was discovered later, the
one-bank holding companies—under the supervision of the Federal
Reserve Board.

Douglas Amendment to the Bank Holding
Company Act: 1956
This prohibits a bank holding company headquartered in one state
from acquiring a bank in another state unless the second state specifically permits the acquisition.

Bank Merger Act: 1960
After a decade of debate over whether to apply existing antitrust laws
explicitly to banking or to incorporate similar competitive standards
into existing banking laws, this legislation plumped for the second
source. It required the bank regulatory agencies (for the first time) to
weigh the possible competitive effects of proposed mergers and acquisitions when considering applications.

---

*From "A Survey of International Banking," *The Economist,* March 14, 1981, p. 19.

Amendment to the Bank Holding Company Act: 1970

This brought one-bank holding companies under the same regulations as multibank holding companies.

International Banking Act: 1978

To bring foreign banks within the federal regulatory framework, the IBA introduced six major statutory changes:

It limited interstate domestic deposit taking by foreign banks. Previously, foreign banks had been free to open full-service branches wherever state law permitted. The new law required each foreign bank to elect a "home state" and restricted domestic deposit taking by offices outside that state.

Existing multistate branch networks of foreign banks were "grandfathered" (allowed to carry on as they were), a major concession since 40 of the 50 largest foreign banks were able to shelter under its wing.

It provided the option of federal licensing for foreign bank agencies and branches. Previously all foreign bank offices had state licenses and some states applied reciprocity rules which effectively barred banks from certain countries.

The federal licensing authority (the Comptroller of the Currency) has permitted foreign banks to establish offices without regard to whether the foreign bank's home country grants equivalent access to American banks.

It authorized the Federal Reserve Board to impose reserve requirements on agencies and branches of foreign banks with worldwide assets of more than $1 billion and to limit the maximum rates of interest such offices could pay on time deposits to the same as member banks.

It required federal deposit insurance (not previously available to foreign banks) for those branches engaged in retail deposit taking.

It amended the Edge Act to permit Edge corporations (which could conduct international banking out-of-state) to compete over a broader range of business and permitted foreign banks to set up such corporations.

It subjected foreign banks to the same prohibitions on nonbanking business as domestic bank holding companies. Once again, existing nonbanking activities (including securities underwriting from which domestic banks are excluded) were "grandfathered."

Depository Institutions Deregulation and Monetary Control Act: 1980

This "omnibus act" had four main aims:

To phase out (over a six-year period) interest-rate ceilings on deposits and to eliminate the 0.25% favorable differential traditionally enjoyed by the thrifts. A Depository Institutions Deregulation Committee, with representatives from the main regulatory agencies, was set up to oversee the process. All the evidence points to the committee accomplishing its task in far less than six years.

To extend nationwide the authority (previously exclusive to the New England states) to offer NOW (negotiable order of withdrawal) accounts. The maximum rate to be offered on NOW accounts has been set initially at 5.25% for all institutions. This ends the prohibition on the payment of interest on demand deposits.

To grant new powers to the federally chartered thrifts. A number of states have passed parallel legislation for state-chartered institutions to discourage desertion from state to federal charter. Most importantly, these powers permit S&Ls to invest up to 20% of their assets in consumer loans, commercial paper, and company securities; to offer credit cards; and to exercise fiduciary powers.

To override state-imposed usury ceilings on mortgages. (Some states have already taken action to raise their ceilings.)

Depository Institutions Act: 1982*

This act was designed to aid failing thrifts and to permit both banks and thrifts to compete immediately for deposits with money funds.

To accomplish the first aim, the act created a scheme under which thrifts whose net worth drops below 3% of their assets can prop up their net worth by swapping paper they issue for promissory notes—to be counted as capital—from the Federal Savings and Loan Insurance Corporation, which insures deposits at S&Ls up to $100,000. For thrifts too sick to survive even with such aid, the act specifically permits takeovers by an out-of-state thrift or even a bank. The act also gives thrifts the new right to make commercial loans up to 10% of their total assets and to accept deposits from firms as well as individuals.

To help banks and thrifts compete with money funds, the new act required the Depository Institutions Deregulatory Committee to estab-

---

*Author's addition.

lish a new account that carried *no* interest rate controls and *no* withdrawal penalties and that permitted a depositor with such an account to make each month three pre-authorized transfers from it and to write three checks on it. The new account, whether at a bank or thrift, was to resemble a money fund account but have the added attraction to depositors of carrying FDIC or FSLIC insurance on deposits up to $100,000. The DIDC responded to this congressional mandate by crediting first the *money market deposit account* (*MMDA*) (December 1982) and then the *Super-Now account* (January 1983).

The law also required that all interest-rate controls on bank accounts as well as the ¼% advantage S&Ls enjoyed over banks on the rates they could pay on time deposits be phased out by January 1984, two years earlier than scheduled in the 1980 Banking Act.

Finally, the act raised from 10% to 15% of capital and surplus the amount that nationally chartered banks may lend to any one borrower. Legal lending limits for state-chartered banks generally equal or exceed those for nationally chartered banks.

CHAPTER 7

THE BANKS: EURO OPERATIONS

According to propagandists on both sides of the Cold War, communists and capitalists are implacable enemies, or at least were pre-Gorbachev. It thus comes as a surprise to find that communist central banks bear as much responsibility as anyone for giving birth to one of the fastest growing, most vital and important capitalist institutions—namely, the international capital market known as the *Eurodollar market*. But then neither communist nor capitalist bankers had much idea of the long-run implications of what they were doing when the Euromarket was born.

EURO TRANSACTIONS IN T-ACCOUNTS

The best way to start a discussion of the Euromarket is by explaining the mechanics of Eurodeposits and loans, about which there is much confusion. First, a definition: *Eurodollars are simply dollars held on deposit in a bank or bank branch located outside the United States or in an IBF.*[1] If a U.S. investor shifts $1MM of deposits from a New York bank to the London branch of a U.S. bank, to Barclays London, or to the London branch of any French, German, or other foreign bank and receives in exchange a deposit denominated in dollars, he has made a *Eurodollar deposit*. Such deposits came to be known as *Eurodollars*

---

[1]International Banking Facilities (IBFs) are described at the end of this chapter.

because initially banks in Europe were most active in seeking and accepting such deposits. Today, however, banks all over the globe are active in the Eurodollar market, and the term *Eurodollar* is a misnomer.[2]

The first important point to make about Eurodollars is that regardless of where they are deposited—London, Singapore, Tokyo, or Bahrain—they never leave the U.S. Also, they never leave the U.S. regardless of where they are lent—to a multinational firm, to an underdeveloped country, or to an East European government. Let's work that out with T-accounts. As noted in Chapter 2, a T-account shows *changes in assets and liabilities* that result from a given financial transaction, as shown below.

T-Account	
Changes in assets	Change in liabilities

To get our example going, suppose Exxon moves $10MM from its account at Morgan in New York to the London branch of Citibank. (You can think of Exxon as writing a check against Morgan New York and depositing it in Citi London, but the transaction is done by wire or Telex.) Clearing of this transaction, which normally occurs on the day after it is initiated, will result in several balance-sheet changes (Table 7–1).

Before we look at these changes, two preliminary remarks are in order. First, Citi's London branch is an integral part of Citibank; and when the bank publishes statements, it consolidates the assets and liabilities of head office and all foreign branches. However, on a day-to-day operating basis, Citi New York, Citi London, and Citi's other foreign branches all keep

---

[2]Some people refer to dollar deposits accepted in Singapore and other Far East centers as *Asian currency units* (ACUs) or *Asian dollars*. The natural extension of this practice would be to refer to dollar deposits accepted in Bahrain as Middle East dollars and dollar deposits accepted in Nassau as Caribbean dollars; that is, to use a multitude of terms to describe the same thing, an offshore deposit of dollars. The logical alternative to *Eurodollar* is *international dollar,* an awkward phrase that has never caught on.

TABLE 7–1
A Eurodeposit is made and cleared

	Exxon	
Demand deposits, Morgan N.Y. −10MM		
(Euro) time deposits, Citi London +10MM		

Citi New York			Citi London	
Reserves +10MM	London office dollar account (a "due to" item, Citi N.Y. to Citi London) +10MM		New York office dollar account (a "due from" item, Citi London to Citi N.Y.) +10MM	(Euro) time deposits +10MM

Morgan New York			New York Fed	
Reserves −10MM	Demand deposits, Exxon −10MM			Reserves, Morgan −10MM
				Reserves, Citi +10MM

separate books. Second, Citibank has just one account at the Fed, that held by Citi New York, the head office.

Now let's look at Table 7–1. It shows that, as a result of the transaction, Exxon exchanges one asset, $10MM of demand deposits at Morgan New York, for another, $10MM of the Eurodeposits at Citi London. To make this exchange, Exxon withdrew funds from Morgan and deposited them at Citi. This means, of course, that when the transaction clears, Morgan must pay Citi the funds Exxon has transferred from one bank to the other. Morgan does this in effect by transferring money from its reserve (checking) account at the Fed to Citi's reserve account at the Fed. Thus, the transaction causes Morgan to lose reserves and Citi New York to gain them. At Morgan, the loss of reserves is offset by a decrease in deposit liabilities.

At Citibank, the situation is more complicated, as Table 7–1 shows. Citi London has received the deposit, but Citi New York has received the extra reserves. So Citi New York in effect owes Citi London money. This is accounted for by adjusting the *New York office dollar account,* which can be thought of simply as a checking account that Citi London holds with Citi New York. To Citi London, as long as this account is in surplus, which it normally would be, the account is a *due from* item that shows up on Citi London's balance sheet as an asset. On Citi New York's balance sheet, the same account is a *due to* item that consequently shows up on Citi New York's balance sheet as any other deposit would. With this in mind, it's easy to follow what happens on Citibank's books as a result of Exxon's deposit. Citi London gets a new $10MM liability in the form of a time deposit, which is offset by an equal credit to its account with home office. Meanwhile, home office gets $10MM of extra reserves, which are offset by a like increase in its liability to its London branch.

Note several things about this example. First, the changes that occurred on every institution's balance sheet were offsetting; that is, net worth never changes. This is *always* the case in any transaction, the consequences of which can be illustrated with T-accounts.

A second and more important point is that, while Exxon now thinks of itself as holding dollars in London, the dollars actually never left the U.S. The whole transaction simply caused $10MM of reserves to be moved from Morgan's reserve account at the New York Fed to Citi's account there (see Table 7–1). This, by the way, would have been the case in any Eurodeposit example we might have used. Regardless of who makes the deposit, who receives it, and where in the world it is made, the ultimate dollars never leave the U.S.

A Euro Loan

In our example, we left Citi London with a new time deposit on which it must pay interest. To profit from that deposit, Citi London is naturally going to lend out those dollars. Suppose that Citi London lends the dollars to Electricité de France (EDF). Initially, this loan results in EDF's being credited with an extra $10MM in deposits at Citi London, as Table 7–2 shows.

TABLE 7–2
A Euro loan is granted to EDF

Citi London		EDF	
Loan, EDF +10MM	(Euro) deposits, EDF +10MM	(Euro) deposits, Citi London +10MM	Loan, Citi London +10MM

EDF of course has borrowed the money, so the $10MM will not sit idly in its account.

Assume that EDF uses the dollars it has borrowed to pay for oil purchased from an Arab seller who banks at Chase London. Table 7–3, which should be self-explanatory to anyone who fol-

TABLE 7–3
EDF uses its borrowed dollars to pay for oil

EDF		Arab Oil Seller	
(Euro) deposits −10MM	Accounts payable −10MM	Accounts receivable −10MM (Euro) deposits, Chase London +10MM	

Citi London		Chase London	
New York office dollar account −10MM	(Euro) deposits, EDF −10MM	New York office dollar account +10MM	Time deposits, Arab oil seller +10MM

Citi New York		Chase New York	
Reserves −10MM	London office dollar account −10MM	Reserves +10MM	London office dollar account +10MM

New York Fed	
	Reserves Citibank −10MM Reserves, Chase +10MM

lowed Table 7–1, shows the balance-sheet changes that will result from this transaction. Note that when EDF pulls $10MM out of Citi London, the latter, since it has no real dollars other than a deposit balance with Citi New York, must in effect ask Citi New York to pay out this money with dollars that Citi New York has in its reserve account at the Fed. As this is done, offsetting changes occur in the New York and London-office dollar accounts at Citibank. Meanwhile opposite but similar changes occur on the books of Chase London and Chase New York.

It's important to note that in this Euro loan transaction, just as in the Eurodollar deposit transaction we worked through above, the dollars never leave New York. The transaction simply results in a movement of $10MM from the reserve account at the New York Fed of Citi to that of Chase. One might argue that we have not yet gone far enough—that the Arab oil seller will spend the dollars he has received and that they might then leave the U.S. But that's not so. Whoever gets the dollars the Arab spends must deposit them somewhere, and thus the spending by the Arab of his dollars will simply shift them from one bank's reserve account to another's. In this respect, it might be useful to recall a point made in Chapter 2. The only way reserves at the Fed can be increased or decreased in the aggregate is through open market operations initiated by the Fed itself. The one exception is withdrawals of cash from the banking system. If the Arab oil seller were to withdraw $10MM in cash from Chase London and lock it up in a safe there or elsewhere, the dollars would have actually left the U.S. However, no big depositor would do that because of opportunity cost: Eurodeposits yield interest; cash in a vault would not.

A Europlacement with a Foreign Bank

In the Euromarket, banks routinely lend dollars to other banks by making deposits with them and borrow dollars from other banks by taking deposits from them. People in the Euromarket and people in New York with international experience always refer to the depositing of Eurodollars with another bank as a *placement* of funds and to the receipt of Eurodollar deposits from another bank as a *taking* of funds. Other people in the U.S. money market are likely to use the jargon of the Fed funds market, referring to placements of Euros as *sales* of funds and to takings of Euros as *purchases* of funds.

To illustrate what happens when a foreign bank ends up holding a Eurodollar deposit, let's work through the mechanics of a placement of Eurodollars with such a bank. Assume that Chase London places a $20MM deposit in the London branch of Crédit Lyonnais.

The special feature of this example is that Crédit Lyonnais, unlike an American bank, is not a member of the Federal Reserve System. This used to mean that the bank, because it was foreign, did not have a reserve account at the Fed and therefore had to keep its dollars on deposit in a U.S. bank. Since passage of the 1978 International Banking Act, foreign bank branches operating in the U.S. are required to hold reserves at the Fed and consequently must have an account there. These branches have, however, continued to make and receive the bulk of their payments through a deposit account they maintain at their U.S. correspondent bank. One reason is that the Fed permits a foreign bank branch to run only a very small daylight overdraft in their Fed account (see Chapter 18).

To continue our example, suppose that the dollars placed by Chase London with the London branch of Crédit Lyonnais are deposited in a Crédit Lyonnais account at Morgan New York. Then, as Table 7–4 shows, the net effect of the transaction will be that Crédit Lyonnais ends up with dollars on deposit in New York, and reserves move from Chase's account at the Fed to Morgan's account. Note again that the dollars remain in New York, even though they are now held by the London branch of a French bank.

In constructing our example, we tried to keep things simple and so ignored an important detail, namely, how Euro transactions are cleared. In the U.S., it is customary for banks to make payments between each other in Federal funds, that is, by transferring funds on deposit at the Fed over the Fed wire; all large payments in the money and bond markets are also made in Fed funds. In contrast, in the Euromarket money transfers are made

TABLE 7–4
A Eurodollar interbank placement

Chase London		Crédit Lyonnais London	
(Euro) time deposit, Crédit Lyonnais London +20MM New York office dollar account −20MM		Deposit, Morgan N.Y. +20MM	Time deposit, Chase London +20MM

Chase New York		Morgan New York	
Reserves −20MM	London office dollar account −20MM	Reserves +20MM	Deposits, Crédit Lyonnais London +20MM

New York Fed	
	Reserves, Chase −20MM Reserves, Morgan +20MM

and settled through the New York Clearing House known as *CHIPS*—an acronym for the computerized Clearing House Interbank Payments System. Payments made through CHIPS used to result in the receipt of *clearing house funds,* which became Fed funds only on the day after receipt. The distinction between Fed funds (good money today) and clearing house funds (good money tomorrow) did several things: It set the stage for banks to engage in profitable technical arbitrages between the two sorts of funds; it also was the source of no end of confusion for foreigners dealing for the first time in the Eurodollar market; and finally, as volume on CHIPS grew, it created an overnight credit risk that both CHIPS and the Fed eventually deemed unacceptable.

Reacting to this risk, CHIPS moved on October 1, 1981, to same-day settlement. Despite a great deal of trepidation by U.S. bankers, who feared a grand-scale, computer snafu, the switch by CHIPS to same-day settlement went so smoothly that all Euromarket participants termed it a nonevent.

For more about CHIPS—its history, method of operation, and relationship to the Fed wire—see Chapter 18.

HISTORY OF THE MARKET

Anyone following Tables 7–1 through 7–4 is likely to wonder what the rationale is for carrying on outside the U.S. huge volumes of dollar deposit and loan transactions in what seems to be a rather complicated fashion. The best way to answer is to describe briefly the stimuli that gave birth to the Euromarket.

Long before World War II, it was not uncommon for banks outside the U.S. to accept deposits denominated in dollars. However, the volume of such deposits was small, and the market for them had little economic significance. During the 1950s, things began to change. One reason was the activities of the communist central banks. Since Russia and other communist countries imported certain goods that had to be paid for in dollars and exported others that could be sold for dollars, the central banks of these countries ended up holding dollar balances. Initially, these balances were held on deposit in New York, but as Cold War tensions heightened, this practice became less attractive to the communists, who feared that at some point the U.S. might block their New York balances. As a result, they transferred these balances to banks in London and other European centers. The value of the dollar goods the communist countries wanted to import often exceeded the amount of dollars they were earning on exports, so these countries became important in the Eurodollar market not only as lenders, but as borrowers.

While the Cold War may have kicked off the Euromarket, other factors stimulated its development. Historically, the pound sterling played a key role in world trade. Much trade not only within the British Commonwealth, but between Commonwealth nations and the rest of the world and between third countries, was denominated in British currency, the pound sterling, and financed in London through borrowings of sterling. After World War II, this began to change. Britain ran big balance of payments deficits (that is, spent more abroad than it earned); and as a result, devaluation of the British pound—a decrease in the amount of foreign exchange for which a pound could be traded—was a constant threat and in fact occurred several times during the period of pegged exchange rates. The chronic weakness of the pound made it a less attractive currency to earn and to hold, which in turn stimulated the trend for more and more international trade to be denominated in dollars. It also caused the British to restrict the use of sterling for financing international trade. Specifically in 1957, the British government restricted the use of sterling in financing trade between non–sterling-area countries; and in 1976, it restricted the use of sterling in financing trade between Commonwealth countries and non–sterling-area countries. Because of the increased use of dollars as the availability of sterling financing decreased, importers began borrowing Eurodollars to finance trade, and the Euromarket emerged first as a nascent and then as a fast-growing and important international capital market.

In the early days of the Eurodollar market, it was British banks, not U.S. banks, that played a leading role. Historically, British banks had a dominant place in financing world trade, so they had expertise other banks lacked. Given that expertise, British banks shrewdly took the view that they could finance international trade in whatever currency was available and acceptable—wampum beads, or, as happened to be the case, dollars.

U.S. banks entered the Euromarket step by step and always *defensively*—their fear being that their London activities would undercut their domestic activities. One U.S. banker, who was in London during the market's formative years, noted, "The story of how the U.S. banks entered the Euromarket reflects rather poorly on us because we did not think out where the market was going. It just sort of grew up on us."

During the early 1950s when the Russian and East European banks began depositing dollars outside the U.S., the London branches of U.S. banks were *not* taking Eurodollar deposits. Several years later, they began to do so hesitantly when some of their good U.S. customers said to them, "Can't you take our dollar deposits in London? The foreign banks do, and they give us better rates than you can in New York because of Reg Q." For several years, this worked satisfactorily because the head offices of the U.S. banks involved could profitably use in the U.S. the dollars deposited with their London branches: in the U.S., the structure of loan and other interest rates was such that U.S. banks could well afford to pay in London higher rates than those permitted under Reg Q.

Then the London branches of U.S. banks began getting 3- and 6-month money, that the head offices of U.S. banks did not want because it did not fit their books (asset and liability structures). So, again *defensively,* the London branches of the U.S. banks began making Eurodollar loans to commercial customers and placements of deposits with foreign banks. In doing so they said, "We are giving you this money but don't count on our continuing to do so because we don't know how long we will continue getting this funny money called Eurodollars." For years, U.S. banks did not view their Eurodollar activities with a customer as a traditional, ongoing banking relationship.

In its initial stages, the growth of the Euromarket was hampered by the myriad of exchange control regulations that all nations except the U.S. imposed on their residents with respect to (1) the use of domestic currency to acquire foreign exchange and (2) the disposition of foreign-exchange earnings. This changed in 1958 when the major European countries, with the exception of the U.K., substantially liberalized their foreign-exchange controls as a first step toward making their currencies fully convertible.

A fourth factor that stimulated the growth of the Euromarket was the operation of Regulation Q during the tight money years of 1968 and 1969. At that time, U.S. money rates rose above the rates that banks were permitted to pay under Reg Q on domestic, large-denomination CDs. To finance loans, U.S. banks were forced to borrow money in the Euromarket. All this resulted in a sort of merry-go-round operation. A depositor who normally would have put his money in, say, a Chase New York CD gave his money (perhaps via a Canadian bank because of U.S. controls on the export of capital) to Chase London, which then lent the money back to Chase New York. In effect, Reg Q forced a portion of the supply of bought money that U.S. money market banks were coming to rely on in funding to move through London and other Eurocenters. The operation of Regulation Q also encouraged foreign holders of dollars who would have deposited them in New York to put their dollars in London. Thus, for example, surplus German dollars borrowed by Italians ended up passing through London instead of New York.

Another important stimulus to the Euromarket was the various capital controls that the U.S. instituted during the 1960s to improve its balance of payments, which was in deficit. The first of these, the Interest Equalization Tax passed in 1964, was designed to discourage the issuance by foreign borrowers of debt obligations in the U.S. market. This measure was followed in 1965 by the Foreign Credit Restraint Program, which limited the amount of credit U.S. banks could extend to foreign borrowers. Finally in 1968, the government passed the Foreign Investment Program, which restricted the amount of domestic dollars U.S. corporations could use to finance foreign investments. Whatever the wisdom and effectiveness of these programs (they were eliminated in 1974), there is no doubt that they substantially increased the demand for dollar financing outside the U.S., that is, for Eurodollar loans.

The persistent balance of payments deficits in the U.S. have often been given substantial credit for the development of the Euromarket; by spending more abroad than it earned, the U.S. in effect put dollars into the hands of foreigners and thus created a natural supply of dollars for the Euromarket. There is some truth to this, but U.S. balance of payments deficits are neither a necessary nor a sufficient condition for a thriving and growing Euromarket. After all, foreigners can deposit dollars in New York, *and* domestic holders of dollars can place them in London. Where dollars are held need not be a function of who owns them. It is often a function of the relative attractiveness of the domestic and the Euromarkets to depositors. What has made the Euromarket attractive to depositors and given it much of its vitality is the freedom from restrictions under which this market operates and in particular the absence of the implicit tax that exists on U.S. domestic banking because of the reserve requirements imposed by the Fed. Eurodeposits taken by U.S. banks are also free from the 8-bp insurance premium imposed by the Federal Deposit Insurance Corporation (FDIC).[3]

A final important stimulus was given to the Euromarket by the hike in the price of oil that occurred in 1974. Due to that rise, member nations in the Organization of Petroleum Exporting Countries (OPEC) suddenly found themselves holding massive balances of dollars, which they deposited in the Euromarket. Meanwhile, many countries that were importers of oil experienced severe balance of payments difficulties and were forced to borrow dollars in the Euromarket to pay for oil imports.

Eurocurrency Deposits

Just as dollars can be deposited in banks and bank branches outside the U.S. to create Eurodollars, the currencies of European countries can be deposited outside their country of origin and thereby give rise to other types of *Eurocurrency deposits*. For example, German marks deposited in London in exchange for a mark balance are *Euromarks*. The major currencies other than dollars in which Eurocurrency deposits are held are German marks, the British pound, Swiss francs (*Swissy* to the irreverent), and yen. There is also a limited market in Dutch guilders and rather difficult markets in other currencies. While the Euromarket is still primarily a dollar market—approximately 70% of Eurodeposits are denominated in dollars—Eurodeposits of other currencies are an important and growing part of the market.

---

[3]This exemption has always existed, but there is currently a proposal in Congress to extend the imposition of FDIC premiums to Eurodeposits taken by U.S. banks. The latter have vigorously argued against this proposal saying (1) that the Euromarket is a wholesale market in which deposit insurance would be meaningless to depositors and (2) that, given the narrow spreads in the Euromarket, the FDIC premium would put U.S. banks at a significant competitive disadvantage vis-à-vis foreign banks. Nonetheless, Congress appeared, in the spring of 1989, determined to impose eventually FDIC premiums on Eurodeposits at U.S. banks.

SDRs and ECUs

Over time, a small proportion of Eurodeposits and Euronotes and -bonds have been denominated in an artificial unit of account. The first was the *Special Drawing Right (SDR)*, a specie of paper gold created by the International Monetary Fund (IMF) back in the late 1960s when people thought that the supply of gold was insufficient for central banks around the globe to have adequate reserves. Originally, the SDR comprised a basket of 16 currencies—X% of this currency, Y% of that, and so on. This made the value of SDRs in terms of dollars or any other national currency tedious to calculate and a nightmare to hedge. Later, the IMF redefined the SDR as a basket of five currencies: the U.S. dollar, the deutsche mark, the yen, sterling, and French francs.

Too little, too late. The *ECU (European currency unit)* had been born. This unit of account is a trade-weighted basket of the currencies of 10 full members of the European Economic Community (EEC). The ECU was launched in the late 1970s, but the first ECU Eurobond was issued only in 1981. ECUs can be hedged, and Eurobanks will thus both accept deposits and lend in ECUs. The Bank of England estimates that currently 2.5% of bank Euro lending and 4% of Eurobonds are denominated in ECUs. At the outset, the ECU was given a boost by the fact that EEC official borrowers, such as the European Coal and Steel Community, were ECU-raisers. More recently, the British and Italian governments have issued bills (government debt just like U.S. T bills) denominated in ECUs. Also, the Australian Wheat Board has started to invoice its clients in ECUs and to sell Euro commercial paper denominated in ECUs.

None of the above makes the ECU a real currency, but central banks like to borrow and hold ECUs as a novel and cheap way of building up foreign-exchange reserves. Also, some investors find the ECU attractive; by acquiring ECU-denominated assets, an investor gets European-currency risk without having to acquire deposits or securities denominated in a variety of currencies.

"Say you want to take a position in sterling or in French francs," noted one Eurobanker, "but you aren't sure you want to do 100% of your position in either currency. As an alternative, you can take a position in ECUs, which pick up some of those currencies but others as well. ECUs is a particularly good position to take when the dollar is weak: if you think that the dollar is going to fall, but aren't sure against which currency, you buy ECUs; also, if you think European interest rates are going to fall, but aren't sure which ones will fall, you buy ECUs.

"The ECU is still not a big currency because there is no central bank behind it. Still, the ECU market is growing. You can lend, borrow, issue bonds in ECU; also, you can hedge an ECU position because most of the currencies in it are dealable. Now, the ECU tends to trade like any other currency; it has an existence of its own."

THE MARKET TODAY

Over time, the Euromarket has undergone great changes: it has grown from meager beginnings into a huge international capital market that deals in increasingly complex and ever more numerous products; one aspect of this market has, however, not changed: the preeminence of London as its center.

The Preeminence of London

From the inception of the Eurodollar market, London has been its biggest and most important center. That this role fell to London is hardly surprising. London has a long history as a world center for a host of financial activities: international lending, trade financing, commodities trading, stock trading, foreign-exchange trading, insurance, and others. In truth, that square mile of London known as *the City of London,* or more often as just *the City,* is and has been since the 19th century the financial capital of the world.

Some of the many factors that contributed to London's development as an international financial center were the freedom and flexibility with which financial institutions were permitted to operate there. That freedom and flexibility still prevail, and because they do, London—with its huge concentration of financial expertise—was the logical place for the nascent Euro-market to develop and flourish. Throughout London's history as a Eurocenter, foreign banks have been permitted to open London branches and subsidiaries with ease and to operate these branches and subsidiaries with a minimum of regulation. The Bank of England has imposed no specific capital requirements on the London branches of foreign banks, and it has imposed no reserve requirements on the Eurocurrency deposits they accept. Britain *taxes the profits* earned by foreign banks' branches and subsidiaries but has imposed *no withholding taxes* on the interest banks pay to nonresident depositors.

While London has remained the preeminent center of the Euromarket, other centers have also developed. The Euromarket is, after all, a worldwide market. In the Far East in particular, Singapore and Hong Kong have both become important centers for Asian trading in Eurodollars. These centers suffer the disadvantage that the natural sources of dollar supply and demand arising from trade and other activities in the Far East are less than those that focus on London, so their role remains secondary.

Banking Centers

From the banks' point of view, one growing disadvantage of basing Euro operations in London is the high taxes that must be paid on profits earned there. Largely to avoid these taxes, *booking centers* have developed in several localities offering favorable tax treatment of profits—Bahrain in the Middle East, Nassau, and Grand Cayman, to name the most important. Banks that operate branches in these centers book there loans negotiated and made in London, New York, or elsewhere. They fund these loans either by having their branch buy money in its own name in the Eurodollar market or by funding the operation with dollars purchased in the name of their London branch. Nassau and Grand Cayman offer one important advantage over Bahrain; they are in the same time zone as New York and only one hour ahead of Chicago. Thus, it is easy for management in U.S. money market banks to direct their operations in these centers during normal working hours.

Federal Reserve figures indicate the importance of Caribbean booking centers to U.S. banks.[4] They show that, in January 1989, the foreign branches of U.S. banks had 496 billion of assets, of which 31.5% were booked in London, 32.7% in the Bahamas and Caymans. The foreign branches of U.S. banks book mostly dollar-denominated assets in the Caribbean; specifically, over 95% of their assets booked in the Caribbean are payable in U.S. dollars, whereas only 70% of their assets booked worldwide are payable in U.S. dollars.

New York and Tokyo

Next to London, the second most important center of the Euromarket is New York. Until the opening of international banking facilities (IBFs) there, New York banks could not accept Eurodeposits, but New York was still an important center in Euro trading for several reasons. First, New York banks and the branches established in New York by major foreign banks are active takers of Euros in the names of their Nassau and Grand Cayman branches. A second reason New York is an important trading center for Euros is that New York and the other banks actively arbitrage between Euro and "domestic" dollars (see Chapter 18). A final reason for the prominence of New York as a Eurocenter is that many of the nation's largest banks direct their worldwide Euro operations from New York.

In the formative years of the Euromarket, U.S. banks felt compelled to establish a London office to participate in this market. So, too, did the other major foreign banks around the world. At that time, London was the preeminent center of the Euromarket. Gradually, the importance of New York relative to London as a Eurocenter increased for all of the reasons cited above. Consequently, in recent years foreign banks, having London branches but no New York branch, have felt compelled to open a New York branch.[5]

---

[4]*Federal Reserve Bulletin,* May 1989, Summary Statistics, p. A57.
[5]The U.S. operations of foreign bank branches are described at the end of this chapter.

The Japanese banks, for example, are major participants in the Euromarket and their activity in the London market is tremendous. Tokyo, however, has never become an important center of this market; the Japanese regulatory and tax environment, unlike that in the U.K., did not favor such a development. (Until recently, Japanese financial markets were subject to tight regulations, which the Japanese are now seeking, with mixed success, to loosen.) Today, Japanese banks and foreign bank branches located in Tokyo may open an entity modeled after a U.S. IBF; it's called a *Japanese Offshore Market* or *JOM*. JOMs are not permitted to issue CDs offshore or to do any security issuance. They may take deposits from offshore entities; these are subject to no reserve requirements, and interest paid on them is subject to no withholding tax. Banks having JOMs may not mingle funds they take in their JOM with funds they take in the Japanese domestic market. These provisions limit the usefulness of a JOM; nonetheless, Japanese banks run sizable JOMs.

Some big U.S. banks have branches and JOMs in Tokyo, but their activities in the Japanese market are limited. They make few loans there, so their funding needs are limited to what they need to carry on money market and trading activities. A typical U.S. bank branch in Tokyo will position, whenever the outlook is favorable, some yen-denominated securities; it will also trade foreign exchange, JGBs (Japanese government bonds), U.S. Treasuries, and Japanese money market instruments—the trading of securities being done through the bank's securities sub. In recent years, the Japanese Ministry of Finance (MOF—pronounced as in Mafia) has sought to deregulate the Japanese money market. In addition to yen CDs, there is now yen commercial paper. The yen BA market, which MOF sought to establish, has so far failed completely. Also, as of June 1989, the opening of a Japanese market in repos and reverses appeared to have been a stillbirth.

Size of the Market

From rather meager beginnings, the Euromarket has developed into a huge market. Unfortunately, it is impossible to say just how huge because there is no worldwide system for collecting data on the Eurocurrency market. The best figures available are the estimates made by the Bank for International Settlements, as extended and modified by the Morgan Bank. Its figures (Table 7–5) cover Eurodeposits in all significant Eurocenters. The gross numbers in Table 7–5 include sizable amounts of inter-bank placements. Using estimates, Morgan eliminates these placements to get figures on the net amounts of Eurodollars and other Eurocurrencies that nonbank depositors have placed with banks in the reporting countries. From these net figures, it is evident that both Eurodollar and Eurocurrency deposits have grown phenomenally over the last decade.

The Major Players: Global Banks

A decade ago, the top 10 American banks were considered crème de la crème credits and consistently ranked high on a list of top world banks. There were of course also European banks—the British clearers, Deutsche Bank, the key French banks, the Swiss banks, and so on—that were big and highly respected players on the world scene and in the Euromarket. In contrast, the Japanese banks were regarded as slightly suspect institutions: they had unfamiliar names, their financials were based on unfamiliar accounting practices, and they often were big buyers of dollars for which they had to pay up.

Today, things have turned topsy turvy. Japanese names dominate the list of top world banks as shown by Table 7–6, which ranks the top 50 world banks by asset size. Citi is the only U.S. bank that makes the top 10. Twenty of the remaining banks, including the top five, are all Japanese. Today, the Japanese banks are recognized by investors in bank paper and by others as massive, highly creditworthy, and highly competitive.

Since U.S. banks have in recent years been under a lot of pressure to pare assets and to improve earnings ratios, one might argue that a ranking of banks by shareholder equity might be a more appropriate and fairer criterion by which to judge the importance on a world scale of U.S. banks. Switching criteria does in fact improve considerably the standing of the top U.S. and European banks, but Japanese names still fill 10 of the top 50 slots when world banks are ranked by shareholder equity.

TABLE 7–5
Eurocurrency market size, end of period ($ billions, end of period)

	1981	1982	1983	1984	1985	1986	1987	1988
Gross claims								
Eurocurrencies, on residents and nonresidents	1,929	2,146	2,253	2,359	2,833	3,578	4,442	
On nonbanks	557	634	665	694	822	1,041	1,300	1,396
On banks	1,372	1,512	1,588	1,665	2,011	2,537	3,142	3,325
In dollars	1,504	1,694	1,797	1,894	2,101	2,545	2,938	3,143
In other currencies	425	452	456	465	732	1,033	1,504	1,579
Gross liabilities								
Eurocurrencies, to residents and nonresidents	1,954	2,168	2,278	2,386	2,846	3,621	4,496	4,814
To nonbanks	372	432	479	497	565	696	820	889
To official monetary institutions	112	91	88	96	112	105	151	147
To other banks	1,470	1,645	1,711	1,793	2,149	2,819	3,525	3,778
In dollars	1,539	1,741	1,846	1,950	2,147	2,586	2,976	3,207
In other currencies	415	427	432	436	699	1,035	1,520	1,604
% in dollars	78.8	80.3	81.0	81.7	75.4	71.4	66.2	66.6
Net market size	892	1,035	1,122	1,150	1,299	1,587	1,861	1,921

Note: Based on foreign-currency liabilities and claims of banks in major European countries, the Bahamas, Bahrain, Cayman Islands, Netherlands Antilles, Panama, Canada, Japan, Hong Kong, Singapore, and IBFs.

Source: *World Financial Markets* (New York, The Morgan Bank).

TABLE 7–6
Top world banks, ranked by asset size

			Assets ($ billions)	Net Income ($ millions)
1.	Dai–Ichi Kangyo Bank	Japan	266.9	680.4
2.	Sumitomo Bank	Japan	250.6	383.4
3.	Fuji Bank	Japan	244.1	571.3
4.	Mitsubishi Bank	Japan	227.5	657.8
5.	Sanwa Bank	Japan	218.2	632.4
6.	Crédit Agricole	France	214.4	404.1
7.	Citicorp	U.S.	203.6	−1,138.0
8.	Norinchukin Bank	Japan	184.9	154.3
9.	Banque National de Paris	France	182.7	563.5
10.	Industrial Bank of Japan	Japan	177.0	380.0
11.	Crédit Lyonnais	France	168.3	441.4
12.	Deutsche Bank	West Germany	165.8	423.1
13.	National Westminster Bank	Britain	162.0	809.3
14.	Tokai Bank	Japan	159.1	298.4
15.	Barclays	Britain	158.0	355.3
16.	Mitsui Bank	Japan	154.1	347.7
17.	Mitsubishi Trust & Banking*	Japan	153.6	412.2
18.	Société Generale	France	153.0	501.9
19.	Sumitomo Trust & Banking*	Japan	144.0	399.2
20.	Taiyo Kobe Bank	Japan	133.2	213.3
21.	Long–Term Credit Bank of Japan	Japan	130.0	288.1
22.	Mitsui Trust & Banking	Japan	129.5	288.1
23.	Dresdner Bank	West Germany	129.0	295.0
24.	Bank of Tokyo	Japan	127.7	386.8
25.	Union Bank of Switzerland	Switzerland	124.6	590.4
26.	Paribas Group	France	122.3	616.3
27.	Yasuda Trust & Banking	Japan	117.7	222.2
28.	Daiwa Bank	Japan	114.5	185.9
29.	Swiss Bank Corporation	Switzerland	113.4	511.6
30.	Hongkong & Shanghai Banking	Hong Kong	106.1	588.9
31.	Commerzbank	West Germany	100.6	267.4
32.	Chase Manhattan	U.S.	99.1	−894.8
33.	Toyo Trust & Banking	Japan	96.2	205.1
34.	Westdeutsche Landesbank Girozentrale	West Germany	94.4	62.8
35.	Bayerische Vereinsbank	West Germany	93.5	148.7
36.	Bankamerica	U.S.	92.8	−955.0
37.	Banca Nazionale del Lavoro	Italy	92.4	39.6
38.	Midland Bank	Britain	90.1	−831.6
39.	Nippon Credit Bank	Japan	88.6	150.9
40.	Algemene Bank Nederland	Netherlands	84.9	296.5
41.	LLoyds Bank	Britain	83.6	−416.7
42.	Kyowa Bank	Japan	83.3	185.2
43.	Crédit Suisse	Switzerland	83.2	431.5
44.	Rabobank Group	Netherlands	81.9	390.4
45.	Bank of China	China	81.4	1,041.1

TABLE 7–6 (concluded)

			Assets ($ billions)	Net Income ($ millions)
46.	Amsterdam–Rotterdam Bank	Netherlands	81.0	272.9
47.	Hypo–Bank	West Germany	78.9	158.1
48.	Deutsche Genossenschaftsbank	West Germany	78.4	111.0
49.	Chemical Banking	U.S.	78.2	−853.7
50.	Shokochukin Bank	Japan	75.8	44.6

Data: IBCA Banking Analysis Ltd.

(Both sets of numbers refer to the latest available figures—end of 1987.)

Overview of Bank Euro Operations[6]

In a very real sense, the Eurodollar market is a true international market without location, which means that for no bank is it a domestic market. Thus, every bank active in the market tends to compartmentalize its activities there, to think in terms of what Eurodollar assets and liabilities it has acquired. In the jargon of the market, every Eurobanker is running a *Eurodollar book*. In the case of foreign banks, the reason is obvious; they are dealing in a foreign currency, the dollar, which has limited availability to them at best. In the case of U.S. banks, the distinction between domestic and Euro operations arises from a less fundamental but still important consideration, namely, the fact that Fed reserve requirements and other factors create a real distinction between Eurodollars and domestic dollars, one that is of varying importance depending on economic conditions and on the maturities of the domestic and Eurodollar assets and

---

[6]For an in-depth discussion of how U.S. and foreign banks run their Eurobooks as well as their books in nonnative currencies (e.g., Morgan's French-franc book at its Paris office), see Marcia Stigum and Rene Branch, *Managing Bank Assets and Liabilities: Strategies for Risk Control and Profit* (Homewood, Ill.: Dow Jones-Irwin, 1982).

liabilities compared. While all U.S. bankers continue to speak of their Eurobook, as distinct from their domestic book, a growing number of them view their job as managing a single, unified *global book*.[7]

Banking ground rules in the Euromarket differ sharply from those prevailing on the U.S. banking scene, with the result that U.S. bank operations in the Euromarket also differ sharply from their operations in the domestic money market. Thus, we will present a quick overview of bank Euro operations before we talk in detail about their deposit-accepting and lending activities in this market.

The first important distinction between U.S. banks' domestic and Euro operations is in the character of their liabilities. In the Euromarket, all deposits, with the exception of *call money,* have a fixed maturity (*tenor* in British jargon) which may range anywhere from one day to five years. Also, interest is paid on *all* deposits, the rate being a function of prevailing economic conditions and the maturity of the deposit. While most bank Euro liabilities are straight time deposits, banks operating in the London market also issue Eurodollar CDs. These instruments carry a fixed rate of interest, are issued for a fixed time span, and are negotiable (only a few oddball tranches of floating-rate, Euro CDs have been issued, mostly by Japanese banks).

For U.S. banks, a second important distinction between their domestic and Euro operations is that no reserve requirements and no FDIC premiums are imposed against their Eurocurrency deposits. Thus, they can invest every dollar of Eurodeposits they receive.

Banks accepting Eurodollar deposits use these dollars to make two sorts of investments, loans and interbank placements. All such placements, like other Eurodeposits, have fixed maturities and bear interest. The market for Eurodollar deposits, nonbank and interbank, is highly competitive, and the rates paid on

---

[7]The practice by some banks of viewing their domestic and offshore books as a single global book is described later in this chapter.

deposits of different maturities are determined by supply and demand. Since the Euromarket operates outside the control of any central bank, there are no Reg Q or other controls limiting or setting the rates that Eurodollars may command. As one might expect, Euro rates are volatile: rising when money is tight, falling when it is easy.

LIBOR, LIBID, LIMEAN

The rate at which banks in London offer Eurodollars in the placement market is referred to as the *London interbank offered rate, LIBOR* for short. The rate at which Eurodollars are bid goes by the acronym *LIBID*. *LIMEAN* is the average of LIBOR and LIBID. Naturally LIBOR, LIBID, and LIMEAN are each a family of rates, one for each tenor quoted; for example, there are separate quotes for 1-, 3-, and 6-month LIBOR. All Europaper used to be priced off LIBOR. Then in the heyday of Euro floating-rate notes, some borrowers were able to achieve sub-LIBOR pricing. Since it seemed silly to quote a rate at a negative spread to LIBOR, the rate on such paper was quoted at a spread to LIMEAN. Normally, the spread between LIBOR and LIBID is ⅛, but it can widen due to market uncertainty or illiquidity. As noted in later chapters, LIBOR, because it is the true global cost of money, has become a key benchmark rate in the U.S. domestic money market. For example, in the U.S. commercial paper market, people now quote and measure relative value in terms of the spread at which such paper trades to LIBOR, not to T bills.

In the Euromarket, unlike the domestic market, all loans have fixed maturities, which can range anywhere from a few days to five years or longer. The general practice is to price loans at *LIBOR plus a spread*. On some term loans, the lending rate is fixed for the life of the loan. By far the more usual practice, however, is to price term loans on a *rollover basis*. This means that every three or six months the loan is repriced at the then-prevailing LIBOR for 3- or 6-month money plus the agreed-upon spread. For example, a 1-year loan might be rolled after six months, which means that the first 6-month segment would be priced at the agreed-upon spread plus the 6-month LIBOR rate prevailing at the time the loan was granted, while the second 6-

month segment would be priced at the same spread plus the 6-month LIBOR rate prevailing six months later. On Euro loans, banks never require the borrower to hold compensating balances.

Running a Bank's Eurobook

Running a bank's Eurodollar book boils down to much the same thing as running its domestic book. The bank must decide what assets to hold and what liabilities to use to fund them. In making these decisions, the bank faces the same *risks* it does in its domestic operations—credit risk, liquidity risk, and rate risk. In its Euro operations, as in its domestic operations, a bank's objective is to maximize profits subject to the constraint that risks are held to an acceptable level.

In a bank's Eurobook, credit risk exists both on ordinary loans and on interbank placements, which—like sales of Fed funds—are unsecured loans. To control risk on ordinary loans, banks impose credit standards on borrowers as well as limits on the amount they will lend to any one borrower. On placement with other banks, credit risk is controlled, as in the case of Fed funds sales, by setting up lines of credit that limit the amount the bank will lend to any other banking institution. As noted below, banks also use lines to limit what is called *country risk*.

Because most of a Eurobanker's assets and liabilities have fixed maturities, it would be possible for a Eurobanker, unlike a domestic banker, to run a *matched book;* that is, to fund every 3-month asset with 3-month money, every 6-month asset with 6-month money, and so on. If he did so, moreover, he would reduce his rate risk to zero because every asset would be financed for its duration at a locked-in positive spread. He would also minimize his liquidity risk; but he would not eliminate it, since on rollover loans he would still have to return periodically to the market to obtain new funding.

While running a matched book would reduce risk, it would also limit the bank's opportunity to earn profits in an important and traditional way: by lending long and borrowing short. Eurobankers are aware of the profit opportunities that a mismatched (*short*) book offers, and to varying degrees they all create a conscious mismatch in their Eurodollar books: one that is carefully monitored by head office to prevent unacceptable risks. How great a maturity mismatch a given bank will permit in its Eurobook depends on various factors: the shape of the yield curve, its view on interest rates, and its perception of its own particular liquidity risk. If a bank is running a global book, the size and nature of the mismatch it wants or can tolerate in its Eurobook will depend partly on the mismatch in its domestic book.

In discussing a U.S. bank's Euro operations, it's crucial to bear in mind that the bank's foreign branches are an integral part of the bank. Thus, the same pressures for change (described in Chapter 6) that operate on the parent also impact its foreign branches. In particular, the diminishing of bank credits in the eyes of investors combined with the trend toward securitization have worked to narrow—in some cases to eliminate—the natural spread banks once enjoyed in Euro lending; this in turn has forced banks to look elsewhere for profits in their Euro operations—especially to fees and profitable dealing activities generated by corporate-finance–type activities. Also, the capital adequacy requirements being imposed by the latest Basel accord are pressuring banks to constrain the size of their Eurobooks. Thus, today, when a Eurobanker talks about creating or closing up a mismatch in his book, his tools of choice are likely to be not, as in the past, cash instruments but rather off-balance-sheet items: Euro futures, FRAs, interest-rate swaps, and option products.

THE INTERBANK PLACEMENT MARKET

The pool of funds that forms the basis for the Eurodollar market is provided by a varied cast of depositors: large corporations (domestic, foreign, and multinational), central banks and other government bodies, supranational institutions, such as the Bank for International Settlements (BIS), and wealthy individuals. Most of these funds come in the form of *time deposits* with fixed maturities.

Call Money

The banks, however, also receive substantial amounts of call money. A *call account* can be a same-day value, a 2-day notice, or a 7-day notice account. On a same-day value account, a depositor can get same-day repayment of his funds if he gets repayment instructions to his bank prior to midday London time. The going rate banks pay for call money is pretty much tied to the overnight Euro rate, which in turn is tied by active arbitrage to the U.S. Fed funds rate. As market rates move, a bank will periodically change the rate it pays on call money. When it does so, it must notify its customers before noon London time.

Normally, Eurobanks sell each other overnight money, not call money. Call deposits come from nonbank depositors; and bank to bank, call deposits vary a lot in amount: on average, call money is likely to equal about 10% of a bank's total deposits. The biggest call account in the Euromarket is probably that of SAMA (the Saudi Arabian Monetary Authority).

The major attraction of a call deposit to the holder is liquidity. Time deposits pay more, but a penalty is incurred if such a deposit is withdrawn before maturity. From a receiving bank's point of view, call money is attractive because, with a positively sloped yield curve, such money is cheap. Also, despite its short-term nature, call money is a fairly stable source of funds, so much so that a big bank might, in running its Eurobook, feel comfortable viewing half of its call deposits as essentially long-term funds.

The Euro Time-Deposit Market

For reasons discussed below, banks receiving Eurodeposits frequently choose to place some portion of these deposits with other banks, often while simultaneously taking deposits of other maturities. As a result of all this buying and selling, a huge and highly active market in interbank placements developed. This market is worldwide. It also has a large number of participants, which reflects two facts. First, banks from countries all over the world participate in the market. Second, every one of a bank's foreign branches—many U.S., European, and Japanese banks have many such branches—participates in this market as a separate entity. Thus, for example, Citibank's foreign branches in London, Singapore, Bahrain, Nassau, and elsewhere all take and place Eurodollars in their own names.

Because there are so many players in the Eurodollar market and because they are scattered over the globe, it would be difficult and costly for them to communicate their bids and offers for deposits directly to each other. To fill the gap, a number of firms have gone into the business of brokering Euro time deposits.

While a high proportion of total Europlacements is brokered, not all such placements pass through the brokers' market. In particular, some money is sold by continental banks direct to big London bidders, with the London bidders quoting rates based on those prevailing in the brokers' market. Also, a bank branch normally won't trade with another branch of the same bank through brokers since the two communicate directly with each other. Today, banks seek more actively than they once did to maximize interbranch transactions—Citi London buys from/ sells to Citi Hongkong; such intrabank transactions permit each branch to meet its specific needs while conforming to the bank's objective of minimizing usage of its consolidated balance sheet.

Risk and Limits

A bank placing funds in the interbank market faces two risks. First, there is the *credit risk,* which banks seek to control through the use of credit lines. In establishing lines to foreign banks, a U.S. bank will look at the normal criteria of creditworthiness, such as size, capitalization, profitability, and reputation. In addition, a bank will be concerned about *country* or *sovereign risk.* Specifically, it will consider various factors about the bank's country of origin that might influence either the bank's viability or its ability to meet commitments denominated in a foreign currency. Of particular interest would be factors such as whether the country of origin was politically stable, whether nationalization on terms unfavorable to foreign depositors was a possibility, and whether the country's balance of payments was reasonably strong.

There's also a second aspect of sovereign risk that banks placing Eurocurrency deposits with other banks worry about. A bank selling Euros to, say, the London branch of the Bank of Tokyo must consider not only the creditworthiness of that bank and Japanese country risk, but also the economic and political climate in London: Is it conceivable that by nationalizing foreign bank branches, freezing their assets, or some other action the British might render it impossible for these branches to honor their commitment to repay borrowed dollars? Questions of this sort are less of a concern with respect to London than to smaller Eurocenters, such as Bahrain and Nassau. Banks seek to limit the sovereign risk to which they are exposed by imposing country limits on their lending and interbank placements.

The administration of these limits is complex. First, two sets of limits apply, country limits and limits to individual banks. Second, for Bank A to track how much credit in the form of Eurodollar placements it has granted to Bank B, it must track the Euro sales of *all* its branches to *all* Bank B's branches. Third, at the same time that Bank A is selling Euros to Bank B, it will also be granting credit to Bank B in other ways, for example, through the sale of Fed funds or via letters of credit.

Granting lines to buyers of Eurodollars was once more casual and less cautious than it later became. In 1974, the Bankhaus I.D. Herstatt, a medium-sized German bank, failed under conditions that left several banks standing in line along with other creditors to get funds due them. This event, along with the difficulties experienced during the same year by the Franklin National Bank, sent shock waves through the Euromarket and caused banks to review with an air of increased caution the lines they had granted to other banks.

The upshot was that many smaller banks lost the lines they had enjoyed and experienced difficulty buying Euros; some were even forced out of the market. *Tiering* also developed in market rates, with banks that were judged poorer credit risks being forced to pay up. In particular, the Japanese banks, consistently big net takers of Euros, had, for a time, to pay up 1 to 2%; and so did the Italian banks because of unfavorable economic and political developments within Italy. Several years after the Herstatt crisis, the Euromarket regained much of the confidence lost in 1974, and lines were again enlarged. Tiering, however, has remained a phenomenon in the market, being more pronounced the tighter money gets and the higher rates rise. Various financial crises, including the failure of Banco Ambrosiano Holdings, that rocked the financial world in 1982 caused tiering to again become more pronounced in the Euromarket and changed its pattern. More about rate tiering in Chapter 18.

Most banks, because of their size, nationality, and customer base, tend to be natural net sellers or buyers of Euros. However, it's important for a bank that wants to buy Euros to sell them some of the time, since one way a bank gets lines from other banks is by placing deposits with them. In the Euromarket, as in the Fed funds market, some banks have to buy their way in.

There is much more to be said about how Euros are quoted and traded in the brokers' market and about arbitrage between Eurodollars and domestic dollars. These topics are covered in Chapter 18.

EURO CERTIFICATES OF DEPOSIT

Because Eurodollar time deposits, with the exception of call money, have fixed maturities, from the point of view of many investors they have one serious disadvantage, namely, illiquidity. To satisfy investors who needed liquidity, Citibank began issuing *Eurodollar certificates of deposit* in London. Its example was quickly followed by other U.S. and foreign banks with London branches.

Because of the liquidity of Euro CDs, banks issuing them are able to sell them at rates slightly below those offered on time deposits of equivalent maturity, 1/4 to 1/8% less when the market is quiet. While Euro CDs were originally designed for corporations and other investors who wanted real liquidity, following the Herstatt incident an interesting development occurred in the Euro CD market. Many smaller U.S. banks and foreign banks as well felt the need for the appearance of greater liquidity in their Eurodollar books. To get it, they started to buy from other banks Euro CDs, which they hold on their books. Some Euro CDs are also purchased by Swiss banks for investors whose funds they manage; these CDs are rarely traded. Most Euro CDs issued in London are, however, sold to investors in the U.S.: corporations, domestic banks, money funds, and others.

Since the major advantage to the issuing bank of writing Euro CDs is that CD money is cheaper than time-deposit money, banks issuing such CDs limit the amount they write so as to preserve the spread between the rates at which they can buy CD money and time-deposit money. To issue CDs, the banks normally post daily rates, the attractiveness of which reflects both their eagerness to write and the maturities in which they want to take money. Occasionally, when the banks are anxious to write, they will also issue through either London CD brokers or U.S. money market dealers who have set up shop in London. These brokers and dealers also make a secondary market for Euro CDs, without which these instruments would have liquidity in name only.

The Euro CD market is not a huge source of funds for U.S. banks. In February 1989, the foreign branches of U.S. banks had liabilities totaling 501 billion, of which 356 billion were payable in dollars. At the same time, the foreign branches of U.S. banks had 30 billion of negotiable CDs outstanding; of these, 25.5 billion were Eurodollar CDs, issued almost exclusively in London; the remaining CDs were presumably part of the foreign branches' native-currency books, for example, their French franc and DM books.[8]

Medium-Term Money

Some banks have raised medium-term Eurodollars in London by selling floating-rate notes. Banks could also raise such money by selling Euro MTNs just as they sell deposit notes in the domestic market—and then do a swap if they want floating-rate money.

---

[8]Source: *Federal Reserve Bulletin,* June 1989.

A bank, however, thinks in terms of its consolidated balance sheet. Domestic medium-term money is cheaper than Euro medium-term money, so if a bank is inclined to buy such money, the place it's likely to do so is in the domestic money market.

EURO LENDING

Today, the Eurodollar market is *the* international capital market of the world, which is very much reflected in the mix of borrowers that come to this market for loans. Their ranks include U.S. corporations funding foreign operations, foreign corporations funding foreign or domestic operations, foreign government agencies funding investment projects, and foreign governments funding development projects or general balance-of-payments deficits.

Euro Bank Loans

Euro bank loans are priced at a spread to LIBOR. Since different banks may be offering Eurodollars at not quite the same rates, the LIBOR rate used in pricing a loan is usually the average of the 11 A.M. offering rates of three to five *reference banks,* the latter always being top banks in the market.

How great a spread over LIBOR a borrower is charged depends on market conditions, who is borrowing, and for what purpose they are borrowing. Loans to finance leveraged buyouts (LBOs) and restructuring are typically done at 2½ or more over LIBOR.

A good corporate credit might, on the other hand, pay only 15 or 20 bp over LIBOR on a 3- to 5-year loan for general corporate purposes. It's hard to generalize because banks today make few such loans. Good credits get from a syndicate of banks a standby line of credit under which they may borrow at an agreed spread over LIBOR. The standby line, for which they pay a fee, may be a *multiple-option facility* (a *MOF*) or some other facility (a NIF or a RUF)—Euro-line names resemble alphabet soup—under which they may bid to their line banks for money when they need it or when they like the market (see Chapters 22 and 24 on Euro commercial paper and Euro MTNs). The advantages to a borrower of getting money using a bid-option facility are flexibility and spreads lower than what it could get on a term loan. A bank asked to bid under a MOF will bid aggressively if the loan fits its book, less aggressively or not at all if the loan doesn't fit its book.

Currently, the credits most likely to do a 5-year, term loan are lesser credits and entities doing special-purpose borrowings—for example, to finance an LBO, a restructuring, or an acquisition that they want to finance first with a term loan and later finance out.

On rollover loans, which most Euro loans are today, the bank normally allows the borrower to choose whether to take 3- or 6-month money each time a rollover date occurs. Banks will also grant a 1-year rollover option to good customers but try to discourage the inclusion of this option in loan agreements because to match fund maturities beyond six months can be difficult due to the thinness of the market in longer-term deposits. What choice of maturity the borrower makes on a rollover date depends on whether he expects interest rates to rise or fall.

The bank may, at the borrower's request, also include in a rollover loan agreement a *multicurrency clause* that permits the borrower to switch from one currency to another—say, from dollars to German marks—on a rollover date. Multicurrency clauses usually stipulate that nondollar funds will be made available to the borrower conditional upon "availability." This clause protects a bank from exchange controls and other factors that might dry up the market and prohibit the bank from acquiring the desired funds, even in the foreign exchange market.

While fixed-rate, fixed-term loans do occur in the Euromarket, they are uncommon. Banks are generally unwilling to make them unless they match fund, a policy that makes such loans so expensive that the borrower is likely to conclude that his funding cost over the life of the loan would be less with a rollover loan. Also, a prime borrower willing to pay up to lock in a fixed borrowing rate is likely to find a Eurobond issue cheaper than a fixed-rate loan. On the other hand, a lesser credit wanting term, fixed-rate financing will probably find that his cheapest route is to borrow variable-rated money from a bank and simultaneously couple that borrowing with an interest-rate swap, variable for fixed rate (see Chapter 19).

Foreign corporates have always been a tough market for the U.S. banks to break into. Such firms have never been big term borrowers; and today, if they want fixed-rate term funds, they are likely either to borrow in the MTN market or to borrow in the U.S. commercial paper market and then swap into fixed.

Often, term loans extended to finance capital projects have an *availability period* during which the borrower receives funds according to some prearranged schedule based on his anticipated needs. The availability period may be followed by a grace period during which no repayment of principal is required. After that, the normal procedure is for the loan to be amortized over its remaining life. Some *bullet loans* with no amortization are granted, but they are the exception not the rule.

On Euro loans, the standard practice has been to disallow prepayment, but some agreements do permit it on rollover dates with or sometimes without payment of a penalty. To gain greater flexibility, the borrower can negotiate a *revolving facility,* which permits him during the life of the loan agreement to take down funds, repay them, and take them down again as he chooses.

The fact that Euro loans are made to borrowers all over the world could create considerable legal complications for lenders, especially in the case of default. To minimize these, Euro loan agreements generally specify that the loan is subject to either U.S. or British law.

Many Euro loans granted to U.S. corporations by U.S. banks are negotiated at the bank's head office in the U.S. This is most likely to occur if the loan is granted to a foreign subsidiary that is kept financially anemic because it is operating in a weak-currency country or if management of the overall firm is strongly centralized. If, on the other hand, the sub is financially strong and its management is largely autonomous, negotiation for a Euro loan will occur abroad, frequently in London because the expertise is there.

Syndicated Loans

Over the 1980s, the Euromarket for syndicated loans changed considerably. There was a big drop-off in volume, although the market has now started back up; according to the OECD, over

$127 billion was raised in the syndicated-loan market in 1988, almost 40% more than in 1987. Also there has been a big change in the roster of borrowers. In 1987, sovereigns and public-sector corporations accounted, respectively, for just 4% and 13% of total syndicated lending.

Back in the 1970s, syndication of Euro loans was a large, growing, robust business. There were various reasons a bank might choose to syndicate a loan. On corporate loans for big projects (e.g., development of North Sea oil), the amount required might exceed a bank's legal lending limit, or the bank might not choose to go to that limit in the interests of diversification of risk. On country loans, the basic chip could be $1 billion or more, and no bank could write that sort of business alone. Country loans often were for such huge amounts because certain borrowers, especially underdeveloped countries, were financing big development projects. Other countries with substantial borrowing needs were financing balance of payments deficits that they had incurred in part because the price of oil had risen, while prices of other raw materials they exported were weak.

The drop-off in syndicated loans was caused by various factors. Sovereigns, in particular, used to do a lot of jumbo loans. As time passed, those sovereign borrowers who remained or who became good credits found that they could borrow more cheaply by issuing securities, particularly Eurobonds. The Kingdoms of Sweden and Denmark are cases in point; so too is Italy, which used to borrow from the banks at LIBOR + ½; Canada too deserted the syndicated loan market. A sovereign that has good access to the Eurobond market but wants floating-rate money can today easily get the latter by coupling his bond issue with an interest-rate swap, and probably he can end up with sub-LIBOR funding to boot.

Latin American and other LDC sovereigns also used to be big borrowers in the syndicated loan market. The international debt crisis that began in 1982 put an end to that.

Like top sovereigns, good corporates found over time that syndicated loans became less attractive as compared to issuing securities. At least until event risk reared its ugly head (see below), investors, disenchanted with bank credits, became much more willing to evaluate corporate credits and to buy the Eurobonds of those issuers that passed muster. This development coincided with a change in the composition of investors in Euro-bonds: once Eurobond investors were principally retail customers, whose ranks included the proverbial Belgian dentist buying Euro bearer bonds to evade taxes; today, the ranks of Eurobond investors include a lot of sophisticated professionals who invest large amounts of fiduciary and other monies.

Another factor that contributed for a time to the decline of syndicated lending was the advent of the market for Euro *floating-rate notes (FRNs)*. Starting with the issuance of perpetual notes, then with subordinated securities, and then with bank securities, this market weakened and lost liquidity. In 1989, one hardly saw any new issues in the FRN market. After the FRN market dried up, a borrower who wanted to raise a lot of floating-rate funds had either to borrow in the fixed-rate market and then do a swap or go to the syndicated loan market.

Current Borrowers

A lot of syndicated lending today is done by big corporates. Often, the loans are related to LBOs, restructurings, and acquisitions of other companies. On such loans, speed and size, both of which banks can provide, are of the essence. Also, such a borrowing is usually based on a quite detailed story by the borrower; the securities market is not the best place for that, especially the Eurobond market in which investors want quality and simplicity.

Some of the above borrowing is what's called *mezzanine finance*. A borrower has gotten his deal together and needs temporary financing to tide him over while he sells assets, reorganizes operations, or whatever he plans to do before he goes public. Mezzanine finance usually pays a couple of points above the rate on junk bonds. Also, the borrower can acquire mezzanine finance any way he wants—in any one of various and funny forms, ranging from preferred stock issues to a loan with an equity kicker in the form of options on the borrower's stock.

The OECD estimates that in 1988 syndicated loans associated with mergers (principally American) exceeded $34.5 billion and accounted for 30% of all new borrowing in the international capital market. The corresponding figures for 1987 were, respectively, $8.3 billion and 12%. With KKR's buy-out of RJR-

Nabisco in late 1988 for $25 billion, the numbers for 1989 promised to be even higher. While American firms are the biggest users of syndicated loans to finance takeovers, British companies also use this market for the same purpose: Grand Metropolitan to buy out Pillsbury, Beazer to take over Koppers.

Mechanics and Fees

Big Euro loan syndication agreements are negotiated in London. Often the lead bank is a top U.S. bank, but big European and Japanese banks have become more aggressive in this area. While many of the banks that participate in a typical Euro syndication are based in London, it isn't uncommon for continental banks and even domestic U.S. banks with no London branch to take a piece of such loans. Doing so may provide them with both a good rate and a chance to diversify their assets.

Loan syndication normally starts with the borrower accepting the loan terms proposed by a bank and giving that bank a mandate to put together a credit for it. Most such agreements are on a *fully underwritten basis,* which means that the lead bank guarantees the borrower that he will get all of the money stipulated in the loan proposal.

Since the amount guaranteed is more than the lead bank could come up with alone, it selects *comanagers* that help it underwrite the loan. Once the lead bank and the comanagers have split up the loan into shares, they have about two weeks to sell off whatever portion of their underwriting share they do not want to take into portfolio. At the end of this selling period, the lead bank advises the borrower as to what banks have participated in the syndication. Then, the borrower and these banks attend a closing at which the final loan agreement is signed. Two days later, the borrower gets his money. From the viewpoint of the lender, participation in a syndicated loan carries a commitment to lend for the life of the loan, since such participations are rarely sold by one bank to another.

Various fees are charged on a loan syndication. First there is a management fee. That fee can fall over a broad range depending on the borrower and the purpose of the loan. If the credit is excellent and the deal is a no-brainer, the fee on a $1-billion deal might be as low as $100,000. In contrast, on a complex LBO or restructuring deal, the management fee might well be over 1% of the total amount borrowed. Normally, the lead bank shares some portion of this front-end fee with the banks that take significant portions of the total loan into portfolio.

A second fee the borrower pays is a spread over LIBOR on whatever funds he takes down. The borrower also pays a commitment fee, generally ranging from ½% down, on any monies committed but not drawn. Finally, there is an agency fee that goes to the bank responsible for interfacing between the lending banks and the borrower, that is, for the receipt and disbursement of loan proceeds and for general supervision of the operation of the credit agreement.

Merchant Banks

While loan syndication can be done directly by a bank, it has become increasingly common for large U.S. banks to do syndicated lending out of separate merchant banking subsidiaries. Loans are also syndicated by consortium banks, that is, by banks set up and jointly owned by several banks, frequently of different nationalities.

A British bank may engage in a much wider range of activities than a U.S. bank may. There has, however, tended to be some degree of specialization between different British banks. In particular, the so-called merchant banks have specialized primarily in providing not loans of their own funds, but various financial services to their customers. These include accepting bills arising out of trade, underwriting new stock and bond issues, and advising corporate customers on acquisitions, mergers, foreign expansion, and portfolio management.

One reason why top U.S. banks have opened merchant banking arms in London is that these subs may engage in activities, such as bond underwriting, that the branch itself could not because of Glass-Steagall. Another reason is that some U.S. banks feel that merchant banking activities, including loan syndication, are a different sort of business from commercial banking—one that requires deals-oriented money raisers and more continuity of personnel than is found in commercial banking. As one banker put it, "Merchant banking is using other people's assets and getting paid a fee for it; the other people in this case may be anyone in the market, including the parent bank. In loan syndications, where we add value is by taking a view on price, terms, conditions, and amounts that can be done for a borrower and by then assembling the group that will manage and sell the issue."

Most U.S. banks' merchant banking subs keep little of the loans they syndicate on their own books. Their objective is to provide the parent bank with the portion of the loan it wants and sell the rest. One reason is that the parent bank has a comparative advantage over the sub in funding. It has a stronger name in which to buy funds, and it has experienced dealers and funding personnel that the merchant bank could duplicate only at considerable expense.

Consortium Banks

A number of U.S. banks, in addition to or instead of setting up a merchant banking subsidiary, have joined with other banks to form consortium banks. These carry out many of the same activities as their merchant banking subs do. The objectives of U.S. banks in joining such groups have been mixed, depending on the size and experience of the bank. Some smaller banks joined to be able to participate in medium-term Euro financings. Other banks joined to gain experience in international financial markets in general, in specific geographic markets, or in new lines of business. Consortia formed by large banks provide a large standing capability for syndicating loans, and these institutions are active in this area.

The Eurobond Market

Between 1983 and 1987, the Eurobond market grew at an explosive pace, with typical new issues rising from about $50MM to almost $200MM. Much of this growth reflected the fact that, for many borrowers who would previously have done syndicated loans, the funding vehicle of choice had become a Eurobond issue.

Deciding just how to structure a borrowing via the issuance of securities involves important and complex questions. Thus, borrowers often turn to investment banks or to the merchant banking subs of big banks for advice. "In doing a borrowing," noted one U.S. merchant banker, "the choice between one instrument and another may save an issuer 3 bp. What really makes a difference is whether an issuer chooses fixed or floating—whether, if he locks in a fixed rate, he chooses the right moment to do so. This second decision may save him tens of basis points. A third decision concerns the currency in which to denominate the issue. A right choice on that question can save an issuer hundreds of basis points. When we are asked to help as an advisor as well as with execution, we start first with the currency decision because it is the most important decision the issuer makes. He needs funds: Does he borrow yen, DM, dollars, or whatever?

"Governments, when they borrow, are likely to be open about making a currency decision if we show them that by doing so they can lower their all-in cost of borrowing. A sovereign, like the Kingdom of Sweden, is used to borrowing in a lot of different currencies, because they couldn't just borrow krona even if they wanted to [the market would not absorb that much krona debt]. Corporates, in contrast, are more difficult. They do not like to make currency decisions. They have certain exposures in certain currencies, and they tend to borrow what they need to cover those cash flows."

The Mechanics

Doing a Eurobond issue resembles somewhat doing a syndicated loan. The issuer awards a mandate to the lead manager; and he and the lead manager agree on the fees, maturity, payment dates, and format of the issue. The front-end fees would be around 1⅛ on 2-year paper, 1⅞ on 5-year paper, and 2⅛ on 10-year paper. Front-end fees obviously also vary depending on the issuer's name and credit.

Next, the lead manager goes out and syndicates the deal with banks and other market makers, allocating each a certain amount of bonds to place. Then, the issue trades in the *grey* market. This important market resembles with the *wi* market in U.S. Treasuries.

Deals are priced at less full fees. So, if a manager brings Canada at 45 over Treasuries, it is 45 over including full fees;

that is, it is not 45 over par, but 45 over at, say, 98⅛. That is where the issue starts trading.

The grey market tells the issuer and the lead manager what the secondary market thinks a new issue is worth, where it should trade relative to existing paper. The grey market has been around officially for six or seven years, unofficially for longer. It used to be that, even if an issue was expensive in a sense, if it had good syndication and people protecting it, it could be sold at the agreed price. Now, the traders in the grey market sell short an issue at the level at which they think they will be able to cover. A lead manager can take exception and *ramp* (take control of) a new issue, restrict his allocations, and say, "Now, you guys who have sold at par less 2¼, I have allocated nothing to you; so when you want to cover your short, you will have to come to me; and my offering price is going to be less 1." This has been done sometimes with, sometimes without success. It depends on how big the issue is and on how strong the selling group is. It only takes a few members of the group to crack, and the grey market gets its paper.

Competition to underwrite Eurobond issues is cutthroat, especially since London deregulated, had its Big Bang (see Chapter 10). "When an interesting issue like the Kingdom of Norway comes along," noted one investment banker, "everyone wants to manage it. One guy says, 'We can do it for 52 over'; another says, '50 over'; another, '49 over'; and so on. If you go beyond a certain price, you are going into your own cost right away, but people have said, 'Well if it costs me 200,000 to do this deal, I need it to be up in the league table, to be one of the big guys.' The competition in London, always fierce, has gotten worse; you have more players coming in—not only the traditional U.S. and U.K. firms, but the Japanese and the Swiss all want to participate in issuing Eurobonds."

Event Risk

U.S. corporate Eurobond issues used to be popular, especially with retail investors who said, "If I know the name, Coca-Cola or IBM, I'll buy the issue. Don't bother me with ratings." In the last few years a lot of professionally managed money has come into the Eurobond market, money managed by people who track market prices and want to trade paper. They have seen Texaco bonds plunge because of a ruling by a Texas judge—judicial lightning at work—and they have seen bonds of other well-related companies plunge in price due to LBOs. All this added a new word to the vocabulary of bond buyers and traders: *event risk*. Suddenly, the bonds of some very good credits were judged as carrying a hitherto unappreciated risk, which is why some corporates wanting funding ended up back in the syndicated loan market. Paper issued by sovereigns is judged to be free from event risk (KKR isn't going to arrange the buy-out of Denmark), so through all the event risk to do, sovereign paper has grown ever more popular with investors.

The Investors
The traditional Eurobond investor bought and held. Today's investor is different. The Swiss are still there, but they have been joined by British merchant banks and other banks that run money for U.S. corporations, U.S. pensions funds—ERISA money. The continued weakness of the U.S. dollar caused a lot of investors to ask, "What currency should I be in?" That's a question European investors had long asked, but it was a new question for U.S. investors such as mutual funds, major insurance companies, and pension funds. Often, their money is managed by professionals, pitted in competition against each other; and if one guy has a tremendous pickup in DM bonds because the mark has appreciated, that doesn't go unnoticed by his peers. A lot of U.S. investors wanting to achieve currency diversification have given money to British merchant banks because the latter have the expertise to run nondollar portfolios, since they've been doing it for a long time. The U.S. investor wanting to get into DM, says, "What do I buy?" The British merchant banks knows the instruments in the DM market.

U.S. banks have also become a new category of investors in dollar and nondollar, fixed-rate securities over the last several years. Banks trade foreign exchange, so it's natural for them to have a view on foreign-exchange rates. Also, they have branches in centers around the globe, so they're in a position to have an informed view not just on the level of German or French interest rates, but on the domestic yield curves there. So big U.S. banks have come to run opportunistic portfolios in gilts, bunds, JGBs, and other nondollar bonds as naturally as they run portfolios in Treasuries. To fund such portfolios, these banks can swap dollars for foreign exchange or they can source local currencies via their local branches.

Professional investors, including banks, are prepared to trade, especially when a change occurs in their view on currencies or rates, so they care about liquidity in a way that the old investor in Eurobonds did not. After liquidity, the new investor wants quality. All of this puts the Eurobond market at a crossroads of sorts. The vast amount of money under management overrides any growth that there has been in the Eurobond market. Certainly, all of the money around can't be invested just in sovereign issues. Also, typical 100MM to 200MM issues by corporates don't go a long way toward sating investors' demands for more paper.

This led one London investment banker to observe: "If the Eurobond market really wants to become a global market, it must grow up now. We have got to have some jumbo issues that have liquidity, are worthwhile to trade in big size at small spreads, and will provide market benchmarks. If we get that, we will eventually have a Eurobond index, a futures contract on that index, and people can then hedge their Eurobond portfolios. That would be useful both to dealers and investors; right now, dealers have to hedge their Eurobond positions using U.S. Treasuries, which puts them at the mercy of spreads.

"Swaps too have had an effect. The swap market means that a lot of deals are done without coming to the public market; the private placement market is fully utilized. Consequently, we don't have these big issues anymore. Without them, the big-gun investors will focus more and more on domestic issues such as gilts, U.S. Treasuries, OATs (French treasuries), bunds, and JGBs. Without benchmark issues that hold the attention of big investors, the Eurobond market is in danger of becoming a second-tier market."

Needless to say, the merchant banking subs of U.S. banks are very active in underwriting new Eurobond issues and in providing swaps, cross currency and fixed floating. In part, what the fight about Glass-Steagall is all about is U.S. banks saying,

"We want the right to do in the U.S. what we've been doing successfully in London for years."

Euro Lines

In addition to granting straight loans, Eurobankers grant lines of credit to a varied group of borrowers, including both domestic and foreign firms issuing commercial paper in the U.S. market.

Euro lines, unlike U.S. lines, are granted on a strict fee basis; no compensating balances are required. Many Euro lines are revolvers that legally commit the bank to provide the line holder with funds if it requests them. Eurobankers, however, have also granted Eurodollar and multicurrency lines on a more or less no-change-in-material-circumstances basis.

Generally speaking, the Euromarket is more transactions oriented than the customer-oriented U.S. market. One result of this is that when money is easy, Euro lines are often cheaper than lines of credit in the U.S. In contrast, when money tightens, Euro lines tend either to dry up in terms of availability or to rise dramatically in price.

In the Euromarket and in foreign banking in general, some of the most important lines granted by banks are not lines to customers but lines to other banks. A French bank operating a dollar book in London or New York is running a book in a foreign currency, and so is a U.S. bank running a French franc book in Paris or a sterling book in London. All these banks worry with good reason about liquidity; that is, about their ability to fund on a continuing basis in a foreign currency the various assets they have acquired that are denominated in that currency.

To reduce the risks in running books denominated in foreign currencies, many major world banks have set up reciprocal line agreements. Under such an agreement a big French bank that naturally has better access than a U.S. bank to the domestic French franc market agrees to provide a U.S. bank with francs in a time of crisis. In exchange, the U.S. bank promises to supply the French bank with dollars. Another way foreign banks operating in the Euromarket enhance their dollar liquidity is by purchasing for a fee backup lines from U.S. banks.

Euro Loans for Domestic Purposes

While the bulk of Euro lending is to foreign borrowers or to U.S. corporations funding foreign operations, a growing number of U.S. corporations have been borrowing money in the Euromarket for domestic purposes. Their major incentive in doing so is to reduce borrowing costs. Frequently, the rate quoted on a Euro loan by a bank's London branch will be cheaper than the *all-in* cost (prime plus compensating balances) quoted by the same bank on a domestic loan, a situation that one top U.S. bank executive described as "sillier than hell."

There are several reasons for this price discrepancy. First, FDIC insurance and reserve requirements, which prevail in domestic banking but not in Eurobanking, in effect constitute a tax on domestic banking that tends to force domestic lending rates above Euro rates. Second, U.S. banks have only a single prime based on 90-day money market rates. With an upward-sloping yield curve from 1 day out to 90, this arrangement naturally penalizes borrowers who want short-term money. In the Euromarket, there is no such penalty. A 1-month loan is priced at LIBOR for 1-month money plus a spread, an all-in rate that may be significantly less than LIBOR on 3-month money plus the same spread. In effect, Eurobankers charge *money market rates* on loans, while domestic bankers until recent years did not.

The potential advantages of borrowing in the Euromarket led some large U.S. corporations to pressure their banks to grant them *either/or facilities,* that is, to permit them to borrow from their bank's head office or a foreign branch as they desire. Generally, the banks resisted, citing the importance of customer relationships, loyalty, and other factors. They did so for two reasons. First, their profit margin was likely to be larger on a domestic loan than on a Euro loan. Second, they knew they could not be competitive in the market for Euro loans. When a U.S. bank lends Eurodollars to a domestic borrower for domestic purposes, it incurs under Reg D a small reserve requirement, which forces it to raise the Euro rate it quotes to a domestic borrower a slight fraction over the rate it quotes to foreign borrowers. Foreign banks lending into the U.S. used to incur no such reserve requirement and thus were in a position to consistently underprice U.S. banks on such loans. Today, foreign bank branches in the U.S. are subject to reserve requirements, and either/or facilities are a common feature of U.S. bank lending agreements to large borrowers.

RUNNING A EUROBOOK

In running their Eurodollar books, the big U.S. banks have taken decades to develop strategies that are sophisticated and with which they feel comfortable. One reason is that the top executives of money market banks were often people with little experience in international business. Also during the early years of the Euromarket, no one really understood it or knew where it was going. Gradually, market expertise developed in London, but that spread only slowly across the Atlantic. Thus, when the London branches of the big U.S. banks began running dollar books, the edict went out from home office that asset and liability maturities were to be matched to minimize rate and liquidity risks.

Learning to Gap
The emphasis on matching continued for some time. In fact, it was only in the early 1970s that U.S. banks became willing to mismatch their Eurobooks aggressively to increase profits. Oddly enough, the Herstatt crisis probably contributed to their willingness to do so. As it blew over, bankers concluded that, if the Euromarket had survived Herstatt, it was sufficiently mature to survive anything.

Today, all the major U.S. banks have several foreign branches running Eurobooks, so their overall exposure to risk in the Euromarket is the sum of the risks associated with several separate branch books. With respect to liability management, head office's main concern is with the rate and liquidity risks that are created through the mismatch of the bank's consolidated Euro position. To control these, management sets up guidelines within which each branch is supposed to operate.

There is no precise way to compare the risk associated with funding, say, a 3-month loan with overnight money versus lending 6-month money and funding the first four months with 4-month money. So head office guidelines take arbitrary and quite different forms. Their purpose, however, is always the same: to limit the mismatch a branch may practice.

Eurobankers often refer to the practice of lending long and borrowing short as running an *open book*. Head office might, for example, control the mismatch on a branch's book by setting limits on the open positions that the branch could assume beyond two months, four months, and six months. An alternative approach is to apply different weights to the mismatches in different maturity ranges (larger weights, the longer the maturity range) and then require that the weighted sum of all mismatches be less than some dollar figure.

The job of operating the branch's book under these guidelines falls to local funding officers. In the London branch of a large U.S. bank, there will be several senior people responsible for making overall policy decisions and a number of dealers under them who actually buy and sell money. Much of the work of the senior people involves formulating a view on what's likely to happen to interest rates and then deciding, in light of that view and current market conditions, what strategies to follow in taking and placing deposits.

If a Eurobanker expects interest rates to stay steady or fall, he will lend long and borrow short, that is, run a *short* book, assuming a positively shaped yield curve. How short depends in part on the slope of the yield curve. As one banker noted, "There's no incentive to take money at call and put it out for three or six months for a 1/4 or 3/8 spread. With a flat yield curve like that, you are taking a tremendous risk for little reward; if rates back up, you are left with a negative carry. But when the yield curve is steep—a 1% spread between call and 1-year rates—there is a real incentive to overlend and take the spread."

When interest rates became high and highly volatile at the end of the 1970s and in the early 1980s, banks began imposing much tighter limits on the mismatch positions branch treasuries could assume. Also, the growing tendency for banks to globalize their world book led to a situation in which the head offices of a number of banks began dictating to their branches the positions the latter should run.

The Dealers

Once a decision about the maturity structure of the branch's assets and liabilities is made, the responsibility for implementing this decision falls on the chief dealer and his assistants. The London dealing room of a large bank is a fascinating and busy place, populated during trading hours by a bevy of time-deposit and foreign-exchange traders engaged in rapid-fire, nonstop conversations with brokers and large customers.

The "book" that is thrust into the chief dealer's care is a sheet of data giving the current amounts and maturities of all the branch's assets and liabilities. The salient features of this book are something a good dealer keeps in his head—the mismatch in different maturities, the amounts of funds he is likely to have to buy or sell in coming days, and when and in what maturity ranges rate pressures might develop from big rollovers. On the basis of this information, the overall guidelines established for the branch, and the strategies set by local funding officers, the dealer's job is to do the necessary taking and placing of funds as profitably as possible. This sounds simple but leaves much room for the exercise of tactics and judgment.

On every Eurodollar loan a bank makes and funds, it has three potential sources of profit. First, there is the spread the bank gets over LIBOR, which compensates it for operating expenses and the credit risk it is assuming. Second, there is the extra $1/16$ or $1/8\%$ that the bank may be able to make if its dealers can pick up the needed funds a little below LIBOR, for example, through astute timing of the purchase. A third way a bank can profit from a loan is through mismatching its book.

Eurobankers take time deposits from two sources, bank customers and the interbank market. A major bank branch in London will have several people whose job is to contact big depositors, such as major corporate customers (e.g., the oil companies), certain central banks, and other big depositors. Unlike the time-deposit dealers, these customer representatives have time to chat with depositors about market conditions and rates. The banks like to pick up money this way, since it saves them brokerage. Also at times, such money may be cheaper than what they could pick up in the interbank market. That depends on the sophistication of the depositor.

Banks that are large takers of funds also try to cultivate direct relationships with other banks. Banks, unlike corporations, can go into the brokers' market to place Eurodollars. Thus, a bank attempting to pick up money direct from other banks to save brokerage normally tries to post fair bid rates for different maturities and to suggest indirectly at least that sellers go elsewhere on days when it is posting noncompetitive rates because it does not need money. A major bank that posts noncompetitive rates may still pick up deposits either because the lender has lines to only a few banks or because his lines to other banks are full.

While large banks prefer to get money direct to save brokerage, brokers are extremely useful to them. Although brokers have to be paid, they save banks money on both communications and personnel. A funding officer of one of the largest U.S. banks estimated offhand that without the brokers, he would need 200 telephone lines and 50 dealers to run the London dealing room. The brokers are also useful to a bank that suddenly discovers it has an hour to raise $200MM of short-dated funds, an amount that might take some time to dig out directly. A third advantage the brokers offer is the cloak of anonymity. As a funding officer at the London branch of one of the largest U.S. banks put it, "Suppose I want to sell $50MM and I call a bank direct, one who would have been prepared to do that transaction in the brokers' market. He sees that it is my bank on the other side and he gets nervous and wonders—what are they trying to do, $50MM or $200MM? So he does a $10MM deal and now not only have I not done the transaction, but I have disclosed the amount I am trying to do." Anonymity in this respect is useful for all the top banks. They are a bit like bulls in a barnyard; whenever they move, their smaller companions get nervous.

Role of Euro CDs

In the Euromarket, a banker can obtain time deposits in a wide range of maturities either directly from nonbank depositors or in the interbank market. Because of the availability of time-deposit money, a bank will issue Euro CDs only if there is a rate advantage in doing so. Also, because the overall market for Euro CDs is thin and the market for any one bank's CDs is thinner still, a bank is cautious about the quantity of Euro CDs it writes: it wants to preserve the spread between the rates it pays for time-deposit and CD money.

U.S. banks no longer issue the volume of Euro CDs they once did. Strictly wholesale banks, such as Bankers Trust and Morgan, still write, but since rate deregulation, domestic banks with big retail bases find they need to buy less wholesale money. Today, the big issuers of Euro CDs are Japanese banks.

"We still issue Euro CDs," noted one U.S. banker in London, "perhaps as much as in the past, but our CD issuance has certainly not increased; as a bank, we are probably overfunded. Still, there is a market for our CDs. Our customers want to hold them; and of course, we do have liquidity requirements—assets to fund. However, our CD issuance is not growing as it was in the 1970s and early 80s. Whatever balance-sheet growth we have had of late probably reflects the fact that we own foreign-currency assets, the dollar value of which has risen in recent years. A lot of our Euro CDs are sold in New York to customers who want to hold London CDs. While our CD issuance is still important, since it's stagnant, its relative importance is declining."

A Brit at a top American bank in London noted: "Our sales of Euro CDs have dropped. We haven't been consistently aggressive in trying to issue as we used to be because we don't need the liquidity. So our volumes have dropped off immensely. Also, a lot more of our business today is being done in small amounts: investors buying 5, 10, or 15MM. Today, the investor demand is not there. Sometimes, we issue Euro CDs just to keep our figures up—our name in the market. Also, investor demand, which is down anyway, is being satisfied by the Japanese.

"In our heyday, U.S. investors wanted top American names. But we have had Contil, banks overissuing, banking scares in the U.S. From the top 10 U.S. banks, it has become the top 8, the top 5, and now virtually the top 3 or 4: Citi, Morgan, Bankers Trust, and possibly Security Pacific; Chase has never been forgiven for overissuing some years ago and still has to pay up a couple of basis points. When the country-debt issue comes up, sometimes we get mentioned and sometimes we don't."

Yet another U.S. banker in London noted: "We try to match

the buyers [of our Euro CDs] in what they want unless the bank has a strong view of where it wants to cover its book. We can issue 1s, 3s, and 6s easily, but once we get beyond 6s, buyers start to run out. Maybe it's that, when we want to sell long-dated CDs, our customers share our view—that rates are going up.

"Our salespeople in London sell our CDs. Also, we get calls from dealers, like Merrill, saying where they would be willing to buy our paper, 1-month to 1-year. If we wish to issue, the bargaining begins: we are triple A and expect to pay less. We are selling CDs at 7 A.M. New York time; the dealer may hedge himself in futures right away, wait for New York to open, then sell to retail and lift his hedge. The competition is hotter than it used to be, and dealers who sell paper for us are getting less than the 05 they once did. Also, today, it is the Japanese, not the U.S. banks, who are the big issuers of Euro CDs."

The Europlacement Book

One of the curious things about the Euromarket, at least to the uninitiated, is that many market participants are busily taking deposits with the right hand and placing them with the left. In the beginning, interbank placements may have been made partly out of a concern for balance-sheet cosmetics. In domestic operations, it's not considered proper for a bank to loan out all the funds it takes in, the idea being that this would leave the bank with no bonds to sell and thus with a potential liquidity problem. For a money market bank, this notion makes little sense, but no U.S. bank, big or small, is going to get caught with no securities on its balance sheet. In their Euro operations, banks used at least to pick up few salable securities unless they ran a Euro CD portfolio. Thus, especially in the early days of the Euromarket when matched funding was the rule, a book in which all assets were loans would have been logical and would have posed no liquidity threat. It would, however, have looked bad according to the traditional criteria of bank management. Placements, which are not classed as loans but can be just as illiquid, do not present this difficulty. Thus, cosmetic considerations were one incentive for Europlacements. Once banks became willing to mismatch, *profits* became another incentive.

A domestic bank that has a strong view on where interest rates are going is hard put to place a big bet based on that view. If it expects interest rates to fall, there is no interbank market in which it can sell long-dated money in volume, and since a savvy corporate treasurer is likely to have the same interest-rate view that the bank does, he will be unwilling to take out a fixed-rate term loan at such a time. If alternatively a domestic banker expects rates to rise, he will want to buy long-dated money, but he has no place where he can do this in volume. Whatever his expectations; his options for structuring maturities are limited.

In the Euromarket, things are different. A bank can't order its customers to take fixed-rate term loans whenever it would like them to, but in the placement market a bank can buy and sell funds in reasonable volume over a wide range of maturities. There are several reasons for the contrast in maturity options between the U.S. market and the Euromarket. First, the Euromarket is traditionally more accustomed to dealing in longer dates. On the deposit side in particular, there have always been some suppliers of funds who were concerned primarily with preservation and safety of principal as opposed to maximizing return and were willing for a spread to supply long-dated funds to creditworthy banks. The ranks of such depositors were joined over the years by oil-rich Arabs, who were willing to offer top banks deposits with maturities as long as five years to stockpile oil income earmarked to finance later investment projects.

The contrast in maturity options between the U.S. market and Euromarket also reflects differences in the positions of banks operating there. The natural customer base of a foreign bank, for example, will include firms that lack the same access to dollar financing that U.S. firms have in the domestic capital market, and that therefore may choose to borrow on terms different from those on which a large U.S. corporation would. Also, because the dollar is not their domestic currency, foreign banks are and should be more anxious to match fund than U.S. banks are. Smaller regional U.S. banks are in a somewhat similar position to foreign banks; they lack the assurance that, say, Citi,

Chase, or Morgan has that they will be able to buy whatever money they need whenever they need it. Liquidity considerations are a final reason that a foreign bank might want to buy long-dated funds whereas a top U.S. bank would not. Especially since the Herstatt crisis, foreign banks operating in the Euromarket have been concerned with liquidity, and one way they can get it is by buying, say, 1-year money and lending it short term.

Placements are generally less profitable than loans because they offer no built-in spread over LIBOR. But because of the maturity options in the placement market, at times they offer attractive possibilities for speculating on interest-rate changes. Assuming a positively sloped yield curve, such speculation is more attractive when interest rates are expected to fall than when they are expected to rise. A bank that expects interest rates to fall will lend long and borrow short. In doing so it gets paid for taking a view (the spread between the long lending rate and the lower short borrowing rate), *and* if the bank is right, it earns something extra as the borrowing rate falls.

Alternatively, if a bank expects rates to rise, the natural strategy is for it to lend short and borrow long. Doing so, however, will cost the bank money, so it will come out ahead only if it is right and rates do rise sharply. Some banks, when they expect rates to rise will, instead of borrowing long and lending short, continue the pattern of lending long and funding short. Or they will fund in a barbell fashion, taking both short and long (6-month and over) deposits. The success of this strategy depends on the speed and extent of the rate rise. Studies have shown that, during a period of rising rates, the barbell strategy often provides funds at the cheapest cost because rates do not rise quickly or sharply enough to offset the advantages of the cheap short-dated funds used.

Oil-Exporters' Dollars

In the Euromarket, the top U.S. banks—because of their size, reputation, and customer base—have always been the recipients of large deposits from nonbank depositors. Both because they could earn profits by laying off such deposits in the interbank market and because the maturity structure of the deposits they received was not necessarily what they desired for their

Eurobook, these banks became big sellers as well as takers of funds. In effect, they came to act as dealers in Eurodeposits.

After the OPEC nations dramatically increased the price of oil in 1974, the dealer banks rapidly became recipients of huge short-term deposits from Arab oil sellers. As they assumed responsibility for recycling petro dollars, their balance sheets changed dramatically, with placements becoming much more important than previously relative to loans.

Their new role as recyclers of petro dollars created problems for the big banks. One concerned liquidity; in taking a lot of short-term money from the Arabs, these banks were violating two basic rules of liability management: (1) a bank should not take a significant portion of its deposits from a single depositor or group of depositors, and (2) a bank should not accept big deposits of volatile short-term (*hot*) money. The one comfort that the big banks could take in this matter was that, regardless of what the Arabs did with their dollars, these dollars could not disappear from the system. If the Arabs pulled a lot of money out of one bank, that bank could certainly buy back the lost dollars in the interbank market from the bank or banks in which the Arabs subsequently redeposited their dollars.

A second problem created by big Arab deposits was credit risk. By taking huge deposits of Arab money and redepositing it with other banks, the dealer banks were forced to assume a credit risk that they thought properly belonged to the original depositor. To compensate for this risk, the dealer banks attempted to buy Arab money as cheaply as possible, a policy the Arabs seemed to understand. A final problem for a bank receiving big Arab deposits was that the resulting $2- or $3-billion increase in deposits and redeposits on its balance sheet tended to perceptibly erode the bank's capital ratios. Such erosion was something that a big bank might willingly have accepted to increase bread-and-butter loan business but not to earn a small margin in the placement market. To cope with these problems, a few big banks sought to limit the size of their Eurodollar book, a policy that offered the side benefit of enabling them to buy money more cheaply than other banks could.

Over time, the problems created by Arab dollars eased, partly because the Arabs gradually became more willing to place funds with the bottom end of the triple-A banks and the top end of the double-A banks. Whereas, in the late 1970s, 10 or 15 banks were receiving the bulk of Arab deposits, the list expanded over time to 50 or 60 banks, and it comprised more non–U.S. names. In addition to expanding the number of banks with which they were willing to place money, the Arabs also became more willing to give top banks longer-term deposits, out to as long as five years.

Eventually, the problems associated with recycling petrodollars diminished. The collapse in the price of oil caused the revenues of oil-exporting countries to fall. At the same time, the expenditures of these countries rose because of huge development programs they had undertaken on the basis of anticipated oil revenues. Thus, the balance-of-payments positions of a number of oil-exporting countries—Mexico and Nigeria to name two—turned from surplus to deficit.

One fact that seems to surprise many people is that, as the Arabs acquired so many dollars, the Middle East did not expand into a major Eurocenter. Bahrain is primarily a booking center funded to a significant degree out of London. Part of the explanation is that the Middle East has always been viewed as an area of political instability, so even people there prefer to keep their funds elsewhere. Also, the Arabs have displayed little talent for the sort of cooperation that would be required to develop a major Middle East Eurocenter. In addition, unlike the Chinese of Singapore, the Arabs have never displayed great interest in or aptitude for banking and finance.

Mismatch Strategies

Because of rollovers, most assets that a bank in the Euromarket is financing have original maturities of three or six months, although some may go longer. In financing these, a bank can mismatch in various ways. The most extreme approach would be to rely on overnight money. Doing so would normally create the greatest positive spread from mismatch, but it would also expose the bank to the greatest rate risk. An alternative would be to fund a new asset for part of its life. For example, a bank might fund a 6-month asset with 4-month money (*buy 4s against 6s* in the jargon of the trade) and then fund the remaining two months with overnight money or a purchase of 2-month Euros. One consideration in plotting this sort of strategy is the maturities that are most actively traded in the Euromarket. Funding a 6-month asset with 1-month money would leave a bank that planned to match fund the tail of the asset in need of 5-month money, a maturity in which the market is thin.

If a bank buys 4s against 6s or pursues some similar strategy, it creates an open position in its book and thereby assumes a rate risk. One way it can eliminate that risk while simultaneously locking in a profit from the mismatch is by entering into a *forward forward* contract; that is, *buying money of a fixed maturity for future delivery*. In the example above, the appropriate forward forward contract would be for 2-month money to be delivered four months hence. In the Euromarket there used to be some trading in forward forwards, but the market was always thin.

The seller of a forward forward assumes a rate risk because he cannot be sure how much it will cost him to fund that commitment. Therefore, he will enter into such a contract only if he is compensated for his risk. In our example, the seller of 2-month money four months hence will want to get something more than the rate he expects to prevail on 2-month money four months hence. For his part, if the borrower is locking up a profit on his mismatch, he might be willing to pay some premium on the forward forward contract. Another reason a buyer and seller might strike a forward-forward deal is that they entertain diverse opinions on where interest rates are headed.

In the game of mismatching, the big U.S. banks have an advantage over their competitors in forecasting Euro rates. One reason is that Euro rates, as shown in Chapter 18, tend to track U.S. rates closely, with U.S. rates generally doing the leading, Euro rates the following. This gives banks that are active in the U.S. money market and have a close feel for developments there (i.e., domestic banks) an edge over their foreign brethren in predicting Euro rates.

Also, the bigger the bank, the better the input it is likely to get from head office and the more intimate the contract between London and head office is likely to be. As the chief dealer in the London branch of a top U.S. bank put it, "We get tremendous input from New York. I speak to people there two hours every afternoon on the phone. Also, the foreign exchange desk next to mine has a direct line open to New York at all times, and we have direct telex, too. All that information permits us to quickly build up a feel for conditions in the U.S. market. There's no way a smaller bank or a foreign bank can get access to the same information. They can read it tomorrow in the paper; we get it right away. That's important because in this market half an hour sometimes makes a crucial difference."

The information flow between London and New York is not one way. At times London sees things New York does not, and the two have differing rate views. For example, at a time when New York anticipated continued ease, a London dealer looking at his book might conclude that both Euro and domestic rates in a certain maturity range were likely to firm up temporarily at least due to a confluence of scheduled Euro rollovers. Alternatively, if New York foresaw an upturn in rates because domestic loan demand was beginning to revive, London might temper that view by arguing that no parallel increase in loan demand was occurring outside the U.S.

A Changing Placement Book

As noted, banks, in running their Eurobooks, face the same pressure they do in running their domestic books—namely, to minimize balance-sheet usage. One casualty has been Euro-placements books. Today, banks are far less willing than they once were to make and take placements of Eurodeposits in the hope of small gains: doing so ties up their balance sheets and it uses up credit lines to other banks. Also, thanks to the Citi-Manila situation (blocked Eurodeposits) and to the problems of Mexico, Brazil, Iran, and so on, banks are now more wary than they were a decade ago not only about what banks they lend to, but about where those banks are situated.

A dealer at one U.S. bank's London branch noted: "The days of calling up Nat West or Barclays and saying, 'Can I have your fixed dates, please?' in which case they would quote you—1/8 wide—3, 4, 6, 9, and 12 months, do not exist any more. We don't get banks calling us up: 'What's 1-month, 3-month, 6-month today?' and we would never think of calling a bank for his run.

An exception is a bank who wishes to borrow and who knows that we have a line to him; he will call and just ask for the period for which he wishes to borrow.

"The volume of our Euro time-deposit book has probably gone up by about ⅓ because we are still free to deal with our branches. Interbranch positions wash out in our bank's consolidated balance sheet, so we have no restrictions on dealing with branches. But we have credit line and sovereign problems in dealing with other banks—restrictions set by New York. We have a good two-way interbranch market going, so the business we do in the interbank market these days is only the tip of the iceberg [of their placement book]."

Today, in mismatching their books, banks use Euro futures, FRAs, interest-rate swaps, and option products with far greater enthusiasm than they use Europlacements. All this is not to say that the interbank cash market in Euros is going away; if anything, this market, after having shrunk, is coming back. There are still banks that have to borrow money to cover assets; and there still are banks that have money that they want to lend. Thus, the cash market in Euros is still there and always will be. Also, as noted in Chapter 18, the Japanese are still very active in the interbank market doing arbitrages.

THE USE OF OFF-BALANCE-SHEET ITEMS

"The degree of mismatch in the book is still an issue," noted one U.S. banker in London, "but now we have many more off-balance-sheet tools with which to do this. By using the latter, we economize balance-sheet usage. We often describe our off-balance-sheet activity as a hedge of our balance-sheet activity, and in some sense, that is true. However, the activity has grown to a point that we and most other banks are actually trading these items. The big volume of trading is in futures, FRAs, and swaps, not in the taking-and-placing market. This is because everyone is in the same boat—wanting to trade off balance sheet.

"In talking about off-balance-sheet activity, you must distinguish between dollars and sterling on the one hand and the other Eurocurrencies, because off-balance-sheet activity is still primarily in dollars and sterling. There is a moderate market in DM FRAs, but less liquidity in the markets for FRAs in other currencies such as French francs and Swissy."

Euro Futures

The principal Euro futures contract that banks trade is the Chicago IMM contract. Euro future contracts are also traded on the *London International Financial Futures Exchange* (*LIFFE*) and on Singapore's *SIMEX*. Initially, the LIFFE contract permitted delivery because the Bank of England and the Exchequer deemed that a no-delivery contract would be a gaming contract. Later, the LIFFE contract was changed to cash settlement and now differs from the Chicago contract only in that it settles at 11 A.M. London time. The Simex contract is fungible with the IMM contract; the LIFFE contract is not. Liquidity is significantly lower on LIFFE than on the IMM; LIFFE has no "locals" as such—the brokers there are just order fillers. Once Chicago opens, London just follows Chicago up and down.

Back in the mid-1980s, as the Euro futures contract was blossoming, banks thought it would be much easier to buy and sell Euros futures for a quick turn rather than to make and take deposits for a small potential gain. Banks love the Euro contract. For one thing, it is cash settlement (there is no delivery), so a bank trading Euro futures cannot get caught long or short in a squeeze. Another attraction of Euro futures is that they are so liquid. In this market, a bank can turn a position—buy or sell 100 or 200 contracts (each for 1MM)—just like that; whereas if a bank were to try to place or take 200MM Eurodeposits, that might take them some time.

A typical London banker noted: "We do some trading [of Eurodollar futures] between Simex and LIFFE; Simex is open until 10 A.M. London time; and so long as the price is right, we will do a deal on Simex even though the volume there is extremely thin; we know that, if need be, we can undo that deal on the IMM. Also, we now have folks in London who stay on until 8 P.M. to catch the Chicago close; we found that often the movement occurred after the LIFFE close, so we were missing a lot of opportunities.

"For sterling-related contracts, LIFFE is the main exchange. We are very active in gilt futures, and the short sterling contract, where volume is high and the contract is very liquid."

U.S. banks are supposed to use futures only for hedging, but in fact they have so many positions that it's easy for them to call just about any futures position a hedge.[9] Still, banks tend not to trade futures for short-term profit, but rather as a way of taking a view over some longer period, for example, the next 30, 60, or 90 days. A banker typifying this attitude noted, "We have never been successful at the trading approach that calls for you to buy futures at 9 A.M., sell them at 11 A.M., and then buy them back in the afternoon. One reason is that our book is so big that it's like an oil tanker. You cannot put it in forward, then reverse, and then forward again. You can try, but it just carries on in the same way. However, we feel we have used futures very successfully in hedging our interest-rate gaps."

Another banker noted: "We have two futures traders in London. They trade and also execute deals that the asset-liability manager asks them to place. We might have a gut feeling that interest rates are going up and maybe decide to hedge our existing overlent position. In that case, we would use futures. In futures, it's easy to execute 50, 100, 200MM within a few minutes. If you try to do that in FRAs, it takes a long time: you have to find a counterparty and check limits. Also, it may be that the bank doesn't want to use cash—it's fairly square in its short positions and wants rather to hedge forward positions."

Despite the fact that the Euro futures market is really a global market that serves other global markets, it still has its peculiar deficiencies. Not all contracts are fungible; and more important, between 3 P.M. and 6 P.M. New York time, when a lot of people are still in their offices, this market—one of the key

---

[9]When a bank uses futures to hedge a position in a cash instrument, it does not mark the cash item to market and it does not take any profit or loss on futures up front. Instead, it accrues everything—flows gains and losses on both the cash and the futures positions over time.

markets of the world—is closed. "This," noted one U.S. banker, "is a major problem, and a lot of firms could have [on October 19, 1987] gone bankrupt just because of that." If the Chicago scheme to computerize trading in Euro futures after hours works, this gap will be closed.

FRAs

Futures are a near perfect way to hedge risks that match the four yearly IMM dates.[10] However, most bank risk is "non-IMM" risk; hence, the development of FRAs.

A *FRA* (*forward rate agreement*) resembles a forward forward except that it's settled not by making or taking a deposit, but rather by making a cash (settlement) payment. For example, if bank A promises to pay bank B a rate of $10\frac{1}{8}$ on a 50MM, 3-month deposit to be received two months hence, bank A will have to make a cash payment to B if two months hence the 3-month rate is below $10\frac{1}{8}$, but bank B will have to make a cash payment to A if two months hence the 3-month rate is above $10\frac{1}{8}$. In this example, the amount of the cash payment would equal the difference between $10\frac{1}{8}$ and the 3-month rate on the day the FRA settled, times 50MM, times the appropriate annualizing factor, which is 3 months/12 months or $\frac{1}{4}$ of a year.

FRAs are easy to trade because the concept is simple. Also, dealers and brokers quickly standardized the terms of the agreement.

---

[10]It may be pedantic to say the hedge is "near perfect," but in fact a lot of hedges that look perfect work out to be slightly less than perfect. The problem is that a measure of 3-month LIBOR on a given morning depends on which banks are sampled at what hour and in what manner; in some fixings, Y banks are sampled, the X highest and lowest quotes are discarded, and the remaining quotes are averaged to get LIBOR. Futures in Chicago and London have their own fixings for LIBOR; FRA contracts incorporate other fixings.

On some days, for whatever reasons, different fixings on LIBOR can produce different numbers. This occurred in March 1989 when there was a $\frac{1}{16}$ difference between where interest rate swaps fixed and where futures fixed; this caused a lot of people to lose $\frac{1}{16}$ on some very big positions.

The obvious advantage of FRAs over forward forwards is that they permit a bank to make the same bet it could with a forward forward, but at settlement they cause neither the making nor the taking of a deposit. A FRA does for a bank the same thing that a forward forward would without impacting at any point the bank's footings.

Also, if a bank becomes unhappy with a position in FRAs—it changes its rate view—it can eliminate its FRA position by doing an offsetting FRA trade, again with no balance-sheet impact. In contrast, if a bank becomes unhappy with a position it has established using cash deposits or forward forwards, it must—to eliminate that position—double up positions, which will impact its balance sheet, either immediately or at a later date.

FRAs: An Example
Here's an example of how a banker might use a FRA. "Suppose," said one bank officer, "that a Middle Eastern customer comes in and wants to give the bank a 100MM deposit for one year. I quote him 8%. Say I start the day with the following funding plan: I want to take 300MM of 1-month money, 200MM of 3-month money, and 100MM of 6-month money. I don't want 1-year money, but I do want 6-month money; so I convert this 1-year money into 6-month money by doing a 6s-against-12s FRA where I place the FRA at 8¼. With this deal, I have converted a 1-year taking into a 6-month taking, and I need take no 6-month money for the day.

"In my example, 1-year money coming in doesn't fit my book—taking it would be against my interest-rate outlook. In the old days, I would have gotten rid of such money by placing it for one year at LIBOR, and I'd have earned a spread, LIBOR minus LIBID. Now, I worry about the balance sheet, so instead I use a deposit in a maturity I don't want as a substitute for a deposit in a maturity I do want."

FRAs, a Precise Hedge
The beauty of FRAs is that they can be dealt for any dates, whereas futures get dealt for only four dates in the year. If a

depositor comes in at the end of April and wants to place 100MM for one year, a bank, by using FRAs, can immediately convert that 1-year deposit into a 6-month deposit. The best a bank could do using futures would be to buy the September and the December contracts, which would create an imprecise—one-month-off—hedge. FRAs owe much of their popularity to the fact that dates in the FRA market are congruent with those in the cash market.

A bank that uses futures, rather than FRAs, to hedge always has basis risk unless the period the bank is hedging precisely matches the period covered by one IMM contract or by a strip of them. Basis risk occurs because the rate locked in isn't exactly the rate being hedged. (For more on basis risk, see Chapters 15 and 16.)

Pricing of FRAs

Euro futures are far more liquid than FRAs because they are an attractive speculative instrument: you can trade them—buy them one day, sell them the next. Because futures are so liquid, they dominate the FRA market. Thanks to ample opportunities for arbitrage involving FRAs and futures, FRAs are always priced off futures. The price of a FRA is the futures price adjusted for the number of days it's removed from a futures settlement date. In other words, FRA prices are an interpolation of the prevailing prices for the June, September, December, and March futures contracts.

Credit Risk on FRAs

Yet another advantage of FRAs is that they expose the contracting parties to minimal credit risk. Said one trader, "A FRA is one of the few transactions in which you never know till you get there who's going to owe whom money. Suppose you deal a FRA and your counterparty goes bankrupt during the period of the FRA. Say you are the seller [the lender] of a FRA at an 8% rate; on the day the FRA settles, you have the bankrupt party's [now worthless] promise of an 8% rate and the market rate is only 6%. What have you lost? Only 2% for a couple of months, since you can still lend at 6%."

One of the stimuli for the takeoff of the FRA market was that FRAs proved extremely useful for lesser-name banks who found it harder than in the past to borrow money in the interbank market. "By using a FRA," noted one banker, "merchant banks suddenly found that they had a way of either trading positions or hedging their existing book.

"For example, a Bearing Brothers can borrow the 3s easier than he can the 1-year. If he wants to position himself in the 1-year [acquire a 1-year asset], it's risky for him to plan to fund himself by borrowing 3s four times in a row, all the while hoping rates won't rise. In the current market, he has a far better alternative: he can borrow 3s and hedge himself by doing a FRA in the 3s–12s; then, 3 months later, he can buy 3s and hedge himself by doing a FRA in the 3s–9s, and so on; he can hedge all the way through.

Jargon, Spreads, the Brokers

Typically, there is a 3- to 4-bp spread in FRAs between the bid and the offer. In FRA-land, the jargon is buy and sell. If you *sell* a FRA, you are lending the rate, and you hope interest rates will fall. If you *buy* a FRA, you are borrowing the rate, and you hope that interest rates won't fall.

FRAs are brokered by the same parties who broker cash Euro time deposits. Fortunately for them, brokering FRAs has taken up some of the slack the latter have encountered due to the decline in interbank trading of Euro time deposits. Currently, traders deal FRAs out to, but seldom beyond, two years.

Nondollar Currencies

Today, a sterling futures contract is traded on LIFFE, and there is also an active market in sterling FRAs. Two 3-month DM futures contracts are traded on both LIFFE and the Paris futures exchange, and DM FRAs are buoyant in Europe. Most other major currency FRAs also trade well; only the French franc FRA trades poorly. There is, today, even limited trading of ECU FRAs.

Liquidity of FRAs
A bank can get a FRA in any date, but the greatest liquidity is found in the 1s against 4s (a 3-month deposit in one month's time); in the 3s against 6s (a 3-month deposit in three months' time); in the 6s against 9s; and in the 9s against 12s. These maturities conform to standard deposit-taking periods.

Banks use both futures and FRAs to hedge over time the risk of movements in interest rates. Futures and FRAs pick up different segments of the yield curve. Also, futures can be done only in multiples of 1MM.

Basically, the FRA market is a London market; liquidity in New York is limited, but U.S. banks are pushing to develop more of a market in New York in order to widen the limited time frame in which they currently can deal.

FRAs as a Speculative Tool
In addition to hedgers, there are in the FRA market speculators who trade FRAs just as they would trade any other instrument: they take positions because they think rates are coming down or going up. If a trader of FRAs has a nice profit and the FRA market is temporarily illiquid—perhaps due to pressure on the dollar rates—he can hedge himself in futures provided, that is, that his FRA dates conform to IMM dates. For this reason, much pure trading in FRAs is done to futures dates.

Interest-Rate Swaps

In Chapter 2, we introduced interest-rate swaps—probably the great financial innovation of the 1980s. Here we focus on swaps principally as a tool in bank asset-liability management. (For more on swaps, see Chapter 19.)

Arbitrage
One interesting aspect of the off-balance-sheet items we are discussing is that, while they appear to be quite different animals,

it's often possible to construct the equivalent of the one out of the other. Thus, lots of opportunities exist to use one off-balance-sheet item to arbitrage against, to hedge, or to substitute for another.

To illustrate, consider a 2-year swap in which one party agrees to pay 2-year fixed and to receive 6-month LIBOR. There is a consecutive set (*strip*) of FRAs that is equivalent to this interest-rate swap. Specifically, for the payor of fixed, the swap is equivalent to getting today's 6-month LIBOR, which is set on the day the deal is done, plus buying three consecutive FRAs: a 6s–12s FRA, a 12s–18s FRA, and an 18s–24s FRA. The equivalence of a short-term swap to a strip of FRAs has led traders to arbitrage between these two markets, which in turn holds rates in the two markets in line with each other.

We mentioned above the equivalence of Euro futures to FRAs done to IMM dates. Naturally, this equivalence has led traders to arbitrage these two instruments, which causes them to trade at almost identical rates. Interest-rate swaps can be hedged not only with a strip of FRAs, but with a strip of futures: specifically, by buying a strip of futures, a trader can accomplish the same thing he would if he did a swap in which he became the receiver of floating.

The above also means that futures can be used to hedge a swap. One trader noted: "There has been an extraordinary increase in the open interest in the Eurodollar futures contract. What I think has happened is that swap desks are now using futures a lot more than Treasuries to hedge swaps in the 1-, 2-, and 3-year range. One consequence is that the spread between the swap market and the futures strip is slowly but surely being arbed out."

Creating a Synthetic, Fixed-Rate, 5-Year Asset

It sometimes occurs that a bank's asset-liability manager takes the view that interest rates are going to go down and, consequently, he'd like to acquire a 5-year, fixed-rate asset. Chances are that his bank is not making any 5-year, fixed-rate loans, and even if it were, such a loan would not be a particularly liquid asset. No problem. The bank's asset-liability manager can use the swap market to create the asset he desires. Specifically, he can enter into a 5-year interest-rate swap in which he receives fixed and pays floating (normally LIBOR). If his bank has a securities affiliate, he may get his swap from that affiliate. The latter is typically in the business of trying to make a profit by trading swap spreads, so it will hedge the swap it has done with the bank by buying, say, 5-year Treasuries until it can trade out that swap at a profit.[11]

A swap is an attractive asset from the bank's point of view. Credit risk is minimal, and capital requirements incurred are small. Another advantage to a bank in taking a position in swaps is, if the bank changes its view on interest rates, it can generally unwind the swap it has put on by doing another swap. "The swap market," noted one London banker, "is an absolutely colossal market. Generally, you can go into the swap market and borrow money back the other way [do a reverse swap] with comparative ease. If I do a swap where I receive 5-year fixed and six months later I want out, I would go back to the swap trader at our affiliate to get an offsetting swap."

Another bank asset-liability manager noted, "We use swaps as a way of creating a position—almost like a cash deal although no cash changes hands. For us, swaps are principally a tool to create interest-rate gaps, rather than to trade or to hedge."

Offsetting a Deposit in an Unwanted Tenor
A swap, like a FRA, can also be used by a bank to offset a deposit that does not fit its funding requirements. Here's an example. "Suppose," said a U.S. banker in London, "that SAMA gives us 100MM of 5-year money. We don't want that 5-year money because we think that interest rates are going down. So we do an interest-rate swap with a merchant bank, say, Morgan Grenfell. Under the swap, we pay 6-month LIBOR and receive a fixed, 5-year rate that's maybe a 5-bp spread over what we're

---

[11]Note that the securities affiliate's hedge does not undo the position put on by the bank. From the point of view of the consolidated balance sheet of the bank holding company (which owns both the bank and its securities affiliate), fixed-rate, 5-year securities—probably funded with repo—have been acquired.

paying SAMA [due allowance made for compounding of the variable 6-month rate]. Effectively, I have converted the 5-year deposit I'm taking into a series of 6-month deposits; thus, I've satisfied my customer by taking his money, but I haven't violated my original funding plan in doing so."

Playing a Swap against Redeposits and FRAs

An imaginative banker can also use an interest-rate swap to enhance his ROA by working the swap in conjunction with his redeposit book. "In the Eurobook," noted one banker, "we do the transformation [gapping] as usual, but there's a new dimension in management of the Eurobook—the development of the swap business. If I see rates going lower but the yield curve is steep, I would, at today's rates, lend 5-year with a swap at 9 and pay 6-month LIBOR which is 7½. That means that, for the next six months, I earn a 1½-point spread if I just do the swap. But I am bullish and think that rates are going down not in six months, but in one month. In that case, I can neutralize my effective 6-month borrowing with a 6-month redeposit and become a taker of overnight funds at 7. By doing so, I increase my spread by 50 bp. That 50 bp does not in and of itself justify the use of the balance sheet, but when I decided to lend 5-year money via the swap, I wanted the 2-point differential between the 5-year rate and the overnight rate.

"At times, I will be happy about the swap repricing I expect to get, and at other times, I will be very upset. I have to have this balance sheet [the placement book] to eliminate the days when I am upset. Ideally, I could buy or sell futures when the risk of an unfavorable repricing upsets me. In practice, however, repricing dates on a swap usually don't match the futures contract dates; and in the current market, you can, from week to week, have a 25-bp differential in yield on the 6-months. So futures are a poor protection for me; and consequently, I must use either the cash market or the FRA market to protect myself when I risk an unfavorable repricing. By trading in either market I can neutralize [over a reset date] the floating-rate portion of my swap."

Options Products

Today, banks also trade caps and floors (recall Chapter 2). They offer these products to their customers as a tool of interest-rate management, and they use them themselves for the same purpose.

The hedges a bank sets on its cap-and-floor positions with customers can also be worked into its gap management. "We have," noted a U.S. banker in London, "one guy trading caps and floors and another trading swaps. So if we were to sell to a customer a 100MM, 5-year cap on 6-month LIBOR, the cap trader would turn around and delta hedge that position with our swap trader.[12] The latter would end up with a 5-year swap where he's receiving and the cap trader is paying fixed. The hedge converts our cap position into an asset-liability position, at least for the amount of the delta hedge. Of course, the delta hedge changes every day as rates change. Suppose our computer program tells us that we are supposed to delta hedge 50% of the 100MM cap we sold; then our swap trader ends up receiving 50MM on the fixed side for five years against 6-month LIBOR. It's up to him to then decide whether he will cover that in the market. If he thinks that U.S. interest rates are going down, he will leave it as a mismatch in his book and trade it. Maybe rates will go down, and he'll be able to cover it at a profit. Maybe rates will rise, and he'll get buried.

"Either way, the point is that any time you do a deal with a customer, you can leverage your trading off that deal. That is what we tend to do. Rarely do we match fund the deals that we do with customers; instead, we use match funding as a tool for pricing. We will match fund if the customer hits us on the side of the market on which we don't want to be. But we try to get the deals that give us positions we want to have, and our pricing reflects that. Once we get those deals, we tend to use them to establish positions against our interest-rate outlook. We can use any one of these instruments [futures, FRAs, swaps, caps, and

---

[12]Delta hedging is explained in Chapter 17 on options and options products.

floors] to create or to hedge interest-rate exposure depending on what we want to do."

Off-Balance-Sheet Items as Substitutes

The Euromarket, like the domestic market, tends to gap trade off economic numbers. "People focus," noted one trader, "on economic releases to the point of virtual paranoia. What you find now is that people will do nothing before a release and react just like that afterwards. If a number comes out and it's much worse than people expected, then the [Euro futures] contract just goes down 10 or 15 points, but then it will bottom out and come back because people were short before the number, and there's profit taking going on. Basically, the market tends to overreact to a number. Once people look at it, they tend to say, in the full perspective, the change is not as good or bad as we thought at first glance. Maybe we should hang a sign in the trading room: 'One swallow doth not a spring make.'"

In any case, a funding officer must react to numbers and, in doing so, he can, depending on market conditions and what he wants to do, use the various instruments discussed above as substitutes for each other. "Say I did my funding plan in the morning," noted a London Eurobanker. "Then at 1:30 P.M., the [U.S.] GNP report comes out and the deflator is lower than expected. What do I do? First, I place more FRAs or receive in a swap. I don't lend cash, I never do that any more. Futures is something I might try to do if I wanted to react quickly, but futures are hard to do after a number because everyone piles into the pits.

"If I wanted to adjust my position in the afternoon, I might put out a few offers in the FRA market and in the swap market, but if I do not get my prices in those markets, and I do not want to go home with the positions I have, I will just go out and buy 100MM futures. I use futures whenever I cannot get the position I want using the other instruments. I always know that I can go to the futures market and get a rough approximation of the position I want. The advantage of futures is that you always have liquidity, so you can readjust your position with ease."

The interplay between different noncash instruments occurs in various scenarios. The same banker noted: "Once I get a load of interest-rate swaps on your book, I'm vulnerable to every 6-month rollover. Maybe one month, before the 6-month repricing, I get worried about interest rates rising. Maybe the Fed is going to tighten and instead of getting repriced at 8, I risk getting repriced at 8¼. The simplest and quickest way for me to hedge against that would be to buy futures. A FRA might be a better hedge, but maybe I can't get a FRA to my date; if not, I have to buy futures."

WORLDWIDE FUNDING

As noted, the major U.S. and foreign banks participating in the Euromarket all have branches running their own separate Eurodollar books in each of the major market centers and in peripheral centers as well. This proliferation of Euro activity naturally raises a question as to how centralized a bank's overall Euro activities should be.

Once, it was typical for a bank's branches in different dealing centers to act in a highly independent way, each creating its own dollar book under guidelines set by home office. Now, some banks see benefits in greater coordination of the Euro activities of their different branches and are attempting to achieve it. Others, however, prefer to stick to decentralization. In this respect, Citibank and Chase are probably at extreme opposite poles: Citi having a reputation for decentralization, Chase for coordination.

One argument for giving branches a high degree of autonomy is that funding at each is headed by senior and experienced officers who expect to accept responsibility and need it to develop. Also, if funding officers in some branches are bullish while others are bearish, letting each put his money where his mouth is has a pro side as well as a con. While the bank will not make as much money as it would have if every branch had acted on a *correct* rate view promulgated by head office, the bank also won't lose as much money as it would have if every branch had acted on an incorrect view. Another argument for branch autonomy is that, in a huge worldwide organization, coordination of what everyone is doing is infeasible or, alternatively, if feasible, would be costly and might take so long that the bank would be handicapped in taking advantage of constantly changing opportunities.

One advantage of coordinating the activities of a bank's individual branches and thereby creating a global Eurobook for the bank is that doing so permits the bank to take its maximum open position in the most advantageous tax areas, for example, to run a very short book in Nassau and compensate by *snugging up* (decreasing the mismatch in) its London book. To the extent that the yield curve is upward sloping, this policy has the advantage of shifting the most expensive funding to the highest-tax areas. A second argument for coordination is that a bank may feel so confident in its rate predictions that it wants to make all its bets in the same direction. A third and, in the 1980s, crucial reason for a U.S. bank to run a worldwide Eurobook was that, because of interest-rate volatility, head office wanted to tightly control the bank's overall interest-rate exposure by running a single *global book* in which its worldwide Euro *and* its domestic dollar books were combined.

Another question concerning the funding of a bank's worldwide Euro operations is the extent to which each branch should be expected to finance its operations by buying funds in its own name. This question arises for two reasons. First, the *natural* (local) supply of and demand for Eurodollars is unbalanced in different Eurocenters; Singapore, Bahrain, and the Caribbean centers, for example, all tend to be big net buyers of funds. Second, lenders of dollars perceive the country risks associated with net buying centers outside London as being greater than those associated with London and are therefore unwilling to lend as much to banks in these centers. Together, these two factors create a situation in which a bank's branches outside London may have to pay more for funds than the same bank's London branch would: whereas the London branch might be able to buy in the middle of the market or at the bid side, the non-London branch might have to buy at the offered side.

While this price differential does not amount to much, $1/16$ to $1/8\%$ typically, to the extent that it exists, there is a natural temptation for a bank to have its London branch buy extra funds in its name and then relend them to its branches in other centers. The only real cost in doing so is that the British Inland Revenue requires that the London branch make some small taxable profit on such transactions. Currently, the minimum acceptable markup is 5/64. Since this figure is modest, many banks do fund—sometimes to a large degree—the operations of their branches in other centers with funds bought in London.

However, there are banks that think every branch should stand on its own feet and do its own funding. One argument is that centers outside London will never be built up as meaningful entities in the global Euromarket unless they are seen to perform in the market in their own names. A second argument is that "sourcing" in London huge quantities of funds that are destined to be used in other centers makes London appear to be a much bigger buyer of Euros than it really is and may thereby impinge on London's sovereign value.

Earlier, we said that there was a lot of dealing in New York and elsewhere in the U.S. in Euros for funding the assets of bank branches located in the Caribbean. This funding is all done in the name of the branch, since if a New York bank bought Euros in the name of head office, these dollars would become "domestic" dollars and as such would be subject to a reserve requirement and the FDIC insurance premium. The fact that the funding and lending operations of the Caribbean branches of U.S. banks are carried out mainly or solely by personnel at head office naturally raised the question of whether the profits of such branches should be treated as domestic income subject to domestic taxation or as foreign-source income. New York State and New York City said, "That's New York income," and they tax it thusly. Tax issues were one reason New York banks had for establishing IBFs.[13]

Eurocurrency Swaps

The bulk of the Eurocurrency market consists of Eurodollar deposits, but it also include Eurodeposits of German marks, sterling, Swiss francs, Dutch guilders, Belgian francs, French

---

[13]See end of chapter.

francs, yen, and other currencies. The uninitiated might think of a bank accepting deposits in all of these currencies as ending up with a mixed bag of different kinds of money. Not so the Eurobanker; he knows that he can turn one currency into another through the simple device of a *swap*. To him money is money whatever its country or origin.

In the foreign-exchange market, currencies are traded for each other on two bases, *spot* and *forward*. In a spot transaction, say, deutsche marks (DM) for dollars, the currencies exchanged are normally delivered two days after the trade is made. In a forward transaction, the exchange occurs at some specified date further in the future, perhaps months later. *A swap is a pair of spot and forward transactions in which the forward transaction offsets or unwinds the spot transaction.* For example, if a holder of marks traded them for dollars in the spot market and simultaneously entered into a forward contract to sell these dollars for marks three months hence, he would have engaged in a swap. Note that the effect of this transaction is to permit the holder of marks to go into dollars for three months without assuming a *foreign-exchange risk*. Specifically, by locking in a selling rate for the dollars he acquires, the swapper eliminates the risk that he might suffer a loss due to a fall in the exchange value of the dollar against the mark while he holds dollars.

Large banks all act as dealers in foreign exchange. The individuals who run this part of the bank's operations take speculative positions long and short in various currencies as part of their normal dealing activities—making markets and servicing customers' buy and sell orders. Also, based on their expectations of probable changes in exchange rates, they will assume speculative positions in foreign exchange designed to earn profits for the bank. Such activities expose the bank to *foreign-exchange risk*. This risk, however, is one that the bank is prepared to assume within limits because the people in the foreign-exchange department are experts in this area.

Funding officers, in contrast, have their greatest expertise in areas other than foreign exchange. As a result, banks in their Euro operations confine their speculation in foreign exchange to the foreign-exchange department and require that funding officers match their Eurobook in terms of currencies (e.g., use dollar liabilities to fund dollars assets). Thus, when a Eurobanker receives a deposit of a currency other than the dollar, he will sell that deposit in the interbank market, swap it for dollars, or use it to fund an asset denominated in that currency. Also, if he's asked to extend a loan denominated in a currency other than the dollar, he will fund that loan either by buying a deposit of that currency or by swapping dollars into that currency.

Most of the time, the spot and forward rates at which any currency trades against the dollar will differ. In particular, the dollar price that a foreign currency commands in the forward market will be higher than the spot rate if this currency can be borrowed more cheaply than the dollar or if it's expected to appreciate in value relative to the dollar. The opposite conditions will cause the currency to sell at a discount in the forward market.

If a currency is selling at a premium in the forward market, a swap out of the dollar into that currency will yield some gain, while a swap out of that currency into the dollar will produce some loss. If, alternatively, a currency is selling at a discount in the forward market, the result will be the reverse. The gain or loss inherent in any swap, the amount of which can be calculated at the time the transaction is arranged, can be expressed as an annualized percentage rate of gain or loss through the use of a simple formula.[14] This rate of gain or loss is a crucial element in a bank's decision about what rates to charge on nondollar loans and to pay on nondollar deposits.

For example, suppose that a corporation offers a bank a 3-month DM deposit and that the forward mark is selling at a premium. If the bank accepts the deposit, it will swap these marks into dollars and in doing so will incur some loss. It will, however, also earn the going 3-month LIBOR rate on the dollars it obtains from the swap. Thus, the rate that the bank offers the depositor will equal roughly 3-month LIBOR minus the annualized rate of loss on the swap. In costing a nondollar loan, the bank follows a similar approach.

---

[14]For a numerical example of a swap, see Chapter 18.

On swap transactions, interest payments generate a residual foreign-exchange exposure. For example, if a bank takes in a 3-month DM deposit and swaps it into dollars, the bank assumes a foreign-exchange risk because it is committed to pay interest in DM on the DM deposit at maturity, while it will earn interest at maturity in dollars on the dollars it has loaned. If the bank chooses to avoid this risk, it can lock in a fixed spread on the overall swap by buying DM (selling dollars) *forward* in an amount equal to the interest to be paid in DM.

Several large banks that receive many deposits of nondollar Eurocurrencies and also have many requests for loans denominated in those currencies actually run books in each of these currencies, matching off deposits in these currencies against loans and placements in the same currencies. Doing so eliminates transactions costs associated with swaps into and out of dollars—the foreign-exchange dealers' spreads between bid and asked prices in the spot and forward markets and some book-keeping and ticket costs. Banks running books in Euromarks and Euro Swissy feel that this reduction in costs permits them to offer depositors and borrowers of these currencies slightly better rates than they could if they consistently swapped all the *natural* DM and Swiss franc business they received into dollar assets and liabilities.

We have talked about banks using swaps to match their Eurobooks (in terms of currencies held and lent). Banks also use swaps another way, to minimize funding costs. Suppose, for example, that a bank wants to fund a 6-month dollar loan. To any funding officer, every Eurocurrency deposit is nothing but a Eurodollar deposit with a swap tagged on. Thus, in shopping for 6-month money, a bank dealer will price out not only 6-month dollar deposits but 6-month dollars obtained by swapping deposits of other currencies into dollars. If 6-month dollars can be obtained more cheaply by buying 6-month Euromarks and swapping them into dollars than by buying dollars, the dealer will go the swap route.

Because all banks in the Euromarket seize every opportunity available to reduce their borrowing costs through swaps, the all-in cost of dollars obtained by swapping any actively traded Eurocurrency into dollars tracks closely the yield on dollar deposits of the same tenor. Thus, the rate saving that a bank can obtain by using a swap to obtain dollars usually amounts to only a narrow spread. However, when the foreign-exchange market moves dramatically, short-lived opportunities for saving ⅛ or ¼% through a swap do occur.

NASSAU AND OTHER SHELL BRANCHES

Initially, U.S. banks set up shell branches in Nassau and Cayman as a way to run in their time zone a Eurobook, the profits on which would be subject neither to foreign nor to New York City and State taxes on their profits. Later, tax rulings freed New York City and New York State to tax bank profits on such books, but the advantages of the books are still such that U.S. banks as a group were, at the end of 1988, running Euro positions of 156 billion and of 243 billion in Nassau and in Cayman, respectively.

While New York and other banks may, as noted at the end of this chapter, run IBF Eurobooks, the profits on which are free from U.S. state and local taxes on profits, a bank's Caribbean branch has a funding advantage over its IBF; as a matter of practice, the Caribbean branches of U.S. banks sell few Eurodollar CDs (1.1 billion were outstanding in February 1989); so the funding advantage of these branches lies not in their ability to sell negotiable CDs, of which they sell few, but rather in the ability of a bank's holding company to raise cheap (maybe 25 bp below LIBOR) money in the domestic commercial paper market and then deposit that money in its Caribbean branch; such deposits are free under Reg D from reserve requirements and also free from FDIC premiums.

The funding advantage enjoyed by a bank's Caribbean branch makes it possible for a bank to earn a spread by booking in Nassau high-quality, short-term, liquid, dollar paper: for example, corporate MTNs, CMOs, and securities backed by auto loans. Note a subtle difference created by Reg D: if a bank makes a loan to a domestic corporation and books that *loan* offshore, the loan—unless offset by an opposite branch-to-head-office dollar flow—is reservable under Reg D at 3%; if, however, a bank buys an MTN issued by a domestic corporation, and books that *security* in Nassau, it incurs no reserve requirement.

Running a carefully selected portfolio of high-quality, liquid securities in a Nassau or Cayman branch offers a bank several advantages. First, since the yield curve in the dollar is normally positively sloped, a bank's foreign branches are likely to do a lot of *transformation*—run *overlent* or *short* books. This practice raises the question of how, if a liquidity crisis were to arise in the Eurodollar market, would head office get dollars to give to its foreign branches as their short-term dollar borrowings ran off faster than their dollar assets. One answer is for a bank to run in Nassau a book of liquid, dollar securities that it could sell maybe not overnight, but over a period of several weeks to a month.

Liquidity is one, but not the only advantage that a bank can glean from running a Nassau book of dollar securities. A second advantage is that, because of transformation, spreads, and timing of positions, such a book can be very profitable. Also, since the reality today for a bank is that it's in securities, not loans, that potential assets exist, a bank that borrows medium term in the deposit note market may well conclude that it can further enhance its profits, without impairing its liquidity, by expanding the size and lengthening the average maturity of its Nassau portfolio.

The Tax-Cushion Problem and Shell Branches

Yet another advantage that a bank can derive from running a *booking center* or *shell branch* derives from what's been dubbed the tax-cushion problem.

A U.S. bank is given a credit against its federal taxes for any foreign taxes it pays on profits it earns abroad. A bank seeking to *maximize* its *aftertax* return must manage its affairs carefully so that it doesn't end up with more foreign tax credits than it can use against its federal tax bill. Because of foreign tax credits, major U.S. banks normally have no trouble working their federal tax liability down to zero. In fact, such banks do so much international business in London and other high-tax centers that they often end up with excess tax credits. In that case, the bank faces what is known as *the tax-cushion problem*.

To illustrate, consider for simplicity a bank that has just three offices, head office and a Tokyo and a Frankfurt branch. If the bank gets into a position where it has booked so much profitable business in Tokyo and Frankfurt that the tax credit it gets from paying a 50% tax on profits in Japan and in Germany exceeds 34% of its *total* taxable income, it will have excess tax credits against its U.S. federal taxes. In this case, the ratio of foreign taxes paid to its total taxable income will exceed 34%, that is,

$$\frac{\text{Foreign taxes paid}}{\text{Total taxable income}} \times 100 > 34\%$$

and the bank has a tax-cushion problem.

The parameters of the tax-cushion problem have changed a lot in recent years due to the slashing of both U.S. and U.K. tax rates on corporate profits. It used to be that London, where banks booked lots of business, was a very high-tax center. Then, the U.K. cut its tax rate on corporate profits from 52% to 34% in roughly the same period that the U.S. federal tax rate on profits was cut from 46% to 34%. The limelight accorded supply-side economics notwithstanding, Japan and Germany left their corporate tax rates at 50%; however, the comparable rate in let's-rev-up-business Hong Kong is a mere 18%.

In any case, a bank that finds itself with a tax-cushion problem needs, in order to solve that problem, to earn more foreign profits without increasing foreign taxes paid. A simple way to do this is for the bank to open a branch in a tax haven, such as Nassau or Grand Cayman, which imposes no profits tax. Such branches are referred to as *shell branches* because no decision making occurs at the branch and no senior bank personnel are stationed there. Instead, the branch is run directly from head office, which books loans and accepts deposits on the shell's behalf. A U.S. bank that has a shell branch in Nassau or some other tax haven will generate a lot of paperwork at the branch; this work is done by some local bank, and the resulting rise in local employment is the benefit the country sponsoring the tax haven gets out of doing so. U.S. banks run a lot of shell branches in the Caribbean because this area is in a time zone that makes it easy for U.S. banks to deal on the shell's behalf during normal working hours.

While some investors feel comfortable placing deposits at the Caribbean branch of a U.S. bank, many do not. This is because most investors don't understand sovereign risk. However, the educational process is ongoing, and the more that people become acquainted with the subject of sovereign risk and realize how small it is with respect to the Caribbean, the more they are encouraged to invest there. Doing so is easier than investing in London because of time-zone considerations.

Sovereign risk has to do with the danger posed to depositors at a foreign branch by possible expropriation of the branch's assets. Many investors fear that, if Nassau or some other tax haven country suddenly turned communist and expropriated the assets of bank branches there, deposits in these branches would not be repayable.

By law, a U.S. bank is responsible for all deposits in its foreign branches unless (1) there is a change in government in a country where it has a branch and (2) the new government is inimical to the U.S. Even if a new government is unfriendly, a U.S. bank is relieved of its liability to repay depositors at the expropriated branch only to the extent that the new government succeeds in seizing or freezing the branch's assets. If 95% of the loans a bank booked in a branch were to major U.S. and multinational companies, these companies would—in the event of expropriation of the branch—pay off their loan obligations not to the branch but to the bank's head office. This would protect 95% of the branch's assets, and thereby 95% of its deposits, from expropriation. If the other 5% of the branch's total loans were to communist countries that recognized the new government's claim on the branch's assets and repaid their loans to the expropriated branch, the maximum loss depositors at the branch could sustain would be 5%. As a matter of practice, the loss would probably be zero since a major U.S. bank would be loath to have depositors lose any money placed with it.

A bank that books assets in a tax haven where the political tide might turn is careful to place only safe loans there—loans to corporations and other entities that would pay off to head office any loans outstanding at an expropriated branch. Because of this, the sovereign risk attaching to deposits in Caribbean tax havens is minimal.

Most U.S. banks book the large loans they make to communist countries at head office or in a branch in a politically stable country; London office is a natural choice.

A GLOBAL BOOK

All U.S. banks running Eurobooks used to think of themselves as running two distinct positions: a domestic book and a Eurobook. In recent years, some banks have departed sharply from this practice and begun to think of themselves as running a single global, dollar book.

One reason for adopting a global-book strategy is that doing so will prevent a bank from getting into a position where it has a natural hedge going for it that it doesn't know about: New York is running a short domestic book; the foreign branches a long book. A bank should also avoid the opposite extreme where both the domestic book and the Eurobook are geared the same way, but so much so that the bank is taking an unacceptable risk against its interest-rate outlook. A bank can avoid either extreme by aggregating its positions worldwide and then implementing strategies with respect to its global position.

A Little History

The head office of every U.S. bank that started operations in the Euromarket in the early 1960s initially instructed its foreign branches to accept *no* interest-rate exposure in their Euro operations. A branch that acquired a 3-month, fixed-rate asset was expected to buy 3-month money against it and then sit tight and earn its spread. This situation lasted until the early 1970s. Then, gradually, U.S. banks began to allow their branches to mismatch. In those days, this almost always meant borrowing short and lending long because the yield curve was usually positively sloped.

As the 1970s progressed, head office at many banks became concerned about the risk to which the mismatch limits it imposed on the branches exposed the bank. Often, these limits were couched in percentage terms. Consequently, as a bank's Eurobook grew, the absolute amounts represented by these percentages became large. The mismatch risk in a bank's Euro-book, which initially had been minimal, became significant.

At this point, the major banks began to track their branches' mismatch regularly from head office and to set tighter mismatch limits based on absolute dollar amounts. By 1975, it was not unusual for a bank to impose a whole set of limits on each foreign branch with respect to various mismatches it could have: overnight against 1-month, 1s against 3s, and so on. Coupled with this, many banks instituted a system whereby all the branches would report to head office weekly on their positions. Head office would then aggregate these reports so that it could determine at a glance the interest rate exposure on its world-wide Eurobook. It would also compare that exposure with the exposure it was taking in its domestic book. For a time, banks permitted their foreign branches to operate more or less autonomously within the confines of the risk parameters set by head office.

Running a Global Book

Then, in the late 1970s and early 1980s, as interest rates became higher and more volatile, a number of banks decided to tighten up still further on the freedom given to the branches: to require that the branches act in conformity with rate views formulated at head office and communicated regularly to them. The path by which banks arrived at this decision was long and less than direct. Nonetheless, the decision itself was extremely important. For the first time, banks were controlling their global book from a central point.

By doing so, a bank got two benefits: better ability to its total exposure and greater flexibility in doing so. For example, a bank that has a lot of floating-rate loans on its domestic book is always vulnerable to a decline in interest rates. If the bank is running a global book, it can offset this vulnerability by running a short Eurobook. For a major bank that fears a fall in rates and wants to run a neutral position, running a short Eurobook is the way to achieve such a position.

At top banks that operate a global book, the absolute limit on running a short day-to-day position in the Eurobook is liberal—several or more billion dollars. If a bank ran just a Euro-book and nothing else, this limit would be so large as to permit the bank to take a tremendous risk. However, when the bank's domestic and Eurobooks are viewed as a whole, the offset to a huge, short Euro position is all the bank's floating-rate loans on which rates can change at the drop of a hat. Given these loans, a short Eurobook can be consistent with a bank's desire to be neutral overall. As this example illustrates, a bank should never look at its domestic book on Tuesday, its Eurobook on Friday. In a volatile rate environment, a global view pays.[15]

Just how a let's-have-a-global-dollar-book approach is implemented varies from bank to bank. The flavor of what's involved is suggested by the remarks of a funding office of a bank espousing this approach: "I have responsibility for coordinating all of the bank's dollar books [U.S. and Euro], which means that I have a dialogue with treasurers in all of the branches. The latter have alternatives in the positions they take: there are limits, lines, and they can do what they want in their dollar books within those guidelines. But we have a close dialogue—exchange ideas, and so on. For the time being, I have a quite different position than our treasurer in Paris. He knows mine and I know his. It puts, as they say in Paris, a little water in our wine. This coordinating role is something I do in a foxy way. The last thing I want is to influence their [foreign branch treasurers'] decisions. I influence a lot the positions that are taken in New York. I do review their positions, but they must assume full responsibility."

BANK OF ENGLAND REGULATION

Since London is the preeminent center of the Euromarket, a look at financial regulation in the London market seems appropriate.

The first point to be made is that regulation of domestic banking has always been far less formal in Britain than in the

---

[15]To properly run a global book, a bank must solve some tricky people problems and appropriately alter its profit-center analysis. See Stigum and Branch, *Managing Bank Assets and Liabilities*, pp. 312–16.

U.S. or on the Continent. Unlike many U.S. bank regulators, the Bank of England proceeds on the assumption that bankers are prudent, honest people who know as much if not more about banking than regulators do. Thus, the Bank's approach, at least during the 1960s and 1970s, was not to impose regulations and ratios on the banks; instead it asked for periodic reports from the banks. On the basis of these, it discussed informally with each bank's top management the quality of the bank's loans, their liquidity, any features of the bank's condition that the Bank of England viewed as unusual or out of line, and any suggestions that the Bank of England might make with respect to the bank's operations.

The Banking Act of 1979

Unlike any other country, the U.K. for centuries had no banking act that regulated its highly developed banking system. Instead, banking in the U.K. thrived under the informally administered Bank of England regulation described above. By the late 1970s, several factors made this situation untenable.

The first was the 1973 banking crisis. In the early 1970s, there was a credit boom, a money supply boom, and a consequent boom in house prices. At the time, a lot of second-tier banks existed merely to take deposits and relend them to property companies with whom they were sometimes affiliated. These banks geared up like crazy, and when the property bubble burst, many were in deep trouble. The resulting mess, dubbed the Banking Crisis of 1973, was dealt with by the Bank of England. To prevent endemic contagion, the Bank nursed back to health those banks that did matter, while letting others fail. The 1973 crisis suggested the need for a more formal system of bank supervision that actually had legislative backing.

A second need for action stemmed from the U.K.'s membership in the *European Economic Community*. *EEC* requirements with respect to banking harmonization mandated that all banks within the EEC be officially licensed before they could do banking business.[16] British banks were not so licensed.

---

[16]This requirement is embodied in the First Banking Directive issued in 1977 by the EEC Commission in Brussels with the approval of the Ministerial Council.

Against this background, the U.K. passed the Banking Act of 1979. This act authorized two forms of deposit-taking institutions, namely, *recognized banks* and *licensed deposit takers*. Either type of institution could provide as many banking services as it wished, but a bank could be licensed as a recognized bank only if, in addition to accepting deposits, it (1) made loans, (2) traded foreign exchange, (3) provided bill finance and handled foreign trade documentation, and (4) engaged in investment management and corporate finance. Both recognized banks and licensed deposit takers came under regulation by the Bank of England, which continued in the main its informal approach to regulation. The many foreign banks operating in the U.K. were treated in precisely the same way as were domestic banks.

Another wrinkle added to U.K. banking at this time was the setting up of a Deposit Protection Fund to protect small depositors in case of a bank failure.

The Banking Act of 1987

The first British banking crisis was quite broad-based. A second bank crisis occurred when a second-tier British bank, Johnson Matthey, failed. This bank failure was regarded as serious because Johnson Matthey was one of the five members of the British bullion market. Thus, its failure could have affected the other banks in the bullion market and thereby the bullion market worldwide. To prevent any such untoward events, the Bank of England bailed out Johnson Matthey, just as the FDIC bails out a failed U.S. bank.

At the time, it was said, rightly or wrongly, that Johnson Matthey ought not to have gotten into the straits it did without the Bank of England having perceived the problem, which it did not. In defense of the Bank, it should be noted that, at the time, the Bank, due to fiscal stringency, had only 50 to 100 people supervising all banks, domestic and foreign, in the U.K.; today, the Bank has over 200 supervisors.

In any case, a new banking act was passed in 1987. This act is broadly the same as the 1979 act except that there is now just one tier of banks, not two. Also, supervision is somewhat tighter, and there have been papers on liquidity, ratios, capital, and so on.

Regulation of Foreign Banks in London

When foreign banks came to London, they were treated in much the same way as domestic British banks. If the Bank of England recognized a bank as reputable in its home country, it permitted that bank to open a London branch with a minimum of red tape. The bank did not have to put in any capital; all it had to do to open an office was to agree to comply with certain regulations, and it was granted the same right to engage in banking that any other bank in the U.K. had. Foreign banks establishing independent entities, merchant banking subs or banking consortia, did have to put in capital, but again if the parentage was reputable, the red tape was minimal. As an executive of a large U.S. bank noted, "When we went to the Bank of England for permission to open a merchant banking arm, they said, 'You need a foreign-exchange trader, someone who knows British exchange control regulations, some capital, and since you are asking to be recognized as a bank, at least a window where you could take deposits whether you do or not. Oh, and one other thing. We'd like you to locate in the City of London. The rents are high which keeps out the riffraff.'"

In justification of the Bank of England's rather casual regulation of foreign banks, it might be added that the Bank operated and still does on the logical assumption that foreign bank branches are an inextricable part of the parent, which implies two things. First, it is difficult if not impossible to regulate these branches as independent entities. Second, the natural assumption is that these branches are being regulated by banking authorities in the parent country, which regulates the activities of the parent bank as a whole.

The ease with which foreign banks could enter the London market and the minimal regulations imposed on their activities there encouraged the entry of several hundred foreign banks into London. It has also permitted the rapid *growth* and constant *innovation* that have characterized the Euromarket.

To a U.S. regulator, the British approach to bank regulation probably seemed like a time bomb guaranteed to create monumental difficulties at some time. Yet, the record shows that the British approach to bank regulation has been at least as successful, indeed more so, than has the U.S. approach. One reason is that there is a lot of mutual respect between banks operating in Britain and the Bank of England. Because of this and because of the real powers the Bank of England possesses, banks don't fight "The Old Lady (of Threadneedle Street)"; instead they take her suggestions seriously. Another reason the Bank of England approach has been so successful is that it is responsible for overseeing the operations of only a limited number of banks, about 100 domestic and several hundred foreign banks. In contrast, U.S. regulators have to cope with over 14,000 banks. As one Bank of England official noted, the limited number of banks in Britain once permitted the Bank of England to know on an almost personal basis the managers of these institutions and thus whether they do or do not need closer supervision.

Naturally with the entry of ever more foreign banks into London, it became increasingly difficult for the Bank of England to pursue its brand of personal regulation. As a result, the Bank of England asked banks to report to it with increasing frequency and visited them more often.

Passage of the 1979 Banking Act and then of the 1987 act put foreign banks operating in London under slightly more formal regulation, but it posed no real problems for them. Basically, Bank of England regulation remained benign. What has, in certain cases, posed problems and red tape for foreign banks operating in London is compliance with the Financial Services Act described below.

LENDER OF LAST RESORT

A question that troubles some Euromarket watchers is: Who is to act as lender of last resort if the market is hit by some event much more shaking than was the failure of the Herstatt? This question really involves two separate questions: Who lends if the supply of Eurodollars dries up? Who lends if the solvency of a major bank or group of banks in the Euromarket is threatened through bad loans or other losses?

As noted, dollars can't disappear, but they can move from

center to center. Thus, it's conceivable, though highly unlikely, that the supply of dollars in the Euromarket could dry up because holders of dollars for some reason decided to move their deposits from banks in Eurocenters to banks in New York or elsewhere in the U.S. Such an eventuality would not cause U.S. banks severe liquidity problems in their Euro operations; they could always buy back in the U.S. market any dollars lost in the Euromarket and use them to fund their Euro assets. The major inconvenience to them in doing so is that they would incur a reserve cost on domestic dollars funneled to the Euromarket. To some extent, foreign banks could do the same thing, but in doing so, they would face a crucial problem: Most would be able to buy in the U.S. market only a fraction of the dollars they were accustomed to buying in the Euromarket. Thus, in the unlikely event of dollars drying up in the Euromarket, foreign banks could face a liquidity crisis. Foreign banks negotiate standby lines with U.S. banks to protect against this risk.

Central banks have discussed at length, in meetings in Basel, Switzerland, the question of lender of last resort to the Euromarket and have reached the conclusion that each looks after his own. Thus, the Fed is the appropriate lender of last resort to a U.S. banker whether its troubles arise from its New York or London operations, and the Bank of England stands behind the operations of its domestic banks both at home and abroad. The logical thrust of this philosophy is that, if foreign banks experienced liquidity problems with respect to their dollar operations, it would be up to their respective central banks to provide them with dollars, something that the central banks of major countries could do either from their own reserves or by obtaining dollars through swaps from the Fed.

With respect to the second question concerning the possible failure by a major Eurobank or group of banks, the comment of a German banker is relevant. In speaking of the Herstatt failure, which sent shock waves through the Euromarket, he said, "The Bundesbank [German central bank] will never admit that they made a mistake, but in retrospect they know they did. They should not have permitted Herstatt to fail; instead they should have merged in into one of the larger German banks. A bank failure on that scale will, I guarantee, never occur in Germany again."

The development of the Euromarket as an international capital market has made a significant contribution over the last several decades to the world economy by providing financing for a huge expansion in international trade and investment. The development of this market has also tied in ways hitherto unknown the economies, capital markets, and fortunes of many free-world countries, including all of the major ones. Thus, to allow this market to falter or fail would create economic havoc on a world scale. Central bankers know this, and the almost universal opinion among bankers is thus that no central bank in a major country will again let one of its key banks fail. Moreover, if a group of banks were threatened, say, by defaults on loans to underdeveloped countries, the central banks standing behind those banks would undoubtedly keep them afloat through individual or coordinated actions. As a foreign banker noted, "No central bank will ever commit itself publicly to keeping all domestic banks above size X afloat, but they know—and we know they know—that, should a major bank be threatened, the economic costs of inaction on their part would *far exceed* the cost of action. Therefore they would act." Another foreign banker echoed this thought, "If any of the top 50 banks in the world went under, none of us would survive. No central bank will say, 'We will support the top X banks.' They do not want to draw a line, but in practice the line is drawn: you'll get central-bank support if you're so big that by failing you would drag everyone else down with you."

The question of who is the lender of last resort in the Euromarket has particularly troubled the Bank of England because of the extensive Euro operations carried out in London by foreign banks. The understanding under which foreign banks are permitted to open branches in London has always been that the parent would stand behind the branch, whatever difficulties it might encounter. In the case of merchant banking subs and consortium banks, this understanding was implicit but perhaps less formal. During the nervous and anxious period after Herstatt failed, the Bank of England acted to formalize this commitment by asking for "comfort letters" stating that each parent of a merchant banking sub or consortium bank would provide support, if required, to that entity up to its share of ownership. For a time, all was quiet on the Western front.

The Failure of Banco Ambrosiano Holdings

Then, in June 1982, the Italian central bank requested that the chairman, Mr. Robert Calvi, of the Banco Ambrosiano, then Italy's 11th largest bank and largest private bank, provide it with details concerning the $1.4 billion of loans that the Banco Ambrosiano Holdings S.A., a Luxembourg financial holding company, had extended through its Latin American subsidiaries to a number of Panamanian companies. Mr. Calvi was later found hanging from a London bridge in a position that suggested that, unless he was an extraordinary athlete, his death was no suicide. From there on, the Ambrosiano story unfolded like a good yarn spun by Paul Erdman. But, unfortunately for Eurobankers, the story was fact, not fiction.

On July 12, the Midland Bank—agent for a syndicate of banks that had lent $40MM to Banco Ambrosiano Holdings (BAH)—declared BAH in default because of long-overdue payments of interest and principal. Other banks in other syndicates followed suit; and on July 14, BAH's assets were frozen by a Luxembourg court.

Subsequent investigations revealed that the $1.4 billion of loans extended in early 1980 by the Latin American subsidiaries of BAH and financed by BAH and other Ambrosiano subsidiaries were to paper corporations, nominally owned by the Vatican Bank. The operations of this bank, the Instituto per le Opere de Religione (IOR), had, until then, been shrouded in secrecy; IOR owned at least 1.58% of the Banco Ambrosiano and was suspected of owning much more. Apparently, in many matters—the full story was never told—the Vatican Bank acted as a *de facto* partner in various ventures with the Banco Ambrosiano. Certainly, Calvi was known in Italian circles as "God's banker."

The declaration by the Midland Bank that BAH was in default and the subsequent disclosure of the irregularities in which the Banco Ambrosiano had engaged (often in confusing partnership with the IOR) caused the Banco Ambrosiano to face a *liquidity* crisis. When it became apparent that this bank could no longer meet its obligations, the Bank of Italy, working with major Italian banks, put together an aid package designed to permit the Banco Ambrosiano to make timely payments on its obligations. This arrangement continued until early August when the Bank of Italy stated that the remnants of the Banco Ambrosiano's assets would be reconstituted into a new bank controlled by the consortium formed to bail out Ambrosiano. By reorganizing the Banco Ambrosiano into a new bank, the Italian central bank permitted that bank to continue activities without interruption.

The support given by the Bank of Italy to Banco Ambrosiano is in line with what one would expect. Since the Herstatt failure, no major free-world country has permitted one of its top banks to fail with losses to depositors. However, in announcing the creation of the Nuovo Banco Ambrosiano, the Italian Treasury stressed that this new bank would assume the liabilities neither of BAH nor of its Latin American subs. The Bank of Italy argued that it was under no legal or moral obligation to pay off the debts of BAH because the company was a holding company located in Luxembourg. For its part, Luxembourg washed its hands of responsibility for BAH's debts on the grounds that BAH was a holding company, not a bank.

All this was troubling to Eurobankers for several reasons. First, they stood to lose hundreds of millions on loans to and noted issued by BAH and perhaps a good bit more on deposits with its Latin American subsidiaries.[17] Second, Eurobankers feared incorrectly that default by BAH might ring the death knell of the Basel concordate, which many of them had viewed as providing a general, lender-of-last-resort underpinning for the Euromarket.

The Basel Concordate

Following the failure of Herstatt, governors of the top 10 central banks of the free world had met in Basel in 1974 and issued, after considered deliberation, the delphic statement:

---

[17]The miasma of intergroup transactions that linked the Banco Ambrosiano, the numerous subsidiaries of its holding company, the Vatican bank, and other Eurodollar market participants are portrayed schematically in the *Financial Times*, August 5, 1982. A lot of the dollar flows in the chart that lead to the Vatican bank are marked with question marks.

> While it is not practical to lay down in advance detailed rules and procedures for the provision of temporary support to banks experiencing liquidity difficulties, the means are available for that purpose and will be used if and when necessary.[18]

The Bank of Italy concluded that this initial statement by the Group of Ten, together with its subsequent dictums, concerned banks; BAH was not a bank; *ergo* the Bank of Italy bore no responsibility for bailing out BAH. Luxembourg also disavowed responsibility for BAH because of its foreign parentage.

All this resulted in much hue and cry in the Euromarket, especially from the 250 banking institutions that had lent BAH a half billion or so, which they stood to lose.

The Aftermath

Post BAH's plunge into bankruptcy, the Euromarket suffered a good case of jitters, but it survived with nothing much worse happening than some cutting back of bank lines and some temporary, if pronounced, rate tiering in the interbank market.

The failure of BAH led to none of the dire consequences initially feared for several reasons. First, sophisticated Euromarket participants took the view that anyone with ears to hear or eyes to read should have known for several years prior to the failure of BAH that Calvi and his foreign operations were in trouble. Said one banker, "If BAH had been a bank and a big bank, its failure would have had a huge impact on credit lines and market liquidity. But BAH wasn't a bank; it was an Italian financing sub operating out of Luxembourg, which everyone accepts as something risky in the first place. If BAH's failure caused you to pull in your reins [cut lines], you must have been shooting without looking. Ambrosiano was to be expected; if you had loans to BAH on your book, I don't want to own shares in your bank."

---

[18]The Group of Ten consists of the U.S., Canada, Japan, the U.K., France, Germany, Italy, Belgium, the Netherlands, and Sweden; Switzerland is an honorary 11th member. The G10 overlaps in membership but is distinct from the BIS whose directors are all governors of European central banks: Belgium, the Netherlands, France, the U.K., Germany, Switzerland, Sweden, and Italy.

While the failure of BAH did not cause even a near crisis in the Euromarket, it imprinted indelibly in the minds of lenders the distinction between a branch and a sub. Lending to a sub in London might be a safe bet because in London, where there are lots of foreign-owned subs in the form of consortium banks, such entities are supervised by the Bank of England, which also has—just in case—a file drawer of comfort letters from their parents. Luxembourg, following the Bank of England's example, asked belatedly—after BAH failed—for comfort letters from the parents of the many foreign-owned financial subs operating in Luxembourg.

Presumably, Luxembourg had no trouble getting such letters from the top German banks, all of whom operate big subs in Luxembourg. These banks do so because the stringent capital and liquidity rules imposed on them by German authorities would preclude German banks from participating on a significant scale in the Euromarket if they did not use the ruse of booking their Eurobusiness on the books of their Luxembourg subs.

Back to Basel

All told, the early 1980s and particularly 1982 were not kind to the Euromarket. In addition to the Banco Ambrosiano debacle, there were the problems of the U.S. Penn Square Bank, the *de facto* nationalization of the failing Continental Illinois Bank, the failures of a passel of U.S. dealers in government securities—Drysdale, Lombard-Wall, E.S.M., and Bevill Bresler & Schulman, to name the most prominent—and of course the East European and later the Latin American debt crisis, which cast doubt on the acumen and ultimately the creditworthiness of a lot of global banks, including some top Americans.

The Bank of England eventually decided the time was ripe for a worldwide effort to achieve uniformity in bank regulation. It went first to the Federal Reserve where it found support. The Japanese and the Germans joined in with rather less unanimity. In any case, subsequent negotiations among the Group of Ten produced the latest Basel accord, described in Chapter 6, which includes, among other points, the imposition on banks of reasonably uniform capital adequacy requirements by 1992.

Observers have assumed that, for the most part, U.S. and British banks wouldn't have too much trouble meeting the new capital requirements, which call for equity capital equal to 4% of adjusted assets. Barclays, Wespac, Citi, and others have taken large sums of new equity capital out of the market with relative ease.

Questions have, however, been raised about how the Japanese banks will raise their capital ratios, which in 1988 were below 2%. Probably, no problem for them. The Japanese banks own a lot of stock that they bought and carry at 50 yen, but which is now worth 5,000 yen. Chances are, they will find ways to sell such stock to sister companies in their zaibatsu and thereby preserve cozy links with customers; avoid depressing the Tokyo stock market; and, if they're sufficiently creative, incur no capital gains taxes. Last but not least, Japanese bank stocks trade at stratospheric price-earnings (PE) ratios. IBJ's was at a PE of 126 when in 1988 it raised, using two rights issues, almost $4 billion of equity capital.

The year 1992 is also the year that the EEC will create a single harmonized market of 323 million consumers. It's not certain what that will mean for Europe's banks. Pan-European superbanks were predicted, but no EEC government seems willing to allow a key national bank to fall into the hands of foreigners. What's more likely is mergers of banks within EEC countries—particularly the emergence of German banking giants—and some acceptable-to-affected-governments, cross-border marriages, such as the one begun between Belgium's La Générale and the Netherlands' AMRO.

The Financial Services Act

The British *Financial Services Act (FSA)*, implemented in 1988, arose out of concern about the protection of investors. The intent was that ordinary retail investors in the U.K. be able to get adequate information about the financial services they were buying and that they be able to boot to get good advice from people professionally qualified to give it. Also, there was the notion that making the provision of financial services in the U.K. squeaky clean would, if anything, enhance London's preeminence as a world financial center.

The whole notion that regulation, however detailed, can protect people from their inherent naiveté, greed, and atavistic inclination to believe in the tooth fairy (especially if an investment house is peddling shares or other participations in said fairy) is itself naive and is moreover daily disproved in the U.S. (read *The Wall Street Journal*). Nonetheless, the British in an uncharacteristic departure from light and sensible regulation produced a massive rule book covering every conceivable investment: life insurance, pension funds, stocks, bonds, and so on. FSA required any firm that was in securities—selling or advising—to seek authorization from a new body, the *Securities Investment Board* (*SIB*), which very broadly was meant to be an SEC. Where possible the SIB delegated its power to *self-regulatory organizations* (*SORs*), such as the stock exchange and the futures market.

The City of London perceived the whole scheme as a dead hand on its business—a most unwelcome change from regulation with a light hand. Some hope for relief appeared when the original chairman of the SIB was replaced by Mr. David Walker, one of the younger directors of the Bank of England. Under Walker, the rules were halved, rewritten largely in English, and derived from straightforward principles of right and wrong, as opposed to the principle of comprehensive administration.

Since FSA was designed to protect the small investor, it should have had little or no impact on the City's wholesale financial activities and in particular on its Eurodollar activities. Not so. The heavy hand of regulation with attendant onerous capital requirements was scheduled to fall on everyone—even Eurodollar brokers who daily act as agents for billions in interbank transactions. Affected firms screamed, "Why us? We've never seen a retail customer; we've never caused a problem; and we deal strictly with professionals who don't need protection. Moreover, all of this onerous regulation will harm, not enhance, the role of London as a financial center."

Finally, the message got through; and in April 1988, the Bank of England issued a revised grey paper. The latter says that any institution that is conducting wholesale, professional business can, if it wishes, be supervised by the Bank of England—not the SIB—in those areas in which it is wholesale and in those markets that are essentially wholesale. This exemption covers brokering between market makers, primary dealings in government bonds, wholesale dealings in money, interbank deposits, foreign exchange, and so on. The Bank of England has put out a list of firms being supervised by it. There's no great cachet to being on the list; a firm need only prove it is in the wholesale business to be on it. For banks, the upshot is that some need no FSA authorization to continue their business as is, while others must get authorizations to cover certain of their activities. For foreign securities firms, there was ongoing dickering and bickering because, besides Britain and the U.S., only a handful of other countries have position-risk requirements with respect to capital.

Another problem on the horizon is that, if City-based firms are to remain competitive within the EEC after 1992, the British government will probably have to modify the FSA to conform to the minimum standards for capital adequacy and conduct of business agreed to and adopted by member states.

SOVEREIGN RISK IN LONDON

Investors, both bank and nonbank, depositing dollars in a bank or bank branch located in a foreign country are always concerned with *sovereign* or *country risk*. U.S. investors, particularly those with little experience in international business, used to display a lot of concern over the sovereign risk associated with making dollar deposits in London. As these investors saw it, at least before the U.K.'s emergence as an oil producer, the periodic crisis through which the pound sterling passed and the chronic weakness of the British economy both suggested that at some time the British might be tempted to block payment on the dollar liabilities of London banks. While one cannot say this could never happen, there is only one conclusion that anyone who has studied the London market carefully can reach: The sovereign risk attached to dollar deposits in London is *very* close to zero.

One practical reason is that Britain would gain nothing from blocking payment of the Eurodollar liabilities of London banks during a sterling crisis. From the end of World War II until the U.K. became an oil producer, the pound sterling was a weak currency; to prop up its value, the British maintained tight controls on the use of sterling by domestic holders. Because of these controls, the Euromarket in London, which would in any case have been largely a market in offshore funds, was strictly a market in offshore funds. With the few exceptions permitted by the British exchange control authorities, all the Eurodollars that flowed into London were owned by foreign depositors, and all the Eurodollars that flowed out went to foreign borrowers. In effect, London acted and still does largely as a conduit through which dollars flow from foreigners to foreigners. Thus, inflows of Eurodollars to London do not add to British foreign-exchange reserves, and outflows do not subtract from them, which means in turn that blocking payment on the Eurodollar liabilities of London banks would have done nothing to stem the loss by Britain of foreign reserve during a sterling crisis. Actually, by 1980, sterling was so strong that the U.K. fully dismantled its exchange control apparatus.

The financial activities centered in the City of London, including Eurodollar transactions, earn Britain large amounts of foreign exchange, provide thousands of jobs, and add vitality to the whole economy. A second reason Britain would not block payment on Eurodollar deposits is that, if it did, it would lose these advantages. As a Bank of England official noted, "If the British interfered with the payout of Eurodollars, nationalized foreign branches, or whatever, that would kill more than the Euromarket, it would kill London. Any action taken against Euro operations in London would immediately spread to London as a banking center; and if London is not a banking center, then it isn't a commodity market, it isn't an international insurance center, it isn't a stock or investment market generally. In London, these things dovetail closely; if you damage one, you damage the lot. The game would not be worth the candle."

Had Britain during a sterling crisis been willing to do something dramatic and potentially dangerous to its economy, the logical step would have been to block the large sterling balances held by Commonwealth nations. That would have directly stemmed the loss by Britain of foreign-exchange reserves by preventing conversion of these balances into foreign exchange. Blocking sterling balances is a course of action that was open to Britain during every sterling crisis. Yet, the British never took it, presumably in part because of the effect doing so would have had on London's role as a world financial center.

FOREIGN BANK OPERATIONS IN THE U.S.

Foreign banks have used various organizational vehicles to enter the U.S. market. A few have set up wholly owned subsidiaries operated under a domestic banking charter. Of these, a handful are long-standing operations like Barclays' banking network in California. Others are of recent origin.

A second way commonly used by foreign banks to enter the U.S. market is to set up *agencies* in U.S. financial centers. By far the largest agencies in the U.S. are those of Canadian banks. An agency can neither accept deposits in its own name nor hold loans on its own books. Instead, it acts as a loan production office and funding agent for the parent bank. It arranges loans and then books them at some branch of the parent, for example, Nassau, or at head office. It also acts as an agent for the parent in the New York money market, buying and selling Fed funds and Euros for the account of head office.

The principal reason why foreign banks initially set up agency offices rather than branches in New York was that, under New York State law, a foreign bank was permitted to set up a New York branch only if its country of origin permitted U.S. banks to establish branches there. Canada precluded foreign banks from establishing branches in Canada, so the big Canadian banks all established New York agencies. Because Canada has since changed its law, Canadian banks could now convert their New York agencies to branches. Four of the top six Canadian banks have done so.

A second reason some foreign banks set up a U.S. agency instead of a branch was to avoid the overhead they would have incurred in setting up a branch with facilities for accepting deposits. Finally, prior to the passage in 1978 of the *International*

Banking Act (*IBA*), foreign bank agencies were subject neither to U.S. regulation nor to reserve requirements. Under the 1978 act, Congress took the view that agencies were, in effect, branches and, as such, should be treated in a fashion similar to that specified for foreign bank branches.[19]

A third way a foreign bank can enter the U.S. market is by setting up a branch. In the early 1980s, the growth of such branches in New York was explosive, but more recently, it has slowed. Prior to the passage of the IBA in 1978, foreign bank branches operated exclusively under state banking laws and were regulated solely by state banking authorities. Most are located in New York, California, and Illinois, which have specific legislation permitting the establishment of branches by foreign banks. Generally, such branches can engage in the full range of domestic banking activities.

Setting up a branch in the U.S. is expensive for a foreign bank in terms of not only overhead, but taxation. Once a foreign bank establishes a U.S. branch, all of its income on loans into the U.S. becomes subject to U.S. taxation. Yet the U.S. market, and more particularly the New York market, has over the years attracted foreign bank branches as surely as a magnet attracts iron filings.

Foreign banks setting up U.S. branches do so for several reasons. First, they are attempting to follow their customers to the U.S. just as U.S. banks followed their customers abroad; the growth of international banking is in part a response to the growth of multinational firms. Second, foreign banks are attempting to develop relationships with large U.S. corporations; most of these have foreign operations, and a foreign bank can thus provide them with special services and expertise. Third, foreign banks set up U.S. branches to obtain access to the huge domestic reservoir of dollars. Finally, the U.S. is a convenient

---

[19]The IBA also granted the Comptroller the power to override New York State's reciprocity restriction by granting a national charter to a nonqualifying foreign bank wishing to establish a New York branch. The Comptroller's power to do so was upheld in court when the Comptroller granted a national charter to an Australian bank wanting to open a New York branch.

place for foreign banks to run a Nassau or Cayman Eurobook.
Foreign bank branches also run IBFs (Table 7–7).

Most foreign bank branches are primarily wholesale operations servicing large as opposed to retail accounts. For example,
the customers of one big foreign bank branch in New York include a large proportion of the Fortune 500, big European corporations, Japanese trading corporations, large firms trading in
commodities, and foreign banks for which the branch acts as a
clearing agent. Foreign bank branches fund themselves much as
domestic money market banks do, by accepting deposits and by
purchasing monies in the Fed funds, Eurodollar, and CD markets. There are, however, differences. First, CDs issued by foreign bank branches have only limited acceptance in the U.S.
market, a fact of life that mattered more when the U.S. CD
market was lively than when it later turned moribund. Second,
prior to passage of the IBA, there was, for a foreign bank branch,
no distinction between Eurodollars and "domestic" dollars because foreign bank branches did not have to hold reserves
against any of the funds deposited with them or purchased by
them.

The position of a foreign bank operating a New York branch
is much the same as the position of the London branch of the
same bank in the Eurodollar market. It is acquiring assets and
incurring liabilities in a foreign currency, the dollar, and it
thinks of itself as running a dollar book. In running this book,
moreover, the New York branch, like the London branch, is
concerned about mismatch and is subject to guidelines from
home office with respect to the degree of mismatch it may run.
One difference, however, is that foreign bank branches in New
York, like domestic U.S. banks, make a lot of variable-rate
loans, so mismatch on their books can't be measured or controlled in quite the same way in New York as in London.

The U.S. is the home of the dollar, so having a U.S. branch
provides a foreign bank with additional funding and liquidity
for its overall Eurodollar operation because the U.S. branch can
tap directly the vast domestic market for dollars. Setting up a
U.S. branch also permits a foreign bank to establish an entity to
which other branches in the bank's international network can
turn to make adjustments in their dollar books; for example, if

TABLE 7-7
Assets of U.S. branches and agencies of foreign banks, December 31, 1988 ($ billions)

Item	All States		New York		California		Illinois	
	Total Including IBFs	IBFs Only	Total Including IBFs	IBFs Only	Total Including IBFs	IBFs Only	Total Including IBFs	IBFs Only
I. Total assets	513.8	247.8	376.3	194.1	74.8	33.7	36.7	12.9
II. Selected assets:								
Total securities and loans	276.9	89.0	187.7	67.6	47.4	14.9	25.5	4.1
Total securities, book value	33.9	10.1	27.6	7.7	4.1	1.8	1.3	0.5
U.S. Treasury	5.8	n.a.	5.5	n.a.	0.1	n.a.	0.1	n.a.
Other bonds, notes, debentures and corporate stock (including state and local securities)	23.3	10.1	17.4	7.7	3.9	1.8	1.2	0.4
Total loans	243.3	78.9	160.3	60.0	43.3	13.2	24.2	3.6
Commercial and industrial loans	124.8	17.6	76.8	14.9	22.3	2.1	15.7	0.3
U.S. addresses (domicile)	103.1	0.3	59.7	0.2	19.3	0.1	15.2	0.0

Source: *Federal Reserve Bulletin*, June 1989.

one of the bank's non–New York branches were getting short-term dollar deposits but had to fund longer-term dollar loans, it might ask the New York branch to lay off its short-term deposits and buy it longer-term money.

A final way in which foreign banks currently enter the U.S. market is by buying U.S. banks: the Hong Kong & Shanghai Banking Co. of London bought Marine Midland of N.Y., and Midland Bank of London bought Crocker National Corp. in San Francisco. More recently, Nat West bought the National Bank of North America and then First Jersey; and California First Bank, 77% owned by the Bank of Tokyo, bought Union Bank of Los Angeles; the latter acquisition gave the Bank of Tokyo a major stake in California's robust economy.

Foreign acquisitions of U.S. banks follow a trend common in other industries. Managers of large foreign firms and of large foreign pension and other funds view the U.S. as an attractive place in which to invest and diversify because—as compared to other countries—the U.S. ranks high in terms of economic and political stability and of potential for continued economic growth. Also, after the collapse in the 1980s of the dollar, dollar assets looked cheap to foreigners when priced in foreign exchange.

Competition with U.S. Banks

When they were able to buy money without incurring a reserve requirement, foreign bank branches had a certain cost advantage over U.S. banks in making loans to domestic firms for domestic purposes. This cost advantage, which disappeared over a decade ago, was always partially offset by the fact that foreign bank branches had to pay up slightly for money they bought in the domestic market and by the fact that any Euros they bought were more expensive than domestic money of the same tenor. Despite this, for years foreign bank branches in major financial centers quoted loan rates to domestic corporations at LIBOR plus a spread, which worked out to a rate below the U.S. prime plus balances. This put pressure on domestic banks in these centers to lend to prime customers at subprime rates and later to offer fixed-rate advances.

Foreign Branches: A Mixed Bag Seeking a Niche

The parents of foreign bank branches in the U.S. are a mixed bag, ranging from a small, London-based, Kuwait-owned consortium bank to major European and Far Eastern banks. The thinking behind why they are here is that, if you are an international bank, you have to be in New York, in London, and in Tokyo. By the late 1980s, most of the foreign banks that were going to open a branch in the U.S. had come. The Australians were the last to do so. One such bank, WestPac, bought a U.S. government securities dealer, Pollack, created a good niche for itself, and is making money.

That, however, is not easy to do. Many foreign banks are finding that, with the playing field level, it's difficult to make money in New York. It's thus typical for foreign bank branches to be seeking a niche. Their initial niche was to go after multinational corporations with a base in their home country—the British banks after British Airlines, BP, and so on. However, the competition for such business is fierce, and these corporations are not really money makers for the banks. Also, a lot of subs of European companies have tended to go with the American banks. So foreign banks got into purchasing corporate loans from U.S. banks; that enabled them to build up their balance sheets in New York without having to build up their staff to go out and search for loans (Table 7–7). It also meshes nicely with the current goal of American banks to minimize balance-sheet usage.

Foreign bank branches, seeking a niche, have also looked at high-net-worth individuals and tried to break into private banking in the U.S., so far without notable success. Some foreign bank branches trade foreign exchange actively and profitably, but they can't *all* make money at it; also, the foreign-exchange market has become so volatile that banks have lost a lot of money in it in recent years. Another niche some foreign banks have tried is real estate. "We have," noted the treasurer of one small foreign bank branch, "built a specialist team of people to look at making loans against shopping malls, buildings under construction, and private homes. We have become a sort of mortgage-type bank, which is the thing our London office did when they set up shop in the mid-1960s."

The Small Fry

Most of the foreign bank branches in New York seem to be making it, but a couple have closed and gone back: Gulf Bank of Kuwait and the Saudi International Bank. At some point, the question arises for a smaller bank if the bank really needs to be in New York, especially given worldwide communications. These days, it's possible to keep a home-country trading room open 24 hours a day. Thus, what a smaller foreign bank may need is a few representatives on the spot in the U.S., but not a trading room.

A small foreign bank finds that its name does not go down well in the U.S., so it has little choice with respect to funding. Basically, it has to buy funds in the interbank market, mostly in Europe, so its cost of funds is LIBOR. One such banker noted, "Where we make our money is buying selected junk bonds—I prefer the term high-yield bonds—because my cost of funds is LIBOR. An American bank's cost of funds is cheaper because he has deposits."

The Bigger Fish

The foreign branches of the big European banks, Swiss Bank Corp., Deutsche Bank, Dresner Bank, Nat West, and so on, have mostly had no trouble finding a niche. A lot of them, like Nat West, have bought into American banks and have become really a domestic-type bank themselves. That's a route open to the bigger foreign banks.

U.S. branches of big foreign banks also have more funding alternatives open to them. By using a dealer to introduce their credit to investors, they can, via an affiliate (a Delaware corporation), borrow a half a billion or more in the U.S. commercial paper market. Also, like U.S. banks, they have the option of issuing fixed-rate deposit notes and swapping them into sub-LIBOR funding. Another factor that counts in foreign-bank funding is country of origin. The big lenders have country or geographic risk limits. "Normally, bank trust departments and Swiss fiduciaries always have large limits to Belgian banks," noted a Belgian banker. "All of the French banks are competing for deposits, but the Belgian banks aren't because there are few of us. So we get money cheaper than the French banks, not necessarily because our credit is better, but because everyone always has limits open to us."

Obviously, the more funding options a foreign branch has, the greater is its ability to seek profits through mismatching its book—a game that the bigger foreign branches often play with success. Speaking of asset-liability management, one foreign banker commented: "My balance sheet is relatively long term on the asset side, and I have a good portion of long-term deposits. With respect to interest-rate risk, we are usually overlent. I have a treasury gap limit I must respect. I would say that 50% of my assets are good quality and readily salable. They may have long maturities, but they are A rated or better, and I can sell them. But just to make my cash position better, I borrow 1-year money—systematically whenever the arbitrage is in place, which it often is—and then do either FRAs or Euro futures to swap 1-year fixed into floating. I may take 100MM of 1-year money and then swap out the next nine months, so I am left with 3-month cash. My interest-rate risk is hedged, but on a liquidity basis, I have 1-year money."

The LBO Niche

When U.S. banks first began to aggressively market their corporate loans, foreign bank branches were prominent among the buyers. However, that lasted only a year or so and then the spread vanished from this business. After that, foreign banks turned to loans generated by leveraged buy-outs.

"We have," noted one foreign banker, "been very successful and made a lot of money on LBOs. Our head office has given us a quite strict definition of what LBOs we may buy: no hostile takeovers, various financial ratios must be satisfied, and what have you. Because of these guidelines and our authorization to do any deals we choose that conform to those guidelines, we can commit very quickly. We will go in and take maybe 100MM of a deal and then sell off 85 of that to other foreign banks. We get this debt directly from the lead banks such as Bankers Trust, Citi, and Manny. In the beginning, we had to go to the lead banks to convince them that we could give them an answer quickly—time is of the essence. Now, they come to us at the early stage of a deal.

"In evaluating a deal, we shave back very much the variables a company gives us; then, we ask what would happen in a deep recession. If, under *our* assumptions, a company would still be able to repay its debt, we will do the credit. While the debt may have a stated term of seven years, it's really bridge financing; this debt is the company's most expensive debt and it gets paid back first.

"Initially, a company may take a 7-year loan; but after a year, they've probably sold some assets, and you get repaid; now, they are a different company—they're profitable—so they reborrow, and we relend at a lower rate. Also, when they refinance, we do what we did on the initial loan—go in for 100MM and sell off 85 to other banks. We are in deals where we are already at the third financing. The business is very profitable—both the margins and the commissions."[20]

Invasion by Buy-Out

As noted, some foreign banks have taken the buy-out route to enter the U.S. market. The trend is particularly noticeable in California where the Japanese are currently plucking off the ripest banks. California is not schedule to open its doors to full interstate banking until 1991. However, in September 1987, it passed a bill reaffirming the right of foreign banks to merge with, or buy, California banks. According to a Federal Reserve survey, Japanese banks held, in mid-1987, 10% of total loan assets in the U.S., 13% of total loan assets in California.

The California market is highly attractive to outside banks; its economy rivals that of the U.K. in size and is expanding rapidly. It irks New York bankers to see Japanese banks buying California banks, while the best they can do is to pick up crumbs left by S&L defaults within the state. This situation doesn't, however, bother California bankers. It seems that many of them would prefer to sell out to Japanese banks, rather than to East Coast banks. The Japanese pay a better price and are viewed as likely to look after staff better.

---

[20]For more on sales of loan participations by banks, see Chapter 23.

Japanese penetration of U.S. banking is far stronger in some areas than in others. Because Japanese banks are highly creditworthy, they have an edge in businesses that involve bank guarantees, such as standby letters of credit, a business in which Japanese banks now have about 50% of the U.S. market. U.S. banks, which are loath to add a lot of contingent liabilities to their balance sheets, may not be sorry to lose such business to Japanese banks, but the latter have their eyes set on juicier pickings.

California is something of a banking backwater; in particular, the corporate banking area is viewed as uncompetitive by people who have experienced the cutthroat conditions that prevail in London and New York. One group that Japanese banks have targeted is lucrative middle-market firms: the broad range of manufacturers, wholesalers, and retailers with annual sales of 10MM to 200MM. Such companies pay up to three percentage points more for loans than do big national firms, and typically they buy from their bankers a wide range of profitable services. California, because of its rapid growth and its highly educated and skilled immigrants, happens to have an unusually large middle market, one that promises tempting profits now and even more tempting profits later as its middle-market companies grow up.

The story is told that, when someone suggested to the chief financial officer of a paper company in America's heartland that he try a lender called the Industrial Bank of Japan, he replied: "I've never heard of them. Do they lend in dollars?" If the Japanese banks have their way, such incidents will wane—the names of Japanese banks will acquire the same familiar ring to financial officers all over the U.S. that they now have to people in the New York money market.

Regulation of Foreign Branch Operations

State regulation of the operations of foreign bank branches in the U.S. has always been stricter and more detailed than the regulation to which foreign bank branches are subject in London. In New York State, for example, foreign banks are subject to all the detailed provisions of the state's banking law. In addition, they are required to hold qualifying assets equal to 108% of their total liabilities (intrabank deposits excepted); of this, 5% must be held in T bills or certain other instruments in a special account with a depository bank. Since the qualifying assets that a foreign bank branch may use to satisfy the 108% requirement include a wide range of instruments—loans on its New York book, CDs bought, deposits at other banks, Fed funds sold, BAs held in its portfolio, and broker/dealer loans—this requirement imposes no cost on foreign banks as do Fed reserve requirements. On the other hand, the 108% requirement does mean that a foreign bank's branch must, net, borrow funds from the rest of the system—funds that constitute, in effect, the branch's U.S. capital base. The New York State 108% rule is designed to ensure that a foreign bank branch will always have sufficient assets to meet its deposit and other liabilities. As such, it has been viewed abroad as a model for foreign bank branch regulation and has been widely copied.

In the eyes of some foreign bankers, however, the New York State regulation is anything but a model. One British bank commented, "It's far too complex and to some extent outdated. In these days when funds can be moved rapidly, a foreign bank in trouble could rape its New York branch before the regulators smelled trouble. The only regulation that makes sense and that is going to be effective over the long run is to grant branch licenses only to banks that are credit- and trustworthy."

One advantage that foreign banks used to enjoy over domestic banks is that they could open branches in several different states, whereas domestic banks were not allowed to engage in interstate banking. Because of this and other issues, a lot of pressure was exerted on Congress to pass new foreign bank legislation putting foreign and domestic banks on an equal footing.

The International Banking Act of 1978

This pressure resulted in passage, in 1978, of the *International Banking Act (IBA)*. The major statutory changes provided by the act with respect to foreign banks are: (1) foreign agencies and branches now have the option of federal licensing; (2) foreign branches and agencies engaged in retail banking are required to buy FDIC insurance; (3) foreign branches and agencies are subject to reserve requirements imposed by the Fed in exchange for which they now have access to the discount window and other services provided by the Fed to domestic banks; (4) foreign banks may no longer branch into more than one state; and (5) the Fed is authorized to act as an examining agency to police the activities of those foreign banks that established multistate branches prior to IBA passage and that were permitted, under a "grandfather clause" in IBA, to keep these branches.[21]

INTERNATIONAL BANKING FACILITIES (IBFs)[22]

On December 1, 1981, domestic banks and foreign bank branches in New York and 11 other states that had passed enabling legislation were permitted to open *international banking facilities (IBFs)*. The hope in New York was that introduction of these facilities would put New York on a par with London as an international banking center; the chance of this occurring, however, was diminished by the restrictions that the Fed imposed on IBF activities.

The concept behind IBFs is to create a species of free trade zone for international money—primarily Eurodollars. An IBF offers a bank several advantages: Deposits in the facility are subject to no reserve requirements, and the IBF need not pay FDIC insurance premiums; also, income earned by the facility enjoys, in New York and certain other states, special provisions for relief from state taxes.[23]

For depositors, one attraction of IBFs is that any interest they pay to foreigners is exempt from withholding taxes; another advantage is that the depositor will get U.S. as opposed to

---

[21]The details of the International Banking Act are spelled out in a mimeographed report by the Board of Governors of the Federal Reserve System entitled *The International Banking Act of 1978* and dated September 17, 1980.

[22]The following section is excerpted in part from Marcia Stigum, "A Free Trade Zone for New York? IBFs to Be Allowed, but Fed Restrictions May Limit Growth," *Pensions & Investment Age,* September 28, 1981, pp. 20–21.

[23]For more details on IBFs and tax provisions covering them, see Sydney J. Key, "International Banking Facilities," *Federal Reserve Bulletin,* October 1982, pp. 556–77.

U.K., Bahrainian, or some other sovereign risk. U.S. sovereign risk won't attract Iranian depositors, but it should attract institutions that are loath to place funds in the shell branches that major U.S. banks have opened in Nassau and other tax havens because they don't like the sovereign risk that they perceive attaches to deposits there.

The origin of IBFs goes back to the days when New York City was tottering on the brink of bankruptcy. At the time, the state and the city zeroed in on the banks as the culprits. The city's problems were the banks' fault because the banks kept selling the city's debt whereas they should have told the city it was bankrupt. To add injury to insult, the city and the state raised their tax rates on bank income earned within New York State, and the city topped off its tax hike with a tax surcharge.

The imposition of punitive state and city taxes gave New York banks a tremendous incentive to book international business in offshore tax havens, primarily Nassau and Grand Cayman, which are located in a time zone that permits New York banks to deal on the shell's behalf during normal business hours. Once this trend asserted itself and serious defections among New York banks became a distinct possibility, the state passed legislation to permit the creation in New York of IBFs. These were supposed to draw huge amounts of business back from London and the offshore shells to New York City.

For the IBFs to get off the ground, the Fed had to give them its blessing. The latter was slow in coming because out-of-town banks opposed New York IBFs as unfair competition. The Fed has a history of not making rules that favor a particular group of banks; to permit the New York IBFs to go ahead, it had to come up with a rationalization: this was that any state could pass the same legislation New York had. A second concern of the Fed was with leakage: the movement of domestic deposits and loan business into the Euromarket. The Fed fears that further leakage would weaken its control over domestic credit and the domestic money supply.

This concern sounds legitimate but is, in fact, somewhat ludicrous since the horse in question left the barn years ago. Today, treasurers at major domestic corporations actively and freely ferry their loan and deposit business between the domestic and the Euromarket on the basis of what best suits their needs. When the Fed, in 1975, wrote a letter to the banks reiterating its instructions to them not to solicit Eurodeposits from domestic depositors, it forgot to send a copy to corporate America, which currently buys a substantial chunk of the Euro CDs issued in London.

Despite the fact that leakage has become a torrent, the Fed—to prevent its further growth—imposed severe restrictions on what IBFs may do; specifically, it ruled that IBFs may not pay interest on overnight money, may not issue CDs, and may not take deposits from or make loans to domestic entities. These restrictions sharply limit the value of IBFs to banks. No corporate depositor will settle for a two-day notice account when he can earn interest on a Euro call account at a London or Caribbean branch. Also, corporate treasurers will not make time deposits with IBFs when they can buy liquid Europaper in London.

Bereft of corporate deposits, IBFs have had to rely for most of their funding on the interbank market for Euros and on deposits from central banks that have large dollar holdings and that, because they wanted to diversify their sovereign risk, were already holding some dollar deposits in the U.S.

This contrasts sharply with the situation at U.S. banks' Caribbean branches where half of the funding comes from U.S. depositors. The restrictions imposed by the Fed on IBFs are sufficiently stringent to make New York unattractive compared with London and other Eurocenters.

Nonetheless, since IBFs were permitted, every major New York bank and a large number of foreign banks with New York branches or agencies have opened such a facility. The banks that have bid most aggressively through their IBFs for Eurodollars are, interestingly enough, not the New York banks who originally wanted the facilities but Japanese banks. The explanation is simple: Japanese banks were not permitted by their Ministry of Finance from running shell branches in the Caribbean and other tax havens; thus IBFs gave the Japanese banks their first opportunity to participate in the shell-branch game that all other banks had been playing for years.

Running an IBF Book Today

A U.S. bank will try to generate as much profit in its IBF as possible because it pays less taxes on profits earned there. However, a bank's IBF operates at a funding disadvantage. It cannot tap, either directly or indirectly, the cheapest sources of funding which are issuing negotiable instruments—deposit notes and commercial paper in the U.S., Euro CDs in London. In particular, a bank's IBF cannot obtain, as can the bank's Nassau or Cayman branch, deposits from the holding company of cheap funds that the latter has raised in the commercial paper market; the reason is that the holding company is a U.S. corporation.

The funding disadvantage at which a bank's IBF operates has severely constrained the growth of such books. At the end of 1988, 310 billion of assets were booked in IBFs, 391 billion in Nassau and Cayman branches. As a group, IBFs run a slightly bigger Euro position than do banks in Singapore, a much smaller one than do banks in Hong Kong.

U.S. banks tend to use their IBFs for limited purposes in which the impact of their funding disadvantage is minimized. One such use is to book cross-currency swaps in an IBF, for example, a swap of floating-rate dollars against fixed-rate DM (or fixed-rate in some other foreign currency). A swap, being an off-balance-sheet instrument, requires no funding.

Another activity that some banks carry on in their IBFs is the running of opportunistic books in French francs, sterling, yen, Canadian dollars, DM, and other currencies. Here, opportunistic means, as one banker put it, "When something happens, we open a book, play the market, and then close the book." An IBF is at less of a disadvantage when it funds assets denominated in a foreign currency—often these assets are readily available securities—than when it funds dollar assets; there is less of a difference between Euro time-deposit and Euro CD rates in foreign currencies than in Eurodollars because, in most foreign currencies, few, if any, Euro CDs are issued. Also, a bank that has privileged access to Eurodollar funding can capture some of that funding advantage for its IBF by buying Eurodollar time deposits at sub-LIBOR rates and then swapping those deposits into foreign exchange, say DM, to create DM funding at 2 or 3 bp below LIBOR (for DM); in the swap, the bank loses some of its funding advantage in dollars because of friction costs.

If the day ever comes when IBFs are permitted to issue negotiable instruments that carry a provision that they cannot be placed with U.S. corporations, the IBF business will presumably boom.

THE NEXT CHAPTER

In the next chapter, we turn to the Treasury and federal agencies, both major issuers of risk-free (near-risk free in the case of agencies) securities. The Treasury market is important not only because of the huge volume of trading that occurs in Treasuries, but because shorts in Treasuries are used to hedge positions in other instruments, such as interest-rate swaps and Euro paper, and rates along the Treasury yield curve serve as benchmarks in a number of other sectors of the money market.

CHAPTER 8

THE TREASURY AND THE FEDERAL AGENCIES

The single most important issuer of debt in the money market is the U.S. Treasury. It is closely followed in importance by federal agencies as a group.

U.S. GOVERNMENT SECURITIES

At the beginning of 1989, the U.S. government had $2.87 trillion of debt outstanding. As Table 8–1 shows, about 4% of the Treasury's outstanding debt is represented by Series E and H bonds, which are *nonnegotiable savings bonds* sold to individuals. The Treasury also issues substantial amounts of special *nonnegotiable* issues (1) to foreign central banks that hold dollars as reserves, (2) to federal agencies and trust funds (including the social security trust fund) that have surplus monies to invest, and (3) to state and local governments.[1]

The remainder of the Treasury's outstanding debt is *negotiable* issues, all of which are actively traded in the money and bond markets. Currently the Treasury issues three types of negotiable securities:[2]

1. Non–interest-bearing *bills* that have an original maturity of one year or less.
2. Interest-bearing *notes* that have an original maturity of 2 to 10 years.

---

[1]The reason the Treasury issues special debt series to state and local governments is explained later in this chapter.

[2]The Treasury once issued interest-bearing *certificates* with an original maturity of one year or less. It has not done so since 1967.

3. Interest-bearing *bonds* that have an original maturity of more than 10 years.

Volume Outstanding

A huge expansion has occurred in recent years in total Treasury debt outstanding (Figure 8–1). The principal cause of the increase is the enormous deficits that the federal government has consistently rung up since 1975 (Table 8–2). Another factor that has contributed to the increase in Treasury debt outstanding is that the Treasury began in 1974 to borrow money in its own name to fund the lending activities of the Federal Financing Bank, discussed below.

The recent sharp increase in Treasury debt has caused a substantial rise in the amount of marketable Treasury securities outstanding (Figure 8–2). Most of this rise has occurred through increases in the amounts of notes and bills outstanding. Negotiable bonds represent the smallest component of the Treasury's total marketable debt (Figure 8–3).

TREASURY DEBT MANAGEMENT: SOME HISTORY

Over the last 25 years, the Treasury has made substantial changes in the types of marketable securities it offers and in the way it sells these securities. These changes were made in re-

TABLE 8–1
Gross U.S. public debt, January 1, 1989 ($ billions)

Bills	414.0
Notes	1,098.4
Bonds	308.9
Total marketable	1,821.3
Savings bonds	107.6
Special issues to U.S. government agencies and trust funds	576.6
State and local government series	151.5
Foreign issues	6.6
Other	208.8
Total gross debt	2,872.4

FIGURE 8–1
U.S. public debt outstanding, total and marketable

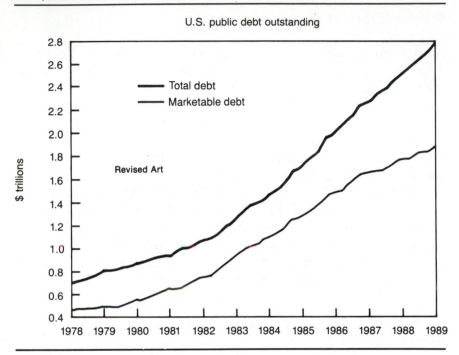

U.S. public debt outstanding

Source: J. P. Morgan Securities, Inc. (U.S. Department of the Treasury).

sponse to several pressures: the Treasury's need to be able to market its debt in the face of increasingly volatile interest rates, its need to be able to market rapidly growing amounts of debt, and its need—perceived by the mid-1970s—to lengthen the average maturity of its outstanding debt (Figure 8–3).

In the mid-1960s, the Treasury funded the debt by selling 3-month and 6-month bills at weekly auctions and 9-month and 1-year bills at monthly auctions; in addition, there was a quarterly financing in the middle of each quarter at which the Treasury sold notes and bonds. The bills were sold as they are today through auctions, the notes and bonds through exchange and subscription offerings.

TABLE 8–2
Federal budget receipts and outlays, fiscal years 1960 to 1990 ($ billions)

Fiscal Year	Receipts	Outlays	Surplus or Deficit (−)
1960	92.5	92.2	0.3
1961	94.4	97.8	−3.4
1962	99.7	106.8	−7.1
1963	106.6	111.3	−4.7
1964	112.7	118.6	−5.9
1965	116.8	118.4	−1.6
1966	130.9	134.7	−3.8
1967	149.6	158.3	−8.7
1968	153.7	178.8	−25.1
1969	187.8	184.5	3.3
1970	193.8	196.6	−2.8
1971	188.4	211.4	−23.0
1972	208.6	232.0	−23.4
1973	232.2	247.0	−14.8
1974	264.9	269.6	−4.7
1975	281.0	326.1	−45.1
1976	299.2	365.6	−66.4
Transition quarter*	81.7	94.7	−13.0
1977	356.9	401.9	−45.0
1978	399.6	448.4	−48.8
1979	463.3	491.0	−27.7
1980	517.1	576.7	−59.6
1981	599.3	657.2	−57.9
1982	626.7	725.3	−98.6
1983	666.1	757.6	−91.5
1984	666.5	851.8	−185.3
1985	734.1	946.3	−212.2
1986	769.1	990.3	−221.2
1987	854.1	1,003.8	−149.7
1988	909.0	1,064.0	−155.0
1989†	975.5	1,137.0	−161.5
1990†	1,059.3	1,151.8	−92.5

*Under provisions of the Congressional Budget Act of 1974, the fiscal year for the federal government shifted beginning with fiscal year 1977. Through fiscal year 1976, the fiscal year ran from July 1 through June 30; starting in October 1976 (fiscal year 1977), the fiscal year ran from October 1 through September 30. The 3-month period from July 1, 1976, through September 30, 1976, is a separate fiscal period known as the *transition quarter*.
†Estimated.

Source: *Economic Report of the President*, January 1989.

FIGURE 8–2

Composition of U.S. government's marketable debt: Treasury bills, notes, and bonds (noncumulative)

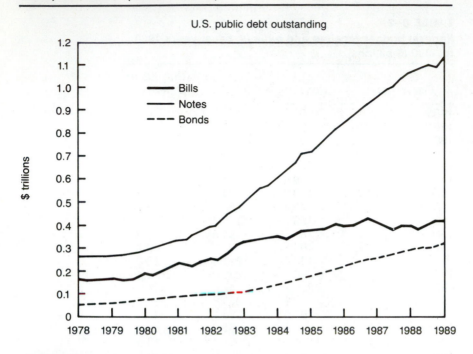

U.S. public debt outstanding

FIGURE 8–3

Average current maturity of privately held, marketable Treasury debt outstanding

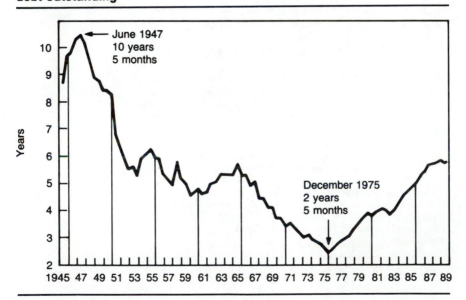

Source: U.S. Treasury.

Bill Auctions

In a bill auction, money market banks, dealers, and other institutional investors who buy big amounts of bills submit *competitive* bids; that is, for the bills they want to buy, they bid a discounted price expressed on the basis of 100. For example, a
dealer who wanted to buy $100MM of 3-month bills might bid a
price of 97.865, which is equivalent to a yield of 8.446 on a
discount basis.[3] The prices dealers and investors bid for bills
depend both on the rates yielded by outstanding money market
instruments and on what (if any) movement they think is occurring in short-term rates.

The less expert investor who is not prepared to work out a
bid to three decimal points can put in a *noncompetitive* bid that
states no price.

> After the auction closes, bids are forwarded to the Treasury
> Department in Washington and tabulated for each issue. First,
> the volume of noncompetitive awards is subtracted from the total
> amount to be issued. Government and Federal Reserve Bank ten-
> ders, which are noncompetitive, are accepted in full. Noncompeti-
> tive tenders of private investors are accepted in full up to [the
> current limit on such tenders]. The remainder is allocated among
> competitive bidders beginning with those that bid the highest
> prices and ranging down in price until the total amount is used.
> The lowest accepted price is called the *stop-out* price. Since a
> number of bids may have been entered at the stop-out price, the
> Treasury may award each of the bidders at this price only a
> portion of the amount requested.

---

[3]Rearranging the formula,

$$D = F \left(\frac{d \times t}{360} \right)$$

which was given on p. 66, we get

$$d = \frac{D \times 360}{F \times t}$$

In the above example, D equals $2.135 per $100 of face value, and t equals 91 (13
weeks × 7 days per week). Thus,

$$d = \frac{2.135 \times 360}{100 \times 91} = 8.446\%$$

After the auction on Monday, the amount and price range of accepted bids are announced, and competitive bidders are advised of the acceptance or rejection of their tenders. Competitive bidders pay the price that they bid while noncompetitive entries pay the weighted average price to three decimals of accepted competitive bids.[4]

Exchange Offerings

When the Treasury sold bonds through exchange offerings, it used two techniques. In a *straight exchange offer*, the Treasury sought to refund maturing securities by offering their holders new securities with the same par value. In an *advance refunding* or *pre-refunding*, the Treasury offered holders of an outstanding issue the opportunity to exchange their securities for new securities of the same par value before maturity.

Holders of eligible securities who did not wish to invest in the new issue could sell their *right* to the new issue to other investors or turn in their maturing securities for cash. The purpose of straight exchange offerings was to encourage existing bondholders to roll their bonds, thereby permitting Treasury refundings to be carried out with minimal disruption to the market. In the case of pre-refundings, an additional objective was to reduce Treasury borrowing costs by taking advantage of the interest-rate cycle; the Treasury would pre-refund when interest rates were expected to rise and pre-refunding looked cheaper than refunding at maturity. Exchange offerings were usually made on generous terms so that issues for which exchange offerings were made rose in value, reflecting the *rights* value they acquired through the exchange offering. The practice of exchange offerings also led to speculative demand for issues that were considered likely candidates for pre-refunding.

Subscription Issues

In a subscription offering [which the Treasury has used to raise new cash], the Treasury announces the amount to be sold, the

---

[4]Margaret Bedford, "Recent Developments in Treasury Financing Techniques," *Monthly Review*, Federal Reserve Bank of Kansas, July–August 1977, p. 17.

interest coupon on the issue, and the price of the issue. The Treasury reserves the right to change the amount sold and the allotment procedures after all subscriptions have been submitted. Additional amounts are issued to Federal Reserve and Government accounts after allotments to the public.

Investors enter subscriptions for the amount of securities they wish to purchase at the Treasury's given price and yield. Since investors may enter subscriptions totaling more than the amount offered by the Treasury, the allotment procedure becomes important for limiting the size of the issue. Allotments can be made by awarding a percentage of the amount of each tender or by setting a maximum dollar amount to be accepted for each tender.

The Treasury usually offers to accept some tenders in full on a preferred allotment basis. Preferred tenders are limited in size (up to $500,000 in recent offerings) and must be accompanied by a deposit of 20 percent of the face value of securities applied for.[5]

The Rate Lid on Bonds

Congress permits the Treasury to pay whatever rate of return is necessary to sell bills and notes but bars the Treasury from paying more than 4.25% on bonds. This rate lid created no problem when long-term rates were below 4.25%. But in the mid-1960s, rates rose above this level, making it impossible for the Treasury to sell new bonds.

In the early 1970s, Congress granted the Treasury permission to sell $10 billion of bonds exempt from this rate ceiling. Congress raised the amount of this exemption on several occasions but always kept the amount small relative to the Treasury's total marketable debt. The 4.25% rate lid, despite its popularity with members of Congress who favor low interest rates, does nothing to hold down interest rates. It does, however, bar the Treasury from competing directly with private corporations and municipal borrowers in the long-term market and from pulling funds directly out of the mortgage market, which explains some of the support for retaining the lid. Nonetheless, the lid was finally removed by Congress in 1988.

---

[5]Ibid., p. 23.

Introduction of Price Auctions

The fact that, for a period starting in the mid-1960s, the Treasury could sell no long-term bonds left it in the position where the longest-maturity security it could sell was a 5-year note. As a result, the average maturity of the debt began to decline at a disturbing rate (Figure 8–3). To counter this trend, the Treasury sought and received from Congress in 1967 permission to raise the maximum maturity of notes from five to seven years.

As interest rates became more volatile in the late 1960s, it became increasingly difficult for the Treasury to issue new debt through subscription issues on which both the price and the coupon were announced several days before the date on which investors tendered for the issue. In a 1970 refunding, the Treasury experimented: for the first time, it used a *price auction* instead of the subscription technique to sell new notes and bonds to the general public.

> In the price auction, the Treasury announces the amount to be sold to the public, and a few days prior to the auction sets a coupon rate and a minimum acceptable price. Competitive bidders state the price they are willing to pay on the basis of 100 to two decimals. These bids may be at par ($100 per $100 face), at a price below par (at a discount), or at a price above par (at a premium). The price bid would reflect the investor's judgment as to how attractive the coupon rate is compared to other market rates. The rate associated with a price of par is the coupon rate, paying a premium will result in a lower effective yield than the coupon rate; and buying at a discount will yield an effective return higher than the coupon rate. As in the Treasury bill market, the noncompetitive tenders are subtracted from the amount to be sold and the remainder is distributed by accepting the highest price bid on down until the amount of the issue is taken. Competitive bidders pay the price that they bid, and noncompetitive bids are accepted in full at the average price of competitive bids. However, since the competitive bids are not necessarily at par, the average price paid by noncompetitive bidders may be more or less than par and thus they will receive an effective yield somewhat different from the coupon rate.[6]

---

[6]Ibid., p. 22.

Switch to Yield Auctions

In 1973, the Treasury further changed its policies of debt issuance. It again sought and received from Congress permission to raise the maximum maturity on notes, this time from 7 to 10 years. Also, because of its increasing cash needs, it discontinued exchange offerings with the February 1973 refunding and began to rely solely on price auction sales. The Treasury also began to issue 2-year notes on a regular cycle but later discontinued this cycle; it also discontinued issuing 9-month bills because of a lack of investor acceptance of this maturity.

The year 1974, which was characterized by high and volatile interest rates, was a difficult time for the Treasury to sell debt. To ease its problems, the Treasury increased the size of the noncompetitive bids that could be tendered for notes and bonds to $500,000 in order to appeal to a wide class of investors. It also began to issue occasionally special longer-term bills for nonstandard periods when it needed additional funds.

The final and most important change that the Treasury made in 1974 was to switch its auctions of notes and bonds from a price to a yield basis. Under the price auction system, at the time a new issue was announced, the Treasury set the coupon on the issue in line with market rates so that the new issue's price, determined through auction, would be at or near par. If rates moved away from the levels prevailing on announcement day, the prices bid on auction day would, reflecting this, move away from par. For example, if rates fell between the announcement of an issue and the auction, bid prices would be above par, whereas if rates rose, bids would be below par. As interest rates became more volatile, deviations of bid prices from par became a problem. In August 1974, one Treasury issue was sold at 101 while another failed to sell out because the Treasury received too few bids at or above the minimum price it would accept. The Treasury feared that above-par prices would discourage some bidders and that below-par prices would place purchasers in an unanticipated tax position (the amount of the discount at issue being taxable at maturity as ordinary income). Another problem with price auctions was that, when the Treasury set coupons, the market tended to move to them, so that price auctions disturbed the market. To solve both problems and to ensure that its issues sold out, the Treasury moved in late 1974 to a new technique in which would-be buyers bid *yields* instead of prices.

In a yield auction for notes and bonds, the Treasury announces the new issue a week or more before the auction. At that time, it tells the market what amount of securities it will issue, when they will mature, and what denominations will be available. *Competitive* bidders bid yields to two decimal points (e.g., 10.53) for specific quantities of the new issue. After bids are received, the Treasury determines the stop-out bid on the basis of both the bids received and the amount it wishes to borrow. It then sets the coupon on the security to the nearest $\frac{1}{8}$ of 1% necessary to make the average price charged to successful bidders equal to 100.00 or less. Once the coupon on the issue is established, each successful bidder is charged a price (discount, par, or premium) for his securities; the price is determined so that the yield to maturity on the securities a bidder gets equals the yield he bid. *Noncompetitive* bidders pay the average price of the accepted competitive tenders.

TABs, Strips, and Cash Management Bills

In 1975, when the Treasury faced the problem both of refunding huge quantities of maturing debt and of financing a burgeoning federal debt, it changed its policies of debt issuance.

From time to time, the Treasury finds it necessary to sell special bill issues to meet short-term borrowing needs. Prior to 1975, the Treasury used *tax anticipation bills* (TABs) and bill strips for this purpose.

> Tax anticipation bills were issued to help the Treasury smooth out its tax receipts, and they would be submitted in payment of income taxes. Commercial banks were usually permitted to make payment for TABs by crediting Treasury tax and loan accounts and thus became underwriters for these issues. About 28 TAB offerings were made during the 1970–74 period, and they ranged in maturity from 23 to 273 days.
>
> A bill strip is a reopening of a number of issues of outstanding bill series. Strips enabled the Treasury to raise a large amount of short-term funds at one time rather than spreading out receipts through additions to weekly bill auctions. In the 1970–74 period, nine strips of bills were issued ranging from additions to 5 series

to additions to 15 series and averaging 22 days to 131 days in maturity.[7]

In 1975, the Treasury discontinued the use of TABs and strips and replaced them with *cash management bills*. Cash management bills are usually reopenings of an outstanding issue and often have quite short maturities. When they are auctioned, the minimum acceptable bid is $10MM, and only competitive bids are accepted. Cash management bills are usually bought by banks and dealers at some spread to their cost of money and held to maturity.

Regularization of Debt Issuance

The year 1975 was important in the evolution of debt management policy. In that year, the Treasury adopted a program of *regularization of debt issuance*. Under this program, the Treasury began to issue 2-year, 4-year, and 5-year notes on a regular cycle. A 2-year note was issued at the end of each month, a 4-year note in the middle of the second month of each quarter, and a 5-year note in the middle of the first month of each quarter. The normal quarterly refunding, at which the Treasury offers a mix of notes and bonds to refund maturing issues and raise new cash, occurs at the middle of the second month of each quarter. Thus, in the late 1970s, the Treasury was issuing coupons on a regular schedule of six dates a quarter.

The Treasury began its policy of regularizing debt issuance for several reasons. First, in the mid-1970s it was obvious, against a background of large and then record deficits, that the government was going to have huge financing requirements for the foreseeable future. Therefore, Treasury officials concluded that, both to minimize the cost of issuing Treasury debt and to maximize the capacity of the market to absorb such debt, it was crucial that debt issuance be made as predictable as possible.

Before the Treasury sought to regularize debt issuance, it operated on a sort of *ad hoc* basis. It used to be that, at a quarterly financing, the Treasury might come with anything from a

---

[7]Ibid., p. 18.

1- to 10-year note or with a long bond if they had authority to sell them. Dealers, never knowing what to expect, had two choices: to come into an auction with a position because they were willing to bet on something or to come in flat (with no position) to avoid risk.

A second reason for regularizing debt issuance was to avoid bunching too much Treasury debt in the quarterly financings. There is a limit on how much debt the market can absorb and dealers can distribute at any time; it was thought that, if the Treasury continued to issue most of its coupon debt on four dates a year, that limit would be breached and the Treasury would consequently be forced to pay higher rates than it would have had to pay if bunching were avoided. Under the current program, the market has a chance to digest one issue before it girds up to take another.

A third reason the Treasury began issuing debt on a regular schedule was that doing so was viewed as a means to lengthen the average maturity of marketable Treasury debt outstanding; in 1977, such lengthening did in fact occur for the first time in years (Figure 8–3).

Exceptions to the General Pattern

Since 1975, the Treasury had relied primarily on yield auctions to sell new coupon securities. It has made exceptions to this practice for several purposes. First, the Treasury sometimes *reopens* (sells more of) an already outstanding note or bond issue. In that case, the coupon on the issue has already been determined in a previous auction; therefore, the new securities offered must carry that coupon and must be sold through a *price* auction.

Second, several times in 1976, the Treasury had so much new debt to place that it feared it would strain the underwriting and distribution capacity of the Street if it used the normal auction procedure; so it issued notes carrying an attractive coupon at a fixed price through subscription offerings. This strategy enabled the Treasury to reach beyond its normal market directly to individual investors. A coupon of 8% was then thought to be a magic number: Whenever the Treasury put an 8% or higher coupon on an issue, individuals—comparing that rate with what they could get on savings accounts and time deposits—would rush out to buy it, and typically they then held the issue to maturity. The last time the Treasury did this was as part of the February 1978 quarterly financing, when it offered a 6-year note with an 8% coupon through a price auction. The Treasury's objective in fixing the coupon instead of using a yield auction was to sell an out-sized issue by appealing to individuals as well as institutional investors. Since then, the Treasury has offered no subscription issues.

While debt regularization offers obvious advantages, critics have suggested that the program may also have drawbacks.

Too Many Issues

Since the Treasury began its program of debt regularization, one question frequently raised on the Street is whether the Treasury is creating a situation in which Treasury issues are too numerous to be tradable. Opinions vary.

One dealer commented, "The Treasury should start reopening issues. Currently, they have so many outstanding that it is impossible to keep track of them all. This puts a premium on active issues; people will buy and be active only in current, on-the-run issues, because to get off the run, is to forgo so much liquidity as to be painful."

A second dealer argued, "Debt regularization is a necessity. You can't have the Treasury just popping in selling 5 billion of this or that and the market never knowing what is coming. It is not good for the market to know that the Treasury has a 15 billion financing job to do in a quarter and to have no idea of where [in the maturity spectrum] or when the issues will come. It would be easier for the traders to have fewer issues, but for the market and the Treasury—it is better to have a debt regularization."

TREASURY DEBT MANAGEMENT TODAY

Treasury officials who are today responsible for debt management are quick to point out that responsibility for making the tax and expenditure decisions that determine the size of the current deficit and of projected deficits belong to other economic policymakers. As one debt manager noted, "We are told what the financing requirements of the federal government are going to be. Our job is to decide, based on our market expertise, what is the least disruptive way of handling that financing requirement."

In recent years, the Treasury has been forced to fund the debt under increasingly difficult circumstances. One third of its marketable debt—currently 1.8 trillion dollars—matures and must be refunded through Treasury sales of new debt each year. In addition, the Treasury must sell new debt to fund the federal government's large current deficits. Selling so much debt would have been no small job for the Treasury under normal market conditions. Money and bond market conditions have, however, been anything but normal since the Fed's switch to monetarism in October 1979. During the period 1979 to 1982, interest rates—short and long—reached historic highs with respect to both level and volatility.

Focusing on Debt Regularization

Throughout this period, debt management has been a nonpartisan issue. The Treasury's agreed-upon objective has been to get its debt sold in the least expensive and the least disruptive way possible, given the constraints placed on it by external forces in the form of congressional mandates and market conditions and by internally imposed constraints, such as its decision to issue no instrument that would compete directly and favorably with savings deposits at banks and S&Ls.

The policy of regularization of Treasury debt issuance, begun in the mid-1970s, has been continued. As noted earlier, the Treasury started its policy of debt regularization by instituting 2- and 4-year note cycles. Over time as the Treasury had more and more debt to finance, it responded by adding more coupon cycles (Table 8–3) and by building up those it already had. To further regularize debt issuance, the Treasury has sought to make its mix of offerings at the quarterly refunding as predictable as possible. Normally, this mix includes a new long bond; on several occasions, however, no long bond was included in a

TABLE 8–3
Quarterly schedule of Treasury coupon offerings

Quarterly Dates	Issue Offered
First month	
Middle	7-year note
End	2-year note
Second month	
Middle	Quarterly refunding (3- and 10-year notes, 30-year bond)
End	2-year note, 5-year note
Third month	
Middle	2-year note
End	4-year note

refunding because the Treasury had at that time exhausted its exemption from the 4¼% lid and was petitioning Congress to increase it.

Since debt regularization was adopted, the major focus of debt management has been on decisions with respect to coupon issues: which coupons and how much of each to issue? This was inevitable given the huge deficits the federal government was running. Whenever the Treasury must meet a big cash drain, it goes first to the bill market (Figure 8–4). Continuing deficits would thus result in an enormous buildup of bill issues if the Treasury made no attempt to expand its coupon issues.

A second objective of debt regularization has been to lengthen the average maturity of the debt, which in 1975 dropped under three years. A short average debt maturity forces the Treasury to sell an enormous quantity of debt each year just for refunding purposes. It also makes the interest component of federal debt service highly sensitive to the current level of market rates. During the period 1979 to 1982, the cost of financing the national debt rose 60% (from 55.5 to 99.1 billion), while the debt itself rose only 21%, in part because the short average maturity of the debt forced the Treasury to constantly refund huge sums of maturing debt at ever-increasing rates.

Debt regularization ought to reduce in several other ways the cost of financing the debt. By reducing uncertainty of the sort that prevailed when the Treasury came to the market on an

FIGURE 8–4
Treasury net market borrowing*

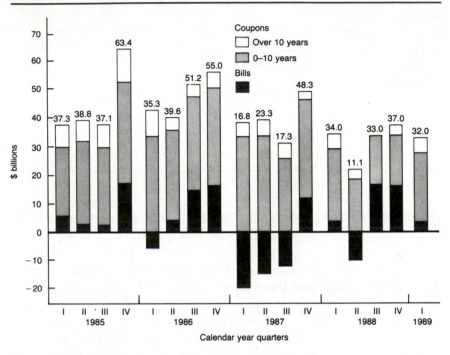

*Excludes Federal Reserve and Government account transactions.

Source: U.S. Treasury.

ad hoc basis, regularization ought to reduce the yields at which dealers and investors are willing to bid for new Treasury issues. It should also decrease borrowing costs because, when the Treasury creates a security and keeps selling it, the security creates its own demand after a time.

For this reason, the Treasury makes it a policy to regularly issue long bonds at each quarterly financing. Its rationale is that, if portfolio managers know the Treasury is coming with a long bond issue once a quarter—as they know that the telephone company does—they will adjust their portfolios so that, when the new government bonds come to market, other bonds will have been swapped out to make room for them. This supposedly will give the Treasury a share of the market under all conditions—a share that the Treasury can increase when conditions are favorable and rates are low.

The Treasury is conscious of the problem of issue proliferation because of debt regularization. Particularly in the case of long coupons, it would like to include in its quarterly financing reopenings of existing issues. Noted one Treasury official, "It makes sense to reopen an issue if possible especially in the longer issues where we normally would have come with an issue of 2 to 2½ billion. That is a rather small issue to develop active trading. By reopening the issue and enlarging its size, we would enhance its liquidity. Unfortunately, we do not often get the opportunity to reopen recent issues because the volatility of rates has been such that the market tends to get away from us [e.g., the rates at which bonds are trading change markedly] between refundings."

Even Keeling

In the old days it used to be that, around Treasury auction dates, the Fed would *even keel,* that is, keep conditions in the money market as stable as possible. Some argued that, if the Treasury kept increasing the number of dates on which it offered coupons, the Fed would be forced to even keel all the time and, consequently, be left with no window during which it could alter monetary policy. In fact, this has not been a problem. Even keeling died an untolled death, one that was facilitated by the Treasury's switch from price to yield auctions and by the Treasury's decision to sell small amounts of coupon debt frequently rather than huge sums quarterly. Today, the Fed pursues monetary policy with little or no concern over the impact of its actions on the success of a particular Treasury offering.

Rate Lid on Bonds

Once the 4¼% lid on the rate that the Treasury could pay on long bonds became a binding constraint, the Treasury issued fewer long bonds than it would otherwise have done. While Congress granted the Treasury exemptions from this lid, eventually up to $300 billion, it refused to remove the lid until the fourth quarter of 1988. Congress wants to retain some control over Treasury debt management policies, to not give the Treasury carte blanche authority to issue long-term securities at any rates. Congress does not want the taxpayers locked in forever at what it views as high rate levels.

Ironically, the moment has never seemed right in the past for the Treasury to sell long bonds, even when by doing so it would have saved a lot of money. Back in the 1950s and 60s, when rates reached cyclical lows, it was argued that the Treasury should not sell long bonds because, by doing so, it would put upward pressure on long rates and thus discourage private capital spending needed to speed economic recovery. On the other hand, when the economy became buoyant and rates moved to cyclical highs, it never seemed appropriate for the Treasury to sell long bonds because at such times rates were always at historic highs due to the upward secular trend in interest rates that has prevailed through the early 1980s.

Under the Reagan administration, the question arose whether the government should continue to sell long bonds at historically high rates when the then new administration was implementing supply-side economic policies that were supposed to generate economic growth while reducing inflation and interest rates. Then undersecretary of the Treasury, Beryl Sprinkel, argued that, by selling long bonds carrying coupons in the teens, the government would demonstrate a lack of faith in its own policies and forecasts.

Those who thought that the Treasury should continue to sell long bonds retorted that the Treasury should not seek, as private borrowers do, to pick its spots in issuing long bonds. The Treasury, they argued, is no more able than anyone else to predict the trend in long rates. Second, due to the inevitable cyclical ups and downs in interest rates, the Treasury, which has so much debt maturing all the time anyway, would have ample opportunity to benefit from low rates when they prevailed. Third, the Treasury must finance somewhere; if they financed less in the long market, they would *have to finance more in the short market,* which would run counter to their intent to lengthen the debt. The Treasury could reconcile heavy reliance on short issues with its intent to lengthen the average maturity of the debt only if the government were running surpluses and the size of the debt were declining.

Some academics countered that the Treasury should not be seeking to lengthen the debt. They argued that Congress would act more responsibly to control inflation if it knew that acting irresponsibly would force up the interest cost of the debt immediately. Scoffed one Treasury official: "What Congressman ever thought of next year's impact of this year's spending?"

Capacity of the Market to Absorb Treasury Debt

The constantly increasing amount of Treasury debt outstanding and the volatility at times of rates have caused some to wonder if Treasury debt issuance might at some point breach the limit on the amount of Treasury debt dealers are able to underwrite or on the amount investors are willing to absorb. So far, Treasury officials have seen no signs that either eventuality is occurring. As one Treasury official noted, "Rate volatility helps make the market because traders make more money when markets are volatile than when they are not. It is true that the Street is taking smaller positions than they once did, but we have had no problem in auctioning our securities. One reason is that unrecognized dealers probably represent a larger proportion of the total underwriting than they did before; you have a lot of speculators who are not primarily government dealers but rather futures market participants who are now bidding directly in government auctions. Also, in bill auctions it is currently not the dealers who are the largest factor but rather the money funds. The amount of government financing has grown rapidly over the last few years, but financial markets have grown with it. Certainly, we have had no problem with coverage in auctions, and there seems to be no shortage of capital to back auction bids."

The Treasury has also had no difficulty finding sufficient investors to buy its debt, though the mix of investors tends to change from period to period. Sales of savings bonds declined until 1982, but this was more than offset by the money that money funds and other mutual funds poured into Treasuries.

Buying of Treasuries by foreign central banks tends to be

cyclical. Pre-1978, when the dollar was weak, foreign central banks accumulated dollars in their efforts to stabilize the rates at which their currencies traded against the dollar. This reoccurred in the 1980s when the dollar plunged in value. Much of the stock of dollars acquired by foreign central-bank operations in the foreign-exchange market ends up in Treasuries. Japanese institutional investors, insurance companies, and others also became substantial buyers of Treasuries in the 1980s, taking at times as much as a quarter of long bonds auctioned.

These observations raise two interesting questions: Thanks to budget deficits, is the U.S. really going broke? And are foreigners acquiring a vast horde of Treasuries that we or some future generation will have, with great pain, to repay? Put another way, are things really as bad as the press makes them out to be?

In these respects, Figures 8–5 and 8–6 are revealing. The first shows that, despite the huge growth in the absolute size of the Treasury's budget deficit, this deficit equaled, at the end of 1988, only 3.2% of *gross national product (GNP)*. In other words, if we allow for inflation and real growth in the economy, which the series plotted in Figure 8–5 does, real growth in the Treasury's deficit relative to national output was a modest 1.45 percentage points between 1958 and 1988. Also, if the budget deficits and surpluses run by state and local governments are included, there was, over this 30-year period, no net change in the *net* deficit run at all levels of government as percentage of GNP.

Figure 8–6 shows an even more surprising result. Despite the much heralded arrival during the 1980s of Japanese and other foreign investors in the Treasury market, the percentage of U.S. marketable debt owned by foreigners peaked not in the 1980s, but in 1978 at 17.5%. Then, during much of the 1980s, this number declined.

On the minus side, the Treasury has lost a number of offbeat sources of funds that used to total a lot of money (Figure 8–7). Sales of savings bonds have diminished; in fact, redemptions have outpaced sales since 1978. Also, until 1978 the dollar was weak, and foreign central banks were always buying dollars to prevent unwanted appreciation of their currencies and then

FIGURE 8–5
U.S. government budget balance as a percent of GNP

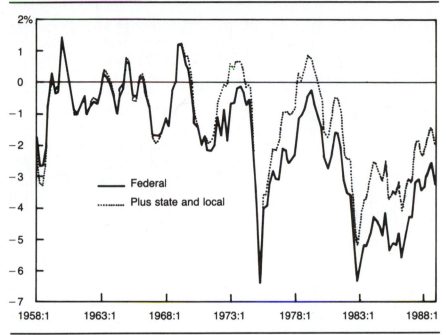

Source: Department of Commerce.

investing these dollars in Treasury bonds. This trend reversed as high interest rates in the U.S. and other factors strengthened the dollar. A third source of funds lost to the Treasury has been investments in Treasury issues by state and local governments. It used to be that, when interest rates declined to cyclical lows, a number of such muni issuers would find it attractive to pre-refund outstanding, high-coupon bonds by selling a new, lower-coupon issue. They would then invest, until the pre-refunded issue reached its refunding date, the proceeds of the new issue in specially tailored, nonnegotiable Treasury issues designed to prevent them from profiting from the potential arbitrage. This source of funds, which accounts in part for the $151.5 billion of Treasury debt that state and local governments held at the beginning of 1989 (Table 8–1), has, because of high interest rates, provided few new funds to the Treasury in recent years.

FIGURE 8–6
Holdings by foreigners of U.S. Treasury securities

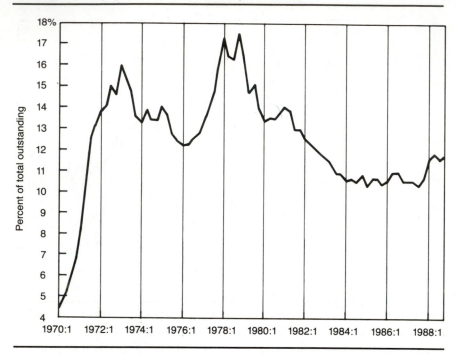

Source: Department of Commerce and Federal Reserve.

Offsetting these losses have been gains from other sources. Money funds, unheard of 15 years ago, today constitute a major source of demand in bill auctions.

Also the innovative zero-coupon securities created out of Treasury long bonds, first by Merrill Lynch and other dealers and then by the Treasury (STRIPs), have created new demand from individuals, especially those having nontaxable IRA and Keogh retirement accounts, for Treasuries, or at least bits and pieces of them.

Despite the fact that the Treasury has experienced no visible difficulty in selling its debt, people keep putting forth to Treasury officials their pet ideas on how the Treasury should borrow. The most conservative—in the sense that it has been done before—is that the Treasury should offer a big subscription

FIGURE 8–7
Treasury net borrowing from nonmarketable issues

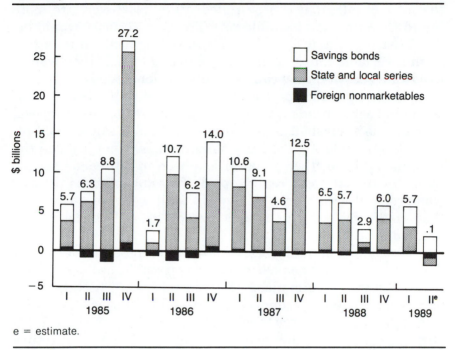

e = estimate.

Source: U.S. Treasury.

issue. The Treasury, which has not utilized the subscription technique since 1978 and has no intention of reviving it, has doubts about the technique, not the least of which is whether it is cost effective. As one Treasury official noted, "We have been able to raise the amount of money needed off the market. From time to time, we pay a concession of 3, 4, or 5 bp, but the market does not appear so overburdened that we should come and offer, say, a 50-bp premium to get off a big subscription issue. That is expensive. Also in doing such an offering, the Treasury would essentially be admitting that the market was too small to accommodate its financing at anything close to current market levels. I have seen no evidence that we are in that sort of environment yet."

It has also been proposed that the Treasury issue a variable-rate security. The Treasury has resisted this idea on several grounds. In its view, it already offers a variable-rate security in the form of bills that can be rolled. Bills, moreover, are more liquid than any new variable-rate Treasury security would be. The Treasury tries to appeal to all market segments. If investors want a variable-rate security, they can buy bills. If they want a fixed-rate security, they can buy notes or long bonds.

Another gimmick proposed to the Treasury has been that it sell gold-backed bonds. The Treasury's answer to that proposal is that it is equivalent to nothing more than a sale of gold attached to the sale of a Treasury obligation; why not just sell the gold outright? Another proposal has been to sell bonds backed by oil in the strategic reserve pool. Treasury officials dismiss this proposal with scorn, "They talk as if we were a company that could not get any money except by selling collateral-secured debt."

Treasury debt managers, who seek to fund the government debt as cheaply and nondisruptively as possible, see no need for what they view as gimmicks. One official said, "The U.S. Treasury is issuing the finest paper in the world in terms of liquidity and credit quality. Every theory I know indicates that the Treasury sells its debt to the investor at the lowest expected return and therefore *a priori* at the lowest expected cost to the issuer of any security in the world. Why should we clutter up this great market by throwing in gimmicks that no one will know how to price—by creating securities that will have limited marketability, at least at first, and for which buyers will therefore demand a higher return?"

Debt Management in the 1980s

The pattern of lengthening the debt, of regularizing debt issuance, and of rejecting new gimmicky securities that was set in the 1970s was continued with only the most minor of changes during the 1980s. "We believe," noted one Treasury official, "that we best serve the long-run interests of the taxpayer by coming to the market with regular, predictable, known amounts and maturities—by generating as little uncertainty as possible. In consequence, debt management has been boring as hell."

A few minor changes have been made. The 20-year bond, which was introduced to replace the 15-year bond, was, like its predecessor, eliminated. "Every time we looked at the yield curve," noted a Treasury official, "there was a hump at 20 years. Either people wanted the longest duration, 30 years, or they did not want to go much beyond 10 years. There were no natural investors for the 20-year bond, just as there were none for the 15-year bond, so we dropped it."

As we noted in our discussion of STRIPs in Chapter 2, Wall Street's TIGRs and related beasts did demonstrate to the Treasury that there was, at times, money to be made in stripping Treasuries. To preempt that profit, the Treasury made more efficient stripping of Treasuries, via the book-entry system, possible; and later, it also permitted traders to reconstitute Treasuries from various pieces previously stripped from Treasuries. Currently, all new issues of Treasury 10-year notes and 30-year bonds may be stripped into zeros.

One price the Treasury had to pay for permitting stripping was eliminating the call feature on new long bonds; to be stripped, new bonds had to have a definite maturity. On older issues, the call feature permitted the Treasury to call a 30-year bond during the last five years of its life. The value to the Treasury of this call was hazy at best, and the option did cost the Treasury something (investors don't grant options for free); so no tears were shed at the Treasury over its loss.

Also, in 1982, the Treasury, to make savings bonds more attractive to individuals, changed the fixed rate they had paid to a market-based variable rate. This made sense, since individuals who wanted a market rate of return had long since learned (1) to buy and roll Treasury bills if they had $10,000 or more to invest or (2) to put their money in a money fund if they had less to invest and wanted less bother.

Finally, the Treasury devised SLUGs, a special series in which state and local government bodies may invest. The origin of SLUGs was that changes in the tax code tightened interest-arbitrage penalties on muni bodies that borrowed at low muni rates money that they then invested at higher Treasury rates. Under the SLUG program, the Treasury calculates the maximum rate that it will pay a muni investor; for its part, the muni investor specifies to the Treasury the rate it is willing to accept. If the latter rate is lower or equals the former, the Treasury sells the muni body securities. Under the SLUG program, the Treasury has taken in about $152 billion of funds from various state and municipal entities (for flows, see Figure 8–7). This amount accounts for about half of the total holdings by state and municipal entities, who also buy marketable governments.

FEDERALLY SPONSORED AGENCIES ISSUING SECURITIES

In Chapter 2, we talked about financial intermediaries, which are institutions that act as conduits through which funds are channeled from consumers, firms, and other spending units with funds surpluses to spending units (consumers, firms, and government bodies) running funds deficits. Most financial intermediaries in the U.S. are private (albeit government regulated) institutions: commercial banks, savings and loan associations, credit unions, life insurance companies, and private pension funds, to name a few.

In addition to these private institutions, a large and growing number of government credit agencies also act as financial intermediaries. These agencies borrow funds which they lend to specific classes of borrowers. The reason for all this government competition to private intermediation is that Congress has periodically taken the position that for some groups of borrowers, the available supply of credit was too limited, too variable, or too expensive. In each instance, Congress's remedy was to set up a federal agency charged with providing a dependable supply of credit at the lowest cost possible to these disadvantaged borrowers. Some federal agencies are owned and directed by the federal government, and their debt obligations are backed by the full faith and credit of the U.S. government. Others are federally sponsored but privately owned. The obligations of federally sponsored agencies presumably have *de facto* backing from the federal government.

The largest government credit agencies specialize in providing mortgage money for housing and agriculture, two favored children of policymakers. In addition, there are agencies that provide credit to small business firms, students, communities financing development projects, and so forth.

Most federal agencies are supposed to set their lending rates so that they at least cover their borrowing costs and perhaps even earn a modest profit. Since each agency's function is to supply funds to borrowers at minimum cost, the rational approach would have been to have the agencies borrow from the cheapest possible source. Because its securities carry zero risk of default and are so liquid, the Treasury can always borrow at lower rates than any other issuer, municipalities excepted (because of the federal tax exemption). Thus, having the Treasury lend to the agencies funds that it had borrowed in the open market would have been the least-cost way to fund agency lending.

This approach, however, was not taken. Instead, until 1974 almost all agencies issued their own securities, each carrying some degree of backing from the federal government. The main reason for taking this approach was that, if the agencies had all borrowed from the Treasury, the Treasury's outstanding debt would have gone up commensurately. Today, it would be $371 billion greater than the $2.68 trillion figure quoted earlier in this chapter.

Such an increase in Treasury debt could have created problems for several reasons. First, Congress legislates a limit on Treasury borrowing. This limit has no perceptible impact on government spending because Congress always pauses—between passing spending bills—to raise it. Nevertheless, Congress has often been stubborn and slow about raising the debt limit, with the result that in practice it might have been difficult for the Treasury to borrow sufficient funds to meet *all* the agencies' needs. Also, there are voters who lose sleep over the size of the national debt. In this respect, it's important to note that agency and federal debts differ sharply with respect to both source and character. Most Treasury debt is the result of government deficits, a true national debt. In contrast, agency debt is incurred to lend, largely to creditworthy borrowers.

THE FEDERAL FINANCING BANK

As federal agencies proliferated, their borrowings from the public caused several problems. One had to do with calendar scheduling. Each year, federal agencies issue substantial quantities of new debt. Agency issues compete with each other and with Treasury issues for investors' funds, and an uneven flow of agency and Treasury issues to the market could result in rates being driven up one week and down the next. To avoid this, the Treasury schedules the timing and size of both its own and agency issues to ensure a reasonably smooth flow of federal issues to the market. In 1973, minor federal agencies made 75 separate offerings, so many that Treasury calendar scheduling of new issues was difficult. Another problem resulting from the proliferation of federal agencies was that the new small agencies constantly being created by Congress were not well known to investors; and because of their small size, their issues were less liquid than Treasury issues. Consequently, small agencies had to pay relatively high borrowing rates.

To deal with these problems, Congress set up in 1973 the *Federal Financing Bank* (FFB), a government institution supervised by the Secretary of the Treasury. The FFB buys up the debt issues of the smaller agencies, and its clientele currently includes about 20 separate agencies.

The FFB was supposed to obtain funds by issuing securities fully backed by the government in a fashion similar to the way the Treasury issues its securities. It tried this approach once with an offering of short-term bills. This issue was bid for by dealers and others at yields close to those prevailing on T bills, but it fell in price in the secondary market, which was discouraging to both dealers and the Treasury. Some dealers felt that, if the FFB had continued to issue its securities, they would eventually have been accepted by investors as equal to Treasury issues and would have sold at yields no higher than those on Treasury issues. The Treasury, however, doubted this; one reason was that FFB offerings would have been smaller than Treasury offerings and consequently less liquid. In any case, the FFB discontinued its public offerings and now borrows from the Treasury. Today, only the major federal agencies still issue new securities to the market.

As Figure 8–8 shows, the FFB's borrowings from the Treasury have risen from a zero base in 1974 to $142 billion in mid-1989, and the trend is steadily upward.

AGENCY SECURITIES

Among the agencies still issuing securities to the public, practices and types of securities issued vary considerably. One can, however, make a few generalizations. Each federal agency establishes a fiscal agent through which it offers its securities, all of which are negotiable. Agency issues are not sold directly to

FIGURE 8–8
Borrowings of the Federal Financing Bank from the U.S. Treasury

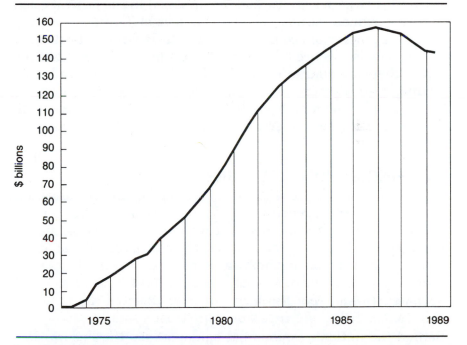

Source: *Federal Reserve Bulletin.*

investors by these fiscal agents. Instead they are sold through a syndicate of dealers, who distribute the agency's securities to investors and participate in making a secondary market for these securities.

Agency securities comprise short-term notes sold at a discount and interest-bearing notes and bonds. Agency bonds are frequently issued with the title *debenture*. Any bond is an interest-bearing certificate of debt. A *mortgage bond* is a bond secured by a lien on some specific piece of property. A debenture is a bond secured only by the general credit of the issuer.

Interest on agency securities and principal at maturity are usually payable at any branch of the issuing agency, at any Federal Reserve bank or branch, and at the Treasury. Agency bonds are typically not callable.

Like Treasury securities, agency securities are issued under the authority of an act of Congress. Therefore, unlike private offerings, they are exempt from registration with the SEC. Typically, agency issues are backed by collateral in the form of cash, U.S. government securities, and the debt obligations that the issuing agency has acquired through its lending activities. A few agency issues are backed by the full faith and credit of the U.S. Others are guaranteed by the Treasury or supported by the issuing agency's right to borrow funds from the Treasury up to some specified amount. Finally, there are agency securities with no direct or indirect federal backing.

HOUSING CREDIT AGENCIES

The major federal agencies still offering securities differ considerably in mission and method of operation, so we have organized our survey of them by function: first the mortgage-related agencies and then the farm credit agencies.

Federal Home Loan Banks

Behind the nation's commercial banks stands the Federal Reserve System, which regulates member banks, acts as a lender of last resort, and otherwise facilitates a smooth operation of the banking system. Behind the nation's S&Ls stands a somewhat similar institution, the *Federal Home Loan Bank* system. The FHLB, created in 1932, is composed of 12 regional banks and a central board in Washington.

S&Ls, savings banks, and insurance companies may all become members of the FHLB system; federally chartered S&Ls are required to do so. Currently, about 3,100 S&Ls belong to the FHLB system; these S&Ls hold almost all of S&L assets.

The Federal Home Loan Banks are owned by the private S&Ls that are members of the system, just as the 12 Federal Reserve Banks are owned by member banks. The private ownership, however, is only nominal since the FHLB, like the Fed, operates under federal charter and is charged by Congress with regulating member S&Ls and with formulating and carrying out certain aspects of government policy with respect to the S&L industry. Thus, the FHLB is in fact an arm of the federal government.

In addition to overseeing member S&Ls, the FHLB also lends to member S&Ls just as the Fed lends to banks. Here, however, the similarity ends. The Fed obtains money to lend to banks at the discount window by monetizing debt. The FHLB must borrow the money it lends to member S&Ls. Most of the money S&Ls lend comes from depositors. The FHLB lends to member S&Ls primarily to augment this source of funds. In a nutshell, the FHLB borrows money in the open market, then relends it to S&Ls, which in turn either reinvest it or, at times, use it to offset deposit outflows.

The purpose of this involved operation is to aid S&Ls with a temporary liquidity problem and to channel money into S&Ls when money is tight. Since the rate S&Ls must pay on FHLB loans is set high enough to cover the FHLB's borrowing costs, such loans are not cheap money for S&Ls.

The main security issued by the FHLB is consolidated *bonds,* "consolidated" referring to the fact that the bonds are the joint obligation of all 12 Federal Home Loan Banks. FHLB bonds have a maturity at issue of one year or more, pay interest semiannually, and are not callable. They are issued in book-entry form and are now sold in denominations of $10,000, $25,000, $100,000, and $1MM. The FHLB also issues discount notes to raise short-term money. These notes have a minimum denomination of $50,000 and maturities under one year.

FHLB securities are backed by qualified collateral in the form of secured advances to member S&Ls, government securities, insured mortgages, and so on. FHLB securities are *not* guaranteed by the U.S. government. However, they are the obligation of the FHLB system, which plays a key federal role in regulating and assisting the S&L industry. Consequently, it's inconceivable that the U.S. government would ever permit the FHLB to default on its securities.

Interest income from FHLB securities is subject to full federal taxes but is exempt from state and local taxation.

FSLIC and the Nation's S&Ls in Crisis

In the 1970s, the saving and loan (S&L) industry was a sleepy province of finance. An S&L was supposed to take deposits from consumers at regulated rates, make fixed-rate mortgage loans to home buyers, and earn a modest spread doing so. This worked fine until inflation and interest rates got out of hand, and money funds, paying high rates, began to drain consumer deposits out of banks and S&Ls. Finally, in 1980 the government lifted rate regulation and permitted banks and thrifts to pay market rates on deposits. However, whereas a bank could capture rising interest quickly on the asset side of its balance sheet, an S&L, saddled with old, fixed-rate mortgages, couldn't; consequently, many S&Ls lost yet more money.

In 1981, the Federal Home Loan Bank Board (FHLBB) allowed most thrifts to offer variable-rate mortgages so that their revenues would fluctuate in step with their cost of funds. In 1982, when 75% of the S&L industry was unprofitable, Congress allowed thrifts to branch out into nontraditional activities such as business loans, consumer loans, and real estate.

As the "S&L problem" came to public attention, FSLIC insurance of S&L deposits, up to $100,000 per deposit, became a big contributor to the problem. To a depositor, putting money in an S&L appeared—so long as he didn't breach the $100,000 mark—as safe as buying Treasuries: both investments had full government backing. Consequently, S&Ls around the country, including the shaky and the sick, found that, if they posted sexy rates, they were flooded with money from wire houses that brokered their CDs and from responses to their advertisements. Depositors cared naught about the financial condition of the institution to which they were giving their money; they just wanted the top rate available on an FSLIC-insured deposit.

With high-cost money rolling in, S&Ls ventured into ever-riskier, higher-yielding investments. It wasn't uncommon for a once-sleepy S&L with a balance sheet whose footings were 5 or 10MM to explode suddenly into a billion-dollar-plus institution that was financing a collection of speculative investments: huge GNMA portfolios repoed to the hilt (a bet on future interest rates), franchises, no-money-down real estate loans, junk bonds, and so on.

A number of entrepreneurial souls, not all Simon pure, saw the S&L game for precisely what it was: a chance to gamble with other people's money on attractive terms—heads I win, tails FSLIC loses. With odds like that, it made no sense to bet 100MM if one could bet a billion. Also, if traditional managers lacked sufficient imagination to see the possibilities, developers and other high-flyers who invaded the industry did, especially those who bought and bloated the balance sheets of little S&Ls in Florida, Texas, and California, where real estate speculation was rampant.

All this led to the peculiar phenomenon of a money-losing industry expanding by leaps and bounds, whereas economic law would have dictated that it contract. Using their considerable political clout, thrifts fought to preserve an illusion of solvency. They obtained from Congress and regulators the right to use accounting gimmicks and relaxed bookkeeping standards to hide losses and capital inadequacy. Many thrifts owed their solvency to special certificates, issued by regulators, that were counted as capital.

As early as 1985, it was evident that FSLIC, which dutifully tried to bail out obviously failed S&Ls, was bankrupt. In 1986, an audit by the Government Accounting Office (GAO) made that official. The spectre of things to come was clear. If FSLIC couldn't reorganize S&Ls operating at a loss, those institutions would continue to grow, their losses continue to mount.

In 1985, the GAO estimated that cleaning up the S&L industry would cost 16 to 22 billion. Congress balked at acting for two reasons. It wanted to try every gimmick possible rather than to spend taxpayer dollars. Equally or more important, House Speaker Wright and other congressmen saw it as their job—thanks to powerful S&L lobbying—to keep the regulators off the backs of S&Ls in their districts. In particular, Texans in government, a numerous and well-placed lot, wanted the regulators to give troubled S&Ls (those in Texas were among the worst) "time to solve their problems." Giving FSLIC additional funds would enable it to require more sick S&Ls to write off real estate loans in default and other sour investments, so many legislators fought successfully to see to it that FSLIC was grossly underfunded.

In the mid-1980s, the Bank Board saw disaster looming, but its efforts to clamp down on S&L abuses were frustrated by the Reagan administration, Congress, and the thrift industry. For its part, the administration, hell-bent on deregulation, denied the Bank Board money to boost its examination staff; apparently, it never dawned on the administration that it was nonsensical for it to treat S&Ls that had, thanks to FSLIC, the right to gamble with public funds the same way it treated airlines that, in setting business strategy, were betting their own money.

FICO

Finally, in 1986, FSLIC ran out of money. In response, Congress passed in 1987 legislation that enabled the FHLBB to set up the *Financing Corporation* (*FICO*). The sole purpose of FICO was to recapitalize FSLIC by making debt offerings and transferring to FSLIC the funds thus obtained. FICO was authorized to borrow 10.8 billion. Its debt is not government guaranteed, but a 3-billion contribution of reserves by the FHLBs was to be used to purchase zero-coupon debt instruments in amounts equal to FICO's outstanding debt. Payment of interest is to be made by regular and supplemental assessments on the nation's 3,100 federally insured thrifts. By July 1989, FICO had issued 3.9 billion of bonds and was expected to issue more once Congress had passed new thrift legislation.

FICO was far too little, far too late. In the fall of 1988, McKinsey, a management consultant, estimated that the liabilities of America's thrifts exceeded their earning assets by 39 billion in 1987 and by 59 billion in 1988; it also reckoned that, by the end of 1989, that figure would swell to $109 billion.

Refcorp

In 1989, the S&L problem was dumped into the lap of the Bush administration, which decided that the time had come to pay up taxpayer dollars to clean up the industry. Those dollars, Bush vowed, wouldn't be spent for nothing; a costly S&L debacle would "never again" occur. Supposedly, under the Bush plan, sick S&Ls would be wiped out before they could accumulate more deficits. However, as that plan worked its way through Congress, it appeared increasingly inadequate.

The Bush plan enacted by Congress assumed that T bill rates would fall to *4.4%*, that the economy wouldn't have a recession for the next *10 years*, and that S&L deposits would *grow* (to bring in more premium income to FSLIC) by 7% a year, whereas S&L deposits were in fact shrinking. Also, by requiring S&Ls to pay higher premiums and to hold more capital, the plan threatened healthy S&Ls with higher costs and constraints on growth. The plan's perhaps most costly shortcoming was that it provided only 35 billion through October 1990 to bail out failed S&Ls. That sounded like a lot, but it was less than the government spent on S&L bailouts in 1987. Also, the new money wouldn't go as far as old money did because, under the new get-tough approach, regulators, in merging sick S&Ls, couldn't continue to use liberal accounting rules, capital certificates, and other gimmicks that formerly permitted them to pare cash outlays.

In any case, the Bush plan called for creation of a new off-budget agency, the *Resolution Finance Corporation (Refcorp)*. Over three years, Refcorp would raise 50 billion by selling 30-year bonds backed by deeply discounted, zero-coupon, nonmarketable Treasuries purchased with thrift industry money. The funds raised would go into the Resolution Trust Corporation (RTC), which would take over and liquidate assets, valued at $400 billion, of failed thrifts. In doing so, Refcorp was to get powers to issue IOUs and loan guarantees—powers that enabled FSLIC in 1988 to issue 40 billion of notes without congressional permission. Industry observers, ranging from ultraconservative to ultraliberal, for once agree on something: Refcorp or maybe Refcorp II and III will rack up a lot more than 50 billion of debt before the S&L mess is cleaned up.

Federal National Mortgage Association

Most money market instruments are extremely liquid. The reason is not simply that these securities are stamped *negotiable,* but more important they have a broad and active secondary market. One of the major factors contributing to the existence of this secondary market is the homogeneity (one unit is just like another) of bills, bonds, and notes. Because mortgages lack homogeneity, a wide secondary market for mortgages never developed in the U.S. The lack of a secondary market for mortgages made these instruments illiquid, which in turn diminished the flow of funds into the mortgage market.

The *Federal National Mortgage Association (FNMA),* popularly known as "Fannie Mae," was set up in 1938 by Congress to create a secondary market in FHA mortgages (mortgages insured by the Federal Housing Administration). Initially, Fannie Mae was wholly government owned, and its funds came from the Treasury. Later in 1954, Fannie Mae was split into three separate divisions: secondary market operations, special assistance functions, and management and liquidating functions.

The secondary market division was supposed to attract money to the mortgage market by providing liquidity for government-insured mortgages. To do so, it bought and sold mortgages insured or guaranteed by the Federal Housing Administration, the Veterans Administration, and the Farm Home Administration. Until February 1977, institutions dealing as buyers or sellers in mortgages with Fannie Mae were required to buy small amounts of Fannie Mae stock, thereby permitting the secondary market division of Fannie Mae to be converted from government to private ownership.

In 1968, Congress completed its partition of Fannie Mae by putting its special assistance and management and liquidating functions into a new government-owned corporation, the *Government National Mortgage Association.* The remaining secondary market division of Fannie Mae, which retained the title Federal National Mortgage Association, was converted into a

privately owned corporation. The corporation's private ownership is, however, to some degree nominal since the government
retains broad powers to direct and regulate the operations of
Fannie Mae through the Secretary of Housing and Urban Development (HUD).

Currently, Fannie Mae's function is to buy government-
insured or guaranteed mortgages (also conventional mortgages
since 1970) when mortgage money is in short supply and to sell
them when the demand for mortgage money slacks off. It does
this through auctions at which it buys and sells some prean-
nounced total of mortgages. Fannie Mae and other agencies created to serve the same purpose have made significant progress
toward increasing the liquidity of mortgages and attracting into
mortgages funds that would otherwise have followed elsewhere.

To finance its mortgage purchases, Fannie Mae relies primarily on the sale of debentures and short-term discount notes.
The latter have maturities ranging from 30 to 360 days, and the
minimum purchase is $50,000. Fannie Mae debentures, which
are not callable, are issued in book-entry form. They pay interest semiannually, and are available in denominations starting
at $10,000 with $5,000 increments thereafter. Fannie Mae debentures are not backed by the federal government, but given
the association's role as a government policy tool and its government supervision, it seems unlikely that the government would
permit a default on Fannie Mae obligations.

Interest on Fannie Mae securities is subject to full federal,
state, and local taxation. The large volume of Fannie Mae securities outstanding makes for an excellent secondary market.

Government National Mortgage Association

The 1968 partition of the old Federal National Mortgage Association spawned yet another financial lady, "Ginnie Mae," more
formally known as the *Government National Mortgage Association (GNMA)*. Ginnie Mae, a wholly government-owned corporation within the Department of Housing and Urban Development, took over the special assistance and the management and
liquidating functions that had formerly been lodged in FNMA.
These functions involve activities that could not be profitably

carried out by a private firm. Ginnie Mae's mission is also to make real estate investment more attractive to institutional investors, which it has done by designing and issuing—partly in conjunction with private financial institutions—mortgage-backed securities, pass-throughs, for which an active secondary market has developed.

Under its special assistance function, Ginnie Mae provides financing for selected types of mortgages through mortgage purchases and commitments to purchase mortgages. Ginnie Mae finances its special assistance operations partly with funds obtained from the Treasury.

Under the pass-through approach, private mortgage lenders assemble pools of mortgages acquired through Ginnie Mae auctions or from other sources and then sell certificates backed by these mortgages to investors. These certificates are referred to as *pass-through securities* because payment of interest and principal on mortgages in the pool is passed on to the certificate holders after deduction of fees for servicing and guarantee. Pass-through certificates have stated maturities equal to those of the underlying mortgages. However, actual maturities tend to be much shorter because of prepayments; the average life on single-family mortgages was estimated to be approximately 12 years back in the mid-1970s and earlier when interest rates were lower and less volatile.[8] On pass-through securities, principal and interest are paid *monthly* to the investor. Because payments made monthly and because the amount passed through varies from month to month due to mortgage prepayment, pass-throughs are issued in registered form only. Pass-through certificates have a minimum denomination of $25,000. They carry Ginnie Mae's guarantee of timely payment of both principal and interest and are backed in addition by the full faith and credit of the U.S. government.

---

[8]Twelve years used to be the standard average life quoted. As interest rates rose—especially in the period 1979 to 1982—and mortgage money became prohibitively expensive or unattainable, home resales declined, and the average life of pass-throughs lengthened reflecting the concomitant decline in prepayments. Later, when interest rates fell dramatically, prepayments soared, and the notion that the 12-year average life was a reliable number was discredited.

Federal Home Loan Mortgage Corporation

The *Federal Home Loan Mortgage Corporation* (*FHLMC* or, more familiarly, *Freddie Mac*) was created in July 1970 through enactment of Title III of the Emergency Home Finance Act of 1970. The organization's purpose is to promote the development of a nationwide secondary market in conventional residential mortgages. To accomplish this, FHLMC buys residential mortgages and then resells them via the sale of mortgage-related instruments. FHLMC's operations are directed by the Federal Home Loan Bank system, which provided the new agency with its initial capital.

To some extent, the FHLMC duplicates the activities of Fannie Mae. But it has a special feature; it may purchase mortgages only from financial institutions that have their deposits or accounts insured by agencies of the federal government. The requirement that it deal with only regulated institutions (whereas Fannie Mae also buys mortgages from mortgage bankers) permits the FHLMC to cut documentation and paper requirements on mortgage purchases and thereby operate at lower cost. Unlike Fannie Mae, which has borrowed over $60 billion to finance its mortgage holdings, the FHLMC has pursued a course similar to that of Ginnie Mae—namely, selling its interest in the mortgages it purchases through mortgage-backed, pass-through securities.

Specifically the FHLMC sells two types of pass-through securities, *mortgage participation certificates* (*PCs*) and *guaranteed mortgage certificates* (*GMCs*). PCs resemble Ginnie Mae pass-throughs. Each PC represents an undivided interest in a pool of conventional residential mortgages underwritten and previously purchased by the FHLMC. Each month the certificate holder receives a prorated share of the principal and interest payments made on the underlying pool. The FHLMC guarantees timely payment of interest on PCs and the full return of principal to the investor. While PCs technically have a maturity at issue of 30 years, their average weighted life is assumed to be 12 years or less.[9]

---

[9]See previous footnote on p. 350.

Guaranteed mortgage certificates also represent an undivided interest in conventional residential mortgages underwritten and previously purchased by the FHLMC. These certificates pay interest semiannually and return principal once a year in guaranteed minimum amounts. The final payment date on GMCs is 30 years from the date of issue, but the expected average weighted life of these securities is around 10 years.[10] Certificate holders may require the FHLMC to repurchase certificates at par 15 to 25 years (the put date varies with the issue) after they are issued.

Both PCs and GMCs are issued in registered form. PCs are sold in denominations of $25,000, $100,000, $200,000, $500,000, $1MM, and $5MM, while GMCs are issued in amounts of $100,000, $500,000, and $1MM. Currently the FHLMC has approximately $19.8 billion of such securities outstanding.

In addition to selling pass-through securities, the FHLMC has also sold $2.2 billion of bonds guaranteed by Ginnie Mae and backed by FHA and VA mortgages.

Finally, in 1981, the FHLMC began issuing its own discount notes and debentures. FHLMC debentures are issued in book-entry form only; they have a minimum denomination of $10,000. FHLMC discount notes are offered with maturities of one year or less and a minimum face value of $25,000.

All securities issued by and through the FHLMC are subject to full state and federal taxation on income.

FARM CREDIT AGENCIES

The production and sale of agricultural commodities require large amounts of credit. So too does the acquisition by farmers of additional land and buildings. To ensure an adequate supply of credit to meet these needs, the government created over time the Farm Credit Administration. This administration, which operates as an independent agency of the U.S. government, oversees the Farm Credit System, which operates in all states

---

[10]See footnote on p. 350.

plus Puerto Rico. Under this system, the country is divided into 12 farm credit districts. In each, there is a Federal Land Bank, a Federal Intermediate Credit Bank, and a Bank for Cooperatives; each bank supplies specific types of credit to qualified borrowers in its district.

Since January 1979, the 36 banks plus a Central Bank for Cooperatives have obtained funds by issuing securities on a consolidated basis under the name of the Federal Farm Credit Bank. These consolidated discount notes and bonds are the secured joint obligations of the 37 Farm Credit Banks. Discount notes are issued with a minimum face value of $50,000 and have maturities ranging from 5 to 270 days; they provide the banks with interim financing between bond sales. Each month, the FFCB issues bonds with maturities of six and nine months. It also issues long-term bonds about eight times a year.

All bonds and notes issued by the Federal Farm Credit Bank must be secured by acceptable collateral in the form of cash, Treasury securities, and notes or other obligations of borrowers from these banks. Although FFCB securities are not guaranteed either directly or indirectly by the U.S. government, nevertheless, given the semiofficial status of the Federal Farm Credit Banks and the government's high sensitivity to farmers' needs, it is inconceivable that the government would permit an FFCB default.

The Farm Credit System in Crisis

During 1985, it became evident that the Farm Credit System was in deep crisis. Thanks to declining crop and farmland prices in the early 1980s, farmers who had gone on a borrowing binge during previous, more prosperous years were increasingly unable to repay loans to the System. In September 1985, the boards of the troubled Farm Credit System's 37 banks agreed to ask for a federal bailout to save the farmer-owned system from a rising tide of bad loans.

Over the next few years, the crisis at Farm Credit went from bad to worse. Outside auditors found the System did not itself know where it stood as it hadn't been following generally accepted accounting practices. Under its home-grown, but legal-for-it accounting practices, some banks had been accruing interest on loans that had been delinquent for three or four years.

While the Farm Credit System's losses mounted *and* the spreads at which Farm Credit System securities traded to Treasuries widened, Congress tried twice to solve the System's problems without putting up any money. First, Congress required strong System banks to share capital with weak System banks, a move some strong banks challenged in court. Then, in 1986 Congress allowed weaker System banks to stretch out the time they could take to write off bad loans—back to bad accounting practices. Between 1985 and December 1987, the System's losses mounted to 4.8 billion. At that point, Congress finally cleared a 4-billion bailout for the System.

The Farm Credit System Financial Assistance Corporation

On January 11, 1988, the *Financial Assistance Corporation* (FAC) was established pursuant to the Agricultural Credit Act of 1987—Congress's bailout bill. FAC was to provide capital to Farm Credit System institutions experiencing financial difficulty. To obtain funds, FAC was empowered to issue during 1988 up to 2.8 billion of 15-year, uncollateralized debt that would be guaranteed as to payment of principal and interest by the Treasury. During 1989, the ceiling on such debt issuance was to increase to 4 billion. Interest on FAC debt is to be paid by the Treasury for the first five years of each obligation's term, by the Treasury and the System during the second five years, and entirely by the System during the final five years.

By early 1989, FAC had issued over 3 billion of Treasury-backed bonds, and the System's problems, whether solved or not, seemed to have been forgotten. In 1989, everyone's attention was firmly focused on the 50- (or is it 100-) billion thrift crisis, which made a 4-billion bailout look like peanuts.

Banks for Cooperatives

The 12 district *Banks for Cooperatives,* organized under the Farm Credit Act of 1933, make seasonal and term loans to cooperatives owned by farmers, purchase farm supplies, provide business services to farmers, and market farm output. These loans may provide working capital or finance investments in buildings and equipment. The Central Bank for Cooperatives participates in large loans made by individual district banks. Initially the Banks for Cooperatives were owned by the U.S. government. Since 1955, however, government capital has been replaced by private capital, and ownership is now private.

Interest income from debentures issued by the Banks for Cooperatives is subject to full federal taxation but is specifically exempt from state and local income taxes.

Federal Land Banks

The 12 *Federal Land Banks* were organized under the Federal Farm Loan Act of 1916. These banks extend first mortgage loans on farm properties and make other loans through local Federal Land Bank (FLB) associations. Mortgage loans must be made on the basis of appraisal reports and may not exceed 65% of the appraised value of the mortgaged property. Although the Federal Land Banks were set up under government auspices, all government capital in these banks has been replaced by private capital, and they are now owned by the FLB associations, which in turn are owned by the farmers who have obtained FLB loans through these associations.

The Federal Land Banks obtain funds to lend out primarily by issuing Consolidated Federal Farm Loan bonds and by occasional short-term borrowings between bond issues. Since 1963, all FLB bond issues have been noncallable. These securities range in maturity from a few years to 15 years. Most have an original maturity of longer than one year. Interest on FLB bonds is payable semiannually. The smallest denominations available are $1,000, $5,000, and $10,000.

S&Ls are placed in an uncomfortable position whenever interest rates rise because the nature of their business is to borrow short and lend long. Federal Land Banks are in a somewhat similar situation since maturities on the loans they extend tend to be longer than the original maturities of the bonds they issue. To avoid the danger inherent in this position, Federal Land Banks now write only *variable-rate* mortgages. This approach enables them to keep loan income in line with borrowing costs whether interest rates rise or fall.

FLB bonds must be backed with collateral in the form of cash, Treasury securities, or notes secured by first mortgages on farm properties. Federal Land Banks are examined at least annually by the Farm Credit Administration. Their securities are not guaranteed either directly or indirectly by the U.S. government. However, their semiofficial status makes it unlikely that the government would ever permit default on their securities.

Income from FLB bonds is subject to full federal taxation but is exempt from state and local taxation.

Federal Intermediate Credit Banks

The 12 *Federal Intermediate Credit Banks (FICB)* were organized under the Agricultural Credit Act of 1923. Their job is to help provide short-term financing for the seasonal production and marketing of crops and livestock and for other farm-related credit purposes. These banks do not lend directly to farmers. Instead they make loans to and discount agricultural and livestock paper for various financial institutions that lend to farmers.[11] These institutions include commercial banks, production credit associations organized under the Farm Credit Act of 1933, agricultural credit corporations, and incorporated livestock loan companies. Originally, FICBs were government owned, but today their ownership is wholly private.

FEDERAL AGENCY SECURITIES

Federal agency securities have been around in significant volume for only two decades, but during that time, the outstanding volume of them has grown rapidly (Figure 8–9). In early 1989, marketable Treasury issues equaled $1.82 trillion, while agency securities (excluding pass-throughs) totaled approximately $0.34 trillion.

---

[11]*Discounting agricultural paper* means buying up farmers' loan notes at a discount.

FIGURE 8–9
Outstanding volume of selected federal agency securities*

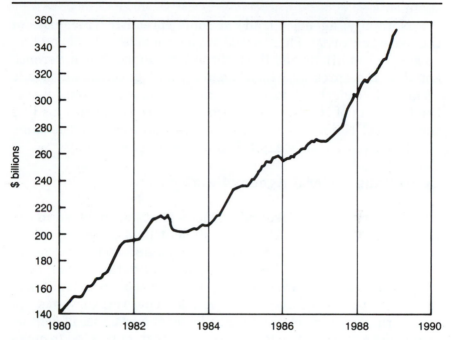

*Issuers covered the Federal Home Loan Banks, the Federal Home Loan Mortgage Corporation, the Government National Mortgage Association, the Federal National Mortgage Association, the Federal Land Banks, the Federal Intermediate Credit Banks, and the Banks for Cooperatives. (Excludes pass-through securities; these instruments are not debts of the agencies through which they are marketed.)

Source: *Federal Reserve Bulletin.*

Attraction to Investors

Federal agency securities are attractive for several reasons. Most agency issues are backed either *de jure* or *de facto* by the federal government, so the credit risk attached to them is zero or negligible. Also, many agency issues offer the tax advantage that interest income on them, like interest income on governments, is exempt from state and local taxation.

A third advantage of many agency issues is liquidity. Agency issues are smaller than Treasury issues so they do not have the same liquidity Treasury issues do, but their liquidity compares favorably with that of many other money market instruments.

Normally, agencies trade at some spread to Treasuries of the same maturity. This spread varies considerably depending on supply conditions and the tightness of money. The difference between the rates at which agencies and governments trade apparently reflects almost solely differences in the liquidity of the two sorts of instruments since capital-rich institutions like the Federal Home Loan Banks must, to borrow, pay the same rates that more poorly capitalized federal agencies pay.

Controlling Federal Agency Debt

There are two sorts of federal agencies that get involved in the credit market: those such as the student loan program, which provide government guarantees of loans, and sponsored agencies such as Fannie Mae, which, although they have been largely "privatized," are regarded by most people who lend them money as the government in disguise. The Treasury has approval rights but no explicit control over the issuance of debt by sponsored agencies. The Reagan administration wanted to make such agencies as close to private as possible. In its view, having sponsored agencies lend, for example, to the housing market makes it appear as if the private sector is doing the job whereas in fact the government really is.

To make the sponsored agencies truly private, the government would have to cut them off from all government ties: no more government borrowing lines, no more government oversight, no more government assistance, implicit or explicit. The government is unlikely to make such dramatic changes because it would meet determined opposition from both the agencies and the sectors they serve. The agencies do not want to be subject to competitive market forces, and the sectors they serve think the current system lowers their borrowing costs.

The Treasury wants to cut back on agency borrowing to pare the government deficit and the amount of government debt offered in the market. Treasury officials also argue that off-budget expenditures and guarantees distort the federal budget, an important function of which is to act as an allocation index for resources used by government.

Congress sees things differently. For congressmen, making sharp distinctions among direct government expenditures, agency loans, and agency guarantees is hard; they think of guarantees in particular as the government just giving a little aid. The unsurprising outcome is that guarantee programs have grown by leaps and bounds.

THE NEXT CHAPTER

In this chapter, we have focused on major issuers of securities traded in the money market. In the next chapter, we turn to the most powerful, and at times most inscrutable, institution in the money market, our central bank—the Federal Reserve. It is current Fed policy, carried out principally on the Open Market Desk of the Federal Reserve Bank of New York, that determines whether interest heads up or down, whether the yield curve has a positive slope or inverts. Naturally, the Fed is secretive about what it's up to, so a tea-leaf-reading industry of Fed watchers has sprung up on the Street. Chapter 9 describes, among other things, just what such watchers watch.

CHAPTER 9

THE MOST WATCHED PLAYER: THE FED*

The Federal Reserve System, the nation's central bank, was established by act of Congress in 1913. The Federal Reserve Act divided the country into 12 districts and provided for the creation within each of a *district Federal Reserve Bank*. Responsibility for coordinating the activities of the district banks lies with the Federal Reserve's *Board of Governors* in Washington, D.C. The board has seven members appointed by the President and confirmed by the Senate.

The main tools available to the Fed for implementing policy are open market operations, reserve requirements, and the discount rate. On paper, authority for policymaking at the Fed is widely diffused throughout the system. In practice, however, this authority has gradually been centered in the *Federal Open Market Committee (FOMC)*, which was established to oversee the Fed's open market operations. Members of the FOMC include all seven governors of the system, the president of the NY Fed, and the presidents of 4 of the other 11 district banks; the latter serve on a rotating basis. Every member of the FOMC has one vote, but it has become tradition that the chairman of the Board of Governors plays a decisive role in formulating policy and acts as chief spokesman for the system, which is why his position is viewed as one of high power and importance.

---

*The author would like to thank Louis Crandall for his extensive collaboration in the revision of this chapter. Mr. Crandall, a professional Fed watcher and resident economist for R. H. Wrightson & Associates, Inc., wrote, in particular, the sections covering the monetarist experiment and developments in Fed policymaking during the 1980s.

In establishing policy, the Fed enjoys considerable independence on paper from both Congress and the executive branch. Members of the Board of Governors are appointed to 14-year terms so that a president has only limited control over who serves on the Board during his term of office. The chairman of the Board, who is designated as such by the president, serves in that capacity for only four years, but his term is not coincident with that of the president, so an incoming president may have to wait until well into his first term to appoint a new chairman.

Congress, like the president, has no lever by which it can directly influence Fed policy or the way it is implemented. In creating the Fed, Congress endowed this institution with wide powers and granted it considerable leeway to exercise discretion and judgment. Having said that, one must hasten to add that the autonomy enjoyed by the Fed is less in reality than in appearance. Presidents who are concerned that the Fed is forcing interest rates too high (presidents *never* seem to be concerned over interest being too low) attack the Fed subtly and not so subtly from the White House. Also, the Fed is aware that Congress, should it become too distressed over high interest rates, might strip away the Fed's autonomy.

The perception that its independence is limited can and has influenced Fed policy. In particular, during times when the Fed was tightening and it appeared that interest rates might reach unacceptable levels, the Fed, more than once in the past, attempted to force a contraction in bank lending while simultaneously preventing interest rates from rising to market-clearing levels. During one such period, 1977, a banker commented. "It is not always politically feasible for the Fed, when it wants to curtail bank lending, to allow interest rates to go where they must to do so. The Fed would never admit this, but they know they are a creature of Congress, and Congress would never let the prime go to 15%—one way or another it would remove in one fell swoop the so-called independence of the Fed." So much for predictions. In the grand monetarist experiment, begun in October 1979, the Fed unhinged interest rates from its control, and the prime soared over 20%. Congress did not "react in one fell swoop" to limit the independence of the Fed, but by 1982, it was tiring of historically high interest and threatening to mandate a change in the focus of Fed policy from controlling money supply back to pegging interest rates. Politicalization of the prime is not unique to the U.S.; it has occurred in Britain and elsewhere as well.

IMPLEMENTING MONETARY POLICY

The primary policy tool available to the Fed is open market operations, the ability to create bank reserves in any desired quantity by monetizing some portion of the national debt.[1] The Fed could in theory monetize anything—scrap metal to soybeans—but it has stuck largely to Treasury IOUs because there has never been any shortage of them; also, they are highly liquid so the Fed can sell them with as much ease as it buys them. In formulating policy, the first question the Fed faces is what macroeconomic *targets* to pursue. There are various possibilities: full employment, price stability, or a "correct" exchange value for the dollar. The achievement of *all* of these targets is desirable. However, since the Fed has only *one* powerful string to its bow—the ability to control bank reserves and thereby money creation by the private banking system—it is often forced to make hard choices between targets, to choose for example to pursue policies that would promote price stability but might increase unemployment.

Once the Fed has chosen its policy targets, it faces a second difficult question: What policies should it use to achieve these targets? If it wants to pursue a tight money policy to curb inflation, does that mean it should force up interest rates, strictly control the growth of the money supply (if so, which money supply), or what?

Not surprisingly, the Fed's answers to the questions of what targets it should pursue and of how it should do so changes considerably over time. One reason is that external conditions—

---

[1]See Chapter 2 for an explanation of debt monetization and a primer on how the Fed creates and destroys bank reserves.

the structure of financial markets, the state of the domestic and world economies—are in constant flux. A second reason is that central banking is an art form that's not fully understood, and the Fed's behavior at any time is therefore partly a function of how far it has progressed along its learning curve.

Before we turn to monetary policy in the last few years, we need to look at the mechanics of and problems in implementing such policy: open market operations and the functions of the discount window.

The Fed's ultimate policy goals today are what they have always been: price stability, high employment, balance-of-payments equilibrium, and a stable dollar. However, as economic conditions shift, so too does the focus of Fed policy. That was demonstrated by the jolt the Fed gave to the capital markets in early 1978 when it tightened, unexpectedly in the face of a sluggish economy, to defend the exchange value of the dollar. It was again demonstrated with far greater vigor when, in October 1979, the Fed switched to monetarism, pure and simple, in a last-ditch effort to wring out of the economy a high and obdurate rate of inflation. By late 1982, the Fed appeared to have taken the pragmatic decision to declare that the inflation battle had been won for the moment and to focus first on stimulating a severely depressed economy, later on sustaining a record-long expansion. Today, the Fed remains, however, sensitive to the danger of renewed inflation as indicated by its tightening in 1988 to 1989. Its mild easing in the spring of 1989 indicated that its current style is fine-tuning; controlling the economy's growth and allowing for an occasional *soft landing*.

Whatever its ultimate macroeconomic goals may be, the Fed currently states its immediate policy objectives in terms of desired rates of growth over several months for the monetary aggregates M2 and M3, a desired range for the Fed funds rate, and, for good measure, a figure for "domestic nonfinancial debt" outstanding (Table 9–1).[2]

---

[2]For the Fed's debt measures, see Table 2–4, p. 29.

TABLE 9–1
The Fed's changing definitions of money supply

Prior to February 1980

M1:   Currency in circulation plus demand deposits.

M2:   M1 plus small-denomination savings and time deposits at commercial banks.

M3:   M2 plus deposits at nonbank savings institutions.

M4:   M2 plus large-denomination CDs.

M5:   M3 plus large-denomination CDs.

February 1980

M1A: Currency in circulation plus demand deposits.

M1B: M1A plus other checkable deposits, including NOW accounts.

M2:   M1B plus overnight repos and money market funds and savings and small (less than $100,000) time deposits.

M3:   M2 plus large time deposits and term repos.

L: M3 plus other liquid assets.

January 1982

M1:   Currency in circulation plus demand deposits plus other checkable deposits, including NOW accounts.

M2:   M1 plus savings and small (less than $100,000) time deposits at all depository institutions plus balances at money funds (excluding institutions-only funds) plus overnight repos at banks plus overnight Euros held by nonbank U.S. depositors in the Caribbean branches of U.S. banks.

M3:   M2 plus large (over $100,000) time deposits at all depository institutions plus term repos at banks and S&Ls plus balances at institutions-only money funds.

L: M3 plus other liquid assets such as term Eurodollars held by nonbank U.S. residents, bankers' acceptances, commercial paper, Treasury bills and other liquid governments, and U.S. savings bonds.

December 1982

The Fed included the new money market deposit accounts (MMDAs) that depository institutions were permitted to offer on December 14, 1982, in M2.

May 1989

See Table 2–4, p. 29.

The FOMC Directive

Eight times a year, the FOMC meets to review economic conditions, its macro goals, and the guidelines it has set with respect to open market operations for achieving these goals. At the end of the meeting, it issues a directive to the manager of the system's open market account in New York. The Fed's *summary* of the directive it reached at its February 7–8, 1989, meeting read as follows:

Record of Policy Actions of the Federal Open Market Committee

At its meeting on February 7–8, 1989, the Committee established ranges of growth for the year of 3 to 7 percent for M2 and 3½ to 7½ percent for M3; no range was set for M1. A monitoring range for growth of total domestic nonfinancial debt was set at 6½ to 10½ percent. In carrying out policy, the Committee indicated that it would continue to evaluate money growth in light of the behavior of other indicators, including inflationary pressures, the strength of the business expansion, and developments in domestic financial and foreign exchange markets.

With regard to the implementation of policy for the period immediately ahead, the Committee adopted a directive that called for maintaining the current degree of pressure on reserve conditions and for remaining alert to potential developments that might require some firming during the intermeeting period. Somewhat greater reserve restraint would be acceptable, or slightly lesser reserve restraint might be acceptable, over the intermeeting period, depending on indications of inflationary pressures, the strength of the business expansion, the behavior of the monetary aggregates, and developments in foreign exchange and domestic financial markets. The reserve conditions contemplated by the Committee were expected to be consistent with growth of M2 and M3 at annual rates of around 2 percent and 3½ percent respectively over the three-month period from December to March. It was understood that operations would continue to be conducted with some flexibility in light of the persisting uncertainty in the relationship between the demand for borrowed reserves and the federal funds rate. The intermeeting range for the federal funds rate, which provides one mechanism for initiating consultation of the Committee when its boundaries are persistently exceeded, was left unchanged at 7 to 11 percent.[3]

The first thing to note about this directive is that target rates of growth are stated not for one monetary aggregate, but

---

[3]*Federal Reserve Bulletin,* May 1989.

TABLE 9–2
Growth of money and debt (percentage changes)*

	M1	M2	M3	Debt of Domestic Nonfinancial Sectors
Fourth quarter to fourth quarter				
1979	7.7	8.2	10.4	12.3
1980	7.4	9.0	9.6	9.6
1981	5.2 (2.5)†	9.3	12.3	10.0
1982	8.7	9.1	9.9	9.0
1983	10.2	12.1	9.8	11.3
1984	5.3	7.7	10.5	14.2
1985	12.0 (13.0)‡	8.9	7.7	13.2
1986	15.6	9.3	9.1	13.3
1987	6.4	4.2	5.7	9.8
1988	4.3	5.3	6.2	8.7

*M1, M2, and M3 incorporate effects of benchmark and seasonal adjustment revisions made in February 1989.
†M1 figure in parentheses is adjusted for shifts to NOW accounts in 1981.
‡M1 figure in parentheses is the annualized growth rate from the second to the fourth quarter of 1985.

Source: 1989 Humphrey-Hawkins report to Congress.

for several. Also, the target rates of growth for the aggregates are stated in terms of *bands*. One reason, is that, as economic conditions change, the public responds by altering the form in which it chooses to maintain its liquidity, and this in turn may distort the relative growth rates of different measures of money supply (Table 9–2). The Fed also states its target rate for Fed funds in terms of a *wide* band.

A second thing to note about the Fed's current directives is that its target bands are so wide and its objectives so hedged that a directive commits the Fed *in print* to do a lot in general— to control money supply growth and control interest rates with due regard to business conditions, inflation, the foreign-exchange market, and so on—but to do nothing specific. The reason why the Fed uses so many words to say so little are discussed at the end of this chapter.

Day-to-Day Operations of the Open Market Desk

As noted, the FOMC gives the account manager in New York several sorts of directives: target ranges for monetary growth, a target range for Fed funds, and so on.[4] As noted later, all evidence suggests that, at least in mid-1989, the constraint that counted was to keep the Fed funds rate within a narrow target range.

Having picked its primary operating target, the desk, with the aid of staff at the Board in Washington and at the NY Fed, estimates what reserves depository institutions will need to support its principal target. The desk then adds to this figure an estimate of the excess reserves that banks will hold and deducts from it an estimate of what appropriate or currently *targeted* borrowings from the discount window will be. The *net* of these figures is the amount of reserves that the desk seeks to supply on average over the week through its open market operations (Table 9–3).

The desk's task sounds straightforward, but in practice it's tricky to carry out. First, the numbers on which its reserves target is based are estimates, which may prove incorrect, of what excess reserves and borrowings at the discount window will be. Second, the quantity of reserves actually available on any day to depository institutions is influenced not only by actions taken on the desk, but by unpredictable changes in Treasury balances, float, currency in circulation, and other *operating factors* that together can easily total several billion.

Treasury Balances

Because of tax collections and securities sales, the Treasury holds huge and highly variable deposit balances. It used to keep these balances primarily in commercial banks in what are called *Treasury tax and loan accounts*. When it did so, the Treasury as it needed to make disbursements, would transfer funds

---

[4]People at the Fed distinguish between quarterly *targets* and *tolerance ranges* that are permissible within any month; the latter are wider because the shorter the period, the more difficult it is to tightly control the rate of monetary growth.

TABLE 9–3
Calculating the desk's reserve target

Reserves needed to support deposits consistent with target
+ Appropriate borrowings at the discount window
− Estimated excess reserves
= Reserve target to be supplied by the desk

from its TT&L accounts into its account at the Fed and write checks against that.

Then in 1974, the Treasury adopted a new policy: It began to hold most of its deposits at the Fed. Its primary reason for doing so was to raise its revenues. By depositing huge sums in its account at the Fed (which drained bank reserves, see Table 9–4), the Treasury forced the Fed to expand its portfolio via additional open market purchases, and the result was that the Fed earned more profit. All Fed profits above a small amount are paid to the Treasury. So by holding its balances at the Fed, the Treasury turned them in effect into interest-bearing deposits.

After the Treasury began holding the bulk of its funds at the Fed, movements of funds into and out of its account there became both huge and difficult to predict. The sheer size of the shifts in Treasury balances created operational problems for the

TABLE 9–4
When the Treasury transfers funds from an account at a commercial bank to its account at the Fed, this decreases bank reserves

The Treasury		Citibank	
	Demand deposits at Citibank −10MM	Reserves −10MM	Treasury tax and loan account −10MM
	Deposits at the Fed +10MM		

The Fed	
	Reserves, Citibank −10MM
	U.S. Treasury deposits +10MM

Fed, which had a hard time offsetting smoothly these flows through normal open market operations. To alleviate this problem, Congress—prodded by the Fed—acted to permit banks beginning in 1978 to pay the Treasury interest on demand balances held with them. For its part, the Treasury started paying banks for services which banks had previously provided free to it in exchange for non–interest-bearing deposits.

Float

Whenever a check is cleared through the Fed, the Fed first credits the reserve account of the bank at which the check is deposited by the amount of the check and then debits the reserve account of the bank against which the check is drawn by a like amount. Sometimes, the reserve credit is made before the reserve debit, which results in a temporary and artificial increase in reserves. This increase is referred to as *float*. Since the size of float can be affected by such factors as the weather (when planes can't fly, movement of checks and reserve debiting are slowed), float has been and remains a difficult variable to estimate.

Currency in Circulation

Whenever the public needs more currency during a peak spending season, such as Christmas or vacation time, it will withdraw extra currency from the banks. The latter get additional currency by buying it from their Federal Reserve Banks. When the Fed ships currency to the banks, it charges their reserve accounts, which in turn reduces bank reserves. Later, seasonal inflows of currency into the banks have the effect of increasing bank reserves. Thus, a third operating factor that affects bank reserves is seasonal variations in the public's demand for currency.

Intervention in the Foreign Exchange Market

A fourth factor that has, at times, a tricky-to-unravel impact on bank reserves is intervention by the U.S. and foreign central banks to influence the exchange value of the dollar. From the desk's perspective, there is no difference between (1) reserves created (or destroyed) via intervention and (2) reserves created (or destroyed) by a rise (or fall) in float. Both factors are folded into the desk's morning estimate of the imbalance in the reserves market and would routinely be offset by the desk through open market operations. Thus, the distinction that some economists draw between sterilized and unsterilized foreign-exchange intervention is fallacious.

Adding and Draining

By comparing its estimate of reserves available to depository institutions with its reserve target, the desk determines each day what amount of reserves it needs to inject or drain from the system. To add reserves, the Fed either buys securities *or* does repos with dealers in government securities. To drain reserves, it either sells securities *or* does reverses with the dealers. As Table 9–5 shows, when the Fed does a repo with a bank dealer, this adds to bank reserves just as an outright purchase of bills would; a repo done with a nonbank dealer would have the same effect on bank reserves. Reverses done by the Fed are repos in reverse gear, they drain reserves.

The securities the Fed buys vary from day to day depending partly on availability. Bills and notes can usually be easily bought in size, and the Fed holds a large proportion of its portfolio in such securities (Table 9–6). Much of the rest is in bonds; which, due to changes in Treasury debt management policy, represent a growing portion of the Treasury's outstanding debt.

The Fed also used to buy federal agency securities, in part because it was directed to do so by Congress in 1971 to help support the market for these securities. However, the agency market matured, and since the early 1980s, the Fed has bought

TABLE 9–5

The Fed adds to bank reserves by doing a repo with a bank dealer

The Fed		Chase Bank	
Bills bought under repurchase agreement +10MM	Reserves, Chase Bank +10MM	Reserves +10MM	Securities sold under agreement to repurchase +10MM

TABLE 9–6
The Federal Reserve's portfolio, May 3, 1989
($ billions)

Loans	2,279
Held under repurchase agreements	
Federal agency obligations—	
Bought outright*	6,654
Held under repurchase agreements	4,446
U.S. government securities:	
Bought outright—Bills	110,002
Notes	92,497
Bonds	30,314
Total bought outright	232,813
Held under repurchase agreements	8,047
Total U.S. government securities	240,860
Total loans and securities	254,239

*These are maturing agencies that the Fed acquired when it was still doing outright purchases of agencies.

Source: *Federal Reserve Board.*

no agencies outright. It does, however, still do repos against agencies (Table 9–6).

The Fed used to buy BAs as part of its program to encourage the growth of the domestic BA market (Chapter 21). However, now that the market has matured, the Fed no longer purchases BAs for its own portfolio.

The Fed sometimes buys governments for same-day settlement; more typically, however, it buys for regular or skip-day settlement because, when it buys on those terms, it gets better offerings from the dealers.[5]

When the Fed wants to reduce reserves by selling securities, it sells securities of short maturity. Said someone on the open market desk, "I do not remember a time in the last 20 years that we have sold coupon issues longer than two years. The market would be shocked and bewildered if we did so; it is taken

---

[5]A skip-day trade is settled two business days after the trade is made. A cash trade is settled on the day it is made.

as a given fact that we do not, so—to do so—we would have to educate the market."

In carrying out open market operations, the open market desk constantly has two objectives in mind: (1) the need to offset short-term fluctuations in reserves due to changes in float and other variables, and (2) the need to gradually and secularly increase bank reserves so that the money supply and bank credit can expand—within the bands set by the FOMC—in step with economic activity and national output. In making day-to-day short-term adjustments in reserves, the desk relies primarily on repos and reverses, which it does against governments and agencies (Table 9–7). Permanent injections of reserves are done through purchases of bills, notes, and bonds.

The line between Fed actions that are a reaction to short-term fluctuations in reserves and those designed to add permanent reserves is difficult to draw because the two often mesh. Also, because of uncertainty with respect to reserve availability, the Fed is often forced to switch gears. Here's a scenario of how things on the desk might go during reserve week: "Our research department does projections of available reserves, and some are done in Washington at the Board. We compare notes on these projections during our morning conference call with the Board. Mostly, we focus on our projections for the current week, but to give perspective to any action we might want to take, we give projections for the next several weeks. Then, we build up a program for the day based on what we think the need is and on the information flowing in from the market.

"Say it is Thursday, and we figure we need $59.4 billion of reserves on average over the week.[6] We think excess reserves will run $1 billion, and the FOMC directive takes $500MM to be an appropriate level of borrowed reserves. Then we have a reserve target of $60.4 billion of which $500MM is expected to

---

[6]As explained in Chapter 12, settlement by the banks is based on their average reserve balances over a two-week settlement period. So the Fed's concern is with the average reserve balances available daily to the banks over the settlement period. Which banks get or lose reserves as a result of Fed open market operations is of no concern to the Fed because banks with surpluses sell funds to banks with reserve deficits in the Fed funds market.

come from borrowings. Say our projections tell us that—unanticipated changes in Treasury balances, float, and currency in circulation aside—there would be $58 billion of nonborrowed reserves in the system if we took no action. That would leave us with $1.9 billion of nonborrowed reserves to add for that week on average.

"We would proceed to add those reserves; and if all went well—the banks did end up with $600MM of excess reserves and so on—that would result in the level of reserves—borrowed and nonborrowed—being just about consistent with the level the committee wanted."

One problem the Fed faces in hitting its reserve target is that the distribution of reserves within a settlement period can be highly skewed, with a lot of reserves being available early or late in the period. Because most banks are unwilling to run big reserve deficits or surpluses on a day-to-day basis, this creates artificial tightness or ease, which the Fed feels compelled to offset and can do only with difficulty. Said one person at the Fed, "A major and not widely recognized problem is the distribution of reserves within the settlement period. If early in the period there is a shortage of reserves, even if we pump in reserves, the market may still be tighter than we like. And by pumping in all those reserves, we may be creating a problem because we are putting in more reserves than we can take out at the end of the period. The market is often incapable of handling a large amount—either because on the repo side they lack collateral or because on the reverse side we have exhausted the supply of banks that want to do reverses.

"Banks who do reverses with us are not as welcome at the discount window as they would be if they did not. So banks are reluctant to do reverses because they fear the money market might tighten and they might have to come into the discount window. The rationale for this policy is that a bank should not borrow from us money that they have in fact lent us. The banks are discouraged from doing reverses and borrowing at the discount window even when they would be taking a loss on the *net* transaction, which at times they would be."

Another difficulty the Fed may experience in trying to hit its target is that it may be forced at times to engage in large

TABLE 9–7
Federal Reserve open market transactions* ($ millions)

Type of Transaction	1986	1987	1988	Aug.	Sept.	Oct.	Nov.	Dec.	Jan.	Feb.
						1988			1989	
U.S. Treasury Securities										
Outright transactions (*excluding matched transactions*)										
Treasury bills										
1. Gross purchases	22,604	18,983	8,223	0	1,280	375	3,599	1,125	0	0
2. Gross sales	2,502	6,051	587	0	0	0	0	0	154	3,688
3. Exchange	0	0	0	0	0	0	0	0	0	0
4. Redemptions	1,000	9,029	2,200	0	0	0	0	0	600	1,600
Others within 1 year										
5. Gross purchases	190	3,659	2,176	0	0	0	0	1,084	0	0
6. Gross sales	0	300	0	0	0	0	0	0	0	0
7. Maturity shift	18,674	21,504	23,854	3,932	1,368	1,669	5,264	1,750	620	5,418
8. Exchange	−20,180	−20,388	−24,588	−4,296	−1,646	−916	−2,391	−1,703	−2,703	−2,308
9. Redemptions	0	70	0	0	0	0	0	0	0	0
1 to 5 years										
10. Gross purchases	893	10,231	5,485	0	0	0	0	1,824	0	0
11. Gross sales	0	452	800	0	0	0	0	0	3	225
12. Maturity shift	−17,058	−17,975	−17,720	−1,821	−1,368	−1,544	−3,088	−1,750	−541	−5,319
13. Exchange	16,985	18,938	22,515	3,971	1,646	639	2,091	1,703	2,492	2,008
5 to 10 years										
14. Gross purchases	236	2,441	1,579	0	0	0	0	562	0	0
15. Gross sales	0	0	175	0	0	0	0	0	20ʳ	0
16. Maturity shift	−1,620	−3,529	−5,946	−2,111	0	−125	−2,145	0	−79	−100
17. Exchange	2,050	950	1,797	325	0	276	300	0	212	200

Over 10 years										
18. Gross purchases	158	1,858	1,398	0	0	0	0	432	0	0
19. Gross sales	0	0	0	0	0	0	0	0	0	0
20. Maturity shift	0	0	−188	0	0	0	−31	0	0	0
21. Exchange	1,150	500	275	0	0	0	0	0	0	100
All maturities										
22. Gross purchases	24,081	37,170	18,863	0	1,280	375	3,599	5,028	0	0
23. Gross sales	2,502	6,803	1,562	0	0	0	0	0	177	3,913
24. Redemptions	1,000	9,099	2,200	0	0	0	0	0	600	1,600
Matched transactions										
25. Gross sales	927,999	950,923	1,168,484	124,875	113,886	98,804	98,618	93,650	94,204	110,393
26. Gross purchases	927,247	950,935	1,168,142	123,220	113,384	97,897	100,680	93,584	94,252ʳ	112,472
Repurchase agreements†										
27. Gross purchases	170,431	314,621	152,613	0	35,800	4,715	17,867	15,575	17,208	0
28. Gross sales	160,268	324,666	151,497	0	30,191	7,727	16,463	14,815	21,969	0
29. Net change in U.S. government securities	29,988	11,234	15,872	−1,655	6,386	−3,544	7,064	5,721	−5,489	−3,434
Federal Agency Obligations										
Outright transactions										
30. Gross purchases	0	0	0	0	0	0	0	0	0	0
31. Gross sales	0	0	0	0	0	0	0	0	0	0
32. Redemptions	398	276	587	10	0	75	14	135	148	40
Repurchase agreements†										
33. Gross purchases	31,142	80,353	57,259	0	12,107	2,223	4,763	7,672	8,980	0
34. Gross sales	30,521	81,350	56,471	0	8,225	4,454	5,132	6,853	11,081	−40
35. Net change in federal agency obligations	222	−1,274	198	−10	3,882	−2,306	−383	683	−2,249	
36. **Total net change in System Open Market Account**	**30,212**	**9,961**	**16,070**	**−1,665**	**10,268**	**−5,850**	**6,681**	**6,404**	**−7,738**	**−3,474**

*Sales, redemptions, and negative figures reduce holdings of the System Open Market Account; all other figures increase such holdings. Details may not add to totals because of rounding.
†In July 1984 the Open Market Trading Desk discontinued accepting bankers' acceptances in repurchase agreements.

Source: *Federal Reserve Bulletin.*

open market operations to offset shifts in Treasury balances or float. The danger is that the large resulting injections or withdrawals of reserves may—depending on market conditions—be mistakenly interpreted by the market as a signal of a shift in Fed policy.

Problems of this sort are the reason the Fed lobbied to have the Treasury hold the bulk of its deposit balances in TT&L accounts at private banks. Despite the Treasury's new deposit arrangements, the Treasury must still keep sizable balances at the Fed. Any time these run below $1 billion, the Treasury runs a risk, unless it puts in more money, of ending up *OD* (*overdrawn*) at the Fed. When this occurs, the Treasury issues the Fed special certificates, which are usually on the Fed's books for no more than a day or two.

A Go-Around

The Fed goes into the market to do open market operations after the morning conference call between the New York desk and the board in Washington. Usually, this is around 11:35 to 11:45 A.M. for repos and MSPs, around 1 P.M. for outrights.

When the Fed goes into the market to do normal, daily, open market operations, the size is usually large. A typical bill or coupon operation for the open market account currently varies from $2.5 to $4 billion. During a peak add period, such as April or December, it is not unusual for the Fed to have $20 billion of repos outstanding on a single day.

Once the Fed decides what it wants to do in the way of open market operations, it does what is called a *go-around*. It calls all of the primary dealers in government securities and tells them that it wants to buy securities, sell securities, do repo, or do reverses and asks them for bids and offers, as the case may be. Technically, the Fed does not do reverses. Instead, it does an almost identical transaction called a *matched/sale purchase* (MSP).[7]

---

[7]For more on the use by the Fed of repos and MSPs and on Fed transactions on behalf

On securities purchases and sales, the Fed compares dealers' bids and offers with current market quotes and determines on which issues yields are most attractive and on which of these issues it has gotten the best quotes. It then does business with those dealers who have given it the highest bids or lowest offers on those issues.

To get current market quotes on government and agencies, the Fed asks five of the primary dealers in governments to give it quotes, hourly or more frequently, for a wide range of securities. Providing such quotes is a nuisance for the dealers, so the Fed rotates the job.

The word that a go-around is being done is flashed out to all the dealers within 30 seconds. Thereafter, the process slows. It takes the dealers time to get back to the Fed with their offerings or bids, and then it takes the Fed time to compare the dealers' propositions and select the most favorable.

In addition to its normal open market transactions with the dealers, the Fed uses transactions with foreign central banks that hold dollars as a way to affect bank reserves. Such transactions are marginal on a long-term basis but can be significant in the day-to-day control of reserves. "Foreign accounts have buy and sell and repo orders everyday," said one person on the desk. "We can choose to be on the other side of any one of those transactions, which gives us flexibility. Say there is a big excess of reserves in the market. If we try to drain reserves, the market may conclude we are tightening further. But if we do transactions internally with foreign accounts, no one sees them, and no one is upset. Such transactions do what a market transaction would do without providing any signal." In early 1989, the Fed held more than $200 billion of marketable Treasuries in custody for foreign official institutions. It also had $4 to $5 billion in its *foreign matched sales pool*—a repo pool in which foreign central banks may daily invest short-term dollar balances.[8]

---

of foreign central banks, see Marcia Stigum's *The Repo and Reverse Markets* (Homewood, Ill.: Dow Jones-Irwin, 1989), chap. 8.

[8]See Chapter 13.

THE DISCOUNT WINDOW

When a bank borrows at the discount window, reserves are created just as they are when the Fed does repos in the course of open market operations (Table 9–8). Back in the 1920s, granting banks loans at the discount window was the Fed's main technique for creating bank reserves. Gradually, this technique of reserve creation was replaced by open market operations, and the primary function of the discount window today is to provide member banks and other depository institutions that encounter any one of a range of possible difficulties with a means to adjust in the short run.[9]

An institution's borrowings at the discount window must be collateralized. According to the old commercial loan theory of banking, it was proper for banks to make only *short-term* loans because their liabilities were short-term in nature. Also, bank loans were supposed to be *self-liquidating;* that is, to fund an activity that would automatically generate funds required to repay the loan. Finally, bank loans were to be *productive;* that is, to fund the production and marketing of goods not, for example, the carrying of securities. Influenced by this doctrine, the authors of the Federal Reserve Act stipulated that only notes arising from short-term, self-liquidating, productive loans were *eligible* as collateral at the discount window. Notes not meeting these conditions are deemed to be *ineligible* collateral.

Currently, the Fed classifies (reflecting various congressional amendments to the Federal Reserve Act) as eligible collateral: Treasury securities, federal agency securities, municipal securities with less than six months to run, and commercial and industrial loans with 90 days or less to run. What banks use as collateral at the window has varied over time. There was a time when banks borrowed at the discount window almost exclusively against governments. Then, large banks began repo-

---

[9]It used to be that just member banks could borrow at the discount window. Then foreign banks were given access to the window by passage in 1978 of the International Banking Act. Finally, all domestic depository institutions were given access to the window by passage in 1980 of the Monetary Control Act.

TABLE 9–8
When a bank borrows $50MM at the discount window, it increases bank reserves by a like amount

The Fed		The Borrowing Bank	
Bank borrowing +50MM	Reserves of borrowing bank +50MM	Reserves +50MM	Borrowing from the Federal Reserve +50MM

ing their government portfolios and using customer promissory notes as collateral. Major banks try to always hold at the Fed adequate collateral against possible borrowings.

When a bank borrows against ineligible collateral, it used to have to pay a rate at least ½% above the posted discount rate. The Monetary Control Act eliminated this penalty rate and thus made the concept of ineligibility historically important but irrelevant for today's discount window. This change pleased the Fed, which viewed the penalty rate as an anachronism and had been asking Congress to eliminate it for a decade or more. Historically, banks made short-term, self-liquidating loans; now banks make many other sorts of loans as well. The Fed's purpose in asking for collateral loans at the window is not to promote short-term lending but to limit its credit risk. Thus, the Fed should be and is more interested, when it takes in loan paper, with the creditworthiness of the borrower than with the maturity of the loan.

In 1974, Congress amended the Federal Reserve Act to exempt 1-to-4-family mortgages used as collateral at the window from the ½% penalty rate. In 1978, the NY Fed facilitated the use of mortgages as collateral for loans at the window by saying that banks in its district need not transfer the physical documents to it; instead, all the NY Fed requires is that a bank segregate mortgages used as collateral at the window and give it a custody receipt. Since 1978, New York district banks with big mortgage portfolios have made substantial use of mortgages as collateral for loans at the window. The NY Fed still requires that other sorts of readily marketable collateral be lodged with it or with a third party. What types of collateral the Fed will take under off-premise custody varies from district to district; generally, Federal Reserve District Banks are viewed as being more lenient the farther west they are.

New Faces at the Window

With passage of the IBA in 1978 and of the Monetary Control Act in 1980, the borrowing constituency of the Fed was raised from 5,000 member banks to 40,000 institutions—the new faces being foreign bank branches and all nonmember domestic depository institutions.

Foreign Banks

Since most foreign banks having U.S. branches or agencies are large, one would have expected them to do at least a test borrowing at the Fed to learn the procedure in preparation for the day they really needed a loan from the window. A few have done so, but the number is small. Most foreign banks still rely on their domestic correspondent bank as a lender of last resort. Presumably, that will change over time as foreign banks learn that the window is truly open to them and, more important, that at times it would be both appropriate and cheaper for them to borrow there.

Since foreign banks must hold reserves at the Fed only against the deposits they book in the U.S., their required reserves are small compared to those of domestic banks of similar size. Whereas a Citi or a Chase might have required reserves of $1 billion, the comparable figure for the Crédit Lyonnais might be only $10MM. Yet when they both need to borrow at the window, the size of the borrowing needs of both classes of banks is likely to be similar. The Fed recognizes this and has said in effect to the foreign banks, "We are as willing to lend you $100MM as we are to lend the same amount to Citi, but since you hold much smaller reserves on average than Citi, we'd expect you to come to the window much less often than they do." That is the Fed's way of respecting the IBA requirement that loans made at the discount window to a bank be related in size to the reserves held by that bank at the Fed.

Nonmember Banks and Thrifts

Most nonmember banks are liquid institutions and are normally sellers, not buyers, of Fed funds. As noted below, an institution that sells Fed funds is not supposed to simultaneously borrow at the discount window as this could result in a profitable arbitrage. The purpose of the window is not to increase profits of depository institutions by creating the opportunity for them to engage in risk-free, for-profit arbitrage.

After passage of the 1980 Monetary Control Act, the Fed published a pamphlet, *The Federal Reserve Discount Window,* to acquaint its new borrowing constituency with discount-window practices.

Bank Attitudes toward Discounting

The Fed takes the position that access to the discount window is a privilege and that institutions should borrow there only when they have a legitimate need and then only for reasonable amounts and periods. The discount rate is sometimes set above money market rates, but often it is set at a level such that it is cheaper for an institution to borrow at the discount window than to buy overnight Fed funds (Figure 9–1).[10] The discount rate, unlike the Fed funds rate, is not typically a major beacon pointing up the direction of Fed policy; it is normally changed only after other short-term rates have moved up or down. However, often a change in the discount rate may be interpreted by the market and intended by the Fed as a signal. An example is the successive hikes that the Fed made in the discount rate from mid-1987 through early 1989 (Figure 9–1).

The Fed's guideline on use of the discount window is vague at best, and not surprisingly there is a wide range of views

---

[10]In 1971, the Fed switched from actually discounting paper at the window to making straight loans against collateral. As a result the discount rate is not quoted on a discount basis as Treasury bill rates are; instead the discount rate is an add-on rate that is directly comparable to the Fed funds rate, which is also an add-on rate. In making the 1971 switch in window practice, the Fed's motive was to simplify lending at the window. The change also permitted banks to borrow more dollars against a given amount of collateral.

FIGURE 9–1

Relationship of the discount rate to the Fed funds rate

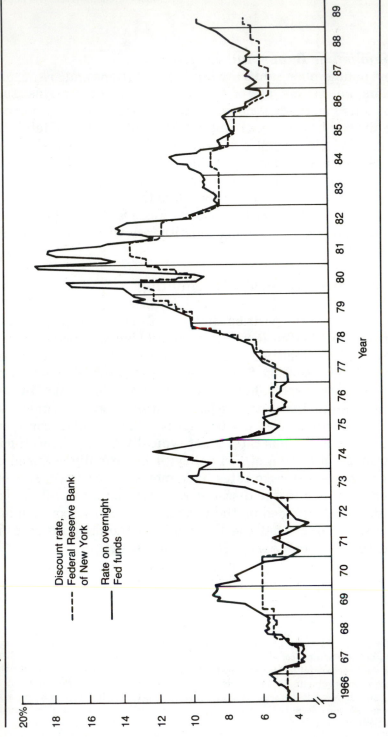

Source: *Federal Reserve Bulletin.*

TABLE 9–9
Discount window administration numerical guidelines

Size of Bank (Domestic Deposits)	Consecutive Weeks Borrowing	Weeks of Borrowing Within:		Borrowing as a Percent of Domestic Deposits
		13 Weeks	26 Weeks	
Under $200 million	4–5	6–7	7–8	2.0
$200 million–$1 billion	3–4	5–6	7–8	2.0
$1 billion–$3 billion	2–3	4–5	6–7	1.5
More than $3 billion	1–2	3–4	4–5	1.0

Source: Board of Governors of the Federal Reserve System, 1985.

among potential borrowers with respect to the window and its proper use. To clarify matters, the Fed has issued guidelines for the amounts and frequency with which banks in different size classes may borrow from the window (Table 9–9).

At one extreme are some small institutions that feel that a stigma is attached to use of the discount window. Other institutions, which take a less extreme point of view, have very conservative senior management who regard it as a signal of weakness to borrow at the window; they are happy and proud to say that they have not found it necessary to borrow at the window in five years, or whatever. This attitude led one bank during the 1974 credit crunch to pay, on a settlement day when Fed funds were tight, 25% for overnight funds rather than go to the window. Such behavior dismays the Fed. Also, it is foolhardy because in paying an exorbitant rate for funds a bank risks raising far more questions in the market than it would do by borrowing at the window.

Still other banks, typically large banks, regard the discount window as what it truly is—a lender-of-last-resort facility that they use occasionally because they experience difficulty in settling on a Wednesday due to an unexpected occurrence: a clearing bank gets hit by dealers loans late on a Wednesday when Fed funds are in short supply; a bank experiences large unanticipated withdrawals; or a bank makes a mistake in tracking its reserve position or has computer problems and ends up short at the end of the day.

Finally, there are banks that will, whenever the discount rate is below the Fed funds rate, borrow at the discount window as much as they feel they can without being criticized by the Fed. A bank that dips its ladle into the bucket every time such a rate advantage exists will eventually get a call from the Fed to say that its borrowing pattern is exceeding that typical for a bank with its characteristics. Once a bank gets such a call, it will withdraw for a time, clean up its record, and then perhaps come back into the window to test the Fed again.

The Fed's Attitude toward Discounting

Today the Fed uses open market operations to make overall adjustments in reserves. The impact of such aggregate actions can differ for individual banks. The Fed views the discount window in part as a safety valve for those banks that are adversely affected by actions taken on the open market desk. From the desk's point of view, it is valuable to know that the discount window is there because it allows the desk to take actions it otherwise might hesitate to take because of the potential impact on individual banks.

Just what, in the Fed's view, is an appropriate use of the discount window for a bank varies depending on the bank's size and position. The Fed knows that big banks have a greater number of short-term borrowing alternatives open to them than smaller banks do, and it takes the view that their need for the discount window should be less frequent than that of smaller banks.

Settlement date is the most likely time for larger banks to come to the discount window. On a Wednesday settlement date, such banks can find their position much shorter than they anticipated, and rates can get out of hand in the Fed funds market on Wednesday afternoon. The reserve period ends on Wednesday so that is the day banks make final settlement with the Fed (Chapter 12). The Fed takes the position that, if the choice facing a bank on a Wednesday is between paying an "exorbitant" rate for funds and coming to the discount window, it should come into the window. This view, however, still leaves room for judgment. If the discount rate is 9 and Fed funds are at 11, is 11 a bandit rate? If not, what about a 3-point spread? Whether use of the discount window is legitimate on a settlement Wednesday also depends on how available funds are in the market, how late in the day it is, how much a bank needs, and the lines available to it in the Fed funds market.

A small bank has less access to the Fed funds market than does a large bank; it lacks access to the Euromarket; and it may have few repo possibilities. When such a bank experiences a sudden runoff in deposits (the school district withdraws balances) or increased local demand for loans, it may be unable to immediately react to that development. It may not have liquid assets to pay off deposits that are running off; it may not have short-term liquidity to fund a big increase in loan demand. In that type of situation, the Fed would view short-term use of the discount window by the bank as appropriate, and it would carry the bank for as long as it took the bank to make the fundamental adjustment required in its asset-liability structure. Normally, the Fed would expect this to take no longer than several months, but that is a flexible number.

"Informational" and Other Calls

To encourage the notion that a loan at the discount window for a legitimate purpose is available on request, the Fed did not used to call an institution that was borrowing for the first time to ask why it was borrowing. Now, the Fed does make this call, partly because it wants to get to know the needs of the many institutions that now comprise its borrowing constituency.

If an institution continues to borrow at the window, the Fed—taking into consideration the amount of the borrowing, the bank's past borrowing record, its frequency of borrowing, and conditions affecting banks of its type at that time—may eventually conclude that the borrowing is getting out of range of the typical need.

Then the Fed would make an *informational call*. This, from the Fed's point of view, has no stigma attached to it. The Fed is trying to get a fix on where the bank is and on how much longer it expects to rely on the Fed. The call lets the bank know that it has reached a point where the Fed is taking an interest in it, and it gives the bank an opportunity to tell the Fed what its problems are and what it is doing to cope with them. Normally this suffices, and within a few weeks the bank will have taken steps to cope with its problems—cut its loans or sought out new deposits.

But if an additional period goes by and no improvement occurs, the Fed will make a second *administrative counseling call*. The purpose of this call is to tell the bank that its borrowing pattern is becoming atypical or excessive and that it is time for the bank to terminate its borrowing. Normally, such a call will end the borrowing. It is rare that the Fed has to make a final call to say that the bank must terminate its borrowing as of a certain date.

Reverses and Loans at the Window

The Fed has an administrative rule that an institution should not do reverses with the Fed if it expects at the time that it might borrow from the Fed during the settlement week. The rationale is to prevent banks from using the window to fund a profitable arbitrage. However, there are qualifications to this rule. If a bank thinks it is in good shape with respect to its reserve position and does reverses and then something changes in the interim—operational problems or whatever—the Fed would not object to the bank borrowing at the window. Also, there is no problem in borrowing if a bank acts as a conduit for customer funds in doing reverses.

The Fed has an additional rule that an institution should not be a net seller of Fed funds during a period in which it borrows at the discount window. This again is to prevent borrowing at the discount window from being part of a for-profit arbitrage.

Seasonal Credit

In 1973, the Fed instituted a program for providing seasonal credit to smaller banks that lack access to the national money market. The purpose of the program was to meet anticipated borrowing needs for banks in resort communities, agricultural regions, and other areas where local businesses need to borrow funds early in the seasonal cycle and make their profits later. To qualify for the program, banks must show a consistent pattern of seasonal borrowing needs over a period of years. The terms of the program were simplified for agricultural banks from 1985 through 1987 in order to channel more credit to areas hit by the farm depression, but the impact was minimal.

The amount of borrowing under the seasonal credit program depends on the spread between Fed funds and the discount rate. In 1988, a year of unusually wide spreads between the funds and discount rates, seasonal borrowing exceeded $400MM a day at its annual peak in late August. In most years, the peak is substantially lower.

Extended Credit

Banks
Besides granting loans at the window to facilitate short-term adjustments, the Fed will grant longer-term financing to institutions encountering fundamental problems. There are two situations in which the Fed provides such emergency aid. One is when an act of God—flood, hurricane, or whatever—adversely affects a group of banks, their borrowers, or their depositors; for example, a hailstorm wipes out a crop and causes farmers to withdraw deposits from local banks. Such a situation would call for prolonged loans to the affected banks and a program to restore them to financial health.

The Fed will also grant emergency long-term financing to a single bank if in the Fed's judgment the risks to the banking system as a whole are sufficiently great to warrant providing credit while another situation is worked out. In 1974, the Fed lent nearly $2 billion to Franklin National at one point while trying to stave off a collapse of that bank. In 1984, the Fed lent as much as $7 billion at times to Continental Illinois while the authorities were putting together a rescue package for that bank.

The financial turmoil of the 1980s has led to an increase both in the number and the size of extended credit loans made by the Fed. The surge in lending to Continental Illinois in 1984

FIGURE 9–2
Extended credit borrowing at the Fed's discount window
(monthly averages)

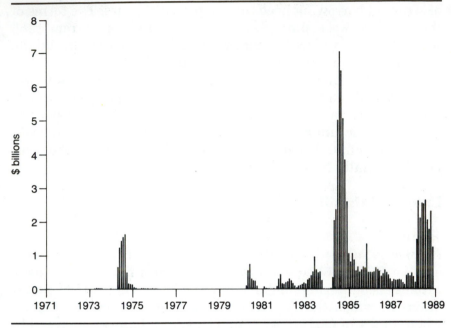

Source: R. W. Wrightson & Assoc., Inc.

still stands as the record, but it is now routine for the Fed to have substantial amounts of extended credit loans on its books (Figure 9–2).

Thrifts
Following passage of the Monetary Control Act of 1980, the Fed instituted an extended credit program for thrifts. The program, however, hasn't been widely used due to numerous Fed restrictions on its use. Thrifts also may borrow from the Federal Home Loan Banks, which serve as their lender of last resort.

One exception occurred in 1985, when some privately insured S&Ls were threatened by deposit runs. Some states, including Ohio, had offered local thrifts state insurance as an alternative to the FSLIC. One member of the Ohio insurance fund, Homestate, failed as a result of the collapse of a government securities dealer (ESM Government Securities) to which it had lent money through repurchase agreements. When this failure threatened to bankrupt the Ohio deposit-insurance fund, other non-FSLIC thrifts in Ohio and elsewhere began to experience massive deposit outflows. The Fed kept these institutions afloat while they adjusted their balance sheets—and applied for FSLIC insurance.

A second exception came in 1989. The beginnings of the congressional debate over the form of the FSLIC bailout finally drove home to many consumers how shaky much of the thrift industry was. This raised the spectre of deposit runs during the interval before the final details of the rescue were agreed upon. In consultation with the Treasury and the Federal Home Loan Banks, the Fed agreed to ease its collateral requirements for specific thrift institutions while awaiting the bailout; for its part, the Treasury agreed to compensate the Fed for a portion of any resulting losses it incurred. Only a few thrifts availed themselves of this opportunity.

Others

The Fed also has limited authority to grant emergency loans to individuals, partnerships, and corporations. This authority was used in the 1930s to grant about 125 loans totaling a mere $1MM; it has not been used since. However, questions have been raised as to whether the Fed could or should use this authority to bail out entities such as the Penn Central, New York City, or Chrysler. The Fed is extremely wary of such lending, save when it addresses the Fed's specific responsibility: to preserve a secure financial system. Other sorts of federal subsidies or assistance, the Fed believes, should be granted only by decisions of Congress and the administration, not by a semiautonomous central bank.

Rates on Extended Credit

Extended credit borrowers do not get the same bargain rates that normal adjustment-credit borrowers do—at least not for long. After 30 days of borrowing at the basic discount rate (and sometimes sooner), the Fed bumps the rate on extended credit up to something like a market rate. The rate on longer-term credits is flexible, and it is reset every maintenance period. In April 1989, the rate on extended-credit advances was 10.45%, versus a 7% discount rate and an average funds rate of 9.84%.

Extended Credit and Deposit Insurance

The Fed's activities as lender of last resort overlap those of the federal deposit-insurance agencies. The Fed's extended credit facility often serves as a way station for banks and thrifts on the road to insolvency (and to an FDIC or FSLIC takeover). A troubled bank often becomes *illiquid* before it becomes *insolvent;* and if it suffers a deposit run, the Fed's discount window is an appropriate, temporary life-support system for it.

Even after the FDIC or FSLIC intervenes, the Fed may still have a role. Today, banks and thrifts are not the only institutions with weak balance sheets; the federal deposit-insurance agencies are undercapitalized as well. Thus, the FDIC and FSLIC often find it convenient to let the Fed lend money to an institution being reorganized rather than to deplete their own cash reserves; then, when the reorganization is complete, the insurance fund often assumes responsibility for the discount-window loans of the bailed-out institution as part of the final workout plan. The Continental Illinois bailout was the largest transaction of this type, but the Fed and FDIC have made other similar deals. The advantage of this mechanism is that it allows FSLIC or the FDIC to inject capital into a failed institution without wiping out its own cash position; instead, the federal insurer mortgages a portion of its future premium income to the Fed to pay off current claims. Such a system is needed only because banks and thrifts have always lobbied successfully to keep deposit-insurance premiums and thereby federal-insurance reserves down to a bare minimum.

SOME HISTORY

Before we look at how the Fed operates today, a few words on history. During World War II, inflation was one extra disruption that the nation could do without. Thus, during the war the appropriate stance for monetary and financial policy would have been for the federal government to raise taxes to cover as much of the war expenditures as possible and for the Fed to pursue simultaneously a policy of restraint to discourage private spending. This, however, was not done. Taxes were held down so as to not discourage incentives, and rationing and price controls were used to contain private spending and control the price level. Meanwhile, the Fed assumed responsibility for pegging interest rates at the low levels that prevailed when the country entered the war. The rationale was to encourage individuals and institutions to buy bonds by eliminating the price risk that would normally attach to holding such securities. The policy had the additional advantage of minimizing the cost to the Treasury of financing the burgeoning national debt.

In guaranteeing to buy whatever quantity of government securities was necessary to peg both long- and short-term interest rates at low levels, the Fed lost all control over the money supply; and its policy permitted a big buildup of private liquidity. In retrospect, this buildup was not totally undesirable because the liquid assets acquired by citizens during the war permitted them to finance at the war's end the purchase of cars and other goods that had been unavailable during the war. The resulting spending spree prevented a much-feared postwar slump.

Inflation, however, did arrive on the scene. By 1948, the Fed was feeling uncomfortable about its obligation to peg bond prices, since that left it with no tool to fight inflation. The recession of 1949 provided some relief, but inflation again became a problem during 1950 when the Korean War broke out. Again, the Fed wanted to tighten but the Treasury resisted, arguing that higher interest rates would disrupt Treasury refundings, increase the cost of financing the national debt, and inflict capital losses on those patriotic individuals and institutions that had bought bonds during the war.

Finally, the Fed threw the gauntlet down to the Treasury in September 1950 by raising the discount rate. The Treasury retaliated by announcing a one-year financing based on the old discount rate of 1.25%. Rather than allowing the financing to fail or rescinding the rate increase, the Fed bought the Treasury's new issue, stuck to its higher discount rate, and then resold the issue to the market at a slightly higher rate. This started a six-month battle with the Treasury, ending in the famous March 1951 *accord* between the Fed and the Treasury, which read:

> The Treasury and the Federal Reserve System have reached full accord with respect to debt management and monetary policies to be pursued in furthering their common purpose to assure the successful financing of the Government's requirements and, at the same time, to minimize monetization of the public debt.

This statement, despite the fact that it appears to be a prime example of "governmentese" that says nothing, was important. Its key phrase, "to minimize monetization of the public debt," gave the Fed the right to henceforth pursue an independent monetary policy. The following year, the Fed, to protect its flank, adopted a policy of *bills only;* in the future, the Fed would confine its purchases of governments largely to bills. In adopting this policy, the Fed was saying to the market and the Treasury that henceforth the market would set the yield curve and in particular the yields on Treasury bonds.

As a price for its accord with the Treasury, the Fed agreed to stabilize credit-market conditions during Treasury financings. This policy, known as *even keeling,* was pursued for years. The reason such stabilization was required was that the Treasury used to fix both the coupon and the price at the time it announced a new issue on Wednesday. Thus, if anything important had happened after the announcement of an issue but before it was sold the following week, that would have killed the auction; that is, the Treasury would have been unable to sell its securities—something that neither the Treasury nor the Fed could risk.

While even keeling prevailed, the Fed tried to plan major moves so that the market would have time to react to them before a Treasury financing. It insisted, however, that Treasury financings meet the test of the market; the Treasury could not rely on direct support from the Fed.

In the 1970s, even keeling gradually died an untolled death. One reason is that the Treasury adopted the policy of selling almost all of its coupon issues through yield auctions. Also, the

Treasury's new policy of auctioning notes of different maturities on a regular cycle created a situation in which the Treasury is in the market twice a month with new coupon issues. If the Fed were to even keel, it would have no "windows" during which it could decisively shift policy.

Before the accord, the Fed was forced to focus almost solely on interest rates. After the accord, the Fed's focus gradually shifted to *free reserves*—excess reserves minus borrowed reserves. The Fed reasoned that the stance of monetary policy would be sufficiently easy during a recession if free reserves were increased, thereby promoting additional bank lending and falling interest rates; and that, during periods of excessive demand for output, the stance of monetary policy would be appropriately tight if free reserves were decreased, thereby promoting a reduction in bank lending and a rise in interest rates.

This reasonable-sounding policy contained a fatal flaw. During a recession, interest rates are likely to fall by themselves as the demand for bank credit diminishes, so increases in free reserves may be consistent with a falling money supply and a tight monetary policy. In an overheated economy, in contrast, limiting free reserves to some small sum need not mean tight money. So long as the Fed continues to supply banks with reserves and the banks use them, a policy of holding free reserves to a low figure is consistent with a rapidly expanding money supply.

After a decade of obsession with free reserves, the Fed in the early 1960s shifted focus to interest rates. At the time, the economy was recovering sluggishly from a severe recession, and the Fed wanted to stimulate investment spending by lowering long-term interest rates. However, the U.S. was also experiencing a big deficit in its balance of payments, and defense of the dollar therefore called for the Fed to maintain high short-term interest rates. In response to both needs, the Fed adopted *operation twist:* It started buying bonds instead of bills in an attempt to force up short-term interest rates while simultaneously lowering long rates.

Whether operation twist was successful in altering the slope of the yield curve, in stimulating investment, or in decreasing the balance of payments deficit has been much debated.

The policy died in 1965, a victim of the Vietnam War, which set off inflationary pressures in the economy and caused the Fed to focus on curbing inflation. In 1966, the Fed introduced the first of several credit crunches that drove interest rates to historical highs.

As fighting inflation came to be a key target of Fed policy, another change was also occurring—a gradual shift in the Fed's attention away from interest rates toward growth of the money supply. The level of interest rates does not necessarily indicate how tight or easy monetary policy is because interest rates respond not only to what the Fed is doing, but to general economic conditions. During a recession, interest rates can fall even though bank reserves and money supply are shrinking. Similarly, during an expansion, rising interest rates are compatible with rapid increases in bank reserves, bank credit, and money supply.

Thus, in the decade following 1966, during which the Fed continued to be concerned much of the time with controlling inflation, it gradually put, in measuring monetary tightness and ease, more emphasis on the rate of growth of the money supply and less on that of bank reserves. This switch in focus was encouraged by Congress, which in a 1975 joint resolution required the Fed to set and announce targets for monetary growth.

Congress's action reflected growing national frustration with the Fed's inability to stem, during the 1970s, the growing tide of inflation. This frustration made people lend a more sympathetic ear to monetarist railings about the Fed's *judgmental* approach to policymaking. Monetarists, most prominently Milton Friedman, had long argued that a judgmental approach invited political meddling and human error; also, it was unnecessary, since a *rigorous* pursuit of publicly announced, money-supply targets would suffice to control inflation. This claim had much appeal and eminent proponents. Given the Fed's poor track record on inflation, many people—even those skeptical about monetarism's easy answers—felt it was time to try a new approach.

Prodded by Congress, the Fed began to set money-supply targets and sought to hold growth of the monetary aggregates within target bands. At the same time, the Fed did not fully accept monetarist doctrine: from long experience, Fed technicians knew that the Fed could not control money supply with the precision envisioned in textbooks.[11] Also, Fed officials feared the instability that rigid monetary control might foster. In any case, the Fed's conversion to monetarism was half-hearted, at least, until October 1979.

THE MONETARIST EXPERIMENT: 1979 TO 1982

The year 1979 was tumultuous; a vicious cycle of rising inflation and a depreciating dollar were undermining confidence in U.S. financial markets. Under pressure to find a strong figure to take the helm at the Fed, President Carter appointed Paul Volcker, then president of the New York Fed, to be Federal Reserve chairman. On Saturday, October 6, 1979, Volcker convened a special session of the FOMC to discuss how to meet the crisis. At day's end, the Fed released a short statement announcing large changes in how it would henceforth implement monetary policy. In doing so, the Fed formally inaugurated what was to become a three-year monetarist experiment.

The "Saturday Night Special"

The Fed's October 6 announcement revealed few details about the FOMC's new policy approach, but it said enough to tell the markets that the financial world had changed suddenly and dramatically. The key words in the announcement were that the new approach "involves placing greater emphasis in day-to-day

---

[11]Because of its difficulty in controlling precisely—even gauging precisely—the size of the money supply by any measure, the Fed had in 1972 adopted as an operating policy target bank *reserves available to support private deposits (RPDs)*. The idea was that, by controlling this aggregate, the Fed could control closely, albeit indirectly, the money supply available to the private nonbanking sector, that is, the total money supply minus Treasury balances at commercial banks and interbank deposits, both of which are excluded from Fed money supply figures. After several years, the Fed gave up on this experiment because RPDs proved as difficult to control and measure as money supply.

FIGURE 9–3
Federal funds rate effective versus monitoring range (monthly levels)

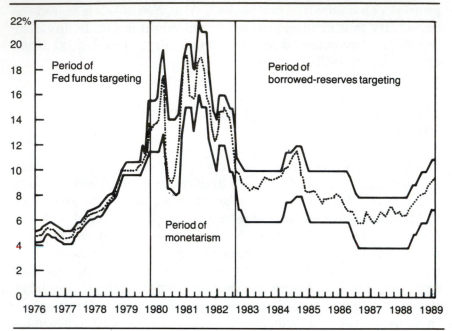

Source: R. W. Wrightson & Assoc., Inc.

operations on the supply of bank reserves and less emphasis on confining short-term fluctuations in the Federal funds rate." That would prove to be the understatement of the decade: the October 6 announcement kicked off a three-year period of extraordinary volatility in the funds market (Figure 9–3). The uncertainties of the new era had an immediate negative impact on bonds prices, which plunged after the weekend. Wall Street traders, feeling as though they'd been mugged, quickly dubbed the announcement *Volcker's Saturday Night Special.*

A Reserves-Oriented Operating Procedure

In a nutshell, the October 6 announcement ushered in a *reserves-oriented* operating procedure designed to achieve tighter control over money supply. The Fed had previously established money-supply targets, but did a poor job of achieving them.

Prior to October 1979, the Fed relied on a *Fed funds-targeting* procedure: the FOMC held the Fed funds rate within a narrow band it established; if money supply grew faster than desired, the FOMC would raise its target band for the funds rate in an attempt to restrain the demand for money and thereby to bring the rate of growth of money supply down into its target range.

By switching to a reserves-oriented procedure, the Fed intended to attack money-supply growth from a different angle. Instead of using marginal changes in interest rates via marginal changes in the rate of growth of bank reserves to influence the demand for money, the Fed would supply just enough bank reserves to support its targeted level of money growth, without regard to how that impacted interest rates. When money supply grows, the need for bank reserves rises as well; in the past, the Fed, desiring to prevent short-run volatility in the funds rate, accommodated such induced increases in the demand for bank reserves through open market operations. Under its new procedures, the Fed would let the increased demand for bank reserves translate immediately into higher interest rates that would persist so long as money-supply growth exceeded target rates.

Why the Fed Acted

Various theories have been advanced as to why the Fed decided to don a monetarist guise in 1979. The simplest explanation— that the Fed believed in monetarism—usually gets the shortest shrift. Comments made by many Fed officials (including Volcker) before, during, and after the monetarist experiment betray a deep mistrust of rigid monetarist doctrine.

The more plausible explanation for the Fed's shift in policy is political. The wide acceptance that monetarism was gaining—among the public, the press, and politicians—put the Fed under pressure to give it a try. Congress, in particular, was taking on an increasingly monetarist cast; and each year, it appeared to be coming a little closer to circumscribing the Fed's autonomy. By taking the initiative in October 1979, the Fed was able to implement monetarism *on its own terms*.

Also, the new operating procedures offered the Fed invaluable political cover for the drastic anti-inflation program it knew was needed. Two things stand out about the monetarist experiment: during its life, interest rates were on average *far higher* and *far more volatile* than they were immediately before or after.

There's no good reason why money growth can't be controlled as easily by managing interest rates as by managing reserves, but doing the former creates a political problem: under a Fed funds-targeting system, the Fed must accept full responsibility for each and every rise in interest rates. Consequently, it's no surprise that the Fed was slow in the 1970s to push interest rates as high as they needed to go. However, by becoming monetarist, the Fed was able to disavow responsibility for spikes and swings in interest rates—the latter were merely unfortunate side effects of the noble quest for a stable rate for growth of the money supply.

On this interpretation, the volatility of interest rates from 1979 to 1982 was an essential part of the Fed's strategy. Had the new operating procedures produced high but stable interest rates, the Fed would have been hard put to argue that it had no control over interest rates. However, by allowing rates to lurch about month to month, the Fed created a convincing picture of an economic variable beyond its control; this picture, perhaps disingenuous, served its purpose. It allowed the Fed to keep rates high enough for long enough to cool the engine of inflation, which had been building up steam for years.

The M1 Game

The volatility that the Fed permitted during the monetarist experiment elevated the Fed's M1 measure of money supply to a position of unrivaled prominence. Of all the Fed's money measures, M1 looked most like the concept used in monetarist models; it consisted (originally) of currency in circulation plus demand deposits at banks; also, it was the money-supply measure most closely related to bank reserves (many of the items in the broader aggregates, M2 and M3, aren't subject to reserve requirements).

Thus, the Fed's weekly release of the M1 number became *the* central event in each week's money and bond market trading. The Fed cautioned that its weekly M1 numbers were tentative and could be highly misleading, but its warning fell on deaf ears. The market knew that, under the Fed's new semiautomatic operating procedures, a $2- or $3-billion deviation from the M1 target might suffice to drive short-term rates up or down. Thus, the market's focus fixed on M1.

The Street put an extraordinary amount of effort into forecasting M1. Economists poured over the money-supply data looking for clues as to the coming week's number. Banks and others developed elaborate deposit surveys designed to allow them to predict the Fed's weekly tabulations. The general quality of private forecasts was poor, but that reflected flaws in the available data, not any lack of effort or ingenuity by those who massaged these data.

End of Experiment

By the summer of 1982, the nation's patience was wearing thin. The economy was falling deeper into the second recession in three years. Financial strains were growing in many sectors, including the LDC debtor nations (Mexico, in particular, appeared to be tottering on the brink of default). Also, and equally important, U.S. inflation indices were turning in their best performances in a decade. Finally, implementation of the new operating procedures had gotten no easier with time; the problems associated with measuring money supply multiplied in the early 1980s as Congress deregulated the financial system.

In August 1982, the Fed, uncertain about how to interpret money-supply numbers and uneasy about the path down which those numbers were leading it, abandoned its reserves-oriented approach. Its retreat from monetarism was not accompanied by the fanfare that greeted its conversion, three years earlier, to monetarism. In fact, some months passed before the Fed formally acknowledged its shift. However, in retrospect, it's clear that a fundamental changed occurred in the summer of 1982: after August of that year, month-to-month swings in the funds rate became far smaller than they had been previously (Figure 9–2); finally, the funds market regained some of its pre-1979 stability.

Measurement Problems

One problem that plagued the Fed throughout its monetarist experiment was the question of how to define and measure money supply: Which money-supply concept is *the* relevant one? Is it narrow M1, currency plus checking accounts? Is it M2, which incorporates a range of *near monies*, such as savings accounts and consumer time deposits? Or is it M3, which adds in large-denomination instruments such as wholesale CDs? Different criteria support different money-supply aggregates: M1 is closest to the monetarists' textbook model, but in recent decades, M2 has shown the most stable relationship to GNP and to the price level. M3 has the advantage of being the most inclusive. An academic economist noted the irony of the situation: "Economists can't figure out how to define money supply, but whatever it is, they're sure it should grow at 3% a year."

When the Fed opted for M1 as its target, its decision making was far from over. The inflationary pressures that prompted the Fed's switch to monetarism also revolutionized the financial system. In the 1970s, as inflation rates and nominal interest rates both soared, a host of new financial instruments were created: money market funds, NOW accounts, Super-NOW accounts, MMDAs, consumer CDs, and so on. To keep pace with the rapidly evolving financial landscape, the Fed had to keep redefining its measures of money supply (Table 9–1). In this environment, M1 quickly ran afoul of Goodhart's Law, which a Bank of England official phrased as follows: "If you create a monetary aggregate and start targeting your system by it, before you know where you are, it will change out of all recognition; and you will have to create another one—exactly what happened in the U.S. and in the U.K."

For the Fed, the introduction of NOW accounts proved to be a classic case in point. During the 1970s, NOW accounts became available in New England; by 1979, they had spread to New York and New Jersey; and beginning in 1981, Congress authorized their issuance nationwide. When NOW accounts were available only regionally, the Fed publish two definitions of the narrow money stock: M1-A, which didn't include NOWs, and M1-B, which did. Then, when NOWs went nationwide, the volume of savings balances flowing into the narrow money supply soared. In response, the Fed published estimates of what its money-supply numbers would have been absent these shifts. Suddenly, four aggregates were competing to fill the shoes of old M1: M1-A, M1-B, shift-adjusted M1-A, and shift-adjusted M1-B. The easy answers promised by monetarists were beginning to look complicated indeed.

IMPLEMENTING MONETARY POLICY TODAY

The 1980s have seen a switch, first dramatic, then gradual, in the procedures followed by the Fed in implementing monetary policy.

A Nonborrowed-Reserves Procedure

During its monetarist experiment, the Fed relied on a *nonborrowed-reserves procedure*. (Nonborrowed reserves are those that the Fed supplies to the banks via open market operations.) During its monetarist period, the FOMC would establish a short-run target for M1. Its staff would then estimate weekly the amount of bank reserves required to support this M1 target. The desk's job was to supply this amount of reserves *minus* banks' anticipated borrowings at the discount window. When M1 deviated from its target path, as it often did, bank borrowings at the discount window had to rise (or fall) which in turn would cause the Fed funds rate to rise (or fall). The Fed's focus on supplying a fixed amount of nonborrowed reserves inevitably led to the erratic movements in the funds rate that occurred from 1979 through mid-1982 (Figure 9–3, p. 396).

A Borrowed-Reserves Operating Procedure

As the 1982 recession deepened, the Fed concluded that the economy was too fragile to support either the level or the volatility of interest rates that had been induced by strict M1 targeting. Accordingly, it shifted emphasis from nonborrowed to borrowed reserves.

Under the Fed's current operating procedure, the spread between the discount rate and the funds rate assumes crucial importance. For the past 25 years, the Fed has typically set the discount rate below the overnight rate for Fed funds. Thus, a bank that borrows reserves at the window rather than in the market gets an instant saving—against which it pays certain nonprice costs: the risk of incurring the Fed's displeasure and the risk that the window might be unavailable on some future rainier day.

The greater is the spread of the funds rate over the discount rate, the greater is the incentive for banks to borrow at the window. Thus, it was no surprise that a quite stable relationship appeared to prevail between the spread of the funds rate over the discount rate and the amount of reserves banks borrowed at the discount window.

Under its borrowed-reserves procedure, the Fed has sought to use this relationship as its handle on the funds rate. Specifically, the New York desk deliberately undersupplies reserves through its open market operations and thereby forces the banks to make up the deficit by borrowing at the window. The amount that the Fed chooses to force the banks to borrow at the window determines how high funds will trade above the discount rate.

Specifically, under its *borrowed-reserves procedure*, the Fed tries to keep banks' borrowings at the window constant by adjusting nonborrowed reserves to meet short-term changes in banks' demand for reserves. The Fed changes its targeted level of borrowing only when it makes a formal decision to change its policy stance. When the FOMC decides to tighten or ease, it may direct the desk to try to induce 100MM more (less) of daily borrowing at the window, knowing that this will likely translate into a 25- or 50-bp rise (fall) in the funds rate—the latter being the Fed's intermediate objective.

There's clearly some irony in all this. The Fed still likes to maintain that interest-rate arbitrage is an inappropriate reason for a bank to borrow at the discount window; yet, the Fed's operating procedures would not work if banks ignored rate incentives. In any case, so long as banks' demand for loans at the discount window is predictable, the Fed can manage the funds rate quite neatly by calibrating the size of the banks' initial reserve deficit.

Pros and Cons of the Borrowed-Reserves Procedure

Since, under the current operating procedures, the level of borrowed reserves is used as a proxy for the funds rate, one might ask why the Fed doesn't simply revert to a straightforward targeting of the funds rate. The answer probably lies in the same political factors that led the Fed to jettison a Fed funds target in the first place. Consider two alternative newspaper headlines, "Fed Raises Interest Rates" and "Fed Borrowing Targets Appear to Rise." Wall Street might perceive the two statements to be equivalent, but Main Street wouldn't.

Also, under the borrowed-reserves procedure, the precise timing of a change in the Fed's borrowing target can be difficult to pinpoint. There has always been a certain looseness, especially in the short run, in the relationship between the Fed funds rate and borrowing at the window. Often it's difficult to tell whether a swing in the funds rate of ⅛ or ¼% reflects a change in the Fed's stance or is simply a blip due to a change in some exogenous factor. The Fed can of course always state publicly what it's up to. However, at times, when it wants to keep its political cover or to keep the market guessing, the Fed may prefer continued ambiguity.

Fed officials offer other rationales for using the borrowed-reserves procedure. One is that the looseness in the relationship between the funds rate and borrowed reserves allows market expectations to play a role in setting rate levels, and that this in turn can provide useful information to policymakers. No doubt, traders' expectations do play a role, in short run, in setting the funds rate, but it isn't clear that those expectations can tell the Fed anything useful. Traders know that the Fed dominates the funds market. Thus, to the extent that traders' expectations influence the funds rate, it is their expectations of future Fed policy that count. For instance, the market will knock the funds rate down if it thinks the Fed is on the verge of easing. In doing so, traders make no judgment as to whether economic conditions are such that the Fed should or shouldn't ease; they just bet that it will. As the Fed well knows, financial markets render traders' judgments about the appropriateness of macro policy in the rates yielded by longer-term securities, not in tightly controlled overnight rates.

The deliberate obscurity of the borrowed-reserves procedure can at times be a drawback. The period following the stock market crash in October 1987 is a case in point. At that time, when market uncertainty put a premium on clear central bank action, the Fed temporarily abandoned its borrowed-reserves target in favor of a policy that approached targeting the Fed funds rate: it instructed the open market desk to bracket the funds rate in a narrow range without regard to the resulting impact on borrowing. Although the Fed never formally described its interim policy as rate pegging, it did admit that it was administering its reserve targets "flexibly" and with considerable importance attached to "money market conditions." Quickly, the market recognized these qualifiers as codewords for a policy of targeting of the funds rate.

Breakdown of the Relationship of Borrowed Reserves to the Funds Rate

Once a sense of stability was restored to the market after the '87 crash, the Fed tried to restore borrowed reserves as its central operating procedure. It succeeded only partially as the once-predictable link between borrowed reserves and the funds rate had, by then, become that latest victim of Goodhart's Law. Once the Fed began to base policy on this relationship, the demand curve for borrowed reserves became unstable.

This problem is illustrated in Figure 9–4, which plots borrowings at the discount window against the average Fed funds rate for each two-week reserve maintenance period from February 1984 through June 1989. Part A shows the maintenance periods prior to the 1987 crash; part B, the periods immediately after the crash. As the charts show, banks became, after the

FIGURE 9–4
The shifting relationship between interest rates and discount window borrowing (reserve maintenance period averages)

A. February 1984–October 1987

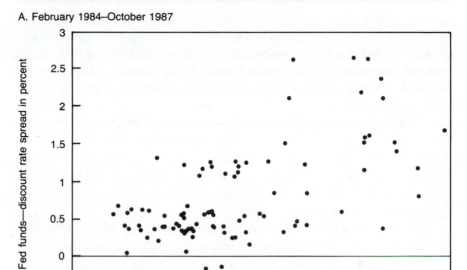

B. November 1987–June 1989

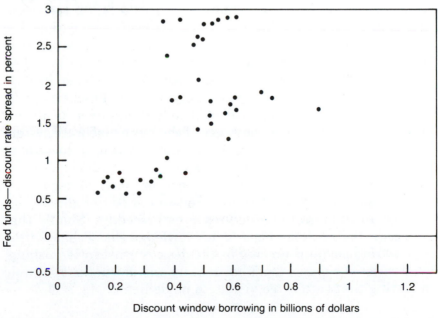

Source: R. W. Wrightson & Assoc., Inc.

crash, much more reluctant to borrow at the discount window. In the first year and a half after the crash, banks rarely borrowed more than an average of 600MM in any one maintenance period despite the existence at times of extremely attractive rate spreads. In the precrash era, similar rate spreads had routinely led to borrowings of a billion or more.

The new caution shown by banks meant that the Fed could no longer use the discount window to fine-tune market conditions. As part B of Figure 9–4 shows, an average level of 600MM of borrowings was as likely to be associated with a 150-bp spread as with a 250-bp spread. Nudging bank borrowing became a blunt tool for controlling rates.

Consequently, the Fed began to focus more directly on the funds rate. The open market desk can easily nudge the funds rate up or down by being more or less generous in its day-to-day open market operations. Since the market knows that the Fed can exercise total control over the supply of nonborrowed reserves, it responds quickly to any hint that the Fed wants the funds rate to change.

Over time, the Fed's operating procedures will undoubtedly continue to evolve. Its borrowed reserves procedure, cobbled together as a temporary expedient during the 1982 recession, proved so useful that this procedure exceeded its original life expectancy. However, the new compromise procedures that emerged in 1988 to 1989 are far from satisfactory. It's pointless for the Fed to establish a borrowed reserves target when its day-to-day operations are directed solely toward bracketing the funds rate within a narrow range. The Fed, however, is always mindful of the political advantages of the more elaborate system it was able to use until late 1987; and it's thus reluctant to discard the last vestiges of that system.

If the demand for borrowed reserves were to regain its former pattern and stability, the Fed would be delighted to go back to a full-dress, borrowed-reserves procedure. Should that not occur, the Fed may have to acknowledge that it has drifted back to rate pegging. So long as the desk is constantly pushing, via a series of signals, the funds rate up and down, the Fed's role in setting that rate is too visible to be denied.

Funds-Rate Targeting with No Target

By 1988 to 1989, one of the few differences that remained between a full-fledged, rate-pegging scheme and the shell of the prior borrowed-reserves procedure was that the Fed had set no explicit target for the funds rate. Even though the FOMC clearly envisioned its policy moves in terms of discrete 25- to 50-bp rate moves, it never said so publicly. During the 1970s, in contrast, the FOMC routinely specified a narrow (50- to 75-bp), short-run, target range for the funds rate. Since 1979, the only formal funds rate target the Fed has published is the *consultation range* set at each FOMC meeting.

This range is a holdover from the Fed's monetarist era. When the FOMC all but abandoned its attempt to influence the funds rate in the short run, it built a safety clause into its operating directives to the desk: it specified a *very* wide band for the Fed funds rate (typically 400 bp) with the proviso that the chairman should consult with FOMC members if the reserve targets seemed likely to drive the funds rate persistently out of that band. The consultation range was in fact breached several times during the chaotic monetarist experiment, but in today's environment, a tolerance range of plus or minus 200 bp for a six-week, intermeeting period constitutes no binding constraint.

Thus, since 1982, the consultation range has been essentially irrelevant; and the monthly average funds rate has certainly never approached either bound of this range. Today, it's unthinkable that, under a borrowed-reserves procedure, the desk would allow the funds rate to swing by much more than 25 bp up or down without a specific FOMC instruction to do so.

While the consultation range now has virtually no bearing on the conduct of open market operations, it does point up the Fed's sensitivity to political considerations. During the period of borrowed-reserves targeting, the funds rate has been more frequently in the upper half of the consultation band than in the lower half (Figure 9–3). When the FOMC is tightening, the upward adjustment in the consultation range usually lags the rise in the funds rate. The Fed is always happier to announce a decline in interest rates than an increase. This does not mean that the Fed objects to tightening; sometimes, however, it prefers not to draw attention to the fact that it's tightening.

TARGETS GOVERNING MONETARY POLICY

So far, we've focused on the ways in which the Fed implements its policy decisions rather than on the reasons for such decisions. The considerations that govern monetary policy are more nebulous than the procedures used to affect them. This was particularly true when, in the late 1980s, the Fed reverted largely to seat-of-the-plants navigation and looked at anything and everything in its attempt to steer a course between inflation and recession.

Macroeconomic and Operating Targets

The Fed sorts the different economic variables it monitors into several categories. At the highest level are macroeconomic targets such as price stability, full employment, and the exchange value of the dollar. These targets constitute the ultimate objectives of monetary policy; they are also the targets that the Fed can control least directly. At the opposite extreme are the Fed's *operating targets* such as the funds rate, free reserves, and borrowed reserves; these targets are easy for the Fed to control directly, but the impact of changes in them on the Fed's macro targets is often indirect and sometimes weak.

Intermediate Targets

Between these two categories of targets lie potential *intermediate targets*. For a variable to be a good intermediate target, it should have a predictable relationship with the Fed's ultimate policy objectives, but be susceptible to relatively close control through changes in the Fed's operating targets. The monetarist experiment provides a classic example of such a three-tiered system: under it, nonborrowed reserves were the operating target, M1 the intermediate target, and the price level the ultimate target.

The 1980s have seen a steady decline in the importance that the Fed accords to intermediate targets. At the end of each of its meetings, the FOMC gives the New York desk a set of economic variables, listed in order of importance, that should guide any intermeeting policy adjustments. Table 9–10 shows the evolution between 1986 and 1989, of the rankings of such targets. In 1986, intermediate targets, such as the money supply and the exchange value of the dollar, still ranked high, even though the Fed was not setting firm, short-run ranges for them. By 1989,

TABLE 9–10
Rankings of key variables in FOMC policy directives: 1986 to 1989

Date of Meeting	Inflationary Pressures	Strength of Expansion	Monetary Aggregates	FX Market Conditions	Financial Market Conditions
Feb 1986	4	2	(1)	3	5
Apr 1986	4	2	(1)	3	5
May 1986	—	2	(1)	4	3
Jul 1986	4	2	(1)	3	5
Aug 1986	4	2	(1)	3	5
Sep 1986	4	2	(1)	3	5
Nov 1986	4	2	(1)	3	5
Dec 1986	4	2	(1)	3	5
Feb 1987	4	2	(1)	3	5
Mar 1987	4	3	2	(1)	5
May 1987	(1)	4	3	2	—
Jul 1987	(1)	3	2	—	—
Aug 1987	(1)	2	4	3	—
Sep 1987	(1)	2	4	3	—
Nov 1987	3	2	5	4	(1)
Dec 1987	3	2	5	4	(1)
Feb 1988	3	2	5	4	(1)
Mar 1988	3	2	5	4	(1)
May 1988	3	2	5	4	(1)
Jun 1988	(1)	2	5	3	4
Aug 1988	(1)	2	3	4	5
Sep 1988	(1)	2	3	4	5
Nov 1988	(1)	2	3	4	5
Dec 1988	(1)	2	3	4	5
Feb 1989	(1)	2	3	4	5
Mar 1989	(1)	2	3	4	5

Source: FOMC minutes.

macro objectives, such as inflation and real economic growth, got the highest rankings. This focus on macro targets amounts, in the words of a former Fed chairman, to no more than "leaning against the wind" of prevailing cyclical pressures: tightening when the economy overheats and inflation threatens, easing when the economy softens.

Rehabilitating Money Supply as an Intermediate Target

An attempt to rehabilitate money supply as an intermediate target began almost as soon as strict targeting of M1 was dropped in 1982. The Fed continued to specify M1 target ranges for some years after its 1982 tactical shift. While unpredictable swings in the monetary aggregates made it impossible for the Fed to hit any of its money targets, the Fed, for a time, still allowed M1 to influence its decisions. As M1 became more erratic, the Fed's attention shifted to the broader and more stable M2. However, that aggregate too became volatile due to financial deregulation; and the Fed was forced, yet again, to look elsewhere for an intermediate target.

With traditional money supply measures misbehaving, Fed economists began to search for a more helpful target by exploring new ways of adding up money-supply components. One early proposal was to weight the different components of money supply according to their "moneyness": less liquid deposit categories, like consumer CDs, were assigned a lower weight than, say, demand deposits. In practice, the appropriate weights proved difficult to gauge, and the proposal was short lived.

In 1989, a more elaborate approach surfaced with the blessing of Fed Chairman Greenspan. In an attempt to look beyond short-run swings in the relationship between money supply and the economy, Fed economists began to look at the price level that would be implied by the current money stock if M2 velocity were at its long-run level. This hypothetical price level, denoted p^* (later dubbed *p-star* by the press), was found to have been a leading indicator of inflation. Specifically, inflation had tended to accelerate whenever p^* had been higher than the actual price level, and vice versa.

The chairman's endorsement of p^* as a useful gauge of the implications of money supply for inflation ensured that the market would pay attention to p^*. However, in 1989, it was too early to tell whether p^* would assume an important role in Fed procedures. Such an approach would rely on arbitrary assumptions, and it would thus lack the intuitive appeal that made monetarism so popular. Its real test, however, will be whether it works; so far, it has had neither to stand up to the pressure of real-time forecasting nor to shoulder the weight of policy shifts. Earlier monetarist prescriptions also looked plausible when tested against historical data, but failed when starred in a real-time drama.

Credit Aggregates as Possible Intermediate Targets

Credit is the flip side of money, so it's unsurprising that one school of thought holds that the true impact on prices and output of the various bank IOUs that comprise money comes from their role in expanding bank credit rather than from their propensity to burn a hole in consumers' pockets. For years, the Fed has monitored various measures of credit. Its emphasis originally fell on bank credit, but securitization of bank debt in the 1980s forced the Fed to broaden its focus: since 1983, the Fed has published formal annual growth ranges for *total domestic nonfinancial sector debt* instead of for bank credit.

The Fed has always distinguished between the types of ranges it sets for money and for debt. Its money bands are *target ranges*, whereas its debt band is a *monitoring range*. If money supply moves out of its target range, there's at least a presumption that the Fed will act. If debt departs from its monitoring range, there's no such presumption.

The Fed picked the *total debt* aggregate that it began to monitor in 1983 because the latter displayed over time a remarkably close relationship to GNP. Not surprisingly, Goodhart's law quickly showed up. During the mid-1980s, growth of total debt showed no correlation to growth of GNP, and this credit aggregate thus failed to assume an important role in Fed policy.

While current debt measures have proved faulty, the notion that credit growth matters still has intuitive appeal; and consequently, interest in credit-based measures lives on. A major obstacle to the adoption by the Fed of credit aggregates as intermediate targets is the lack of a sophisticated body of macroeconomic theory that would support its doing so. Much of the macro theory that links money supply to the price level depends on concepts that have little relevance to the workings of a modern financial system, but at least such a theory exists and has even earned a Nobel prize. No comparable macroeconomic theory for credit aggregates yet exists.

Market Judgments as Intermediate Targets

Yet another school of thought says that the Fed ought to be guided, about the prospects for inflation, by private-sector judgments, as reflected in market prices. The late 1980s might seem an odd time to advance such an argument, given the poor track record of market prices as a predictor—especially in October 1987. Still, the Fed can't ignore market developments, since traders have access to a broader range of information than policymakers can hope to review. More important, markets render their judgments instantaneously, a useful feature to central banks struggling to keep abreast of events. Finally, most analysts and policymakers agree that market expectations with respect to inflation deserve special attention because they have a nasty propensity to be self-fulfilling. An economy that expects low inflation tends to resist rises in individual prices; whereas an economy that expects inflation has no such defense mechanism: on the contrary, when inflation is expected, a price hike becomes a signal to buy now to beat later, larger price hikes.

The CBR Index
A trio of diverse market-based indicators is sometimes mentioned as an appropriate early-warning system for the Fed. The first of these is commodity prices. Some studies have shown a strong linkage between commodity price indices (such as those published by the Commodities Research Bureau [CRB] and the *Journal of Commerce*) and lagged movements in the general

price level. A few Fed officials have advocated greater reliance on such measure in policymaking. The Fed, however, has a strong tradition of viewing labor costs as a key determinant of future inflation, and it's thus unlikely to concentrate exclusively on commodity prices.

The Exchange Value of the Dollar

A second indicator is the exchange value of the dollar. An inflow of capital that causes the dollar to appreciate can be interpreted as a sign that investors view current U.S. interest rates as being so high that they offer large real returns even after allowing for inflation. However, currency markets are notoriously volatile; and they are influenced by many political, psychological, and international factors that are unrelated to the U.S. rate of inflation.

The Slope of the Yield Curve

A third indicator that some Fed officials would like to emphasize is the slope of the yield curve. Normally, the yield curve slopes upward because liquidity preference and risk aversion make investors willing to accept lower returns on less volatile short-term securities.[12] However, expectations with respect to inflation also play a role in shaping this curve: if investors feel that current conditions are such that inflation is likely to decline, they will accept lower yields on long-term bonds, causing the yield curve to *invert*. Alternatively, if investors feel that inflation is likely to accelerate, they will demand exceptionally high yields on long-term bonds, causing the yield curve to become exceptionally *steep*.

This suggests that the slope of the yield curve can be viewed as an indicator of just how tight monetary policy is at a given time. That information may be useful for the Fed since it often has difficulty quantifying the easiness or tightness of its current policy. Also, an unusually steep yield curve may indicate that self-fulfilling expectations of inflation are a threat.

---

[12]Recall Chapter 4.

There are, however, many caveats that must be taken into account in interpreting the slope of the yield curve. Changes in real interest rates, as opposed to shifts in the expectation of inflation, can impact the curve; so too can an attempt by the Treasury to change the average maturity of its debt; finally, legal and regulatory factors affect relative demands for securities of different maturities.

The Risk of Overkill

When available theories—monetarist and other—are found to be lacking, the Fed has no choice but to be pragmatic—a strategy not without danger. One problem is that monetary policy operates with a lag. To illustrate, suppose that indications of a strong economy persuade the Fed to tighten for a time. Eventually, the economy will experience lower growth, but delays in the collection and uncertainties in the interpretation of economic data mean that the Fed probably won't know for several months that the economy has changed trend. And when the Fed does find this out, the lags with which its policy operates mean that its previous tightening will continue to depress an already weakened economy for some months to come. Experience has made the Fed painfully aware of the risk that its policies will overshoot a turning point in the business cycle. To avoid doing so, the Fed now monitors the full range of data available to it for hints on economic trends, current and future.

A FINAL NOTE: GREENSPAN'S AND VOLCKER'S DIFFERENT ENVIRONMENTS

In watching the Fed today, a key point to bear in mind is that Greenspan, when he became chairman, was operating in a totally different economic environment than did Volcker when he became chairman. In 1979, the U.S. had had two consecutive years of double-digit inflation, and polls showed that inflation was the public's number one concern. Thus, Volcker had public support, and as soon as Reagan was elected, political support for doing—in fact an absolute mandate to do—whatever was necessary to break inflation, even if that meant, as it did, inducing a recession.

Volcker understood that, and by the time Reagan took office, the Fed had pushed interest rates to their highest levels in history, ensuring that any comparison of economic conditions prevailing in January 1980 with those that would later ensue could only be favorable. The economic environment Volcker inherited was primed for a traditional recession. The Volcker recession, like many that preceded it, clearly would be, and in fact was, a cleansing vehicle—a plus for the financial system as a whole because it weeded out the poorly managed, the inefficient, and the excessively speculative.

Greenspan, in contrast, to Volcker, inherited a *fragile* economy, a financial system *in crisis*. When Greenspan came to office, there loomed in every direction huge, lingering, sectoral problems that might easily take a decade or several to work out. These included the 100-billion—or would it be more?—thrift crisis; the 400-billion of LDC debts on which banks realistically would likely get paid 50 cents, 20 cents, maybe 0 cents on the dollar; lingering bad loans in the domestic agricultural and energy sectors; and big splotches of weakness in the heavily mortgaged real estate market. To make matters worse, consumer and corporate debt were at historically high levels, and the LBO borrowing-and-lending spree was continuing unabated.

All this made for a financial system so fragile that the economy looked as if it could tolerate only one condition, continued economic growth; only such growth would permit the economy to work off its huge legacy of debt—good debts, shaky debts, and just plain bad debts. In the economic environment Greenspan faced in 1989, a recession to fight inflation couldn't be a healthy, cleansing affair; the vulnerability of entire sectors of the economy was such that any downturn would risk a cascading of foreclosures and failures.

Greenspan could never say this publicly, but presumably he sensed it as he took office. Certainly, the gingerly manner in which his Fed initially moved suggested that he was fully aware that he was dealing with a very vulnerable, very fragile system—that his bottom line was that the Fed couldn't fight inflation with a recession because the economy couldn't afford a recession. To pay the cost of past excesses—forget the cost of a current recession—the economy would require a long, steady stretch of growth.

If Greenspan had a mandate, it was: Do something about inflation if you can, but *above all* don't kick the economy off the cliff.

WATCHING THE FED

The Fed shrouds its policymaking in secrecy. As a result, the Street employs a small army of professional *Fed watchers,* who seek constantly to figure out what the Fed's up to. The first rule of Fed watching, at any time and under any operating procedure, is to pay attention to what the Fed does rather than to what it says. The Fed's words and deeds sometimes match, but not always. During the 1980s, the Fed publicly understated the extent to which its policy sought to restrain the economy. The bias, however, doesn't always run that way: during the 1970s, the Fed talked a good anti-inflationary game, but pursued policies that culminated, by 1979, in double-digit inflation.

Fed open market operations are the best guide to what the Fed's doing in the short run, but interpreting these requires considerable care. It's important to remember that the vast majority of all desk operations are *defensive* rather than *dynamic*— intended to correct for movements in the operating factors rather than to shift interest rates. Thus, the significance of a given Fed operation can only be judged in the context of the banks' seasonal reserve needs. Generally, a system repo is bullish and matched sales are bearish, but not always. At times, the Fed can tighten by doing a smaller repo than it otherwise would have, or ease by doing smaller matched sales than it otherwise would have. Fed watchers regularly estimate the Fed's technical *add* or *drain* job; these estimates provide useful baselines against which to measure Fed operations.

A second important source of information is the condensed set of minutes for its previous meeting that the FOMC publishes a few days after each of its meetings. This information, roughly 60 days old when it becomes available, isn't much help in anticipating short-run changes in Fed policy, but it does shed light on how the FOMC is operating in general. In particular, it helps to convey the degree of consensus or lack of it within the Committee. The FOMC has a tradition of producing near-unanimous votes on its final policy stance. However, not all members are equally enthusiastic, and the policy record summarizes (anonymously) the concerns of the least persuaded. This can help a Fed watcher to assess the likelihood of a shift in the balance of opinion within the Committee in response to changing economic conditions.

Each set of FOMC minutes includes the policy directive given to the NY Fed at the end of the meeting. In recent years, this directive has included a brief summary of the economic environment as viewed by the FOMC, and a summary of recent money supply developments, and an "action paragraph" to guide the desk until the next FOMC meeting. This action paragraph specifies whether the desk should take any immediate action; it also lists the factors that should govern any intermeeting adjustments in policy. (These are the key policy variables that were summarized in Table 9–10.) The action paragraph in the directive issued at the meeting on March 28, 1989, read as follows:

> In the implementation of policy for the immediate future, the Committee seeks to maintain the existing degree of pressure on reserve positions. Taking account of indications of inflationary pressures, the strength of the business expansion, the behavior of the monetary aggregates, and developments in foreign exchange and domestic financial markets, somewhat greater reserve restraint would, or slightly lesser reserve restraint might, be acceptable in the inter-meeting period. The contemplated reserve conditions are expected to be consistent with growth of M2 and M3 over the period from March through June at annual rates of about 3 and 5 percent, respectively. The Chairman may call for Committee consultation if it appears to the Manager for Domestic Operations that reserve conditions during the period before the next meeting are likely to be associated with a federal funds rate persistently outside a range of 8 to 12 percent.

Several things about this paragraph are noteworthy. First is the fact that the FOMC voted for an unchanged policy: it sought "to maintain the existing degree of reserve positions." The Committee, however, was biased toward tightening further: in Fed-speak, to say that "somewhat greater . . . pressure would" be acceptable is a far stronger statement than "slightly lesser restraint might" be needed. The desk was being told to be prepared to nudge rates upward, depending on the strengths of inflation and of business activity.

The paragraph also illustrates the Fed's habit of retaining obsolete, boiler-plate text in its official documents. In early 1989, the FOMC persisted in including interim money supply growth rates in its directives, despite the fact that its list of priorities in the very same paragraph ranked the monetary aggregates third behind the outlook for inflation and the strength of the economy. As matters turned out, M2 fell at an annual rate of 2% between the March and May FOMC meetings, while M3 grew at only a 3% rate. This severe shortfall in monetary growth had *no* impact on the conduct of monetary policy during the period, despite the prominent position of the aggregates in the directive.

The tenacity of boiler-plate language is even more obvious in the concluding sentence about the funds rate. The directive says that the FOMC wants to be consulted if the desk's manager feels that the funds rate might move out of the 8 to 12% range. During the two-month intermeeting period that followed, the weekly average funds rate was frozen in a range of 9.71 to 9.95%. Under the operating procedures that the Fed, by 1989, had used for nearly seven years, it was virtually unthinkable that the funds rate might stray much further than that absent a shift in Fed policy.

Prior to each FOMC meeting, the Fed also publishes one policy document called the *tan* or *beige* book. This book compiles regional economic assessments sent in by the staffs of the 12 Federal Reserve Banks before each FOMC meeting. It is one of three regular reports put together for each meeting; all are known by the color of their covers. The other two are the *green book* and the *blue book,* both of which are written by the staff of the Fed Board in Washington. The green book assesses current economic conditions and makes economic projections for the next year or two; the blue book outlines the implications of the various short-run policies the FOMC might implement.

The fact that the Fed chooses to publish only the tan book says much about the latter's relative importance. If the Fed felt that the tan book said much relevant for policymaking, it would be classified as the other books are. As it stands, the tan book is composed of impressionistic, anecdotal evidence; no attempt is made to impose a common perspective on the brief regional reports it contains. The market pays much attention to the tan book, when it's published, perhaps more than the FOMC itself does.

There's one formal report that Congress requires the Fed to publish. Under the Full Employment and Balanced Growth Act of 1978 (known more familiarly as the Humphrey-Hawkins Act), the Fed must report semiannually on monetary policy to Congress. This requirement dates back to the peak of Congress's affaire du coeur with monetarism; originally, the report was intended to give Congress an opportunity to chide the Fed for not keeping M1 under control. Despite the fact that emphasis on M1 has waned, the Fed chairman still troops to Capitol Hill twice a year to explain monetary policy to the congressional banking committees.

His report contains a mixed bag of material. Its primary audience is Congress, not the bond market or the general public. Thus, the reports are designed to make as few waves as possible. They do, however, often convey the tone of the Fed's thinking on the economy. Also, they are sometimes used to announce innovations in Fed procedures: such reports have included first mentions of both the total debt aggregate and p^*. The market always pays close attention to the Humphrey-Hawkins reports, and on occasion, it's rewarded with a new insight into what the Fed's up to.

FORECASTING INTEREST RATES

Every bank, dealer, and investor is busy predicting interest rates over various time spans. Money market participants base many of their decisions on short-time horizons and are most concerned with and have most confidence in short-term rate predictions. Many believe that interest rates can be predicted with better than 50% accuracy for short periods—one, two, or three months—but that somewhere beyond that predictability diminishes sharply.

In predicting short-term interest rates, Fed watching is a big input in everyone's calculations. There are, however, other inputs. Interest-rate predictors are voracious readers of every bit of news on economic trends, on the ups and downs of economic indicators. In addition, they estimate the funds that borrowers are likely to demand and lenders are likely to supply; more demand than supply means that rates will likely rise. One important element in such estimates is the Treasury's projected borrowing needs. The Treasury estimates them, but the Street feels that the Treasury's figures are often unrealistic: because of political considerations, the Treasury must stick with the official projections of both GNP and the inflation rate in predicting its revenues and expenditures. Other problems also crop up. For example, Defense Department expenditures may run for months below projected levels due to delays in procurement.

Street predictors of interest rates also plug into their calculations the forecasts produced by major economic models, constructed by Wharton, Data Resources, and others. Also, many banks, dealers, and even large investors have sophisticated in-house models for making interest-rate predictions. The time span of econometric projections of interest rates tends, however, to be much longer than that on which money market participants base their decisions. So the economists and econometricians employed by banks and dealers—and they are legion—are by and large kept politely but firmly out of the trading room.

The Yield Curve as a Predictor of Rates

Another predictor of interest rates that many Street people look at is the yield curve. The argument for the yield curve as a predictor of interest rates is best illustrated with an example, taken from a period in the 1980s when the slope of the yield curve was *positive*. At that time, the 3-month bill was trading at 7.62, the 6-month bill at 8.00, and the 9-month bill at 8.40 (see Figure 9–5). Presumably, many people holding the 3-month bill had longer-term money to invest and could therefore have bought the 6-month bill, which was yielding 38 bp more than

FIGURE 9–5
The yield curve in the bill market has a *positive* slope

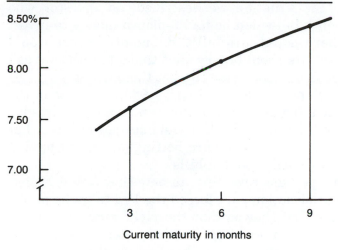

Current maturity in months

the 3-month bill. For them not to have done so implies that they expected that the 3-month bill three months hence would yield 8.38, that is, that by rolling the 3-month bill they could earn the same *average* return over six months as they could by buying the 6-month bill.[13] Similarly, the fact that the 9-month bill yielded 8.40 implies that investors expected the 3-month bill six months hence to also trade at 8.80. This sort of argument can be applied to any stretch of the yield curve, so that, throughout its length, the shape of this curve reflects the Street's expectations as to what future interest rates will be and thus provides implicit consensus predictions of future rates.

The value of these predictions is debatable. Presumably, they have a *bearish* cast, because the farther an investor extends on the maturity spectrum, the greater the price risk he assumes. The amount of that bearish bias can't be measured, but the assumption used to be that in ordinary times it works out to be 1% over the length of the yield curve. Since 1979, ordinary times have not prevailed.

---

[13]For the formula to precisely calculate the *forward* rates implied by cash bill rates, see Stigum's *Money Market Calculations,* pp. 54–57.

Whether the yield curve is a good or bad predictor of interest rates, an investor can't ignore the implicit rate predictions made by it. In the situation we described, an investor who bought the 3-month bill when he had 6-month money to invest *bet* implicitly that the 3-month bill three months hence would yield at least 8.80. He should know that that's his bet and ask whether it's a good bet, not make the bet thoughtlessly.

At times, such as late 1988 to early 1989, the slope of the yield curve in the bill market is *negative:* an investor must give up yield to extend maturity. Such a yield curve indicates that investors expect rates to fall and are betting on this by buying relatively expensive, longer-dated bills.

It's amusing, perhaps revealing, to note that Ralph Nader, in a freedom of information suit, forced the Fed to make public an internal memo that showed that the yield curve had had a better track record at predicting interest rates than did the Fed's own model. From this, one might conclude that econometric models are abysmal at predicting interest rates, that the yield curve is a better predictor of interest rates than most people believe, or that interest rates can't be predicted!

The Experts at Work

Twice a year, *The Wall Street Journal* asks a group of experts for their predictions on where the 3-month bill and the 30-year bond will trade six months hence. Then, six months later, the *Journal* repeats its survey; at the same time, it also compares prevailing bill and bond yields with the experts' predictions six months earlier as to what those yields would be. Typically, the experts' predictions turn out to be so bad that an investor, had he been forced to bet on the basis of "expert" opinion, would have done best had he bet that the experts would be wrong with respect to not only magnitude of change in yield, but direction of change.

A survey reported in the *Journal* on July 5, 1989, provides a case in point. It indicated that an individual who followed the experts' predictions at the end of December 89 would have totally missed the late spring bond rally in 89 because he would, looking at the experts' average prediction, have expected the yield on the long bond to be 121 bp higher than it actually was in

June 89. As one might expect, the experts did better in predicting in December 88 what 3-month bills would yield at the end of June 88: the experts' average forecast in December 88 was that 3-month bills would yield 8.28 at the end of June 89, whereas they actually yielded 7.89 at that time.

The problem with expert predictions is that experts display a herd instinct: no one wants to be the guy who was way-out-of-line wrong. So, if rates are going up, the expert feels a compulsion to predict that rates will go up some more or maybe stay flat. To predict that rates will fall is to go out on a limb where, if one is wrong, one is going to be wrong in a big, obvious way. A forecaster who follows the herd when the herd is wrong can always say, "Yea, I was wrong, but this and that fooled us all." (Read: "My prediction was no worse than most everybody else's.")

To be fair to experts, one should add that so many exogenous shocks constantly impinge on the economy that it may be that God Himself could not predict the long-bond rate six months hence—at least not unless He predetermined at creation all that has happened and all that shall happen.

Lacy Hunt of the CM&M Group (a primary dealer's expert) was honest enough to say that bond yields are inherently unpredictable. Amitai Etzioni, a professor at George Washington University, put it another way: "The lesson [of the *Journal* survey] is, if you believe economists can predict the future, then you also believe in the Tooth Fairy and Santa Claus."

THE NEXT CHAPTER

In the next chapter, we turn to the dealers and brokers who through their constant buying, selling, and communicating make liquid markets for money market securities. It is because of them that a Ford or a World Bank can pick up a phone and say, "Bid me 150MM of the long bond," and get a bid. It is also because of them that a U.S. or foreign borrower can, in a few hours, sell tens of millions of MTNs or commercial paper to investors. Dealing is always potentially profitable, always risky, and definitely never dull.

CHAPTER 10

THE MARKET MAKERS: DEALERS AND OTHERS

The collection of markets described in this book is called *the* money market. This suggests that the market's participants trade in a single market where at any time one price reigns for any one instrument. This description is accurate, but startling. Money market instruments, with the exception of futures contracts, are traded not on organized exchanges but over the counter. Moreover, money market participants, who vary in size from small to gargantuan, are scattered over the whole U.S.— *and* throughout Canada, Europe, the Middle East, and the Far East. Thus, one might expect fragmentation of the market, with big New York participants dealing in a noticeably different market from their London or Wichita counterparts. However, money market lenders and borrowers can operate almost as well out of Dearborn, Michigan (Ford), Washington (the World Bank), Tokyo, or Singapore as they can from Wall Street. Wherever they are, their access to information, bids, and offers is (time zone problems excepted) essentially the same. That the money market is a single market is due largely to the activities of the dealers and brokers who weld the market's many participants into a unified whole and to modern communication, which makes this possible.

THE DEALERS

First, a few definitions. In the U.S., commercial banks, prior to the slow and continued crumbling of Glass-Steagall, were institutions whose mission, according to law and regulation, was to

424

accept deposits in one form or another, to make loans, and if they so chose, to trade exempt securities. In their native countries, foreign banks often have broader powers; Japan is an exception, as it acquired, thanks to the American occupation after World War II, its own version of Glass-Steagall.

Nonbank dealers fall in the category of *investment bankers*. An investment banking firm is permitted to trade and to underwrite both exempt securities and corporate stocks and bonds as well—any paper that it or others can devise and bring to market. Investment banking, like commercial banking, requires a lot of capital. Among firms in the business, there are huge differences in size, capital, and range of products covered.

The British also have *merchant banks* whose principal mission is to earn fees by playing an advisory role and by setting up deals—often with an investment of their capital in the equity of the deals. To add to the confusion, all of the above institutions play a lot or a little on each other's turf. Also, the British have a confusing habit of referring to investment bankers as "banks," so when a Brit talks about a bank, it may turn out to be Merrill Lynch.

This is a book about the money market. Consequently, in speaking of *dealers,* our principal focus will be on the activities of investment banks and of commercial banks in the issuance and trading of money market securities. However, we can't ignore the many other markets in which some dealers are active because how well or poorly dealers fare in these markets can and has impacted their money market activities; for example, firms that suffered crippling losses when the stock market nosedived in October 1987 were in no mood or position to continue to be active market makers and position takers in Treasuries, money markets, or mortgage-backed securities.

Agent and Principal Roles

In dealing in money market paper, dealers may wear one of two hats, agent or principal. If a dealer acts as an *agent,* he gets a *fee* from an issuer for showing and selling the latter's paper to investors. Goldman, Merrill, and Shearson, all big dealers in commercial paper, wear their agent hat almost all the time when they sell commercial paper. So too do dealers when they sell new medium-term notes (MTNs) for issuers. We say "almost all the time" because occasionally an issuer, with a special financing need, will ask a dealer, who is his agent for selling commercial paper or MTNs, to position for him a specific chunk of paper to a specific date—always with the understanding that that paper is the dealer's to trade as he chooses.

When a dealer puts on his hat as *principal,* that means he is buying for and selling from his own position; put another way, in a trade, he is the customer's counterparty, not his agent. Dealers act as principal in many sectors of the money market. For example, when dealers bid on, distribute at issue, and later trade Treasury and federal agency securities, they always act as principal.

To say that a dealer acts as an agent in a particular market does not preclude his also trading in that market as a principal. For example, Merrill, which took the lead in creating the MTN market, made a commitment to investors, at the time it did so, to always be there to bid, at no more than an 05 off the offer, for any MTNs that investors had bought and now wanted to sell. Thus, in the MTN market, Merrill and other dealers who entered this market act as agent, most times, when new paper is issued; but equally important, they act as principal in creating a lively secondary market for such paper.

Dealers as Market Makers

While their motive is profit, the crucial role dealers play in the money market is as market makers; and in performing that role, they often trade off their own positions. Part of the dealers' role as market makers involves *underwriting new issues.* Most large municipal note issues are bought up at issue by dealers or syndicates of them who take these securities into position and sell them off to retail. In the market for governments, there is also underwriting, though of a less formal nature; frequently, dealers buy large amounts of new government issues at auction and then distribute them to retail.

In the *secondary market,* dealers act as market makers by constantly quoting bids and offers at which they are willing to buy and sell. Some of these quotes are to other dealers. In many sectors of the money market, there is an *inside market* amongst dealers. In this market, dealers quote price *runs* (*bids* and *offers* for securities of different maturities) to other dealers, often via interdealer brokers. Since every dealer will *hit* a bid he views as high and *lift* an offering he views as low, trading in the inside market creates, at any time for every security traded, a prevailing price that represents the dealers' consensus of what that security is worth.

Dealers also actively quote bids and offers to retail. In doing so, they consistently seek to give their customers the best quotes possible because they value retail business and know that other shops compete actively with them for it. This competition ensures that dealers' quotes to retail will never be far removed from prices prevailing in the inside market. Thus, all of the money market's geographically dispersed participants can always trade at close to identical bids and offers.

As the above suggests, through their trading activities, the dealers give the secondary market for money market instruments two important characteristics. First, they ensure that at any moment a single price level will prevail for any instrument traded in it. Second, by standing ready to quote firm bids and offers at which they will trade, they render money market instruments liquid.

SOURCES OF DEALER PROFITS

Dealers earn profits from various, often interrelated, activities: agent fees, trading, doing customer business, positioning, carry (when it's positive), arbitrage, the sale of proprietory products, and so on.

Agent Fees

Currently, commercial paper outstanding dwarfs the amounts outstanding of every other money market instrument and even outstrips T bills outstanding. Also, the MTN market is, for money market dealers, the big success story of the current decade. Thus, agent fees, for dealers who are top players in the commercial paper and MTN markets, amount in the aggregate to a tidy and dependable source of profit. Also, those fees are a profit source that commercial bankers have eyed with envy as they fought to break down barriers that prevented them from expanding further into investment banking.

Trading

What a trader is supposed to do depends on what he trades and what firm he works for—also, on market environment. In the past, traders were often expected to make money actively trading their sector of the market, short-term, even intraday, and often interdealer. When the CD market was alive and well, the big traders at Sali and Merrill might be heard saying, "Hit your bid for 100[MM]," "Lift your offering for 50."

Today, while short-term trading of cash instruments to earn trading profits still occurs, it's less lively in many markets than formerly. Part of the reason is in the change in what's out there to trade: the domestic CD market is dead; the BA market is shrinking; and the commercial paper market never was a trading market. Also, the mood of the dealing community has changed over the last decade. Bouts of historically high and historically volatile interest rates as well as major losses at a number of houses have caused firms to put more focus on building up dependable, steady sources of profit and on controlling risk.

Some years ago, a trader described the Street as "the last frontier." In a sense, it still is for the right person in the right place. However, dealers, unlike Clint Eastwood, are not eternally primed to shoot from the hip whenever an opportunity arises. Dealers go through cyclical mood swings that are heavily dependent both on their past results and on the current market environment.

Still, over time, dealing rooms have become populated with ever more traders. There has been a proliferation of products; a dealer probably has fewer, perhaps far fewer, traders now trading strictly money market instruments. But he now has basis traders trading the basis between various cash and futures instruments, options adjusted traders who arb OTC options against Treasuries if yield on the latter looks relatively cheap or rich, swap traders, and all sorts of other arb traders. With the advent of globalization and the 24-hour markets, there are more and more instruments to arb and more and more hours in which to do it. Thus, it is not surprising that the Primary Dealers Association's 1988 directory listed over 760 traders at the 41 dealers covered—many of whom have offices not only in New York, but in London, Tokyo, and Hong Kong; and this list is far from all-inclusive.

Servicing Customers

An important part of a trader's job has always been to service his firm's retail base: to acquire, at attractive rates, paper for his firm's sales force to show and sell to investors. Sometimes, that is most or all of what a firm wants certain traders to do. For example, Merrill, with its superb distribution, wants its money market traders to concentrate on acquiring paper for distribution; they are not paid to make an 02 here or there trading.

In governments, a dealer also tries to make a 1/32 by buying in the *inside,* interdealer market and then selling to retail. However, competition to capture big retail accounts is often so fierce that such profits prove illusive. Nonetheless, dealers keep competing to do retail business because, even if it's not particularly profitable, it gives them valuable information on how customers view the market, on what they are doing—buying or selling.

"One of the most important factors in our positioning," noted one dealer, "is what our customer base is doing. If we see a tremendous amount of customer selling, we will do the business, but our traders must be adept at buying securities and immediately dumping them back into the Street through the brokers and ending up, ideally, short the market. That information [on customers] is really valuable; it is why we develop those relationships."

Proprietary Products

When the glamour of doing big deals in governments, agency paper, or money markets is stripped away, running a dealership is not so different from running a supermarket: a dealer's competitors all have pretty much the same products at pretty much the same price. It is tough to get rich peddling catsup; equally, it's tough to get rich selling plain vanilla governments.

Hence, dealers are always on the outlook for a new proprietory product—something they can sell to retail *at a spread* because they are the only or the first suppliers of that product. Some years back, dealers, led by Merrill, started setting up trusts backed by Treasuries through which they sold to retail TIGRs and a zoo of other homemade, zero-coupon Treasuries. That game was so profitable for the dealers that the Treasury preempted the profit in it by permitting a more efficient stripping of Treasuries via the book-entry system. Dealers, undeterred, went on to other pastures: used mortgages to back yet new sorts of hybrid paper; created hedged transactions in foreign currency-denominated paper; created, priced, and sold interest-rate caps, collars, and floors; and so on and on.

One way to make money on customer business is via financial innovation. Seeing this, dealers combed the universities and other institutions to find people with strong backgrounds in math and finance—*quants* or *rocket scientists* as they were quickly dubbed—paid them astronomical salaries, and asked them to engineer new derivative products, including options and other hybrids, that could be sold to retail at a spread. Such innovation proved, however, to carry its own risks, noted below.

Yet another way dealers seek to profit from customer business is by having its traders develop and pass on to retail good ideas on trades to be done—on what is cheap and what is expensive. This tack works better in complex securities, such as mortgage-backs and their derivatives, than in Treasuries. In the former market, the implied prepayment option in a mortgage often causes mortgage-backed products to trade in unexpected ways, as rate levels move and the yield curve shifts.

Also, Merrill, by selling—perhaps mistakenly—its Bloomberg system to big customers, gave them access to reams of historical data and the capacity to examine spreads between securities and over time spans of their choosing. One result was that sophisticated customers were soon, on their own initiative, trying to sell to Merrill what was expensive and buy from Merrill what was cheap—not the sort of customer business for which a dealer nightly prays.

Position Profits

A dealer, depending on the product, the market, and his mood—
"I'm bullish" or "Ouch, I just took a *big* hit"—may look to *position taking* to make big profits. If customers are in a mood to buy and if a dealer thinks the market will rally or continue to rally, he might want to add 100MM or whatever to his positions with the intent to hold those positions for some time until he can sell them out at a tidy profit.

Traditionally, the appetite of some shops to position, *to speculate,* has been stronger at some shops than at others.[1] One might argue that positioning done specifically to speculate, as opposed to positioning that arises out of a dealer's daily trading activities with retail and with other dealers, is not an inherent part of being a market maker. Such speculation serves, however, useful functions. It guarantees that market prices will react rapidly to any change in economic conditions, in demand, in supply, or in rate expectations. Also, and more important, the profits dealers can earn from correct position plays are a prime incentive for them to set up the elaborate and expensive operations that they daily use to trade with retail and each other. In effect, position profits help to oil the machinery that dealers need to be effective market makers.

Dealers possess no crystal balls enabling them to perfectly foresee the future. They position on the basis of carefully formulated expectations. When they are right, they can make huge profits; when they are wrong, their losses can be staggering. Thus, the successful shops, the ones that survive, are right on the market more often than wrong.

As noted, dealers' appetite for positioning changes in part with economic conditions. In the early 1980s, when interest rates were high and highly volatile, one dealer in governments

---

[1]The term *speculation* as used here and throughout this book is *not* meant to carry any pejorative connotation. *Speculation is taking an unhedged position, long or short.* A homeowner who buys a house financed with a mortgage is assuming a speculative, leveraged position in real estate. A dealer who buys governments with repo money is assuming a speculative, leveraged position in governments. The only difference between the two is that the dealer *knows* he's speculating; the homeowner used not to think of it that way.

commented, "For us to make money, we have to focus on the real nuts and bolts of the business—service. We look at our business as one in which we provide our clients access to the market, investment advice, risk transfer, and execution." Put another way, "We are trying to make money servicing retail." In the late 1980s, another dealer in governments commented: "Spreads have shrunk to the point where it is questionable how much profit there is in doing customer trades. Thus, there is an increased necessity to position because to do customer business alone does not make you successful."

Another factor in a shop's appetite for position plays is the way it is organized. Banks, as highly visible, publicly owned institutions, have always operated under a lot of pressure from bank analysts to generate a *steadily growing* profit stream; they earn no brownie points for making big capital gains this quarter and none the next. Big nonbank dealers organized as partnerships used not to be under the same pressure, but when they went public, they began to sound and act like banks. Said one such nonbank dealer, "As a highly visible public firm, we have had to begin to look at leverage and consistency of earnings because we want to maintain the high perceived value our debt has in the market, and we want the market to view our stock not as cyclical, but as blue chip." That's a precrash of 1987 quote.

The Numbers

Table 10–1 presents some interesting numbers on the positions that dealers have taken in recent years. The growth over time in the figures on line 7, which records dealer positions in federal agency securities, correctly suggests that dealers have been operating in a rapidly expanding market. Agencies are awkward to short as markets for them are often illiquid compared to those for Treasuries. If a dealer thinks that the market is due to head South, the instrument to short is Treasuries, not agencies, CDs, BAs, or commercial paper.

The big shorts that dealers have at times run in Treasuries overall, and in particular maturity sectors of the Treasury market, reflect several things. First, dealers short Treasuries if they expect the market to drop; second, dealers have, in recent years, shorted huge amounts of Treasuries to hedge positions in other instruments—in particular, but not only, interest-rate swaps; third, dealers often short Treasuries as part of an arbitrage.

The massive numbers for repos and reverses recorded under the *Financing* heading of Table 10–1 reflect not only the financing by dealers of positions, but more important, the running by dealers of matched books in repo and reverse (discussed below).

HEDGING

No dealer can stand ready to make markets to customers without holding inventory and being willing to position securities on which a customer wants a bid. Shops that stress making markets to retail realize this and emphasize techniques to minimize the risk inherent in being a market maker. One technique is hedging. Hedging, once a sometimes affair, currently gets a lot of attention, especially now that large and liquid futures markets exist for governments and Euro time deposits. Using these markets, a dealer can transfer the risk generated by customer business back into the markets far faster than formerly, and dealers do just that.

Over time, hedging has evolved into an art form and is, for some products at some shops, an automatic response to position taking done to facilitate customer business. Not so long ago, a dealer wanting to hedge a position in cash securities had basically two choices: short a like cash instrument or short futures. Now that the menu of both products and derivative products has grown, new hedge trades have become routine. For example, a dealer might use an interest-rate swap to hedge a position in MTNs, a short of cash Treasuries to hedge an interest-rate swap, a short of Euro futures to hedge commercial paper, a cap to hedge a floor, and so on and on. The possibilities keep growing.

Most times, a trader doing a hedge does not completely eliminate risk, because the item he sells differs somewhat from the item he bought. In that case, the hedger has residual spread risk: during the time of his hedge, the spread between the yields on the items he's long and short might move against him. On a well-constructed hedge, residual spread risk is far less than the

TABLE 10–1

U.S. Government securities dealers positions and financing (averages of daily figures, in billions of dollars)[1]

							1989	
Item	1984	1985	1986	1987	1988	Jan.	Feb.
					Positions			
Net immediate[2]								
1. U.S. Treasury securities	5.4	7.4	13.1	−6.2	−22.7	−32.3	−31.7
2. Bills	5.5	10.0	12.7	4.3	2.2	−3.5	−3.7
3. Other within 1 year	0.06	1.0	3.7	1.6	−2.2	−1.8	−3.5
4. 1–5 years	2.2	5.1	9.3	0.6	−3.0	−10.1	−8.8
5. 5–10 years	−1.1	−6.2	−9.5	−6.5	−9.7	−8.5	−8.2
6. Over 10 years	−1.2	−2.7	−3.2	−6.2	−10.1	−8.3	−7.3
7. Federal agency securities	15.3	22.9	33.1	31.9	28.2	26.7	30.1
8. Certificates of deposit	7.4	9.2	10.6	8.2	7.3	6.8	6.3
9. Bankers' acceptances	3.9	4.6	5.5	3.7	2.5	2.2	2.2
10. Commercial paper	3.8	5.6	8.1	7.5	6.1	8.6	6.5
Futures positions								
11. Treasury bills	−4.5	−7.3	−18.1	−3.3	−2.2	−1.6	4.6
12. Treasury coupons	1.8	4.5	3.5	6.0	6.2	3.3	2.8
13. Federal agency securities	0.2	−0.7	−0.2	0	0	0	0
Forward positions								
14. U.S. Treasury securities	−1.6	−0.9	−2.3	−1.2	0.3	0.1	0.9
15. Federal agency securities	−9.2	−9.4	−11.9	−18.8	−16.3	−12.8	−14.8

Financing[3]

Reverse repurchase agreements[4]							
16. Overnight and continuing	44.1	68.0	99.0	126.7	136.3	150.5	127.4
17. Term agreements	68.3	80.5	108.7	148.3	177.5	198.8	172.6
Repurchase agreements[5]							
18. Overnight and continuing	75.7	101.4	141.7	170.7	172.7	193.4	163.8
19. Term	57.0	70.0	102.6	121.2	137.1	139.5	126.0

[1]Data for dealer positions and sources of financing are obtained from reports submitted to the Federal Reserve Bank of New York by the U.S. Treasury securities dealers on its published list of primary dealers.

Data for positions are averages of daily figures, in terms of par value, based on the number of trading days in the period. Positions are net amounts and are shown on a commitment basis. Data for financing are in terms of actual amounts borrowed or lent and are based on Wednesday figures.

[2]Immediate positions are net amounts (in terms of par values) of securities owned by nonbank dealer firms and dealer departments of commercial banks on a commitment, that is, trade-date basis, including any such securities that have been sold under agreements to repurchase (repos). The maturities of some repurchase agreements are sufficiently long, however, to suggest that the securities involved are not available for trading purposes. Immediate positions include reverses to maturity, which are securities that were sold after having been obtained under reverse repurchase agreements that mature on the same day as the securities. Data for immediate positions do not include forward positions.

[3]Figures cover financing involving U.S. Treasury and federal agency securities, negotiable CDs, bankers' acceptances, and commercial paper.

[4]Includes all reverse repurchase agreements, including those that have been arranged to make delivery on short sales and those for which the securities obtained have been used as collateral on borrowings, that is, matched agreements.

[5]Includes both repurchase agreements undertaken to finance positions and "matched-book" repurchase agreements.

Note: Data on positions for the period May 1 to September 30, 1986, are partially estimated.

Source: *Federal Reserve Bulletin.*

market risk inherent in the position hedged. Thus, whenever hedging does not eliminate position risk, it at least substantially reduces it.

DEALER FINANCING AND CARRY

The typical dealer is running a highly leveraged operation in which securities held in position may, depending on whether he's a bank or a nonbank dealer and on the types of securities he trades, total 40, 50, or 100 times capital. Dealers used to rely heavily on dealer loans from New York banks for financing, but now, as one dealer commented: "The state of that art is that you don't have to."

Repo money is cheaper, and dealers rely chiefly on it to meet their primary financing needs. For such dealers, the need to obtain repo money on a continuing basis and in large amounts is one additional reason for assiduously cultivating retail customers. The money funds, corporations, state and local governments, and other investors that buy governments and other instruments from dealers are also big suppliers of repo money to them.

Much of the borrowing dealers do in the repo market is done on an overnight basis (Table 10–1). The overnight rate is typically the lowest repo rate. Also, securities "hung out" on repo for one night only are available for sale the next day. Nonbank dealers have to clear all their repo transactions through the clearing banks, which is expensive. As a result, they also do a lot of *open repos* at rates slightly above the overnight rate. Open or demand repos have an indefinite term, either the borrower or the lender can, each morning, choose to terminate the agreement.

Banks prefer to do overnight repos with customers who will permit them to safekeep the securities bought. This saves clearing costs and ensures that the bank will have the securities back at 9 A.M. the next day. If repoed securities are transferred out of the bank, there is always the possibility that the securities will be delivered back to the bank too late the next day for the bank to repo them again or to make timely delivery if they have been sold. To make repo as convenient an investment as possible, some banks have minimum balance arrangements with customers under which any excess deposit balances the customer holds with them are automatically invested in repo. In effect, what such a bank is doing is getting around Reg Q and paying the customer interest on any demand deposits he holds in excess of any minimum compensating balance the bank requires him to maintain.

The financing needs that nonbank dealers do not cover in the repo market are met by borrowing from banks at the dealer loan rate. Even dealers who look primarily to the repo market for financing will use bank loans to finance small pieces they hold in inventory. A typical nonbank dealer commented, "The smallest repo ticket I will write is 2MM. On a transaction of less than 2, writing the tickets and making deliveries is not worth the cost and trouble. I can combine small pieces, but generally I let such junk just sit at the bank."

In financing, bank dealers have one advantage over nonbank dealers—they can finance odd pieces they do not repo by buying Fed funds.

While much dealer financing is done using open or very short repos, dealers will sometimes finance speculative positions they anticipate holding for some time with term repo, taking in money for 30, 60, or 90 days, or even longer (Table 10–1).

Fails and the Fails Game

If, on the settlement date of a trade, a seller does not make timely delivery of the securities purchased, delivers the wrong securities, or fails in some other way to deliver in proper form, the trade becomes a *fail*. In that case, the buyer does not have to make payment until proper delivery is made, presumably the next day; *but* he owns the securities as of the initially agreed-upon settlement day. Thus, on a fail the security buyer (who is *failed to*) receives a one-day free loan equal to the amount of the purchase price, that is, one day's free financing. And if the fail persists, the free loan continues. Fails occur not only in connection with straight trades, but in connection with repos; on a repo, the lender has to make timely return of the collateral he is holding to unwind the transaction and get his money back.

Dealers often play some portion of their financing needs for a fail; that is, they estimate on the basis of past experience the dollar amount of the fails that will be made to them and reduce their repo borrowing accordingly. If their estimate proves high, more securities will end up in their box at the clearing bank than they had anticipated, and that bank will automatically grant them a box loan against that collateral.[2] On such last-minute loans, the clearing banks charge the dealer a rate that's a tiny margin above their posted dealer loan rate to encourage dealers to track their positions and run an orderly shop. A dealer who plays the *fails game* is in effect using his clearing bank as a lender of last resort.

A DEALER'S BOOK

A dealer who takes big positions is operating like a banker. He acquires assets of varying types and maturities and incurs liabilities of varying maturities to finance them. And like a banker, he faces *risks:* credit risks, a rate risk, and a liquidity risk.

Because dealers confine themselves to buying high-grade paper, as opposed to making loans to LDCs, dealers assume fewer and smaller credit risks than banks do. But because they borrow so much short-term money and are so highly leveraged, the rate risk they assume is substantial. This is especially true because the classic way dealers make a bullish bet is not only to buy *more* securities, but to *extend* to longer maturities where they get more bang for the buck from rate movements.

Every dealer, because he is exposed to a large rate risk, is conscious that he is running a large *unmatched book.* Moreover, he seeks, like a bank, to profit from that mismatch while simultaneously monitoring it to ensure that it does not become so large that it exposes him to *an unacceptable level* of risk. Noted

---

[2]See the discussion of dealer loans by clearing banks at the end of this chapter.

one dealer, "Any guy who can run a large dealer operation on leverage could run a bank, not the esoterica of loans to Zaire, but the nuts and bolts of asset and liability management."

While bankers talk about managing the mismatch in their book, dealers talk about *tail management,* by which they mean the same thing. Dealers also talk about *indices,* where an index is some average of asset and liability maturities that indicates the rate risk to which they are exposed.

One difference between dealers and banks is that there is much more pressure on the dealer to be right and to be right in the short run. One reason is that dealers mark their assets to market daily and track daily their profits and losses overall and by instrument. A second reason is that dealers' annual compensation is tied closely to performance through bonuses or other devices. As one dealer noted, "If we buy at the wrong moment, we cannot hold a 2-year note, let alone a 10-year bond, to maturity not only because of profit considerations, but because of the emotional and psychological damage that holding that security and marking it to market would have on the work group. We have to be right on balance, and we don't have the luxury of being able to wait for the long run to prove us right." A bank, in contrast, while it marks its dealer and trading portfolios to market, may or may not track the performance of its investment portfolio daily, and it certainly does not attempt to mark its loans to market. Thus, in managing its overall position, a bank can brush under the carpet the consequences of at least some ill-conceived plays by lumping their impact on profit in with overall profits instead of isolating them.

Interest-Rate Predictions

The key rate in the money market is the Fed funds rate. Because of the role of this rate in determining dealers' cost of carry (the repo rate is usually slightly below the funds rate), other short-term rates key off the Fed funds rate in a fairly predictable way (Figure 10–1). Thus, when a dealer positions, he does so on the basis of a strongly held view with respect to where money supply numbers and Fed policy are headed; and *every long position he assumes is, in particular, based on an implicit prediction of how*

FIGURE 10–1

Other short-term money rates key off the Fed funds rate

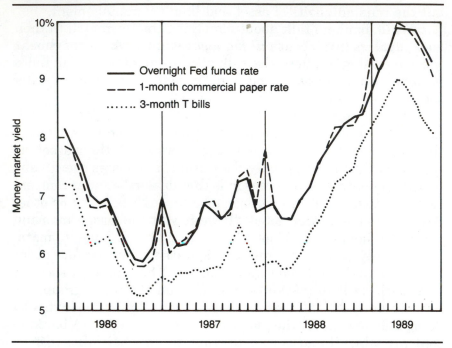

Source: *Federal Reserve Bulletin.*

high Fed funds and other money market instruments might trade within the time frame of his investment. In formulating expectations about the funds rate, dealers engage in constant and careful Fed watching of the sort described in Chapter 9.

Confidence Level in Positioning

Positioning is a form of gambling, and the dealers most skilled in this art attempt first to express their expectations about what might occur in terms of probabilities of various outcomes and second to estimate the payoff or loss that a given strategy would yield if each of these outcomes were to occur. Then, on the basis of these numbers, they decide whether to bet and how much to bet.

Probabilists who have theorized about gambling like to talk about a fair gamble or a *fair game*. A fair game is one that, if played repeatedly, will yield the player neither net gains nor losses. For example, suppose a person plays the following game: A coin is flipped; if it lands heads up, he wins $1; if it lands heads down, he loses $1. The probability that the coin will land heads up is ½. So half the time he bets our player will lose $1; half the time he will win $1; and his *expected winnings or return,* if he plays the game repeatedly, is *zero*.

There is nothing in it for a dealer to make a fair bet. What he looks for is a situation in which expected return is *positive;* and the more positive it is, the more he will bet. For example, if a dealer believed: (1) that the probabilities that the Fed would ease and tighten were 60% and 40%, respectively, and (2) that a given long position would return him $2 if the Fed eased and would cause him to lose $1 if the Fed tightened, then his *expected* winnings would be

$$0.6 \times \$2 - 0.4 \times \$1 = \$0.80$$

In other words, the gamble is such that, if the dealer made it 10 times, his expected winnings would be $8. That degree of favorableness in the bet might suffice to induce the dealer to position.

If the game were made still more favorable, for example by an improvement in the odds, then he would gamble still more. For example, if the dealer believed: (1) that the probabilities that the Fed would ease and tighten were 70% and 30%, respectively, and (2) that a given long position would again return him $2 if the Fed eased and lose him $1 if the Fed tightened, then his expected winnings would be

$$0.7 \times \$2 - 0.3 \times \$1 = \$1.10$$

In other words, the gamble is such that, if he made it 10 times, his expected winnings would be $11. That's the sort of gamble that might cause the dealer to pull up the delivery trucks and position securities in size.

All this may sound a bit theoretical, but it is the way good dealers think, explicitly or intuitively; and such thinking disciplines them in positioning. As one dealer noted: "The alternative is a sloppy operation in which a dealer runs up his position because he sort of likes the market now or runs it down because he doesn't like the market."

Quantifying his thinking about the market also helps a dealer provide retail with useful suggestions. Most customers can find fair bets on their own. What they appreciate is a dealer who can suggest to them a favorable bet, that is, one on which the odds are out of synchronization with the payoff and the expected return is therefore positive.[3]

In quantifying expectations and payoffs and acting on them, fleet-footedness is essential. Everyone on the Street is playing the same game, and the market therefore frequently anticipates what the Fed is going to do. Thus, the dealer who waits until the Fed is ready to move will probably be too late to make money, the market having already discounted much or all of that move.

The Maturity Choice

We suggested that the more favorable the gamble a dealer faces, the more securities he's likely to position. And this is precisely the way dealers talk about what they do; specifically, dealers frequently comment, "The higher our *confidence level,* the more we will position." Translated into the jargon we've used, this means simply that the higher the probability associated with gain and the lower that associated with loss (that is, the higher the expected return), the more the dealer will bet.

There is, however, one more wrinkle to the dealer's positioning decision. As noted, a classic part of a bullish strategy is for a dealer to extend to longer maturities. The reason he is tempted to extend is that the longer the maturity of the securi-

---

[3]To keep things simple, we assumed in our examples that only two interest-rate outcomes were possible. More might be, each with its own associated payoff; Let p_1 equal the probability of the first interest-rate outcome and x_1 the associated payoff; p_2 the probability of the second interest-rate outcome and x_2 the associated payoff; and so on. Then, the expected return or value (E) on a bet in which it is assumed that the Fed might peg Fed funds at any one of three possible levels would be:

$$E = p_1x_1 + p_2x_2 + p_3x_3$$

Using this approach, one can easily generalize the technique to any number of possible outcomes.

ties he positions, the more price play he will get. To illustrate, suppose that a dealer believes that the probability that the average Fed funds rate will *fall* by 1 point is 70% and the probability it will *rise* by 1 point is 30%. If the dealer positions the 90-day bill, which has a yield that is likely to move roughly as many basis points as the Fed funds rate does, he will be making a bet on which his potential gains and losses per $1MM of securities positioned are $2,500. If alternatively—to make the example extreme—he invests in the 9s of 2018, his potential gains and losses will be in the range of $49,000 per $1MM even if a 1-point move in the Fed funds rate is assumed to move the yield on these securities only 15 bp. Whether he positions 90-day bills or the 9s of 2018, the dealer is making a favorable bet. However, positioning the 9s of 2018 is a much *riskier* bet because, if rates rise, the dealer will lose much more owning the 9s of 2018 than he will owning the 90-day bill.

Dealers are very conscious that extending to longer maturities exposes them to greater *price risk*. They also tend to think that extending to longer maturities exposes them to greater risk for another reason; namely, the predictability of long-term rates is less than that of short-term rates. Short rates relate directly to Fed policy; long rates do so to a much lesser extent because they are also strongly influenced by the *slope* of the yield curve. Thus, the dealer who extends must be prepared not only to predict Fed policy, but to predict shifts in the slope of the yield curve—an art that is separate from and, in the eyes of many dealers, more difficult than successful Fed watching.

To protect against the risks posed by extending maturity, some dealers confine their unhedged positions largely to securities of short current maturity. A dealer typical of this group noted, "We are accused of being an inch wide and a mile deep— the mile deep being in securities with a maturity of a year and under. There are various arts in this business: predicting spreads, predicting the yield curve, predicting the trend in interest rates. You go with the learning curve of the organization you have, and ours is very strong in predicting short-term spreads and yields."

Other dealers are more willing to extend maturity to reach for gains, but in doing so, they seek to control carefully the price

risk they assume. The guidelines used to control price risk—
frequently they take the form of smaller position limits on
longer maturities—vary considerably from shop to shop. One
reason is that there is no certain way a dealer can compare the
risk he assumes in holding 6-year notes to that he assumes in
holding 6-month bills. Another is that, in establishing position
limits by instrument and maturity, a dealer is inevitably making subjective judgments about the ability of each of his traders.

SHORTING

When money market dealers are bullish, they place their bets
by positioning securities: when they are bearish, they do so by
shorting. One might expect that the quantity of securities a
dealer would short, if he believed that the probability of a fall in
securities prices was 80%, would be as great as the quantity of
securities he would position if he believed that the probability of
a rise in securities prices was 80%. But in fact dealers will, at a
given confidence level, short smaller amounts of securities than
they would position. There are several reasons. First, the only
instruments dealers can short are governments and agencies;
other instruments, such as commercial paper, MTNs, Euro CDs,
and muni notes, are too heterogeneous with respect to name,
maturity, and face amount to short. Second, shorting securities
tends to be more cumbersome and expensive than going long
because the short seller must find not only a buyer, but—since
the shorted securities must be delivered—a source of these securities.

Over time, it has become increasingly common for dealers
to *reverse in* securities shorted rather than to borrow them. One
reason is that the reverse may be cheaper. When a dealer borrows securities, he gives up other securities as collateral and
pays the lender a borrowing fee, which typically equals 1/2 of 1%
but may be more if many people want to short an issue at once.
On a reverse, the dealer obtains the securities shorted by buying
them from an investor with an agreement to repurchase. In
effect, the dealer is extending a collateralized loan to the owner
of these securities. The owner takes the loan because he needs

cash or, more typically, because he can reinvest the loan proceeds at a higher rate, and the reverse thus becomes to him part of a profitable arbitrage.

Whether a dealer borrows securities or reverses them in, he must make an *investment*—in the first case in collateral, in the second case in a loan to the institution on the other side of the reverse. To figure which investment would yield more, he compares the rate he could earn on the collateral *minus* the borrowing fee with the reverse rate. For example, suppose a dealer has some short-dated paper yielding 9.25% he could use as collateral. If he did so, he would own that paper at 9.25% minus the 0.5% borrowing fee; that is, at an effective rate of 8.75%. If the reverse rate were 9%, he would do better on the reverse.

A dealer's overall cost on a short is (1) the interest that accrues on the securities shorted (rise in value in the case of a discount security) over the period the short is outstanding *minus* (2) the yield on the offsetting investment he makes. If the reverse rate exceeds the net rate he could earn on collateral backing a borrowing, reversing will be the cheaper way to support his short.

A dealer who borrows securities to support a short never knows with certainty how long he can have those securities because borrowed securities can be called by the lender on a day's notice. If, alternatively, a dealer reverses in securities for a fixed period, he knows he will have the securities for that time. Thus, a dealer who anticipates maintaining a short for some time may choose to cover through a reverse rather than a borrowing because it offers him certainty of availability.

REPO AND REVERSE BOOK

A large dealer who is known to the Street can borrow more in the repo market and at better rates than can a small dealer or a corporate portfolio manager. Thus, a large dealer finds knocking at his doors not only customers who want to give him repo money, but would-be borrowers who want to reverse out securities to him because that is the cheapest way they can borrow. In response to the latter demand, large dealers have taken to doing repo and reverse not just to suit their own needs but as a profit-making service to customers. In providing that service, the dealer takes in securities on one side at one rate and hangs them out on the other side at a slightly more favorable (lower) rate; or to put it the other way around, the dealer borrows money from his repo customers at one rate and lends it to his reverse customers at a slightly higher rate. In doing so, the dealer is acting like a bank, and dealers know this well. As one noted, "This shop *is* a bank. We have customers lining up every morning to give us money. Also we are in the business of finding people who will give us securities at a little better rate than we can push them out the repo door. So we are a bank taking out our little spread, acting—if you will—as a financial intermediary."

A dealer who seeks to profit by borrowing in the repo market and lending in the reverse market ends up in effect running a *book* in repo. And, like a bank, he can mismatch that book to increase his profit, that is, borrow short and lend long. A dealer who runs a short book in repo incurs not only a rate risk, but other risks as well.[4]

ARBITRAGES

Arbitrage is another activity from which dealers seek to develop consistent profits—not spectacular gains but 10 bp here and 20 there earned by observing an anomaly in the market, taking a position against it, and then having the patience to wait until natural market forces eliminate that anomaly and permit the arb to be unwound at a profit.

Strictly defined, the term *arbitrage* means to buy at a low price in one market and to simultaneously resell at a higher price in another market. Some arbitrages in this strict sense do occur in the money market. For example, when a Japanese bank sells deposit notes at 50 over (Treasuries), swaps the proceeds at 80 over to get funding at LIBOR minus 30, and simultaneously buys other banks, Euro CDs at LIBOR flat, it is engaging in

---

[4]See numbers in Table 10–1; also Chapter 13.

arbitrage in the strict sense of the term[5]. Another example of pure arbitrage would be a dealer who takes in collateral on a reverse for a fixed period and repos at a lower rate for precisely the same period, that is, a matched transaction in repo.

Money market participants use the term *arbitrage* to refer not only to pure arbitrages, but to various transactions in which they seek to profit by *exploiting anomalies* either in the yield curve or in the pattern of rates established between different instruments. Typically, the anomaly is that the yield spread between two similar instruments is too wide or too narrow; that is, one instrument is priced too generously relative to the other. To exploit such an anomaly, the arbitrageur *shorts* the expensive instrument and goes *long* in its underpriced cousin; in other words, he shorts the instrument that has an abnormally low yield relative to the yield on the instrument in which he goes long.

If the arbitrageur is successful, he will be able to unwind his arbitrage at a profit because the abnormal yield spread will have narrowed in one of several ways: (1) the security shorted will have fallen in price and risen in yield, (2) the security purchased will have risen in price and fallen in yield, or (3) a combination of the two will have occurred.

In the money market, yield spread arbitrages are often done (1) between identical instruments of similar maturity (one government is priced too generously relative to another government of similar maturity) and (2) between different instruments of the same maturity (an agency) issue is priced too generously relative to a government issue of the same maturity).

Note that in strictly defined yield spread arbitrage (the long and the short positions in similar maturities), the arbitrageur exposes himself to *no market risk*. If rates rise, the resulting loss on his long position will be offset by profits on his short position; if rates fall, the reverse will occur. Thus, the arbitrageur is not basing his position on a prediction of the direction of market rates; he is concerned about a possible move up or down in inter-

---

[5]This example is taken from Chapter 24.

est rates only insofar as such a move might alter yields spreads in the money market.

An arbitrage in the purest sense of the term involves *no* risk, since the sale and purchase are assumed to occur simultaneously or almost so. An arbitrage based on a yield spread anomaly involves, as noted, no market risk, but it does involve risk of another sort: The arbitrageur is speculating on a yield spread. If he bets that a given spread will narrow and it widens, he will lose money. Thus, even a strictly defined yield spread arbitrage offers no locked-in profit.

Money market dealers actively play the arbitrage game. They have stored in a data base all sorts of information on historical yield spread and have programmed a computer to identify anomalies in prevailing spreads as they feed into it data on current yields. Dealers used the resulting "helpful hints to the arbitrageur" both to set up arbitrages themselves and to advise clients of arbitrage opportunities.

Generally, in a dealer shop, arbitrage is done in an account that is separate from the *naked trading* account. Arbitrage and naked trading are distinctly different lines of business. The trader who seeks to profit from a naked position long or short is a specialist in one narrow sector of the market, and the positions he assumes are based on a prediction of interest-rate trends and how they are likely to affect yields in his sector of the market. The arbitrageur, in contrast, has to track yields in a number of market sectors, and if he engages in strictly defined yield-spread arbitrage, he is not much concerned with whether rates are likely to rise or fall.

Anomalies in yield spreads that offer opportunities for profitable arbitrage arise due to various temporary aberrations in market demand or supply. For example, if the Treasury brings a big 4-year note issue to market, it might trade for a time at a higher rate than surrounding issues because investors were loath to take the capital gains or losses they would have to in order to swap into the new issue. In this case, the cause of the out-of-line yield spread would be, for the time it persisted, that the new issue had not been fully distributed. Alternatively, an anomaly might be created by a particular issue being in scarce supply.

Example of an Arbitrage

Here's an example of an arbitrage along the yield curve. The dealer put it on at a time when the yield curve was flat. His general expectation was that the Fed would ease causing the yield curve to steepen. Also, he anticipated that the spread between the 3- and 4-year notes would widen because the Treasury normally now includes a new 3-year note in its quarterly financing, the announcement of which was scheduled for early November.

In late October 1981, the yield curve in the 3- to 4-year area was relatively flat. Thus, buying the current 3-year note and shorting the current 4-year note appeared to be an attractive arbitrage. Here's how one dealer did this arbitrage. On October 21, for settlement on October 22, he bought the current 3-year note, 13⅛s of 8/15/85, at a yield to maturity of 10.95. Simultaneously he shorted the current 4-year note, 12¼s of 9/30/86, at a yield to maturity of 11.00.

The current 3-year note was trading at a dollar price of 105− 3+, and the yield value of ⅓₂ on it was 0.126. The current 4-year note was trading at a dollar price of 103−28+, and the yield value of ⅓₂ on it was 0.0096.[6] The smaller yield value of ⅓₂ on the 4-year note meant that, for a given movement up or down in interest rates, the 4-year note would move 131% as far up or down in price as the 3-year note would.[7] This in turn meant that, if the arbitrage were established on a dollar-for-dollar basis, that is, if the amount of 4-year notes shorted equaled the amount of 3-year notes purchased, the arbitrage would expose the dealer to market risk. In particular, if rates should fall while the arbitrage was on, the dealer would lose more on his short position in the 4-year note than he would gain on his long position in the 3-year note. To minimize market risk, the dealer set the arbitrage in a *ratio* based on the yield values

---

[6]The + in the quote equals 1/64.
[7]The calculation is

$$\frac{0.0126}{0.0096} = 131\%$$

of 1/32 on the two securities; this procedure insulated the arbitrage against general movements up or down in yields but not against a relative movement between yields on the two securities.

Table 10–2 shows precisely how the arbitrage worked out. The dealer bought for October 22 settlement $1.31MM of the current 3-year note and financed these securities by repoing them at 7.50%. Simultaneously, he reversed in $1MM of the 4-year note at the lower 7.15 reverse repo rate and sold them. Thirty-one days later when the dealer's expectations had come true—the Fed had eased, and the yield curve steepened—the dealer was able to unwind his arbitrage, which he put on at a 5-bp spread, at a 16-bp spread (Step 2, Table 10–2). The dealer's total return on the arbitrage was, as Step 3 in Table 10–2 shows, $2,611 per $1MM of securities arbitraged.

On an arbitrage of this sort, risk is limited to the spread relationship, so the size in which dealers do such arbs depends only on their ability to finance the securities purchased and to borrow the securities shorted. In practice, such arbs are commonly done for $50 or 100MM.

Arbs of the sort illustrated in Table 10–2 are routinely done today; the only special thing about this arb was that it was done in a volatile market. If the same type of arb had been done in early 1989 when markets were less volatile, it would likely have yielded not 11 bp, but only 5 bp.

Today, a dealer's arb trader is often referred to as a *curve trader* because he is taking positions, long and short, along the *yield curve*—making bets as to how two securities at different points along the yield curve will move relative to each other. For more examples of yield-curve arbitrages, see Chapter 14, "Curve Traders."

Risk: The Unexpected Occurs

When a strictly defined yield spread arbitrage fails to work out, the reason is usually that something unexpected has occurred. Here's a dated but still valid example. On several occasion in the spring of 1977, the old 7-year note and the current 7-year note, whose maturities were only three months apart, traded at a 10-

TABLE 10–2

An arbitrage along the yield curve

Step 1: Set up the arbitrage for settlement October 22, 1982.

    A. Buy $1.31MM of the current 3-year note, 18⅛ 8/15/85, at 105−3+ (10.95 yield)

Principal	$1,376,933
Accrued interest	31,771
Total purchase price	$1,408,704

    Repo these securities at 7.50.

    B. Reverse in and sell $1 MM of the 4-year note, 12¼ 9/30/86, at 103−28+ (11.00 yield)

Principal	$1,038,906
Accrued interest	7,445
Total sale price	$1,046,351

    Reverse rate 7.15.

Step 2: Unwind the arbitrage for settlement on November 22, 1982.

    A. Sell out the long position in the 3-year note at 106−2+ (10.49) yield:

Principal	$1,389,623
Accrued interest	46,255
Total sale price	$1,435,878

    Pay financing cost at 7.50 repo rate for 31 days: $9,098.

    B. Cover the short position in the 4-year note at 105−1 (10.65 yield):

Principal	$1,050,323
Accrued interest	17,935
Total purchase price	$1,068,258

    Receive return on reverse at 7.15 for 31 days: $6,442.

Step 3: Calculate net return on arbitrage.

    Return on long position in the 3-year note:

Sale price	$1,435,878
Purchase price	−1,408,704
Cost of repo	−9,098
Total return	$ 18,076

    Return on short position in 4-year note:

Sale price	$−1,068,258
Purchase price	1,046,351
Income on reverse	6,442
Total return	$ −15,465

    Net return on overall arbitrage:

Return on long position	$18,076
Return on short position	−15,465
	$ 2,611

bp spread. This made no sense since it implied that, at the 7-year level, the appropriate spread between securities differing by one year in maturity was 40 bp—an impossible yield curve. One dealer successfully arbitraged this yield spread three times by shorting the high-yield, current note and going long the old note. On his fourth try, the unexpected occurred. In his words, "We stuck our head in the wringer. We put on the 'arb' at 10 bp, and while we had it on, the Treasury reopened the current 7-year note. That did not destroy the productive nature of the arbitrage, but it did increase the time required before it will be possible to close it out at a profit. The costs of shorting the one issue and being long the other (especially delivery costs on the short side) are high so that at some point we will probably have to turn that arbitrage into a loss trade. Had the Treasury reopened some other issue, we would have made $200,000 bang. Instead we're looking at a $40,000 paper loss."

The arbitrage in this example comes close to being a strictly defined yield arbitrage. Many money market arbitrages do not. Dealers will often go long an issue of one maturity and short another issue of quite different maturity. An arbitrage of this sort resembles a strictly defined yield-spread arbitrage in that it is a speculation on a yield spread. However, it is more risky than such an arbitrage because, if interest rates move up or down, the price movement in the longer-maturity security will normally exceed that in the shorter-maturity security; thus, the arbitrage exposes the investor who puts it on to a *price risk*.

Dealers are aware of this and attempt to offset the inherent price risk in an arbitrage involving securities of different maturities by adjusting the sizes of the two sides of the arbitrage, as in the arbitrage example above. If, for instance, the arbitrage involves shorting the 2-year note and buying the 7-year note, the arbitrageur will short more notes than he buys. Such a strategy, however, cannot completely eliminate market risk; a movement in interest rates may be accompanied by a change in the slope of the yield curve, and the difference in the price movements the two issues would undergo if interest rates changed can therefore only be estimated.

Bull and *bear market arbitrages* are based on a view of where interest rates are going. A bull market arbitrageur anticipates a fall in interest rates and a rise in securities prices. Thus, he might, for example, short 2-year Treasuries and go long in 10-year Treasuries on a one-for-one basis, hoping to profit, when rates fall, from the long coupon appreciating more than the short coupon. If, alternatively, the arbitrageur were bearish, he would do the reverse: short long governments and buy short ones.

An arbitrage can also be set up to profit from an anticipated change in the slope of the yield curve. For example, an arbitrageur who anticipated a flattening of the yield curve might buy notes in the 7-year area for high yield and short notes in the 2-year not necessarily on a one-to-one basis. If the yield curve flattened with no change in average rate levels, the 7-year note would appreciate, the 2-year note would decline in price, and the arbitrage could be closed out at a profit.

Money market practitioners are wont to call any pair of long and short positions an arbitrage; however, as the maturities of the securities involved in the transaction get further apart, price risk increases, and at some point, the "arbitrage" becomes in reality two separate speculative positions, a naked long and a naked short.

Money market arbitrageurs normally put on both sides of an arbitrage simultaneously, but they rarely take them off simultaneously. As one dealer noted, "The compulsion to *lift* a leg (unwind one side of an arbitrage before the other) is overwhelming. Hardly anyone ever has the discipline to unwind both sides simultaneously. Instead they will first unwind the side that makes the most sense against the market. If, for example, the trader thinks the market is going to do better, he will lift a leg by covering the short."

Arbitrage Today

Once futures markets opened—first in bills, later in bonds, notes, and Euros—arbitrages between cash and futures markets mushroomed. To an arbitrageur, a sale of a futures contract is a substitute for a short position in a cash security, and a purchase of a futures contract is a substitute for a long position in a cash security. Thus, the introduction of futures opened up new ways to do arbitrages that were once done strictly in the cash market.

A good arbitrageur is always alert to opportunities for trading around one leg of his arb to pick up a few basis points here or there. Before futures, that trading around used to involve moving from one cash security to another; now, it may involve moving from cash to futures or vice versa depending on how spreads move.

If the arbitrageur has any problems these days, it is that there are so many cash securities on the quote sheet and so many futures contracts that the choice among alternatives is getting hard. Said one trader, "Say I want to do a yield-curve trade—long on the front end, short on the back end: Do I go long bill futures, cash bills, BAs, the repo market (collateral), or bond spreads; and on the back end, do I short the 10-year note, the note contract, bond futures, or cash bonds—and if cash bonds, do I choose current coupons or the discounts out there." The arrival of options on fixed-income securities and of other new instruments including interest-rate swaps, has further widened the menu of opportunities and made the choices more difficult.

Support personnel play an important part in any arbitrage operation. As one dealer noted, "The one thing in an arbitrage account that can force a paper loss to become a realized loss is if you lose control of your ability to support your short side. You don't want your traders worrying about when securities are due back, so you need someone else who assumes responsibility for making sure that people doing repo and reverse keep the needed supply of securities you have shorted on hand."

Money market dealers seek out promising arbitrage opportunities not only because they can profit from them in their own trading, but because arbitrage suggestions passed on to customers are a source of customer business. As one dealer commented, "We're in a competitive business, and the customer looks for the guys with the best ideas and information. If we supply them, he trades with us."

The persistence with which dealers and their customers arbitrage every out-of-line yield spread they find has an important impact on the money market; it ensures that spreads relationships never get far out of line or, to put in another way, that the differences in the yields on instruments of different types and maturities consistently mirror differences in the liquidity of and credit risk, if any, attached to these instruments.

Given all the arbitrage on the Street, the question arises: How can there be anything left to arbitrage? The answer seems to be that opportunities continue to exist partly because of the constantly increasing size of the market, partly because of the constant entry of new investors, some of whom are unsophisticated players, and, finally and most important, the constant introduction of new products. As would be expected, opportunities for arbitrage increase noticeably in volatile markets.

TAILS

Dealers who were bullish used to create tails as a way to pick up a profit if rates did in fact fall or, in some cases, just stayed flat. When carry is positive and the expectation is that rates won't rise, traders still do this. As often or more often, however, traders create tails as part of what has come to be known as a *cash-and-carry* or *basis trade*: the purchase of a cash security which is simultaneously sold in the futures market and financed until expiration of the futures contract with term repo.

Tails can be confusing. The easiest way to explain them is with an example. We will do so here with a cash-market trade. In Chapters 15 and 16, we work out cash-and-carry trades involving futures.

Assume a dealer is operating in an environment in which 90-day BAs are trading at a rate ⅛ below the Fed funds rate. Assume also that Fed funds are trading at 8.075, 90-day BAs at 7.95, and 30-day term repo at 7.50.

If in this environment the dealer were to buy a 90-day BA and finance it with 30-day term repo, he would earn over the 30-day holding period a positive carry equal to or a profit equal to 45 bp over 30 days. He would also have created a *future* 60-day BA, namely, the unfinanced *tail* of the 90-day BA purchased.

If he thought, as dealers do, of the carry profit over the initial holding period as raising the yield at which he in effect buys the future security, then by purchasing a 90-day BA at

7.95 and repoing it for 30 days at 7.50, he would have acquired a future 60-day BA at a yield of 8.05.[8] The 45-bp carry, which is earned for 30 days, adds only 10 bp to the yield at which the future security is effectively purchased because the latter has a maturity of 60 days, which is twice as long as the period over which positive carry is earned.

Faced with this opportunity the dealer would ask himself: How attractive is it to contract to buy a 60-day BA at 8.05 for delivery 30 days hence? Note the dealer would precisely break even, clearing costs ignored, if he were able to sell that future BA at a rate of 8.05. Thus, contracting to buy the future BA will be attractive if he believes he can sell the future BA at a rate below 8.05.

The dealer's answer to the question he has posed might run as follows: Currently, the yield curve is such that 60-day BAs are trading 15 bp below the rate on 90-day BAs. Therefore, if the 60-day BA were to trade at 8.05 one month hence and if yield spreads did not change, that would imply that a 90-day BA was trading at 8.175 and Fed funds at 8.30, that is, at a level approximately 1/4 above the present rate. I do not believe that the Fed will tighten or that yield spreads will change unfavorably, therefore I will do the trade.

If the dealer were correct—the Fed did not tighten and yield spreads did not change—he would be able to sell 30 days hence the future 60-day BA he had created at 7.80, which is the rate that would be the prevailing rate at the time on the 60-day BA, if his predictions with respect to yields and yield spreads were correct.[9] In doing so, he would make a profit equal to 1/4 (the purchase rate 8.05 minus the sale rate 7.80) on a 60-day security.

Of course, the dealer's predictions might prove to be favorable. Note, however, he has some built-in margin of protection. Specifically, if he is able to sell his future BAs at any rate above

---

[8]Note that the *higher* the yield at which a discount security is purchased, the *lower* the purchase price. So buying the future security at 8.05 is, from the dealer's point of view, better than buying it at 7.95.

[9]Recall a 60-day BA was assumed to be trading at a rate 15 bp below the rate on a 90-day BA, at $7.95 - 0.15 = 7.80$.

7.80 but still below 8.05, he will make some profit, albeit less than he would if he sold at 7.80. If, on the other hand, rates or rate spreads move so unfavorably that he ends up selling his future 60-day BA at a rate above 8.05, he will lose money.

For the benefit of those who like to look at dollar numbers rather than yields, we have reworked the example presented in dollars in Table 10–3. Recall a 60-day BA was assumed to be trading at a rate 15 bp below the rate on a 90-day BA, at 7.95 − 0.15 or 7.80.

In deciding whether to buy securities and finance them for some period, dealers invariably "figure the tail," that is, determine the effective yield at which they are buying the future security created. Whether the security financed is a discount security or an interest-bearing one, this yield can be figured approximately as follows:[10]

$$\begin{pmatrix} \text{Effective yield} \\ \text{at which future} \\ \text{security is} \\ \text{purchased} \end{pmatrix} = \begin{pmatrix} \text{Yield at} \\ \text{which cash} \\ \text{security is} \\ \text{purchased} \end{pmatrix} \times \begin{pmatrix} \dfrac{\text{Rate of} \\ \text{profit} \times \text{Days} \\ \text{on carry} \quad \text{carried}}{\text{Days left to maturity} \\ \text{at end of carry period}} \end{pmatrix}$$

Applying this formula to our example, we get:

$$7.95 + \frac{0.20 \times 30}{60} = 7.95 + 0.10 = 8.05$$

Risk

A dealer who engages in the sort of transaction we have just described incurs a rate risk. He might end up with a loss or a smaller profit than anticipated because the Fed tightened unexpectedly; because BA rates rose relative to the Fed funds rate due to, say, increased supply; or because a shift in the yield curve narrowed the spread between 60- and 90-day BAs. Thus, when a dealer who thinks such a transaction would be profitable

---

[10]There is a bias in this approximation. For a formula giving the precise yield calculation on a tail, see Stigum and Mann, *Money Market Calculations* (Homewood, Ill.: Dow Jones-Irwin, 1981), pp. 41–45.

TABLE 10–3
Figuring the tail: an example*

Step 1: The dealer buys $1MM of 90-day BAs at a 7.95% rate of discount:

Discount at which BAs are purchased $= \dfrac{d \times t}{360} \times F = \dfrac{0.0795 \times 90}{360} \times \$1,000,000$

$= \$19,875$

Price at which BAs are purchased $= F - D = 1,000,000 - 19,875$

$= \$980,125$

The dealer finances the BAs purchased for 30 days at 7¾%

Financing cost† $= \dfrac{0.0775 \times 30}{360} \times \$1,000,000$

$= \$6,458$

Step 2: At the end of 30 days, the dealer owns the BAs at a net cost figure. Determine what yield this cost figure implies on the future 60-day BAs created:

Net cost of future 60-day BAs $=$ Purchase price $+$ Financing cost

$= \$980,125 + \$6,458$

$= \$986,583$

Net discount at which 60-day BAs are owned $= F -$ Net cost

$= \$1,000,000 - \$986,583$

$= \$13,417$

Rate at which future 60-day BAs are purchased‡ $= \dfrac{360 \times D}{t \times F} = \dfrac{360 \times 13,417}{60 \times \$1,000,000}$

$= 0.0805$

$= 8.05\%$

Step 3: Future 60-day BAs created are sold at 7.80% discount rate. Calculate dollar profit:

$$\text{Discount at which BAs are sold} = \frac{d \times t}{360} \times F$$

$$= \frac{0.0780 \times 60}{360} \times \$1{,}000{,}000$$

$$= \$13{,}000$$

$$\begin{aligned}
\text{Profit} &= \text{Net purchase discount} - \text{Discount sale} \\
&= \$13{,}417 - \$13{,}000 \\
&= \$417
\end{aligned}$$

Step 4: Figure the annualized yield on a discount basis that $417 represents on a 60-day security:

$$d = \frac{360 \times D}{t \times F} = \frac{360 \times \$417}{60 \times \$1{,}000{,}000}$$

$$= 0.0025$$

$$= \tfrac{1}{4}\%$$

*For explanation of formulas used, see p. 66.
†Actually, less than $1MM has to be borrowed, which is one reason why the dealer's approach to figuring the tail is only an approximation. A second reason is that the BA rate is a discount rate, the repo rate is an add-on rate.
‡Solving the equation

$$D = F\left(\frac{d \times t}{360}\right)$$

for d, gives us

$$d = \frac{360 \times D}{d \times F}$$

459

decides to take the position, the size in which he takes it will depend both on the confidence he has in his rate and spread predictions and the amount of risk to which he thinks it would expose him. The same sort of transaction could also be done in other short-term securities.

RELATIVE VALUE

We have said that a dealer will position securities if he is bullish. In choosing which securities to buy, he considers relative value.

Every rational investor is interested in risk, liquidity, and return. Specifically, he wants maximum return, maximum liquidity, and minimum risk. When he shops for securities, however, he finds that the real world presents him with nothing but trade-offs; securities offering higher returns tend to be riskier or less liquid than securities offering lower returns. That is as true in the money market as elsewhere, and it is the reason money market dealers think first of *relative* value when they decide to position.

If the spread at which one security is trading relative to another more than adequately compensates for the fact that the high-yield security is riskier or less liquid than the low-yield security, the high-yield security has greater relative value and should be bought in preference to the low-yield security. If, alternatively, the spread is inadequate, then the low-yield security has greater relative value and should be bought in preference to the high-yield security. When dealers talk about relative value, they are really talking about the management of credit risk, market risk, and liquidity.

Relative value considerations arise not only in choices between different instruments, but in choices between different maturity sectors of the same market. A dealer might ask whether he should position 6-month or 1-year bills. If the yield curve were unusually steep out to one year and the dealer expected it to flatten, then the year bill would have more relative value than the 6-month bill.

Relative value analysis, besides guiding a dealer in deciding what securities to position or short, is also useful for generating business with customers, and dealers use it that way constantly. To take an example, suppose BAs and bills in a given maturity range are normally spread X bp. The spread is now X + 15 bp, which more than compensates for the extra risk and lesser liquidity of the BAs. Moreover, the dealer anticipates that the spread at which BAs trade to bills will narrow. Then the BAs have greater relative value than the bills, and by pointing this out to retail customers holding bills, the dealer could probably induce some of them to *swap* for a yield pickup out of their bills into BAs (to sell their bills and buy BAs).

TECHNICAL ANALYSIS

In the days before futures were around and later when they were still a mystery to lots of people, money market traders focused on fundamentals exclusively: How are economic conditions changing? What is the Fed doing? Where is relative value in light of the above?

With the advent of futures, money market traders imported charting and *technical analysis* from the futures markets. While technical analysis comes in a multitude of forms, it purports to be a method for gleaning information about *future* price movements from *past* price movements. People into technical analysis do various moving averages of prices, look at point and figure charts, identify heads, shoulders, support levels, and so on (Chapter 14). The *efficient market hypothesis*, developed by economists studying stock prices, claims, depending on how strongly the hypothesis is asserted, that the current price of a security reflects all that is known and knowable about the value of that security, and what is knowable includes its past price performance. The clear implication of this much-tested and oft-sustained hypothesis is that technical analysis is worthless: the past behavior of a security's price has *no* predictive value with respect to the future behavior of that security's price.

That may be so, but nonetheless technical analysis has spread like a rampant virus through the trading community.

Today, almost every trader has a point and figure chart of some sort in front of him.

One believer in technical analysis commented: "What technicals do is to show you a picture of price action and of levels of entering and exiting the market that are most efficient. Today, securities, foreign exchange too, are all commodities. If everyone knows that a certain level is important, then whether it is, ultimately, the correct level at which to buy or sell the market, it will be a level at which lots of securities trade, simply because the charts identify that level as important.

"It has gotten to the point now that, on some days in a highly volatile environment when the market happens to be going down for whatever reason—maybe a bad piece of fundamental news—a lot of trading will occur at a particular level identified by the charts; and if that level fails, the market will just gap down to the next such level."

Having said the above, the same trader went on to add: "Whether you assume that technical analysis, in and of itself, has any merit is irrelevant. It is followed by so many traders that, whether you believe the message you get from a chart or not, enough people do so that charts have an effect. There is *no* fundamental reason for charts to be correct. Still, I could not imagine doing business without the technical analysis that our firm has."

Charts it would seem are here to stay. Whether a trader believes in them or not, he can't ignore them, since so many other traders follow and act on them. To a believer in the efficient market hypothesis, the trading community appears less than 100% rational. However, that view is perhaps undemocratic. In a country whose most recent president consulted an astrologer, traders too surely have the right to be mildly loony— to engage in collective chart gazing if that pleases them.

RUNNING A DEALER OPERATION

We have talked a lot about how money market "dealers" operate, but a dealership, of course, consists of many people. At its heart are a position manager, who is invariably a highly savvy

Street person, a group of specialized traders, and a sales force that contacts retail.

The position manager (or managers—in large firms responsibility is layered) has various responsibilities. First, he has to establish guidelines to limit the total risk the firm assumes at any one time. Second, it is his responsibility to develop a forecast of short-term interest rates—using inputs from his resident Fed watcher, his traders, and retail activity. Then, he must decide, based on the level of confidence he has in that forecast, whether his firm should make a market play, how big that play should be within the firm's position limits, and the instruments and maturity range in which the play should be made.

Establishing Position Limits

As interest rates became more volatile and position risks concomitantly greater, dealers—with their limited capital—began to pay a lot more attention to risk management and in particular to the setting of position limits overall and at different points along the yield curve. Since risk defies precise measurement, different dealers set such limits in different ways. A typical approach is for a dealer to start by saying: The most we are willing to lose in one day is XMM. Next, for securities at different points along the yield curve, the dealer constructs volatility indices based on the past price behavior of these securities or on their respective durations. The firm might then use indices to establish maximum positions it is willing to assume at different points along the yield curve. Or, alternatively, the firm might say: "Given the current market environment, the maximum total position we will assume is $1 billion. Our index tells us that long bonds are seven times as volatile as the year bill, so if we make our play the short end, we are willing to go up to a billion, but if we make our play in long bonds, we'll do only 1/7th of that."

One change that has occurred in recent years is that dealers, in gauging the risks associated with positions in different securities, focus frequently on duration rather than current maturity. The rationale behind doing so was described in Chapter 5.

Position guidelines are arbitrary at best, which is not to say that they are without purpose. Said one dealer, "We know our position limits are arbitrary, but they give us the comfort of knowing, when we go home at night, that we will still be in business tomorrow."

In implementing position limits, a dealer faces a delicate task. If he wants good traders, he has to give them some freedom, but he can't give them so much that he loses control over the size and composition of the firm's position. One manager described the problem well, "Every trader is entitled to trade his markets, to have a certain degree of free hand. Traders are big boys. Sometimes, however, I find, much to my dismay, that our bill futures trader is short, our bill trader long, our swap trader even to a little long, and our coupon trader short. Thanks to the grace of God, it often all works out because our traders know their markets and the technicals in them. But when we are making a major position play, my allowance for each trader doing his own thing in his own market no longer holds. Then, I have to set the positions and the limits."

The Traders

Because there are so many types of money market instruments, because they trade so differently, and because they vary so in maturity, money market dealers all have a bevy of traders, each trading a single *narrow* sector of the market: short bills, long bills, 2- to 4-year notes, Euro CDs, BAs, short agencies, MTNs, and so on.

Trading on an hour-to-hour, day-to-day basis is a fine art that those with the inherent knack pick up through on-the-firing-line training. A good trader bases every trade he makes on his feel about the levels at which every instrument in which he deals ought to be trading. That feel will tell him, for example, that a 6 bid for one instrument is the same as a 13 bid for another, in other words, that he should be *indifferent* between selling one instrument at 6 and the other at 13; also if his market trades at a ²⁄₃₂ spread, he should be indifferent between buying the one instrument at 8 and the other at 15. So the trader will quote these two markets, 6–8 and 13–15. If someone hits his bid at 13 and takes his offer at 8, he will, if his indifference levels are correct, have earned $2/32$ and established a position (long in the one security and short in the other) that he can with patience unwind for another $2/32$. The unwinding is, of course, likely to occur one leg at a time. Retail might pick up the securities in which he is long, then he would have to buy something else to keep his *net* book even. And if such *chain trading* caused a maturity gap in his book, he would seek out other trades to close it—tell the sales force to look to buy this or sell that. The essence of successful trading is to be able to set correct indifference levels and then keep the position moving—buying here, selling there, and picking up 32nds along the way.

Of course, at times the firm may take a strong view with respect to where interest rates are going and want the trader to run a net long or short position in his book. To establish that position, he will have to be a net buyer or seller, but once he has established the position, trading again becomes calculating indifference levels and trading off them in a fashion that keeps his book where he wants it.

A trader is a highly paid professional whose life is his market. Most traders are young; they have to be since they operate under a lot of pressure, both because of the hectic pace of the market and because the results of what they do get thrown at them daily in the form of a profit and loss statement on their previous day's trades. Most traders are also highly competitive. As one dealer noted, "A trader is the archetype I-will-kill-you player of tennis, backgammon, and other games. He knows this is a killer business, and to him winning is everything—it's his mission in life, and when he wins, he won't even be nice about it."

A trader's job is to work not to manage. He has to quote markets, write tickets, and make things happen, all the while interjecting his personality into what he is doing. Today, more and more traders have MBAs, but as one dealer noted, such training does not make a guy a trader: "There are a lot of bright guys down here with degrees, and they construct models on the computer of future interest rates, but when Sali's trader says to them, 'The 6-month bill is 29–28, what do you want to do?' they face a whole different class of decision. There may be beneficial sorts of training that could be given them beforehand, but there is no possible training for meeting that sort of situation well."

Creating a Trading Team

In the recent environment of high rate volatility, it has become increasingly important to dealers seeking to control risk closely to achieve a high degree of discipline among their traders. In a firm that wants both to service retail and to limit risk, there is a natural, constant conflict between the firm and its traders. Traders do not want to be functionaries who buy here and sell there to satisfy either the needs of the firm's retail customers or the demands of its position manager. Traders want to be creative people who earn money by taking big positions and by being right on the market; they also have sensitive egos that get them into trouble.

One position manager, describing his efforts to control both risk and his traders, said, "We thought having a bunch of traders along the yield curve all trying to decide whether the market was cheap or expensive was a poor way to manage risk. We had to retrain our traders—to get them a lot more comfortable with a team environment where we tell some guys that they have to sit out a rally because we are not going to make our play in their sector. I think we now have the most effective trading desk on the Street. To get it, we had to get traders to think that the good trader is not the guy who buys a billion, but the guy who makes consistent profits during the year. We found that a trader feels a need to belong; he does not want to be out there all alone. As management, we share the risk with him all the way, which reduces the stress in his job. We want our traders around for a long time. The most disruptive thing to a trade or sales organization is continuous turnover—a condition endemic on Wall Street—that we have stopped temporarily.

"Steinbrenner's Yankees are a good model for what you find in a lot of undisciplined trading outfits. There are a lot of high-priced ball players all trying to wing a home run, but the team has not won too many games. Our objective is not to have one winning season, but to build a number of steady revenue streams. If you don't have such revenue streams, you are always going to be speculating instead of having the freedom to pick your spots. Since we have tried to speculate less, our record of making good speculations has improved. This year was our best ever."

The last comment throws an interesting perspective onto our earlier observation that rate volatility has shifted the focus at more than one dealer shop from earning profits on speculation to finding consistent sources of revenue. The discipline of doing the latter may improve a dealer's ability to do the former.

Sales Force

There is a lot of variability from dealer to dealer in the size of the sales force and its function. At one extreme are houses that are big in commercial paper and put their sales force to work selling Amco Credit and have them do repo as an afterthought. At the other extreme are the position houses that look to their sales force first as sellers of repo, second as a source of information on how retail is behaving in and views the market, and third as an outlet to retail business when the firm wants it. A few such firms even reward their sales force according to the amount of repo they do, which is fairly unusual.

The level of sophistication among sales personnel varies considerably. It takes little expertise to sell commercial paper to the average corporate treasurer but a lot to deal with some of the sharper players in the market.

In most corporations, running the short-term portfolio is a rookie job, in a scant few it is done by highly paid professionals. The dealers staff accordingly; rookies talk to and advise rookies, and pros talk to pros. Said one dealer, "It works fine hiring a rookie to talk to a rookie. They relate to each other and have a good time. I can't have a hotshot trader of mine talking to the money trader of some average corporation. They're separated by an unbridgeable cultural gap."

DEALERS THAT GOT IT WRONG: CASES AND CONSEQUENCES

In 1975, Eldin Miller's Financial Corp., a fledgling government securities dealer, went belly up with estimated losses of $15 to $25MM to investors. At that time, one could hope that some lessons had been learned: know thy counterparty in a repo; ensure that repos and reverses are properly collateralized; and so on. Alas, memories are unfortunately short. A few years later, there were lots of new faces in the money market—*and* they were people who had never heard of Eldin Miller.

From the late 1970s on, when interest rates were often far higher and far more volatile than they had ever been, a number of smaller dealers—some new, some who had been around for awhile—went bankrupt with large losses to investors. It is estimated that the failure of Drysdale Government Securities in 1982 cost banks and investors $270 to $290MM, that the failure of Lombard-Wall, Inc., in 1982 cost investors $20MM, that the failure of Lion Capital Group in 1984 cost investors $40MM, that the failure of RTD securities in 1984 cost investors $1.7MM, that the failure of E.S.M. Government Securities in 1985 cost investors $300MM, and that the failure of Bevill, Bresler and Schulman in 1985 cost investors yet another $150MM.

These bankruptcies and others followed a variety of patterns. However, a reasonable generalization is that losses to customers typically resulted from one or both of several practices: (1) the failing firm treated securities, including repo collateral, that it was holding in safekeeping for customers loosely to say the least—sometimes such securities were hypothecated more than once, sometimes they were sold; and (2) the failing firm gave inadequate collateral to customers when it repoed securities out to customers and/or it demanded excessive collateral when it reversed in securities from customers.

It's important to note, with respect to the above failures, that no investor ever lost so much as a penny due to credit and other problems at a major dealer. While the big boys may at times have lost a lot of money due to market turbulence, they stayed, to a man, squeaky clean in their dealings with customers. Another point to note is that, with the exception of the losses by Chase and several other NYC banks during the Drysdale bankruptcy (losses due, at least in the case of Chase, to an admitted failure of the bank's internal controls), no major investor or dealer lost a penny because of the bankruptcies we have listed. It was small investors—school districts, S&Ls, and so on—who saw their money vanish as small dealers in governments went down the tubes. The big, sophisticated players had all protected themselves by following old and respected rules of prudence. To the extent that they dealt at all with the second- or third-tier dealers that failed, the big players to a man had said, "We will buy securities from you, sell securities to you, and do repo with you, but only on a strictly DVP (delivery versus payment) basis and on a basis of reasonable margin." It's hard for a market player to lose big bucks because of a dealer bankruptcy if his rules are these: never give a dealer money except against securities due; never give him securities except against money due; and never do repos or reverses with him except when margin is set and maintained at a reasonable level consistent with accepted market practices.

The Fed Acts

Naturally, the problems outlined above raised a brouhaha in Washington and elsewhere. Despite the fact that recent bankruptcies of government securities dealers raised only a rather narrow issue—how to protect *smallish* investors from hanky panky by *smallish* dealers in exempt securities—cries went up for imposing new rules and regs on *all* dealers in governments.

The Fed took a crack at solving the perceived problem by coming up with complex "voluntary" guidelines on capital adequacy, which were supposed to apply to all dealers in governments except the primary dealers whose activities the Fed was already overseeing. The Fed's guidelines, which are extremely complex, require that a dealer maintain sufficient capital to cover (1) the credit risk of its receivables and (2) the market risk of its securities inventory where the latter is calculated, for different types of securities, on the basis of the historic volatility of the prices of those types of securities. This sounds reasonable. There is, however, as a wise banker once noted, a fallacy in this approach: risk can be accurately gauged only *ex post*. A glance at how various money market participants have lost big sums of money suggests the truth in this dictum. In the mid-1970s, thrifts lost money by selling GNMA puts because neither they nor their regulators appreciated that this means of garnering *fee income* involved placing a risky bet on the direction of interest rates. Wiser firms have lost bundles learning the risks inherent in *new* products and, when markets were volatile and changing, in *old* products as well. If capital requirements alone sufficed to keep financial institutions afloat, a lot of now defunct banks and thrifts would still be around.

Congress Acts: The Government Securities Act of 1986

While the Fed was experimenting with new capital rules, Congress, in a typical political response, was debating what *it* should do about dealer bankruptcies. Despite the fact that only a narrow group of dealers had caused losses to investors—by lying about their financial strength, by double pledging securities in the repo market, by demanding excessive collateral on reverses, and by playing other games—Congress felt called on to focus on the "great problems with respect to *unregulated* government securities dealers"—*all* of them.

After much debate and delay, Congress finally passed, in October 1986, the Government Securities Act of 1986. This act ostensibly fixes a lot of things, many of which were not broken in the first place.

The act requires a number of things. First, all government securities brokers and dealers except registered broker/dealers and financial institutions (domestic and foreign banks, and federally insured thrifts) are required to register with the SEC. Primary dealers as a class are not excepted from this registration requirement. Registered broker/dealers and financial institutions that deal in governments are required to file a notice with their appropriate regulatory agencies (ARAs).

Second, the act requires that the Secretary of the Treasury, in consultation with the SEC and the Fed, promulgate rules regarding the activities of brokers and dealers in governments. These rules relate principally to capital adequacy, custody and use of customer securities, the mechanics of repos and reverses, the carrying and use of customer deposits or credit balances, financial reporting, and recordkeeping.

Capital Requirements

Under the new regulatory regime, broker/dealers who deal directly (not through a GSI) in governments will continue to be subject, as they were before, to the capital requirement imposed by the SEC under 15c3-1 of the Securities Exchange Act of 1934; banks that deal in governments will be subject to capital requirements imposed by bank regulators; and other dealers will be subject to new capital requirements fashioned by the Treasury, which used as its model the complex, voluntary capital guidelines created by the Fed for government securities dealers. SEC capital requirements follow a different format than Treasury capital requirements, but one is not clearly more onerous than the other.

Financial Reporting

Besides respecting a new net capital rule, dealers who were previously unregulated will now be required to have annual audits of their financial statements, a procedure that will be overseen by the National Association of Securities Dealers (NASD).

Repos, Reverses, and Safekeeping

Several things were done by the Treasury and the SEC in their regulations to pare the risks associated with repos and reverses. In particular, both the Treasury and the SEC imposed complex capital charges on repos and reverses. One purpose of these requirements was to create incentives to encourage dealers doing repos and reverses to operate as follows: collateral is to be reasonably priced; the amount of money that changes hands is to be a reasonable percentage of the collateral's market value; and finally, margin calls are to be made if significant changes occur in that market value.

Also, under the new regs, a dealer, before doing repo with a customer, must send to the customer a written agreement that includes a specifically worded disclosure regarding the dealer's right to substitute collateral. A dealer must also send to a customer confirms on all transactions, including repos and reverses. Also, a dealer *must* segregate in a safekeeping account at his clearing bank and on his books any customer securities, including repo collateral, that he holds for customers. On hold-in-custody repos, a dealer, on his confirms to customers, is supposed to list collateral separately—he can no longer write "various." Also, he is supposed to state the market value of the securities that he is giving to the customer as collateral.

The difficulties that regulatory authorities experienced in setting up new regulations under the Government Securities Act of 1986 suggest that such regulations will be subject to evolution over time.

BLOOD ON THE STREET

In the mid-1980s, mention of dealer losses and problems would have brought to mind the then recent failures of BBS, ESM, and others. By the late 1980s, mention of the same thing would have brought to mind a quite different constellation of events: the huge losses, the firings—in sum, the blood on the Street—that followed the stock market crash in 1987.

The Dealer Community B.C., Before the Crash

Over time, the dealing community has gone through cycles of prosperity and slump. The last major downswing occurred in the late 1960s. At that time, a pattern occurred (repeated in major respects in the years immediately following the October 1987 crash of the stock market): big initial losses, followed by numerous closings and mergers. Also, in the late 1960s, a time when most Street firms were partnerships or proprietorships, a generation of men who had gotten rich as partners in Wall Street firms said, "The party is over, I am going to withdraw my capital."

Gradually, as the 1960s became the 1970s, the crisis began to pass: dealers began to get new blood, some creativity, and best of all, a huge step-up in volume associated with the burgeoning of government, municipal, and other debt. In the early 1970s, the Street started to rebuild from the ashes. Unfortunately, however, it stubbed its toes several times—a good example being the way the Street got caught in the 1975 near-bankruptcy of New York City. These events led to the institution of much tighter credit and risk controls on the Street, which in turn gave firms a framework from which to take off again. Thereafter, there were some huge infusions of capital on the Street both from money generated in the business and from outside sources. In the 1980s, some major firms went public and others were bought, often by foreigners.

For a time everyone—the banks and others—wanted to get into the securities business. The result was a tremendous buildup in personnel, capital, and for awhile, the trading volume to support it. During the 1980s, stock market volume doubled yet again, and with the Reagan administration, deficits doubled also. In addition, innovation kept adding to the volume of products to be issued and traded; new products of the 1980s included interest-rate swaps, various options products, and MTNs—all of which, once launched, grew explosively.

Globalization

The 1980s were marked not only by significant increases in the number and volume of financial products traded, but by a trend toward globalization of financial markets. Globalization is a multifaceted phenomenon. At its simplest level, it can be taken to mean the trading of certain financial instruments 24, or nearly 24, hours a day, where the instruments traded include foreign exchange; Euro time deposits, cash, and futures; and governments, cash, and futures. At a deeper level, globalization means the trend in major economies toward deregulation and securitization, a trend that permits entities native to one national capital market to operate with ease in another.

It is, for example, evidence of globalization that the big four Japanese securities dealers—Nomora, Nikko, Diawa, and Yamichi—all opened shop in the U.S. and all became, during the 1980s, primary dealers in governments. Foreign dealers from other countries also came to the U.S. market—some via subsidiaries, some via the purchase of U.S. dealers. Meanwhile, U.S. dealers, nonbank and bank, expanded during the 1980s their foreign activities, particularly in London and Tokyo.

Seen from a different perspective, globalization means that major borrowers worldwide perceive as potential investors in their paper not just native institutions, but institutions worldwide. In particular, the Treasury has come to rely on Japanese institutional investors to snap up a goodly chunk of its new debt issuance. The U.S., however, is not the only country needing to issue a lot of new debt. Debt has grown pretty much everywhere, except most recently in the U.K., which in the late 1980s was paying off its debt (*gilts*); it, thus, became efficient for countries such as France, Italy, Sweden, and from time to time Germany and Japan, to come up with mechanisms that would make it easy for investors to make a quick and dirty comparison of their debt with that of the big dog borrower, the U.S. The French, for example, went from having a rigidly controlled market for their debt, Obligations Assimilables du Trésor (dubbed OATS), to a system that cloned in many respects the issuance and trading of U.S. Treasuries. The French now have a group of 13 primary dealers, instead of just a few French banks, distributing their debt; they also have auctions of their debt, standard maturities, and both a futures market and a market for options on futures. The result has been to increase the liquidity of French Treasuries and to make them much more attractive to foreign investors.

As they say, it takes two to tango. For markets to become truly global, it is not sufficient that borrowers seek to sell their paper to investors in other countries. The flip side is that previously parochial investors around the globe must experience a change in attitude. Not so many years ago, U.S. investors used to reason: I get dollars in; sooner or later, I will have to pay dollars out; therefore, I shall invest only in dollars, and I need pay little or no attention either to the exchange value of the dollar or to what goes on in other national capital markets. Today, that attitude is changing: U.S. investors are becoming more like European and certain Asian investors; the latter have long been very currency conscious and also knowledgeable about sovereign risk; consequently, they were and continue to be willing to hold a broad basket of investments and to make short-term distinctions about where value lies.

Nation by nation, deregulation and securitization have been catalysts for the globalization of capital markets. Another catalyst has been swaps: plain vanilla, one-currency coupon swaps, and cross-currency swaps. Swaps permit financial alchemy, both nationally and internationally, on both assets and liabilities.

True globalization of financial markets is a situation in which all participants, regardless of their country of origin and regardless of what currency they take or pay in their normal course of business, have equal access and equal discretion over denominating their securities bets—asset or liability—in any currency and in any capital market. The world is not there yet, but it's moving in that direction.

Big Bang, London, October 1986

Prior to October 1986, domestic British markets for equities and gilts were neatly cartelized with the result that cartel members could count on a steady and attractive stream of monopoly profits. At this time, stock brokering commissions were fixed, jobbers (market makers) could sell only to brokers, and brokers could sell only to retail. No nasty competition in the stock market. In the gilt market too, there was a cartel of sorts: five or six jobbers, who did all of the business. The Thatcher government decided to break all this up, to create competition in the interests of efficiency and lower transactions costs.

British deregulation in October 1986, dubbed *Big Bang,* occurred when it was boom time in world financial markets and when globalization was on the march. Add to that that British cartels had generated excessive profits for insiders, and what occurred was the inevitable: too many people came to the party. It is a simple law of economics that, where there is high profitability, capital will, if permitted, move toward that profitability to the point where there is too much capital and therefore unprofitability. That, essentially, is what happened in both the British stock and bond markets as a result of Big Bang.

To cite one example, the British gilt market, which in size is a fraction of the U.S. Treasury market and which is currently contracting, attracted 27 market makers where comparison with the U.S. suggests that 12 to 15 would have been a viable number. All in all, a lot of dealers—British, American, Japanese, and others—invested a lot of money and hired a lot of expensive personnel to position themselves to become, post-Big Bang, big players in one area or another of the British stock and bond markets. However, after Big Bang, many of these firms found themselves in markets in which too many firms were chasing too little business; consequently, they were experiencing losses—hemorrhaging money every day they stayed in the fray. Some beat a hasty retreat; others scaled back their operations but hung in the hope that their competitors would leave and thereby permit margins to improve. In many cases, that hope proved vain, and even in 1989, the exodus from certain London markets was continuing.

October 19, 1987

In a sense, Big Bang was a harbinger of things to come. When stock markets crashed worldwide in October 1987, there was suddenly a lot of blood on Wall Street. Some firms, E. F. Hutton and L. F. Rothchild to name two, suffered big initial losses; Hutton was almost immediately bought by Shearson, Rothchild was later bought by a Kansas thrift. Other firms that managed to get through October 19 relatively unscathed suffered a predictable aftershock.

In the preceding years of prosperity, dealers had built continuously; and in the process, they had acquired tremendous levels of overhead that they could cover only if they continued to do a high volume of business. However, after the crash, trading volume in securities markets contracted. In August 1987, average daily volume of trading on the NYSE was 193,000 shares; by May 1988, it had fallen to 154,000 shares. Volume also plummeted in the government market despite the fact that the initial impact of the crash on governments was to cause them to rally because it was widely and correctly anticipated that, in response to the crash, the Fed would ease. In October 1987, average daily trading in the government market was 138 billion; by July 1988, it was down to 92 billion; and by January 1989, it had recovered only to 107 billion.

After the crash, the volume of business necessary to cover the levels of overhead that had been established on Wall Street in headier days was simply *not* there; for this reason, yet more firings—thousands of them—and other measures to cut overhead were inevitable.

During the months following the crash, typical headlines read:

"Prudential Unit Had Loss in 87 of 100MM"

"Salomon Posts 4th Period Loss of 74MM"

"Merrill Plans Layoffs, Cutbacks to Save 370MM"

Another sign of the times: just prior to the crash and after a bad spell in the bond market, once proud Salomon announced that it was quitting the municipal bond, the commercial paper, and other money markets—all areas in which Sali once played a prominent role.

A Time for Change

One reason that the cycle in securities markets hits dealers so hard is that they are notoriously bad at strategic planning. All too often, dealers expand without restraint when times are good, contract with great pain when times are bad. In particular, faced with prosperity, dealers typically try to be all things to all people: add every new product that comes along on the theory that there is or eventually will be some synergy that makes doing so pay off. Often, in expanding, dealers get into a new area without benefit of a business plan, without asking: What are the risks in trading this new product? If we trade it, how much capital should we allocate to it? What target rate of return should we require on that capital?

OTC options is an example of a product that the Street got into without adequate analysis. A dealer, acting as a broker, can't make money selling listed options at $20 a round turn. If there is money to be made, it is in OTC options where the dealer can charge his customer a spread. But it is precisely on the OTC side of the business that dealers have gotten severely hurt. "Wall Street," noted one dealer, "has lost millions and millions of dollars trying to participate in the options market. Despite the time and effort it has put into developing this market, the market has yet to make anyone any money. Firms sit there and grind out some earnings as an industry and then First Boston drops 100MM on one trade. That wipes out the career earnings of the rest of Wall Street forever.

"There is no money in the product because there are no buyers of options. In Treasuries, government-plus bond funds are a natural long; they buy Treasuries and then sell options [write covered calls] to get some extra yield. The dealers buy these options and then can find no buyers for them, so the Street ends up long options, which is bad use of capital. Options positions are time and hedging intensive. The only time I [a dealer] can sell an option is to cover one that I sold you: the market is up two points, and you want to change the strike; so you ask me to offer the option you previously sold me and to buy the new option you now want to sell me."

A common comment on the Street is that dealers are good at risk management but bad at general business management. What is more, compared to managers in other lines of business, they are grossly overpaid.

One MBA trader, describing the industry's problems commented: "Like General Electric, we [the dealers] are really just manufacturing and moving inventory. Our markups are bigger than GE's and so too are the risks we take. Yet, we do well to match GE's return on capital"[11]

Inevitably, there exist lots of differences dealer to dealer in management style and in ROEs attained. In 1987, an admittedly bad year, Sali earned an ROE of 3.7%. That number looked good compared to the ROEs racked up by a number of other shops. But in the same year, Morgan Stanley, reputed to be the best-run firm on the Street, earned 25.3% on capital. Morgan Stanley succeeds by stressing profitability over market share, by emphasizing teamwork over superstars, and by limiting risk taking to a few areas it thinks it knows best. Goldman is another dealer known for good management. Goldman tends not to

---

[11]Ironically, GE actually bought a dealer, Kidder, Peabody & Co. Kidder had been profitable but not so well managed. Management was supposed to be GE's ace in the hole. After two years, the upshot was that—thanks to big differences in culture and squabbles over turf—GE was earning, on the 600MM it paid for 80% of Kidder, more headaches than money.

be the first in a new business, but when it has studied the new product and thinks that it's a good bet and a good fit, Goldman makes a tenacious and determined effort to be a top dealer in it. That is not to say that nurturing a new product cannot be good business. Merrill has surely profited handsomely from its MTN business, which it pioneered and now dominates.

One beneficial effect of the crash of 87 and the pressures put there at and thereafter on dealers' profits is that dealers have responded by trying to manage their businesses more professionally. One manager of a government-bond-trading operation, speaking of 87 and its aftermath, observed: "Wall Street is known for expanding in good times and then being too big when the market retreats. In October 87, we were positioned in fixed-income securities for a fall in rates and that balanced the money we lost on risk arbitrage and the equities side, so our trading gain/loss was a wash. But what happened afterward was that business came to a standstill in junk bonds, new equities, retail, and so on. All of those revenues stopped, so even if we didn't lose money trading, we lost it just being open until we cut our overhead down to the size of our diminished revenues. Suddenly, dealers, me included, have to act like real businessmen, which is probably for the good; we are asked to worry not just about which way the market is going, but about the bottom line, accounting, interest costs, real estate expenses, and so on. Look at our trading room, at our regional offices. Someone must pay for that. You grow dependent on constant revenues. That's OK so long as everything keeps going, but when it stops, there's another story."

Exit to Boutiques and Fizzle Out of the Quants

Several other postcrash developments on Wall Street are worthy of short note: the exit of superstars to boutiques and the fading aura of rocket scientists. So long as volume and profits were rising on Wall Street and everyone was getting richer, people at multiline firms did not squabble much about how to divide power and profits. After the crash, that changed. Securities trading has become so efficient that it is nigh impossible for a trader to make lots of money unless he can guess volatility correctly. So the talented superstars have gone where the real spread is—anything from commercial real estate to mergers and acquisitions (M&A). Such business is rich business: there is a spread, and overhead does not choke profits because the business itself does not require a lot of analytics, support groups, and operations people.

After the crash, a number of superstars doing rich business for big dealers left to set up their own boutiques. The reason was principally money. A real estate guy might reason, "I am doing a 100MM deal for my firm and there is a 2⅓-point, maybe 3-point, spread, in that deal. If I do it as part of a big dealer, most of that spread will go to pay overhead and to make up for losses in other divisions. Why don't I get some financing and start a boutique so I can keep a lot more of the spread I earn?" First Boston's Wasserstein and Perella, big M&A stars, reasoned that way and they were not the only superstars on the Street who did.

Rocket scientists is not the very accurate title accorded to mathematically sophisticated people whom Wall Street imported from other fields to develop new products. For a time, there was no amount too great for a big securities firm to pay a rocket scientist or *quant* as such folks are also called. Among other things, the Street's quants developed and priced options products and created exotic mortgage-backed hybrids. After the crash, the quants lost a touch of their aura. In the harsh light of reality, firms realized that their quants had helped them produce products that were great for the customer—just what he asked for—but not always so great for the dealer: the products were not always fully understood by risk managers; they often lacked liquidity; and sometimes they did not make that much sense for the industry to trade. Examples are OTC options and Merrill's principal-only, mortgage-backed POs on which Merrill lost a cool quarter of a billion.

Interestingly, the big Japanese dealers, who are regarded as good at doing commodity-type business as opposed to business that is at the cutting edge of sophistication, appear to be using the current pause in the Street's love affair with quants to employ quants of their own and play catch up. A few years ago, a domestic dealer with a hot new product knew that it would be just a matter of months before some domestic competitor offered clients a creative imitation. No one even thought about the Japanese. Now, however, by acquiring the infrastructure to innovate, Japanese firms will, at the very least, be positioned to be fast followers in the marketplace.

MONEY MARKETS: DEAD OR ALIVE?

A decade ago, trading in money market securities—bills, BAs, CDs, and so on—was an important business for every major dealer. A startling change that has occurred over time is the diminution of trading that money market dealers do, as opposed to principally shoveling out paper to investors as is done in the commercial paper and several other markets.

The change reflects partly the dramatic changes that have occurred in product mix at the short end of the market. It also reflects the fact that, before the crash, dealers went through a period in which trading in money markets was not particularly profitable. Some dealers then, some later, either got out of the money markets business or de-emphasized it: Sali closed down its money markets business; Hutton, a good player, got bought out, so they are out of the business; Dean Witter de-emphasized money markets and so too did First Boston, which cut half its trading desk. Today, there are only three firms on the Street who are increasing their participation in money markets: Drexel, Merrill, and Shearson.

This struck one old-time trader—always in money markets—as odd. "There has never been," he noted, "a better time to be in the money market than now: since October 1987, there has been a real move in the direction of increasing liquidity, the flow of funds into money funds has gone up tremendously. There is a growth curve in the short-term market, but everyone is getting out because they haven't made any money at it lately. At just the time they could start making money, they close up.

"A lot of professionals who manage billions of money market assets are scared to death that there will be no one to trade with. The number of quality issuers is declining, and the number of dealers who can bid and offer paper in size is 50% of what it once was.

"Recently, the money market business has been a bonanza. Dealers who want to be in it should do well. However, if people who have been in the business only four or five years need retooling in any area, it is in money markets because that is not what they learned. In the old days, you used to start out in money markets and work your way up, someday be a long bond trader. Today, for the trainees, it is just the opposite. They start out as a GNMA, corporate bond, options, or basis trader; and they don't learn the money market. Most folks who came into the market in recent years don't have a clue as to how CDs, BAs, bills, and so on work; how Fed policy interacts with all of that; how repos, spreads, cost of carry, riding the yield curve, and bills rolls work. And that is where the big growth is right now."

At times, the world doth turn, right back to where it started.

Global Dealers?

In the aftermath of Big Bang, a British regulator made an interesting comment: "In London, there was a notion afloat, prior to Big Bang, that deregulation worldwide and globalization of capital markets would eventually lead to a situation in which a few big securities firms would dominate capital markets worldwide. The experience of Big Bang suggests that maybe after all native firms have advantages in their native countries that are hard for foreign competitors to overcome." One of these advantages is certainly that native securities firms have, in New York, in London, and in Tokyo, strong and long-standing relationships with big, native, institutional investors—and also with individuals too which counts in the stock market and other markets in which individuals are important buyers: munis, CDs, and so on. Put another way, U.S. securities houses are finding that relying on cross-border business can be, in Tokyo and elsewhere abroad, a recipe for starvation; to become profitable, they must behave like domestic securities houses and seek out local investors.

Whatever the future may hold, it is clear that, as the 1980s close, foreign securities operations, started earlier in the decade with high hopes, are, if they had not already been, written off and closed, typically awash in red ink. Between 1983 and early 1989, the number of foreign securities houses operating in Tokyo rose from 6 to 47. Thanks partly to the fact that land and administrative costs in Tokyo are, according to American firms, often double those in New York, only 6 of those 47 firms were profitable in 1988. Meanwhile, the Japanese Big Four were faring no better in New York—all were losing money and paring staff. Other foreign firms too—the U.K.'s County NatWest Government Securities Inc. to name but one—found the New York market tough sledding and eventually closed shop. And in London, the story continued much the same as it had been since Big Bang: every week, some foreign firm was either pulling out or paring some facet of its London operations. This is not to say that no foreign securities firms were making money in London in the aftermath of Big Bang. Disastrous experiences there were had by firms such as Citicorp, Chase, and Sec Pac, which bought London stockbrokers and tried to enter an area in which they lacked experience. Other firms that were well established in the Euromarkets, that did not buy stockbrokers, and that grew internally—Morgan Stanley, Goldman, and Japan's big four securities houses to name several—have fared far better and, in some cases, are continuing to expand.

A clear lesson of the 1980s is that securities firms seeking to expand internationally need to pick their niches with great care.

THE CLEARING BANKS

We have described the role of dealers as market makers in the money market. There are also other institutions that play a vital role in this process—the clearing banks and the brokers. The *clearing banks* clear, for nonbank dealers, trades in governments, agencies, and other money market instruments. The banks with the largest clearing operations are Manufacturers Hanover Trust (*Manny Hanny* or just *Manny* to all who know her), Security Pacific, the Bank of New York (*BONY*), and the Irving Trust (in 1988, BONY bought Irving in a hostile takeover). Many other banks routinely clear trades for investors who hold securities in custody with them, but not for dealers.

In acting as a clearing agent, a clearing bank makes payments against securities delivered into a dealer's account and receives payments made to the dealer against securities delivered out of its account. It also safekeeps securities received by a dealer and makes payments into and out of the account that the dealer holds with the bank. Finally, a clearing bank provides dealers with any financing they require at its posted *dealer loan rate*.

Volume

Clearing, which sounds simple in theory, turns out in practice to be a huge and complex operation because of the tens of thousands of trades and repo transactions that occur daily in the New York market. The vast majority of money market instruments traded in the national money market are payable in New York regardless of where the issuer is located and are safekept in New York regardless of where the investor is located.

The volume figures at a big clearing bank are staggering. Manny's average trade is approximately 10MM. On an average day, Manny clears over the Fed wire 22,000 transactions; and on a record day, it has cleared 38,000 transactions, 20% of which are pair offs. A pair off occurs when, for example, Sali and Merrill, which both clear through Manny, do a trade with each other; Manny clears such trades simply by moving securities from desk A to B through its internal system. On an average day, Manny alone processes $90 billion of transactions to its general ledger, and the figure on some days has been in excess of $125 billion of which $30 billion might reflect the trades of a single dealer!

The Fed Wire

Thanks to the fact that governments and most agencies were put into book-entry form and can be transferred over the Fed wire, huge volumes of transactions in these securities are cleared, each business day, with relative ease. There is congestion, at times, on the wire; computers do go down at the Fed and at the banks it serves; and the Fed wire rarely closes on the schedule it is supposed to; still, these are relatively minor inconveniences. Without the wire and book entry, clearing would be chaos.

Large dealers have a computer-to-computer linkup with their clearing bank. Smaller houses deliver trading tickets by hand to their clearing bank, often the night before clearing if the trade is for regular settlement. As securities are delivered to a clearing bank, the bank matches them up with a dealer's purchase tickets, and payment is made against receipt. When securities go out, the procedure is reversed.

Despite the computerization that has been applied to securities clearing (all governments have long been delivered and paid for over the Fed wire), a clearing operation used to require a lot of staff. In 1977, Manny Hanny had 11 people on its Merrill desk handling receives to and delivers from that account; by 1982, Manny's Merrill desk had 14 people handling twice as many trades. Today, thanks to continued automation, Manny in general handles significantly more transactions with a greatly reduced staff. Currently, Merrill's transactions in wireable securities are handled 80 to 90% on a fully automated, *remote* basis by Merrill Lynch personnel. This arrangement, not uncommon for a big dealer, puts that dealer's fate—When, to whom, and *at the risk of what fails,* do I deliver out securities?—squarely in its own hands. Automation notwithstanding, the size of Manny's clearing floor, which is jammed with computer terminals making and receiving messages, still rivals that of a football field.

The Fed wire is supposed to close at 2:30 P.M. for buys and sells and at 3 P.M. for reversals to correct mistakes. If those deadlines are not met, which is most of the time, extensions are granted. Said the head of one clearing operation, "Extensions are one of the reasons I have a lot of turnover of personnel. Many of our clerks begin work around 9:30 to 10 A.M., and they must stay until the close. In the last three months, the system has rarely closed prior to 5 P.M. And once the system closes, our clerks have one to three hours of work left to process. Consistently, we have 10 to 20 people who work 50 to 55 hours a week because the Fed wire closes late.

"All this costs money. My department spends about $35,000 a month on overtime and another $10,000 on taxis to get home people who work three hours or more past their normal quitting time." The same frustrated clearing banker went on to note, "In the last 15 months, the Fed has met its 2:30 close only three times: once for a hurricane, once for Good Friday, and once by good luck."

As noted in Chapter 12, such extensions inevitably cause frequent late closings of the wire for funds transfers. Congestion on the Fed wire and the movement to same-day settlement of funds have combined to convert the workweek of Fed funds traders and brokers, who used to view their jobs as fun, into a series of unbearably long days.

Turnaround Times

Years ago, it was common for dealers to get securities into their clearing bank on time but for that bank to be unable to make timely redelivery of those securities. The dealers asked for and got a two-minute turnaround time from their clearing bank. Then the issue went to the Fed, which finally decided that dealers deserved some privilege as makers of the market in governments and adopted a formal *turnaround time* in those cities where it was considered necessary: New York, Chicago, San Francisco, and Los Angeles. Now a customer in those cities has until 2:15 P.M. to deliver securities to a dealer, and a dealer has until 2:45 P.M. to deliver securities to a customer or to a dealer bank in those cities.

Dealer Loans

Extending dealer loans is an inherent and important part of a bank's clearing operations. When securities come into a clearing bank for a dealer's account, the banks pay for them whether or not the dealer has funds in its account, and it takes in any payment made to the dealer on security sales. Then at the end of the day, the bank net settles with each dealer. Since payments out of a dealer's account are made against the receipt of securities and payments in are made against the delivery out of securities, if a dealer ends up net short on cash for the day, he will have bought more securities than he sold, and the bank will have collateral against which to lend to him. Dealer loans are always made on an overnight basis. The collateral is returned to the dealer's account the next morning, and his account is charged for the loan amount plus interest. Because overnight repo is cheaper than dealer loans, most dealers use dealer loans only to finance odd pieces and securities they hold because they failed on a delivery.

The clearing banks are happy with the relatively small reliance dealers place on dealer loans for their financing; in fact, they tell the dealers not to think of them as a primary supplier of position financing. The size of dealer's positions is so huge that these positions could not be financed in toto by the clearing banks or even by the whole New York banking community. Despite the fact that dealers eschew bank financing, dealer loans can reach large proportions. A big clearing bank lends on average as much as $150MM overnight to dealers. Some days, however, the figure goes as high as $700MM, of which—top side—$400MM might go to a single dealer.

Normally, clearing banks post their dealer loan rate at around 11 A.M. It runs 1/4 to 3/8 above the Fed funds rate when money is easy and as much as one point above Fed funds when money is tight. This rate typically prevails for the rest of the day, but if the level at which Fed funds trade alters sharply, it will be changed. This occurs most often on Wednesdays when the banks are settling with the Fed.

Clearing banks attempt to get estimates from the dealers of their anticipated borrowings as early as possible so that they can adjust their Fed funds positions accordingly. A dealer may end up needing much less financing than he anticipated or significantly more. Thus, a clearing bank does not know the full size of its loans to dealers until after the national money market has closed, the Fed wire has closed, and sometimes the bank itself has closed. This causes the major clearing banks no problem in settling with the Fed because they have automated their wire to the Fed and know their reserve balance instantaneously even if they can't identify as quickly the sources and uses of funds that led to that balance.

If a clearing bank gets hit with big dealer loans late on a

Wednesday and Fed funds are very expensive, it may go to the discount window for funds. This is something about which the Fed used to be quite understanding but no longer is. The clearing banks manage to accommodate the wide fluctuations that occur in their loans to dealers only because they are large banks with big reserve positions and the ability to buy huge and highly variable sums of money in the Fed funds market. A smaller bank without that ability could not function as a major clearing bank.

On dealer loans, the clearing banks normally require collateral plus some margin, 2% on most short-term instruments and maybe 5% on a longer-term instrument, such as a Ginny Mae pass-through. If a dealer ends up with insufficient collateral, the clearing bank still makes all payments due out of his account and gives him an overdraft, for which it charges a rate higher than its normal dealer loan rate.

Clearing banks are not the only banks that provide dealers with overnight money. If other banks happen to find themselves with excess funds, perhaps because they have been hosed with money by correspondent banks that sell them Fed funds, they will call the dealers and offer them dealer loans at an attractive rate. Foreign banks also lend to dealers caught short too late to do more repo; the rate they change is a small spread over the rate at which they can buy Fed funds.

Clearing charges represent an important part of every dealer's costs. Clearing banks used to set their fees on the basis of the par value of the securities cleared. Then, as automation reduced their costs, they switched to a per-ticket pricing structure, and as they did, the net cost of clearing to dealers fell. Fees for clearing vary from bank to bank, and also at a given clearing bank they may vary for different dealers. As one dealer noted, "We have a sweetheart relationship with our clearing bank, and whatever the banks may say, such relationships are common."

Mistakes

Clearing banks make mistakes. Sometimes the problem results from delivery instructions. Said one clearing officer, "What is a good delivery instruction? Chase Manhattan Bank, 1 Chase

Plaza, 43rd floor, Att. Al Clark. That is terrific, it says everything, but it does not fly on the wire. I need something that says Chase/Cust or Chase/Dealer, a system-recognizable mnemonic. Problems with respect to delivery instructions arise when a dealer gets a new salesperson who sends something back to operations, which sends us God knows what. Sometimes a dealer has to take a fail for us to make the point to him. At a lot of shops, the operations side tends to be ignored in terms of resources until things start to go not so well."

"Also, we make mistakes, maybe half a dozen on a 12,000-trade day. An operator pushes the inquire button instead of transmit. We hope the mistake is on a 1MM not a 20MM trade. Naturally, 100MM problems always arise on Fridays or before a long weekend. On the day before Labor Day weekend, we found a 65MM problem because an operator failed to push *transmit*. The trade was an outright sale to a receiver who had the securities going out to seven or eight different places. Fortunately, we saved about 40MM of it. In a situation like this, we end up giving someone a free dealer loan on whatever we can't save; that can be a big hit."

THE BROKERS

A broker is a firm that brings buyers and sellers together for a commission. Unlike dealers, brokers by definition do not position. Brokers are everywhere in the money market. They are active in the *interdealer* markets in governments, agencies, CDs, Euro CDs, BAs, repo, and reverse, and in the *interbank* markets for Fed funds and Euro time deposits.

Volume and Commissions

The volumes of funds and securities that are brokered each business day are staggering. Unfortunately, because statistics on brokered trades are not collected in most sectors of the market, it is impossible to put precise dollar figures on these amounts. It is possible, however, to give a few suggestive numbers. On an average day one of the top Fed funds brokers, who is in competition with a number of other brokers of varying size, may broker over 20 to 25 billion of funds! Currently almost all interdealer trades in governments and agencies are done through brokers.

Brokers could not survive without a huge volume of trades because the commissions they receive per $1MM of funds or securities brokered are so small. In the bill market, brokerage on 90-day bills works out to $12.50 per $1MM in the Fed funds market, on overnight trades it's only $0.50 per $1MM. In some sectors of the market (Fed funds and Euros), brokerage is paid by both the buyer and the seller; in others (governments and agencies), it is paid only by the dealer who initiates a trade by either hitting a bid or taking an offer quoted by the broker.

The Service Sold

Much of what a broker is selling his clients is a fast information service that tells the trader where the market is—what bids and offers are and how much they are good for. Speed of communication is thus crucial to a money market broker, and each has before him a board of direct phone lines through which he can contact every important trader he services by merely punching a button. Over those lines brokers constantly collect bids and offers throughout the day. They pass these on to other traders either by phone calls or more commonly over display screens, referred to throughout the industry as *CRTs*—short for cathode ray tubes.

In many sectors of the market (governments, Euro time deposits), the broker gives runs: bids and offers for a number of issues or maturities. In others (the market for overnight Fed funds), just one bid and offer are quoted. In some sectors of the market, bids and offers are good until withdrawn; in others they are understood to be good for only a few minutes.

The pace at which brokering is done in all sectors of the money market is hectic most of the time and frantic at certain crucial moments—in the Fed funds market, on Wednesday afternoon when the banks settle with the Fed; in the government market, after key numbers (indicators) are released.

A broker has to be not only quick, but *careful* because he is normally expected to substantiate any bid or offer he quotes.

This means that if he quotes a market inaccurately to a trader, he must either (1) pay that trader an amount equal to the difference between the price he quoted and the price at which the trade can actually be got off or (2) buy securities from or sell securities to that trader at the quoted price and then cover, typically at a loss, his resulting long or short position.

The ethics of brokering are strict in all sectors of the money market. A broker is not supposed to and never will give up the names of the dealers or banks that are bidding or offering through him. He simply quotes prices and size. However, in certain markets, once a bid is hit or an offer taken, names are given up. In the Fed funds market, for example, before the seller can agree to a trade, he must know to whom he is selling because he has to check that he has a line to the buyer and that it is not full. Also, the buyer has to know who the seller is because the two institutions clear the transaction directly with each other over the Fed wire. In many brokered securities trades, in contrast, the seller never knows who the buyer is, and vice versa.

There are certain rules of ethics that brokers' clients are expected to observe. In particular, in markets in which names are given up, the customer is not supposed to then go around the broker and do the trade direct. Also, brokers feel it is unfair of a trader to use them as an information service and just do small trades through them. Traders who make a practice of this get to be known and ignored by brokers.

Usefulness of Brokers

In recent years, brokerage has been introduced to almost every sector of the money market; and in those market sectors where it did exist, the use of brokers has increased dramatically. One reason is that in all sectors of the market the number of dealers has expanded sharply; as a result, it has become increasingly difficult for a trader to know where other traders are quoting the market and to rapidly disseminate his own bids and offers other than through the communications network provided by the brokers. In the government market, there are over 40 primary dealers, and no bill trader can possibly keep in touch with his counterparts at other shops by talking to each of them directly.

Another important reason brokers are used is anonymity. A big bank or dealer may operate in such size that simply by bidding or offering, he will affect either market quotes or the size for which they are good. A trader who would be willing to buy $15MM in bills through a broker might, for example, be leery of buying the same amount at the same price from a big-position house for fear that the latter might have a lot more of these bills to sell.

A second reason anonymity is valued by traders is the "ego element." In the words of one dealer, "Anonymity is very important to those giant egos on Wall Street. When they make a bad trade, they just do not want the whole world to watch them unwind it at a loss."

Still another reason the brokers are used is because a lot of traders literally hate each other, usually because of some underlying ethical issue, real or perceived. As one trader noted, "There are guys I would not deal with personally, but if it happens through a broker, well OK. Money is green whatever the source."

A final reason brokers are used, particularly in the government market, is that the brokers' screens provide an arena in which a trader can paint pictures and play other trading games.

Consolidation of Brokers

Over the years, there has been a strong tendency for brokers to merge. The reasons are various. For a big blind broker, a marriage that adds to capital can look extremely attractive. A second reason for broker mergers is that a shop that handles a wide menu of securities has a better chance of getting its foot into a dealer's door and, once there, can better service the dealer's needs. Institutions that reverse out securities often do so, for example, as part of an arbitrage in which they invest in another security; a broker that offers one-stop shopping can put together the whole arbitrage package.

In Euro and foreign exchange brokering, both cross-market and trans-Atlantic mergers made sense. The foreign-exchange and Euromarkets could not be separated, and no broker could provide an international service without having an office or tie of some sort in at least both New York and London.

Going Abroad

As a number of U.S. dealers in Treasuries and agencies began to trade these securities out of offices in London and Tokyo (globalization on the march), several brokers of governments followed them to these foreign centers. How profitable doing so has been for them is questionable. Both centers are expensive places to operate, and the volume of trading in U.S. governments done in those centers (Tokyo especially) during local business hours has been a disappointment to both dealers and brokers. London trades more actively once New York opens, but a lot of the trading of Treasuries done in London involves unwinding which was done earlier in Tokyo. It has developed over time, that big foreign investors in Treasuries, such as Japanese insurance companies, prefer to trade such securities during the hours when the U.S. market is open, that is, when the market has the greatest depth and is most liquid. (For more on brokers of governments, see Chapter 14.)

Personnel

Brokering is much more than quoting rates. As brokers are wont to note, it's a highly professional business. The broker is often required to make split-second decisions about difficult questions. If a trader offers at a price and the broker has X bids at that price on his pad, with which buyer does he cross the trade? Technically, he attempts to decide who was there first, but the choice is often complicated by the fact that the offer is for one amount, the bids for others.

Also, in some sectors of the money market, a broker does more than quote rates. The buyer or seller may look to him for information on the tone of the market, and it's the broker's job to sense that tone and be able to communicate it—to say, for example, to a bidder, "The market's 5/16–3/8, last trade at 5, but I think it could be worth 3/8."

Being a broker is also part salesmanship—to get a buyer or seller who has done one trade to let the broker continue to work for him. This is especially the case in markets, such as those for Fed funds and Euros, where a dealer who does a trade is likely to have a lot more business to do in the same direction during the day. In one area of brokering, the reverse market, salesmanship is crucial. To get a bank or an S&L to reverse out securities, the broker often must point out a profitable arbitrage and then sell the institution on doing that arbitrage.

Being a good broker requires a special mix of talents. As noted, salesmanship is one. In addition, a broker has to be able to listen with one ear on the phone and keep the other tuned to bids and offers coming in around him, to maintain a feel for his own market and for other related markets as well. A good broker also has to be able to think on his feet and often use his own personality to put trades together. As one broker noted, "Brightness is not enough; anyone can quote a market."

Many brokers are ex-traders, people who have the advantage when they come to brokering of knowing a market and how traders in it operate. One reason traders become brokers is the pressure under which traders operate. Another is their own inability to do what many good traders do, forget their position when they go home. Said one successful broker, "Trading is a problem. You track the things you think might impact the market and then buy. All too often the unexpected—war in the Middle East—happens and you end up being right for the wrong reason, or vice versa. Once as a trader, I was down three quarters of a million. I made 2MM the next month, but accepting the fact that I had done something stupid at one point was too much. It's part of the reason I became a broker."

The Government Securities Clearing Corporation (GSCC)

Currently, the dealers, brokers, and clearing banks are working to establish a still more efficient means of clearing book-entry through the *Government Securities Clearing Corporation* (*GSCC*). The principal objective of GSCC is to achieve more netting in clearing. Doing so would reduce traffic and congestion on the Fed wire, reduce perceived credit risks by various parties, and make possible some reduction in the multibillion-dollar daylight overdrafts that clearing banks now run in their reserve accounts at the Fed due to their clearing activities. GSCC was slow to get started because the parties involved had difficulty resolving their conflicting interests, but in early 1989, it looked as if they would have their new system up and running by the end of 1989. A rough estimate is that GSCC will eliminate a quarter of the business now done by clearing banks. Certainly, all trades done by brokers will be netted rather than cleared through a clearing bank as is presently the case.

COMMUNICATIONS

In a discussion of the makers of the money market, ignoring the phone company, Telexes, CRTs, computers, and other communications facilities would be a serious omission. Without Ma Bell and her foreign counterparts, the money market would be an utterly different place. That the money market is a single market that closely approaches the economist's assumption of perfect information is currently due in no small part to the fact that New York brokers and traders are one push of a direct-phone-line button away from the B of A and often only a four-digit extension from London, Singapore, and other distant spots. All this is extremely expensive. Banks spend well over half a billion on phone bills; and the nonbank dealers and brokers spend huge amounts in addition to that.

The phone bill is one reason for the concentration of the money market in New York. The brokers in particular have to be there to minimize communications costs. It is cheaper to be in New York with one direct phone line to the B of A than to be in San Francisco with 40 direct lines to New York.

Thanks to deregulation of communications and advances in technology, including communications satellites, a number of U.S. securities firms with branch networks have found that setting up a private communications network makes sense; it saves them money, makes them more nimble, and enables them to communicate increasing amounts of data with increasing rapidity.

With the globalization of markets, instantaneous communication worldwide is, for a big securities firm, vital. Thus, it is not surprising that Merrill's private network is, today, at the forefront of what securities firms are doing. At home, U.S. securities firms have great freedom in setting up a private communications network: they can rely on satellites and on microwave networks, and hook in this and that new gizmo. Abroad, things are far tougher. State-run post, telephone, and telegraph authorities (*PTTs*) inhibit, in most of Europe and in much of the Third World, the development of private networks by strictly controlling what equipment can be used and by whom. In Europe, leased phone circuits cost on average four times what they do in the U.S.; local PTTs force companies to use locally made modems and faxes; and private microwave networks are virtually outlawed; satellites are OK, but only if a company uses the local PTTs' equipment and transmits over the International Telecommunications Satellite Organization (Intelsat), jointly owned by the U.S. and 113 other countries. Among major countries, Germany is probably the worst offender, whereas Britain has opened its communications market to competitors of British Telecom, the national phone company. Interestingly, Germany is beginning to bend. The easiest way to ensure that the local PTT is profitable is to maintain its monopoly over the widest area possible, but countries are beginning to realize that this conflicts with their desire to be competitive not just in finance, but in other areas as well. Also, they are beginning to realize that the setting up of private communications networks generates big sales of equipment and transmission lines; also, since most of the voice-and-data messages carried by this equipment eventually go over local phone company lines, private networks generate significant traffic on such lines.

There is nothing new about the difficulties firms face in setting up private communications networks that span the globe. What is new is that, with the globalization of financial markets, financial firms find vast new demands being made on them in terms of their ability to transmit price and other data on any one of a host of different markets instantaneously from one part of the globe to another.

The Information Vendors

Two decades ago, the only way money market participants could get current quotes was by calling brokers and dealers. Moreover, to get a range of quotes they had to make several calls because no quote system covered the whole market. In 1968, a new organization, *Telerate,* began to remedy this situation by quoting commercial paper rates not on the phone, but on a two-page, *cathode-ray-tube* display system (*CRT*); it then had 50 subscribers. From this modest start, the system was quickly expanded because people wanted more information.

Today, several hundred pages of information on credit market quotes and statistics are available to Telerate subscribers; the subscriber gets the page he wants by pressing a series of numbered buttons. Information on current quotes, offerings, and bids are inputted into the system through computers around the country, and the system is dynamically updated; that is, if GMAC changed its posted rate while a viewer is looking at the commercial paper quotes, the quotes change as GMAC inputs its new rates into the system. A wide range of institutions—dealers, investors, and borrowers—now use Telerate; its advent has not only eliminated a lot of phone calls, but vastly improved communications within the money market. On the international scene, there is a similar *Reuters* system that flashes information on the Euromarket, the foreign-exchange market, and other related markets into foreign countries and the U.S. Since the money market is international in scope, it was to be expected that both Telerate and Reuters invaded each others' turf both geographically and in terms of information provided.

Telerate and Reuters are highly profitable and a natural duopoly. Others would like to move into the market areas where these two firms are strongest, but two factors militate against this: setting up a competing system—getting access to data and setting up all the needed hardware and software—would be extremely expensive. Second, since brokers today all use CRTs, the typical trader's desk is already cluttered with as many CRTs as can fit. To displace a Reuters or Telerate screen on a trader's desk, a competitor will have to offer something better. The strongest competitors of Telerate and Reuters have niches in other markets: Quotron, owned by Citicorp, feeds out quotes on U.S. equities; ADA sells similar information.

It is estimated that, today, the vending of financial information, a market that did not exist 15 years ago, is worth $3 billion a year worldwide. Two obvious ways competitors in this business can improve their screens are (1) to add analytics and (2) to turn their screens into interactive systems over which trades can be executed. Starts have been made in both directions.

As noted, the Bloomberg system is crammed with analytics, but it is blocked from logical expansion by a 1984 agreement with its backer, Merrill; under that agreement, Bloomberg may not sell terminals to a dozen of Merrill's biggest rivals until January 1, 1991. Today, Bloomberg is begging Merrill to let it break this covenant: to sell screens to Merrill's biggest competitors and to permit those competitors to post on the system their own bond quotes. Bloomberg envisions how sweet it would be for Merrill if, all over the world, bond sellers and buyers were getting price data from a Merrill-controlled screen. This, in Bloomberg's vision, would give Merrill advantages akin to those that American and United gained from introducing proprietory airline reserves systems that are widely used by travel agents. Playing on the name of American's reservations system, Bloomberg speaks of his ambition to "Sabre-ize" the Bloomberg terminal.

Turning dumb terminals into trading systems is not a new idea. Twelve years ago, a London-based dealer in Euro CDs rhapsodized about how his firm was going to have such a system to sell Euro CDs back into the States—put its offerings on a screen and let investors lift them electronically. Nonetheless, screen trading has been slow to get off the ground for several reasons. First, organized exchanges (including those trading financial futures) are naturally opposed to being put out of business, though the Chicago Mercantile Exchange is planning, with Reuters, to try a new, *off-hours* screen-trading system called Globex. Second, while it's possible to program a computer to execute simple trades—"Lift your offering for 1MM," "Hit your bid for 2MM"—it's far more difficult to program it to handle "workup" trades of the sort commonly done by brokers of governments. A major dealer bidding for Treasuries via a broker doesn't want to show his hand: he might bid for 1MM, get it, and then say "Make it 5MM," "Make it 10MM," "Make it 22.5MM." Current automated systems are too cumbersome to handle well that sort of trade.

Finally, there are vendors of back-office systems who have visions of breaking down the barriers between back-office and dealing-room computer systems and competing with vendors of data, maybe more. CRTs arrived on the Street in the late 1970s; now the time seems ripe for further innovation and automation—just what sort isn't, however, yet clear.

THE NEXT CHAPTER

In this chapter, we focused on dealers, brokers, and others who are active in making what are today often not only national, but global, financial markets. In the next chapter, we focus on buyers in these markets, on money market investors.

FURTHER READINGS

For more on clearing, see Marcia Stigum, *After the Trade: Dealer and Clearing Bank Operations* (Homewood, Ill.: Dow Jones-Irwin, 1988).

CHAPTER 11

THE INVESTORS: RUNNING A SHORT-TERM PORTFOLIO

Money market investors include a wide range of institutions: commercial banks, savings and loan associations, insurance companies of all sorts, mutual savings banks, other financial institutions, federal agencies, nonfinancial corporations, international financial institutions, such as the World Bank, foreign central banks, and foreign firms—financial and nonfinancial. Also, when interest rates get sufficiently high, individual investors make forays into certain sectors of the money market.

One might expect most institutional portfolios to be managed with considerable sophistication, but "the startling thing you would find, if you were to wander around the country talking to short-term portfolio managers [not the Fords and the World Banks], is the basic underutilization of the portfolio." These are the words of the sales manager of the government department in one of the nation's top banks. Another dealer described portfolio management practices similarly but in slightly different terms, "Most portfolio managers would describe themselves as 'conservative,' by which they mean that the correct way to manage a portfolio is to look to your accounting risk and reduce that to zero. The opportunities thereby forgone are either ignored or more frequently not even perceived." Many short-term portfolios are poorly managed, most are not managed at all. Before we talk about that, let's look first at how a liquidity portfolio should be managed.

CONTRAST OF A PORTFOLIO MANAGER
WITH A DEALER

In Chapter 10, we noted that dealers' biggest profits result over time from well-chosen position plays and that a crucial ingredient in a successful dealer operation is therefore the ability to manage a highly levered portfolio well.

Much of what we said in Chapter 10 about how a good dealer manages his portfolio applies to bank and corporate portfolio managers as well. There are, however, important differences in perspective between the two. First, a dealer is likely to be *much* less risk averse than the typical manager of a liquidity portfolio because it is the dealer's job to speculate on yields and yields spreads, whereas the portfolio manager's job is first to ensure that the funds he invests will be available whenever his firm needs them and only second to maximize the return he earns on these funds. A second difference in perspective is that, whereas the portfolio manager has free funds that he has to invest, the dealer has no such funds, and his decision to invest is therefore always based on a view of the market. A third difference in perspective is the time horizon. A dealer often buys securities on the expectation that he will be able to resell them at a higher price within a few hours or a few days. The portfolio manager, in contrast, is normally looking for instruments that he would be comfortable holding for some longer period—how long depends on the type of portfolio he is running.

THE PARAMETERS

A liquidity portfolio is always managed within certain investment *parameters* that establish limits with respect to: (1) the types of instruments the portfolio may buy; (2) the percentage of the portfolio that may be invested in any one of these instruments (in T bills the limit might be 100%, whereas in BAs, which are less liquid, it might be much lower); (3) the kind of exposure to names and credit risk the portfolio may assume (which banks' paper and which issuers' commercial paper it may buy and how much of each name if may buy); (4) whether the portfolio may invest in Euros and foreign names; (5) how far out on the maturity spectrum the portfolio may extend; (6) whether the portfolio may short securities or repo securities; (7) whether the portfolio may use futures and options; and (8) whether the portfolio may take foreign-exchange risk or must always hedge.

The investment parameters within which every liquidity portfolio operates are set by top management. Because senior management delineates the portfolio manager's playing field and thereby the kinds of winnings—return on investment—that he may seek to earn through managing the portfolio, it is important that management take time to learn what the game is about before establishing such guidelines. Another input in this decision should be an evaluation of the kind of money that the firm is likely to have to invest short term: How big is it likely to be? How variable will it be? A third important input is the firm's management style. There are swinging corporations and there are very conservative corporations, and that difference should be reflected in their styles of portfolio management. A fourth factor is the caliber of the personnel the firm hires to manage its short-term portfolio. The more qualified they are, the wider guidelines should be set and the greater the latitude the portfolio manager should be given to exercise judgment.

MANAGING A LIQUIDITY PORTFOLIO

In large institutions, a portfolio manager is often given several portfolios to manage—one for the firm itself, another for its financing sub, still others for self-insurance funds, and so forth. With respect to each portfolio, the manager must ask: What are the size, variability, and predictability of the money I am investing? The answer obviously depends in part on the purpose for which the funds are held. For example, the short-term portfolio of a manufacturing firm that experiences big seasonal fluctuations in cash flows, as auto firms and food packers do, will be more variable and less predictable in size than a portfolio supporting a self-insurance fund. A second element in the portfolio manager's evaluation of the sort of money he is investing is the cash forecasts the firm gives him—their frequency, the periods for which they are available (these might be tomorrow, the next week, the next month, and the current quarter), and the confidence that experience suggests he can place in these forecasts. The portfolio manager's assessment of the sort of money he is investing tells him how long he is likely to be able to hold securities he buys and thus the planning horizon—30 days, 90 days, 1 year, or longer—on which he should base investment decisions.

Relative Value

Once he has determined his planning horizon, the portfolio manager asks, just as a dealer does: *Where is relative value?* Answering this question requires knowledge, experience, and feel for the market.

On a purely technical level, the portfolio manager must first face the problem that yields on money market instruments are not quoted on comparable bases. The problem is not just that yields on discount securities are quoted on a discount basis whereas yields on interest-bearing instruments are quoted on another basis. There are also all sorts of other anomalies with respect to how interest accrues, how often it is paid, whether the security is U.S. or Canadian (Canadian CDs trade on a 365-day-year basis, domestic CDs on a 360-day-year basis), whether it is a leap year, whether a security happens to mature on a holiday, and other factors. Often, these anomalies are *not* reflected in the yield to maturity figures on dealers' quote sheets.[1]

A number of portfolio managers, who run such large sums of money that the cost is justified, have developed sophisticated computer programs that permit them to calculate yields on a wide range of securities on a comparable basis. One such portfolio manager noted, "I developed a program that incorporated a day algorithm that I got from a mathematician. I wanted the computer to know when a weekend occurs and to skip it in evaluating yield on a Friday trade I do for regular settlement. I also wanted the computer to recognize that in agencies July 31

---

[1]See Marcia Stigum and John Mann, *Money Market Calculations: Yields, Break-Evens, and Arbitrage* (Homewood, Ill.: Dow Jones-Irwin, 1981).

is a nonday [no interest accrues], that Feb 29 exists whether or not it actually does, and so too does Feb 30; there's an arbitrage from Feb 28 to March 1 in agencies, and I want the computer to recognize this. The computer also knows a Canadian security from a U.S. security."

In evaluating the relative value of different instruments, being able to calculate their yields on a comparable basis is just a starting point. In addition, the portfolio manager must have a good feel for the *liquidity* of different instruments, under both prevailing market conditions and those he foresees might occur. This can involve subtle distinctions. The manager of a large portfolio commented, "I buy only direct issue [commercial] paper that I know I can sell to the dealers—GMAC but not Prulease. It's a question of liquidity, not quality. Also, I buy paper from dealers only if they are ready to take it back."

To determine relative value among different instruments, the portfolio manager must also have a good feel for *yield spreads*: what they are, and how and why they change. This too involves subtleties. Here's an example of one investor's thinking at one point: "Lately, the 6-month bill has been trading way above Fed funds. I ask, 'Why?' The technical condition of the market has been excellent with little supply on the Street [in dealers' hands]. So the 6-month bill should have done better, but it didn't. The reason is that we've got a pure dealer market. The retail buyer, who is scared and going short, is simply not there."

Finally, to determine where relative value lies among different *maturity* sectors of the market, the portfolio manager must explicitly predict interest rates *and* the slope of the yield curve over at least the time span of his planning horizon. Such predictions will, as noted in Chapter 9, be based on a wide range of factors, including a careful tracking of the Fed's stated objectives and whether it is currently achieving these objectives.

Relative value, in addition to depending on all the factors we have enumerated, may also depend partly on the temperament of the portfolio manager—whether he has the psychology of a trader, as some do, or whether he is more inclined to make a reasoned bet and let it stand for some time. As one investor noted, it makes a difference, "The 9-month bill will, except in very tight markets, trade at yield levels close to the corresponding long issue, which is the year bill. So if you are looking for the most return for your dollar on a buy-and-hold strategy, you buy the 9-month bill and ride it for three months. If, however, you want to trade the portfolio—to buy something with the idea that its price will rise—you are better off staying in the active issue, which would be the current year bill."

Credit Risk

Most companies, when they have money and are trying to increase yield, will start reaching out on the credit spectrum—buying A-2 or P-2 paper.[2] A few do so in an intelligent and reasoned way, devoting considerable resources to searching out companies that are candidates for an upgrading of their credit rating to A-1 or P-1 and whose paper thus offers more relative value than that of A-1 and P-1 issuers.

The average firm, however, would probably be well advised not to take this route. As the sales manager of one dealership noted, "We tell a company doing this, 'It's the wrong thing for you to do because you do not know how to do it. You have no ability to track these companies. Also, their financial statements are not worth much, and you of all people should know this because you know what you do to your own.' They sort of look at us with jaundiced eyes, and say, 'Oh, yes, I guess that's so.' "

Many of the ablest portfolio managers tend to steer clear of credit analysis. As one commented, "We are not interested in owning anything that does not have unimpeachable credit because, on an instrument that does not, credit will tend to dominate the performance of the instrument more than interest rates. Also, I am a one-man band, and I simply do not have to evaluate credit risk."

The exception to this attitude is most often found in portfolio managers working for insurance companies. They are a different breed: far more comfortable than most with credit expo-

---

[2]Commercial paper, as noted in Chapter 23, is rated by several rating services. A-2 and P-2 paper are a grade off top-rated A-1 or P-1 paper.

sure. This is an offshoot of their purchases of long corporate bonds. Because of these purchases, portfolio managers at insurance companies follow many corporate credits, and, consequently, can and do knowledgeably buy a lesser-grade commercial paper that other portfolios wouldn't touch.

Maturity Choice

While a good portfolio manager can, as many do, refuse to get into credit analysis, he *cannot* avoid making explicit interest-rate predictions and basing his maturity choices on them. As one portfolio manager pointed out, "The mistake many people make is to think that they do not have to make a forecast. But buying a 90-day bill and holding it to maturity *is* making a forecast. If you think that rates are going to move up sharply and soon, you should be sitting in overnight repo; and then when rates move up, you buy the 90-day bill."

Making rate predictions is important not only because an implicit rate prediction underlies every maturity choice a portfolio manager makes, but because good portfolio managers feel as a group that the way yield on a large portfolio can most effectively be increased is by positioning correctly along the maturity spectrum: by recognizing which maturity sectors of the market are cheap (have relative value) and which are expensive, and by buying or selling accordingly.

Riding the Yield Curve
The best way to illustrate the kind of dividends yielded by maturity choices based on an explicit prediction of how interest rates might move is with a few examples. Let's start by illustrating how a technique commonly used to raise return—namely, *riding the yield curve*—must be based on an explicit prediction of how short-term rates might change. Riding the yield curve is a strategy to increase return when the yield curve is positively sloped; it calls for buying a security out on the shoulder of the yield curve and holding that security until it can be sold at a gain because its current maturity has fallen and the yield at which it trades has consequently decreased. The main threats to the success of such a strategy are (1) that short-term rates might

FIGURE 11–1
Yield curve in an example of riding the yield curve

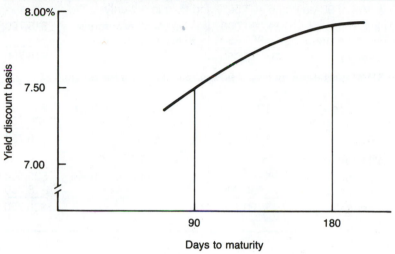

rise across the board and (2) that the yield curve might invert at the short end.

Assume that an investor has funds to invest for three months. The 6-month (180-day) bill is trading at 7.90, and the 3-month (90-day) bill is trading at 7.50 (Figure 11–1). The alternatives the investor is choosing between are: (1) to buy the 90-day bill and mature it and (2) to buy the 6-month bill and sell it three months hence. To assess the relative merits of these two strategies, the investor does a *break-even analysis*.

On $1MM of bills, a 90-day bp (a basis point earned for 90 days) is worth $25.[3] If the investor bought the 6-month bill, he would earn 40 bp more than if he bought the 3-month bill. Thus,

---

[3]The formula used (see p. 66) is:

$$D = \left(\frac{d \times t}{360}\right)(\$1,000,000)$$

The calculation is as follows:

$$\left(\frac{0.0001 \times 90}{360}\right)(\$1,000,000) = \$25$$

TABLE 11–1

Dollar calculations of return in example of riding the yield curve

I. Buy $1MM of 90-day bills at 7.50% and hold to maturity.

Face value	$1,000,000	Discount at purchase	$18,750
−Purchase price	981,250	−Discount at maturity	0
Return	$ 18,750	*Return*	$18,750

II. Buy $1MM of 180-day bills at 7.90% and sell at break-even yield of 8.30%.

Sale price	$979,250	Discount at purchase	$39,500
−Purchase price	960,500	−Discount at sale	20,750
Return	$ 18,750	*Return*	$18,750

III. Buy $1MM of 180-day bills at 7.90% and sell at 7.50%.

Sale price	$981,250	Discount at purchase	$39,500
−Purchase price	960,500	−Discount at sale	18,750
Return	$ 20,750	*Return*	$20,750

he could sell out the 6-month bill after three months at a rate 40 bp above the rate at which he bought it, that is, at 8.30, and still earn as many *dollars* on his investment as he would have if he had bought and matured the 3-month bill (Table 11–1). Therefore, the rate on the 3-month bill three months hence would have to rise above 8.30 before holding the 6-month bill for three months would pay out fewer dollars than buying and maturing the 3-month bill.

How likely is this to occur? Due to the slope of the yield curve (a 40-bp drop between the 6-month and 3-month bill rates), the rate at which the 3-month bill trades three months hence would be 7.50 if no change occurred in interest rates, that is, 80 bp below the break-even rate of 8.30. Thus, the investor has 80 bp of protection, and the question he must ask is: How likely is it that the Fed will tighten in the next three months so sharply that yield on the 3-month bill will rise 80 bp from 7.50 to 8.30? If his answer is that it is highly unlikely, then he would buy the 6-month bill and ride the yield curve.

Note that if the investor buys the 3-month bill and matures it, he will earn $18,750 on each $1MM of bills he buys (Table

11–1). If, alternatively, he opts to ride the yield curve and does so successfully (i.e., buys the 6-month bill and is able, because the Fed does not tighten, to sell out at 7.50), he will earn $20,750, which exceeds $18,750 by $2,000. This $2,000 equals the extra 80 90-day bp he earns: 40 because the 6-month bill is bought at a 40-bp spread to the 3-month bill and 40 because he is able to sell it three months later at a rate 40 bp below the rate at which he bought it.

Actually, the investor riding the yield curve in our example has more protection than we indicated. The reason is that, when he buys the 6-month bill, he invests fewer dollars than when he buys the 3-month bill. So on a *simple interest basis,* he would earn an annualized return of 7.75 if he bought and matured the 3-month bill, whereas if he bought the 6-month bill at 7.90 and sold it as the break-even level of 8.30, he would earn an annualized return, again on a simple interest, 365-day-year basis, of 7.92, which is greater.[4] To earn an annualized return of only 7.75 on the funds invested in the 6-month bill, the investor would have to sell it out after three months at a discount of 8.46, which is 96 bp above 7.50. The first break-even calculation we made on a dollar-return basis is easier, but the second more accurate.

Another Maturity Decision

Here's a second example of how a conscious prediction of interest rates over the investor's time horizon can help an investor increase yield. The example is dated; the point it makes is *not.* When it appears that the Fed might tighten, the reaction of many portfolio managers is to retreat in panic to the base of the yield curve. Whether doing so is wise depends on the opportunities available and on how fast and how far the Fed is likely to tighten.

In April 1977, it was felt that the Fed was tightening. Funds were trading at 4¾ and no one was sure where the rate was going. It was the feeling in the market that a ¾ point move

---

[4]The formula for return (in decimal form) is:

$$\left(\begin{array}{c} \text{Annualized return on a} \\ \text{simple interest basis} \end{array} \right) = \left(\frac{\text{Dollar return}}{\text{Principal invested}} \right) \div \left(\frac{\text{Days held}}{365} \right)$$

was needed and that 5½ would probably be the top side, but some in the market suggested 5¾. Just prior to this period, 6-month BAs had risen in yield from 5.20 to 5.85 because of a lack of demand on the part of investors; the yield on 3-month BAs was 5.45. At this point, a portfolio manager with 3-month money to invest faced a choice. One alternative, assuming he was managing an S&L portfolio, would have been to adopt the bearish strategy of selling overnight Fed funds in anticipation of eventually getting a 5½ overnight rate.[5] Alternatively, he could have decided to buy 6-month BAs and sell them after three months.

Using the same sort of break-even analysis illustrated in the previous example, one investor facing this choice concluded that if he bought 6-month BAs at 5.85, he could after 90 days sell them at 6.30, and do as well as he would have if he had invested in overnight Fed funds and the Fed funds rate had in fact immediately moved to 5½.[6] In other words, he could sell 6-month BAs three months hence at 85 bp above the rate at which 3-month BAs were then trading and still earn as many dollars as he would have by rolling funds overnight at 5½. That 85 bp protection seemed more than sufficient, so he bought the 6-month BAs. As things turned out, the Fed's target for funds was only 5¼–⅜, so the BAs were by far the better investment. An investor who did not use this analysis would have missed this opportunity.

Asymmetric Positions of the Investor and the Issuer

The two maturity-choice examples we worked through involved a choice between riding the yield curve and making an alternative investment: in one case buying and maturing the 3-month bill and in the other case rolling overnight funds.

---

[5]The alternative facing a corporate portfolio manager would have been to invest in overnight repo or in overnight Euros.

[6]The calculation assumes that the same number of dollars would have been invested in both instruments. It also allows for the fact that an investor selling funds gets daily compounding of interest. The funds rate is quoted on a 360-day-year basis.

With respect to riding the yield curve, note that a bank or S&L issuing CDs or a firm issuing commercial paper is playing precisely the opposite ball game from the investor—one is trying to minimize interest paid, the other to maximize interest earned. If the issuer of paper finds that, from a cost point of view, it makes sense to roll 3-month paper, then the investor should be buying 6-month paper and holding it for three months rather than rolling 3-month paper.

Stability of Return

As one good portfolio manager after another will note, "Real money is to be made by positioning correctly along the maturity spectrum—by making conscious market judgments and acting on them."

Such positioning does not, however, guarantee *steady* high return. One reason is that sometimes the portfolio manager will be wrong in his rate predictions. A second reason is well described by one manager, "If you can invest out to two years and you feel strongly that rates are going to fall, you might choose to have an average 9- or 12-month maturity—not everything out in the longer spectrum. If you are correct and the market rallies, the proper response is to shorten the portfolio—not just to sit there and hold this apparent book yield, but to recognize it. The reason you sell is that the market eventually gets to a point where you think it has reached a peak and might go lower. If after you sell you decide that you were wrong and believe—on the basis of a new rate forecast—that rates are likely to go still lower, you buy in again long term."

It's hard to produce a stable income pattern with this sort of portfolio management, and it would thus be criticized by some. But the basic assumption is that the firm is a going concern. Therefore, the portfolio manager's primary goal should be long-term profitability, not stability of income.

In this respect, the track record of the World Bank's liquidity portfolio is interesting. The managers of this portfolio have for years constantly been making maturity choices of the sort described above. In February 1977, their treasurer noted that over the previous 29 months, they had earned on their dollar portfolio a high average return, 9.32%, but their monthly annualized returns had fluctuated from a low of -0.67% in one month to a high of almost $+32\%$ in another.[7]

As this track record suggests, in evaluating the performance of a managed portfolio, monthly figures are meaningless. A portfolio manager needs to look at this average record for six months or longer to get a true feel for his performance.

Time Horizon and Maturity of Securities Purchased

In our example of why the return on a managed portfolio is likely to fluctuate from month to month, the portfolio manager—believing that rates were likely to fall—might well have extended maturity into the 2-year area. Such an extension need not imply that either the portfolio manager's planning horizon or his interest-rate forecast extends anywhere near two years. It simply implies that he is confident that rates will fall over some shorter period and that he is willing to sell and realize his gain once rates fall.

A few managers of short-term portfolios, who have wide parameters, even buy Treasury notes and other longer-term instruments in the hope of realizing short-term gains. Said an ex-portfolio manager, "If I liked the market, I'd buy a 10-year note even if I needed the money tomorrow." That's an extreme example, but this portfolio manager had the inborn instincts of a successful Street trader, which he eventually became.

Changing Relative Value

The search for relative value is not a one-time affair. The money market is dynamic; changes in demand, supply, expectations, and external events—announcements of the latest money supply figures, changes in tax laws, the souring of country loans, or

---

[7]Today, the World Bank is still regarded as tops in managing a liquidity portfolio.

the failure of a dealer—are constantly impacting it; and, as they do, yield spreads and rates change. Thus, relative value may reside in one sector today, in another tomorrow.

Tracking changes in relative value takes time and effort, but as a portfolio manager gains experience, it becomes almost second nature. Also, a portfolio manager can rely on the dealers for help. Once a portfolio manager recognizes that a change in relative value has occurred between instruments or maturity sectors, his response should be to *swap* or *arbitrage*.

As one portfolio manager with wide parameters observed, "Arbitraging a portfolio is one way to make money, whether it's a complete arbitrage or a swap between sectors of the market. Money market instruments oscillate in relative value for good reasons; and as you get experienced, you can with not too much time keep asking why one sector of the market is out of line with where it should be—the latter judgment being more than an extrapolation of a historical average. Once you have convinced yourself that the reason is transitory, then not to own the instrument that is undervalued and be short in the other instrument that is out of line is foolhardy."

Extension Swaps

We discussed various arbitrage strategies in Chapter 10. One simple swap strategy many portfolio managers use, when markets are calm, is to do *extension swaps*. They pick a maturity sector of the market they like, say 2- or 3-year governments, and then, for example, adopt the strategy of *extending* (lengthening maturity) a few months whenever they can pick up 5 bp and of *backing up* (shortening maturity) a few months whenever that costs only 3 bp. If market conditions are such that many such swaps can be done, a portfolio manager can pick up basis points this way. Note that, whereas a 90-day bp is worth only $25 per $1MM, a 3-year bp is worth $300.[8]

---

[8]The calculation is:

$$3(0.0001)(\$1,000,000) = \$300$$

A similar practice used by some investors in bills to pick up basis points is to roll the current 3-month or 6-month bill each week when new bills are auctioned. If conditions are such that new bill issues, which the market must absorb, are priced in the auction cheap relative to surrounding issues, then by rolling his bills, the investor may be able to pick up each week two or three $25 or $50 bp by doing this. A second advantage of this strategy is that it keeps the investor in current bills, which are more liquid than off-the-run issues.

Leverage

Like a dealer, a portfolio manager can repo securities he owns.[9] If the portfolio is that of a fair-sized bank, the portfolio manager will probably be able to repo securities directly with retail customers. If, alternatively, the portfolio is that of a corporation or other institution that does not have direct contact with suppliers of repo money, the portfolio manager can always repo his securities with the dealers, who will in turn hang them out on the other side (see Chapter 13 on matched book).

The ability to repo securities can be used by a portfolio manager in various ways. If an unanticipated, short-term need for cash arises at a time when the portfolio manager has established a position he wants to maintain, he can bridge that gap by repoing securities instead of selling them. Said one corporate portfolio manager, "We never fund to dates. We fund to market expectancy—what we think is going to happen to interest rates. We can repo the portfolio so we never have problems raising money for short periods. If we have to raise money for a long period to meet a portfolio embarrassment [securities in the port-

---

[9]Jargon in this area is confusing. Dealers talk about "doing repos" when they are financing their position and about "doing reverses" when they are taking in securities and lending money. Some portfolio managers who use repurchase agreements—just as dealers do—to lever, talk about doing repo, others talk about doing a reverse (i.e., reversing out securities). We have opted to use the word *repo* when the initiative comes from the side wanting to borrow money, and *reverse* when the initiative comes for the side wanting to lend money and/or to obtain specific collateral.

folio can only be sold at a loss], that means we made an error and had better face up to it."

Another way a portfolio manager with wide parameters can use the repo market imaginatively is to buy a security, finance the first part of its life with term repo, and thereby create an attractive future security. That is a technique of portfolio management, the rewards and risks of which we discussed in Chapter 10. A corporate manager can use it as well as a dealer, and some do.

Still another way a portfolio manager can use the repo market is to out and out lever his portfolio—buy securities at one rate, turn around and repo them at a lower rate, and then use the funds borrowed to buy more securities. Or the portfolio manager can simply buy securities for which he has no money by doing a repo against them at the time of purchase. A portfolio manager who uses this technique commented, "I repo the portfolio as an arbitrage technique everyday and probably run the biggest matched sale book in American industry. We repo anything we can, even corporates. In doing repo, I am either financing something I have or buying something I don't have any money for. We take the repos off for quarter ends because they might comprise the aesthetics of our statement." Avoiding repos across the quarter ends is common among those corporations that use repos, so it is impossible from looking at corporate financial statements to determine who does it.

To the corporate portfolio manager who can use repo, it is, in the words of one such manager, "the most flexible instrument in the money market. You can finance with repo, you can borrow using it, and you can ride the yield curve using it—buy a 2-month bill, put it out on repo for a month, and then sell it or do a 30-day repo again. And you can use repo to create instruments: put a 6-month bill out on a 2-month repo, and you have created a 4-month bill two months out."

Despite the many ways in which the ability to borrow in the repo market can be used, it is uncommon for a corporate short-term portfolio manager to be able to repo any of his portfolio.

In large banks, the practice of repoing the government portfolio is almost universal. As noted in Chapter 6, such a bank views its government portfolio as a massive arbitrage rather than as a source of liquidity. Among smaller banks, practices with respect to the use of repo vary widely.

Arbitrages Based on a Term Repo

With respect to the use of repo by portfolio managers, a distinction should be made between portfolio managers who use the market consciously to borrow and lever, and those who are, so to speak, coaxed into doing reverses. As noted in Chapter 10, when dealers want to short securities they will often cover their short by reversing in securities. If the security is not readily available, the dealer will go to a broker of repo who knows what securities various banks, S&Ls, and other institutions have in their portfolios. The broker will attempt to get an institution that holds the needed securities to reverse them out by showing that institution an attractive arbitrage. Such a transaction looks like an ordinary repo, but the initiative comes not from the institution that is borrowing, but from the dealer who wants to cover a short. Many banks, S&Ls, and other institutions that would never use repo to meet a temporary cash need or to lever will reverse out securities that they intend to hold indefinitely, probably to maturity, to pick up, say, 50 bp on a short-term arbitrage.

Break-Even Rate on a Reverse to Maturity

Frequently an institution that holds a government note or bond in its last coupon period will find that, by swapping out of that security term Fed funds or some other instrument, it can pick up 50 bp or more. On a $1MM swap, a pickup of 50 bp is worth approximately $2,500 if earned over six months, half as much if earned over three months. Thus, such swaps are attractive. Many institutions, however, cannot do such a swap on an outright basis if the security they want to sell is trading, due to a rise in interest rates, below the book value their accountant assigns to it.

Institutions in this situation have to resort to doing swaps indirectly. Instead of selling the maturing notes or bonds, they *reverse them out to maturity* to a dealer; that is, they borrow money against the securities. Then, they invest that money in a higher-yielding instrument, often one that matches in current maturity the security being reversed out. An institution that does this type of transaction is in effect arbitraging between the low term repo rate at which it can borrow on a collateralized basis and the higher rate at which it can invest.

Normally, a dealer who is doing a reverse to maturity will try to charge a reverse rate at least 10 bp above his break-even rate. When a security's true yield to maturity—which measures the dealer's cost on the reverse—is significantly less than its yield to maturity on the quote sheet, the dealer will try for more. Thus, it is worth an investor's time to calculate a dealer's *break-even reverse rate*. When a short government is sold and the proceeds are reinvested in some higher-yielding instrument, some $X of extra earnings will be picked up; how many to go the dealer and how many go to the investor will depend on where the reverse rate is set.

This point can perhaps be made with more punch by using a dollars-and-cents example. In one riskless-to-both-sides trade that a dealer made with a sleepy S&L, there was an $8,000 profit to be divvied up. The dealer set the reverse rate so that $5,000 went to him, $3,000 to the S&L doing the arb. Had the S&L treasurer known how to calculate the dealer's break-even reverse rate, he would have been in a position to bargain for a more equitable arrangement. Probably, he could have captured another $3,000 of the profit to be made on the trade, leaving the dealer with $1,000—not bad pay to the dealer for selling a security at the bid side of the market and writing a few tickets.[10]

Caveat

As we note in Chapter 13, a repo or a reverse always exposes both sides, the supplier of money and the supplier of collateral, to credit risk. Thus, a portfolio manager who does either transaction should check carefully both the credit of his counterparty in the trade and the way the trade is arranged. In particular, no portfolio manager should do nondelivery repo (*letter repo*) except short-term with a top-credit-quality dealer.

---

[10]For an off-the-quote-sheet example that illustrates a reverse to maturity and the calculation of a dealer's break-even reverse rate, see Stigum and Mann, *Money Market Calculations*, pp. 93–95.

Use of Futures, Options, and Swaps

Portfolio managers who may use futures, options, and interest-rate swaps are currently in the minority, but to those who may, these instruments offer an array of opportunities to lock in yields and borrowing costs, to arbitrage, to hedge, and to speculate. We discuss these opportunities in later chapters.

Shorting Securities

It's unusual for the manager of a corporate portfolio to be authorized to sell securities short but less rare than it used to be. The ability to short securities can be useful to a portfolio manager in several ways. First, it permits him to arbitrage as dealers do—going long in an undervalued security and short in an overvalued security—as a speculation on a yield spread. A few corporate portfolio managers do this quite actively.

A second reason a corporate portfolio manager might want to short is because borrowing through a short seems less expensive than selling an attractive investment. Said one portfolio manager, "If we decided, yes, the market is in here [in a given maturity sector], then we would look for the cheapest thing [the instrument with most relative value] on a spread basis—Euro CDs, BAs, or bills—and buy that. Even though bills might yield less than, say, Euro CDs, we might buy them because the spread on Euros into bills was too tight. We'd decide whether to buy or not and then buy the cheapest thing. When we decided to sell, we would sell the most expensive thing. But we could not short so we were sort of up against it at times when we had to sell. I had already bought the cheapest thing around, so generally I had to sell something cheap. It bothered me a lot not to be able to short when we needed cash, but it might have raised questions with stockholders."

The Big Shooters

We have drawn in this chapter and the last a distinction between dealers and portfolio managers that is perhaps too sharp. There are in the U.S. money market a number of large liquidity portfolios that take positions that rival those taken by more than one dealer, and a few of those portfolios are very actively managed. The people who run them utilize every tool of portfolio management that the dealers do—from creating future securities and figuring tails to shorting in order to do arbitrages. Some also trade their positions as actively as a dealer does. Said an individual who ran one such portfolio, "I sometimes bought securities today that I knew I would have to sell for cash the next day. I might even buy if I was bullish for the next few hours—I have bought securities on the day cash was needed and sold them later in the day if I thought the market would go up a couple of 32nds." The major differences between portfolios of this sort and a dealer operation are first that retail business is important to a dealer, and second that, whereas dealers are highly levered, a leverage ratio of 3 to 1 is highly unusual and probably top side for a standard liquidity portfolio. In a dedicated portfolio, however, leverage may, as noted below, be used extensively and routinely.

Fit the Strategies to the Times

A number of the portfolio strategies we have described make sense in "normal" markets when rates display some stability and predictability and when the yield curve slopes upward. In the period October 1979 to at least late 1982, investors were playing in a different ballpark. Rates were historically high, historically volatile, and cyclically unpredictable; also, much of the time the yield curve was negatively sloped.

Noted one portfolio manager in the fall of 1981, "Riding the yield curve and tails are no longer interesting. One had better forget them. I have resisted the temptation to extend maturities, and I have been amazed when I compare my rate of return to what it would have been had I attempted to extend and either hold to maturity or ride the yield curve. During periods of intense rate volatility, what you must do is to make the proper maturity decision because the impact of that decision on total return dwarfs that of all others; right now the correct decision is to opt for the shortest maturity you can. If you can live with day-to-day rollovers, you should do it even though you may have to accept lower rates occasionally on a Wednesday."

By the late 1980s, the world faced by the fixed-income investor was totally different. Rates were far lower than at the start of the decade, and at times, the yield curve was unusually flat. In that environment, it made no sense to ride the yield curve because there was no curve to ride. What plays or strategies are appropriate for a portfolio manager depend on market environment, which—as recent history proves—can change dramatically.

Compounding

Until the turn of the decade, 1970s to 1980s, neither investors nor borrowers thought much about the impact of frequent rolling of investments or borrowings on the return earned or the cost incurred. To fail to do so in a period of high rates can be an expensive mistake, since the impact of compounding on a rate earned or paid increases not only the more often compounding occurs, but the higher the rate being compounded is.

To illustrate, suppose that the yield curve is flat at 14% from overnight to six months. If an investor opts to buy 6-month paper and roll it once, his total return over the year will be 14.49% assuming no change in interest rates. If, alternatively, he rolls overnight funds on the 255 business days that typically occur during a year, he will—again assuming no change in rates—earn a total return of 15.02%, 53 bp more than by rolling a 6-month CD. On a $20MM investment, this would amount to $106,000 of extra earnings over a year.

Our simple example is not meant to suggest that interest rates, when they reach a given level, are likely to stay there for a year and that a portfolio manager should act accordingly. Rather, our intent is to illustrate the power of compounding to raise total return when rates are high and to suggest that, during such periods, the portfolio manager, in making maturity choices, should start by making benchmark calculations of the sort we did to get a feel for how compounding would affect his total return under different rate and maturity-choice scenarios.

Also, a rate of 14% is not necessary for compounding to make a difference. A rate of 8% will do quite well.

Marking to Market

In well-run short-term portfolios, it is common practice to mark the whole portfolio to market each day. The objective of running a portfolio is to maximize over time not interest accrued, but *total financial return*—interest earned plus capital gains realized minus capital losses realized. If a portfolio manager who has this objective, buys a 2-year note with a 9% coupon and then finds that yield on that note has risen to 10%, he will view his decision to have bought the 9% coupon as a serious mistake. Moreover, if he anticipates that rates will rise still further, he will sell that security at a loss (convert his paper loss into a realized loss) and wait to recommit long term until he thinks rates have stabilized.

The use of this tactic in portfolio management calls for a willingness to book capital losses, and that willingness is a hallmark of every good portfolio manager. Realizing losses is, however, difficult to do psychologically; it is something a trader must discipline himself to do. One advantage of marking a portfolio to market each day is that it helps get the focus of those who buy and sell for the portfolio off book value. As one portfolio manager noted, "If market value declines today and you book to market, tomorrow you start at that market value. And your gain or loss will be a function of whether tomorrow's price is better than today's." Said another, "If you mark to market, the past is gone. You've made a mistake, and the point now is not to make another one."

Tracking Performance

Active management can substantially increase yield on a short-term portfolio. "You can as much as double yield on a short-term portfolio," said one practitioner of the art, "by arbitraging sectors and by changing maturities in response to interest-rate forecasts."

In an institution where the short-term portfolio is actively managed, there are always people in top management who understand the credit market and who are therefore comfortable with creative management of the institution's portfolio. It is also the case that the focal point in management of the portfolio is on yield earned rather than on when money is needed. In other words, the portfolio manager's main concern in investing is with where relative value lies, not with when he needs cash; specifically, he does not *fund* to dates—buy 3-month bills because he needs money three months hence.

Performance in every liquidity portfolio managed to maximize return is carefully tracked. A key element in this tracking is marking the portfolio to market so that the return-earned calculation incorporates not only realized but unrealized capital gains and losses.

Once performance is tracked, it is compared against various yardsticks. A portfolio manager might, for example, compare his performance with what he could have achieved had he followed any one of several naive strategies: rolling overnight funds, rolling 3-month bills, or rolling 6-month bills. If the portfolio invests longer-term funds, the yardstick might be the yield on 2- or 3-year notes.

Another standard often used is the performance achieved by various money funds, each of which runs in effect a large-liquidity portfolio. Comparing the performance of two portfolios is however, difficult; one must ask about the differences in parameters: in maturity restrictions, in percentage restrictions, and in name restrictions. Also, differences in the time flow of funds through two portfolios may affect their relative performances.

Still another approach used in evaluating performance achieved is to compare actual results with the optimal results that could have been achieved. In other words, to ask: How high was the return we earned compared with what we could have earned if our market judgments had always been correct?

Tracking performance and comparing it against various yardsticks are important; doing so gives the portfolio manager a feel for how well he is doing; it also gives management some standard against which to evaluate his performance. As one portfolio manager noted, "I'm a money market specialist working for an industrial concern so it's hard for management to evaluate what I do unless I give them some frame of reference."

In a few rare cases, the portfolio manager is not only judged but paid, according to how well he performs. That sort of arrangement is typically found only in a corporation or a bank that has a large short-term portfolio and has recognized that, to get professional management, it must hire a Street-oriented person who will never do anything but run money or work at a related job.

THE STREET'S VIEW OF THE WAY IT'S DONE

We've discussed so far how an elite minority of portfolio managers who have wide latitude in what they may do and who possess the skill and judgment to make good use of that latitude manage their portfolios.[11]

Most liquidity portfolios—be they owned by corporations, banks, S&Ls, or other institutions—are managed with little sophistication; perhaps it would be more correct to say they are barely managed at all. A frequent problem is that top management has never focused on what portfolio management is all about and how it should be done. In the case of corporations, management will often adopt the attitude: We're in the business of manufacturing widgets, not investing. Having done that, they fail to apply to managing of their short-term portfolio the principles they daily apply to managing the whole corporation. Some banks and S&Ls that daily assume carefully calculated credit risks in the course of their normal business operations simultaneously run their securities portfolios according to the guiding principle: Buy Treasuries and mature them.

Restrictive Guidelines

When top management fails to be interested in and to have knowledge of what managing a liquidity portfolio involves, it establishes, almost invariably, extremely tight guidelines on what the portfolio manager may do; such guidelines reflect, as

---

[11]The Ford portfolio is universally viewed on the Street as being aggressively and astutely managed. Another portfolio that consistently gets kudos from the Street is that of the World Bank.

one portfolio manager noted, "the attempt of a bunch of guys who know nothing about securities to be prudent."

Tight guidelines make it impossible for a portfolio manager to use almost any of the strategies of portfolio management discussed earlier in this chapter. Another problem with tight guidelines is that they are sometimes written in terms of amounts rather than percentages. This can make a large portfolio difficult to manage and may lead to false diversification; an extreme example is provided by a corporation that went so far as to limit the amount of T bills its portfolio could hold.

The Accounting Hang-Up

The failure of top management to understand or interest itself in the management of the liquidity portfolio also results in what might be called the *accounting hang-up*. Specifically, it has created a situation in which the majority of portfolio managers, all of whom would describe themselves as *conservative,* believe that the correct way to manage a portfolio is to reduce their accounting risk to *zero*. In other words, they attempt to run the portfolio in such a way that they will *never* book a loss.

This means that they can take no market risk: They can't do swaps that would produce a book loss regardless of how relative value shifts; when they need cash, they can't decide what to sell on the basis of relative value; they can't arbitrage; in fact, they are literally reduced to rolling overnight money and buying securities they intend to mature.

To fully appreciate how the decision never to take a loss restricts a portfolio manager, it is necessary to understand that when a portfolio acquires a discount security, such as bills or BAs, each day the accountant accrues interest income on that security at the discount rate at which it was purchased, so when the security is redeemed at maturity for full face value, all of the difference between the purchase price and the face value (i.e., the discount at purchase) will have been accrued as interest. This seems reasonable, but it means, for example, that if a portfolio manager buys 6-month bills at 7.90 and resells them three months later at 8.30, that is, at a rate *above* that at which he bought the bills, *he will have incurred a capital loss even though in dollar terms he has earned money.* Table 11–2 spells out the mathematics of this. By buying $1MM of the 6-month bill at 7.90 and holding it for 90 days, the portfolio has actually earned $18,750; the $1,000 accounting capital loss occurs only because the accountant has accrued $19,750 of interest over the holding period.

The yields and maturities in this example were purposely chosen so that they are identical with the yields and maturities used in the example of riding the yield curve presented earlier in this chapter (Table 11–1). Once these numbers are seen in the context of that example, it is clear that the unwillingness to take an accounting loss (to expose the portfolio to an accounting risk) rules out even the most basic investment strategy based on market judgment: namely, riding the yield curve. In this respect, note that in our example the portfolio manager who rode the yield curve stood to gain—if interest rates did not rise—an extra $2,000 of return, *and* he had a lot of protection against losing in terms of dollars earned but *not* against incurring an accounting loss.

Portfolio managers preoccupied with accounting losses and gains are frequently encountered by dealers. Said one, "It cracks me up when someone comes to me with BAs or bills and says, 'What's your bid?' and I say, '8.60,' and he says, 'I can't sell because I bought at 8.50 and I can't take a loss.' It makes no

TABLE 11–2

Accounting treatment of $1MM of 6-month bills bought at 7.90 and sold three months later at 8.30

Book value at purchase	$960,500
+ Interest accrued over 90 days	19,750
Book value at sale	$980,250
Price at sale	$979,250
− Book value at sale	980,250
Accounting capital gain (loss)	$ (1,000)
Price at sale	$979,250
Price at purchase	960,500
Actual gain	$ 18,750

sense if he has held the instrument for awhile, but I do not question people any more. I figure they just don't understand the concept. Still it's crazy, if you have to generate cash, to say that you cannot sell the instrument it is best to sell because you cannot take a 10-bp loss." Said another dealer, "I talk to portfolio managers about this problem and encounter nothing but resistance. They do not care if they could earn more money, they are just not going to take a loss. It's an organizational, not a rational constraint."

The whole accounting problem applies not only to discount securities, but to Euro CDs and other interest-bearing securities, because the accountant accrues interest on them just as he does on discount securities; in addition, he amortizes over the time to maturity the premium on coupons purchased at a price above par and accretes over the time to maturity the discount on coupons purchased below par.

A Negative-Sum Game

The aversion to book losses and the failure to track performance that are characteristic of many institutions create a negative-sum game for the portfolio manager. If he invests on the basis of market judgment, he ends up in a position where, if his judgment is wrong, the resulting losses—even if they are losses only by accounting standards—will be highly visible and criticized, whereas if his judgment is correct, the resulting gains will not be perceived by senior management.

The obvious response of the portfolio manager put in this position is to make no attempt to predict interest rates and to invest so as to avoid all market risk. If such a portfolio manager reaches for yield at all, he does so by buying P-2 paper or Euro CDs because they offer relatively high yields without asking whether they have *relative value*. Such portfolio managers think of themselves as sophisticated because they know a lot about many different markets, *but* when they need cash three months hence, they buy a 3-month instrument instead of making a conscious market decision.

Opportunity Cost

The typical "conservative" portfolio manager thinks of himself as never having lost a penny or at least as not having lost very many, and his accountant will confirm this. But in fact an institution with a portfolio run on the principle that it funds to dates and never takes a market risk incurs a large *opportunity cost,* namely, the earnings forgone because the responsibility to manage funds in the portfolio has been abnegated. An example is provided by the example of riding the yield curve given earlier in this chapter. The portfolio manager who rides the yield curve with a lot of basis points of protection built into his gamble need not be right more than half the time to noticeably increase yield. Thus, to refuse to do so to avoid the risk of an accounting loss implies a cost, one no less real because it goes unperceived at many institutions.

There is also a more subtle aspect to opportunity cost. As one portfolio manager commented, "Most people you talk to will buy a 6-month bill and hold it to maturity and say that they are taking no risk because they know what they are going to earn. That is farcical. They *are* taking a risk, one that is not measured by the accounting system but is measured in terms of opportunity cost. And the institution may in reality be affected by this risk. If rates rise sharply and the money invested could have been used elsewhere, there is a cost to having bought those securities. Either the institution must finance them somehow or it may be forced into other suboptimal business decisions."

Many common portfolio practices can be pursued only at considerable opportunity cost. One is to say that, if money is needed in 30 days, cash on hand should be invested in a 30-day instrument even though predictable cash flows will more than suffice to cover that need. Another is to invest a large sum of money in short-term instruments when it is clear that most of that money will not be needed in the short run or even in the long run. A corporation that pursues such a strategy, as some triple-A credits do, pays a large premium year in and year out to ensure that it can survive even a severe credit crunch without mild discomfort.

It is sometimes suggested that the reason some large corporations do not manage their portfolios is that they have too much money; that is, it is impossible within the confines of the money market to actively manage $3 or $4 billion. Sums of that magnitude are, however, actively managed; the World Bank's multibillion-dollar portfolio is a prime example. So, too, are the actively traded portfolios of some huge money funds.

As noted, there is an opportunity cost to not managing money. The counterpart is that it costs money to have someone manage a portfolio; consequently, there is some level below which benign neglect—rolling commercial paper or investing surplus cash in a money market fund—is the preferable alternative. That cutoff point is hard to pinpoint; estimates put it anywhere from $40 to $60MM. Somewhere up from that, between $100 and $150MM, there are solid benefits to be reaped from having someone watch the market daily.[12]

For the firm at the opposite pole, one with hundreds of millions to be managed in one or a number of portfolios, the optimal solution may be one that a few institutions in this position have adopted—namely, to hire a professional, give him wide guidelines, monitor his performance, and pay him on an incentive basis so that making market judgments is for him a positive-sum game. A side benefit of doing so is that the same individual can be used, as is done in many corporations, to manage the parent's or its financing sub's commercial paper operations. Anyone who can manage a short-term portfolio well can manage a commercial paper operation equally well, since the latter is nothing but a *negative* portfolio.

Ignorance of opportunity cost and extreme risk aversion are not the only reasons why many large institutions have failed to opt for professional management of their portfolios. Another is that they would have to pay a professional money manager in toto what a senior executive earns. A third reason is that corporations, especially if they are headquartered in outlying places, have difficulty attracting and holding Street-oriented people.

---

[12]See Chapter 26 for more on this point.

For a large corporation that wants to aggressively manage its portfolio, the commonly practiced alternative tactic of having one fast-track rookie do the job for awhile and then train another to do it does not always work out. Said a portfolio manager who traveled that route, "Trading is an art form which I could not succeed in teaching my peers who had come through the system as I did. I would have done better to take on some kid hustling on the streets of Marrakesh."

THE CONTRARIAN VIEW

Our remarks above reflect strongly the Street's view of how well—or better, of how poorly—institutions manage their liquidity portfolios. In that view, there tends to be a bias in favor both of trading and of position taking based on a view on interest rates. A contrarian case to be made that many portfolio managers are wise to limit how much they do either of the above.

Too Harsh a Judgment?

Currently, there are over 15,000 commercial banks, 20,000 S&Ls, tens of thousands of municipal bodies, and a host of nonfinancial business firms—the majority of whom are running rather small liquidity portfolios.

In smaller institutions, it is common for the liquidity portfolio to be managed by someone who wears several hats and who, in particular, is not a money market specialist. If such a person tries to be aggressive, he runs a nonnegligible risk of getting, at some point, into deep trouble, since he will lack the time and expertise to develop a reasoned view on interest rates.

A second problem facing the small portfolio manager who is willing to be aggressive is that at least some Street salespeople are likely to advise him to try new and/or complicated products that they themselves, maybe even the Street, do not yet fully understand. In the past, a number of portfolio managers who played around with various then-new instruments—selling GNMA puts to take an extreme example—experienced serious financial losses because they had no inkling of the risks inherent in the new product that was sold to them. The small portfolio manager is probably well advised, because he is not a money market professional, to keep things simple and, in particular, to avoid new products until all of the quirks and bugs in them are apparent from the costs—losses—that others have incurred to get up the learning curve in them.

NEW DEVELOPMENTS IN MANAGING CORPORATE LIQUIDITY PORTFOLIOS

Some savvy managers of large corporate liquidity portfolios argue that the objective that a portfolio manager who invests his firm's *working capital* is paid to pursue is to provide liquidity, safety, and yield in that order. Thus, for such a portfolio manager to trade or to otherwise take bets with monies in such a portfolio is inappropriate. Moreover, to do so is, for the portfolio manager personally, a negative-sum game: if he makes money on his bets, his winnings may be ignored, whereas if he loses money on his bets, his losses—if large—will surely mean that someone must go; and that someone is likely to be him.

A Unified Treasury

The above is not to say that a good corporate portfolio manager thinks today that his job is to twiddle his thumbs and to invest in bills only. Major corporate investors are trying to exploit more fully opportunities open to them, but in their own way, at their own pace.

One development worthy of note is that a number of major corporations, each of which comprises a parent plus various subsidiaries, have moved to unify their treasury operations. In particular, they have moved to consolidate all short-term funds held by the parent and its subsidiaries into a single pool run out of head office. Such pooling makes sense on several counts. First, a corporation doing so increases the professionalism with which it manages, companywide, its funds while it simultaneously reduces the cost of managing such funds. Second, it can more easily implement one corporate risk attitude. Third, it can diversify more easily: the pooling approach would, for example, call for just one, not many limits on Chrysler paper or on deposits at a given bank. Also, running a consolidated portfolio might permit a corporation with subsidiaries outside the U.S. to invest more heavily in, say, Euro commercial paper than it could if every entity within the corporation ran a separate portfolio; and that in turn would give the company the option to buy, for example, Chrysler paper in the market in which it was cheapest: the Euromarket. Finally, running a consolidated portfolio is likely to markedly reduce the transactions costs that a big corporation incurs in keeping its funds fully invested; in the money market, an institution tends, partly due to economies of scale, to get better rates and better prices the bigger the pool of money it invests.

Dedicated Portfolios

In recent years, the tendency for corporations to pool funds in a single liquidity portfolio as well as the increasing skill that corporations have developed in predicting cash inflows and disbursements have contributed to both the ability and the willingness of corporations to create *dedicated portfolios* in which they are willing to assume risk to raise yield and in which liquidity becomes a secondary consideration. Specifically, corporations have, in recent years, become more willing to carve out a portion of what they normally call their working capital pool of funds and dedicate that portion to more aggressive management.

More aggressive management can mean one or more of several strategies. One might be to engage in dividend capture programs. A second might be to buy, when the yield curve was upward sloping, 5-year Treasuries with the intent either to hold them only so long as the rate outlook was favorable or to hedge them as necessary. A third aggressive strategy would be to make short-term forays, unhedged, into high-yield paper denominated in a foreign currency, for example, into paper denominated in New Zealand or Aussi dollars; obviously, currency depreciation is a risk in the latter strategy, but the rewards can be handsome if the investor is not caught in a major downturn of the local currency.

Leveraging

Another aggressive technique some corporations have adopted
is to borrow when an opportunity arises for a good arbitrage.
Said one portfolio manager who does this: "It is a fulfillment of
the responsibilities that an investment manager has today to
look at his opportunities not only on the asset side, but on the
liability side." Debt incurred by a corporation as part of a financial arbitrage is most typically put on the balance sheet of the
parent company, but could be done on a smaller scale in, say, a
finance company subsidiary.

Corporations that borrow funds to reinvest in money market instruments are typically circumspect about the amount of
such borrowing they will do. In its charter, a corporation states
its business; and if it has not stated that it is in the finance
business, big borrowings to do money market arbitrages might
be viewed as an *ultra viris* act.

A conservative corporation might, if rates are correct, add
1% to its total borrowings in order to do money market arbitrages. Less conservative corporations—said to include some
electronics firms and a big breakfast food company—are willing
to borrow far more. A company that borrows to finance money
market arbitrages makes this activity a profit center, rather
like a bank running a Eurobook or a dealer running a book in
repo and reverse. A few nonfinancial firms may be running arbitrage books into the billions. More typically, the numbers run in
the hundreds of millions, and then there are the smaller players
with books running 5, 25, or 50MM.

A corporation running a leveraged portfolio may borrow in
various ways: from banks or by issuing domestic commercial
paper, Euro commercial paper, medium-term notes, or even
long-term debt. Its arbitrage might, for example, be to borrow in
the Euro medium-term note market and to turn around and buy
slightly weaker credits in the same market. The spread on such
a transaction might be from 10 to 50 bp. Naturally, the runner
of a corporate arbitrage book could match or unmatch his asset
and liability maturities. As we note in later chapters, there are
many ways to play the "book game."

Another strategy a corporation doing a money market arbitrage might use would be to invest in quality credits out to five years and to source the required funds in short-term markets. This would be attractive in a period when interest rates were softening; should rates reverse direction, the corporation might dispose of its long-term assets and unwind its liabilities or it might hedge.

LET'S SEE THE NUMBERS, PLEASE

In answer to the Street's position that corporations (and others as well) ought, across the board, to manage their liquidity funds more aggressively, one astute corporation portfolio manager made some telling remarks: "I have watched the results of banks' and dealers' own trading departments, and these results have been up and down. I am not sure that, *net,* banks and dealers have had strong positive results over a long period. If a dealer is going to make a case for trading, he should show total rates of return that have been earned from trading over a 5-, 10-, or 15-year period: a period sufficiently long to display performance in a number of different market environments.

"People talk about their performance, but often they do not specify on what basis they calculate return earned. For dealers and portfolio managers to compare returns earned using different investment approaches, we must all speak the same tongue: use the same methodology. I don't know if some dealer investing short term has beaten my results, but I do know that, over a 15-year period, I have beaten the results of my company's pension fund; and it invests long-term money."

THE NEXT CHAPTER

In the next chapter, we begin our discussion of the individual sectors of the money market. The first sector we consider is the Fed funds market; daily, banks and certain other financial institutions borrow and lend in this market, on an unsecured basis, hundreds of billions of dollars.

PART 3

THE MARKETS

CHAPTER 12

THE FEDERAL FUNDS MARKET

Scene: Late Wednesday afternoon on the Fed funds desk of a major New York bank.

"Where is that 150MM we bought?"

"The bank swears they sent it."

"Then why the hell hasn't the transfer gone through the San Francisco Fed?"

"The bank says their computer broke down. They had to deliver the transfer request by hand."

"Is that money coming or not? Call the New York Fed! Ask them if they'll keep the wire open or let us do an 'as of' tomorrow. Damn! This is enough to make an atheist out of a priest."[1]

SETTLING WITH THE FED

Wednesday afternoon settlement with the Fed creates a lot of tension for bankers, brokers, and the Fed. To understand why requires some knowledge of the rules by which banks settle.

All banks that are members of the Federal Reserve System, and since 1980 other depository institutions, are required to

---

[1]This actual situation resulted from something happening that was *never* supposed to happen. A wire transfer of Fed funds got lost in the Fed's computer network. The San Francisco Fed sent out the notice of the transfer of funds, but that message was not received by the New York Fed; it simply disappeared in the Fed's switching center at Culpepper, Virginia. Later, when the Fed upgraded the Fed wire, the Culpepper switching center was eliminated. Now, district Fed banks communicate directly with each other, *but* individual Feds still "go down"—their computers, that is.

maintain reserves in the form of deposits at the Fed. Any vault cash such institutions hold also counts as reserves.[2]

In the old days, pre-1984, the reserves that a bank had to maintain during the current settlement week were based on the average daily deposits it held over a seven-day period two weeks earlier. Monetarists pushed for *contemporaneous reserve accounting* on the theory that it would reduce short-term fluctuations in money supply by forcing banks to adjust their reserves and thereby their lending to their current, not their previous, deposits. This was a naive notion based on some Econ 101 text's outmoded description of banking: a bank gets a deposit, and says, "Gee, I automatically make a loan."

In real life, banks did not and do not operate that way. When loan demand was strong, money center banks adjusted their loans not to what deposits they received, but rather to the level of loans that their valued, creditworthy customers demanded of them; these banks then funded their loans, to the extent necessary, by buying money in the money market. Today, the problem money center banks face is a paucity of demand for C&I loans from good corporate credits; their principal concern is not how to fund their loans; instead, they focus on ROE, ROA, and capital adequacy.

In any case, at the time of the switch to contemporaneous reserve accounting, banks objected on the grounds that the switch would be operationally expensive for them and, to boot, serve no useful purpose. A second problem bankers saw with contemporaneous reserve accounting was put succinctly by one banker, "I pay $145 billion everyday. If my error rate is ½%, which is reasonably good, I have made $750MM of mistakes. If I don't have time to identify and correct those errors, all my reports to the Fed will be wrong. The Fed tells me they are going to fine tune control of the money supply by getting information faster from me. They are wrong. They are going to get more current, but less accurate, information."

Despite bank protests, the Fed went ahead in 1984 with contemporaneous reserve accounting, some said as a sop that

---

[2]For the reserve requirements currently imposed by the Fed on depository institutions, see Table 6–4.

then Chairman Volcker felt he had to throw to the monetarists, who were at the time a vocal, in-fashion group.

Today, the reserves that a bank must maintain during the current settlement period are based on the average daily deposits it held over the immediately previous 14 days. Also, settlement now occurs not every Wednesday, but every other Wednesday.

For reserve calculation purposes, the reserve period begins on Thursday and ends on Wednesday. In settling with the Fed, a bank starts with a certain *required* average daily level of reserves. It need not hit its required level every day, but its average daily reserve balances over the reserve period must equal this figure.

To make it easier for banks to settle, the Fed permits a bank to offset a deficiency (up to 2% of its required) in one reserve period with a surplus run in the previous or following period.[3] The carry-over privilege is, however, limited to one period. A bank cannot go *red* (have a reserve deficiency) two periods in a row; and if it goes *black* (runs a reserve surplus) two periods in a row, the second period's surplus becomes excess reserves for which it gets no credit. Thus, a bank's settlements with the Fed tend over time to follow a pattern, alternating red and black settlement periods.

Some years ago, activity in the Fed funds market could be accurately summed up as follows. With the exception of the B of A, the dollar total of the assets most large banks chose to fund far exceeded their deposits. The reverse was true of most smaller banks. Thus, large banks had a chronic need to obtain funds to settle with the Fed, whereas smaller banks had a chronic need to invest excess funds to avoid running a surplus. The needs of both sorts of banks were well met in the Fed funds market. In this market, reserve-short banks bought Fed funds (funds on deposit at the Fed), and reserve-rich banks sold them. Since the

---

[3]The 2% surplus or deficiency that a bank may carry forward equals 2% of the *total* reserves it must hold over the reserve period, which in turn equals the bank's required reserves times 14; this is so because a bank's required refers to the *average* balance it must maintain over a 14-day period. Thus, if a bank's required were, for example, $1 billion, it could carry forward a reserve surplus or deficit equal to:

$$\$1 \text{ billion} \times 14 \times 2\% = \$280\text{MM}$$

open market desk at the NY Fed worked hard each settlement period to ensure that the quantity of reserves that the banks needed to settle was provided to them, all the banks managed—via the mechanism of the Fed funds market—to settle, on each settlement date, more or less within a whisker of where they meant to be.

The above description still gives a quite accurate idea of what the Fed funds market is all about and of how it operates. However, as noted later, some new players have entered the market in a big way, and the positions of some of the older players have changed. Also, over time, volume has increased dramatically.

THE FED WIRE

The operation of the Fed funds market and related activities requires tens of thousands of transfers of dollars daily among thousands of banks and other depository institutions. This is possible in large part because of the Fed wire system. Under this system, an individual bank's computer is linked by wire to the computer at its district Federal Reserve Bank, which in turn is linked by wire to the computer at every other district Fed bank.

When a commercial bank wants to transfer funds from its reserve account to that of another bank, it types out a computer message that goes directly to the Fed, and the required payment is automatically made. For example, if the B of A sold $50MM of Fed funds to Fuji Bank, N.Y., it would send through its computer the appropriate message to the San Francisco Fed, which would debit B of A's account and relay the payment message to the NY Fed, which would credit Fuji's account and notify Fuji (Table 12–1).

The Fed wire began to assume its present form several decades ago. Before that, even the big New York banks had to exchange checks to make payments to each other. Now, they are linked by wire to the NY Fed, and all interbank payments in New York, with the exception of Euro transactions (see Chapter 18), go over the Fed wire. The NY Fed was the first district bank to be linked by wire to member banks within its district.

TABLE 12–1
The B of A sells Fuji N.Y. 50MM of Fed funds

Bank of America		Fuji	
Reserves −50MM		Reserves +50MM	Fed funds
Fed funds sold			purchased
+50MM			+50MM

San Francisco Fed		New York Fed	
	Reserves, B of A		Reserves, Fuji
	−50MM		+50MM

Until 15 or 16 years ago, the way the principal banks in St. Louis, which were across the street from the St. Louis Fed, communicated with the Fed was to walk across the street and deliver a slip of paper. Now all the Federal Reserve District banks and most of their branches have extended access to the Fed wire to member banks having volumes of transactions justifying such access.

Banks use the Fed wire not only to handle their transactions in the Fed funds market, but for other transactions. Each major bank has hundreds of correspondent—domestic and foreign—banks that keep accounts with it, and it keeps accounts at other banks. Throughout the day, monies are constantly being paid into and out of these accounts over the Fed wire in connection with securities transactions, collections, and so forth.

Also, corporations and nonbank financial institutions are constantly requesting banks to *wire transfer* funds for them. For example, a large corporation might wire money from its account in a West Coast bank into its account at Citibank and then later in the day have those funds wired from that account to the account at Manny Hanny of a nonbank dealer from which it had bought governments. The money market, which is largely a cash-settlement market (payment is made on the day of a trade with "good"—*immediately available*—funds), generates a huge volume of traffic on the Fed wire.

Congestion on and Reliability of Fedwire

Because of the vast number of messages that pass daily over the Fed wire (funds transfers and transfers of Treasuries and other book-entry securities), it is essential, if the banking system and the money market are to operate efficiently, that every Fed computer and every bank computer keep up and running and that no backlog of transactions develop anywhere in the system. Unfortunately, this isn't the norm.

The Fed's wire used to be a major offender. In the early 1980s, it was taxed to its limit with the result that it was often subject to "throttle," took messages from the banks at lower than its normal speed. From a user's point of view, throttle was like being put on hold every time one sent a message to the Fed. In 1983, the Fed made a major upgrade of the automated system it uses to support Fedwire. Today, the system is able to handle far more messages and far more book-entry issues.

However, computers at the district Fed banks, including the NY Fed, still go down from time to time. When this occurs, certain interdistrict transfers of funds and of wireable securities (typically versus Fed funds) cannot be made until the downed computer is gotten up again. For various reasons, including its disinclination to grant banks "as of" credits (discussed below), the Fed in such situations often keeps the Fed wire open past, sometimes long past, 6:30 P.M. EST, the hour at which the wire is supposed to close for funds transfers. Speaking of the problem, one broker noted, "A week ago Monday, the Philly Fed went down in the late afternoon and never came up again. The Fed's response was to keep extending the closing of the wire in half-hour increments. We fiddled our fingers until 11:15 P.M. when the Fed finally gave up and closed the wire."

Late closings of the wire force banks and brokers to keep personnel on the job—often doing nothing but waiting for a computer somewhere to come up so that messages already in the pipeline can get through. This is costly for the affected firms who end up having to pay to folks they must keep on the job past normal closing time not only overtime, but dinners and taxi rides home.

Because the major banks could not tolerate a long breakdown in their computer operations, they have all designed their internal systems so that the maximum down time for a break-down is no more than a few minutes, or hours at most. Amusingly, the big New York banks, which had all supplied their computer systems with emergency generators years ago, woke up one day to ask, "What the hell would our computer centers, humming away in the midst of a blackout, be working on with the rest of the bank shut down in darkness?" So they supplied auxiliary power to all the major departments that provide inputs to their computer system: check collections, money transfer, and the trading room. Said the manager of one bank computer operation, "We have got that capacity and," reaching into his desk, "I keep a flashlight, too."

HISTORY OF THE MARKET

In 1921, some member banks were borrowing at the discount window, while others had surplus reserves for which they had trouble finding an outlet due to depressed market conditions. After informal discussion, the banks that were borrowing from the Fed began purchasing balances from the banks that had excess reserves, and the Fed funds market was born.

Trading in Fed funds continued throughout the 1920s but fell into disuse during the 1930s, when most banks had excess reserves for a long period. During the early 1940s, the banks purchased large amounts of the $400 billion of new government debt issued to finance the war, and they adopted the practice of settling their reserve positions by trading short-term Treasury bills for cash settlement.

Gradually, it became clear that there was an easier way for the banks to settle—instead of selling bills among themselves, they began in the early 1950s to sell 1-day money among themselves.[4] And as they did, the Fed funds market—dormant since the 1920s—was revived. Another reason for the revival of the funds market was that, as interest rates started to rise after the Treasury-Fed accord, everyone became more conscious of the value of money left idle, and banks in particular began to see the

---

[4]This development was fostered by Garvin Bantel (now Garvin GuyButler), a firm that once brokered call loans to brokers and was an important broker of list bonds. Garvin is now a major broker of several money market instruments, both domestic and Euro.

merit in keeping their excess funds fully invested. The revival of the Fed funds market was particularly attractive for retail banks with a customer base consisting largely of consumers. These banks needed an outlet for their surplus funds, and they took up the practice of selling Fed funds everyday to their large-city correspondents.

By 1960, these developments led to a situation where the big New York and Chicago banks began to deliberately operate their basic money positions so that they were always short, on the ground that they needed room to buy all the Fed funds that were coming into them from smaller correspondents. This was an attractive situation for the large banks because Fed funds were the cheapest money around, and they naturally asked: Why not use it for 10% of our overall needs?

In the late 1950s when the big banks sold to their correspondent banks the "service" of buying up the latter's excess funds, they said, "Of course if you ever need Fed funds, we will be happy to sell them to you." This commitment came back to haunt them in 1963 when interest rates started to take off in the aftermath of the Kennedy tax cut. By then, the smaller correspondent banks had developed an insight into the money market; they began buying Treasury bills, which were then trading at a higher yield than the discount rate, and financing them first with their own surplus funds and then by purchasing Fed funds from the big banks.

At that time Fed funds had *never* traded higher than the discount rate. Since banks bought Fed funds only to settle their reserve positions and then only as an alternative to borrowing at the discount window, bankers feared that any bank that was willing to pay more than the discount rate for Fed funds would be subject to the accusation that for some reason it could not borrow at the window.

Gradually, the situation became critical for the big banks because all their correspondents were buying T bills at 4%, financing them with Fed funds purchased at 3½% (the level of the discount rate), and raking in the spread. This continued for more than a year, during which time the big banks became huge net sellers of Fed funds. To fund the sale, these banks were issuing CDs at rates higher than the rate at which they were selling Fed funds to their "valued" correspondents.

Something had to give. Finally, on 1964, Morgan decided that if any bank could get away with paying more than the discount rate for Fed funds, it could; and on October 4 of that year, it bid 3⅝ for funds at a time when the discount rate was 3½ and funds were trading at 3½. The $500MM estimated to have been traded at this higher rate that day was a small sum by today's standards, but the gambit succeeded and began a new era in the funds market. Rapidly funds began to trade at a market rate that was determined by supply and demand and was affected by the discount rate only insofar as that rate influenced demand.

After funds began to trade at a market rate, the Fed funds market mushroomed, and more and more banks got into it. Regional banks that at the inception of the market were selling funds to large banks began to operate their own regional markets. Before this development, most trading in Fed funds was done in New York and Chicago, with perhaps a little in San Francisco. Small outlying banks with only a little money to sell were excluded from the market because it made no sense for a bank with $100,000 of overnight money to sell to telephone New York when the rate it would get was 3 or 3½%.[5] However, when the regional banks began to buy Fed funds, it paid for a bank in Joplin, Missouri, to call St. Louis for $0.30 to sell even $50,000 of Fed funds. In the Fed funds market now, regional banks buy up funds from even tiny banks, use what they need, and resell the remainder in round lots in the New York market. Thus, the Fed funds market resembles a river with tributaries: Money is collected in many places and then flows through various channels into the New York market.

As the Fed funds market developed, some regional banks that entered it felt they were not in close enough contact with the market to call the last ¼ or ⅛; they adopted the practice of asking brokers to sell or buy money for them at whatever price the brokers thought was the best available. The amount of such *discretionary money* amounted at one time to a sizable sum. To-

---

[5]At a 3½% rate, $100,000 of overnight Fed funds is worth $9.72.

day, that money has vanished; the regionals have become more sophisticated.

"In the days when Fed funds were first traded, the market was," said one ex-trader from a large bank, "a travesty, a joke as far as being a real market. There were six or eight real decision makers in the entire market—a couple of brokers and the guys on the money desks of the top banks. When a top broker walked in on Thursday morning at the start of a new settlement week and said, 'Funds are 11/16–3/4,' the market pretty much formed up around that. Few people would challenge that view because they knew a lot of banks had given that broker money to buy or sell at his discretion. On Broadway the *New York Times* drama critic can close a show. In every area you have opinion makers, and the Fed funds market was no exception."

Controlling the Fed Fund Rate versus Controlling the Money Supply

Over time, the Fed funds market had evolved considerably. Initially, Fed funds traded at 1/4s of a percent; then, as more participants entered the market and it became more competitive, funds began trading at 1/8ths and then at 1/16ths. For a time, the Fed let the funds rate fluctuate in a wide band. Then, in the late 1960s, it began to peg that rate tightly. How tightly is indicated by a comment made in 1977 by a person on the Fed desk, "When we are in a period when our Fed funds target is not changing, money supply is growing at a steady rate, and we are at peace with the world, we are inclined to be more relaxed about the funds rate and to let it fluctuate within a 1/4 band. But in a delicate situation where we want to give signals to the market— when they are misunderstanding our posture and we want to be sure they get the message—we might narrow that spread to 1/16."

All that changed in October 1979 when the Fed switched to monetarism pure and simple. At that time, the Fed decreed that the rate at which funds traded would be wherever market forces took it, which turned out to be all over the lot. Whereas in pre-1979 days a move during the day, other than Wednesday, in the Fed funds rate of one quarter was unusual, intraday swings of

200, 300, even 400 bp in the rate became common after the Fed switched the primary focus of its policy from tight control of the funds rate to tight control of the rate of growth of money supply.

As noted in Chapter 9, there are good grounds for doubting whether the Fed was ever a serious convert to monetarism; more likely, it viewed a public profession of monetarism as a sort of temporary expedient. By declaring that its goal was to control money supply, the Fed was able to fight inflation by allowing interest rates to rise to market-clearing levels—levels that proved so high that they would have been politically unacceptable had not politicians too bought monetarism.

Once inflation was quelled, the Fed gradually moved away from its monetarist stance. Having changed its definition of money supply as often as Elizabeth Taylor changes husbands— there was M1 to M5, M1A, M1B, and L—the Fed more or less admitted that, in a constantly changing world, there was no measure of money supply that it could control and, more important, no measure that it made sense, theoretically or practically, to control.

Today, the Fed is back to behaving quite as it did before its fling with monetarism. In December 1988, one funds broker observed: "The Fed is pretty much pegging the Fed funds rate these days. We are not affected by money supply; the funds rate is where the Fed wants to put it. The Fed likes to publicize in their minutes a half-point band for fluctuations in the funds rate, but in actuality, the band is generally a quarter. Lately, funds have been trading at 8¼; so 8 flat and 8¼ are OK. Beyond that, the Fed will come in and do repos or reverses. Today, funds are trading on the high side. Everyone has *disco fever:* they anticipate a rise in the discount rate."

The Effective Fed Funds Rate

Time out for a definition. People often speak of *the* Fed funds rate, but on any given day, funds trade from early morning until late afternoon; and the rate at which they trade has plenty of time to bounce around a bit. To get a single number for the rate at which funds traded on a particular day, market statisticians have to construct an average rate. The average rate they use is a weighted average of the funds rates that prevailed during the day where the weights used are the amounts of funds that traded at each of the funds rates that prevailed. This weighted average is called the *effective Fed funds rate* or some contraction thereof.

Fed Control over the Funds Rate

Given that there are so many players in the funds market, that the composition of these players and even their stance—as buyers or sellers—keep changing, and finally, that so many factors—including the operating factors described in Chapter 9—affect supply and demand in the funds market, the Fed's task of pegging the funds rate is tough.

"Today," noted one funds broker, "the Fed seems to do a better job of hitting their target rate for funds than they did in the past. You can see this best by looking at the weekly effective or even the biweekly effective funds rate. A lot of folks look at that number, and you can peg it as close as an 02."

The reasons for the improvement in the Fed's ability to control the rate at which funds trade are several. "For one thing," continued the same broker, "the Fed now has better control over float. Also, the Fed now has better numbers; they clarified a lot of their forms so banks now give more meaningful and consistent numbers to the Fed than they did in the past. In addition, the Fed monitors the market more closely than they used to. We get called [by the Fed] maybe five times a day, and so too do the other brokers. During the morning call, the Fed asks us, 'What does the market look like today? What does it expect of us today?' After the Fed intervenes, they call to ask if the market was happy with what they did. The Fed also calls the money center banks and other major players in the market. Thus, the Fed has a pretty good handle on what everyone expects and on what everyone has to do [to buy or to sell].

"Ten years ago, Sternlight [Chief of the Open Market Desk] said, 'If you want to hang your hat on something, hang it on the average effective funds rate over the settlement period.' That is as true now as it was then. The Fed is doing things now the same way they always did; they have not changed. People try to attribute complex motives to the Fed, but they are not there. The Fed has improved on what they do, but they do it the same way."

RUNNING A FED FUNDS DESK

The primary job of the manager of a bank's Fed funds desk is to ensure (1) that the bank settles with the Fed *and* (2) that in doing so it holds no more excess reserves than the amount, if any, that it can carry into the next week. This is a tricky job at a major bank because each day such a bank experiences huge, highly variable, and difficult-to-predict inflows and outflows of funds. These all influence the bank's balance at the Fed and so they must be carefully monitored by the desk, which at the same time is buying or selling funds as necessary to develop the balance it wants for the day at the Fed.

The flows that affect a major bank's funds position come from various sources. Its correspondents sell it huge sums of money, and sometimes they will ask to buy funds from it. Additional flows result from changes in correspondent (domestic but more especially foreign) bank deposit balances, changes in customer deposit balances (firms wiring money into and out of the bank), changes in the Treasury's balance in its tax and loan account, big loans coming on or going off the bank's books, purchases and sales made by the bank's portfolio and by the bank's dealer department, changes in the amount of CDs the bank has outstanding, changes in the level of repos it does, flows from and to foreign branches, and—in the case of clearing banks—fluctuations in dealer loans.

Normally, a bank's Fed funds desk starts the day with a sheet on which it projects the inflows and outflows that will affect its bank's reserve account at the Fed during the day. Some, such as flows generated by maturing repo and big loans going on or off its books, are known. The rest it estimates on the basis of past experience and any additional information available. The desk *heads out* (adds up and compares) all these figures to get its first estimate of what money it will need to buy or sell during the day. Then, as the day progresses and actual inflows and outflows occur, someone on the desk tracks these flows and their effect on the bank's balance at the Fed. This is boring and tedious work, but it must be done if the bank is to keep a handle on its position. As one Fed funds trader after another will note, the traders on the desk are only as good as their backup people. When one of the latter makes an error, the bank may inadvertently end up way black or way red, a situation that can create a problem on any day and a major bust on a Wednesday.

At most major banks, the Fed funds desk is managed conservatively. The desk has a good idea of what average daily balance it must have to settle for the period, and it attempts to be each day within 10% of that figure. One reason is that, since Fed funds trade in a narrow band—except when the Fed is moving the rate, there is not much incentive to play the rates, go long on a day when funds seem cheap and short on a day when they seem expensive.

A second reason for a Fed funds trader to be conservative is that his bank has only two ways to evaluate his performance: Is the bank covered? How does the average rate he paid compare with the Fed effective? No funds trader wants to hear his management say: "The Fed effective was this, you had to be an idiot not to at least hit it."

Yet another reason banks are disinclined to play around on the Fed funds desk is that most of them are either big natural sellers or buyers of funds, and they work best—because of line problems—when operating from their natural stance. With the exception of B of A, most large banks are net buyers of funds. A bank will sell funds only to a bank to which it has extended a line and only up to the amount of that line. Thus, if a bank that is normally a net buyer of funds accumulates a big surplus position, it may have difficulty working off that surplus because it has insufficient lines to sell it.

Some state-chartered banks have an additional problem. The Comptroller of the Currency has ruled for national banks that funds purchases and sales are not to be treated as borrowings and loans for purposes of regulation. Thus, there is no legal limit on the amount of Fed funds a national bank may sell to another bank. In some states, however, sales of Fed funds are treated as a normal loan. In such states, a state-chartered bank can extend to another bank a line equal to only a small percentage of its capital.

A bank that cannot get rid of excess funds because of line problems can always sell these funds in the repo market, that is, provide dealers with secured loans. But in doing so it will typically get a lower rate than it would by selling funds, and it may end up selling off excess funds at a rate below that at which it purchased them from its correspondents.

Line problems can also constrain the amount by which even the largest and most well-thought-of banks can go red early in the week. When Franklin and Herstatt failed, banks were suddenly reminded of something they had almost forgotten—that the sale of Fed funds is an unsecured loan. In response, banks cut back on their lines for selling funds, which in turn diminished the leeway banks have to vary their daily purchases of Fed funds.

Today, thanks to more recent bank problems—Contil, LDC debt, the woes of the Texas banks, the real estate problems of certain regional banks—sellers of Fed funds are, if anything, more credit conscious than ever: *no one wants to get hurt*. "If a bank gets downgraded to a C," noted one broker, "the first lines to go are the Fed funds lines. Fidelity's being downgraded to a C [in late 1988] probably lost them 300 to 450MM of liquidity that was available to them the day before. When Contil's problems hit in 1984, liquidity for them dried up overnight. Now, they have built themselves back up to the point where they are back in the market and are able to buy some monies, but they are a much smaller institution and do not need anywhere near the size they needed prior to their problems."

More conservative lines put pressure on banks to stay close, daily, to their anticipated reserve needs. Said one dealer, "If you think, at the beginning of the reserve period, that the Fed is going to do a lot of adding and that funds are going to trend down, you might borrow a little less than you otherwise would have. But at a large borrowing bank, you have such a big job to do that you cannot get far behind and hope to make it up at the end of the reserve period. It cannot be done."

Conservative Fed funds traders, while they will not try to make money by dealing aggressively in funds, attempt to do what they can for the bank's profit and loss (P&L) statement in other ways. Said one typical of the breed, "We are not supposed to be a profit center. We do, however, usually make money if we sell funds or finance dealer loans. The dealer loan gives us a better spread ³⁄₁₆ to ¼ over Fed funds, and it's a secured loan. But the real nature of our game is to buy cheaper than the effective funds rate. We make the bank money by saving it. A 16th is only $1.74 on $1MM, but with the amounts we borrow, 16ths can mount up."

Dealing Aggressively

While most Fed funds traders are conservative, and well advised to be so because that is what management wants, there are a few sharpshooters in the crowd. One trader of this genre, who was quite comfortable going above or below his daily required by 50%, commented, "I don't like to just pick up the phone and buy or sell. If I feel that there is strength in the market, I will wait to sell even if I have a lot to sell. Then in the early afternoon, there is the moment of truth. I have to make some sort of decision. You get a good sense of accomplishment when you wait and it turns out you were right. When it does not, you have to scramble. But that is part of the fun of doing it. The fun is to have a conviction and at times buy yourself long or sell yourself short."

Said a trader who liked to play even more: "Some guys act as if they settled every night. That is what you call a *day position*. I have a different philosophy. Say I need $100MM a day for seven days, that is, a $700MM cumulative. If I think rates are high one day, I might buy just $50MM and then pick up $150MM the day after if rates are more reasonable. Also I go where the money is cheapest. If it is cheaper to buy Euros, I buy Euros, not Fed funds. If Euros are cheap, I will buy Euros and sell Fed funds.

"When I got this job, they tended to think that you need $100MM a day. I said, OK, if I can get money cheap, I will buy $200MM and sell $100MM off at a profit and reduce my effective cost of funds. Not many people do that. I ask: How can a bank not leverage down their cost of funds by using this route? It takes extra work to buy and sell, but in the end you reduce your cost of money. Over the first quarter of this year, if I had just bought money all the time from our correspondents, as I should have, I would have had an effective cost on the $500MM to $1 billion, which I had to buy, that was 25 bp higher than the actual effective cost of money I achieved. And I managed that savings in a market in which you have a ⅛ spread.

"A lot of banks look at the Fed funds guy as custodian of a checking account whose prime function is to make sure that the bank does not go OD at the Fed. The Fed funds market has not progressed as far as other markets have, and it should. This is where the action is, where the basic position of your bank is settled.

"Too many people are stodgy. The way I look at it, Babe Ruth only hit .342, and he was a superstar. Ty Cobb, who had the best batting average ever, hit .367. So if you are right 75% of the time, you are going to make a lot of money. If you are gambling, you have to take the big loss to make the big win. Lots of guys say to me, 'I never took a big loss,' but they never made a big win either."

This quote illustrates well an attitude that is common on the Street and characteristic of aggressive traders, dealers, and portfolio managers: There are plenty of gambles around in which you can count on being right more than half the time; if you are, you'll make money, so to not gamble is expensive and foolish.

Personnel and Sophistication

Most of the traders on the funds desks of large banks have no special academic training for their job. They are people with a good memory, which a Fed funds trader requires, who started out in operations and just picked up trading. In a few banks, the trading slot on the Fed funds desk is one that fast-track MBAs are passed through for a year.

At small banks, the Fed funds desk is often run with much less sophistication than at large banks because the person who does the job is the treasurer of the bank and also has to handle governments, repos, and whatever. Sophistication, however, is not only a function of size. A trader at a bank that ranks 150th may be quite sophisticated, whereas one at a somewhat larger bank is merely an order clerk—when he has $10MM to sell, he calls the broker, gets a quote, hits the bid, writes a ticket, and thinks of himself as a trader.

Glamor

While a Fed funds trader may handle huge sums everyday, there is little glamor or recognition attached to the job, as is the case with most money market jobs. Said one trader who handles several billion dollars everyday, "I went out to dinner the other night with a fellow from Price Waterhouse. He said, 'What do you do?' I said, 'Trade overnight funds.' He said, 'Oh, how does your wife like your working nights?'"

Overnight Money

The bulk of the money sold in the Fed funds market is overnight money. Much of this money is traded directly between the selling and buying banks.

Because they depend heavily and persistently on purchases of Fed funds to cover their basic funding needs, most large banks go out of their way to cultivate smaller correspondents that find it convenient to sell their surplus funds on an ongoing basis to one or several large banks. A smaller bank could, of course, shop in the brokers' market and try to pick up an extra 1/16, but most don't because the amounts they sell are so small that the cost of trying would outweigh the potential gain. Overnight 1/16 on $10MM is only $17, and that's before the phone bill is paid.

To cultivate correspondents that will sell funds to them, large banks stand ready to buy whatever sums these banks offer, whether they need all of these funds or not. If they get more funds than they need, they sell off the surplus in the brokers market. Also, they will sell to their correspondents if the latter needs funds, but that occurs infrequently. As a funding officer of a large bank noted, "We do feel the need to sell to our correspondents but we would not have cultivated them unless we felt that they would be selling to us 99% of the time. On the occasional Wednesday when they need $100,000 or $10MM, OK. Then we would fill their need before we would fill our own."

When the Fed funds market was younger and less competitive and the smaller players were relatively unsophisticated, it was not uncommon for buying banks to pay their smaller correspondents a rate well below the New York rate. Today, however, most large banks pay correspondents that sell to them regularly some formula rate—the opening rate, the average rate for the day, or whatever. And even though they know that they may well have to sell off some of the funds they purchase from correspondents, they do not try to arbitrage—buy low and sell high. A banker typical of this attitude said, "We will pay a bank in Cedar Rapids the same rate for $100,000 that we would pay the B of A selling us $100MM. We do that because we want the bank in Cedar Rapids to be coming back to us. Relative to other sources of funds, Fed funds are cheap, and we try to cultivate this funding source."

A few big banks, however, still see a potential arbitrage, "trading profits," in selling off funds purchased from smaller banks and attempt to profit from it to reduce their effective cost of funds. Also a few tend to bid low to their correspondents. Said a trader typical of the latter attitude, "We have a good name in the market so I often underbid the market by a 1/16. A guy with a few million to sell doesn't care. He's happy to get his money sold and get on with other banking business." The tendency to shave rates is particularly pronounced on Fridays because a Friday purchase is for three days. At the opposite end of the spectrum are majors who will offer a small bank an extra 1/4 to pick up correspondent-bank business with them.

One of the striking things about the Fed funds market is the wide access all banks have to it. A tiny bank with $50,000 of overnight money to sell won't be able to sell to one of the top money market banks because such a bank would not bother with such dribbles. But at a rate slightly off the market, it can sell its funds to a regional bank that is happy to take in small amounts either to fund its own position or to resell in larger blocks. Even S&Ls have gotten into the Fed funds game. Small thrifts sell funds through their Federal Home Loan Bank; small credit unions sell funds through a private institution, the *U.S. Central Credit Union,* which acts as a central depository for credit unions. The national market for borrowing CD money is open in real volume only to the top 25 banks or so in the country.

But regional banks much smaller in size can and do buy large sums in the Fed funds market. The market is also open to foreign bank branches who are now major players in the market.

There is some tendency in the Fed funds market for banks to expect banks they sell to be willing to sell to them, and a handful of banks will sell funds only to banks with whom they have reciprocal lines. However, the need to "buy one's way in" is less pronounced in the Fed funds market than in the Euromarket because banks in the Fed funds market tend to be one way most of the time—either consistent buyers or consistent sellers.

THE BROKERS' MARKET

In addition to the large volume of funds traded *directly* between big banks and their correspondents, there are huge amounts of overnight funds traded through *brokers*. Large banks lay off any excess funds they take in from their correspondents in the brokers' market. Also, if their needs exceed the amounts they receive from their correspondents, they will buy funds through brokers. There are many regional banks, foreign banks, and foreign agency banks that also buy and sell funds through brokers. And those few funds desks manned by traders who *deal* in funds—buying and selling to pick up ⅛—add to the volume in the brokers' market.

The major brokers in the market are Fulton Prebon, Garvin GuyButler, Lasser Brothers, and Noonan, Astley, and Pierce. In addition, there are several minor brokers.

Brokerage

The Fed funds rate is an add-on rate quoted on a 360-day-year basis. Thus, if funds were trading at 9¾, a purchase of $50MM of overnight funds would cost the buyer

$$0.0975 \times \$50,000,000 \times \left(\frac{1}{360}\right) = \$13,541.29$$

In addition, he would pay brokerage costs equal to $0.50 per $1MM per day, which works out to slightly less than ¹⁄₅₀ of 1 percentage point. Brokerage is paid by both the buyer and the seller.

The volume going through the brokers varies from day to day. Friday transactions are particularly attractive to a broker because he earns a 3-day commission on them; a Friday sale is unwound on Monday. On an active day, a top broker with a staff of 30 may handle more than $20 billion of overnight funds.

Function of the Brokers

The major function of the Fed funds brokers is communications. There are so many participants in the brokers market—all the top 500 banks plus a lot of foreign banks plus various quasi-government bodies—that, in the absence of brokers, the banks would need a host of traders and telephones on their Fed funds desk to get their job done.

Each broker has a particular set of names that use him. There is, however, considerable overlap between the clients of the top brokers, since many banks use two or even three brokers on a regular basis. The brokers put in direct phone lines to any bank having a volume of trading through them that justifies the cost. They communicate with the rest over WATS lines. The phone bill for a broker is necessarily huge: He is providing a communications network, and doing so is costly.

In addition to communications, brokers also provide the banks with anonymity. A top bank that has a big job to do values this because it fears that, if it were a bid for or offer huge sums in its own name in the market, it might move the market.

The brokers' market is really open to only those banks that buy and sell in volume. In Fed funds, anything under $5MM is an odd lot. A small bank in Iowa that wants to buy $500,000 is better off going to its regional correspondent, since the New York brokers are not set up to handle trades of that size. Noted one broker: "We have a guy who sells through us $300,000 to $1MM everyday. He asks, 'What is the market?' We say, '5/16–3/8.' He says, 'What do I get for $1MM?' We have to say, '1/8.'"

Today the average trade in the brokers' market for overnight funds is $25MM. A few of the major banks won't take 5s [$5MM] any more, and some won't even take 10s. A lot of regionals, however, both take and give 10s.

Trading the Sheet

A Fed funds brokering operation today is a rather impressive sight to view: 28 or 30 people sitting around a desk, each constantly talking on one of a battery of direct phone lines facing him, and each constantly scribbling down bids and offers on a sheet of paper. That sheet, however bedraggled it may look, is a key part of the operation since each person on the desk, by glancing at it, can see what banks are bidding and offering through the firm and what the amounts are.

Brokers will often describe what they do as *trading the sheet*. "We do not," said one broker, "trade in the sense of taking a position. But when someone acts in the market, how do we react? That is our trading decision. The first day after a settlement always used to be difficult because it was a slow day. We'd end up with a sheet cluttered on both sides with bids and offers. If a name then came in and said he wanted to sell $20MM at the bid, we might have 25 names to choose from; ethically, the best we could do was to decide who was there first. When the market is moving, you do not have to worry about this because everyone will be satisfied. A settlement Wednesday is easy because it moves so fast."

Brokering is very much a team effort. Commented the head of one brokering operation, "This job takes concentration and coordination. To run an efficient shop, you cannot have two people on the phone saying that the market is going down and three others saying that it's going up. Avoiding that is hard because our thoughts on the market may change 20 times a day."

Many Fed funds brokers come out of the banks, and a number are ex-Fed funds traders. Such experience is valuable: an ex-trader knows how to quote the market and understands how to react to what the banks do.

Quoting the Market

BROKER:

Hello, ¾ bid on 50. I am offered at 6 in two spots, 75 firm, 50 under reference.

BANK:

I'll take 50.

BROKER:

OK, 50 done. Can I make it a C note?

Brokering occurs at a breakneck pace. The top New York banks do not want a lot of information, and a broker makes a fast quote to them. In a minimum of words, he attempts to convey the tone of the market. He might, for example, quote the market: "5/16–3/8, last at 5/16," or "5/16–3/8, quiet," or "Market last at 3/8 looking like it might go to 9." Some regional banks want a slower quote and a little more information on market developments. Said one broker, "The worst even ask what the *handle* is."

In the Fed funds market, banks, in addition to putting *firm* bids and offers into the brokers, will also make *subject* bids and offerings. When a bank's bid or offer is subject or *under reference,* before the broker executes a trade for that bank, he has to go back and ask it if they will make their bid or offer firm. When the Fed goes into the market to do open market operations, it creates uncertainty, and the brokers, in courtesy to their customers, treat all bids and offers as subject until they are renewed.

Part of the fun and the frustration of brokering funds is that the market changes constantly throughout the day. Thus, an important part of a broker's job is to get a line on the market, a feel for its tone and where it is moving. In doing so, he looks not only at his own market, but at related markets. What is the rate on overnight repo? Where are Euros trading? The top Fed funds brokers also broker Euros, repo, and various other instruments, so their people have constant and easy and immediate access to information on developments in related markets.

Fine-Tuning Quotes

In the Fed funds market, whenever a buyer takes a seller's offering, the broker has to go back to the seller and tell him the name of the buyer and ask him if he will do the trade. The ethics of the game are such that the seller is supposed to do the trade unless he does not have a line to the buyer or his line to the buyer is filled. If the seller can do the trade, the broker then tells the buyer the seller's name, and the buyer and the seller clear the trade directly over the Fed wire. Brokerage bills are sent and paid at the end of the month.

Line problems and other subtleties make brokering more than just quoting two rates. A good broker knows what lines various banks have extended to other banks and how big they are. And he tries to guess during the day how much of those lines have been used up. Said one broker: "I know the B of A's lines better than they do. It's not that they tell me, but if they keep selling some guy XMM day after day, I know pretty quickly what their line to him is."

"Because of line problems," commented the same broker, "the quote to each bank is individualized." Line problems become especially acute on a Wednesday when the banks settle and trading is active. "The quote will be one thing to Fuji if they have been in the market all day long buying up everything in sight and another story to Chase if they have been selling all day. A broker is foolish if he says, '9¼–⅜,' when there is nothing on the offer side good to the guy on the phone who wants to buy. We may have an offering but we say none. Or I can say, 'I am 9¼–⅜, but my offer is not good to you. I will work for you at that price.'"

Part of being a good broker is the ability to be a good salesman—to anticipate a customer's needs and to nudge him subtly into a trade. One broker noted, "This is a pattern market in the sense that many names do not change their posture in the market very much. They are constantly one way or the other. You often know with a good customer what he is going to do and when he is going to do it. A good broker will anticipate what the bank is going to do without letting the bank know and without being pushy. The minute you see a borrowing bank's line ring, you get your people on the phones with the accounts that are going to be selling. So when the bank says, 'I will take 200,' you have the offers all lined up and can say, 'Sold 25,' 'Sold 50,' and so on."

The same broker went on to observe that "when you have a big buyer on the phone, you try to get a round number out of him. If he asks me how much I might be able to bring down [get for him] and I say 350, my next question might be: 'Do you want 500?' This is a volume market; we can put through a single trade for half a billion a lot easier than we can do five $1MM trades."

Knowing what a bank might want to do is also important because some big banks fear that showing all they want to do might distort the market. So a bank that is looking for $1 billion might bid for only $100MM. When a broker sells money to such a bank, he always tries to keep the trade going by asking: "Can I work some more for you?"

The Garban, Telerate, and Reuters screens show constantly updated quotes on Fed funds so that buyers and sellers can use them to track what the market is doing.[6] However, a given broker's quotes may at any moment differ from those on the screen because the market moves so fast. Also, each broker has a somewhat different clientele so that quotes coming out of different brokers may vary slightly.

The Banks

It costs a bank money to buy and sell through a broker, but using a broker saves the bank time and cuts its phone bill. Said one trader: "When I have funds to sell, it is easier for me to go into the brokers and hit 10 or 15 bids than for me to call individual banks." Also there is the human factor. The same trader continued: "If I sell through the broker and then the rates fall, I feel, well, that bank was in there bidding at that rate. If I go in and sell direct and then the rate falls off, often the guy who sold will feel I knew something he did not. And the next time I call, he bids below the market."

Most large banks use several brokers. One reason is that the more brokers a bank uses, the more exposure it gets. An-

---

[6]Garban brokers governments and agencies. See Chapter 14.

other is that a bank with a big job to do may be able to operate faster by using several brokers.

A third reason some sharp traders use two brokers is that now and then the quotes at two major brokers will differ long enough to allow a profitable arbitrage. Said one trader: "The last time the Fed did reverses, Garban was at 3/16, Fulton Prebon at 1/8. I bought through Fulton Prebon, sold through Garban, and picked up 1/16 on every buck I passed through."

Finally, there is the embarrassment factor. One dealing trader commented: "If on a Wednesday I buy funds at 10 through Fulton Prebon and now want to sell at 8, I will go to another broker. I made a mistake and it's embarrassing. The guy at Garban says, 'Hey, you are going to sell before the bottom falls out.' He does not know I took in the money at 10."

The banks will also use the brokers to play games with each other. A bank may try to influence where funds are trading by posting high bids when they want to sell and vice versa.

The Opening

In the early morning, the chatter in a broker's office is likely to run:

"Work for you? OK, I show you out."

"1/4–5/16, with the Japanese paying 5. No opening yet."

"Light opening at 5/16, a regional name. I am at 1/4–5/16."

Calling an opening is a touchy affair for a major broker because a lot of big banks pay their correspondents the opening rate. Years ago the big New York banks tried on occasion to distort this rate. One broker said: "They were paying correspondents the opening rate at Mabon or Garvin. So to ensure they were not getting ripped off, they used to come into the market and hit the bids, and they had an official opening. That was a distortion since the market opened on the bid side. We stopped that because we thought it was unethical. They might sell $100MM at that price when they had $500MM that they were committed to buy at that price. We told the banks that, if they satisfied every bidder on our sheet, we would call an opening. If not, we would not. That stopped that."

Sometimes, the major brokers open ⅛ apart because one opens on the bid side of the market, the other on the offered side.

THE HEAVIES: BUYERS AND SELLERS

Years ago, the big takers of funds were the money center banks in New York and Chicago, while the B of A, with all its branches, was consistently the biggest net seller. Today, the brokers' market for funds had a new cast of heavies.

The Big Takers

The Japanese banks are big takers of funds; they are sellers only occasionally. On a typical day, the Japanese can be counted on to take a third to over 40% of funds sold through the brokers. "For the Japanese," commented one broker, "there is almost never enough. They always seem to find something to finance at a spread to funds. If you do 20 to 22 billion a day in total volume, you can assume that out of that you have done about 7 billion just with Japanese banks. That's a safe bet day in and day out."

The superregionals have also become big takers. These new movers and drivers of the market are primarily in New England and the Southeast. Their ranks include NCNB of Charlotte, Connecticut Bank and Trust, Connecticut National Bank, Shaumett Bank, Bank of New England, and Bank of Boston.

The New York money center banks still buy, but not in the volume they used to. Thanks to rate deregulation, some New York banks with big retail divisions don't need the outside money they once did to fund their wholesale operations. Also, some of the old "top 10 U.S." banks have credit and line problems. Contil's days of being a huge taker have passed, and lines to Manny are, as noted below, meager. Finally, big banks have developed other more attractive sources of funding; when market conditions are such that a top-name bank can swap medium-term money into sub-LIBOR funding and avoid the liquidity concerns that come with rolling daily billions of overnight funds, buying the latter loses its allure. Still, a bank, such as Morgan, that is a modest taker when the yield curve is flat may, if they think rates are coming down, buy 5 or 6 billion of funds as a rate play.

The Big Suppliers

Supply too has changed in the funds market. The biggest single seller used to be the B of A; in the past, when the B of A was in the market, everyone used to react; now, the B of A is just another seller. Currently, for the B of A, being a seller of funds is a conscious decision based on credit considerations. With their low rating, they would have a hard time buying in the national market.

The big lenders in the brokers' market today are quasi-government bodies: the regional Home Loan Banks, Freddie Mac, Fannie Mae, Sallie Mae, and the U.S. Central Credit Union. Together, they supply about 40% of the funds traded in the brokers' market; and on a given day, any one of them can be huge.

The Federal Home Loans hold reserves and deposits of S&Ls; also, they may be investing funds they have borrowed through the sale of their securities and that they have not yet lent to S&Ls or otherwise invested. The mortgage crew, Freddie and Fannie, are huge 100-billion institutions; when they sell debentures they may end up with float for four or five days, which they sell off in the funds market.

The Home Loans and their ilk will sell to everyone if they are good quality and meet certain capital requirements. A lot of smaller regionals are also suppliers of funds; typically, they can't sell Japanese, which can create problems for them on days when, say, Freddie Mac has a big float and is more than 50% of the market. As the smaller regionals hit the domestic bids, the latter dry up. However, if the Japanese banks still need money, they get it: a superregional or a non-Japanese foreign bank will come in, buy extra funds, and resell them to the Japanese.

Tiering

The current high sensitivity of funds sellers to credit quality shows itself both in lines granted in rates. Say the market is 1/8–1/4, with the handle at 8. A top-rated Morgan can buy 300MM on the bid side, a billion on the offered side, whereas Manny can buy nothing on the bid side and be lucky to buy 200MM on the offered side. Amongst big domestic banks, Morgan and Manny are night and day in terms of the size they can buy and the rate they must pay.

The Japanese, depending on the liquidity of the market, will pay anywhere from 1/16 to 1/8 over the low bid side; if there is lots of liquidity, they can buy at the offered side. Normally, if the market is 5/8–11/16, with the regionals paying 11/16, the Japanese can buy almost anything they need at 3/4. Major non-Japanese foreign banks, such as Barclays, can buy at the offered side of the market, as they are not huge takers. Lesser regional names, good in quality but lacking exposure in the national market, will have to pay the offered rate.

Size

With big buyers and big sellers so prominent in the brokered market for funds, it is not uncommon for large sums to change hands in a single trade. "A regional will come into the market and say," noted one broker, "'Give me a block, I will pay up.' He reasons, 'Why buy 10 pieces of 10 or five 20s when I can get one piece of 100 from a Home Loan?' We also get bids from the Japanese: 'Give me 100MM+'; or 'Give me the biggest ticket out there.' Mitsubishi is a classic; he comes into the market, buys three big tickets, picks up a billion, and is gone for the day."

Volume

While the cast of characters who play big in the funds market keeps changing, one constant remains in the market: volume constantly rises. One broker estimates that the brokered market for overnight funds now averages 70 billion a day.

THE DAILY PATTERN

On October 1, 1981, the Fed required that CHIPS go to same-day settlement.[7] At that time, the Fed introduced a new schedule of cutoff times for money transfers over the Fed wire; it also changed the old pattern under which the Fed wire closed for interdistrict and intradistrict transfers on a geographic basis: early in New York, later on the West Coast. Today cutoff times apply nationally.

CHIPS is scheduled to settle by 4:30 P.M. New York time, and by 4:35 P.M. the New York Clearing House banks and other participating members should have a printout indicating their bank's gross and net positions with CHIPS, the gross and net positions for each bank for whom they settle, and finally their *net net*—the dollars they must send out or will receive due to CHIPS settlement.

At the same time that CHIPS settles, the Fed wire closes for commercial (nonsettlement) transactions. From 4:30 to 6:30 P.M. is *the settlement period;* a *settlement transaction* is one in which both parties are subject to reserve requirements under the 1980 Banking Act.

Together with same-day settlement of CHIPS, the new Fed wire schedule has turned daily trading in Fed funds into a sort of two-phase affair. From the opening of the market at 8:30 A.M. until about 2 or 2:30 P.M., banks busily trade funds to get themselves roughly into the position in which they want to end the day.

Then at 4:30 P.M., the CHIPS figures hit the major banks, and a new burst of activity occurs. No small amount of this activity is on the part of foreign bank branches and agencies, which make and receive most of their payments through an account at a correspondent bank, typically a top New York bank. Once these banks get their CHIPS figure, they will have at their clearing bank either a surplus that they want to unload or a deficit that they must cover. As foreign banks make transfers into and out of their clearing bank accounts—for French

---

[7]For reasons, see Chapter 18.

and Japanese banks the sums can be huge—each clearing bank must in turn buy or sell funds to fine-tune its reserve position which is affected both by its net net from CHIPS and by subsequent transfers into and out of foreign bank and other correspondent bank accounts held with it. The cutoff time for transfers out of correspondent bank accounts is traditionally 6 P.M. The time from then to 6:30 P.M. is reserved for banks on line with the Fed to adjust their accounts there by buying and selling amongst themselves.

The above scenario of trading hours and cutoff times sounds well organized and reasonable, except perhaps to New York traders for whom it means a 10-hour day: 8:30 A.M. to 6:30 P.M. In practice, however, the schedule is more fantasy than fact since, as noted earlier, it is a rare day when all cutoff times are respected. Also, the Fed has agreed that, if CHIPS settles late due to machine problems, it will extend wire hours to accommodate banks that settle through CHIPS.

A second, more common problem is that the Fed wire gets so jammed in the early afternoon with securities traffic that the cutoff times cited in Chapter 10 for securities transactions have to be extended. This in turn requires that the banks be given more time to settle. Consequently New York traders and brokers of Fed funds frequently work until 7 to 7:30 P.M., and on really bad days the Fed wire closes *hours* later than that.

All this leaves the New York banks and funds brokers with a big staffing problem. No institution can expect employees regularly to work 50-hour weeks. Yet a 10-hour day is awkward to break into shifts. Noted one broker, "If they went to 24-hour-a-day trading, that would make my job easier. Right now I am in limbo. The pace of the desk is such that you just do not sit down; 8:30 A.M. to 6:30 P.M. is a *long* day."

WEDNESDAY CLOSE

The most exciting and volatile time in the Fed funds market occurs every other Wednesday afternoon when all depository institutions settle.

On a settlement Wednesday, a bank's Fed funds trader will try to determine as early as possible what the bank's position is. At 5:30 P.M. he starts putting numbers together. He knows his final net CHIPS number and his number for securities transactions; everything else is pretty well cleaned up and steady. The big unknown—a hardship same-day settlement has imposed on the clearing banks—is what monies foreign banks will transfer into and out of the bank late in the day. Foreign banks, who—after they get their CHIPS position—do a lot of volume to work off that position, can cause tremendous changes late in the day in a clearing bank's position. Sometimes on a settlement Wednesday, this will create real problems for such a bank.

Extensions and As ofs

On a settlement Wednesday, the loss of a transaction in the system, a mistake by a bank, or a mistake by a broker can set off a panic on a bank's Fed funds desk; they thought they had settled and suddenly find they have not. A bank in this position may ask the Fed to hold the wire open until the mistake is righted or may ask the Fed to permit them to do an *as of* transaction, that is, to do a transaction the next day and be credited for it as if the transfer had occurred on the previous day.

In the scenario that introduced this chapter, a bank was searching wildly for $150MM that had been lost in the system. The Fed is tough about doing "as of" transactions in such situations because, as someone at the Fed noted, "The way things work out is that if a West Coast bank is supposed to have sent Chase money and Chase did not get it, through no fault of either bank [something went wrong with the wire system or a computer], and if we then credit Chase as if the transfer had been made, there will be no offsetting debit for the West Coast bank; it will be a one-sided adjustment, and we end up giving money away free. The reason is that the West Coast bank will argue that they knew they had sent the money, and when they saw their balance [at the Fed], they assumed that this money had already been taken out and managed their balance accordingly.

So to take the money from them now would cause them to end up short through no fault of their own."[8]

"When people reported things by hand, there was no such thing as 'as of' adjustments. The advent of computers gave rise to them—obliged us to give money away free because of mistakes that lie with the technology. The same thing occurs when governments and agencies [securities] are transferred over the Fed wire."

A slightly different situation in which a bank might ask for an "as of" transfer is if it had made a mistake in tracking its own balance or if a mistake had been made by a broker. Here is an example of the latter. When the Fed wire still closed by districts, a broker commented late one Wednesday afternoon, "We are in trouble. We thought a bank was willing to give up 1/8 to sell. He says he was not. They misunderstood me and I misunderstood them. Now we have a bank that is short $25MM. We will try to find someone outside the district and arrange an 'as of' sale.

"The Fed can be a son of a bitch about this sort of thing. This is an ethical business, so it is sad that when an honest mistake is made, they do not give much leeway. But if they are not strict about cutoff times, abuses occur. Still, they do make allowances for size.

"For a small bank in Tulsa, losing $5MM is like Chase losing $250MM. The Fed thinks of the small banks as less sophisticated so it is more likely to let them do an 'as of' to cover a mistake than they are to let a New York bank do so."

It is the current understanding of the major banks that the Fed will not permit them to do an as of (*reserve adjustment*) transaction unless failure to do so would cause the bank to be OD at the Fed. A bank that is overdrawn at the Fed at the end of the day incurs a stiff penalty.

---

[8]Because of the huge volume of transfers being made into and out of a major bank's account at the Fed, it is not uncommon for such a bank to reconcile its balance at the Fed, which it can track throughout the day, with transfers into and out of that account after both it and the Fed have closed. Thus, a bank could make the honest mistake of assuming that its closing balance reflected an outward transfer that had not gone through.

On a Bank's Desk

Settling on a Wednesday is tricky for a bank's funds desk. A bank can offset large and unanticipated inflows to or outflows of funds from its reserve account right up to the moment the Fed wire closes by selling or buying additional Fed funds. However, the Fed funds rate sometimes gets out of hand late Wednesday when either bids or offers may be scarce. This has been particularly true for the large New York banks, which clear for major international banks. The latter may, after they get their CHIPS figures at 4:30 P.M., make tremendous transfers into and out of their clearing bank account until the 6 P.M. cutoff for such transfers. That leaves the clearing banks only half an hour to clear up their own positions at the Fed.

A bank that finds itself unexpectedly in the red can, in addition to buying funds, go to the discount window. But if it is way red, it may have a collateral problem, that is, need to borrow more than the amount of collateral it has at the Fed. In that case, it either must scurry to find funds or, if worst comes to worst, ask for an unsecured advance at the window. In the short run, the Fed has to grant such an advance, but asking for it is a black mark against a bank, and the Fed will expect that bank to be more careful and conservative in the future.

The fact that a bank can run 2% short or long on its reserve balance and carry that over into the next 2-week settlement period gives it some leeway in settling. How much depends on whether it settled on the nose during the previous period. If, for example, it was red in the previous period, then in the current period it has to settle on the nose or run an excess.

Sometimes on a Wednesday, many banks end up with reserves imbalances in the same direction—they are all red or all black. This occurs because the Fed has misestimated the reserves available to the banks, and there are either too many or too few in the aggregate. When this occurs, the funds rate will start to move.

Late on a Wednesday, when the Fed can no longer act, the Fed funds rate can go anywhere and sometimes does. As one trader noted, "Yesterday was a prime example of how the funds rate can still bounce on a settlement day: we stayed within a narrow band [a bit over 8%] till 5 P.M.; then, swoosh, funds ran up to 12%, bounced first down, then up a couple of points; we finally closed at 8¼%. At times, the range of bounce will be only a half a point. Then there are Wednesdays when, at the close, you cannot give funds away. It happened within the last month that funds were offered at ½ of 1%, and there were no takers. Those lenders 'spilled it.' Maybe a bank got dumped on late several hundred million that it it did not expect to come in; the bank, 'Thought I was square, now who pays?' The answer was no one."

Part of the reason the funds market becomes so volatile late on Wednesday is that volume can get so *thin* that a $10MM purchase will move the market up ½. A bank may also have to pay high rates late in the day because, while funds are still offered in the market, they are not being offered by banks with lines open to it.

That the funds rate sometimes falls so low on Wednesdays is due to the way the carry-over provision operates. Suppose a few banks end up late on a settlement Wednesday way black due to bad numbers. As they pump out money, the funds rate will start to fall; this ought to attract buyers because banks can carry a reserve surplus from the current settlement period forward into the following settlement period, and sometimes the banks will bid for the surplus funds to carry them forward. It may, however, happen that most of the big banks were black the previous settlement period, if so, then if they go black again, they will get no credit for the current settlement period's surplus. A bank in this position will bid for additional funds only if the rate is very low and only if it can buy more money than the black it is erasing. For example, if a bank were $80MM black in the previous settlement period and planned to be $80MM short in the current settlement period, it would pay it to decrease that short only if it bought more than $80MM and only if it bought that money very cheaply.

If a bank in such a position bids for funds, it will probably put in an *all or none* (AON) bid. An AON bid does not mean that the money all has to come from the same source, only that it has to equal in total the amount bid for and be offered at the rate bid.

Weekly Pattern in Excess Reserves

Because banks can carry forward reserve deficiencies and excesses in limited amounts, one would expect a pattern in banks' excess reserves; namely, that if they were *positive* one week, they would be *negative* the next. In 1980 (the last year for which the Fed collected such data), precisely such a pattern existed in the excess reserves run by *large* banks in New York, Chicago, and elsewhere. However, for the banking systems as a whole, excess reserves are consistently positive (Table 12–2, line 7). The reason is that there are many smaller banks in the system that consistently run excess reserves either because they don't find it worthwhile to sell off the last penny of their surplus reserves or because they do not ever want to end up at the discount window and so manage their funds positions very conservatively.

THE FORMER FORWARD MARKET

So far we have been talking mostly about the market for overnight funds for *immediate* delivery. Before CHIPS went to same-day settlement, there was a lot of trading in overnight funds for forward delivery (a sale on Friday for delivery on Monday) in connection with Euro arbitrages. One of the Fed's objectives in mandatory same-day settlement on CHIPS was to eliminate the possibilities for technical arbitrages between Euros and Fed funds that next day settlement of CHIPS created. Such arbitrages, which were profitable and therefore were carried out for huge sums, cost the Fed money on lost reserve balances; they also resulted in big overdrafts in clearing house funds and therefore a big potential risk.[9]

TERM FED FUNDS

Most transactions in the Fed funds market are for overnight (over the weekend in the case of Friday sales) funds. There is, however, a market for what are called *term Fed funds*. On term

---

[9]See Chapter 18.

TABLE 12–2
Reserves and borrowings, depository institutions ($ millions)

	Biweekly Averages of Daily Figures for Weeks Ending									
	1988				1989					
	Nov. 16	Nov. 30	Dec. 14	Dec. 28	Jan. 11	Jan. 25	Feb. 8	Feb. 22	Mar. 8	Mar. 22
1. Reserve balances with Reserve Banks[1]	38,143	35,981	38,363	37,106	38,724	36,514	32,260	32,455	34,485	34,720
2. Total vault cash[2]	26,219r	27,259	26,316	27,927	27,904	27,414	31,488	29,739	27,581	26,738
3. Vault[3]	25,022	25,814	25,128	26,525	26,679	26,243	29,318	27,838	25,962	25,335
4. Surplus[4]	1,198r	1,446	1,188	1,403	1,225	1,171	2,170	1,901	1,620	1,403
5. Total reserves[5]	63,165	61,795	63,491	63,631	65,403	62,757	61,578	60,293	60,446	60,055
6. Required reserves	61,562	61,160	62,515	62,550	64,256	61,786	60,035	59,278	59,490	59,304
7. Excess reserve balances at Reserve Banks[6]	1,603	635	976	1,081	1,147	972	1,543	1,016	957	751
8. Total borrowings at Reserve Banks	3,233	2,562	2,014	1,347	2,048	1,527	1,270	1,477	1,800	1,586
9. Seasonal borrowings at Reserve Banks	180	178	131	137	94	61	78	99	116	136
10. Extended credit at Reserve Banks[7]	2,838	1,863	1,529	968	1,208	1,028	792	1,111	1,250	1,164

[1]Excludes required clearing balances and adjustments to compensate for float.

[2]Dates refer to the maintenance periods in which the vault cash can be used to satisfy reserve requirements. Under contemporaneous reserve requirements, maintenance periods end 30 days after the lagged computation periods in which the balances are held.

[3]Equal to all vault cash held during the lagged computation period by institutions having required reserve balances at Federal Reserve Banks plus the amount of vault cash equal to required reserves during the maintenance period at institutions having no required reserve balances.

[4]Total vault cash at institutions having no required reserve balances less the amount of vault cash equal to their required reserves during the maintenance period.

[5]Total reserves not adjusted for discontinuities consist of reserve balances with Federal Reserve Banks, which exclude required clearing balances and adjustments to compensate for float, plus vault cash used to satisfy reserve requirements. Such vault cash consists of all vault cash held during the lagged computation period by institutions having required reserve balances at Federal Reserve Banks plus the amount of vault cash equal to required reserves during the maintenance period at institutions having no required reserve balances.

[6]Reserve balances with Federal Reserve Banks plus vault cash used to satisfy reserve requirements less required reserve.

[7]Extended credit consists of borrowing at the discount window under the terms and conditions established for the extended credit program to help depository institutions deal with sustained liquidity pressures. Because there is not the same need to repay such borrowing promptly as there is with traditional short-term adjustment credit, the money market impact of extended credit is similar to that of nonborrowed reserves.

Source: Federal Reserve Bulletin.

transactions the funds are normally sold for a period of time, normally in the range of a week to six months. Occasionally, longer-term transactions also occur.

There is no way to measure the size of the term market. "It is," noted one broker, "an elusive number, since a lot of the term deals that are done are done direct. Occasionally, we will see a Japanese bank buy term funds to fund, say, its Singapore branch or to do an arbitrage: buy 1-year funds, sell a [1-year] strip of Euro time deposits and pick up an 03 or an 04."

In recent years, the term market seems to have shrunk for several reasons. Banks, domestic and foreign, that are buyers of term funds now have attractive new opportunities to get medium-term, reserve-free, floating-rate monies. Thus, the term market lacks the allure it once had for them as a source of funds. Prolonged uncertainty over where rates are going is another factor that, in recent times, has driven buyers to stay in overnight funds.

The supply side of the term market has also dried up. Before rate deregulation, thrifts could sell CDs, reinvest the proceeds in term funds, and earn a spread on the arb. After deregulation, a thrift had to pay 10½ for 6-month CD money, and it might get only 9½ on 6-month term funds; so, for a thrift to write a CD and invest in term funds would be a *"Polish arb."*

THE NEXT CHAPTER

The market for Fed funds is one in which *immediately available* funds are lent on an *unsecured* basis. A market closely related to the Fed funds market is the *repo* market, in which immediately available funds are lent on a *secured* basis. We turn to the repo market in the next chapter.

CHAPTER 13

THE REPO AND REVERSE MARKETS

Over the last several decades, the repo market has become one of the biggest sectors in the U.S. money market. This is hardly surprising, given the current market environment: today, there is so much debt to be financed, so many arbs to be done; also, new strategies are constantly being developed in which repo and reverse play a key role; finally, dealers' matched books have become in many shops a significant trading and profit center in which the vehicle traded is term collateral.

There are no regularly collected statistics on volume transacted in the repo market.[1] According to the best estimates of one repo broker: "The *overnight brokered* market in repo runs about 10 billion a day. In terms of what is traded on *a direct basis,* the number could be astronomical; if there is a trillion of debt outstanding, overnight repo is certainly up in the hundreds of billions. Only a small percentage of that is brokered; the lion's share is done direct: every little retail bank is placing repo directly with their dealer or bank.

"A conservative estimate for the term market is 100–150 billion outstanding. When it trades, the *forward market* [described below] runs around 10 billion, but that varies a lot from one *wi* period to the next."

---

[1] See page 630 for *SIPC (Securities Investor Protection Corporation)* Repo Task Force's estimates, released in September 1989, on repo market size.

DEFINITIONS AND SOME JARGON[2]

Repurchase agreements (*repos for short*) are contracts involving the *simultaneous sale and future repurchase* of an asset, most often Treasury securities. Typically, the seller buys back the asset at the same price at which he sold it; also, on buy-back date, the original seller pays the original buyer *interest* on the implicit *loan* created by the transaction. Interest due on a repo at maturity is at the stated *repo rate* for the stated maturity of the repo.

Transactions in the repo market are referred to by various terms: a *sale-repurchase agreement,* a *repo* (or *RP* for short), or a *reverse.* The term *sale-repurchase agreement* accurately describes how the transaction is typically done. First, a deal is struck on the phone between the dealer and his customer. The dealer then sends his customer two separate *confirmations* (*confirms*): the first confirms the *sale* of securities for current settlement; the second confirms the *repurchase* of these same securities for settlement at some later date (Figures 13–1 and 13–2).

Because the term *sale-repurchase agreement* is a mouthful, Street people talk about doing repos and reverses. While the terms *repo and reverse* slip easily off the tongue, they can be confusing because the Street uses them with little consistency. The essential point is this: A repo or a reverse—one *firm's repo is necessarily another's reverse*—is a loan secured by collateral in the form of securities. One side lends money, the other side lends (or *reverses out*) securities. At the risk of adding confusion, we note that the party lending money is sometimes said in Street-speak to be *reversing in* securities.

To help keep all this straight, bear this in mind: when a dealer says he is going "to repo securities," he means that he is going to finance securities he owns *or* securities he has reversed in; in contrast, when an investor says he is going "to do repo," he means he is going to invest in repo, that is, to finance someone else's securities.

---

[2]Much has already been said in this book about repos, reverses, and their uses. This chapter builds on and amplifies this earlier discussion.

FIGURE 13–1

Merrill confirmation to Federated of an overnight repo: *Leg 1*, the *sale* of T notes to a Federated mutual fund

---

```
                                        CONFIRMATION
  Merrill Lynch
  Government Securities Inc.                        PAGE        OF
  One Liberty Plaza 165 Broadway New York New York 10080 (212) 766-3000
                                        TIME OF EXECUTION OF TRANSACTION
                                        WILL BE FURNISHED ON WRITTEN REQUEST

  ┌                          ┐        ┌                              ┐
     TRUST FOR US TREAS OBLIGATION
     ATTN: KATHY LANI
     FEDERATED INVESTORS TOWER            RECEIVE FROM
     PITTSBURGH, PA  15222                MANUFACTURERS HANOVER TRUST

  └                          ┘        └   NOTE011000028               ┘
  AS PRINCIPAL WE CONFIRM THE FOLLOWING TRADE.
  ┌─────────────┬───────────────┐  ┌──────────┐  ┌──────────────┐
  │ TRADE DATE  │ SETTLEMENT DATE│  │ ACCOUNT  │  │ REFERENCE NO.│
  │             │               │  │   NO.    │  │              │
  │  12/09/87   │   12/09/87    │  │ 869-70279│  │ R7343051420  │
  └─────────────┴───────────────┘  └──────────┘  └──────────────┘
                                                  TKT NO. F101
```

```
REPURCHASE AGREEMENT RATE    6.750

         SECURITY RATE          Due
UNITED STATES TREAS NOTES      13 3/4    05/15/1992

PAR   100,000,000.00                 PRIN    $118,000,000.00
CPN/INTEREST      $0.00 INT    $0.00  TOTAL   $118,000,000.00

SUMMARY                 TOTAL PRINCIPAL     $118,000,000.00
                        TOTAL CPN/INT                 $0.00
                        TOTAL INTEREST                $0.00
                        TOTAL MONIES        $118,000,000.00
```

CUSTOMER'S COPY

CODE 5504 REV. 2/84 PRINTED IN U.S.A.

Receive from Manufacturers Hanover Trust tells Federated what clearing bank will be delivering securities to it.

Despite the fact that repos and reverses take the form of sequential sales and repurchases of securities, everyone on the Street agrees that the *economic essence* of the transaction is that it is a *collateralized loan,* not a pair of securities trades. Specifically, on the day the transaction is initiated, securities are sold against money; on the day the transaction is unwound, these flows are reversed—the money and the securities are returned to their original holders with the initial money holder getting something extra in the form of interest for the use of his money during the term of the transaction (Figure 13–3).

FIGURE 13–2

Merrill confirmation to Federated of an overnight repo: *Leg 2,* **the**
repurchase **of T notes from a Federated mutual fund**

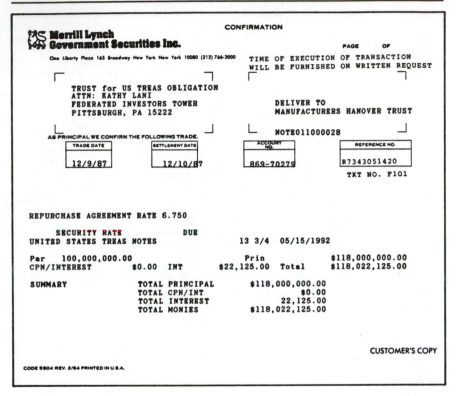

Deliver to Manufacturers Hanover Trust tells Federated to which clearing bank it must
send Merrill's securities.

Interest Due on a Repo

Repos are always quoted in the market in terms of the interest
rate paid—the *repo rate.* This jibes with the interpretation of a
repo (or a reverse) as being a secured loan to the seller of the
securities with the securities "sold" serving as *collateral.*

The repo rate is a straight add-on interest rate calculated on
a 360-day-year basis. So interest due is figured as follows:

FIGURE 13–3
Money and securities flows in a repo: *Leg 1* **can be viewed as a collateralized borrowing or as a "sale" of securities;** *Leg 2* **reverses this transaction and provides for payment of repo interest**

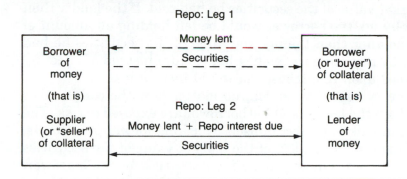

$$\text{Interest due} = \left(\begin{array}{c}\text{Principal} \\ \text{amount}\end{array}\right) \times \left(\begin{array}{c}\text{Repo} \\ \text{rate}\end{array}\right) \times \left(\frac{\text{Days repo is outstanding}}{360}\right)$$

Applying this formula to the example of overnight repo presented in Figures 13–1 and 13–2, we get

$$\$118,000,000 \times 0.0675 \times \frac{1}{360} = \$22,125$$

that is, precisely the dollar amount of *interest due* shown in Figure 13–2; this confirm closes out the one-day transaction initiated by the confirm in Figure 13–1.

CREDIT RISK AND MARGIN

In a repo transaction, the lender is exposed to risk. Interest rates might rise, forcing down the market value of the securities he has taken in; if the borrower then went bankrupt and the repurchase were not executed, the lender might be left holding securities with a market value less than the amount he had lent. Assuming the securities repoed have not been trading above par, the lender could make himself whole by maturing these securities, but if he needed the money he had lent, that might be impossible or it might be expensive because it would force him into other suboptimal decisions.

The borrower in a repo transaction also incurs a risk. Interest rates might fall during the life of the agreement, forcing up the market value of the securities he had sold. If the lender then went belly up, the borrower would be left holding an amount of money smaller than the market value of the securities he had sold. So by retaining the money lent to him instead of effecting the agreed-upon repurchase, he would incur a loss.

In every repo transaction, no matter how the collateral is priced, both the lender and the borrower are exposed to risk. The lender can seek to protect himself by asking for *margin,* that is, by lending less than 100% of the market value of the securities he takes in; but in doing so, he *increases* risk for the borrower. Alternatively, the borrower might seek to reduce his risk by asking for *reverse margin,* that is, by asking the lender to buy his securities at a price above their market value, but that would increase risk for the borrower. No strategy exists to simultaneously reduce risk for both the borrower and the lender.

Margin in Practice

Traditionally on a repo transaction, the lender of money, because it is lending the more liquid asset, receives margin. To provide that margin, securities used as repo collateral are priced at market value minus a *haircut;* the size of the haircut varies depending on the maturity, scarcity value, and price volatility of the underlying collateral, on the term of the repo, and on the creditworthiness of the customer. The standard haircuts prevailing today are given in Table 13–1.

GROWTH OF THE MARKET

Dealers first began to use the repo market to finance their positions shortly after World War II. Later, as large banks began to practice active liability management, they joined the dealers in the repo market, using it to finance not only their dealer positions, but their government portfolios. Over the years, the mar-

TABLE 13–1
Standard haircuts (margin) prevailing in the repo market*

	Length of Repo		
Type of Collateral	One Week	One Month	Three Months
T bills	10 bp	20 bp	75 bp
Governments and agencies			
(notes and bonds)	1/8	1/4	3/4
Mortgage-backed securities	2.0	3.0	5.0

*On governments and agencies, the haircuts all refer to *yield*. The value, as repo collateral, that a lender would assign to a such a security equals the price it would command at a yield equal to the rate at which it's *bid* in the market *minus* the haircut. On mortgage-backed securities, the haircut is *points* deducted from the *dollar price* at which the security is trading; for example, if a mortgage-backed security, trading at 101-26 (100 and 26/32), were repoed for three months, its value as collateral would be 101-26 less 5 points, or 96-26.

ket, which was initially small, grew dramatically. In 1969, the Fed amended Regulation D to make clear that repos done by banks against governments and agencies (banks were already doing them) were borrowings exempt from reserve requirements. The same amendment also specified that repos done by banks against other instruments—CDs, BAs, and loans in particular—were subject to reserve requirements; the amendment thus killed banks' use of the repo market to finance such instruments.

A second factor that contributed to the rapid growth of the repo market was the Treasury's decision in 1974 to shift the bulk of its deposits from TT&L accounts at commercial banks to accounts at the Fed. This shift freed billions of dollars worth of governments and agencies that the banks had been holding as collateral against Treasury deposits for use as collateral in the repo market.

Acceptance by investors of repo as a money market instrument grew in step with the increased use of the market by borrowers. The historical highs to which the Fed pushed interest rates on several occasions beginning in the late 1960s made corporate treasurers acutely aware of the opportunity cost of holding idle cash balances. In response, they became big investors in repo, which offered them a way to invest highly variable amounts of money on a day-to-day basis. By the mid-1970s, most corporations, including many that a few years earlier did not know what repo was, had amended their bylaws to permit them to invest in repo.

State and local governments and their agencies have also become huge investors in repo. Such government bodies are frequently required by law to hold their excess cash in bank deposits or to invest it in governments and agencies. Also, they are typically not permitted to take a capital loss on their investments, which means that they cannot invest in a security that they are unsure they will be able to hold to maturity. Repo collateralized by governments and agencies offers state and local governments—whose regulations permit them to use it instead of outright purchases of governments—a way to invest tax receipts and proceeds of note and bond issues in *any* amount for *any* period. The volume of money going into the repo market from state and local governments can be huge. If New York State sells $3 billion of bonds, all that money is immediately invested in the repo market and stays there until it's needed.

Today, foreign central banks are also big investors in the repo market. Often, they invest in repo by putting their short-term excess dollars in a repo pool run by the FRBNY. However, a number of foreign central banks also do repo through money center banks. Supranational entities, like the World Bank, also supply funds to the repo market.

Currently, one of the biggest classes of investors in repo is money funds, who collectively have the job of keeping several hundred billion of funds invested short term. It isn't uncommon for a single such fund to do on a single day with a single dealer a repo trade for 800MM or more.

Dealer Repos and Reverses

While the Fed collects no marketwide statistics on repo, it's possible to glean an idea of what goes on in the repo and reverse markets from Fed figures on the repos and reverses done by U.S. dealers in government securities. Currently, dealers' total repos and total reverses differ little month to month (part A, Figure 13–4). This reflects the fact that, on a *net* basis, dealers in

FIGURE 13–4
Average daily financing by U.S. Government securities dealers
($ billions)

A. Total repos and reverses

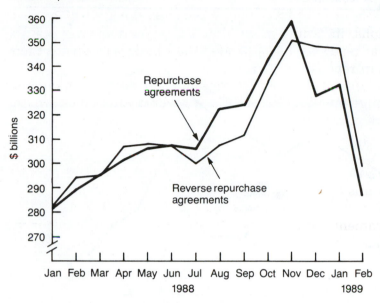

B. Overnight and open repos

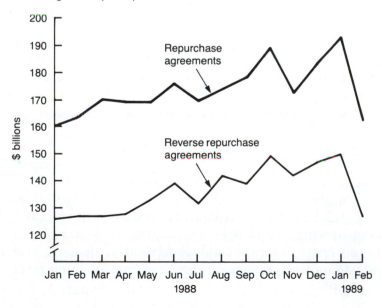

FIGURE 13–4 (concluded)

C. Term repos and reverses

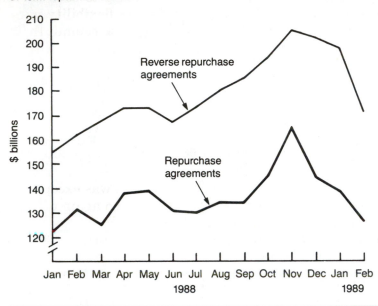

Source: *Federal Reserve Bulletin.*

governments—during the period considered—did not have large, if any, positions to finance; consistently, dealers' large *short* positions in governments roughly equaled their *long* positions in agencies and other money market securities (recall Table 10–1, pp. 434–35).

The large amount of reverses dealers do reflects not only their covering of shorts, but the substantial growth, discussed below, of the matched books they run in repo and reverse. Parts B and C of Figure 13–4 show that dealers tend to run *short* books in repo and reverse: consistently, dealers borrow more money doing overnight and open repos than they lend doing overnight and open reverses; and consistently, dealers lend more money doing term reverses than they borrow doing term repos.

Repo and Market Decisions

The repo market gives investors who are willing to base their investments on market judgments tremendous flexibility with respect to where along the yield curve they want to commit their funds. If the answer is at the very base of the yield curve, they can roll overnight repo indefinitely.

At times doing so can be very attractive. In early 1982, when yields were high and looking as if they might go higher, Fed funds and repo traded in the range of 14 to 15% while short bills were yielding only 12 to 13%. Thus, at that time, a portfolio manager who owned short bills could have picked up 200–300 bp in yield by selling his bills and investing in the same instrument under repo. In 1988, when the yield curve was exceptionally flat, and in early 1989 when it *inverted,* repo again offered an attractive investment to portfolio managers who felt, as many did, uncertain as to where longer-term rates might be headed.

THE OVERNIGHT REPO RATE

The overnight repo rate (Figure 13–5) normally lies slightly below the Fed funds rate for two reasons. First, a repo transaction is in essence a secured loan, whereas the sale of Fed funds is an unsecured loan. Second, many investors—corporations, state and local governments, and others—who can invest in repo cannot sell Fed funds.[3]

An institution that can't sell Fed funds could invest short term by buying securities due to mature in a few months or even a few days. Doing so, however, is usually unattractive. In recent years the yield, even on 3-month bills, has consistently been well below the repo rate (Figure 13–6); and on still shorter bills, the yield discrepancy has been even greater. The reasons are several. First, many investors, including some state and local

---

[3]Such institutions can't sell Fed funds because banks are not permitted under Reg Q to pay interest on overnight money they take domestically from nonbank sources.

FIGURE 13–5
The overnight repo rate tracks the overnight Fed funds rate closely

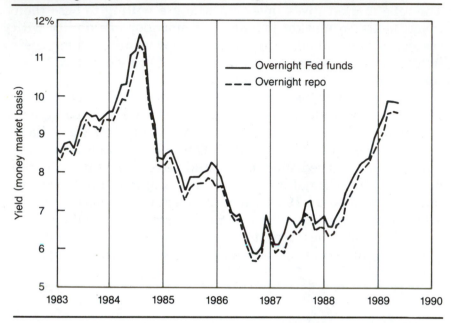

Source: J. P. Morgan Securities, Inc.

government bodies, can't invest in repo; they have to own the securities outright. Second, short bills are often used by dealers as collateral for short positions (holding short bills for collateral exposes a dealer to no significant price risk). Third, many short bills are held by investors who intend to roll them at maturity and who never consider the alternative of selling out early to pick up additional basis points. Fourth, money funds tend to sop up any short paper, including bills, that they can find to keep the average maturity of the securities in their portfolio short. Fifth, foreign central banks invest in bills a lot of the dollars they sop up whenever the dollar sinks below their target rate.

The spread between the Fed funds rate and the repo rate can be anything from several points to just a few basis points. How wide it is depends partly on the supply of collateral available. At times, when the Fed is doing a lot of adding—for exam-

FIGURE 13–6

The overnight repo rate and the 3-month bill rate (money market yield)

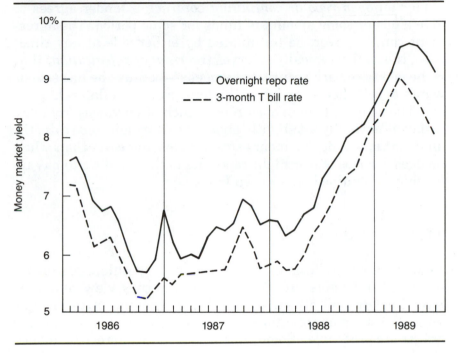

Source: J. P. Morgan Securities, Inc.

ple, to offset a shift in Treasury balances—the supply of collateral on the Street will dry up, and the spread between the repo rate and the funds rate will widen. At other times, when the Treasury has just sold a large amount of new debt that has yet to be fully distributed, dealers will have a lot of collateral, and the spread between the funds rate and the repo rate will narrow.

Most of the borrowing done in the repo market is collateralized by governments and agencies. Dealers, however, also repo other money market instruments, including BAs and commercial paper. The spread between the repo rate on governments and that on other securities can be negligible if there is a shortage of collateral on the Street, but normally this spread is 5 to 10 bp, and it can widen to 15 bp.

OPEN REPO

Under an *open repo* or *continuing contract,* a lender agrees to give a dealer some amount of funds for some period. The agreement can, however, be terminated by either side at any time. Also, the dealer typically reserves the *right of substitution;* that is, he can take back securities he needs—because he has sold or wants to sell them—and give the lender other collateral.

The rate paid on an open repo, which often varies from day to day, is normally set slightly above the overnight repo rate. On an open repo, a dealer incurs smaller clearing costs than when he does a series of overnight repos; he is thus willing to pay up for money obtained on an open basis.

TERM REPO

Dealers enter into term repo agreements to speculate—to create (as noted in Chapter 10) future securities they view as attractive. Dealers and others also do huge amounts of term repo, when the structure of interest rates is such that cash-and-carry trades are profitable.[4] Some large banks use term repo to finance the longer governments in their portfolios to keep their book from being too short. Other large banks, however, rely strictly on overnight repo to finance their portfolios. Said one banker typical of the latter group, "We do mostly overnight repo and feel comfortable with that because the demand placed on us for collateral far exceeds the supply we have. We could repo our government portfolio two or three times over everyday."

In recent years, there has been an extraordinary increase in the amount of funding to dates—tax dates, dividend dates, oil payment dates, and so on—that corporations do, and corporations as a result have become big lenders in the term repo market. Public bodies are another big source of money in the term repo market. For the investor wanting to fund to a specific date, a big attraction of term repo is that he can usually do it in size to

---

[4]For examples see Chapters 15 and 16 on futures.

any date he chooses; this eliminates the need for him to scour the world for short paper maturing on his date.

Many investors, including municipalities and some financial institutions, cannot take a capital loss because of legal or self-imposed restrictions, but they can take an interest loss. Suppose such an investor has money that he thinks will be available for six months but that he might need sooner. He can't invest in 6-month bills because, if he did, he might incur an accounting loss if he sold them. He can, however, take the same or similar securities in on a 6-month reverse repo; that is, invest in 6-month term repo. If three months later the investor finds that he needs his money and the bill market is in the "chutes" (prices are down), he can repo out the collateral he has taken in. In doing so, he may incur a *loss of interest* because the rate on the repo he does to borrow exceeds the rate on the term repo in which he invested (i.e., he may have negative carry on his offsetting repo transactions), *but* he won't incur a capital loss. Often, municipalities can repo securities they have obtained on a reverse but not securities they own outright. So a number of municipalities invest in term repo to get the protection and flexibility described in the example above.

On a term repo, as on an open repo, a borrower of money often would like to be able to substitute one batch of collateral for another. Maybe the borrower is a dealer who's financing inventory for some number of days; if so, he'd like to be able to sell from his inventory; and to do so, he must be able to give the lender of money new collateral for the old collateral he's sold and wants to deliver out. For a slightly sweeter repo rate, a number of investors will grant a dealer *the right of substitution.* "Instead of 6.60, we might," noted one big dealer, "pay 6.62 to get the right of substitution. Some accounts will give us that right, others won't."

THE YIELD CURVE IN REPO

In the repo market, as in other markets, the yield curve normally slopes upward, but at the very short end of the market, the curve frequently inverts; in particular, the overnight rate is often a few basis points higher than the rate on 1- or 2-week repo. The reason is that short-period repo competes with commercial paper for investors' dollars, while the overnight repo rate relates to the frequently higher dealer loan rate, which in turn keys off the Fed funds rate. Precisely what relationships exist among repo rates of differing maturities depend on the availability of financing to dealers and on the amount of collateral they have to finance.

BROKERING OF REPO

It used to be that little brokering of *stock* repo was done; that is, the repo normally done by dealers and banks to finance their positions and portfolios. Banks and dealers have a customer base with which they can do such transactions directly and efficiently. Also they view repo as part of their customer line—one more thing they can show customers.

This has changed a great deal over the past decade. Today, dealers are using repo much more actively and not just as a financing tool. This latter branch of the market is known as the *term-specials* market; it involves the trading of specific issues on repo, discussed below. Half of the multibillion-dollar matched books (discussed below) that most dealers run are necessarily repo transactions. Dealers can do that volume of trading efficiently only by relying on brokers for a lot of interdealer trading.

Noting the change in the way repo is used by dealers today, one broker, whose volume is 20% greater than what it was only two years ago, noted, "Dealers now view the repo market just like any other market. Their matched-book traders will give you bids against securities and rates at which they will offer securities based on their expectation of rates. Today, our market is as actively traded as other sectors of the money market."

Currently, the top brokers of repo and reverse are RMJ, Eurobrokers, and Fulton Prebon. Garvin and FBI are also active in the business.

THE FORWARD MARKET IN REPO

There used to be no forward market in either overnight repo or term repo. Occasionally, however, a dealer or a bank would negotiate a forward repo deal with, for example, a government body that knew money would be coming in on a tax date.

Today, the situation has changed. Dealers have for years traded a coming Treasury issue on a wi basis. More recently, dealers have started trading a forward repo rate that settles the day a new Treasury issue that's been trading wi settles. Thus, on each Treasury issue, dealers now trade both their position and their financing rate as of the settlement date. For wi issues, forward trading of repo starts on the auction, sometimes the announcement, date and ends on the settlement date. Forward trading of repo, once small and occasional, is now huge and occurs for every Treasury issue that trades wi.

REPOS IN FED OPEN MARKET OPERATIONS

As noted in Chapter 9, the Fed is a significant and frequent player in the repo market. In its open market operations, the Fed uses *outright purchases* of government and agency securities to make permanent additions to bank reserves. Over the last decade, the Fed has added roughly $13 billion a year to bank reserves through increases in its portfolio. To do so, the Fed need not do outrights often, and it doesn't. It's in the market no more than half a dozen times a year.

Repos

Repos are by far the most frequent transaction the Fed does in connection with open market operations. Doing repos is the only way that the Fed can offset temporary drains on bank reserves; these occur frequently, but according to no set pattern. Thus, the Fed, during a given reserve period, may be in the market day after day doing repos, or it may be out of the market for days.

MSPs[5]

When the Fed wants to drain reserves temporarily, it can do so by doing MSPs with the Street. Because the Fed must secularly raise bank reserves, it finds that the occasions on which it wants to do MSPs with the Street are far fewer than the occasions on which it wants to do repos with the Street.

Today, the Fed does repos and reverses only against government and agency collateral.

THE REVERSE MARKET

Many smaller banks that won't trade their portfolios will occasionally reverse out securities for various reasons: because repo money is cheaper than buying Fed funds, because—in the case of term repo—they expect the funds rate to rise and they need cash, or because they see an attractive opportunity to arbitrage.

S&Ls are also active in the reverse market. S&Ls will put securities out on repo when they are shown an opportunity to reinvest the funds they obtain at a higher yield in some other instrument—term Fed funds, BAs, or Euros. The big West Coast S&Ls are most active in the arbitrage game. They have large portfolios and big lines to New York banks. So, if the rates are there, they will do trades in size.

When the yield curve is flat, banks and S&Ls may reverse out securities as part of an arbitrage for as little as a ³⁄₁₆ spread, but when the yield curve is steep, they are likely to demand ½. *Term reverses,* which are typically done for a period ranging from one to six months, may or may not permit substitution. An *open reverse* is normally initiated by a dealer to cover a short, and there is no right of substitution; the closing of such a reverse

---

[5]MSPs (matched sale purchases) are the Fed's version of reverses. See section below, "Fed Use of Repos and Reverses Today."

is determined by the borrower of securities: either he buys the securities he's short at a profit or he says, "I've made a mistake," and closes out his short at a loss.

For a bank or S&L that has securities a dealer wants, an alternative to reversing out these securities would be to do a straight loan—give the dealer the securities, take in other securities as collateral, and pick up a ½% borrowing fee. This second alternative is less attractive if the institution wants cash, which it may if it anticipates a rise in interest rates.

Most states and municipalities are strict investors of cash. They will do repos but not reverses. There are some municipalities that will lend out securities in their portfolios; the majority, however, either don't have the right to do so or don't understand the transaction.

Risk and Liquidity

There is no liquidity in a term repo; it is not an asset that can be sold, and the underlying agreement cannot be broken. Thus, one might argue, as some have, that banks and S&Ls that put securities in their liquidity portfolios out on term repo are impinging on their liquidity. In all probability, however, they are not. Most of the time they are reversing out securities that they would in almost no circumstance consider selling. Also, if worse comes to worse, they can raise cash by selling or repoing the asset they have acquired as the other leg of the arbitrage.

One real risk in this game is that an unsophisticated portfolio manager might, when the yield curve is steep, buy long bonds as a basis for arbitraging and not realize how great a price risk he's assuming. As one dealer noted, "Buying the 9¼s of 98 at a book yield of 10 and repoing them at 7½ can look attractive to a small investor when the idea is presented to him. But should interest rates rise, he may get burned on this strategy because he loses more money selling these bonds than he has earned arbitraging against them." Note that risk arises here because the securities are purchased as part of an arbitrage rather than as a long-term investment.

Brokering of Reverses

Reverses—other than those done by dealers as part of their matched book—are often proposed to an institution by a broker who, because his firm brokers a range of money market instruments, is in a good position to point out attractive arbitrage opportunities—to provide "one-stop shopping." A broker of such reverses is a salesman as opposed to someone who is just fast on the phone; he has to convince the customer to take in money and then to put it out elsewhere.

"We do not," commented one such broker, "just go in and say: 'Hi, 30, 60, 90 days at 30, 45 and 55. Do you want to do $25MM?' We have to show people a reason to do a reverse. To be a good reverse broker you have to know as many alternative uses as possible for money, to have a working knowledge of and a feel for more areas than in any other money market job.

"You do not just walk in and do a trade with a guy, and you do not take no for an answer. There is some rate at which a trade will go. To put together a trade on which you make money takes time and work. You have to know what your customer can do in terms of investments and what the lender is going to demand in terms of margin. Every trade that is agreed upon with respect to amount and rate is done subject to *pricing*.[6] Different accounts demand different amounts of margin. Sometimes we can't get a trade off because the two sides are half a point away on the pricing. If we get in a bind on pricing, we just start all over again."

In the brokers' market for repo and in the market in general, trades are agreed upon for round-lot sums, for example, $25MM. Then the precise amount of the loan is calculated, taking into account pricing and the way the agreement is set up. Thus, on a $25MM trade, the dollars lent might be more or less than $25MM.

---

[6]*Pricing* refers here to the value that will be assigned to the securities reversed out. Margin is created for the lender in a reverse transaction by pricing the securities below market value plus accrued interest.

Reverses to Maturity

As noted in Chapter 6, some bank portfolio managers are loath to sell high-coupon securities that are trading at a premium and recommit their funds to another instrument because, if they sell these securities, they will reduce the interest income they are booking. The repo market gives the portfolio managers a way to get around this predicament.

One dealer gave an illustration, "Say a bank owns the 11½s of Oct '90, which have nine months to run. If the portfolio manager sells them, he won't be able to get a comparable coupon, so he refuses to sell. What he can do, however, is to put these securities out on repo until maturity, book the interest income on them, and use the cash he has generated to invest in some other attractive instrument. That's a common transaction now. A couple of years ago, no one had heard of it."

THE SPECIFIC ISSUES MARKET

Dealers go short for various reasons: as a speculation, to hedge a long position in a similar security, or to reduce their position so that they can make a big bid in a coming Treasury auction. The theory behind going into an auction short is that the new issue will, until it's distributed, yield more than outstanding issues; that, however, doesn't always occur when the Treasury is paying down its debt as it sometimes does on a seasonal basis. Whatever his motivation may be, a dealer who shorts a given issue has to obtain those securities somehow to make delivery. Normally, he does so by reversing them in rather than borrowing them.[7] Some widely placed issues are easy to find. Others he must hunt up on his own or with the help of a firm that brokers reverses.

---

[7]The economics of reversing in securities are discussed below.

The Borrowers

The market for reverses to cover shorts is often referred to as the *specific issues* market because dealers shop in it for specific issues. Typically, a dealer won't find another dealer who has the particular issue he needs and who also wants to finance it for some period. So dealers are only a minor supplier of collateral to the specific issues market. There is also a second reason for this. Said one dealer, "I deal in specific issues only for myself. I will give them to some of my dealer friends but only because they will do the same for me. I try not to support the market for specific issues because I know that, if I give a guy $50MM year bills, he is shorting them and that is going to drive the market down. So all I am doing is hurting myself. If I can get an issue that is likely to be shorted in the future, I will hold it for myself."

The major suppliers of securities to (borrowers of money in) the specific issues and the general reverse markets are banks. This accounts for the fact that the top banks in the country, and in particular the top New York and Chicago banks, all borrow substantial sums from the dealers. Because banks reverse out, especially via their trust or custody departments, so many securities to dealers, their net loans to dealers are much smaller than their total dealer loans.

S&Ls and certain other financial institutions are also large suppliers of collateral in the specific issues market. So too are a few municipalities and a few corporate portfolios. Reverses are, as noted, not well understood except by those who do them, so it isn't surprising that one corporate portfolio manager commented, "I reverse out securities to dealers, but I *never* refer to it around the company as 'lending out' our valuable securities."

Reverses in the specific issues market usually have a term ranging from a week to a month. Activity in this market is greatest during a bear market because dealers increase their shorts in a declining market.

The Reverse Rate

When a dealer lends out money as part of a transaction in which he is reversing in securities to cover a short, the rate he gets on his money is often significantly *less than* the going rate for financing general collateral with repo. "The rate on a reverse depends," noted one dealer, "on the availability of the securities taken in. In the reverse market, there are no standard rate relationships; it's entirely a question of demand and supply. Today, funds traded at 8⅝ to 9—a wide band indicating that the Fed is probably readying a rise in the discount rate. The current 2-year note, the 8⅞s of Nov 90, was *hot,* definitely a special: the reverse rate on it ranged from 2 down to ¾. A bank that had that issue, reversed it out at 2, and invested the proceeds by selling Fed funds at 8⅝, made 6⅝ on that arb.

"That's important for a guy who speculates on what might become a hot issue. Thrifts do that. So too do the Japanese—not the dealers trading—but the portfolio side; in selecting an issue, they consider—besides coupon, maturity, and liquidity—whether the issue might become hot."

The Brokers

Dealers who want to reverse in a specific issue will often turn to a broker of reverses. The brokers make it their business to know where various special issues are and at what rate they might be available. A repo broker acts in effect as a commission salesman for the dealers; if he finds bonds, he earns a commission or a spread; if he does not, he is paid nothing for his trouble.

The brokers try not to take bonds from one dealer and give them to another. The dealers talk to each other and could arrange trades of this sort themselves. As a rule, the brokers will try to pull specific issues out of regional banks, S&Ls, and other smaller portfolios. In doing so, they are using their own special knowledge and thus providing a real service to the dealers.

When they have arranged a trade, some brokers of repo will give up names to the institutions on both sides of the trade, charge both sides a commission, and leave it to them to clear the trade. Other brokers act as a principal in transactions they broker, taking securities in on one side and lending out money on the other. In doing so, a broker is acting as a credit intermediary, and he incurs risk on both sides of the transaction. Brokers who act as principals in repo and reverse trades are, like all participants in the repo market, extremely careful to deal only with institutions whose credit they know to be unimpeachable.

When a broker acts as a principal in a reverse transaction, he works for whatever spread he can get; normally it ranges from an 01 to ⅛, with the average being 1/16. If, however, the broker finds a firm that wants to repo stock collateral and another that wants to borrow the same collateral as a special, he might be able to earn ¼.

BORROWING VERSUS REVERSING IN SECURITIES

We have said that a dealer who is short governments can either reverse them in or borrow them. There are pros and cons to each procedure.

To begin, we make a simple and *very* helpful observation: *in a securities lending, the investor swaps collateral for collateral; in a reverse, he swaps collateral for money.*

Reversing in Securities

Generally, a dealer will reverse in securities on an *open* basis, which means that the transaction can be terminated at the request of either party; and, if the party wanting to terminate the transaction calls before 10 A.M., the securities become returnable the same day. Most securities lending programs operate this way, but some have requirements for next-day termination.

Sometimes, a dealer will do a *term* reverse: take an issue that he thinks—hopes—will become hot and tie it up on term for at least a week. Often, the trader who does this is speculating that the issue will become hot, be shorted by traders, and therefore become *tight* in supply; if this occurs, the issue becomes what is known as a *special:* an issue that is in such demand that it can be reversed out (used to borrow money) at a rate below— perhaps full points below—the repo rate. The trader who wins on such a speculation ends up lending money, when he reverses in securities, at a rate well above the rate at which he borrows money when he subsequently reverses out those same securities. In other words, he ends up earning a positive spread on a two-legged arbitrage.

Borrowing Securities

When a dealer borrows securities, it is often from a very conservative portfolio that wants full protection from risk. The standard arrangement is that the dealer borrowing, say, $10MM of Treasuries gives the lender of securities $10.2MM of other securities as collateral for his borrowing. He also pays the lender of securities a fee of 50 bp.

A special aspect of a borrowing of securities is that the margin resembles that on a repo, but it goes to the lender not of money, but of securities. The reason that the borrower of securities ends up becoming the giver of margin is that the transaction is driven by his need to borrow securities. A dealer, if he wants to have a viable program for borrowing to cover shorts, must be able to go to an institution holding securities and say, "Look, if you will lend me your bonds, I will make that an extremely safe and attractive transaction for you. I will pay you a fee of 50 bp so that you don't have to worry about arbitrage, market conditions, reinvestment, timing, moving monies, and so forth. Also, I will give you protection in the form of collateral equal to 102% of the value of the bonds you lend me; and I will maintain that 102% level of collateralization over the life of the transaction."

Which to Do and Why

Some years ago, the market swung in favor of reverse repos over borrowing securities. The primary advantage of a reverse repo over a borrowing of securities is that a reverse is operationally simpler: A reverse requires only *one* delivery of securities, whereas a borrowing requires *two* deliveries. Just the same, both types of transactions commonly occur depending on the particular circumstances under which a deal is struck.

Normally, an investor dealing directly with a dealer won't want to go to the bother and cost of doing a reverse unless he can pick up at least 50 bp on the deal. Often, an investor holding securities has an arbitrage lined up where he expects to get at least a 50-bp spread between the rate at which he borrows money from the dealer and the rate at which he can invest that money. Such an investor will want to reverse out, rather than lend, securities to a dealer. In the alternative case, the investor says, "Give me collateral, not money, and I'll take my 50 bp as a fee." Some investors won't do reverses because they lack reinvestment capabilities and don't, therefore, want cash.

Some investors are set up both to reverse out and to lend securities. They will go the reverse route if the spread on the arb is more than 50 bp. If it is not, they will go the securities-lending route.

A dealer wanting to cover his shorts must be prepared to go both ways, to reverse in securities or to borrow them. How a given deal is struck involves both an investor, who holds securities, and a dealer, who wants securities, responding to relative rates and to availability in deciding what they want to do.

Since a lot of borrowing of securities by dealers is done to prevent "fails to receive" from creating "fails to deliver," a lot of dealers borrow securities from other dealers 10 minutes before the close of the Fed wire or during the *reversal period* (at the end of the day, banks are given a half-hour period to DK any incorrect deliveries that may have been made to them).

Dealers caught in a pinch can also reverse in securities from the Fed.

MATCHED BOOK

The term *matched book* describes offsetting positions in repos and reverses that a dealer creates by reversing in securities and simultaneously "hanging them out" on the other side: by matching his *reverses-in* of securities with *repos-out* of the identical securities. Part of the impetus for the development by big dealers of huge matched books came from the failure of Financial Corp.; this failure made investors wary of engaging in a repo transaction with a firm whose name and credit were not well known to them. Firms that subsequently experienced some difficulty in borrowing directly from retail in their own name began to borrow from big dealers.

Fed Statistics on Dealers Repos and Reverses

Today, the running of matched books has become a big business, one that accounts for many billions of the assets and liabilities on the books of every major dealer. While no statistics are collected on matched book per se—a feat that would be difficult, since different dealers tot up different things in measuring their matched books—Fed statistics on dealer repos and reverses are revealing (recall Figure 13–4). These statistics show that the reporting dealers were, on an average day in February 1988, borrowing in the repo market $290 billion, while at the same time, they were lending in the reverse market $300 billion.

Those big and nearly identical numbers reflect two things. First, dealers were running huge matched books. Second, in February 1989, dealers had a *net* short position of $31.7 billion in governments that was largely offset by two *net* long positions that they also held: $30.1 billion in agencies and $14.8 in CDs, BAs, and commercial paper.

Functions of Matched Book

Strictly speaking, matched book refers to a dealer's lending and borrowing against identical securities. In practice, however, dealers tend to regard a wider range of transactions as part of their matched book. Also, dealers have learned to *mismatch* their *matched* books: to mismatch asset and liability maturities in their books in order to turn those books into a play on the direction of interest rates. The upshot is that a dealer's repo desk may regard its "matched-book" responsibilities as comprising as many as five distinct things.

Financing the Dealer's Position
Typically, a dealer's repo desk is first responsible for financing as much of the dealer's long position, normal inventory plus trading positions, as possible. For dealers, repo is the cheapest money around; the overnight repo rate on government collateral is normally a spread *below* the Fed funds rate, whereas the dealer loan rate at New York clearing banks is a spread *above* the funds rate (recall Figure 13–5). Most big dealers work the

repo market hard, financing there every bit of inventory they can. A good dealer will finance at this clearing bank at its posted dealer loan rate only odds and ends that cannot, often because of transaction costs, be economically repoed.

Sometimes a trader will borrow (or reverse in) securities not because he is short those securities, but because he thinks he might want to short those securities in the future as the market breaks; if he does this, he will cover his cost of borrowing (recoup the money he has lent) by relending (repoing) the securities he has taken in until he decides to short them. Running a matched book gives a dealer tremendous flexibility.

Covering Shorts

A second responsibility of a dealer's repo or matched-book desk is to cover the dealer's shorts by reversing in securities that the dealer then uses to make good delivery of securities that he has sold, but does not own. When a dealer does a reverse to cover a short, his obvious objective is to obtain control over a specific amount of specific collateral.

A reverse to cover a short contrasts sharply with most repos. Normally, control over collateral is not a key element in a repo trade; the lender of money demands collateral only to limit his credit risk, and any concern he has over which collateral he gets, bills or 30-year bonds, exists only because of a credit-risk concern.

Acting as a Financial Intermediary

When dealers moved from using repos simply to finance their positions to using repos to run matched books, they took a giant step: they diversified in a big way into a new-to-them business, financial intermediation. A *financial intermediary* is an institution that (1) solicits funds from funds-surplus units in exchange for claims against itself and (2) passes on those funds to funds-deficit units in exchange for claims against the latter. Banks, S&Ls, credit unions, life insurance companies, mutual funds, and other financial institutions are all financial intermediaries; so too is a dealer to the extent that he does matched book.

The matched part of matched book is taking in collateral (any collateral will do), hanging out that collateral on the other side, and "taking the middle." Borrowing funds at one rate and relending them at a *higher* rate to earn a spread—that's what dealers running matched books do—is pure and simple, for-profit financial intermediation.

Primary dealers include among their ranks firms such as Discount, Sali, Goldman, and Merrill, who can borrow with ease many billions of dollars apiece in the national repo market. The big lenders in the repo market know the names and the credits of these dealers; and they are happy to deal with and make secured loans to them. The same is not true for many other would-be borrowers in the repo market: small dealers, small banks, and S&Ls.

The aversion of short-term portfolio managers to credit risk combined with the desire of many smaller institutions to borrow in the repo market created the opportunity for major dealers to become, as part of their matched-book operations, credit inter-mediaries.

Actually, large dealers assume little credit risk in lending, in part, to smaller borrowers. These dealers are protected not only by their credit departments, but, more important, by the collateral they require borrowers to deliver to them and by their practice of taking and monitoring margin.

Capturing the middle is not the only benefit a big dealer gets from providing repo money (via reverses) to smaller institutions. Large dealers get additional business, trading and retail, from the smaller dealers and financial institutions to whom they provide credit.

Matched Book as a Facilitation Device

Over the years, as their matched books made dealers in effect a source of credit, one function of their matched books became to facilitate sales of securities by providing credit to would-be buyers. Here's an example. An S&L wants to bolster its earnings by adding to them some positive carry. So it buys high-yield, mortgage-backed securities, reverses them back to the selling dealer, and earns the difference between the yield on them and the reverse rate. This can be dangerous, because the S&L is assuming a lot of price risk to earn just a little carry.

Generating Borrowed Funds

It used to be that dealers running a matched book regularly did trades in which they borrowed on the repo side half a point or more than they lent on the reverse side. A well-run matched book could and did generate borrowed funds for the firm that ran it. Today, however, that has changed. Because of the well-publicized losses that investors in repo have sustained in recent years, big investors in repo often demand, even when they are dealing with highly creditworthy dealers, more margin than they used to. Also, dealers realize that, in some cases at least, the more margin they give a customer, the lower the repo rate the latter will require.

Profit on a "Matched" Matched Book

If a dealer repos out securities for the same period that he reverses them in (for example, hangs out on repo for 30 days any collateral he reverses in for 30 days), he is running a "matched" matched book: he has no mismatch of maturities. Spreads on matched-maturity repos and reverses are narrow, but a dealer doing such trades can make money by doing a large volume of them. Also, he can live with a small spread because he incurs no interest-rate risk and only minimal credit risk.

TRADING COLLATERAL—MISMATCHING THE BOOK

Money market dealers have long used standard, cash-market instruments to establish bets of various sorts. They have gone long money market instruments when they were bullish; used bills and BAs to establish tails; put on arbs in the government market; and so on. Matched book gave them yet another game to play, "trading collateral" of different maturities—mismatching their books in bankers' parlance.

To understand what's involved, one must visualize precisely what it means for a dealer to run a book in repo. Part A of Figure 13–7 shows the flows that occur when a dealer reverses in securities on one side and repos them out on the other. As we've said,

FIGURE 13–7
Running a book in repo and reverse

A. Reversing in securities and repoing these securities creates a new asset and a new liability on a dealer's book

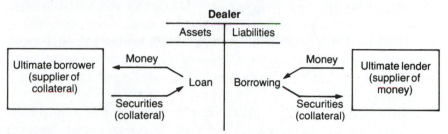

B. The dealer's book in repo and reverse

Dealer

Assets	Liabilities
Collateralized *loans* of varying maturities	Collateralized *borrowings* of varying maturities

the essence of a repo transaction is *not* that securities are being sold, but that *secured loans* and *borrowings* are being made. If the securities "sold" are thought of simply as *collateral,* it becomes clear that, when a dealer takes in securities, he is making a *loan* that is an *asset* to him; *and* when he repos these same securities, he is creating a *borrowing* that is a *liability* to him. Thus, a dealer's book in repo and reverse consists of a collection of collateralized loans and borrowings (part B of Figure 13–7). All of these loans (assets) and borrowings (liabilities) are, moreover, *fixed in term* and *fixed in rate.*

The real money to be made in running a "matched book" comes from *mismatching* the book with respect to maturity. By adjusting the maturity of the loans and borrowings in his matched book, a dealer can *contrive* bets on future interest rates that expose him to pure *interest-rate risk.*

For example, a bullish dealer, anticipating a fall in rates, might reverse in the 2-year note for 60 days and do a 30-day repo against that position. If his interest-rate forecast proves correct, the 30-day financing rate will be lower 30 days hence, and he'll make money. The dealer in this instance does not have market risk because he does not own the 2-year note; instead, he has interest-rate risk which derives from a possible rise, during the initial 30-day financing period, not in the yield to maturity of the 2-year note, but in the 30-day financing rate. On a matched-book trade, the interest-rate risk created is only occasionally, and then only by accident, close to—it's *never* identical with—the market risk associated with holding the underlying collateral.

In this example, the bullish dealer is taking in *long collateral* relative to the repos he puts on. Having long collateral differs from having long securities in several ways. A long position in Treasuries can be sold at any time, whereas a long position in collateral can't. Also, being long Treasuries creates market risk specific to the securities held.

The flip side to having long collateral is to have *short* collateral, reverses that are short in maturity relative to one's repos. For example, a bearish dealer might reverse in securities for 30 days and do a 60-day repo *with a right of sub;* in this case, the dealer's risk is that 30 days from now, when he must again reverse in 30-day collateral to complete his trade (when he must substitute new collateral for "maturing" collateral), he'll find that the 30-day reverse rate, which he's going to earn on the tail of his trade, has fallen, not *risen.*

The position in money market instruments equivalent to having long collateral would be a *forward short* created by a *forward short sale* of securities. Most money market paper, such as BAs, is heterogeneous; consequently, the only money market instrument a bearish trader can short is bills. An advantage of using a matched book to create bearish bets is that a dealer can create such a bet using any money market instrument as his underlying security in the trade.

Profit in Trading a Mismatched Book

Training a *mismatched* book in repo and reverse is a trickier game to understand and to play than is trading bills, CDs, or BAs. Also, the matched-book trader has the advantage, which a

CD or BA trader does not, of being able to short the market when he is bearish by lending money short term and taking in collateral for a longer term. For both of the above reasons, the profits to be gleaned from running a mismatched book are high when a trader is good at the game. Noted one such trader, "In every place I have worked, I have traded matched book like any other money market security, and my book has always been the most profitable individual item for the firm except for trading Ginnie Maes."

Growth in Matched Book

The figures in Table 13–2 on dealer's positions, repos, and reverses are revealing. The small positive to net short positions that dealers take in Treasuries, together with the modest positions they take in agencies and in money market paper, contrast sharply with the huge amounts of repo and reverse, term and overnight, that they do. Dealers' matched books are big and growing.

One broker of repo and reverse attributed this growth to several factors: "First, screen brokering was introduced, and the PSA standardized across brokers the rules and regs of screen brokering. Second, whereas credit lines used to be very loose,

TABLE 13–2

U.S. Government securities dealers Positions and Financing (averages of daily figures, in billions of dollars)

				1987						
Item	1984	1985	1986	Apr.	May	June	July	Aug.	Sept.	Oct.
					Positions					
Net immediate										
1 U.S. Treasury securities	5.4	7.4	13.1	−7.0	−13.5	−8.0	−8.9	−10.9	−23.3	−15.4
2 Bills	5.5	10.0	12.7	−.8	−5.9	2.3	5.0	5.6	2.40	7.3
3 Other within 1 year	.06	1.0	3.7	3.1	3.5	2.1	1.3	.5	−.76	−.6
4 1–5 years	2.2	5.1	9.3	2.5	1.1	.4	−2.3	−6.0	−10.1	−4.9
5 5–10 years	−1.1	−6.2	−9.5	−5.9	−7.6	−7.5	−7.0	−5.7	−8.1	−8.7
6 Over 10 years	−1.2	−2.7	−3.2	−5.8	−4.5	−5.2	−5.8	−5.0	−6.7	−8.4
7 Federal agency securities	15.3	22.9	33.1	32.9	32.8	31.9	33.2	33.3	33.7	34.0
8 Certificates of deposit	7.4	9.2	10.6	8.5	9.0	8.6	7.4	7.9	8.0	7.5
9 Bankers' acceptances	3.9	4.6	5.5	3.7	3.7	3.8	3.2	3.4	3.0	2.9
10 Commercial paper	3.8	5.6	8.1	6.3	6.6	7.2	6.5	5.8	6.4	7.4
Futures positions										
11 Treasury bills	−4.5	−7.3	−18.1	−5.0	1.8	−.6	.9	−2.0	−.2	2.5
12 Treasury coupons	1.8	4.5	3.5	3.9	2.6	3.2	6.2	6.3	7.3	8.8
13 Federal agency securities	.2	−.7	−.2	−.095	−.098	−.1	−.1	−.95	−.09	−.1

Source: *Federal Reserve Bulletin.*

credit has become probably the number one consideration; that development made repo a real trading vehicle, and matched books expanded after 1986 [the year regulation of dealers in governments was, as noted below, introduced]."

FED USE OF REPOS AND REVERSES TODAY

From insignificant beginnings, repos and reverses have grown in the post–World War II period, to be a key part of Fed open market operations.

The Tools of Open Market Operations

Whenever it buys securities or does repos, the Fed adds to bank reserves and that is so regardless of who its counterparty in the trade is. Conversely, whenever the Fed sells securities or does reverses, it drains bank reserves.

The New York Open Market Desk

The Federal Open Market Committee (FOMC) in Washington sets, at its eight meetings per year, the targets to be pursued by the Fed in its open market policy. Money supply is to grow within a specified percentage band; Fed funds are to trade at such and such a rate. The FOMC's directive is today carried out by the open market desk of the New York Fed.

Over time, the Fed has accumulated a portfolio of over $240 billion of government and federal agency securities through outright purchases of securities designed to create permanent bank reserves. The Fed at the end of January 1989 also had on its books 4.7 billion of repos it had done to create temporary bank reserves.

Influencing Bank Reserves

In implementing the FOMC's directive, the desk has two jobs. First, as the economy grows over time, a secular increase in bank reserves is required to prevent upward pressure on interest rates and to permit adequate growth of money supply. One job of the desk is thus to add slowly to the permanent supply of reserves available to banks. Doing that job alone doesn't require that the Fed be in the market often.

However, bank reserves are influenced not only by the Fed's actions, but by various *operating factors* such as the size of Treasury balances at the Fed, the amount of currency in circulation, Federal Reserve float, and the size of foreign central bank balances at the Fed. These operating factors constantly fluctuate by sizable sums, so if the Fed did nothing to offset them, the amount of reserves available to banks would also fluctuate, often unpredictably. To prevent this, the Fed tries to offset fluctuations in the operating factors.

An increase in certain operating factors (e.g., Treasury balances at the Fed, currency in circulation) *drains* bank reserves, whereas an increase in other of these factors (e.g., float) *adds to* bank reserves. Thus, to offset the impact on bank reserves of a rise in Treasury balances, the Fed might do billions of repos. Conversely, to offset the impact on bank reserves of a rise in float or of a seasonal decline in currency in circulation, the Fed might do reverses.

The Advantages of Doing Repos and Reverses

To offset fluctuations in operating factors, the Fed needs to take temporary, tactical actions. We emphasize "temporary," because most changes in operating factors that affect bank reserves are short-lived. It snows; planes do not fly; checks do not move and clear; and float rises. The weather improves, and float falls.

In theory, the Fed could offset the impact on bank reserves of all short-term changes in the operating factors by doing *outright* purchases and sales of Treasury bills or coupons. The Fed, however, does not do this; instead, to make temporary adjustments in bank reserves, it uses repos and what it calls *matched/ sale purchases (MSPs)*; the latter transactions resemble reverses. Repos and MSPs have proved to be much more versatile tools than outright trades for the Fed to use for temporarily adjusting bank reserves.

The Beginning: Matched-Sale/Purchase Transactions

The Fed has been doing repos since the 1920s. In contrast, it devised MSPs only in the late 1960s. Someone on the desk described the Fed's first matched sale/purchase as follows: "The Fed did its first MSP because it anticipated an airline strike. A strike would cause bank reserves to rise, since checks, to be delivered by air, would not move and consequently would not clear. We tried to devise a transaction that would permit us to drain reserves on a temporary basis. We could not do what the market called a reverse repo because it looked too much like a borrowing. We had to do an outright sale of securities we owned. So we came up with MSPs, which we book as a sale of securities out of our portfolio."

Fed MSPs resemble, but are not identical to, Street reverses.

A Repo Go-Around

When the Fed does a go-around for repos, it asks the dealers to bid a repo rate; to say, "We bid to do XMM of repo with you at rate Y." Dealers, besides bidding for financing for their own positions, may also pass along to the Fed bids of their customers for repo money. Once the Fed has the dealers' bids, it "hits," starting with the highest bid, however many bids it must to do the total of repos it wants to do. The lowest bid rate that the Fed accepts is known as the *stop-out rate*.

An MSP Go-Around

When the Fed does a go-around for MSPs, it offers to sell to dealers one or several bill issues at the rates at which these issues are trading in the market. It then asks the dealers to offer a rate at which they will resell these bills to the Fed. The Fed expects the dealers to set the buy-back (repurchase) rates they offer so that they earn some reverse rate on the money they lend to the Fed. In doing MSPs, the Fed hits those bids that give it the lowest implied reverse rate. Remember, the Fed in this transaction is borrowing from the dealers.

MSPs versus Street Reverses

The substance of Fed MSPs is the same as that of Street reverses. However, the mechanics of the trades differ. Normally, dealers do reverses at a reverse rate they quote to customers. In contrast, the Fed does MSPs at the rate implied by those dealer bids of buy-back rates that it accepts.

MSPs, unlike repos done by the Fed, are not subject to withdrawal since they are literally outright sales from the Fed's portfolio matched by specified *forward* purchases to be added to that portfolio.

Characteristics of Fed Repos

Term of Fed Repos
In practice, the Fed rarely does repos with a term of over seven days. Most often, it does overnight repos; but over a weekend, it may do 3- or 4-day repos. The reason that the Fed does such short repos, and short MSPs as well, is that short repos and MSPs are the most flexible tools the Fed can use to deal with a highly variable and often difficult-to-forecast situation, namely, the ever-changing level of bank reserves.

When it does multiday repos, the Fed will often do more than it really needs to because it anticipates that, before the repos mature, dealers will withdraw some of the collateral they delivered to the Fed at the start of the repo.

Margin
The Fed always takes margin when it does repos. It won't publicly state how much except to say that it takes 2½ to 3 points on longer issues. The Street thinks that the margins the Fed takes are "biggies."

The Fed reprices each day the collateral dealers give it when it does repos with them. The reason that the Fed takes big margins is that it wants sufficient margin on repos so that it will not be required by any likely rise in market rates to call for additional margin. Apparently the Fed succeeds; it has never happened, in the memory of people currently at the desk, that the Fed had to call for additional margin.

Right of Substitution

When it does a repo for several days, the Fed permits the dealers to substitute collateral on the first day of the repo. The Fed realizes that the dealers may sell, unexpectedly, securities that they had said they would deliver to it, and the Fed wants to ensure that it does, regardless of such sales, the volume of repos it contracted to do in the go-around. After the first day, the Fed does not permit substitution on repos done with it.

Counterparties

Dealers are not the only counterparties that the Fed has in doing repos and reverses. The Fed also does a lot of MSPs with foreign central banks, and, since the mid-1970s, the Fed has permitted dealers to show customer money to it when it was doing reverses and customer collateral to it when it was doing repos. Many dealers' customers, however, are unaware of this possibility.

Transactions for the Accounts of Foreign Central Banks

Foreign central banks hold short-term balances of dollars for a number of reasons. One is that the dollar is a reserve currency, a currency that foreign central banks hold, instead of or in addition to gold, as part of their foreign-exchange reserves. Also, when the dollar is weak, some foreign central banks will buy dollars in an attempt to stabilize foreign-exchange rates.

The Fed offers to invest, in either bills or repos, any dollar balances that foreign central banks hold with it. Foreign central banks with long-term dollar balances often invest these balances in Treasury bills.

Normally, foreign central banks will have at least some temporary balances sitting at the Fed, funds that they will need in several days to make a payment. To permit foreign central banks to earn a return on such balances, the Fed offers them an investment facility: it permits them to invest dollars short term in a *pool of funds* that it in turn invests in the repo market by doing System MSPs with dealers; investments in this pool pay a return determined by current repo rates.

The Fed takes the expected size of the foreign-central-bank repo (MSP to the Fed) pool to be an operating factor, like currency in circulation or Treasury balances. If the pool turns out to be larger than anticipated, that drains bank reserves and vice versa. Either eventuality may force the Fed to take additional action to hit its reserves target.

BACKGROUND OF THE GOVERNMENT SECURITIES ACT OF 1986

In the early 1980s, bankruptcies of a number of smaller dealers cost investors, mostly smallish, hundreds of millions of dollars, principally as a result of the failed dealers' misdeeds in the repo and reverses markets. This led in 1986 to the regulation of the government securities market. In this section, we discuss the background that opened the door to market abuses and the steps that have been taken to ensure that they do not reoccur.

Dealer Safekeeping of Repo Collateral

At the end of the 1970s and in the early 1980s, there were numerous dealer failures, which resulted in multimillion-dollar losses for investors doing repo and reverses. These losses were unnecessary and developed almost entirely from two sources: the switch to sloppy pricing of collateral and the failure of investors in repo to take delivery of collateral. In the following sections, we discuss these issues and actions that were taken to tidy up repo-market practices.

While delivery of collateral to the lender of money was common in the early repos done between big dealers and big investors, some customers, instead of taking delivery of repo collateral or even of securities purchased outright, have long left such securities with their dealer for safekeeping.

Reasons for Dealer Safekeeping

Some dealers offer to safekeep securities for customers at no charge. One reason a dealer may do this is to nurture customer relationships by providing to his customers, at no cost to them, a service that they would otherwise have to buy. A second reason some dealers prefer, on overnight repos, to safekeep customer securities, especially physical securities, is that delivery would, relative to the interest paid on the repo, be costly to both parties. A third reason some dealers prefer to safekeep customer securities is risk of a subsequent fail. Dealers reason, "If I deliver out, as collateral for an overnight repo, 10MM of bills to XYZ Corp., I must worry about whether XYZ will return my collateral tomorrow in time for me to redeliver it to another repo customer or to an outright buyer. If, alternatively, I safekeep, overnight, for XYZ his collateral, I know that, tomorrow when my repo with XYZ comes off, I'll have my bills in time to make good delivery of them to another customer."

Exempt versus Regulated Securities

In discussing dealer safekeeping, one must distinguish between regulated and exempt securities. The SEC legislation passed in the 1930s brought under federal regulation trading in corporate stocks and bonds, but not trading in most money market instruments. Today's roster of exempt securities comprises government and federal agency securities, BAs, CDs, commercial paper with an original maturity of 270 days or less, and municipal securities. Regulation of municipal securities, introduced in 1975, is carried out by the Municipal Securities Rule-Making Board (MSRB), not the SEC. Regulation of government securities, introduced in 1986 to 1987 with the passage of the Government Securities Act (GSA) of 1986, is now carried out by the SEC, the Treasury, and bank regulators.

Regulated Securities. Any broker/dealer who deals in regulated securities is required by Rules 15c2-1 and 15c3-3 of the Securities Exchange Act of 1934 and by Article III Section 19(d) of the Rules of Fair Practice of NASD to hold all fully paid-for securities that he safekeeps for a customer in a denominated, segregated account in which the customer is afforded significant protection. In particular, a broker/dealer holding securities in such an account may neither hypothecate nor negotiate such securities unless he is specifically instructed by the customer to do so. Also, a customer who holds fully paid-for securities with a regulated broker/dealer for safekeeping may, at any time, demand immediate delivery of those securities.

Exempt Securities. Prior to passage of the Government Securities Act (GSA) of 1986, firms that dealt solely in exempt securities, including the *Government Securities, Inc. (GSI)* subsidiaries that some broker/dealers created to deal in exempt securities, did not have to conform to any rules with respect to the safekeeping of customer securities. With the passage of GSA in 1986, various rules and regulations, both new and existing, were applied to dealers in governments.

Operation of Dealer Safekeeping

Prior to GSA, dealers who dealt solely in exempt securities and who offered dealer safekeeping could and did use various arrangements for holding customer securities. Some such firms, mainly smaller ones, simply held customer securities in their clearing account. Doing so saved a dealer money, because a clearing bank charges a fee each time a dealer moves securities between his clearing account and his safekeeping account.

Despite the fees that a dealer incurs when he opens a safekeeping account for customer securities, most unregulated dealers who were, prior to 1986, safekeeping securities for customers did have a safekeeping account at their clearing bank. However, the dealer was and still is free to move securities into and out of this account at will. The clearing bank had and still has *no* information about which customers' securities are in the dealer's safekeeping account; the clearing bank knows the account solely as one of several accounts the dealer maintains and over which he exercises *sole* control.

Dealer safekeeping of this ilk is referred to as *trust-me* safekeeping; and with good reason.

Responsibilities of the Clearing Bank

When a dealer in exempt securities sets up at his clearing bank a safekeeping account, the dealer's bank has *no responsibility under securities law* to police movements of securities into and out of that account. Since the latter point has been the subject of several suits and a source of misunderstanding to many investors, the point is worth emphasizing.

Fraud Associated with Dealer Safekeeping

At the turn of the decade, a string of dealer bankruptcies shook the government market. The list of firms no longer with us includes the following once familiar names: Drysdale Government Securities, Lombard-Wall, Lion Capital Group, Comark, RTD Securities, E.S.M. Government Securities, and Bevill Bresler and Schulman. While not all of these firms used precisely the same techniques for getting their fingers into other people's pockets, a number of them discovered that unverifiable dealer safekeeping combined with the trusting nature of many of their smaller customers provided them with an easy means of generating, via various frauds, hundreds of millions of dollars to enhance their capital and to cover, sooner or later, their cumulative trading losses—losses that each firm had and that each firm earnestly prayed would vanish, if not today, then tomorrow.

It is likely that no dealer in government securities ever set up shop specifically to make a living from defrauding his customers. Probably in every case, a dealer who eventually engaged in fraud started out intending to make money running an honest business; then, due to his incompetence and/or to a few unfortunate bets he made on the market, he lost money and ended up broke. At that point, he succumbed to the temptation to reason, "I'm bankrupt at the moment, *but,* if I just borrow from customers for a little while, I can recoup my losses." And, thus, started the fraud, the creative accounting, and the deceit. Noted one dealer, "Covering up widespread fraud is such a time-consuming and troublesome chore that it's hard to believe that any dealer would, in a market where it's possible to make money honestly, choose, except under duress, to be dishonest."

Perfection of Interest: Who Owns That Collateral?

An investor who has left securities for safekeeping with a dealer who goes bankrupt may, to his great shock, find that thanks to dealer safekeeping he faces not one but two sequential problems: Are his securities there? If so, does he in fact own them in the eyes of the law?

Under a state's *Uniform Commercial Code (UCC)*, which state to state is anything but uniform, a good case can be made that an investor who leaves securities in safekeeping with a dealer instead of requiring that his dealer deliver those securities to him, has failed to *perfect his interest* in the securities. In plain English, the code seems to say that, if an investor does not bother to take possession of securities he bought, either via a purchase or via a repo, he will not be recognized in bankruptcy court as owning those securities. This, for example, is true regardless of whether the bankrupt dealer's records show that a specific security in its possession at the time of its bankruptcy was being held by it in safekeeping for a specific customer.

Any investor who, to obtain securities he thinks are due him, gets into a dispute in bankruptcy court (1) over whether his interest in certain securities is perfected (i.e., over whether he is a secured or general creditor of his bankrupt dealer) or (2) over whether repo is a securities transaction or a collateralized loan will soon recognize that he has fallen into a slough of legal complexities. There are, moreover, few broad precedents to indicate whether he will win in his struggle to emerge, securities in hand, from this slough. The one sure thing is that he, the investor, will rack up legal bills that he'll not soon forget.

Letter Repo

The problems we have been discussing with respect to dealer safekeeping occurred almost exclusively between small (read unsophisticated) investors and small dealers. Nondelivery repo, or *letter repo* as it's frequently called, has never caused problems when practiced between sophisticated investors and large, creditworthy dealers.

Nondelivery repo goes under a lot of names. Some dealers shops call it *letter repo,* others call it a *due bill,* and still others refer to it as *hold-in-custody (HIC)* repo. Whatever it is called, the reasons for and characteristics of such repos tend to be pretty much the same at major dealers.

Dealer Reasons for Doing Letter Repo

The principal reason that dealers use letter repo is to achieve operational efficiencies.

An operations person at one major dealer—a Cadillac credit—described how his firm got into letter repo, "Ten years ago, when we did repo it was always DVP (delivery versus payment), and delivery on a repo was just like delivery on an outright sale. Typically, at the end of the day, we have very large money amounts of securities in small pieces. We used to dump that stuff into a bank loan at the end of the day, which was expensive. Then one of our guys said, 'Why can't we repo this stuff without having to do all of this paper work?'

"Today, the way our system works is that we enter into our computer all day the dollar values of the letter repos customers want to do with us; the computer knows what classes of securities each customer will accept. At 3:30 or 4 P.M., we press a button and say, 'OK computer, allocate.' The computer spits out confirms to customers and instructions to our clearing bank. The bank then takes the collateral we have assigned to letter repo and moves it out of our clearing account into a customer safekeeping account.

"We know that our bank knows that the collateral is pledged to a customer as part of a letter repo. We next make up a letter of confirmation to each [letter] repo customer, slap onto it a listing of paper collateralizing his repo, and then send that confirm off in the mail to the customer. When the customer gets his paper confirm, he reads that, on Monday, he lent us 100MM and that this was the collateral. The customer can use that document to go back to the bank and ask if that collateral was really in our customer safekeeping account. Occasionally, customers send in an audit guy to do just that."

The incentive for dealers to use letter repo is greatest when the collateral that the dealer wants to finance could be delivered out only with a lot of cost both to the dealer and to the investor. For this reason, dealers have traditionally done letter repos to finance their holdings of various physical securities and their holdings of odd lots of wireable securities as well. Firms that deal in commercial paper have, in particular, used letter repo to finance overnight unsold paper they have positioned.

Investor Reasons for Buying Letter Repo

A repo investor who leaves his collateral in safekeeping with a dealer is—the recent safeguards of GSA notwithstanding—doing the risk equivalent of extending an *unsecured* loan to his dealer. Whether doing so is advisable depends on who is lending to whom.

Many big, sophisticated investors routinely buy commercial paper, which is the equivalent of their making short-term *unsecured* loans to corporations, financial and nonfinancial. Rarely have investors in commercial paper lost money. Commercial paper is sold on the basis of its being exactly what it is—a short-term, *unsecured* note; thus, the first thing that an investor in commercial paper considers is *credit risk:* Who is the issuer? How good is his credit rating?

A sophisticated investor in letter repo will apply exactly the same reasoning: Is the credit of a Merrill or a Sali good enough for me to extend to them what might prove to be an unsecured loan? Letter repo is most often done short term, overnight, or over the weekend. Consequently, it is not difficult for a sophisticated investor with the capacity to evaluate credit to conclude, "If I can accept the credit risk inherent in buying commercial paper from, say, GMAC, I can accept the credit risk inherent in doing letter repo with, say, Merrill. Neither investment will cause me to lose sleep at night."

Tri-Party Repos

While some large investors are willing to do letter repo, others aren't. To do a variant of hold-in-custody repos with such customers, certain big dealers and their clearing banks invented *tri-party* repos.

It is becoming increasingly common for large investors to negotiate with their dealer and with their dealer's clearing bank tri-party repo agreements in which the clearing bank not only knows both sides of a repo transaction, but holds the repo collateral put up by the dealer in custody for the investor for the life of the repo. Such an agreement has several advantages. It obviates the need for delivery of collateral, while protecting the interests of the investor whose credit risk becomes that of a major bank rather than that of the dealer. A tri-party repo also reduces the clearing costs associated with a large repo and makes substitution of collateral on such a repo cheaper and simpler for both the dealer and the investor.

On a tri-party repo, the dealer pays the clearing bank a fee, but the investor does not. Typically, tri-party repos are done for large sums; such repos may amount to hundreds of millions when the investor is a money fund.

Big investors, who do tri-party repos, may and sometimes do send their auditors around to check whether the clearing bank has in fact segregated their collateral. On such a repo, the dealer's collateral does not come back to him until he repays his loan from the investor.

Third-Party Custody

While many small portfolio managers rely pretty much on their dealer to clear their securities trades and to safekeep their securities, major investors, including those who do some letter repos and tri-party repos, almost always hire a *custodial agent bank* both to clear their securities trades and to hold certain or all their securities for them. The custody-bank approach, which totally eliminates the portfolio manger's credit risk vis-à-vis the dealer, costs money; it also involves, relative to dealer safekeeping, extra steps for both the portfolio manager and the dealer.

The Agreement and the Mechanics

Institutional investors that aren't depository institutions cannot hold book-entry securities themselves, and most of them don't, for various reasons, want to hold physical securities themselves. Thus, large, sophisticated investors, financial (e.g., life insurance companies and money funds) and nonfinancial, use an *agent bank* or banks to clear their securities trades, to hold securities for them, and to collect and credit to their accounts monies due them when the securities they own pay interest or dividends or, in the case of fixed-income securities, when they mature.

Safety of Bank Custody

An overriding concern of all large, sophisticated portfolio managers who open bank custodial accounts is safety for their valued securities, and such safety is precisely what they think bank custody affords them. With third-party custody, as opposed to dealer safekeeping, the investor gets a separate custodial account and clear identification of the securities in that account as his.

The manager of a major U.S. corporate portfolio, who's a most conservative fellow, explains what he believes are the safeguards of bank custody: "When I enter into a custodial-agency agreement with say Chase or Citi, that bank acts, under that agreement, as a fiduciary for me. They examine the authenticity of the securities upon advice from me, confirmed in writing; *they also will act only on my specific instructions.* If I tell them that I expect $100MM in government repo coming in from dealer X, they will not pay out until that occurs."

Margin and the Pricing of Collateral

Back when dealers and investors first started doing repos after World War II, they priced collateral precisely; that is, they priced discount securities at market value and coupon securities at market price plus accrued interest. Also, in calculating the amount to be loaned, they normally haircut by some small percentage the value of the collateral that was to secure a repo loan, that is, they took margin.

Evolution Away from Precise Pricing

Precise pricing of collateral was a safe way to do things, but it was inconvenient because it led to crazy, odd amounts of money. An investor who had a million to invest did not want a dealer coming back at him with a number like $968,132.23. Many investors were more concerned about getting *all* of their money invested than about getting adequate protection against credit risk. So gradually, dealers got away from precise pricing of collateral. Dealers would borrow 100 against 90-day bills trading at 96 or they would borrow against coupons at "par flat"; that is, they'd price coupons at some round price flat (e.g., at 98 flat) and ignore coupon interest. For the sake of convenience, market practices deteriorated.

Abuses of Imprecise Pricing

Imprecise pricing of collateral was an invitation to dealers who were short on capital and integrity to engage in abuses of two sorts. If they were bullish, they were tempted to follow the strategy Eldin Miller made famous: buy bills at 95, repo them for 100, and use the temporary funds thus generated to provide margin for buying more bills.[8] Alternatively, if they were bearish or at least did not anticipate a market rally, they were tempted to follow Miller's strategy two: reverse in high-coupon securities nearing a coupon date and then sell those securities for full market value, including accrued interest. The dealer might then use the extra funds he had generated to cover trading losses, to cover current operating expenses, and/or to finance additional speculations.

The above strategies, while neither illegal nor immoral, are dangerous. A dealer who uses either risks getting into a situation in which he is so highly levered that the only bets he can afford to make are winning bets. One bad bet—that rates are rising when in fact they are falling—and he's bankrupt.

Tidying Up Market Practices

The Drysdale, Lombard-Wall, and later dealer bankruptcies finally forced some tidying up of repo-market practices. That this took so long reflects in part opposition to new rules and regulations by the big dealers. These dealers argued, correctly enough, that no customer had ever lost a penny doing repos and reverses with them and that new rules and regs would stifle innovation and impose costs on sectors of the market in which there had never been a problem.

One suggestion was that the dealers doing repos and reverses introduce some form of self-regulation. Several problems

---

[8]See story of the failure of Financial Corp., Chapter 10.

effectively barred this approach. First, the history of the dealer community's efforts to adopt any sort of standardized practice is that they have a hard time agreeing to do anything: dealers are human; they are competitors; and they have sizable egos. Second, at least some of the senior statesmen of the dealer community felt that self-regulation, however nobly begun, would eventually become counterproductive. Noted one: "Self-regulatory groups start out with the best of motives; they intend to make as few rules as possible, just those that are obvious and to which the dealers with integrity would adhere to in any event. Then, there are the second, third, fourth, and fifth years; the founding fathers revolve off; the five chairmen of their respective companies who started off the self-regulatory body are no longer very interested in it. In their place, you now have a bunch of young do-gooders out to make a name for themselves. The next thing, these guys make all sorts of rules and start changing market practices; among them, there is a tendency for self-aggrandizement, which is human nature."

Since dealers failed to standardize and to tidy up repo market practices, a need was created, at least in the eyes of some, for regulatory action. In due course, both the Fed and the Congress acted.

Full Accrual Pricing

The Drysdale bankruptcy, perhaps because it caused a large loss to a bank, the Chase, finally stirred the Fed into action. The Fed recommended, in a letter to the primary dealers, that they henceforth price repo collateral at market price *plus* accrued interest *minus* a reasonable haircut. Under this method of pricing, known as *full accrual pricing,* any coupon interest received by the holder of collateral is still transferred on the coupon data to the ultimate owner of the securities serving as collateral; for high-coupon securities repoed with a lot of accrued interest, this transfer leads to an offsetting adjustment in the dollar value of the repo loan, one that reflects the fall to zero in accrued interest on the repo collateral.

Repricing Collateral. Typically, term and open repos and reverses have included a right to reprice collateral. Some dealers track daily the value of collateral that they have taken in; if such securities fall in value, they want more collateral. Prior to passage of the Government Securities Act of 1986, not all dealers used, however, to bother to reprice collateral regularly. A common attitude used to be this: we don't reprice collateral because to do so would be a lot of trouble; besides we wouldn't want to insult or inconvenience our valued customers.

A dealer's attorney noted, "Because we are a small shop, we have always marked to market. We found out, however, that a lot of people out there did not used to mark to market with us. We would ask for margin, if appropriate, but we would never send out additional margin unless they asked for it. Lots of times, people would not ask us. Consequently, we were ahead of the game."

Standardizing Haircuts

Prior to the spate of dealer bankruptcies that began in earnest in the early 1980s, a lot of people on the Street—dealers, investors, and others—were rather casual about margin. Depending on who the contracting parties were, haircuts could be just about anything: a big positive number, a small positive number, zero; in some cases, margin was even a negative percentage of the money lent (i.e., the money lent exceeded the value of the collateral).

Today, in contrast, there is more standardization in margin practices: margin is likely to run ¼ of a point per month on Treasury bills, notes, or bonds (⅜ of a point on a 45-day repo); the same on agencies; 2% on letter repos of commercial paper and other securities; and much more on mortgage-backed securities—3 points on a 1-month repo, 4 points on a 2-month repo, and 5 points on a 3-month or longer repo. The figures for margin on repos on Treasuries that we cite here refer to interdealer trades.

Repo Agreements

Today, parties doing repos or reverses with each other frequently exchange a letter of agreement that spells out the terms of the trade: the names of both parties; a description of the asset traded; the pricing of the asset; the rate of interest to be paid to the lender of money; the term of the agreement; and, if the collateral is not to be safekept, where it is to be delivered.

Evolution in Market Practice.

Repo agreements were more common at the start of the repo market than later. As time passed, market participants took the view that *all that had to be said by way of a contract was said in the buy and sell confirms.* Strange as it may seem now, people, primary dealers included, were not terribly concerned about perfecting a lien, provisions of the UCC, and so on.

My Word Is My Bond.

The lack of concern that money market people displayed about dotting the legal *i*'s and *t*'s with respect to repo reflected not only their notion that repo contracts could be and were established by virtue of *an exchange of confirms,* but their notion that they were afforded much protection by the standards of the business in which they operated. Money market folk felt, at least until recently, that they are in a business in which people say, "My word is my bond," and mean it; a business in which, if someone says something is "done," it is done. Money market folk also felt protected by the knowledge that people on the Street are generally people of integrity; and just in case they are not, every Street person's rule one is "Know thy customer," which translates to: check everything about the counterparty, including first and foremost, his financials.

The Lombard-Wall Ruling.

Lombard-Wall came tumbling down in August of 1982. It was school districts and other investors, not the big dealers, who lost money due to Lombard-Wall's failure. Consequently, this failure, like that of Financial Corp., might in time have been forgotten by the Street, but this was not to be. A new bankruptcy code had been adopted in 1978, and there was no definitive history as to how a bankruptcy court would characterize a repo transaction.

When Lombard-Wall filed for bankruptcy in early August 1982, it argued that the federal bankruptcy code prohibited its customers from selling securities it had delivered to them as repo collateral. Specifically, Lombard-Wall asked the court for and got a stay in bankruptcy; this means that the firm received the protection of the court and that all of its transactions were *stayed*. This ruling set off alarm bells on the Street. If the repo collateral received from a suddenly defunct dealer were perchance long bonds, one wanted, in the interests of minimizing market risk, to be able to sell those bonds immediately: today, not tomorrow.

The *Lombard-Wall* case offered the first opportunity for a court to characterize repo under the new bankruptcy code. Since the new code contained no specific provisions about how to treat repo, the court had to look for some characterization of repo; its choices were a secured borrowing or a purchase and sale. The court ruled that repo was a secured borrowing; and once it did, the automatic stay provisions of the bankruptcy code became applicable. This ruling, together with the application of the automatic stay, "scared," noted one dealer's counsel, "the hell out of the industry."

Basically, dealers and banks could not care less what repos and reverses are, so long as they can do them in big volume and with *no* problems. For primary dealers with their huge matched books, the Lombard-Wall ruling created a problem. Said one dealer, "What if you were involved with [had the collateral of] an outfit that got into bankruptcy? You were hung out to dry." Suddenly reverses, one half of their big matched books, were seen by dealers as leading to possible market risk; and dealers do *not* want market risk except when it's volitional— when they get to choose the timing and the tune of the market play.

Prior to Lombard-Wall, the Street had always operated on the assumption that, if A did a repo with B and if B went broke with A holding B's collateral, A could sell that collateral, and it could do so *mui pronto*. So long as this assumption appeared tenable, dealers viewed the credit risk inherent in reverses as something with which they could live, provided that they paid attention to margin. Noted one dealer, "If I do a reverse with you, my responsibility is to see that this transaction is properly margined, that we are basically at par in terms of the dollars involved, and that the agreed-upon financing cost is all that is out there. If you go bankrupt, I want to sell out those securities immediately. I don't worry about the credit of the issuer, but I do worry about market risk; there's a volatile market out there."

Amending the Bankruptcy Code.

Amending the Bankruptcy Code. Post Lombard-Wall, the industry said, "Let's get the uncertainty—What kind of trade am I doing? What may I do with collateral?—out of this." They lobbied, through the *Public Securities Association (PSA)*, a trade association of which they are a division, for an amendment to the bankruptcy code that would permit a holder of repo collateral to immediately sell out that collateral if the other party defaulted. The Fed, sensing the danger that the Lombard-Wall ruling posed to dealers and thus to the operation of the government market, supported the dealers; and it was the Fed's lobbying in the end that caused Congress to pass the 1984 amendment to the bankruptcy code. This amendment, which has some exceptions, was not all the dealers wished for, but it was all the Fed would go to bat for.

While the Lombard-Wall ruling certainly touched off a panic among dealers, it is possible that a similar ruling might in subsequent cases go the other way. In the *Lombard-Wall* case, there was a written repo agreement, which, at the time, was in itself quite unusual. Also, the Lombard-Wall agreement, said one lawyer, "was worded so that it sounded like a collateralized loan." This lawyer continued, "In the *Lombard-Wall* case, the judge was looking at one particular repo. Depending on the type of participant and the type of agreement, another judge could choose to characterize repo in another way," as the BBS bankruptcy judge did.

Writing a New Agreement. Basically, the dealers viewed the amendment to the bankruptcy code as a form of insurance. Once dealers got it, they reasoned: maybe we need a written agreement for repos and reverses. Having such an agreement might put us in a better position if we ever end up in court making claims against a defaulting party. Also, so long as we are going to write an agreement, let's write it so that it gives repos and reverses all possible *indicia* of a securities trade. Then our first line of defense against a default on a repo or a reverse will be a document stating that we and the other party contracted to do a pair of securities trades. If the judge respects this expressed intent, we are home free; either we have got money or we have got securities that we can sell immediately; and if we margin properly, our losses will be minimal. On the other hand, if the judge rules that a reverse done by a party in default is a collateralized loan, we will have in most cases protection from the bankruptcy code amendment, and again, if we have margined properly, our losses will be minimal.

Enter the Lawyers. The above reasoning led the dealers, one by one, to call down to their corporate counsels and say, "Write us a repo agreement that will *protect us* in all eventualities."

Naturally, every dealer had produced a multipage repo agreement that he wanted other dealers to sign while he himself was unwilling to sign their agreements because the latter were not—so said his counsel—evenhanded. The contest over whose agreement was going to be signed was bound to end in stalemate.

The only possible solution, and the one finally adopted, was for the primary dealers to form within the Public Securities Association a committee charged with drafting a standard repo agreement. Finally, after much effort, the PSA produced such an agreement.

Naturally, the dealers wanted their customers to sign this agreement. Most did, but there are still some holdouts. Municipalities and state government bodies often have their own agreements mandated by law, and they are loath to ask their respective legislatures for any changes. Mutual funds have also resisted signing the PSA agreement; their trade association, the Investment Company Institute (ICI), has written its own repo agreement, and for reasons unique to their industry, mutual funds prefer that repo agreement to the PSA agreement.

The Government Securities Act of 1986

The PSA agreement was designed principally to protect the dealers. Meanwhile, investor losses due to failures of dealers in governments was creating a brouhaha in Washington. As noted in Chapter 10, the upshot was the passage of the Government Securities Act of 1986. This act contained a number of provisions designed to protect customers doing repos and reverses with dealers.

Repos, Reverses, and Safekeeping

Several things were done by the Treasury and the SEC in their regulations to pare the risks associated with repos and reverses. In particular, both the Treasury and the SEC imposed complex capital charges on repos and reverses. One purpose of these requirements was to create incentives to encourage dealers doing repos and reverses to operate as follows: collateral is to be reasonably priced; the amount of money that changes hands is to be a reasonable percentage of the collateral's market value; and, finally, margin calls are to be made if significant changes occur in that market value.

Also, under the new regs, a dealer, before doing repo with a customer, must send to the customer a written agreement that includes a specifically worded disclosure regarding the dealer's right to substitute collateral. A dealer must also send to a customer confirms on all transactions, including repos and reverses. Also, a dealer *must segregate* in a safekeeping account at his clearing bank and on his books any customer securities, including repo collateral, that he holds for customers. On hold-in-custody repos, a dealer, on his confirms to customers, is supposed to list collateral separately—he can no longer write "various." Also, he is supposed to state the market value of the securities that he is giving to the customer as collateral.

The difficulties that regulatory authorities experienced in setting up new regulations under the Government Securities Act of 1986 suggests that such regulations will be subject to evolution over time.

POSTSCRIPT: RESULTS OF SIPC SURVEY OF THE REPO-REVERSE MARKET

In November 1988, the Securities Investor Protection Corporation (SIPC) surveyed various entities, including dealers and banks, that were doing repos and reverses in an attempt to measure the size of the repo-reverse market and to determine certain of that market's characteristics. The response rate to SIPC's questionnaire was generally quite high.

Aggregating responses, SIPC estimates the size of the repo-reverse market in the fall of 1988 at $755 billion. Presumably, this number involves a great deal of double counting: if dealer A reversed out securities to dealer B, a common transaction in matched book, the trade was reported and counted twice in the SIPC survey—once as a repo, again as a reverse.

Another interesting finding was that, of the total repos done by dealers, only 3% were hold-in-custody (HIC) repos. For all other entities doing repo, the percentage was significantly higher, 24.6%.

THE NEXT CHAPTER

In the next chapter, we turn to the markets for governments and agencies, huge markets in themselves and markets that have spawned new markets for a host of derivative products—the most prominent being futures markets and markets for various option products.

FURTHER READINGS

Stigum, Marcia, *The Repo and Reverse Markets* (Homewood, Ill.: Dow Jones-Irwin, 1988). This book contains a bibliography on the repo market.

CHAPTER 14

GOVERNMENT AND FEDERAL AGENCY SECURITIES

The government market, which used to be stuffy and humdrum, has evolved over the last three decades or so into one of the most active and innovative sectors of the money market. The reasons are several. In 1961, Congress amended the tax law so that bank capital gains, which had been taxed at the capital gains rate, were taxed as ordinary income. "Overnight, that change," one dealer noted, "converted 6,000 stodgy bankers into portfolio managers who were supposed to make a profit." At about the same time, tightening and easing by the Fed began to create wide swings in interest rates. "Back in the old days," noted the same dealer, "bonds had no sex appeal. They were not going to change much in price so you bought them, clipped the coupon, and matured them. Then, suddenly, because of big fluctuations in interest rates, it became possible for portfolio managers and dealers to make money positioning and trading governments."

Another stimulus to the development of the government market was the decision by the SEC to force stock exchange firms to negotiate commission rates. That change effectively cut stock house commissions by 75% so they began looking for something new to do. They searched just at the time big money was being made by dealers in governments, and many decided to open government bond dealerships. A few lost a lot of money, but a number prospered and stayed.

The huge and consistent growth of the federal debt has also contributed to the evolution of the government market by creating more supply and by attracting more players, both domestic and foreign, into the market. So, too, did the freedom in which the government market operated; ironically, the government market, unlike other securities markets, was not subject to regulation until the passage of the Government Securities Act of 1986.

This act, which among other things imposed capital requirements on dealers in governments and restricted just how they might do repo, still left dealers with lots of room to innovate, something they had been doing for years. For example, over the last several decades, the development of the reverse market and the specific issues market has made transactions by dealers and portfolio managers, unheard of 20 years ago, now commonplace. The government market is one of the few markets in which it is possible to run large short positions—to make money on a negative attitude—and growth of the reverse market has made shorting simpler, cheaper, and more attractive. Also, introduction of trading in bill, note, and bond futures and options has opened up a host of new strategies for dealing, investing, and speculating in governments; and it has attracted many new participants to the market. Finally, it was innovation by dealers that led the Treasury to introduce STRIPs and stripping.

BILLS, NOTES, AND BONDS

Negotiable Treasuries come in three principal varieties: bills, notes, and bonds.

Bills

The Treasury currently issues bills in 3-month, 6-month, and 1-year maturities. Bills are issued in denominations of $10,000, $15,000, $50,000, $100,000, $500,000, and $1MM. A round lot in the interdealer market is $5MM, and a retail customer who buys bills from a dealer will get a quote somewhat off the market unless he bids for size.

Bills used to be issued by the Treasury in the form of bearer certificates. The Treasury and the Fed then made it possible to hold bills in *book-entry* form (described below), and since 1977, the Treasury has offered bills in book-entry form only.

Notes

The Treasury currently auctions 2-, 4-, 5-, and 7-year notes on a regular cycle. It usually includes a 3- and a 10-year note during quarterly refundings. Notes are now available in book-entry form only.

When the Treasury wants to encourage individuals to invest in a new note issue, it sets the minimum denomination at $1,000. At other times, it sets it at $5,000. In the interdealer market for notes, $1MM is a round lot, trades for $5MM occur routinely, and trades for even larger amounts are common. Money market investors typically trade notes in size. The note market is a wholesale market, except for sales to individuals and small portfolio managers who typically buy to hold to maturity.

Bonds

As part of its strategy of lengthening the average maturity of the debt, the Treasury has wanted in recent years to offer a new 30-year bond in each of its quarterly refundings. However, Congress long ago imposed a 4.25% lid on the coupon that the Treasury could pay on new bond issues. Consequently, for years the Treasury could issue long bonds only to the extent that Congress exempted an increasing dollar amount of its bonds from this restriction. Congress was always loath to take such action; and for this reason, the Treasury was able, in a number of years, to offer only two, not four, new long bonds. In the fall of 1988, Congress finally abolished its anachronistic lid on the coupon that the Treasury may put on new long bonds.

Treasury bonds used to be callable during the last five years of their life. The last such issue that the Treasury sold was the 11¾s of 2014, callable in 2009. Starting in 1985, the Treasury eliminated the call feature from its bonds to facilitate the stripping of these securities into zeros (see STRIPs below).

Flower Bonds

A number of old *low-coupon* government bonds that currently sell at prices well *below par* carry a special feature. They are acceptable at par in payment of federal estate taxes when owned by the decedent at the time of death. In 1977, the capital gain realized at the time of the holder's death was made taxable. Currently, flower bonds maturing on the following dates are available: February 1990, August 1992, February 1993, May 1994, February 1995, and November 1998. Some of the issues are callable; all are available in minimum denominations of $500.

Settlement

Trades in Treasuries can be done either for *cash* (same-day) settlement or for *regular* (next-day) settlement. The norm is regular settlement, and probably 95% of note and bond trades are done for regular settlement. Cash settlement, which must be agreed upon by both the buyer and the seller, is more common in bills. Trades in Treasuries can also be done for skip-day settlement or later—maybe because the buyer is doing something against a corporate issue that settles on a corporate basis.

Attraction to Investors

Treasury securities offer the investor several attractive features. They expose him to zero credit risk, and while they yield less than other market instruments except for municipals, they are the most liquid instruments traded in the money market. Governments owe their liquidity to the fact that most individual issues are extremely large, and governments are thus not discrete heterogeneous instruments, like BAs or MTNs. In the spring of 1989, individual bill issues outstanding ranged from $7 billion to over $15 billion; the smallest note issue was $4 billion, but most note issues were much larger and several were in the $6 to $9 billion range. Bond issues are also substantial, $3.6 to $18.5 billion on recent issues.

Another advantage of Treasuries is that interest income earned on them is *not* subject to state and local taxation. Also, interest earned by holding a T bill to maturity can be treated for tax purposes as having all been earned in the year the bill matures.

A final attraction of governments is the wide array of these securities available. In early 1989, the Treasury had outstanding 35 different bill issues ranging in current maturity from a few days to a year, 131 note issues, and 68 bond issues. The current maturities of these note and bond issues ranged from a few days to almost 30 years. Also, as noted below, investors can buy a wide array of STRIPs.

Ownership

Table 14–1 shows how ownership of the government debt is split between different classes of investors. The top part of the table, which refers to *marketable* Treasury debt, is of most interest for present purposes. It shows that the Fed is the biggest domestic investor in marketable governments. It is closely followed by

TABLE 14–1
Public debt of the U.S. Treasury, third quarter 1988 ($ billions)

Type and Holder	
Federal Reserve Banks	229.2
Commercial banks	203.0
Insurance companies	135.0
Money market funds	10.8
Other corporations	86.0
State and local governments	286.0
Individuals	72.0
Foreign and international	333.3
U.S. government securities dealers	−25.8*
Other (including federal agencies)	473.4
Marketable Treasury debt	1,802.9
U.S. government agencies and trust funds	550.4
Individuals (savings bonds)	10.0
Other	239.0
Nonmarketable Treasury debt	799.4
Total public debt	2,602.3

*The *negative* holdings of dealers represent a *net* short position.

Source: *Federal Reserve Bulletin.*

commercial banks. State and local governments are also sizable investors. Among domestic investors, the next most important holders of governments are other corporations and individuals.

One key entry in Table 14–1 is the $333.3 billion of governments held by foreigners. As this figure suggests, foreigners are at times important investors in Treasury debt. Whether they are in or out of the market can affect the rates at which the Treasury is able to sell new issues. In the period 1979 to 1982, foreigners were big buyers of governments because rates were high, the dollar was strong, and the U.S. promised political stability.

BOOK-ENTRY SECURITIES

In 1976, the Treasury announced that it would move over time to a system under which virtually the entire marketable federal debt would be represented by *book-entry securities* instead of engraved pieces of paper. *Under the book-entry system, banks that are members of the Federal Reserve hold securities at the Fed in accounts on which record keeping is computerized.* All marketable governments may be held in book-entry form, and the bulk of the Treasury's marketable debt is now held in this form.

A bank typically has several different book-entry accounts at the Fed. For example, it may have one account for securities in which it has an interest: securities in its dealer position, securities in its investment portfolio, and securities it has taken in on repo; a second account for securities it is safekeeping for corporate and other investors; and a third account for securities it holds for dealers for whom it clears.

The Fed's computer tracks the amounts and types of securities every bank has in each of its accounts. Each bank's own computer tracks for the investors and dealers for whom it holds securities what issues and amounts of these issues each such institution has placed with it.

In New York, the major banks are linked by wire to the Fed, and all securities transfers among them are made by *wire*. If Bankers Trust were, for example, to sell bills to Citibank, it would make delivery by sending a wire message to the Fed, whose computer would debit Bankers' account for X bills and credit Citi's account for the same number. Simultaneously, the Fed's computer would automatically transfer money equal to the purchase price of the bills out of Citi's reserve account at the Fed into Bankers' reserve account.

The movement to book-entry securities and wire transfers was precipitated in 1970 by the refusal of several major insurance underwriters to underwrite government securities held by dealers. Treasury notes and bonds (but not bills) could be registered, but in fact dealers and most major investors held them, as well as bills, in bearer form. So there was a huge volume of valuable bearer paper being stored and constantly moved about on the Street, thus inviting theft.

Faced with an insurance crisis, the dealers began to hold their securities in accounts at the major banks. At the same time, the Fed initiated a system that made it possible for banks to wire securities between each other during each business day. At the end of the day, however, the banks had to show up at the Fed and take physical delivery on any issues on which they had been *net* receivers over the day and to make physical delivery of issues on which they had made *net* deliveries over the day. This procedure eliminated much messenger traffic in governments, but hundreds of millions worth of them still had to be carried between the banks and the NY Fed at the end of the day to effect net settlements. The introduction of book-entry securities eliminated these end-of-day movements.

Now that literally billions of dollars of governments are stored in the Fed's computers, the Fed faces a classic records protection problem. It undoubtedly has considerable backup to make its system fail-safe. Such backup can be provided in various ways; for example, by writing records out to disks or tapes and storing them in off-site locations.

The book-entry system for governments was designed by the Treasury in haste and under pressure, but it has worked efficiently and has been accepted with enthusiasm by dealers, banks, and most investors.

To move to book entry, the Treasury set up an enabling regulation that had the effect of law and, to the extent that it conflicted with portions of the uniform commercial code in regard to transfers and pledges, had the effect of overriding that law.

Since the Treasury moved to book entry, all federal agencies still issuing securities to the public have come up with their own versions of the Treasury's enabling regulation. And today most agency securities, with the exception of discount paper, can be held in book-entry form and are eligible for wire transfer.

Physical movements of BAs, commercial paper, MTNs, and certain other securities still occur between banks whenever trades are cleared. Everyone in the industry agrees that eliminating movements of physical paper would be a good idea, since it would simplify and reduce the cost of clearing trades in such paper. Remaining physical paper could be gotten off the street either by enlarging an existing depository, for example, the Depository Trust Company (DTC), which immobilizes corporate stocks and bonds, or by creating some new depository. To date little progress has been made in this direction, although by 1989, the MTNs of at least one issuer, Chrysler, had gone book entry via DTC.

PRIMARY DEALERS

Any firm can commence dealing in governments and federal agency securities. The Fed, however, will deal directly only with *recognized* or *primary dealers*.

In recognizing a dealer, the Fed looks for capital, character in management, and capacity in terms of trained personnel. Specifically before the Fed will do business with a firm, it wants to ensure: (1) that the firm has adequate capital relative to the positions it assumes; (2) that the firm is doing a reasonable volume (at least 1% of market activity) and that it is willing to make markets at all times; and (3) that management in the firm understands the government market—particularly the risks involved—and is making a long-term commitment to the market.

When a firm expresses an interest to the Fed in becoming a primary dealer, the Fed first asks it to report its trading volume and positions on an informal basis. If the firm appears to meet the Fed's criteria, the Fed then puts it on its regular reporting list. After a time as a *reporting dealer* if the firm still appears to meet the Fed's criteria, the Fed recognizes that dealer and does business with it.

While the Fed expects a primary dealer to make markets at all times, it recognizes and accepts the fact that some shops tend to specialize at either the long or the short end of market.

The big profits primary dealers make in good years and the decline in brokerage income on stock trades were two reasons many firms set up dealerships in governments. Another was that firms specializing in corporate bonds felt it was important to get into the government market to obtain firsthand knowledge of this market, which they could use as a tool in marketing new corporate bonds: sell corporates, for example, by swapping customers out of governments.

Setting up a dealership in governments is time-consuming, difficult, and costly. Talented personnel, usually in scarce supply on the Street, must be hired and then welded into a team that works. Firms entering the government market normally expect to lose millions before they create an organization capable of producing profits.

Recent Growth in the Number of Primary Dealers

Despite the considerable effort and costs associated with becoming a primary dealer, there was a rush, starting around 1986, of new firms, often foreign, that sought this status. One lure of the Treasury market, then and now, is that it is the biggest and most liquid securities market in the world. In 1986, a second lure was that the market was bullish and pleasantly volatile, which is good for traders' profits.

At the end of 1985, there were 36 primary dealers in governments, only a handful more than there had been years before. By the end of 1986, that number was 40; by the end of 1987, it was 43; and by the end of 1988, it was 46.

As the number of primary dealers grew, there was a marked increase in the number of such dealers who were foreign firms or subsidiaries of foreign firms. By early 1989, 13 of the 44 primary dealers in government securities were foreign owned. A number of foreign firms became primary dealers in governments by buying up shops that already had that status: Kleinworth Benson bought ACLI; Midland Montague took over Crocker Bank's primary dealership when that bank was sold to Wells Fargo; the Bank of Montreal bought Harris Bank, a primary dealer; the Hongkong Bank controls Marine Midland, which in turn owns the CM&M Group, a primary dealer; and Westpac, an Australian Bank, bought Pollock.

Others foreign firms sought to gain primary dealer status by setting up shop and trading under their own banner in New York. The Japanese big four did this. Because of their obviously Japanese names, the aggressive way in which they traded to gain market share, and their awesome capitalization (the market capitalization of Nikko Securities is twice as large as the combined market caps of Merrill Lynch, American Express, and Manny Hanny), there was some resentment at the way the Japanese big four pushed their way into the primary dealer club. Congress went so far as to direct the Fed to revoke the primary dealer status of Japanese securities firms in the U.S. if U.S. dealers were not given similar standing in Japan. The Japanese responded by taking steps to open up the market in Japanese Government Bonds (JGBs) to U.S. and other foreign dealers.

Big U.S. dealers who set up shop in Tokyo were anxious to trade there not only U.S. Treasuries, but JGBs as well. That was natural, since the market for JGBs is second only to the U.S. Treasury market in terms of size and liquidity. The Brits for their part certainly opened up the market for gilts to U.S. dealers on Big Bang day, but then they played a dirty trick on the many dealers who came to the party: the Brits actually started to pay down their debt, something U.S. dealers were culturally ill prepared to face, since back home national debt outstanding moved in only one direction—up, and fast up at that. An interesting development that we discuss at the end of this chapter is that, in general, non-native dealers have not made the money they hoped to (or have even lost money) trying to trade foreign government debt on its native soil.

In any case, faced with a flood of would-be primary dealers, the Fed in November 1988 tightened the rules for becoming a primary dealer. The NY Fed announced that it thought that

"50 or so" primary dealers would meet its needs in conducting open market operations (at that time there were 46 primary dealers). The Fed also said that each primary dealer's customer transactions in Treasuries and agencies should average 1% (up from 0.75%) of total primary-dealer volume with customers and that a primary dealer should have more than $50MM of capital (up from the previous minimum of $25MM). Thanks to losses related to the 1987 crash of the stock market, and the subsequent doldrums in the government market, County NatWest Government Securities and L. F. Rothchild resigned their primary dealerships, reducing the number of primary dealers to 44.

AUCTION PROCEDURES

Currently, the Treasury sells all of its marketable debt through auctions.

Bills

The Treasury offers new 3- and 6-month bills each week and a new year bill (actually a 364-day bill) every four weeks. The new 3-month bill is always a reopening of an old 6-month bill, and every fourth week the new 6-month bill is a reopening of an old year bill. Except when holidays interfere, the size of the new bill issues to be offered is announced on Tuesday, the securities are auctioned the following Monday, and they are paid for and issued on the next Thursday.[1]

Banks and recognized dealers may submit tenders at the auction for the accounts of their customers as well as for their own account. Other bidders may submit tenders for only their own accounts. The Treasury accepts tenders from commercial banks, trust companies, and securities dealers without deposits; payment for securities purchased by these institutions must be made in immediately available funds on settlement day. All other bidders must submit the full face amount of the book-

---

[1]For a description of how the auction works, see pp. 317–18.

entry bills for which they apply; the Treasury remits to such bidders the difference between the face value of the bills they purchase and the purchase price they pay.

Any institution bidding for bills may pay for them with maturing bills, that is, by what is called *rolling bills*: In this case, the Fed pays to the bidder on settlement day the difference between the value of its maturing bills and the price at which it has purchased new bills.

Competitive bidders in the auction submit tenders stating the quantity of bills they are bidding on and the price they bid. A subscriber may enter several bids, stating the quantity of bills for which he is bidding at each price. The price bid is based on 100 and is stated to three decimal places. An investor who, for example, bids 92.485 is offering to pay $92.485 per $100 of face value on the quantity of bills for which he bids.

Between the day on which bills are auctioned and the day on which they are issued, the new bill issue, which has been sold but not yet delivered, is traded among investors and dealers on a *when-issued* basis. Securities traded on this basis are denoted *wi* on dealers' quote sheets.

Notes and Bonds

The Treasury presently offers a mix of coupon issues at each of its quarterly refundings; these occur in February, May, August, and November. The Treasury's current schedule calls for the quarterly refunding to include three issues: a 3-year note, a 10-year note, and a 30-year bond. These issues are generally sold on consecutive days, with the security of longest maturity being sold last. In addition to its refundings, the Treasury also offers a 2-year note every month, and 4-, 5-, and 7-year notes every quarter.

In note and bond auctions, the normal practice (Figure 14–1) is for investors to bid yields to two decimal places.[2] As in the case of bills, banks and recognized dealers may submit bids for notes and bonds for the accounts of their customers as well as

---

[2]See Chapter 8.

FIGURE 14–1
Tender for 2- and 3-year T notes

FORM PD 5174-1
(January 1988)

OMB No. 1535-0069
Expires 01-31-92

TREASURY DIRECT

TENDER FOR 2-3 YEAR TREASURY NOTE

TENDER INFORMATION

AMOUNT OF TENDER: $ _____

TERM _____

BID TYPE (Check One) ☐ NONCOMPETITIVE   ☐ COMPETITIVE AT ▢▢.▢▢ %

ACCOUNT NUMBER ▢▢▢▢ – ▢▢▢ – ▢▢▢▢

INVESTOR INFORMATION

ACCOUNT NAME

ADDRESS

CITY   STATE   ZIP CODE

TAXPAYER IDENTIFICATION NUMBER

1ST NAMED OWNER ▢▢▢ – ▢▢ – ▢▢▢▢ **OR** ▢▢ – ▢▢▢▢▢▢▢
SOCIAL SECURITY NUMBER   EMPLOYER IDENTIFICATION NUMBER

TELEPHONE NUMBERS

WORK (▢▢▢) ▢▢▢ – ▢▢▢▢   HOME (▢▢▢) ▢▢▢ – ▢▢▢▢

PAYMENT ATTACHED

TOTAL PAYMENT: $ _____

CASH (01): $ _____   CHECKS (02/03): $ _____
SECURITIES (05): $ _____ $ _____
OTHER (06): $ _____ $ _____

DIRECT DEPOSIT INFORMATION

ROUTING NUMBER ▢▢▢▢▢▢▢▢▢

FINANCIAL INSTITUTION NAME

ACCOUNT NUMBER

ACCOUNT NAME

ACCOUNT TYPE (Check One) ☐ CHECKING   ☐ SAVINGS

AUTHORIZATION

For the notice required under the Privacy and Paperwork Reduction Acts, see the accompanying instructions.

I submit this tender pursuant to the provisions of Department of the Treasury Circulars, Public Debt Series Nos. 1-86 and 2-86 and the public announcement issued by the Department of the Treasury.

Under penalties of perjury, I certify that the number shown on this form is my correct taxpayer identification number and that I am not subject to backup withholding because (1) I have not been notified that I am subject to backup withholding as a result of a failure to report all interest or dividends, or (2) the Internal Revenue Service has notified me that I am no longer subject to backup withholding. I further certify that all other information provided on this form is true, correct and complete.

_____ SIGNATURE   _____ DATE

FOR DEPARTMENT USE

TENDER NUMBER
912827

CUSIP

ISSUE DATE

RECEIVED BY

DATE RECEIVED

EXT REG   ☐
FOREIGN   ☐
BACKUP   ☐
REVIEW   ☐

CLASS   ☐

NUMBERS

☆ U.S.GOVERNMENT PRINTING OFFICE: 1989—620-344

for their own account. Bids from commercial banks, trust companies, and securities dealers need not be accompanied by a deposit. Other bidders must accompany their bids with a deposit, normally 5%, and must pay the remaining amount due with a check that will clear on or before settlement day or with immediately available funds on settlement day. Notes and bonds bid for in an auction may also be paid for with maturing securities.

During the 1- to 2-week period between the time a new Treasury note or bond issue is auctioned and the time the securities sold are actually issued, securities that have been auctioned but not yet issued trade actively on a *when-issued* basis. They also trade *wi* during the announcement to auction period.

Secondary Market

Little trading in outstanding notes and bonds occurs on organized stock exchanges. The New York Stock Exchange lists a few issues, and the American Exchange (AMEX) offers odd-lot trading in a few others, but neither exchange moves much volume.[3] The real secondary market for bills, notes, and bonds is the dealer-made market, in which huge quantities of bills, notes, and bonds are constantly traded under highly competitive conditions at small margins. Before we turn to that market, let's look at the brokers.

THE BROKERS

Dealers in government securities actively trade with retail and with each other. In recent years, the volume of trading in governments has become so huge and the pace so fast that almost all interdealer trades are done through brokers.

Table 14–2 shows this. In February 1989, for example, primary dealers did $106.6 billion of trades in Treasuries. Only $42

---

[3]AMEX trading in odd lots of governments is primarily for the convenience of brokers. If the broker uses a dealer to execute a small buy or sell order, the dealer's fee eats up most of the commission that the broker charges the investor. In contrast, on bond trades executed on an exchange by a member firm, transaction costs to the broker are minimal.

TABLE 14–2

U.S. government securities dealers transactions (par value; averages of daily figures, $ millions)

Item	1972	1975	1978	1979	1980	1981	1982	1983	1984	1985	1986	1987	1988	February 1989
U.S. government securities	**2,933**	**6,027**	**10,286**	**13,183**	**18,332**	**24,728**	**32,261**	**42,135**	**52,778**	**75,331**	**95,447**	**110,050**	**101,634**	**106,560**
By maturity														
Bills	2,259	3,889	6,173	7,915	11,413	14,768	18,393	22,393	26,035	32,900	34,249	37,924	29,393	29,500
Other within 1 year*	—	223	392	454	421	621	810	708	1,305	1,811	2,115	3,271	3,427	3,202
1–5 years	422	1,414	1,889	2,417	3,330	4,360	6,271	8,758	11,733	18,361	24,667	27,918	27,780	39,240
5–10 years	189	363	965	1,121	1,464	2,451	3,555	5,279	7,606	12,703	20,455	24,014	24,941	21,029
Over 10 years	63	138	867	1,276	1,704	2,528	3,232	4,997	6,099	9,556	13,961	16,923	16,093	13,589
By type of customer:														
U.S. government securities dealers	726	885	1,135	1,448	1,484	1,640	1,770	2,257	2,919	3,336	3,670	2,936	2,762	2,957
U.S. government securities brokers	411	1,750	3,838	5,170	7,610	11,750	15,794	21,045	25,580	36,222	49,558	61,539	59,849	61,625
All others†	1,794	3,392	5,312	6,564	9,229	11,337	14,697	18,833	24,278	35,773	42,218	45,575	39,023	41,977
Federal agency	**527**	**1,043**	**1,894**	**2,723**	**3,258**	**3,306**	**4,140**	**5,576**	**7,846**	**11,640**	**16,747**	**18,084**	**15,900**	**14,873**

Note: Averages for transactions are based on number of trading days in the period. Transactions are market purchases and sales of U.S. government securities dealers reporting to the Federal Reserve Bank of New York. The figures exclude allotments of, and exchanges for, new U.S. government securities, redemptions of call or matured securities, or purchases or sales of securities under repurchase, reverse repurchase (resale), or similar contracts.

*Not given in earlier *Federal Reserve Bulletins.*

†Includes—among others—all other dealers and brokers in commodities and securities, foreign banking agencies, and the Federal Reserve System. Also includes commercial banks.

Source: *Federal Reserve Bulletin.*

billion of this business was done direct, most with other dealers, and $61.6 billion was done with the brokers.

The most important reason brokers are used in the government market is ease of communication. In addition to the 44 primary dealers in governments and agencies, there are also a number of *reporting* or *aspiring dealers* as they're also called. (A dealer who aspires to become a primary dealer goes through a process whereby he reports his trading figures, first monthly and then daily, to the Fed; hence, would-be primary dealers are dubbed by some "reporting dealers," by others "aspiring dealers." With so many primary and reporting dealers, no government trader can keep in touch directly with all of his counterparts at other shops; he needs the brokers. Also, different shops split responsibility for different issues in different ways. Thus, a trader who covers 2- to 4-year notes at one shop might have to call two different traders at another shop to get quotes in his area.

The principal brokers of governments and agencies are RMJ, FBI (Fundamental Brokers Inc.), Cantor Fitz, Garban, Liberty, Hill Farber, and Chapdelaine. Of these, the big four (listed first) probably do 90 to 95% of the business. Currently, 52.4% of the business done by primary dealers is done with the brokers, 42.1% is done with retail, and only 5.4% is done dealer to dealer.

A large dealer is likely to have one or two bill traders, a number of traders of Treasury coupons, several traders of STRIPs, a basis trader or two, an options adjusted trader, a number of arbitrage traders, and a number of agency traders. Today, there are probably 1,200 to 1,300 (maybe more—it's hard to do a head count) traders in governments and agencies among the primary dealers and at least as many brokers to cover them. Each broker staffs for periods when volume is at a peak because he must service his clients adequately then to get their business when the volume is down.

The Brokers' Screens

In 1979, Garban became the first dealer to replace quotes over the phone with CRTs. Now, all of the brokers use screens to disseminate quotes.

A broker displays bids and offers placed with it for bills, Treasury coupons, and agencies on several different screens. When a new bid of offering comes in, the broker receiving it types it into his computer, and the new quote appears on its screen in the dealers' trading rooms within seconds. Generally, a broker considers a bid or offer placed with it good until canceled. However, a good broker will come back to his customer and check periodically. If a bid or offering is stale, he will say, "Can we freshen this up?"

Under what conditions bids and offers in the government market will go *off* or *subject* (to reconfirmation) is a matter left up to individual brokers. Usually, when the Fed comes into the market, all bids and offers go subject. However, when some key economic number is released, some brokers make the market subject, others don't; in this area, there are no formal rules. The practice of having the brokers' screens go subject whenever the Fed comes into the market or an important economic number comes out gives everyone a shot at reacting to such developments and thus protects traders from getting picked off.

One interesting change in the brokers' screens is that they now contain a lot more information. Today, the prices at which Treasuries trade are sharply influenced not just by the Fed funds rate and what the Fed is doing, but by oil prices, commodity prices, exchange rates, the size of the trade deficit, whether the stock market happens to be crashing, and so on.[4] Reflecting this, a bill trader now finds on various brokers' screens quotes not just on Fed funds, but on the Dow Jones average, the bill contract, the Euro contract (that is the global short hedge), the oil contract, sister securities such as the 2-year note, the long bond, the long-bond contract, the dollar/yen and other exchange rates, and so on.

Screens have now been around in the government market for well over a decade. "A lot of guys did not like the screens at the beginning," said one broker. "The Salis, Morgans, and Merrills were used to getting preferential treatment—first phone

---

[4]When the stock market crashed on October 19, 1987, there was a massive rally in the Treasury market, which prior to the Crash had been bearish. The Crash caused a flight to quality. Also, people correctly reasoned that the Fed would respond to the Crash by easing, which it did.

call from the brokers." The screens endured, however, and they have given traders one more way to play trading games. Also, as one trader noted, "a lot of this market is psychology, and when those CRTs start blinking hit, hit, hit, it has tremendous impact."

Volume and Size of Trades

Bill quotes in the brokers' screens are all good for 5MM unless otherwise indicated. Five million is a round lot and the minimum block anyone wants to trade. Currently, the average bill trade in the brokers' market is around 10MM, but trades far larger than that are done. A money fund or a central bank might come in and ask one of the bigger dealers to bid or offer 500MM bills, a goodly bit of which the dealer might lay off in the brokers' market. In notes, the average trade in the brokers' market is probably 7 to 10MM depending on the broker, and in the long bond it is 3 to 4MM.

Today, the brokers together broker about $6 to $14 billion of governments a day—the number varies a lot depending on how active the market is (Table 14–2). This big volume reflects several factors. The Treasury's outstanding marketable debt keeps growing; Treasury futures have created opportunities for traders to do a variety of new trades. Also, the development of new products, such as interest-rate swaps and MTNs, has increased trading in Treasuries, since the quick and dirty way for a dealer to hedge positions in these instruments is to short Treasuries, cash or futures. Finally, in some years, yields on Treasuries have been highly volatile; such volatility creates opportunities for traders to make big profits and thus encourages a surge in trading volume.

Because of the speed with which big trades can be executed through them, brokers, by their very existence, have contributed to the growth of new trades and trading techniques. Noted one bill trader, "It is now more efficient, for the cash-and-carry business against futures, to use the brokers when you want to buy size. Rather than call dealers to find out who has the bill I want, I can put a bid into the brokers' market and get execution almost immediately. In the old days, it would take me 10 or 15 minutes to buy 100MM. These days, I can do that in a second or two. The pace of this business had gotten a lot more frenetic."

When brokers talk to traders, they do not give advice. Brokers have inside information on what large dealers are doing, so it would be unethical for them to express opinions on what the market is likely to do.

If a trader has a bid in the market, he gets the right of first refusal on any new offering. Thus, for example, if a trader had a bid in at 6 and someone else came in with a $1MM offering at 7, a Garban broker would call the bidder and say, "6–7, a million. Your bid." The trader could then say, "I bought them," or just, "OK," the latter indicating that he has no interest. The bidder has 30 seconds to pick up his phone and take the new offering; after that, it is fair game for anyone. During the first 30 seconds a quote is on the Garban screen, it blinks to show that it is new.

The practice of giving the last seller first crack at the next bid is one reason why every trader needs to deal with several brokers. Say Merrill has a big selling job to do. They will hit a broker's bid in the issue they want to sell and every bid that comes in after it. Meanwhile, nobody else can hit a bid with that broker for the issue Merrill is selling.

Whenever a trade is effected through Garban, their screen flashes "hit" or "tak" (for taken) so that the market can see what trades are done and the prices at which they are done.

Commissions

The commission rates brokers charge on bills are 1/4 of an 01 on the year bill and 1/2 an 01 on the 6-month bill, both of which work out to $25 per 1MM. On 3-month bills, brokers charge 1/4 of an 01, which works out to $12.50 per 1MM.

The commission rate brokers used to charge on coupons was 1/128, which equals $78.12 per 1MM. Dealers thought this too much. Over the years prior to 1986, several developments occurred that increased brokers' profits. First, there were technological changes that lowered the cost of brokering. Second, brokers were able to accommodate the huge increases that occurred in the average size and number of brokered interdealer trades at limited additional cost. Despite these developments, no broker cut his rates; interbroker price competition was nil. The upshot was that brokers earned increasingly high profits, profits that dealers came to regard as absurd. A dealer's definition of what constituted an absurd level of brokers' profits was simple; at the brokerage rate of $78.12 per 1MM on coupons, a big broker who assumed *no risk* was earning on an $80 billion-volume day, more profit than was the average dealer who—to make any money—had to assume *lots of risk*.

To introduce some price competition to the world of government brokering, Salomon Brothers in 1986, together with a group of 30 other dealers, formed a new government bond broker, Liberty Brokerage, Inc. The advent of Liberty caused brokerage rates on government notes and bonds to fall immediately to $\frac{1}{256}$, one half their old level.

Liberty has never become much of a factor in the market. After three years in the business, it was doing only 2 to 3% of all brokered trades and was said to be losing money. The dealers never put the resources into Liberty to build it into a really professional operation. Perhaps all the dealers ever wanted was to put Liberty in place and keep it there to prevent the dealers from raising their commissions in the futures. Perhaps also, the dealers, who know the dealing but not the brokering side of the business, thought that it would be far easier than it is to build from scratch a professional brokering operation.

Traders at shops that have an interest in Liberty have themselves no interest in favoring Liberty over other brokers. Any money that Liberty makes goes not into a trader's pocket, but into his firm's general account. What a trader cares about in his own P&L, and, consequently, he judges brokers by one criterion, the quality of execution they provide.

Brokerage is paid only by the side that initiates a trade, so *locked markets,* markets in which the bid and offer are identical, can and do occur in governments. At times, when there is little interest in the market—no one wants to do anything—a locked market will persist for some time.

Risks in Brokering

With the exception of Cantor Fitz, brokers of governments deal only with primary and aspiring dealers who have already been well vetted by the Fed. This—plus the money market motto: "my word is my bond"—gives brokers and dealers a high degree of comfort with respect to the huge volume of trades executed through the brokers. Everyone expects everyone else to deal in good faith and to be able and in fact to settle trades on the agreed terms, even trades on which a trader has a big loss.

To a broker, the major risk in his business is that he may make a mistake. This might occur in several ways.

First, a broker has to be careful about what rates he quotes on his screen, since he must stand up to them. Said one, "If we put a wrong number on the screen, most traders are good about it and tell us. But there are others who like to hang us. When their [direct phone line] buttons light, you almost know that there is something wrong on the screen."

A second and bigger risk to a broker is that he and a client with whom he has done a trade may not both *know* that trade the same way: the security, the face amount, or the price. Because of tight controls, mistakes of this sort are infrequent, but even one such mistake can wipe out a broker's profits on a whole day's trades. To avoid errors, brokers employ double- or triple-check, in-house systems to record accurately all trades they do; also, they check back with each client to make sure that both sides know every trade they have done the same way.

It used to be that errors would rarely occur when dealers talked with brokers or with other dealers on the phone because they knew how to go through the reconfirm on the phone so no misunderstanding would occur. Describing this process, one dealer said, "If I call on the phone and say, 'I have a par bid for $10MM on the 2-year, are you interested?' and the other guy says, 'Yes, I will sell you 10MM at the buck,' then I say, 'I buy 10MM at par.' We have said it a few times and, when we hang up, we both write the tickets right away." Errors occur more often when salespeople talk to customers because many customers are unprofessional on the phone; so too are some junior salespeople.

Out Trades

Despite the care that brokers take, out trades do occur. Say a broker does a trade at 10 A.M. and when he later checks out with his counterparty, he says, "I sold you 10MM 10-years," and the counterparty says, "I did not buy 10MM, I bought 5MM." Or maybe the broker and the trader both know the trade as 10MM 10-years, but they don't know the same price. Either way it's an *out trade*.

In years past, when a dealer and a broker were faced with an out trade, they would sort of try to reconstitute the trade, and if they could not agree on what it was, the broker, more often than not, ate the cost of the out trade. When a broker ends up long or short due to an out trade, he always immediately covers that position, regardless of whether he has a gain or a loss in it.

Today, out trades have become more common, but, commented one broker, "Compared to the amount of business we all do, it is not a big problem." Still, continued the same broker, "In recent years, as the markets grew and became more volatile, the dealers put kids on the phone who lacked experience and knowledge of the business and its jargon. Also, dealers came to view the brokers as just one more place, along with the Chicago pits, to trade—just another place to get business done. Dealers no longer have, toward brokers, a big brother attitude: you do not screw your broker because he is your friend. Consequently, we came to the conclusion that we had to *tape* our conversations with traders."

Agent versus Principal

Brokers never give up names on trades done through them. They used to clear their trades through their respective clearing banks. Now, trades done through brokers are to be cleared via a netting process run by the Government Securities Clearing Corporation.

By not giving up names on trades done through them, by acting as *blind brokers,* brokers in the government market assume in effect the role of principal. However, brokers in this area think of themselves "as just rolling through a trade from, say, Sali to Merrill." Put in legal terms, brokers think of themselves as acting in fact as *agent, not principal*.

The brokers believe if there were a hit, failure to settle by one party to a brokered trade and consequent loss to the other party, the injured party would look through the broker to the other party who defaulted for restitution of his losses. Thus, the brokers' attitude is, "If there's a hit, don't [dealer] look at me, look at them [the defaulting dealer]." The Government Securities Act of 1986 sort of defines government brokers as agents, but the issue has never been tested in court.

Although most people don't notice, all of the principal brokers of governments are currently owned—via merger and acquisitions—by British firms. Thus, to the U.S. brokers' long-standing conviction that they act as agents is added the mind set of their British parents; the Brits have been brokering for over 200 years, and when the Brits think brokering, they think agent, agent, agent.

While dealers have not contested, so long as things went smoothly, the notion that interdealer brokers are agents, one broker noted, "People will tell me that they do a lot of wi business with our firm because its parent has deep pockets. And that after we have hammered home that we are agents. Every time we add a new customer, we send out a letter stating the definition in the Securities Act of 1986 of an interdealer broker as an agent, and so on."

The agent/principal question was brought to a head when dealers and brokers tried to agree on the Government Securities Clearing Corporation, designed to make the clearing of governments more efficient. The dealers wanted the brokers to both put up capital and assume risk. The brokers said no on both counts but finally reached a compromise that probably made no one terribly happy.

GSCC, by netting trades, will eliminate the need for brokers to clear trades. To the brokers, that cut in their costs sounds dandy, but they are less keen on the notion that an industry-owned cooperative is going to know exactly who is doing what business and that, in addition, the dealers might say, "Your costs were cut by X, now cut your rates by Y."

Going National

Cantor Fitz, the one government broker that has *gone national*—allowed major retail customers access to its screens—has enjoyed tremendous success and is currently the single biggest broker of governments. Its example has naturally led other brokers to think of going national.

Noted one dealer, "The possibility of the brokers going national is the fear most dealers live with because there is a proprietary advantage to being part of that system. That advantage is the biggest advantage in being a recognized [by the Fed] dealer. Most everyone else trades without their headlights on.

"There is an incredible differential in the information available to an institutional investor in Okefenokee who is looking at one not very well used [by the dealers] broker's markets [Cantor Fitz's] and that available to a recognized dealer who has five brokers' TVs and is plugged in with 120 phone lines to all the other dealers and to all the exchanges where they trade futures. That information differential is how dealers outtrade their customers."

Who May Tune In

Brokers will give a screen to any primary dealer. Also, any time a firm that says it's an "aspiring" dealer and has good credit comes to a broker, the broker will put them on its system.

A long-threatened suit by Lazard Freres raised the issue of whether it violates antitrust laws for brokers and big dealers to have a network that generates valuable market information for a limited circle of firms. For years, investigations have been going on; Justice has been saying that maybe there should be wider access to the screens, while Treasury has been saying, "The market works very well, fellows."

One upshot of this was that two of the major brokers set up a joint venture to sell the last price to an information vendor. In the mid-1980s, all of the vendors wanted such information. Thus, the brokers thought that selling price information might turn out to be a 40 or 50MM industry. Things did not turn out that way. Telerate is the only game in town; they already publish Cantor Fitz's quotes, so they are unwilling to pay anyone else for prices. Reuters is strong in foreign markets, but their philosophy is that they do not pay for prices. Knight Ritter is a smaller player; and Quotron, now owned by Citi, can't make up its mind what it wants to do.

A related issue is whether bids and offerings should be made public. That issue raises yet another question: Who owns that information, the brokers or the dealers?

Automated Trading

The government brokers run what amounts to an unlicensed exchange. In the 20-odd years that governments have been brokered, the way in which that exchange operates has slowly changed. At the outset, brokers phoned runs to dealers. Then, in 1977 to 1978, the era of screens began. Now, a decade later, the market seems ripe for further change, perhaps a switch to an automated system, since many of today's traders grew up using computers.

Reuters has spent millions of dollars developing the Reuters 200, an automated trading system with voice recognition. The system is impressive, but noted one broker, "On *workup trades,* the 5s, the 10s, the 25s, and so on, the computer falls short. If you want to buy 1MM and the other guy wants to sell 1MM, the system is fine; but it cannot cope fast with a typical [workup] situation: a guy puts a bid into the screen for 1MM; his bid is hit, and he says [as his successive bids are hit], 'Make it 5,' 'Make it 10,' 'Make it 22.5MM.' The automated system is too cumbersome for that sort of trade." Yet, that is how large trades typically get done. When a dealer has a sizable job to do, say in coupons, he typically bids for or offers 1MM because he doesn't want to show his hand.

More Dealers Going National?

Probably for reasons suggested above, one more broker of governments, RMJ, made public in early 1989 plans to go national. The big primary dealer-only brokers have long yenned to do so, figuring there was a lot of money to be made dealing with big institutional customers. Still, they didn't do it because they feared that, if they did, their dealer customers would "put them in the penalty box": stop doing business with them.[5]

RMJ's initial decision to go national may simply confirm a trend that has been going on. A big institutional investor does not invest warm-blooded money with "its" dealer. It shops the dealers with a determination and finesse that is turning governments into *a commodity*. When dealers and brokers talk about governments becoming "a commodity," what they mean is that there's *no spread* for them in trading governments with big accounts to whom price alone matters. But if that's so, then in the end perhaps dealers won't mind, might even like, having one or more of the interdealer brokers go national, since that would permit them to get along without some of their expensive salespeople who currently aren't generating much net revenue.

That's not to say that the dealers would be left with no function toward big retail accounts. For example, most large accounts would probably find it more cost-effective to have a dealer work a big swap for them (especially in off-the-run issues) than to take the risk and use the resources they'd have to in order to do the job themselves. Also, a big account that wanted to buy zeros of a certain maturity in size probably wouldn't want to get into the business of stripping bonds itself. Finally, many accounts surely value the flow of information they get from a good dealer: his views on relative value in the market, on possible changes in the shape of the yield curve, on the meaning of recent economic numbers, and so on.

A big problem for a broker going national is capital. Once he does that, he can't say he's just an agent. He becomes a principal; no matter how high the credit standards he sets for permitting retail customers on his system, neither dealers nor customers will want to deal through him unless he is viewed as having the resources to make good on a trade where one party defaults. That's why Cantor Fitz has a 75MM balance sheet at risk.

---

[5] Apparently, that happened to RMJ and was one reason RMJ reversed, later in 1989, its decision to go national.

THE BILL MARKET

The bill market is the one sector of the government market that is truly part of the money market, since short coupons are not traded actively as are bills of similar current maturity.

Bill Auctions

The cast of bidders in a typical bill auction is varied. The Fed currently holds in portfolio well over 100 billion of bills, some portion of which matures each week. The Fed replaces some or all of its maturing bills by *rolling* them in the auction; it never bids for bills in the auction to increase the size of its portfolio. To add to its portfolio, the Fed buys bills in the secondary market from dealers.[6]

Currently, foreign central banks have huge holdings of dollars. Those of countries with strong currencies have accumulated dollars defending the dollar. However, even central banks of Latin American countries may gather up sizable dollar balances prior to making interest payments on their foreign debt. The favored place for foreign central banks to put their dollars to work is the bill market. In particular, foreign central banks are currently large bidders for 6-month bills, much smaller bidders for 3-month bills, which they already own as a result of earlier purchases of longer bills (Table 14–3, *Foreign official*).

Besides the dealers, other major players in bills are money funds, state and local governments, and—when rates are right—individuals. Since they were introduced to money funds, individuals have become extremely rate conscious. Consequently, in a period such as early 1989 when the yield curve was inverting and bills probably outpaid any money fund, individuals flock to the bill market.

---

[6]To prevent the Fed from becoming a money-printing machine for the Treasury, the Fed has long been forbidden to buy—except on a rollover basis—other than small amounts of new Treasury debt directly from the Treasury. This prohibition has, under current institutional arrangements, *no* effect whatsoever on the size of the Fed's portfolio or on the amount of bank reserves it creates.

TABLE 14–3
Results of a weekly bill auction held February 13, 1989

	Tenders Applied for and Accepted ($ millions)			
	3-Month Bills		6-Month Bills	
Type of Bidders	Total Applied for	Total Accepted	Total Applied for	Total Accepted
Federal Reserve	2,584.0	2,384.0	2,300.0	2,100.0
Foreign official	14.8	14.8	1,173.5	1,473.5
Noncompetitive	1,577.0	1,577.0	1,290.0	1,290.0
Subtotal	4,175.8	3,975.8	4,763.5	4,863.5
Net to the Street	24,762.2	3,229.0	19,128.0	2,349.0
Total issue	28,938.0	7,204.8	23,891.5	7,212.5

Before the auction, there is a buzz of auction talk among the dealers. Dealers know the size of the issues the Treasury is offering, and they try to assess the retail interest in these issues and what amounts other dealers are likely to bid for. That is the sort of information a trader requires to hone his bid down to the last decimal point.

Much of the talk between dealers before the auction focuses on what are going to be the *top* and the *tail* in the auction; in a bill auction the top is the highest price (lowest yield) bid in the auction and the tail is the lowest bid (highest yield) accepted in the auction. Dealers bidding on bills all want to hit the tail, which takes skill. On an auction day, one dealer noted: "Today I do not want to buy much. I am just trying to bid for where I think the tail will be. I am bidding for practice, to see if my market reading is accurate. You have to keep in touch because, when you really want to buy, you need to have the confidence."

The final moment of decision for a dealer comes at about 1:25 Eastern time. Then time runs out. He has to pick a price, grab a phone, and call a runner stationed in a special room at the Fed; the latter has a tender form all made out except for the bid prices, which he inks in at the last moment.

Once the Fed receives all the bids—the cutoff time is 1:30 P.M.—it determines what bids it will accept; it announces the result of the auction at 6:00 P.M. in the evening.

Table 14–4 shows the results of a bill auction held March 27, 1989. Note that on the 3-month (13-week) bill, the top and the tail were separated by only 0.015 in price and by only 6 bp in yield. The difference between the top and the tail in auctions of Treasury notes and bonds is also usually small.

Supply in Treasury auctions varies from week to week and from month to month. At times when the Treasury is paying down the debt seasonally or extending the maturity of the debt, it will sell fewer bills than the amount maturing. At other times, it will increase the size of the regular weekly bill auctions. Supply offered also varies from one note or bond auction to another.

Dealers act in part as distributors of the Treasury debt. How much distribution is required on a new issue depends on the relationship between the supply offered and demand by retail. When the Treasury is adding, it is likely that the new issue will sell at a fractionally higher yield than surrounding issues until it is distributed, and dealers consequently have a profit incentive to bid aggressively in the auction. When the reverse is true—for example, the Treasury is reducing the size of a bill issue—there is both less need for the dealers to act as distributors and less profit incentive for them to bid aggressively in the auction.

TABLE 14–4
Results of a weekly bill auction held March 27, 1989

	13-Week	26-Week
Applications	$25,046,775,000	$19,783,925,000
Accepted bids	$7,220,940,000	$7,203,790,000
Accepted at low price	68%	11%
Accepted noncompetitively	$1,219,435,000	$1,171,750,000
Average price	97.700 (9.10%)	95.389 (9.12%)
High price (rate)	97.712 (9.05%)	95.399 (9.10%)
Low price (rate)	97.697 (9.11%)	95.374 (9.15%)
Coupon equivalent	9.44%	9.69%

Both issues are dated March 30. The 13-week bills mature June 29, and the 26-week bills mature September 28.

Bill Shortage

These days, people sometimes talk about the *shortage* of bills
There is no shortage in the sense that bills can't be bought at
any price. However, due to the Treasury's policy of lengthening
the average maturity of the debt, bills represent a declining
percentage of marketable Treasury debt. Also, the scarcity of
bills is reflected in what's happened to carry: some years back,
the 3-month bill often traded at positive carry; now, the 3-month
bill trades almost always at negative carry, the 6-month bill
even to carry, and only the year bill at positive carry.

In gauging the shortness of the supply of bills, it isn't useful
to look at total bills applied for in an auction. That number is
meaningless; the Fed expects primary dealers to give a bid, but
their bid needn't be close to the market. Thus, a dealer who
doesn't want to buy bills might bid 8.75 for bills he expected to
come at 8.73. A number that is meaningful is how many of the
bills sold in an auction get to the Street. Table 14–3 shows that,
in the auction on February 13, 1989, the Fed, foreign official
institutions (often central banks), and noncompetitive bidders
took big chunks of the new 3- and 6-month bills sold. (Noncompetitive bids—now limited to 1MM or less—include bids by individuals and others who take bills out of the market and are
unlikely to put them back in.) *Net,* in the auction described in
Table 14–3, only 3.2 billion of the 3-month bills and 2.3 billion
of the 6-month bills sold found their way to the Street. If these
amounts were split evenly among the primary and aspiring
dealers, each would end up with peanuts. That's one sense in
which there is a bill shortage.

To put the above numbers in perspective, note the long- and
short-bill traders at a big shop might together easily trade 3 to 4
billion of bills on an average day. While only a portion of these
trades would be with retail, these traders are likely, during the
course of a day, to do many 10 to 25MM trades with corporations, trades with money funds, each of which might run 250MM
or more, and big trades with state and local government bodies
and with foreign central banks.

Another point of interest in Table 14–3 concerns what the
Fed did. The Fed may apply in an auction for sufficient bills to
roll its maturing bills, but nothing requires it to buy that many

bills. In the 2/13/89 auction, the Fed failed to roll 400MM bills, a tack it had been taking for three weeks. Bills that the Fed does not roll the Street ends up buying, and such buying drains bank reserves. By failing to roll all of its maturing bills over the three weeks in question, the Fed drained, without benefit of open market operations, 1 billion of permanent reserves.

Runs

Runs in the brokers' market and between dealers are for *current* issue, that is, those most recently auctioned. In 3-month and 6-month bills, an issue stays current for a week. During that period, the new issue is distributed to people who don't have it but want it and vice versa. After that activity in this issue dies down, a new issue is auctioned and becomes current, and action again picks up.

Bills are quoted in 01s. Thus, a trader's market in a given bill might be 9.10 offered and 9.12 bid. In the interdealer market, traders often refine their bids and offers to half an 01 by using pluses; a bid of 12+ means that the trader is bidding 12½ bp. The *handle,* 9 in the above illustration, is never quoted.

A broker's run in the bill market might be: "3-month, 50–49, 2 by 5; 6-month at this juncture 70 locked, 10MM up. On the year bill, 96–95, 10 by 1." When a broker quotes the size of the market as "2 by 5," he means that 2MM is bid and 5MM offered. When size is "10MM *up,*" that means both the bid and the offer are good for 10MM. Sometimes, dealers will make their bids and offers on an all-or-none basis. If the dealer bids for 5MM AON (all or nothing), no one can hit that bid for less than 5MM. Sometimes, there will be a bid on an issue but no offer. In that case, the broker would quote the market, for example, as "70 bid without."

Currently, the bid-off spread in the brokers' market is an 01 in the active bills, an 02 in the off-the-run bills.

The Real Market

Bids in the brokers market may or may not reflect the *real market,* that is, the bid and offered prices at which size could be done. One trader commented: "I think in part of the real market as the market away from the brokers. If I were to go to a retail account who owns bills I want, what would I have to pay to buy them on a swap, what would it cost me to get them from him to me?

"At times, quotes in the brokers' market are distortions of the market because they are created to be misleading. Suppose I want to buy 100MM of a particular bill. I know that everyone is looking at the brokers' market. So what do I do? I make a one-man market. I make them 85 locked, 5 up on both sides. Now I go around and call the dealers and ask them for a market in that bill and they will make it 85–83 or 86–84. I will buy them at 83 or 84 and then I will take my market out [of the brokers' screen] after I have bought what I needed. Then, if I want, I can put another market in, and that becomes the market. These are the games played by traders. If you want to buy or sell, you try to distort what you really want to do. Depending on the market, this can be done at times with some success.

"Of course, when I put a locked bid with the brokers I have to stand up to both sides. It might not work. I might lock the market and get myself immediately lifted. If I wanted to buy, that would ruin that act; and now I would have to buy another 5MM. You cannot lock too far from the real market. But remember, we are talking about distorting the market an 01 or half an 01. That pays because I am trading big volume.

"If a dealer does not know if the market on a broker's screen is the real market, he has to spend some money to find out—to buy or sell to find out how real the bid or offered side is in terms of size. If he spends 10MM on bills and they are reoffered, then he knows that there is a genuine seller there. If he buys 5 and that is all he can buy, then maybe that is not the real market. Maybe the market is just holding up because the bid is stronger than the offer."

Trading wi

Bills have long been traded on a when-issued (*wi*) basis between the auction and settlement dates. Some years ago, the custom developed of trading bills wi after they are announced but before they are auctioned. Because of this practice, the most recently announced *and* the most recently auctioned 3-month bill will both trade wi for several days in the middle of each week. During this period, traders refer to the most recently announced 3-month bill as the wi bill even if the most recently auctioned 3-month bill is still trading wi.

In bills, wi trading is very active both between dealers and between dealers and retail. For a trader who wants to short the market, selling bills trading wi is more attractive than shorting an outstanding issue, because on a wi sale delivery need not be made immediately and a wi sale is thus simpler and cheaper than an ordinary short sale. Also, a bill trader who remains bearish and wants to keep on his short can do so by constantly rolling that short, week to week, in the wi market. That way he never gets involved in the cost of borrowing, which eats into the profitability of a short.

For a dealer who wants to trade 3-month bills, buying them wi is at times the only way he can do so without incurring a negative carry. Suppose, for example, that Fed funds are 8.40, the repo rate on governments at 8.20, and the 3-month bill is trading at 8 on a discount basis, that is, at 8.10 on a bond equivalent yield. If a trader buys that bill and finances it, he'll have negative carry. Still, a lot of people like to trade that bill, so they will trade it in the wi market where carry is in effect zero.

Trading on a wi basis before the auction serves other useful purposes. Noted one dealer, "A lot of regional firms trade the wi market actively. Before the advent of such trading, the recognized dealers with brokers' wires were able to engineer auctions because people outside the New York dealer community were not sure where the market was. So if three guys got together, they could—in the talk before the auction—push it an 01 or an 02 and buy most of the auction. Now with wi trading, the regionals know where the market is because the bill has been trading wi three or four days before the auction.

"Also, a lot of times people who do not like the market will build up a short going into the auction, so half the issue is really taken care of before 1:30. That really stabilizes the market when you bring in a new issue."

Weekly Cycle

There tends to be something of a weekly cycle in the way the bill currently being auctioned trades. "On Monday," one trader noted, "you have the auction. Then Tuesday, right after the auction, you generally do not see too much price improvement unless it was a very aggressive auction or some extraordinary event affects the market; on Tuesday, the market performs sloppily because you have people who can sell the issue whether they have it or not. On Wednesday, there is a day to go, and people who are short start to think—shall I take my short in or not; and the market tends to behave a little better. Then Thursday, you have demand. The shorters have to cover or borrow, which is expensive. Also, the previous bill matures and people who have not rolled over in the auction have to put their money to work, so they go and invest in the new bills. This is the busiest day. Then Friday it tails off a bit."

Technicals

These days, bill traders, like other traders of governments, engage in technical analysis. Ask a bill trader at a major shop about this, and he will likely pull out a dog-eared, Scotch-taped roll of paper on which he charts daily price activity in the bill market.

"I have to look at technicals," noted one bill trader, "because other people do. However, you don't get the same gapping in bills that you do in bonds when rates reach a certain level. Bills are more placed where the bond is more traded by speculators. If you were inclined to speculate in the bill market, it would be easier and cheaper to speculate in Euro futures. So you will see the bills just sit still and the bonds jump eight ticks; Euros trade that way too—almost follow the bonds.

"In bills, fundamental supply and demand are more important. If there is a dramatic amount of buying, no matter what the technicals say—even if they say 'Don't buy'—I have to buy if retail is buying. Right after the stock market crash in 1987, the year bill rallied. Part way into the rally, some technicians said, 'This move down in the rate is half the prior move up, so that is as far as the market should go.' They shorted and lost a lot of money. Twice, the chartists tried to stop the rally in the year bill; nonetheless, highs were made on Thursday of that week. You can follow the technicals, but you also have to look at fundamentals."

Swaps in the Brokers' Market

In doing big trades with retail, bill traders rely partly on the liquidity afforded them by the brokers' market. In working trades with retail, traders will use this market not only to do straight buys and sells, but to swap out of offsetting positions created, say, by an account that asks the dealer for a swap out of one bill issue into another. "Recently, things in the brokers' screens are more often than not hooked together," said one trader as he finished a successful trade. "I told the broker that I would sell the Aug 10 bills at 8.49 if I could buy Aug 17s at 8.52, and I told him my size. When he got a customer who wanted to buy the Aug 10s, he automatically did the other side of the trade. I was trying to undo a swap with a customer and make some money out of it. That was the last 15MM I had to unwind. I just made half a basis point—not a big deal but I did 50MM."

A Place to Build Volume

To become a primary dealer, a dealer must do 1% of retail business as measured by the Fed. The easiest and cheapest way to do such business is in the bill market because profits and losses there are so small. When the dealer community was growing from 36 to 46, the bill market became very difficult to trade. "A customer would ask for an offering," commented one trader, "and I wanted to sell them because I owned them, so I would offer at the bid side, at 46½, and I would miss at 47½. Someone was paying an 01 to buy that business."

This has changed recently. New dealers have got their Fedwires and they have experienced a period of losses. Now, new dealers, particularly the Japanese, who were huge in the bill market, are expecting their bill trader to make money as opposed to buy retail business. Said one trader, "The market is now a lot saner, you do not have to sell through the market to do business with retail."

Quotes to Retail and Protocols

When a good trader gives quotes to retail he will not simply *bracket* the brokers' market—quote a bid slightly above that in the brokers' market and an offer slightly below that in the brokers' market. He will quote on the basis of his own perception as to where the real market is.[7] Also, his quotes will be influenced by the size he wants to do or retail wants to do.

One dealer commented, "Say I wanted to buy size in an issue. The bid in the brokers' market is 20–18, 10 by 5. I might bid 17 to retail for 50MM. That's an 01 less than the offered rate in the brokers' market, but there I can buy only 5 not 50."

If a retail customer has a lot he wants to buy or sell and he wants to get the job done properly, there are certain protocols he should follow. Say he is a big seller; he should be reasonably open with a single dealer and get that dealer to work for him—to try to retail what he is selling piece by piece to people who might be buyers. Sometimes, a big seller will hit every bid around for 10 or 20MM, the market gets swamped, and the dealers all end up competing with each other to unload these securities. A customer who sells that way gets a reputation and won't get the same treatment from dealers the next time.

The dealer is also expected to be fair with retail. Said one, "A professional dealer won't move the market on a customer who tells him he's a big buyer or seller." Another dealer commented, "Say I want to sell 100MM of an issue; the World Bank comes in and wants to sell to me and the market is 84–3; I will make him 86–5. He will know right away I am not his person. He will know I am trying to sell. I will be open with him—tell him I am not in a position to help him because I too have a position to unwind."

The protocol of openness does not apply between dealers. If a dealer is trying to sell in size, he will attempt to hide that from

---

[7]Recall the discussion of trading in Chapter 10.

other dealers—to try, for example, to play the games described above to distort the market and cloak his true intent.

The 90-Day Bill Rate

The Fed directly influences a single interest rate, the Fed funds rate. In doing so, however, it strongly affects the level and pattern of other short-term interest rates. It used to be that the 90-day bill rate was coupled to the Fed funds rate and other rates keyed off it; as the Fed funds rate changed, the whole structure of short-term interest rates would change.

Today, the linkage between the Fed funds rate and the rate on 3-month bills is far less tight than it once was; and as a result, the 3-month bill rate is no longer the bellwether rate it once was. One reason is that foreign central banks that have intervened to support the dollar have used the dollars thus acquired to buy huge amounts of bills. At times, such buying causes bills to way outperform other money market instruments. In consequence, securities that used to be spread off bills have become unsalable. Today, investors will not buy bill-based floaters or anything that is indexed off bills.

As Figure 14–2 shows, a rate that has in recent years tracked closely the Fed funds rate is the rate on 3-month Euros. As would be expected, the spread of Euros to Fed funds tends to narrow when rates are falling and to widen when rates are rising.

Today, the rates at which money market instruments trade are all evaluated in terms of the spread at which they trade to Euros of similar maturity. Euro rates have thus replaced bill rates as the benchmarks that investors use to gauge relative value.

Short Bills

Short bills used not to be very actively traded, perhaps because the principal buyers of them were corporate treasurers, banks collateralizing government deposits, bank trust departments, and other investors who tended to be hold-until-maturity investors. Of these, the corporate treasurer at least is likely to have

FIGURE 14–2

Yield comparison: Fed funds, 3-month T bill, 3-month LIBOR

(monthly averages, through April 1989)

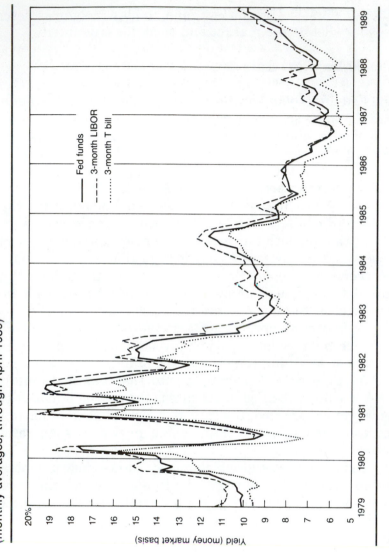

Source: J. P. Morgan Securities, Inc.

moved out of short bills into commercial paper where he gets a much better rate.

Today, the yield curve in bills still tends to be steep at the very short end due to people putting away short bills—their doing so dries up supply. However, a lot of other people are out there trading huge amounts of bills right up until they mature. In particular, central banks have large holdings of short bills, and as soon as they own a bill that is rich to the bill next to it, they will swap. So too will money funds.

Short bills do especially well whenever there is uncertainty in the market. A flight to quality will always drive down the rates on such bills. Even if the Fed appears to be tightening at the time of a flight to quality, investors like short bills; they reason that, if they are in something that is very short, a rise in interest rates won't hurt them that much.

In a dealership, the job of trading short bills is often given to a trainee. The market for short bills is quite stable so he can't lose much money, and trading these bills gives him an opportunity to learn the lingua franca and other fundamentals of bill trading before he goes on to trade longer bills, which is where the action and risk is.

TREASURY NOTES

The activities of a note trader closely resemble in some ways those of a bill trader but differ sharply in others, because notes trade differently from bills. In the note market, yields are quoted in 32nds, but quotes can be refined to 64ths through the use of *pluses;* an 8+ bid, for example, means that the bid is eight and one-half 32nds, which is $17/64$. On dealers' runs for notes with less than a year to run, the normal spread between the bid and asked is $1/32$. On notes in the 1- to 2-year area, the spread widens to $1/16$, and on notes beyond one year, it is typically $1/8$, except on new issues that are very actively traded. Quotes on notes are normally good for $1MM, but trades much larger and smaller are also done.

Most large shops have a number of people trading notes. A junior trader may be responsible for trading notes with a current maturity of 0 to 18 or 21 months, an area where it is hard to lose a lot of money. Several more senior people will trade longer notes. Often the person working with short coupons will do trades of coupons against bill futures.

Trading Notes

Over the years, big changes have occurred in the way dealers bid for and deal in notes and bonds because of the huge increases that have occurred in the number and sizes of outstanding issues and because of the increased volatility of rates.

A fair, if oversimplified, way to describe how shops used to trade coupons would be to say that they bought notes when they were bullish, shorted them when they were bearish, and had a specialist arbitrageur who sought at all times to profit from rate anomalies.

Today talking to coupon traders, one hears them again and again speak about positioning and trading on a hedged basis where the hedge is often *generic:* The trader buys something— often a new issue at auction and sells something else so that he views his net position as zero and to boot has established an arbitrage or spread that promises to yield profits. The process is best described by quoting a few traders.

Said one, "A few years ago a major shop would easily run a billion position unhedged. Now the dealers have become arbitrageurs. For example, when the government sells 4-year notes, the Street sells 2s and 6s or 2s and 5s. Then they cover their shorts in the coupon area by buying the 4-year note. Last week the Treasury sold 5 billion 5-years, and all of a sudden 2-years, 3-years, and 4-years were all over the place. The supply of these securities was created by shorts dealers put on so as to bid on the new 5-year note. Once we got done with the 5-year note auction, the 2s and 3s were still not going any place because the next auction down the pike was the year bill.

"Whereas big shops used to go long 500 or 600 of a new issue, they are now more likely to go short and long in ratio and rightly or wrongly to consider their net position zero. For example, at current interest rate levels, the yield value of $\frac{1}{32}$nd on a 2-year note is 0.018 whereas on a 10-year note it is 0.005. If a dealer buys 4MM 2-year notes and shorts 1MM 10-year notes, he considers his net position zero.

"Actually, there is a lot of risk in being long one area and short another. In 1980, Citi, for example, had a lot of 2-year notes and was short the long bond. When the note market rallied, Citi covered its short in the long bonds, let its long position in notes ride, and made 100MM." As this quote indicates, the plays dealers refer to as hedges are anything but pure hedges. Also, the lines between hedging, arbitraging, and trading have become fuzzy.

Another dealer, speaking of how dealer trading has changed said, "I think you are seeing more generic hedging: 'I like the yield curve or I like the market, so I will buy the short end of the curve and sell the longer end,' or 'I like the curve and the market and there is supply coming in the longer end, so I will buy the short end and short the long end.'

"Last week, the year bill came and people were buying them. What were they selling? Everyone was selling the 2-years, because they expect them to come tonight. There is more of that hedge-type trading now. It is trading because there is considerable risk to this sort of thing. It is a hedge in the sense that, if the 2-year comes cheaply, the year bill will go down. What a trader is betting is that the 2-year note will go down faster than the year bill because $6 billion of the new 2-year is coming in the auction. Consequently, the 2-year should decay faster in yield than the year bill. Currently, the year bill is trading 10.10–10.12; no one expects the year bill to be 10.10 and the 2-year note to be down half a point.

"On this sort of hedge, you would expect to lose money on one side and to make it on the other. You hope to make more than you lose. That is not like the old game of selling the old 2-year and buying the new 2-year and letting that work out. In the past you could do that trade in considerable size; it is less easy now.

"It has also become common for dealers to use futures as a hedge, often generically. You have bought something, and you want to sell something. If it is cheaper to sell the futures market than to short the cash market, you sell futures. Which is cheaper at a given point will depend on several factors: the spread of cash to futures, transactions costs, and the cost of carrying a short [the reverse rate].

"Today, it is hard to separate arbitrages and hedges. No one consciously sits down and says, 'I want to buy 2-years and sell long bonds.' They might say, 'I am going to buy the 2-year in the auction when they come, and if I have to sell something, I will sell the longer end because supply is coming there next week.' Those are not arbs. They are generic plays along the yield curve based upon supply. They may or may not work."

Hedging and arbitraging are practiced not only by coupon traders, but by bill traders. Said one, "Market volatility has led people to do a lot more arbitrage trading than outright risk trading. They still do the latter when market conditions seem right. However, there are now a lot more people doing spread trades. Traders, for example, will buy a spread. Currently, the spread of the year bill to the 2-year note is roughly 105 bp. When the spread was 60 bp, traders were buying the year bill and selling the 2-year note. They did this trade because they anticipated that the slope of the yield curve would turn positive and thought that that would widen this spread. Now that the spread has gotten to 105, traders sell the year bill and buy the 2-year. Or if they do not have to trade on, they will sell the year bill and buy the 2-year because the year bill will be auctioned next week so they expect this spread to come in at least temporarily.

"There is a lot of spread trading going on in the cash market. Traders also do spread trades between the 6-month and the year bill and between the 3- and 6-month bills."

In absorbing new supply, the Street still takes risks by not taking the big naked positions it used to. By learning to hedge its bets, the Street has become more efficient in distributing the debt. This explains in part how the market managed, even in years of highly volatile rates, to smoothly absorb ever-increasing amounts of new Treasury debt in all maturity ranges.

Wi Trading

Notes have always been traded wi from auction to settlement. The Treasury used to forbid the trading of coupons wi during the period between announcement of a new issue and auction of that issue. The Treasury feared that such trading would be speculative and leave room for investors to be injured. Such fears were probably always groundless. In any case, the Treasury has switched its thinking. It concluded that it might save money by permitting new coupons to trade wi after announcement, so it rescinded its ban on such trading.

This was a big innovation in the coupon market. Now, new coupon issues are routinely traded wi before they are auctioned. Since the Treasury auctions all its new coupons through yield auctions, traders who trade (on a yield basis) coupons wi before an auction are trading securities on which they don't know what the coupon will be. After the auction, they have to *back into prices* on the basis of the coupon established in the auction and then write tickets on all such trades they have done. If anyone has been inconvenienced by the new wi trading in coupons, it is the back-office people who have to deal with a big hassle every time a coupon is auctioned.

Current Issues

In the note market, an issue is current from the time it is auctioned until it is replaced by a new issue. Thus, the new 2-year note is current for a month, and new 4-year note for a quarter. A current issue trades much more actively than other issues until it becomes distributed or is replaced by a new issue. Although notes range in original maturity from 2 to 10 years, there are at any time only five or six current issues that are relatively new and actively traded at narrow spreads. Moreover, before the Treasury undertook its program of regularization of debt issuance, there were even fewer.

Many investors roll notes to stay in the current issue, just as they roll 3- or 6-month bills. Sometimes, they will even give up coupon just to stay in a note that is active enough so that they can get a bid on size in a market that is quiet or going down. Staying in the current note allows the investor to increase yield by moving out on the yield curve while still maintaining liquidity. Dealers, too, like to position current issues. As one noted, "When I go long or short, I like to stay as current as possible because that is where most people have buying and selling interest."

In longer notes, the market used to sometimes go for months without a new issue, something that would be unimaginable in the bill market. When this occurred, trading in this market area tapered off. Where and when the Treasury chooses to issue its new debt also affects the yield curve. For example, before the 3-year note was added to the issues sold in the quarterly refunding, a trader of long notes commented, "We are going 6 months with no auction of a 3-year note. That will drive down the yield on the 3-year note relative to yields on other issues around it."

Another factor that may affect how well an issue trades is how closely it trades to par. "Old 10-years trade cheap to the new 10-year," noted one trader. "Recent off-the-run 10s—the 2nd, 3rd, and 4th previous issues—trade cheap to the active issue because they are less liquid. However, if an issue trades at par, that makes it attractive to a lot of people. Par seems to be a magic number for money managers. To me as a dealer trying to make $1/32$, par means nothing."

Profit in Trading with Retail

Today, big accounts will often put three or four dealers in competition when they want a big bid or offering. When this occurs, the winning dealer will often be hard put to make any profit on the trade. Yet dealers do this sort of business. One 10-year note trader observed: "I do a lot of business at no profit. Why? I want to make the customer know that I am not an odd-lot trader. I can do the business, and I can get these guys to come back for other stuff when I am really involved. A lot of business in Treasuries is done for no profit, sometimes at negative profit. One reason is that a big shop like ours wants market share. Also, we want to see the customer business overall.

"Today, there are so many dealers, and we've all squeezed each other out. Consequently, Treasuries trade like a commodity, and there's little profit to be made unless you are a tick trader like me."

Short Coupons

Coupons with a current maturity of a year or less are not actively traded. One reason is that brokerage is much less on bills than on coupons. Also, the bill market naturally tends to be active because there are so many bill auctions.

Another reason short coupons trade inactively is that it's difficult for government dealers to staff all their major chairs, so they put rookie trainees on short coupons—in a bank, it might be someone who has graduated from the Fed funds desk.

Seasoning and Trading

Not all issues trade strictly on the yield curve. One of the reasons is that varying reception that different issues receive in the auction.

"It takes time," one dealer noted, "for an issue to get well distributed, *seasoned*. How long depends on how well the auction went. Some auctions are sloppy and some are good. If in an auction, retail steps up and takes half or three quarters of an issue and they never intend to reoffer these securities so they are put away right off the bat, the float cleans up in a hurry. In other auctions, you have the opposite; the dealer fraternity by and large buys up the issue, it does not have anyone to sell them to, and it takes forever to get rid of them. That causes anomalies in the yield curve. You will see in the 2-year note area situations where the current 24-month and 20-month notes are trading at the same rate, and the 19-month note is trading for 10 bp less. Why the 10-bp jump over one month and no jump over the next four? It is because there are dog issues out that never get as seasoned as the issues surrounding them."

Another trader noted, "If there is a lot of interest in an issue when it comes out, if it is large in size, and if it is widely distributed, it will continue to be actively traded. Profits can be taken, the issue becomes popular, and people buy and sell it. What counts is that there is sufficient size in trading hands—not necessarily dealers but investors who are willing to trade. It is also important that traders be able to borrow the issue. If they can't, no one will short the issue, and it won't be actively traded."

Trading Notes

A note trader is responsible for a large number of note issues, more than one person can actively follow. So the typical trader concentrates on a few issues in his area. "Once you know the issues you follow closely," commented one trader, "there are relationships. In the 2-year area, if you know where the Junes are, you know where surrounding issues should be. Even if you do not trade the Julys for a week and you have a trade a day in the Junes, you know, if you are worth your salt, where the Julys should be."

Prices are much more volatile in the coupon market than in the bill market because maturities are longer. For this reason, dealers take smaller positions in coupons than in bills, and the coupon positions they assume become smaller the longer the current maturity of the securities positioned. One dealer commented, "If our bill trader is sitting there with 100MM in bills, that might be equivalent in terms of risk exposure to a 50MM position in 2-year notes and—in a normal market—to a 10MM exposure in long bonds."

Because a trader in governments is responsible for only a limited maturity spectrum, he is not in a position to arbitrage one sector of the market against another. That is a function typically carried on in a dealership in a separate arbitrage account. However, a trader can and does attempt to arbitrage temporary anomalies along the yield curve in the sector he trades. "If I see a blip in the yield curve—the Julys are out of line with the Augusts—I will short the overpriced issue and buy the other," noted one trader. "Generally, the payoff on this sort of thing is $1/32$ or $1/16$."

Technicals

A coupon trader has to be concerned about more than Fed policy and the Fed funds rate. He also has to consider any factors that might affect the yield curve, and he has to follow closely the *technicals—factors that affect supply and demand—*in his market.

At times, the dealer community will go net *short* in coupons. When dealers, as a group, short an area, they eventually must buy securities from retail to cover that short. Dealers put on shorts in anticipation of a decline in coupon prices; as part of an arbitrage (for example, they might short the 2-year note and buy the 7-year note—a *bull market arbitrage*); or as part of the hedge-type trades described above.

Table 14–5 shows dealers' net positions in different areas of the Treasury curve yield curve. One treads dangerous ground if one tries to infer from such data just what dealers' views on the market are: Are they bullish or bearish? Do they expect the yield curve to steepen, flatten, or invert? The reason is that so many different factors may cause a dealer to short a given issue. One factor we didn't mention above is that traders of non-Treasury instruments often short Treasuries as a hedge. For example, a trader of mortgage-backs may short 10-year or shorter Treasury notes as a hedge. Also, a dealer who runs a book in interest swaps will routinely short Treasury bonds as a hedge whenever he does with a customer a coupon swap that makes him a receiver of fixed; he lifts his hedge when he finds a home for the flip side of the swap.

Whatever the reason for a given short, a lack of securities of the Street and a need to cover that short can cause a *technical rally* in coupons. "Things in my part of the market," commented a trader of intermediate coupons, "can be technically bone dry in a way that never occurs in the bill market."

One of the technicals a note trader must constantly consider is what arbitragers might be doing in his area of the market. Commented one note trader: "Whenever something important— an economic or political development—that affects the market occurs, I have to think as much about what the arbitrages are going to do as about where the market in general is going. If I think our arbitrage guy is sitting there getting ready to buy 3-year notes and sell 7-year notes, I sure don't want to be short the 3-year note even if I think that the market is going down."

TABLE 14–5
Positions of U.S. government security dealers (par value; average of daily figures, $ millions)*

Item	1974	1975	1976	1977	1978	1979	1980	1981	1982	1983	1984	1985	1986	1987	1988	1989
U.S. government securities	**2,580**	**5,884**	**7,592**	**5,172**	**2,656**	**3,223**	**4,306**	**9,033**	**14,769**	**14,224**	**5,538**	**7,391**	**12,912**	**–6,216**	**–22,742**	**–31,729**
Bills	1,932	4,297	6,290	4,772	2,452	3,813	4,103	6,485	8,226	10,800	5,500	10,075	12,761	4,317	2,250	–3,718
Other within 1 year	–6	265	188	99	260	–325	–1,062	–1,526	1,088	921	63	1,050	3,705	1,557	–2,223	–3,548
1–5 years	265	886	515	60	–92	–455	434	1,488	3,293	1,912	2,159	5,154	9,146	649	–3,015	–8,827
5–10 years	302	300	402	92	40	160	166	292	–318	–78	–1,119	–6,202	–9,505	–6,564	–9,662	–8,825
Over 10 years	88	136	198	149	–4	30	665	2,294	2,026	528	–1,174	–2,686	–3,197	–6,174	–10,082	–7,385
Federal agency securities	**1,212**	**943**	**729**	**693**	**606**	**1,471**	**797**	**2,277**	**4,169**	**7,313**	**15,294**	**22,860**	**32,984**	**31,911**	**28,231**	**30,055**

*Net amounts (in terms of par values) of securities owned by nonbank dealer firms and dealer departments of commercial banks on a commitment, that is, trade-date basis, including any such securities that have been sold under agreements to repurchase. The maturities of some repurchase agreements are sufficiently long, however, to suggest that the securities involved are not available for trading purposes. Securities owned, and hence dealer positions, do not include securities purchased under agreements to resell.

Note: Averages for positions are based on number of trading days in the period; those for financing, on the number of calendar days in the period.

Source: *Federal Reserve Bulletin.*

Technical Analysis

Every Treasury note trader keeps an eye on one sort of technical analysis or another, but not all have the same degree of faith in such analysis. One 10-year note trader commented, "I keep an eye on such analysis. But to me, it is important only insofar as it influences other people. By influence, I mean: Does it inspire fear or confidence?

"Almost everyone believes in certain formations on a technical chart. If everyone is short at the second formation of a head and shoulders [looks sort of like a capital M], how can the market go down? If the market is at that point and it stays there for a period X of time, I usually buy, especially if I have talked to seven dealers and six are short. Also, I consider speed. Maybe it took half an hour to get up one side of the formation, half a day to fall, then two days to get up the other side, and we are still there at the top for half a week. Then I fade the market. I am more of a contrarian. A contrarian does well in *range markets*— markets with lots of sidewise motion. He does terribly when there is a clear direction in the market."

Recent markets have been range markets. The same trader noted: "I always look at the bond and the 10-year. Except for around the Crash, you have seen the bond trade within 50-bp ranges for the last three years: within certain 6-month intervals, a 7-day moving average would never go more than 23 bp over sold or 23 bp over bought [*over bought* means that current yield is lower than the yield over the last seven days]." Traders who gained their experience, confidence, even hybris, when there was a clear direction in the market made a lot of money from 1980 to 1985, but they have faced difficult times since then. The same trader continued, "In my few years in the business, I have seen the effect of hybris on one's P&L. The more conviction one has, the more money I have seen people lose. People, however, now seem to realize that the markets have changed. There are no gunslingers anymore. You can't power trade the market anymore. It's too easy to lose a year's, a lifetime's worth of work in five minutes."

Brokers

Traders of government notes and bonds use the brokers fully as much as bill traders do and for the same reasons. In the government market, as in other markets, one of the most important features of the brokers' market is that, whenever something occurs to cause a break in market activity, it serves as the arena in which trading is reestablished. It is part of the protocol of the dealer fraternity that whenever something big—such as a move by the Fed—has an impact on the market and causes uncertainty as to where issues should trade, dealers do *not* call each other and ask for runs. They do, however, look to the brokers' market for bids and offers, and generally someone is doing something there. Gradually, as a few trades are done through the brokers, more bids and offers are put into the brokers, and a semblance of order in trading is reestablished.

Games

Traders play the same trading games in the brokers' market and elsewhere that bill traders do. "Trading is much like a poker game," said one note trader. "You try to bluff, to sound like a buyer when you are really a seller. You tell the guy you are in great shape for the market to go down when you are, in fact, long and hope he will buy some of your securities. When my boss says, 'Let's get down in position,' the first thing I will do is put a bid in the brokers. The only way to get down is to find some help [create some buyers]. Sometimes, my bid will be low, and sometimes it will be good; if I get hit, I have a bigger job to do.

"I have the ability to use two brokers at a time. Say the market is 11+ 12+; I have notes offered at 11+ and can't sell them. I will go out and buy them at 12+. Say I started with 30MM I bought at 10. By buying 5MM from another broker at a higher price than where I am willing to sell, I might lose 1/32 on that 5MM, but I now am much more likely to be able to get the other 30MM I own off and make one or one and a half 32nds on them."

BONDS

Treasury long bonds extend in maturity well past the year 2000 and are not part of the stock-in-trade of the money market.

Long bonds are much more volatile in price than short instruments, and the risks in positioning them are commensurately greater. As a result it was always typical for traders of long governments to hedge the bulk of their positions. Especially before the advent of bond futures, many bond traders, if they bought a million long bonds from a customer and could not immediately resell them, would short a similar active issue and then wait and unwind the position when they could. In the view of some traders, such trading is wasted activity. Said one, "You should never end up with a security you do not want. If you buy such a security, you should sell it immediately. If you can't because the issue is illiquid, you may have to sell another issue. Doing so, however, puts you in a poor position because you now have two issues that you can trade only when someone else has a need to trade them."

Spreads and Active Issues

In recent years, spreads in the bond market have narrowed because individual issues are so much bigger these days, because the Board (Chicago Board of Trade bond futures) provides traders with so much liquidity, and because so much volume is transacted in the market. These days it is not unusual for a big shop to trade well in excess of a billion of bonds a day. Before the crash in October 1987, the volume of bonds traded increased roughly in line with the increase in Treasury long debt outstanding. After the Crash, volume slackened off somewhat (Table 14–2).

Because of all the volume transacted in bonds, in any active issue there is always virtually a locked market in the brokers' market. There will be a 10 lock, a 14 lock, or whatever. Locked markets occur because neither side is willing to take the initiative and pay brokerage. The widest spread that a bond trader is likely to see is half a basis point.

In long bonds, virtually every issue is active because customers have positions in virtually all of them. They do a lot of
swaps between securities to increase their total rate of return by
1 or 2% over a year. This is in sharp contrast to the situation in
the note market. In the 10-years and under area, there are only
two active issues for a given maturity that the Treasury sells:
two 10s, two 7s, two 5s, two 4s, two 3s, and two 2s. The premium
placed on active note issues is phenomenal compared to that
placed on more active long issues. The premium on active note
issues is created by speculators who prefer to always trade the
most active issues because they can get in and out of them with
the greatest ease.

The end users of securities, buyers who intend to hold them
to maturity or at least stay with a given security for some period, will buy off-the-run securities on which they can get some
pickup in yield.

Trading Bonds

Volatility has declined in bond prices and yields from what it
was in the early 1980s, and now bonds, like notes, have tended
to trade in compressed ranges. Consequently, many primary
dealers, with the exception of the largest, aren't willing to take
much of a position in bonds. "A lot of guys," noted one bond
trader, "will go into a big number, like employment, flat. That
takes liquidity out of the market, because if the market rallies
strongly, they have no bonds to sell. There is not that composition of longs and shorts in there that gives the market some
equilibrium when it has to face an economic number. So what
happens is that you get strong-movement days right after a
number and then settle into periods of narrow-range days. The
latter don't give you a chance to get anything going, which in
turn becomes one more reason for volume to dry up. It feeds on
itself. Until we get a fundamental break in information—say,
that the economy is starting to slow down—volume is not going
to pick up."

Range markets influence how a trader trades. "My attitude," noted one bond trader," is that, if you look at where the market closes every night, 85% of the time at some point during the next day, you trade back to that close. Out of the 15% that you do not, 10% is because you have a big number coming up that is going to skew the market to a new level. Consequently, unless a big number is coming out, I should not take a big position home overnight, and I should not ride a trade for three or four days. I should try to reduce my exposure and think about it the next day."

Technical Analysis

Like traders of other instruments, long-bond traders are deep into technical analysis. Technical analysis comes in many flavors, and when a trader says he finds technical analysis useful, he may have a quite specific flavor in mind. "I don't," said one bond trader, "find standard technical analysis like chart formations, relative strength indicators (RSI), moving averages useful. The market moves from one level to another very fast, and once it gets there, the speed slows down and it tries to turn around. I think about elasticity with respect to market moves. When price moves to the bottom of the trading range, you've stretched that rubber band a lot. Technical analysis becomes an analysis of human psychology, and people's reactions are always constant."

Risk Analysis

Now that every trader thinks in terms of duration, which permits him to say that the directional risk in 10 bonds (10MM bonds) is the same as the directional risk in 100MM year bills, it's easy to find a bond trader who prefers to measure his risk as being long or short XMM year bills and a 10-year note trader who prefers to measure his risk as being long or short YMM long bonds. Traders seem to be most comfortable gauging their risk in units of whatever it was they first traded or traded longest, not necessarily in what they currently trade.

Dealing with Retail

The big buyers of long bonds tend to be insurance companies, pension managers (including certain state and local government bodies running pension funds), bond funds, and money managers out to maximize duration. Bank trust departments, to the extent that they buy Treasuries, typically buy them in the 5- to 7-year range.

In trading with retail, a dealer's job is to facilitate flows. Since he is both the bid and the offer vis-à-vis retail, he has a good chance to pull out a spread between the bid and the offer; and the more customer flow he handles, the better are his chances of earning that spread.

In dealing with retail, it is important that a dealer, if he wants to see activity by big accounts, be as big as the market—be able to deal in the size his customer wants to deal in. An occasional account might ask a dealer to bid on 250MM of long bonds—maybe five traders in the business could handle such a request. "When I buy 250MM from a customer," said one bond trader, "I have to reduce my exposure. Probably I bought those bonds in competition with two or three other dealers who know that those bonds have come into the market. So I pretty much have to get out. I bid them on an assumption about where I could get out. If I think it is down 2/32, I bid them down 2/32 from the bid side of the market at the time. If I think that I need to sell maybe only 50 or 100MM of them, I take that into consideration. If I buy something and do not want it, I have got to get out of all of it. I cannot half hedge it because I am either right or wrong; so, either I want to hold on to it all or to sell it all.

"Say I bought the long bond at 102½. The Board [bond futures] is trading at 89½. If I figure that I can sell only 50MM bonds around 102½ before I start to drive the bond down, I will, at the same time I start selling cash bonds, start selling the Board at 89½. I can probably sell more of the futures than I can of the cash. Say I sell 100 bonds 1,500 bond contracts.[8] My *net*

---

[8]In bond-land, "100 [*cash*] bonds" is understood to be 100MM face value. However, since the bond futures contract is for bonds having a $100,000 face value, 1,500 contracts equals 150MM face or 150 bonds.

position is now flat; but I am long bonds and short-bond futures, so I have basis risk [risk that the relationship of cash to futures prices may move]. My goal is to be flat bonds and flat the Board. To do that, I have to sell the basis." (For an example of a basis trade, see Chapter 16.) There are many traders who will trade bond basis with our trader, all of the dealers' long-bond traders as well as basis traders, spec accounts who play around in basis rather than in bonds.

The Distribution of Bonds

Initially, the Treasury and the Fed viewed the initiation of trading in bond futures with a jaundiced eye; they feared various imagined abuses and undesirable consequences to which this new market might lead. In fact, the Board has been tremendously helpful in the distribution of new Treasury bond issues. If in any period there is 1 billion of open interest, in most cases the billion short is the Street, the billion long is customers: dentists in Des Moines and other individuals to whom the Board offers the opportunity to speculate on interest rates. The willingness of these individuals to speculate and their preference for taking long positions has permitted the Street to hedge huge positions on the board. The ability to establish such hedges enables dealers to buy a new issue when the Treasury wants to sell it and to sell the issue—sometimes at a significantly later date—when retail wants to buy it.

CURVE TRADERS

Traders have always understood that there is a difference between the risk that the yield curve might shift up or down and the risk that the relationship between two yields along the yield curve might change. Traders position to profit from the first sort of risk, do arbitrages to profit from the second (recall Chapter 10).

    With the widespread use of duration in figuring and hedging market risk, jargon is changing. Duration-weighted hedging is likely to leave a dealer long and short quite different maturities. It eliminates *directional risk:* protects the dealer against a *parallel shift* in the yield curve (e.g., rates in all maturities going up or down an 01). However, a dealer who is flat from the point of view of duration-weighted hedging can have a big and risky curve trade on: he could be short at the front end of the curve and long at the back end or vice versa. If so, he has *curve risk*. A dealer can always gauge his curve risk by looking at his position sheet, which tells him exactly where he's long and short. If he doesn't like his curve risk, he can alter his positions along the curve. On the other hand, if he likes his curve risk—it's a bet he wants to make—he'll let his positions stand.

These days, the traders at a shop whose job it is to make bets on relationships along the yield curve—that is, do arbs along the yield curve—are often referred to as *curve traders*.

In periods when market volatility is low and it's therefore tough to make a lot of money on position plays (this was so in 1988 and early 1989), dealers tend to do a lot of arbitrage. In the words of a curve trader, "Range markets lead the way for a little more value trading and less speculation. By value trading I mean this sort of thing: I think the 5-year note, which is being auctioned today, will come cheap; that is not to say that I am just going to buy the 5s and have a long position. It means I should buy the 5s and sell 10s or something else around it because I think that the 5s are cheap to other issues—have value relative to other issues. Speculating is just saying, 'Let's buy them.' "

Curve traders prefer to deal in active issues, but they sometimes get involved in off-the-runs. Because these issues are less liquid, it may take longer for them to get back into line; also, it will take a curve trader longer to get into and out of off-the-runs.

Sometimes, a curve trader will have two separate accounts. In one, he day trades, which eliminates the need to finance positions overnight. In the second, which is a desk proprietory account, he puts on trades for longer term. When he trades the second account, he has to borrow securities for term to cover his short, and therefore he has to take more interest in conditions in the finance market. He certainly does not want to short something that's on special.

Using Technical Analysis

The majority of spread (curve) traders keep some sort of histori-cal data. Figure 14–3 shows the daily spreads—between the 2s and the 5s, the 2s and the 10s, and the 2s and the bond—as plotted by one curve trader during the period early 1988 to early 1989. The straight lines added to this figure were drawn by the trader to indicate the ranges within which each spread appeared to be trading.

One interesting observation about Figure 14–3 is that hav-ing a perspective on spreads is entirely different from having a perspective on where the market is going. That spreads are de-clining tells you, for example, nothing about how the level of the yield curve is changing.

Figure 14–3 represented to the trader who drew it technical analysis. "The charts," he observed, "are a really helpful tool. However, you have to put charts and fundamentals back to back. A chart is more a tool to support a fundamental idea or to tell you *when to enter or exit a trade.*"

A 2s/Bond Curve Trade

When markets and spreads are not highly volatile, the best way for a curve trader to make money is to do the extremes, pro-vided, of course, that he has a strong opinion on how the shape of the yield curve is likely to change. Commented one curve trader, "You do something like the 2s/bonds [the 2-year note versus the long bond], which is a nice volatile spread. On October 27 [1988], I put on a trade—sold 58MM 2s and bought 10MM bonds, which is roughly the equivalent [measured in yield values of $\frac{1}{32}$].[9] I put on the trade at a spread of 53. The long bond outperformed the 2s significantly—by 43 bp. So I was able to take the trade off at a spread of 10; and I made 43 bp, which is about 120 32nds on 10MM long bonds or $430,000." The profit calculation could just as well have been made in terms of the 2s instead of the bond; 43 bp on 58MM 2s also works out to a profit of $430,000.

---

[9]Recall the arb example in Chapter 10, pp. 449–51.

FIGURE 14–3
A trader's charting of spreads in the Treasury market

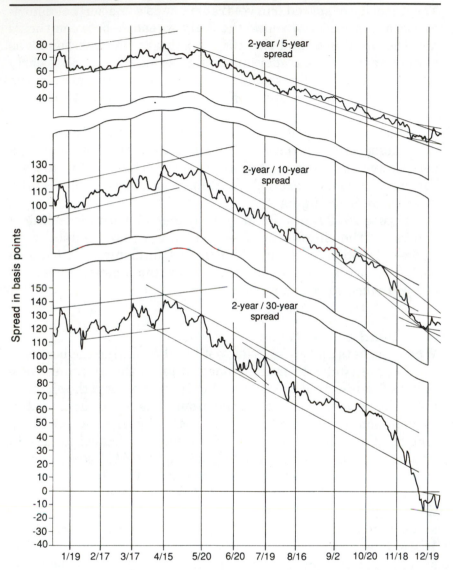

Actually, our curve trader does not care whether he made or lost money on his position in the 2s; ditto his position in the bond. His bet was that the yield curve would flatten, not that it would move up or down. In fact, the yield curve over the period flattened and rose, so our trader lost some money being short 2s and made more than $430,000 being long bonds.

One can see in Figure 14–3 the flattening and then inverting of the yield curve. In particular, when the 2-year–30-year spread reached zero, this meant that the yield curve was flat over the 2- to 30-year range; when the same spread went *negative*, this meant that the yield curve had *inverted*.

A 2s/5s Curve Trade

The above curve trade took a little over a month to work out. Here's an example of a day trade done by the same curve trader late in February 1989. Our trader came in in the morning with the premise that the 5-year notes were cheap. So he bought 35MM wi 5 years at an average yield of 9.45 and sold 80MM 2-years at an average yield of 9.515 (he established the weights using yield values of $\frac{1}{32}$, 0.0081 on the most recently issued 5-year, and 0.0176 on the 2-year). Note the trade was a "give 6½" because the trader gave up yield in putting it on.

The trade worked out as well or better than planned. In the trader's words, "Fortunately for me, the Fed did matched sales [reverses to drain reserves], which wasn't really expected, and the front end traded down a lot further than the rest of the market did. I bought the 2s back at an average yield of 9.59 and sold the wi 5s at 9.48, a difference of 11 bp. So my gain on the trade was 4.5 bp—roughly $60,000 on 35MM 5-year notes."

A Losing Curve Trade

Not every curve trade has a happy ending. In early 1989, when the yield curve was inverted, Sali was reported in *The Wall Street Journal* (March 23, 1989) as having put on, in its fixed-income arbitrage group, which uses complex mathematical models and employs six PhDs in math and science, a complex curve trade involving Treasury bonds, mortgage securities, and related futures and options. Sali's bet was that short-term rates would remain relatively stable while long-term rates would rise. Instead, both short-term and long-term rates rose further, and the spread between the two, instead of narrowing, widened. As a result, Sali had a loss of over a 100MM, and it had yet to close out all of its positions.

Prior to this trade, Sali's "rocket scientists" under John Meriwether were reported to have been so successful in making risky interest-rate bets that Meriwether was "the firm's biggest rising star." All told, March 1989 was a bad month for rocket scientists. A few days after Sali's loss, the Navy launched a Trident rocket (missile) that it had to blow up seconds after launch, creating king-sized fireworks for TV viewers.

THE ZOO

In recent years, *zero coupons* (note and bond issues carrying a zero coupon) have found a ready market both in the U.S. and Euromarkets. A big attraction of zeros to buyers is that they provide a guaranteed reinvestment rate over the life of the bond. For investors, this guarantee significantly reduces uncertainty over what total return a bond will yield over its life. The offset to this advantage in the U.S. is that taxable investors must pay taxes on interest that accrues to them on zeros as that interest accrues whereas they actually get interest years later when bond matures. Consequently, in the U.S. zeros are most attractive to tax-exempt or low-taxed investors: pension funds and individuals investing IRA or Keogh monies.

In August of 1982, Merrill, banking on the idea that Treasuries packaged as zeros could lure into long-term government bonds many investors who would not otherwise buy them, came up with an idea of how to do this packaging: buy long bonds, put them into a bank, and issue receipts against all coupon payments and the principal repayment that the Treasury is scheduled to make. Packaging a Treasury long bond this way creates a series of zero-coupon Treasuries, one maturing on every coupon date including the final principal repayment date.

Merrill sold its Treasury Investment Growth Receipts (*TIGRs,* pronounced tigers) at the present values of the principal amount the investor would get. Since zero coupons appealed more to long-term investors than to short-term investors, in pricing its TIGRs, Merrill, to attract shorter-term investors, offered investors buying short TIGRs a guaranteed yield to maturity slightly above the yield to maturity offered by regular Treasuries of similar maturity; on long TIGRs Merrill offered a guaranteed yield to maturity below rates on the yield curve.

On its first venture into coupon stripping, Merrill bought, cut up, and banked half a billion of the 14s of 2011; it then sold, on the basis of these securities, $2.565 billion of TIGRs. That venture—viewed with considerable trepidation by some executives at the firm—was such a success that Merrill followed it up with a new TIGR issue: $1.39 billion of TIGRs backed by $300 million of the 12¾s of 2010.

While Merrill was the first to wave its wand over interest-bearing Treasuries and create zero-coupon bonds from them, Merrill's TIGRs were soon followed by Sali's CATs and Lehman Brothers' LIONs.

It is estimated that, by the end of the summer of 1982, Wall Street firms had stripped and resold nearly $14 billion of Treasuries to an array of buyers including big tax-exempt institutions, parents looking to fund junior's college education, holders of IRA and Keogh plans, and foreign investors; the latter are estimated to have snapped up as much as ¼ of Merrill's TIGRs.

STRIPs

The zoo that grew on Wall Street did not go unobserved by the Treasury. It decided to preempt for itself the profits earned plus the high expenses incurred by the dealers in creating proprietory zeros. To do so, the Treasury declared in late 1984 that henceforth any 10-year note or any 20- or 30-year bond that it issued could be stripped via the book-entry system.[10] To make this possible, the Treasury gave a separate CUSIP number to the corpus (principal) of each bond or note that could be stripped

---

[10]The Treasury used to issue a 20-year bond. It stopped doing so because it decided that 20-year bonds appealed to no natural class of investors and that it therefore had to pay up to buy 20-year money.

and a separate CUSIP number to each date on which coupon payments on such securities were to be made. The Treasury dubbed its new do-it-yourself zeros *STRIPs* (for *Separate Trading of Registered Interest and Principal*). The long bond issued in the November 1984 refunding was the first bond to be strippable under the new Treasury program; it was also the last callable issue offered by the Treasury.

STRIPs have a lot of appeal to a wide array of investors. They are a pure product about which an investor needn't do a lot of thinking. He knows that, if he invests X dollars today, he will get Y dollars at the end of some known time, T. That's certain, and there's no reinvestment risk to worry about. However, an investor buying zeros should be aware that a zero coupon displays much greater price volatility than does a coupon security having the same current maturity (recall Chapter 4). This feature of zeros is unlikely to disturb the hold-until-maturity investor, and it may well entice the speculative investor who'll get a lot of bang for his buck playing with long zeros.

Zeros have been used for all sorts of things: auto dealers have offered zeros as an incentive to buyers of new cars; state lotteries have used zeros to defease payoffs to winners; and owners of baseball teams have used zeros to fund multiyear, multimillion-dollar player contracts.

On a more pedestrian level, zeros appeal to mom and pop as a good investment for IRAs, Keoghs, and funding junior's college tuition. Also, the crash of October 19, 1987, drove a lot of frightened consumer money into zeros: a stock market that could fall 500 points in a day made a certain investment look awfully attractive. The big demand for zeros from consumers tends to be in the 13- to 20-year maturities.

There is also a large institutional demand for zeros from pensions funds, insurance companies, and other big investors wanting long duration and certain return. Such investors are often looking for zeros with a duration of 15 to 20 years.

The appeal of zeros across the maturity spectrum is indicated by the contrast in the yield curves pictured in Figure 14–4. Generally, STRIPs sell at a lower yield to maturity than do unstripped Treasuries of the same maturity; also, the discrep-

FIGURE 14–4
Yields on STRIPs are generally lower than those on Treasury coupons

A. U.S. Treasury STRIPS yield curve, pricing date 03/21/89

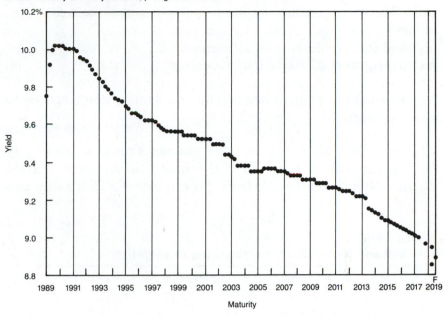

B. U.S. Treasury yield curve, pricing date 03/21/89

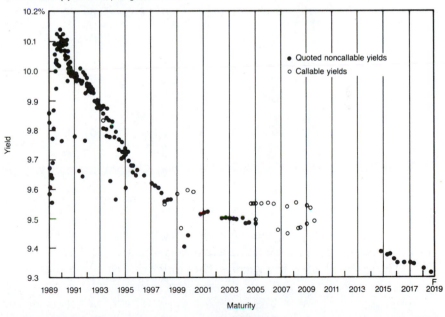

Source: Goldman Sachs & Co.—Financial Strategies Group.

ancy becomes greater the longer the current maturity considered.

Stripping and STRIPs Outstanding

Since the Treasury permitted stripping, dealers—in response to investor demand—have been busily at it. Table 14–6 shows the total outstandings of STRIPs, corpus and coupon, as of January 31, 1989. Not all maturities are shown; Treasury bonds pay coupon interest on the 15th of the month in January, March, August, and November. So the total number of STRIPs that can

TABLE 14–6
Principal and coupon STRIPs outstanding as of 1/31/89

	A. Principal STRIPs Outstanding ($ millions)				
	Feb	*May*	*Aug*	*Nov*	*Year*
1993	0	0	0	0	0
1994	0	0	0	1,160	1,160
1995	664	1,678	951	526	3,820
1996	270	126	0	340	737
1997	0	145	0	90	235
1998	0	0	0	0	0
1999	0	0	0	0	0
2000	0	0	0	0	0
2001	0	0	0	0	0
2002	0	0	0	0	0
2003	0	0	0	0	0
2004	0	0	0	5,610	5,610
2005	0	2,535	3,024	0	5,559
2006	0	0	0	0	0
2007	0	0	0	0	0
2008	0	0	0	0	0
2009	0	0	0	4,530	4,530
2010	0	0	0	0	0
2011	0	0	0	0	0
2012	0	0	0	0	0
2013	0	0	0	0	0
2014	0	0	0	0	0
2015	9,954	0	5,203	3,637	18,794
2016	2,108	5,264	0	8,555	15,927
2017	0	9,705	3,667	0	13,372
2018	0	2,767	0	896	3,664
Total					73,408

TABLE 14–6—*Concluded*

	B. Coupon STRIPs Outstanding ($ millions)				
	Feb	*May*	*Aug*	*Nov*	*Year*
1989–1993	1,358	2,241	1,358	2,241	7,198
1994	1,358	2,241	1,358	2,241	7,198
1995	1,358	2,173	1,321	2,079	6,931
1996	1,271	2,054	1,259	2,049	6,633
1997	1,259	2,037	1,259	2,031	6,586
1998	1,259	2,027	1,259	2,027	6,572
1999	1,259	2,027	1,259	2,027	6,572
2000	1,259	2,027	1,259	2,027	6,572
2001	1,259	2,027	1,259	2,027	6,572
2002	1,259	2,027	1,259	2,027	6,572
2003	1,259	2,027	1,259	2,027	6,572
2004	1,259	2,027	1,259	2,027	6,572
2005	1,259	1,701	1,259	1,549	5,767
2006	1,097	1,549	1,097	1,549	5,292
2007	1,097	1,549	1,097	1,549	5,292
2008	1,097	1,549	1,097	1,549	5,292
2009	1,097	1,549	1,097	1,549	5,292
2010	1,097	1,282	1,097	1,282	4,758
2011	1,097	1,282	1,097	1,282	4,758
2012	1,097	1,282	1,097	1,282	4,758
2013	1,097	1,282	1,097	1,282	4,758
2014	1,097	1,282	1,097	1,282	4,758
2015	1,097	1,282	537	1,282	4,198
2016	260	1,103	163	912	2,438
2017	163	591	163	167	1,083
2018	0	167	0	40	207
Total					139,201

Source: Merrill Lynch, Government Debt Research.

be outstanding is 4 times 30 coupons plus corpus for every strippable bond.

In the land of STRIPs, a distinction is made between STRIPs that correspond to *principal* (*corpus*) and those that correspond to *coupons*. One reason the Treasury made this distinction initially was to appeal to Japanese investors who, prior to a change in their tax laws, were not taxed on income from a zero corpus until it matured.

Whether a dealer can make money stripping a given bond depends on the relationship between the market value of that bond and the market value of the sum of its parts. Every dealer has a program geared to make this calculation. The arbitrage is obvious: if the value of the bond is less than the value of the sum of its parts, then strip. Also, the reverse is true: if the value of the bond is more than the value of the sum of its parts, then *reconstitute* the bond. The arb works both ways.

Since the arb is so obvious, there is rarely money to be made either in stripping or in reconstituting bonds. For example, on February 21, 1989, the number-crunching Bloomberg System showed that if a dealer were to buy 100MM of the 9s of November 18 and strip them, he would make 770,000 if he could sell all of the pieces at the offered side of the market, but lose 267,000 if he could sell them only at the bid side of the market.

Usually, the stimulus to strip or reconstitute is a big request from retail. "What really happens," noted one trader, "is that you have a customer who wants to buy the corpus of, say, the 09 bond and another customer who wants to buy part of the strip of coupons. So you tell your sales force, 'If you get rid of these and those coupons, then we can work this order: buy this bond; strip it; and sell this piece to one guy, that piece to another guy, and so on.' Or it could work the reverse: somebody wants to sell me all of these coupons relatively cheap, so if I could just go and get this corpus and this and that coupon, I could reconstitute the bond cheaper than the market is."

Given that tax laws are such that, for most investors in STRIPs, it makes no difference whether they own corpus or coupons, it would seem pointless to continue to distinguish between the two. However, doing so does prevent dealers from, say, reconstituting a 10-year bond from bits and pieces of 20- and 30-year bonds that have been stripped. Thus, the Treasury need not fear that stripping and reconstituting will change the structure of its outstanding debt. Also, coupon and corpus STRIPs trade differently because STRIPs corresponding to corpus are much bigger and thus have more appeal to institutional investors.

Stripping continues apace mostly in the outstanding 20- and 30-year bonds (Table 14–7, Parts A and B). The 10s can be stripped but tend not to be because investor demand is strongest for zeros with current maturities in excess of 10 years. In 1988, the Treasury offered a new long bond in only two of its four refundings because it ran up against the now-repealed lid on the amount of bonds it could issue with a coupon above 4¼, so its issuings of bonds totaled only $18 billion. During the same year, dealer stripped 22 to 23 billion of the eligible long bonds. So net during 1988, outstanding Treasury bonds declined and STRIPs expanded. "I can," said one trader, "see that happening for years."

One effect of stripping is to reduce the liquidity of the long bond. "What you have seen," noted a dealer, "is that the long bond is no longer the trading vehicle it was three years ago. I think that now the 10-years is becoming the major trading vehicle. On Wall Street, your best government trader used to be the 30-year trader; he is now more often the 10-year trader. We traders of zeros have become by default the long-bond traders. We dictate how rich or cheap it gets. We buy bonds when they are too cheap and take them apart; and when they get too rich, we buy zeros, reconstitute them, and sell long bonds."

The STRIPs Market

Of the many primary and reporting dealers, probably less than 10 do 70% of the business in STRIPs. Also, not all of those dealers see the same demand. A wire house like Merrill sees a lot of demand from consumers and institutions whereas a shop like Goldman sees only institutional demand.

Table 14–8 gives quotes on selected STRIPs. Normally, STRIPs are quoted in terms of yield. STRIPs are brokered by the major brokers of Treasuries. In the brokers' market for STRIPs, 1MM is a round lot, and the usual spread between the bid and the offer is 2 or 3 bp. There is one broker of odd-lot STRIPs, M.K.I. Securities Co.

A dealer who is big in STRIPs will have a desk of traders— maybe a trader for short STRIPs, a trader for long STRIPs, a trader of proprietary zeros, and maybe a couple of traders for agency paper that has been stripped and agency bullet issues (see below).

TABLE 14–7
Stripping activity, October 1988 through January 1989

A. Stripping Activity in Strippable Treasury Notes and Bonds ($ thousands)

1/31/89		Total Outstanding	Net Stripped		In January 1989			Net Stripped		
					Recons.	Stripped	Net Stripped	In December	In November	In October
11.625	11/94	6,658,554	1,160,000	17.42%	16,000	83,200	67,200	70,400	4,800	(17,600)
11.250	2/95	6,933,861	664,480	9.58	0	0	0	(9,600)	0	(40,000)
11.250	5/95	7,127,086	1,678,240	23.55	16,000	28,960	12,960	133,980	(10,460)	(55,200)
10.500	8/95	7,955,901	950,800	11.95	1,200	0	(1,200)	(10,400)	0	(11,600)
9.500	11/95	7,318,550	526,000	7.19	18,000	30,000	12,000	(31,200)	0	(16,400)
8.875	2/96	8,410,929	270,400	3.21	0	209,600	209,600	0	0	0
7.375	5/95	20,085,643	126,643	0.63	0	86,400	86,400	40,000	0	0
7.250	11/96	20,258,810	340,000	1.68	0	229,600	229,600	110,400	0	0
8.500	5/97	9,921,237	145,200	1.46	0	85,200	85,200	0	0	0
8.875	11/97	9,808,329	89,600	0.91	0	89,600	89,600	0	0	0
11.625	11/04	8,301,806	5,609,600	67.57	0	48,000	48,000	0	67,200	(1,600)
12.000	5/05	4,260,758	2,535,150	59.50	0	16,000	16,000	0	(16,400)	(3,300)
10.750	8/05	9,269,713	3,024,000	32.62	220,000	771,200	551,200	72,800	147,200	44,000
11.750	11/14–09	6,005,584	4,530,400	75.44	24,000	16,000	(8,000)	(24,000)	(24,000)	(32,800)
11.250	2/15	12,667,799	9,954,080	78.58	17,600	0	(17,600)	9,600	0	(92,000)
10.625	8/15	7,149,916	5,203,200	72.77	0	19,200	19,200	0	0	(24,320)

Coupon	Maturity	Amount Issued	Net Stripped	%	Recons.	Stripped	Net Stripped	In December	In November	In October
9.875	11/15	6,899,859	3,636,800	52.71	19,200	126,400	107,200	32,000	188,800	233,600
9.250	2/16	7,266,854	2,108,000	29.01	36,800	332,000	295,200	760,000	0	100,000
7.250	5/16	18,823,551	5,264,000	27.96	512,800	300,800	(212,000)	1,778,400	271,200	202,400
7.500	11/16	18,864,448	8,555,360	45.35	234,560	331,360	96,800	(366,080)	216,080	948,960
8.750	5/17	18,194,169	9,704,800	53.34	186,400	328,480	142,080	130,880	1,022,080	88,320
8.875	8/17	14,016,748	3,667,200	26.16	0	76,800	76,800	444,800	171,200	544,000
9.125	5/18	8,708,639	2,767,200	31.78	43,200	939,200	896,000	1,026,400	844,800	0
9.000	11/18	9,032,850	896,400	9.92	50,400	449,800	399,400	350,000	147,000	0
Total		73,407,310			1,396,160	4,597,800	3,201,640	4,518,380	3,029,500	1,866,460

B. Stripping Activity in Strippable Treasury Notes and Bonds by Maturity ($ thousands)

1/31/89	Amount Issued	Net Stripped		In January 1989			Net Stripped		
				Recons.	Stripped	Net Stripped	In December	In November	In October
10-year issues	163,219,777	5,951,120	3.65%	51,200	842,560	791,360	303,580	(5,660)	(140,800)
20-year issues	26,588,193	11,168,750	42.01	220,000	835,200	615,200	72,800	198,000	39,100
30-year issues	127,630,417	56,287,440	44.10	1,124,960	2,920,040	1,795,080	4,142,000	2,837,160	1,968,160
Total	317,438,387	73,407,310		1,396,160	4,597,800	3,201,640	4,518,380	3,029,500	1,866,460

Source: Merrill Lynch, Government Debt Research.

TABLE 14–8
Quotes on selected Treasury STRIPs as of 03/20/89

Maturity	Price	Yield (bid)	Modified Duration	Gain from Convexity	Value 0.01 (decimal equivalent)	Value $1/32$ (bps)	Change from (in basis points)	
							Day Ago	Month Ago
Coupons								
11/15/89	93.88	9.93	0.6237	0.0034	0.59	5.34	8.00	58.00
02/15/95	57.12	9.71	5.6352	0.1722	3.22	0.97	5.00	33.00
11/15/00	33.80	9.53	11.1246	0.6461	3.76	0.83	2.00	28.00
05/15/06	20.76	9.38	16.3862	1.3828	3.40	0.92	1.00	24.00
05/15/12	12.27	9.27	22.1290	2.5015	2.71	1.15	1.00	21.00
08/15/16	8.79	9.07	26.2198	3.4983	2.31	1.36	1.00	22.00
Principals								
11/15/94	58.61	9.68	5.3936	0.1583	3.16	0.99	3.00	37.00
02/15/19	7.55	8.83	28.6442	4.1714	2.16	1.45	-2.00	N/A

Source: Goldman Sachs.

Dealing with Retail

A zero trader may try to generate business with retail in several ways. He might show investors that, by coming out of a central maturity, say, the 2011s, 12s, or 13s, and going into 07 paper and 16 paper in weighted amounts, they could pick up yield or take out dollars and turn up where they wanted to be in terms of duration. That's called a *barbell trade*.

A zero trader might also show an account that has the flexibility to be in, say, Feb 10 or Nov 10 [i.e., 2010] an opportunity to do a spread swap between those maturities that would permit the account to pick up a basis point and maybe next time reverse the trade to give up only half a basis point. Street dealers who work on their inventory also do such *maturity basis swapping*.

Trading STRIPs

The spread movements in zeros are very sensitive to changes in the shape of the yield curve. "So we do," observed a zeros trader, "a fair amount of arbitrage both for ourselves and as we buy from and sell to customers. If I sell something to a customer, I am unlikely to be buying back that exact issue in the next 10 minutes. So I have to buy something else back against it. I try to sell what I think is expensive and buy back what I think is cheap. That entails setting up some sort of arb; it can be just a spread arb within a sector—meaning, if I sell Feb 99s, maybe I buy May 99s and try to swap them with a different customer; it can also mean a yield-curve trade: I sell Feb 99s and buy 30-year bonds. A 10-year zero and a 30-year bond have about the same duration. I am trying to match durations at all times—to take directional risk out of my position but still have a spread trade on."

Another trader of zeros noted that, since zeros range all over the lot in maturity, he might, to hedge positions in zeros, use an offsetting position in similar zeros, use the long-bond contract against 15- to 30-year stuff, and maybe use the old 3-year, the old 7-year, and the old 10-year against shorter paper.

One feature that makes trading zeros difficult is that the reverse and bonds-borrowed market in zeros is only a couple of years old; and by the standards of the Treasury coupon market, it is still small. "The repo market in zeros isn't," noted one trader, "like the repo market in Treasuries. Outstandings of individual maturities in zeros are a lot smaller, so it isn't uncommon to find issues [of zeros] that you cannot borrow or that trade at very tight repo spreads. Also, it isn't uncommon to have fails, although things are a lot better than they were two years ago. To the extent that Wall Street as a community keeps stripping 3 billion bonds a month, things will keep getting better."

Treasury Issuance of Zeros

Some people, looking at the STRIPs-yield curve in the spring of 1989 asked, "Why shouldn't the Treasury issue 30-year zeros? That's the most expensive [lowest cost to the Treasury] paper it can sell." There are several good reasons why not. First, in the spring of 1989, 30-year zeros were trading at around eight cents to the dollar. Thus, to raise—by selling STRIPs—the kind of money it gets from selling 30-year coupons the Treasury would have to issue securities having a face value 12 and a half times bigger, and that would bump the Treasury right up against the statutory debt ceiling. Also, Congress and many others would surely oppose having the Treasury issue 30-year debt that would have *no* cost to any administration in the near future.

FEDERAL AGENCY SECURITIES

The major federal agencies that issue securities to the market have over 230 billion of *coupon* securities outstanding (Table 14–9). Most agency issues are much smaller than comparable Treasury issues. The Treasury has a few bond issues outstanding that are less than 1 billion, but since 1984, its new bonds issues have been running in the 2- to 18-billion range, its new note issues in the 7- to 9-billion range. The biggest agency coupon offerings are done by the Federal Home Loan Banks (FHLB).

TABLE 14–9
Major federal agency coupon securities (as of January 12, 1989)

Issuer	Number of Issues	Amount ($ billions)
Federal Home Loan Banks (FHLB)	140	108.2
Federal National Mortgage Association (FNMA)	102	72.0
Federal Farm Credit Banks (FFCB)	53	35.3
Student Loan Marketing Association (SLMA)	18	4.5
Federal Insurance Corp. (FICO)	9	5.5
Federal Land Banks (FLB)	4	1.6
Federal Assistance Corp. (FACO)	2	0.7
Total Federal agency coupon issues	328	227.8

Source: J.P. Morgan Securities, Inc., quote sheet.

New Members of the Club

A big problem in the market for agency paper is that there are so many issuers and so many small issues that illiquidity is a constant problem. That, however, fails to deter Congress from adding new members to the club of borrowers.

The Financial Assistance Corporation (FACO)

From 1985 on, it was clear that the Farm Credit System was in deep trouble; and for a period, its securities traded at rates reflecting investor distrust of the agency's credit. Farm Credit's problems reflected a number of factors. Back in the go-go 1970s, system bankers urged farmers to borrow more; inflation would take care of repayments. Later, in the early 1980s, declining farm prices and accelerating inflation caused the collateral backing farm loans to decline in value, and at the same time, some farmers fell behind in payments. To add to the system's woes, it is composed of 37 primary banks and hundreds of local lending outlets run by local boards with no central guidance. Finally and astonishingly, the system did not begin to track its quarterly earnings until 1984, and it wasn't until 1985 that it let an outside auditor inside its doors. They and others found at

Farm Credit a set of home-brewed accounting standards that masked bad lending and lax regulation—system bankers were recording interest payments, and thus profits, on loans that were three or four years delinquent.

After much foot dragging and debate, Congress reached the obvious conclusion that it could not let the Farm Credit System fail. In December 1987, Congress finally approved a $4-billion rescue package for the tottering system. This bailout surpassed in size previous federal bailouts of NYC, Chrysler, and Lockheed.

The rescue package chartered a new agency, the *Federal Assistance Corporation. FACO* is authorized to issue 3 billion of bonds in 15-year maturities. Interest on these government-backed bonds will be paid by the Treasury over the first five years, split by the Treasury and the system over the second five years, and paid by the system over the third five years. FACO securities are issued by the staff of the Office for finance of the Federal Farm Credit Bank and the funds raised are funneled into the Farm Credit System.

Congress's rescue package for the Farm Credit also provided for the securitization of farm mortgages and rural housing loans. This program has yet to be implemented, but when it is, its securities will surely be dubbed *Farmer Macs*.

Today, Farm Credit securities are back to trading at respectable rates, investors' faith having been restored. That, of course, guarantees nothing about what the future will bring.

The Federal Insurance Corporation (FICO)

A crazy patchwork of regulation that required S&Ls to pay depositors fixed rates and to make fixed-rate mortgages in a rising rate environment first got S&Ls in trouble. By the time deposit rates were deregulated in the early 1980s and adjustable-rate mortgages were permitted, many S&Ls were already deeply in the red. To help them out, they were given various goodies including new investment powers which helped a number of them lose money in previously forbidden ways. Finally, large-scale fraud entered some areas of what was once a solid, if sleepy, industry.

By mid-1988, the total assets of "unhealthy" thrifts—those having a net worth of less than 3% of assets—equaled $423 billion, which was 34% of the industry's total assets; and these figures may be meaningless due to the questionable value of many S&L assets.

The Federal Savings and Loan Insurance Corporation (FSLIC) lacked sufficient cash to bail out big insolvent thrifts, so it invented FSLIC promissory notes as a substitute for cash. So far, the Bank Board has issued more than 10 billion of such notes to induce investors to take over insolvent thrifts. The thus "rescued" thrifts may count FSLIC notes as capital, but this capital is dummy capital, since FSLIC may lack the income to pay interest, let alone principal, on these notes. In 1988, FSLIC asked Congress for a federal guarantee for its notes, but didn't get it. Since FSLIC has for a number of years been technically bankrupt—if its contingent liabilities are added to its balance sheet—the American Institute of Certified Public Accountants has cast a dubious eye on the practice of S&Ls carrying FSLIC notes on their balance sheets at par.

To staunch the losses being incurred by sick thrifts, FSLIC needed funds to recapitalize. Begrudgingly, Congress in 1987 created a new federal agency, the *Financing Corporation. FICO* was authorized to sell $10.8 billion of bonds over three years and funnel the cash thus raised into FSLIC. That money was a meager fraction of what FSLIC needed, but House Speaker James Wright, well financed by the Texas thrifts, was determined that FSLIC not get sufficient funds to close down Texas's huge and ailing thrifts, who needed time to "work out their problems," which meant, euphemisms aside, time to lose a few more tens of billions of what ultimately were clearly going to be taxpayers' dollars.

To defease principal on FICO bonds, the 12 district Federal Home Loans Banks pool funds from retained earnings to buy Treasury zeros that match in maturity and face whatever bonds FICO issues. Interest on FICO bonds is to be paid out of FSLIC insurance premiums.

One troubling aspect of FICO bonds is that FSLIC is now required to make, from the insurance premiums it collects, interest payments on both FSLIC notes and FICO bonds. Standard accounting analysis of FSLIC suggests that a crossover point will be, maybe already has been, reached at which the interest FSLIC must pay out on these two types of securities will exceed the premiums it takes in from S&Ls whose deposits it insures. FSLIC could raise its insurance premiums, but that would only encourage the drive already on by healthy S&Ls to convert into banks in order to get lower-cost FDIC insurance.

Distribution

Federal agencies usually distribute new coupon issues through selling groups. An agency will announce the size of a new issue to be offered. At that time, the member of its selling groups—maybe 140 dealers for bigger agencies—begin to distribute the issue by determining (*circling* in Street jargon) customer interest in it. Small banks and other investors who aren't rate conscious will often put in a *market order* for the new issue—agree to buy it before it is priced. Other buyers will make a *subject bid*—agree to buy some amount of the issue if its coupon is set at rate X or better.

Dealers are each allocated a specific share of the total issue to be sold. They attempt to presell that share, and if they are more successful at this than other dealers, the agency increases their allocation.

The day after an agency announces a new issue, it starts to think about pricing. It makes its own reading of the market, talks to people at the Treasury, and inquires of a cross section of dealers how presales of its issue are going and where they feel the coupon should be set. The agency seeks to price its issue so that the latter will trade close to par. Once the agency announces its pricing decision, its new issue begins to trade wi.

Dealers in a selling group get a fee, which ranges, depending on the issuer and the size and maturity of the issue, from $3 to $3.50 per $1,000 on whatever securities they sell. Their function is to get the securities into the hands of a wide range of investors, not to position the new issue. However, in a sale characterized by poor retail demand, the major dealers would if necessary underwrite—buy for their own position—the new issue to get it sold.

The dealers who participate in the selling group are also market makers, and in that capacity they assume long and short positions in agencies. Sometimes after the sale of a new issue, dealers who like the issue will go back into the market as buyers and position it. This is easy to do if an issue goes immediately to a premium of a few 32nds; some buyers will want to sell out and take their profit and that will create a floating supply. How long distribution takes depends on the initial reception an issue gets in the market. If it is poor, the securities may overhang the market for a long period.

Agency securities trade wi for a week or two after they are priced and sold. The wi period used to be longer because of the time required to print certificates. Now, however, virtually all new agency issues are sold in book-entry form.

Competitive Bidding on New Issues

In early 1989, FICO set what might become a precedent: it sold an issue through a competitive-bid process. The winning bid came at a very attractive rate which led FHLB to suggest that it too might try the competitive-bid route. Dealers argue that, while competitive bidding may work well for agencies at times, it could work to their detriment in periods when demand is slack. The selling concessions that dealers get on new agency issues are the vigorish that makes so many firms commit to maintain agency trading staffs. Without that vigorish, many smaller dealers would have little incentive to stay involved in agencies.

Firms that have good corporate bond departments—like Sali, Goldman, and Merrill—would continue their commitment to distribute and trade agencies, but such firms are few in number. If over time, agencies came to be viewed as just another corporate-bond-type product, that might hurt the agencies' ability to price their paper as expensively as they have in the past.

One way agencies have long cut out the underwriting concession on some of the paper they issue is by reopening outstanding issues. When an agency does that, it calls around to a handful of firms and asks them to bid in competition for 50, 100, or 150MM of some issue.

The Secondary Market

The secondary market in agency securities, like that in governments, is made by dealers trading with retail and with each other. There are, however, significant differences between the two markets. These result largely from the fact that agency issues are smaller than Treasury issues and are traded less actively (Table 14–2).

Several primary dealers in governments are in the market everyday trading agencies, but many others are sometimes players who will position when they like a spot in the agency market and otherwise ignore it.

Dealers feel comfortable shorting agencies only when the issue is new, actively traded, and large. Consequently, dealers' net positions in agencies, unlike their net positions in governments, are always positive (Table 14–5).

Interdealer quotes in agencies are good for only 500,000, and many trades of that size are done. A 5MM trade is a big trade in the agency market except on a new or short-term issue. A 10MM trade is a rarity.

In agencies, the bid-offer spread tends to be wider than in Treasuries. Just what it is depends on the name, the newness, the size, and the maturity of the issue. Most active agency issues are traded at no more than a 2/32 spread, and most off-the-run issues should be available at a 1/4-point spread.

Many agency investors are bought by trust accounts, state and local governments, commercial banks, and foreign accounts, who never sell or swap the issues but rather mature them. Also, some issues get bought largely by investors, particularly foreign accounts, who won't lend securities. A dealer can't, in response to a bid from retail, sell short such an issue and figure he can make delivery by borrowing the issue until he can buy it. Because some agency issues get so well *seasoned* (really put away), it occurs in the agency market that one issue that has the same name and a similar coupon and maturity as some other issue will, nonetheless, trade expensive to that other issue.

In recent years, agencies have become, if anything, less liquid than they used to be. A problem with agency securities is that the agencies issuing them have not increased the size of their issues as the Treasury has done. On 500- and 800-MM agency issues, once an issue gets distributed, it gets illiquid. Noted one trader, "I would like to see the agencies reopen issues and build up an issue to 2 or 3 billion in size. People have offered this concept to the agency fiscal agents who have rejected it. There are so many agency issues that it is hard to keep track of them, and many are so small. What develops a really liquid market is the ability to short an issue because then you always have someone—an arbitrageur—there willing to buy it back at a price. But an arbitrageur has to be crazy to short agency issues. You can't borrow enough of them to do it. Whereas I can short almost any Treasury issue on the list and know I can borrow it at a price, I can't do that in agencies."

The illiquidity of agency paper is reflected in the fact that in inactive issues spreads can be virtually anything. Noted another trader, "You will even get bids on agency paper that trades infrequently. People will say, 'We know where the 5-year note is. These things should trade 60 bp off the note, so if 5-year notes are trading at 9.50, we will bid 10.10 for this agency paper.' "

Agency traders use brokers just as traders of governments do but less extensively. FBI is the major broker of agencies. The market in off-the-run agencies is so thin that when a dealer wants to buy or sell such an issue, he will often be quite open about his position with other dealers to see if they can help him find securities he wants to buy or a buyer for securities he wants to sell. Said one dealer, "Look at my position. I have 940,000 of this issue, I am short 90,000 of that one, and I need 290,000 of this other issue. I am not going to go into the brokers market to clean up all that. I will go to other dealers and talk to them, to Sali and Merrill. They will help me, and I help them."

Foreign-Targeted Paper

Several federal agencies have targeted special issues to foreign markets: Japan, Australia, and the Euromarket. Of the agencies, it is Sallie Mae (SLMA) who has pursued this tack most aggressively.

Agency Zeros

There are several sorts of agencies zeros. First, Freddie Mac, Fannie Mae (FNMA), and Sallie Mae have between them issued six zero bullets, some of which are quite long in term. Agency zeros have also been created by the stripping of FICO paper. At one point, FICO 30-year coupons were trading at a 115-bp spread to Treasuries, and the corpus was very attractive to institutional investors. There was thus spread to work with, and dealers, Sali first, began stripping FICOs. Several dealers have also stripped the FNMA 9s of 18. Most agency issues aren't attractive to strip because they are relatively small and offer a dealer little spread to work with.

Agency Discount Notes

In addition to selling medium- and long-term securities, the major federal agencies also sell discount notes (*dizzy notes* to traders), which resemble Treasury bills. Currently, agency discount notes outstanding probably total something over 70 billion (Figure 14–5). The World Bank's *whirlie birds* get lumped in with agency discount paper because dealers typically trade World Bank securities on their agency desk.

These notes are sold through dealers who get an 05 for their effort. An agency selling notes will decide what rate to offer on its notes after conferring with dealers in its selling group about market conditions. Some post rates all the time but post competitive rates only when they want to sell. Agencies invest any excess funds they raise through the sale of discount notes in repo. That's a negative carry for them so they are careful not to raise more short-term money than they need.

Agencies use funds raised through the sale of discount notes to provide bridge financing to a date when they intend to issue longer-term securities. They also issue discount notes when money is tight and they need to borrow but do not want to borrow long term at high rates. The FHLB, for example, experiences a substantial demand for loans from S&Ls when money is tight, but this demand tapers off rapidly as interest rates fall. Thus, if the FHLB borrows long term at high rates, as it has

FIGURE 14–5
Federal agency discount notes outstanding ($ billions)

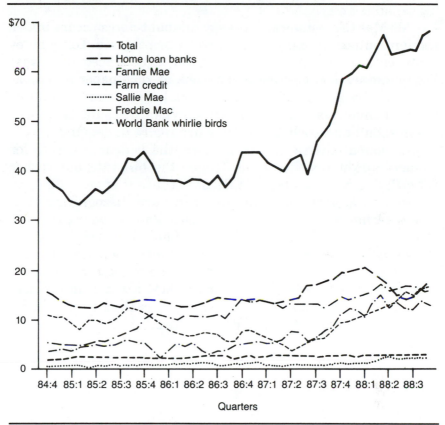

Source: 1988 Survey by FHLB, updated April 1, 1989.

done on occasion, it is likely to find that is has locked up for a long period expensive money that neither it nor member S&Ls later want.

Outstanding agency discount paper is traded less actively than bills are and is somewhat less liquid than bills. When the agencies are writing a lot of new paper, the dealers will bid for old paper to get customers to swap into new paper, and activity in the secondary market for such paper picks up. At other times when the agencies are not writing, activity drys up. A dealer will always give retail a bid on old paper, but getting an offer out of a dealer may be more difficult because, to supply old paper, a dealer must go out to an account that has the paper and try to bid it away.

Most of the issuance of agency discount notes occurs under six months and in many cases in the 3-month area. Dizzy notes trade at a spread over bills and used to be priced that way. Today, however, investors tend to look at such paper not vis-à-vis bills but vis-à-vis LIBOR, commercial paper, and other alternative money market investments. When discount notes get cheap relative to such paper, they are really in demand.

As noted earlier in this chapter, the benchmark rate for money market investor is no longer the bill rate but rather LIBOR. Everyone quotes off LIBOR because it is viewed as the purest indicator of where interest rates are. Recognizing this, Home Loan developed a LIBOR-based floater, whereas some years back it would naturally have sold a bill-based floater.

Money funds and state and local governments are big buyers of dizzy notes. An average trade in this market might be for 5 or 10MM, but trades for 50 and 100MM are not uncommon. The market for dizzy notes is huge, larger than the BA market—something most people don't realize.

GLOBALIZATION OF THE GOVERNMENT MARKET

The 1980s have been the decade of globalization. Despite the long slide of the dollar beginning in September 1985, Japanese investors tripled their investment in Treasuries in 1985 over what they had bought in 1984. Net, in 1985, the Japanese purchased 19.2 billion of Treasuries. One stimulus to foreign investment in Treasuries was the repeal in 1984 of the U.S.'s 30% withholding tax on interest income paid on governments to nonresidents.

During the 1980s, signs of globalization were everywhere. Initially, the Japanese, before they became more value-and-trading minded, just bought, bought, bought the Treasury long bond. They became so big, that a lot of auction talk before a refunding focused on how much of the new long bond to be sold would be gobbled up by Japanese investors. Would they take 30% as previously or would they be deterred by the continuing decline of the dollar, fear of the bear market, and so on? Nicholas Brady, who led the task force that investigated the causes of the October 1987 stock market crash even went so far as to blame the Japanese for touching off the Crash by selling Treasury bonds. Meanwhile, American investors began to daily eye developments in foreign stock and bond markets, especially those in Tokyo and London. Morning news told where the Tokyo markets had closed and where had London opened, and market quotes in *The Wall Street Journal* acquired a new international flavor. Want to know how Bunds and JGBs are doing? Look in the *Journal*.

Dealers: Ship Ahoy

For various reasons, including just plain size of outstandings, U.S. Treasury securities came to be the flavor of governments that seemed destined to be actively traded 24 hours a day. U.S. dealers who had been operating in London's Euromarket for years, set up shop in Tokyo, and prepared to deal in Treasuries 24 or near 24 hours a day. ("Near" because there is a quiet time from New York's close to Tokyo's open.)

At the time, the view of globalization was that people would trade U.S. Treasuries just as actively in non–New York hours as during New York hours. So the U.S. dealers said, "If Japanese and other foreign players want to trade Treasuries round the clock, we will bring the government market if not to their doorstep, at least to their time zone. To do this, U.S. dealers in governments set up trading operations in Tokyo, to cover Japan and the rest of the Far East, and in London to cover the U.K., the rest of Europe, and even Africa.

Meanwhile, of course, Japanese and European dealers were opening up shop in New York.

Organizing for 24-Hour Trading

When people thought that Treasuries would eventually be actively traded 24 hours a day, it seemed logical for U.S. dealers to organize worldwide trading activities by *passing the book*: New

York at its close would pass its book (positions) to traders in Tokyo who would take over trading the book and then at their close pass it on to London, which would trade it and then pass it on to New York.

Passing the book wasn't a great success. One reason was that, to a trader, the one thing that is really important is his position; thus, to have someone else making subjective decisions on the market and doing customer trades that impacted his position and his P&L went down poorly with New York traders.

As foreign business grew, U.S. dealers tried a second tack: they sent senior traders to London and Tokyo with the autonomy to trade on their own within limits. As this occurred, passing the book became dated. There is sufficient liquidity in Tokyo, for example, so that a trader for a U.S. dealer can sell governments and, if he can't buy back the same issue, he can at least hedge by buying a similar active government. That creates an arb that the New York curve trader can later unwind. Also, traders in New York leave, for traders in Tokyo to try to work, standing orders for their accounts and for customer accounts: "At these levels, buy 2s and sell 5s, buy bonds and sell 10s." At the Tokyo close, traders there pass on similar standing orders to traders in London. Esoterics, such as agencies, STRIPs, and proprietory zeros, have to be traded off the New York book.

One interesting aspect of 24-hour market in the U.S. governments is that it wreaks havoc with the sleep patterns of a lot of folks. Traders in Tokyo are in at 7:15 A.M. catching up on what happened in New York during the day, and from 8 A.M. to 11:30 A.M. they get some extra liquidity because the CBT is running its evening session for the Treasury bond contract. After the Board closes, it's just cash trading. The Tokyo market reacts as much as New York to economic numbers. In Tokyo, nonfarm payroll comes out at 10:30 P.M., so Tokyo traders will on certain days see more market flow in the late evening, after a break for dinner, than they have seen all day.

Brokers of governments, such as FBI, RMJ, Garban, and Cantor, followed their dealer clients to Tokyo and London. "We have," noted one broker, "18 bodies in London, 12 in Tokyo. Most of my New York brokers come in at 8 or 8:30 A.M. We broker in New York from 9 A.M. to 5:30 or 6 P.M. At 8 P.M. New York time, it's 9 A.M. in Tokyo, and trading there starts to pick up. Tokyo brokers until 3 or 4 A.M. New York time. Then London takes over. When it is 4 A.M. in New York, it's 9 A.M. in London; so basically, London has five hours before New York kicks in. The only hiatus is the two hours between the New York close and the Tokyo open. The Australian market is supposed to kick in then, but so far nothing has happened down there." While the brokers show pictures in New York not just for active issues, but for off-the-runs and exotics, the bids and offers posted with them in foreign centers are pretty much limited to active Treasuries.

The Reality of the 24-Hour Market

The U.S. dealers clearly have the apparatus in place to cope with and profit from active Treasury markets 22, even 24, hours a day. Unfortunately, the 24-hour market they set up shop for never really came to pass. The London and Tokyo markets in Treasuries never grew sufficiently to handle size comfortably. Big orders did and still do move these markets. "If a customer buys 100MM long bonds, the market will," noted a Tokyo trader, "go up a lot easier over there than it does in New York. Our market is thinner despite all the dealers who are here fighting and climbing over each other to get business."

Gradually, big traders in Tokyo and London concluded that the place and the time to trade size was New York during business hours there. Thus, the biggest of the Japanese institutional investors set up investment operations in New York, which only further diminished and confirmed the illiquidity of the Tokyo market.

While Tokyo and London offices may not produce the volumes of business once hoped for, they produce some shocking costs. Musing over the cost of living in Tokyo, one broker noted, "In Tokyo, a Johnny Walker Black and water is $14, an apartment is $4,000 a month, and a steak is $47." Office space and other expenses are commensurately high.

Tokyo has been a big disappointment to the brokers; it is costing them a fortune, and no volume is being done. Said one trader, "800MM to 1 billion bonds a night is a lot. Overall, our volume is 93% in New York, 4 to 5% in London, and 1 to 2% in Tokyo."

In everybody's view, the dealers are faring no better. They are incurring huge expenses, doing so-so volume, and net losing money on trading governments in foreign centers. The problem is certainly not lack of effort and money spent on their part. More likely, the reality is that, no matter what anyone says or does, the market for U.S. governments is always going to be more liquid and more profitable to trade during the hours when U.S. markets are open. A similar statement could also be made of Gilts, JGBs, Bunds, and OATS, although they too have big nondomestic followings.

Staying Home

The third stage in the evolution of how U.S. dealers organize to trade round-the-globe markets in Treasuries may well prove to be that they keep salespeople stationed in Tokyo, Singapore, Hong Kong, London, and wherever else they are needed, but they bring their traders home. "Clearly in 1984 to 1986, the tremendous growth of foreign participation in the Treasury market—both the volumes and the potential profitability that we all saw and felt in those markets, particularly Tokyo, as well as London, swayed," noted a Citibanker, "a lot of firms into rushing to expand their operation into those times zones. In late 1988, we brought back our traders from Tokyo and London and have created a 24-hour trading staff here in New York. We did this for a number of reasons. One is cost, which in Tokyo is incredible. We still have salespeople in Citibank offices throughout the world, but the trading of U.S. governments is done only in New York. We have a 'hoot-and-holler' system that goes, in addition to the U.S., into Toronto, Tokyo, Hong Kong, Singapore, and London, which has a link desk to all of our other European operations. A salesperson in Singapore can easily get a quote in their daylight time by shouting into the hoot-and holler system and getting a quote from our trader in New York who has the government brokers' screens right in front of him. At night, he can access those screens as if he were in Tokyo.

"So long as we have our salespeople out there close to the customer, it is the same thing as being in all three time zones. But it's better with respect to cost and ability to manage risk in a more centralized fashion. Also, we are utilizing our plant 24 hours a day. We have on the New York trading side, a trader of governments who comes in at 5 P.M. and stays through Tokyo hours; he crosses over with another trader who comes in about 3 A.M. to trade London and stays until 11 A.M. We also have sales assistants round the clock who get out information to our other sales units and who also treat other of our offices as clients. With our swap books and hedging around the world, we have a substantial amount of trading that is done in house. We have also sent all our domestic clients an 800 number they can call any time during the night to find out what is going on, to leave orders, or to trade. Our counterparties that are used to dealing with us during the daytime now think of us as being 24 hours here in New York. It is working beautifully."

While some may and do view Citi's centralization of trading in New York as a step back from globalization, the officer quoted is convinced that others will follow in Citi's steps. The brokers for their part have also started to come home. They are not running profitable operations abroad, and what's more, they are doing nothing that they could not now do in New York. Today, communications technology is such that governments could just as well be dealt and brokered on a Pacific island as in New York. The current role of New York as market center is simply a product of history.

Globalization versus Internationalization

It's useful to distinguish between internationalization and globalization of markets, which are two different things. Internationalization implies that people become much more aware of what goes on in other countries and how it affects what goes on in their country—also, that for investing and borrowing, there are more than domestic markets. Globalization assumes more seamless global markets in which there are not the pockets of activity that exist in today's markets worldwide.

One problem that dealers from every country face is that, to make money in a foreign market—except the London Euromarkets, which have no native home—one must almost become a native dealer with a native staff. It's tough for a Japanese dealer whose New York activities are directed by Japanese executives to get major business from big U.S. institutions just as it is tough for U.S. dealers to garner business from the Japanese insurance companies, trust banks, and others. Some big U.S. and European banks have foreign branches and subs that locals view as native institutions; however, it took decades and decades to create such a presence—to have local beginners mature into executives who are part of and in tune with the local scene, but who can also work well with head office. Some British banks, for example, grew up to serve an empire that they outlasted.

THE NEXT CHAPTER

In this chapter, we focused on the cash market for governments. In the next two chapters, we explore futures markets for governments and for Euros. These markets, which were a what-do-we-do-with-them novelty in the 1970s, have today become a major factor that permeates trading, one way or another, in every market we talk about.

APPENDIX TO CHAPTER 14
OFFICIAL TIME OUT FOR A LAUGH

The FSLIC Paper Goes Round and Round*. . .

You could set your beeper by the time the intercom buzzed on a Monday, and Cadwallader was ready to pick up the handset even before he heard the sound.

"Morning, Cadwallader," said the voice.

"Morning, Harry."

"Have a good weekend?"

"Wonderful. I got out of the office for an hour on Sunday. You?"

Continued

"Vineyard great as usual. What's new on the calendar, Cadwallader?"

There was a thick document on Cadwallader's desk, messengered in on Saturday from Washington. "Biggest thing," he said, "is an offer to tender for these new Federal Home Loan Bank Board bonds. The FSLIC rescue package? Competitive Equality Banking Act? Remember reading about it a couple of weeks ago?"

"Sure."

"Good deal for us, I think," said Cadwallader. "Congress okayed ten point eight billion dollars of this stuff to be issued in the next three years, and the guys who do the first issues will have the inside track later. First cut is about seven hundred million. Good discount for the underwriter."

"Federally guaranteed paper?"

"Well, no," said Cadwallader. "No guarantees."

"How do they pay it off?"

"Well, there's two different sources, one for the semiannual coupon, one for the principal."

"Segmented values, eh? Strips. I/O, P/O. Government's beginning to do that itself these days, eh? Cut out hard-working fellas like us."

"Not exactly. These are straight bonds, Harry. What's segmented is the source of payment to the holders."

"What does that mean?"

"It's thirty-year paper," said Cadwallader. "The district Federal Home Loan Banks take care of the repayment of principal out of their accumulated surplus. Safe, one hundred percent. They purchase zero-coupon Treasuries now and pledge them irrevocably to the bonds. They can buy a million bucks of thirty-year zeroes for about $80,000. Means that for $80,000 out of pocket the Home Loan Banks get $920,000 available now to pay off depositors in busted S&Ls. It also means—that's why Congress liked it—that nothing has to be put on the budget or the debt."

"And who pays the coupon?"

"FSLIC pays the coupon."

"No government guarantee?"

"No government guarantee."

Continued

There was an edge on Harry's voice. "I thought they were issuing the bonds because the wheels had come off FSLIC."

"That's right. Terrible wreck, FSLIC."

"Then how is FSLIC going to pay the interest?"

"Bank Board says the thrifts are going to get well, clean up all those bum assets, take advantage of all the new opportunities under deregulation. And the S&Ls will be paying larger fees to FSLIC to service the bonds."

"Wait a minute, Cadwallader. Can't S&Ls convert from FSLIC to FDIC, which ain't broke so nobody's fixing it?"

"Yes, after a one-year moratorium. But only the best of them have the net worth that allows them to join FDIC. And Congress okayed the exit tax for FSLIC, two years' premiums."

"How much do you figure the FSLIC premiums will have to go up to pay the interest on these bonds at the same time they have to pay off the busted S&Ls?"

"Well, you sort of double and start off from there. Congress okayed two and one-half times."

"So if you're an S&L in good enough shape to shift to FDIC, you recoup the exit tax in two years?"

"Maybe less."

"I see," said the voice in the handset.

"What makes it really safe," Cadwallader said, "is that if worst comes to worst they can pay the coupons on the last set of bonds by selling the next set of bonds."

"Cadwallader," said the voice, now with a touch of irritation, "that's known as a Ponzi game."

Cadwallader made a face at the intercom. "It's what the federal government does every quarter," he said.

"Who do you think will want to buy this paper?" said Harry.

"There's a guaranteed market," Cadwallader said.

"Who's that?"

"S&Ls. It's a legal investment for them. They gotta buy it."

"Sure," said the voice consolingly. "The problem is, the executive committee met yesterday and decided we have to worry a little more about the image of the firm. Need a little prestige in the markets, right? Don't want to be associated with too much junk, eh? World's turning more conservative, Cadwallader, for

Concluded

better or worse. And there's a limit to the number of deals we can buy with our capital."

"Yes, sir."

"There's some paper out for bids you haven't heard about, Cadwallader, because you do only domestic. Colombian government bonds, with the coupon indexed to the street price of cocaine. Solid investment, but intriguing. I think we're going to spring for that."

"Whatever you say, Harry. You're the boss."

"Yep," said Harry, with obvious feelings of comfort and relief. "You can explain it to the Home Loan Bank Board, can't you, Cadwallader? They won't have hard feelings, will they?"

"Strictly business, sir?"

"That's the ticket, Cadwallader. Strictly business."

*Mayer is speaking of FICO paper.

CHAPTER 15

FINANCIAL FUTURES: BILLS
AND EUROS

Forward transactions are common in many areas of economic activity including the markets for commodities. *In a forward transaction a seller agrees to deliver goods to a buyer at some future date at some fixed price.* For example, a farmer growing onions might, before the harvest, sell some portion of his crop to a buyer at a fixed price for delivery at harvest. For the farmer, this transaction reduces risk. To grow onions, the farmer incurs various costs; by selling his onions forward, he guarantees the revenue he will receive for his onions at harvest, and he thus locks in a profit on his operations. That profit may be more or less than what he would have earned if he had waited to sell his crop at harvest at the *spot* price then prevailing in the *cash market* (market for immediate delivery) for onions.

**FORWARD TRANSACTIONS IN THE
MONEY MARKET**

Forward transactions are common in the money market. For example, all wi trading of Treasuries is trading for forward settlement. Other forward trades of Treasuries are also done. To illustrate, suppose that an insurance company sells a *guaranteed income contract* (*GIC*) for a principal amount of 10MM to be paid to it three weeks hence; the insurance company, having sold the GIC, now needs to protect itself against a fall in interest rates over the coming three weeks. One way this company could lock in today's rate levels would be by buying for settlement three weeks hence, say, 10MM of 10-year notes. Assume it does so. Then when the money due it from the sale of the GIC comes in, the insurance company will pay for and take delivery of the

10-year notes it previously purchased for forward delivery. Next, it would probably sell these notes to acquire more exotic, higher-yielding assets.

This example suggests an interesting question: What relationship is likely to prevail between spot and forward prices? For physical commodities such as gold or wheat, forward prices always exceed *spot* (*cash-market*) prices because goods stored for forward delivery must be financed; also, storage and insurance costs must be paid. In financial lingo, *carry on physical commodities is always negative,* and for this reason, one would expect the forward price of a physical commodity to exceed its spot price. The fact that consecutive (more distant) gold futures contracts always trade at higher and higher prices relative to the spot price of gold reflects the positive cost of financing, storing, and insuring physical gold (Table 15–1).

The logic that dictates that forward prices will exceed spot prices for commodities does *not* apply for financial instruments. In the above example, a dealer was asked to offer 10MM of 10-year notes for forward delivery; under normal market conditions—the yield curve slopes upward—he would offer 10-year notes for forward delivery at a price *less than* their spot (cash-market) price because *carry* on the notes would be *positive:* the term (3-week) repo rate would be less than the yield at which

TABLE 15–1
Gold prices: spot (cash) and futures as of 03/31/89

Gold (100 troy ounces)	Price: $ per Troy Ounce
Spot	383.20
CMX futures	
Apr 89	383.50
June	387.60
Aug	393.50
Oct	399.50
Dec	405.00
Feb 90	410.00
Apr	416.60

Source: *The Wall Street Journal,* April 3, 1989.

the notes were trading. The forward price of a financial instrument may equal, be less than, or exceed its cash-market price. Which it is depends on the sign and size of carry whenever the instrument traded for forward delivery is a security that has been issued and is trading in the cash market.

Other sorts of forward deals are also struck in the money market. A bank may agree to do a 3-month Euro time deposit with another bank three months hence at an agreed rate that reflects both parties' expectations as to the direction of interest rates. Such a transaction is called a forward forward. A FRA resembles a forward forward except that on settlement date, no deposit changes hands; instead there's a cash payment between the contracting parties based on the relationship between the rate at which the trade was done and the market rate at the time of settlement. In a FRA, both parties are betting on a future interest rate. If rates move such that one party loses X on his bet, the other party wins X (FRAs are a zero-sum game). Forward forwards and FRAs are, in effect, over-the-counter (OTC) versions of formal futures contracts; forward forwards are forward contracts settled with delivery, whereas FRAs are forward contracts settled with a cash payment.

Interest-rate swaps are also sometimes done for forward settlement, particularly in what's called the IMM swap (Chapter 19). Finally, we recall that repo financing is traded for forward delivery during the period when a Treasury issue trades wi. This permits a trader to lock in both the yield he will receive on the issue and the financing rate he must pay when the issue settles and securities are delivered to him. In the case of wi securities, forward repos, FRAs, and interest-rate swaps done for forward settlement, the long in such a trade has nothing to carry (no security to finance); consequently, the forward price established in the market presumably represents simply the consensus view of traders as to what a specific rate or price will be on a specific forward date.

Often, money market participants assume forward positions to reduce risk. However, they also can and do take forward positions to assume risk—to make bets on future rates or prices—and to put on one leg of a sometimes complex arbitrage.

FUTURES VERSUS FORWARD CONTRACTS

Most *futures contracts,* like many forward contracts, specify that the seller of the contract will deliver to the buyer a specific amount of a specific item at a specific price on a specified future date. However, some financial futures contracts call for cash settlement as does the Euro contract discussed below. Any forward or futures contract can be settled equitably with either delivery or a cash payment. Which method is used is pretty much a matter of history—which method was initially adopted for reasons of legality, custom, or convenience.

While futures contracts are similar to forward contracts in certain respects, they differ from the latter in other important respects. First, whereas forwards are normally custom-tailored contracts, *futures are standardized contracts made and traded on exchanges that are chartered, designated, and licensed to serve as a trading arena in specific futures contracts.* Second, whereas forward contracts are normally made with the intent that either delivery or a cash payment shall be made at expiration of the contract, *delivery is usually not made in connection with a futures contract even if the contract contains specific delivery provisions.* Instead, *a buyer* of a futures contract will typically close out his position before the contract matures by making *an offsetting sale* of the same contract, *a seller* by making *an offsetting purchase.*

The reason delivery is not made is that people typically enter into futures contracts not to buy or sell an item, physical or financial. Instead they want either (1) *to offset risk on a long or short position, that is, to hedge that position by taking an equal and offsetting position in futures;* or (2) *to speculate on a change in the price of an item or in the spread (measured in price or yield) at which it trades to some other item.* The hedger attempts to put himself in a position where any losses he incurs on his cash position (e.g., he is long X and the cash-market price of X drops) will be offset by an equal gain on his futures position. As shown in examples below, the hedger can accomplish this by establishing a position in futures and later closing it out. The speculator, who neither owns nor desires to own the underlying commodity or financial instrument, can also realize whatever gain or loss he makes on his speculation simply by closing out his position in futures.

For a hedger, a transaction in futures is often a temporary substitute for a transaction in the cash or spot market. For example, a bond trader at a big shop might, as noted in Chapter 14, be asked to bid on 250MM bonds. He bids and his bid is hit, but he does not want such a big and risky long position in bonds. Maybe he can sell right away in the brokers' market 100MM of the bonds he has just bought, either at a small profit or at least at no loss. To cover the other 150MM, he would short bond futures, the market for which is deep and liquid. This trade (Chapter 16) leaves our bond trader long the basis (between cash bonds and futures). As the basis fluctuates, our trader hopes he will next be able to sell the basis at a profit and thus end up (1) being flat both bonds and the basis and (2) having made a small profit to boot.

FINANCIAL FUTURES

In January 1976, the *International Monetary Market* (*IMM*), now part of the Chicago Mercantile Exchange (CME), opened trading in futures contracts for 3-month Treasury bills. The trading of futures contracts for financial instruments was not new. In October 1975, the Chicago Board of Trade opened trading in futures contracts for Ginnie Mae pass-throughs, and prior to that, the IMM had introduced trading in futures contracts for major foreign currencies. Still, introduction of the bill futures contract was an important innovation for the money market because trading in Ginnie Mae pass-throughs and foreign exchange lies at the fringe of what could strictly be called money market activities.

In contrast, the bill market is a key sector of the money market, and as part of their normal investing or borrowing activities, every money market participant could find potential uses for sales or purchases of bill futures.

The initial reception of bill futures by the Street was marked by uncertainty and coolness. The dealers looking at the new market all groped for the "right numbers"; they asked what the relationship between spot and futures prices should be and how they could profit from trading in the new market. Many investors were confused about the nature of the contract and uncertain as to how they might or should use it. Also, some felt that a contract traded by "commodities speculators" next to the pork belly pit was suspect.

Nonetheless, the volume of contracts traded in the bill futures market rose (Figure 15–1) through 1982 rapidly and dramatically; in fact, for a time, the market in bill futures came to be used more widely than any futures market ever had been. One reason was that dealers in governments quickly became active participants in the new market, following a pattern well established in other futures markets where dealers who position

FIGURE 15–1

Average daily volume of the IMM Treasury bill futures contracts (thousands)

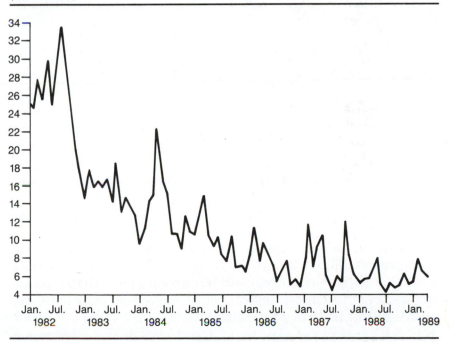

Source: Donaldson, Lufkin & Jenrette (Chicago Mercantile Exchange).

the commodity traded are big buyers and sellers of futures contracts.

By the summer of 1982, daily volume in the bill futures market averaged $32 to $34 billion; in contrast, the volume of bills traded daily in the cash market by all recognized and reporting dealers in governments averaged only $20 to $22 billion. This comparison was impressive for a futures market that was only six years old.

The success from the start of the Treasury bill futures contract spurred introduction by several exchanges of a host of other futures contracts on different financial instruments. Some of the new futures contracts, in particular the *Chicago Board of Trade's (CBT's)* bond futures contract, filled a real need and were highly successful. However, most new financed futures contracts quickly failed. For example, the CBT's futures contract for 90-day, A-1, P-1 commercial paper never attracted much interest because the real market in commercial paper is for paper with an original maturity of 30 days or less; also, when delivery occurred at the maturity of this contract, the least attractive paper meeting delivery specifications was always delivered.

In 1981, the New York Futures Exchange (NYFE) introduced futures contracts in currencies, bills, and bonds with much fanfare and high hopes that these contracts would succeed since New York, not Chicago, is the capital of the money market and in particular the center of the cash market for money market instruments. In fact, all these NYFE contracts failed partly because NYFE never had the strong locals Chicago did to build up and maintain liquidity in its contracts. Also, the initial NYFE contracts met no unfilled needs, since all—with the exception of the bond contract—were me-too imitations of contracts already traded in Chicago.

Introduction of some contracts that appeared to be obvious winners was delayed by slow-moving regulators. It was not until 1981 that trading in domestic CD futures was permitted. Unfortunately, not long after, investors came to regard some of the top 10 American banks as far better credits than others (Chapter 20). As a result, a variant of Gresham's law—good money drives out bad money—came into play: shorts delivered consistently the least well-thought-of and thus the cheapest CDs that were deliverable under the contract. This ploy killed off the new CD contract in short order.

In 1982, trading in Eurodollar futures was finally permitted. Settlement of this contract by delivery would have been a nuisance and, more important, would have invited quick death, again at the hands of a variant of Gresham's law. Wisely, regulators permitted cash settlement of the Euro contract, even though to some, the idea of a futures contract with cash settlement smacked of high-stakes gambling.

That a contract trades well initially is no guarantee that it will continue to do so. The GNMA contract, at first a big success, has all but died because its delivery mechanism provided market participants with some nasty surprises when interest rates became high and volatile. Today, it appears that the bill contract too is dying due to circumstances noted below.

REGULATION

Currently, futures trading in bills and other financial instruments is regulated by the *Commodity Futures Trading Commission (CFTC)*, which first authorized trading in bill futures in November 1975. At that time the SEC, which regulates trading in most securities and in securities options, argued that contracts for the future delivery of securities were securities and that it should therefore have jurisdiction over the futures market in Treasury bills and other financial instruments. The CFTC countered that regulation of trading in such contracts fell within its purview because the law creating the CFTC gave it exclusive jurisdiction over trading in contracts for future delivery.

The dispute between the two agencies resurfaced in 1978 when the SEC recommended to Congress that it take over the CFTC's authority to regulate futures trading in securities. The SEC's concern over futures trading in securities was heightened by the difficulties that arose in the dealer-made, off-the-board forward market for Ginnie Mae pass-throughs, when a small dealer, Winters, whose operations had been irregular, failed.

Under Chairman James Stone, the CFTC was slow to approve new futures contracts, it demanded from exchanges proposing new contracts extensive documentation that economic justification existed for these contracts. When Philip Johnson took over as chairman of the CFTC in the summer of 1981, he took a more free-market philosophy; in his view, exchanges should be permitted to introduce new contracts meeting standard regulatory requirements with less *a priori* proof of economic justification. *A posteriori* the market would demonstrate whether introduction of a new contract was justified: If the new contract traded well, it fulfilled a need; if it failed, it did not.

In the summer of 1981, the CFTC finally approved not only a domestic CD futures contract, but the first of several stock index futures contracts; the latter provided for *cash settlement,* an innovation that had been proposed by industry participants for years.

While the CFTC began to move, its underlying jurisdictional dispute with the SEC remained; the SEC continued to argue that a futures contract on an exempt security was a security and therefore subject to SEC jurisdiction. Finally in the fall of 1981, Chairmen Johnson of the CFTC and Shad of the SEC reached a jurisdictional accord spelling out each agency's area of regulatory authority (Table 15–2). This agreement, passed into law in 1982, gives the industry guidance as to where jurisdiction lies and thus provides more certainty to would-be proposers and users of new contracts.

The accelerated pace at which federal regulators began to approve new contracts led to a rapid expansion in the menu of securities—financial futures, options on fixed-income securities, and options on futures—being traded. The specifications of the principal financial futures contracts and of options on those contracts that are traded on U.S. exchanges are outlined in Table 15–3.

BILL FUTURES

To begin our discussion of financial futures, we examine the bill contract: the basic contract terms, how the contract is quoted, the clearing function of the exchange, how margin is handled,

TABLE 15–2
SEC-CFTC jurisdictional accord in 1981

I. SEC jurisdiction
    Options on any security including:
        U.S. government and other exempt securities
        Certificates of deposit
        Any index of securities
    Also options on foreign currencies

II. CFTC jurisdiction
    Futures contracts including:
        U.S. government and federal agency exempt securities
        Broad-based indexes of securities
        All currently traded futures
    Also options on:
        Futures contracts
        Foreign currencies

III. Prohibited
    Futures contracts on corporate and municipal securities
    Futures contracts on narrowly based indexes of securities

---

how the market for the contract is made, and how the contract may be used for hedging and other purposes.

With respect to basics, the futures contracts for all fixed-income securities work and are traded—with the exception of cash settlement—in pretty much the same way, so much of what we will say about the bill contract applies to other futures contracts as well. The peculiarities of the bond and note futures contracts are described in Chapter 16.

The Bill Contract

The basic contract traded on the IMM is for 1MM of 90-day Treasury bills. Currently, a contract matures once each quarter—in those weeks of March, June, September, and December when the newly auctioned 3-month bill is a reopening of an old year bill. There are eight contracts outstanding, so when a new contract starts to trade, the furthest delivery date stretches 24 months into the future. Traders refer to the farthest out contracts as *red;* for example, in November 1990 contracts for December 1991 bills were in pit jargon the *red Decs.*

TABLE 15-3
Contract specifications for principal financial futures and options on financial futures

Contract Specifications for Financial Futures and Options (Actual and Proposed) as of 1989

Contracts	Exchange	Symbol	Hours Chicago Time	Trading Unit	Minimum Price Fluctuation	Daily Price Limits
Financial futures						
T bond	CBT	US	7:20–2:00	$ 100,000	1/32 of 1% = $31.25/contract	3 pts = $3,000/contract
T note 5 yr.	CBT	FV	7:20–2:00	100,000	1/64 of 1% = 15.63/contract	3 pts = 3,000/contract
T note 10 yr.	CBT	TY	7:20–2:00	100,000	1/32 of 1% = 31.25/contract	3 pts = 3,000/contract
Muni bond	CBT	MB	7:20–2:00	100,000	1/32 of 1% = 31.25/contract	3 pts = 3,000/contract
30-day int. rate	CBT	FF	7:20–2:00	5,000,000	.01 (1 basis pt) = 41.67/contract	150 pts = 62,500/contract
Euro 90-day time dep.	IMM	ED	7:20–2:00	1,000,000	.01 (1 basis pt) = 25.00/contract	No limit
90-day U.S. T bill	IMM	TB	7:20–2:00	1,000,000	.01 (1 basis pt) = 25.00/contract	No limit
T note 5 yr.	FINEX	FY	7:20–2:00		1/64 of 1% = 15.63/contract	No limit
T note 2 yr.	FINEX	TW	7:20–2:00	200,000	1/4 of 1/32 = 15.64/contract	No limit
Currencies						
Australian dollar	IMM	AD	7:20–2:00	100,000AD	.0001 (1 pt) = $10.00/contract	150 pts = 1,500/contract
British pound	IMM	BP	7:20–2:00	62,500	.0002 (2 pt) = 6.25/contract	400 pts = 2,500/contract
Canadian dollar	IMM	CD	7:20–0:00	100,000CD	.0001 (1 pt) = 10.00/contract	100 pts = 1,000/contract
Deutsche mark	IMM	DM	7:20–2:00	125,000DM	.0001 (1 pt) = 12.50/contract	150 pts = 1,875/contract
French franc	IMM	FR	7:20–2:00	250,000Ff	.00005 (5 pt) = 2.50/contract	500 pts = 1,250/contract
Japanese yen	IMM	JY	7:20–2:00	12,500,000JY	.000001 (1 pt) = 12.50/contract	150 pts = 1,875/contract
Swiss franc	IMM	SF	7:20–2:00	125,000SF	.0001 (1 pt) = 12.50/contract	150 pts = 1,875/contract
Stock indexes						
S&P 500 Index	IMM	SP	8:30–3:15	$500 × index	.05 (5 pt) = 25.00/contract	Limits in place§
NYSE Composite Index	NYFE	YX	8:30–3:15	500 × index	.05 (5 pt) = 25.00/contract	No limit
Major Market Index	CBT	BC	8:15–3:15	250 × index	.05 (1 pt) = 12.50/contract	No limit
CBOE 250 Index	CBT	JV	8:30–3:15	500 × index	.05 (1 pt) = 25.00/contract	{+50 = 1,250/contract {−30 = 750/contract
Options for financial futures						
T bond	CBT	CG, PG	7:20–2:00	$100,000 face value CBOT U.S. T bill futures contract of a specific delivery month	1/64 (1 pt) = $15.63/contract	3 pts = 3,000/contract

TABLE 15–3—(continued)

			Last Day of Trading†		Initial Margins‡		Contracts
T note 10 yr.	CBT	TC, TP	7:20–2:00	$100,000 face value CBOT T note futures contract of a specific delivery month	1/64 (1 pt)	= 15.63/contract	3 pts = 3,000/contract
Muni bond	CBT	QC, QP	7:20–2:00	One CBOT muni bond index futures contract deliverable	1/64 (1 pt)	= 15.63/contract	3 pts = 3,000/contract
Euro	IMM	ED, CE, PE	7:20–2:00	One ED futures contract	.01 (1 pt)	= 25.00/contract	No limit
T bill	IMM	T1, CQ, PQ	7:20–2:00	One T bill futures futures contract	.01 (1 pt)	= 25.00/contract	No limit
Options on currency futures							
Australian dollar	IMM	AD, KA, JA	7:20–2:00	One AD futures contract	.0001 (1 pt)	= $10.00/contract	Option ceases trading when corresponding future locks limit
British pound	IMM	BP, CP, PP	7:20–2:00	One BP futures contract	.0002 (2 pt)	= 12.50/contract	Option ceases trading when corresponding future locks limit
Canadian dollar	IMM	C1, CV, PV	7:20–2:00	One CD futures contract	.0001 (1 pt)	= 10.00/contract	Option ceases trading when corresponding future locks limit
Deutsche mark	IMM	D1, CM, PM	7:20–2:00	One DM futures contract	.0001 (1 pt)	= 12.50/contract	Option ceases trading when corresponding future locks limit
Japanese yen	IMM	J1, CJ, PJ	7:20–2:00	One JY futures contract	.000001 (1 pt)	= 12.50/contract	Option ceases trading when corresponding future locks limit
Swiss franc	IMM	E1, CF, PF	7:20–2:00	One SwFr futures contract	.0001 (1 pt)	= 12.50/contract	Option ceases trading when corresponding future locks limit
Options on index futures							
S&P 500 Index	IMM	SP, CS, PS	8:30–3:15	One S&P 500 futures contract	.05 (5 pt)	= $25.00/contract	All S&P options series close when future locks limit
NYSE Composite Index	NYFE	YX*		One NYSE composite index futures contract	.05 (5 pt)	= 25.00/contract	No limit

TABLE 15–3—(concluded)

	Last Day of Trading†	Initial Margins‡	Contracts
Notes bonds	Seven business days prior to the last business day of the delivery month.	$2,000	T bond
		1,500	10-yr T note
		1,250	5 yr T note
	Last business day of the delivery month	800	30-day interest rate
	Eighth to last business of the delivery month	1,250	Muni bond
	Second London business day before third Wednesday	900	Eurodollar
	Business day prior to issue date	800	90-day T bill
		1,200	Australian dollar
		2,000	British pound
		1,400	Deutsche mark
Currencies	Second business day before third Wednesday	1,700	Swiss franc
		1,700	Japanese yen
		700	Canadian dollar
		700	French franc
	Third Thursday	4,000	S&P 500 Index
	Thursday before third Friday of the contract month	4,000	NYSE Composite Index
	Third Friday of the delivery month	4,000	Major Market Index
	First business day prior to the first	4,000	CBOE 250 Index
	Saturday which follows the third Friday of the month.	(All options must be paid in cash. Options writes are margined differently.)	
	Third Friday of the option month		T bond futures
	Third Friday of the option month		T note futures
	Last day of trading in Muni Bond Index futures of the corresponding month.		Muni Bond Index
	Second London business day before third Wednesday of contract month.		Eurodollar
	Friday which precedes by six business days first business day of contract month.		90-day T bill
	Second Friday prior to the third Wednesday of contract month.		Currencies
	Business day prior to the third Friday.		S&P 500
	Quarterly expiration—Thursday before third Friday of the contract month.		NYSE Composite Index
	Non-quarterly expiration—third Friday of the contract month.		

*See individual vendors for codes.
†See individual exchanges for rules concerning holidays.

‡Subject to change by the CBT, IMM, NYFE, and Finex exchanges.
§Contact the IMM exchanges for limit specifications

Source: Donaldson, Lufkin & Jenrette. The information set forth above has been obtained from sources believed to be reliable; however, we make no representations as to its accuracy.

Price Quotes

Bills trade and are quoted in the *cash market* on a yield basis; consequently, the bid always exceeds the offer; also, when yield rises, price falls, and vice versa. This seems reasonable to a person accustomed to trading discount paper, but it's confusing to a person who's accustomed to trading commodities or stocks. The IMM therefore decided not to quote bill contracts directly in terms of yield. Instead, it developed an *index system* in which a bill is quoted at a "price" equal to 100.00 minus yield; a bill yield of 8.50 would thus be quoted on the IMM at 91.50. Note that in this system, when yield goes down, the index prices rises: and a trader who is long futures profits. This conforms to the relationship that prevails in other commodity futures markets, where longs profit when prices rise and shorts profit when prices fall.

Price Fluctuations

Price fluctuations on bill futures are in multiples of an 01, one basis point. Because the contract is for delivery of 90-day bills, each 01 is worth $25.

The maximum price fluctuation permitted in any one day is 60 bp above or below the preceding day's setting price.[1] However, if on two successive days, a contract closes at the normal daily limit in the same direction (not necessarily the same contract month on both days), an expanded daily price limit goes into effect: On the third day, the daily price limit on all contract months goes to 150% of the normal daily limit. If on that day, any contract month closes at its expanded daily price limit and in the same direction as the preceding daily limit price change, the daily price limit expands to 200% of the normal daily price limit and remains there as long as any contract month closes at this expanded daily price limit.

---

[1]The *setting price* is the average of the highest and lowest prices at which trades occur during the last minute of trading.

Clearing Function of the IMM

Whenever a trade occurs on the IMM, there must be a buyer and an offsetting seller. Each trader's contractual obligation, however, is not to his counterpart in the trade but to the IMM. The IMM stands between the principals in a trade; it is the opposite side of every trade effected on the exchange, even though it never itself assumes any net position long or short in bill futures. The IMM's purpose in acting as what might be called a supervisory *clearing house* is to guarantee the fiscal integrity of every trade made on the exchange.

Margin

An important part of the IMM's job is to oversee the enforcement of margin requirements and the monetary transfers they require. When a trader buys a contract on the IMM, he does not pay for it immediately, and if he sells a contract, he does not receive payment immediately. Both the buyer and the seller, however, must put up *margin*. Currently, the minimum margin required by the IMM is $800 per bill contract on an outright position. On a special position it is less. (A brokerage house through which an individual trader deals may require more.)

When a trader assumes a long or short position, he will incur gains and losses each day thereafter as price fluctuates. The amount of each day's gain (loss) is added to (subtracted from) his margin account at the end of the day. For example, if a trader bought a contract at 92.20 and the settling price at the end of the day on that contract was 99.20, he would have incurred a loss equal to $750 (30 bp times $25), and that money would be subtracted by his broker from his margin account. Some other trader would necessarily have made an equal and offsetting gain, and money equal to the amount of that gain would be added to his margin account. This adding and subtracting is done through the IMM, which collects money from brokers whose clients have incurred losses and transfers it to brokers whose clients have earned profits. Because margin balances are adjusted through the IMM at the end of each business day, a trader starts each day having realized, through additions to or deductions from his margin account, the net gain or loss he has made on his position since he established it. The IMM margin system converts on a daily basis what would be *paper* gains and losses into *realized* gains and losses.

If the balance in a trader's margin account falls below the current *maintenance margin* limit, which is less than the initial margin, he must immediately deposit additional funds (variation margin) in this account to bring it up to that level. If he fails to do so, his broker is required to close out his position. If, alternatively, a trader has earned profits and his margin account has therefore risen above the margin he's required to maintain he may withdraw the excess margin.

The IMM's requirements with respect to margin maintenance guarantee that a trader's losses on a given day are unlikely to significantly exceed the amount in his margin account and thus make it improbable that any investor would end up in a position of being unable to honor a contract he had made either by liquidating his position through an offsetting trade or by making or taking delivery of securities.

If a trader takes offsetting long and short positions in the two contracts closest to maturity, he is required to put up only less initial margin, and the minimum margin he must maintain is also smaller. On offsetting long and short positions in contracts farther out on the maturity spectrum, the trader must maintain margin equal to any loss he has incurred on that position. If there is none, he need not put up any margin.

Collateral in the form of securities may be used as initial margin so that the effective cost of putting up such margin can be reduced to close to zero.

End of Trading

Trading in a bill futures contract terminates in the week of the delivery month on the second business day following the weekly auction of the 3-month bill, which is a reopening of the old year bill. This would normally be a Wednesday. Settlement of futures contracts outstanding at the time trading is terminated is made on the following day, Thursday. This is also the day on which settlement is made on the 3-month cash bill just auctioned.

Thus, there are always new 3-month bills available for delivery on the day an outstanding future contract is settled.

Buyers of futures contracts do not normally take delivery, but it can be done.[2] The buyer who wants to take delivery instructs the IMM that he wants delivery to be made at a particular Chicago bank. The IMM then instructs the seller's bank to make delivery there, and delivery is effected against payment in Fed funds.

Commissions

Since well over 90% of all buyers and sellers of financial futures close out their positions by doing an offsetting trade, *futures commission merchants (FCMs)* charge, on an initial buy or sell of futures, a *round-turn* commission: if a customer's initial trade is a *buy,* his FCM charges him a round-turn commission on that buy, but *no* commission on a later offsetting *sell.*

FCMs used to charge a high minimum, round-turn commission; it was phased out with a switch to negotiated commissions. Currently, on wholesale trades, the commission on the bill and Euro contracts is around half a basis point ($12.50) round turn per contract traded; and on big trades, it goes down from there. On bond futures, a round-turn ticket might be $8 or $10, with $6 or $7 being absolute bottom.

How the Market Is Made

The market in cash bills, as noted in Chapter 14, is made by dealers in geographically disperse institutions who keep in contact through direct phone lines and through the brokers, and who are required to quote bid and asked prices to each other and to retail.

In bill futures, in contrast, all trades are made during regular trading hours in the bill pit on the floor of the CME in Chicago; the futures market is thus a single central market.

---

[2]Normally, not more than 5 to 10% of outstanding futures contracts are settled by delivery.

Traders in the bill pit make their bids and offers known by crying them out. In the pit, all that is heard is the highest bid and the lowest offer. Anyone with a lower bid or higher offer remains silent until the market moves to his level. The face-to-face market in the bill pit is akin to the market that dealers in cash bills would make if they were jammed in the same physical place shouting and signaling to each other instead of dealing over the phone with brokers.

There are three types of traders in the bill pit. First, there are employees of brokerage houses who execute trades for retail customers and for the brokerage house's own account. Many of these brokers also trade for their own accounts; a broker who does this is required to execute customer business before dealing for his own account. The second type of trader in the pit is the *"deck holder."* Deck holders sell a service to brokers; they handle limit orders (e.g., customer orders to buy at 20 when the market is at 22) and stop-loss orders (a customer orders to sell if price falls to a certain level). A deck holder files all orders given to him by brokers according to price and then, as the market moves, executes those orders he can. Finally, there are private persons (*locals*) in the pit who trade for their own account on an outright speculative basis or more often on a spread basis; an individual who wants to trade bill futures on the CME floor can do so by buying a seat on the exchange.

A dealer who calls another dealer in cash bills and gets a quote 65–64 can say to the dealer, "You sold bills at 64." He can't do that in the futures market. He can call a broker on the floor and get information on the price at which the last trade occurred and on what bids and offers currently are. But if he asks the broker to execute an order at the current bid or asked price, he can't be sure that the broker will be able to. In a fast market, the five yards from the broker's phone to the pit can be a long way, and the market may have moved by the time the broker gets there. Thus, a retail customer has to deal differently with a broker in the futures market than he does with a dealer in the cash market if he wants to get orders in size executed.

The major dealers are all members of the principal exchanges on which financial futures are traded, and on each such exchange, they have two separate desks for trading futures—

one to handle trades for house accounts and one to handle trades for customers.

Technically, bids and offers in the futures market do not go subject when a big number is being announced or when the Fed is in the market. However, futures do not trade through a number. "For the five-second interval that a number is coming out," noted one trader, "all eyes are glued to the Dow Jones screen. This morning we had a number. Our [cash] markets and the futures markets traded right up to 8:29 [A.M.] and 55 seconds, and they started trading again at 8:30 and 5 seconds. Officially, the futures market has to be open at 8:30 because it never closes [during trading hours] unless it is closed by its board of governors. But, for those 10 seconds, it does not trade because everyone is waiting for that number."

Market Participants

The principal participants in futures markets are speculators, hedgers, arbitrageurs, and spreaders. About speculators there is little need for explanation: these individuals buy or sell futures contracts in the hope of gain. When futures prices rise or fall sharply, to the dismay of one group or another, the blame is often placed incorrectly on speculators. Actually these much maligned individuals perform a function essential to any futures market; they assume risks that others—including hedgers and arbitrageurs—seek to shed.

HEDGING

A portfolio manager who sells bill futures to limit the risk on a long position in bills and a portfolio manager who buys bill futures to lock in a rate at which he can invest an anticipated cash inflow are both managing risk by *hedging*. *To hedge using financial futures is to assume a position in futures equal and opposite to an existing or anticipated position, which may be short or long, in cash or cash securities.*

Delivery

An important point to note about hedging through the purchase or sale of either commodity or financial futures contracts is that delivery need not be and usually is not made or taken in connection with a hedge. Normally, hedges and speculative positions as well are closed out by making an offsetting trade in the same contract. Also, as noted, some newer futures contracts (Euro and stock index contracts) do away with delivery by specifying cash settlement.

The hedger attempts to put himself in a position where any loss he incurs on his cash position in the commodity (e.g., he is long and price in the cash market drops) will be offset by an equal gain on his futures position. He can do this by establishing a position in futures and later closing it out. The speculator who neither owns nor desires to own the underlying commodity can also realize whatever gain or loss he makes on his speculation simply by closing out his futures position.

If a hedger, speculator, or other futures market participant wants to make or take delivery, he is—unless cash settlement is specified—free to do so. A trader who maintains an open position in such a market at the expiration of a futures contract must settle by making or taking delivery.

A Long Hedge with No Basis Risk

To illustrate hedging, we will consider a few examples. First, a *long hedge* with no basis risk.[3] Suppose that an investor's cash-flow projections tell him that he will have a lot of cash to invest short term in the future; that is, he is going to be *long* investable cash. He can wait to invest until he gets the cash and take the then prevailing rate, or as soon as his projections tell him how much cash he will have, he can lock in a lending rate by buying bill futures.

---

[3]As illustrated below, the outcome of a hedge may depend on how the spread between two rates moves. If so, the hedger incurs *spread* or *basis risk*.

Table 15–4 illustrates this. We assume that our investor knows in June that he will have 10MM of 3-month money to invest in September and that when September arrives he will invest that money in bills. In June, the September bill contract is trading at 10.50. If our investor buys 10 of these contracts, he will earn 10.50 on the money he invests in September, regardless of the rate at which the cash 3-month bill is then trading.

One way he could get the 10.50 rate would be to take delivery in September of the bills he purchased at 10.50. But to see the nature of the hedge, we assume that, in September when his cash comes in, he closes out his futures position and buys cash bills.

As the September contract approaches maturity, it must trade at a yield close to and eventually equal to the rate at which the 3-month cash bill is trading. If a divergence existed between these two rates as trading in the contract terminated, potential for a profitable arbitrage would exist. For example, if, a few days before the September bill contract matured, it was trading at a much higher yield than the cash bill, traders would buy the contract, sell cash bills on a *when issued* basis, take delivery in Chicago to cover their short position in the cash bill, and profit on the transaction.[4]

In Outcome 1 (Table 15–4), we assume that, as the September contract matures, the 91-day cash bill trades at 10.20 and the futures contract consequently also trades at 10.20. At this time, our investor sells his September contracts and buys the cash 3-month bill. He purchased his futures contracts at 10.50 and sells them at 10.20, a lower rate. Since the delivery value of the contracts is higher the lower the yield at which they trade, our investor makes (Table 15–4) a $7,500 profit on his futures transaction.

When his profit on futures is deducted from the price at which he buys cash bills, he ends up paying an effective price for

---

[4]In practice, a maturing bill futures contract will trade during the last few days of its life at a yield a few basis points higher than the deliverable cash bill. The difference reflects the extra commission and other transaction costs that an investor would incur if he bought bill futures and took delivery instead of purchasing 3-month bills in the cash market.

TABLE 15-4

A long hedge using bill futures: no basis risk; 10MM face amount

Step 1 (Thursday, third week of June): Purchase 10 September bill contracts at 10.50.
   Put up security deposit.
   Pay round-turn commission.

Step 2 (Wednesday, third week of September): Sell 10 futures contracts; buy cash bills.

Outcome 1: Cash 91-day bill trading at 10.20.

Sell September contracts at 10.20.	
Delivery value of futures at sale	$ 9,745,000
−Delivery value of futures at purchase	9,737,500
Profit on futures transactions	$ 7,500
Buy 91-day cash bills at 10.20.	
Purchase price of cash bills	$ 9,742,167
−Profit on futures transactions	7,500
Effective price of 91-day bills	$ 9,734,667
Calculate effective discount at which bills are purchased:	
Face value	$10,000,000
−Effective purchase price	9,734,667
Discount at purchase	$ 265,333

Calculate effective discount rate, d, at which cash bills are purchased.

$$d = \left(\frac{\text{Discount}}{\text{Face}}\right)\left(\frac{\text{Annualization}}{\text{factor}}\right) = \left(\frac{\$265,333}{\$10,000,000}\right)\left(\frac{360}{91}\right)$$
$$= 0.1050$$
$$= 10.50\%$$

Outcome 2: Cash 91-day bill trading at 10.80.

Sell September contracts at 10.80.	
Delivery value of futures at sale	$ 9,730,000
−Delivery value of futures at purchase	9,737,500
Loss on futures transaction	$ (7,500)
Buy 91-day cash bills at 10.80.	
Purchase price of cash bills	$ 9,727,000
+Loss on futures transaction	7,500
Effective price of 91-day bills	$ 9,734,500
Calculate effective discount at which bills are purchased:	
Face value	$10,000,000
−Effective purchase price	9,734,500
Discount at purchase	$ 265,500

Calculate effective discount rate, d, at which cash bills are purchased.

$$d = \left(\frac{D}{F}\right)\left(\frac{360}{91}\right) = \left(\frac{\$265,500}{\$10,000,000}\right)\left(\frac{360}{91}\right)$$
$$= 0.1050$$
$$= 10.50\%$$

these bills that is $7,500 less than the actual price he pays. And this lower effective price implies that the yield he will earn on his investment is not 10.20, the rate at which he buys *cash bills,* but 10.50, the rate at which he bought bill futures.

Because the prevailing yield at which the cash 3-month bill was trading in September was lower than the rate at which our investor bought bill futures in June, he earned a higher yield, when he invested in September, than he would have had he not hedged.

There is, however, a counterpart to this. As Outcome 2 in Table 15–4 shows, if in September, the cash 3-month bill were trading at 10.80, our investor would have lost so many dollars on his hedge that he could have earned only 10.50 on the money he invested.

Calculating in Basis Points

It's instructive to work out a hedge example in dollars and cents. However, it's quicker to do it in terms of basis points earned and lost. In our example, the investor buys September contracts at 10.50 and, according to Outcome 1, sells them at 10.20. On this transaction, he earns on each contract for 1MM of bills 30 90-day basis points (bp).[5] By buying the 3-month bill at 10.20 and maturing it, he earns 1,020 90-day bp per 1MM of bills purchased. So *net* he earns 1,050 90-day bp per 1MM of bills purchased, a yield of 10.50 over 90 days.

Actually, the basis points earned on the cash bill are 91-day bp, and those earned on the futures contract are 90-day bp. This difference, however, is not reflected in the numbers in Table 15–4 because it affects yield earned only beyond the third decimal point.

The example we presented was a *long hedge* with no basis risk because the investor bought a futures contract for the precise instrument and maturity in which he planned to invest.

A Second Hedge with No Basis Risk

The hedge illustrated in Table 15–4 calls for the investor to *buy* bill futures. Here's a second example in which the investor, to

---

[5]Recall from Chapter 4 that a 90-day bp is worth $25 per 1MM.

lock in a higher return, *sells* bill futures (this hedge too involves no basis risk). On 3/9/89, an investor wants to put money into bills for three months. Suppose that he could buy the 3-month bill at 8.40 and mature it. Suppose also that he has a second alternative: buy the 6-month bill at 8.55 and sell, also at 8.55, the June bill contract, which settles on 6/1/89. If our investor took alternative 2, he'd know with certainty that he'd earn 8.55 over the 3-month holding period, and he'd pick up 15 bp more then he would if he took alternative 1: buy the 3-month bill at 8.40 and mature it. Those extra 15 bp would be worth to him per 1MM of 6-month bills purchased:

$$15 \times \$25 \times 91/90 = \$379.17$$

The factor 91/90 comes into the above calculation because our investor would be earning 15 bp on 91-day cash bills.

The trader we have just described is referred to as a *basis trade*. A good question is whether an investor would want to do this trade for such a small yield pickup. Maybe a governments-only money fund that could do futures would because they have to be in bills. Other investors with wider parameters would be attracted to this trade if the yield curve were steeper and they could, consequently, get a 40-bp or better pickup in yield. Later, we give, from a slightly different perspective, an example of this trade where rates are such that they yield pickup is much greater.

In both of the hedge examples we've presented so far, we neglected the small round-trip commission costs our investor would incur on his futures transactions. We also neglected the possibility that he might receive or have to pay out variation margin. If he received variation margin and invested the money thus received, he'd earn a bit more; conversely, if he had to pay out variation margin, he'd earn a bit less.

Hedges with Basis Risk

Hedges are common, but hedges involving *no basis risk* are not. The standardization of futures contracts required for them to be actively traded and to have liquidity is such that the hedger is normally unable to find a futures position that will give him a perfect offset to his position, actual or desired, in the cash market. Thus, to use futures, he must settle, if you will, for a ready-made rather than a tailor-made suit; and often, he will willingly do so for good reasons: the ability to strike a trade, the liquidity of the position he assumes, and the protection against risk of default that dealing on a futures exchange affords him.

Often, a hedger using financial futures will find that the hedge he establishes carries basis risk for one or both of two reasons: (1) the contract's settlement date does not match precisely the time horizon in which he anticipates dealing (e.g., he fears that interest rates might decline and wants to lock in a rate at which he can buy bills in May, a month in which no bill futures contract settles), or (2) he wants to hedge a position, actual or anticipated, in a security other than the deliverable security (e.g., he sells bill contracts to hedge a position in BAs or some other money market paper). Hedging a position in one security by assuming a futures position in a different but similar security is known as a *cross hedge*.

The precise outcome that a hedger will attain from a cross hedge is always clouded with some degree of uncertainty. How closely his gain (loss) on futures will track his loss (gain) on his cash-market position will depend on how the *spread (basis)* between the rate on the futures contract he's using and rate on the instrument he's hedging changes over the life of his hedge.

When a hedge carries basis risk, the hedger shifts the nature of his speculation from a speculation on a *rate level* to a speculation on a *spread:* he assumes *basis risk*. He does so because he believes, generally with good reason, that the uncertainty of outcome generated by spread risk will be substantially less than *rate-level* risk (i.e., general market risk) to which he would have been exposed had he not hedged.

Example of a Cross Hedge and Resulting Basis Risk

We can illustrate the basis risk that arises from a cross hedge by changing several assumptions in our second example of a hedge (buy 6-month bills and sell bill futures that settle precisely three months hence). Suppose our investor wants to invest in BAs for three months and faces the following alternatives: (1) he can buy domestic, 3-month BAs at 9.25; or (2) he can buy domestic, 6-month BAs at 9.35 and sell 3-month bill futures at 8.55. At the moment he makes his choice, 3-month bills are trading at 8.48, that is, BAs are 77 bp cheap to bills. If that spread were to stay constant, our investor, by taking alternative (2) rather than (1) would earn an extra 10 90-day bp, each worth $25 per 1MM.

However, the BA-bill spread is not written in stone. Another scenario could occur: the dollar weakens sharply; foreign central banks are forced to sop up dollars, which they invest in bills; that in turn drives the 3-month bill rate down to 8.33, but it has no impact on the 3-month BA rate. Under this second scenario, our investor must, at the end of three months, buy back at 8.33 the 3-month bill futures he earlier sold at 8.48; doing so gives him a loss on his position in bill futures of 15 90-day bp:

$$8.33 - 8.48 = -0.15 = -15 \text{ bp}$$

At the same time, our investor sells his 6-month BAs, after holding them for three months, at the unchanged 3-month BA rate of 9.25. By being in 6-month BAs rather than in 3-month BAs, our investor has picked up 10 90-day bp,

$$9.35 - 9.25 = 0.10 = 10 \text{ bp}$$

but he's lost 15 90-day bp on his position in bill futures. Thus, *net,* by choosing a cross hedge over a straight investment in 3-month BAs, our investor has lost 5 90-day bp, or $125 per 1MM of BAs bought. In this example, our investor took on *basis risk,* put himself in the position where a widening of the BA-bill basis in the 3-month area would lower his net return, and that is precisely what happened.

It might be argued that no investor is going to get involved in the above trade in the hope of picking up a mere 10 90-day bp or that our investor would have done better to hedge using Euro futures. Both points may be well taken. However, our purpose was simply to illustrate the nature of basis risk in a cross hedge, and our example—whatever its realism—does that.

Also, one can imagine circumstances in which the above trade would be more attractive to an investor. The yield curve in the 3- to 6-month area is *steeper,* so our investor gets a bigger yield pickup by extending from a 3- to a 6-month maturity. In addition, our investor might reason, "The dollar is strengthening so *the spread of BAs to bills should narrow,* which will add to my profit on the trade." That's speculating on the basis with the hope of profiting from a favorable change in the basis.

A Cash-and-Carry Trade with No Basis Risk

So far we have considered examples in which an investor with cash to invest uses bill futures as a tool to hedge absolute rate risk. There are also various arbitrages that dealers and spec accounts can put on using bill futures that require the arbitrageur to put up little or no cash; basically, such trades, depending on their complexity, constitute a bet on one or more rate spreads.

A trade that is done in bill futures in huge volume when rates are right and that tends to link rates on cash and futures bills is one that has been dubbed the *cash-and-carry trade.* This trade could be done by many investors, but it is most commonly done by professional speculators and large dealers, who watch the relationship among cash, futures, and term repo rates and put on this trade in size whenever that relationship makes the trade profitable.

For a leveraged investor, an attractive tactic is to buy a cash bill, finance it with term repo, and cover the rate risk on the resulting tail by selling that tail in the futures market.[6] Whether doing so will be profitable depends on the relationship among the term repo rate, the rate on the long cash bill, and the futures rate. There must be some term repo rate at which a dealer who does the above transaction will just break even; this break-even *rate* has been dubbed the *implied repo rate.* Whenever the prevailing repo rate is less than the implied repo rate, putting on a cash-and-carry trade yields a profit.

In the inverted-yield curve environment that prevailed in early 1989, the cash-and-carry trade was unprofitable, so to illustrate it, we use rates that prevailed in an earlier period. The example is important because it introduces a widely used con-

---

[6]The concept of tails and how they are created was discussed in Chapter 10.

cept, the implied repo rate, which we will encounter again in Chapter 16.

On October 28, 1982, the 3/24/83 bill, which was the deliverable bill for the December 1982 bill futures contract, was trading at 8.26. On the same day, the December bill contract, which expired 56 days hence, was trading at 8.28.

The repo rate is an add-on, 360-day rate. Thus, to calculate the implied repo rate on a cash-and-carry trade based on the above cash and futures rates, one must calculate the holding period yield (HPY) on a 360-day basis that an investor could have earned if he had bought the 3/24/83 bill at 8.26 and simultaneously sold that bill at 8.28 for delivery 56 days hence in the futures market.

That calculation, worked out in Table 15–5, shows that holding period yield—the implied or break-even repo rate—was 8.51.

TABLE 15–5
Calculating the implied repo rate which equals the holding period yield earned on a 360-day basis on the bill*

Step 1: On 10/28/82, purchase 1MM of the 3/24/83 bill at 8.26.

$$\text{Purchase price} = (\$1,000,000)(0.0826)\left(\frac{147}{360}\right)$$

$$= \$966,271.67$$

Step 2: On 10/28/82, simultaneously sell the December 1982 bill futures contract at 91.72, which corresponds to a yield of 8.28.

$$\text{Sale price} = (\$1,000,000)(0.0828)\left(\frac{91}{360}\right)$$

$$= \$979,070.00$$

Step 3: Calculate holding period yield (HPY), which equals the *implied repo rate.*

$$\text{HPY} = \text{Implied repo rate} = \left(\frac{\text{Sale price} - \text{Purchase price}}{\text{Purchase price}}\right)\left(\begin{array}{c}\text{Annualization}\\ \text{factor}\end{array}\right)$$

$$= \left(\frac{\$979,070.00 - \$966,271.67}{\$966,271.67}\right)\left(\frac{360}{56}\right)$$

$$= 0.0851 = 8.51\%$$

*For a simple formula for calculating the implied repo rate on a bill trade, see Stigum's *Money Market Calculations* (Homewood, Ill.: Dow Jones-Irwin, 1981), pp. 161–66.

Had the actual term repo rate for a 56-day repo been 8.25 on October 28, 1982, then by buying the 3/24/83 bill, financing it for 56 days at 8.25, and selling the resulting tail in the futures market at 8.28, a trader could have picked up $3,908.03 per 10MM of the trade he put on (Table 15–6).

Comparing the 8.25 term repo rate with the 8.51 implied repo rate suggests that this trade offers a locked-in profit of 26 bp on the amount invested for 56 days. In fact there are a few slips twixt the cup and the lip: a few things that might or will happen to alter the spread earned on the trade. First, a small commission must be paid on the futures trade.

Second, if bill rates rise sharply over the holding period, variation margin in the form of investable dollars will be paid into the trader's margin account, which—assuming he invests these dollars—will raise his return on the trade. Our trader's 26-bp profit spread would conversely be threatened by a rally in bills, which would result in margin calls that he would have to meet in cash. How much of a threat do potential margin calls pose to our trader? Relatively little. Even in the unlikely event that bills rallied 100 bp on the day the trade settled (10/28/82), the extra margin he would have to put up over 56 days would, assuming a 8.25 financing rate, cost him only 2¼ bp of his profit spread.

A third factor that might marginally affect the profit earned by our trader is the price at which the 3/24/83 bills and the December bill futures contract *converge* at expiration of the fu-

---

TABLE 15–6
Calculating the profit on a 10MM cash-and-carry trade if rates were those in Table 15–5 and the term repo rate were 8.25

A: Formula

Profit = (HPY − Term repo rate)(Amount invested)(Fraction of year invested)

B: Profit calculation

$$\text{Profit} = (0.0851 - 0.0825)(\$9,662,716.70)\left(\frac{56}{360}\right)$$

$$= \$3,908.03$$

tures contract. The bill futures contract is for $1MM of 90-day bill on which a basis point is worth $25. The deliverable bill is in fact a 91-day bill on which a basis point is worth $25.2777 per million. The trade thus calls for selling bills on which a basis point is worth $25 and delivering bills on which a basis point is worth $25.2777. If the convergence price on the trade is below the price level at which the trade is put on (i.e., if rates rise), the trader will have lost some of his profit because he will have lost on his cash position basis points worth $25.2777 while gaining on his futures position a *like amount* of basis points worth only $25. Much can be made of *convergence-price risk,* but in fact if the cash and futures prices converged 100 bp above the price level at which the trade was put on, the trader would lose only two of his 26 bp profit margin on the trade. Alternatively, if cash and futures converged at a price level well below that at which the trade was put on, the trader would add a couple of basis points to his profit margin on the trade.

A final factor affecting profit on the trade is transaction costs—back-office costs or whatever. Usually, these are so small that no one bothers to incorporate them into return calculations.

To sum up, a trader putting on a cash-and-carry trade does not lock in a certain rate of return. However, on a short trade of the sort illustrated, even a 20% rise in bill prices, which is big, would leave most of his profit intact.

We have been talking about the signal that the relationship between the implied repo rate and the actual term repo rate gives the leveraged trader. The strictly cash investor who is investing money into December also gets a signal from the relationship between these rates. If the implied repo rate *exceeds* the term repo rate, then the cash investor will earn more by investing in the long bill and selling December futures than he would by investing in term repo and probably more than he would by investing in the bill maturing at expiration of the futures contract. If, alternatively, the reverse is true and the leveraged cash-and-carry trade (Tables 15–5 and 15–6) is unprofitable, the short-bill trade offering the cash investor the highest return would probably be to buy the 56-day December bill and mature it.

An Unleveraged Cash-and-Carry Trade

In an example above, we noted that, for a cash investor wanting to invest short term, the structure of rates is at times such that his holding period yield will be greater if he does a cash-futures trade—buys a longer bill, sells the nearby futures contract, and makes delivery—than if he does a strictly cash-market trade: buys the short bill and matures it.

Table 15–7 illustrates such a situation: By doing the cash-futures trade, an investor, faced with this rate matrix, can pick up 95 bp more in yield than he would have had he operated strictly in the cash market—bought the short bill and matured it.

Note the 95-bp yield pickup is not locked in stone. All the factors that we said would or might affect the outcome of the trade described in Tables 15–5 and 15–6 come into play in this example too. Futures commissions will reduce the yield pickup slightly. Also, a rally in the bill market will cost the investor a few basis points of his yield pickup both because of margin calls and because of the cost implied by the convergence of cash and futures prices at a higher level. These factors, even if they all work to lower yield pickup, are, however, too small to alter the fact that this is a productive, attractive trade for the alert cash investor.

Spreading

A hedger is typically shifting his risk from a speculation on rate levels to a speculation on spread variation. A speculator with no position in cash or cash securities to hedge can also speculate on spread variation. Such speculation, which is referred to as *spreading,* calls for the trader to short one contract and go long in a neighboring contract on the expectation that the spread between the two contracts will either narrow or widen. Here's an example. In normal markets, the yield curve is steep at its base and then gradually flattens. Suppose, for illustration, that, in the futures market, the yield curve has the shape pictured in Figure 15–2. The yield spread between the two contracts nearest maturity is 40 bp; there are 30 bp between the second and

TABLE 15–7

An unleveraged cash-and-carry trade: no basis risk

Strategy A: Buy long bill, sell futures, and make delivery.

1. Buy, on 11/15/82 at 8.43, $1MM of the 3/24/82 bill, which matures in 128 days.

$$\text{Purchase price} = (\$1,000,000) \left(1 - \frac{0.0843 \times 128}{360}\right)$$

$$= \$970,026.67$$

2. Simultaneously sell, on 11/15/82, $1MM of December 82 bill futures at a price of 91.76 (8.24 yield).

3. On 12/21/82, deliver the 3/24/82 bill, the current maturity of which is now 91 days, against the December futures contract, which is assumed to settle at 91.76.

$$\text{Sale price} = (\$1,000,000) \left(1 - \frac{0.0824 \times 91}{360}\right)$$

$$= \$979,171.11$$

4. Calculate rate of return on purchase and resale

$$\text{Rate of return} = \left(\frac{\text{Sale price} - \text{Purchase price}}{\text{Purchase price}}\right)\left(\begin{array}{c}\text{Annualization}\\\text{factor}\end{array}\right)$$

$$= \left(\frac{\$979,171.11 - \$970,026.67}{\$970,026.67}\right)\left(\frac{360}{37}\right)$$

$$= 0.0917 = 9.17\%$$

Strategy B: Buy short cash bill and hold to maturity.

1. Buy, on 11/15/82 at 8.15, $1MM of the 12/21/82 bill which matures in 37 days. Hold the bill until maturity.

$$\text{Purchase price} = (\$1,000,000) \left(1 - \frac{0.0815 \times 37}{360}\right)$$

$$= \$991,623.61$$

2. Calculate the rate of return on holding bill to maturity

$$= \left(\frac{\$1,000,000 - \$991,623.61}{\$991,623.61}\right)\left(\frac{360}{37}\right)$$

$$= 0.0822 = 8.22\%$$

Calculate yield pickup by doing Strategy A, not B:

$$\left(\begin{array}{c}\text{Yield pick up from}\\\text{doing A, not B}\end{array}\right) = 9.17 - 8.22$$

$$= 0.95$$

$$= 95 \text{ bp}$$

On a $10MM trade, the extra return earned would be:

$$(0.0095) \left(\frac{37}{365}\right) (\$10\text{MM}) = \$9,630$$

---

*The formula for calculating the discount on a bill was given in Chapter 4. For a formula to calculate holding period yield on a bill sold before maturity, see Stigum's *Money Market Calculations* (Homewood, III.: Dow Jones-Irwin, 1981), p. 53.

FIGURE 15–2
Yields on bill futures contracts expiring in 3 to 15 months

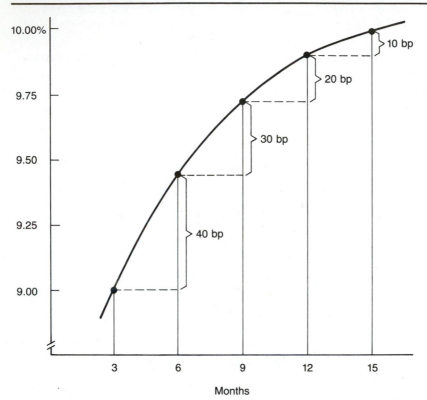

third contracts, 20 between the third and fourth contracts, and 10 between the fourth and fifth contracts. The spreader assumes that, as the more distant contracts approach maturity, spreads between them will widen. Given this expectation, he might short the contract maturing in 12 months and buy the contract maturing in 9 months. If, over the next six months, the spread between these contracts widened from 20 to 40 bp, he would be able to close out his position at a 20-bp profit.

He earns a profit because, if the spread widens, the price of the futures contract in which he has a long position will rise in value relative to that in which he has a short position. Whether yields rise or fall over the holding period is immaterial to whether he profits or not. What counts is that the spread widens. His principal risk of loss is thus that the yield curve will flatten (or invert) so that the spread between the contracts that he's long and short will narrow (or turn negative) rather than widen.

Spread traders are an important and permanent component of futures pits. A spreader who sees selling in the March contract but knows that there is a bid in the Junes will buy the Marches, sell the Junes, wait until the pressure is off the Marches, and then turn the position around. Spreaders account for over half of all trading in the longer contracts. In doing trades of the above sort, spreaders perform an important market function—they provide liquidity to the longer (*back*) contracts.

Curve Trades or Calendar Spreads

As Table 15–8 shows, there was on April 5, 1989, open interest in only the first four of eight possible bill futures contracts. Normally, one thinks of a spreader as a local who isn't keen to assume outright risk in a back contract. For example, on April 1989, he'd be unwilling to assume an outright position in March 90 bill futures, but he'd do a Dec89–Mr90 spread trade, since the latter exposes him to only limited risk, which—given his rate view—he'd be willing to assume, at least for the time it took him to trade out of it.

A dealer's *curve trader* is a different sort of animal. He might use futures to put on a bet as to how the shape of the yield curve will change—a trade that's also called a *calendar spread*. To illustrate, suppose that a dealer reasoned, "The economic environment is such that it's a good bet that the short end of the yield curve is going to invert even further." Then his curve trader might buy the June89 contract at 8.78 and sell the Mr90 contract at 8.67—betting that the spread between the two would widen. Because of the illiquidity of the back bill contracts, to get into the Mr90 contract, the curve trader would surely have to do a spread trade, in bills or Euros to bills, and then close out the leg of that spread trade that he did not want to hold. From the point of view of liquidity, the Euro contract, discussed below, is far more attractive for doing curve trades.

TABLE 15–8
Bill and Euro futures markets quotes, April 5, 1989

TREASURY BILLS (1MM)—$1 million; pts. of 100%

	Open	High	Low	Settle	Change	Discount Settle	Discount Change	Open Interest
June	91.18	91.28	91.17	91.22 +	.02	8.78 −	.02	14,679
Sept	91.09	91.17	91.08	91.13 +	.03	8.87 −	.03	3,606
Dec	91.02	91.09	91.01	91.07 +	.04	8.93 −	.04	1,283
Mr90	91.24	91.33	91.24	91.33 +	.07	8.67 −	.07	331

Est vol 10,140; vol Tues 11,499; open int 19,924, −1,229.

EURODOLLAR (1MM)—$1 million; pts. of 100%

	Open	High	Low	Settle	Change	Yield Settle	Yield Change	Open Interest
June	89.62	89.67	89.56	89.60 −	.03	10.40 +	.03	282,867
Sept	89.52	89.57	89.46	89.52 −	.01	10.48 +	.01	158,974
Dec	89.47	89.54	89.44	89.49 +	.01	10.51 −	.01	102,620
Mr90	89.78	89.84	89.77	89.81 +	.03	10.19 −	.03	65,656
June	90.03	90.08	90.01	90.07 +	.03	9.93 −	.03	33,065
Sept	90.18	90.23	90.17	90.23 +	.03	9.77 −	.03	27,220
Dec	90.20	90.23	90.17	90.23 +	.03	9.77 −	.03	24,899
Mr91	90.33	90.36	90.30	90.36 +	.03	9.64 −	.03	15,108
June	90.41	90.42	90.36	90.43 +	.03	9.57 −	.03	12,763
Sept	90.45	90.46	90.41	90.47 +	.03	9.53 −	.03	21,028
Dec	90.46	90.48	90.42	90.48 +	.02	9.52 −	.02	10,832
Mr92	90.49	90.53	90.46	90.52 +	.03	9.48 −	.03	2,532

Est vol 203,840; vol Tues 227,733; open int 757,564, +7, −351.

EURODOLLAR (LIFFE)—$1 million; pts. of 100%

	Open	High	Low	Settle	Change	Lifetime High	Lifetime Low	Open Interest
June	89.60	89.67	89.56	89.60 +	.09	91.10	88.76	28,394
Sept	89.51	89.56	89.47	89.50 +	.08	91.83	88.72	12,308
Dec	89.46	89.53	89.45	89.48 +	.11	91.67	88.93	6,955
Mr90	89.77	89.79	89.76	89.79 +	.09	91.37	88.88	1,753
June	90.02	90.02	90.02	90.03 +	.05	90.63	89.31	347
Sept	90.16	90.16	90.16	90.16 −	.04	90.64	89.89	484
Dec	90.17	90.17	90.17	90.17 −	.14	90.36	90.23	107

Est vol 11,671; vol Tues 11,010; open int 50,348, −882.

Source: *The Wall Street Journal.*

Bill Futures: A Dying Contract?

As Figure 15–1 shows, average daily volume in bill futures is far down from what it was in the 1982 heyday of the contract. The reasons are several. Today, rates on short-term paper other than bills track Euro rates much more closely than bill rates (Figure 15–3). Thus, a dealer who keeps core positions in BAs, Euro CDs, and other short paper and who ends up holding some commercial paper now and then, gets a better hedge by shorting Euros futures than by shorting bill futures. Also, if he shorts bills futures, he can react to economic developments or to selling and buying via the Tokyo or London office only during the limited hours that Chicago trades. In contrast, if he shorts Euros, he can adjust his position by trading Euro futures on SIMEX in Singapore or on LIFFE in London.

FIGURE 15–3
Over time, short-term rates move together: 1-month LIBOR, 3-month Euro commercial paper, 6-month Euro CD, 3-month U.S. T bill (weekly averages, through May 19, 1989)

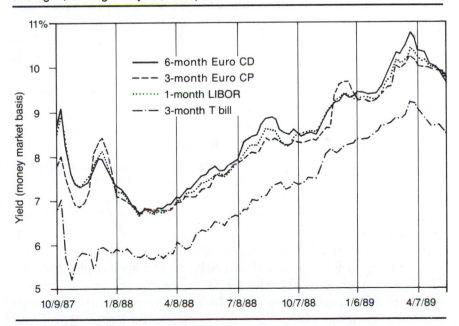

Source: J. P. Morgan Securities, Inc.

A second problem with bills futures is that the contract has been squeezed on several occasions. The fact that the deliverable bill is a reopening of an old bill does not really help much. Bills have a tendency to get put away, and only a portion of the new supply coming to market just before settlement of a bill futures contract actually gets to the Street. In a reopening of an old year bill in the spring of 1989, of the 7 billion of new 3-month bills auctioned, 4.4 billion were gobbled up by "noncomps," so only 2.6 billion got to the Street. With numbers like that, it's tempting for a dealer, working perhaps in cahoots with a big money fund, to buy a lot of contracts plus a lot of the floating supply of the deliverable bill. The game is this: when the contract settles, shorts will be unable to get their hands on deliverable bills; fails to deliver will occur; and so long as these fails last, the squeezer—who's long unsettled bill futures—will earn the bill rate on bills he hasn't yet had to pay for.

The problems we've mentioned have discouraged people from trading bill futures which has led to a decrease in the liquidity of the contract; the latter has in turn further decreased the attractiveness of the contract to hedgers, curve traders, and others.

The risk of a future squeeze in the bill contract could be eliminated by rewriting this contract with provision for cash settlement. However, the IMM seems undisposed to make this change. Thus, there's no development in sight that seems likely to stem the continuing decline in the trading of bill futures.

THE EURO FUTURES CONTRACT

For the many banks, domestic and foreign, that operate in the Euromarket, LIBOR has long been the marginal cost of funds. This led many to think that a Euro futures contract had the potential to be the most widely used and traded of all financial futures contracts; consequently, futures exchanges were eager to introduce a Euro contract. Finally, in the spring of 1982, the IMM was authorized by the CFTC to begin trading a futures contract for 3-month Euros. The *London International Financial Futures Exchange* (*LIFFE*), when it opened in September 1982, introduced a similar contract for 3-month Euro time deposits.

The Euro time-deposit contract introduced by the IMM resembles the bill contract in that it is also for 1MM of a 90-day instrument. Also, like the bill contract, the Euro contract can be used in a wide array of trades: to put on long and short hedges, to create synthetic securities, to put on spread trades, and to do an ever-expanding list of arbitrages. However, the two contracts differ in that the IMM Euro contract provides for cash settlement.

Given the heterogeneity of bank credits and the tendency of investors to overreact to any problems, even temporary, that a bank may experience, a futures contract for money that banks buy (i.e., for deposits at different banks) might well have fared no better than the domestic CD contract had not its originators insisted on cash settlement.

The idea of cash settlement on a futures contract had been around for a long time, but until the introduction of the IMM Euro contract, it was never incorporated in any futures contract. Those opposed to cash settlement of a futures contract argued either that such a contract was suspiciously close to gambling or that a mechanism for delivery of the commodity or instrument underlying the futures contract was required to assure convergence of cash and futures prices. Those favoring cash settlement saw it as a means to create a viable futures contract in an instrument on which delivery would be difficult or impossible to effect smoothly. They also saw cash settlement as the simplest of innovations to introduce.

Thus, the IMM proposed and the CFT accepted a futures contract for a 3-month Euro time deposit with the settlement price (100 minus yield) being established off 3-month LIBOR quotes prevailing in London on the day of settlement. By authorizing cash settlement on the IMM Euro contract, the CFTC, in its role as federal regulator of futures markets, overcame a practical barrier that had existed to cash settlement of futures contracts: by its action, it preempted state gaming laws under which a futures contract providing for cash settlement might have been judged to be an unenforceable gaming contract.

Gaming laws also exist in the U.K. and other countries. Because of them, LIFFE opted for a Euro time-deposit contract with provisions for delivery at settlement of the contract or optional cash settlement. In doing so, LIFFE had little choice. U.K. futures markets are regulated informally by the Bank of England, which lacked the power, even if it had chosen to do so, to take any action that would have insulated a futures contract providing for cash settlement from U.K. gaming laws.

Initially, the IMM Euro contract got off to a slow start (Figure 15–4). As with the bill and bond contracts, the entry of natural end users into the new market was slowed—in some cases temporarily precluded—by various constraints: regulatory dictates on what different classes of institutions—banks, thrifts, insurance companies, and others—might and might not do, accounting practices that caused successful hedges to threaten desired earnings stability, and lack of expertise.

From the outset, the IMM contract has several crucial advantages of the LIFFE contract. First, the IMM contract was

FIGURE 15–4
Average daily volume in the IMM Euro futures contract (thousands)

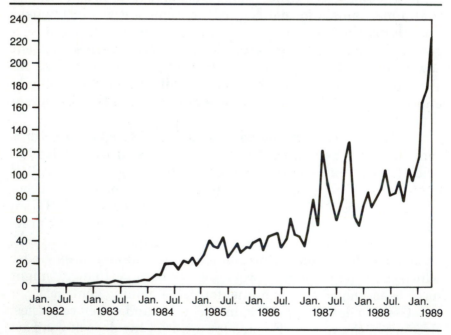

Source: Donaldson, Lufkin & Jenrette (Chicago Mercantile Exchange).

traded near the bill pit, which encouraged a natural low-risk trade to get volume in Euros going—spread trades between the bill and Euro contracts. Also, the IMM had the advantage of having an active body of locals that was accustomed to trading financial futures and keen to take on a new one; LIFFE lacked such locals and the liquidity that trading by locals immediately gave to IMM Euro contract.

Over time, as Figure 15–4 shows, the IMM Euro contract has become a fantastic success that has only one near rival, the CBT long-bond contract. On April 5, 1989, contracts for $204 billion of Euros were traded on the IMM and open interest at the IMM in this contract totaled $757 billion. LIFFE volume in its Euro contract was a little over 1/20 of that in the IMM contract, and LIFFE's outstandings of its Euro contract were less than 1/10 of that of the IMM contract. Meanwhile, at the CBT bond pit, traders exchanged contracts for $18.5 billion of long bonds, and open interest in the bond contract totaled $29 billion. Trading in contracts for all other financial futures pale when compared to trading in Euros and the long bond. One measure of the strength of the IMM Euro contract relative to both the LIFFE Euro contract and the bill contract is the number of periods for which it is actively traded (12) and the fact that liquidity exists not just in the front or in the front two contracts. Currently, the IMM Euro contract goes out three years, and it's expected to go five as trading in the contract increases.

A Euro contract is also traded on the *Singapore International Monetary Exchange (SIMEX)*.[7] The SIMEX and IMM Euro futures contracts are fungible, a big convenience to round-the-clock traders, but the LIFFE and the IMM contracts are not; however, prices on the latter two exchanges track each other closely, since the contracts traded are so similar. A U.S. dealer who does a trade on LIFFE and then wants to transfer his position to the IMM (where he can trade in New York hours) now typically uses a spread broker who for a small concession will work to sell LIFFE and buy Chicago or vice versa; at the end of

---

[7]A Eurodollar futures contract is also traded on the Sydney exchange in Australia, but volume is negligible. Tokyo, in addition, launched a Eurodollar futures contract in 1989, but it got off to a *very* slow start.

the day, the broker comes back to the dealer and reports where he got the trade done.

The alternative is messy. Noted one trader, "If you do a trade on LIFFE and want to clean it up, you have to have LIFFE on one phone, Chicago on the other, and try to get offsetting trades done at the same price level. To move your position from one market to the other is a big pain."

Trading Hours

Trading in Euro futures used to start at the civilized—for Chicago traders—hour of 9 A.M. New York time when the cash-market trading opened. At that time, the Treasury and other departments tracking important numbers adopted the practice of announcing many of those numbers at 8:30 A.M.—the idea being to give the market time to absorb the numbers before it opened. In fact, what happened is that people started to trade earlier: cash in New York or London and Euro and Treasury bond futures on LIFFE in London. Thus, on early-number days, the half hour or more before Chicago opened provided a great window of opportunity for LIFFE, which often saw more trading during this period than during the rest of its day. Responding to the business being lost to LIFFE, the IMM and the CBT moved up the opening of trading in the bill, Euro, and bond futures contracts to 8:20 A.M.

Currently, the Euro contract can be traded in Chicago from 8:20 A.M. New York time to 3 P.M. SIMEX opens about 7:30 P.M. New York time and runs until 3 A.M., at which time London is open. London trading hours overlap New York trading hours, so the only real gap during which Euro futures cannot be traded occurs between the Chicago close and the SIMEX opening. Tokyo is thinking of trying to close that gap, and Chicago is talking about night sessions at the Merc. Also, as noted below, futures trading is moving in the direction of computers, which removes all reason for a key market to ever close. Liquidity, however, has two dimensions: it is not just a matter of what hours trades can be transacted, but of the size that can be done at a given hour. "The Singapore market is not," noted one trader, "as liquid as Chicago is; they try but the amounts are smaller."

Hedging

It's easy to take the Eurodeposit-market curve and calculate from it implied Euro forward rates for periods that match the IMM contract periods. Comparing such rates to actual IMM rates, one finds that Euro contracts typically trade a little cheap to (at a higher yield than) the corresponding implied forwards. One reason is that dealers in money market instruments, which can't be shorted, use Euro futures to hedge. A dealer in commercial paper, BAs, Euro CDs, and other short paper is always long inventory, and if he fears that the market is going down, the natural thing for him to do is to sell Euros; however, if he thinks that the market is going up, he doesn't buy Euros, he buys inventory.

As noted below, dealers sell Euros to hedge not just money market inventory that they hold, but interest-rate swaps that they warehouse, interest-rate caps that they write, and other exotics as well.

Liquidity

"The Euro futures market is," in the words of one trader, "an amazing market—extremely liquid. Especially if you are just trading the front contract as a speculator, you can get in and out at any time at one tick. Two years ago, the typical size in the market was that people would quote maybe 50 or 100 lots. Locals now make quotes good for 100 lots, and frequently you see trades of 500 lots and up in the market. Nowadays, a thousand can trade and it does not really move the market much, whereas a 1,000 lot used to move the market 3 or 4 bp. The Euro contract is a great thing to spec in—you can get in and out all you want."

To put the above quote in perspective, note that a 1,000 lot corresponds to $1 billion of Euros. A tick in Euros, as in bills, is worth $25. So a 5-bp move on a 1,000 lot in Euros would be worth 125,000. Since Euros are traded in big size and the rate is at times quite volatile, speculators get a lot of bang for their buck going naked long and short the Euro contract.

Calendar Spreads in Euros

For a spec who does not particularly like to take outright positions in the market but likes to trade relative values between calendar months, the Euro contract is also excellent. After the front four contracts come four *red* contracts and then four *green* contracts. In Euros, there is good liquidity in the front contracts and in the reds, but the greens can get a little thin (Table 15–8). For a spread or curve trader, the place to be is Euros, not bills. "In Euros," noted one trader, "you might be able to do 300 or 400MM of a year spread—the June contract against the next June contract or Sept against Sept—without moving the market. If you wanted to do 1,000 in a year spread, you might move the market three ticks or so."

On a year spread, a trader can make or lose lots of money. Here's an example. Starting in 1988 and continuing into 1989, the yield curve, which had a positive slope, got progressively flatter and then progressively more inverted. One would have expected Euros to follow a similar pattern. They did, but in an exaggerated way: some calendar spreads in Euros moved over 200 bp and then back 50 bp. Figure 15–5 tracks one such spread.

Two things caused the severe inversion of the Euro futures curve indicated by the plunge in the spread plotted in Figure 15–5. First, in the whole market, the yield curve flattened and then inverted. Second, some special factors were driving spreads. One was interest-rate-swap activity. Suppose a dealer does a big 3-year interest-rate swap and warehouses it while he looks for people wanting to take the other side; the swap puts the dealer temporarily at risk; and to hedge, he's likely to sell a 3-year *strip* of Euros if his customer swapped floating rate to fixed rate or to buy a 3-year strip of Euros if his customer swapped the other way (for swaps, see Chapter 19).

Such hedging is a large source of demand and supply in Euro futures. At times, it can cause spreads to get out of line because the open interest is much smaller in the back contracts than in the front contract. In early April 1989, the open interest in the June 89 contract was 283,000 contracts ($283 billion), while in the March 91 contract it was only 15,000 contracts.

In that sort of environment, a big LBO deal (like KKR's

FIGURE 15–5
Eurodollar futures calendar spread (June 1989–March 1991)

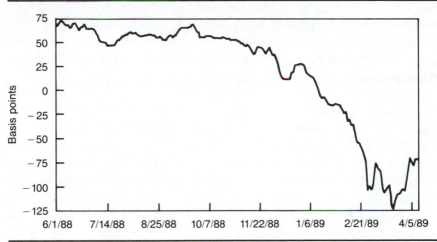

Source: Goldman Sachs.

$25-billion buy-out of RJR Nabisco) that generates a huge amount of floating-rate debt can affect for a time Euro futures spreads. The borrower might hedge directly his interest-rate risk by selling a big strip of Euro futures or he might do a huge interest-rate swap, floating to fixed, with a dealer; if he did the latter, the dealer would be selling a strip of Euros to hedge.

Suppose that either way a deal results in the selling of a 15-billion strip of Euros. That size won't affect the front contract, but it's going to double the back contract or take it all away. Thus, hedging a huge swap can have a big impact on prices in the back contracts.

If the borrower has done a swap with a dealer who hedges by selling a strip of Euros, later as the dealer is able to find the other side of the swap, he will buy back, a bit at a time, the Euro strip he previously sold. So first there's a big flow one way, and then a flow the other way. The front contract absorbs this nicely, but the back contracts don't.

A curve trader who, in September 1988, anticipated that the yield curve would invert further and who sensed the impact that hedging of the debt created by the KKR RJR Nabisco deal would likely have on the Euro curve might well have done the trades outlined in Table 15–9. Note the first trade profits from the severe inversion of the Euro curve shown in Figure 15–5; the second trade profits from the snap back in the June 89–March 91 spread from −124 bp to −77 bp as the distortion of the Euro futures curve caused by a bulge in hedging along the curve diminished.

Another thing that a Euro curve trader must keep an eye on is activity in interest-rate caps (Chapter 17). A big LBO borrower who's taken on a lot of floating-rate debt might reason, "I can live with rates going to 12%, but after that I want to be capped out." A dealer will write such a cap, but doing so puts him at substantial risk. He can hedge by buying Eurodollar put options, but maybe the dealer thinks they are too expensive and anyway he could trade them in size only for the front three, maybe four, months. If so, the dealer might opt to just delta hedge. If the dealer's option starts at the money, his hedge ratio is 50%, which means that for 10MM of options, he needs to short a 5MM strip of Euros.

In 1988, dealers had written about 175 billion of interest-rate caps. If 40% of these were delta hedged, that's about 70 billion to be hedged; and if dealers start off with a 50% hedge, that alone is 35 billion of shorts in Euro futures. Most of these delta hedges are stacked in the front contract (and later rolled) because the front contract is so liquid that dealers can do huge size in it.

If the market goes down (i.e., if rates rise) while dealers have delta hedged a lot of caps, their delta hedges will call for them to sell yet more Euros just to maintain those hedges and that will impact spreads. "Yesterday, the front Euro contract was up 24 bp," observed one trader. "You could say that short interest rates were down 24 bp, but they weren't; LIBOR rates came off about 1/16 to 1/8; some of the bills rallied about 10 bp. The only thing that went 24 up was the front Euro contract. One possible explanation is that you have all these people delta hedging. It's similar to portfolio insurance: you get additional buyers when the market goes up, additional sellers when the market goes down."

TABLE 15–9
Two consecutive Euro curve trades (calendar spreads)

Step 1: On 9/21/88, sell 100 June 89 Euro futures at 91.17 and buy 100 March 91 Euro futures at 90.51.

The June89–Mr91 spread is *sold* at:*

$$91.17 - 90.51 = +66 \text{ bp}$$

Step 2: On 3/20/89, unwind trade put on in Step 1 and put on the reverse trade; to do so, buy 200 June 89 Euro futures at 88.82 and sell 200 March 91 Euro futures at 90.06.

The June89–Mr91 spread is now *bought* at:

$$88.82 - 90.06 = -124 \text{ bp}$$

Step 3: On 4/4/89, unwind the second spread trade by selling 100 June 89 Euro futures at 89.63 and buying 100 March 91 Euro futures at 90.40.

The June89–Mr91 spread is now *sold* at:

$$89.63 - 90.40 = -77$$

Step 4: Figure profit on the two consecutive spread trades: Basis points earned on first spread trade—selling and then buying the spread—equals:

$$66 \text{ bp} - (-124 \text{ bp}) = 190 \text{ bp}$$

Basis points earned on second spread trade—buying and then selling the spread—equals:

$$-77 \text{ bp} - (-124 \text{ bp}) = 47 \text{ bp}$$

Profit earned on the two trades (each for 100 contracts worth $25 per tick) is figured as follows:

$$\text{Profit} = (100 \text{ contracts}) (\$25/\text{bp/contract}) (190 \text{ bp} + 47 \text{ bp})$$
$$= \$592,500$$

*Since the index price at which Euros futures trade equals 100 minus the appropriate Euro rate, the price at which the spread is initially sold is figured as follows: let

r_{Mr91} = the rate on the Mr91 contract
r_{Ju89} = the rate on the June89 contract
S = the spread traded

Then,

$$S = (\text{Price of June89 futures}) - (\text{Price of Mr91 futures})$$
$$= (100 - r_{Ju89}) - (100 - r_{Mr91})$$
$$= r_{Mr91} - r_{Ju89} = 9.49 - 8.83 = 66 \text{ bp}$$

The TED Spread

A classic spread trade for which the Euro futures have been used since day one of the contract is the TED spread. This spread is defined as the price of the bill futures contract minus the price of the Euro futures contract. Let

d = discount rate implied by the bill futures price

r_E = Euro rate implied by the Euro futures price

Then the TED spread can be written as

$$(100 - d) - (100 - r_E) = r_E - d$$

That is, it reduces to the rate on Euros minus the bill rate and is thus naturally positive, since 3-month Euros trade at a spread above 3-month bills.

In market jargon, a trader *buys the TED spread* when he buys bill futures and sells Euro futures, and he *sells the TED spread* when he sells bill futures and buys Euro futures. (A mnemonic hint: When you buy the spread, you buy the instrument that starts with a *b*, namely, bills.) Normally, the TED spread widens when rates rise, narrows when rates fall.

The story we told above about the severe steepening of the Euro futures curve goes a long way toward explaining what happened, in early 1989, to the June 1989 TED spread (Figure 15–6). A trader sensitive to market developments might well have done the consecutive trades outlined in Table 15–10: first go short the spread, then go long the spread.

The size in which traders do the TED spread varies. A small account might do 25 or 50 contracts. A dealer might do 500 to 1,000 contract, and a large dealer with a strong view might do as much as 10,000 contracts—that's a $10-billion bet.

An interesting aside is that liquidity is so bad in the bill contract that a trader who wants to do size in the third and sometimes even in the second bill contract will often be better off doing a TED spread and then getting out of the Euro side than he would be simply doing bill futures. Spreaders make the market for the TED spread more liquid than is the market for bill futures.

FIGURE 15–6
June 1989 TED spread (TBM9–EDM9)

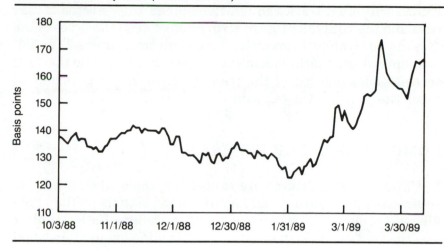

Source: Goldman Sachs.

TABLE 15–10
A TED spread

Step 1:   On 2/1/89, buy 500 June 89 bill futures at 91.66 and sell 500 June 89 Euro futures at 90.43.

The spread is *bought* at:*

$$91.66 - 90.43 = 123 \text{ bp}$$

Step 2:   On 3/20/89, sell 500 June 89 bill futures at 90.56 and buy 500 June 89 Euro futures at 88.82.

The spread is *sold* at:

$$90.56 - 88.82 = 174 \text{ bp}$$

Step 3:   Figure profit on first buying and then selling the TED spread:

$$\begin{aligned} \text{Profit} &= (500 \text{ contracts}) \,(\$25/\text{bp/contract}) \,(174 \text{ bp} - 123 \text{ bp}) \\ &= \$637,500 \end{aligned}$$

*Recall what we said above: the TED spread equals the price of the bill contract minus the price of the Euro contract, which in turn equals the Euro rate minus the bill rate, a difference that is quoted in basis points.

Today, the TED spread is being extended. Traders, instead of just doing a TED spread (3-month bills against 3-month Euros) will often track the relative spread between the 2-year note and the equivalent Euro strip and between the 3-year note and the equivalent Euro strip. Spreaders trade these 2- and 3-year spreads in a fashion similar to the way they trade the TED spread—only one leg of the trade is done in the government securities market, the other in Euro futures.

COMPUTERS IN THE FUTURE?

In Chicago today, futures are traded by people who crowd into octagonal pits shouting and flashing hand signals as they haggle over price. All that may be about to change. Both the Merc and the CBT plan to try computerized trading on an after-hours basis.

A lot of exchange members are dismayed, thinking that once computers are there to match up orders, there will be no reason to have traders jostling and shouting in the pits to execute orders: everyone can trade sitting in their office or at home in front of a CTR. Locals don't like this vision of the future, but big institutional members, such as Merrill and First Chicago, are said to be pushing for computerization, which could easily be tied into their own automated systems.

The exchanges, for their part, have promised to turn the computers off during daytime hours. But everyone wonders if that will be just for starters. Computerized trading appeals to the Merc and the CBT as a way to compete more effectively for global business with exchanges in Tokyo, London, and Zurich, which currently are automated or are about to be. Also, computerized trading would provide audit trails that could be used to uncover the types of trading abuses that the FBI in 1989 alleged it had found during a 2-year probe of the Chicago markets.

After working on its system, Globex, for several years, and persuading three other exchanges to join with it, the Merc planned to start automated trading in late 1989. The CBT's Aurora system probably won't be finished until 1990. Globex is to automatically match buy and sell orders according to price and time. Aurora is being designed to let traders interact using "mouses."[8]

The day of automated futures trading is sure to come, but whether it is here yet or not is another question. One New York trader mused, "I fear that with Globex, we may end up shooting ourselves in the foot. People do not realize how important the locals are until they are not there anymore. When dangerous moments occur, the locals have to give you a price, even if it is a silly price. With a computer, they can just shut it off."

THE NEXT CHAPTER

In this chapter, we looked at futures for 3-month instruments. In Chapter 16, we turn to futures for Treasury long bonds and notes. Thanks to multiple deliverables, bond and note contracts display quirks and complexities that have no parallel in the straightforward bill and Euro contracts.

---

[8]In a surprise move, the CBT and the Merc announced, on May 26, 1989, plans to merge the electronic trading systems that each is developing. Impetus for the move came from several sources. Big clearing members of both exchanges complained that duplication of after-hours electronic trading systems would mean huge, unnecessary expenses for them. Also, the Chicago exchanges would like to develop a trading system that would eventually become a worldwide industry standard; such a feat would help them reverse the current downward trend in their share of the world's futures business, which now stands at 60% and looks to fall lower if Chicago can't capture a growing share of futures trading in Japan.

CHAPTER 16

TREASURY BOND AND NOTE FUTURES*

In 1977, the *Chicago Board of Trade* (*CBT* or *Board* to Street folk) introduced a futures contract on Treasury bonds, which became successful and is today the most heavily traded of the contracts for financial futures. In the spring of 1989, over 250,000 bond futures contracts were traded on an active day, and open interest ranged from 300,000 to 400,000 contracts (Figure 16–1 and Table 16–1). The bond contract, as well as the T note contracts subsequently introduced, are all for securities having a face value of $100,000.

In Chapter 15, we described the functions of a futures exchange, how margin is handled, and how a futures contract can be used to speculate, to hedge, and to arbitrage. These remarks all apply, with certain obvious modifications, to the Treasury bond and note contracts. (For the specifications of the bond and note contracts, see Table 15–3, p. 732. The phenomenal growth of trading in the bond contract is pictured in Figure 16–1.)

Treasury bond and note futures, like cash Treasury bonds and notes, are traded on the basis of price. Consequently, longs profit when the prices of bond and note futures rise, shorts when they fall. Prices of T-bond and of 10-year note futures are quoted *in 32nds*; those of 5- and 2-year notes *in 64ths*.

On a *bond* or *10-year note* futures contract, a price of 94-17 should be read 94^{17}/32; and the minimum price movement or *tick*, as it's called, is 1/32. In the cash market, in contrast, active Treasury bonds are traded in 64ths. Addition of 1/64 to a cash-

---

*The author extends many thanks to Franklin Robinson, Ph.D. University of Pennsylvania, Vice President, Citicorp Securities Markets, Inc., for his valuable insights and, in particular, for the numerical examples, based on market quotes, that he contributed to this chapter.

FIGURE 16–1

U.S. Treasury bond futures contracts, average daily volume (thousands)

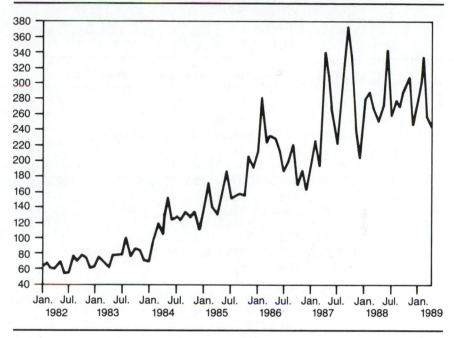

Source: Donaldson, Lufkin & Jenrette (Chicago Board of Trade).

TABLE 16–1

Wall Street Journal* quotes on Treasury bond and note futures, April 25, 1989.

FUTURES

	Open	High	Low	Settle	Chg	Yield Settle	Chg	Open Interest
TREASURY BONDS (CBT)—$100,000; pts. 32nds of 100%								
June	89-16	89-21	89-10	89-15	+ 1	9.157	− .004	241,608
Sept	89-16	89-18	89-09	89-13	....	9.165	....	40,388
Dec	89-14	89-17	89-08	89-11	....	9.172	....	14,385
Mr90	89-10	89-10	89-07	89-09	....	9.180	....	5,725
June	89-06	89-07	89-05	89-07	....	9.187	....	3,652
Sept	89-04	89-04	89-04	89-04	+ 1	9.199	− .004	1,369
Dec	....	....	....	89-00	+ 1	9.214	− .004	309
Mr91	....	....	....	88-27	+ 1	9.233	− .004	97
June	....	....	....	88-22	+ 1	9.252	− .003	196

Est vol 85,000; vol Fri 146,317; op int 307,738, −16,713

TABLE 16-1 *(concluded)*

FUTURES

	Open	High	Low	Settle	Chg	Yield Settle	Chg	Open Interest

TREASURY BONDS (MCE)—$50,000; pts. 32nds of 100%

	Open	High	Low	Settle	Chg	Settle	Chg	Open Interest
June	89-14	89-17	89-10	89-14	− 1	9.161	+ .004	9,157
Sept	89-12	89-13	89-11	89-12	− 2	9.169	+ .008	129

Est vol 1,400; vol Fri 2,733; open int 9,332, −186.

T BONDS (LIFFE) U.S. $100,000; pts of 100%

	Open	High	Low	Settle	Chg	Settle	Chg	Open Interest
June	89-18	89-18	89-10	89-11	− 0-01	89-26	86-10	7,025

Est vol 1,028; vol Fri 2,809; open int 7,035, +277

10 YR TREASURY NOTES (CBT)—$100,000; pts. 32nds of 100%

	Open	High	Low	Settle	Chg	Settle	Chg	Open Interest
June	92-28	93-00	92-22	92-27	....	9.105	....	78,765
Sept	92-28	92-30	92-26	92-30	....	9.090	....	5,614
Dec	....	....	....	93-00	....	9.080	....	190

Est vol 12,000; vol Fri 12,862; open int 45,923, +228.

5 YR TREAS NOTES (CBT) $100,000; pts. 32 of 100%

	Open	High	Low	Settle	Chg	Settle	Chg	Open Interest
June	95-065	95-08	95-035	95-075	+ 0.5	9.21	− .01	45,078
Sept	....	....	....	95-105	+ 0.5	9.19	....	845

Est vol 2,121; vol Fri 1,917; open int 45,923, +228.

5 YR TREAS NOTES (FINEX) $100,000; pts. 32 of 100%

	Open	High	Low	Settle	Chg	Settle	Chg	Open Interest
June	95-015	95-04	94-31	95-035	+ 1.5	9.24	− .02	17,371
Sept	95-055	95-07	95-045	95-07	+ 1.5	9.21	− .02	320

Est vol 2,000; vol Fri 1,805; open int 17,691, −5.

−OTHER INTEREST RATE FUTURES−

Settlement prices of selected contracts. Volume and open interest of all contract months.

30−DAY INTEREST RATE (CBT) $5 million; pts. of 100%

May 90.06 −03; Est. vol. 275; Open Int. 3,348

2 YR. TREAS NOTES (FINEX) $200,000; pts. 32nds of 100%

Jun 97-07 −0.5; Est. vol. 300; Open Int. 4,628

CBT–Chicago Board of Trade. FINEX–Financial Instrument Exchange, a division of the New York Cotton Exchange. IMM–International Monetary Market at Chicago Mercantile Exchange. LIFFE–London International Financial Futures Exchange. MCE–MidAmerica Commodity Exchange.

*As Table 16–1 indicates, the successful CBT bond contract has stimulated the introduction of look-alike contracts on LIFFE (trying to capitalize on T bond trading in Europe) and on the MCE. Trading in 5-year and 2-year notes futures currently doesn't amount to much. Since a successful futures contract is a big money maker, futures exchanges, in their search for a winner, are constantly introducing new contracts and new versions of existing contracts. Unfortunately, few of these entrants to the lists survive to make any money for their promoters.

market price is indicated by adding a *plus*. Thus, a quote for cash T bonds of $121-18+$ equals 121 plus $18/32$ plus $1/64$, which sums to $121^{37}/64$.

THE CONTRACT

Once a quarter (subject to the congressionally imposed debt ceiling), the Treasury markets a new long bond in the refunding. It does so through a yield auction, which establishes the coupon on the new issue. In recent years, this procedure has, due to the volatility of interest rates, created a situation in which outstanding Treasury long bonds are a heterogeneous mix: they have varying current maturities; they have radically different coupons; older issues are callable, but recent issues aren't.

To create a successful, liquid contract for Treasury bond futures, the CBT could not, given the heterogeneity of outstanding Treasury bonds, design its futures contract around a single issue that would be deliverable against the contract. Instead, it had to design its contract so that a wide and changing array of bonds would be deliverable on equitable terms against it. To see how the CBT did this, we examine the delivery provisions of the contract.

DELIVERY PROVISIONS

Someone who had sold bond futures and is thus *short* the contract may liquidate his position by *offset*: by buying bond futures. (In practice, *most bond futures positions, both short and long, are liquidated by offset*). However, a short may, alternatively, elect to liquidate his position by delivering, during a specified delivery period, contract-grade T bonds.[1] Although delivery is used to settle only 5 to 10% of bond futures positions,

---

[1]In this chapter, the term *short* refers to an entity that has *sold* bond futures and is thus short bond futures; conversely, the term *long* refers to an entity that has *bought* bond futures and is thus long bond futures.

the delivery provisions of the futures contract are crucial because they play an important role in determining the relationship between the price at which bonds trade in the cash market and the price at which bond futures trade.

The Delivery Period

A Treasury bond futures contract is identified by the month in which it expires, for example, the December 1991 contract, the March 1992 contract, and so on. A short may deliver bonds to cover his short on *any* business day during the delivery month corresponding to the contract he's short, but on the last business day of that month, he must deliver if he hasn't done so previously.

A short who decides to deliver bonds must notify the CBT of his intent to do so by 8 P.M., Chicago time. The next day, the CBT designates a long to whom delivery will be made, informs the designated long that he will be receiving bonds, and instructs the seller to deliver bonds to that long. The long, for his part, has *no* option as to whether or when to receive bonds; he is chosen because, at the time of notification to deliver, his long in the expiring bond contract is, among such positions still outstanding, the one that was put on at the earliest date. The day after the CBT designates a long to receive, the short delivers bonds to that long versus payment in Fed funds.

A bond futures contract may be traded during the delivery month except during the last seven business days of that month.

Deliverable Bonds

A Treasury bond is called *contract grade* if it's eligible for delivery in settlement of a short position in futures. The CBT contract provides that a contract-grade bond must have, from the first day of the delivery month, at least *15 years remaining to maturity* if it's not callable and at least *15 years remaining to call* if it's callable. Older Treasury bonds are callable five years from maturity; such bonds are contract grade only so long as they have a current maturity of 20 or more years.

THE INVOICE PRICE

The CBT contract is for bonds having a face value of $100,000. Thus, a trader who is short 10 contracts must, to liquidate his short, deliver bonds with a par value of $1MM. How many dollars the trader will get for his bonds depends on the price at which these bonds are invoiced in the futures-market delivery process. This invoicing procedure takes a little explaining.

Calculating the Principal Amount

Under the CBT contract, a *contract-grade bond carrying an 8% coupon* would (if there were one) be invoiced at the futures price that prevailed on the exchange at the 3 P.M. close on the day the short gave notice to deliver. Thus, if futures closed at $80^{24}/_{32}$ on the day the short gave notice, he would receive for his 8% bonds a dollar price of 80.75 or $80,750 per $100,000 of bonds delivered; the short would also receive interest accrued through the settlement date on his bonds. However, a short will rarely, probably never, find himself delivering bonds with an 8% coupon. Currently, no such deliverable-grade bond exists.

The Delivery or Conversion Factor

To enable shorts to deliver a contract-grade bond with any coupon—high or low—on equitable terms, the CBT introduced what's called a *conversion* or *delivery factor* into the invoicing of contract-grade bonds. *The factor associated with any bond is calculated by dividing by 100 the dollar price that the bond would command if it were priced to yield 8% to maturity (or to call).*

In Chapter 5's discussion of duration, we introduced the concept of present value. *The price at which any bond trades in the cash market equals the present value of the cash flows it will throw off over time discounted at its yield to maturity.* There is nothing mysterious about this. It follows from the definition of a bond's yield to maturity as *the rate* at which future payments from the bond must be discounted in order that they sum to the bond's current market price.[2]

If we discount at 8%, the cash flows that a bond will throw off over time, we obtain *the bond's present value in the 8% world of futures*—the price at which the bond would trade if its yield to maturity were 8%. If we next divide this present value by 100, we obtain the bond's *factor*.[3] If a bond carries a coupon greater than 8%, its present value—discounted at 8%—will exceed 100; and its factor will therefore exceed 1.

To illustrate, it suffices to consider a $100, 1-year note with a 12% coupon; the present value of this note, discounted at 8% and allowing for semiannual compounding of interest to reflect the semiannual payment of coupon interest, is given by

$$PV = (100) \left[\frac{(0.12/2)}{(1 + 0.08)^{1/2}} + \frac{(1 + 0.12/2)}{(1 + 0.08)} \right]$$

$$= 100(1.0780) = 107.80$$

$$= 107 \frac{25.6}{32}$$

which rounds to

$$PV = 107 - 25 +$$

As expected, the present value obtained exceeds 100. If we discounted at 8% a 12% bond with a current maturity of 15 years or

---

[2]A problem with this classic definition of a bond's yield to maturity is that it assumes that all cash flows thrown off by a bond prior to maturity will be reinvested at a rate equal to the bond's yield to maturity. Since different bonds trade at different yields to maturity, this assumption cannot hold for all bonds even at one point in time; and in a world of changing yield levels, it will not hold even for one bond over many time periods. The definition of a bond's yield to maturity is arbitrary and necessarily so: in a world where the future is uncertain, future reinvestment rates cannot be known with certainty.

An attraction of zero-coupon securities is that, because they pay no coupon, they expose the investor to no reinvestment risk. However, even on a zero, the *real rate of return* (the *nominal rate minus the rate of inflation*) is uncertain because future rates of inflation cannot be known with certainty.

[3]The need to divide a bond's present value, discounted at 8%, to obtain its factor results from the bond-market convention of quoting price as dollars per $100 of face value. This convention, along with the convention of expressing yields as percentages rather than as decimals, causes conventional bond-market formulas to be strewn with needless and confusing divisions and multiplications by 100.

more, we'd find that its present value exceeded 100 and that its factor therefore exceeded 1.

If, alternatively, we discounted at 8% a bond carrying a coupon less than 8% we'd find that its present value was less than 100 and that its factor was therefore less than 1.

Let's put our definition of the factor in symbols.[4] Let

$$\mathscr{F} = \text{the factor}$$

Then, for any bond,

$$\mathscr{F} = \left(\frac{\text{Dollar price at 8\% yield to maturity (or call)}}{100} \right)$$

$$= \left(\frac{\text{Present value discounted at 8\%}}{100} \right)$$

To sum up, the factor associated with a bond having a *coupon greater than 8%* always *exceeds 1*. Conversely, the factor associated with a bond having a *coupon less than 8%* is always *less than 1*. Here are two examples. Vis-à-vis the March 1988 bond futures contract, the 10⅜s of 2012 had a factor of 1.2326 (greater than 1); the 7¼s of 2016 had a factor of 0.917 (less than 1). For further examples, see Table 16–2.

The farther a bond's coupon diverges from 8%, the farther its factor will diverge from 1. For example, a seller would receive more for delivering a bond with a 12% coupon than he would for delivering a bond with a 10% coupon; this makes sense because, in the 8%-yield environment of futures (or in any positive-yield environment for that matter), the present value of a 12% bond will exceed that of a 10% bond.

The value of any coupon, high or low, depends on how long an investor will receive that coupon. Thus, a bond's time to maturity (or call) enters into the calculation of the dollar price that the bond would command at a given yield to maturity (or call). Specifically, as a bond's current maturity declines, its fac-

---

[4]Actually in this definition, a bond's time to maturity (or to call) is its current maturity rounded down to the years plus the number of whole 3-month increments remaining in its life as of the first day of the delivery month.

TABLE 16–2

Selected bonds, bases as of February 17, 1988, and March 17, 1988, which are respectively the start and end dates of examples worked through later in this chapter; a comparison of numbers in the two tables shows the process of convergences, as described below

A. Selected Bond Bases as of Close of Business on February 17, 1988

Contract: Mar 88 Futures Price: 93- 3
Settlement Date: 02/18/88
Repo Rate: 9.600%
Delivery Date: 03/31/88

Issue	Price	Factor	Delivery Price	Price Basis	Carry Basis	Forward Price	Value Basis	Implied Repo Rate
11.875–11/15/03	127–10	1.3408	124–26	80	12+	126–29+	67+	− 7.450%
12.000–05/15/05	129–14	1.3682	127–12	66	12+	129– 1+	53+	− 4.407
9.375–02/15/06	107–11	1.1283	105– 1	74	9	107– 2	65	− 9.844
11.750–02/15/10	129–17	1.3425	124–31	146	12	129– 5	134	−21.229
10.000–05/15/10	112–18	1.1841	110– 7+	74+	9	112– 9	65+	− 8.763
14.000–11/15/11	153– 7	1.5743	146–18	213	14	152–25	199	−27.567
10.375–11/15/12	116–28	1.2326	114–24	68	10	116–18	58	− 6.674
12.000–08/15/13	133–21	1.3976	130– 3+	113+	12	133– 9	101+	−13.881
13.250–05/15/14	146–29	1.5299	142–13+	143+	13	146–16	130+	−16.872
12.500–08/15/14	139–15	1.4560	135–17+	125+	13	139– 2	112+	−15.252
11.750–11/15/14	131–28	1.3820	128–21	103	11	131–17	92	−11.857
11.250–02/15/15	128– 4	1.3561	126– 8	60	11	127–25	49	− 3.881
10.625–08/15/15	122– 4	1.2892	120– 0+	67+	10	121–26	57+	− 6.219
9.875–11/15/15	113–27	1.2073	112–12+	46+	8+	113–18+	38	− 2.333
9.250–02/15/16	107–14	1.1383	105–31	47	8	107– 6	39	− 3.224
7.250–05/15/16	86–13	0.9167	85–11	34	5+	86– 7+	28+	− 2.216
7.500–11/15/16	89– 4	0.9442	87–29	39	6	88–30	33	− 3.348
8.750–05/15/17	102–10	1.0841	100–29+	44+	7	102– 3	37+	− 3.145
8.875–08/15/17	104– 7	1.0981	102– 7	64	8	103–31	56	− 8.044

B. Selected Bond Bases as of Close of Business on March 17, 1988

Contract: Mar 88 USH Futures Price: 92- 1
Settlement Date: 03/18/88

Repo Rate: 9.600%
Delivery Date: 03/31/88

Issue	Price	Factor	Delivery Price	Price Basis	Carry Basis	Forward Price	Value Basis	Implied Repo Rate
11.875–11/15/03	125–20	1.3408	123–13	71	4	125–16	67	– 5.634%
12.000–05/15/05	127–18	1.3682	125–29	53	4	127–14	49	– 1.793
9.375–02/15/06	105–22	1.1283	103–27	59	3	105–19	56	– 6.156
11.750–02/15/10	127– 5	1.3425	123–18	115	4	127– 1	111	–14.989
10.000–05/15/10	110–20	1.1841	108–31	53	3	110–17	50	– 3.800
14.000–11/15/11	150–10	1.5743	144–28	174	4+	150– 5+	169+	–21.149
10.375–11/15/12	114–21	1.2326	113–14	39	3	114–18	36	– 0.181
12.000–08/15/13	131– 1	1.3976	128–20	77	4	130–29	73	– 6.654
13.250–05/15/14	144– 1	1.5299	140–25+	103+	4	143–29	99+	– 9.866
12.500–08/15/14	136–21	1.4560	133–32	85	4	136–17	81	– 7.578
11.750–11/15/14	129–13+	1.3820	127– 6	71+	3+	129–10	68	– 5.668
11.250–02/15/15	125–26	1.3561	124–26	32	3+	125–22+	28+	1.991
10.625–08/15/15	119–26	1.2892	118–21	37	3	119–23	34	0.471
9.875–11/15/15	111–23	1.2073	111– 3+	19+	3	111–20	16+	3.925
9.250–02/15/16	105–13	1.1383	104–24	21	3	105–10	18	3.293
7.250–05/15/16	84–21	0.9167	84–12	9	2	84–19	7	5.440
7.500–11/15/16	87– 8	0.9442	86–29	11	2	87– 6	9	4.956
8.750–05/15/17	100–13	1.0841	99–25	20	2	100–11	18	3.166
8.875–08/15/17	102– 3	1.0981	101– 2	33	2+	102– 0+	30+	– 0.083

tor changes: from one successive contract to the next, the factor approaches, ever so slowly.[5]

Invoicing Principal

Bonds delivered via the CBT are invoiced at a price that equals *the price at which bond futures close* on the day when the short gives notice of intent to deliver times the bond's *factor*; this product represents the value the CBT assigns to the bond's *principal*; the seller also receives interest accrued on the bonds through the settlement date.

Let's put that in symbols. Let[6]

$$P_F = \left(\begin{array}{l} \text{The price (\textit{per \$1 of face value}) of bond futures,} \\ \text{i.e., the price quoted in the market \textit{divided by 100}} \end{array} \right)$$

Then

$$\left(\begin{array}{l} \text{The invoice price of} \\ \text{a bond's principal} \\ \text{per \$1 of face value} \end{array} \right) = P_F \mathscr{F}$$

Adding Accrued Interest to the Invoice Price

The short delivering bonds under the CBT contract receives not only dollars for principal, but dollars for *accrued interest* on his bonds. Let

c = a bond's coupon rate (stated as a decimal)

B = the number of days in the bond's current coupon period (it may range from 181 to 186)

t = the days during the current coupon period on which interest has accrued as of the settlement date

a_i = accrued interest on the bond, per \$1 of face value

---

[5]There's a term for this, *factor slippage.*

[6]We adopt, in the remaining equations presented in this chapter, the practice (1) of quoting all bond prices—cash, futures, and forward—in terms of dollars *per \$1 of face value* and (2) of quoting yield as a decimal. Doing so permits us to state key relationships in their simplest form. Note, it makes *no* difference whether we take a bond's price to be dollars per \$100 of face value or dollars per \$1 of face value so long as we are consistent when, for example, we figure the invoice price of \$100,000 of a specific issue.

Then, in invoicing a bond, accrued interest is calculated as follows:[7]

$$a_i = (c/2)\,(t/B)$$

Using the above expressions, let's work through an example. Suppose that, on 3/16/88, a short notified the CBT that he intended to deliver the 10⅜s of 12, which had a factor of 1.2326 against the March 88 contract. On this date, futures closed at 92-22. Thus, the short would have received for his bonds, per $1 of principal value delivered,

$$P_F\,\mathscr{F} = (92^{22}\!/_{32})\,(1.2326)/100$$
$$= 1.1424661$$

As of March 18, 1988, 58 days had elasped in the current, 182-day coupon period of the 10⅜s of 12; thus, on this date, accrued interest on this issue per $1 of face value was:

$$a_i = 0.03534341$$

From the above numbers, it follows that a short who delivered, on March 25, 1988, $100,000 of the 10⅜s of 12, would have received for his bonds

$$(\$100{,}000)\,(1.1424661) = \$114{,}246.61$$

for *principal*; and

$$(\$100{,}000)\,(0.03534341) = \$3{,}534.34$$

for *accrued interest*. Summing these amounts, we get

$$\text{Invoice price} = \$114{,}246.61 + \$3{,}534.34$$
$$= \$117{,}780.95$$

BASIS

For a trader or investor to use bond futures to hedge or to arbitrage, he must understand how the price of futures relates to the cash-market prices of outstanding, contract-grade bonds. To describe this relationship, we begin with the concept of basis.

---

[7]The *2* comes into the formula because the T bonds pay interest twice a year. Thus, accrued interest due is figured as one half the coupon rate times the fraction of the current coupon period that has elapsed as of settlement.

A deliverable bond's *basis* is the difference between the price at which a bond trades in the cash market and the (invoice) price at which it is valued (could be sold) for forward delivery in the futures market. In other words, basis is *the difference between a bond's cash-market price and its (forward) present value in the 8% world of futures.* Let

$$P = \text{a bond's price in the cash market}$$
$$\beta = \text{a bond's basis}$$

Then in symbols,

$$\beta = P - P_F \mathscr{F}$$

For example, on 2/17/88, the 10⅜s of 12 was trading in the cash market at a price of 115-20 for settlement on 2/18/88. Its March 1988 factor was 1.2326, and the futures price was 93-3; so the basis, β, of the issue was:

$$\beta = 115^{20}/_{32} - (93^{3}/_{32})(1.2326)$$
$$= 28.^{1}/_{32}$$

A bond or basis trader would simply say that, on 2/17/88, the basis of the 10⅜s of 12 was 28.1. *In bond-land, it is understood that basis is always quoted in 32nds.*

At any one time, many bond issues will be contract grade. If one were to calculate, during a period when carry was *positive,* the basis for each of these issues, one would find that all issues had a *positive* basis; some large, some small. (Table 16–2 provides examples.)

CARRY

A bond's basis is composed of two principal elements, the first of which is carry. Recall *carry* is the profit or loss a trader earns by holding a fixed-income instrument, the purchase of which he has financed with borrowed money; if a bond has a current yield of, say, 10% and can be financed with 8% repo, a trader who buys and finances this bond will earn, exclusive of any capital gain or loss, approximately two points of carry. The carry rate is an *annual* rate. To calculate actual carry earned, one must know the *holding period:* one year, 90 days, 30 days, or whatever.

Also, carry can be calculated *ex ante* only if a trader locks in a term repo rate for his full holding period. Alternatively, a trader might reason: "The yield curve is upward sloping; interest rates are unlikely to rise; so I'll take my chances and finance day to day." In that case, a trader can't know with certainty what carry he'll earn over his holding period.

A Bond's Carry-Determined Forward Price

If one party agrees to sell a specific bond at a specific price to another party at a specified future date, that trade is referred to as a *forward contract,* and the contract price is referred to as a *forward price.*

For any bond issue, carry (which depends both on a bond's current yield and on the relevant term repo rate) determines, for each forward date, a unique forward price. This (carry-adjusted) price is called the bond's *forward price.*

To illustrate, assume that a bond that yields 10% can be financed with term repo for three months at 8%. The bond's forward price equals its current cash-market price *minus* the profit a trader could earn by buying the bond, financing it for three months, and simultaneously selling it for delivery three months hence.

Whenever carry is positive, a bond's forward price will be *less than* its current market price, whereas if carry is *negative* the *converse is true.*

Given a complete term repo market, the possibility of risk-free arbitrage will ensure that a bond trades for forward settlement at its carry-determined forward price. For example, if a bond's quoted forward price exceeded its carry-determined forward price, that would elicit the following arbitrage: traders would buy the bond in the cash market, finance it, and simultaneously sell it for forward delivery. Because this arbitrage is risk-free, it would continue until the forward price at which the bond was offered had fallen to its carry-determined forward price. Thus, arbitrage guarantees that a bond's quoted forward price will not exceed its carry-determined forward price.

Consider now the flip situation: the forward price at which a bond is quoted is *less than* is carry-determined forward price. Such a low forward price would encourage holders of the issue to do the following risk-free arbitrage: sell the issue in the cash market, invest the proceeds in repo, and repurchase the issue for forward delivery. This arbitrage would drive a too-low forward price up to its carry-determined level.

Carry as an Element of Basis

Since a futures contract is just an exchange-traded forward contract, a fundamental component of a bond's basis to futures must be carry. To see this, note that, if the bond contract were for a specific issue, the delivery value of this issue would, neglecting transaction costs, always precisely equal the issue's forward price for delivery on the last day of the futures contract.

From this, it follows that, when a futures contract still has some time to run, carry must be one element in a bond's basis. In thinking about carry, it's best to begin with the case where the yield curve is positively sloped and carry is therefore also positive. That's the normal situation and the one that's easiest to grasp. However, carry may in practice also be negative or zero. The sign and size of carry will depend on the slope and steepness of the yield curve. When the yield curve inverts and carry is *negative,* the basis of some or all contract-grade bonds may be *negative.* On the other hand, when the yield curve slopes upward and carry is *positive,* then the bases of all contract-grade bonds must, as shown below, also be *positive.* Put another way, when carry is positive, futures prices are lower than cash prices by at least the value of carry.

VALUE (OR CARRY-ADJUSTED) BASIS

If we calculate a bond's basis and subtract from it the bond's carry (positive or negative) to the last delivery day of the futures contract, we are typically left with a positive sum. This sum varies from one deliverable bond to another, and sometimes it can be quite large (Table 16–2). A logical term for this second component of basis is *carry-adjusted basis*. However, that's a bit of a mouthful, so we'll use a shorter term, *value basis*.

A bond's value basis, regardless of the market conditions under which it's measured, is never negative. Thus, value basis appears to reflect factors that give cash bonds value relative to bond futures. Also, as noted below, no risk-free arbitrage exists to elminate *positive* value basis.

One reason that futures tend to trade somewhat cheap to cash bonds probably lies in the fact that bond futures are heavily used to hedge not only Treasuries, but interest-rate swaps and other instruments as well. Presumably, some portion of the value basis of deliverable bonds reflects the dominance in the market for bond futures of dealers and investors who seek to reduce market risk from various sources by shorting bond futures.

CONVERGENCE OF CASH AND FUTURES PRICES

We next turn to what it means to say that the prices of cash bonds and of bond futures converge at delivery. First, we recall that a bond's basis has two elements: carry and value basis. The strict meaning of *convergence* relates to the convergence of the carry basis, that is, to the fact that carry goes to zero as the time to futures expiration goes to zero.

The value basis will converge to zero only in the sense that *the delivery option* tends to zero. However, this will occur only for those issues that are "cheap enough" to deliver, that is, for those issues for which the delivery option *will probably not* be exercised. However, given that various other delivery options exist, even for the cheapest to deliver issue or issues, the value basis of such an issue will be positive until the last couple of days of the month.

Tenable Values of a Bond's Value Basis

Negative Value Basis

While a bond's "overall" basis may be negative so long as carry is negative and significant, a bond's *value basis* must be *positive*. A negative value basis, which implies that cash is cheap to futures, would invite the following risk-free arbitrage: a trader could buy a bond having a negative value basis at its cheap cash-market price, simultaneously short futures, and eventually deliver that bond at its more expensive, futures-market invoice price. Such arbitrage would tend to lower the futures price, raise the cash-market price of the bond having a negative value basis, and thereby drive the value basis of that bond toward zero.

Zero and Positive Value Basis

A value basis of zero on a deliverable bond is sustainable over time because it creates *no* opportunity for riskless arbitrage. The same is true of positive value basis; no arbitrageur would sell a bond having a high value basis and simultaneously buy futures in the hope that, at the expiration of futures, the high-value-basis bond he had sold or some similar bond would be delivered to him. The latter will never occur.

No alert trader of bond futures would deliver, to cover a short in futures, bonds having a high value basis. That would be to throw away basis. If a bond is trading at a high value basis, its cash-market price exceeds the invoice price at which it could be delivered to cover a futures short. Thus, if an owner of a high-value-basis bond wanted to cover a futures short by delivering, he would be better off selling his high-value-basis bond in the cash market, buying a zero-basis bond in this same market, and then delivering that bond to cover his short. That way, he'd end up receiving the full cash-market price for his high-value-basis bond rather than the bond's lower invoice price.[8] Because traders do not deliver high-value-basis bonds at the expiration of a

---

[8]If an investor owned and wanted to keep high-value-basis bonds (maybe, he'd been hedging them), he could cover his futures short by *offset:* by buying futures.

futures contract, there's *no* arbitrage that works to eliminate *positive* value basis on individual, contract-grade bonds.

Having said that, we hasten to add that, at or near the delivery period of a futures contract, not all deliverable bonds can trade at a positive value basis. If they did, then a trader could profit by selling the futures contract and taking delivery of whatever issue a short chose to deliver to him. Arbitrage of this sort will work to drive at least one contract-grade bond to a zero or near-zero (there are always transaction costs) value basis.

Summary

During the delivery period of a futures contract as carry decays to zero, at least some contract-grade bonds will trade at or near-zero basis, none will trade at a negative basis, and some will trade at a positive basis. When these conditions hold simultaneously, cash and futures prices are said to have *converged*. (Convergence does not imply that, during the delivery period, futures will trade at a price equal to the cash-market price of every or even of one deliverable bond.)

As cash and futures prices converge, a movement in the price of a high-value-basis bond will have *no* impact on the price at which futures trade, since high-value-basis bonds are irrelevant to the delivery process. However, if a bullish development (the dollar strengthens, oil prices fall) were to raise the prices of all deliverable bonds and thus their bases, arbitrage would force up the futures price if the latter had not moved up *pari passu* with cash-market prices.

The Value of Delivery Options

A second and far more important reason that a bond's value basis is never negative is the various options imbedded in the bond futures contract; these options have value only to a short who might make delivery. Thus, a seller of futures purchases delivery options from the buyer, and the premium he pays for them lowers the price of bond futures relative to the prices of cash bonds.

An analyst who's willing to pull out his scalpel and really dig and delve can uncover as many as seven options imbedded in the bond futures contract. Some are more valuable than others; also each option will prove profitable to exercise only under a particular constellation of market conditions—a constellation whose probability of occurrence at the expiration of a given contract may be highly probable, highly improbable, or something in-between.

The Day to Which Carry Is Calculated

Before we turn to the most important options, there's one more technical question to consider. A seller of futures may delay making delivery from the outset to the end of the delivery period. If carry on the bonds he plans to deliver is positive, the longer he waits to deliver, the lower will be the effective cost of the bonds he delivers. That's not to say that the short will surely make more or lose less to the extent that he delays delivery; so long as the short delays delivery, the economic outcome of his position remains uncertain because the futures price continues to fluctuate.[9]

The existence of a choice as to when to deliver raises a question: What delivery day should be used in calculating carry and a bond's carry-determined forward price? On a cash-and-carry trade, the standard is to calculate carry to the rational last delivery day of futures. So if carry is positive, it's the last business day of the month; if carry is negative, it's the first day. However, even when carry is negative, it's a rare short who delivers on the first business day of the month because, in doing so, he would give up roughly 29 days worth of other delivery options. What's rational isn't so easy to define *ex ante*. In any case, a lot of people say, "Let's just use the first and last days of the month whether they are business days or not, since a day or two of carry won't significantly affect our analysis." Thus, it's the first and last days of the delivery month that go into the Street's computers.

---

[9]Exception: the CBT bond futures contract does not trade during the final seven business days of its delivery period.

The Option to Choose Which Bond to Deliver

If the value basis of a particular issue is high during the delivery period, much of that basis may be viewed as the value assigned by the cash market to a short's option to deliver not that issue, but some other contract-grade issue. The value of the option to *not* deliver a particular issue will vary from one contract-grade issue to another; also, it will be greater (1) the greater the relative volatility of bond prices and (2) the greater the time remaining to settlement of the futures contract.

Greater relative price volatility in the cash market for bonds enhances uncertainty about relative cash-market prices in the future and hence about which issues will be economically deliverable as the contract expires; such uncertainty, since it works to the advantage of a short, will raise the discount at which futures trade to cash and thereby enlarge the value bases of deliverable issues. Also, the longer the remaining life of a futures contract, the greater will be the uncertainty about which issues will be economically deliverable as futures expire, and the greater will be the value bases of at least some cash bonds.

The "Wild Card" Option

Yet another option available to a trader who's short futures is the right to time—down to the hour, the minute—his declaration of intent to deliver. On any day during the delivery period, a short may elect to declare his intent to deliver up to 8 P.M. Chicago time. During the period 3 to 8 P.M. of a delivery day, the futures price that will be used to invoice a delivery is the price at which futures closed at 3 P.M. The cash market, however, continues to trade after futures close. Thus, it might occur that, after the futures close, cash-market prices drop significantly on bearish news. In that case, an alert trader who was short futures and chose to deliver might make some money.

To illustrate, consider a trader who is short, say, 10 futures contracts. If he's an arbitrageur betting on how the basis will move, he will (for reasons noted below) have a long position in bonds but it will equal only a fraction, roughly $1/\mathscr{F}$, of his position in futures. If the delivery factor, $\mathscr{F}$, is significantly greater than 1, say, 1.4 or 1.5, our trader must to deliver *buy in* a big *tail*—buy a lot more cash bonds, since the par value of the cash bonds he's long is significantly less than the par value of the futures he's short. It is partly by permitting a trader to buy in a big tail at a cheap price that the so-called *wild card option* may profit a short.

It also increases a short's profit if the move in the cash market causes the economically deliverable bond to change from one with a low factor such as 1.1 to one with a high factor such as 1.6. In the early 1980s, market conditions—rate levels, rate volatility, and so on—were such that at times exercising the wild card option could be highly profitable to a short. However, in the late 1980s, market conditions were such that a short was unlikely to profit much from exercising this option.

An arbitrageur who is short futures and long, in ratio, a cash bond having a factor *less than 1* will own more bonds than he can deliver. Thus, should he elect to deliver, he must sell some of his bonds. For such a trader, the wild card option has no value.

The Switch Option

A third delivery option works as follows: different bonds are trading pretty close together. During the last week of the delivery month, when futures have ceased to trade, the price spread between the bond a trader owns and the next economically deliverable bond changes such that the second bond becomes relatively cheaper; in this case, it is more profitable for the trader (1) to sell the bond he owns and (2) to buy and to deliver the second bond.

Dissecting all of the options embedded in the bond contract and analyzing when they will and won't have value leads to a lengthy and sometimes tedious discussion. For the reader who wants to know all, there's a book: *The Treasury Bond Basis* by Burghardt, Lane, and Papa (Probus, 1989); see especially Chapter 3. (See also the forthcoming revision of Stigum's *Money Market Calculations*).

Technical Factors Affecting the Value Basis

It used to be fashionable to say that *all* of a bond's value basis represented the value of delivery options. But, studies that attempted (using the Black-Scholes model) to place dollar values on the delivery options associated with various bonds relative to various futures contracts suggested that the value bases of some bonds exceeded any rational value that could be assigned to associated delivery options. Thus, the Street now thinks of a bond's value basis as the *maximal value* of the relevant delivery options but recognizes that these options need not be worth that much. "The value basis," noted one trader, "has meaning only to the extent that it is saying how relatively expensive or cheap an issue is. You could get the same meaning by saying, 'Well, the 14s of 11 are in certain environments very expensive to other issues.' That would mean exactly the same thing."

Unusual Investor Demand

Various technical factors may also be at work causing a bond's value basis to go in or go out. One is unusual investor demand. "Suppose an insurance company suddenly decides," commented a trader, "that it needs a long-duration instrument to hedge something. And, say, it's a very much off-the-run issue—the 9¼s of 16. If they start buying that issue, that makes the 9¼s expensive in the cash market; and if the issue is expensive in the cash market, by definition—since futures have not changed—the issue's basis expands. That does not necessarily mean that the issue's associated delivery options are now more expensive. In fact, nothing has changed except for a temporary dislocation of supply and demand for one issue."

Stripping and Scarcity

Also, some issues have been so widely stripped and other high-coupon issues are so well buried in mutual fund and other portfolios that don't lend them out that they rarely trade; for such an issue, a wide basis simply reflects that futures are cheap to the issue. The 14s of 11 are an example. No one would think of delivering them: first, a trader could not get enough of them to deliver; second, the market would have to rally 200 to 300 bp for the issue to become economically deliverable.

One can argue that such issues have a value basis only mathematically. A trader knows the cash price of the issue, its factor, the futures price, and carry. So he can calculate the issue's value basis, but to say that that basis represents the value of the issue's delivery options lacks meaning.

Tightness in the Repo Market

Tightness in the repo market means that an issue goes special. Say, only 5 billion of an issue is in public hands, and the dealers collectively short 3 billion of it. Now buyers expect delivery of an extra 3 billion of the issue; and if the investors who own the original 5 billion refuse to lend it out, then that issue becomes suddenly scarce in the collateral market: it becomes special. Tightness means specialty and a *very low* reverse rate.

Here's a famous example: Starting in February of 1986, the Japanese bought and held onto a large part of the 9¼s of 16. They did not realize that it is standard practice to lend out bonds because, at the time, they had no experience in the repo market. This situation persisted into the second quarterly refunding that occurred in May of 1986; at that time, U.S. dealers, expecting the Japanese to swap out of the 9¼s into the new long bond, shorted the issue. The Japanese, however, failed to do this swap with the result that the 9¼s became extraordinarily special and traded, for a time, at near-zero to negative reverse rates.

An issue's value basis can go in and out depending on how tight the issue is in the repo market. If an issue goes on *special,* its basis will tend to expand even though its carry (over the full term to futures expiration) is not *expected* to change markedly: the trade in the issue may be for a 3-month period, and the issue itself may become special for only three days; still, the issue's basis will go out for those three days.

Summary

During the delivery period of a futures contract as carry decays to zero, at least some contract-grade bonds will trade at or near-zero basis; none will trade at a negative basis; and some will trade at a positive basis (Figure 16–2). When these conditions hold simultaneously, cash and futures prices are said to have *converged.* (Convergence does not imply that, during the delivery period, futures will trade at a price equal to the cash-market price of every or even of one deliverable bond.)

As cash and futures prices converge, a movement in the price of a high-value-basis bond will have *no* impact on the price at which futures trade, since high-value-basis bonds are irrele-

FIGURE 16–2
The bases vis-à-vis the March contract 10⅜s of 12 and of the 7¼s of 16 shrank toward zero as the March bond futures contract expired

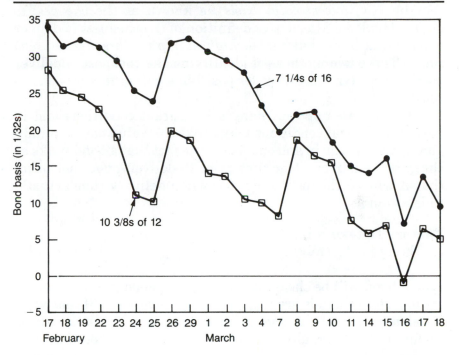

vant to the delivery process. However, if a bullish development (the dollar strengthens, oil prices fall) were to raise the prices of all deliverable bonds and thus their bases, arbitrage would force up the futures price if the latter had not moved up *pari passu* with cash-market prices.

THE CHEAPEST TO DELIVER BOND

The bond contract provides for *multiple deliverables*—at any point, as many as 30 bonds are technically deliverable under it. However, only one or several of these bonds will be *economically deliverable*. Since a trader who delivers a bond having a positive value basis is simply giving away basis, he will always make the economic choice to deliver the issue or issues that have—during the delivery period—the smallest value basis. The issue that seems, at a given time, most likely to be delivered (i.e., the issue that has the *lowest value basis*) is known as the *cheapest to deliver* bond. An alternative definition of the cheapest to deliver bond is that issue that has the *highest implied (break-even) repo rate*.[10] These two methods of identifying the cheapest to deliver bond are equivalent except for possible small differences due to rounding.

As we noted above, changes in market conditions and in various technical conditions may cause the value bases on individual bonds to go in and out. Thus, the fact that a bond ranks as cheapest to deliver, some time prior to delivery, does not mean that it will be cheapest to deliver when delivery time actually rolls around.

Factors Determining Which Bond Is Cheapest to Deliver

Which bond will be cheapest to deliver depends on duration and yield. Suppose bonds are trading at the same yield; if that yield is *below 8%,* then the bond with the *shortest duration* will be cheapest to deliver; alternatively, if that yield is *above 8%,* then the bond with the *longest duration* will be cheapest to deliver. Among bonds having the same duration, the bond with the highest yield will be the cheapest to deliver.

Factor Bias

Sharp changes in the level of current yields will tend to cause a change in the cheapest to deliver bond or bonds. The reason is

---

[10]For any deliverable bond, the *implied repo rate* is the repo rate at which a cash-and-carry trade (buy and finance cash and sell futures) would just break even. The higher a bond's value basis, the lower the repo rate a trader can afford to pay to carry that bond and still break when he delivers the bond to cover a short in futures. Hence, just as the value basis cannot be negative, the implied repo rate cannot exceed the market repo rate without engendering a risk-free arbitrage.

that the CBT factor is biased. When yields are below 8%, the CBT factors favor delivery of high-coupon, short-duration bonds. On the other hand, when market yields are above 8%, CBT factors favor delivery of low-coupon bonds with long durations. Only when yields are at 8% are the CBT factors unbiased.

An *unbiased* factor could be constructed for a deliverable bond. It would be the present value of that bond, discounted at current market yields, divided by the present value of a 8% bond, also discounted at current market yields. An obvious disadvantage of such an unbiased factor is that its value would constantly change; and consequently, a trader who put on a trade today would have to reweight that trade tomorrow using tomorrow's factor. A switch to an unbiased factor, which would be possible and has been proposed, would destroy the constancy of the factors and thereby probably also destroy basis trading, reduce the liquidity of the futures market, and reduce the efficacy of using futures to hedge.

One basis trader noted, "The biases in the factors are well known. So when you are at certain yield levels, you can say, 'Well, I am at 9.10, and 7¼s are cheapest to deliver; but I am only 30 bp away from where a higher coupon would suddenly become cheapest to deliver.' If we were down at 7.80, I'd say, 'I want to deliver 12s of 13 or 12½s, but I am only 20 bp away from where the 87⁄8s or the 8¾s—something like that—would be cheapest to deliver.' All of this is of course complicated by what's happening in the cash market. If they are stripping the 7½s or the 7¼s, that may mess up my calculations. Suddenly, those issues will get premiums of several basis points. You cannot just say that because you have this factor bias, this bond is definitely going to be delivered. If it were that simple, we basis traders wouldn't make any money.

"At the level when the cheapest to deliver switches from the 7¼s to medium- to high-coupon issues, it is almost rapid fire from the 103⁄8s, to the 12s, to the 12¾s. Well, if the *theoretically* cheapest to deliver bond happens to be an issue that is not readily available and the matched-book guys find that out, supply will just dry up. People will be forced to cover their shorts in the cash market, which in turn will drive out the basis on the issue." That's why some of the key issues, such as the 7¼s, the 10⅜s, are so preferred. They are large issues, and it's harder to play games with them.

HEDGING WITH BOND FUTURES

Bond futures offer an investor in cash bonds a means to hedge the market risk inherent in his position. In discussing hedging, we will assume that our portfolio manager's strategy is to maintain a running hedge for his position: each time the contract that he is short nears expiration, he *rolls* that contract—*buys* the expiring contract to offset his short and *sells* the next contract. Alternatively, our portfolio manager might decide to hedge only when it's his view that a rise in interest rates is likely; our remarks on hedging apply with an obvious modification or two to that tack as well.

Presumably, the objective of a portfolio manager who hedges is to reduce—preferably to zero—his risk of capital loss on his bonds. He could do that—create a situation in which his losses (gains) on his cash bonds precisely matched his gains (losses) on his position in futures only if he were hedging a bond with a constant value basis of zero, that is, a bond whose basis exactly equaled carry. Note, doing this could only appeal to a fully funded investor; a leveraged investor, having no funds to invest, could gain nothing from this strategy—neither capital gains nor carry.

The above assumptions hardly describe the real world. Consequently, our hedger will find that hedging entails both costs and risks. To investigate these, we will look at the effect of relaxing the above assumptions. We begin with carry. Suppose that carry is positive and that the other assumption holds. Each time, our hedger rolls his hedge, he will be "selling" his bonds at a futures price equal to their forward price. With positive carry, that means that he will lose money each time he rolls his hedge and the amount he will lose will equal the difference between the current yield on his bonds and the rate he could have earned had he invested his capital in term repo (3-month repo, if he's rolling his hedge from one futures contract to the next). Moral:

all else constant (forgetting our other assumption), an investor who runs a rolling hedge will tend to earn not the current yield on his bonds, but rather the term repo rate. If the yield curve is upward sloping, this lowers the rate of return he earns. Conversely, if the yield curve is inverted, this raises the rate of return he earns.

Note it makes sense that our investor will earn on a continuously hedged bond portfolio—when basis risk is assumed away—simply the term repo rate. Our investor is making a short-term riskless investment, and on it, he's earning precisely the return that a short-term riskless investment pays.

Next, let's relax the assumption that the value basis is zero and constant; specifically, we allow for multiple deliverables. Now our hedger will find that the basis at which he puts on his hedge will contain two elements—carry and value basis. The value basis at which he puts on his hedge is not written in stone. It may go in or out during the time he's hedged. If it goes in, our hedger will lose value basis and thus money. If it goes out, our hedger will gain value basis and thus money. Whatever happens, our hedger, by shorting futures, has assumed *basis risk*.

Our hedger's risk of losing a lot of value basis will be least if he happens to be hedging the cheapest to deliver bond and if that bond stays cheapest to deliver throughout the life of the contract. In that case, he'll lose any value basis that his bonds had when he hedged them, but by definition, these bonds had, at that time, the smallest value basis of any deliverable issue.[11]

Choosing a Hedge Ratio

Another issue our hedger confronts is choosing a ratio in which to put on his hedge. In the real world of multiple deliverables, a hedger, in choosing a hedge ratio, often looks to the bond factor. The fact that bonds delivered to cover a short in futures will be invoiced at a price equal to the futures price times a bond's factor means (assuming that the factor exceeds one) that, if the price of his cash bonds changes by one point, the price of futures

---

[11]At the expiration of futures, the value basis of the cheapest to deliver bonds must be at or near zero.

will change less—by only $1/\mathcal{F}$ of that amount. But if this is so, then to get a good hedge—one where any capital losses (gains) on his bonds are matched by capital gains (losses) on his short in futures—the hedge should short $\mathcal{F}$ times as many futures as the face amount of the bonds he wants to hedge. A similar argument holds if the factor is less than one; only it tells the hedger to short an amount of futures less than the face amount of the bonds he wants to hedge.

While hedgers often use a bond's factor to set their hedge ratio, there's a problem with this approach: because of factor bias, this approach exposes a hedger to *more basis risk* than necessary. In Chapter 4, we introduced the concept of the yield value of $1/32$. Let

v_{32} = yield value of $1/32$

CDT = the cheapest to deliver bond

A lower-risk approach for our hedger would be to set his hedge ratio as follows:

$$\left(\begin{matrix}\text{Hedge} \\ \text{ratio}\end{matrix}\right) = \left[\frac{(v_{32} \text{ on the CTD})(\mathcal{F} \text{ of the CTD})}{(v_{32} \text{ on the issue to be hedged})}\right]$$

Hedge Example

In Table 16–3, we outline the results of a hedge of the $7\frac{1}{4}$s of 16 using the Dec88 bond future. The hedge was established on March 1, 1988, and liquidated on December 8, 1988. Chicago Board of Trade delivery factors and yield values of $1/32$ were used to determine the hedge ratios. In the latter case, we reset the hedge on April 8, 1988, to adjust for a change that occurred in the cheapest to deliver instrument.

Over the life of the hedge, the price of $7\frac{1}{4}$s of 16 declined by 5-24, or \$57,500 per 1MM. By comparison, the net loss on the hedged portfolio was approximately \$30,000 per 1MM of bonds. Over the same period, the Dec88 basis of the $7\frac{1}{4}$s collapsed approximately 109/32, or \$34,000 per 1MM of bonds. Thus, by substituting basis risk for market risk, the investor was able to reduce his losses by approximately \$23,000 per 1MM of bonds held.

TABLE 16–3
Using bond futures to create a 9-month hedge*

Step 1:   Purchase the bonds:

On 03/01/88, buy for settlement on 03/02/88, 1MM of the 7¼s of 05/15/16 for 88-1.

Principal amount $880,312.50

Step 2:   Determine hedge using Chicago Board of Trade weighting:

The hedge ratio is the CBT delivery factor for Dec88, that is, 0.9171. To hedge using CBT factors we would, on 03/01/88, sell 9 CBT Dec88 bond futures contracts at 92-5.

Step 3:   Determine hedge using yield-value-of-a-32nd weighting against the current cheapest to deliver bond, which is the 10⅜s of 12:

Using the formula for the hedge ratio derived in the text, the hedge ratio is:

$$(0.00291/0.00322)(1.2284) = 1.1$$

To hedge using yield-value-weighting, we would, on 03/01/88, sell 11 CBT Dec88 bond futures contracts at 92-5.

Step 4:   Reset hedge using value of an yield-value-weighting against the "new" cheapest to deliver bond, which is the 7¼s of 16:

Since we are hedging the cheapest to deliver, we can use the Dec88 delivery factor of 0.9171 for the hedge ratio. To reset the hedge using CBT factors, we would, on 04/08/88, buy back 2 CBT Dec88 bond futures contracts at 89-2. We are now short only 9 Dec88 contracts.

Step 5:   Unwind the hedged investment:

On 12/08/88, sell for settlement on 12/09/88, 1MM of the 7¼s of 05/15/16 at 82-9.

Principal amount $822,812.50

On 12/08/88, buy 9 CBT bond futures contracts at 89-19.

Step 6:   Calculate hedge results using CBT-weighted hedge investment:

Loss on purchase and sale of the 7¼s of 16:
Proceeds from sale on 12/08/88	$822,812.50
−Cost at purchase on 03/01/88	880,312.50
Loss on principal	$ 57,500.00

Gain on CBT-weighted hedge of 9 CBT bond futures:
Value when sold on 03/08/88	$829,406.25
−Value when purchased on 12/08/88	806,343.75
Gain on futures	$ 23,062.50

TABLE 16–3 (continued)

Net gain:	
Loss on principal	$ 57,500.00
+Gain on futures hedge	23,062.50
Net loss	$ 34,437.50

Note: The Dec88 basis for 7¼s of 16 was 112.5 32nds on 03/02/88 and 3.7 32nds on 12/08/88. The loss (in 32nds) from being *long the basis of the 7¼s of 16* was:

$$(112.5 - 3.7) = 108.8, \text{ or } \$34,000$$

which, as should be expected is approximately the same as the loss on the hedged portfolio using CBT weights ($34,437.50).

Step 7: **Calculate hedge results using yield-value-weighting against cheapest to deliver without resetting the hedge:**

Loss on purchase and sale of the 7¼s of 16:	
Proceeds from sale on 12/08/88	$ 822,812.50
−Cost at purchase on 03/01/88	880,312.50
Loss on principal	$ 57,500.00
Gain on yield-value-weighted hedge using 11 CBT bond futures:	
Value when sold on 03/08/88	$1,013,718.75
−Value when purchased on 12/08/88	985,531.25
Gain on futures	$ 28,187.50
Net gain:	
Loss on principal	$ 57,500.00
+Gain on futures hedge	28,187.50
Net loss	$ 29,312.50

Step 8: **Calculate hedge results using yield-value-weighting against cheapest to deliver with resetting the hedge:**

Loss on purchase and sale of the 7¼s of 16:	
Proceeds from sale on 12/08/88	$822,812.50
−Cost at purchase on 03/01/88	880,312.50
Loss on principal	$ 57,500.00
Gain on repurchase of 2 CBT bond futures:	
Value when sold on 03/08/88	$184,312.50
−Value when purchased on 04/08/88	178,125.00
Gain on futures	$ 6,187.50
Gain on yield-value-weighted hedge of 9 CBT bond futures:	
Value when sold on 03/08/88	$829,406.25
−Value when purchased on 12/08/88	806,343.75
Gain on futures	$ 23,062.50

TABLE 16–3 (concluded)

Net gain:	
Loss on principal	$ 57,500.00
+Gain on futures hedge (2 contracts)	6,187.50
+Gain on futures hedge (9 contracts)	23,062.50
Net loss	$ 28,250.00

*Our example illustrates a hedge of principal. Therefore, we do not consider coupon interest, which of course the investor will earn.

BASIS TRADES

When an investor hedges a long position in bonds, he ends up, because of the way the contract is written, speculating on the basis, which can move up or down over time subject to certain constraints: (1) carry must approach zero as futures expire; (2) the value basis of one or of several cheapest to deliver bonds must approach zero as futures expire; and (3) if convergence affects the prices and yields at which the cheapest to deliver bond or bonds trade, the prices and yields of other bonds must move *pari passu* so that all bonds trade at reasonable relationships to each other, given the market environment.

To a trader, basis is simply a *synthetic security,* the price of which is quoted in 32nds.[12] Anything whose price fluctuates attracts traders. Thus, it isn't surprising that traders began to trade the basis. Formerly, doing so was awkward: a trader might buy 1MM or 2MM bonds and then try to sell futures where he thought the contract was. Then, RMJ, Liberty, Garban, and others began brokering bond bases, and in doing so, they created a tight, liquid market. Today, the quote in a broker's screen for a given basis might be bid 12, offered 12¼; the trades of 25, 50, 100MM a crack are common.

While a lot of basis traders probably think of themselves not as arbing between cash and futures, but rather as buying and

---

[12]A basis price of 0-16.6 should be read $16/32 + 0.6/32 = 16.6/32$, whereas a price of 1-16.6 would be $32/32 + 16.6/32 = 48.6/32$.

selling a *synthetic security,* in fact no such security exists. When the trader's back office clears a buy or a sell of the basis, it must clear two trades, a cash trade and a futures trade. Normally, the futures trade will clear on the trade date, the bond trade the following day.

To illustrate, suppose that a trader *sells the basis (sells bonds and buys futures)* through a broker. The trader on one side of the transaction might say, "Clear my trade through Citicorp. Futures Corp. (CFC) [which is a futures commission merchant (FCM)]," and the guy on the other side might say, "Clear me through Merrill." Since what has been traded is the basis at 12, prices must be assigned to the cash and futures legs of the trade in order to clear them. Two constraints limit the prices that may be assigned: (1) the futures price must be within the day's range of prices, and (2) the two prices must together determine a basis of 12.

The futures transaction, which is executed outside the pit, is known as an *exchange for physical (EFP)*. On an EFP, a trader pays his FCM the normal commission, $7 per contract or whatever, and the latter clears the trade for him. One beauty of EFPs is that they may be done any time: 24 hours a day, 7 days a week. In an EFP, the party who is selling cash instruments and buying futures is required, for the deal to be legal, to actually own the cash instrument to be delivered. However, dealers are exempt from this requirement. Typically, a dealer who sells the basis, ends up short bonds (since he had no bonds to begin with), and, consequently, he must reverse in bonds via his financing desk to cover his short. The reverse rate he'll get from his financing desk, next day when the cash trade settles, is one of the uncertainties he must face.

A trader will sell (short) the basis when he expects it to go in, buy it when he expects it to go out. Tables 16–4 and 16–5 present two examples in which a trader first sells, then buys the basis. These examples show how two instruments, having quite different durations and coupons, both converge as futures expire. The trade in Table 16–4 is in the popular, short-duration 10⅜s of 12, which were in early 1988 cheapest to deliver. The trade was put on in the middle of February 1988 and taken off a

TABLE 16–4

Cash-futures bond arbitrage with a "short-duration" instrument

Step 1:   Put on the trade:

1.   On 02/17/88, sell for settlement on 02/18/88, 1MM of the 10⅜s of 11/15/12 at 115-20.

Principal amount	$1,156,250.00
Accrued interest	27,077.61
Total proceeds	$1,183,327.61

2.   On 02/17/88, buy 12 CBT bond futures contracts at 93-3.

3.   Invest proceeds from bond sale in a term repo at 6.40% for 29 days to 03/18/88.

Note: the above transactions are equivalent to *selling the basis of the 10⅜s of 12* at a price (in 32nds) of 0-28.1.

Step 2:   Unwind trade:

1.   On 03/17/88, buy for settlement on 03/18/88, 1MM of the 10⅜s of 11/15/12 at 115-7.

Principal amount	$1,152,187.50
Accrued interest	35,343.41
Total cost	$1,187,530.91

2.   On 03/17/88, sell 12 CBT bond futures contracts at 93-10.

3.   On 03/18/88, close the term repo:

$$\text{Interest income} = (\$1,183,327.61)(0.0640)(29/360)$$
$$= \$6,100.71$$

Note: the above transactions are equivalent to *buying the basis of the 10⅜s of 12* at a price (in 32nds) of 0-6.5.

Step 3:   Calculate gain on trade:

Gain on sale and purchase of the 10⅜s of 12:		
Proceeds from sale on 02/17/88		$1,156,250.00
−Cost at repurchase on 03/17/88		1,152,187.50
Gain on principal	$	4,062.50
Carry loss:		
Interest earned on reverse repo	$	6,100.71
−Coupon interest paid		8,265.80
Carry loss	$	2,165.09
Gain on purchase and sale of 12 CBT bond futures:		
Value when sold at 03/17/88		$1,119,750.00
−Valued when purchased on 02/17/88		1,117,125.00
Gain on futures	$	2,625.00

TABLE 16–4 (concluded)

Net gain:		
Gain on principal	$	4,062.50
−Carry loss		2,165.09
Gain on futures		2,625.00
Net gain	$	4,522.41

The above transactions are equivalent to the following basis trade (all prices in 32nds):

Gain (in 32nds) on sale and purchase of the basis of the 10⅜s of 12:	
Sell the basis on 02/17/88 for	0-28.1
Buy the basis on 03/17/88 for	0- 6.5
Gain on basis	0-21.6
Carry loss (in 32nds):*	
Interest earned on repo	0-19.5
−Coupon interest paid	0-26.4
Carry loss	0- 6.9
Net gain (in 32nds):	
Gain on basis	0-21.6
−Carry loss	0- 6.9
−Value of 0.326 futures†	0- 0.2
Net gain in 32nds	0-14.5
Net gain in dollars‡	$4,531.25

*The value of a 32nd is $31.25 per contract.
†A *tail* of .326 futures arises because we cannot transact fractional amounts of futures. In this case, we can only buy 12 CBT contracts, not the 12.326 contracts implied the delivery factor.
‡The difference in the two calculations, $4,522.41 versus $4,531.25, is due to rounding.

month later in the middle of the delivery month.[13] During this period, the basis in the 10⅜s collapsed from 28.1 to 6.9 as carry and the time value of the delivery options decayed. When the trade was unwound on March 17th, the futures contract had only four days left to trade and final settlement was less than

[13]The dates in this and following examples were selected to illustrate a typical period in which the slope of the yield curve was positive and, thus, so too was carry. A year later, the yield curve had inverted; convergence was still occurring but less clearly, because the resulting moves in basis reflected the decay of both *negative* carry and the *positive* value basis.

TABLE 16–5
Cash-futures bond arbitrage with a "long-duration" instrument

Step 1:   Put on the trade:

1. On 02/17/88, sell for settlement on 02/18/88, 1MM of the 7¼s of 05/15/16 at 86-13.

Principal amount	$864,062.50
Accrued interest	18,921.70
Total proceeds	$882,984.20

2. On 02/17/88, buy 9 CBT bond futures contracts at 93-3.

3. Invest proceeds from bond sale in a term repo at 6.40% for 29 days to 03/18/88.

Note: the above transactions are equivalent to *selling the basis of the 7¼s of 16* at a price (in 32nds) of 0-34.2.

Step 2:   Unwind trade:

1. On 03/17/88, buy for settlement on 03/18/88, 1MM of the 7¼s of 05/15/16 at 85-31.

Principal amount	$859,687.50
Accrued interest	24,697.80
Total cost	$884,385.30

2. On 03/17/88, sell 9 CBT bond futures contracts at 93-10.

3. On 03/18/88, close the term repo:

$$\text{Interest income} = (\$882,984.20)(0.0640)(29/360)$$
$$= \$4,552.27$$

Note: the above transactions are equivalent to *buying the basis of the 7¼s of 16* at a price (in 32nds) of 0-13.7.

Step 3:   Calculate gain on trade:

Gain on sale and purchase of the 7¼s of 16:	
Proceeds from sale on 02/17/88	$864,062.50
−Cost at repurchase on 03/17/88	859,687.50
Gain on principal	$ 4,375.00
Carry loss:	
Interest earned on repo	$ 4,552.27
−Coupon interest paid	5,776.10
Carry loss	$ 1,223.83
Gain on purchase and sale of 9 CBT bond futures:	
Value when sold at 03/17/88	$839,812.50
−Valued when purchased on 02/17/88	837,843.75
Gain on futures	$ 1,968.75

TABLE 16–5 (concluded)

Net gain:	
Gain on principal	$ 4,375.00
−Carry loss	1,223.83
Gain on futures	1,968.75
Net gain	$ 5,119.92

The above transactions are equivalent to the following basis trade (all prices in 32nds):

Gain (in 32nds) on sale and purchase of the basis of the 7¼s of 16:	
Sell the basis on 02/17/88 for	0-34.2
Buy the basis on 03/17/88 for	0-13.7
Gain on basis	0-20.5
Carry loss (in 32nds):*	
Interest earned on repo	0-14.6
−Coupon interest paid	0-18.5
Carry loss	0- 3.9
Net gain (in 32nds):	
Gain on basis	0-20.5
−Carry loss	0- 3.9
−Value of 0.326 futures†	0- .1
Net gain in 32nds	0-16.5
Net gain in dollars‡	$5,156.25

*The value of a 32nd is $31.25 per contract.
†A *tail* arises because we cannot transact fractional amounts of futures. In this case, we can only buy 9 CBT contracts not the 9.167 contracts implied the delivery factor.
‡The difference in the two calculations, $5,119.92 versus $5,156.25, is due to rounding.

two weeks away, so most of the convergence that was going to occur had occurred.

Note that the trade was put on using CBT factors to weight the trade. Some basis traders and many investors may, because of factor bias, prefer to use the approach based on values of ¹⁄₃₂ that we described above when we talked about hedging; or he might work with yield values of an 01 which amounts to the same thing (recall Chapter 5).

Table 16–5 shows a similar basis trade done in the long-duration 7¼s of 16. Although this issue was not cheapest to deliver under the March contract, its basis too was affected by convergence. The cheapest to deliver issue cannot trade independent of all other issues; whatever happens to futures, yields on cash bonds must trade in reasonable relationship to each other. If one issue converges, they all must, unless some development affects just a certain issue or issues; for example, in a high-yield environment, high-coupon issues become very expensive, so a high-coupon issue might start to converge and then have its basis go back out due to a rise in yields. Conversely, the basis of a low-coupon issue might move out with a fall in yields.

Basis Trading by a Fully Funded Investor

Our basis-trade examples describe a dealer who must fund with repo any bonds he buys. A portfolio manager who owns bonds can also do basis trades. According to one view, a basis trade is the same trade whether it's done by a leveraged dealer or by a fully funded investor such as an insurance company. The truth is that it is and it isn't. For a fully funded investor, the current "in term" for a basis trade is that it's a *yield-enhancement* trade. This is a slight euphemism: there is always risk associated with a basis trade; and consequently, there's no guarantee that such a trade will only enhance, never lower, yield.

Basis Trading and Bond Liquidity

Basis traders started trading the basis to make money. Incidentally, they changed profoundly the way bonds are traded. *BF,* before futures, a bond trader asked to bid on some off-the-run issue would, if his bid were hit, immediately hedge by shorting some similar issue. Typically, this left him with an illiquid long and an illiquid short, which he'd hope some other bond trader would help him unwind.

Today, a trader can, in the cash market, do huge blocks in current issues without moving the market much if at all. Not so in off-the-run issues. Say a big insurance company comes in and asks a dealer to offer 200MM of the 7¼s of 16. If the dealer makes an offer and gets lifted, he's now short; and there's no way that he can go to the cash screens and buy 200MM 7¼s. However, he can go to the basis screen, buy 200MM of the basis in the 7¼s, and then try to buy futures at a price that leaves him a (positive) spread.

Because liquidity is so great in the basis market, it's common for traders to price bonds, not just cheap to deliver issues but any issue, on a basis. Dealer to dealer, traders are, today, more likely to trade bonds on a basis than to trade them outright. Most customers still want cash bids and offers, but asking for them may not be the way to get the best price. Suppose that the price at which an issue's basis is trading and the futures price together imply that the issue should be priced at 110- 4. A dealer might say to a counterparty who wanted an offering and who was willing to trade the basis, "If you want me to offer 100MM of this issue, the price is 110- 8, but if you want it on the basis, the price is 110- 5." Here the dealer is saying in effect to the counterparty, "It will cost you 3⁄32 if you put me at risk; as I have to go into basis-land, cover, get out of my futures, and do all that other stuff."

Today, a bond trader must also be a basis trader. Recall the example we gave in Chapter 14 of a bond trader who was asked by retail to bid on a huge block of bonds—250MM of them. Since the trader could not immediately sell all those bonds in the cash screens, he immediately shorted some futures. Note once he did so, he had on *a basis trade*. The only difference between a basis trader who buys the basis and a bond trader who buys bonds and then sells futures, is that the basis trader trades just once through a basis broker whereas the bond trader whose bid is hit is—for the 30 or 40 seconds it takes him to sell futures—at risk that futures might move against him.

Trading in Foreign Government Bonds

A person not favorably disposed toward finance—and there are such folks—might well look askance at basis trading and related fancy stuff. "What," he might ask, "is the contribution of these new instruments and techniques other than to complicate and add new risks to what was once a simple business: buying and selling cash instruments having no credit risk?"

In this respect, events in the markets for the debt of foreign governments are instructive. One by one, those markets—from

Tokyo, to Bonn, to Paris—are aping or have aped the mechanisms used in the U.S. to trade Treasuries. Thanks to gaming laws, Germany did not permit domestic trading of futures in Bunds, so futures and basis trading of Bunds sprang up in London, and the liquidity of Bunds was better for it. Not until 1989 did Japan begin work on setting up a domestic market in repo and reverse. The lack of such a market impaired the liquidity of Japanese government bonds (JGBs) and in particular precluded arbitrage that would have held rates along the yield curve in line. Because of the lack of a market in repo and reverse, traders in JGBs concentrated their activities in a few active issues which traded at a significant yield concession to the curve. Meanwhile, when other off-the-run issues became expensive, they stayed that way; traders couldn't short such issues as they would have in the U.S. because they could not cover a short in JGBs with a reverse.

A CALENDAR SPREAD

Another trade people frequently do with bond futures is *calendar spreads*—here, they are making bets about the relative steepness of the yield curve over say a 3-, 6-, or 12-month period. They are saying, "I think that the curve is going to invert, so I want to be short [sell] certain calendar spreads," or, "I think that the curve is going to steepen, so I want to be long [buy] certain calendar spreads."

Here's an example. In June 88, a trader could observe that the curve had been getting flatter and he might have reasoned that the curve was likely to continue to flatten and then invert. This conviction might in turn have led him to sell the Sept–Dec spread in, say, July at 29, that is sell Sept futures and buy Dec futures. Then in September, he might have bought back Sept–Dec at 19 for a $10/32$ profit and have sold Dec–March at 18. Then in December, he might have closed Dec–March at 11 for a $7/32$ profit and have sold March–June at 11. Finally in March 89, he might have decided to get out of the spread of -2. All told, he would have made $10 + 7 + 13 = 30$ 32nds on his successive, calendar-spread trades.

Alternatively, our trader might, in July 88, have reasoned that the curve was going to invert and to stay that way for some time. Suppose that, at that time, he decided that the thing to do was to sell a 1-year spread six months forward. He knew that the September contract was going away soon, so he sold the Mar89–Mar90 spread—a profitable move. During the period when the succession of 3-month calendar spreads moved down 30 ticks, the Mar–Mar spread moved down approximately 80 ticks.

In Table 16–6, we work through the profit and loss calculation for a calendar spread trade. Lest the reader think that traders of futures always make money, we picked for this example a trade that lost money. Figure 16–3 shows how this spread moved during the period covered by the example.

FIGURE 16–3

The March 88–June 88 spread in bond contract over the period covered in the example shown in Table 16–6

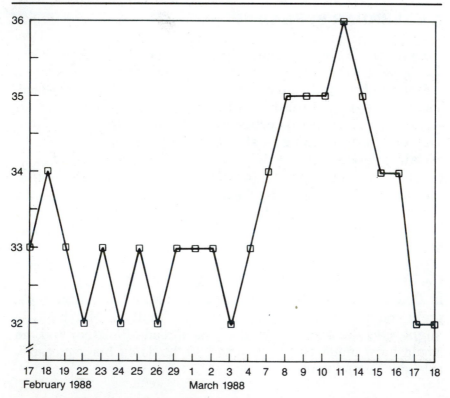

TABLE 16–6
Buying ("going long") the March–June CBT bond calendar spread

Step 1:   Put on the trade:

1. On 02/17/88, buy 10 CBT March bond futures contracts at 93-3.

2. On 02/17/88, sell 10 CBT June bond futures contracts at 92-2.

Note: the above transactions are equivalent to *buying the March-June calendar spread* at 1-1.

Step 2:   Unwind the trade:

1. On 03/17/88, sell 10 CBT March bond futures contracts at 93-10.

2. On 03/17/88, buy 10 CBT June bond futures contracts at 92-10.

Note: the above transactions are equivalent to *selling the March-June calendar spread* at 1-0.

Step 3:   Calculate gain on trade:

Gain on purchase and sale of the 10 CBT March bond futures:	
Sell on 03/17/88 for	93-10
Buy on 02/17/88 for	93- 3
Gain per bond future	0- 7
Gain on 10 bond futures*	$2,187.50
Loss on purchase and sale of the 10 CBT June bond futures:	
Sell on 02/17/88 for	92- 2
Buy on 03/17/88 for	92-10
Loss per bond future	0- 8
Loss on 10 bond futures	$2,500.00
Net loss:	
Gain on March bond futures	$2,187.50
−Loss on June bond futures	2,500.00
Net loss	$ 312.50
Note: The above net-loss calculation is equivalent to:	
Net loss:	
Buy the spread on 02/17/88 for	1- 1
Sell the spread on 03/17/88 for	1- 0
Loss per contract	0- 1
Loss on 10 contracts	$ 312.50

*The value of a 32nd is $31.25 per contract.

THE NOB TRADE

The *NOB* (*notes over bonds*) trade is a spread trade between note and bond futures. To buy the spread, one buys note futures and sells bond futures; to sell the spread, one does the reverse. Maturity of deliverables excepted, the 10-year note contract is identical to the bond contract. However, it is much less liquid than is the bond contract (Table 16–1); in note futures, there's virtually no liquidity after the front two contracts.

The note contract is used by the same sorts of people that use bonds futures: specs, hedgers, spreaders, and basis traders. However, speculators prefer the bond to the note contract because it is more liquid and because it offers a bigger bang for the buck if a spec is right.

The 5-year note contract is sort of a slimmed down (in terms of trading volume) version of the 10-year note contract. It has however, one trick: the most recently issued 5-year note is deliverable, and it is issued literally in the month of delivery. That imparts a special aspect to the game of basis trading this contract. A trader must guess what coupon a note that's going to be issued several months hence will have; he must also guess whether that note will be the cheapest to deliver.

While note futures are often used by dealers to hedge positions in cash instruments—mortgage-backs, MTNs, and so on—a lot of the open interest, especially in the 10-year note contract, comes from spreading in the NOB. One way to establish a position in 10-year note futures is to buy or sell the NOB and then close out the bond futures leg of the spread. A local may be unwilling to be in 10 years, but he will do a NOB. The same goes for muni bond futures, only the trade there is called the *MOB* (*munis over bonds*).

Tables 16–7 and 16–8 present, respectively, examples of NOB trades, weighted and unweighted, and Figure 16–4 shows the movements in the NOB over the relevant period. Going long the NOB is technically going long the curve—it is equivalent to buying 10s and selling 30s. In the first example, a NOB with a weight of 1.5 to 1, the weight is roughly the weight of 10 years to 30 years in terms of the value of an 01. Weighted and unweighted NOBs will produce slightly different price action.

TABLE 16–7
Buying ("going long") the weighted NOB using a weight of 1.5 on CBT notes

Step 1: Put on the trade:

1. On 02/17/88, buy 15 CBT note futures contracts at 97-10.
2. On 02/17/88, sell 10 CBT bond futures contracts at 93-3.

Note: The above transactions are equivalent to *buying the unweighted NOB* at 4-07 and purchasing a "tail" of 5 CBT note contracts at 97-10.

Step 2: Unwind trade:

1. On 03/17/88, sell 15 CBT note futures contracts at 97-24.
2. On 03/17/88, buy 10 CBT bond futures contracts at 93-10.

Note: The above transactions are equivalent to *selling the unweighted NOB* at 4-14 and selling the "tail" of 5 CBT note contracts at 97-24.

Step 3: Calculate gain on trade:

Gain on purchase and sale of the 15 CBT note futures:	
Sell on 03/17/88 for	97-24
Buy on 02/17/88 for	97-10
Gain per note future	0-14
Gain on 15 note futures*	$6,562.50
Loss on purchase and sale of the 10 CBT bond futures:	
Sell on 02/17/88 for	93- 3
Buy on 03/17/88 for	93-10
Loss per bond future	0- 7
Loss on 10 bond futures	$2,187.50
Net gain:	
Gain on note futures	$6,562.50
−Loss on bond futures	2,187.50
Net gain	$4,375.00
Note: The above net-gain calculation is equivalent to:	
Net gain:	
Gain on unweighted NOB†	$2,187.50
+Gain on 5 contract "tail"	2,187.50
Net gain	$4,375.00

*The value of a 32nd is $31.25 per contract.
†See Table 16–8 for calculations.

TABLE 16–8

Buying ("going long") the unweighted NOB

Step 1: Put on the trade:

1. On 02/17/88, buy 10 CBT note futures contracts at 97-10.
2. On 02/17/88, sell 10 CBT bond futures contracts at 93-3.

Note: The above transactions are equivalent to *buying the unweighted NOB* at 4-07.

Step 2: Unwind trade:

1. On 03/17/88, sell 10 CBT note futures contracts at 97-24.
2. On 03/17/88, buy 10 CBT bond futures contracts at 93-10.

Note: The above transactions are equivalent to *selling the unweighted NOB* at 4-14.

Step 3: Calculate gain on trade:

Gain on purchase and sale of the 10 CBT note futures:	
Sell on 03/17/88 for	97-24
Buy on 02/17/88 for	97-10
Gain per note future	0-14
Gain on 10 note futures*	$4,375.00
Loss on purchase and sale of the 10 CBT bond futures:	
Sell on 02/17/88 for	93- 3
Buy on 03/17/88 for	93-10
Loss per bond future	0- 7
Loss on 10 bond futures	$2,187.50
Net gain:	
Gain on note futures	$4,375.00
−Loss on bond futures	2,187.50
Net gain	$2,187.50
Note: The above net-gain calculation can be done more simply as follows:	
Net gain:	
Gain on unweighted NOB per contract	0- 7
Net gain on 10 contracts	$2,187.50

*The value of a 32nd is $31.25 per contract.

Also, in a weighted trade, the weights are, because of convexity, good only around where the trade is put on; if the market trades way away—yields rise or fall significantly—the weights change, and a weighted NOB must be reweighted.

FIGURE 16–4
Movements in the NOB over the period covered in the example shown in Tables 16–7 and 16–8

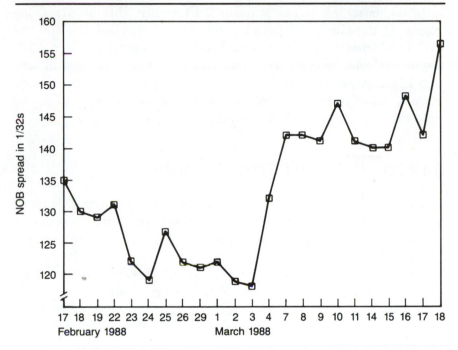

A trader can weight a NOB to be bullish or bearish. He can put the trade on saying, "I am bullish, so I'll weight it as a bullish trade," which means that he goes long slightly more. A trader always has to round the factors he used to the nearest millions, and he can round them up or down.

A trader might buy a NOB for either of two reasons. First, he might want to mimic a curve trade: he thinks that the curve is going to steepen between 10s and 30s, so he wants to be long 10s and short 30s; that is more a weighted NOB trade. Second, he thinks the market might sell off, and he wants to take advantage of the difference, between the 10s and the 30s, in the value of an 01—of the fact that, if the market sells off, bonds will tend to drop in price faster than 10s. The unweighted NOB trade is more directional: the trader is saying, "If the market is rallying,

I want to be short the NOB, but if the market is going to sell off, I want to be long the NOB."

In our examples of a NOB, the market rallied, but the NOB gets wider which is not standard. Probably, this occurred because, at the time of the trade, the market was bearish and the NOB reflected this bearishness even though prices rallied a little due to a technical correction. Once the curve started to flatten big time in the spring of 88, the NOB tended to collapse regardless of market direction—whether the market rallied or sold off, the curve kept flattening.

JARGON IN BOND-FUTURES-LAND

No one speaks standard English in the money market, least of all futures traders. First, if a trader refers to a futures contract by just its month of expiration, it's understood that he's speaking of one of the four nearby contracts, not all of which may expire during the current year; in April 1989, *the March contract* was understood to be the March 90 contract.

Also, *the bond* is always understood to be the most recently auctioned bond, which is also the most actively traded issue. *The old bond* is the previously auctioned bond, and *the old, old bond* is the bond auctioned previous to the old bond.

THE NEXT CHAPTER

Not so long ago—the mid 1970s and earlier—the money market, to the extent that it dealt in securities, dealt strictly in cash securities, except for an occasional forward trade tailored to meet the need of a customer. Now futures are ubiquitous and so too are options. Today's money market trader is likely to be dealing in puts, calls, caps, floors, collars, and even something called swaptions. In Chapter 17, we turn to options—puts and calls—and related esoterica.

CHAPTER 17

OPTIONS: IN THE FIXED-INCOME WORLD*

SOME DEFINITIONS

Options come in two flavors, *puts* and *calls;* and to every option transaction, there are two parties, a *buyer* and a *seller,* usually referred to as the *holder* and the *writer,* respectively. The *holder* of a *call* option has the right to buy the *underlier* (a commodity, a financial instrument, or the notional principal on a rate agreement) from the counterparty (the *writer*) at a specified price (the *strike price*) until the end of a specified period (the *expiration date*).[1] In contrast, the *writer* of a *call* option has the *contingent obligation* to sell the underlier of the option to the counterparty at the *strike price* until the *expiration date*.

Puts work the other way round from calls. The *holder* of a *put* has the *right* to sell to the counterparty, whereas the *writer* of a *put* has the *contingent obligation* to buy the underlier from the counterparty (Figure 17–1).

Note that a put is not somehow the reverse of a call. Puts and calls are *two distinct* instruments, each of which may be bought or sold. Thus, whereas futures quotes give just one price per instrument per period, options quotes give—for each strike price and for each expiration date traded—*two* prices: one for the relevant put, one for the relevant call. For example, Table 17–1 shows that *The Wall Street Journal* quoted, for August 11,

---

*I would like to thank Franklin Robinson, James Mehling, and Philip Ginsberg for their help and for their ideas on what constitutes a proper introduction to options in the fixed-income world. Since most of this chapter's writing is mine, responsibility for any errors or omissions is mine alone.

[1] *Underlier* is a nice generic term for the thingamabob, whatever it is, that an option may be on. Today, listed options are traded on commodities, securities, futures contracts, interest-rate indices, and so on.

FIGURE 17–1
Puts and calls: Rights, contingent obligations, and features

A. Rights and contingent obligations

		PUT	CALL
		Type	
	BUYER	Contingent right to sell	Contingent right to buy
Party	**SELLER**	Obligation to buy	Obligation to sell

B. Identifying features of an option

1. Is the option a put or a call?
2. What's the underlier—land, a stock, a bond, whatever—that the option is written on?
3. What's the option's strike price?
4. What's the option's expiration date?
5. When can the option be exercised?

1989, one *settle* price each for the Sep 89, Dec 89, and Mar 90 T-bond futures. However, for this same day, the paper quoted under the heading, "Futures Options" (short for *options on futures contracts*), 36 prices at which puts and calls on these three T-bond futures—each having one of six different strike prices and one of three different expiration dates—traded.

In options-land, a distinction is made between American and European options. An *American option* may be exercised on any day up to and including its expiration date. In contrast, a *European option* may be exercised only on its expiration date. An American option, because it offers multiple opportunities for exercise, is generally worth more than its European cousin. All options traded on U.S. exchanges are American options. However, U.S. parties to an OTC option are free to agree to whatever terms they choose.

TABLE 17–1

Quotes on listed interest-rate instruments: options on cash bonds, futures, and options on futures

OPTIONS

Friday, August 11, 1989

For Notes and Bonds, decimals in closing prices represent 32nds; 1.01 means 1 1/32. For Bills, decimals in closing prices represent basis points; $25 per .01.

Chicago Board Options Exchange

U.S. TREASURY BOND—$100,000 principal value

Underlying Issue	Strike Price	Calls—Last Aug	Calls—Last Sep	Calls—Last Oct	Puts—Last Aug	Puts—Last Sep	Puts—Last Oct
8 7/8% (yba)	103	....	....	....	....	0.05	....
due 2/2019	106	4.09	....	....	....	....	....
	107	3.11	....	....	....	....	....
	107 1/2	....	....	....	0.02	....	....
	109	1.09	....	....	....	....	....
	110	....	....	2.07	....	....	....

Total call vol. 1,035 Call open int. 2,113
Total put vol. 72 Put open int. 467

OPTIONS ON SHORT-TERM INTEREST RATES

Strike Price	Calls—Last Aug	Calls—Last Sep	Calls—Last Oct	Puts—Last Aug	Puts—Last Sep	Puts—Last Oct
70	....	8 1/8	....	....	5/16	....
75	....	3 1/4	....	....	3/4	....
77 1/2	....	2 1/2	....	5/16	....	....
80	1	1 7/16	....	1 1/4	3 1/4	....
82 1/2	....	9/16	....	....	....	....

Total call volume 864 Total call open int. 3,515
Total put volume 260 Total put open int. 3,691
IRX levels: High 79.50; Low 74.60; Close 79.50, +0.90.

OPTIONS ON LONG-TERM INTEREST RATES

Strike Price	Calls—Last Aug	Calls—Last Sep	Calls—Last Oct	Puts—Last Aug	Puts—Last Sep	Puts—Last Oct
75	....	4 1/8	....	....	....	....
77 1/2	3 5/8	....	....	....	9/16	13/16
80	1 3/8	1 1/2	....	1/2	1	....
82 1/2	....	5/8	....	....	....	2 7/8

Total call volume 398 Total call open int. 1,511
Total put volume 277 Total put open int. 2,045
LTX levels: High 81.36; Low 78.51; Close 81.32, +0.93.

FUTURES

TREASURY BONDS (CBT)—$100,000; pts. 32nds of 100%

	Open	High	Low	Settle	Chg	Yield Settle	Yield Chg	Open Interest
Sept	98-04	99-15	96-26	97-02	– 26	8.304	+ .086	245,791
Dec	98-00	99-10	96-24	96-31	– 25	8.313	+ .082	64,661
Mr90	97-26	99-00	96-20	96-24	– 24	8.337	+ .080	13,438
June	97-19	98-24	96-16	96-16	– 24	8.363	+ .079	5,897
Sept	98-03	98-08	96-09	96-09	– 23	8.387	+ .077	3,899
Dec	97-05	98-03	95-30	96-02	– 22	8.410	+ .073	1,250
Mr91	97-22	97-22	95-26	95-26	– 22	8.437	+ .074	289
June	....	....	....	95-18	– 22	8.464	+ .074	123

Est vol 525,000; vol Thurs 392,115; op int 335,380, +4,735.

	Open	High	Low	Settle	Chg	Discount Settle	Discount Chg	Open Interest
Sept	92.48	92.57	92.21	92.32	– .09	7.68	+ .09	13,431
Dec	92.93	93.16	92.64	92.73	– .16	7.27	+ .16	9,584
Mr90	93.18	93.38	92.90	92.93	– .16	7.07	+ .16	1,617
June	93.15	93.25	92.83	92.84	– .17	7.16	+ .17	350

Est vol 14,446; vol Thurs 5,760; open int 24,989, +451.

MUNI BOND INDEX(CBT)$1,000; times Bond Buyer MBI

	Open	High	Low	Settle	Chg	High	Low	Open Interest
Sept	94-05	94-31	93-03	93-10	– 19	96-08	78-06	13,014
Dec	93-31	94-24	92-26	93-00	– 18	96-01	81-10	3,361
Mr90	93-00	93-05	92-19	92-20	– 18	95-23	85-19	307

Est vol 5,000; vol Thur 5,334; open int 16,803, –468.
The index: Close 93-30; Yield 7.29.

EURODOLLAR (IMM)—$1 million; pts of 100%

	Open	High	Low	Settle	Chg	Yield Settle	Yield Chg	Open Interest
Sept	91.50	91.62	91.25	91.32	– .15	8.68	+ .15	221,952
Dec	91.88	92.12	91.54	91.59	– .24	8.41	+ .24	227,800
Mr90	92.09	92.30	91.76	91.80	– .23	8.20	+ .23	87,468
June	92.01	92.20	91.67	91.72	– .22	8.28	+ .22	43,191
Sept	91.82	92.01	91.53	91.58	– .18	8.42	+ .18	34,850
Dec	91.56	91.76	91.33	91.38	– .15	8.62	+ .15	27,919
Mr91	91.53	91.70	91.33	91.37	– .13	8.63	+ .13	22,305
June	91.49	91.70	91.32	91.36	– .12	8.64	+ .12	22,736
Sept	91.60	91.67	91.32	91.36	– .11	8.64	+ .11	18,443
Dec	91.55	91.62	91.27	91.31	– .11	8.69	+ .11	14,869
Mr92	91.58	91.65	91.33	91.34	– .11	8.66	+ .11	12,422
June	91.56	91.63	91.31	91.32	– .11	8.68	+ .11	5,538
Sept	91.48	91.48	91.27	91.27	– .11	8.73	+ .11	2,447
Mr93	91.42	91.42	91.20	91.21	– .11	8.79	+ .11	2,708

Est vol 512,418; vol Thur 144,538; open int 744,648, –2,818.

EURODOLLAR (LIFFE)—$1 million; pts of 100%

	Open	High	Low	Settle	Change	Lifetime High	Lifetime Low	Open Interest
Sept	91.50	91.65	91.48	91.52	+ .13	91.85	88.72	31,614
Dec	91.88	92.11	91.84	91.92	+ .20	92.26	88.93	12,432
Mr90	92.07	92.27	92.05	92.12	+ .22	92.34	88.88	3,947
June	91.98	92.15	91.96	92.05	+ .25	92.31	89.31	1,716
Sept	91.79	91.81	91.79	91.88	+ .25	92.11	89.89	638
Dec	91.55	91.55	91.55	91.64	+ .24	91.88	90.02	317
Mr91	91.49	91.49	91.49	91.56	+ .19	91.81	91.56	119

Est vol 10,027; vol Thurs 6,799; open int 50,801. –160.

–OTHER INTEREST RATE FUTURES–

Settlement prices of selected contracts. Volume and open intrest of all contract months.

30–Day Interest Rate (CBT) $5 million; pts. of 100%
Sep 91.20 –.07; Est. vol. 250; Open Int. 1,846
Mortgaged-Backed (CBT) $100,000, pts. & 32nds of 100%
Sep Cpn 9.0 99-24 –1; Est. vol. 150; Open Int. 1,466

CBT—Chicago Board of Trade. FINEX—Financial Instrument Exchange, a division of the New York Cotton Exchange. IMM—International Monetary Market at Chicago Mercantile Exchange. LIFFE—London International Financial Futures Exchange. MCE—MidAmerica Commodity Exchange.

FUTURES OPTIONS

T-BONDS (CBT) $100,000; points and 64ths of 100%

Strike Price	Calls—Last Sep-c	Calls—Last Dec-c	Calls—Last Mar-c	Puts—Last Sep-p	Puts—Last Dec-p	Puts—Last Mar-p
94	3-08	3-50	4-08	0-04	0-52	1-34
96	1-21	2-27	2-62	0-17	1-29	2-15
98	0-16	1-28	2-00	1-10	2-27	3-15
100	0-03	0-49	1-16	3-00	3-44	4-28
102	0-01	0-25	0-55	4-60	5-17	5-60
104	0-01	0-14	0-36	6-60	7-06	....

Est. vol. 220,000, Thur vol. 72,680 calls, 57,146 puts
Open interest Thur; 396,454 calls, 393,694 puts

T-NOTES (CBT) $100,000; points and 64ths of 100%

Strike Price	Calls—Last Sep-c	Calls—Last Dec-c	Calls—Last Mar-c	Puts—Last Sep-p	Puts—Last Dec-p	Puts—Last Mar-p
97	2-11	2-54	....	0-03	0-43	....
98	1-16	2-09	....	0-09	0-63	1-34
99	0-35	1-35	....	0-29	1-22	....
100	0-10	1-04	....	1-02	1-54	....
101	0-04	0-48	....	1-59	2-30	....
102	0-02	0-29	0-60	2-58	....	....

Est. vol. 10,000, Thur vol. 4,714 calls, 4,813 puts
Open interest Thur; 47,932 calls, 42,055 puts

MUNICIPAL BOND INDEX (CBT) $100,000; pts. & 64ths of 100%

Strike Price	Calls—Settle Sep-c	Calls—Settle Dec-c	Calls—Settle Mar-c	Puts—Settle Sep-p	Puts—Settle Dec-p	Puts—Settle Mar-p
90	....	....	....	0-05	....	....
92	1-36	2-05	....	0-17	1-06	....
94	0-25	1-01	....	1-06	1-63	....
96	0-05	0-36	....	2-47	3-29	....
98	0-01	0-10	....	....	5-02	....
100	....	....	....	....	....	....

Est. vol. 203, Thur vol. 41 calls, 132 puts
Open interest Thur; 6,123 calls, 6,814 puts

EURODOLLAR (IMM) $ million; pts. of 100%

Strike Price	Calls—Settle Sep-c	Calls—Settle Dec-c	Calls—Settle Mar-c	Puts—Settle Sep-p	Puts—Settle Dec-p	Puts—Settle Mar-p
9075	0.60	0.92	1.16	0.03	0.11	0.15
9100	0.38	0.74	0.96	0.06	0.17	0.20
9125	0.19	0.57	0.79	0.12	0.24	0.26
9150	0.09	0.42	0.63	0.27	0.33	0.34
9175	0.04	0.29	0.48	0.47	0.45	0.44
9200	0.02	0.19	0.36	0.70	0.59	0.56

Est. vol. 44,569, Thur vol. 8,025 calls, 13,826 puts
Open interest Thur; 175,426 calls, 202,098 puts

EURODOLLAR (LIFFE) $1 million; pts. of 100%

Strike Price	Calls—Settle Sep-c	Calls—Settle Dec-c	Calls—Settle Mar-c	Puts—Settle Sep-p	Puts—Settle Dec-p	Puts—Settle Mar-p
9100	0.55	1.00	1.23	0.03	0.08	0.11
9125	0.32	0.80	1.03	0.05	0.13	0.16
9150	0.15	0.60	0.84	0.13	0.18	0.22
9175	0.05	0.43	0.67	0.28	0.26	0.30
9200	0.03	0.30	0.52	0.51	0.38	0.40
9225	0.02	0.20	0.38	0.75	0.53	0.51

Est. Vol. Fri , 150 Calls, 120 Puts.
Open Interest Thurs 6,263, Calls, 6,547 Puts.

–OTHER INTEREST RATE OPTION–

Final or settlement prices of selected contract. Volume and open interest are totals in all contract months.

Mortgage-Backed (CBT) $100,000; pts. and 64ths of 100%

	Aug-c	Sep-c	Oct-c	Aug-p	Sep-p	Oct-p
Cpn	9.5	9.0	9.0	9.5	9.0	9.0
99	0-42	0-12	....	0-01	....	....

Est. vol. 90. Thur vol. 95. Op. Int. 4,041.

Treasury Bills (IMM) $1 million; pts. of 100%

Strike	Sep-c	Dec-c	Mar-c	Sep-p	Dec-p	Mar-p
9225	0.12	0.62	....	0.05	0.15	....

Est. vol. 14. Thur vol. 11. Op. Int. 1,627.

CBT—Chicago Board of Trade. CME—Chicago Mercantile Exchange. FINEX—Financial Instrument Exchange, a division of the New York Cotton Exchange. IMM—International Monetary Market at Chicago Mercantile Exchange. LIFFE—London International Financial Futures Exchange.

Source: *The Wall Street Journal*, August 14, 1989.

THE RISE OF OPTIONS TO PROMINENCE

Options are hardly a new instrument. Put and calls on equities were long traded on the alleys of Pine Street to which the New York Stock Exchange crowd relegated such trading. Also, callable bonds have a long history; and that ubiquitous instrument, the home mortgage, has traditionally incorporated a right to prepay without penalty.

Nonetheless, options gained wide attention and usage and also became the subject of relentless analysis only after several developments brought them to the fore. One was the creation in 1973 of the *Chicago Board Options Exchange (CBOE)* to trade listed options on equities.

A simultaneous development that pushed options to the fore was the derivation and publication by Messrs. Black and Scholes of a model for pricing European calls on non–dividend-paying equities. This model allowed for the consistent valuation of options, which in turn facilitated trading of options. Second, the notion that options had calculable values, and more important, that traders could profit by using such values to determine which options were cheap, which expensive, did much to add to the allure of trading options. Third, the techniques used to derive the model were so complex as to suggest that someone who had sufficient background in math and in probability theory to follow the derivation of the model and to adapt it to yet other types of options and circumstances might—as they say on the Street—"gain an edge" and thereby make a bundle. This proved a great motivator for quants to push forward the complex analysis of options pricing.

A final factor that did much to increase awareness of and interest in options was the rising volatility of interest rates after 1979. In particular, participants in the markets for mortgages and for mortgage-backed securities suddenly became aware, sometimes to their great pain, that the no-penalty, prepayment clause in a home mortgage was an imbedded option, one that consumers in refinancing high-rate mortgages were not in the least loath to exercise. Also, when rates turned volatile, financial institutions learned, often at great cost, that financing long-term, fixed-rate assets with short-term, floating-rate funds was a high-risk proposition. Consequently, in the volatile-rate environment that prevailed from the late 1970s on, options on fixed-income instruments would probably have been widely traded even had there been no Black-Scholes model. After all, pre–Black-Scholes, options were traded for years even though, at the time, there was no model that gave even the foggiest notion of how options should be valued.

Today, in the fixed-income world, options are ubiquitous and no longer go half noticed. Exchanges have created listed options on Treasuries and listed options on financial futures. Also, the Street's dealers—bank and nonbank—produce, price, and sell to entities ranging from highly leveraged LBOs to staid regional banks a wide range of *over-the-counter (OTC) options,* custom-tailored to meet each client's specific needs.

Dividing the Turf

The old OTC market in puts and calls had, like OTC forward markets, several disadvantages. First, every trade struck was necessarily a contract between a single buyer and a single seller, and as such, it exposed both sides to credit risk—the risk that the other side would fail to fulfill its obligation under the contract. Also, like forward contracts, OTC puts and calls were heterogeneous, and, consequently, were difficult to trade and illiquid.

To overcome these difficulties, the CBOE proposed and was permitted by the SEC to establish a market in *listed* stock options. In this market, the heterogeneity of options was substantially reduced because only a limited number of options were listed. Also, a new institution, the *Options Clearing Corporation (OCC),* was created to interpose itself between buyers and sellers of options; the OCC, functioning much like a clearing corporation on a futures exchange, assumes the other side of every buy and sell on the exchange and, by doing so, gives its guarantee to the trade.

These two innovations, limiting the number of options traded on a stock and creating the OCC, made it possible for greater liquidity to develop in the new standardized options and thereby set the stage for explosive growth in the trading of stock options. The example of the CBOE was imitated by the American Stock Exchange (AMEX) and by various regional exchanges, which were also permitted by the SEC to list and trade stock options.

Until the early 1980s, neither options on commodities nor on exempt, fixed-income securities were listed and traded on U.S. exchanges. Commodity options had gotten a bad name in the U.S. because London and other commodity options were peddled by bucket shops to U.S. investors, many of whom lost a lot of money due to the improper practices these shops employed; the latter included charging inflated prices, failing to execute buy and sell orders, and manipulating markets. In 1978, Congress reacted to these abuses by outlawing for a time the sale of commodity options in the U.S. Not until the fall of 1982 did the CFTC partially remove this ban by introducing a pilot program under which it authorized commodity exchanges to trade options on a limited number of commodities beginning with gold and sugar.

The arrival of options on exempt, fixed-income securities was stalled by a jurisdictional dispute between the SEC and the CFTC. Futures exchanges—always on the lookout for a promising new contract—eyed their success with futures contracts on GNMAs, T bills, and T bonds, and the CBOE's success with listed stock options, and proposed that they be permitted to trade options both on the securities underlying their futures contracts and on the futures contracts themselves.[2] The CBT, home of the T-bond and GNMA futures contracts, was particularly eager to snare for itself the right to trade options on T bonds and GNMAs. It faced competition, however; both the AMEX and the CBOE also wanted to trade options on these securities.

The upshot was that the CBT applied to the CFTC for permission to trade options on GNMAs and Treasuries, while the AMEX and the CBOE applied to the SEC for the same permission. These competing applications raised the question of which

---

[2]Later, the once successful GNMA futures contract died out (though efforts to revive it in a new form continue); trading in options on GNMAs never took off.

commission was to regulate these new options—whose OK would count. As noted, the CFTC and the SEC, having sparred over turf for years, finally reached, in the fall of 1981, the accord outlined in Table 15–2. This accord gave the SEC jurisdiction over options on governments and other exempt securities, including agencies, while reserving for the CFTC jurisdiction over options on futures contracts for securities, commodities, and foreign exchange.

In September 1982, Congress finally ratified the SEC's jurisdiction over options on governments and agencies. During the intervening year, the CBT fought, through repeated court actions, the authorizing by the SEC of options exchanges to commence trading options on governments and GNMAs. Thus, it was not until October 1983 that, with the blessings of the SEC and the courts, the AMEX began to trade options on T notes and T bills and the CBOE options on T bonds. While unsuccessful in its attempt to gain the right to trade options on Treasuries and GNMAs, the CBT did, in October 1982, initiate with CFTC approval trading in options on its T-bond futures contract.

Under the terms of the SEC–CFTC accord, the futures exchanges appeared to be the losers; ironically, however, it was they who, over time, were the winners. Securities exchanges got the right to trade options on exempt securities, which turned out to have next to no appeal to investors and traders. Futures exchanges, in contrast, got the right to trade options on futures contracts, which turned out to be extremely popular with traders and investors (contrast the relevant figures on open interest and trading volume in Table 17–1).

Classes of Options

In a market for listed options, it's common to trade a *class* of options on a single *underlier,* which may, *inter alia,* be an *actual* (actual security or commodity) or a *future* (futures contract); this class consists of options on the underlier that expire on different quarterly dates and that have different strike prices. The more interest investors have in options on a particular underlier, the wider the class of options on it that can be traded without impairing liquidity in the option.

When options on an underlier are traded at different strike prices, the width of the bands set between these prices will depend partly on the volatility of the price of the underlier: the more volatile its price, the wider the bands that the exchange will set. Also, if the price of the underlier moves sharply, the exchange will normally respond by introducing new options on the underlier, ones having strike prices that bracket the underlier's current market price.

The classes of *listed* options on futures for interest-rate instruments are all equally broad; however, among these classes, in only two are all or almost all options within the class actually traded; these are options on the popular T-bond and Eurodollar futures contracts (Table 17–1). There is, however, also a lot of activity in listed options on T-note futures and in listed options on foreign exchange, cash and futures; the latter are not shown in Table 17–1. This table also gives no hint of the deep and liquid markets that exist in OTC options on fixed-income instruments.

VALUE OF AN OPTION

The price, *premium* in options jargon, at which a put or call trades consists of two parts: *intrinsic value* (Figure 17–2), which may be positive or zero, and a *time-value premium* (Figure 17–3), which also may be positive or zero.

A *call option* has *positive* intrinsic value if the market price of the underlier *exceeds* the strike price of the option; it has *zero* intrinsic value if the market price of the underlier *equals or is less than* the strike price of the option. A *put option* has *positive* intrinsic value if the market price of the underlier is *less than* the strike price of the option; it has *zero* intrinsic value if the market price of the underlier *equals or exceeds* the strike price of the option.

An option, call or put, is said to be *in the money* if its intrinsic value is *positive*. It is said to be *out of the money* if its intrinsic value is *negative*.

The price at which an option trades will depend on several factors, the most important of which are the price of the under-

FIGURE 17–2
Intrinsic value of a call option

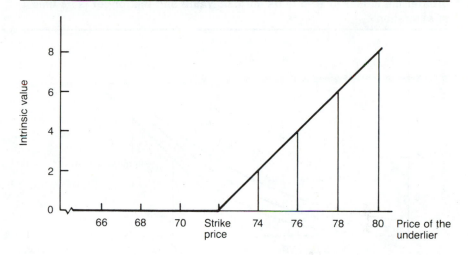

lier, the volatility of that price, the strike price of the option, and the time to expiration of the option.

Every option is a *wasting asset:* its value declines as time passes and it approaches expiration. Thus, an option's time-

FIGURE 17–3
Intrinsic value of a put option

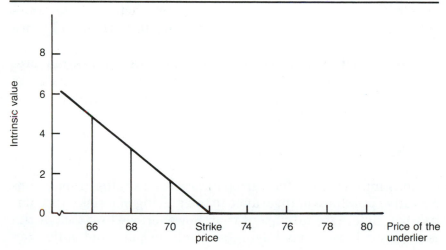

FIGURE 17–4
The time-value premium—price minus intrinsic value—on an option is greater the closer to zero is its intrinsic value and the longer is its time to expiration

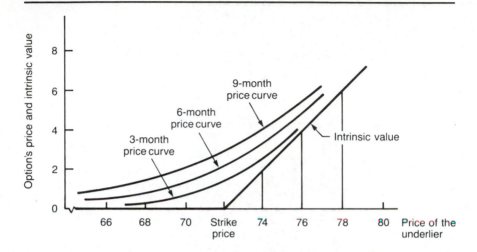

value premium will be greater the farther the option is from expiration. However, an option's time-value premium also depends on the relationship between the price of the underlier and the option's strike price. Normally, an option's time-value premium will, for a given time to maturity, be greatest when the price at which the underlier is trading is at or near the strike price of the option. The impact of these two factors on the time-value premium commanded by an option is illustrated in Figure 17–4.

As an option approaches expiration, its time-value premium is said to *decay*. The rate at which it decays increases as time passes and the option's time to expiration decreases.

BASIC USES OF OPTIONS

Options may be used for various purposes ranging from a conservative purchase of insurance to the placing of a risky speculative bet. Before we talk about that, however, we first look at the profits and losses that buying and selling puts and calls may produce.

Profit from Being, at Expiration, Long or Short a Call or a Put

The least complex option strategy is to simply buy or write (go long or short) an option, and that's where we begin. Suppose that A (an entity who might be an individual, a dealer, a corporation, whoever) buys a call with a strike price of X. For his call, A pays a premium, P_c, so he's immediately out of pocket P_c dollars (Figure 17–5).

A's gain or loss by the time his call expires depends on the price at which the underlier is trading at that time. At expiration, the value of A's call will equal its intrinsic value; and A's profit or loss on the call will equal the intrinsic value of the call *minus* the premium, P_c, he paid for it. From this it follows, that, if—at expiration—the underlier of A's option is selling at a price, $X + P_c$, A will just break even: his call will have an intrinsic value precisely equal to P_c, the premium he paid for it. Should the price of the underlier exceed, at expiration, the break-even price, $X + P_c$, A will have a gain on his call; and that

FIGURE 17–5
Profit (loss) curves at expiration of a *call*

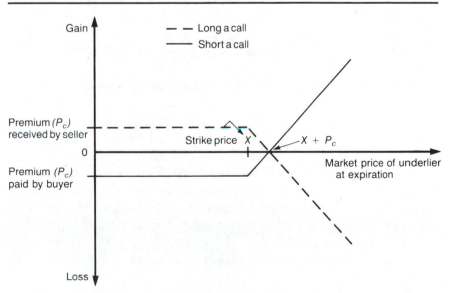

gain will *fully reflect* any further increase that has occurred in the price of the underlier beyond the level $X + P_c$.

Alternatively, the price of the underlier might at expiration lie *below $X + P_c$*, but *above X*. In that case, A recoups some, but not all, of the premium, P_c, he paid for his call. Finally, at expiration, the price of the underlier might be below the strike price, X. In that case, A's call expires worthless; and A loses the full amount, P_c, he paid for his call.

All this is shown by the *hockey-stick* profit profile for being long a call that's pictured in Figure 17–5. Together, Figures 17–5 and 17–6 show the profit profiles for the four simplest option strategies: being long or short a call or a put. Each profit profile has a hockey-stick shape, but the risk implications of these similarly shaped profiles differ sharply.

A *buyer* of a *call* cannot lose more than the premium he pays, and if the price of the underlier *rises* above the strike price by more than the amount of that premium, he will participate *fully and to his profit* in any further *rise* in the price of the underlier. Similarly, a *buyer* of a *put* cannot lose more than the premium he pays, and if the price of the underlier *falls* below the strike price by more than the amount of that premium, he will participate *fully and to his profit* in any further *fall* in the price of the underlier.

Life is *riskier* for the *writer* of either a put or a call (see again Figures 17–5 and 17–6). The *most* the writer of a call or a put can gain is the *premium* for which he writes his option. If he has written a call and the price of the underlier starts to rise, there's no limit on the loss he might experience if he holds his position to expiration (that's so because there's no limit on how high the price of the underlier might go by expiration). To illustrate, suppose that A writes at a strike price of 55 a call on Fly-Me Airways stock, which is currently trading at 50. Then, alas for A, Ride-Us Airways, backed by some LBO big hitters, makes an offer of 100 a share for Fly-Me. With Fly-Me now *in play*, its stock will soar; and A, who's sold a call at 50, will be out a bundle of money whether he covers (buys back) his short call right after the Ride-Us bid is announced or he hangs in until the call he's short expires.

The writer of a put similarly risks a substantial loss (Figure

FIGURE 17–6
Profit (loss) curves at expiration of a *put*

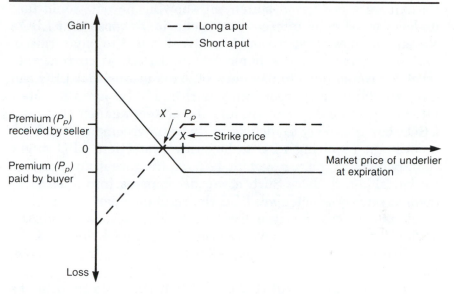

17–6). The most he can gain is the premium, P_p, at which he writes his put. However, should the price of the underlier fall below $X - P_p$, the only limit on the amount he might lose is the bound imposed by the fact that the price of the underlier cannot fall below zero.

Buying Puts as Insurance

Given the conditional or *contingent* nature of an option, it's easy to see how an entity might buy an option as a form of *insurance*. One example would be an investor who has carefully assembled a portfolio of bonds that meets his needs—good credits, good diversification, and so on. He fears a dip in the market, but he doesn't want to sell his bonds and have to recreate his portfolio. In this case, he might find it attractive to insure his portfolio by buying some puts on T bonds or on T-bond futures. Either way, he'd have basis risk; also, as with any insurance policy, he'd lose his premium if the insurance were not used, that is, if rates stayed flat or fell.

A classic example of a borrower who's likely to buy options as insurance is an LBO. It's standard for an LBO to prepare for its lenders a *pro forma* statement showing how it would fare under a worst-case, interest-rate scenario. Suppose that LBO's statement shows that it would be OK if it had to pay a rate of 12.5 on its variable-rate bank debt and that, at current rate levels, it would have to pay only 11. This means that LBO can live, according to its reckoning, with a 150-bp jump in rates; after that, it would be in trouble. To protect against this risk, LBO's bank is likely to include in its loan agreement with LBO a covenant requiring LBO to buy rate protection. LBO might comply by buying a *cap,* say, at 12.5, on the rate it must pay on its variable-rate debt. Such a cap decomposes into a *series of options,* each of which gives LBO the right on a particular (rate) reset date to opt to pay a fixed rate of 12.5 rather than the variable, formula rate it would otherwise pay. Obviously, LBO will exercise its option to pay 12.5 fixed only if the variable, formula rate it's paying is reset above 12.5.

To obtain an overall risk profile that they and their banks can live with, many LBOs will do some interest-rate swaps (floating to fixed) and cover the rest of their variable-rate exposure by buying interest-rate caps. In recent years, LBOs have been a significant portion of the cap market on the corporate side.

Buying a Call as a Leveraged Investment

A second way an investor can use a long call position is to establish a highly leveraged position in the underlier. An advantage of this approach is that the investor gets almost all of the upside potential that he'd have if he owned the bond—almost all because he pays a call premium—but his downside risk is limited to losing the call premium. To illustrate, suppose that, for a 2-point premium, an investor can buy a 3-month call with a strike price of 100 on a bond that's currently trading at 100. Further, suppose that three months hence, at expiration of the call, this bond is trading at 110. An investor who bought the bond for cash would have earned over three months a 10% return, that is, 10/100, whereas an investor who leveraged by buying a call would have earned over the same three months a 400% return, that is, $(10 - 2)/2$.[3]

There is of course a flip side to this story. If, over the life of the option, the price of the bond had gone not from 100 to 110, but rather from 100 to 90, the cash investor would have lost 10% on his investment, while the buyer of the option would have lost 100% of the premium he paid for his option.

Availability of Alternative Strategies

At this point, the alert reader may have noted that a fixed-income-market player contemplating the use of financial options often has a range of strategies he might employ. For example, if an institutional investor wants to lock in a rate at which he can invest funds due in the future, he can buy call options, buy futures, or buy cash bonds forward (the last is equivalent to buying cash bonds and repoing them). Similarly, if an investor or trader wants to hedge bonds, he can buy a put or sell futures.

Typically, no one strategy dominates. Which a person chooses to use will depend on various factors: What are his parameters, for example, can he do futures? How do the profit profiles of alternative strategies compare? Does he want the basis risk and the risk of margin calls that come with using futures? How do the different markets in which he might operate compare in terms of liquidity and transaction costs? If he has to report to management, what's easier to explain: buying a put or selling futures?

Actually, it's rare for a manager of an institutional bond portfolio to buy puts as insurance against a feared market decline. Most times, such a manager views the purchase of a put as an automatic loss to the portfolio. Thus, if he fears a market downturn, he'd rather shorten the duration of his portfolio or sell futures. If he sells futures and the market doesn't go down, he isn't out anything, except maybe the time value of the money he's put up as margin, about which he tends not to worry. In

---

[3]At expiration, the value of a call with a strike price of 100 on a bond that is selling at 110 must be 10. If it were less, risk-free arbitrage would drive up its price.

contrast, if he buys a put for 2 points and the market doesn't fall, he's out 2 points, about which he does worry.

Writing a Call

As noted, writing a *naked* call (i.e., without owning the under-lier) can expose the writer to great risk. In contrast, a "conserva-tive" strategy investors sometimes use "to enhance the yield" on assets they own is to *write covered calls,* that is, sell calls against assets they own. The idea is that the investor will earn the yield that the asset pays plus a succession of call premiums.

Normally, a professional who writes covered calls writes them right above the market. If his bonds trade up and get called, such a writer figures, "I can buy the bonds again, so it will be as if I hadn't written the call." Also, the writer has the time-value of the option for some period, and that is worth some-thing whether his bonds are called or not. Professionals are very good at doing covered writes and not losing money at it.

Writing a Put

As noted, writing a *naked* put (i.e., without being short the underlier) is risky, but someone who is confident that the price of the underlier is going only one way, up, may regard doing so as a good bet. For example, an investor in the last stages of a bear market in bonds might reason: "The Fed must ease—look at the economic numbers, the thrifts in crisis, and so on. I will write naked puts on T bonds."

Many options strategies call for taking several or more op-tions positions simultaneously: strangles, straddles, and so on. We'll mention these later, but first, we turn to the pricing of options.

VALUING AN OPTION

The question of what constitutes a fair value for an option is one that's bound to interest some players in options more than others. An LBO shopping for interest-rate protection may well shop around to get a cap at the cheapest price available, but it's unlikely to delve into the mysteries of options pricing any more than an individual buying life insurance is likely to study actuarial calculations.

On the other hand, a trader, arbitrageur, and especially a firm writing OTC options needs a handle on what constitutes a fair market value for an option. He's also going to want to know on what factors that value depends and how that value will change as those factors change. All of which brings us to the Black-Scholes model for pricing options.

Probability Distributions

To develop their model, Messrs. Black and Scholes first made some assumptions that might be viewed as amazing by many people but are in fact common in economics and finance. Then they applied some high-powered math to derive their path-breaking result. (Later researchers showed that the Black-Scholes result could be derived using simpler math.) We can't go through the Black-Scholes derivation here, but we can sketch some of the background for it.

An option is a contingent claim, for example, the right to pay 12.5 fixed if LIBOR + an agreed spread exceeds that level. Thus, to determine what a particular option is worth, one must first ask: How likely is the occurrence of a certain event or events?

The field of mathematics that deals with likelihoods is known as probability theory. Here's a simple example. We have a *fair* coin, which we define to be a coin that, when flipped, will come up heads half the time (i.e., with a probability of $\frac{1}{2}$) and tails half the time (i.e., with a probability of $\frac{1}{2}$). We flip the coin three times—do three *trials*. The probability that we get heads, H, on the first trial is $\frac{1}{2}$. If our coin is fair, the probability that we get heads on the second flip is the *same* as it was on the first flip, $\frac{1}{2}$; so the probability of our getting HH is $(\frac{1}{2})(\frac{1}{2}) = \frac{1}{4}$. Consider level 2 of the *probability tree* in Figure 17–7. Four outcomes are possible—HH, HT, TH, TT—and the probability of each occurring is $\frac{1}{4}$.

FIGURE 17–7
A probability tree illustrating possible outcomes of flipping a fair coin
three times. On each flip, the possible outcomes are heads, H,
and tails, T*

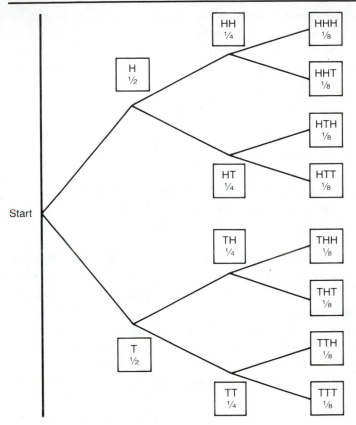

*The boxes at each branching of the tree show the outcome, for example, HH, and below it the probability of that outcome, ¼ for HH.

In a situation in which differing outcomes are possible, the probabilities across all outcomes must sum to *1*. Put another way, as we do each trial something must occur, so if the probabilities of possible outcomes don't sum to 1, our list of possible outcomes must be incomplete.

Level 3 of the probability tree drawn in Figure 17–7 shows the possible outcomes when a fair coin is flipped three times.

From it, we can deduce that the probabilities of getting, after three *trials* (flips), the outcomes of 0, 1, 2, and 3 heads are those given in Table 17–2.

Table 17–2 shows a simple probability density function. We could create a wider range of possible outcomes by doing more trials. If we did so, we'd be extending an example of what's known as the *binomial distribution*.

The number of trials undertaken is a parameter of the binomial distribution. By letting this number approach infinity and simultaneously permitting the range of possible outcomes to become *continuous,* as opposed to *discrete,* one can obtain the familiar, bell-shaped *normal distribution*. In studies of natural phenomena—such as people's heights, weights, and IQ—researchers often assume that the variable under study is normally distributed.

Imagine, for a moment, that we were to collect data on the heights of a large sample of adult women in the general population and then to plot what's called a *density function:* number of observations for each height observed. Our density function would be a bar chart that might show, for example, that we'd observed 10,321 women who were 5′ 5½″, 11,000 who were 5′ 5″, and so on. If we then drew a smooth curve through the tops of all of the bars in our chart, we'd get a curve that resembled the *normal distribution* (Figure 17–8 shows a normal distribution with mean 5′ 4″). Next, imagine that we were to repeat this

TABLE 17–2

Probability density function of the number of heads obtained when a fair coin is flipped three times

Possible Outcomes: Number of Heads Obtained	Probability of Each Outcome
3	⅛
2	⅜
1	⅜
0	⅛
$\left(\begin{array}{c} \text{Sum of the} \\ \text{probabilities of} \\ \text{possible outcomes} \end{array} \right) = 1$	

FIGURE 17–8
Probability density function of the height of adult women in general; the mean is 5′4″

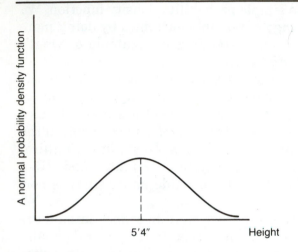

procedure, but this time we measured the heights of high-fashion models only; the latter are picked partly on the basis of height, since clothes are thought to look better on tall women. A curve drawn though the tops of the bars comprising our new

FIGURE 17–9
Probability density function of the height of high-fashion models; the mean is 5′9″

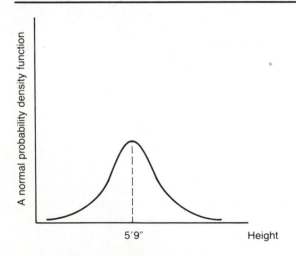

density function would again have the bell shape of a normal distribution, but its shape would differ from the first one we drew in *two* respects: (1) the mean of our new density function would be higher, say, 5′ 9″ instead of 5′ 4″; and (2) the bell would be more pointed, less squat—there's less *variability* in height among fashion models than among women in general (Figure 17–9).

This observation suggests something important. A key parameter of random variable is its *variance*. Are the outcomes near the mean or more disperse? Figures 17–8 and 17–9 both show normal distributions, but the variance of the second random variable is smaller than that of the first. All of the attention focused on volatility by traders of options results from the fact that a key number in the valuation of a specific option is the variance of the price of the underlier.

Assumption that the Price of the Underlier Is Lognormally Distributed

One of the key ingredients that goes into the mathematical mix master that produces the Black-Scholes option-pricing model is the following assumption: the price changes of the underlying asset are distributed according to the *lognormal distribution*. Figure 17–10 pictures a lognormal distribution.

Put-Call Parity

The next ingredient that Black-Scholes threw into their mathematical mix master was a no-arbitrage condition. A *no-arbitrage condition* simply says that the relationship between two or more prices must be thus and so because if it weren't there'd be opportunity for profitable, risk-free arbitrage that would push prices into the configuration dictated by the no-arbitrage condition. Elsewhere, we've encountered no-arbitrage conditions, even if we haven't called them that. Specifically, calculation of the implied forward prices that we talked about in Chapter 16 was based on a no-arbitrage condition; so too was our conclusion that a deliverable bond could not trade at a negative value basis to the bond futures contract.

FIGURE 17–10
A lognormal probability density function

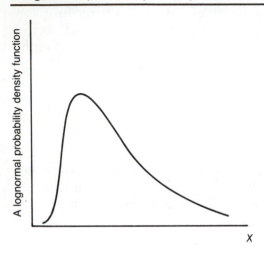

Put-call parity is the no-arbitrage condition Black and Scholes used; it applies in options-land to *European options* (options that can be exercised at expiration only). To derive put-call parity, we consider two alternative investment strategies. Strategy I calls for the investor to buy a call and write a put on an underlier; the put and the call are both written at the same strike price, X, and both expire on the same date. Observing parts I to III of Figure 17–11, we note that the profit profile of strategy I, which requires an investment equal to the call premium paid *minus* the put premium received ($P_c - P_p$), has a profit profile *identical* to the profit profile that would be produced by shorting the underlier at price X and having it trade, at expiration of the put and the call, at a price equal to B.

Consider now a second strategy: buy the underlier on a leveraged basis, where the amount borrowed equals the discounted value of the strike price and the rate of discount equals a short-term, risk-free rate, that is, borrow on a discount basis an amount such that the sum to be repaid at expiration of the option equals the strike price, X. Strategy II requires an investment equal to the current price of the underlier, B, minus the discounted value of the strike price, X.

FIGURE 17–11
The put-call parity theorem—the profit profile of strategy I: buy a call and write a put on an underlier, both with strike price, X, and both expiring on the same date

I. Profit profile of buying a call at P_c

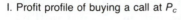

II. Profit profile of writing a put at P_p

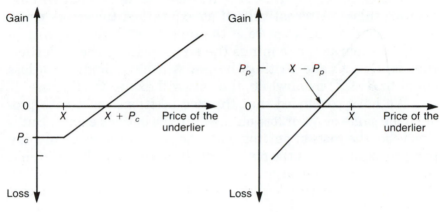

III. Overall profit profile of strategy one, where B equals the price of the underlier at expiration of the put and the call

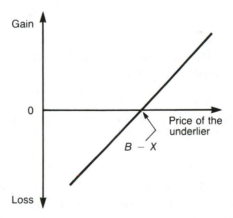

Now, an interesting observation. If strategies I and II are both unwound on the date the options expire (not before), each produces the same profit or loss, namely $B - X$; this amount, which may be positive (a profit) or negative (a loss), equals the market price of the underlier on the date the options expire minus the strike price. That this is so for strategy II is obvious. That it is also true for strategy I follows from what happens to the intrinsic values of the put and the call at expiration. If at expiration, the market price of the underlier, B, exceeds the strike price, X, the call will be worth the market price of the underlier minus X, that is, $B - X$; meanwhile, the put will expire worthless. Alternatively, if at expiration, the strike price, X, exceeds the market price of the underlier, B, the put will be worth the market price minus the strike price of the underlier, that is, $B - X$; and writing the put will have produced a loss equal to $B - X$; meanwhile, the call will expire worthless.

We have concluded that the two positions must both produce the same profit or loss on the date the options expire. But if this is so, the costs of putting on these two positions on any day prior to expiration of the options must be equal; if they weren't, there'd be a risk-free arbitrage: money could be made by buying the position that cost less and shorting the position that cost more.

This equivalence of investments and outcomes is called the *put-call parity theorem*. Using symbols, we can state the theorem as follows:
Let

P_c = the value of a call at a strike price X expiring at T
P_p = the value of a put at a strike price X expiring at T
Xe^{-rt} = the present value of the strike price X at time t[4]
B = the value of the underlier on the expiration date, T

Then, the put-call parity theorem states that, at expiration,

$$P_c - P_p = B - Xe^{-rt}$$

The put-call parity theorem leads to two interesting observations. First, put-call parity basically says that two two-part positions will have the same profit-loss result. By manipulating

---

[4]Here, because of the Black-Scholes assumption of continuous time, the discount factor used is e^{-rt}. Otherwise, the notion of present value is the same as the one we used in Chapter 5 and later chapters.

algebraically the four elements comprising these two positions, one can restate put-call parity to show various other equivalencies between pairs of positions established using these four elements. For example, one can show that a long call position is equivalent to a leveraged position in the underlier plus a long put. Similarly, a position comprised of a long call and an investment in a risk-free discount instrument that matures at expiration of the option position is equivalent to a position comprised of being long the underlier and long a put.

Put-call parity also leads to another interesting observation: the prices of puts, calls, the underlier, and the risk-free lending rate must always have a relationship to each other such that the put-call parity theorem holds.[5]

The Black-Scholes Model: Home Stretch

Economic theory cannot put an absolute price on a commodity or asset; it can only determine relative prices—for example, the price of a commodity relative to the price of labor. What Black and Scholes sought to do was create a model for *valuing* an option relative to the price of its underlier. Such a model is not necessary for options to be traded. The market will *price* options, regardless of whether economic theory has a model to *value* them. Also, a model for valuing options must, to be widely accepted, pass the test of producing values that have some reasonable relationship to market prices.

In constructing their original model, Black and Scholes considered a European option (one that can be exercised only at expiration) on an underlier that paid no return. To construct their model, they made a number of assumptions, including the following: (1) the price of the underlier at expiration is lognormally distributed with standard deviation equal to volatility

---

[5]In our discussion, we assumed implicitly that the underlier pays no interest or dividends. The theorem can be restated to allow, for example, for payments of coupon interest on a bond. Doing so doesn't change the gist of the theorem; it just adds a term.

times the square root of t, time; (2) the risk-free rate of interest is constant over the life of the option; and (3) the markets for both the underlier and an option on it are *frictionless, are competitive, are continuous,* and allow for *short sales.* The latter are *strong* assumptions, but they are typical of the assumptions made in economics and finance; and strong assumptions are the stuff on which theorems that get somewhere are based.[6]

In constructing their original model, Black and Scholes drew on the put-call parity theorem, described above. They also drew on a range of results from economic theory, finance theory, and capital allocation theory, all of which makes it difficult, if not impossible, for someone unfamiliar with these fields to follow their arguments. To further complicate matters, Black and Scholes used some high-powered mathematics to solve the valuation problem they had posed.

In discussing the Black-Scholes model, one needs to distinguish between the model presented in Black and Scholes' seminal paper and the model as it stands today. The wide interest aroused by Black and Scholes' original work stemmed in part from the earlier publication of related work by Merton. Thus, the original model is often referred to as the Black-Scholes-Merton model. After publication of Black-Scholes' paper, other researchers worked on a range of refinements and extensions of the basic model. Thus, what is today called *the Black-Scholes* (*BS* for short) *model* is the work of many people: Black, Scholes, Merton, Cox, Ross, Rubenstein, and others.

A key part of Black-Scholes' original argument was the notion that one could constuct a *hedged* portfolio, comprised of *long* a call and *short* a *fraction* of its underlier, such that (1) the value of the portfolio could be preserved under all conditions and (2) the portfolio itself would therefore yield the risk-free rate of

---

[6]A later-famous student of Schweinger, the reknowned Harvard physicist, paraphrased the typical opening line of a Schweinger lecture as follows. "While 1 is not precisely equal to zero, for the purpose of this argument. . . ." That should ring a bell with and bring a smile to the lips of anyone who has sat through lectures in theoretical economics or finance.

return. Black and Scholes then showed that, under certain assumptions, it was possible to construct such a portfolio; from there, they went on to demonstrate how an option could be valued.

All or most investors are assumed to be *risk averse*. Consequently, they require a *risk premium* to buy a *risky* asset, and an option *is* a risky asset. After publication of the original BS model, one question raised was: Shouldn't investors require some risk premium to buy an option? Put another way, weren't Black and Scholes implicitly assuming that investors were *risk neutral* (indifferent to risk)? If the answer were yes, then more information would be required to value an option.

Cleverly, and relying again on arguments from economic theory, finance theory, and capital allocation theory, Cox and Ross constructed a risk-neutrality argument, which, as used in options valuation, eliminates the need to know, in valuing options, investors' risk preferences. While the Cox-Ross argument considers how risk-averse investors would value the Black-Scholes portfolio in a *risk-neutral* world, in no sense does the risk-neutrality argument state that investors in options are risk neutral; also, although the risk-neutrality argument has imbedded in it an assumption that the value of the underlier increases at the risk-free rate, the argument only says that the underlier and an option on it can be valued as if this assumption were true, not that it is true. The real import of the risk-neutrality argument is that, in valuing an asset, one can act as if all assets increased in value at the risk-free rate, from which follows the importance of assuming, in valuing an option, that the risk-free rate is constant over the life of the option. Basically, the risk-neutrality argument asserts that a crucial assumption made by Black and Scholes is reasonable.

For our purposes, it isn't necessary to write down the precise equation in which the BS model is now stated. Most practitioners rely on a programmed calculator or computer to generate option values, just as bond-market people all use a programmed calculator or computer to generate bond yields and duration numbers. However, for completeness, we state the BS model in an appendix to this chapter.

AN OPTION'S VALUE AS THE PRESENT VALUE OF ITS INTRINSIC VALUE AT EXPIRATION

What is interesting about the options-pricing model is what it says about delta, the hedge ratio, and about how various factors, including the price of the underlier and the passage of time, will affect an option's value. However, before we turn to these topics, it's helpful to look at the value of an option from a second perspective, namely, as the *present value* of its *expected value*. That concept, unlike the math used by Black and Scholes, is within the realm of understanding of most people.

Expected Value

In Chapter 5, we introduced the concept of *present value*. Here, the only new concept we need is that of expected value. If we are speaking about a *discrete* distribution, like the one that describes the likelihood of heads coming up when a fair coin is flipped N times, the concept of expected value is straightforward. Specifically, *expected value, E,* equals the sum of the value of each possible outcome times the probability that that outcome will occur.

   To illustrate, we apply this concept to the probability density function in Table 7–2, which shows the number of heads that three flips of a fair coin might produce and the likelihood of each such outcome. The expected value (E) of heads observed is as follows:

$$E = 3(\frac{1}{8}) + 2(\frac{3}{8}) + 1(\frac{3}{8}) + 0(\frac{1}{8})$$
$$= \frac{12}{8} = 1.5$$

   In our heads-tails example, it's easy to interpret the meaning of expected value. It's the average value one would obtain if one repeated many times the experiment of flipping a fair coin three times and then calculated the average number of heads observed per trial. Clearly, one could never observe heads coming up 1.5 times in any *one* 3-flip trial, but one could observe, after doing, say, a hundred 3-flip trials, that the average number of heads observed per 3-flip trial was 1.5.

An Example: The Impact of Variance on an Option's Value

In this example, we calculate the expected value of an option under two sets of assumptions. Our objective is to show that the value of an option will be greater, the greater the variance is of the probability distribution of the value of the underlier at expiration.

The June Eurodollar futures contract has just expired, and we want to value a position in a put option on the Eurodollar contract that expires the following December. We ring up the 800 number of the omniscient creator to get the probability density function of the possible values at which the contract might expire. An answer, Table 17–3, arrives by fax.

Assume that the strike price is 90.50. If at expiration, the contract were trading at 90.00, which corresponds to a rate of 10.00, our position in the put would be worth:

$$50 \text{ bp} \times \frac{1}{4} \times \$1\text{MM} = \$1,250$$

Alternatively, our position would be worth \$2,500 if the contract were trading at 89.50 at expiration; and it would be worth \$0 if the contract were trading at 90.50, 91.00, or 91.50 at expiration, that is, if our put expired worthless.

TABLE 17–3
Probability density function of possible values for the price of the December Eurodollar futures contract at expiration*

Price of Eurodollar Futures at Expiration	Probability of This Outcome
91.50	0.1
91.00	0.2
90.50	0.4
90.00	0.2
89.50	0.1

*This probability density function is assumed to be centered on the price at which the December Eurodollar futures contract is trading today.

Using the probability density function in Table 17–3, we can calculate the expected value of our position in the put as follows:

$$E = 0.1(\$2,500) + 0.2(\$1,250) + 0.4(\$0) + 0.2(\$0) + 0.1(\$0)$$
$$= \$500$$

The number we have just calculated is the expected value of our position in the put at expiration of the contract, that is, six months hence. The price we must pay for the put is dollars *today*. Clearly, we would be overpaying for the put if we paid today the expected value, six months hence, of our position in the put. A fair market value to pay for the put today would be the *present value* of that sum. Assume that the appropriate rate of discount is 10%. Then the fair value today of our position in the put is calculated as follows:[7]

$$PV(E) = \$500/(1 + 0.1)^{0.5}$$
$$= \$476.73$$

Next, let's suppose that, in response to our ring to ye olde 800 number, we were told that each of the five possible outcomes listed in Table 17–3 was equally likely, that is, that the probability of each occurring was 0.2. As Figure 17–12 shows, this new probability density function, when plotted, is squatter than the plot yielded by the probability density function in Table 17–3. This corresponds to the fact that the variance of the new probability density function exceeds that of the former. If we stick to our assumptions about forward prices and that the strike price is 90.50, then the expected value of our position in the put is, under the new probability density function, as follows:

$$E = 0.2(\$2,500) + 0.2(\$1,250) + 0.2(\$0) + 0.2(\$0) + 0.2(\$0)$$
$$= \$750$$

---

[7]The 0.5 comes into the equation because we are discounting $500 to allow for a 6-month, not a 1-year, waiting period.

FIGURE 17–12
Two probability density functions for the price at expiration of a Eurodollar futures contract

A. Initial probability density function

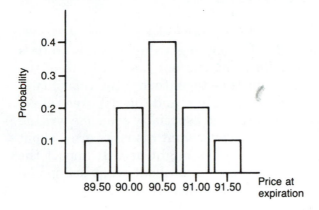

B. Second probability density function with greater variance

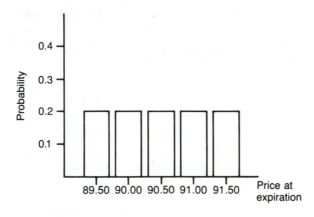

and today's fair market value of our position in the put is:

$$PV(E) = \$750/(1 + 0.1)^{0.5}$$
$$= \$715.10$$

Our example illustrates an important point: *the greater the variance of the probability density function of the price at expira-*

tion of the underlier, the greater, all else constant, will be the value of an option.

THE KEY RISK SENSITIVITIES OF AN OPTION

According to the BS model, the option's value depends on (is a function of) several variables: the current market price of the underlier, the strike price, the time to maturity, the volatility of the price at expiration of the underlier, and the risk-free rate of return. Anyone trading options, and especially someone writing options, needs to be concerned about what his risks are—about how changes in the above variables might or will impact the value of options he's long or short and about what actions he might take to hedge or otherwise reduce his risk.

Delta

The first question an options trader is likely to ask is: "How will the value of my option change if the price of the underlier changes, *all else constant*?"[8] The number he's looking for is *delta* (Δ), which is the slope (rate of change) of the value of the option with respect to the price of the underlier at the current market price of the underlier (Figure 17–13). For calls, delta ranges from 0 to +1, for puts from −1 to 0 (Figures 17–14 and 17–15).

For a call that's at the money, delta is 0.5. It's more for a call that's in the money, less for one that is out of the money. On an

---

[8]When a trader asks how the value of an option will change if the value of just *one* of its *arguments* (variables it's a function of) changes, that's equivalent, in mathematical terms, to asking: What is the value of the *first partial derivative* of the Black-Scholes expression for the option's value? Thus, *delta* is the first partial of the option value with respect to the price of the underlier. *Gamma,* discussed below, is the first partial of delta, with respect to the price of the underlier; that's equivalent to saying that gamma is the second partial, with respect to the price of the underlier, of the Black-Scholes expression for the value of the option.

Other variables discussed below are also first partials. *Theta* is the first partial of the option value with respect to time: *rho* the first partial of the option value with respect to a change in the risk-free rate of return.

FIGURE 17–13
A change in the market price of an underlier, ΔP_u, causes a change, ΔP_c, in the value of a call on that underlier. The call's *"delta"* equals $\Delta P_c/\Delta P_u$. Here delta is approximately 0.5.

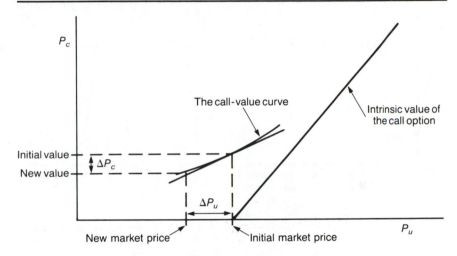

option that is *deep in the money,* delta is very close to (approaches asymptotically) 1; such an option, when it's on a bond, is sometimes described as a *mini bond* because its value changes almost one for one with the price of the underlier. For an option

FIGURE 17–14
Delta and gamma of a call

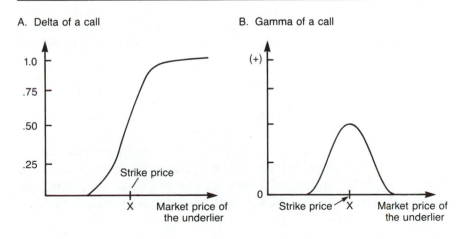

A. Delta of a call

B. Gamma of a call

FIGURE 17–15
Delta and gamma of a put

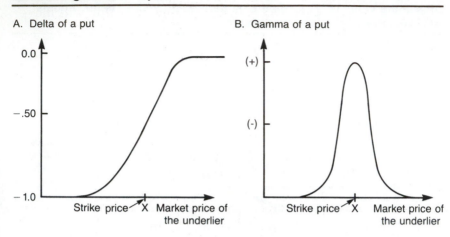

A. Delta of a put

B. Gamma of a put

that is way out of the money, delta approaches zero for obvious reasons.

Recall that earlier, in discussing risk neutrality, we talked about a hedged portfolio, long a call, short a fraction of the underlier. Delta is the fraction of the underlier that a trader who's long a call should be short the underlier to be fully hedged. Such a short is called a *delta hedge,* and traders refer to a hedged position in an option as *delta-neutral.*

The delta of an option is always *nonlinear* with respect to the price of the underlier (recall Figure 17–13). However, the delta of a fractional position in the underlier is always a *constant.* Consequently, delta hedging an option by going short or long a fraction of the underlier will create a portfolio in which gains (losses) on the option are precisely offset by losses (gains) on the position in the underlier only if the change in the price of the underlier is very small.

If a *long* position in puts or in calls is delta-hedged with an appropriate position in the underlier, a perceptible change in the price of the underlier will result in a *profile* on the hedge. Also, since the option delta will change as a result of a change in the price of the underlier, there will be slippage in the hedge; consequently, the delta hedge will have to be rebalanced.

A delta hedge will be almost perfect and will also result in almost no slippage only at an extreme option value. For example, if a long call is *very* deep in the money, its value will move almost *pari passu* with that of the underlier; and the delta hedge ratio, which will be close to short one underlier for each long one call, will result in an almost perfect hedge; also the hedge ratio will be almost insensitive to changes in the price of the underlier. If, alternatively, a long call is way out of the money, a delta hedge will display maximum slippage.

If a *short* position in puts or in calls is delta-hedged with an appropriate position in the underlier, a perceptible change in the price of the underlier will result in a *loss* on the hedge. This is called the *gapping problem* for short options. The only way a real-world trader who was short options could prevent an adverse change in the price of the underlier from inflicting a loss on his position would be to correctly anticipate that price move and put on an appropriate anticipatory hedge. Hedges of short positions in puts and calls also exhibit slippage as the price of the underlier changes.

To say that a trader who has delta-hedged a long position in an option will profit if the price of the underlier moves doesn't mean that he can't lose money on his position. Quite to the contrary, he must worry about the passage of time and about possible decreases in volatility, both of which will diminish the value of his option. Like a successful juggler, a successful options trader must keep his eye not on *the* ball, but on *several*—specifically, on each of the several factors that may cause the value of his option to change.

The problems associated with hedging an option crop up whether the option is on a bond, a future, or a rate. The difference among these options is in the instrument used to hedge the option: *an option on bonds is typically hedged with bonds; an option on futures with futures; a cap or a floor with an appropriate FRA.*

The only perfect hedge for an option is an opposite position in the same option. For example, if a dealer were able to sell one party a cap at rate Z and then to buy a cap from a second party, also at rate Z, he'd be perfectly hedged.

Gamma

Gamma (Γ) is defined as the rate of change of delta with respect to a change in the price of the underlier (Figures 17–14 and 17–15).[9] A trader has to track the gamma of an option because it tells him by how much he must change his delta hedge whenever the price of the underlier changes. Gamma is not a constant but changes both as the price of the underlier changes and as time passes.

Theta

An option is a wasting asset; as it approaches expiration, its time value almost always decays. The rate of change of the value of an option with respect to time remaining to expiration is known as *theta* (Θ).

For any option, the value of theta depends on several factors. One is the market price of the underlier in relationship to the strike price of the option (Figures 17–16 and 17–17: part A).

An option's theta also varies depending on other factors: its time to expiration; whether it's in the money, out of the money, or at the money; and whether it's a put or a call (Figures 17–16 and 17–17: part B). Clearly, a trader of options must keep his eye on theta, since its value, which changes over time in a complex fashion, is one determinant of how his profit (loss) in his options position will change over time.

Theoreticians express theta in terms of a 1-day rate of decay in time value. Often, however, the 1-day rate is so small that traders look at the 7-day rate of time decay. Time decay is not a linear function; instead, it increases rapidly in the final four weeks or so of an option's life. This make sense intuitively. If an option has 100 days to expiration, the passage of one day will decrease its time to expiration by 1%, whereas if an option has 10 days to expiration, the passage of one day will decrease its time to expiration by 10%.

---

[9]Gamma is simply the slope of the curve that plots delta as a function of the market price of the underlier. Gamma achieves its *maximum* value at the price of the underlier at which the delta passes through a point of inflection.

FIGURE 17–16
Theta of a call

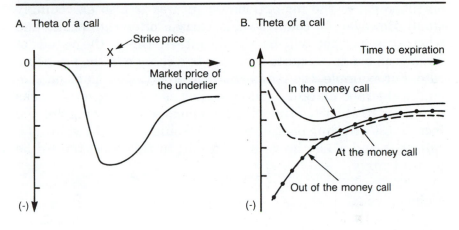

A. Theta of a call

Strike price

X

Market price of the underlier

0

(-)

B. Theta of a call

Time to expiration

0

In the money call

At the money call

Out of the money call

(-)

Rho

Rho (P) measures the rate of change of the value of an option as the risk-free rate of interest changes. How sensitive the value of an option is to the risk-free rate depends on what the underlier is.

FIGURE 17–17
Theta of a put

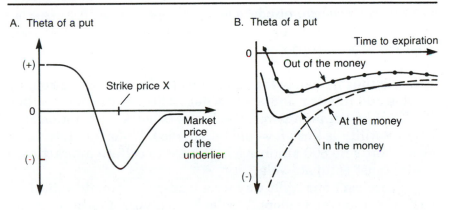

A. Theta of a put

(+)

Strike price X

0

Market price of the underlier

(-)

B. Theta of a put

Time to expiration

0

Out of the money

At the money

In the money

(-)

Option values are sensitive to the carry profit on the underlier from today to expiration. Because carry is exceedingly small on futures, the rho for options on futures is also exceedingly small. However, for coupon bonds, carry is often significant; and when it is, rho too will be significant. At times, the values of options on bonds are quite sensitive to a change in the financing rate. For example, the long bond has, on occasion, gone on special in the repo market, trading as low as 1% for several weeks at a time. If, at such a time, the long bond were yielding 8%, the fact that it's trading on special at 1% would lower the value of a call on it and raise the value of a put; in this case, there'd be positive carry.

Vega

Traders sometimes also speak of *vega*. It's the change in the price of an option due to a change in the *volatility* of the price of the underlier. If a change in volatility from 9 to 8% produces a change in the price of an option on a bond from 1-28 to 1-22, the vega of that option is 6/32. Vega is large for price changes in at-the-money options and for percentage price changes in out-of-the-money options. Also, an option's vega is greater, the longer the time to expiration of the option.

VOLATILITY

The BS model assumes that the volatility (sigma) of the underlier's price is *constant* and *known*.

Historical Volatility

It would thus be handy for an options trader if he could ring up ye olde 800 number and ask: "What's true volatility for option XYZ?" If he got an answer, the Black-Scholes assumption that true volatility is known would be satisfied. Unfortunately, however, there's no 800 number for a trader to call; so in practice, a trader must estimate volatility.

There isn't one right way for a trader to estimate volatility; basically, the way traders do so is by applying a formula for an unbiased estimator to some slice of historical data on the price of the underlier. The number they get is referred to as *historical volatility*.

Implied Volatility

Inevitably, some options trader said, "I know, for option X, the strike price, the price of the underlier, the option's time to expiration, *and* the price at which the option is currently trading. From these, I can calculate *implied volatility,* the value that the volatility of the price of the underlier must have in order that its market price be what it is." There's no doubt that every price of an option implies a specific level of volatility and that that implied volatility can be calculated.

Some traders go further and seem to take the view that volatility is a *variable* as opposed to the *constant* assumed in the model's derivation. To be correct, one needs to distinguish between volatility, a presumed constant related to the variance of the price distribution and implied volatility, a number derived from market price. The BS model *values* options using an assumed value for volatility, while the market *prices* options and thereby generates a derived value for volatility, that is, implied volatility. For example, if one looks at the implied volatilities of options on bond futures at multiple strikes and across multiple dates, what one is seeing is the market's perception of price changes in the underlier over specific periods.

For example, near-term options might be trading at 10% volatility, whereas far options might be trading at 5% volatility. A person might ask, "What is the market telling me here? Does the market think that volatility is declining over time?" The latter is one view, but more likely, the correct view is that the market is saying: "There's a lot of uncertainty about price changes in the near term, which increases the demand for short-term relative to long-term options. There isn't necessarily less uncertainty about price changes over a long period, but the pricing equation has other things to take care of that; for example, there is huge time value in the price of a long-dated option." A trader who is long or short an option that will expire in two weeks has little time value to play with. He likely compensates for his uncertainty by adjusting up the price (the implied volatility) of the option. That doesn't mean that the volatility of the price of the underlier has changed; rather it means that the trader must be compensated for his uncertainty.

An analogy is the bid-offer spread in bonds. If people are uncertain as to where the market is, there may be a 3-tick spread, whereas if people are more certain and the market is calm, the spread may be half a tick. A 3-tick spread in bonds doesn't mean that the market has become chaotic (more volatile); it means that market participants have temporarily become unsure of where things are priced; and when uncertainty increases, traders widen spreads. The same thing happens in options, only there, the way a trader prices his short-term uncertainty is to up the option's price (the premium for insurance). It is one thing to say that the underlying process has become more uncertain (that the underlying volatility and hence the variance has changed), another to say that traders have temporarily become more uncertain.

That is not to say that the variance of the underlying process cannot change. Anyone who says that some real-world variable is distributed according to a particular probability distribution really ought to add *given the current state of the world* (a term of art used by statisticians and others). The state of the world can change, and if it does, so too may the distribution of the price of the underlier. For example, if uncertainty with respect to a firm's future earnings suddenly increases—due to a regulatory change, the death of a founding father, whatever— the state of the world, at least with respect to the probability distribution of the price of that stock, will certainly have changed, and the variance of its distribution will presumably have increased.

Future Volatility

Traders also have a notion of future volatility. If they expect a particular option to trade at a higher volatility in the future, they will want to buy the option or *to buy volatility* as traders are wont to say. Conversely, if they anticipate a fall in implied volatility and therefore in options prices, they will want *to sell volatility*.

In trying to estimate future volatility, traders will, for one thing, look at current implied volatility and ask whether it's high or low relative to where historical volatility has been. They may also look at what economic events are coming up. In particular, implied volatilities on short-dated options tend to be higher just before the announcement of an economic number than right after. This reflects the uncertainty traders associate with the announcement of an economic number and the fact that, in today's markets, which gap trade, the announcement of a number may cause a big market move.

Hedging against a Change in Volatility

The value of an option changes in a curvilinear fashion as its volatility changes. No *linear instrument*—a bond, a future, an interest-rate swap—will display such price changes. Consequently, the only way to hedge a position in options against a change in volatility is with another position in options (Figure 17–18).

OTHER OPTIONS STRATEGIES

If a trader is long a call and long a put at the same strike price, he's said to *long a straddle* (Figure 17–19). Alternatively, if he's long a call above the market and long a put below the market, he's said to be *long a strangle* (Figure 17–20). Either trade creates a wasting asset, but each can be profitable if the market has been quiet for some time, and it seems poised to break out of its trading range. Such a breakout should be accompanied by an increase in implied volatility; if so, increased implied volatility will offset time decay if the market moves either way.

In either trade, the trader doesn't care whether the market moves up or down so long as it moves some distance. For a long straddle to be profitable, the market price of the underlier must move outside a range equal to the strike price plans or minus the premium paid for the straddle. For a long strangle to be profitable, the market price of the underlier must move either below the put price minus the premium paid or above the call strike plus the premium paid.

FIGURE 17–18
The only way to hedge a position in an option against a change in volatility is with an opposite position in the same option

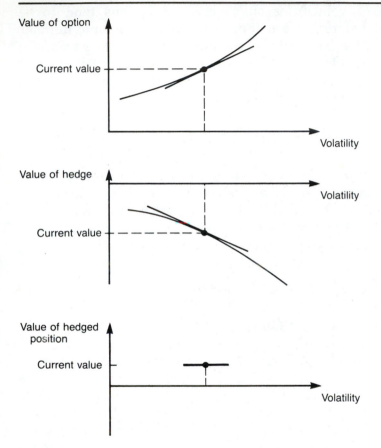

A trader who *shorts* a *strangle* or a *straddle* is betting that the price of the underlier won't have changed much by expiration (Figures 17–19 and 17–20). Both time decay and declining volatility will help these trades, although profit on each is limited to the premium received at sale.

Many guaranteed-investment-contract (GIC) portfolios that are invested in corporate bonds are naturally *short* a strangle: if the market rallies (interest rates decline), the corporate bonds will be called away by the issuer; while if the market declines

FIGURE 17–19
Profit profiles: long and short a straddle

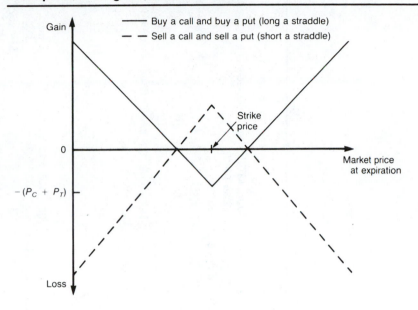

FIGURE 17–20
Profit profiles: long and short a strangle

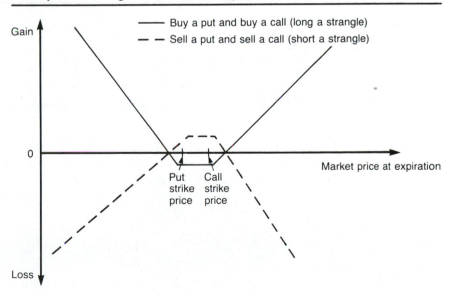

TABLE 17–4

A buy write on bond futures*

A. Step 1: Put on the trade

Buy 100 Sept 89 futures contracts at 97-03.

Value = (100 contracts)(100,000/contract)(97³⁄₃₂ per $100 face)

= $9,709,375 (only *margin* need be paid)†

Sell 100 Sept 89 calls at a strike of 98 at a price of 0-32.

Premium earned = (100 calls)(100,000)(³²⁄₆₄ per $100 face)

= $50,000

B. Possible outcomes

I. If, at expiration of the option, the futures price is 98 or above, the trade profits. Assume futures settle at 98.

Selling price of futures		98-00
Minus Purchase price of futures		97-03
Profit/contract in 32nds		0-29

II. Figure profit in $S:

Gain on futures = (29 ticks)($31.25/tick)(100 contracts)		$ 90,625
Plus Premium earned on sale of put		50,000
Total gain		$140,625

C. Figuring downside break even for futures

  I. The break-even price:

	Purchase price for futures	97-03
Minus	Options premium (in 32nds)	0-16
	Break-even price for futures	96-19

  II. The break-even calculation on dollars:

	Call premium earned = (0-32)/contract)(100 contracts)($15.625)	= $50,000
Minus	Loss on bond futures = (0-16/call)(100 calls)($31.25)	= 50,000
	Net gain	= $ 0

*Note bond futures are quoted in 32nds, bond futures in 64ths.
†In August 1989, initial margin on bond futures was $2,000/contract for a hedge account, $2,500/contract for a spec account.

(rates rise), the customers who have invested in GICs will cash them in (*put* them back to the company running them) and invest their funds elsewhere.

SOME NUMERICAL EXAMPLES OF OPTIONS TRADES

In this section, we work through four short examples of options trades involving bond futures and options on bond futures: a buy write (Table 17–4, pp. 862–63), a bull spread (Table 17–5), long a strangle (Table 17–6), and short a strangle (Table 17–7). These examples are largely self-explanatory. The one thing to

---

TABLE 17–5

A bull spread in options on bond futures

A.   Step 1: Put on the trade*

Buy 100 Sept 89 calls at a strike price of 96 at a price of 1-34.

Sell 100 Sept 89 calls at a strike price of 98 at a price of 0-32.

Net cost of the spread = [(1 + 2⁄64)/$100]($100)($100,000) = $103,125

B.   Possible outcomes

1.   Maximum profit will be if futures close above 98.

2.   Downside break-even equals the lower strike price plus the net cost of the spread, that is,

Downside break-even = (96) + (1-02) = 97-01*

3.   Illustrative outcomes:

| | Futures at Expiration | Corresponding Value of | | Net Proceeds in Dollars |
		96 Call	98 Call	
Prices	96-00	0-00	0-00	
Profit/loss		−$153,125	+$50,000	−$103,125
Prices	97-01	1-02	0-00	
Profit/loss		+$50,000	−$50,000	+$0
Prices	98-16	2-32	0-32	
Profit/loss		+$96,875	+$0	+$96,875
Prices	100-00	4-00	2-00	
Profit/loss		+$246,875	−$150,000	+$96,875

*Note again that bond futures are quoted in 32nds, calls on bond futures in 64ths, which is why (96) + (1-02) = 97-01.

TABLE 17–6
Long a strangle on bond futures

A. Step 1: Put on the trade*

Buy 100 calls at a strike price of 98 at a price of 0-32.

Buy 100 puts at a strike price of 96 at a price of 0-27.

B. Possible outcomes

1. Upside break-even = Upper strike + Premiums = 98+0-59 = 98-29+.
2. Downside break-even = Lower strike − Premiums = 96−0-59 = 95-02+.
3. Maximum loss is limited to total premium paid and will occur if market at expiration is anywhere between lower and upper strike prices.
4. Illustrative outcomes:

	Futures at Expiration	Corresponding Value of		Net Proceeds in Dollars
		96 Put	98 Call	
Prices	94-00	2-00	0-00	
Profit/loss		+$157,812	−$50,000	+$107,812
Prices	95-02	0-60	0-00	
Profit/loss		+$51,562	−$50,000	+$1,562
Prices	97-00	0-00	0-00	
Profit/loss		−$42,188	−$50,000	−$92,188
Prices	100-00	0-00	2-00	
Profit/loss		−$42,188	+$150,000	+$107,812

*Note bond futures are quoted in 32nds, puts and calls on bond futures in 64ths. A quote of 98-29+ means the quote is 98 + $^{29}/_{32}$ + $^1/_{64}$.

look out for is that bonds are quoted in 32nds, whereas options on bond futures are quoted in 64ths.

TRADES USING SYNTHETIC SECURITIES

Options are also used to create what are called *synthetic* instruments. For example, being long a call written on a futures contract and short the futures creases a synthetic long put position. Alternatively, being short a call and long a futures creates a synthetic short put position.

Similarly, by combining puts and calls, a trader can create synthetic futures positions. For example, being short a call written on a futures contract and long a put creates a synthetic short

TABLE 17–7
Short a strangle on bond futures

A. Step 1: Put on the trade*

Sell 100 calls at a strike price of 98 at a price of 0-32.

Sell 100 puts at a strike price of 96 at a price of 0-27.

B. Possible outcomes

1. Upside break-even = Upper strike + Premiums = 98+0-59 = 98-29+.
2. Downside break-even = Lower strike − Premiums = 96−0-59 = 95-02+.
3. Maximum profit occurs if market at expiration is anywhere between the lower and upper strikes and is equal to the premium received.
4. Unlimited loss potential.

C. Illustrative outcomes:

	Futures at Expiration	Corresponding Value of		Net Proceeds in Dollars
		96 Put	98 Call	
Prices	94-00	2-00	0-00	
Profit/loss		−$157,812	+$50,000	−$107,812
Prices	95-02	0-60	0-00	
Profit/loss		−$51,562	+$50,000	−$1,562
Prices	97-00	0-00	0-00	
Profit/loss		+$42,188	+$50,000	+$92,188
Prices	100-00	0-00	2-00	
Profit/loss		+$42,188	−$150,000	−$107,812

*Note bond futures are quoted in 32nds, puts and calls on bond futures in 64ths. A plus sign following a bond quote means "add $1/64$," for example, 98-27+ = 98 + $27/32$ + $1/64$ = 98 + $55/64$.

futures position, whereas being long a call and short a put creates a synthetic long futures position.

Liquidity, transaction costs, and margin requirements vary among markets. Consequently, it sometimes pays a trader to create a synthetic position by using several markets, rather than to create a direct position by using one market only.

SHORTCOMINGS OF THE BLACK-SCHOLES MODEL

The original BS model values a European option on a call written on a stock that pays no dividends, whereas traders of options want to value a range of options, which includes American puts and calls written on dividend-paying stocks, on coupon-bearing bonds, and so on. This has led to considerable tinkering with the BS model. Some adjustments turn out to be easier than others; American puts are particularly tough to value.

The Black-Scholes assumption that the price of the underlier is lognormally distributed is close for stocks, but fundamentally wrong for bonds. Theoretically, the price of a stock could go to infinity over time (a possibility permitted by the lognormal distribution), but the price of a bond is bounded: at maturity, it must, if the bond isn't in default, equal 100. When the underlier is a bond, the appropriate distribution of price is a generalized beta distribution. However, in valuing a short-term (3- to 6-month) option on a long-term bond, it actually doesn't make much difference which distribution is used; where the choice of distribution is crucial is in valuing longer-term options on bonds and in valuing short-term options on bonds nearing maturity (e.g., a 3-month option on a 6-month bond).

Another problem with the BS model is that it doesn't work for deep-in-the-money or deep-out-of-the-money options. At extreme values of delta, the model blows up and fails to give correct hedgeable values.

Also, even on stocks, the BS model doesn't value long-term options well. The reason is that the assumption that stock prices are lognormally distributed isn't really correct, although it works well enough for valuing short-term options on stocks.

People attack the problem of valuing long-term options by using Monte Carlo (by chance, as in gaming) simulations. They don't try to guess whether the distribution of the price of the underlier is lognormal or this or that; instead they impose certain boundary conditions and then generate literally thousands and thousands of possible rate or price outcomes (paths). They then calculate the expected value of the option by assuming that each outcome is equally likely or maybe by doing stratified sampling—by saying it's more likely for rates or prices to be within certain bounds that they place on the end value.

Usually, Monte Carlo simulation is done for a portfolio containing both the underlier and options on it; what people calculate is hedge ratios. They ask: How much of the underlier do I need to hedge this option under all of these different outcomes?

Some people have been quite successful at developing techniques for valuing long-term options. All such techniques require a vast array of calculations; also, all are, for obvious reasons, proprietory products. People may say they've got a good procedure for valuing long-term options, but they aren't going to tell anyone precisely what it is.

THE NEXT CHAPTER

In the next chapter, we turn to the market in which Euro time deposits and a novel and increasingly popular instrument, forward rate agreements (FRAs), are traded. We also talk about the swapping of Eurocurrency deposits and the hedging of foreign-exchange risk, the trick that makes possible covered interest arbitrage.

APPENDIX: STATEMENT OF THE BLACK-SCHOLES MODEL FOR PRICING AN OPTION ON A BOND

The assumptions underlying the derivation and use of the simplest version of the BS model for valuing European type options are:

1. The markets for the option and the underlying asset are frictionless, competitive, and continuous, and they allow short sales.
2. The risk-free rate of interest, r, is constant over the life of the option.
3. The underlying asset pays no dividend or coupon.[10]
4. The price of the asset at expiration is distributed lognormally with mean μt and standard deviation $\sigma \sqrt{t}$.

---

[10]This assumption is easily relaxed, and hence the BS model is routinely used to price dividend-paying stocks and coupon-bearing bonds.

Let

C = the price of a call option

B = the price of the underlying bond

t = current time

T = expiration date

K = the strike price

r = the risk-free rate of return,

σ = standard deviation (volatility)

$\tau = T - t$ (time to expiration of the option)

Then, according to Black-Scholes,

$$C(B, t; T, K, r, \sigma) = BN(h) - Ke^{-r\tau}N(h - \sigma\sqrt{\tau})$$

where

$$h = \log(B/Ke^{-r\tau})/\sigma\sqrt{\tau} + (\sigma\sqrt{\tau})/2$$

and

$N\,(\cdot)$ is the standard normal distribution function

The notation for the value of the call, $C(B, t; T, K, r, \sigma)$, has been amended to show explicitly that the value of the call is a function of two *variables, B* and *t*, whereas *T, K, r*, and volatility, σ, are all *parameters that are fixed for the life of the option.*

SUGGESTED READINGS

Option Volatility and Pricing Strategies by Sheldon Natenberg, published 1988 by Probus Publishing Co., Chicago, Ill. This excellent book gives a readable explanation of the effects of volatility on option pricing. It also gives a detailed, easy-to-read explanation of some of the theories of option pricing. It includes some mathematical equations, but the text and examples are aimed at the user who wants to know what is going on in the option model without getting bogged down in the mathematical derivation.

Options Markets by John C. Cox and Mark Rubenstein, published 1985 by Prentice-Hall, Inc., Englewood Cliffs, N.J. This is an academic treatise for those who interested in the underpinnings (mathematical and from the theory of finance) of pricing options on common stocks. Those of an academic bent will be able to apply this information to other options. The graphs showing the effects of the various elements of option pricing, such as volatility, time decay, interest rates, etc., are excellent. The book has an extensive bibliography on options.

Option Pricing by Robert Jarrow and Andrew Rudd, published 1983 by Dow Jones-Irwin, Homewood, Ill. This book is especially designed for those academics and practitioners who are looking for a thorough presentation of general option pricing using several models, including the Black-Scholes formula, Roll's American-call option formula, and Merton's jump-diffusion formula. There are no graphs in this book; it is all mathematical formula. The book gives a complete analysis of the influence of dividends on options pricing.

In addition, the major option exchanges publish numerous pamphlets explaining details of their particular contracts as well as some useful strategies.

CHAPTER 18

EUROS: CASH TIME DEPOSITS AND FRAs

BROKER:

I'm ⅞–¾ in the one month. Do you do anything?

DEALER:

I'll support you at ⅞, and I'm in there for size.

Such is the chatter that fills the phone lines over which Euro time deposits are traded.

ROUND THE GLOBE MARKET

The market for Eurocurrency deposits follows the sun around the globe. Due to the position of the international date line down the middle of the Pacific, the market starts, between 8 and 9 A.M. local time, in the Far East centers of Tokyo, Singapore, and Hong Kong.

Singapore owes its importance to its strategic geographic position and to the favorable access and tax treatment it accords foreign bank branches; beginning in 1976, Singapore changed its banking and tax laws with the aim of becoming the Zurich of the Far East. Also, Singapore has the distinction of having a futures exchange, SIMEX, that trades in decent volume a Euro contract that's fungible with the IMM contract.

Japanese and foreign banks operating in Tokyo can't book Eurodeposits on shore except in a Japanese version of an IBF. However, the top managements of Japanese banks who are major players in the Euromarkets are domiciled in Tokyo, and that lends importance to Tokyo as a Eurocenter. Some trading of Euros also occurs in Kuala Lumpur.

Banks that are active in the Far East market, including foreign banks and in particular the big U.S. banks, do some trading there that is "a natural" against business in Far East: funding loans to finance and accepting deposits generated by economic activity in that area. However, such trading, while it's growing, is still smaller than that done in Europe and in the U.S.

Singapore is instrumental in starting off each trading day. It is the first center in which the banks can react in volume to anything that might have happened after the New York close— a late economic announcement in the U.S. or an international incident such as new warring in the Middle East. Also, much of the trading by banks in Singapore involves position taking against what will happen later in the day.

According to one broker's estimates, Tokyo accounts for 50% of the Euro business done in the Far East, Singapore for 25%, and Hong Kong for 25%. This is a big change from a few years ago when the role of Tokyo was nonexistent.

After the Euromarket opens in Southeast Asia, the next centers to enter the market are those in the Middle East, Bahrain in particular. Here again, natural activity is limited; and in recent years, it's actually declined due to the fall in oil prices and in consequent money flows. The principal role of Bahrain has always been as a booking center.[1]

Both Eurodollars and Euroyen are actively traded in the Far East. In contrast, Euro sterling and Eurodeposits denominated in other European currencies are traded mostly in Europe, very little in the Far East.

London and other European centers, which are the next to open, do so early to catch the Singapore close. Singapore tends to

---

[1]Bahrain replaced Beirut as the financial center of the Middle East after civil war in 1974 destroyed Beirut and the then flourishing Lebanese economy. Beirut, because it was a prosperous business center and had an indigenous supply of traders, had a natural and better base for becoming a major financial center than Bahrain has or is ever likely to have.

be a net taker of funds, and as a result, the London market often opens on the firm side due to borrowing interest from Singapore.

Because of the huge volume of natural activity and, more important, because of the ability of banks in London to book Eurodeposits on shore, the New York market used to lean on the markets in London and other European centers. In the late 1970s, U.S. banks opened their Euro desks at 5 A.M. New York time and closed them for all intents and purposes at 12 noon when London closed. Gradually, this changed; one important factor was the setting up by the head offices of U.S. banks of Caribbean shell branches in which they could book huge amounts of Euro loans and deposits; a second factor was the emergence in Chicago of a highly successful Eurodollar futures contract.

In talking about the relative importance of different Euro-centers, the key question is: In what centers and at what times of day, is there liquidity? Nowadays, the answer is that there is good liquidity in the mornings in London, but the best liquidity of the day is during the hours when the IMM is open, between 8 A.M. and 3 P.M. New York time. This is so because so much Euro business done goes back to interest-rate swaps and other derivative products.

SIMEX adds some liquidity to the trading of Euros in the Far East, LIFFE to the trading of Euros in London. However, the size that a trader can do on SIMEX or even on LIFFE is much lower than what he could do in Chicago: there are days when a trade of 200 or 300 contracts might affect price on SIMEX. Also, Chicago has far better liquidity than either LIFFE or SIMEX not only in the front, but in the back, contracts; consequently, a trader can do futures strips in size on the IMM, which he can't really do in either of the other time zones. To hedge an interest-rate swap or to arbitrage futures against cash or FRAs, a trader needs to do a strip of futures.

The timing of liquidity in the Euromarket causes senior officers of Japanese financial institutions, who are a major factor in the interbank market, to lead somewhat disrupted lives. Particularly on days when a U.S. economic number is being released, a senior Japanese banker in Tokyo will typically go out to dinner at 5 or 6 P.M. his time with a broker or another banker, and then return to his office at 9 P.M., which is 8 A.M. New York time, to be ready for that number. Then he may stay in his office another two, three, or four hours making decisions based on what that number is and on how the market reacts to it. Thus, it's not unusual in the interbank, time-deposit market for a New York trader to find that he's trading, during the early morning, not only with the London and New York branches of a Japanese bank, but directly with its head office. The fact that the Japanese believe that the best liquidity in Euros is during IMM hours and adjust their behavior accordingly makes that belief self-fulfilling and bodes poorly for the future of the Tokyo Euro-dollar contract, which got off in 1989 to a *very* slow start.

From the time New York closes until Singapore opens, the Euromarket goes through its "dark hours." Some trading occurs in San Francisco and other centers, but the volume is so small that banks cannot react in size to any major development until the Far East opens.

FRAs

Back in the late 1970s and early 1980s, the big banks used to run huge Euro time-deposit books on which they sought, with quite consistent success, to make money on maturity transformations, gapping, and trading for small spreads. If the yield curve was positive, a bank might position itself by lending 1-year Euros and borrowing 3-month Euros. Also, banks routinely did forward forwards, for example, committed to lend or borrow 3-month Euros X months hence. Then, for reasons discussed in Chapter 6, banks came under increasing pressure to shrink their balance sheets and to increase their return on equity. As a result, banks pared their Euro time-deposit books, and when they wanted to position, their instrument of choice was futures, not cash.

A *forward rate agreement* [FRA] is simply an OTC variant of futures. It is a contract in which the *buyer* promises to pay the *seller* some specified rate of interest during some specified future period on some specified *notional sum*. On the *settlement date*, the start date of the notional loan or deposit, no principal changes hands; instead, the contract is settled by a *cash payment* from one party to the other; the direction and size of the payment depend on the difference that prevails on settlement day between the contract rate and the market rate for the relevant time period.

In 1984, FRAs were introduced first in Switzerland by the Compagnie Financière et de Crédit, then in the U.K. by its money brokering subsidiary, the Tradition Group. By the end of 1984, an interbank market in FRAs had been started in London. Interest in FRAs then spread to continental Europe and later to the U.S.

An Example

A *buyer* of a FRA might be a *borrower* who seeks protection against a rise in interest rates; a *seller* might be a *lender* who seeks protection against a fall in interest rates. The precise mechanics of a FRA are best illustrated with an example.

Suppose that Bank X buys a 3-month FRA from Bank Y. Specifically, Banks X and Y do 2s against 5s, which means that X promises to pay Y a specified rate for 3-month Eurodollars, two months hence. Suppose that rate is 9, that the notional amount of the FRA is 5MM, and that the contract period is April 1 to June 30. Bank X is getting protection against or betting on a rise in the 3-month rate to a level above 9; Bank Y is doing the reverse.

Suppose that on settlement day, 3-month Eurodollars are trading at 9.10, 10 bp above the contract rate. Basically, Bank Y must pay, on settlement day, to Bank X a sum equal to ten 3-month bp *times* the notional principal of 5MM. Actually, the calculation is slightly more complex; since settlement on a FRA is made in advance (at the start of the notional loan or deposit period), the settlement sum is calculated by *discounting* the interest differential due from the maturity date to the start date using the relevant market rate.

The basis used in discounting is actual/360 for dollars, actual/365 for sterling. The formula used for discounting is familiar; we derived it in Chapter 4 to calculate the price of a T bill.

Let

r_c = the contract rate (as a decimal)
r_m = the market rate (as a decimal)
t = the tenor of the notional deposit in days
F = the face (principal) amount of the notional deposit
S = the sum due at settlement

Then, the interest differential due the buyer before discounting is (assuming r_m exceeds r_c) given by:

$$(r_m - r_c)F\left(\frac{t}{360}\right)$$

The discount factor is given by:

$$1 - \frac{r_m t}{360}$$

And S is thus calculated as follows:

$$S = \left[(r_m - r_c)F\left(\frac{t}{360}\right)\right]\left[1 - \frac{r_m t}{360}\right]$$

Plugging the numbers from our example into this formula, the precise settlement sum that Bank X is owed by Bank Y can be calculated as follows:[2]

$$S = \left[\$5,000,000(0.0910 - 0.0900)\left(\frac{91}{360}\right)\right]\left[1 - \frac{0.0910(91)}{360}\right]$$
$$= (\$1,263.89)(0.97699)$$
$$= \$1,234.81$$

The market rate used in calculating the sum due on a FRA when it settles, dubbed FRABBA (pronounced fraa-baa), is LIBOR for the relevant time period as calculated by the British Bankers' Association (BBA) and published on both Telerate and Reuters. FRABBA is calculated as follows: the offered rates quoted by eight BBA designated banks for the contract currency

---

[2] If on settlement day, the contract rate exceeds the market rate, the sum due the seller is the *absolute value* of S, calculated using our formula.

for the contract period to prime banks in the London interbank market are collected at 11 A.M. on the settlement date; the two highest and the two lowest quotes are eliminated, and the remaining four quotes are averaged and rounded, if necessary, to five decimal places.

Features of FRAs

FRAs tend to be done in the 3-month to 12-month maturity range, but they can be done for longer periods. The contract period of a FRA may be one of the standard periods for which Euros are quoted, such as 3, 6, 9, and 12 months, or it can be for a *broken date,* a nonstandard period.

To make it easier to deal in FRAs and to ensure that FRAs were not subject to the 10% U.K. tax on gaming, the BBA laid down, in September 1985, standards for FRA contracts. These apply to all interbank dealings in London unless otherwise stated. The BBA also created a standard, fill-in-the-blanks contract for FRAs.

FRAs, since they are an OTC product, can be traded in any currency in which people want to strike a deal. Dollar FRAs top the list in volume; sterling FRAs are actively traded in London, DM FRAs in London and on the continent. "Yen FRAs are not bad," noted a broker, "and they will probably take off with the opening of the Euroyen contract in Tokyo. There are occasional amounts in Swissy and bits in Swissy and ECU but very small."

Advantages of FRAs

The quick acceptance achieved by FRAs reflects the fact that they are an off-balance-sheet item. Also, FRAs offer some decided advantages over futures. First, FRAs are not locked into IMM dates; instead, they can be custom tailored to meet a specific buyer's or seller's needs with respect to both start date and tenor. Thus, a trader who uses a FRA to hedge isn't exposed to much, if any, basis risk.

Second, a trader who strikes a FRA deal doesn't have to put down any initial margin, nor does he have to worry about variation margin calls as he would if he bought or sold futures. Third, since the amount at risk in a FRA deal is only the potential settlement sum, never the principal amount (which is only notional), a bank doing a FRA uses only a small bit of its credit line to its counterparty, whereas it would use a big bit if it committed to do a cash deposit. This is consistent with the fact that doing a FRA exposes a bank to minimal credit risk, since only the settlement sum is at risk and then only if rates go one way—make it a receiver at settlement.

Perhaps the best feature of FRAs is that they are strictly a no-brainer. This is particularly attractive to corporate traders who can explain to management in two minutes max that, by doing a FRA, they are locking in a future borrowing or lending rate. If the same trader wanted to use futures, the explanation would be much longer; the trade would have more of a speculative ring ("You're going to buy what they trade next to pork bellies?"); and he'd probably have to explain margin, margin calls, and basis risk.

The FRA Market Today

Today, the undisputed center of the FRA market is London. The FRA market is growing in New York but isn't as liquid there as in London. One broker observed: "A year ago [mid-1988], there were only 40 or 50 banks in the States involved in FRAs. Now, the number is probably 75, 80, or 100; and one or two new players a week are entering the New York market. All of the big Americans, all of the major Canadians, and most of the foreign banks are involved. The only two factors that haven't really gotten too involved are regional Americans and the Japanese."

The problem for the Japanese is that the Bank of Japan has restricted banks in Tokyo from trading FRAs. No one knows why. The BOJ restriction does not, however, apply to Japanese bank branches outside of Japan. Some of these branches have done FRAs in London and New York, but most haven't because their head office can't do FRAs. In 1989, it was generally expected that when trading in Euroyen began in Tokyo, BOJ would lift its restrictions on Japanese banks trading FRAs and that that in turn would lead to a second wave of growth in the FRA market.

In interest-rate swaps, liquidity tends to be primarily in New York. However, in FRAs, liquidity is still generally in London and from the Continent; thus, New York lacks a bit in liquidity during the afternoon when London has gone home. "Then," said a broker, "we find we struggle a little. If it's a regular period such as the 6s–12s, we'll find a price OK, but in some of the odd periods, it's harder to get support than when London is in. However, that's changing. We're getting a few banks who are market makers, and they'll make a two-way dealing price in the afternoon. Also, the IMM hours definitely influence liquidity. Perhaps 35 to 40 of our FRA players are running hedged books, where they are hedging all of their FRA transactions against futures. When the IMM closes, it takes those banks out of the market; so after 3 P.M., when futures are closed, the market is very quiet."

Banks use FRAs in various ways. Some banks do 70% of their FRA business against a futures hedge. They will work out (compound) the rate on a futures strip and compare it with the rate at which they can do a FRA. Sometimes, they can pick up, say, a 6s–12s FRA 6 or 7 bp below the corresponding futures strip. If so, they buy the FRA and buy the futures strip as a hedge. Then, they look for an opportunity during the life of that transaction to lend the FRA back at the rate on the futures strip. At that point, they close their futures position by selling futures, and in theory they've locked in 7 bp minus transaction costs. That's a small spread, but the players make money by doing volume. A lot of banks play this game.

Also, a number of banks use FRAs on a purely speculative basis, to gap. The banks like FRAs because they're off balance sheet and reasonably liquid.

A bank may also use FRAs to generate cheap funds, whereas in the past, they might have used a forward forward. For example, a bank might find that, by taking 1-year dollars and then lending a 6s–12s FRA, it can provide itself with much cheaper 6s than it could pick up in the market. One problem with this is that, because the bank is taking 1-year money, it ties up a line for a year to create what's really only a 6-month position. Some Japanese banks, who don't seem to have balance-sheet concerns, do this. Despite having done a 6s–12s FRA, the bank, when the second 6-month period rolls around, must still lend, since its 6s–12s FRA placed no funds, just locked in a rate. Because the FRA settles in six months at LIBOR, if the bank can lend at LIBOR, it will be breaking even on the back half of the deal, but if it can only lend at LIMEAN, it will lose 6 bp for six months. Sometimes, deals of this sort can produce 6-month dollars at 15 to 18 bp below where a bank could pick up 6-month dollars. But the trade is a sometimes affair; it will work for several months and then go away.

At times, a bank can work the other way round. Say a bank is looking for 6-month dollars and can't find a cheap source; a customer comes in and offers the bank some cheap 3-month dollars. If it takes them, then maybe by borrowing a 3s–6s FRA, the bank can produce some cheap 6-month dollars as well.

A lot of banks are also doing FRAs against their corporate customers. Corporate America and corporate Europe as well have caught on to the FRA, and they do a lot of FRAs with their banks, sometimes huge ones. For a corporate with seasonal fluctuations in cash flows—it anticipates that it will be borrowing or lending Euros during certain periods—a FRA is a perfect instrument. A corporate can lock in a rate for a period that matches his dates and not have to worry about margin as he would with futures. A corporate can't come directly into the brokers' market; he does his deal with his bank, which in turn lays it off in the brokers' market.

THE BROKERS

The major banks in London post rates at which they are willing to take Eurodollar deposits in different maturities, and they do pick up some money directly, particularly from banks on the Continent. Much interbank trading in Euros—cash and FRAs—is, however, done through brokers. Brokers are a necessity in the Euromarket because participants in this market are so numerous and because they are scattered around the globe.

In the late 1970s, the Eurobrokers were limited to brokering cash Euros. Then, as interbank trading of Euro time deposits fell off somewhat, the brokers picked up brokering first interest-rate swaps and then FRAs. Over time, the brokers' off-balance-sheet business (or capital-markets business, as they call it) has probably grown to a greater extent that the drop off in their cash business; so net, their volume and income are up. One London broker noted that 50% of his firm's business in dollar deposits is FRAs; and that overall, 50% of his firm's business is in brokered cash, 40% in FRAs, and 10% in interest-rate swaps.

Today, the principal brokers of Euros are Tullet & Tokyo Forex; Garvin Guy Butler; Godsell, Astley & Pearce; Fulton Prebon; and Eurobrokers. They're followed by shops such as Lasser Marshall and Tradition. The brokers all operate world-wide—have operations in all of the principal Eurocenters. Many of the brokers have been formed by trans-Atlantic, even trans-Pacific, mergers and amalgamations; and their ownership is strongly British. However, Eurobrokers, after being bought with British money, bought themselves back with Canadian money. There's also some German and Swiss ownership in the brokering community.

Today, a broker of Euros, FRAs, and swaps may also broker foreign exchange or Fed funds and repo. Also, some of the brokers are FCMs (futures commission merchants), which makes sense, since being an FCM enables a broker to provide his customers with, if they want it, one-stop shopping for FRAs and a futures hedge.[3] Thus, the biggest of the brokers have huge staffs; one, for example, has 200 brokers in New York plus 50 back-office staff, another 20-odd brokers and staff in Toronto, several hundred people in Tokyo, and even more than that in London.

Brokerage Rates

Brokerage rates on Euros used to be identical in London and New York. Originally, the London rates were set by the Bank of England, and New York basically just went by London rates. Then, some of the banks in New York—it started in foreign

---

[3]The big U.S. banks have all opened a holding-company subsidiary that's an FCM, but a lot of other banks need to go to an FCM to execute a futures trade.

exchange—negotiated volume discounts. Some time later, the Bank of England told the U.K. brokers, "You can charge what you like." Currently, the basic rates for everyone in both places are an 02 for cash (both sides pay) and an 01 for FRAs and interest-rate swaps. But the bigger players have all negotiated discounts, often the same package in both New York and London. The discount may kick in when they get to $10,000 a month in commissions, increase when they get to $20,000 a month, or whatever. The basic rates have not changed, but active players get deals.

Speaking of net income, a New York broker noted: "At the moment, in the capital-markets area (FRAs and interest-rate swaps) and in the cash Eurodollar area, we are running fairly similar. Where the cash used to be far ahead of the other two, FRAs and swaps have caught on over the last year and a half, and both areas now generate around the same commission volume."

The Brokers' Market

Each brokering firm is selling to its client banks a vast, fast-operating information network, which no bank could duplicate with its own resources. In this respect, it's interesting to note that the British, perceiving the importance of good communications to London as a financial center, long ago created excellent and relatively cheap phone and Telex facilities to link London with the rest of the world—that at a time when domestic communications were quite another matter.

In Euro time deposits, as opposed to FRAs, there's a lot of activity in a wider range of currencies—dollars, sterling, and all of the major European currencies. Also, the market in Euroyen is big. While some banks, like Citi and Chase, have a big deposit base and are not the active takers of funds in the brokers' market that they once were, there is still a lot of activity in this market. Some of the big globals are always in buying or selling. Also, in the interbank market, there are always small banks who don't have a big deposit base and who are takers because they need money to fund their loan books: the small Spanish banks, the Italian banks, U.S. regionals, and the small English banks.

On the taking side, however, it's the Japanese who dominate. The Japanese are such active takers of dollars, often to do one arbitrage or another, that one gets the impression that they have yet to hear three words that the other banks have heard loud and clear: capital adequacy requirements. Constantly, the Japanese are in the market doing, in huge size, arbitrages (involving time deposits, Euro CDs, futures, swaps, whatever), typically at far smaller spreads than the big Americans, given their balance-sheet concerns, require.

In the Eurodollar market, there are maybe 400 substantial players. In the Euroyen market, in contrast, 25 Japanese banks dominate: they're so big that no one wants to go in and tangle with them in their own currency. "We did," noted one broker, "an analysis of the business we generate in Euroyen: 93% was with Japanese banks, 7% with non-Japanese banks. The Japanese are unique in that they dominate their own Eurocurrency market by a big margin. The Euromark market, for example, is not dominated by the German banks. Also, the Swiss banks do not dominate the market in Euro Swiss francs, although other banks dealing in Euro Swissy do keep a close eye on what the big Swiss banks are doing."

Pace and Professionalism

Brokering Euros, like Fed funds, is a rapid-fire, bang-bang game. It requires total concentration on the part of the broker and an ability to simultaneously listen to the phone with the right ear and keep track with the left of any changes in quotes other brokers in the room shout out. Brokering requires thinking but only of the quickest sort. "The thing that comes closest to it in the United Kingdom," said the director of a big brokering outfit, "is a British turf accountant [bookie] calling rates across the wire."

In London and in other centers as well, most of the Euro brokers and bank dealers as well turn out to be British and more specifically to be cockneys. For some reason the east end of London, a working-class area, seems, like similar areas in many big cities, to breed the sort of person that brokering and dealing require—one who is quick-witted and has a sense of humor that keeps him from going barmy at the end of a day of pressure.

Brokering of Euros, cash and FRAs, is an extremely professional operation. One advantage to a bank of using a broker is anonymity. A big bank can bid for large sums in this market without moving price, something it mightn't be able to do if it went direct.

To preserve anonymity, it's a cardinal rule among brokers that they never give up the name of a bank bidding for or offering funds until one bank actually initiates a transaction. At that point, the broker tells the lender the borrower's name so that the lender can check whether his line to the borrower is full. If it isn't, the ethics of the game are that the lender must sell the funds he has offered to the bidding bank; in particular, he is not to go around the broker and sell directly to the bidding bank.

In FRAs, as in cash, the size banks want to do can, at times, be huge. "Now and then," noted a broker, "a bank might want to do half a billion or a billion of dollar FRAs in a certain period—perhaps against his cash book or against a corporate, perhaps as a hedge or a speculation. A month ago, a big American lent a billion in 1s–4s. There has been some huge size done by corporates—oil companies, multinationals, and the like. Over several weeks, one big British corporate has gone into the banks several times and done several billion in a single FRA period."

In New York, 50% of the FRA business done by banks is done on a direct basis. Generally, banks will quote each other markets having a 4- or 5-bp spread. That's the basic width of quotes in the FRA market.

Market liquidity is good in FRAs. One broker noted: "If someone asked us to quote a price in a period in which we have nothing, we'd feel confident about quoting a 5-bp spread and being able to support it. In the more popular periods, such as the 3s–6s, 6s–12s, we'd like to think we could quote as low as a 3-bp spread and be able to support it. If a bank needs a price for 200 or 250MM in a certain period, generally in that kind of size, we could supply him with a 4- or 5-bp dealing price. We don't trade that size often, but we can do it."

Because Eurobrokers have a reputation (one not shared by some continental brokers of foreign exchange) for not "blowing around" information on who's bidding and offering in their market, some large banks are willing to be quite open with their broker about what they want to do. A bank dealer, for example, might say to a broker, "In the 6s, I want to do a lumpy piece. What's that market really like? If I took 500MM, would it move against me?" Since a broker monitors the market minute by minute, that's a question to which he can give an informed reply. Thus, in the eyes of many bankers and brokers, an open relationship should exist between a good bank and a good broker. However, many are of another opinion; they never tell their broker what they *really* want to do.

Working a Trade

A big part of the broker's job is to provide the banks with an information network, a vital service, since no large bank would start dealing in the morning without first calling the brokers to get a feel for levels and tone in the market. A good broker does more, however, than just quote prices. He works to narrow spreads and create trades by persistence, cajolery, pleading, humor—any ploy that works.

If, for example, the 1-month were quoted at 8⅞ to ¾, the broker might call a bank and say, "Can you close that price for me?" If the bank dealer answered, "I'll pay 13," the market would be at 7⅜–^{13}/16, and the broker would start calling around to find a bank that would offer below ⅞. Suppose he found an offer at ^{27}/32. Now, the bid and the offer would be only 1/32 apart. At that point, the broker and his colleagues, each of whom might have direct phone lines to a dozen banks, would start "banging around the board" (punching those direct phone line buttons) saying, "Anything in the 1s? Nice close price." Eventually, some bank would probably bite, and a trade would have been created and done.

"Our job," observed another broker, "is not just quoting rates; it may require bringing about a deal between guys who want to do slightly different things. Say 3s are 5/16–¼ and 4s are ⅜–5 [a 1/16 spread in each tenor]. If someone asked me to quote 3½ months, I'd say ^{11}/32–9/32; and if they take me, I go to the guy who is giving 3s at 5 and say, 'How about lending longer at 11?' or to the guy lending 4s and say, 'How about lending shorter at 11?'

"It's easier than it sounds; there's lots of liquidity, lots of players, so you don't really get caught. Most of the dealers know where it is anyway, so they are just saying, 'Go get it.'"

The Mechanics of Brokering

The big brokers speak to a wide range of banks, including most of the bigger banks and most of the medium-tier banks. "We have," noted one New Yorker, "direct lines and facilities to talk to most banks. There are a few banks a broker doesn't talk to because of real or perceived past problems; that's always going to happen. We speak to every Japanese bank in New York, to all of the Americans, to all of the clearers, to most European banks, and to a cross section of regionals. Some of the brokers have a better handle on the regionals, especially those who have a big Fed funds desk, like Prebon or Garvin. A regional bank always has its Fed funds to do, and if occasionally it wants to do something in 3-month dollars, it will go to one of those brokers."

When a bank puts a bid or an offer into a broker, it's understood in London, where the primary participants in the market are international banks with traders who do at most deposits and foreign exchange, that the quote is good until a trade is made or the bank calls back to say, "I'm off." In the U.S., a trader at a regional bank may be responsible for not only Euros and foreign exchange, but a number of domestic instruments as well; for that reason, a broker, depending on the customer, may feel the need to call him back if some time (a half hour or more) has passed to reconfirm his bid or offer.

The broker, for his part, can be held to any price he quotes as firm provided that a line problem does not tie up a trade. If, for example, Chase London offered to sell 6-month money at the bid rate quoted by a broker and the bidding bank then told the broker he was off and had forgotten to call, the broker would be committed to *substantiate* his bid by finding Chase a buyer at that price or by selling Chase's money at a lower rate and paying a *difference* equal to the dollar amount Chase would lose by selling at that rate. Because activity in the Euromarket is hectic, mistakes do occur, and they can be expensive: On 5MM for six months, even 1/16 of 1% works out to $1,562.50. Since brokers operate on thin margins, a broker wouldn't be around long if he got "stuffed" often; so good brokers take care to avoid errors.

It used to be that whenever some important news hit the market—Citi raised its prime or whatever—the banks would call the brokers to shout "Off, Off!" on their bids and offers, and a broker would quote rate on an "I suggest," "I think," or "I call" basis, which meant that a bank could not hold him to these quotes. A sharp break in market activity put a broker back in the position in which he started the day, with a blank pad. To get trading started again, he had to call around to the banks to find out where they anticipated money would now trade and then try to find banks that would substantiate these new levels by making even small, but firm, bids and offers. Today, with the large presence of U.S. banks—there are over 200—this is less true. Americans tend to keep trading with other Americans pretty much regardless of what news hits the market.

Quotes and Maturities

In the market for overnight Federal funds, money normally trades for immediate delivery. In the Euromarket, in contrast, the delivery date, or *value date* as it's called, is two days hence unless otherwise specified. The reason is that foreign exchange settles two days forward. If a Euro spot transaction is dealt on, say, a Tuesday it results in funds being delivered on Thursday. The Euromarket, however, also deals in overnight funds for immediate delivery and for delivery the next day. The former sort of transaction is referred to as a deal in *overnight* funds or as *dealing over today;* the latter is referred to as a *tom next* (for tomorrow next) transaction in London and as a *rollover* or as *dealing over tomorrow* in the U.S.

Eurodollar deposits are quoted in the interbank market in a wide range of maturities: overnight, tom next, spot, the week, 1 to 6 months, 12 months, and one to five years. The Euromarket is a short-term market; depending on rate expectations, 50% or more of trading volume occurs in the 3-months-and-under range. Most of the rest occurs in the 3-months-to-1-year range. Trades of 2- to 5-year money occur but are uncommon.

While the Euromarket actively trades 1-, 2-, 3-, 6-, and 12-month deposits, it is, like the repo market, a flexible-date market in which participants may do any number of days they need. Odd-day, off-the-run deposits (e.g., for 26 days) are referred to as *broken* or *cock dates*. Brokers quote them by saying, for example, "We want early 2s out to the 15th [a deposit for less than 2 months that ends on the 15th]" or "We have 1 week short of 2s to go." Depending on the time a call is put into a broker, dealing over today may be a hassle, but dealing over tomorrow is not.

Euro Feds

It's possible to carry out Eurodollar transactions over the Fed wire when both sides have a Fed account. Such transactions, dubbed *Euro Feds,* are the exception rather than the rule. A foreign bank branch in Los Angeles that's doing a trade with a regional American in Minneapolis or a Japanese bank in Seattle might rather pay and receive funds via its local district Federal Reserve Bank than via a New York bank. One broker estimates that only 1 to 2% of the Euros they broker are done in Euro Feds; the rest go through CHIPS.

It used to be that clearing house funds differed from Fed funds in that they turned into immediately available funds, that is, Fed funds, only on the day after the delivery or value date. The distinction that existed in the Eurodollar market between the value date and the date on which good funds were available to the recipient created the basis for some actively pursued technical arbitrages between Fed funds and short-dated Euros.[4] All that ended when CHIPS moved to same-day settlement.

Size and Quotes

On occasion in the Euromarket, one encounters a situation in which the bid and asked rates are identical—what a Eurobroker

---

[4]For a description of the technical arbitrages that occurred between Fed funds and overnight Euros before CHIPS moved to same-day settlement, see Chapter 17 of edition one of this book.

would call an *either-way market*. Since brokerage is paid by both the buyer and the seller in the Euromarket, an either-way market can occur only when the market in a given tenor gets "hung up on lines." Suppose Dresdner were offering 20MM of 1-month money through a broker and that Toronto Dominion decided to take this money. The broker would call Dresdner and say, "OK, we will pay at your price." Dresdner would then ask, "Who is it?" and the broker would say, "Toronto Dominion." At that point, Dresdner might say, "Done for 20," or "I'm full on that name," or "All I can do for him is two." In either of the last two cases, Dresdner would still have dollars to sell, Toronto Dominion would still have dollars to buy, and the two might end up quoting identical bid and offer rates.

In quoting Euro rates, London quotes the rates "tops and bottoms"; that is, the offered rate and then the bid rate. New York does the reverse for reasons now shrouded in history.

Speaking of the bid-offer spread in Euros, a broker observed: "In the cash market, the basic outside of the market would always be quoted at a ⅛ spread, the spread between where you have a lot of lenders and the prime buyers bidding. It's common to have difficult lenders lending in the middle at 13 and some of the smaller names paying up to 13; so if the quote's, say, ¾–⅞, it's pretty general that you have an either-way [*13-across* or *13-choice*] market, but the credit would not be as good as ¾–⅞. Basically, it comes down to whom you are talking to: if you are talking to someone who wants his prices based on real tip-top credits, you might make him a market 1/16 or ⅛ wide."

The minimum size in which brokers of Eurodollars will deal is 1MM, but most trades are larger. In the market for overnight and short-dated funds, trades of 10, 20, 50, and even 100MM are common. In the fixed dates, trades of 20MM are considered good size with the average being more like 5 or 10MM.

Normally, activity in the Euromarket is heaviest in the 6-month-and-under maturities, since most of the assets Eurobankers are funding are either short in tenor or roll every three to six months. When borrowers anticipate that rates might rise and the yield curve is not too steep, activity will be centered in the 6-month area because borrowers will opt for a 6-month roll. Alternatively, if rates are expected to drop or remain stable, activity will be strong in the 3-month area. Trades of long-dated funds, up to five years, occur in the interbank market, but normally they are done direct because brokerage is high on a big trade of long-dated funds.

Naturally, brokers prefer trades in the long dates to those in the short dates. But they try to give all their customers, including heavy traders of overnight funds, good service on the theory that if they support a bank in the short dates, they will occasionally get in on the gravy train when the bank trades long-dated funds in the brokers' market.

TIERING

Eurodollar deposits are a heterogeneous commodity. They differ with respect to not only maturity, but credit risk—the name of the buying bank and the center he's in. Thus, there is a tiering of quotes according to banks' names and to the centers in which they operate.

"With respect to tiering, a lot depends," observed one broker, "on who is tiering the banks. A Japanese bank will tier all the Japanese banks at the top and then the rest of the world. An American or European bank would probably start with the top Americans—whereas you once had the top 10 Americans, there is now tiering within that 10—and the top Europeans. Their first tier would be the really prime Americans, the British clearers, perhaps the big German and the big Dutch banks; their second tier would be the French, the bigger Australian banks, the bigger Japanese banks; and their third tier would be second-tier Americans along with medium to smaller European names and some Japanese names.

"However, tiering is extremely varied. Some banks still have no credit lines to any Japanese banks: a few regionals will put offers into the market, but say, 'I can't do any Japanese names.' Regional Americans tend to be very conservative; they are looking either for a prime American or a top European—that's all they can lend to because they have very restrictive credit lines. Most of the bigger Europeans and Americans now have fantastic credit lines to the Japanese—as big as they have to each other.

"Sometimes, the Japanese have to pay up not because of credit concerns, but because they buy so much. Often, you might have five or six Europeans lending for a certain period for a certain price; there are three or four Japanese paying the price; and not one of these Europeans can lend to any of the Japanese—their credit lines to them are all full because the Japanese are so active. Say a bank has a 50MM credit line to Dai-Ichi Kangyo. Dai-Ichi is trading out of Tokyo, Hong Kong, Singapore, Paris, Dusseldorf—he might have branches in 15 different centers; if all 15 branches are bidding in the market, it doesn't take a lot for a bank to fill up its credit lines to him."

Today, the rate differentials due to tiering are subtle. "Say," continued the same broker, "that 3-month Euros are 3/4–7/8. At the 3/4s, you would have the big Americans and the clearers paying. If for some reason they were willing to pay more, they'd issue commercial paper. In the middle, you will find the Japanese and the medium-type European names—perhaps the Belgian and the Scandinavian banks—paying 13/16. At the top of the market, you will find the small names (perhaps your Korean banks and some small London and European names), subsidiaries, and such paying 7/8.

"But every now and again, the Japanese step up to pay 7/8 because they are not getting any funds at 13—if there are lenders at 13, they are full with Japanese. Occasionally, the bigger French banks, which are actively traded from many different branches, will pay the top because so many people are full with them. The tiers do not always work in terms of quality of name; sometimes, they work in terms of credit availabilities.

"Today, there is less tiering than in the early 1980s. Then, for example, some of the regionals' credit lines were so strict that they could lend only to other Americans. Some of the big Americans used to bid 1/8 below the market and still receive money from regionals. The Japanese almost always had to pay up top to get money. Nowadays, the Japanese can pick up money in the middle of the market; the Americans have to put more marketable prices in; things have closed up a bit."

Tiering by Center

If lenders weren't conscious of sovereign risk, the Citi-Manila saga and the Panama story made them so. Apparently all lenders to foreign bank branches got their money out of Panama, which wasn't the case with Citi-Manila, but today no bank will place funds with a bank in either center. Among other centers, there's some tiering, but slight. "Bahrain," continued our observant broker, "is still reasonably active as a center, and they sometimes have to pay up a little for the center; some banks have strict credit concerns and can't lend to Middle Eastern centers—probably more than in the early 1980s. However, a large number of banks are prepared to deal with a bank in Bahrain, and banks there do not have much trouble raising funds. Very occasionally, you see someone out of Abu Dhabi, out of Dubai, out of Riyadh, or out of Kuwait; but 85 to 90% of the Middle East business is Bahrain center. All of the foreign banks that have opened branches in the Middle East are in Bahrain.

"Grand Cayman and Nassau are still quite active centers. All of the U.S. banks and all of the foreign banks in the U.S. have Nassau or Cayman branches. However, since introduction of the IBF, a lot of them are using their IBFs rather than Cayman or Nassau. Some of the Dutch, French, and German banks do have credit concerns about lending into Cayman and Nassau. Overall, however, most banks are as happy to lend into these centers as to an IBF. A Bankers Trust can, 99% of the time, get money as cheaply in the name of his Caribbean branch as in the name of his IBF."

Tiering in FRAs

In FRAs, there's little tiering as credit concerns are much less. "Also," our broker added, "in the *cash market,* price might be 3/4–7/8, and you might have 25 bids and 25 offers at various levels. That gives a bank leeway to be a little choosy. If a big American and smaller names are paying the same price, the lender will do the American; and the smaller names will have to pay up, which causes tiering. In FRAs, we are looking at so many periods and at so many different combinations of dates, that you've probably got only one bid or one offer in any given period; consequently, a bank can't be too choosy about who they'll lend to because only one bank may be paying in their period. Also, the credit risk is too small to justify real tiering."

While brokers never divulge the names of the banks that have placed bids and offers with them, to cope with the problems posed by lines, names, and locations, they sprinkle their runs with bits of information that can be helpful to the bank to whom they are quoting a run. For example, a broker might note that the bid in a given tenor was by a "prime name out of Hong Kong" or that the offer in some other tenor was from a "rather difficult lender," that is, one with lines to only a few banks.

To be as informative as possible, the brokers also throw in with their regular quotes some hints as to what is being done or could be done in the market. For example, a broker might note, "The 3s are 3/16–5/16 but may come at 1/4," or "Overnight funds are bid 7/16 out of London and Bahrain and come OK at 1/2." The variations are endless. A good broker does more than just quote rates: He gives his client banks, at a rapid-fire pace, all the useful information he can.

SETTLING THROUGH CHIPS

In Chapter 7, to keep things simple, we ignored the fact that most Eurodollar transactions clear not over the Fed wire but through the New York Clearing House. The New York Clearing House, the oldest and most prominent clearing house in the country, was set up to provide a mechanism for clearing both customer checks and bank official checks. Since the institution of the Fed wire, the bulk of the domestic funds New York banks exchange among themselves now go over that wire, but the Clearing House has assumed a vastly more important function, *clearing Eurodollar payments* amongst domestic and foreign banks.

Almost every Euro transaction creates the need for an interbank payment. In the old days, New York banks made such payments by issuing official checks, which were cleared through the New York Clearing House. A big New York bank might both issue and receive 1,500 or more official checks a day. Thus, clearing involved a huge amount of tedious, expensive, and labor-intensive paperwork. Despite the enormity of the job to be done, checks received by the Clearing House were normally *cleared* on the same day so that *settlement* in Fed funds could be made between the banks on a timely basis the next day. Sometimes, however, checks got lost, and clearing them took three, even four, days.

To reduce the unnecessary float such delays caused, the Fed strongly urged the New York Clearing House banks to set up a computerized communications network to handle interbank money transfers. This system, *CHIPS,* an acronym for *Clearing House Interbank Payments System,* went on-line with live transactions in April 1970. Participants in the CHIPS system include 11 of the New York Clearing House banks (12 before the BONY-Irving merger) and 128 other New York banking institutions, two thirds of whom are foreign; the ranks of the latter include foreign bank branches and agencies as well as Edge Act corporations set up by domestic banks.[5] Another two or three banks, mostly foreign, apply each year to join the system.

Every participant in CHIPS has a terminal computer, linked by leased telephone lines to the central CHIPS computer, through which it can directly send and receive payment messages. The central CHIPS computer immediately processes all such messages. Then, at 4:30 P.M., it produces for each participating bank item-by-item detailed reports of payments made to and received by it and by institutions holding accounts with it; the printout also indicates the bank's gross position with CHIPS, the gross and net positions of any banks for whom the bank settles, and finally, if the bank is a *settling bank,* its *net net*—the dollars it must send out or will receive due to CHIPS settlement. Also, by netting debits and credits, CHIPS figures each participating bank's net position vis-à-vis every other participating bank and the system as a whole.

The settlement system from there on is both efficient and swift. Of the 139 banks that participate in CHIPS, 22 have

---

[5]U.S. Trust, a New York Clearing House Bank, does not participate in CHIPS.

become, with the Fed's permission, *settling banks*.[6] After the CHIPS figures come out at 4:30, CHIPS participants who are not settling banks settle their account at one of the settling banks. Each settling bank that, on a net-net basis, has a debit balance with CHIPS sends over the Fed wire to the account that CHIPS maintains at the Fed the sum required for it to settle. After CHIPS has received these monies, it in turn wires out, again over the Fed wire, all monies it owes settling banks who have ended the day on a net-net basis with a credit balance at CHIPS. Monies are supposed to flow into CHIPS' account from settling banks with a net-net debit balance by 5:30 P.M. and to go out to settling banks with a net-net credit balance by 6 P.M.; at that time, the balance in CHIPS' account at the Fed should return to *zero*.

CHIPS strives mightily to stick to the above time schedule, but sometimes it doesn't make it. Occasionally, its computer system goes down, causing delays. More commonly, the computer of a participant goes down making it impossible for that bank to get out all its payments due to CHIPS participants by the 4:30 deadline. In such a situation, CHIPS no longer grants extensions except in extraordinary situations. An extraordinary situation would be if the bank having a computer problem were, say, Morgan and if Morgan owed another settling bank so much money that the other bank could not settle with CHIPS without getting its money from Morgan; in that case, so as not to jeopardize settlement, CHIPS would remain open until Morgan got its computer up and its payments out.

Volume through CHIPS

The volume of funds flowing through CHIPS each day has grown steadily and, today, is staggering. On an average day, CHIPS handles between 130,000 and 150,000 transactions (Figure 18–1). The average amount per transaction is nearing 5MM (Figure 18–2). In total, CHIPS clears payments whose value has

---

[6]The Fed permits banks to become settling banks if, in its view, they have the size and financial strength to handle huge payment volumes.

FIGURE 18–1
Average daily number of transactions of CHIPS*

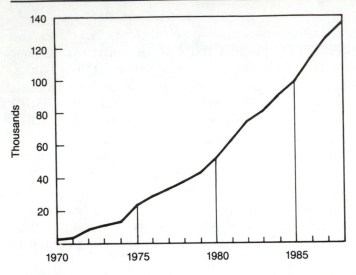

*First day on-line was April 6, 1970.

Source: CHIPS.

FIGURE 18–2
Average dollar amount per transaction on CHIPS*

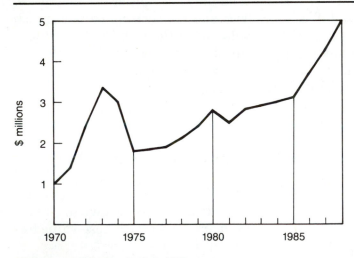

*First day on-line was April 6, 1970.

Source: CHIPS.

FIGURE 18–3
Total dollar volume of settlement of CHIPS by year*

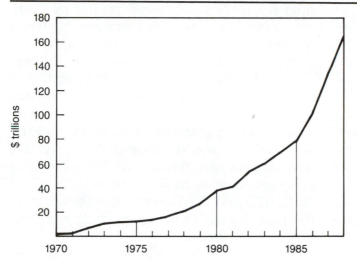

*First day on-line was April 6, 1970.

Source: CHIPS.

risen to over 165 *trillion* a year (Figure 18–3). On its record day during the first half of 1989, CHIPS cleared 268,894 transactions, having a dollar value of 1.26 trillion.

Why CHIPS Is Still with Us

Since CHIPS moved to same-day settlement, Fed funds and what used to be called clearing house funds have become fungible in the sense that a payment made through either system results in the receipt of good funds on the day the payment is made. To the outsider, this raises the question of why CHIPS continues to be used. There are several compelling reasons.

All payments mechanisms are bound by the payer's technical capability to execute payments which in turn depends on how execution has traditionally been done. Originally, money market participants in New York made payments to each other by check. Messengers delivered these checks to the New York

Clearing House, where they were cleared and settled on the next day. Then, the Clearing House switched to a computerized system, which automated the settlement procedure, but by tradition, these checks were next-day money. So there was in place a next-day settlement system with which everyone was happy. Also, and more important, there was an infrastructure in place for using this system; participants had both a computer linkup to CHIPS and people trained to use it; the system worked; and everyone used it.

Then, participants in CHIPS gradually became uncomfortable with the huge overnight or worse still over-the-weekend risk to which next-day settlement exposed them. CHIPS solved this by moving to same-day settlement. Now, the value date of the funds paid over both CHIPS and the Fed wire are the same. In this respect, they are fungible, and in theory, participants could use either network to transfer funds.

In practice, foreign banks make and receive the bulk of their payment through CHIPS because their pattern of making and receiving payments tends to create huge daylight overdrafts in the accounts that they keep with settling banks. The Fed will not permit foreign banks to run big daylight overdrafts with it. It reasons: Why should we take the risk? The big New York banks are willing to take this risk for foreign banks who are their customers because they feel that they are compensated for assuming it through customer relationships.

Domestic banks are also heavy users of CHIPS. A typical money center bank probably makes about 40% of its transfers over the Fed wire, 40% through CHIPS, and another 20% through *book transfers* (a book transfer is a transfer of funds from the account of one depositor at a bank into the account of another; it is done through internal bookkeeping entries).

Given his choice, an operating man will always use a more efficient and cheaper system. In the early 1980s, CHIPS had, but Fedwire did not, a formatted-transaction type, which meant that, on two out of three transactions, no clerical labor was required to post to a customer's account items received over CHIPS. Also, CHIPS was cheaper, about 31 cents versus 65 cents per transaction per party. Today, the Fed wire has instituted a formatted-transaction type akin to CHIPS', but CHIPS remains cheaper: 20 cents versus 50 cents (prices on both networks have fallen).

Cost is not the only reason CHIPS remains popular with users; saving 30 cents may in fact have little bearing on how a bank chooses to transfer 5MM. A second advantage CHIPS offers banks is that it's faster than Fedwire. Also, it has more bells and whistles. A bank can make inquiries into the CHIPS database: for example, if bank A has told bank B that B will be getting money from A, B can inquire into the CHIPS system and find that, yes indeed, that payment is stored there. If a bank is ordered to pay, it's a help if it can peek at its hold card and see that a payment it has been promised is really stored there, ready to come to it. One of the reasons that foreign banks use CHIPS is that they have greater latitude with respect to running daylight overdrafts on CHIPS than they do on Fedwire.

Daylight Overdrafts

Currently, there are huge *daylight overdrafts* at three levels in the payments system: in the accounts of major domestic banks at the Fed, in the accounts of some participants in CHIPS, and in the accounts of correspondent banks, particularly foreign banks, at their domestic correspondent bank.

These overdrafts are, under the current system, operationally unavoidable because banks and bank customers are making and receiving huge payments leveraged on the basis of small balances. The average demand deposit at one major New York bank turns over 7,000 times a year! Noted an officer of this bank, which has an institutional—as opposed to retail—client base, "I pay and receive on an average day 145 billion. The assets of my institution are 55 billion. I roll those assets every 2½ hours, and I roll the bank's capital 70 times a day—roughly every 10 minutes. Operations of this size mean that I must at times experience large extremes in my net debit or credit positions at CHIPS and at the Fed. There is no way we can regulate the flow of these payments so everyone stays in balance so long as so many payments are made on the basis of such small balances."

One of the problems facing this bank and others is that in real terms demand deposits at U.S. banks declined by 50% between 1971 and 1981 while the volume of payments being made by bank depositors mushroomed.

Every morning, someone has to start making payments to get the system going, and the people who do will probably end up OD for a time. These people will either be those who borrow the most and, thus, owe the most (e.g., a bank returning Fed funds bought overnight) or those banks with the most efficient system who can execute payments the fastest.

Daylight overdrafts create credit risk for the Fed, for settlement of CHIPS, and for banks at which other banks run them. All of these institutions are concerned about this risk. However, it's impossible to impose the simplistic solution of banning daylight overdrafts. Solving the credit problem posed by overdrafts by banning them, at one or all levels, would put the payments system into *gridlock*—bank X could not pay bank Y because it had not received payment from bank Z, and so on.

A payment system and a credit control system are in direct conflict. This reality notwithstanding, the Fed has campaigned with some success to limit the huge daylight overdrafts that domestic banks used to run with it. The Fed's latest move on this front was to announce on May 31, 1989, that it proposed to limit the daylight overdrafts of domestic banks to their capital and those of foreign banks to 5% of their U.S. liabilities. Lawrence Uhlick, executive director of the Institute for International Banks, correctly observed, "The [Fed's] proposal represents an awfully negative view of the fundamental strength of global institutions and is inconsistent with how the market treats them."

The Fed is also proposing to charge banks 68 cents for every $1,000 of daylight overdraft they run beyond certain threshold amounts. This move will again raise costs for entities whose payments force the banks to go OD at the Fed. In particular, the added costs could be phenomenal for securities dealers because they are the biggest users of daylight overdrafts—a phenomenon that falls naturally out of the clearing of governments and of other money market securities.

Fedwire routinely handles 300 to 400 billion a day in payments and securities transfers; and banks' daylight overdrafts at the Fed hit, at times, 120 billion. Much as it would like to, the Fed cannot totally eliminate the daylight overdrafts banks run with it. So long as huge payments are leveraged on a small deposit base, big daylight overdrafts will continue. Knowledgeable and responsible bank officers who understand the system at an operational level—as well as operational people at the Fed—know that this cannot be done. They agree that "the best solution is that, if there is a bad guy in the system, you have to identify him and get him off the system before he has an opportunity to create trouble."

Initiatives by CHIPS to Limit Credit Risk

The CHIPS's network, like Fedwire, produces big daylight overdrafts. To reduce the credit risk inherent in this, CHIPS has taken several steps. First, in 1981, it changed from next-day to same-day settlement, thereby reducing—from as much as four days over a holiday weekend to hours—the time during which an overdraft at CHIPS can be outstanding.

Since it went to same-day settlement, CHIPS has instituted three other steps to reduce the credit risk inherent in its payments system. The first of these, begun in 1984, was *receiver, bilateral, net-credit limits*. This mouthful of words means that each bank on the system puts into the CHIPS computer, for every other participant, a limit on the dollar amount it will go long against (be owed payments by) that other participant. For example, bank A might put a 500MM limit in the CHIPS computer for bank B; by doing so, it would be saying, "B can be committed to send me up to 500MM, but no more, until I commit to send B some funds; then B can commit to send me more funds." Note, even though CHIPS settles only once a day, late in the day, banks are making payments back and forth throughout the day, and they are sending each other advices of these payments; thus, A can track, throughout the day, the total payments B owes it and the total payments it owes B; A's exposure, if any, to B is the *net* amount B owes it. The limits that major New York money center banks set on each other may run in excess of a billion.

The next credit-risk-limiting step CHIPS took was to institute in 1986 *debit caps* (really sender net-debit limits). These caps are derived by formula from the bilateral credit limits banks on the system post vis-à-vis each other. These caps prevent a bank from going deficit into the CHIPS system by more than X dollars. Net-credit limits permit receivers of funds to protect against deficits; debit caps permit the system to do likewise.

Most recently, CHIPS has approved a fourth safeguard called *settlement finality*. The concept is simple. CHIPS is asking its users to join with it in a loss-sharing arrangement under which each participant promises to make up a pro rata part of any failed participant's balances. In addition to that contractual obligation, CHIPS is asking its participants to pledge with it collateral, in the form of U.S. government securities, equal to the full amount of their respective obligations. If there's ever an emergency—some bank cannot settle its debit with the system—CHIPS will take those securities and sell them for Fed funds.

Settlement finality will require CHIPS participants to post as collateral an estimated 4 billion of securities. For the banks, the chief drawback of having to do this is that they won't be able to repo such securities; instead, they'll have to tie up their own funds in financing them. Settlement finality is scheduled to become operational around July 1990.

Failure of CHIPS to Settle

CHIPS functions on confidence. When the German authorities closed Herstatt, confidence drained out of the system even though Herstatt was not a participant in CHIPS, only an account number at a participating bank. The loss of confidence in CHIPS caused *gridlock*; bank X would not make a payment to Y until it got cover which deprived another bank of cover with the result that everything froze in the system. Fortunately, a fast meeting and some fast decision making sufficed to restart the system.

This illustrates an important point. It's crucial for CHIPS to limit access to the system to New York–based entities because when a problem—real or potential—arises, proximity of the major participants is required for a quick solution to be reached and for the market, easily disturbed by rumors, to be calmed. While regional banks would like CHIPS to provide nationwide access to CHIPS, CHIPS is and will remain a New York institution because both the markets and the key players in them are there.

While CHIPS has always settled, the possibility exists, at least until settlement finality becomes operational, that it could not, and rules are in place to cope with this contingency. If a settling bank informs CHIPS that it will not settle for a participant because that bank does not have, say, 50MM to settle and the settling bank will not lend the money, the clearing house has authority to take one of several actions. It can settle on the positions that exist, which means that some bank will go unpaid. It can come up collectively with a loan for the bank that cannot settle. Or it can rerun the day's transactions as if the nonsettling bank had never existed. This will produce new settlement figures that could conceivably put some other bank—for example, one supposed to receive the bulk of the 50MM that now will not be paid—in the position where it cannot settle, which would put CHIPS again in the position of being unable to settle.

CHIPS has never failed to settle. Said one officer who oversees his bank's operations on CHIPS, "If CHIPS fails to settle, I jump out of my [14th-story] window. CHIPS cannot not settle because, if it were to do so, it would destroy confidence in the money market internationally—create a worldwide financial panic, perhaps worldwide depression."

So long as huge deposits are leveraged on a small deposit base, big daylight overdrafts will continue to put at risk a system that cannot be permitted to fail. Senior people at the Fed want to eliminate this risk by eliminating the daylight overdrafts. Knowledgeable and responsible bank officers who understand the system at an operational level—as well as operational people at the Fed—know that this cannot be done. They agree that "the only solution is that, if there is a bad guy in the system, you have to identify him and get him off the system before he has an opportunity to create trouble."

SWIFT

It used to be common for banks to use Telex and other common carriers to transmit payment advices and instructions for international transactions that were eventually cleared through CHIPS. In 1973, the leading international banks began planning a *private* bank communications network called SWIFT, an acronym for Society for Worldwide Interbank Financial Telecommunications. SWIFT, a computerized message switch, was designed to rationalize the transmission of bank messages. It is owned by the hundreds of banks—located around the globe—that currently subscribe to the system. SWIFT first went live on a limited basis in Europe in 1977. It was then extended to North America, after that to the Far East, and finally in 1984, to the Middle East.

The major advantage of SWIFT is that it has a strict format requirement for messages. This enables subscribing banks to construct a computerized interface that keys messages transmitted via SWIFT directly into the CHIPS system or into Fedwire, as appropriate. Doing so eliminates clerical processing of Telex messages and thus streamlines, for subscribing banks, the making and receiving of payments through CHIPS and through Fedwire.

Today, a major problem for SWIFT is the success with which it has grown. In September 1977, SWIFT handled 400,000 messages; by 1986, it was handling that amount of traffic in half a day; it had 2,164 banks on its network, and network traffic was growing at an annual rate of 24%. To cope with escalating volume as well as to add new bells and whistles to its basic service, SWIFT embarked on an ambitious project—creating a new system, SWIFT II, that would have more capacity and flexibility than did the initial SWIFT system. Like many vendors, banks, and government bodies, SWIFT overestimated its ability to complete on time a very large software project; as a result, SWIFT II still hadn't appeared in 1989, seven years after it was announced and work was begun on it. By adding switches to its existing system, SWIFT has been able to keep its capacity well above its peak-day traffic figure; and in 1987, it announced that brokerage houses, central depositaries (such as DTC), and investment exchanges would, for the first time, be allowed to use the SWIFT network—a move that many banking members had resisted.

Using its existing network, SWIFT has also been able to offer other services to its subscribers. One of its subs, SWIFT Terminal Services (STS), produces terminals that interface with the network and now has over 50% of that market. Another subsidiary, SWIFT Service Partners (SSP), sells a cash management system, much to the chagrin of those banks that have spent freely to perfect their own systems. SSP also offers STREAM, a global risk management system; at the time SSP developed its system, only about 20 banks had the ability to manage risk on a global scale. Yet another SSP product is an ECU netting system that SSP developed in response to the needs of 18 European banks who found it time-consuming to track all of their ECU deals. Dollar netting systems are the preserve of large U.S. banks.

SWIFT's repeated failures to get SWIFT II up and running have caused continued fear that traffic on the network would outrun capacity—a fear that has deterred some would-be members from joining the system. In July 1989, it was said that, by the fall of 1989, SWIFT would make good on its promise to have SWIFT II up and running, but in recent years, SWIFT has made and broken many promises.

EUROCURRENCY SWAPS—THE MECHANICS

A substantial part of the total Eurocurrency market represents deposits of nondollar currencies (see Table 7–5). Eurodeposits denominated in currencies other than the dollar are actively traded in the interbank market in the same way that dollars are. The only significant difference is that trading volume is much smaller in them than in dollars.

Some trading in Eurocurrency deposits is generated by swaps, which as noted in Chapter 7, are extensively used by banks to match assets and liabilities in their Eurobooks by currency and to create deposits in a desired currency as cheaply as possible. Not surprisingly, the movement from fixed to floating exchange rates has somewhat changed the environment in which swaps occur. The increased volume of hedging improved forward markets, and bid-asked spreads in the foreign exchange market diminished. These developments favor the use of swaps. However, floating rates have also created a situation in which adjustments occur more rapidly. If a rate gets out of line, creating a possibility for profitable arbitrage, someone will hit it quickly and put it back in line. Thus, the opportunities available to a bank to cut funding costs by using swaps to create currency deposits are more evanescent than they once were, and where they are varies tremendously.

In Chapter 7, we described how a swap (*switch* to the British) operates in intuitive items, but we did not derive a formula for calculating the all-in interest cost of funds generated through a swap. The easiest way to do so is with an example.

Swap: Dollars into DM

Suppose a bank commits itself to lend 6-month Euro DM and now must fund this loan. It could take in the funds *natural,* that is, take a 6-month DM deposit, or it could take 6-month dollars and swap them into DM. To determine which is cheaper, the bank dealer must calculate the *all-in* rate of interest (cost) he would have to pay on DM obtained through a swap and compare that with the interest rate on a natural DM deposit.

The all-in interest cost on a currency deposit obtained by swapping another currency into that currency is the interest rate on the original deposit *minus* the gain (*plus* the loss) on the swap calculated as an annualized percentage rate. A swap is a sell-now-buy-back-later transaction, for example, like shorting Ford stock in February and covering in June. On a swap transaction, the percentage rate of gain or loss is calculated as follows:

$$\frac{\text{Selling price} - \text{Buying price}}{\text{Selling price}}$$

Since in the swap at hand (dollars into DM), the bank is going to sell dollars spot and buy them back forward, the percentage rate of gain or loss on the swap can be expressed as follows:

$$\frac{\left(\begin{array}{c}\text{Selling price of \$s}\\ \text{in the spot market}\end{array}\right) - \left(\begin{array}{c}\text{Buying price of \$s}\\ \text{in the forward market}\end{array}\right)}{\left(\begin{array}{c}\text{Selling price of \$s}\\ \text{in the spot market}\end{array}\right)}$$

This expression gives the percentage rate of gain or loss on the swap over the life of the swap. If the swap is for less than a year, as in our example, this figure will understate the annualized rate of gain or loss. To see why, note that, if it were possible to earn a 2% gain on a 6-month swap, then by repeating that swap twice during a year, one could earn 4% over the year. To calculate the *annualized* rate of gain (loss) on a swap that's outstanding less than a year, we divide the percentage gain or loss on the swap by the fraction of the year that it's outstanding.

Let

t = days the swap is outstanding

Then with rates quoted on a 360-day-year basis,

$$\left(\begin{array}{c}\text{Annualized \% gain or loss}\\ \text{on a swap of \$s into DM}\end{array}\right)$$

$$= \frac{(\text{Selling price of \$s}) - (\text{Buying price of \$s})}{(\text{Selling price of \$s})} \div \left(\frac{t}{360}\right)$$

If the spot rate for DM is quoted in the U.S. as 0.52397, that means it takes $0.52397 to buy a deutsche mark.[7] Since the spot rate for DM is expressed in units of dollars per DM, it is the

---

[7]When a foreign currency is quoted in terms of the amount of local currency required to buy a unit of foreign currency, that's called a *direct quote*. In our example, 0.3886 is the U.S. direct quote for DM; the German direct quote for dollars would be *inverse:*

$$\text{German direct quote for \$s} = \frac{1}{0.52397 \text{ \$/DM}} = 1.90851 \text{ DM/\$}$$

In most countries, foreign-exchange (fx) rates are direct quotes. The U.K., however, is an exception. There fx rates are *indirect* quotes which means that a British fx trader would quote the exchange rate between dollars and pounds as the number of dollars needed to buy a pound, which corresponds to the U.S. direct quote for pounds.

buying price of DM. To get the selling price of dollars, which we need to calculate the cost of the swap in our example, we have to invert the spot rate. For example, with the spot rate at 0.52397, the selling price of dollars is

$$\frac{1}{0.52397 \text{ \$/DM}} = 1.90851 \text{ DM/\$}$$

Let

$S = spot\ rate$ for DM quoted in U.S. terms
$F = forward\ rate$ for DM quoted in U.S. terms

Then, in a swap of dollars for DM,

$$\text{Selling price of \$s} = \frac{1}{S}$$

$$\text{Buying price of \$s} = \frac{1}{F}$$

Substituting these values into the formula derived above, we get

$$\begin{bmatrix} \text{Annualized \% gain or loss} \\ \text{on a swap of \$s into DM} \end{bmatrix} = \begin{bmatrix} \dfrac{\dfrac{1}{S} - \dfrac{1}{F}}{\dfrac{1}{S}} \div \dfrac{t}{360} \end{bmatrix}$$

$$= \left(1 - \frac{S}{F}\right)\left(\frac{360}{t}\right)$$

As we said, the all-in interest cost of DM obtained through a swap equals the interest paid on the dollars borrowed *minus* the annualized rate of gain on the swap. Let

i_{DM} = all-in interest cost of the DM generated through a swap of \$s into DM

$r_\$$ = interest rate paid on the dollars swapped into DM

Then, in symbols,[8]

$$i_{DM} = r_\$ - \left(1 - \frac{S}{F}\right)\left(\frac{360}{t}\right) = r_\$ + \left(\frac{S}{F} - 1\right)\left(\frac{360}{t}\right)$$

---

[8]This formula does not take into account the impact of hedging interest that is earned in DM, but paid in dollars.

To illustrate, we consider a numerical example in which 6-month dollars are swapped into 6-month DM. Assume that the spot rate is 0.52397; the forward rate is 0.52865 (the forward mark is at a premium); the interest cost of 6-month Eurodollars is 8¾%; and the bid-asked quotes on 6-month Euro DM are 6¹⁵⁄₁₆–7%. Plugging the first three of these numbers (all quotes that prevailed on July 21, 1989) into our formula, we get:[9]

$$i_{DM} = 0.875 + \left(\frac{0.52397}{0.52865} - 1\right)\left(\frac{360}{184}\right)$$
$$= 0.0875 - (0.0088527)(1.95652)$$
$$= 0.0875 - 0.01732$$
$$\cong 7.02\%$$

Because the forward DM is selling at a *premium,* the swap results in a gain. Thus, the annualized cost of the swap is negative, and adding it to $r_\$$ reduces i_{DM} below $r_\$$; still, borrowing dollars and swapping them into DM turns out to be 2 bp more expensive than buying 6-month DM at the offered rate of 7%; in this case, taking the swap route doesn't pay.

Often, in actively traded currencies, the cost of a Eurocurrency deposit obtained through a swap lies in the midrange of the bid-offered quotes in the interbank market for deposits of that currency in that tenor.

Swap: DM into Dollars

Swaps, of course, are done not only out of dollars into a foreign currency, but out of a foreign country into dollars. For example, had the swap been DM into dollars, then we would have been interested in the all-in interest cost of the dollars obtained through the swap. That rate can be calculated as follows. Let

$i_\$$ = all-in interest cost of the dollars generated by a swap out of DM

r_{DM} = interest rate paid on the DM swapped into dollars

---

[9]The 6-month period quoted on Friday, July 21, 1989, contained 184 days.

Then

$$i_\$ = r_{DM} + \left(\frac{F}{S} - 1\right)\left(\frac{360}{t}\right)$$

In discussing swaps, we assumed that the mark was the foreign currency involved in the swap. The formulas we've derived are, however, valid for a swap between dollars and any Eurocurrency.

Arbitrage

Arbitrage, strictly defined, involves buying at a low price in one market and selling simultaneously at a higher price in a second market. Swaps in the Eurocurrency deposit market are nothing but a form of arbitrage, one so widely practiced that it creates, except under unusual conditions, a very consistent relationship in each maturity range between (1) the interest differential at which deposits of a given currency trade relative to Eurodollar deposits and (2) the premium or discount at which the currency trades relative to the dollar in the forward market for foreign exchange.[10]

While it's true that a dollar is a dollar, there are, as noted in Chapters 6 and 7, subtle differences to U.S. banks between

---

[10]The difference between the spot and forward rates at which a currency trades ($S - F$) is called the *swap rate*. Whenever short-term interest rates are lower on deposits of a nondollar Eurocurrency than they are on Eurodollar deposits, the swap rate on that currency quoted in U.S. terms will be *negative*, that is, that currency will trade at a forward premium. Moreover, because of the activities of arbitrageurs—institutions seeking to borrow at one rate and lend at a higher one—the size of the premium will be such that the cost of borrowing that currency and swapping it into dollars will equal or nearly equal the cost of borrowing dollars. Note that in our example of swapping dollars into DM, the interest rate on 6-month DM was lower than that on 6-month dollars, and the swap rate was accordingly negative:

$$0.52397 - 0.52865 = -0.00468$$

Because the swap rate is the difference between the spot rate and a specific forward rate, its size depends on the *tenor* of the swap transaction.

Whenever short-term interest rates are higher on deposits of a nondollar Eurocurrency than on Eurodollar deposits, the arbitrage will work the opposite way, making the all-in cost of borrowing dollars and swapping them into that Eurocurrency approximately equal to the cost of borrowing that currency directly.

Eurodollars and domestic dollars because of reserve requirements and FDIC premiums. Thus, to some degree the Eurodollar market is separate from the domestic money market, a situation that creates the possibility for arbitrage between the two markets.

ARBITRAGES BETWEEN THE U.S. AND EUROMARKETS

In different maturity ranges, Euro rates tend to be higher than U.S. rates most of the time. However, the tracking between U.S. and Euro rates is extraordinarily close over time (Figures 18–4 to 18–6). Spreads widen and narrow, and sometimes rates cross, but the main trends up and down are always the same in both markets. There's no doubt that this consistency in rates is the work of arbitrage, but that still leaves open the question of where the major impetus for rate changes typically comes from. Are changes in U.S. rates pushing Euro rates up and down, or vice versa? A British Eurobanker's succinct answer: "Rarely, does the tail wag the dog. The U.S. money market is the dog, the Euromarket the tail."

The truth of this statement has created a foreign contingent of Fed watchers—in London, Paris, Singapore, and other Euro-centers. Much as some bankers, especially foreign ones, would like to think of the Euromarket as an international market that responds largely to developments external to the U.S. economy, experience has taught them that whenever the Fed moves, its actions immediately impact the Euromarket. Consequently, to be successful, Eurobankers must understand the workings of the U.S. money market and follow closely developments there.

Two sorts of arbitrages are used to link U.S. and Euro rates, *technical* and *transitory*. Technical arbitrages were most important at the short end of the market, and opportunities for them occurred because of the way Euro transactions affected, due to institutional arrangements, the reservable deposits of U.S. banks buying and selling Eurodollars. Opportunities for technical arbitrage vanished with the movement of CHIPS to same-day settlement.

FIGURE 18–4
Overnight rates: Euros and Fed funds (money market basis, monthly averages)

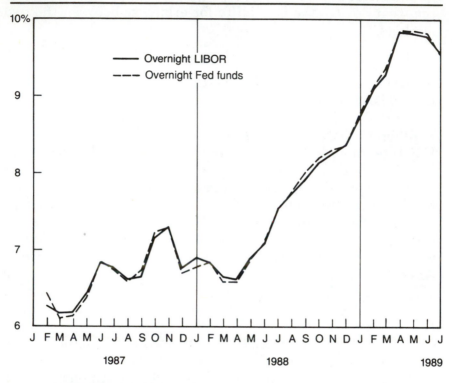

Source: J. P. Morgan Securities, Inc.

Transitory arbitrages, in contrast, are money flows that occur in response to temporary discrepancies that arise between U.S. and Euro rates because rates in the two markets are being affected by differing supply and demand pressures. Much transitory arbitrage used to be carried on by banks that actively borrow and lend funds in both markets. Another group whose activities tend to pull together U.S. and Euro rates are investors who shift from domestic to Euro instruments and back in response to changing yield spreads. Finally, a growing number of borrowers, domestic and foreign, shift between the domestic and the

FIGURE 18–5
One-month rates: commercial paper and LIBID (money market basis, monthly averages)

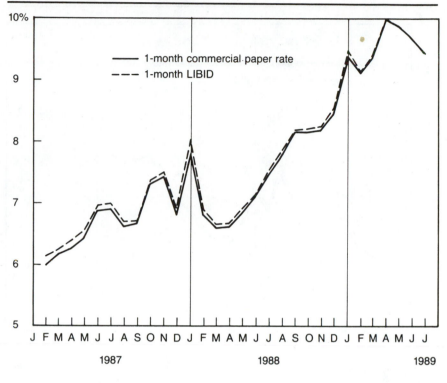

Source: J. P. Morgan Securities, Inc.

Euromarkets in response to changes in the relationship between lending rates in the two markets. Their activities too hold rates together.

The Banks: Soft Arbitrage

In making funding choices, domestic versus Euro, U.S. banks always compare relative costs on an *all-in* basis. To a U.S. bank, the all-in cost of funds it raises in the domestic market exceeds the nominal rate it pays by the FDIC premium, if any, it incurs

FIGURE 18–6
Three-month rates: commercial paper and LIBID (money market basis, monthly averages)

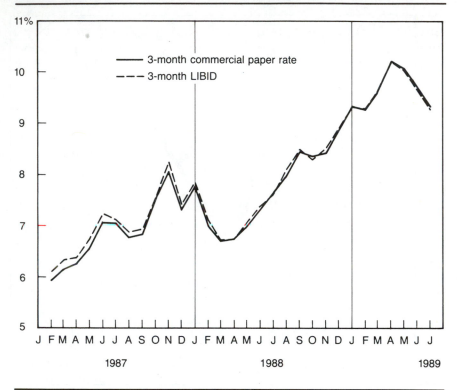

Source: J. P. Morgan Securities, Inc.

and by the cost, if any, of reserve requirements. Currently—although Congress is proposing to change this—a U.S. bank incurs *no* FDIC premium when it takes Eurodollar deposits. Also, it incurs *no* reserve requirement on taking Eurodollars per se; however, the heart of the Fed's Reg D, much amended over time, is that a U.S. bank must hold reserves equal to 3% of its *net borrowings* (over a seven-day averaging period) from the Euromarket.

In the late 1970s and early 1980s, when U.S. banks were still funding themselves to a significant degree through the sale of 3- and 6-month CDs and when balance-sheet concerns were still minimal, U.S. banks would actively arbitrage between the U.S. and Euro markets even when doing so would enlarge their balance sheets. Early in such bygone days, when CD rates were low, one U.S. banker noted, "Today, 6-month Euros are at 6⅛. I could buy 6-month money in New York at 5¾, but the all-in cost would be 6.03. That sort of arbitrage [buy at 6.03 and sell at 6.125] is probably not worth the bookkeeping. But if the domestic all-in rate fell to 5.70, I might do the arbitrage in size— provided I had sufficient unused credit lines to sell [redeposit in the Euromarket] the money I raised in New York."

That sort of arbitrage no longer occurs much if at all. For one thing, banks, as noted, today sell few wholesale domestic CDs in the once prime and popular maturities of three and six months. Instead, banks much prefer, for reasons discussed in Chapter 6, to sell fixed-rate deposit notes that have a minimum maturity of 18 months and on which they therefore incur no reserve requirements. Whenever they sell such notes, banks then slap on an interest-rate swap to convert the proceeds of the note sale from fixed-rate to floating-rate funds. Using this technique, a prime American bank can achieve sub-LIBOR funding and simultaneously ease its liquidity concerns.

A second factor that deters old-style, active bank arbitrage is the fact that all of the big U.S. banks have balance-sheet concerns. Banks used typically to think first of their reserve-requirement constraint; in considering a ploy, they'd ask: Will it pay when reserve costs are taken into account? Today, banks face a second binding constraint: every asset a bank acquires has a capital cost; so a ploy, no matter what it earns, doesn't pass muster unless it pays an attractive return on the now-scarce capital that capital-adequacy requirements say the bank must assign to it.

Thus, today, the arbitrage that banks do between the domestic and Euromarkets is what one U.S. banker refers to as *soft arbitrage*. "What tends," said this banker, "to tie domestic and Euro rates together is that some banks have consolidated their funding operations into a unified operation that looks at sources of funds, both onshore and offshore, as alternatives. That is a form of soft arbitrage in that we are looking for the cheapest available source of funds. If we have a situation in which domestic rates are atypically low relative to Euro rates, the bank will look at the domestic market as a temporarily cheaper source of funds, and vice versa. Also, we don't look just at domestic versus Euro funding opportunities at the bank level, but at opportunities for funding via commercial paper [at the holding-company level]."

Soft arbitrage is imprecise for several reasons. First, not every bank has unified its funding into one operation. Second, even a bank that has must be cognizant of certain constraints it faces in terms of market share and customer relationships. For example, a bank might feel compelled to take money that was a tad expensive out of one market as opposed to another so as to maintain its presence in the first market and so as not to floor the second market. Also, a bank might feel compelled to take money that was a tad expensive from a customer in order to maintain its relationship with that customer.

Spread in Overnight Rates: Fed Funds and Euros

Without looking at actual spreads, one would expect the overnight rate on Fed funds to lie a slim spread below that on overnight Euros. A lot of the domestic entities that use the sale of overnight funds as a source of liquidity are small institutions who, because of concerns about credit and sovereign risk, have probably never established lines that would permit them to sell overnight Euros; also, at least some sellers of funds may be barred from selling Euros because they operate under rules that deem such sales to be prohibited "foreign" investments.

Still, at times Euro overnights do trade expensive to overnight Fed funds (Figure 18–4). For example, in July 1989, overnight Euros had, at one point, been trading for several weeks at 1/16 below where overnight Fed funds were trading. The explanation comes down to supply and demand. Sometimes, banks in Europe and the Far East end up long Euros: maybe they have taken a rate view that led them to borrow 6-month Euros; they are now long all this money and have to lend it short term until the rise in short rates that they anticipate occurs. Banks located outside the U.S., as opposed to foreign bank branches situated in the U.S., can't sell Fed funds as can domestic banks; so they lend overnight Euros and, in doing so, may push the overnight Euro rate below the rate on overnight Feds.

In any case, there are enough globals who are free to operate in sufficient size in both markets so that the overnight rates on Euros and Feds cannot get too far out of line except on days when some temporary technical factor causes an aberration in one of these rates.

The Spread of Commercial Paper Rates to LIBOR

To show the tracking between longer money market rates in the domestic and Euromarkets, one would, in an earlier period, have compared rates on, say, 3-month and 6-month CDs, domestic and Euro. Today, with domestic banks selling few, if any, wholesale 3- and 6-month CDs, a comparison of such rates would be meaningless.

A better comparison to make is between commercial paper rates and LIBID. Today, a number of borrowers and investors are sensitive to this spread. During the years that the domestic CD market was contracting, the commercial paper market was exploding (Chapter 22). More and more investors were drawn into the commercial paper market, which offered higher yields than did prime bank CDs, and once accustomed to those higher rates, they were loath to buy a domestic CD unless it paid a competitive rate. Banks, however, were loath to pay higher rates on domestic CDs, which also cost them the FDIC premium plus reserve requirements.

One result was that banks began to look more and more to the issuance of commercial paper at the holding company level as a way to fund certain of their operations. If a bank's holding company deposits in its bank monies raised through the issuance of commercial paper, those deposits, just like any other deposit, are reservable and subject to the FDIC premium. However, if those monies are used to fund offshore operations of the bank, such funds are not reservable. In Chapter 7, we gave an example of one bank strategy for using funds raised by selling commercial paper to fund bank operations offshore: it called for the bank holding company to sell commercial paper and then deposit the funds thus raised in its bank's Caribbean branch, which in turn used those deposits to fund a profitable portfolio of short- to medium-term securities, principally corporate. A bank that does this is clearly keeping a close eye on the rate at which it could raise Euros of comparable maturity.

Also, U.S. banks are not the only banks to have discovered the commercial paper. Issuance in this market by foreign banks is, as noted in Chapter 22, substantial. Borrowing of this sort by prime global banks clearly tends to pull U.S. commercial paper rates toward LIBID.

Another phenomenon that exerts a similar pressure, one that began years ago and has continued to grow, is the issuance of U.S. commercial paper by prime European corporates and government agencies, such as Électricité de France and Gaz de France. The alternative of such borrowers is clearly to borrow in the Euromarket at some spread to LIBOR.

More recently, a market in European commercial paper (ECP) has sprung up in London (Chapter 22). U.S. dealers were quick to point out to their clients that it was in their interest to set up a global program that would permit them to issue not only domestic, but Euro commercial paper. Doing so would permit them to get the cheapest rate worldwide and to enhance their investor base. Obviously, ECP trades at a spread to LIBOR. (U.S. dealers have also been pushing global programs in the burgeoning medium-term note (MTN) market, using the same pitch to issuers that they do in the commercial paper market. MTNs, as noted in Chapter 24, are a logical extension of the mode of commerical paper issuance to longer maturities.)

Investors too play their part in wedding domestic and Euro money market rates. U.S. investors are the principal buyers of Euro CDs. Also, while ECP cannot be sold on shore to a U.S. investor, it can be and is bought by U.S. firms with foreign operations. If treasury at the head office of such a company runs its worldwide short-term portfolio on a consolidated basis, as some companies do, then the company can load up its offshore portfolios with ECP and reason justifiably that its consolidated portfolio is adequately diversified in terms of names held, sovereign risk assumed, and so on.

Given what we've said, the close relationships that prevail between commercial paper rates and LIBID in the 1-month and 3-month areas is not surprising (Figures 18–5 and 18–6). Today, most commercial paper is issued in the 30-days-and-under range, so the 3-month commercial paper rate is sometimes regarded as a bogus rate. However, some big corporate finance companies do issue, at times in size, paper with 3- and 6-month maturities; also, bank holding companies would like to stretch some of their issuance to longer maturities, and they're doing so with some success as commercial paper investors gradually become more willing to extend to longer maturities.

A part of the problem of showing the closeness of U.S. and Euro rates is that the instruments sold in the two markets are not exactly parallel. Also, with the advent of interest-rate swaps, a borrower can get to a bogy rate he wants to pay, say, LIBOR plus or minus a spread, by borrowing in the commercial paper market or by borrowing medium-term, fixed-rate and by then doing an interest-rate swap. The latter is precisely what banks do: they issue in the domestic market medium-term, fixed-rate, deposit notes and then do a swap fixed-rate to LIBOR. As an indication of the synchronization of domestic and Euro rates in a longer maturity, we have plotted, in Figure 18–7, 2-year LIBID against the rate paid on 2-year deposit notes by a prime American bank, Morgan. Not surprisingly, the two rates track each other closely; in fact, during the last two months covered by the chart they were identical.

While people may argue about just what Euro-U.S. rate comparisons are most telling, it's clear that, today, borrowers and investors, both domestic and foreign, regard LIBOR, LIMEAN, or LIBID, as the case may be, as the benchmark rate against which they compare every short-term rate that they pay or receive.

THE NEXT CHAPTER

In Chapter 19, we turn to interest-rate swaps. This new market is fascinating on a number of counts: it's growing at an explosive rate; it has been put to an incredibly wide range of uses by both borrowers and investors; and amazingly, the swaps it produces,

FIGURE 18–7
Two-year rates: Morgan deposit notes (domestic) and LIBID
(monthly averages)

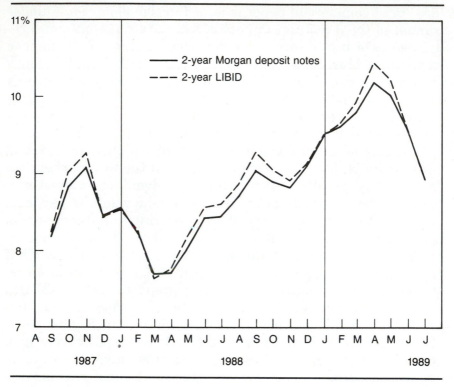

Source: J. P. Morgan Securities, Inc.

sometimes piled one on top of another, are capable of transforming a liability or an asset from its original form into a quite different form, one that fits the needs of the borrower or investor, but gives him a better rate than he could have gotten without his swap or swaps. Interest-rate swaps are the closest the 20th century has come to achieving alchemy.

CHAPTER 19

INTEREST-RATE SWAPS

An interest-rate swap is a contract between two parties to pay and receive, with a set frequency, interest payments determined by applying the differential between two interest rates—for example, 5-year fixed and 6-month LIBOR—to an agreed-upon notional principal.

Put more intuitively, an interest swap is a trade that produces, over time, the same cash flows that would be produced if party A were to say to party B, "You and I have different liabilities with the same maturity—let's swap," and the swap were done.

SOME HISTORY

A peculiar feature of interest-rate swaps is that they evolved out of more, not less, complicated instruments, namely, parallel loans and currency swaps.

Parallel Loans

The easiest way to describe a *parallel loan* is with an example. We'll use dollars and sterling.

In the post–World War II years before oil gushed from the North Sea, sterling was chronically weak; and to prop its value, the Bank of England imposed controls on the external use of sterling. One aspect of these controls was that a U.K. corporation that wanted to invest in the U.S. had to pay a premium price ($/£ rate of exchange) to obtain dollars to do so.

Nothing spurs innovation like a regulation. Somewhere, probably London, some creative financial soul said, "There are, in this world, not just U.K. corporations that need dollar financing, but U.S. corporations that need sterling financing. Couldn't a $/£ swap be arranged between such firms on terms advantageous to both?"

The answer was yes, and the parallel loan was born. Sticking to essentials only, we can illustrate how such a loan worked as follows. Suppose that British Petroleum (BP), which has sterling balances, has a U.S. sub that needs dollars to fund an investment in the U.S.; assume also that IBM, which has dollar balances, has a U.K. sub that needs sterling to fund an investment in the U.K. Finally, assume that the rate at which sterling trades in the *spot* market (market for immediate delivery) is $1.80 per British pound.

One way BP could get dollars for its U.S. sub to invest without paying a premium would be for it to strike the following deal with IBM: BP agrees to lend to IBM's U.K. sub £10MM; in exchange, IBM agrees to lend to BP's U.S. sub $18MM. That's a parallel loan in a nutshell (Figure 19–1). Normally, a parallel loan has a fixed maturity, typically 5 to 10 years, and is structured as a *bullet loan* (all principal is repaid at maturity). Suppose in our example that the parallel loans made are for seven years at fixed rates. Then, IBM's U.K. sub would pay interest to

FIGURE 19–1
A parallel loan

A. Flows of *principal* at the outset of the loan; reverse flows occur when loan matures.

B. Directions of *interest* flows during the life of parallel loans.

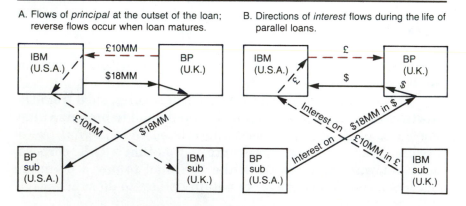

BP on the £10MM the latter has lent it at the rate prevailing in the sterling market for 7-year, fixed-rate money. Similarly, BP's U.K. sub would pay IBM interest on its $18MM loan at the going U.S. rate for 7-year, fixed-rate money. Normally, the payments of interest due on the two loans would be timed to occur at the same intervals, say, semiannually, and would, in practice, occur simultaneously.

Sometimes, parallel loan agreements also contain a *ratchet clause* that calls for the interest rates paid on the loans to move, up or down, in tandem with interest rates in the countries whose currencies are involved, U.K. and U.S. interest rates in our example. The credit risk associated with a parallel loan is that one party will fail to make a payment of interest due or, at maturity, of principal plus interest due. To mitigate this risk, a parallel loan agreement typically contains a *right of offset* clause that gives each party the right to offset payments due it but not received against payments due from it. Prepayment provisions on parallel loans, if they exist, must be negotiated, since prepayment by one party of its loan would leave that party with an unsecured loan to the other party.

In our example, if the $/£ exchange rate were to change over the life of the parallel loans, say sterling were to weaken, then the dollar value of BP's loan to IBM's U.K. sub would fall below the dollar value of IBM's loan to BP's U.S. sub. That in turn would cause IBM to suffer a foreign-exchange loss on its loan of sterling to BP; it would also expose IBM to credit risk. To preclude these consequences, BP and IBM could include, in their loan agreements, a *topping-up clause:* a clause that required that additional advances or repayments on one of the loans be made if the $/£ spot rate were to move beyond some trigger point.

In our example, there is no reason why it must be the respective subs of IBM and BP that need local-currency funding. It might be that it is IBM and BP themselves that need, respectively, sterling and dollar financing. In that case, IBM lends BP sterling and vice versa, and the deal is called a *back-to-back loan*.

The beauty of a parallel loan agreement is that it may enable one or both parties to use surplus balances of their native currency to finance an investment by a sub of theirs in a non-native currency. A possible disadvantage of such an arrangement is that it puts a liability on the balance sheet of each party involved, thus making them appear more leveraged. This disadvantage disappears if the parties instead do a currency swap.

A Currency Swap

To illustrate a *currency swap,* let's continue with our BP–IBM example, only this time we will assume that the agreement struck between BP and IBM calls for IBM to *sell*—no liabilities this time—$18MM to BP, which BP onloans to its U.S. sub and for BP simultaneously to *sell* sterling 10MM to IBM, which it onloans to its U.K. sub. The assumed exchange rate is again $1.80/£, so the two transactions are equal in value. Concomitantly, the parties agree to buy back the dollar and sterling amounts sold at the same exchange rate at a fixed future date. Over the life of the swap, which again might be 5 to 10 years, one party will make periodic net interest payments to the other at a rate that approximates the differential between specified sterling and dollar interest rates. These rates can be either fixed or floating depending on the ratcheting clause, if any, in the agreement. We set our example in a period when sterling was a weak currency; consequently, the presumption is that sterling interest rates will be higher than dollar interest rates and that net interest will therefore flow in our example from BP to IBM.

The reader may find it helpful to note that a currency swap is structured similarly to a repurchase transaction. Recalling Chapter 13, we know that IBM, by entering simultaneously into a spot purchase and a forward sale, could reverse in governments; a currency swap boils down to IBM reversing in not governments, but sterling. The flip side of the transaction is that BP repos interest-bearing sterling balances and receives, as collateral, interest-bearing dollar balances.

In a currency swap, risk is minimal: the right of offset is implied by the structure of the agreement; and exchange-rate risk can be handled, as in a parallel loan, through the inclusion of a topping-up clause.

As a comparison of Figures 19–1 and 19–2 shows, a cur-

FIGURE 19–2
A currency swap*

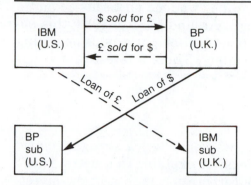

*At expiration of the swap agreement, the IBM-BP *sale* (swap) of £ for $ is reversed: IBM gets back its $ and BP gets back its £ on the terms negotiated at the outset of the swap.

rency swap can be structured so that it accomplishes exactly the same thing that a parallel loan agreement would. A currency swap offers, however, several advantages over a parallel loan: it's mechanically simpler, and it puts no liability on the balance sheet of either of the contracting parties.

A company might opt to do a currency swap for any of several reasons: to mitigate exchange control regulations, to unlock a blocked currency balance, to lower its cost of borrowing a foreign currency, or to obtain financing in a currency that it is unable to borrow long term.[1]

A COUPON SWAP

Analytically, the outcome of a currency swap is as if two parties had swapped liabilities denominated in two different currencies; in our example, it is as if BP had swapped with IBM a sterling

---

[1] If a company acquires a balance of a foreign currency that it cannot, due to the host country's exchange controls, convert into its native currency, that balance is said to be *blocked.*

liability of its own for an IBM, dollar liability. Conceptually, there is no reason why two liabilities need be denominated in different currencies in order to be swapped on terms advantageous to the contracting parties. Around 1981 to 1982, this notion dawned independently on several bright groups operating in different world financial centers. Thus, interest-rate swaps were born.

An Example

The first type of interest-rate swap done was a straight *coupon swap,* a specie of swap that's easy to explain. To illustrate, let's assume that Triple B, a U.S. corporation with a below-investment-grade credit rating, wants to finance in dollars an investment in plant and equipment. Dollar interest rates are volatile, so to permit long-term budgeting and to protect itself against interest rate exposure, Triple B wants to obtain medium-term, say, 5-year, financing at a fixed rate.

Unfortunately, Triple B finds that, because of its low credit quality, investors are none too eager to acquire its paper. In fact, if it were to float a 5-year, fixed-rate Eurobond, it would have to pay a rate of 11.70. Triple B's alternative is to get a term loan from its bank at a floating rate, say 6-month LIBOR + 3/8.

Meanwhile, there exists a foreign bank—call it Fuji—that wants to borrow floating-rate dollars; from 1979 on, Fuji has learned in the school of hard knocks that, to minimize its interest-rate exposure, it ought to make only floating-rate loans funded with floating-rate money.[2] Fuji is well liked by Euro investors and could sell 5-year, fixed-rate notes at 10.75. Alternatively, it could borrow 6-month floating-rate dollars in the interbank market at LIBOR + 1/4.

At first glance, it would appear that there is not much Fuji could do for Triple B except to lend it 6-month money at LIBOR + 3/8, fund that loan at LIBOR + 1/4, and thereby make a

---

[2]The first bank to do a coupon swap was not a Japanese bank, but Japanese banks eventually did tons of this business.

scant ⅛ for itself. Not so. There's a more interesting deal Fuji and Triple B can strike.

Note Fuji can borrow fixed-rate, 5-year dollars in the Euronote market at a rate of 95 bp below the rate that Triple B would have to pay, whereas it can borrow 6-month, floating-rate money at a rate only 12.5 bp below the rate that Triple B would have to pay. Clearly, relative to Triple B, Fuji has privileged access to fixed-rate money. This correctly suggests that the cheapest way for Fuji and Triple B to borrow *jointly* (i.e., each borrows the same sum) $10MM of 5-year, fixed-rate money and $10MM of 5-year, floating-rate money would be for Fuji to be the borrower of fixed and Triple B to be the borrower of floating.

This course of action has the disadvantage that it leaves each borrower with precisely the type of funds it did not want to borrow: Fuji with fixed-rate dollars, Triple B with floating-rate dollars. But, no problem. Enter the coupon swap. Fuji says to Triple B:

> I will offer you the following deal. You borrow at LIBOR + ⅜ and sell me that debt at LIBOR flat. I, in turn, will borrow 5-year, fixed-rate money at 10.75 and sell it to you at 11. You'll lose ⅜ on your sale of LIBOR funding to me, but when you add that ⅜ to the 11% I am going to charge you for 5-year, fixed-rate money, you end up with an *all-in cost* of funds of only 11.375; that's 32.5 bp better than you could do if you borrowed 5-year, fixed-rate money in your own name.

Fuji is not being altruistic. As Table 19–1 shows, the deal enables Fuji to shave 50 bp off the rate it must pay for 6-month money—to get such money at LIBOR − ¼ instead of at LIBOR + ¼.

A Free Lunch?

The example we have just worked through, which, however the deal is worded, is the economic equivalent of Fuji and Triple B selling each other their respective liabilities at prices that make the deal advantageous to both, seems to violate the "no-free-lunch" principle so dear to the heart of every economist. Actually, it does not. In the 19th century, a famous British econo-

TABLE 19–1

The Fuji–Triple B swap, based on comparative advantage, produces a savings pie of 82.5 bp, which the two split: 50 bp to Fuji, 32.5 bp to Triple B

A. **(1)** *Saving* on 5-year, fixed-rate funds if Fuji borrows them:

Rate to Triple B:	11.70
− Rate to Fuji:	10.75
	.95 bp saving

(2) *Extra cost* on floating-rate funds if Triple B borrows them:

Rate to Triple B:	LIBOR + 3/8
− Rate to Fuji:	LIBOR + 1/4
	12.5 bp extra cost

(1) − (2) *Net saving* on paired borrowings:

95 bp − 12.5 bp = **82.5 bp**

B. **(3)** Saving to Fuji on the swap:

Cost to Fuji of floating-rate borrowing	LIBOR + 1/4
− Net cost after the swap (10.75 − 11 + LIBOR):	LIBOR − 1/4
	50 bp

(4) Saving to Triple B on the swap:

Cost of a term borrowing	11.70
− Net cost after the swap (LIBOR + 3/8 − LIBOR + LIBOR):	11.375
	32.5 bp

(3) + (4) Total savings earned by Fuji and Triple B on the swap:

50 bp + 32.5 bp = **82.5 bp**

---

mist, Ricardo, demonstrated that, even if country A enjoys an absolute cost advantage over country B in the production of both wine and cheese, if A's absolute cost advantage over B is greater in wine than in cheese, then it's possible for both A and B to be better off (drink more wine, eat more cheese) if A specializes in the production of wine (in which it has a comparative cost advantage), B specializes in the production of cheese (in which it has a comparative cost advantage), and A and B trade: A's wine for B's cheese. That in a nutshell in the classic argument for free trade in *goods*.

What applies to goods also applies to money. Fuji has a comparative advantage over Triple B in the borrowing of fixed-rate money, whereas Triple B has a comparative advantage over Fuji in the borrowing of floating-rate money. If each borrower specializes in borrowing what it can borrow best, they reduce their aggregate borrowing costs by the 95-bp advantage that Fuji enjoys in the fixed-rate market *minus* the 12.5-bp disadvantage that Triple B suffers in the floating-rate market. Subtracting 12.5 bp from 95 bp, we get 82.5 bp. By borrowing along lines of their respective comparative advantages and then trading via a swap the liabilities thus created, Fuji and Triple B create a 82.5-bp pie of savings that they can carve up between themselves. That, moreover, is precisely what Fuji's proposed deal does. It shaves Triple B's borrowing cost by 32.5 bp and Fuji's by 50 bp. Summing these savings, we get 82.5 bp, precisely the pie of rate savings to be split.

Trade based on a difference in comparative advantage, be it in goods or liabilities, is a *positive-sum game*.

EVOLUTION OF THE DOLLAR, INTEREST-RATE-SWAP MARKET

The U.S. dollar, interest-rate-swap market began in late 1981 with custom-tailored deals, often arranged by one or more intermediaries. The earliest such swap to achieve wide publicity was a swap of fixed for floating between Deutsche Bank Luxembourg and a lesser credit; through this swap, arranged by Merrill Lynch and Crédit Suisse, First Boston, Deutsche Bank was able to obtain sub-LIBOR funding.

From this point on, interest-rate swaps looked like a great deal to everyone who could get involved. This group included intermediaries—banks and dealers—who, for a fee (1) arranged such swaps and (2) *guaranteed* both sides of the swap. Major U.S. banks with their expertise in analyzing U.S. corporate and other credits were a natural for the intermediary business; such banks could with comfort accept the credit risk of dealing with many lesser credits, and at the same time, their name was acceptable to all potential swap parties.

Inevitably, it occurred that an intermediary would have a customer who wanted to do one side of a swap but no customer who, at that precise moment, wanted to do the other side of the swap. To get real business done, intermediaries took to *warehousing* swaps: doing one side of a swap and holding the second side on their books until a customer came along who wanted that second side. To make warehousing practical and to minimize the risk inherent in this practice, swaps had to be made more tradable and thus at least a somewhat liquid product; this was done through *standardization* of swap terms.

The Plain Vanilla Swap

Standardization produced the *plain vanilla,* also known as *generic,* swap. A plain vanilla swap is a swap of fixed-rate for floating-rate dollars with a maturity ranging from 2 to 10 years. The floating rate is 3-month LIBOR, and the fixed rate is quoted at *a spread to Treasuries*. For example, if the swap were done for five years, the fixed rate might be quoted as 5-year Treasuries *plus* 90 [bp].

Payments of fixed-rate and floating-rate interest due under the swap are due on the same day and are *netted*. Specifically, on each payment date—these occur *semiannually*—the party who is called, on that date, to pay the higher rate of interest must make a net payment of interest to the second party. Since the floating rate in a swap may float above as well as below the fixed rate, the party who pays net interest in one period may well receive net interest in the next. Netting of interest payments in a swap achieves two important purposes: it reduces credit risk for all parties to the swap, and it reduces as well the usage by these parties of the credit lines that they have extended to each other.

BBA and ISDA Documentation

In the early days of the swap market, would-be parties to a swap had to call in their lawyers who would then scratch their heads and try to think of all of the *i*'s that had to be crossed and *t*'s that had to be dotted in the negotiation and documentation of the swap agreement in order for their client to get the deal they wanted. This was inefficient.

Today, most swaps, plain vanilla and other, are done using standard documentation, which itself comes in two varieties.

The lite variety is *British Bankers' Association (BBA)* documentation. Under BBA documentation, swap participants basically agree to do telex confirmations, to select U.K. law as the law governing the swap, and to use BBA or ISDA references rates (found on Telerate and Reuters) in calculating interest due. The need to specify precisely what reference rate will be used is necessary because many rates are quoted by a variety of sources, not always on exactly the same basis. BBA documentation is technically good for only a swap of two years or less, but some people will do trades using BBA documentation out to five years.

The *International Swap Dealers Association (ISDA)* provides the full-calorie variety of swap documentation. Specifically, ISDA has produced a fill-in-the-blanks, master swap agreement that, when completed, becomes a signed contract. The clauses in the ISDA agreement and the blanks to be filled in cover every conceivable aspect of a swap: What are the dates on which payments shall be made? What are the dates on which the floating rate shall be *reset?* What is a default event? How shall it be handled? Whose law shall govern, U.K. or New York State? If the floating rate is 3-month LIBOR, what reference rate shall be used? (ISDA lists four possible reference rates for LIBOR as well as TIBOR, which is the dollar deposit rate quoted in Tokyo at 10 A.M. Tokyo time.) And so on and on. The ISDA interest-rate-swap agreement runs 13 pages, and ISDA takes many more pages to explain elsewhere just what is said in those 13 pages.

Swaps with Bells and Whistles

We described above the plain vanilla swap, which is much used. Frequently, however, a would-be swapper wants a swap with particular bells and whistles to fit their particular needs. This leads to the creation of swaps in flavors more numerous than those in which Howard Johnson dishes out ice cream. There are swaps of prime against LIBOR (one of several species of floating-to-floating swaps), annual-pay swaps in which the floating rate is 3-month LIBOR compounded over a year, and so on. Fortunately, ISDA documentation is so flexible—has so many blanks to fill in—that it can be used to document swaps of all flavors.

Street-Speak in Swap-Land

The generic coupon swap is an absolute no-brainer—so simple that it is incredible that no one thought to do it long ago. Jargon in swap-land is, however, another matter: most confusing at best. To help the reader, we have produced Table 19–2.

The best way to fix in one's mind that a *bidder* for a swap is bidding for the right to *pay fixed* and that the *payor of fixed* is the *buyer* of (i.e., *long*) the swap is to recall the origin of the coupon swap: good old Triple B, the weak credit, was struggling to *buy* fixed-rate money, which in some circumstances it might not be able to do directly at any rate; Fuji, in contrast, had attractive borrowing alternatives and got into the deal only because it saw an opportunity to get funding at LIBOR flat.

The principal amount for which a swap is done and on which interest payments are due is referred to as the swap's *notional principal*—notional because this amount is neither received nor paid.

Another memory jogger is to think of swaps in *spread* terms. *Payors* [of fixed] benefit when spreads go out because they are *long* the spread. *Receivers* benefit when spreads come in because they are *short* the spread.

THE BROKERS

Brokers got into the business of brokering swaps as early as 1983, and today brokers' screens show an active interdealer market in swaps. The principal brokers of swaps are Tullet & Tokyo, Eurobrokers, Garban, and Prebon.

Brokerage on interest swap is currently 1 bp per annum, and each side pays. It is, however, common for dealers to negotiate about the maximum amount with their broker. Brokerage is paid up front.

Brokers broker both money market swaps and coupon swaps. Thus, a broker's run might go: "Spot 1 year, 8.80–83; Dec–Dec, 1 year, 9.03–9; March–March, 1-year, 9.15–20; 2 years on the spread, 67–70; there is an offering in the market at 9.18, which is about 69 over; 3 years, 70–76 . . ." and so on. In

TABLE 19–2
Street-speak in swap-land*

Bid/offered
- A *bid* is for the right to *pay fixed* (and to receive floating).
- An *offer* is for the right to *receive fixed* (and to pay floating).

A payor of fixed†
- Pays fixed and receives floating.
- Is said to have *bought* and thus to be *long* the swap.
- Changes his interest-rate exposure as if he had incurred fixed-rate rather than floating-rate debt.

A payor of floating
- Pays floating and receives fixed.
- Is said to have *sold* and thus to be *short* the swap.
- Changes his interest-rate exposure as if he had incurred floating-rate rather than fixed-rate debt.

Notional principal amount
- The dollar amount (e.g., $5MM) to which the swap applies; this amount is neither paid nor received. Thus, the term *notional principal.*

Dates
- *Spot start:* a spot-starting swap starts two days forward because LIBOR settles two days forward.
- *Trade date:* date on which counterparties agree to do the swap.
- *Effective date:* date on which agreed-upon fixed and floating rates start to accrue.
- *Maturity date:* date on which agreed-upon fixed and floating rates cease to accrue.
- *Reset date:* date on which the floating rate is reset.

Quotes on dollar coupon swaps
- *Money market swaps:* the *fixed rate* is an *absolute* rate quoted for some fixed period such as one year from "now," one year starting in December (that's Dec–Dec, pronounced deess–deess), and so on. The *floating rate* is typically 3- or 6-month liability LIBOR.
- *Term swaps:* the *fixed rate* is Treasuries plus a spread, e.g., 5-year Treasuries + 40 (basis points). The *floating rate* is some money market index (e.g., 3-month LIBOR), usually *flat* (i.e., no spread).
- *A basis swap:* one floating rate against another, e.g., the commercial paper rate against LIBOR.

*Some of these terms are introduced later in the chapter.
†To reduce confusion, the terms *a payor* or *a receiver* have come always to refer to fixed. *A payor* (of fixed) may also be described as overbought, *a receiver* (of fixed) as overlent.

the longer maturities, brokers give a run that is akin to the run of active issues that someone will give in governments (except there's this difference: in swaps, bids and offers are quoted in terms of yield, whereas in Treasury notes and bonds, bids and offers are quoted in terms or price: $\frac{1}{32}$s or $\frac{1}{64}$s). Brokers post their runs on Telerate or Reuters.

A broker's run for term swaps produces a yield curve that, while it is quoted at a spread to Treasuries, is independent of the Treasury yield curve. One view of a swap (the fixed-pay side) is that it is a *synthetic corporate bond*. This view leads to interpreting the swap yield curve as a yield curve for synthetic corporates. Another interpretation of the swap curve is that it is the Euro yield curve for long dates.

The brokers' biggest clients are top swap houses, such as Citi, Bankers, Morgan, Chase, Sali, and First Boston: players that warehouse and actively trade swaps. When a swap trade is arranged through a broker, the scenario might go as follows: first, the two parties agree, through the broker, to trade, say, a 2-year swap in the middle of the bid-offer spread. Next, the broker passes names to the counterparties so that they can do a credit check. That might be instantaneous or it might take a little time: a guy might say, "I have to send this deal to my credit department to see if we can do it." Noted one broker, "Citi and Morgan trades are automatic. But today we have a trade involving First Chicago and Hambros. It is not the trading side of First Chicago, but the First Chicago Capital Markets division that is trying to do a 7-year swap with Hambros; they may have to create a new credit line." As credit lines are checked, Treasuries trade up and down, so when the counterparties come back and say, "The credit's OK. Let's price the swap," they then have to get a quote; generally, they ask their bond desk, "Where can I buy or sell [for example] 25MM of the 2-year?" Sometimes, they come back with different numbers and have to negotiate about what price to use; if they can't agree on price, the deal falls through. Suppose the contrary. The counterparties, who first agreed to trade at 69 *over,* now agree to price the 2-year at 8.46; that sets the fixed rate on their swap at 9.15, and they're ready to write an agreement.

Because interest-rate swaps are brokered on a give-up-name basis, swap brokers act strictly as *agents*. Unlike blind brokers of governments, swap brokers never acquire even momentary positions in the instruments they broker.

DEALER BOOKS IN SWAPS

When a dealer warehouses swaps, he creates positions, a *book,* in swaps: he's long swaps A, B, and C; short swaps X, Y, and Z. By running a swap book, a dealer incurs certain risks. He does so to earn a reward, profits. Just how makes an interesting story.

Risks in a Swap Book and Hedging

So long as a swap is in a dealer's book, that swap creates some *credit risk* for him, just as his being an intermediary in a swap does. Whether the dealer sheds that credit risk when he trades out the swap depends, as noted below, on how he does so.

When he positions a swap, a far more important and immediate risk for a dealer is *market risk*. To *sell* a swap, be the receiver of fixed, is equivalent to being *long* a bond. Consequently, if interest rates *rise* (*fall*), the market value of the swap will *fall* (*rise*), just as the market value of an equivalent bond would. A similar but opposite market risk devolves from being long a swap.

The market value of a 5-year swap that pays a fixed rate of 8.50 would, if the bid on the swap rose 25 bp to 8.75, fall by an amount approximately equal to the change that would occur in the market value of a 5-year note with an 8.50 coupon if the yield to maturity at which that note traded were to rise from 8.50 to 8.75; the latter amount works out to $1.0415 per $100 of face value, $10,415.62 per $1MM of face value.[3] Clearly, a dealer

---

[3]The calculation is precise only if there is an exact date match.

who runs a swap book containing hundreds of millions of swaps can easily incur lots of market risk.

To be a dealer in swaps does not, however, necessarily call for having guts, balls, a rate view, and an affinity for taking positions and concomitant market risk. Dealers who run swap books—all big swap dealers have them—are of the opinion that they are neither paid to nor supposed to incur a lot of market risk. Dealers *hedge* their swap books. To hedge a long position in a particular swap, a dealer can go long a Treasury of similar duration (recall Chapter 5). Conversely, to hedge a short position in a particular swap, a dealer can short a Treasury of similar duration.

Sometimes dealers do precisely this, but often they hedge using a pool concept. A long position in one swap may hedge a short position in another, so all a dealer really need hedge is his *net* exposure—the pools of fixed- and floating-rate money that will come in or go out in different future periods as a result of his swap positions. This approach to hedging is called the *zero-coupon approach* because in theory all cash flows in different periods could be hedged through purchases and sales of appropriate zero-coupon securities. Easier said than done. The first problem a would-be hedger finds is that he has these little mismatches of dollars, in and out, all over the place going out to 10 years. So he must aggregate his cash flows over reasonable time periods, say quarters, and then hedge his remaining mismatches. A second problem is supply and liquidity; as one trader noted, "It is ludicrous to assume that you can use zero-coupon securities to hedge yourself because in practice there are too few of them out there." There's a good case that the swap market is forward LIBOR. Thus, Eurobonds ought to make a better (less basis risk) hedge than T bonds and notes. However, Eurobonds have associated credit risk; also, the issues are too small to be tradable. So a hedger of medium-term swaps is left using Treasuries because they're there and they're liquid. For short-term swaps, Euro futures are, as noted later, the best hedge: they're for the same instrument, they're quoted on the same basis, and they're liquid.

When a swap-book trader hedges using Treasuries, he is left with residual spread risk because the spread at which swaps trade over Treasuries is not written in stone; it can and does change, sometimes significantly and unexpectedly. For example, when Citibank surprised the market by announcing in 1987 a 3-billion write-off (increase in its loan-loss reserves) of its LDC debt, the Treasury curve did not budge, but the swap yield curve moved up sharply. The upshot was that swap traders who had sold swaps and shorted Treasuries as a hedge lost a bundle.

An Aside

At this point, the reader may be a trifle confused. In Chapter 6, we spoke about banks using unhedged swap positions as a part of asset and liability management. Here, we are talking about dealers, nonbank and bank, hedging swap positions. Actually, a big bank is likely to be doing swaps in a big way in at least two different areas: the Treasury division and the capital markets or corporate finance group, which—at least in the London sub—is guys doing investment banking activities, mergers and acquisitions, asset and liability management for clients, underwriting of new issues, and so forth.

If a Treasury officer has the opportunity to sell a swap at a fixed rate of 9, what interests him is the *absolute level* of the rate he can get. He thinks of such a swap as a synthetic corporate bond financed at LIBOR and asks whether, given his view on rates, the swap is an attractive "asset" to acquire as opposed to buying straight Treasuries, buying corporate medium-term notes, or maybe doing nothing. His view on the value of the swap depends on his assessment of whether rates are likely to fall and on his assessment, if he's inclined to take on fixed-rate assets, of where relative value lies.

A bank's corporate finance division generates a lot of new swap supply in connection with its various activities; in particular, swap issuance, at least in longer maturities, is often driven by securities issuance: a big borrower, maybe a sovereign, might issue 250MM of bonds in the Euromarket and promptly do one or more swaps to create, on favorable terms, a *synthetic security* that has the characteristics it desires with respect to maturity, rate (fixed or floating), and currency of denomination.

When a bank's corporate finance group proposes a swap to a client, its objective is to sell product and services for a fee, explicit or implied in the pricing of the products sold. A bank's corporate finance officer neither has nor is supposed to have a view on whether the flip side of a swap he proposes to a client would be viewed as having value by a bank Treasury officer. A swap generated by the bank's corporate finance group ends up in the bank's swap book.

When the bank's swap-book trader looks at a swap, he is interested not in absolute rate level, but in *spread*. Assume that the market in the 5-year swap is 82 bid, 88 offered and that 5-year Treasury notes are trading at 8.10. A swap that pays 9 fixed is offered to the swap-book trader. He sees value in that swap not because it pays an absolute rate of 9, but because it pays 90 over Treasuries, whereas the offer in the swap market is 88 over Treasuries. In the prevailing market environment, a swap that pays 9 gives the trader 2 bp of protection.

A well-managed bank will try to coordinate its swap activities, so it does not end up running one swap book here and another there. Some banks succeed better at this than others. Also, it is common for a Treasury officer wanting to position a swap to ask his own swap desk for quotes; however, to keep that desk "honest," he's likely to ask for quotes from other dealers as well. Suppose a bank's Treasury wants to sell, say, a $200MM, 5-year swap for asset-liability-management purposes, and that it does this trade with its swap book. The trader responsible for the latter would in turn view that buy either as an offset to an existing position that he would otherwise have hedged or as a new position needing to be hedged. If the trader hedges the position, *net* the bank's new position is the hedge (a long position in Treasuries); but once the swap trader sells the swap and lifts the hedge, *net* the bank's position is the position that its Treasury initially put on, short the swap.

Above, we were speaking principally of money center banks who also may generate a lot of swaps out of their IBF. The superregionals are not active market makers in swaps. They are situation-driven institutions that will do swaps for their own asset-liability management and to cover business they do with their own customers. Consequently, such an institution may be in the brokers' market one day, then out for several weeks.

Trading Spreads and Making Profits

A swap-book trader is likely to say that his job is to trade spreads. What he means is that, when he sells or buys a swap, he is looking to reverse that trade (buy what he has sold or vice versa) at a rate such that the basis-point spread he picks up on his trades into and out of the swap exceeds most times the narrow bid-offered spread that prevails in the interdealer market in swaps. "To make money on the swap desk," noted one swap trader, "you must beat the market."

Profiting from a Swap Book

An example: Again, suppose that the 5-year swap market is 82 bid, 88 offered. (If the *handle* were 9, this would translate to 9.82 bid, 9.88 offered.) That means that there is strong support from fixed-rate payers at around 82 *over* [Treasuries], and there is support from fixed-rate receivers at around 88 *over*.[4]

In taking on positions in his swap book, a trader will likely be dealing with customers, not other dealers. So one way he can seek to profit is by trying first to buy a swap at the offered side of the market or better and to then sell it at the bid side of the market or better. In our example, if he did just that, he would pick up as profit at least the bid-offered spread of 6 bp. (Note, if the trader buys Treasuries at the bid side of the market and sells at the offered side, as he does when he puts on and takes off swap hedges, he would lose the bid-offer spread. This difference in outcome reflects the difference in how the swap and Treasury markets are quoted, yield versus price.)

To run a swap book, a dealer must incur a variety of costs, including the 1/32s he loses putting on and taking off hedges; he also must commit capital. A well-managed dealer will want

---

[4] The market in a Treasury note might be 21 bid 22 offered. That is consistent with our saying that being short a swap is equivalent to being long a bond. Whereas the swap market is quoted in terms of *yield*, the Treasury market is quoted in terms of *price*. Thus, 21 bid and 22 offered for a 5-year Treasury note might be equivalent to 17 bid, 16 offered if the bid and the offered for the notes were quoted in terms of yield, not price.

traders in various areas to earn some minimum risk-adjusted rate of return on the capital they are allocated. Thus, a swap trader might end up needing to earn 10 bp on positions he runs through his book in order to meet his firm's bogy for ROK. To do that calls for knowledge of who might want to do what, finesse, and patience. Also, even a 10-bp spread provides little margin to compensate a dealer for the real, if small, credit risks his swap desk incurs vis-à-vis its counterparties.

Achieving the Bogy

The whole idea of running a swap book is for a trader to create positions in which the rate he is getting has value itself because it is better than the market offers. Put another way, the swap business is all about recognizing valuable cash flows and being able to hedge them.

To illustrate, we assume that the trader's firm is engineering an interesting transaction for or giving good advice to a client; and as part of the deal, the client does a 5-year swap in which the dealer receives 90 over Treasuries at a time when the 5-year swap is 82 bid, 88 offered. Now, the swap trader has received a cash flow with value because it pays 2 bp more than the rate at which he could turn that trade in the brokers' market.

Maybe the swap trader received this cash flow with value because the payor of fixed had done a large bond issue and wanted a chunky—200MM or more—swap (fixed to floating) that probably could not be turned in the market in one shot without moving the bid-offer.[5] Or maybe the treasury division of his own bank wanted to put on the swap, quickly, to make an interest-rate play.

To meet his 10-bp bogy, our trader must trade out of the swap he sold at 90 over by buying it at 80 over. Doing that may require time; enter spread-risk management. Immediately, our

---

[5]In the brokers' market, trades are routinely done at or near quoted rates for 10MM, more often for 25MM. A trade of 100MM might or might not move rates; a trade of 200MM surely would.

trader hedges by shorting 5-year Treasuries at 8.10. He now has residual spread risk: the spread of the swap curve to the Treasury curve might widen, but he has acquired a valuable cash flow giving him some protection against this.

To short Treasuries, our swap trader reverses them in from his repo (matched-book) desk and pays the latter the reverse or repo rate. Thus, while the swap remains in his position, he must pay out the coupon on the securities shorted and LIBOR; at the same time, he is receiving the fixed rate of 9 and the repo rate. Assume that the overnight repo rate is 6, and that 6-month LIBOR is 7.50. On the fixed-rate side, our trader is making 90 bp (9 on the swap minus 8.10 on the Treasuries). On the floating-rate side, he is losing 1.50 bp (7.50 minus 6). So *net* he has negative carry on his position of 60 bp. He is willing to accept this negative carry, because he is holding and hedging a cash flow with value. However, he is conscious that he has yet another risk: the LIBOR-repo spread might move against him, thereby increasing his negative carry. (The 90 bp that he's earning on the fixed-rate side is written in stone.)

Because of negative carry and spread risks, our swap trader wants to turn his position, immediately if he can, by going the other way. To do so, he needs to acquire a fixed-rate liability at Treasuries plus 80. Maybe a big corporate is doing a floating-rate bond issue that they would be willing to swap, fixed to floating, at 80 over. Or maybe the swap will have to be turned in small pieces. To be successful in the swap business, it is essential that a dealer have a strong marketing presence. "You really depend," observed one trader, "on your knowledge of what clients need to do. You cannot sit in an ivory tower and look at absolute rate levels and developments in the macroeconomy and say, 'Here is where rates are going,' because you are not trading absolute rates. You are trading those spreads, and you have to know what everyone else in the market wants to do. Otherwise you cannot do big deals of the sort we do.

"If we underwrite an issue for the Kingdom of Sweden and they want to swap [fixed to floating] as part of the deal, we will probably warehouse part or all of the swap because we don't have clients coming in the door wanting to go the opposite way in such size everyday. We get some very chunky deals. We may sit on 250MM of the swap. We will split it up into little pieces, maybe to European corporates. We may end up running Sweden against Gaz de France. Meanwhile, we have these repo-LIBOR risks that we have to manage. GDF might want to sell the swap because they have outstanding floating-rate notes that they want to swap into fixed rate or maybe because two years ago, they had sold fixed-rate Eurobonds, swapped the proceeds into floating-rate, and now want to get back into fixed rate because fixed rates have come down."

The Beauty of a Hedged Swap Book

The marketing, investment banking side of the business is terribly important to running a swap book profitably; the latter in turn enhances a dealer's ability to do other businesses such as underwriting. "One big advantage we have," noted one swap trader, "is that we can reduce absolute rate risk to zero, so we can stand there and make a price to our client. We do not depend, should a sovereign do a big bond issue, on the availability of a counterparty who is interested in acquiring that sovereign's fixed-rate liabilities at exactly the rate level at which that sovereign is issuing. We can warehouse these things, sit on them for a time. We can make these positions, less our profit margin, available to our clients when it suits them rather than when it suits us and our rate view. That is the beauty of our fully hedged business."

Assignment Brokering

Early on, dealers taking in and then trading out a swap would assume the position of swap counterparty to both the buyer and the seller of the swap; in doing so, the dealer guaranteed each side's performance. Playing the role of credit intermediary exposes the dealer to credit risk and puts contingent liabilities on his balance sheet. Over time, swaps have become a much more negotiable instrument than formerly. Also, as the swap market has become liquid, especially in dollar swaps, margins attainable have narrowed. Consequently, dealers have difficulty getting the spread they require if they are to both deal and be a credit intermediary. Therefore, it is becoming common today for dealers to do *assignment brokering* rather than play the role of credit intermediary.

Here's a dealer's example: "We will do a swap with Sweden. Then, Gaz de France comes along and says, 'We are interested in this position.' We say, 'Fine, you can take [have a credit line to] Sweden. Here is the price.' We end up putting the two together direct. We step out entirely—do not guarantee the other side's credit anymore. Obviously, in this case, we will work for a smaller margin."

Lifting a Leg

A bank tries to make money on its swap book by engineering a transaction with a client with whom it has a relationship and having that client pay by letting the bank receive at, say, 90 or 92 over rather than at the inside rate of 88. The engineering may involve structuring an interesting transaction and giving good advice on rates—adding value in some way. With swap spreads narrowing and competition becoming tougher, this is becoming harder to do, which tempts a swap trader to try to enhance his margin by speculating. Like arbitrageurs and other traders, swap traders are tempted to lift a leg now and then. Take, for example, a bank dealer who has sold a big swap that pays fixed and has bought Treasuries to hedge. If his bank suddenly forms the view that rates are going up 50 bp, he is not going to then sit on 250MM of Treasuries. He will sell some of them. "The positions that are created as a result of doing client swap business are," noted one trader, "also positions that we can now start to manage based on outright rate views. We have those positions anyway. That is why swap teams in most banks are now organizationally part of the trading division and report to the senior risk manager of the bank. Swaps are a natural way of taking positions and using those positions either for spread trading or for speculative purposes. Our business is developing into a business where we do both."

A Global Swap Book

Swaps are really a global business. A lot of foreign entities do dollar swaps, and a lot of that business is done in London and Tokyo, especially highly structured deals. The top swap dealers all have offices in New York, London, and other financial centers. Thus, running *a global* swap book calls for some coordination. One dealer described his firm's approach as follows: "The actual running of our dollar-swap book sits in New York. When London and Tokyo are open, we talk to them. They have authority to trade, but pricing and hedge recommendations are always sent out from New York to give them guidelines. Early in the morning, London office may have a client who wants to do a dollar-interest rate swap. Our traders in London know more or less where the market is. The day before, we were talking to them late in their day; and we will have sent them an overnight fax saying: this is what went on in New York, and these are the prices at which we would deal. So our London traders take that information, make a decision about the client, do the trade, and execute a hedge in Treasuries. But the trader who's responsible for signing off on the portfolio of swaps and hedges sits in New York."

Dealers as Market Makers in Swaps

Above, we focused on how dealers in swaps seek to profit by working customer business, which is not so different from a trader of governments of some other securities seeking from a chain of trades in one or a related set of securities to end up with a profit. In addition, the big dealers in swaps also trade actively with each other in the brokers' market in standard flavor swaps, Treasuries-over-versus-LIBOR, and others we mention below.

Often, an end user or trader of swaps who has a swap on that he wants to unwind will simply enter into the mirror image of that swap. Say he does a 5-year swap, fixed to floating; if a year later he does a 4-year swap, floating to fixed, he's back, if rates haven't changed, to where he started except that he has used up, for the four years his two swaps have to run, some of the credit lines he has to others and that others have to him. If rates have changed, either one party will have to make a cash payment to the other in order for a mirror swap to fly, or the party unwinding will have to do a mirror swap at a new fixed rate that reflects his gain or loss on his initial swap.

Bank versus Nonbank Dealers in Swaps

While the ranks of top swap dealers include both bank and nonbank dealers, bank dealers have certain natural advantages. First, banks are able to analyze and deal with a broader range of clients than can investment banks who lack the facilities to do that kind of credit analysis. Second, banks have a vast natural funding capability; they are funding and gapping all the time, and consequently, they have a natural layoff for a lot of ancillary market products that investment banks do not have. Third, customers generally prefer the credit of a top bank to that of a top nonbank dealer; some will not even take the latter.

That is why a lot of investment banks are heavily involved in "brokering" swaps. They have the underlying corporate finance deals; they are the guys who bring new corporate issues to market; they are involved in LBOs and M&A activity, both of which require swaps. An investment banker might shop the swap dealers to get the best prices he can on each piece of a trade for a client, then package those pieces and present the package to the client as a pass-through. A bank that gets involved in such a package is taking the name not of the investment bank, but of the client. For packaging various financial products into a single structured deal that meets the precise needs of his client, the investment bank gets a fee. Generally, the investment bank would prefer not to get involved in managing the client's swap position; he is a structurer.

MONEY MARKET SWAPS

Swaps originated as a medium-term instrument, and our discussion of swaps so far has focused on such swaps. However, there's also lots of activity in short-term money market swaps, much of it with a pronounced Euro flavor. Money market swaps are widely used in the classic way (to reduce or lock in borrowing costs), as a tool for speculation, and as part of an arbitrage.

The IMM Swap

In discussing money market swaps, we will focus first on what's called *the IMM swap*. The IMM swap, which by one trader's estimate represents 50% of short-term swaps, is a swap of a 1-year fixed rate against 3-month LIBOR, where the 3-month rate floats. The swap is dubbed the IMM swap because the start, end, and three intermediate reset dates are set to coincide with the dates on which four successive IMM contracts for 3-month Euro-dollars settle. The IMM swap itself has *no* futures component.

The popularity of IMM swaps reflects the fact that, besides being a tool for doing classic swaps, they are also a great speculative instrument and a great arbitrage tool. IMM swaps are often done for *forward* dates; for example, in September, one might do the Dec–Dec (pronounced *dees–dees*) swap or even the March–March swap (recall the broker's run we quoted earlier).

One beauty of the IMM swap is that there is no cost of carry provided the swap is closed out before it becomes effective. A second advantage is that there is a lot of liquidity in 1-year swaps done to IMM dates. Thus, someone who put on, in September, a Dec–Dec swap for *forward* settlement and wanted to close out that swap in, say, November would have no trouble doing the precise *mirror swap* (recall that a trader closes out a swap by doing the mirror swap). A trader who does a 1-year swap that starts on a *cock, broken,* or *stub* date—all three terms denote a non-IMM date—will, if he tries to do a mirror swap, likely end up having to do a swap whose dates lag the dates in his initial swap; if so, his mirror swap will leave him with a small basis risk because he'll be in long and short swaps that aren't quite identical. Most times, an IMM swap is put on as a *forward swap;* a swap that is put on for immediate settlement is called a *spot swap.*

A Money Market Swap Used in the Classic Way

The 1-year rate in the IMM swap is not 1-year anything. However, the rate will be close to 1-year LIBOR in the cash market, if the swap happens to be a spot-start swap, because if it were ⅛ above or below that rate, opportunities would open up for arbitrage.[6] Cash-market, 1-year LIBOR is not the only rate on which IMM-swap traders keep one eye glued. A second is the 1-year rate obtained by *compounding* the rates at which four consecutive IMM contracts are trading, that is, the 1-year rate implied by a specific *futures strip*.

Unlike American banks, such as Chase, Citi, Chemical, and the B of A, which have customer bases that provide them with enormous deposits, the big Japanese banks have no dollar-deposit base. If they need dollars to fund themselves or to do arbitrages, they have to buy them. Thus, despite their triple-A status, Japanese banks often have to pay up slightly in the Euromarket to get funds. On a day when Chase could fund itself at no worse than LIBID, a Japanese bank might have to pay LIMEAN or even LIBOR. Thus, Japanese banks have a special incentive to do deals that will shave their cost of funds.

Suppose that, on a given day, a Japanese bank takes a 1-year deposit at 8.75 and is looking to do a swap, 1-year fixed against 3-month LIBOR. Chase, a market maker in swaps, observes that the 1-year rate on Euros implied by the nearby futures strip is 8.96, so it figures that it ought to be able to find a customer who would be a willing payer of that rate or something close to it. So Chase offers the Japanese bank—again call it Fuji—a swap in which it will pay Fuji 8.87 fixed and receive 3-month LIBOR. Immediately, Chase hedges by buying the futures strip and thereby locking in a compounded annual rate of 8.96. It has done, warehoused, and hedged a swap. Next, Chase looks for a final-demand customer who'd be willing to pay fixed. That customer might be an LBO (leveraged buy-out) borrower

---

[6]On an IMM swap (for one year) that starts one or three months forward, the IMM swap rate can differ radically from 1-year LIBOR.

who wants relatively short-term debt because it anticipates selling off, over the short run, various assets of the corporation it is buying (Chapter 23 speaks briefly on the whys and hows of LBO deals). The borrower—we'll call him LBO—being a below-investment-grade credit, gets a bridge loan that is priced at a spread above 3-month LIBOR. LBO would like to fix its borrowing costs over the year; the margin between its anticipated net cash flows and the cost of servicing its debt is none too wide, so LBO doesn't want to run the risk of having to roll 3-month LIBOR in a rising rate environment. Accordingly, LBO is happy to do the following swap with Chase: LBO pays Chase 8.95 fixed for one year (1 bp below the rate implied by the futures strip) and receives from Chase 3-month LIBOR (Figure 19–3). The moment this swap is done, Chase closes out its futures hedge and, assuming no movement in futures, is looking at a 8-bp margin for its role as intermediary.[7]

Several things are interesting about this example. First, everyone seems to win. Fuji has shaved its funding costs to 3-month LIBOR minus 12; and if it can pick up some paper yielding LIBOR, maybe some bank CDs or a floating-rate loan, it will have locked in a spread of 12 bp—perhaps a few basis points more or less depending on the precise rate it gets on its investment. LBO is also happy because it has turned floating-rate funding into fixed-rate funding at a rate below what it would have had to pay if it had borrowed (providing it could) 1-year, fixed-rate money. This example, except for the maturities of the liabilities involved, is no different from the Fuji–Triple B example presented early in this chapter. Fuji, as a triple-A bank, has a comparative advantage in issuing fixed rate, but wants lower-cost, floating-rate money. LBO has a comparative advantage in issuing floating rate, but wants to reduce its interest-rate risk. Each borrows according to its comparative advantage; Chase intermediates a swap between the two; and everyone walks

---

[7]If, however, futures have moved up, Chase will have lost on its futures hedge, but, presumably, it will have profited from a matching increase in the fixed rate LBO is willing to pay it.

FIGURE 19–3
Paired money market swaps: Chase earns 8 bp; Fuji gets funding at LIBOR minus 12 bp; and LBO locks in a fixed rate of 8.95 for one year*

*Labeled arrows indicate directions and rates of interest flows. (See text.)

away happy. *This is as classic an example of why the swap market exists as one can find.*

Chase of course is running a swap book. When Chase does the swap with Fuji, it warehouses that swap; and it does so with no guarantee that some customer will come along wanting the flip side of that swap. Still, Chase is not running a big risk: it is in the market and has a good origination staff who are in touch with LBO and other players. The key to running a successful swap book, whether the swaps are short or medium term, is to have a nice two-way flow of both triple-A credits who issue fixed but want to pay floating and of lesser credits who borrow floating but want to pay fixed. For a market maker, the principal difference between the short- and medium-term swap markets is that the cast of players varies somewhat between the two markets.

Also, we should note that Chase in meeting customers' needs for money market swaps will not always be dealing in *clean* swaps, that is, swaps done to IMM dates. Probably 50% of short-term hedges are spot swaps done to cock dates or odd dates. Thus, part of the spread a market maker in swaps earns is a payment for assuming and managing the small basis risks that arise in its book because many customers want to do a cock-date swap, which the market maker covers two or three days later by doing a second odd-date swap that isn't quite the mirror image of the first swap.

Amending a Swap with a FRA

Suppose LBO is happy with his swap whether it is for one year or five years. Remember he is paying fixed and both receiving and paying LIBOR—a wash. Thus, to him where LIBOR goes is immaterial. Nonetheless, LBO might suddenly entertain a strong view that LIBOR is likely to drop in the short run. He does not want to undo his swap, but still, he wants to profit from the drop in LIBOR he predicts. Easily done. The next LIBOR reset is one month off, so LBO does a 1 by 4 FRA, which locks in the 3-month LIBOR he will receive at the next reset. By doing a FRA, LBO is reversing—for *one* reset period only—his initial decision to put on a swap. In fact, if LBO wanted to, he could, by doing a strip of FRAs, reverse his swap for *all* remaining reset periods.

This example suggests an interesting and correct observation: *A swap is a strip of FRAs, and a FRA is a single-set swap* (except for differences in settlement features). The first part of this statement says that, just as one can build a swap out of a strip of futures, one can also build a swap out of a strip of FRAs; the reason is that, just as one can calculate a 1-year fixed rate by compounding the rates on four consecutive IMM contracts, one can also calculate a 1-year fixed rate by compounding the rates on four consecutive FRAs (e.g., a 1 by 4, a 4 by 7, a 7 by 10, and a 10 by 13).

To see that a FRA is a single-set swap, consider the following example. A borrower paying 6-month LIBOR on a 1-year loan does a swap, fixed for floating. By the time, he enters the transaction, he knows the first 6-month LIBOR rate he will get. Say it is 8½ and the fixed rate he is paying is 8.88. Basically, what the borrower's swap does is to lock in an implied 6-month LIBOR rate, six months hence (all other rates are known with certainty). Thus, the borrower could accomplish the same thing by doing a 6 by 12 FRA.

Actually, the FRA and the swap are not quite the same thing. With the swap, there is a net cash flow at the end of the first 6-month period. For a pure speculator or arbitrageur, that cash flow translates to a cost of carry of about 38 bp. Normally, arbitrage between the FRA and the swap will bring the rates on the two instruments into a relationship such that a trader will be indifferent between which he does. However, since different factors drive prices in the two markets, opportunities for profitable arbitrage occasionally arise.

This, by the way, is a classic case of arbitrage. Effectively, the same product, 6-month money six months hence, is being sold in two different markets as two different products and, occasionally, at two different prices. Only rarely, however, does an arbitrage between the 1-year swap and the 6 by 12 FRA yield a profit. The markets for both products are closely watched, and both are constantly traded in size. Also, many people track this arb because it's attractive: both sides of it leg off-balance-sheet instruments, no money need be put down, and credit risk is minimal.

The IMM Swap as a Speculative Vehicle

Suppose an individual holds strongly the view that short-term interest rates will shortly fall and wants to bet on that happening. He could buy bills or BAs, repo them, and wait for rates to fall, at which time he could sell his paper at a profit and pay off his repo borrowing. Speculation in the cash market is simple, but it costs the speculator the bid-offer spread in the instrument he trades, and he must get financing. Alternatively, our trader might use futures to speculate—sell bill or Euro futures. To do so, he would have to pay transaction costs. More important, he would also have to put up margin; and, if rates should move much—even temporarily—against him, he would have to make additional variation margin payments, perhaps substantial ones.[8] Yet a third way our trader could position for a fall in

---

[8]The risk in variation margin calls is not one that a trader should treat lightly. Often, a trader will do an arb using one or more positions in futures in which he reasons: "Rates are out of whack; A exceeds B; but, as time passes, A must come to equal B." That that is true is no protection against A and B getting further out of whack in the short run and the trader having, consequently, to meet huge variation margin calls. Should this occur, the risk to the trader is that he will exhaust his funds before A and B move into line. A scenario of rates getting more, not less, out of whack over the short run has caused sleepless nights for—even bankrupt—more than a few professional traders. Similarly, a correct view that short-term rates are coming down shortly does not preclude their taking, to a trader's peril, one more big bump up.

short-term rates would be to enter into an interest-rate swap. He could, for example, do a swap in which he would receive 1-year fixed and pay 3-month LIBOR.

The forward IMM swap is a great speculative vehicle—an ideal trading instrument. There is no cost of carry on an IMM swap provided the trader closes it out before it becomes effective. Also, so long as a trader does a *clean* swap (one to IMM dates), he will have no mismatch when he does a mirror swap. Because of these factors, the IMM swap has excellent liquidity. The only drawbacks to buying or selling an IMM swap and then doing a mirror swap are that the trader ends up with two credit exposures and he also increases, by a small amount, his capital requirements. When a trader sells an IMM swap, he is making the same sort of bet that a bank's treasury does when it sells a 5-year swap; the difference is that the seller of a 5-year swap is betting that medium-term rates will fall, whereas the seller of an IMM swap is betting that short-term rates will fall.

Suppose a trader sells in September an IMM swap at 9; his view is that short-term rates will fall, and behold, the 1-year rate does fall to 8.50. Now, he does the mirror swap and pays 8.50 fixed. On the swap at 9, he is paying 3-month LIBOR; on the swap at 8.50, he is receiving 3-month LIBOR; so the LIBOR flows wash. Thus, thanks to his offsetting swaps, he has net, with no rate risk, a 50-bp, through-the-middle profit.

The trader could just as well have bet that rates would rise. In that case, he would have bought the swap at 9 and hoped that the 1-year rate would rise to 9.50. If it did, the trader would again be able to take out a 50-bp profit.

A beauty of the IMM swap is that it allows a trader to assume one year's worth of risk in a single transaction; using futures, he'd have to buy or sell a strip of four futures contracts to get the same risk. Also, on the IMM swap, there is no initial margin and no margin calls.

The IMM Swap as the Leg of an Arb

In talking about money market swaps, we first looked at a classic swap (Fuji–LBO) in which the market maker, Chase, determined what fixed rate it was willing to pay and what fixed rate it thought it could get by calculating a benchmark rate, namely, the rate obtained by compounding a strip of four consecutive IMM rates. By taking a position in a swap and hedging it, Chase created an arbitrage and made 9 bp.

A common arb that dealers and spec accounts do is to arb the IMM swap against a strip of IMM contracts. To illustrate, suppose that, in late September, Hill Samuel, a British merchant bank, figures that the Dec–Dec strip is trading on a compound-basis at 8.90; he also observes that the Dec–Dec IMM swap is trading at 8.80. He buys the strip as the asset side of his arb and buys the swap as the liability side of his arb. He has thus set himself up to receive, December to December, 8.90 and to pay 8.80. If he rides that arb through that period, he will make a 10-bp profit minus transaction costs and minus any costs he may incur as a result of margin calls. What happens to 3-month LIBOR is to him immaterial. If it rises, he will lose money on his position in futures, but that will be matched by an increase in his net cash flow from the swap on quarterly reset dates. However, Hill Samuel's hope is that, sometime before his swap becomes effective, the compounded strip rate and the 1-year rate in the IMM swap will trade on top of each other. If that occurs, he will close out his position in futures by selling his strip, close out his swap by doing the mirror swap, and be left with a 10-bp profit.

To illustrate, suppose that, in November, the compounded rate on the Dec–Dec strip equals 8.85 and the Dec–Dec swap is also trading at 8.85. Hill Samuel bought his futures strip at an effective rate of 8.90; by now selling that strip at 8.85, he makes five 1-year bp.[9] Simultaneously, Hill Samuel sells a swap that's a mirror to the one he bought. In that swap, he was to receive 1-year fixed at 8.80. Now, he sells a more valuable swap in which the receiver of fixed is to be paid 8.85. Again, Hill Samuel picks up five 1-year bp, for a total of 10 1-year bp.

Money market swaps occur in what could rightly be called artibrage-land. Traders arbitrage swaps against futures, swaps against cash, swaps against FRAs, FRAs against futures, and so on. Arbitrage opportunities keep arising because these related

---

[9]Recall from Chapter 15 that futures are priced in terms of an index: 100 minus yield. Thus, when yield falls, futures prices rise.

markets are constantly impacted by many different events. Maybe a Japanese does a big cash-and-swap arbitrage, which drives up the swap market; this creates profit in the swap-FRA arbitrage, so someone does the swap-FRA arbitrage, which drives up FRAs; this creates profit in the FRA-futures arbitrage, so someone does the FRA-futures arbitrage, which drives up futures. An event that moves one rate causes a rate-ripple that creates 5 bp for every player except maybe the futures player if he is an unhedged spec. Clearly, someone loses, usually the spec player in the futures pit.

Needless to say, every active player in the markets we have been describing—swap, cash, futures, FRA—requires at least one person to constantly monitor rates in these related markets and a computer programmed to crunch rates and to identify arbs.[10]

The brokers love arbs between FRAs, cash, futures, and swaps, because so many of them are done and because, each time one is done, the arbitrageur must do at least two things at the same time—buy this, sell that. Sometimes, a dealer will leave a standing order with a broker: "If you can get me 10 bp between X and Y, do the trade."[11] The Japanese do that in New York and in London. Thus, when a broker says, "There is interest by the Japanese in the 1-year CD switch [swap]," a market maker knows things are going to happen. (The Brits call a swap a switch.)

Basis Swaps: Floating to Floating

Swaps are done not only fixed to floating, but floating to floating. Whenever a swapper does a *floating-to-floating or basis swap,* he is, in effect, *swapping spreads.*

---

[10]Anyone wanting to identify and do money market arbs of the sort we've been describing needs to be concerned with things such as day-count problems, residual basis risk, and cost of carry where it arises. For break-even formulas and benchmark calculations, see the forthcoming revision of Stigum's *Money Market Calculations* (Homewood, Ill.: Dow Jones-Irwin).

[11]The above scenario, described by a trader, may already be dated as traders today basically price everything—FRAs, swaps, even 1-year cash for the most part—off the futures market; also, such prices adjust with corresponding rapidity.

In Chapter 23, we talk about the use of commercial paper to provide not only construction financing for a building, but to provide long-term financing, in lieu of conventional mortgage financing. An issuer whose paper was regarded by investors as top-notch might reason, "I can do this and not worry about liquidity; also I do have bank backstop lines. However, short-term rates can be pretty volatile, so maybe I had better do a swap, floating to fixed, to cut my interest-rate risk." The workhorse swap, fixed to floating or vice versa, is of course the LIBOR-versus-Treasuries-over swap described earlier. Our commercial paper issuer does this swap, but finds that he now has a new problem. He is now paying Treasuries plus (a fixed rate) receiving LIBOR, and paying the commercial paper rate: thus, he has basis risk: if the spread of LIBOR to the commercial paper rate narrows, that will cost him money. So he does another swap to reduce the uncertainty associated with his funding costs: he swaps, at a spread, LIBOR for the commercial paper composite index. His paper may sell a touch above or below this index, but at least he knows that it is not going to sell far from it. By *cocktailing* two swaps, our commercial paper issuer has fixed his funding costs long term, presumably at a spread below the Treasuries-plus rate he is paying, since commercial paper normally trades at a spread below LIBOR.

Here's a second example complete with market maker. The Kingdom of Sweden wants to issue fixed to take advantage of its good name to get sub-LIBOR funding, but it wants to pay floating because it thinks that rates are going to fall. So he issues Eurobonds at Treasuries +45 and simultaneously does a swap with Chase; under the swap, Chase pays Sweden Treasuries +75, and Sweden pays 6-month LIBOR, which net gives it funding at 6-month LIBOR minus 30 (Figure 19–4).

Chase now has a swap to work off. Next in the door comes Ford Motor Credit. FCM has a contrary view: rates are going up—it takes two views to make a market. FMC, a big direct issuer of commercial paper, does a swap with Chase where it pays Chase Treasuries +60, and Chase pays it the 30-day commercial paper index.

Now Chase is warehousing two swaps that don't match up, but customers keep coming in the door. The next is a spec ac-

FIGURE 19–4

Chase, a market maker, does offsetting swaps—fixed to floating, floating to fixed, and floating to floating—to earn net 15 bp*

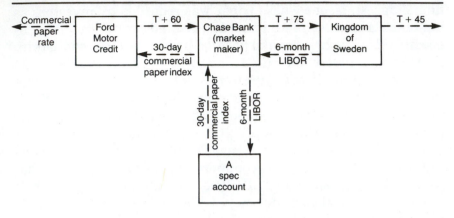

*Labeled arrows indicate direction and rate of interest flows. (See text.)

count; he thinks that the commercial paper–LIBOR spread, which is normally 20 to 30 bp (with LIBOR being the higher of the two rates), is going to widen to, say, 40 bp, that is, that LIBOR is going to rise relative to the commercial paper rate. So he does a swap with Chase in which he receives 6-month LIBOR and pays the 30-day commercial paper composite rate +30. If he's right and the commercial paper–LIBOR spread widens to 40, he'll do a mirror swap and take out a 10-bp profit.

Alternatively, the fourth party might be a bank that had previously done a swap under which it is paying 6-month LIBOR and getting the commercial paper rate +40. Now it wants to lock in a 10-bp profit on that swap by doing the mirror swap at the commercial paper rate +30.

In any case, Chase makes net 15 bp, assuming all payment and resent dates are semiannual. To earn that, Chase has had to do some interim managing of spread risks, has had to use up some of its credit lines, and has had to allocate some capital to support its swap business.

Deposit Notes and Other MTNs

Bank issuers of deposit notes (domestic and foreign) are big swappers. Often, they will issue fixed-rate deposit notes with a minimum maturity of 18 months to reduce applicable reserve equipment to zero. What they really want, however, is floating-rate money. So they do a plain vanilla, LIBOR-versus-Treasuries-over swap to get sub-LIBOR funding.

Depending on market conditions and on their name, corporates and other nonbank issuers of MTNs might go either way; sell fixed and swap to floating or vice versa.

SWAPTIONS

Whoever said "There's nothing new under the sun" was not a devotee of money market jargon. "Swaption" is not in Webster's *yet,* but it is the talk of the Street. A *swaption* is an option on a swap. Most swaptions are capital-market products that arise out of the issuance of medium- or long-term securities; for this reason, we will limit our discussion of swaptions to one example.

Suppose a U.S. corporate wants to issue 7-year paper. Also, it wants to add a 5-year call feature to that paper so that, if rates fall, it can reduce its funding cost. Adding that call feature will increase by, say, 10 bp the rate that our corporate must pay for 7-year money. That's not much, but the typical investor in corporate paper, especially in the U.S., does no sophisticated analysis of what granting a call option is worth. He reasons, "It's 7-year paper that they might call in 5 years. I am getting 10 bp extra; and if they call the issue, I'll buy something else." That is his level of analysis.

Assume our issuer sells 7-year paper with a 5-year call feature. Next he does a swap, fixed to floating. On a straight 7-year swap, the fixed rate he would receive would be Treasuries + 70. However, he makes the swap callable after five years (i.e., if he throws in a swaption), and the fixed rate he receives is not Treasuries + 70, but Treasuries + 90. In other words, by selling as a swaption the option that be "bought" when he issued callable paper, he gets 10 bp more for it than he paid for it, which reduces by a like amount his all-in funding cost. Great deal, but how does this occur in efficient markets? The answer is that, whereas the buyer of corporate paper fails to analyze the value of the option he is granting, the receiver of the swaption is knowledgeable about volatility, Black-Scholes pricing, and all that, so he assigns to the swaption a value in line with its true economic worth.

Our corporate issuer had reduced by 10 bp his all-in cost of funding. Also, he isn't concerned about the impact of the call feature on his liquidity. He wouldn't be doing this deal if he were not a good credit; so he reasons: "If rates fall, and the swap is called in five years, I will call my bonds and issue new 2-year notes, which I'm confident I can do."

If what our corporate really wanted to do was to pay fixed, he could issue fixed-rate callable paper, do a fixed-to-floating swap with a call feature to garner 10 bp, and then do a second swap, floating to fixed.

Note the principal involved in our swaption example is the same principle on which banks rely in selling capped CDs: there are basis points to be made whenever an option or a series of them (i.e., a cap) is underpriced in one market, but correctly priced in another.

Paring funding costs is not the only reason a party might want to do a swaption. A second may be to hedge an asset or a liability that may or may not materialize within a certain time. Finally, a spec might want to buy or sell a swaption as an outright punt on rates.

CROSS-CURRENCY SWAPS

A *cross-currency swap* occurs, for example, when a borrower wants to borrow, say, fixed-rate DM and swap them into fixed-rate dollars. Cross-currency swaps are a simpler, more sophisticated, and more flexible version of the back-to-back and parallel loans people did years ago. Generally, cross-currency swaps are done off bond issuance, and for that reason, we will confine our discussion of them to several short examples.

A successful cross-currency swap, like a generic coupon swap, usually turns out to be based on differences in the comparative advantages in borrowing of two or more entities. To illustrate, suppose that Lufthansa wanted to raise 500MM to buy some airplanes in the U.S. As the German flag airline they have unique access to the DM sector of the Eurobond market. Also, from a technical point of view, they have strong loyalty from their underwriters—more leverage with them than they would have if they did a U.S. dollar-denominated Eurobond issue. Thus, for Lufthansa, the cheapest way to get fixed-rate, medium-term dollars would surely be to borrow fixed-rate DM in the Eurobond market, and then swap them for fixed-rate dollars of the same term. A market maker, such as Chase, Morgan, whomever, would through its market presence be able to find a party wanting to do the flip side of this swap.

Another factor that often plays a role in cross-currency swaps is government rules and regs of one sort or another. Here is an example. The government of Spain had a rule that no one could issue Europeseta bonds. At one point, it partially relaxed this rule and said that supranationals, such as the World Bank, the EEC, the European Investment Bank, the Interamerican Development Bank, and a few others, could issue such bonds. Some of these supranationals did just that, and their issues—a scarce commodity—commanded excellent terms. However, none of these borrowers wanted pesetas. It thus turned out that the few banks that had good underwriting ability for peseta bonds, good swap capability, and sufficient local presence in Spain to find end users of long-term pesetas were able to earn fat spreads. Actually, finding demand for long-term pesetas was easy for a bank with the right contracts; Spanish corporates had an enormous, unmet demand for long-term, fixed-rate pesetas, since no long-term bond market exists in Spain outside of the government bond market. The upshot was that the World Bank swapped the pesetas they raised into long-term Swiss francs, Eurofirma swapped their pesetas into floating-rate DM which they onlent to Deutschebank, and so on. The flip side of these swaps was taken by Spanish corporates. Spain's action resulted in windfall profits to outsiders, but Spain got what it wanted: prestige borrowers to open the Europeseta bond market. Spain's view was, "We are liberalizing our economy. This is a first. We want no disasters, please."

To *cocktail* means to string swaps together. Often cross-currency swaps call for cocktailing. A borrower with good access to the Swiss bond market may really want floating-rate dollars. If so, it will borrow fixed-rate Swissy; then, it will either swap (1) to fixed-rate dollars and then to dollar LIBOR or (2) directly to dollar LIBOR.

When a market maker in cross-currency swaps arranges such a swap it goes into his book of cross-currency swaps which he seeks to manage much as he manages his dollar-swap book: without interest-rate risk and without currency risk. Dealers do take lots of currency risk, but they try to confine their taking of it to their foreign-exchange desks. To be a market maker in cross-currency swaps, cocktailed or straight, a dealer needs a wider market presence and even sharper risk management and hedging skills than he does if he just runs a dollar-swap book. For one thing, a dealer who books a swap denominated in a foreign currency such as Swiss francs, ECU, yen, or gilder, finds that there is no active government bond market in which he can hedge. So he ends up punting every time, like it or not.

Still, dealers keep pursuing cross-currency swap business. An amazing thing about plain vanilla, dollar, coupon swaps is that, transparent as the inherent arbitrage is, it still has not been arbitraged away. However, in this business, a market maker's spread is narrowing, where is cross-currency swaps it can still be juicy. To earn a good spread, a market maker will work a little, even a lot, harder.

If one were to diagram a cocktailed cross-currency swap, one would likely find the market maker dealing with at least three counterparties, as did Chase in Figure 19–4. Cross-currency swaps eat a market maker's lines; also, since they are less amenable than dollar swaps to assignment brokering, they eat a market maker's capital assigned to swaps.

END USERS OF SWAPS

Swaps can prove useful to just about every class of borrower: sovereigns, supranationals, government agencies, banks and corporates (domestic and foreign), thrifts, insurance companies, real estate developers, and so on. One reason for the popularity of swaps with end users is that swaps are a non–zero-sum game and, as such, can have inherent value to all parties.

Another attraction of swaps is that they are a *no-brainer*. An entity condemned by the market to borrow at a floating rate could conceivably control much of its resulting rate risk through an adroit use of futures. However, an institution that uses futures to hedge rate risk needs a skilled trader, as a maladroit trader may get it into worse trouble than that which it sought to avoid through hedging; the unfortunate experiences that numerous institutions have had with futures hedges attest to this. A swap, in contrast to a futures hedge, takes no skill or tending on the part of the end user. He says, "I'd rather pay rate A than B," signs an agreement, and that's that. If he wants to pay fixed rate so that he can budget interest expenses and sleep at night, all that is required is the stroke of a pen. If he has contracted to pay 10 and rates go to 30, he still pays 10. Of course, if rates go to zero, he still pays 10 too, but that is the nature of fixed-rate debt: it protects at a price.

PRESENT SUCCESSES

Because it filled so many needs so well, the swap market has experienced unprecedented growth over the eight years that have passed since interest swaps were born. The International Swap Dealers Association (ISDA) estimates that, in mid-1988, interest-rate swaps outstanding totaled $1.1 trillion (Figure 19–5); of these, dollar swaps amounted to $0.7 trillion.

Also, market growth continues apace. Of the $311 billion of new swaps arranged in the first half of 1988, interest-rate swaps accounted for $251 billion (150 billion of these being new interest-rate swaps in dollars). Swap dealers reckon, moreover, that the swap market may have grown from 25 to 50% in the second half of 1988.

Currently, the swap market dwarfs the Eurobond market. A U.S. bank that's a top player in swaps has been known to arrange $1.5 billion of swaps in a single day. Good size in a new corporate Eurobond issue is a mere $200MM, and the Eurobond market is reported to generally choke when it must swallow $500MM of bonds in a day.

FIGURE 19–5

Estimated swaps outstanding in mid-1988 totaled $1.1 trillion: $879 billion of interest-rate swaps and $198 billion of currency swaps

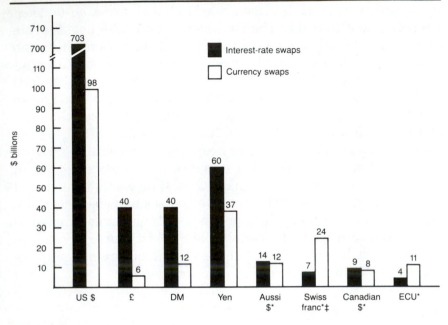

*Estimated.
‡End 1987.

Source: International Swap Dealers Association (ISDA).

THE FUTURE

The new capital adequacy guidelines that the Fed and other central banks are imposing on banks have an impact on all swaps, but the impact is greater on cross-currency swaps than on single-currency swaps. These guidelines are, thus, crimping the growth of the cross-currency swap business.

Yet another cloud on the horizon in the swap market is the fact that 70 or so swap houses (bank and nonbank) did swap and swaptions deals, totaling $10, maybe nearer $20 billion, with British local council (municipal authorities). These bodies, mostly payors of floating, were hard hit when interest rates started to rise and the yield curve to invert though 1988 and early 1989. The affected muni bodies were in no position to ante up a lot of extra interest, since they got into the swap-swaptions game to generate extra revenue they needed but couldn't get due to limitations on their taxing authority. In the spring of 1989, the British government was refusing to bail the local councils out of their predicament and was threatening to declare such deals *ultra vires* (beyond the councils' legal powers). That, in turn, was threatening to leave the banks with estimated losses of over $330MM.

Yogi Berra would have commented, "It's *déjà vu* all over again." Dealers, U.S. at least, tend to regard anyone running "institutional money" as a *sophisticated investor*. In the case of some credit unions, small S&Ls, school districts, sewer districts, and so on, the sophisticated investor may turn out to be an ex-welder, a lawyer who's ignorant—as most lawyers are—about investments, Aunt Minnie, whomever. Let a sales rep get such an institution to sell naked Ginnie Mae puts, play in swaptions, or do swaps to pick up some "free money," and big trouble (lawsuits in the U.S.) is bound to ensue: a financial time bomb has been set; the only uncertainty concerns precisely when it will detonate.

Asset Swaps

The above problems notwithstanding, the prospects are that the swap market will continue to grow rather than contract. We have been talking in this chapter about liability swaps and the creation of synthetic liabilities. There is plenty of room to apply the same principals to the opposite side of the balance sheet, assets.

Say an investor has a U.S. dollar asset. He likes the credit, the maturity, but not the currency. He'd prefer Canadian-dollar assets because his view is that the Canadian dollar will appreciate. Or maybe he wants Aussi-dollar assets because they pay high yields and he thinks that the Aussi dollar isn't going to depreciate that much more. In any case, by using a swap, an investor can turn a U.S.-dollar asset into a synthetic Aussi-dollar or Canadian-dollar asset. The Japanese have been doing this for some time. In particular, Japanese life companies swapped into synthetic, Canadian-dollar assets some years ago; then when the Canadian dollar has staged a nice recovery, they swapped out into synthetic DM and other assets. "We say to the Japanese," noted one dealer involved in such swaps, " 'Your Canadian dollar swaps are now worth XMM —present value. You do not want a check, but would you like some high-yielding DM assets?' Instead of continuing to pay the Japanese interest and principal in Canadian dollars, we give them DM assets instead.

"The swap business," continued the same dealer, "has swung from being a liability-driven tool to being an asset-management-driven tool. The reasons are several. Our client base includes a lot of pure investors. Also, the asset-swap requirements of our client base have been neglected, so there is some good margin available in that business."

In recent years, asset swaps have fueled an increasing amount of the swap business—to the point where they can be a major reason for swap spreads moving in and out. Corporates have become less dominant on the pay side of the market. They're still there, but one of the major ways for a swap desk to receive, besides doing structured transactions with corporations, is to asset-swap bonds: to find bonds that on a fixed basis are unattractive and perhaps illiquid, to swap those bonds into floating, and to then sell them to money market players at a spread to some money market rate (LIBOR, commercial paper, or Fed funds). A recent favorite for asset swappers has been Japanese ex-warrant bonds (mostly dollar-denominated) that Japanese companies have issued against the backdrop of their spiraling stock market.[12] Some issuers are double-A or triple-A credits; other, weaker credits get a guarantee from a Japanese

---

[12]Usually, companies issue *warrants* (a negotiable instrument that's been around for years) to lower their cost of borrowing. In recent years, Japanese companies have issued dollar-denominated bonds bearing warrants. The value of these warrants, which are priced in dollars and allow warrant holders to purchase Japanese shares at a fixed yen price, has permitted Japanese companies using them to borrow at less than a quarter of the rates they'd otherwise have had to pay. Also, almost as a by-product of raising capital, Japanese borrowers have created a vibrant new sector of the Euromarket—the Japanese equity-warrant market.

One reason most of the issuance is done in London, not Tokyo, is that Article 65 (the Japanese version of Glass-Steagall) prevents Japanese banks from participating in underwriting such paper in Tokyo, but not in London. Another problem for Tokyo issues is that they are yen denominated, which removes a swaps opportunity at the underwriting end. It's estimated that total warrants issued through July 1989 added 6 percent to corporate Japan's equity—Japanese equity warrants are BIG business.

bank. The bonds are issued with low coupons and trade at a steep discount once the warrants have been stripped off.

"For us," noted a swap dealer at a money center bank, "besides doing cross-currency swaps, the asset-swap business produces a huge amount of our fixed-receive deals. The resulting assets, which have 2- to 5-year maturities, are sold primarily by our money market sales force at, depending on the quality of the assets, LIBOR flat to LIBOR + 50. That's attractive because it's hard for corporates to get LIBOR-based assets, especially at a positive spread.

"On our funding desk, we receive on swaps five times as much as we pay. When we pay on swaps, we generally do so based on our interest-rate view. When we receive on swaps, we sometimes also do so based on our interest-rate view, but more often, we're offsetting medium-term liabilities. A problem for a swap desk is that generally its business flow calls for it to pay fixed more often than it wants to. Consequently, the desk actively seeks, especially in bull markets, ways to receive; asset swaps, mostly in 4- and 5-year maturities, are a big way for us to do this."

The Ted Spread in Swap-Land

Another growth area in swap-land is in the TED spread. Currently, one of the major reasons for the explosion in swaps and in the number of players in this market is the growth of volume in Euro futures. In 1987, there were only eight (two years' worth of) Euro futures. Today, people can pay fixed against a 4-year strip, and 5-year strips are in the works.

The expanding Euro strip has also led traders to do a TED-spread arbitrage. It's not the TED spread of bills versus Euros. It's buying eight contracts in weighted amounts and buying 2-year T notes against them or doing a similar arbitrage using 3- or 4-year T notes. That arb closely replicates a swap. "Suppose," noted one swap trader, "that you can't find anyone to pay you fixed, and you think that swap spreads are coming in in the 2- and 3-year area. You can sell 2- or 3-year notes, buy Euros, and have a synthetic swap—one that will take you out of your risk and allow you to profit from narrowing swap spreads. This arbitrage technique has made both swaps and Euro futures (off of which swaps are priced) much more liquid; and in doing so, it's brought more players into the market.

"Unfortunately, it's also taken some of the skill out of pricing swaps. Today, everyone says, 'Well, the strip is at 9, so I'll make an 8.95–9.02 market.' When everyone figures out a game, that game is pretty much up and you're left with just a commodity market. The swap market is a mature market except for structured deals, but it will stay a good market because you can do so much with swaps."

Swapping Swaps

Another likely source of continued growth in the swap market is the growing tendency of financially sophisticated people to view a swap not as a once-and-for-all deal, but rather as a deal that they are willing to reverse or to alter whenever their views on markets change and they consequently feel the need to fine-tune their assets, their liabilities, or both. Sovereigns, corporate treasurers, and others of this ilk are active *swappers of swaps*.

A corporation that has in the past done a swap that it now wants to unwind often has a profit in that swap. If the counterparty is willing, the initial agreement can be torn up and a cash payment made reflecting the current market value of the swap. More often, a swap must be unwound via a mirror swap. For example, a corporation's position might be that it had swapped fixed to floating when fixed rates were 10 and that rates have risen to 11; in that case, if the corporation does a "mirror" swap, it will probably end up receiving at 11 and so realize its profit on its initial swap over the remaining life of that swap.

Whatever the future holds for swaps, it's a safe bet that life in swap-land will continue to be hectic and full of unexpected twists and turns—nary a dull moment.

THE NEXT CHAPTER

In the next chapter, we turn to the CD market. During the 1980s, this market, once a major source of funding for money center banks, has gone through a dramatic slimming and a change of character.

CHAPTER 20

CERTIFICATES OF DEPOSIT: DOMESTIC, EURO AND YANKEE

The first domestic negotiable CDs backed with a dealer commitment to make a secondary market in them were issued in 1961 by Citibank. Throughout the 1970s and early 1980s, short-term, fixed-rate CDs became a major money market instrument; in their funding, money market banks came to rely so heavily on the sale of such paper that it became impossible to imagine how these banks could manage their liability positions without them.

Today, the market for short-term, fixed-rate CDs is moribund. This abrupt change is due to several factors: credit problems at certain major banks, rate deregulation, changes in reserve requirements, the shift of money center banks toward investment banking, and the emergence of other, more attractive modes of bank financing.

This chapter thus serves three purposes: it describes briefly the market for old-style CDs; it tells of innovations in the CD market; and it serves as a preface to Chapter 24's discussion of MTNs, a major subclass of which are bank deposit notes.

THE INSTRUMENT

Banks have long needed some dependable source of longer-term funds (maturities measured in months, not days) to maintain their liquidity and to manage their interest-rate exposure. Most money center banks have always received some large time deposits from individuals, partnerships, and smaller corporations.

The total of such deposits was, however, small relative to the banks' needs for longer-term deposits. To fill the resulting gap, the banks turned to the one sector of the money market in which they could buy longer-term funds in volume, the CD market.

A certificate of deposit is a negotiable instrument evidencing a time deposit made with a bank at a fixed rate of interest for a fixed period (Figure 20–1). CDs bear interest and are quoted on an interest-bearing rather than a discount basis. Normally, interest on a CD, which is calculated for *actual days on a 360-day-year basis,* is paid at maturity. However, on CDs issued with a maturity beyond one year, interest is paid semiannually.

CDs are normally issued in 1MM pieces. While technically negotiable, smaller pieces have poor marketability and have always traded at a concession to the market. Most CDs, regardless of the issuer's location, are payable in New York.

When first issued, CDs were subject to a rate lid under the Fed's Reg Q. In 1969, this lid became binding as money market rates pushed through the Reg Q ceiling. As a result, money moved from domestic time deposits into Eurodeposits, and U.S. banks lost 14 billion of CD money. In response, they promptly borrowed the 14 billion back from the Euromarket; the Fed's ill-conceived attempt to limit bank lending by cutting off the bank's access to bought money failed. After 1973, the Fed imposed no lid on the rate that banks might pay on time deposits of

FIGURE 20–1
A specimen CD

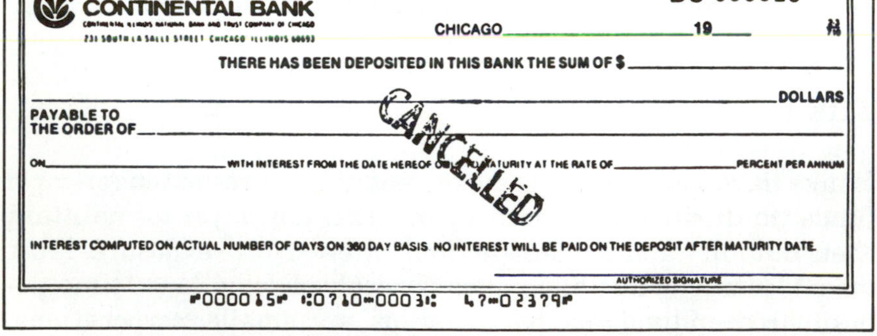
NEGOTIABLE TIME CERTIFICATE OF DEPOSIT
BC 000015
CONTINENTAL BANK
CONTINENTAL ILLINOIS NATIONAL BANK AND TRUST COMPANY OF CHICAGO
231 SOUTH LA SALLE STREET CHICAGO ILLINOIS 60693
CHICAGO ____________ 19____
THERE HAS BEEN DEPOSITED IN THIS BANK THE SUM OF $ ____________
____________ DOLLARS
PAYABLE TO THE ORDER OF ____________
ON ____________ WITH INTEREST FROM THE DATE HEREOF ON MATURITY AT THE RATE OF ____________ PERCENT PER ANNUM
CANCELLED
INTEREST COMPUTED ON ACTUAL NUMBER OF DAYS ON 360 DAY BASIS. NO INTEREST WILL BE PAID ON THE DEPOSIT AFTER MATURITY DATE.
____________ AUTHORIZED SIGNATURE
⑈000015⑈ ⑆0710⑉0003⑆ 47⑉02379⑈

100,000 or more. In the final heydays of the domestic CD market (early 1980s), New York City banks were borrowing about 35 billion in this market; all large U.S. banks about 135 billion. (Current numbers on large-denomination CDs outstanding are unavailable as the Fed has discontinued this series.)

Variable-Rate CDs

In the late 1970s, largely in response to demand from dealers who sold CDs to money funds, banks began to sell a new type of negotiable CD, *variable-rate CDs*. The two most prevalent types were 6-month CDs with a 30-day *roll* (on each roll date, accrued interest was paid and a new coupon was set), and 1-year CDs with a 3-month roll.

The coupon established on a variable-rate CD at issue and on subsequent roll dates was set at some amount (12.5 to 30 bp depending on the name of the issuer and the maturity) above the average rate, as indicated by the *composite* rate published by the Fed, that banks were paying on new CDs with an original maturity equal to the length of the roll period.

The major buyers of variable-rate CDs were money market funds. In calculating the average maturity of their portfolios, these funds treated variable-rate CDs as if they matured on their next roll date. One reason was that such paper must trade at or above par on a roll date. Second, and more important, the dealer selling the CD gave the buyer a *put* (the right to put the paper back to him); the buyer could exercise this put on each roll date.

Volume

After the removal of Reg Q on CDs, changes in the volume of outstanding CDs occurred largely in response to variations in the level of loan demand experienced by banks. This was to be expected, since banks viewed CD money as a *marginal source of funds* to be drawn upon when an increase in loans had to be funded.

Another factor influencing the volume of CDs outstanding was the need that issuing banks felt to have a continuing presence in the market. As a funding officer of one large bank said, "It would be unthinkable for us, whatever our needs might be, to be totally out of the market." For regional and foreign banks, the need to be in the market on an ongoing basis was especially acute, since these banks had to keep selling to establish and maintain their names on investors' approved lists.

Risk and Return

Because FDIC insurance offers a depositor protection on only the first 100,000 of deposits with a bank, it is meaningless for corporate and other large depositors. Thus, the investor who puts one or many millions into bank CDs assumes some small credit risk. For this reason, and also because of their lesser liquidity, CDs have always yielded somewhat more than bills of the same maturity, with the spread becoming, in recent years, much wider and much more variable. Today, 3-month domestic CDs really trade at a spread off (below) 3-month LIBOR (Figure 20–2).

The yield spread between CDs and bills widens when money tightens for the following reasons. First, there is the familiar, if irrational, tendency of investors to back away, when money market rates rise, from risks, that, when rates were low, they willingly assumed to raise return on their investments. Second, the condition of the banking system appears to worsen when the nation's financial system is under strain; thus, the risks associated in the eyes of many investors with holding bank CDs tend to be positively correlated with the rates yielded by such instruments.

Investors in Bank CDs

When CDs were first issued, a lot of them were bought by cash-rich corporations. Later, however, many corporations went from the position of being cash-rich to being big borrowers of short-term money. Soon, over half of bank CDs were being bought by money funds. CDs have also been bought by state and local governments and by other financial institutions. Generally, banks do not invest actively in CDs other than when they position them as part of their dealer operation. In this respect, it

FIGURE 20-2

Today, domestic, 3-month CDs trade at an increasingly tight spread to 3-month LIBOR

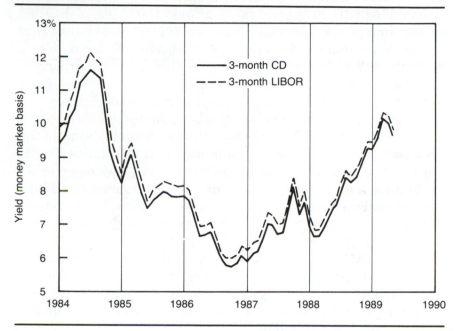

Source: J. P. Morgan Securities, Inc.

should be noted that a bank may not invest in or buy back one of its own CDs, as the Fed would view this as violating the condition that legally permitted the bank to issue the instrument, namely, the receipt of a fixed-maturity, time deposit.[1]

Because CDs expose the holder to a credit risk, large investors in CDs seek to assess the creditworthiness of different banks. On the basis of such assessments, each investor establishes a list of banks whose paper it is willing to buy and sets limits, *undisclosed lines* in Street jargon, on the amount it will

---

[1]A few money market banks have traded their own paper in their role as *dealers* in CDs. The Fed has never challenged their doing so. No one wants to open the issue because it would get the banks and the Fed back to discussing whether a CD is a security or a deposit; and reopening that discussion would again raise the question of state blue-sky laws and other issues that were considered in 1961 when Citi first began issuing *negotiable* CDs.

place with individual banks on its approved list. The analysis investors put into deciding which banks they will invest with and in what amounts ranges from casual to elaborate. At the elaborate end are investors who pour over the reams of detailed information on the financial conditions of individual banks that is provided in publications put out by Sheshunoff & Co., Keefe Bruyette & Woods, and other bank analysts. Not surprisingly, the sale of such publications rose dramatically as one major bank after another had its own particular serious problem.

While many investors worry about the possibility that a major bank issuing CDs might fail, others, including some of the most sophisticated, completely discount that possibility. In the words of one investor typical of the latter group, "Money market banks are agents of the central bank. The Fed knows it and they know it, and the Fed is not going to let one of them fail so long as they play ball. A bank that doesn't may end up closing or being merged with another bank, but depositors are not going to lose money. I do not worry about problems at the Chase versus those at Morgan because the truth is that the Chase has no more chance of failing than Morgan. Moreover, if either were to fail, conditions would be such that other worries would preempt my concern over lost CD dollars."

To such an investor, the main reason for tracking the problems of individual banks closely is that other investors' reactions to these problems create market premiums and discounts, which in turn create opportunities for investors. The same individual went on to say, "If bad news comes out about the Chase, I know that the market is going to overreact. So I check with the dealers on the spreads at which Chase CDs are trading. If liquidity is still there, I dump my Citis and buy Chases. Experience has proved me right." Certainly, the later government bailout (nationalization) of Contil supported this investor's position, enunciated years earlier.

Tiering

Prior to 1974, tiering in the CD market was modest, and CDs of all the top banks traded at roughly the same level. Then problems emerged at the Franklin and other banks, and things changed.

Investors began to look more closely at the condition of individual banks issuing CDs, and tiering became a pronounced condition. Who had to pay up changed constantly as investors' perceptions of the financial strengths and weaknesses of individual banks changed. When New York City appeared to be on the verge of bankruptcy, the top New York banks, all of which had substantial holdings of New York City securities, had to pay higher rates than top Chicago banks to issue CDs. Several years later the situation reversed.

The year 1974 was particularly hard on regional banks. At that time, many CD investors reacted to the troubled state of the banking industry by paring regional banks from their lists of acceptable names. This forced some regional banks out of the New York market and caused others to have to pay up. Later, as money eased, customers began looking at a wider range of names and found that some regional banks were strong credits compared with some of their big New York sisters; and gradually, more regional names became acceptable to investors in the national market.

The tiering that developed in the mid-1970s among CDs issued by top banks gradually worked itself off. As this occurred, management in certain top banks came to the dealers and reminded them that their banks provided the dealers with financing and other business. They then added that they saw no reason why their CDs should not trade as well as those of any of the other top 10 banks. The dealers said, "OK, we will trade the top 10 names on a no-names basis." This meant that a dealer's bid or offer to another dealer would be good for any of the top (by asset size) 10 banks.

Initially, this change tended to improve trading in domestic CDs. By making heterogeneous paper more nearly homogeneous, it increased the ease with which CDs could be traded, and that in turn increased the attractiveness of CDs as a trading vehicle and, thereby, liquidity in the CD market.

However, no dealer agreement—written or, in this case, understood—could make paper trade for long at a level other than that at which the forces of supply and demand determined it should trade. The events of 1982 clearly demonstrated this; when both Chase and Contil experienced severe, well-publicized difficulties, no dealer or sophisticated investor thought either bank was in danger of failing. Nonetheless, suddenly a lot of investors did not want to touch either Chase or Contil paper. They feared that the paper of both banks would become less liquid. Also, a corporate portfolio manager might want to get out of such paper to avoid having to defend his holding it to his board.

Maturities

Most CDs issued in the U.S. used to be in the 1- to 3-month area. There was a market in 6-month paper, but beyond that, no issuing was done in real size. The reasons were several. One was demand. Money funds (see Chapter 26) are required to maintain a short average maturity on the securities they hold. Many other investors buying CDs were corporations funding tax and dividend dates that were at most 90 days in the future. Such investors needed liquidity, and many preferred to obtain it by buying short paper that they could hold to maturity.

A second reason for the thin market in CDs with a maturity at issue of six months or more is that, in normal times when the yield curve is upward sloping, it's cheaper for banks to buy longer-term money by rolling 3-month CDs. "Six-month money is high-cost money," noted one banker. "So you have to believe that the Fed is going to move dramatically to justify buying it on rate considerations alone. If you buy it at all, it's likely to be to improve—at an acknowledged cost—your liquidity."

The All-In Cost of CD Money

When a bank evaluates the cost of CD money, it thinks in terms not of the rate it posts, but of its *all-in* cost—reserve requirements and FDIC insurance included. The Fed used to be concerned over the short average maturity of bank CDs outstanding. To induce banks to issue long-term CDs, the Fed first raised Reg Q ceilings on CDs of longer maturity and then cut reserve requirements on them. However, when money tightened and interest rates rose—precisely the time when the Fed wanted to see banks buy longer-term money, the average maturity of CDs outstanding declined. During such times, the banks wanted to issue longer-term CDs, but as a practical matter, investors refused to buy them. The Fed's old structure of reserve requirements—lower requirements on longer CDs—probably had little impact on CD maturities because it was outweighed by the impact of investors' preferences with respect to maturities.

Today, the Fed reserve requirement on bank sales of short-term CDs is 3%. The impact of this on the all-in cost to a bank of money raised via the sale of short-term CDs is easy to calculate. For such a bank, the all-in cost of CD money is 1.0309 times (103.09% of) their posted rate *plus,* of course, 8.33 bp for FDIC insurance.[2] To illustrate, if a bank is posting a rate of 9.15 on 3-month CDs, its all-in cost on that money (including the FDIC premium) will be:

$$(1.0309 \times 9.15) + 0.0833 = 9.4327 + 0.0833$$
$$= 9.516$$

The New Issue Market

In the heyday of the CD market, banks preferred to place as much of their CDs as possible directly with customers through their own sales forces. A bank felt that the less visible borrowing it did through dealers, the better its credit would appear. Also, a bank feared that the CDs it issued through dealers might end up back on the Street just at the time it wanted to borrow additional funds, thereby creating a situation in which it had to compete with itself to write new CDs.

---

[2]Calculating the all-in cost of CD money to a bank that must hold non–interest-bearing reserves at the Fed is simple. Let

r = the quoted rate paid on the CD
r^* = the all-in rate paid when required reserves are taken into account

If a bank must keep 3% reserves against time deposits, then the amount of money available to it will be, per dollar taken in, only $1.00 - 0.03; and the all-in cost of this money will be r^* in the expression

$$r^*(1.00 - 0.03) = r$$

which simplifies to

$$r^* = \frac{r}{0.97} = 1.0309r$$

Despite their predilection for writing directly to customers, banks did issue a lot of CDs through dealers. As a funding officer whose attitude was typical noted, "All things being equal, we would rather place the deposit ourselves. But if a dealer is willing to take our CDs at a competitive rate and it fits our needs, we sell to them." Often, a dealer got an 05 for distributing a bank's CDs, especially if the bank was trying to do a big program.

Over time, banks came to rely less on dealers to distribute their CDs. Banks expanded their own money market sales forces. Also, money funds started coming directly to banks. Said one bank officer, "The money funds just sop up enormous amounts of paper. Every time we post a rate, the money funds are the first buyers we see. Much of that money comes direct because the funds figure that the dealer, if he does the trade, will have his 02 or 05, whereas if they [the fund] come direct, they can get the full rate."

YANKEE CDs

Foreign banks open branches in the U.S., the natural home of the dollar, to expand their liability base in dollars for several reasons: to finance loans made to U.S. and foreign corporations operating in the U.S., to finance other dollar-denominated paper they acquire, and to be able to arbitrage between the U.S. and Eurodollar markets. Like U.S. banks, many foreign banks also run a Caribbean branch and an IBF.

A foreign bank that makes a reasonable attempt to cultivate relationships with domestic banks can easily gain access to money in the Fed funds market. However, since this market deals primarily in overnight funds, foreign banks wanting to obtain financing for longer periods had to rely on the sale in the New York market of their CDs, dubbed *Yankee CDs*.

While dealers could be helpful to U.S. banks in writing CDs, particularly second-tier banks, they were a necessity to U.S. branches of foreign banks. A foreign bank branch trying to sell

CDs in the U.S. market faced several problems. To many investors, its name was not well known. Second, even investors who had heard of a particular foreign bank often failed to perceive that, say, Barclays or Crédit Lyonnais was a giant on the world banking scene just as was Citi or Chase. Third, many sophisticated investors felt that they didn't know enough about French, Japanese, or other foreign accounting practices to read intelligently the financial statements of foreign banks.

In issuing CDs in the U.S., a foreign bank branch started with a few U.S. commercial customers who, because they had dealt with that bank abroad, knew it, and were willing to buy its CDs. To sell beyond this limited customer base, a foreign bank branch had to turn to a dealer who for an 05 would push that bank's paper by acquainting other investors with its name and credit. The resulting education took time, so a foreign bank branch normally started out having to pay substantially more than a domestic issuer, a condition that gradually diminished as its name became accepted.

Lack of familiarity with foreign names is not the only problem foreign banks face in selling their paper in the U.S. As the manager of the New York branch of a big French bank noted, "Foreign banks, in bidding for dollars, face two limits: one is set by investors on the basis of the institution's financials; the other is set by dollar holders on the country risk they are willing to accept." With respect to the second limit, French banks compete with each other and with corporate bidders for dollars, such as Gaz de France, which is a big issuer of commercial paper through Goldman Sachs. Finally, the growing number of foreign banks that are issuing commercial paper through a U.S. holding company may be raising cheap dollars, but such paper competes with the bank's CDs for an investor's limit on the bank's name.

The early buyer of CDs issued for foreign banks was always *a yield buyer*. To get that yield he incurred what he perceived as some extra risk, and he accepted limited liquidity. Since many foreign banks issuing CDs in the U.S. market worked through an exclusive dealer, the primary—often the only—place where the holder of such a CD could get a bid on it was from the selling dealer.

DEALER OPERATIONS

At the height of the CD market, there were about 35 dealers in CDs, though the number of dealers who were big players and active market makers in both good and bad markets was much smaller. The key dealers were those that were in the market pretty much from the start: Salomon Brothers, Goldman Sachs, Discount Corp., First Boston, Lehman Brothers, and Merrill.

Part of a dealer's job was distribution, getting new CDs that banks wanted to write out into investors' hands. A second and equally important part of a dealer's job was creating a secondary market for CDs. Dealers did this by standing ready at all times to quote bids and offers both to retail and to other dealers. Because of the diversity of names and maturities in the CD market, dealers could not short CDs, but they could position them, and sometimes did so in size.

The Inside Market

CD dealers operated and still do in two markets, *the retail market* in which they do business with customers and the *inside market* in which they trade with each other.

In the interdealer market, bids and offers are good for 5MM with the understanding that good delivery is 5 by 1: five pieces for 1MM each.

The Brokers

In January 1976, one firm started brokering dealer trades in CDs, and after that a number of other firms entered the business. Brokers were and are actively used by CD traders for the same reason they are used by traders in governments—they provide anonymity and speedy communication with other dealers.

TERM CDs

There was no way banks could sell CDs in any maturity range without a viable secondary market because investors demand liquidity, which can be provided only through active market making and positioning by dealers. Positioning CDs eats dealer capital, and the capital attrition becomes larger the longer the maturity of the CD and the more accrued interest it carries. Thus, dealers were slow to make a market in *term CDs,* that is, in CDs with maturities ranging from two to five years.

In the fall of 1976, however, dealers started to look seriously at this market, and they did sell several fair-sized term issues for Citi and Chase. Partly because of pricing and market conditions, these issues were anything but successful; and dealers were left, in a thin market, holding big positions at a loss. Term CDs never caught on, and subsequently, they were issued only infrequently under special conditions.

One problem with term CDs was that basically they were done on a privately placed basis. Corporation XYZ would be looking to placed 25MM, so a bank would do a deal with them if it fit the bank's needs. Alternatively, a bank might have a program to do, say, 300MM out in three years; they might do 5MM with one investor at an 8.90 coupon with an October 17 maturity, 10MM with a different investor at a different coupon with a different maturity, and so on. The result was a thin mix of heterogeneous CDs that were not tradable: CDs that lacked any common denominator that would provide liquidity to anyone.

In a sense, the same problem always existed in the market for short-term CDs. But in the heyday of that market, there was a lot of product flow into that market; consequently, it was always active, and dealers dealt with the plethora of maturity dates by quoting CDs on the basis of early and late Octobers, and the same for every other month.[3]

DEATH OF THE OLD CD MARKET

So far we have been speaking of the market for short-term, fixed-rate CDs, which reached its apogee in the early 1980s and then proceeded to die off with greater rapidity than any market pro would have thought possible. While no one anticipated the

---

[3]For further comment on the market for fixed-rate, medium-term CDs, see Chapter 24.

near demise of the old CD market, in retrospect it is easy enough to identify the factors that killed it off.

Credit and Name Problems

1982 saw the Mexican debt crisis which weakened the credit of banks, particularly Manny Hanny, that had significant amounts of Mexican debt on their balance sheets. Then followed the sudden and severe Contil crisis and subsequent bailout. Naturally, people began to take a dimmer view of bank credits; certainly, being one of the top 10 American banks no longer meant investors automatically wanted to own your paper.

CD Futures

Just as the CD market was reaching its top, CD dealers finally got what they had long been clamoring for, a domestic CD futures contract. CDs futures were, among other things, supposed for the first time to give CD dealers an efficient way to hedge their CD positions and to do cash-futures arbs. CD futures were also supposed to permit banks to become even more sophisticated in asset-liability management; finally, CD futures were supposed to give corporate borrowers a more efficient means to hedge their cost of borrowing short term from banks.

A big problem with the CD futures contract was that it allowed for delivery, not cash settlement. Therefore, to ensure a sufficient supply of deliverable paper and that delivery not disrupt the cash market, the contract had to specify: (1) that CDs written by a number of banks be deliverable at expiration of the contract, and (2) that delivery might be made on any day over a rather long period (two weeks was selected).

In mid-1981, the domestic CD futures contract got off to a slow but reasonable start, but in mid-1982 volume first peaked, then plunged. Once the paper of deliverable-name banks started to trade at significantly different levels, the contract was doomed. No one wanted to get stuck taking delivery, because they knew they would be paying full market price for the worst paper in the cash market. The CD version of Gresham's law— bad money drives out good money—worked with a vengeance.

Rate Deregulation

A second factor that killed the wholesale CD market was rate deregulation mandated by the Monetary Control Act of 1980. In the fall of 1982 banks were permitted to start offering *Money Market Demand Accounts (MMDAs)*, which permitted them to pay consumers T bill–related rates on what were essentially restricted-use demand deposit accounts. Suddenly, banks were able to bid back from money funds a lot of money that they had earlier lost to them. Then, in the fall of 1983, banks were permitted to offer retail CDs. By then, the wholesale CD market was staggering, and the retail CD just toppled it over the edge. With the advent of retail CDs, banks could go out and pay a reasonable rate to Joe Smith for his dippy $5,000. Money center banks with big retail businesses—Chase, Chemical, and Citi to name several—could and did do just that; they lapped up consumer deposits. As a result, the need of these banks for wholesale CD funding dropped dramatically, especially since this new money came in at a time when banks were under pressure to improve both their ROA and ROE—something they sought in part to do by paring their balance sheets. In the end, what really killed the wholesale CD market was lack of supply.

The 1983 Change in Reserve Requirements

In 1983, the Fed made a change in bank reserve requirements that drove yet another nail in the coffin of the old, short-term CD market. On 4/29/82, the Fed set the following reserve requirement on bank time deposits (remember wholesale bank CDs are negotiable time deposits): 3% if the original maturity was less than 3½ years; 0% if original maturity was longer. On 10/6/83, the Fed lowered the original-maturity cutoff: the reserve requirement on a CD became 0% if its original maturity was 18 months or longer.

Lucky was the bank that still wanted some wholesale CD funding. In no time, that bank was negotiating with great success with money funds to buy variable-rate CDs with a minimum maturity of 18 months. The bank struck a deal with a money fund; the money fund then selected a dealer with a roll-date *put feature* that it liked; finally, the bank struck a deal with that dealer to add, for a small fee, its put to the CD that the bank was selling to the fund. For everyone, the deal was great: the dealer got a fee for his put; the bank got reserve-free, medium-term funds; and the money fund got an above-market yield for in effect agreeing—but not with absolutely no out—to make a series of short-term deposits with the bank.[4]

Today, the only area where the domestic CD market is truly alive is for CDs with a maturity at issuance of 18 months and over. The big wholesale banks like Morgan and Bankers, that have no consumer business, issue out there. So, too, do all of the Yankee banks (U.S. branches of foreign banks). The exception is the Japanese banks: they are good quality and typically go right to the deposit note market.

Deposit Notes and MTNs

As noted in Chapter 6, U.S. banks used to live with a constant tension between their need to add to liquidity and their need to avoid excessive interest-rate exposure. Thanks to financial innovation, this is no longer so. Today, banks routinely sell 2- to 5-year, fixed-rate deposit notes and immediately swap the proceeds into variable-rate money. By doing so, a top-credit bank can obtain sub-LIBOR funding, avoid reserve requirements, substantially add to its liquidity, and simultaneously avoid enlarging its interest-rate exposure. Now that banks have this option for raising money, it isn't surprising that selling old-style, 3-month CDs holds little allure for them. Thus, financial innovation is another reason for the drying up of supply in the traditional CD market.

When a bank wants to raise medium-term money at the bank level, it sells deposit notes. When it wants to do so at the

---

[4]The issuing bank couldn't itself offer a put to the money fund buying its CD because, if it were to do so, it would endanger the reserve-free status of the money it was raising. The CD, being negotiable, could be sold and maintain its reserve-free status, but only if the buyer were *not* the issuing bank.

holding-company level, it sells MTNs. We'll talk more about the deposit and medium-term note markets in Chapter 24.

Decreasing Profitability for Dealers

The demand for funds in the CD market during the years 1978 to around 1983 or 1984 was basically from money center banks. Most of the asset growth of the regionals—Mellon, First Minneapolis, the Texas banks, and a few others excepted—was being funded by increases in core deposits. Also, during this period, no one wanted to hear about an S&L CD. The S&L industry was collapsing; and its asset growth was funded, not through increases in core deposits, but through FHLB advances and through repos.

The above was not particularly good news for dealers. The big money center banks who were the ones issuing CDs had over the years developed their own in-house sales forces, so they had no need for dealers to place most of the paper they sold.

Also, the dealers were getting murdered on their CD trading because they had not developed futures sufficiently to hedge their positions. "If you got hit," noted one dealer, "with 5- and 6-month Morgans, and the Fed tightened, which they were doing pretty regularly during that period, you were in jail—just throw away the key until the damn things matured. Often the yield curve was inverted, which just added to the misery."

The severe cost of carry, competition from banks' sales desks, and heavy competition among nonbank dealers to get paper of known credits that were on everyone's approved list— all these factors made trading CDs unprofitable or only marginally profitable for dealers. The upshot was that, one by one, a lot of nonbank dealers, including mighty Sali, either got out of the business of selling CDs and other money market instruments or sharply scaled back their activities in money markets.

CDs and other money market instruments are bull-market products—a dealer can make money positioning them when rates are falling, but he can't make money shorting them when rates are rising. The bull markets of the mid-1980s may have permitted some dealers to overlook their low margins or losses on money markets, but 1988 was all bear market; and it drove a lot more dealers out of the money market business. That is perhaps ironic. The year 1988 also saw an unprecedented buildup of liquidity; thus, it may prove in retrospect that 1988 was the year dealers should have been devoting more, not less, resources to beefing up their money market desks.

THE CD MARKET TODAY

While the old CD market has shrunk dramatically, there are still niches where it shows life. The top wholesale banks, who have no need to sell such paper, still sell, often at below the Fed index rate, small amounts of short-term, fixed-rate CDs, often to special customers—smaller banks with whom they have relationships, trust department customers, and so on.

To get dealers to focus on selling an institution's CDs, the Street must understand that that institution is going to be a regular name; once they expect a certain amount every month, they funnel it through, and get the business done. An example is Boston Safe, a nonbank bank; they have huge programs and the majority of their funding comes from the domestic CD market: some direct, some via dealers.

Also, the Street and investors are beginning to realize that, while the thrift industry may overall be a disaster, certain thrifts are some of the best-run financial institutions around. Their core deposits equal or exceed their loans; they have no interest-rate risk and little credit risk; they just print money. Firms of this ilk—Great Western, World S&L, Cal Federal, and Sears Saving—are getting on investors' approved lists and regularly selling large amounts of CDs. This is a big change from the past. Not so long ago, no thrift had a chance of selling unsecured paper in the *national* market (as opposed to selling federally insured CDs for $100,000 or less to mom-and-pop investors). Now, the best of the thrifts have been looked over, rated, and accepted by at least some institutional investors.

Currently, thrift CDs trade cheap to good bank CDs, rather like Japanese CDs. They are attractive to certain yield-conscious investors.

MARKET MAKING IN CDs TODAY

Today, what remains of the CDs market is a very illiquid market. For reasons explained, supply is down. Consequently, no one focuses on the market, and there is therefore little interest by dealers, and little demand. When CDs were a top money market instrument, when there was supply in the market, it was not uncommon for members of the CD trading fraternity, guys who would trade size, to say, "Hit your bid for 100," or "Lift your offering for 50." That era is dead.

Today, there is no longer even a run in domestic CDs; the credits have changed so much, and dealers are being very specific about what is offered. In the interdealer market, such as it exists, 5MM is still a round lot, and the bid-offer spread is 2 to 5 bp. When new issues of domestic CDs do come to market, it is often in large pieces; when a bank wants to issue, they might well want to issue 50MM and get that funding done, bang.

There are still brokers' pages for CDs, but since just a smattering of banks are active in this market, such pages are not active. For example, there is a section of the Garvin screen that shows bids and offerings of S&L CDs, domestic CDs, domestic BAs, and regional BAs. Thus, there is that outlet, *but* there might be just one offering up there.

EURODOLLAR CDs

Eurodollar CDs were first issued in the London market in 1966 by Citibank. The new instrument was quickly and readily accepted by the market, and volume outstanding rose rapidly. It is impossible to get precise figures on Euro CD outstandings, but Bank of England figures indicate that outstandings in this market, which were about $10 billion in 1974, have ranged over the years 1985 to 1988 between $60 and $70 billion.

Characteristics

A Euro CD, like a domestic CD, is a negotiable instrument evidencing a time deposit made with a bank at a fixed rate for a fixed period (Figure 20–3). Euro CDs bear interest, and Euro CD

FIGURE 20–3
A Euro CD issued by Chase London

rates are quoted on an interest-bearing basis. Interest, which is calculated for actual days on a 360-day-year basis, is paid at maturity on Euro CDs with an original maturity of one year or less, and annually on those with an original maturity of more than one year.

Traditionally, all Euro CDs were denominated in dollars, but recently some have been denominated in yen. Over time, there has been demand by investors for CDs denominated in German marks and Swiss francs, but the German and Swiss central banks have requested that the Bank of England not permit the issuance in London of CDs denominated in their currencies. Their objective has been to discourage any innovation that in their view might create additional opportunities for speculation in their currencies or encourage the use of their currencies as a reserve currency. The Bundesbank has also discouraged the issuance of Euromark CDs outside London.

For all intents and purposes, the market in Euro CDs is a London market. Eurodollar CDs are issued in centers outside London, but their numbers are small, and the liquidity and marketability of non-London CDs are limited. Today Morgan, Bankers, and maybe some other banks issue CDs out of Nassau. On such Euro CDs, payment and physical delivery occur in New

York. What is actually delivered in New York is not the Nassau CD but a *negotiable receipt of deposit,* dubbed *NERD*. Only a few dealers—Merrill, First Boston, and Morgan—make a market in NERDS.

Sales of Euro CDs issued in London are normally made for settlement two days forward, although settlement on a same-day basis can be arranged. Settlement is made by payment of funds in New York, but the actual securities are issued and safekept in London.

Eurodollar CDs issued in London are subject to British regulations. These specify that payment at maturity must be authorized by the issuing bank in London, but actual payment is made in New York for value the same day the CD is presented in London for payment.

One problem both for banks issuing Euro CDs and for investors in these instruments is that, because of the difference in time zones between New York and London, it's impossible to synchronize—as is normally done in money market transactions—delivery of and payment for Euro CDs. To cope with this difficulty and to minimize the physical movement of securities, the First National Bank of Chicago has set up in London a *CD Clearing Centre,* which assures participants payment and delivery on any transaction they make with another member of the Centre.

Euro CDs, like domestic CDs, are normally issued in 1MM pieces. However, Euro CDs for 500,000 have always traded at less of a concession to the market than have domestic CDs of similar size. Because most Euro loans are rolled every three or six months, the bulk of Euro CDs issued are in the 3- to 6-month maturity range. However, Euro CDs with maturities as long as five years are common; the proceeds of such term CDs might be used to match fund an asset of similar maturity or to do one leg of an arbitrage.

Issuers

The major issuers of Eurodollar CDs used to be the branches of all of the top U.S. banks. Other issuers were the British clearing banks, the British overseas banks, and London branches of Canadian, continental, Japanese, and regional U.S. banks.

Today, many of the top American banks still issue in the market depending on their credit and on their need for funds. Since no reserve requirement applies to Euro CDs issued by U.S. banks, the most recent change in reserve requirements did not deter U.S. banks from issuing short-term Euro CDs, as it deterred them from issuing domestic short-term CDs.

In recent years, the Japanese banks have become increasingly important issuers of Euro CDs, both short term and as long out as five years. The Japanese banks use 5-year money to do interbank switches and arbs versus Euro interbank which goes out to five years. Since the advent of bank deposit notes, the Japanese have pared their issuance of medium-term, Euro CDs. Often, Japanese banks will now write deposit notes as a substitute for doing 50MM or 100MM of 5-year, Euro CDs. Investors prefer deposit notes to Euro term CDs, which are annual pay, actual over 360. Also, there are more dealers in the deposit note market and they are more active; so most times, the Japanese can get funding cheaper there.

The Investors

There has always been a chunk of the money invested in Euro CDs that comes from banks in the expatriate money belt of Switzerland: Geneva, Lausanne, and Lugarno. The money invested is customer money, and the Euro CDs acquired are almost never traded because the customers for whom Swiss banks invest are interested in avoiding taxes and in obtaining safety, not in earning 16ths and 8ths through trading. Sometimes, such a customer needs cash; if so, the Swiss bank simply lends to him against his CD rather than sell the instrument.

Overall, today, the Euro CD market is driven by New York retail. The biggest investors are money funds, bank trust departments, insurance companies, and corporate liquidity portfolios. One big change in New York retail is that, in recent years, money funds, loaded with cash, have become very credit conscious as opposed to prospectus conscious. They want to deal with triple-A banks, so Euro CDs issued by top Japanese banks are a natural for them, and they buy tons of them.

With time, the concerns about the sovereign risk attached to London CDs and about funny, unfamiliar foreign names that once deterred conservative U.S. investors from buying Euro CDs, especially ones issued by non-U.S. banks, have diminished considerably. Today, sterling is again a strong currency and Japanese names are becoming increasingly familiar to Americans. If Smith can drive a Honda, he is unlikely to get upset if he finds that his money fund is holding Bank of Tokyo Euro CDs. Smith may not know much about Bank of Tokyo, but at least he's sure it's not a troubled Texas bank.

Rates on Euro CDs

The Fed has ruled that Euro CDs issued by foreign branches of U.S. banks are exempt from Reg Q because they are liabilities of the branch. Thus, U.S. bank branches in London have always been free to pay the going market rate for CD money, a situation that led, in 1969, to substantial gaps between the rates paid on CDs in New York and London. Today, with Reg Q in abeyance on all large-denomination CDs, rates on Euro CDs track domestic CD rates closely, as Figure 20–4 shows. Normally, Euro rates are higher than U.S. rates, with the spread between the two being wider the tighter money is and the longer the maturity of the securities compared.

The gap between yields used to reflect the fact that Euro CDs were less liquid than domestic CDs. Today, that is no longer true. However, some investors still view Euro CDs as a riskier investment than domestic CDs. In this respect, it should be noted that any Eurodollar CD issued by the London branch of a U.S. bank is a direct obligation of that bank, and *the credit is thus that of the parent*. Also, with respect to sovereign risk, it is true that some sticky legal questions would arise should the British stop payment on Eurodollar CDs issued in London, but as noted in Chapter 7, the likelihood of their doing so is zero.

Also, one should note that the Fed index for domestic CD rates is a less meaningful number today than it was in the past. Today, the number is derived from a vanishing market in which some regional banks are able to buy money at sub-market rates while others are paying up because of credit problems.

FIGURE 20–4
Yields on 3-month CDs, Euro and domestic

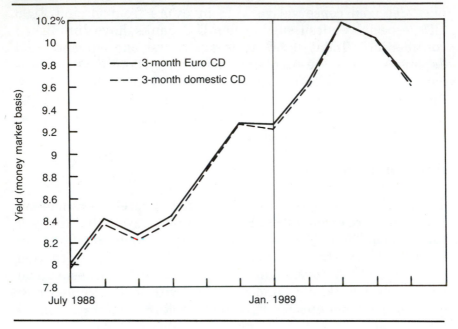

Source: J. P. Morgan Securities, Inc.

For investors, the crucial rate comparison to determine whether to buy a Euro CD is usually how the CD is priced relative to interbank.

Tiering

Tiering always reflects strongly the problems that a particular bank or that banks in particular countries have encountered recently. Today, the top Euro CD market is all tiered. There are only four domestic banks that trade well anymore: Citi, Bankers, Sec Pac, and Morgan. Everyone else is tiered. Regionals will sometimes trade better than some New Yorkers, sometimes worse, depending on their scarcity value. Of the British clearers, Nat West is considered tops; the ranking goes Nat West, Barclays, Lloyds, then Midland.

A big change from the past is the elimination of the wide spread at which Japanese Euro CDs used to trade to domestic U.S. Euro CBs. Today, there are instances where some of the better traded Japanese names will trade better than a First Chicago or a Manny Hanny Euro CD. That did not used to happen. In the early 1980s, there were spreads of 25 to 40 bp between domestic and Japanese names that now trade on top of each other.

There is, however, one emerging problem with Japanese names. Japanese banks have in recent years been taking a lot of Euro time deposits in regional offices that they have set up around the U.S.: Atlanta, Seattle, Los Angeles, San Francisco, and New York. The attraction of a Euro time deposit is that it is generally a bit cheaper to the customer: Fuji might pay 8.12 on a Euro time deposit but do the corresponding Euro CD at only 8.08 or 8.10; generally, Japanese Euro CDs trade LIBID to LIBID minus 5 bp. That relationship stays intact partly because it is slightly cheaper for the bank to do a Euro time deposit than to hit the Street with Euro CDs; on the CDs, there is some brokerage and some First Chicago clearing costs.

A money fund manager with a billion to invest may figure that he wants to keep 500MM in negotiable paper, but that the other 500MM he can fix out in a time deposit at a slightly better rate. As a Japanese bank gets customers to give it Euro time deposits, it fills those customers' lines to it, which in turn limits sales of its Euro CDs to those customers. As more Japanese banks do this, they create more popularity in the Euro CD market for European names.

Another emerging problem is that there is beginning to be tiering among Japanese names. It used to be that the 12 Japanese city banks all traded on the run. Now some Japanese trust banks are coming into the market, something which used to be taboo, and the market is becoming very name selective, especially out of New York.

The New-Issue Market

How Euro CDs get issued varies from bank to bank. J. P. Morgan Securities will bid for and typically get the lion's share of any new Euro CDs issued by Morgan Bank. Bankers Trust, in contrast, will not position, in its securities subsidiary, any of its own new paper. Instead, it simply posts rates and sells off the shelf to retail.

The Japanese banks often use dealers and are very rate sensitive in what they will issue. "The Bank of Tokyo will," noted one New York dealer, "ask me for my Euro CD run, my Yankee CD run, my term CD run, my deposit note rate run, and my Yankee term CD run." The same dealer continued, "I will be most aggressive on my Euro CD run and on my deposit note run because those are the two most liquid markets."

The major dealers in Euro CDs today are Merrill, Shearson, Goldman, Drexel, First Boston, Morgan, Bankers Trust, First Chicago, and Contil. Currently, 80% of the business in Euro CDs is done by the top 10 to 20% of the many dealers who operate in this market.

The Secondary Market

There are a number of interdealer brokers of Euro CDs. Of these, the main players are today Garvin Guybutler, Tullet and Tokyo, and Eurobrokers. The same is also true for Euro time deposits.

While there is still liquidity in Euro CDs, the traditional dealers in the market have pared their staffs or simply gotten out of the business. Sali, Paine Webber, DLJ, CM&M, and Citi have all done this. Morgan, a prime dealer, has two Euro CD traders and is thinking of cutting back to one.

The main reason for the cutbacks is the declining profitability of trading Euro CDs. Euro CDs, like other money market instruments, are bull-market products because a trader can't short them. The bull markets of the early 80s brought forth a lot of new competition, but the 1988 bear market hurt the dealers. To compound their problems, there are now boutiques and niches of European banks coming to New York and setting up small firms. If Dreyfus's money fund wants Morgan Euro CDs, they will go first to J. P. Morgan Securities, since the latter is most likely to have the product. Similarly, if they want Credit Anstalt paper, they will go directly to them, and maybe Credit Anstalt will be able to peddle some other stuff to Dreyfus. Since they create product, banks have a natural advantage over non-bank dealers in trading Euro CDs.

One surprise is that, after U.S. dealers who were big in Euro CDs cut back, the big four Japanese dealers made no real effort to come in and make a presence in the market. The big Japanese dealers have the capital and presumably the contacts with Japanese banks to get a lot of inventory and to hire an astute trader to hedge it. Had they done that, they might well have been able to penetrate New York retail and especially the cash-rich money funds who are always hungry for paper, especially in big blocks.

Today, the interdealer market in Euro CDs is thin. It used to be, at least in Japanese Euro CDs, that a trader could call different people and say, "Give me a market," and they would give him a 2-point market, 52–50, and the trader could hit them for 25MM. Now, they will take 5 or 10MM and back up their bid.

"The Euro CD market is much more of a placement market now," noted one London trader at a U.S. shop. "There is no longer an interdealer market in which Goldman sells to Bankers who sells to Merrill who sells to Sali. Instead, today, we would phone up a bank, take in as inventory any CDs we bought from them, and then sell those CDs through our distribution network."

Also, today's trader is afraid of getting hit with paper from a Japanese bank that has issued a lot of Euro CDs or Euro time deposits to retail. If, say, Tokai has to issue 500MM, all of a sudden there may be a lot of restricted bids on the screen. It is not a liquid market if a broker's screen is full of bids and they are all ex-Tokai. In such a situation, if a dealer ends up with some Tokai Euro CDs and retail cannot take them, he has nowhere to go.

Commenting on liquidity in today's Euro CD market, one trader said, "The Japanese Euro CD and the Japanese BA markets are about equal in terms of liquidity. On a liquidity scale of 1 to 10, they used to have a liquidity of 8. Now that number is down to 7."

The Eurodollar Futures

We have said that Eurodollar CDs are a bull-market product; a trader can't short them. Presumably, he could short the Euro futures contract.[5] "However," noted one CD trader, "the futures market can be very volatile, emotions take over, and so many different types of people with different objectives are dealing in futures that it's not the same thing—being short futures as being short cash Euro CDs."

THE NEXT CHAPTER

In the next chapter, we discuss the market for bankers' acceptances, an instrument that has long been used for the financing of imports, exports, and the storage of goods abroad. In recent years, the Japanese have become big issuers of dollar BAs; nonetheless, the BA market overall is today in decline.

---

[5]Recall Chapter 15's discussion of Euro futures.

CHAPTER 21

BANKERS' ACCEPTANCES

Bankers' acceptances or bills of exchange, as they are also called, are an old financial instrument dating back to the 12th century when early forms of this instrument were used to finance international trade. For the two centuries prior to creation of the Fed, world trade was denominated and financed primarily in sterling, and a market in sterling bankers' acceptances flourished in London.

The founders of the Federal Reserve System, created in 1913, felt that a domestic bankers' acceptance market patterned after the London market should be developed to enhance New York's role as a center of international trade and finance, to promote U.S. foreign trade, and to improve the competitive position of domestic banks. The Fed's founders thus empowered national banks to accept time drafts, which these banks were previously unauthorized to do. They also took other actions to support the growth of this infant market, including permitting the Federal Reserve to rediscount and purchase eligible acceptances.

By the late 1920s, with the Fed's help, a domestic market in bankers' acceptances had become well established, and more than $1.7 billion of acceptances were outstanding. Then due first to the Depression and later to World War II, acceptances outstanding declined sharply. In May 1945, they totaled only $104 MM. After the war, as international trade revived, acceptance financing again became popular; and by the end of 1973, the total volume outstanding was $8.9 billion. Since that time, this volume first grew exponentially; then it tapered off (Figure 21–1).

FIGURE 21–1

Through 1984, the volume of BAs outstanding expanded; then market growth tapered off

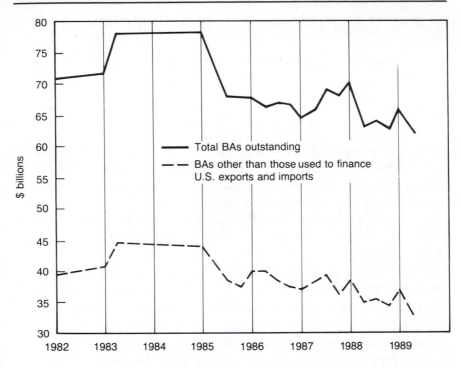

Source: *Federal Reserve Bulletin.*

THE INSTRUMENT

A *bankers' acceptance (BA) is a time draft;* that is, an order to pay a specified amount of money to the acceptance holder on a specified date. BAs are drawn on and accepted by a bank that, by accepting the draft, assumes responsibility to make payment on the draft at maturity.

Creation

Under current Fed regulations, BAs may be created by accepting banks to finance foreign trade, the domestic shipment of goods, domestic or foreign storage of readily marketable staples, and the provision of dollar exchange credits to banks in certain countries.

In Chapter 3, we gave one example of how a BA might be created. A U.S. importer wants to buy shoes from a foreign seller and pay for them several months later. To obtain the necessary financing, he has his bank write a letter of credit for the amount of the sale, which it sends to the foreign exporter. When the shoes are exported, the foreign firm, using this letter of credit, draws a time draft on the importer's U.S. bank and discounts the draft at a local bank, thereby obtaining immediate payment for its goods. The exporter's bank in turn sends the time draft along with proper shipping documents to the importer's U.S. bank. This bank accepts the draft—making it an irrevocable obligation of the accepting bank—and pays out the proceeds of the draft to the exporter's bank. The accepting bank may then hold the accepted draft as an investment, or it may sell it in the open market. When the draft matures, the drawer is responsible for paying the accepting bank the face amount of the draft.

If a U.S. firm uses BAs to finance exports, the process is the reverse. For example, a Japanese firm that wanted to purchase U.S. goods on credit might arrange for a letter of credit from a New York bank under which this bank would agree to accept dollar drafts drawn by a U.S. exporter to cover specified shipments to the Japanese importer.

While the drawing of BAs is frequently preauthorized by a letter of credit, in many instances BAs also arise out of contractual arrangements that are less formal than a letter of credit and are later supported by appropriate documentation. In effect, BAs can be created in various ways. Precisely how a given BA is created depends on who the participants in a transaction are and on the nature of that transaction.

Creating BAs requires much specialized knowledge on the part of the accepting bank. Consequently, it is done only by banks that have foreign departments staffed by personnel who are knowledgeable about the market.

A large proportion of BAs used to be originated by Edge Act corporations, which are specialized subsidiaries set up by banks to engage in international banking. Top money market banks established Edge Act subs in financial centers around the country to service local business. It used to be that a bank, like Morgan, would issue Edge Act paper out of each of its subs: its Houston Edge, its San Francisco Edge, and so on. The trouble with this approach was that each sub had only limited capital. To solve this problem, Congress in 1982 permitted banks to merge their Edge Act subs into a single corporation; one sub took over the role of head office, the others became branches. After that, U.S. banks began to issue all of their Edge Act paper, wherever it is originated, out of a single head office—Miami in the case of Morgan. This change enhanced the creditworthiness of Edge Act paper by enlarging the capitalization of the corporations issuing it. Currently, the use by U.S. banks of Edge Act subs for originating BAs is declining. Japanese banks now do a large share of BA origination in the U.S.; also, U.S. banks have shifted more of the remaining BA origination they do onto the books of head office.

The Goods Financed

Bankers' acceptances used to be created principally to finance domestic exports and imports. This changed in 1974 when the price of oil rose dramatically. At that time, the Japanese and others began to borrow in the domestic BA market to finance their imports of oil. As a result, the BA market grew sharply. Also, as Table 21–1 shows, it changed in character. Currently, more than half of all BAs outstanding are created to finance the storage or shipment of goods between foreign countries; these BAs represent financing of *third-country trade:* transactions in which neither the exporter nor the importer is a U.S. firm.

The prominence of third-country financing in the U.S. acceptance market reflects the fact that the U.S. market is the only world financial center in which there's a wide market for

TABLE 21–1
**Bankers' acceptances outstanding according to the nature of the
transaction financed, February 1989** ($ billions)

Imports	15.6
Exports	13.9
Goods stored in or shipped between foreign countries	33.3
Total	62.8

Source: *Federal Reserve Bulletin.*

dollar-denominated acceptances. There was talk in London of
starting a market there in Eurodollar BAs, but nothing came of
it. The mix of commodities financed in the BA market has not
changed much in recent years; "grains," which in bankers' lingo
covers wheat, corn, soybeans, and sorghum, are by far the largest single item; other big items are cotton and oil.

Characteristics

BAs, like T bills, are a *discount* instrument, and yields on them
are quoted on a discount basis. Most BAs are backed by documentation such as invoices, bills of lading, or independent terminal or warehouse receipts. This documentation is held by the
accepting bank, so the instrument sold to investors is a simply
drawn note (Figure 21–2). This note describes the nature of the
transaction being financed and has been stamped "accepted" by
the accepting bank. BAs are generally issued in *bearer* form.
They may be drawn for varying maturities, but the largest volume of BAs traded in the market is in the 3-month area.

The amount of BA financing required by a borrower depends on the transaction he is financing. Five million is a round
lot in the brokers' market, and typically BAs are issued in
blocks of at least that size. Occasionally, an issuing bank will
sell off a block as large as 50MM.

Maturities of BAs at issue range from one to six months. A
BA with an original maturity of more than six months becomes
"ineligible" (see below), and it therefore trades at a concession to
the market.

FIGURE 21–2

Specimen bankers' acceptance, Harris Bank

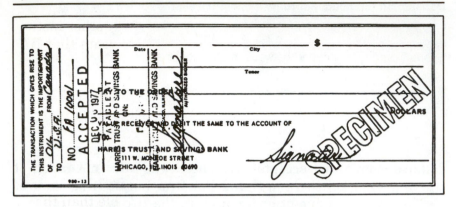

FIGURE 21–3

Today, the BA rate tracks LIBOR

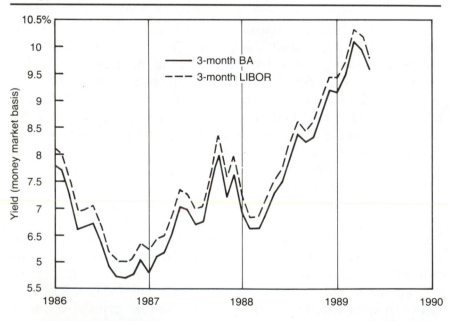

Source: J. P. Morgan Securities, Inc.

The credit risk to an investor of holding a BA is minimal. The instrument not only constitutes an irrevocable primary obligation of the accepting bank but is typically a contingent obligation of the drawer; it is also an obligation of any other institutions that have endorsed it. During the 70-odd years that BAs have been traded in the U.S., no investor in BAs has suffered a loss of principal.

BAs trade at a spread above bills. Traditionally, this spread was 15 to 25 bp in the 3-month area, but for reasons noted in earlier chapters, bills currently trade expensive to other money market instruments; as a result, the BA-bill spread is today often a point or more. This spread widens markedly when rates are rising, narrows when rates are falling. Currently, the spread of BAs to LIBOR is narrower and more predictable than that of BAs to bills (Figure 21–3).

ELIGIBILITY REQUIREMENTS

A high official of the New York Fed, now retired, recalled that, when he first came to the bank, one of the first questions he had to answer was: Are yak tails readily marketable? That's not common knowledge, but fortunately he was able to come up with a quick answer, "Yes, they are"; he'd just read that yak tails were used in the U.S. to make high-quality Santa Claus beards. And why, one might wonder, did the New York Fed care about the marketability of yak tails? The answer is that it determined whether a particular BA was or wasn't eligible.

To understand the BA market, one has to know something about eligibility requirements. The initial Federal Reserve Act specified that BAs eligible for discount at or purchase by the Fed had to meet certain requirements. These, as noted in the second column of Table 21–2, are complex. Generally their spirit is that, for a BA to be eligible, it should finance a short-term (no longer than six months), self-liquidating commercial transaction of one of several specified types.

The implications of this set of criteria for eligibility have changed considerably over time. The initial intent and practice were that banks experiencing a temporary need for funds would

TABLE 21–2
Bankers' acceptances: Eligibility and reservability

Type of Bankers' Acceptance	Eligible for Purchase*	Eligible for Discount†	Exempt from Reserve Requirements If Sold‡
Export-import, including shipments between foreign countries:			
Tenor—6 months or less	Yes	Yes§	Yes
6 months to 9 months	Yes	No	No
Domestic shipment, with documents conveying title attached at the time of acceptance:			
Tenor—6 months or less	Yes	Yes§	Yes
6 months to 9 months	Yes	No	No
Domestic shipment, without documents conveying title:			
Tenor—6 months or less	Yes	No	No
6 months to 9 months	Yes	No	No
Shipment within foreign countries:			
Tenor—any maturity	No	No	No
Foreign storage, readily marketable staples secured by warehouse receipt:			
Tenor—6 months or less	No	Yes§	Yes
6 months to 9 months	No	No	No
Domestic storage, readily marketable staples secured by warehouse receipt:			
Tenor—6 months or less	Yes	Yes§	Yes
6 months to 9 months	Yes	No	No

Domestic storage, any goods in the U.S. under contract of sale or going into channels of trade and secured throughout its life by warehouse receipt:			
Tenor—6 months or less	Yes	No	No
6 months to 9 months	Yes	No	No
Dollar exchange, required by usages of trade, only in approved countries:			
Tenor—3 months or less	No	Yes	No||
3 months to 9 months	No	No	No
Finance or working capital, not related to any specific transaction:			
Tenor—any maturity	No	No	No

Tenor refers to the full length of time of the acceptance from date of inception to maturity. To be eligible for discount, a bankers' acceptance must be endorsed by at least one member bank, as provided in Section 13(6) of the Federal Reserve Act.

*Authorizations announced by the Federal Open Market Committee on April 1, 1974.

†In accordance with Regulation A of the Federal Reserve Act.

‡In accordance with Regulation D of the Federal Reserve Act.

§Providing that the maturity of nonagricultural bills at the time of discount is not more than 90 days.

||According to revised Regulation D, these acceptances are reservable, but the Federal Reserve Board's legal staff has expressed an opinion that the exemption from reserve requirements is also applicable to dollar exchange acceptances.

Source: Jean M. Mahr and William C. Melton, "Bankers' Acceptances," *Quarterly Review*, Federal Reserve Bank of New York, Summer 1981, p. 53. In constructing this table the authors relied on an unpublished paper by Arthur Bardenhagen.

sell to the Fed (that is, rediscount at the discount window) BAs and other eligible paper. Later, open market operations replaced the discount window as the Fed's primary tool for creating bank reserves, and the Fed's view as to what was an appropriate use of the discount window changed. Now, no bank would ask the Fed to rediscount a BA to maturity to raise funds because doing so would violate the spirit in which loans are currently extended at the discount window.

The key importance today of the eligibility requirements stated in the original Federal Reserve Act (see the third column of Table 21–2) is that only acceptances that are deemed eligible according to these requirements may be sold by member banks without incurring a *reserve requirement*.

Currently, banks can and do create some ineligible acceptances. If they sell such acceptances, they incur a reserve requirement. The resulting reserve cost is passed on by the bank to the borrower. Thus, a borrower who requires ineligible as opposed to eligible BA financing pays a higher rate.

Eligibility at the Fed

In the early 1970s, the Fed was active in the BA market in four ways: It bought BAs for its own portfolio and did repo with BA dealers as part of its normal open market operations; in addition, it lent to banks at the discount window against BAs as collateral, and it bought—adding its own guarantee to them—BAs in the open market for the account of foreign central banks.

Buying BAs for its own portfolio on its own initiative was nothing new for the Fed. To encourage growth of the BA market, the Fed did this continually from the inception of the BA market after World War I. By 1974, a big change had occurred in the composition of the BAs that were being created by the banks. At this time, the Fed decided to modernize its rules on what BAs it could purchase as part of its open market operations; responsibility for setting eligibility requirements for purchase was passed from the Board of Governors to the Federal Open Market Committee. The new eligibility requirements relative to purchases issued by the FOMC are summarized in column 1 of

Table 21–2. One major change was that BAs with a maturity of up to nine months, provided they met other eligibility requirements, became eligible for purchase even though they were ineligible for discount.

At this time, when the Fed bought BAs, it did not usually ask a dealer to tell it in advance which bank's paper the dealer was offering; the Fed made no attempt to distinguish gradations in quality among different banks' paper. Instead it asked the dealers only that they offer it *prime* paper. The Fed's main criterion for determining that a bank's paper was prime was that it be traded in reasonable volume and with reasonable frequency in the secondary market: that the paper was acceptable to the market.

In the market's view, however, there were and still are quality gradations in paper, and tiering exists in the rates paid by different institutions. To avoid acquiring undue amounts of paper considered by the market to be less attractive, the Fed instructed the dealers to offer and deliver to it a reasonable mix of acceptances created by prime banks. If the Fed's holdings of any one bank's paper became unduly large, it would temporarily refuse to accept that name until its holdings were reduced to an acceptable percentage.

The Federal Reserve Bank of New York has for years purchased for foreign correspondents (mainly other central banks) government securities, agency securities, and BAs.

Prior to November 8, 1974, the Federal Reserve guaranteed the acceptances it purchased for its foreign correspondents. The policy of guaranteeing acceptances held by foreign correspondents was developed in the process of working out reciprocal correspondent relationships with other central banks during the early years of the Federal Reserve System. Such guarantees were at that time considered useful in encouraging the development of the bankers' acceptance market. In part, due to the favorable rate spread between acceptances and Treasury bills, foreign correspondent holdings of bankers' acceptances guaranteed by the Federal Reserve increased rapidly during 1974 to a level of about $2 billion. Against this background, officials of the Federal Reserve concluded that there was no longer justification for extending a guarantee favoring a particular private market instrument or a particular group of investors.[1]

Because of the Fed's decision to stop guaranteeing BAs, the number of foreign banks buying them dropped by about two thirds, and the holdings of remaining foreign customers fell to about $300MM in 1975. To cushion the effect on the BA market of this large drop in foreign purchases, the Fed temporarily increased its purchases of BAs by a like amount.

Then, gradually, the Fed let its BA holdings drop. Finally, in March 1977, when the Fed was buying for its portfolio only an insignificant amount of BAs—$1 or $2MM daily—it determined that the BA market was sufficiently mature so that it no longer needed the Fed's support, and it stopped buying BAs for its portfolio.

Eligibility requirements with respect to purchases used, however, to still have significance. BAs that were eligible for purchase were also eligible for repo, and the Fed continued to do repo with BA dealers until July 1984. At that time, it discontinued such repos.

Currently, banks may use as collateral for loans at the discount window any BAs that are eligible for purchase by the Fed and any other paper that meets the general eligibility standards established by the window.

BANK PRICING AND SALE

When a bank creates an acceptance, it prices the BA as follows. First, it checks the rate at which paper of the maturity it is creating and carrying its name is trading in the dealer market; that is, the rate at which it could sell the acceptance. To this rate it adds any reserve cost it would incur in selling the acceptance if the latter is ineligible.

To the sum of these two costs, the bank adds on a commission for its services. Back in the mid-1970s, the standard accep-

---

[1]Ralph T. Helfrich, "Trading in Bankers' Acceptances: A View from the Acceptance Desk of the Federal Reserve Bank of New York," *Monthly Review,* Federal Reserve Bank of New York, February 1976, p. 53.

tance fee was 1.5%. Time and competition changed this. Today, U.S. banks charge a better credit 25 to 30 bp, while Japanese banks take a commission of as little as 10 to 15 bp.

Selling versus Holding

Once a bank creates a BA, it can either hold the paper as part of its loan portfolio or sell it. Bank attitudes on this point vary considerably. It used to be that, when the Fed was tightening and banks were short on reserves, they would normally choose to sell BAs to be able to fund more straight loans. In contrast, when money was easy, there was more variability in bank behavior. Some banks consistently sold a large proportion of the BAs they created to investors. For other banks, the decision whether to sell BAs was strictly an investment decision.

Noted one such banker, "We will hold BAs if we think that rates are coming down and will sell them if we think that rates are going up. However, our decision on BAs is usually weighted toward selling them out rather quickly because, if you have a profit in them and you sell them out fast, you get the profit for sure and right away for the whole maturity of the BA. If you wait, you are speculating on what will happen to the cost of funding. BAs are a relatively low-yield instrument, and spreads are narrow, so it doesn't take much of a rise in rates to take you from a profitable to an unprofitable position in BAs. Also, the cost of funding BAs is higher for a bank than for a dealer because a bank incurs a reserve requirement when it repos acceptances unless it does the repo with another bank. Because of this, the cheapest way for us to fund BAs is usually with Fed funds."

Another banker made the same point more succinctly, "Whenever we position BAs, it is a rate decision. I tell our trader, any time we think it is a good idea to buy 90-day money, he had better not build up any assets—just sell the BAs we create out to the market."

The environment in which banks currently operate—heightened concern over capital ratios, balance-sheet usage, and return on capital—has further diminished the meager appetite banks once had for positioning BAs.

Borrowing via the BA Route

Years ago when rates were lower and less volatile, a firm with a financing need that could be covered in the BA market faced a relatively simple choice: go the BA route or borrow at a floating-rate prime. The advantage of BA financing was that it was cheaper, and a firm's decision to use BA financing was typically a rate decision.

As rates rose and became more volatile, the spread of prime over the lower commercial paper rate got as wide as 350 bp, and borrowers began to view prime as a punitive rate. To retain borrowers, banks changed their lending terms dramatically (Chapter 6). Today, a firm financing a commodity transaction will—depending on its size, credit, and relationship to its bank—have a menu of borrowing alternatives from which to choose: a loan at a floating prime, a Euro loan, a fixed-rate advance, or BA financing. Also, it may have access to the commercial paper market.

A firm with a financing need will seek to borrow as cheaply as possible. Thus, today as before, a borrower's choice as to which financing method to use is typically a rate decision. The commercial paper market remains the cheapest source of short-term financing available to firms. Borrowing via the BA route is a way for a firm that lacks direct access to the open market—because it cannot sell commercial paper—to obtain indirect access to this market; the access is more expensive because the firm must pay the accepting bank a fee for opening the door for it to this market.

Many domestic firms that use the BA market are financing commodity imports and exports—grains—frequently huge amounts. These firms have tremendous financing needs. Also, due to the extreme variability of commodity prices, their financing needs are equally variable and also unpredictable. Therefore, such firms, besides trying to minimize their borrowing costs, feel the need to maintain as many sources of financing open to them as possible. Thus, some top firms finance part of their needs in the commercial paper market, part in the BA market, and part with bank loans.

Bank loans become an attractive alternative to BA financing when spreads are reasonable and the borrower is unsure how long he will need financing. If a borrower repays a BA early (as Fed regulations require him to do if the underlying transaction is terminated early), no proportion of the bank commission on the BA is repaid to him. He does get a pro rata rebate on the discount fee but minus ¼ or so.

MARKET STOCK IN TRADE

Prior to 1984, BAs outstanding grew phenomenally, and all signs indicated that this trend would continue. More cost-conscious firms wanted to use the BA market to shave their borrowing costs, and bankers—always inventive—were looking for new ways in which BA financing might be used.

One impediment to continued growth of the BA market was an antiquated and economically hard-to-defend rule incorporated in the Federal Reserve Act. This rule limited the amount of BAs a bank could have outstanding to 100% of its capital and surplus. With Fed permission, granted semiautomatically, this limit could be extended to 125%. In mid-1982, the 125% rule, which never had been a binding constraint on BA creation, became so for many major banks, some of whom sought to get around the rule by issuing more Edge Act paper. In the fall of 1982, Congress passed legislation permitting banks to issue eligible acceptances equal to 150% of their capital and surplus. Congress also made it easier for banks to use acceptances to finance domestic trade. Both changes seemed likely to stimulate BA creation by the major domestic banks.

However, BAs originated by domestic banks actually declined thereafter. One reason was intense competition from Japanese banks, who now originate over 50% of the BAs sold in the U.S. market. Other foreign banks also originate dollar BAs, but only in relatively small amounts. Because BAs, even if sold, remain a contingent liability of the originating bank, one that must be backed by capital, and because of the importance banks today attach to improving their capital ratios, it's not clear that

U.S. banks were overly pained to lose a lot of BA business to Japanese banks. Certainly, they weren't prepared to work for the low commissions that Japanese banks find acceptable.

A second reason for the decline in the origination of BAs by U.S. banks was the general decline in size of the BA market. The latter reflects the fact that, for an issuer, BAs were always a cumbersome financing tool; and, today, the typical borrower is likely to have more financing alternatives, especially given the growth of the commercial-paper market. Perhaps, for example, the borrower is an A-2, P-2 issuer; if so, he'd be comparing the all-in BA rate he'd have to pay with rates on A-2, P-2 paper, maybe with the cost of a bank loan obtained via a bid feature in his backstop facility, and maybe with a Euro loan at LIBOR plus a spread.

INVESTORS IN BAs

Today, the biggest investors in BAs are municipal bodies and money funds. Then come pension funds, some thrifts and savings banks, insurance companies, and assorted other smaller investors.

Whereas five years ago, some muni bodies might have regarded Japanese BAs as unfamiliar, foreign paper that carried a funny (please don't ask me to pronounce it) name, today such provincialism has largely disappeared. Municipal investors, especially but not only West Coast ones, have no problem with Japanese BAs. They recognize that the top Japanese banks are the largest and among the strongest banks in the world and that Japanese BAs have good liquidity. Also, muni investors have never experienced any problems with their investments in Japanese BAs; finally, muni investors find that the maturities of Japanese BAs, like those of commercial paper, often fit well the periods for which they wish to invest. With respect to the attitude of big money funds toward Japanese BAs and their experience with such paper, we need only say ditto; like muni investors, money funds have come to have a hearty appetite for Japanese BAs.

To limit credit exposure vis-à-vis any one bank and to ensure diversification, major investors in bank paper, BAs and other, set up lines limiting how much paper of each sort they will take that bears any one bank's name. A big investor might have large lines to all of the top 13 Japanese issuers of BAs but none to Manny or Contil. Investors' lines are a fundamental determinant of current rate-tiering in the BA market, something we discuss below.

CHANGES IN HOW THE MARKET IS DEALT

In the early 1970s, when the BA market was small—$6–8 billion of outstandings—dealers did not position much, and activity in the market was light. At that time it was a tradition, respected by all dealers, that the spread between their bid to the banks and their offer to retail was 1/4. Thus, if the banks were creating BAs at 5, the dealers would automatically resell them to retail at 4 3/4. With all the dealers posting and bidding the same rates to the banks, which dealers got what was strictly a function of their relationships with particular banks. To break this pattern, Merrill and Sali in 1970 began quoting competitive rates; and once they did, all the other dealers followed.

By 1983, when the volume of BAs outstanding was soaring, 30 firms had access to the brokers' market in BAs, and most recognized government dealers traded BAs. Dealers got into the business because BAs were there in growing volume and retail wanted them. Also, BAs, particularly Japanese BAs, were actively traded among dealers. At that time, there were some firms, Merrill, at one extreme, that focused on profiting from *distribution to retail*. Merrill was and remains a breed apart: complete buyers from issuing banks and from the Street. At the other extreme, were large *trading* shops, like Sali, that sought to make big profits by taking successful positions.

At that time, the BA market was actively brokered by FBI and Garvin. Brokerage was an 01 on every trade done through the brokers, and BA brokers were making a tidy profit on heavy volume.

Today, with the BA market in decline, things have changed dramatically. Sali, once a big trader of BAs, has left the market, and so too have many other dealers. One big difference between past and present is that outstandings are down, from 78.4 billion at the end of 1984 to 62.8 billion in early 1989. Another problem with domestic BAs, besides declining issuance, is that credit problems at a number of domestic banks have destroyed the run that once existed in top-name, domestic BAs. When *the run* prevailed, dealers made bids on and offers of top-name domestic BAs on a *no-name* basis, the paper of all such issuers was regarded as sufficiently equal in quality to trade at the same rate.

The Run in Domestic BAs

"The domestic market," noted one BA trader in early 1989, "has changed a lot even since I started to trade BAs a few years ago. Then, there used to be a brokers' run where you could trade money center names; and 13 top names traded on that run. Then, the number got down to eight: Contil, First Chicago, Manny, and others had their problems. Gradually, the run got whittled down to practically nothing. Now, the names that trade on the [brokers'] screen are Bankers, Citi, Chase, Security Pacific, the B of A, and then the regionals. Morgan BAs rarely get on the screen; they trade so well that they vanish to retail and are never seen on the Street. The run is for all intents and purposes dead. Now, a broker will call and say, 'I have 5MM Chases.' You no longer put up a bid against an offering unless you know what is offered. If it's a Manny, you are going to bid 15 or 20 back from the rate on a Bankers or a Morgan BA."

Regional Names

Prior to 1974, the Fed supported the market for regional bankers' acceptances by buying such paper for the account of foreign buyers and adding its guarantee to it. When the Fed stopped this practice, some of the regional banks took a beating. The year 1974 was characterized by tight money and well-publicized difficulties in the banking industry. Investors then became very credit conscious. Prior to that time, most big investors would buy the paper of any $1-billion bank. But in 1974, some investors began to revise their criteria and decided that size wasn't equal to quality. With a number of them saying they would take only the top 10 or 15 banks' paper, the regionals were forced to pay up, and tiering developed.

Later, thanks partly to the credit problems at certain money center banks, investors began looking more at regional BAs; and in a number of cases, they liked the quality they saw. Thus, today, there is more regional paper around that dealers trade. However, there is no run in regional names. Brokers always list on their screens any offerings of regional BAs by size and by name of the issuing bank.

Despite the growth in Japanese and regional paper in the BA market, "Activity is nothing like in 1983," commented one dealer. "Then, spreads were wider, and you made more profit. It was the start of the bull market. There was more volume, more volatility. Whenever there is volatility, brokers make money, regardless of whether the market goes up or down. When brokers have pictures on their screens, they have the opportunity to earn their commissions. In a dull market—nothing is trading; the brokers starve. Years ago, when there was more volume and volatility and more dealers were involved, a trader could always turn to the Street—to the brokers—to get out of product he did not want. Now, unless you are a retail-oriented shop, you cannot be a big player in BAs."

Japanese BAs still trade on their own run, and liquidity for them is good in the sense that a retail customer can always get bids from dealers on any Japanese BA he might want to sell. However, interdealer trading in Japanese BAs is less active than formerly. Still, it is far better than in domestic BAs. "When retail isn't buying," noted one trader, "you have some liquidity. You can hit a bid in the brokers' market or hit Chemical's or Lehman's bid. We dealers exchange runs in Japanese BAs. If, in bidding on a big block of BAs, I missed, I will know 90% of the time who owns those BAs. The product will show up in someone else's run."

A part of the decline in interdealer trading in the BA market must be attributed to the fact that, while supply has declined, demand has not. Today, it seems that a lot more BAs, once they are created, get sold immediately—either directly by the issuer or via a dealer—to a retail customer who, 9 times out of 10, holds the paper to maturity. Thus, there's little floating supply in the market for dealers to trade; consequently, there are fewer dealers; and those who are there are leery of taking big positions unless they can count on retail, as opposed to other dealers, to buy the paper they've positioned.

THE BA MARKET TODAY

Today, the BA market is segmented into four parts: a few money center names, some regional names, the Japanese issuers, and the *Yankee issuers* ("Yankee issuers" are non-Japanese, foreign bank branches, e.g., French, Swiss, German bank branches).

The top money center banks that issue BAs—Morgan, Bankers, Chase, Citi—all have their own sales forces selling Treasuries to and doing repo with retail. Given the declining volume of BAs they issue, these banks do not need to use non-bank dealers to sell their BAs; their own sales forces can easily do most or all of the job. "I can sell," noted a trader at one such bank, "all of the BAs we create to our retail. Rarely, do I sell to the Street, except to help someone out."

Currently, some of the regionals are cutting back on their issuance of BAs, but others are going to stay big in the business: Pit Nat (Pittsburgh National Bank), Rep NY (Republic Bank of New York), Philly Nat, Harris Trust, Maryland National. The regionals, like the money center banks, have their own sales forces, and the only BAs they offer to dealers are those that they cannot sell themselves. Net, the market in regional BAs is not that active for dealers, and only a few dealers do much in it. Merrill is of course there because Merrill has retail *everywhere* in the country; consequently, they can find a buyer for just about any paper, including even a Manny BA (currently, a lot of investors have no line for Manny BAs).

A regional who wants to sell BAs it's issuing will call a dealer for a bid. Some regionals will deal with just one dealer exclusively because they like and trust that dealer. Other regionals wanting to sell will call every dealer out there and try to get the best bid.

Right now, Yankee names issue rather few BAs. However, there is a lot of demand from investors for these names, so in the future, Yankee banks may issue more BAs.

The top Japanese city banks are the big issuers of BAs today. Unlike domestic banks, the Japanese banks lack sales forces; consequently, they must rely on the dealers to distribute their paper. A typical dealer observed, "I call the major Japanese issuers every morning and give them a *bid run* [bids for different maturities]. They also get bid runs from other dealers. Then, depending on how aggressive my bids are and also on the relationship, they will come back and show me individual pieces of paper on which I make them a firm bid.

"We trade off—at a spread to—interbank. That is the way we make our markets whether it is CDs, BAs, or commercial paper. So, when I come in in the morning, I get a feel for what interbank has done overnight, how it is in the morning. I see if there is any activity on the screens—any bids. Sometimes, there will be no bids, so I have to go basically on spreads and on how I feel about the market. That's how I come up with my bid run."

"To the Japanese," commented another dealer, "my run must be a good indicator. If I am an aggressive buyer, have an ax to grind, really want to have them call me back and to buy their paper, it's very important to give them good runs." Another dealer commented, "To get paper from an issuer, I must bid inside the bid. If the market is 8.07 bid, 8.05 asked, I would make the market 7–5 to another dealer; but for me to get paper from an issuer, I would have to bid an 06—go to the middle; and often, retail wants better than an 05. It's getting more and more difficult to take a basis spread out of this market."

Daichi is the biggest issuer of Japanese BAs. Other Japanese banks issue less and their issuance may be sporadic. "You will hear," noted one trader, "nothing out of an issuer, and then, all of a sudden, he will sell you a 50MM block. Some issuers will do 5MM pieces several times a week. Still others will do nothing for a time and then come down with two 50MM and one 100MM piece all in the same day."

The Dealers

In domestic BAs, Merrill, because of its distribution, is king. Its mission is to buy from issuing banks and from the Street to obtain product for its sales force to distribute to retail. Accordingly, Merrill's BA trader is paid for servicing the banks from whom it buys product and its retail investors; he is not paid to make right decisions on rates and position plays. What positions he inevitably ends up holding overnight are hedged using the nearby Euro futures contract. In the current market, Merrill's BA trader has no liquidity so far as the brokers are concerned because no other dealer has distribution for such a wide range of domestic names. However, for Merrill, the problem is more typically to find supply than to find retail. In domestic BAs, compared to Japanese BAs, there is just not that much business to be done by the dealers.

Today, the list of active BA dealers is far shorter than it was just a few years ago. Besides Merrill, there are Lehman, Bankers, Morgan, the B of A, Chemical, First Chicago, and Citi. They are the players who have paper all of the time and who are continually in the market. When a big block is traded, 90% of the time, it will be to one of the above dealers. In addition, there are dealers who are sometimes players.

Speaking of the market in domestic BAs, one dealer said, "I used to talk to six or eight different dealers and give them my bid-to-offer spreads. Now, Bankers will call me and say, 'Do you have paper in the early 3s?' I'll say, 'Yea, five Pit Nats at such and such a level.' It is not an active, trading, dealer-to-dealer market any more. You can still make trading plays, but it's less than in the past. If you are bullish and think you can place paper eventually, you can position a lot of BAs if you have the network and know where to go to buy. However, because of the lack of market liquidity, the risk is that your retail is not going to want to buy; if not, you will have to hold your position and sell out gradually."

In Japanese BAs, Merrill has lots of competition. Even there, however, it is retail that separates the big players from the smaller ones. A dealer with retail who buys BAs at the bid side or a little better and then wants to get out of them can probably do so at the offered side of the market rather than having to hit bids in the brokers' screens and lose his spread. In Japanese BAs, the bid-offer spread in the interdealer market is an 02; and it is the guy with retail who is most likely, each time he buys and resells paper, to be able to take out an 02 or an 01.

Years ago, a dealer could deal in BAs without retail, just with other dealers. He could buy paper from Daichi, show it to the Street, and get lifted. Today, a dealer needs retail; spreads are narrower than they used to be, and it's tough to make money trading dealer to dealer.

The Brokers

Garvin and FBI still broker BAs; and Eurobrokers recently entered the market more recently. Brokerage, as before, is still an 01.

"Usually," commented one trader of domestic BAs, "there are three or four things up there [on a broker's screen]. The most active part of the screen is the part devoted to regional paper. No one wants to put in a bid for 'on the run paper' because you don't know what you are going to get hit with. You will see an occasional offering up there—someone wants to get out of something. Everyone knows what it is. Maybe three or four regional names trade actively. If one of us wants to get out of our positions, we will put them up there. If everyone hates the market, the bottom part of the screen keeps decreasing, and offerings in the regional part of the screen get bigger and bigger."

When there is a bid on the screen, it influences, but does not set, a trader's bid run. "I always make a two-way market," noted one trader of Japanese BAs, "but I do not have to be as good as the best bid on the screen. My bid can be worse, but my offer must still be 2 bp from my bid, in which case other dealers can buy paper from me at a cheaper level."

Maturity Distribution of BAs

A lot of things affect the maturity distribution of outstanding BAs, including concerns of issuing banks about the aesthetics of their balance sheet at end-of-quarter. There is definitely more paper three months and in, and that is the most liquid area of the curve by far. In the 3-months area, there are both new 3-month BAs and 6-month BAs that have been outstanding for three months. BAs trade the same whether they are fresh or have been outstanding for some time.

Since BAs are issued on every business day of the month, to give them more homogeneity for trading purposes, BAs maturing in a given month are quoted for early and late dates in the month, for example, a bid or an offering might be for early or late Jans. Also, paper that is exactly six months from maturity is actively traded and trades on the run. The least liquid BAs are the 4s and 5s. Eligible BAs do not go beyond six months in maturity.

Average Size of Trades

It's difficult to generalize about the size of BA trades; one could almost say anything goes from half a million to 50MM.

In the brokers' market, 5MM is a round lot, but given that BAs often do not come in nice round pieces—5 or 10MM, 1 by 1, it is understood that a bid or offer in the brokers' market is good for anything from 5MM to 6MM 250. An average-size trade in the brokers' market is 10 to 15MM; 50MM is a big trade. Typically, dealers prefer to buy blocks of at least 5MM, and those with good retail hanker to get blocks of 20, 35, 50MM. There are muni bodies and money funds who love blocks of that size and who will even pay up to get them. However, only a few banks issue blocks as big as 50MM. "You see few of those big deals," noted one trader, "so when one comes to market, you want to jump on it." The majority of trades, whatever their size, are not for even amounts; they may be for 10.5MM, 12.37MM, or some round amount plus an *odd tail*.

A dealer, like Merrill, that has lots of little as well as big clients is happy to get the odd tail because among its retail are buyers looking to invest just a small amount. Commented one trader: "I find it helpful when I have some small pieces because there is more liquidity from my standpoint. Our retail is large, so if I buy 50MM 6-months and have a lot of half-million increments in it, I can sell the 1MM ½s, the 2½s, and the 3½s, whereas if I had just 1MM pieces, I would be more limited in the trades I could do with retail. I will always ask the bank from whom I am buying for some half million lots, but they won't always oblige. Then, I explain why I want the halves and that there is even the possibility that I could pay a little better if I got some. That entices them to do it. If I can get a 20MM block, 5 by 1MM, 10 by 5, I can have it sold away before you know it."

TIERING

Once upon a time, investors wanted just BAs issued by money center banks, and consequently, such paper traded expensive relative to all other paper in the BA market. Today, tiering is a lot more complex because investors pay more attention to an individual issuing bank's credit than to its class—whether it's regional, Yankee, or whatever.

Money Center Names

Today, amongst money center banks, Morgan trades best; Bankers trades between Morgan and Citi; Chase trades several basis points back; B of A—their BAs are dubbed BOAs (as in boa constrictor)—also trades back. Mannys just do not trade except maybe to Merrill. If Contil is issuing any BAs, they do so to local retail as their BAs do not show up in the New York market.

Regional Names

As problems surfaced with respect to money center names, investors became more interested in regional names. In general, investors perceive strong regional issuers to be as good or better credits than money center banks. NCNB and First Charlotte are aggressive banks that are getting better and better. BAs of these banks, of Pit Nat, of Philly Nat, and of other regionals that have no Latin American debt on their balance sheets trade better than some money center bank BAs. However, regional names do not, as noted above, trade on the run; thus, to buy these names, a dealer needs retail that will also buy them.

Japanese BAs trade pretty much on interbank, sometimes a little more expensively than interbank. It depends: BAs tend to be expensive in the front end, in the 1- and 2-months, which retail really likes; in that area, the Japanese banks can often arrange financing at 5, at times even 10, bp below interbank; however, if Euro CDs and commercial paper are trading cheap to interbank, investors won't want to go into 6-month Japanese BAs, and such paper may then trade cheap to interbank.

Japanese BAs

While the run has virtually vanished from interdealer trading to top domestic BAs, the run for Japanese BAs is still alive and well: currently, BAs issued by 13 Japanese banks trade on a no-name basis in the interdealer market, that is, dealers' bids and offers are good for any Japanese name so long as all of the paper delivered is the same name: not a bit of this and a bit of that.

Despite the fact that Japanese banks issuing BAs are all triple-A credits and the fact that their BAs have good liquidity, Japanese BAs generally trade at an 8- to 10-bp spread to top, on-the-run domestics. This spread may be due in part to the unfamiliarity factor: most investors now accept Japanese BAs, but some have more of an appetite for such paper than others; West Coast investors tend to have big lines to Japanese banks, whereas portfolios in more conservative companies and in more conservative regions like the Midwest have smaller lines for Japanese paper. Also, the spread, top-Japanese-to-top-U.S., may be simply a matter of supply and demand; in 1989, 13 Japanese banks alone were issuing over half of all BAs issued in the U.S. market.

Historically, the spread, Japanese to top domestic, has been as high as 20 to 25 bp. At other times, Japanese BAs have traded on top of top domestic BAs. In the view of one, not atypical, trader, "When you consider relative quality and relative liquidity, the normal spread should be no more than a nickel."

Yankee Issuers

The Yankee issuers of BAs—Deutsche Bank, Allgemaine, the Swiss banks, Crédit Lyonnais, West Pac (Australian)—are all triple-A credits and are well perceived by domestic investors.

Also, their BAs have scarcity value, since there are fewer non-Japanese foreign names in the market than there used to be. Typically, Yankee BAs trade at a spread below Japanese BAs; for example, Deutsche Bank usually trades 4 expensive to the Japanese run, Allgemaine maybe 2 or 3 expensive to the Japanese run. "In a bull market, Yankee paper can trade at quite a wide spread to the Japanese BA market;" noted one trader, "a lot of investors have all of the good domestic and foreign names on their approved list; and toward the end of a month in which they have done a lot of buying, they may get filled up on Japanese names. Then, if they see some esoteric name, a regional or a Yankee, they'll grab that paper; that is when you see Yankee BAs trade pretty rich to the Japanese run."

Ineligible BAs

A BA may be ineligible for various reasons: for example, it lacks a bill of lading or it's longer than 180 days. Years ago, there was a lot of trading in ineligible BAs. Today, that market has pretty much disappeared. An ineligible BA that did come to market would currently trade 10 to 15 bp cheaper than an eligible BA.

THE FINANCING OF DEALER POSITIONS IN BAs

Banks usually finance any BAs they position with Fed funds, because if they repoed them, they would incur a reserve requirement.

Nonbank dealers can finance BAs they position with repo or with dealer loans. Since repo is cheaper, dealers normally use it. Delivering out collateral would be expensive for a dealer repoing BAs, so normally he does short-term, typically overnight, *letter* (also called a hold-in-custody) repo: he holds the physical BAs and gives the investor a list of those BAs that serve as collateral for his repo.

On a normal day when government repo is 1/8 to 3/8 below funds, a dealer with good retail and thus good access to repo money, can repo BAs at maybe a nickel or a dime below funds.

The spread will be smaller the fewer the BAs a dealer is looking to finance; it will also be smaller if there is a shortage of government collateral in the repo market.

THE NEXT CHAPTER

In the BA market, banks sell short-term corporate paper that they have guaranteed. In the next chapter, we turn to the sale of unsecured, corporate, short-term notes—of commercial paper. Once sleepy and small, the market for commercial paper has, in recent years, been put to a host of innovative uses. One upshot is that, today, commercial paper outstanding outstrips T bills outstanding.

CHAPTER 22

COMMERCIAL PAPER: DOMESTIC AND EURO

Commercial paper is an unsecured promissory note with a fixed maturity. The issuer promises to pay the buyer some fixed amount on some future date but pledges no assets, only his liquidity and established earning power, to guarantee that promise. Commercial paper is exempt from SEC registration if the issuer meets one of several alternative sets of requirements.

Back in 1970, the commercial paper market was a parochial market that tended, by investment banking standards, to be populated by less sophisticated, less intense, less motivated people. The paper sold was also mundane, definitely plain vanilla. Also, in 1970, the commercial paper market, judged by outstandings, was just one of several important sectors of the money market (Figure 22–1).

Today, all that has changed dramatically. The wholesale market for short-term CDs is dead; volume in the BA market is on the decline; meanwhile, the commercial paper market has expanded to the point where commercial paper outstanding outstrips bills outstanding, and both dwarf BAs outstanding. A measure of the growth in importance of the commercial paper market is that, whereas in 1970, commercial paper accounted for 23% of the total outstandings of the major money market instruments included in Figure 22–1, by the beginning of 1989, the corresponding number had soared to 66%.

As noted below, the commercial paper market has grown not only in size, but in diversity of issuers and in types of paper issued. Today, U.S. commercial paper trades at a spread off LIBOR, the international cost of money to borrowers (Figure 22–2); and a variety of foreign players are active in the market. Also, sophisticated market players are keenly attuned to any factors that might affect interest-rate levels, and they routinely

FIGURE 22–1
U.S. money market instruments outstanding

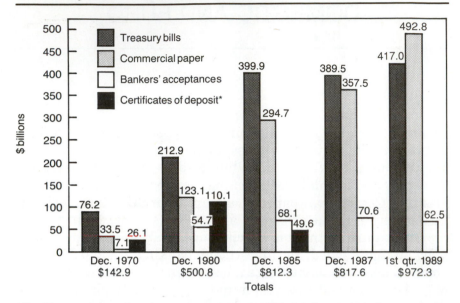

*Certificates of deposit no longer represent a significant dollar amount of money market instruments outstanding.

Sources: Federal Reserve Bank of New York and The Bureau of Public Debt. Prepared by Goldman Sachs.

use sophisticated tools: foreign-exchange swaps, interest-rate swaps, and options (in the form of a cap on rates paid).

Commercial paper is typically issued in *bearer* form (Figure 22–3), but it can also be issued in registered form. Rates on commercial paper, like those on bills and BAs, are quoted on a *discount* basis. A small amount of commercial paper is issued in interest-bearing form; the rate paid on such paper is the quoted discount rate converted to the equivalent simple interest rate.

The commercial paper market is definitely a wholesale market; typically, the minimum sale, specified by the offering memorandum, is 100,000 to 250,000. A corporate liquidity portfolio might do a trade for 250,000, a money fund for 50MM to 100MM. At one big dealer, the average size of all sales consistently falls around 5MM.

FIGURE 22–2
Today, commercial paper trades at a spread off LIBOR

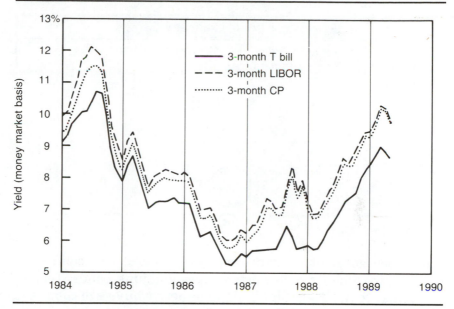

Source: J. P. Morgan Securities, Inc.

INVESTORS IN COMMERCIAL PAPER

Investment companies, principally *money funds,* are the single biggest class of investors in commercial paper (Figure 22–4). For money funds, commercial paper is a natural: it is short in maturity and low in credit risk; also, because the number of issuers is large, it offers opportunities for diversification of credit risk. Other important buyers of commercial paper are banks' trust departments, insurance companies, corporate liquidity portfolios, and state and local government bodies (including pension funds run by such bodies for their employees).

Thrifts are, depending on rate spreads, sometimes buyers of commercial paper. If such paper carries a rating of A-2, P-2 or better, thrifts may count it as part of their liquidity reserves. Given their high cost of funds, it would have been a Polish arb for thrifts to buy such paper at the rates such paper paid in early 1989. If thrifts buy lower-rated or unrated commercial paper,

FIGURE 22–3
A commercial paper specimen, Ford Motor Credit Company

that paper goes into another portfolio where it is compared
against instruments such as mortgages and junk bonds. Today,
the yields are not there for thrifts to be active buyers of commercial paper, but they used to be major buyers in the late 1970s
and early 80s when rates were high and quality-yield spreads
were consequently wide.

ISSUERS OF COMMERCIAL PAPER

The large market for commercial paper in the U.S. was, until
the early 1950s, unique to the U.S. Its origins trace back to the
early 19th century when firms needing working capital began to
use the sale of open market paper as a substitute for bank loans.
Their need to do so resulted largely from the U.S.'s unit banking
system. Elsewhere, it was common for banks to operate
branches nationwide, which meant that seasonal demands for
credit in one area of the country, perhaps due to the movement
of a crop to market, could be met by a transfer of surplus funds
from other areas. In the U.S., where banks were restricted to a
single state and more often to a single location, this was difficult. Thus, firms in credit-scarce, high-interest-rate areas
started raising funds by selling commercial paper in New York
and other distant financial centers.

For the first 100 years or so, borrowers in the commercial paper market were all nonfinancial business firms: textile mills, wholesale jobbers, railroads, and tobacco companies, to name a few. Most of their paper was placed for a small fee by dealers; the principal buyers were banks. Then in the 1920s, the market began to change. The introduction of autos and other consumer durables vastly increased consumers' demand for short-term credit, which in turn led to the creation and rapid growth of consumer finance companies.

One of the first consumer finance companies was the General Motors Acceptance Corporation (GMAC), which financed consumer purchases of General Motors cars. To obtain funds, GMAC (*Gee Mack* in Street argot) began borrowing in the paper market, a practice that other finance companies followed. Another innovation by GMAC was to short-circuit paper dealers and place paper directly with investors; this made sense because GMAC borrowed such large amounts that it could save money by setting up in-house facilities to sell its paper.

FIGURE 22–4
Investors in U.S. commercial paper

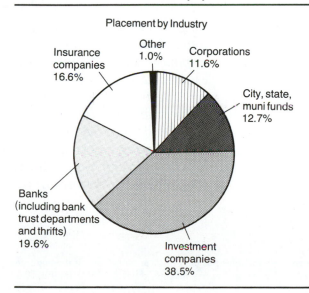

Placement by Industry

Insurance companies 16.6%

Other 1.0%

Corporations 11.6%

City, state, muni funds 12.7%

Banks (including bank trust departments and thrifts) 19.6%

Investment companies 38.5%

Source: Goldman Sachs' estimate.

Despite the advent of finance company paper, the paper market shrank during the 1920s, stagnated during the 1930s, and then slumped again during World War II; by 1945, commercial paper was a relatively unimportant instrument. Since then, the volume of commercial paper outstanding has grown steadily. One reason is the continuing growth since World War II in the sale of consumer durables, often on credit.

A second factor was the Fed's decision to pursue tight money with a vengeance on a number of occasions starting in the mid-1960s. In 1966 and again in 1969, firms that were accustomed to meeting their short-term borrowing needs at their banks found bank loans increasingly difficult to obtain. On both occasions, money market rates rose above the rates banks were permitted to pay on CDs under Reg Q, and banks therefore had difficulty funding new loans. Once firms that had previously borrowed at banks short term were introduced to the paper market, they found that most of the time it paid them to borrow there because money obtained in the open market was cheaper than bank loans except when the prime rate was being held by political pressure at an artificially low level.

Industrial and Finance Company Paper

Today, nonfinancial firms—everything from public utilities to manufacturers to retailers—still issue paper, and their paper, which is referred to as *industrial paper,* accounts for about 22.1% of all paper outstanding (Figure 22–5). Such paper is issued, as in the past, to meet seasonal needs for funds and as a means of interim financing; that is, to fund the start-up of investment projects that are later permanently funded through a long-term bond issue. In contrast to industrial borrowers, finance companies have a continuing need for short-term funds throughout the year; they are now the biggest borrowers in the commercial paper market.[1]

---

[1]"Other financial" in Figure 22–5 includes not only finance companies, but companies engaging in mortgage banking, factoring, finance leasing, other business lending, and other activities.

FIGURE 22–5
The U.S. commercial paper market: Issuer profiles*

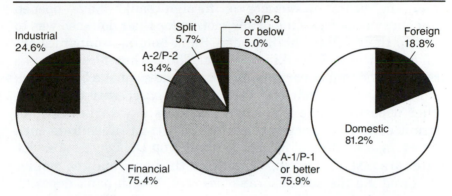

*Ratings classification calculated by number of issuers. Issuer classification calculated by percent of outstandings.

Sources: Federal Reserve Bank of New York, Moody's Short-Term Market Record, Standard & Poor's Commercial Paper Record. Prepared by Goldman Sachs.

Domestic Bank Holding-Company Paper

In tight-money years, domestic bank holding companies have joined finance companies as borrowers in the commercial paper market. Many U.S. banks are owned by a holding company—an arrangement offering the advantage that the holding company may, by law, engage in activities in which the bank may not. Initially, bank holding companies borrowed in the commercial paper market partly to fund bank operations by purchasing a portion of the bank's loan portfolio. In August 1970, the Fed ruled that funds channeled to a member bank that were raised through the sale of commercial paper by the bank's holding company or any of its affiliates or subsidiaries were subject to a reserve requirement. This ruling eliminated the sale of bank holding-company paper for such purposes. Today, bank holding companies, which are, as Figure 22–5 shows, active issuers of commercial paper, use the money obtained from the sale of such paper to fund nonbank activities in areas such as leasing and credit cards, to fund offshore branches, and for sundry other purposes that vary bank to bank.

Foreign-Bank Commercial Paper

Over the years, a number of foreign banks have opened branches in the U.S. One prime motive for their doing so was to expand their dollar liability base. Bank holding companies are unique to the U.S. banking system. Thus, when foreign banks issue commercial paper in the U.S. they do so at the bank level; and the buyer gets paper that ranks *pari passu* with the bank's other deposits. Some municipal investors and thrifts are not permitted to buy foreign securities. To attract funds from such investors, a number of foreign banks set up Delaware subs. The latter are just a borrowing conduit for the bank, and the monies borrowed via the sub also rank *pari passu* with bank deposits. To make the sale of commercial paper a cost-effective way to raise dollars, foreign banks avoid reserve requirements by investing offshore any dollars thus obtained.

Some foreign-bank commercial programs are now as big as 3 or 4 billion. The largest issuers include the big French banks (Crédit Lyonnais, Societé Generale, BNP), Toronto Dominion, and even the Union Bank of Finland. Merrill, Goldman, and other dealers are active sellers of foreign-bank commercial paper.

Own-Name Dealer Paper

Most of the principal dealers in commercial paper, Merrill and Goldman to name two, also sell their own commercial paper. Doing so increases their liquidity by giving them one more source of short-term funds; it also increases their range of choice with respect to the maturity structure of their short-term liabilities; and probably, it decreases their average cost of funding— certainly, it does so to the extent that it enables a dealer to avoid financing his positions at high-cost, bank dealer-loan rates.

Paper Sold to Garner Foreign Exchange

Years ago, foreign companies in the U.K., France, Germany, and other countries found that the cheapest way for them to raise short-term funds in their native currency was to borrow Eurodollars and swap them into that currency.[2]

Goldman led several such borrowers in the U.S. paper market; it showed them that they could shave 50 to 150 bp off their short-term borrowing costs by selling U.S. commercial paper for dollars and then having Goldman swap those dollars into their native currency. A private British company began the parade of foreign borrowers into the U.S. commercial paper market. It was followed by several French companies, including Gaz de France and other French utilities, whose paper carries a government guarantee.

Today, Goldman, Merrill, and other dealers do a brisk business in foreign-name paper. The list of issuers has expanded to include firms from Sweden, Norway, Finland, Luxembourg, Belgium, and various other countries. It has also expanded to include major *sovereign borrowers*, such as the Kingdom of Sweden, which is a sophisticated user of every debt market—U.S., Euro, and other—in which it can borrow to its advantage. The rate of increase of foreign borrowers in the domestic commercial paper market has, however, slowed for two reasons. First, most of the big foreign borrowers who are willing to go through the rating-agency process and the market-development process that it requires for a foreign borrower to access the U.S. commercial paper market have already done so. Second, those who have not may find that, for them, issuing in the new Euro commercial paper market is more attractive than issuing in the U.S. market.

Today, foreign issuers—sovereign, bank, industrial, and other—account together for 20% of the total paper issued in the U.S. commercial paper market (Figure 22–5).[3] While some foreign issuers still swap dollars borrowed in the U.S. commercial-paper market into their native currencies, many others, including most foreign banks, borrow in this market to satisfy a natural need for dollars.

---

[2]For foreign-exchange swaps, see Chapter 18.
[3]The number gets bigger the broader one defines "foreign."

Municipal Commercial Paper

It was not until several years after taxable money funds had been successfully launched that *tax-exempt money funds* were begun. One reason for the slow start of the latter was the scarcity in the market of short-term, tax-exempt paper. Once tax-exempt money funds opened shop, they grew rapidly; and their growth created a demand for the invention of new short-term instruments that would be attractive to municipal borrowers. One such instrument was muni commercial paper; another was muni 7-day demand notes (Chapter 25).

Muni borrowers were attracted to the idea of issuing commercial paper because it permits them, when the yield curve is upward sloping, to borrow at cheaper rates than they could if they sold muni notes, which usually have an original maturity of 6, 9, or even 12 months. The first muni commercial paper was issued by the same types of borrowers who issue revenue bonds: A power authority might use commercial paper to finance an inventory of fuel, a corporation to finance construction that it would later fund long term by issuing industrial revenue bonds. Later, general obligation (GO) issuers—Connecticut, Massachusetts, Oregon, Big Mac, and Columbus, Ohio, to name a few—came into the market and began issuing commercial paper as a permanent alternative to other financing sources.

All muni commercial paper is top rated. Most issuers back their paper with revolving credits, some with straight bank lines, a few—the minority—with letters of credit or a guarantee from a group that insures, for a fee, municipal bonds.

Currently, Goldman, Lehman, and First Boston—all big dealers in commercial paper—have a lock on the municipal paper market.

Today, there is not much *tax-exempt* commercial paper around. To a great extent, muni bodies lost their ability to issue such paper due to recent tax reform. Also, muni bodies found that it ran counter to their conservative fiscal management to sell a lot of commercial paper, as doing so added volatility and unpredictability to their borrowing costs. There are, however, a few municipal commercial paper programs still up and running that issue paper, the interest on which is *taxable*. Today, such programs finance things like nuclear fuel for power plants.

BANK LINES

While commercial paper may have an initial maturity as long as 270 days, many issuers stick to the 30-days-and-under maturity range.

Because of the short average maturity of commercial paper outstanding, issuers must currently pay off billions of dollars of maturing paper each month. An individual issuer is sometimes able to pay off maturing paper on a seasonal basis with funds generated from his operations, and sometimes he pays it off with funds generated by the sale of long-term debt. But by far the bulk of all maturing commercial paper is paid off by *rolling* that paper: the issuer sells new paper to get funds to pay off maturing paper.

This creates a risk for both the issuer and the investor; namely, that some adverse turn in events might make it extremely expensive, even impossible, for the issuer to sell new paper to pay off maturing paper. To obviate this risk, all issuers back their outstanding paper with *bank lines of credit*.

An issuer who did not pay the insurance premium, which the cost of bank lines really is, might at some point find himself in a position where difficulties in marketing new paper forced him to sell off assets at fire sale prices or to cut back on the volume of his business. Issuers' concern over this eventuality has a basis in fact. When the Penn Central went bankrupt with $82 million in commercial paper outstanding, this created difficulties for all issuers, particularly those in weak financial condition. Tight money has at times also created difficulties for issuers lacking a top credit rating.

A second reason commercial paper issuers pay to acquire bank lines, whether they think they need them or not, is that investors will buy only paper backed by bank lines.

Amount of Lines

Most issuers attempt to maintain 100% line backing for their paper or a figure close to that. There is, however, much variability among issuers and even for individual issuers over time.

An issuer who has a big seasonal need to borrow, say, at Christmas, will allow his percentage of line backing to fall temporarily during his peak borrowing period. Also, an issuer who pays down the amount of commercial paper he has outstanding because he had funded some of his debt with a new long-term issue may go *overlined* for a period; that is, have line backing in excess of 100%. Banks that grant a firm a line do not like to have that firm terminate the line after one month and ask to have it extended again six months later; so going overlined at times is a price issuers pay to maintain good relations with their banks.

The biggest single issuer of commercial paper, the General Motors Acceptance Corporation, has less than 60% line backing for its paper because it borrows so much that it would have difficulty getting 100% line backing even if it used every bank in the country. Also, other huge top-grade issuers have line backing well below 100%.

How much line backing is really needed by an issuer as insurance depends on its position. Top issuers have had to pay up at times for money, but they never experienced real difficulty in selling their paper even during periods of crisis (Penn Central) or when money was tight.

Types and Cost of Lines

Commercial paper issuers use different types of lines to back their paper. Under a standard line agreement, if the issuer activates his line, his borrowing automatically turns into a 90-day note. Issuers also use *swing* lines that permit the issuer to borrow one day and repay the next if he chooses. Swing lines are attractive to issuers because issuers occasionally experience short, unanticipated needs for cash; on a given day an issuer may not sell as much paper as he expected to, but he may be able to cover this deficiency on the next day.

It used to be normal practice for issuers to pay for lines with compensating balances; and the standard formula was a 10% balance against the unused portion of the line and 20% balance against any monies taken down under the line. Today, those numbers have the ring of ancient history.

Over the years, it became increasingly common for issuers to pay a fee instead of balances for lines, or a fee plus reduced balances. Banks initially resisted the trend toward fee lines but gradually gave in on that point. Except when money is very easy, it is cheaper for an issuer to pay a straight fee of ⅜ or ¾% for a line than it is for him to hold compensating balances with his bank. Foreign banks entering the U.S. encouraged the trend toward fee lines by offering U.S. companies cheap fee lines as a sort of loss leader—to obtain some business and to justify their existence here.

A number of commercial paper issuers back some small portion of their outstanding paper with *revolving lines of credit*. Under a revolver, the bank customer pays a commitment fee of ¼% on top of the normal compensation he pays the bank for the line. In exchange for that commitment fee, the bank guarantees that it will honor the line for some number of years. The big advantage such a line offers the customer is that it guarantees that, no matter how tight money gets or what happens to his position, he can borrow from his bank. As icing on the cake, the issuer obtains a second advantage—because he can turn any borrowing under the line into a term loan, he may treat commercial paper backed with a revolver as long-term debt for statement purposes.[4]

Most firms that take out revolvers do not have a top rating and want to ensure that money will be available to them from their banks under any circumstances. Some years ago, one such issuer noted, "In the latest period of market tightness, the commercial paper market had problems. There was the failure of W. T. Grant and the difficulties of the REITs [real estate invest-

---

[4]Some multiyear credit lines give the lender a chance to take a second look at a company before permitting them to take down funds under their line. If a multiyear line agreement contains a "no change in material circumstances" clause, borrowing under it may not be treated as long-term debt.

ment trusts], and the banking community itself was experiencing shock waves. Because of all that, there were questions within and without the banking industry as to how good bank lines were, particularly annual credit lines. Some companies attempted to activate credit lines without success. They got either a direct refusal or a refusal on the basis that a material adverse change had occurred in their condition. So being an A company [A bond rating] in a market dominated by AA and AAA companies, we felt it was prudent to strengthen ourselves in the minds of investors and one way we did this was to put together a multiyear credit."

A few issuers of commercial paper have used Eurodollar revolving lines of credit to back some portion of their outstanding paper. REITs in particular established a number of such lines in London with the understanding that they would never be used, but when the REITs fell upon hard times some of these lines were used. A few U.S. utility companies have also used Euro lines to back their commercial paper.

Competition from the Sale of Bank Loan Participations

As we note in Chapter 23, money center banks have started structuring into most committed, commercial paper–backstop lines what is called a *bid option:* in addition to borrowing at the committed, formula rate, the line holder can come in and ask its banks to bid for paper at a rate less than the committed rate. At times, a commercial paper issuer can, using such bid options, get money cheaper than in the commercial paper market.

Such loans, which typically range in maturity from 30 days to nine months, are made by banks at razor-thin margins. Thus, to make money on them and to protect their ROA, banks sell out the bulk of such loans, in the form of loan participations (a new money market instrument), to corporate liquidity portfolios and other investors.

From our quick preview of bank loan participations, it should be clear that this new business competes directly with the issuance of commercial paper via dealers. A natural question is thus: does one borrowing method have an inherent cost advantage over the other? One dealer noted: "Bank loan participations do impact the use of commercial paper. Supervalue Stores in Minneapolis and a number of other companies use both markets: sell commercial paper and write loan participations. It is our understanding that banks, to generate product, often misprice—pay too much for—loan participations. At those times, we encourage our borrowers to use them." A big investor saw things slightly differently: "The banks are getting business from the [commercial paper] dealers by being willing to work for less, which they can do because they pay their people substantially less. There is no need for a guy at a dealer who just sells commercial paper to get a six-figure salary plus a big bonus."

Yet another dealer observed: "It's primarily A-2, P-2 credits who find borrowing from a bank that sells loan participations to be competitive [with selling commercial paper]. All industrial companies rated A or better can raise funds in the commercial paper market at rates below where banks fund themselves; rarely do such borrowers find bank loans competitive. For a borrower, the primary advantage of a bank loan is that he doesn't need back-up facilities because the rating agencies aren't technically rating loan participations, a loophole that probably won't last much longer."

RISK AND RATINGS

Since the early 1930s, few issuers of commercial paper have defaulted. In the case of dealer paper, one reason is that, after the 1920s, the many little borrowers that had populated the paper market were replaced by a smaller number of large, well-established firms. This gave dealers, who were naturally careful about whose paper they handled, the opportunity to examine more thoroughly the financial condition of each issuer they dealt with.

Since 1965, the number of firms issuing at any time a significant quantity of paper to a wide market has increased from 450 to over 1,600; of these, several hundred are currently non-U.S. borrowers.

Only five issuers of commercial paper have failed over the

last 15 years.[5] Three were small domestic finance companies that got caught by tight money; in each case the losses to paper buyers were small, $2–$4MM. The fourth firm that failed was a Canadian finance company that had sold paper in the U.S. market; losses on its paper totaled $35MM. The fifth failure, one that shook the market, was that of the Penn Central, which at the time it went under had $82MM of paper outstanding.

One positive result of the Penn Central's failure is that rating of paper became more widespread and rating standards were tightened. Today, close to 100% of dealer and direct paper is rated by Moody's, Standard & Poor's, and Fitch.

Paper issuers willingly pay the rating services to examine them and rate their paper, since a good rating makes it easier and cheaper for them to sell paper. The rating companies, despite the fact that they get fee income from issuers, have the interests of the investor at heart because the value of their ratings to investors and, thereby, their ability to sell their rating services to issuers depend on the accuracy of their ratings. The worth to an issuer of a top rating depends on the track record of borrowers who have held that rating.

Each rating company sets its own standards, but their approaches are similar. Every rating is based on an evaluation of the borrower's management, earnings, and balance sheet. Just what a rating company looks for depends partly on the borrower's line of business; the optimal balance sheet for a publishing company differs from that of a finance company. Nonetheless, one can say in general that the criteria for a top rating are strong management, a good position in a well-established industry, an upward trend in earnings, adequate liquidity, and the ability to borrow to meet both expected and unexpected cash needs.

Since companies seeking a paper rating are rarely in imminent danger of insolvency, the rating agencies' main focus is on *liquidity*—can the borrower come up with cash to pay off its maturing paper? Here the rating company looks for ability to

---

[5]In June 89, Integrated Resources, an issuer of "junk" commercial paper (sold via Drexel) defaulted. That default rattled the $5-billion market for junk commercial paper, but not the near-$500-billion market for A-1, A-2 paper. See more on junk paper below.

borrow elsewhere than in the paper market and especially the ability to borrow short-term from banks. Today, for a company to get a paper rating, its paper must be backed by bank lines.

Different rating firms use different classifications to grade borrowers. Standard & Poor's rates companies from A for highest quality to D for lowest. Also, it subdivides A-rated companies into three groups according to relative strength, A-1 down to A-3. Moody's uses P-1, P-2, and P-3.

Investors in commercial paper are a conservative lot, and reflecting this, the vast majority of issuers have, today, top ratings from both Moody's and Standard & Poor's (Figure 22–5).

Rating Tiering

In the early 1960s, when the commercial paper market was small, all issuers paid similar rates to borrow there, in part because of the homogeneity of issuers. Then, after the Penn Central's failure, periods of tight money, and the entry of far more names into the market, investors became far more credit conscious; they wanted top names, and rate tiering developed in the market. This tiering became a function not only of an issuer's commercial paper rating, but of its long-term bond rating. Many investors wanted to buy only unimpeachable credits and looked to an issuer's bond rating as a quick way to check the credit of an issuer with whom they were unfamiliar. Today, the market still distinguishes, although less than formerly, between A-1+ issuers with a triple-A bond rating and those with only an A+ bond rating; now, the typical investor takes the view that, since commercial paper is short-term paper, it is the commercial paper rating that is more important because it focuses on an issuer's current liquidity: on his ability to repay short-term debt.

The spread at which A-1+, P-1 paper trades to A-2, P-2 paper varies depending on economic conditions. When money is tight, investors become more concerned about credit risk and the spread widens (it reached 200 bp in the summer of 1982). After a period of tight money, investors, seeking to maintain past portfolio yields, tend, as rates fall, to become *yield buyers:* they switch out of low-yielding, top-rated paper into higher-yielding, second-tier paper; and as they do, they drive down the spread

FIGURE 22–6
Historical interest-rate comparison, 1-month instruments

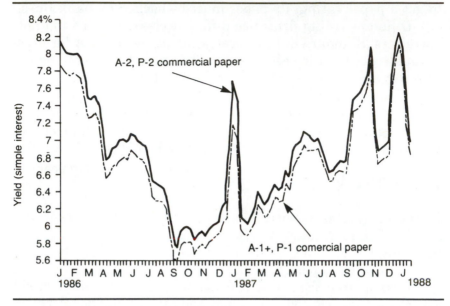

Source: Goldman Sachs' Financial Strategies Group.

between A-1 and A-2 paper to the point where it may be only ⅜, ¼, or less (Figure 22–6). Whether money is easy or tight, only a limited number of investors will buy P-3 or unrated paper from the few dealers, including Drexel, who sell it (Figure 22–5). Investors willing to buy low-quality paper include some insurance companies who, because they hold large portfolios of long-term corporate paper, publicly offered bonds, and private placements, track on an ongoing basis the earnings and condition of a wide range of firms.

The appeal of junk commercial paper is that paper sold by a single-B credit may, depending on market conditions, pay 1% or more than the rate paid on paper issued by an A-1, P-1 credit. Issuers in the junk market include such well-known names as Avis and Navistar. Belying its name, junk commercial paper had no default before the downfall of Integrated Resources.[6]

---

[6]See note 5 on p. 1038.

Commercial Paper versus Other Yields

Today, commercial paper yields far more than Treasury bills of comparable maturity (Figure 22–2). Normally, the spread is widest when money is tight—first because commercial paper exposes the investor to credit risk; second, because it is less liquid than bills. The spread between the yields on commercial paper and bills can also be severely impacted by other factors. For example, the widening of this spread after October 1987 reflected not only a flight to quality by investors, but (1) the Treasury's paydown, due to debt management policy, of bills outstanding and (2) a large demand for bills from foreign central banks who, to support the exchange value of the dollar, were selling their currencies and buying dollars, many of which they then invested in U.S. T bills.

The really interesting thing that Figure 22–2 shows is that, in recent years, the rate that the commercial paper rate has really tracked closely (on an apples-to-apples, simple-interest basis) is LIBID, the international cost of short-term money. That's globalization of markets on the march.

TYPES OF COMMERCIAL PAPER SOLD

Due in large part to the efforts of commercial paper dealers to expand their business and the inflow of funds into money market funds, which created a huge new demand for commercial paper, the menu of commercial paper available has gone from one flavor, plain vanilla, to many. Most commercial paper, whatever its flavor, is exempt from registration according to one of the sections of the Securities Act of 1933, has a maturity at issue of 270 days or less, and is high in credit quality.

3(a)(3) Commercial Paper

Most commercial paper in the market is still plain vanilla, 3(a)(3) paper. Such paper is exempt under section 3(a)(3) of the Securities Act of 1933, which exempts from registration paper that is used to finance "current transactions" and that has a maturity at issue of nine months or less.

4(2) Commercial Paper

Section 4(2) of the Securities Act of 1933 and rule 506 promulgated thereunder exempt what is called "4(2) paper" from registration. Such paper must meet various conditions, the most important of which are that it be sold only to "accredited" investors, that it not be publicly offered or sold, that it not be purchased by an investor with the intent to resell, and that an investor who does resell do so in an exempt transaction.

Borrowers who sell 4(2) paper do so to finance noncurrent transactions such as acquisitions, stock repurchase programs, and other long-term assets. When 4(2) paper was first introduced, it traded cheap to plain vanilla paper because it was viewed by investors as less liquid. Investors then changed their view, and 4(2) paper now trades at the same level as other commercial paper of the same credit quality.

Goldman, Merrill, and Shearson are the biggest dealers in 4(2) paper, also known as *privately placed* paper.

LOC Commercial Paper

A number of firms, domestic and foreign, borrow in the commercial paper market by issuing *LOC (letter of credit) paper*. This paper is backed by a letter of credit (LOC) from a bank. In the LOC, the bank gives an irrevocable and unconditional guarantee either that it will in all cases pay off the paper at maturity or that it will do so if the borrower lacks sufficient funds to do so. Either way, the investor is fully protected. LOC paper is exempt from registration under section 3(a)(2) of the Securities Act of 1933, which exempts securities "issued or guaranteed by any bank."

An LOC is a form of credit enhancement, one that substitutes the credit of the bank writing the LOC for that of the issuer. In rating LOC paper, the rating agencies analyze not the credit of the commercial paper issuer, but the credit of the bank issuing the LOC and the precise guarantee provided by that LOC. Thus, by obtaining a letter of credit, an issuer might, for example, get a P-1 rating on its paper, whereas the same paper with no LOC would get only a P-3 rating or no rating.

The first LOC-backed commercial paper program was established in 1969, but this financing technique did not blossom until the later 1970s and early 80s. At that time, LOC paper grew in response to several factors. One was the huge appetite of the burgeoning money funds for high-quality, short-term paper, an appetite that bank liabilities, which were growing slowly due to sluggish loan demand, could not sate. Also, at this time the nature of banking was changing; money center banks were looking for sources of fee income; and fee income was precisely what writing an LOC provided a bank.

During the 1980s, LOC paper became a successful money market product, and it now represents 5 to 10% of total commercial paper outstanding.

LOC paper is issued principally by four categories of borrowers. First and largest are domestic borrowers who either are a less-than-investment-grade credit or prefer not to disclose their financials fully and publicly. Next in importance are nuclear fuel trusts. Since the mid-1970s, more and more utilities have been accessing the commercial paper market via LOCs to finance their nuclear fuel cores. Typically, a utility doing so sets up a single-purpose corporation to issue commercial paper and purchases nuclear fuel with the proceeds. This structure provides the utility with off-balance-sheet financing. However, the issuing corporation, being only nominally capitalized—its equity might be as little as $100—needs a bank LOC to be able to sell commercial paper. The third most important group issuing LOC paper is real estate developers for whom the sale of LOC paper is a cheaper source of funding than are bank loans. Finally, many foreign companies use LOC paper to raise funds in the U.S. They may do so to reduce their need to provide additional capital to a U.S. sub, to avoid full disclosure of their financials, or to be able to use the proceeds to finance long-term capital rather than current transactions.

When LOC paper was first introduced, virtually all LOCs were issued by large domestic banks. Over time, this changed. Today, LOCs are written mostly by foreign banks because the LOCs of some U.S. banks trade less well; also, most U.S. banks do not want the contingent liability of an LOC on their balance sheet. Under the current tiering of bank credits, LOCs of top

European banks—UBSC, Crédit Suisse, Suisse Bank, and the like—carry the highest value; the next grade would be the Japanese banks and top regional banks like Sec Pac; their LOCs would out-trade those of any money center bank except Morgan.

The fee for an LOC is about 50 bp. This fee depends both on the credit of the issuer and on the bank giving it. For example, a Japanese bank that is aggressively pursuing the business will charge less than does a Swiss bank.

Other Forms of Commercial Paper

We have already mentioned the sale by foreign companies of U.S. commercial paper to obtain, via a foreign-exchange swap, proceeds in their native currencies. In discussing dealer paper, we describe two more innovative forms of commercial paper that dealers have created recently. Finally, there is Euro commercial paper, which we cover at the end of this chapter.

DEALER PAPER

U.S. commercial paper is issued both via dealers and direct by issuers. Due to the aggressive efforts of dealers to develop new products that are attractive to both investors and borrowers, dealer paper outstanding has, over the years, grown somewhat more rapidly than direct paper outstanding, and today, it represents over 50% of total commercial paper outstanding (Figure 22–7).

Fed figures have no detail in their breakdown of total dealer paper by type of issuer. However, Figure 22–8, which breaks down Goldman's issuers by type and by domicile, domestic or foreign, probably gives a good general profile of the issuers who use dealers. Industrial issuers are by far the biggest. Also, foreign issuers loom largest in three categories: sovereign/government agency, banking, and industrial.

Competition amongst Dealers

Traditionally, Goldman was the leading dealer in commercial paper. Merrill came to equal Goldman in size when it acquired

FIGURE 22–7
U.S. commercial paper outstanding: Dealer and direct

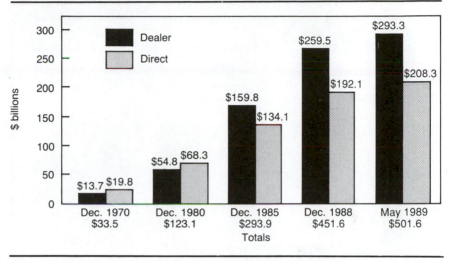

Source: Federal Reserve Bank of New York.

A. G. Becker. Today, Merrill and Goldman remain the top dealers in commercial paper. Shearson, First Boston, Morgan Stanley, and Drexel are also active in the market, and so too are several fledgling bank dealers—Bankers, Citi, and Morgan. At the moment, the market shares of the top dealers are so big that the market is highly concentrated.

It used to be that some dealers, certainly Goldman, insisted that their clients work exclusively through them. Merrill, in contrast, started out aggressively on a multiple-dealer track; its pitch to issuers was: "Include us among your dealers." In September 1987, Goldman changed its policy on sole dealerships, and a month later, Sali chopped out its commercial paper business. Goldman's decision thus proved fortuitous as it put Goldman in an excellent position to pick up new clients, which it and other dealers did.

Sali's exit from the commercial paper business caused the market to become more concentrated; it also caused issuers to become, with good reason, concerned about whether their dealer would stay in business for the long haul. While the commercial paper business is concentrated, competition amongst dealers is

FIGURE 22–8
Goldman Sachs commercial paper issuer profile, April 1988

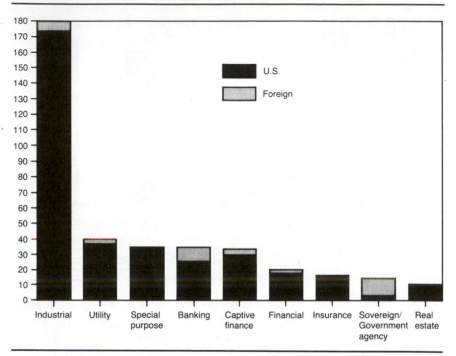

Source: Goldman Sachs Research Portable.

fierce, and the pressure on margins is, said one dealer, "incredible."

The same dealer went on to equate running a dealing operation in commercial paper with running an oil refinery: "If you are not running volume through the system, you cannot make it in this business. At a 70% utilization rate, you maybe break even or are losing a bit of money. At 80%, 85%, or 90% utilization, you begin to make real profits, profits that justify the allocation of more resources to and continued investment in the business. Sali was always a player in commercial paper, but never really big—4th or 5th in terms of market share. They got out of the business because they concluded that they didn't have and couldn't get, without a big investment, the critical mass of business a commercial paper dealer needs to make profits on a fully allocated basis."

To an investment banking firm or to a big bank moving in that direction, an attraction of being a successful commercial paper dealer is that being a client's dealer in commercial paper often becomes for a dealer the core of many investment banking relationships; certainly, a commercial paper dealer has to be in daily contact with most of his clients and they with him. A dealer who walks away from the commercial paper business is going to aggravate a lot of clients, and that in turn will impact other of the dealer's businesses, such as underwriting new corporate issues. Sali proved this.

Fees

Traditionally, commercial paper dealers charged their client a fee of 1/8, which works out to $3.47 per 1MM per day. Today, that number is under pressure. On the one side are dealers who reason that they invest too much in the way of people, technology, whatever to budge much on rates and stay profitable over the long run. On the other side are dealers whose pitch to clients is: "We may not have the broadest distribution, but we will work for only 5 bp." For major issuers, the full 1/8 fee is a thing of the past, but not for the traditional cyclical issuer of 100MM to 150MM.

Monitoring Credit

In recent history, there have been no bankruptcies amongst prime commercial paper issuers. This is due in part to the rigorous credit monitoring that goes on at Goldman and other major dealers. "We have," noted one dealer, " a senior and a junior analyst responsible for following every one of our credits and a credit policy committee that monitors all of our issuers. In most cases, our issuers are also investment banking clients of our firm. So we have corporate or global finance coverage, which gives us intimate knowledge of what a firm's financial condition is at any given time. If we were to fear that a company might be dramatically downgraded or in the worst case go bankrupt, we would take that company out of the market well before that time. That is the theory of the liquidity backup lines that go with commercial paper issuance."

Several dealers sell unrated paper. Issuers of unrated paper typically come to Drexel first. Drexel has 50 or 60 such issuers—all of the Millikan guys. These issuers are mostly industrial, but sometimes it's a finance sub of a highly leveraged manufacturer; also, there is Golden Nugget. For Drexel, selling unrated commercial paper is a natural offshoot of its philosophy on high-yield bonds. Some dealers will not touch the stuff; said one, "Even if you charge 25 bp to sell shaky paper, the risk/return just is not there. You have to invest more in credit monitoring, which carries costs; and if one of your shaky issuers goes under, you have to have sold a lot of paper for 25 or 50 bp to recoup the costs and the anguish of resolving that."

Risk and Market Liquidity

Despite the presence of a few questionable credits in the commercial paper market, evidence suggests that, today, it would take a lot to shatter confidence and liquidity in this market as occurred, for example, after the failure of the Penn Central. In particular, after the stock market crash in October 1987, there was tremendous volatility in the money markets and a marked widening of quality spreads; nonetheless, all sectors of the commercial paper market continued to display tremendous liquidity. Also, the likelihood of a major player going bankrupt is, today, small; Texaco, for example, withdrew from the commercial paper market in an orderly fashion. Failure of a junk issuer occurred, but impacted only the junk end of the market, which is small.

One striking difference between the commercial paper market, past and present, is that, now, there are many hundreds of billions of dollars out there that must be invested short-term everyday. Thus, investors as a practical matter cannot say en masse, "I am not going to invest in commercial paper." For all practical purposes, the U.S. money market is, today, commercial paper, T bills, and term repo; these three instruments dwarf all else in outstandings.

Issuance of Dealer Paper

An issuer's dealer does several things for it. First, the dealer, who is in close contact with market conditions, will each day advise the issuer, if the latter wants such advice, on what rates the issuer should post that day on the various maturities of his paper that he wants to sell. Second, the dealer will post the issuer's offerings—maturities, rates, and amounts—to his salespeople. The latter, who have contacts with a wide range of investors, will then seek, via calls to investors, to sell the issuer's paper.

A dealer's final responsibility to an issuer may be to position any paper that the issuer tried but failed to sell that day. Generally, dealers are not keen to position paper. Said one, "We are like a candy store: we buy it [commercial paper], we sell it, we have *no* interest in owning it." Still, if an issuer takes a dealer's advice in pricing his paper—sets what the dealer thinks are reasonable rates for reasonable amounts of paper—the dealer will agree, as part of his relationship with the issuer, to position any of the issuer's paper that remains unsold. The amounts involved are usually small, and the positions assumed are usually only overnight.

In the old days, the dealer's trader who had responsibility for a given issuer just posted rates and took orders. Today, he is much more of a true trader. "There is," noted one dealer, "a real tactical game going on. The trader has to be able to manage the pricing intraday, to know when to take opportunistically more or less money out of the market. If the trader is doing a good job, he will have said to his client at the beginning of the day, 'We think that producer prices could do this, and if that happens, this is where the market will be.' Also, if during the day, Fed funds or currencies move, the trader will instantly go back to the client and say, 'The market is going against us, and I think we ought to do thus and so.' Most clients give the trader discretion: he can sell paper within bands anywhere he wants.

"A trader has to be on his toes all the time, because issuers monitor our performance on a retrospective basis. There is the Fed composite index for commercial paper and all of the other indices against which issuers can spread the rates they pay to see if they are getting improving, deteriorating, or constant price performance. We also monitor our performance daily." With the fierce competition that exists among dealers, every dealer is under intense pressure to get the best rates he can for each of his clients.

Along with the shift to commercial paper traders being true traders, there has occurred a big, concomitant change in technology. "We now have," noted one dealer, "a computer optimization plan for our issuers into which they are linked. Also, we are putting in a system where we have no tickets. Trading is all done on what we call a 'Burger King board'; the trader punches in what the trade is going to be and it shows up on a screen; also, we have automatic inventory adjusting.

"Today, our traders have screens, just like a government bond trader, showing what is going on in various money markets around the commercial paper market. As they price commercial paper and advise clients, our traders are following commodity prices, currencies, interbank, and all of those other products."

Maturities

Traditionally, the market for commercial paper was a market for paper with a maturity at issue of 30 days and under. Today, a lot of issuers are still unwilling to extend further, primarily because they are afraid to make a decision. The cash manager issuing paper is paid to get the lowest rate. If he extends to six months, he is taking a risk. If he is wrong, he hears about it for the next six months. If he is right, he is not rewarded. To him, 30-day paper is sort of neutral gear.

Still, things are changing. Today, more issuers than ever are willing to look out to 60, even to 270, days; and a good and growing part of commercial paper outstanding is for 60 days or longer. Some more sophisticated issuers are willing to take a view on interest rates. Also, issuers, recalling the late 1970s and early 1980s, when a lot of them got badly burned, do realize that, at times, by staying 30 days and under, they are making a decision on interest rates, even if at the time they may not think they are. The more senior is the decision maker, the more likely he is to extend at times.

Foreign banks are willing to offer their commercial paper at all maturities, one to six months, at a level. They know where they can arb the market; for example, on a given day, a foreign bank might be willing to take 100MM for six months at 6.95 because they know they can turn around and lay off that money, perhaps in the interbank market, at 7 or 7.05. In the early

1980s, foreign banks wanted to make ⅜ to ½ a point on an arb. Now, they are willing to play with bigger numbers for spreads that are at most 5 or 10 bp. The new Basel capital guidelines will probably cut down on that.

There is no dearth of investors willing to buy longer-term commercial paper. Some money funds tend to stay 60 days and in, but others are willing to extend out on the yield curve. Also, insurance companies are always very willing to look at longer dates, and so too are some muni investors. Corporations looking to do an arbitrage will also sometimes make a play out there.

The Secondary Market

A commercial paper trader's primary responsibility is to assist issuers, but he also has a second responsibility, to provide liquidity for investors. More than any other aspect of the commercial paper market, it is the secondary market that has, in recent years, been developed.

Every dealer who sells commercial paper stands ready to buy back paper sold through him. The dealer's bid used to be the going market rate for paper of that grade and current maturity plus ⅛. Now, the plus is more likely to be 5 bp. Liquidity was poor in the secondary commercial paper market when the bid-offer spread was in effect ⅛. It's a lot better now that that spread has been whittled down to an 05.

Over time, the dealers had tried to contribute to the liquidity of the secondary market for commercial paper for the obvious reason that it made commercial paper more attractive to investors in general. A less obvious reason is that, while the commercial paper market was exploding in recent years, a drop occurred in the outstandings of other short-term instruments, such as CDs and BAs. Thus, investors who traditionally had bought other types of paper when they wanted to extend and to trade the market became more willing to look at 6- or 9-month commercial paper. Gradually, the commercial paper market changed from being a market in which the buyer typically wanted to hold to maturity. Now certain buyers, when they see an opportunity, will position longer-maturity commercial paper and trade it for profit.

For their part, the dealers not only will take back commercial paper for an 05, but at times, they will go back to investors, bid aggressively to buy back paper, and then trade it. They do that to make money, to provide liquidity to all sectors of the market, and to get a feel for correct pricing in each sector of the market.

Some dealers will position unsold paper for longer than overnight. Said one: "We will buy unsold commercial paper for longer than overnight if the client so desires. Maybe the client has a specific need to a specific date or maybe he fears that rates are rising and does not want to risk meeting higher rates in the market next day. Whenever we position a client's paper, we do so with his knowledge. We are not in the market to trade against our clients, and we do not want to give the impression of doing so. However, when we take in paper for longer than over-night, that paper is ours to do with as we please—to hold to maturity or to trade. Any paper we buy we will try to sell out, but we try not to put that paper in competition with any other paper that the client might be trying to sell: if I hold 30-day paper of a client and he comes in wanting to sell more in the same area, I try to sell the customer's new paper first. Honestly, however, if it's a bad market, we are going to try to get out of any securities we own."

A Broker of Commercial Paper

One innovation in the secondary market for commercial paper is that FBI began, in 1986, to broker such paper. FBI will show any offering a holder of paper wants to make. Now, the primary paper offered on the FBI screen is that of the big direct issuers: Citibank, GMAC, Ford, and Sears. Also, some other bank names, including foreign names, get offered there occasionally. "We will use the broker," said one dealer, "from time to time if, for example, we go out and buy Citi paper in their auction and then feel we cannot resell it quickly via our regional offices."

New Borrowers

Commercial paper dealers are always seeking new business: cultivating new classes of issuers they can put into the market. In the last several years, they have met success on several fronts.

Universal or Multicurrency Commercial Paper

In the late 80s, with the dollar chronically weak and short-term rates much higher in countries such as Australia and New Zealand than in the U.S., a venturesome investor of dollars was tempted to make unhedged investments in foreign-currency-denominated, short-term paper. However, he faced potential hassles and risks: he might have to buy unfamiliar names; he had to deal with foreign settlement practices and foreign custodians; in some countries, he had to pay withholding taxes; and then, he had to worry about country risk.

All this led Goldman to a novel idea: if investing in Aussi-dollar paper in Australia was awkward, why not create and trade *synthetic* Aussi-dollar paper right in New York and the same for paper denominated in numerous other currencies? Goldman dubbed its new product *universal commercial paper (UCP)*. The way it works is simple: Goldman finds U.S. investors who are willing to purchase UCP in a specific foreign currency; a U.S. company then agrees to borrow the U.S. dollar equivalent at a specified rate; two business days later, the investor remits the foreign currency to the issuer via Goldman; Goldman sets up a currency swap with the issuer, who thus has no foreign-exchange risk; at maturity, the issuer pays principal and interest to Goldman in dollars; and the investor is repaid in the foreign currency.

For the investor, selling UCP is just like selling U.S. dollar-denominated paper except that the transaction settles with a two-day lag to permit settlement of the foreign-exchange transactions required at issuance of the paper. UCP had an enthusiastic reception with borrowers who felt it permitted them to shave a few basis points off their cost of funds. Said one, "We'd do rubles, if we could hedge them." Investors in UCP are not the traditional buyers of commercial paper. They might be overseas mutual funds that want to invest internationally or high-yield funds that want to diversify. The UCP buyer takes a currency risk, but his reward is higher yield and the opportunity for appreciation. One satisfied buyer, a fixed-income manager at a major insurance company, said, "What makes this paper unique is that you can decide which foreign exchange you want to take your risk in, deal with credit risks you're familiar with, and be paid for that risk—all without foreign custodians."

Merrill has a product similar to Goldman's UCP, which it calls *multicurrency commercial paper (MCCP)*. With respect to this sort of program, one dealer noted: "In my opinion, such programs have become sexy and glamorous in the U.S. over the last few years because, with the volatility of the dollar, U.S. money managers have finally realized that there is a play to be made dealing in currencies. I started in this business in 1972 in Canada; and at that time and prior to it, there was what was in effect universal commercial paper being issued by Canadian dealers. Take a company like International Harvester with a Canadian sub that needed Canadian dollars. Sometimes, the foreign-exchange markets were such that you could do a fully hedged transaction—raise Canadian dollars for IH, credit Canada—20 bp cheaper by doing a U.S.-pay note and selling it to U.S. investors than by selling a Canadian-pay note to Canadian investors. So UCP or MCCP is just a jazzed-up name for something that has been around for years. Today, there is not that much foreign-denominated commercial paper done. It amounts to less than 5% of total outstandings."

The reason is interesting. "The foreign-exchange market," continued the same dealer, "is more precise than it used to be. When I was working in Canada, the foreign-exchange market was such that a window would open because of particular strengths or weaknesses in U.S. and Canadian dollars; that window might be there for two or three weeks creating tremendous opportunities. But, as more players, especially foreign-exchange banks, became conscious of the relationships between money market rates and forward foreign-exchange rates, the opportunities got arbed out. The 2- to 3-week window became a 1-week window, then a 1-day window, and now a 15-minute window."

Some observers have expressed doubts about the need for either UCP or MCCP: it accomplishes nothing that borrowers and investors could not do on their own, so why pay a dealer to do it? Clearly, there are some money market players who like the challenge of dickering around in the foreign-exchange market and of coping with foreign settlement and custodians. Others, however, feel they lack the expertise in-house for all that. One reason for Goldman's and Merrill's success with UCP and MCCP is that they have astute and respected traders of foreign exchange.

Asset-Based Commercial Paper

Asset-based commercial paper is paper that is issued by a shell company whose sole purpose is to purchase assets, from one company or many, of a specific type and quality and to then fund these assets by borrowing in the commercial paper market. Usually, the assets purchased are either (1) *trade receivables* or accounts receivable due from buyers of a company's products (Michelin tires or Mattel toys) or (2) *term receivables* such as auto loans and credit card bills. Both types of financial assets are either liquid or have short maturities, and term receivables generate a return.

An example of such a structured transaction is CAFCO, which is Goldman's biggest single issuer. This special-purpose corporation, which is a joint venture between Citicorp Industrial Credit and Goldman, finances receivables for corporations that for some reason—perhaps they are not big enough—do not want to issue commercial paper, but also do not want to pay the higher costs associated with bank financing or with *factoring*— selling for immediate cash trade receivables to an intermediary known as a *factor*. CAFCO commercial paper, of which there was 4 billion outstanding at the beginning of 1989, is rated A-1+, P-1 and trades well.

Commercial paper sold to finance real estate receivables is another form of asset-based commercial paper that has grown dramatically in recent years. When building its new headquarters, Goldman sold, via the 85 Broad Street Corporation, commercial paper as it needed funds. That sort of transaction is common now. When the borrower has completed his building, he can pay off his commercial paper outstanding by obtaining long-term financing or he can continue to roll his commercial paper *but* pay a fixed rate by doing a pair of interest-rate swaps: swap one is pay a fixed rate set at a spread over Treasuries and receive floating-rate LIBOR; swap two is pay LIBOR and receive the commercial paper composite rate.[7] By cocktailing swaps, the

---

[7]The *composite commercial paper index* is the arithmetic average of the offered rates on A-1, P-1 industrial commercial paper. It is published weekly by the FRBNY in report H 15.

issuer can transform, at little or no basis risk, his commercial paper borrowings into a synthetic, term, fixed-rate borrowing.

The use of commercial paper as a permanent or more sophisticated financing vehicle has grown dramatically. In fact, the paper-rate-versus-fixed-rate swap is now the second most common to the LIBOR-based swap. A good 15 to 25% of the commercial paper market growth over the last few years has been swap related.

Commercial Paper with a Cap

With the increasing sophistication in the market—interest swaps, caps, collars, and floors—some commercial paper dealers have begun doing maturity extension programs in which they sell an issuer a cap on the rate he will have to pay over some period. Capped commercial paper is really *two* products: a regular commercial paper trader sells the issuer's paper; a second trader of caps and floors prices and sells the issuer a cap (recall from Chapter 18 that a cap is a series of options).

"We tell the borrower," said one dealer in capped commercial paper, "that, for an up-front premium of X basis points, we will cap out a certain dollar amount at some rate, Y. The borrower can name his rate, and on the basis of that rate, we calculate the price of the option." A rate cap looks most attractive to borrowers when it looks as if rates might be moving up and becoming more volatile. "It's a bit of a shock to issuers," added the same dealer, "to see the premium that they have to pay out in cash for a cap, but once they understand the idea, it makes sense to many of them to take a look at the product. Everyone has a budget, and a cap permits the issuer to budget the cap rate plus the premium." The toughest question, the most mysterious calculation for a corporate treasurer contemplating the use of a cap is: Is the cap priced fairly or excessively? Ask God or Jeane Dixon, foreseer of the future.

Bank Dealers in Commercial Paper

In 1978, Bankers Trust became the first bank to attempt dealing in commercial paper. During the decade-long court battles that ensued, the Securities Industry Association, acting for nonbank dealers, disputed the right of banks to deal in commercial paper. Eventually, Bankers, Morgan, Citi, Chase, the B of A, and other top banks were all in the market selling commercial paper strictly as *agents*.[8] The banks acted as agents—no dealing as principal and no positioning of paper—because that was, at first, what the courts told them they were permitted to do.

"We were told," said one bank dealer, "that we could not underwrite commercial paper. So we developed honestly selling it. People would ask me, 'How do you do all of that volume?' I would say, 'We sell it. We do exactly what we tell the Fed we are doing: we act as agent, not underwriter. We have no friendly third parties. We are not stuffing it in the holding company.'

"Now that our dealing in commercial paper has been approved, what is great is that we grew up in the business with the discipline that you cannot underwrite commercial paper. It's the worst thing you can do. The dealers do not underwrite commercial paper, but not all the banks understood that. If you underwrite what you think is the last 200MM of an issuer's paper, I guarantee that he will have another 200MM coming tomorrow. Commercial paper is really a placement business. We were lucky that we did not have to learn that economically. We started with one issuer with a 60MM program. I think he was doing us a favor as he did not really want to issue. Our outstandings are now over 5 billion."

Bank dealers are still small potatoes relative to the principal nonbank dealers in commercial paper. However, they are competition to the latter. Yet, noted one dealer, "The banks do not seem to be the ones who are pushing fees down. It is the smaller nonbank dealers. They may think that this is their last chance: if they do not capture a certain critical mass—market share—now, then when the banks really figure out what to do, they will have no chance.

"The banks have not fared well in this time of uncertainty," continued the same dealer. "They themselves are not in favor as institutions. Also, issuers seem to be gravitating toward proven

---

[8]See Chapter 6 for a description of the Glass-Steagall litigation.

distribution capability—they do not want to have an experience like they had with Sali.

"We guarantee our clients liquidity. In the minds of many of them, we are their lender of last resort. In fact, because of backup lines and all that, we are not. Still, when we take on a commercial paper account, we tell them, 'If you need money, we will get it for you.' On occasion, we have gotten a call at noon, 'I need 400MM.' Kodak raised billions in a matter of days to pay for Sterling Drug. We roll over 5 billion of paper a day downstairs now. It is a machine, fabulous to watch for someone who understands it."

ARBITRAGE IN THE DOMESTIC COMMERCIAL PAPER MARKET

One thing that distinguishes the commercial paper market today from its sleepier past days is the amount of *arbitrage* that goes on in the market. We have mentioned several forms such arbitrage takes. There is dollar-to-dollar arbitrage: a foreign bank sells domestic commercial paper to raise dollars and then lays them off in the Euromarket at a positive spread. There is also dollar-to-foreign exchange arbitrage: a foreign borrower, to shave his borrowing costs, sells dollar-denominated commercial paper and then swaps the proceeds into his own currency. Finally, there is the reverse of that arb: a domestic borrower, also to shave his borrowing costs, sells foreign-denominated paper, and then swaps the proceeds into dollars. Arbs of the latter two sorts are also done in the Euro commercial paper market, described below.

One arb we haven't discussed so far is the following: an issuer, say an A-1, P-1 industrial company, uses some portion, small to all, of the proceeds of its sales of commercial paper to invest in higher-yielding paper. In the early 1980s, Kellogg (of corn flakes fame) obtained a no-action letter from the SEC permitting it to sell 3(a)3 paper for arbitrage purposes. Kellogg began the game; Arco, Atlantic Richfield, and others followed.

At the outset, a double-A issuer could issue its paper, turn around and buy A-2, P-2 paper, and pick up 200 bp. Eventually, however, that spread fell to a mere 10 or 15 bp. One reason was that more commercial paper issuers began to do the arb. Also, in the early 1980s, a lot of A-2, P-2 issuers had, for rating reasons, to fund themselves out of the commercial paper market; they did this by issuing new long-term debt or equity; and, consequently, arb players found themselves investing in a shrinking market.

In the early 1980s, commercial paper issuers also arbed into foreign-bank commercial paper. At that time, they could pick up triple-A, foreign-bank paper at a yield that was high relative to the rate they were paying to borrow, since U.S. investors demanded a high yield to take a non-U.S. name. However, as more people did that arb and also as foreign names became more acceptable to U.S. investors, spreads in this arb too came down.

Now, if a commercial paper issuer wants to profit from arbitrage, he must mismatch maturities: issue 3s and invest in 1s because the yield curve is going up or whatever. Obviously, there is risk in this, since the arbitrageur is making a bet that his view on rates is correct. Another ploy open to commercial paper arbitrageurs is to invest in highly speculative paper—take credit risk.

Today, the sale of commercial paper solely for the purpose of arbitrage is declining because available spreads do not justify the costs of such a program. To sell paper, an issuer must pay the rating agencies, pay issuer and paying-agent fees, and pay the cost of administering his program. Also, companies that were doing this arb realized that it could blow up their balance sheets and distort their ratios. On second thought, some concluded, "We are in the business, not of arbing commercial paper, but of manufacturing widgets."

DIRECT ISSUE PAPER

Currently, about 43% of all commercial paper outstanding is placed directly by the issuer with investors. Firms issuing their paper direct—about 20 to 25 do—are mostly large finance companies and bank holding companies. Some of these finance companies, such as GMAC, Sears Roebuck Acceptance Corp., and

Ford Motor Credit (FMC), are captive finance companies that borrow primarily to finance the credit sales of the parent industrial or retailing company. Others, such as Household Finance, Beneficial Corp., and Associates Corporation of North America, are independent finance companies.

Growth in Outstandings

Over the last five or six years, the auto finance companies and most other direct issuers have experienced dramatic increases in the amount of paper they have outstanding. This, however, has not been true for all directs, Sears being a case in point. Table 22–1 gives outstandings for the 17 largest directs; note

TABLE 22–1
Major direct issuers

Company	Ratings	Commercial Paper Outstanding 9/30/87 ($ millions)
American Express Credit	A-1+, P-1	3,182
Associates Corp. of North America	A-1+, P-1	2,802
Barclays American Corp.	A-1+, P-1	1,492
Beneficial Corp.	A-2, P-2	1,492
Chrysler Financial	A-2, P-2	8,909
CIT Group Holdings	A-1+, P-1	3,126
Ford Motor Credit	A-1+, P-1	14,018
GE Capital Corp.	A-1+, P-1	17,686
General Motors Acceptance Corp.	A-1+, P-1	28,965
Heller Financial	A-1+, P-1	2,713
Household Finance	A-1+, P-1	3,061
ITT Financial	A-1, P-1	2,804
John Deere Credit	A-2, P-2	1,331
Merrill Lynch	A-1, P-1	8,977
Prudential Funding	A-1+, P-1	3,295
Sears Roebuck Acceptance Corp.	A-1+, P-1	7,440
Westinghouse Credit	A-1, P-1	3,242
Average for all 17 issuers		6,737
Average excluding auto finance companies		4,475

Source: Moody's Short-Term Market Record. Prepared by Goldman Sachs.

that the auto finance companies, especially GMAC, stand among the directs, all of whom are large, as giants.

Diversification into Financial Services

A second striking change in direct issuance over recent years has been the expansion, especially by the auto finance companies and/or their parent companies, into other related finance services: mortgage servicing, insurance, the thrift business, leasing, and so on. Such diversification made sense on a number of counts: the auto companies had strong earnings and could thus finance acquisitions of firms in financial services; the auto business is cyclical and thus produces profits that swing cyclically; diversification into related financial services appeared to offer the auto companies and their finance subs attractive, stable earnings. The auto finance companies are not the only finance companies that have diversified into financial services; GE Credit, now called General Electric Capital Corp. (GECC), has also done so.

A number of the financial-services firms that the big finance companies acquired already had their own commercial paper programs. Thus, a natural trend for the big finance companies has been, as they diversified, to begin to run a number of independent commercial paper programs—to act rather like a commercial paper dealer. ITT Finance runs, for example, four separate commercial paper programs, including programs for ITT Finance, for the parent corporation, and for Hartford Insurance, a subsidiary of the parent. FMC issues commercial paper for Ford Credit, for Ford Motor Company of Mexico, and for Ford Credit Canada; it is also thinking of doing so for other affiliates.

A related development, one likely to continue, is for a finance company that runs a number of programs for different affiliates to rename itself something like Ford Financial Services and then to consolidate some or all of its commercial paper issuance: to issue commercial paper in one name for a number of affiliates and to then downstream the money raised to the affiliates for whom it is borrowing.

The Payoff to Going Direct

The big directs sell their paper direct to investors to save money by eliminating dealer fees. Direct issuance involves, however, substantial costs. Thus, direct issuance is cost-effective only for a big issuer. "If I were setting up shop," observed an executive of one big direct, "I would be hard-pressed to want to have a direct program if it were less than 1 billion on average; thus, if my seasonal bottom were 500MM, my top would have to be 2 billion. You can do business with the dealers on a small program for 7 to 10 bp. On a billion, that is 1MM. To run a 1-billion program, you'd probably need several traders, several clerical and salespeople, a travel budget; and right there, you've probably already spent 200 to 400MM. If your total costs amount to 5 or 6 bp, you might as well give the business to a dealer." The fact that the dealers have become more competitive (lowered their fee from the old standard ⅛) has raised the size at which it pays to go direct; so too has the fact that banks are getting into the business and are, if anything, more competitive than the dealers.

A giant direct can, however, save a lot of money by selling its paper direct. One big issuer estimates that its all-in cost of issuance runs 1 bp.

Running a Direct Commercial Paper Operation

While different directs have different setups, a look at how one sells its paper gives a good idea of what's involved. "We have," noted an executive of one big direct, "several traders. Every morning, these traders, I, and my boss meet to chart our overall objectives—What are our cash needs? In what maturities do we want to raise money?—and to set our initial rates. After 9 A.M., our traders, who follow developments in all markets, have total responsibility for making any rate changes required during the rest of the day. We have 15 clerical people, mostly part time, and 10 salespeople who call out rate changes to customers, take transactions, and see that settlement occurs—that notes get delivered and all that. The difference between our clerical people and our salespeople is that the latter, besides having responsibilities in the office, are also responsible for visiting existing customers and for developing new customer relationships. We divide the U.S. into six regions; in each, we have an office with a manager, at least one salesperson, and several clerical people. Since a salesperson's responsibility is to do as much business as he can in his geographic area, it's unwise to let salespeople set rates; we permit only our traders to do that."

While directs have their salespeople call customers to give them their posted rates and any changes in them, they also post their rates on Telerate and Reuters. Some big directs also post their rates with bank money desks. When banks were forbidden by Glass-Steagall from acting as dealers in commercial paper, they could and did post rates for direct issuers and arrange sales of such paper to investors. The banks did this partly so that they could offer their clients a full menu of money market instruments; also, direct issuers typically purchase large backup lines from banks that post their paper rates. It still occurs that some directs sell a portion of their paper through banks, but the volume of paper sold this way is far less than it was formerly, especially in the New York area. Now that banks are permitted to deal in commercial paper, banks that do so have a natural incentive to sell first paper on which they get a fee.

Some direct issuers, especially those who are just entering the market, will break rates for a large investor if they want money. Others won't. "We do," said an established issuer, "little of that. It happens once in awhile, usually on what we call a *reverse inquiry*. Say we don't want much, if any, 90-day money today. We may have a customer call who says, 'I need to put 100MM away; it must be for 90 days; and your quote is off the market.' Say we are quoting 9½ at 90 days and the market is 9¾. The guy might say, 'If you can show me 9⅝, I will give you the money.' Chances are we would do that. I view that as being attentive to a customer's needs. However, if we are quoting a market rate and someone comes in and tries to hold us up for another 05, we will never break rates. Our traders are paid to know where the market is, so we are sticky about that."

Backup Lines

Typically, the big directs are not 100% lined. They don't feel they need that quantity of lines, and at least the biggest direct, GMAC, probably couldn't get credit facilities equal to its total commercial paper outstandings even if it wanted to. Directs purchase backup lines from both domestic and foreign banks. In addition, they also do other sorts of deals to give them liquidity. "We have," noted one direct, "standby receivables agreements where, at the snap of a finger, we can sell a block of receivables to a bank. That is part of the 10 billion we count as lines. We could do a lot more such deals. Also, we could probably have the same sort of arrangement with insurance companies—do a billion with each of the 10 largest insurance companies."

As noted in Chapter 23, big banks that extend backup lines to issuers of commercial paper often include in the line agreement a bid option under which the bank can bid to make a short-term loan to the issuer. Banks making such loans often sell them out to investors in the form of loan participations.

Prepayments

The big direct issuers of commercial paper will all prepay on paper they have issued if the investor needs money before the paper he has purchased matures. Some issuers do this at no penalty. Others will give the investor who requests prepayment the rate that he would have gotten on the day he purchased his paper if he had brought paper for the period he actually held it. The no-penalty system would seem to invite abuse—to encourage investors to buy, whenever the yield curve is upward sloping, paper of a longer maturity than that for which they intend to invest in order to get a higher rate. Issuers, however, figure that game out quickly and don't let an investor get away with it for long.

One reason issuers are so willing to prepay is that most do not want investors to sell their paper to a dealer for fear that the dealer's later resale of that paper might interfere with their own sales. Still, a few of the largest issuers, GMAC in particular, will occasionally sell longer-term paper to dealers who position it for carry profits and as a speculation.

Secondary Market

Secondary-market trading occurs with increasing frequency in direct-issue paper. Big finance companies, such as GMAC, and big bank holding companies, such as Citicorp, have huge amounts of paper outstanding, some of which has been issued in large blocks that mature on a given day.[9] Money market dealers sometimes position such paper as a rate play. This practice has become so common that one broker brokers blocks of such paper among dealers.

Master Notes

Bank trust departments have many small sums to invest short term. To provide them with a convenient way to do so, the major direct issuers of commercial paper offer bank trust departments what are called *master notes*. A master note is a variable-rate demand note on which the issuer typically pays the rate he is posting for 180-day money, that rate plus 1/8, or some similar formula rate.

A bank trust department with whom an issuer has opened a master note invests monies from various trust accounts in it. Then, each day, the bank advises the issuer what change, if any, has occurred in the total amount invested in the note. From a trust department's point of view, a master note provides such a convenient way for investing small sums to any date that it typically keeps the balance in any note issued to it close to the limit imposed by the issuer on the size of the note; daily variations in the size of a large master note—say, one for $15MM— might be no more than $100,000.

For the issuer, master notes provide a dependable source of funds and reduce bookkeeping costs. Money obtained through a

---

[9]Taking its cue from the Treasury, Citi's holding company auctions 150MM of its commercial paper every Wednesday.

master note, however, is expensive for the issuer because the rate paid is based on the 180-day rate; most issuers limit the amount of master notes they issue.

A and B Notes

Because bank trust departments keep master notes filled up most of the time, some direct issuers said to them, "Look, you have a master note for XMM, and most of the time you have it 90% full. Let's call the top half of that note an *A note;* you can take money out of it on demand. The bottom half of the note we will call a *B note;* on that part you have to give us a 13-month notice to withdraw funds."

The advantage to the issuer of this arrangement, which is common among direct issuers, is that the issuer gets cheap money that he can record on his balance sheet as *long-term* debt. From the trust department's point of view, the arrangement provides a high rate on what is really short-term money because different monies are constantly being shifted into and out of the overall note. Issuers of B notes take the position that such debt is not commercial paper but rather a private placement. Still, such debt is recorded in money market statistics as commercial paper.

Prior to its getting into serious financial difficulties, W. T. Grant had a number of master notes outstanding with bank trust departments. While it had closed out these before its bankruptcy, that event did cause a number of bank trust departments to question whether they should not invest cash balances in trust accounts in an institutional money fund rather than in a master note. An institutional money fund offers a bank trust department the same convenient subaccounting that a master note does and a comparable yield. In addition an institutional money fund has the advantage over a master note that it offers, instead of exposure to a single credit risk, *diversity of credit risk.*

Laying off Money

It is difficult for the big direct issuers to borrow on a given day precisely the quantity of money they need. Typically they borrow slightly more; and at times, if they are not quick in cutting rates, they may be hit with a lot of unwanted funds because rates elsewhere in the market are falling. Direct issuers all run a short-term portfolio to lay off excess funds. Their investments include a wide range of money market instruments and are made with varying degrees of sophistication.

Because they can borrow short-term at very low rates, the big directs with prime names could arbitrage—buy short-term money in the commercial paper market and lay it off at a positive spread elsewhere. Most do not do so, however, out of concern for the aesthetics of their balance sheet. One individual responsible for investing excess funds raised by a large direct issuer observed, "We would not take on money to lay it off at a profit. But as a matter of policy we stood on a posted rate, and sometimes we got hosed with excess money. Then we'd lay that off. I wanted to look at it differently: We can raise money at 8 and lay it off at 9, let's make a million. But management wanted the ratios of the credit company to conform to what people analyzing the company's credit wanted. Maybe they were overly conservative, but we never borrowed as an arbitrage."

While the above attitude is prevalent, some big directs (not the auto finance companies) do borrow in a big way to arbitrage when a profitable opportunity arises. Such activities do not make these arbitrageurs popular with directs who don't play the arb game. Said one of the latter, "When issuers are arbing, they do not necessarily act rationally in the market. For example, if your market level at 30 days is 8½ and you have some big participant in there who has an arbitrage opportunity and it suits his purpose to pay 85∕8 or even 8¾ for 30 days, he will go in and do that. It just screws up the market for everyone else."

MTNs

Direct issuers of commercial paper are typically also big issuers of MTNs (Chapter 24). Directs can and do sell some of their MTNs directly to investors, but usually such sales amount to only a small percentage of their total sales of MTNs, 5% or less. Like other issuers of MTNs, direct issuers of commercial paper sell most of their MTNs through dealers, who for their part commit to make an active secondary market in such paper.

With respect to the MTN market, one big direct commented, "We like the MTN market, and we participate in it a lot. We arb that instrument versus a public offering. Any time we get a debt deal offered to us by an underwriter—some dealer says, 'We can do 100MM for you for five years (swaps, options, and all that junk), and this is the all-in rate,' I go to the MTN market and ask what it would cost us to issue 5-year debt there. If it's cheaper to do MTNs, we tell the dealer to get lost. If it's not, we tell the dealer, 'Hey, we'll do it.' For us, MTNs are a good benchmark."

ECP

Some directs issue Euro commercial paper, the market for which is described below. In London, the directs sell their paper through dealers. Right now, the ECP market is often unattractive to the top-rated directs because Euro rates tend to be higher than U.S. rates. The ECP market is, however, an important market for, as an example, Chrysler; in 1989, Chrysler had an A-2, P-2 rating and, consequently, faced limits as to how much it could do in the domestic market. One A-1, P-1 issuer commented, "We are expanding our ECP program. We like the market, and we think it may become important for us: one day, size may get to us; also, we think that U.S. and Euro rates are going to come together, perhaps when the Japanese commercial paper market opens up to foreign borrowers." The parent companies of some big directs also have foreign subs that issue ECP; one parent company has, for example, an Australian sub that issues ECP out of Hong Kong.

Canadian-Dollar and Other Foreign-Denominated Commercial Paper

Many of the big domestic finance companies also have Canadian operations that they finance partly with commercial paper. Also, some U.S. industrial firms operating in Canada issue commercial paper.

When interest rates are significantly higher in Canada than in the U.S., much Canadian paper is sold in the States. The investors who buy such paper do not want to assume a foreign-exchange risk by holding on an unhedged basis commercial paper denominated in Canadian dollars, so they hedge typically in one of two ways. A few large investors will arrange their own hedge: buy Canadian dollars spot, invest in Canadian dollar paper, and sell the proceeds forward.[10] The other approach is for issuers or dealers to hedge large amounts of Canadian paper and sell it to investors for U.S. dollars. Such paper is referred to as *dollar pay paper*.

When Canadian rates are higher than U.S. rates, covered interest arbitrage forces the Canadian dollar to a discount in the forward market and the U.S. investor loses on his swap; as a result, the rate he earns on hedged Canadian paper will typically exceed by only a small margin the rate offered on U.S. paper of similar maturity.

Big directs, especially those that have branched out into related financial services, may find themselves selling not only Canadian-dollar paper, but other foreign-denominated paper as well: Aussi-dollar commercial paper, sterling commercial paper, sterling CDs, and so on. Also, because of dealer-arranged swaps, some of the paper they sell in London, while it yields them U.S.-dollar proceeds, is denominated in various other currencies.

Right now, there is a market in London in Euroyen paper. In terms of rate, this market is not especially attractive to U.S. issuers wanting to borrow U.S. dollars on a fully hedged basis. However, at least one U.S. direct issuer is fascinated by the possibilities that may arise when the yen commercial paper market in Tokyo opens up to foreign borrowers. "Within the next five years," he commented, "the yen market in Japan will be open to foreign issuers. When that happens, I want to be there because the Japanese have all the money in the world; and I want to be able to access it. We will probably have a Euroyen program in place soon. One reason I want such a program is to develop a working relationship with one or two of the Japanese houses. Then, when the Japanese domestic market opens up, they can just waltz me right in there."

---

[10]Recall the discussion of swaps and hedges in Chapter 18.

Globalization

The globalization of financial markets will affect the operations of direct issuers just as it will affect the operations of other big financial entities. One direct issuer commented: "Our philosophy is that we are a pretty big issuer of debt of all kinds: short, medium, and long term. Our overriding concern is not only the availability of money, but also the cost of it. We want to go wherever it is cheap, and we have all sorts of nutty stuff we are thinking about that will make sense at some point.

"Globalization is the key. Eventually, further deregulation in Europe and in Japan will bring markets together from the point of rates. When that occurs, the big problem we, as an issuer of debt, are going to have—and this is purely mechanical—is: How in the heck do you handle the time zones? We can handle our London activity; it is not big at all. But how are we going to handle things if five years down the road we are also issuing in Tokyo? There is a different day over there, so we are going to end up having a round-the-clock kind of issuance. It will be a real challenge, and I don't yet know how it's going to work."

EURO COMMERCIAL PAPER

Beginning in the mid-1960s, when exports of capital from the U.S. were restricted by taxes and other measures, several corporations began to issue dollar-denominated commercial paper through U.S. dealers in London. The market for Europaper, which offered investors an opportunity to diversify out of Eurodollar time deposits, started small, but showed signs of promise. By the early 1970s, this market had grown to $100MM in outstandings; then, in 1974, the U.S. eliminated the Interest Equalization Tax and related measures. Again, it became cheaper for corporations to borrow in the U.S., and the market for Europaper died. In the 1980s, it was born again due not to divine intervention, but to vastly changed economic circumstances plus some Darwinian-like evolution.

Evolution: Syndicated Loans to ECP

Darwin wrote of animals and plants. Money market instruments too are subject to evolution: what instruments evolve and survive depends on what's viable, which in turn depends on economic circumstances; the latter can be counted to do, with certainty, only one thing, change constantly. In 1978, when the first edition of this book was published, domestic bank CDs appeared to be a permanent feature of the money market, a survivor; so too, Euro syndicated loans. The former is now an endangered species, the latter far less robust than it once was.

Euro commercial paper (ECP), in its second life, evolved out of the securitization of bank syndicated lending. In the late 1970s and early 1980s, investors considered the top 10 American banks to be the finest credits; the spread between U.S. and Euro rates was wide; and top American banks could issue Euro CDs at a significant saving to LIBID. A big change occurred post-August 1982, when the Mexican debt crisis hit. Investors became concerned about the credits of U.S. money center and other banks that had Latin American and other LDC debt on their balance sheets. Nothing that has occurred since has eased investors' concerns about bank credits.

When banks were regarded as the highest-quality credits, syndicated lending thrived because it was easy for banks to build in a spread. However, as investors altered their appraisal of credits, they turned away from bank paper and opted to buy more sovereign and corporate paper. Gradually, sovereigns and corporates found that they could achieve finer and finer borrowing rates, rates that rivaled those that banks could achieve. This in turn eroded the natural spread in bank-syndicated lending and set the stage for disintermediation of such lending. A second contributing factor was the pressure banks were feeling, at the time, to reduce their leverage by getting low-margin business off their balance sheets.

NIFs and RUFs

In the early 1980s, dealers, Merrill in the lead, saw an opportunity. Under a *note issuance facility (NIF)* or a *revolving underwriting facility (RUF)*—these amount to the same thing—a borrower could strike a deal with its banks under which it would issue 3- or 6-month notes and place them via an agent or agents; if the latter failed to place all the notes that the borrower wanted to sell, the banks that had granted the RUF or NIF would underwrite the unsold notes at a formula cap rate. A RUF or a NIF is a committed, medium-term (3-, 5-, 7-year) bank line with an inbuilt, note-issuance mechanism. Borrowers issuing notes under a RUF or a NIF could commonly do so at as much as half a point below the rate they would have had to pay for a syndicated loan. Economic conditions favored disintermediation.

Firms such as Merrill and Crédit Suisse, First Boston (CSFB) had a global infrastructure for distribution—contacts with buyers of floating-rate notes, CDs, and other paper. So it was a natural for them to distribute the paper issued under RUFs and NIFs. This paper was a CD if the borrower was a bank, a *Euronote* if the borrower was some other entity. Initially, the banks that underwrote NIFs and RUFs were principally interested in facility fees, not in distributing paper, particularly as they did not know where to sell it. Meanwhile, Merrill and CSFB began to call around to more and more institutions with a view to getting them to invest in Euronotes. A lot of the buyers they found turned out to be commercial banks. This woke up the banks writing NIFs and RUFs; they thought, "Why don't we get involved in selling Euronotes? It seems to be a profitable business." Little did they guess that the investment bankers in the business were at the time making not $\frac{1}{18}$ or even $\frac{1}{16}$, but more like 3 or 4 bp, and they were beginning to depend very much on volume.

In any case, it came to pass that a lot of commercial banks tried to get into the distribution of Euronotes—they were earning something on the lines and wanted to earn something more on distribution. Consequently, some banks would say, "If we grant part of the line, we want part of the paper issued under it to sell." One way Euronotes were distributed to banks was via *tender panels*. A would-be note issuer would agree with its line banks to submit notes it wanted to issue to them for bids; in doing so, the issuer knew that the worst that could happen is that he would have to pay the formula cap rate incorporated in his RUF or NIF. The Kingdom of Sweden was a classic example of a user of the tender panel. They would announce, "Next Wednesday, we want our tender panel members [which are 40 banks] to bid for our 6-month paper. The auction is next Wednesday. You will hear Wednesday afternoon what paper you bought. The paper settles the following Monday. We are going to show 100MM." The banks would give their bids, the best of which would be hit. In a functional sense, the tender panel was like Sweden's Euro primary dealers.

For an issuer, tender panels presented certain problems. The banks bidding never knew if or how much paper they would get, so they could not make firm commitments to investors wanting to buy paper. Also, some tender panel members lacked distribution capability and, sometimes, they would end up dumping an issuer's paper in the secondary market at rates below what they had paid for it. Finally, the tender panel approach forced the issuer to wait not two days, but as much as a week before he got his money; and it locked him into 3- or 6-month maturities.

Enter ECP. As time passed, top-quality issuers began to say, "Hey, the market for Euronotes is growing and here to stay. We no longer need to issue our paper under the umbrella of a NIF or RUF with a built-in, bank-underwriting mechanism. Instead, we will use agent dealers and do a *tap offering:* a continuous offering with different rates posted for different maturities." The dealers said, "Fine, we will call that Euro commercial paper."

Legally, Euronotes and ECP are the same thing: unsecured, short-term paper. Issuers that use ECP prefer it to Euronotes because they can back all or some portion of their ECP issuance with general revolving lines of credit. There's a small cost saving in this, but not much. More important, ECP gives the issuer greater flexibility—he can post attractive rates at the maturities he finds most attractive. Also, he has more control over the rates he pays. Finally, an issuer can custom-tailor maturities to fit an investor's need: give him paper maturing in two months and seven days if that's what he wants.

Today, the ECP market is young and fast-growing. Issuers like it because they can borrow relatively cheaply there and with flexibility. Dealers have less reason for cheer; they are selling a lot of ECP but not making any money doing so.

Dealers in ECP

Since there is not now and never was a Glass-Steagall Act in the U.K., the top dealers in ECP are a combination of commercial and investment banks: Citi, Swiss Bank Corp., Merrill, Morgan, and Crédit Suisse, First Boston. Other firms, such as Shearson, Morgan Stanley, Bankers Trust, Chase, First Chicago, and SG Warburg (a U.K. house), are there but are lesser players.

The nonbank dealers got into the market because it was a natural extension of their business in the U.S. commercial paper market. If there was going to be an ECP market, the top dealers regarded themselves, with their global distribution networks, as a natural choice of agent by issuers. Commercial banks had their own motives for getting into the market. In 1984 to 1985, the main reason that the banks entered the market was that they saw that, unless they maintained a relationship with a borrower in the ECP market, they could be walking away from a lot of other business, including other types of loans. They did not want to do this, so begrudgingly they took on ECP business.

In 1986, things changed; it was becoming increasingly apparent that Glass-Steagall could easily fall within a few years. Thus, the big American banks saw the ECP market as a perfect platform from which to launch an assault on the domestic commercial paper market, which happens to be, for U.S. commercial paper dealers, a very profitable business: profitable in itself and a source of strong relationships with corporates for other sorts of business. During the period around 1987, there was a massive buildup in the efforts made by top U.S. banks to become major players in the ECP market. Citi and Morgan, in particular, went out of their way to develop a dedicated structure through which to sell ECP. This was doable, if expensive; banks have strong global corporate relationships, and corporates are strong buyers of the debt of other corporates; so for the banks, it was a matter of edging corporates away from the interbank deposit market and into other people's commercial paper.

Over time, a major problem arose for dealers in ECP; too many of them had come to the party. At one point, 78 dealers (obviously many only minor players) were scrambling for ECP business, business that amounted and still does to only a small fraction of total commercial paper sold in the U.S. As noted, for a dealer to make money selling commercial paper, he must push through volume, as margins—even in the U.S.—are thin.

Issuers of ECP

Dealers trying to build volume were soon scouting for potential issuers of ECP; they looked just about everywhere—from Australia to Iceland—and at just about anyone—corporates, governments, government agencies, banks. What currency the borrower wanted was immaterial; most ECP is denominated in dollars, but dollars can be swapped into other currencies.

A lot of ECP is unrated, although that is beginning to change. For foreign borrowers looking at the rating and other costs of issuing in the U.S. market, the all-in cost of issuing ECP worked out on many days to be virtually the same as issuing in the U.S. So they said, "Let's go the ECP route."

Today, there are 700 to 800 issuers in the ECP market, and *every one* is there from triple-A corporates to single-B, equivalent-rated, Korean companies; the best to the worst banks in the world; sovereigns ranging from the Kingdom of Sweden to Indonesia and Aman. Said one London dealer, "There are no barriers here." Recognizing that investors wanted to get away from the interbank market because they were worried about banks with Latin American exposure, dealers in particular sought out as issuers European banks that had no Latin American exposure— Dutch banks, Finnish banks, Austrian banks, and so on.

For each new issuer, the dealers prepare an information memorandum and then send it to investors around the globe. The issuers said, "Hey, for no money, these guys are going to run around the world getting me new money. Let's go for it." The ECP market is an easy market for the issuer to say yes to. Actually, "no money" is inaccurate; an issuer setting up a group of dealers to sell his ECP would probably pay around $15,000 to set up his program; he doesn't necessarily need a rating and documentation is minimal. For that money, he is ensured that at least 400 investors around the globe will get an information memorandum on him. Not surprisingly, some entities have issued ECP because they planned to do, within a few years, some other Euromarket public offerings and wanted to get their name better known in Europe. For that purpose, no cheaper form of marketing exists than selling ECP.

From the start, it was common for an issuer to use more than one dealer. If an issuer does, either he can post rates on a screen, and it is first come, first served, or he can phone up a dealer he likes and say, "What's your bid for 20MM 6-months?" The ECP market is a global market in which business is not done just during London hours. "A lot of our Far Eastern borrowers will," noted one dealer, "phone up our Hong Kong or Singapore office and do business with them while we are still asleep. That office hedges our interest-rate risk with futures in Singapore, and then we sell the paper when we get in. Our U.S. borrowers will post as they go home at night; we will sell their paper here in Europe, but we protect them—if rates decline, we are expected to stop selling at the rates they posted."

Some of the big U.S. directs, such as GMAC and Chrysler, issue ECP, but they do so through dealers. Currently, there is no direct issuance of ECP.

Figure 22–9 gives a profile of today's issuers of ECP.

Investors in ECP

The market in Euronotes and later in ECP started out without anyone having much idea of who the investors were going to be. Initially, the market was borrower or supply driven, and to a large extent, it still is. Investors never queued up to buy the paper, whereas borrowers were queueing up to issue.

Buyers of ECP turned out to be pretty much who one would have expected them to be: corporations outside the U.S., some money funds and investment advisors, central banks, banks, and pension funds (Figure 22–10). Product propinquity, which presumably leads to familiarity and ease of clearing, appears important as 50% of ECP is sold in the U.K.; this number may,

FIGURE 22–9
Euro commercial paper market by type (by number of facilities)

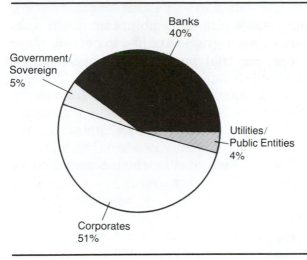

Banks
40%

Government/
Sovereign
5%

Utilities/
Public Entities
4%

Corporates
51%

Source: Goldman Sachs International Corp., July 1989.

FIGURE 22–10
Euro commercial paper market: Profiles of Goldman Sachs' investors

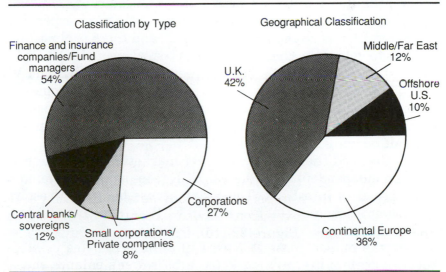

Classification by Type

Finance and insurance
companies/Fund
managers
54%

Central banks/
sovereigns
12%

Small corporations/
Private companies
8%

Corporations
27%

Geographical Classification

Middle/Far East
12%

U.K.
42%

Offshore
U.S.
10%

Continental Europe
36%

however, be misleadingly large because so much Euro activity occurs in London.

ECP is not sold to U.S.-based investors for several reasons. First, a lot of Yankee issuers also have programs in the U.S. commercial paper market, where rates are lower. Second, there are potential withholding tax problems. Third, the SEC does not want the paper sold in the U.S. unless it is registered. Offshore U.S. entities, such as foreign subs of U.S. companies, can and do, however, buy ECP (Figure 22–10). Thus, for a large U.S. corporation that runs a globalized treasury (recall Chapter 11), the inability of the parent to buy ECP may not be a binding constraint: by buying ECP via its foreign subs, the company may be able to fully sate its appetite for such paper.

Rates and Ratings

At the outset, ECP traded around interbank, which caused some investor resistance. Investors thought they should get a spread to interbank. Dealers countered, "You are getting liquidity and a chance to diversify credit risk. Also, EDF and Sweden may well be better credits than a bank." Today, the majority of ECP is issued below LIBOR. However, the spread between the rates that different borrowers pay is wide, reflecting the fact that a wider range of credits can access the ECP market than can access the U.S. commercial paper market. The most expensive sovereign ECP is issued 20 below LIBID, and there is almost no limit as to where the cheapest paper is issued over LIBOR. Still, the vast bulk of ECP is issued between 15 below LIBID and 1/8 over LIBOR. (For a comparison of average ECP and domestic commercial paper rates, thumb back to Figure 22–2; it shows that domestic commercial paper trades at a consistently negative but varying spread to LIBID.)

In the U.S., the commercial paper market is large enough to have an independent rate whereas ECP rates are always quoted at a spread to interbank. The latter occurs because investors view their alternative to investing in ECP as investing at interbank.

At the outset, most ECP was unrated. This was possible because dealers literally marketed a borrower's balance sheet, and there were a lot of asset-hungry investors who were willing to take the trouble to analyze a credit in order to buy its paper. Today, more ECP is rated than previously, but 40% of ECP still has no rating, and another 15% has only an affiliated rating (maybe, the issuer has sold a rated Eurobond). Small banks love unrated paper and its high yield; analyzing credits is after all a core business for a bank. Also, a small subsidiary bank in Luxembourg may buy unrated paper because the parent bank has a relationship with the issuer.

Maturities, Liquidity, and Currency of Denomination

Average maturities are longer in ECP than in domestic commercial paper. The average maturity in ECP is near 90 days, whereas in the U.S., it is near 35. Dealers who sell ECP are willing to bid for it, but the liquidity of ECP is still not as good as that of U.S. commercial paper. While most ECP is issued in U.S. dollars, some is also issued in yen, Dutch guilders, ECUs, Aussi dollars, Kiwi dollars, and Hong Kong dollars. The sterling commercial paper market, which is free from withholding taxes and sales restrictions, is actually both a domestic market and part of the global ECP market, although no one calls paper traded in it Eurosterling commercial paper.

Outstandings

Currently, ECP outstandings are around 40 to 50 billion. The growth of this market has been very much at the cost of the Euronote market in which outstandings have stagnated at around 15 billion (Figure 22–11). Despite the rapid growth of the ECP market, total outstandings of ECP still amount to only $1/10$ or so of total outstandings of domestic commercial paper.

Fee Structure and Dealer Profits

Currently, in the U.S. commercial paper market, there is a fee structure. Dealers hang tight and demand 5, 7, or 10 bp from an issuer depending on his name and volume. In the ECP market,

FIGURE 22–11
Euro money market instruments outstanding

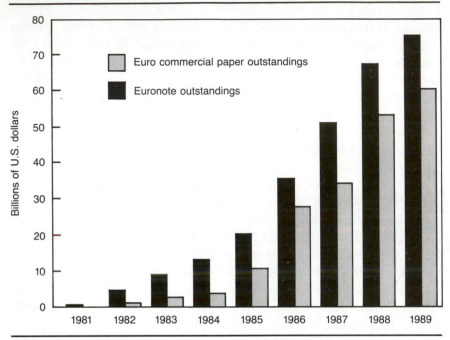

Source: Goldman Sachs (based on Bank of England data).

it was, at least at the beginning, the issuers who were dictating to the market. Said one dealer, "An issuer would start off posting at LIBID; a month later, he would drop to LIBID minus 2 bp and he'd say, 'If you want to argue about it, we will fire you.' At the time, we [dealers] were all paranoid about being fired because we had market share and were fighting to keep it. So we said, 'This can be a loss leader for three months.' Now, everyone's market share is more or less established, and there's a hardening of attitude by us dealers—the investor has had his free ride, and we want to make a little money. Now, when the issuer says, 'We will fire you,' we say, 'Do it.'"

Gradually, the dealers have gone from the point at which they were placing paper at a loss of maybe at a 1- or 2-bp spread to the point where they are getting maybe 3 or 4 bp. Whether that covers anyone's fully allocated costs is another matter. In any case, it is in the interest of borrowers to see further consolidation among ECP dealers and some widening of their spreads as no dealer will pursue forever a market in which he's losing money. Also, an important part of a dealer's function is to provide secondary-market liquidity, and he is certainly not going to make a strong and continued commitment to doing that in a market in which he is losing money on issuance. Some borrowers seem finally to understand that.

FOREIGN COMMERCIAL PAPER

Over time, the American investment markets, which had the luxury of evolving really from the depression on in relative stability, have proved to be the most efficient and resilient markets around. Thus, it is unsurprising that other countries have copied U.S. markets. This occurred in Treasuries, and it has also occurred in commercial paper.

There has been a commercial paper market in Canada for years. More recently, commercial paper markets have also been established in the U.K., Sweden, France, Japan, and Australia. Like the ECP market, these foreign commercial paper markets all ape in large degree the long-established U.S. commercial paper market. Also, at least some of them fill a real need: the yen commercial paper market, established in October 1987, had a year later outstandings that outstripped those of the ECP market.

Because of the global currency mix that now exists, given the various national markets in which commercial paper is issued and the various currencies in which ECP is denominated, any investor or issuer can now start in any one of a number of currencies and get back, via a swap, to his own currency if he wants to. Dealers see this as an opportunity to generate business.

Merrill, for example, has an arbitrage program that hunts for anomalies in foreign-exchange spot and forward rates. The moment a dollar asset yields a fully hedged investor of DM more than LIBID, their German desk will start calling German corporates looking for one that wants a better return than interbank.

"At times," noted one dealer, "we have been able to turn dollar-LIBID paper in DM-LIBOR paper. We have done deals with a 2- or 3-bp advantage in them for both the issuer and the investor: the currency that the issuer wanted was sterling, the currency that the investor had was DM, and the currency in which the paper was issued was dollars. That is a truly global commercial paper market and it was not possible two years ago."

THE NEXT CHAPTER

In the next chapter, we turn to the loan participation market, a market that competes, at its high-quality end, with the U.S. commercial paper market.

CHAPTER 23

BANK SALES OF LOAN PARTICIPATIONS

Today, *the* top priority in the strategic planning of most money center banks is (recall Chapter 6) the switch from commercial banking to investment banking. The selling by money center banks of loan participations is one manifestation of their commitment to evolve out of old-style banking into investment banking. In old-style banking, the buzzword was *lending;* in new-style banking, the buzzword is *distribution.* For a money center bank, one natural product is to create and distribute loans.

SOME HISTORY

Up to the mid-1960s, banks were happy lenders. In those good, bygone days, banks had a large share of the market for corporate external financing. Banks lent to their C&I clients at prime, often at prime plus a spread. In addition, banks required borrowers to keep substantial compensating balances of demand deposits with them. In this environment, banks were able to earn fat, net-interest margins on their principal business, lending.

   Over time, several factors disturbed the comfortable position in which banks had been operating. One was *securitization.* Entities that traditionally had borrowed from banks found that they could borrow at cheaper rates by selling their own IOUs directly to cash-rich investors. The sale by former bank borrowers of commercial paper, a trend that developed swiftly from the early 1960s on, was the first wave of disintermediation, induced by securitization, to wash away a part of the banks' traditional lending base. Subsequently, and thanks in part to the trend, both domestic and worldwide, toward deregulation—a trend that made capital markets freer and securities issuance ever easier—other waves of disintermediation followed, each wave further eroding the banks' lending base.

As the years passed, former bank borrowers found a whole array of different IOUs that investors were willing to buy from them at attractive rates: Eurobonds, Euronotes, domestic MTNs in umpteen flavors (plain vanilla to peanut crunch), Euro MTNs, Euro commercial paper, and so on. Beginning in the early 1980s, the growth of the swap market expanded by a large multiple the options open to a would-be raiser of funds: often, with swaps, a borrower could cut his funding costs by first selling securities to get one sort of money and then swapping, on attractive terms, that money into money of another sort: he could borrow fixed and swap to floating, borrow Swissy and swap to dollars—the possibilities became endless.

The changes we have described were clearly structural, not temporary. Once the genie of securitization was let out of its bottle no one or no force was going to squeeze it back and cork it firmly there.

To add insult to injury, a number of the problems that one or all money center banks experienced from the early 1980s on began to cast a cloud over bank credits, obviously a far thicker cloud for some bank credits than for others. In any case, the upshot was that certain borrowers, top sovereigns like the Kingdom of Sweden and other triple-A (nonfinancial) credits, found they could borrow funds as cheaply or more cheaply than could banks themselves.

All this put the banks in an unpleasant position. If they could lend at all to a good credit, it was at a razor-thin margin, one that might not even cover their full costs. While this phenomenon may have hit first in the domestic market, eventually, it also caused a sharp decline in syndicated Eurobank loans—a once attractive bread-and-butter, even caviar, business for the banks.

At first, the money center banks responded by increasing their leverage: they tried to increase earnings by making a slightly lower ROA on a lot more assets. For a time, that permitted these banks to maintain their ROEs despite the unfavorable climate for banking. However, by 1980, the average capital-asset ratio at top New York banks was approaching the unheard of level of 30; at that point, regulatory and market pressure dictated a reversal.

Banks had to find a way of shrinking their assets without shrinking their earnings. One alternative always open to them was to make more loans to sub-investment-grade credits. The numerous new routes to disintermediation presented far fewer attractive opportunities to poor credits than to top credits, since nonbank buyers of corporate IOUs are by and large extremely credit conscious. However, the last thing big banks needed was to further degrade the quality of their loan portfolios: to add loans of sub-investment-grade credits to their already heavy holdings of questionable loans, LDC and other.

Wholesale banking was a bankrupt business, but investment bankers who were in a business that overlapped in many respects traditional bank activities were on average doing quite nicely: in good years, the largest of them were, on average, attaining twice the steady 15% ROE that the biggest of the money center banks were, on average, able to hit. Hence, the strategic decision by money center banks to evolve out of old-style banking into investment banking.

Distribution of Loans: An Appropriate Tactic

One big part of investment banking is distribution. Banks had been dealing in and distributing exempt securities for years. Thus, quite naturally, the idea occurred to them that one step they could take to become more like investment bankers would be to get out of their old make-a-loan-and-hold-it business into a new business, namely, the make-a-loan-and-distribute-it business.

If such loans could be made at low cost and sold at a reasonable spread, this switch in businesses would help banks to simultaneously both lower their assets and raise their ROEs—just what they, the regulators, and the market wanted.

Loan sales promised to produce what amounted to *fee income* even if some banks chose to book it as net interest income as it accrued over time. Fee income is a big element in the earnings of investment banking firms. Thus, to banks, loan sales looked like a tactic appropriate to their strategy of evolving in the direction of investment banking.

Distribution of Loans: A Natural Evolution

The making and distributing of loans is a natural for money center banks. Such banks have long-standing relationships with a wide range of corporate and other potential borrowers, often multifaceted relationships: as a lender, as a source of lines, as a supplier of the various exempt securities in which banks may deal, as a source of foreign exchange, as an advisor on strategies for the use of new and exotic instruments such as options and swaps, as a supplier of leveraged leases, as an advisor on mergers and acquisitions and on leveraged buy-outs, and as a provider of various other banking services.

On the flip side, money center banks have a wide range of contacts with investors: through their sales forces, they have for years been selling investors bank products (BAs, CDs, and, most recently, bank deposit notes), various exempt securities, and some privately placed securities, and, for a fee, investment management. Also, offshore, where Glass-Steagall does not apply, money center banks have for decades been active in investment banking as underwriters and distributors of a wide range of securities, particularly Euromarket paper, but also securities originating in foreign capital markets and denominated in the currencies native to those markets.

Perhaps most important, loan selling is not a new business for banks. For years, banks have sold, participated, placed, and syndicated their loans, usually, however, only with other banks. In selling commercial loans to a far wider range of investors, money center banks have simply dusted off and redesigned a long-standing business tactic to serve their current strategic planning.

BANK CHANCES TO LEND TODAY

Big money center banks have *two* chances to lend these days. Thus, the loans they have to sell are of two sharply differing sorts, with each sort being sold to a quite different group of investors.

Loans Made under Commercial Paper, Backstop Lines

When companies sell commercial paper, the rating agencies want to see, as liquidity insurance, bank lines backing that paper. Depending on the issuer, the rating agency might want the lines to be *committed* lines, that is, legally binding commitments on the participation of the lending bank, or they might permit just *advised* lines, saying the bank will give the commercial paper issuer a line for XMM, under which it may borrow from the bank at some mutually agreeable rate. A lot of the lines that banks have on their books are legally binding commitments where, for a period of seven years, the bank agrees to lend to the commercial paper issuer at a formula rate, LIBOR + 1/4 or whatever.

Commercial paper, backstop facilities tend to be huge, 1 or 2 billion, and they are syndicated amongst a wide group of banks. The pricing on such lines is razor thin, LIBOR + 1/8 with maybe a 1/16 facility fee. Thus, this business is uninteresting to a bank looking to get a decent return on its balance sheet.

In the past, the only return that banks got out of issuing commercial paper, backstop lines was a small fee for making a commitment to lend. In practice, corporations that took down committed lines from banks never borrowed under those lines at the stipulated formula rate, because the commercial paper market was so strong that they could always borrow in that market or in other markets for less than they could under their bank line.

Recently, money center banks started structuring into most commercial paper, backstop facilities what is called a *bid option:*

in addition to borrowing at the formula rate, the line holder can come in and ask its committed lending group to bid for paper on a *non–pro rata* basis—at a rate less than the committed rate. At times, a commercial paper issuer can, using such bid options, get money less expensively than he could in the commercial paper market.

Today, a large part of the loan sales money center banks make are advances extended to borrowers under the bid options on committed commercial paper backstops. Most typically, the loans sold range in maturity from 30 days to 9 months: under 30 days, corporations can usually borrow most cheaply in the commercial paper market, which is really a market for paper 30 days and under; over 9 months, corporate borrowers can go directly to the MTN market.

Thus, the loan participations we are speaking of here are short in maturity, very high in credit quality, and low in yield—basically paper appropriate for a conservatively managed liquidity portfolio.

LBO Loans

A second type of loans that big banks have an opportunity to make these days are LBO loans, loans whose characteristics are the direct opposite of loans generated under commercial paper backstops. LBO loans are long in term, low in credit quality, and high in yield. LBO loan participations are *not* a money market instrument, but for completeness, we discuss them at the end of this chapter.

SELLING SHORT-TERM, HIGH-QUALITY LOANS

In discussing loan sales by banks, we begin where banks began the business, namely, with the sale of short-term, high-quality, low-yield loans to conservative investors. High quality generally means that the borrower's commercial paper is rated A1, P1 or A2, P2. Sometimes, high quality is achieved through some form of credit enhancement. An issuer who did not want to release his numbers might buy a surety bond from an insurance company or get his debt backed by a letter of credit from a bank. Also, a subsidiary of a corporation might borrow with the parent's guarantee.

The Beginnings

The sale of short-term, high-quality loans by banks is a recent development. It began in 1983; and by 1984, all money center banks were either involved in or had plans to enter this business. Bankers Trust and Citicorp are credited with pioneering the business; Morgan and Chase followed close at their heels.

In describing the mood and attitude with which banks entered this business, one banker noted: "We saw that increasingly our corporate business was moving away from us: our issuers were either in the commercial paper market, which is a cheaper way to raise working capital or, alternatively, they were getting cheap money from foreign banks who were willing to buy corporate loan business. Once we recognized that, plus the fact that new constraints, external and internal, were impinging on our balance sheets, two things became obvious: first, our balance sheets probably could no longer carry the marginal business we were getting from our corporate clients; second, even if it could, that business was not going to yield us the new and higher ROE and ROA we had targeted. The only logical conclusion was that, if we were to continue to lend, we had to lend not for ourselves, but for someone else—*to act as a loan intermediary.*"

The Loan Participation Agreement

In the discussion that follows, we take loan sales to mean *subparticipation* of loans, that is, situations in which loans on a bank's book are sold, *to maturity* and on a *nonrecourse* basis, to another institution, which might, for example, be an insurance company, a pension fund, or a corporate liquidity portfolio.

The Mechanics of Selling Loan Participations

Money center banks sell loans only to sophisticated investors. Since there is no legal requirement for sophistication, a bank's test of sophistication must be completely subjective. One bank culls out unsophisticated buyers by saying it will sell only to entities having at least a billion in assets and a portfolio of 250MM. That at least keeps out the local fire departments and other small investors who would probably sue if a loan sold to them went sour.

After an investor has been vetted, he is asked to sign a loan-participation agreement that is quite standard across the market. This short agreement, which is signed by both the investor and the selling bank, says basically that the agreement obligates neither the investor to buy, nor the bank to sell, loan participations, but if the bank offers the investor something he agrees to buy, the terms under which the sale will occur are thus and so. In particular, the bank often represents to the investor that it will administer any loan it sells in the same way it administers a loan it holds for itself. Also, the agreement indemnifies the selling bank for any legal expenses it might incur in the enforcement of the loan. The agreement often states, in addition, that the buyer *may not resell* the loan to another investor without the consent of the selling bank. Finally, the agreement refers to a certificate that would evidence an individual loan participation if the bank were to sell one to the investor.

Once the bank and the investor sign the agreement, the bank and the investor would talk daily, weekly, or however often the investor wants to talk, and the bank would offer the investor whatever loan participation it had to sell. Say it was a 1-month Masco corporate at 8½%. If that looked attractive to the investor, he would wire the selling bank money and in return get a loan participation certificate; the latter, *nonnegotiable* piece of paper would say, "You, ABC investor, have purchased from us 5MM in our loan to Masco Corporation. We will pay you 8½%; principal and interest are due on X date, if, as, and when we receive funds due from the borrower."

Dual Risk

The investor in a loan participation has a dual credit risk, to the borrower and also to the selling bank. The second risk arises because it is the selling bank that collects interest and principal and sends it on to the investor. For whatever time interest and principal collected by the selling bank are in the hands of that bank, those funds are not held in legal trust. Thus, if the selling bank were to go under, the investor would be in trouble—probably find himself a general, unsecured creditor of the bank. Thus, in determining the relative value of a loan participation offered to him, the investor needs to consider that he gets a higher rate on a loan participation than on commercial paper, but on commercial paper he has only one credit risk.

Size of Trades

In the market for high-quality loan participations, the average trade is probably around 25MM, and it is easy for banks to do trades of 100MM. Smaller trades are unattractive. "You do not want," noted one banker, "trades of less than 5MM or 10MM because operations costs will kill you. The margins in this business are razor thin, just slightly better than selling commercial paper."

Bank Attitudes in Selling

Banks approach the sales of short-term, high-quality loans in two different ways. Probably most typical are banks who generate such loans for resale only and who, once they have generated them, will sell them at almost any price. The objective of such banks is to increase volume and not to carry any of the paper they generate on their balance sheets. A bank operating this way is typically feeling a severe capital constraint.

That is really how the business began in 1983 to 1984. Today, a bank lucky enough to have a strong capital position can take a slightly different tack. Most money center banks tend to have a loan portfolio that has, over time, become—thanks to LDC and other problem loans—illiquid and weak, one that is short on good corporate assets. Thus, a bank that over the past several years has strengthened its capital position and reduced its leverage is likely to be actively looking for good-quality assets it can book. Such a bank can go into the public market and purchase securities, public MTNs or public, receivables-backed deals. However, if it does so, it loses the dealer commission, which on MTNs is substantial, 20 to 40 bp; also, in a public receivables transaction, the bank loses all the underwriting fees and commissions. In sum, a bank that buys securities in the public market gives away a lot and gets no credit from the customer.

Thus, a bank that has adequate capital to want to acquire additional high-quality loan assets prefers, to the extent it can, to generate product internally at levels higher than it could buy product in the public market. In such a bank, an asset-liability officer is likely to say to the bank's lending officers, "Make whatever loans and receivables deals you want, but when you go to sell them, give me a chance to bid. If paper you generate happens to fit my [the bank's] needs, I want it, provided my bid is as good as any other bid you get. If it isn't, give the paper to any guy who bids an 05 more."

Sales Volume and the Leaders in Sales

Currently, the Fed requires banks to record loan sales on their call reports and it publishes data on total loan sales by banks. However, this series is misleading to useless. The Fed's explanation of how and what banks are to record under loan sales is so confusing that probably no two banks report comparable numbers. Also, today the numbers reported surely confuse two very different things, sales of high-quality loan participations, money market instruments, with sales of LBO loan participations.

In any case, the leader in the business is today regarded as Sec Pac. Bankers Trust is second, followed by Chase and Morgan. After the top five, there are two or three others, and then volume numbers drop off sharply. That is where the regionals start coming in; they are in the market, but they are small.

An American Banker newsletter on loan sales and securitization, "Asset Sales Report," noted in its issue of October 10, 1988, that, in early October 1988, the total C&I loan sales of "10 major banks" amounted to 16 billion short-term (one year or less) and 44 billion long-term, for a total of 60 billion. This newsletter also reported that, at the time, the spread on such loans offered ranged from 13 to 39 bp over the average rate sought by commercial paper dealers, with the lowest yield spread being on 5-day loans of issuers rated A1, P1, and the highest yield spread being on 90-day paper of issuers rated A2, P2. Presumably, such yields spreads aren't written in stone, but they do indicate that, as one would expect, loan participations offer the investor some yield pickup over a straight investment in commercial paper.

Investors in High-Quality Loan Participations

Money center banks used to sell a lot of loans to their correspondent banks in a very expensive-to-them way: they would sell down such loans at full fees and full prices. This meant, for example, that if a money center bank which was earning LIBOR + ¼ on a loan and had gotten an arrangement fee of 100,000, sold 10% of that deal to a correspondent bank, the latter would get 10% of the up-front fee and a pro rata share of the commitment at full LIBOR + ¼. Today, the market has evolved so that the selling bank would take a *skim,* certainly from the up-front fee and also a second skim which is the difference between the LIBOR + ¼ that the borrower pays, and the LIBOR + 20 at which the bank might sell the loan to another bank. Whatever it may have been that banks thought they were getting out of selling loan participations to correspondents with no skim, today it is the skim that greases, at all money center banks, and all loan sales business regardless of who the buyer is.

When money center banks first started selling high-quality, short-term loan participations, foreign banks accounted for 100% (or close to it) of the loans sold. Now this group is down to roughly 10 to 15% of the investment-grade loans sold by money center banks. Nonbank buyers account for the remainder. The ranks of the latter include bank trust departments (often investing for pension funds), insurance companies, and corporate liquidity portfolios. Money funds are not buyers of loan participations; such funds can buy a small basket of private placements, but they presumably can find higher-yielding assets to fill that basket, if they do, than loan participations.

Liquidity of Loan Participations

As indicated, in a loan participation sale, a nonnegotiable certificate is issued to the investor. Thus, there are no dealers and brokers in this market as there are in the BA and CD markets, and the liquidity of loan participations is limited.

Making loan participations liquid is a problem. Loan participations are not exempt securities, as are BAs, so if a bank sold negotiable loan participations, it might run afoul of the law and be accused of selling unregistered securities. A selling bank can tell an investor, as they do, "If you need to sell, we will try to find another buyer and act as an intermediary." However, a bank selling a loan participation cannot tell the investor, as would a commercial paper dealer, that it commits to buy back such paper at the market minus some spread whenever and if ever the investor should want to sell it; if the selling bank were to do that, it would not have made a *nonrecourse* sale of the loan and, consequently, the loan would remain on its balance sheet.

In theory, investor X, having bought a loan participation from say, Morgan, might ask Morgan for permission to sell that loan participation to investor Y. However, it is difficult to see why Y would want to buy. If he did, he'd have a triple credit risk: For Y to get his money at the end of the deal, the borrower would have to pay off Morgan who in turn would have to make payment to investor X, who in turn would have to make payment to Y. Contorted, to say the least.

Future of the Business

The market for short-term, high-quality loan participations is an interesting one, but it is uncertain just how long it will be around. Usually, corporations that issue commercial paper can get funding more cheaply directly in the commercial paper market; also, more and more corporations are issuing commercial paper. Thus, the market serves only a small niche, and as time passes, the number of investment-grade issuers that money center banks can effectively reach is dwindling. Where the market is currently growing is in terms of sub-investment-grade investments, say single and double B issuers. In that market, an issuer can find money cheaper than has been traditionally available to him by having a money center bank act as an intermediary between him and a foreign bank. More about that later. The investment-grade side of the market is tough, and it is shrinking.

BANK SALES OF ASSET-BACKED PAPER

Asset-backed paper is any paper, public or private, whose payments depend largely on the cash flows generated by dedicated financial assets, such as automobile loans, credit card loans, franchise agreements, and so on. Such paper is neither a general unsecured corporate debt obligation nor a secured corporate debt obligation. The paper is repayable out of the cash payments from the named assets and typically has only limited recourse to the corporate originator.

Asset-backed paper can be issued publicly or privately. Chrysler Financial Corp. might, for example, have a lot of auto loan receivables that they want to finance. They could go to J. P. Morgan Securities and have them create and sell a registered asset-backed security for them. That route works fine, but can be expensive for Chrysler.

An alternative is for Chrysler to go to a bank like Morgan and arrange a bank-purchased deal. Morgan, for its participation, may be interested in working with Chrysler on two counts: first, it might want to generate some high-quality assets for its own portfolio at a better rate than it would get if it bought publicly offered paper on which the underwriting dealer was making his cut; second, Morgan probably would plan to sell off parts of the deal in the form of loan participations.

The Mechanics of Issuance

The mechanics of bank-purchased asset-backs are simple. A money center bank goes to a Ford, a Chrysler, or whomever, that has some receivables to finance. The bank, say it is Morgan, buys the receivables through a formal *receivables purchase agreement* from the borrower, say, Chrysler. This agreement, which looks somewhat like the pooling and servicing agreement that a publicly offered, asset-backed security would contain, spells out the understanding between the bank and Chrysler. Under the agreement, Chrysler continues to collect interest and principal on the auto loans sold and forwards those collections to the bank. Should Chrysler be deficient, negligent, or go away as a servicer, the bank can replace them with someone else, just as the trustee in a public offering of asset-backs could do.

In buying receivables, Morgan does not examine each loan, but rather looks at Chrysler's past experience with similar loans (e.g., loss and delinquency experience) and to Chrysler's representations about the characteristics of the pool of loans sold (information that would be in the prospectus of a public deal): that the loans are all current; that they are all aged 90 days; that they are for new, not used, cars; and so on. Morgan then makes a filing under the Uniform Commercial Code to perfect its interest in (ownership of) the body of car loans sold.

To allow for the fact that some auto loans are not paid off, that some cars do get repossessed, there is, in private as in public deals, credit enhancement provided by either the seller's contingent repurchase obligation or an overcollateralization. The recourse can be structured in many ways; which way is used depends on the creditworthiness of the seller and on the seller's accounting objectives. Under the repurchase obligation, Chrysler says, "I will repurchase the first 7% of any loans that go bad." With overcollateralization, Chrysler says, "I am going to sell you the first 93% of collections on XMM of receivables; for this you have to pay me only 93 cents on the dollar." Both approaches have the same effect of protecting the buyer of the receivables.

The one difference is that the reserve is payable out of the loan contracts themselves, whereas the contingent repurchase obligation is a general corporate obligation. That is why the accounting treatment differs for the two. Historically, Chrysler's losses have run less than half a percent, but Chrysler typically gives 7.5% as a reserve, that is, it gives a reserve that is 15 times historical losses, which is pretty good protection to the investor.

In a public deal, to simplify the story to an investor, a receivables seller typically wraps the repurchase obligation or the overcollateralization with a letter of credit from a bank, such as United Bank of Switzerland (UBS). The public security buyer looks to the LC for his protection, while the provider of the LC looks to the repurchase obligation or the overcollateralization to reimburse any draws under the LC.

In other words, the credit enhancement provided by the seller is the same in both the public and private markets. What differs between the two markets is that, from the buyer's perspective, the public market recourse provision generally has someone else's name on it (the LC issuer), and it is rated. In a private bank deal, typically the recourse provision has no LC slapped on it, and it is not rated.

Selling Participations in Asset-Backed Loans

If Chrysler has a $1-billion pool of receivables to sell, Morgan might buy the whole pool under a receivables purchase agreement and then, after the fact, sell participations in that loan—100MM to BONY, 100MM to Sumitomo, and so on. Alternatively, a group of banks might agree to purchase together Chrysler's receivables, with each participating bank taking down, say, 100MM of the deal. In practice, banks do private receivables deals both ways.

Yield

The principal advantage to investors of a private, asset-backed deal is yield. While conditions in the public and private markets are constantly changing, the investors' yield on a bank deal can be 20 to 30 bp better than on a public deal. The trade-off is that participation in a private deal is less liquid than are publicly offered securities.

LBO LOAN PARTICIPATIONS

Participations sold in bank LBO loans are definitely *not* a money market instrument. However, since they are huge, much discussed, and a cousin—albeit distant—of the loan participation sales we've been discussing, we conclude this chapter with a short discussion of LBOs and of bank loans to finance them.

LBOs in a Nutshell

For the reader who knows that an *LBO* is a *leveraged buy-out,* but is a touch vague on what that means, we begin by sketching the *bare bones* of such a deal.

An LBO is a buy-out, sometimes by management, sometimes hostile. Say the stock of XYZ Corp. is selling at 50MM, and management decides to make a bid of 100MM for the company. Management, which probably has little or no cash to invest, and their LBO group—Kohlberg Kravis Roberts & Co. (KKR) or one of the other buy-out partnerships or funds they manage—might put up, say, 10MM of equity and borrow the other 90MM, making the deal leveraged 10 to 1. The buy-out group might borrow 40MM from the banks *long term* and do a 50MM *bridge financing,* that is, borrow from the banks short-term 50MM to tide them over until they sell 50MM of *junk (sub-investment-grade) bonds.*

The motive of management in an LBO deal may be to prevent a hostile takeover. Often, it's to enhance their own wealth—sometimes their power and prestige. That isn't to say that, economically, LBOs are always a bad idea. To pay off the mountain of high-cost debt with which it has saddled itself, management will have to cut costs, operate more efficiently, and frequently sell healthy operating divisions; otherwise, it's going to end up bust.

Normally, an LBO deal would be structured such that management, having put up no money, ends up—assuming the banks and the junk bonds get paid off—with 20% of XYZ, which is now a privately held company. The other 80% of XYZ ends up being owned by the LBO group, say, KKR and the various LBO funds that together have put up 10MM in equity. KKR, Merrill, and others manage huge specialized LBO funds that do nothing but invest in LBO deals, so there's no dearth of equity funds available for doing such deals. In our assumed deal, KKR might put up 1MM of its own money, and its own LBO fund or others might put up another 9MM of equity.

In an LBO, part of management's strategy for paying off its heavy debt may be to sell off divisions of the company. Such divisions may be sold to another company or they may be sold via a *spin-off* LBO to the management of the division being sold. Playtex was sold off thusly to its management, and today it's making a fortune.

The rationale behind LBOs is that mature public companies often sell at a substantial discount from the price they would command if they were private. Growth companies are an exception; they sell at a premium.

Private ownership has a different value than public ownership. For one thing, the job of the president of a large public company is not just to enhance stockholders' wealth; he must satisfy various constituencies—consumers, the workers, the stockholders—and then he must take care of himself and his friends; to do the latter, he builds up an empire with perks, planes, a suite at the Waldorf, a hunting lodge in Texas, and a fishing lodge in Canada. If such a company goes private, it can pare such frills and cut costs: management can become like a Sam Walton, run around in a pickup truck, have a billion, and it's your own billion. Also, management in an LBO typically sees ways to operate more efficiently, which isn't surprising. For a public company to be efficiently run, it must have a strong private content, as Ford did and as most public companies don't.

There are also tax advantages to private ownership. First, management can pay itself big salaries instead of double-taxed dividends so long as the compensation isn't so large that IRS deems it to be "unreasonable" (in which case, the portion of compensation deemed to be unreasonable is taxed as if dividends had been paid). Second, a private company can leave in the company monies that would have been paid out as dividends, but again a *caveat:* there can be a tax on "excess retained earnings" if the monies retained aren't needed for business operations (this creates no problem for a growing company that's reinvesting retained earnings). Third, monies left in the firm get taxed only once as part of an inheritance, and the heirs end up, in the best case, with the whole company; naturally, any dividends received by the heirs are taxable income to them.

Management of a company that's been taken private may also take an alternative route. Once it's trimmed costs and made operations more efficient, management's number one priority is to use the monies thus saved to pay down the company's bank loans and junk bonds. Then, management may choose to make its bundle by taking its now-private company *public* once again.

Bear-Hug LBOs

Normally, an LBO firm, like KKR, will work hand in glove with management. However, things can get messy, and the LBO outfit might decide to do the LBO and replace existing management with its own handpicked team of managers. In this case, it is the new, not the former, managers who end up with an equity stake in the now-private company. There is a danger in an aggressive move such as KKR made on RJR Nabisco. Formerly, companies perceived KKR as a friend of management. By having played an at least uninvited, if not hostile, role in the RJR Nabisco LBO, KKR risks limiting the number of CEOs who will be willing to sit down and talk with it in the future.

Buyers of Junk Bonds

It was estimated in mid-fall 1988 that the junk-bond market has swollen to 175 billion and that another 8 to 16 billion bonds were in the pipeline headed to market before year-end. By July 1989, *The Wall Street Journal* was describing the junk-bond market as a 200-billion market. Junk bonds, being sub-investment grade, pay a high yield, and there seem to be numerous investors who believe that they can evaluate the risks inherent in such paper and pick issues that will turn out to be good investments.[1] In any case, insurance companies, mutual funds,

---

[1] The seminal work on junk bond defaults was done by Edward I. Altman of New York University and Scott A. Namacher of Pepsico, Inc. (Drexel Burnham Lambert has also devoted significant resources to the analysis of yields and default rates on junk bonds.) The thrust of this work is that yields on these bonds are higher than required by their true risk. In April 1989, a controversial, unpublished study by Paul Asquith et al. from Harvard indicated that true default levels have been substantially higher than those calculated by Altman and Namacher. The nature of the disagreement between the two studies lies in their methodologies, n.b.: Are losses to be looked at on a coincidental or cumulative basis? Many observers consider the issue of the true risk level of junk bonds to be unresolved.

pension funds, and, most recently, the Japanese have become big buyers of junk bonds.[2] Thrifts, too, bought junk bonds but are now reducing their holdings of them.

One reason for investors' enthusiasm about buying junk is that most studies to date show that junk outperforms high-quality bonds in the long run. However, in the second quarter of 1989, when the economy was slowing, prices of junk, not surprisingly, trailed prices of Treasuries, which had rallied. The reason for the contrast was that junk bonds of some issuers, Integrated Resources and Resorts International to name two, had turned to *trash*—showed losses of more than 37%.

LBO Loans

Originally, banks provided the bridge financing for LBO deals, but they would do so only if an investment banker had made a firm commitment to underwrite the junk-bond issue that was to finance the deal long term. Then, certain investment banking firms, starting with First Boston, said—as a tactic to break Drexel's lock on LBO business—"We'll do the bridge financing and then worry about selling the bonds." Other investment bankers followed suit to provide some or all of the bridge financing on certain deals. The risk in providing bridge financing is that, if the junk bonds fail to sell during a specified period, the short-term bridge loan may convert, depending on how it's structured, into long-term securities conferring equity rights in the LBO; that might leave the lender a reluctant investor.

A big part of the debt assumed in an LBO is senior bank debt with a term of around seven years. Banks love this sort of lending for several reasons. They get large origination fees for committing themselves. These fees can be as much as 2.5% of the overall facility, which works out to 100MM on a 4-billion facility. Another attractive feature of such debt to banks is that currently LBO lending accounts for a large percentage of new

---

[2]Purchases of junk bonds by insurance companies and by pension funds are subject to statutory limits.

bank lending to corporations; also, this lending is at a generous spread, around 2.5 points over LIBOR.

Finally, lead banks in an LBO make money by selling loans to other banks. The process of going from a large to a smaller underwriting commitment varies from bank to bank. Some big banks take the position that you find primary lenders, buyers who sign in on the agreement and are in there with full rights; such banks sub-participate as little as possible. Other banks prefer to whittle down their underwriting commitment by selling to maturity participations in the underlying loan. Banks that take the latter route try to retain some skim on the amount of the sale. Thus, the mechanics of such loan sales resemble those we described earlier with respect to the sale of sub-participations in commercial paper, backstop loans. A bank that does not try to get a skim in distributing its underwriting commitment on an LBO loan still gets agency fees, a relationship with the customer, and visibility as a big player.

Most sales by banks of LBO loans are to other banks. Traditionally, most nonbank buyers bought only investment-grade credits. Today, however, insurance companies and the like are getting into participating on a primary basis in some highly leveraged debt.

An LBO loan is complicated and risky, and the accompanying documentation is long and involved. Consequently, sub-participations in such a loan can only be sold to buyers who understand such things.

Sub-participations in an LBO loan may also be quite illiquid as limitations on resale are likely to be built into the sale agreement; any number of limitations are possible. In particular, to resell, the buyer of the debt may need to get permission from either the borrower or its agent bank.

Sales of sub-participations in an LBO loan are done with no recourse. Also, the buyer of a sub-participation buys *with full rights,* which means that he gets all voting rights under the agreement with regard to changes in the covenants, interest rates paid, and so on. A structured deal, like an LBO, will contain a series of financial covenants—promises that the borrower makes to the lenders who must vote on any changes, amendments, or waivers of those, amongst other things.

The LBO also makes, in the indenture of its junk-bond issue, certain promises to the buyers of its bonds. This bond issue, like any bond issue, has a trustee, one of whose responsibilities is to track whether the LBO company is in compliance with the promises it made to holders of its public debt.

In an LBO, the complex debt agreement that management makes with bank lenders is likely to trigger default before covenants made to public debt holders do; however, the public debt (the junk-bond issue) may contain a cross-default provision saying that, if the LBO defaults on its bank debt, that default will automatically trigger a default on its publicly issued debt.

In an LBO deal, the bank debt is generally senior debt, the junk bonds subordinated debt. The distinction between senior and subordinated debt is a matter of priority of payment. In theory, senior debt holders are supposed to get paid off before subordinated debt holders do; that's one reason why, if an LBO calls for 7-year, senior bank debt, the subordinated debt will have a longer maturity, maybe 10 years. As a matter of practice, in bankruptcies, theory and practice often turn out to differ. In a bankruptcy, it's not unusual for senior debt holders to get 70 cents on the dollar, while subordinated debt holders get 30 cents on the dollar.

A Fiasco in the Making?

Recalling REITs and LDC loans, some banking observers fear that banks, in their LBO lending, are taking on excessive risks that will come home to haunt them. In late 1988, Chairman Greenspan of the Fed and William Seidman of the FDIC both sounded warnings about the risk posed to banks by LBO lending. Also, in 1989, Akira Nagamshima, the senior Bank of Japan representative in the U.S., warned Japanese banks to approach leveraged buy-outs with caution and, in particular, not to lend a disproportionately high amount in any one deal.

These warnings notwithstanding, bankers with LBO portfolios seemed, in early 1989 at least, well pleased with them. They felt they had evaluated risk carefully and were getting an excellent return relative to risk assumed.

Foreign banks are big buyers of LBO loan participations; some even get into the loan resale game. One European banker noted that his head office permitted him to take down big underwriting commitments because he had demonstrated his ability to sub-participate the bulk of them to other foreign banks who needed more time to get approval from head office to buy in.

A second attractive feature of the loan-underwriting business is that, since term bank loans are an expensive part of an LBO financing package, they are often refinanced, perhaps several times, as the fortunes of the company that has been bought out improve. Each time this occurs, the initial loan is repaid, and a new loan is floated at a lower rate. Thus, each such refinancing gives banks a chance to earn yet more underwriting profits.

THE NEXT CHAPTER

In the next chapter, we turn to one of the newest, fastest growing, and dynamic markets in the money market—the medium-term note (MTN) market. In this market, corporates, top-quality sovereigns, and others obtain medium-term funds they used to obtain via bank loans; and banks, domestic and foreign, obtain medium-term funds to replace short-term funds they used to obtain via the sale of CDs. Belying its name, the MTN market is—as maturities lengthen—replacing a chunk of the corporate bond market.

CHAPTER 24

MEDIUM-TERM NOTES

The burgeoning *medium-term note (MTN)* market is a product of the 1980s. In part this market is a dynamic continuation of the trend toward securitization, one whose roots trace back, distantly, to the origins of the commercial paper market. The MTN market also provides a dramatic illustration of how financial markets evolve in response to changing economic stimuli. Finally, the MTN market is a natural counterpart to the swap market; these two markets enjoy a symbiotic relationship: both originated at the same time, and the growth of each has fed that of the other. Whatever view one takes on the source of the MTN market's vigor, indisputably MTNs are one of the securities success stories of the 1980s.

THE BEGINNINGS

The giants of the commercial paper market, GMAC, FMC, and other big finance companies, have long sold their paper direct to investors. In 1972, GMAC began also to sell medium-term notes direct to investors as doing so was an ideal way for it to match fund auto loans. However, the market for such MTNs was small; consequently, the paper was illiquid, and investors demanded a relatively higher yield to buy it.

Shelf Registration and Rating

Any corporate debt having a maturity at issue of more than 270 days (the cutoff for exempt commercial paper) must be registered with the SEC. In March 1982, the SEC adopted *Rule 415* on a temporary basis and finalized it in November 1983. This path-breaking rule permitted *shelf registration* of new corporate debt issues. Under shelf registration, all a would-be issuer need file with the SEC is its historical and current financials and a description of the type and amount of securities it plans to issue under its shelf.

Rule 415 made life easier for issuers of MTNs: before it, every time an issuer experienced a material change in condition and every quarter when it had new financials, it had to rewrite and reprint the documentation it had submitted to the SEC, a procedure that cost time, money, and legal fees; after 415, an issuer was permitted to incorporate changes of the above sort "by reference" into its initial filing with the SEC. An issuer of MTNs always had the right to change the rates it offered on new paper whenever it chose to—GMAC did so from 1972 on—so the procedure of continuously offered MTNs was in place prior to 415.

When a would-be issuer files with the SEC, it typically obtains, at the same time, a rating for its shelf from one of the rating agencies. That rating would be for some specific amount of possible new debt.

A rated shelf merely puts the SEC and the rating agency on notice as to what debt the filer of the shelf might issue. Basically, what the SEC wants to track is what is going on in the debt market, whereas the rating agency is interested in the worthiness of this happening.

Once a company has filed a shelf and gotten that shelf rated, it need not sell immediately, or even ever, the full dollar amount of securities for which it has filed. Alternatively, the company might decide that it wants to sell more securities than it initially filed for—not 200MM, but 300MM. In that case, the issuer must inform both the SEC, which would amend the shelf, and the rating agency, which would review its rating of the shelf.

Originally, the MTN market was designed to fill the gap between the commercial paper and corporate bond markets. Also early on, most of the companies issuing shelf paper were finance companies such as GMAC and FMC. These companies, with their great appetites for cash, needed to widen and deepen, to the extent possible, their access to the debt market. Some of the early sales by such companies of MTNs represented match funding, but such companies are now so sophisticated in managing their assets and liabilities that they not only match fund but frequently mismatch, making calculated interest-rate plays.

Merrill: Market Midwife

What really got the MTN market off the ground was not 415; rather, it was Merrill's vision that GMAC's MTNs need not trade like diseased animals, but could instead trade consistent with GMAC's other notes of similar maturity. For this to occur, Merrill had to and did commit itself to creating a new market.

In the old days, when an investor who had bought MTNs direct from GMAC wanted to sell those notes, he was told by GMAC to go to a dealer. The latter wasn't much interested in making a good bid on such notes for two reasons: he hadn't sold the notes at issue and he wasn't involved in the market—had no ready contact with investors who'd want to buy the notes.

Merrill's idea was that a dealer of its strength could, on its own if it so chose, render MTNs liquid by committing itself to making good bids at all times to any investors who wanted to sell notes issued through it. This notion was both novel and bold, since previously people had equated liquidity to the presence of many dealers in a market; and in the beginning, Merrill was alone in the MTN market.

Merrill's strategy for creating a market in MTNs was simple: ape the commercial paper market, but make a far stronger commitment to developing and maintaining an active secondary market. To this end, Merrill set up a trading desk dedicated to MTNs; people on that desk daily contacted issuers, posted their rates, and interacted with salespeople. Merrill also made a commitment to provide liquidity because lack of liquidity was the principal reason why MTNs had traded at a higher yield than similar corporate underwritten notes. Specifically, Merrill promised to dedicate a significant portion of its capital to taking positions and to making markets in MTNs—all to provide liquidity to investors. Merrill reasoned, correctly, that today's seller of MTNs would be tomorrow's buyer.

The starting gun in the MTN market was sounded in 1981

when Ford Motor Credit began to sell MTNs, first through Goldman and later also through Merrill as agent. In 1983, GMAC also began to sell MTNs through Merrill as agent, and Chrysler Financial did so shortly thereafter. These big issuers paved the way for others (general finance companies, industrial companies, and banks) to enter the MTN market and for a secondary market to develop in MTNs.[1]

Once MTNs began to take off, other dealers saw the promise in this market and promptly entered it.

MTNs: THE PRODUCT

Over time, the product sold in the MTN market has evolved. MTNs began as fixed-rate, medium-term, unsecured corporate obligations offered on a continuous basis in a range of maturities at yields reflecting the shape of the yield curve and the appetite of the market for the issuer's paper. Today, the stock in trade of the market is far more diverse.

Banks and bank holding companies (domestic and foreign), thrifts, sovereigns, foreign government agencies, and others have joined the original group of issuers, which comprised mostly domestic finance companies. In addition to unsecured senior debt obligations, the market now deals in paper that is credit supported: LOC paper, collateralized paper, and so on. Also, a goodly proportion of MTNs are, today, medium-term bank deposits created through the sale of *deposit notes*.

Maturities of MTNs range from nine months to over 30 years, and the investor generally has the option to choose the exact maturity date he desires. MTNs pay interest on a 30/360-day basis, and most are noncallable and nonrefundable. Fixed-rate MTNs generally pay interest semiannually on two preestablished interest-payment dates, regardless of their maturity

---

[1]Some big finance companies still sell MTNs not only via dealers, but direct to investors. However, the amounts of MTNs sold direct are small because issuers use the same people to sell their MTNs that they use to sell their commercial paper, and such people lack the accounts, the contacts, and the know-how to sell medium-term securities.

date. Floating-rate MTNs pay interest at specified floating rates, which reset at various intervals and may be set at a spread to any one of various indices such as LIBOR.

MTN programs are usually rated by nationally recognized credit-rating services such as Moody's, Standard & Poor's, Fitch, and Duff and Phelps.

Figure 24–1 shows a specimen MTN. The issuer is Merrill Lynch & Co., Inc., and the paper is sold on Merrill's MTN desk. Dealers are one more type of entity that has joined the ranks of firms issuing MTNs.

FIGURE 24–1
Specimen MTN: Issuer Merrill Lynch & Co., Inc.

DISTRIBUTION OF NEW ISSUES

Today, a typical issuer of MTNs has two, three, or four dealers whose duty is, as in the commercial paper market, to represent the issuer. Daily, or from time to time, the issuer posts rates with the dealers who represent him. He might say, "At two years, I will take money at 50 off the [Treasury] curve," or whatever. The dealers would then market his paper in the amounts he wanted, confirm trades with him, and take their fee.

The near-standard fee for the industry is 12.5 to 75 bp depending on the maturity, rating, and novelty of the paper sold; by "novelty" we mean whether the issue is a first or has some unusual feature that means that the dealer will have to hold the issuer's hand and also do a lot of explaining to investors. One of the advantages of a standard commission is that the selling dealer has no vested interest in selling, say, Ford over Chemical Bank. A standard fee gives the market more of a commodity flavor for dealers selling MTNs, which in turn works to the benefit of issuers.

LATENT INVESTOR DEMAND

The money market provides investors with a wide array of short-term instruments that vary with respect to credit, yield, maturity, and degree of liquidity. At the opposite extreme are corporate bonds, long in term and normally not actively traded once they are distributed. The investor who wants something in-between is left with relatively low-yield Treasuries and agencies, many of which, especially agencies, are not particularly liquid.

Until the advent of MTNs, what the market lacked was high-quality, corporate paper in the short end. As indicated by the eagerness with which buyers of MTNs eventually snapped up such paper, there were a lot of banks, bank trust departments, insurance companies, thrifts, investment companies, and muni bodies that had a large and unsated appetite for such paper (Figure 24–2).

FIGURE 24–2
Investors in the medium-term note market, June 30, 1989

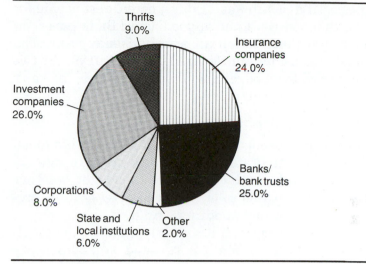

Source: Goldman Sachs.

It is indicative of the latent demand for medium-term paper that, today, 20 to 30% of the issuance of such paper is investor driven: that is, the investor calls a dealer saying, "I need 10MM of 6-year paper. What can you find for me?" The dealer then scouts around for an issuer who wants to write such paper.

The 30/360 versus Actual/360 Hurdle

Some people would have said: "What's the big problem with respect to medium-term paper? For years, banks have been offering, off and on, to sell fixed-rate, medium-term CDs—with little success."

One problem with bank medium-term paper is that it lacked liquidity. That problem in turn reflected the fact that large classes of investors, including insurance companies, would not buy medium-term bank paper in what had been its standard packaging. The reasons were several. One, hard to believe, is that insurance companies found it difficult to cope with the way bank paper accrued interest.

Many institutional investors, particularly insurance companies, buy a lot of corporate paper, which pays interest on an 30/360-day basis. (If a month has 31 days, no interest is paid for the last day of the month—a not-so-good deal.) Bank paper, on the other hand, pays interest on an actual/360-day basis. The fraction 365/360 equals, to four decimal points, 1.0139; thus, if 3-year corporate and bank paper are both offered at 9, the bank paper pays

$$9 \times 1.0139 = 9.125$$

that is, 9⅛ on a corporate bond basis. That calculation is a touch rough because a fully accurate comparison must take into account the day and month on which the paper is bought, whether a leap year is coming up, and so on. But computers can be programmed to take care of such diddling things.

With or without a computer, it's easy to see that an actual/ 360-day yield *grows bigger* when it is restated on a 30/360-day basis. One would have thought that that simple insight would have spurred insurance companies and other traditional bond buyers to reprogram first their thinking and then their computers; doing so would have permitted them to compare, on an apples-to-apples basis, yields on bank and corporate paper and thus to make investment decisions on a more rational basis. Not so. "I would have difficulty," noted one dealer, "overestimating the occasional laziness of bond investors. For many of them, the problem of 30/360 versus actual/360 is insurmountable. They would not buy a term CD because they could not compare its yield to that of a corporate bond.

"By and large, 99.8% of the securities bought by the typical corporate investor are 30/360. He does not want to deal with any security that pays actual/360. To him, such securities are a nuisance to buy and to periodically mark to market. Also, on a swap, he wants to be able to figure, with no fuss, whether he is getting a yield pickup or give-up."

In defense of the investor in corporates, since he is not alone in his aversion to actual/360-pay securities, the latter are in the term market much less liquid than are 30/360-pay securities. Thus, in selling a term CD, the investor might easily give up, in the *dime bid-offer spread,* more than the extra interest he had earned by buying that CD because it yielded an extra 20 or 30 bp.

In any case, when MTNs were set up, there was no contest about how yield should be fixed. From day one, MTNs paid on a 30/360 basis.

Pick Your Moment to Invest

MTNs proved to have another advantage from the viewpoint of investors in corporates. Once the market became established, there were lots of issuers, and consequently, there was always paper that an investor, once he had funds, could immediately draw down from some issuer's shelf on a more or less custom-tailored basis—pick his maturity date. The same investor, if he chose to buy an underwritten corporate bond, would have to wait for a deal he liked, and his latitude to pick a maturity that suited him would be far more limited.

LATENT BORROWER DEMAND

Borrowers for their part found MTNs a boon. Documentation was simple, a lot simpler than negotiating loan-by-loan indentures for a series of bank loans. MTNs put money on tap for borrowers. Moreover, it was flexible money: they could draw it down as they needed it *and* in the specific maturities they needed.

Finance companies may have been the first big borrowers in the market, but others soon followed: industrial corporations, utilities, thrifts, and sovereigns, including the Kingdom of Sweden, a big and sophisticated borrower, who seems to find a way—swap or whatever—to make borrowing in every debt market invented a good deal for it; also, the World Bank has been in the market offering its COLTS. As Figure 24–3 shows, bank borrowers, too, form a big segment of total MTN issuance. The bank borrowing shown in Figure 24–3 includes issuance at both the bank and the bank-holding-company levels. We discuss such borrowings below.

FIGURE 24–3
Public MTNs: Issuer profile (1985—2nd quarter 1989)*

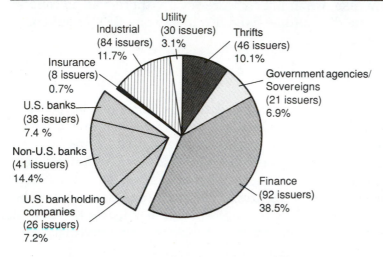

*Based on $ volume of program filings; total issuers, 386.

Source: IDD Information Services, Inc., September 30, 1988. Prepared by Goldman Sachs.

In the fall of 1987, one major bank thought interest rates were about to fall and instructed its bankers to offer fixed-rate, medium-term loans to its better-rated clients. It is indicative of the attractiveness of the MTN market to issuers that every company polled responded, "If you want to lend to us medium-term, buy our MTNs."

GROWTH OF THE MARKET

As they fitted the needs of both borrowers and lenders, domestic public MTN programs outstanding expanded from 2.6 billion in 1981 to over 60 billion by early 1989. The most rapid expansion of the market occurred after 1984 (Figure 24–4).

The MTN market fills the needs of companies with varied borrowing needs. Almost 50% of the 232 public programs outstanding in the fall of 1988 fell in the 100MM to 300MM cate-

FIGURE 24–4
Public medium-term note programs*

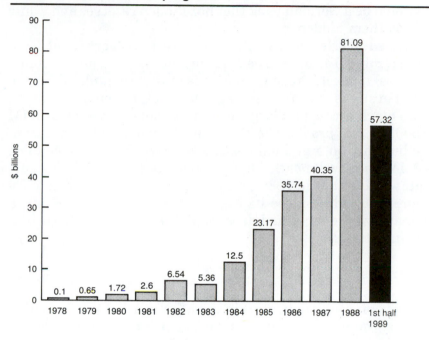

*Chart excludes programs designed exclusively for the EMTN Market.

Source: IDD Information Services, Inc., June 30, 1989. Prepared by Goldman Sachs.

gory; another 35% fell in the 500MM to 600MM category; finally, 30 borrowers had programs of a billion or more.

Borrowers who have used the MTN market are almost without exception investment grade. Over the period 1985 to 1988, 90% of these borrowers had ratings of triple A to single A from one rating agency or several. Borrowers with triple-B ratings were in the distinct minority.

Privately Placed Paper

The MTNs we have been talking about so far, and to which all figures in this chapter apply, are rated, publicly offered paper. There is also a *private* MTN market. An issuer in this market might not choose to get its paper rated, perhaps because it doesn't want to divulge sufficient information to do so; an example would be a German bank that has hidden reserves and wants to keep them hidden.

Rated MTNs are, as noted, all investment grade (above a triple B minus) at issue. The MTN market is not a junk (double-B or less) market. Probably, one reason that no junk MTNs are issued in size is that, in a leveraged buy-out, the buyer-borrower needs quick access to a large amount of money: may be 300MM or 500MM *mui pronto*. The MTN market can handle that sort of size but only on a gradual basis; a borrower may be able to do 300MM over two months, but not over two days. Having said that, we note that in 1988 Philip Morris filed a $3-billion MTN program to help finance its $13-billion acquisition of Kraft, a company whose large and dependable cash flows made such financing attractive.

Maturities

At the beginning, maturities in the MTN market ran from nine months, the cutoff for commercial paper, out to several years. Since then, maturities have lengthened dramatically. First, investors bought short paper, then as they came to believe that there was indeed liquidity in 2- and 3-year MTNs, they became willing to move a bit further out on the yield curve, and then again a bit further. Today, MTN maturities of 5, 10, and 15 years are common, and maturities as long as 30, even 40 years, are not unusual.

Issuers for their part were often eager to lengthen maturities. Those that issued floating-rate MTNs could hedge their interest-rate risk with Euro futures, which now extend to four years, or lock in a fixed rate with an interest-rate swap, routinely done for five years and further.

The lengthening, over time, of the maturities of MTNs issued has contributed substantially to the growth of MTNs outstanding. Year to year, issuance of MTNs has increased, but outstandings of MTNs have risen far faster.

In 1981, 70% of MTNs issued through Merrill had a maturity of nine months to two years; the remainder had a maturity of two to five years. By the late 1980s, the numbers had flipped: only 22% of MTNs issued through Merrill had a maturity of nine months to two years, and 21% had a maturity of more than five years.

Book-Entry MTNs

Once all securities were physical. Getting a physical security makes an investor feel good, safe: he has something to tuck in his safe or in that of his custody bank. The problem with physical securities is that they are troublesome and expensive to clear; also, if they are in bearer form, they pose the risk of theft.

To obviate the above problems and risk, the U.S. Treasuries and most agencies come in *book-entry* form: there are no physical securities, and ownership is tracked by computer records. The Depository Trust Company (DTC) and the National Securities Clearing Corporation (NSCC) have, by immobilizing physical securities, managed together to create a book-entry environment for the clearing of corporate stocks and certain other securities.

In 1985, Merrill and Chrysler began negotiations with DTC to develop a book-entry system for Chrysler's MTNs. This was a challenging job as MTNs, unlike underwritten corporate bonds, do not come in nice big lumps of 100MM or more. If, on a given day, Chrysler twice issues notes that both carry the same rate but have maturities of 2 years and 2 years and 5 days, it has issued two separate securities. Similarly, if on a given day, Chrysler twice issues notes that both have a flat 2-year maturity but carry slightly different rates, it has issued two separate securities. Thus, Chrysler's outstanding MTNs, like those of any big issuer, represent thousands of separate securities.

After three years' work, DTC finally created a book-entry system that could handle MTNs at a reasonable cost, and in March 1988, Chrysler's MTNs finally went book entry. This change, which is likely to signal a movement to book entry over time of many, if not most, MTNs, will save money for everyone: issuers, agents, and investors. Currently, it costs $25 to $30 to clear a trade in a physical security, whereas DTC's fee will be around $1.50.

The creation of book-entry MTNs should vastly enlarge the base of investors who are willing to purchase this paper. In particular, there are huge bank trust departments that won't buy a physical security. They want book-entry securities that have an identifying CUSIP number. Their reason is that, periodically, they mark to market all securities they are holding for customers; securities that have a CUSIP number can be marked to market simply by purchasing a computerized pricing service from Merrill, Sali, Morgan Stanley, or some other source; physical securities, however, must be marked to market by hand, something some big investors refuse to be bothered with.

YIELDS ON MTNs

Yields on fixed-rate MTNs are always quoted at a spread off Treasuries. How large that spread is varies depending on the credit of the issuer, the maturity of the note, and the general level of interest rates. Invariably, credit spreads widen as rates rise, contracts as rates fall.

For a number of years, banks have generally traded wide to industrials, a phenomenon that reflects investor demand; due to the money center banks' well-publicized problems with LDC loans, to the Texas banks' problems with energy and real estate loans, and so on, investors are inclined to take a dim view of bank credits. Thus, in August 1989, investors were demanding, in the 5-year area, 70 off for a triple A bank, only 45 off for a triple A industrial.

The big LBOs of 1988—KKR buying out RJ Nabisco and so on—sent shock waves through the corporate bond market. Thanks to leveraged buy-outs and recaps, investment-grade corporate bonds turned, on more than one occasion, into junk overnight. The Street's term for the risk of this occurring is *event risk*. The specter of event risk caused conservative corporate bond buyers to flee to quality—to seek out bonds issued by entities who either couldn't be bought out or whose buy-out wouldn't cause its bonds to be downgraded.

The MTN market is a subset of the corporate bond market.

Therefore, anything that impacts demand by sector and thus sector-yield spreads in the bond market impacts similarly, if less strongly because of shorter maturities, the MTN market. So long as big LBOs continue, companies in highly regulated industries, such as utilities and banking, and the sovereigns also (KKR can't buy the Kingdom of Sweden) are going to have a heyday, yieldwise, in the MTN market.

Floating-Rate MTNs

Currently, about 5% of all MTNs issued pay a floating rate. An entity might want to issue floating-rate paper because it was financing assets that paid some indexed short-term rate, because it could do an attractive swap—floating for fixed, or because it thought it a good bet that, over the life of its borrowing, floating-rate debt would prove cheaper than fixed-rate debt.

A floating-rate MTN pays interest at a specified floating rate. That rate paid is a spread, positive or negative, off one of several well-recognized money market indices; these include LIBOR, the commercial paper index, the Federal funds composite, the prime rate, and the bill rate. On floaters, reset intervals are generally weekly, monthly, quarterly, or semiannually. The frequency with which interest is paid is established by the issuer in response to the issuer's needs and investor preferences. Floaters require a yield premium for longer maturities; while the buyer of a floater is not subject to interest-rate risk, he's subject to more risk with respect to credit and basis changes than he would be if he bought short-term paper.

Floating-rate paper constitutes probably no more than 5% of the total MTN market. It is the typical market investor who buys such MTNs. Some corporate floaters are issued with puts. An investor, such as a money fund, may be able to treat, for purposes of meeting restrictions on the maturities of the assets it may hold, an MTN with a put as having a maturity equal to its time to next put date, rather than its time to maturity. This is attractive to a money fund that must keep tens of billions of dollars invested short-term.

BANK DEPOSIT NOTES

Over time, the composition of the MTN market is changing. The finance companies really started the market. Later, banks became, at both the bank and the holding-company level, big issuers in the MTN market (Figure 24–3).

Please, Quack Like a Corporate Bond

Over the years, banks have frequently had a hard time convincing some institutional buyers to buy medium-term CDs. This is a cultural thing. First, most eligible buyers of medium-term, bank funding products are insurance companies. The latter typically buy only rated securities. A bank is rated, but a CD is not. What is the difference? For an answer, ask an insurance company. Also, when shown bank medium-term CDs, buyers of corporate paper ask questions that are difficult to answer intelligently such as: "How big is the deal?" What can a dealer say other than, "Well he's got 80 billion of CDs outstanding; he's writing today; and he'll probably write more tomorrow, next week, or some time in the future." Buyers of corporate paper also want a prospectus.

So Wall Street said we will create *bank deposit notes*. We will call them the 8¼s of 90 at par; they'll be double-A rated; and, of course, the paper will pay 30/360. This little drill did not come free; it cost maybe 25 bp. Perhaps half of those basis points went to the issuer to pay them to get their notes rated and to come up with some sort of offering circular (a stand-in for a prospectus); the other 12.5 bp went to the dealers who sold the paper.

When the Street created deposit notes, it operated on the assumption, which proved correct, that the average bond buyer believes that, if it talks like a duck, walks like a duck, and quacks like a duck, it's a duck. However, decking out a bank deposit to look like a corporate security does *not* make it a corporate security. A deposit note is an FDIC-insured bank deposit that ranks *pari passu* with all of a bank's other deposits and that yields, on an apples-to-apples basis, often as much as 25 bp less than a medium-term CD of the same bank for the same maturity.

The Banks: For Money, We Will Quack

For a bank, issuing deposit notes is simple. The bank pays a small fee to a rating agency to rate its issue. No documentation is required by any government body, but it has become traditional in these deals for a bank to provide an offering circular that gives the bank's current financials, that defines a deposit note, that tells where such a note ranks in terms of a bank's liabilities—that the buyer is a depositor, not a creditor, and so on. Such a circular is *much* less comprehensive than a prospectus, but it's something that the buyer can file in his drawer labeled "Prospectuses." Many banks will not put together any document, in which case the selling dealer may do a circular and get the bank's OK on what it says. Finally, a bank wanting to issue deposit notes negotiates with some group of dealers the terms on which it will offer its paper.[2]

Maturities of Bank Deposit Notes

A bank's offering circular typically says that the bank may issue paper ranging in maturity from 9 months to 15 years. Banks, however, have never offered deposit notes with a maturity at issue of less than 18 months—the cutoff that reduces reserve requirements to 0%. Currently, maturities on bank deposit notes range from 18 months to 5 years, with the average being from 2 to 2½ years. There have been some 7- and 10-year issues, but banks tend to think of 5 years and longer as long term.

Advantages Offered to Issuing Banks

Naturally, a bank wanting to finance floating-rate assets with floating-rate liabilities finds that deposit notes have the disadvantage of paying a fixed rate. However, not to worry. A bank with a good credit rating can easily swap fixed-rate money raised in the bank deposit market into *sub-LIBOR funding*.

---

[2]A bank holding company issuing MTNs, as opposed to a bank issuing deposit notes, must register its issue with the SEC and make normal disclosure. Bank deposit notes, because they are a *bank liability,* are an *exempt* security.

A bank like Morgan with a *top* credit rating has, vis-à-vis other banks, a privileged access to funds: it can buy money cheaper than other banks. How much cheaper depends on the maturity of the funding. The average investor won't take less or much less for the honor of lending *overnight* to Morgan rather than to Manny. But if the loan is for five years, the spread between the rates at which the two banks can sell paper widens appreciably. Thus, the better a bank's credit, the lower the rate at which it can obtain floating-rate money by selling fixed-rate deposit notes and swapping fixed for floating.

For banks with good credit, the invention of the deposit note was a great deal. By using this new instrument, such a bank can reap a number of advantages: source funds in size from nontraditional buyers of bank paper; avoid reserve requirements; reduce its traditional tension between concern over liquidity and concern over interest-rate exposure; and finally, get funding at a rate below that at which it could roll 3- or 6-month liabilities in the Euro interbank market.

The acceptance by major banks of deposit notes is indicated by the fact that, currently, 40% of the continuously offered deposit note and MTN filings by banks are in the 500MM-to-600MM range, 10% in the 600MM+ range.

Growth of the Market

Insurance companies, pension funds, and other institutional investors turned out to be enthusiastic buyers of deposit notes; and the market, which began only in 1986, took off (Figure 24–5). By the second quarter of 1989, continuously offered bank deposit notes and MTN programs totaled an estimated 23.5 billion.

The deposit note market has not by any means been the sole province of the U.S. money center banks. In recent years, certain regional banks have been getting a lot of good press: some are great credits and have the capital to grow. Such banks are welcome in the MTN market.

There is a point at which the size of a bank dictates its possibilities for growth. NBNC, which was in 1978 a $2.2-billion, and is now a $55-trillion bank holding company, is an example. Today, NBNC has both the size and the capital to make big loans and is thus doing some heavy lending. The good

FIGURE 24–5

Growth in continuously offered medium-term and deposit note programs (dollar volume filed)*

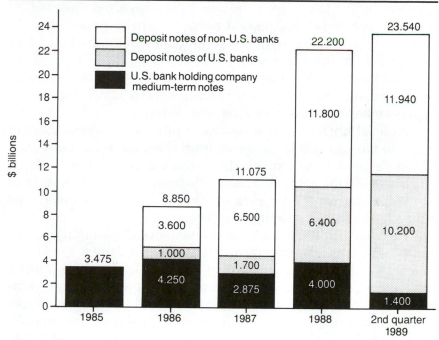

*Filings refer to filings with the SEC. A filing must precede issuance, and a borrower need not issue the full dollar sum for which he has filed.

Source: IDD Information Services, Inc., June 30, 1989. Prepared by Goldman Sachs.

superregionals who are at that point buy funds in every market open to banks, the MTN market included.

Also, big foreign banks, many of whom are excellent credits, are finally being perceived by more and more U.S. investors as such. Almost all of the long-term deposits and subordinated debt of foreign banks is denominated in their native currencies, but these banks hold a lot of dollar assets; so to them, a source of medium-term dollar funding that is both readily available *and* reasonably priced is an attractive opportunity for funding diversification. Hence, the big usage of this market by foreign banks (Figure 24–5). Generally, the holding-company structure that obtains in U.S. banks is not applicable to foreign banks; thus, foreign-bank issuance of MTNs is generally at the bank level.

Japanese Bank Deposit Notes

Of the foreign-bank users of the deposit note market, the Japanese are by far the largest. In late 1988, there were around 30 non-U.S. banks issuing deposit notes. Of these, approximately 10 to 12 were Japanese; and together, they accounted for 55 to 60% of the foreign-bank slice of the deposit note market. Japanese bank deposit notes never have a maturity of more than five years because the Ministry of Finance (MOF) will not permit Japanese banks to issue beyond five years.

At least until capital adequacy requirements forced them to begin to pare low-ROA business from their balance sheets, the Japanese banks were using the deposit note market to do as much as 500MM a day of a neat arbitrage. We tell the story to illustrate that markets, even in the U.S., are not always as efficient as some are wont to believe.

In early 1988, the big Japanese banks, all highly rated, could issue term floating-rate CDs at LIBOR minus ⅛. At the same time, deposit notes issued by triple-A banks were trading at 40 over Treasuries, and the swap market was 80 over Treasuries. Looking at this rate constellation, the Japanese banks saw a great arbitrage. They offered to issue deposit notes at 50 over. To investors, those notes looked 10 bp cheap to the curve, so they bought billions of them. Meanwhile, the Japanese promptly swapped the proceeds of their deposit note sales at 80 over, which gave them 3-year money at LIBOR minus 30. The difference between LIBOR minus ⅛ and LIBOR minus 30 is 17.5 bp. Simply by going the deposit-note-cum-swap route versus issuing floating-rate CDs, the Japanese were able to reduce their funding costs by 17.5 bp.

For Japanese banks, it was easy to invest money obtained at LIBOR minus 30 at a profit. They would buy CDs issued by other banks at LIBOR flat or finance loans at LIBOR flat and pick up a profit of 30 bp, 17.5 bp more than they could have had they financed the same investments by selling floating-rate CDs.

For a time, Japanese banks were pumping out 500MM of deposit notes a day at 50 over. Meanwhile, investors were saying, "Hey, I bought this paper last week at 50 over which was 10 cheap to the curve. Why doesn't the spread narrow? Instead, it's now 55 over." The dealer's answer was, "Those spreads will never ever narrow. The Japanese banks do not need to raise 300MM to buy a piece of equipment or to build a plant; they are borrowing money to lay it off at a profit; consequently, they will sell you, at 50 or 55 over, as many billions of those notes as you can buy. Every time you buy those notes, you are just giving the Japanese banks free money."

Bank Notes

Banks pay an insurance premium of 8.125 bp to the FDIC on all deposit notes they issue. A bright banker at Republic New York said, "We are a good bank. Why do we have to issue insured deposit notes? Why can't we just issue unsecured bank notes at the bank level, the way any corporation issues notes? On such plain vanilla notes, we won't owe the FDIC any insurance premium."

The product Republic New York pioneered is known as *bank notes*. Technically, such notes are unsubordinated liabilities with 2- to 5-year terms, and banks sell them strictly to institutional investors to whom deposit insurance means next to nothing, since (except in the case of pension funds covering more than one individual) it covers only the first $100,000 of a deposit.

By selling over a billion of bank notes, Republic New York saved itself over $800,000 a year in FDIC premiums. Other banks soon followed Republic New York's lead. In particular, Morgan Bank, Banker's Trust, and State Street Boston began selling bank notes.

The issuance of bank notes did not escape notice by the FDIC. In November 1988, this agency proposed that its insurance premiums be extended to cover bank notes. The FDIC is naturally concerned about losing premiums. It is also concerned that, in a bank bankruptcy, bank notes might be held to be covered by FDIC insurance. There is a precedent: In 1985, Golden Pacific National Bank, a small New York bank in Chinatown, failed with 14.5MM of outstanding promissory notes on its books. These notes, called "yellow certificates" because they were printed on yellow paper, had been treated by the bank as uninsured funds. A federal judge ruled, however, that the certificates were nonetheless covered by FDIC insurance, and the FDIC had to pay off the holders.

Bankers countered the FDIC proposal by saying that a bank note looks like a bond, pays like a bond, and so should not be treated like a deposit. Also, bank notes are sold only to sophisticated investors who presumably know what they are buying.

To a bank, an advantage of issuing a bank note at the bank level rather than at the holding-company level is that bank notes can be sold with a one-page offering circular, whereas bank-holding-company notes would have to be registered with the SEC. Also, any money raised at the holding-company level and funneled into the bank via holding-company deposits with the bank would be subject to FDIC insurance premiums.

Bank-Holding-Company MTNs

Actually, a number of U.S. banks do issue MTNs at the holding-company level (Figure 24–3). The holding company may use the proceeds of such note issuance to fund its credit-card business, its leasing business, and various other holding-company activities.

Foreign-Currency-Denominated Bank Deposit Notes

In the past, the Fed prohibited U.S. banks from denominating deposits held in the U.S. in a foreign currency. The Fed ruled twice on this. One ruling goes back to McChesney Martin, and is a bit of a howler; it said that U.S. banks could issue only dollar-denominated deposits in the U.S. because, if banks were to accept nondollar-denominated deposits in the U.S., the Fed would lose its ability to track the U.S. money supply. In a second ruling, the Fed said that, if U.S. banks were to issue deposits denominated in currencies other than the dollar, the banks would be betting against the U.S. dollar, something bank foreign-exchange traders have done rather often in recent years.

Banks would like to be able to issue, in the U.S., deposits denominated in currencies other than the dollar and pressed yet again this issue with Fed Chairman Greenspan. Also, several U.S. dealers tried to get the Fed to change its mind on this issue. Finally, at the end of 1988, the Fed ruled that banks in the U.S. could begin accepting deposits denominated in currencies other than the dollar, but not until 1990. At that time, it will be possible for U.S. banks to run a universal deposit note program whereby a U.S. bank could, on a given day, say to its MTN dealers: "I will issue 2-years at 50 off Treasuries, I do not care how you do it—Kiwi dollar plus a currency swap or whatever."

How wide the appeal of nondollar-denominated deposit notes will be to investors is less clear. Most U.S. investors who play currency markets want all the liquidity that they can get, so if they want to make a DM play, they want to own Bunds (German government bonds). The investors most likely to buy a foreign-currency-denominated deposit issued in the U.S. are yield buyers; such investors might, for example, be tempted to buy deposit notes denominated in Aussi dollars or in other soft currencies; that is, notes that would pay a high nominal interest rate to compensate for the foreign-exchange risk inherent in holding them unhedged.

Thrift MTNs

Today, thrifts are significant players in the MTN market (Figure 24–3). So far, all of the medium-term notes that thrifts have issued have been in the form of MTNs, on which the thrifts pay no deposit insurance. Since the FSLIC premium is 21 bp, thrifts have a big incentive to avoid paying it whenever and however possible. FSLIC, unlike the FDIC, has not raised the issue as to whether thrifts should be required to pay insurance premiums on MTNs issued at the thrift level. It is easy for a thrift to argue that such paper is not a deposit, but in bankruptcy court, FSLIC might have difficulty making the same case.

It is not surprising that thrifts have been big issuers of MTNs. A top-quality thrift such as First Nationwide can issue at a spread in the MTN market such that, if they do a swap, they can, under favorable market conditions, get funds at LIBOR flat. That is also where they can issue floating-rate CDs. Naturally, they are not going to issue CDs when they can issue MTNs at the same rate and save 21 bp on insurance.

Thrift issuance of medium-term notes falls into two categories, secured and unsecured. It is only in the last three years that unsecured thrift paper has been rated. Prior to that, selected thrifts could issue CDs but they had to pay up. The MTN market did not used to be liquid for them. Now that has changed. Once the rating agencies confirmed that the top thrifts such as Great Western, First Nationwide, and Sears were good quality—they have no LDC debt, and, hopefully, never ever again are they going to be as mismatched as they were in 1981 to 1982—investors came to understand thrifts better. In particular, some less credit-sensitive investors have taken time to look at thrift paper as an alternative to typical corporate or domestic bank paper, and they feel comfortable with certain thrift credits.

Less creditworthy thrifts also issue MTNs, but they must back them with collateral. The latter might be Fannies, Freddies, Ginnies, or commercial mortgages; some thrifts even use high-yield junk bonds to collateralize their borrowings. Thrifts issuing collateralized paper can access funds on an unsecured basis by selling short-term CDs, but in the institutional marketplace, they cannot access 2-, 3-, and 4-year money without putting up collateral.

As investors have become more comfortable with thrift paper, the dealer community has become more aggressive in pursuing business with thrifts. Merrill was first; it has been followed by others—Goldman Sachs, Sali, Shearson, First Boston, Morgan Stanley, and Drexel.

Yield and Liquidity

Through their success, bank deposit notes have virtually eliminated the market, small as it was, for fixed-rate, medium-term CDs. Yet, the yield on the latter was in the past and still is somewhat higher than the yield on deposit notes carrying the same name and having the same maturity.

Part of the explanation is investor lethargy. "I offered a guy," noted one dealer, "a swap out of top Japanese deposit notes into top Japanese medium-term CDs; I offered to pay him 60 over for his deposit notes and to put him into medium-term CDs—same maturity—at 90 over, and the CDs I was trying to sell were new stuff. The investor would not do the swap." So much for the thesis that investors are never willing to give money away.

Defenders of bank deposit notes see things differently. Said one, "The medium-term CD market has always had a problem; it was an illiquid market for several reasons. The deposit note market has tried to address this situation—to enhance liquidity. People should be willing to pay something for that enhanced liquidity; therefore a deposit note should yield slightly less than a similarly rated CD."

DEALERS AS MARKET MAKERS

The principal dealers in the MTN and deposit note markets are Merrill, Shearson, Sali, Goldman, First Boston, and Morgan Stanley (Figure 24–6). There are also peripheral players who make occasional runs—take a shot at getting into the market for a year and then usually fall off for one reason or another.

The New-Issue Market

As noted, dealers in MTNs began by acting as agents, just as they do in the commercial paper market. They posted rates for their clients and took a fee, pretty well standardized, for what they sold. At the outset, they did not and were not expected to underwrite their clients' paper as do dealers who underwrite corporate bond issues.

Distribution of Bank Deposit Notes

Distribution has evolved differently in the bank deposit note market. Big banks like Morgan that have securities subsidiaries with distribution capability normally do not use dealers except

FIGURE 24–6
Domestic MTN programs: Leading agents of MTNs (1/1/88–1/1/89)*

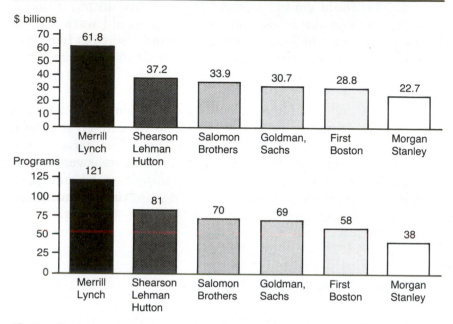

*Full credit given to each agent for principal amount.

Source: Prepared by Merrill Lynch (based on data from IDD Information Services, Inc.).

when they want to do something big in a hurry. If such a bank needs to do, say, 300MM in 2-year notes pronto, they will call around to the dealers to get bids. Such banks do not use the dealers on a continuing basis. It is the superregionals and others who lack good, national-market access who need dealers to represent them in the market and to guarantee the liquidity of their paper. No one worries about the liquidity of paper issued by Bankers Trust, Morgan, or Citi. A Fleet or a Bank One is a great institution, but not a household name. Such a bank, therefore, generally uses a dealer.

Ideally, the deposit note market works best on an agency basis. However, thanks partly to the operations of the big banks, distribution in this market is changing. It is becoming more common for new paper to be underwritten by the dealers. The old view was that, when dealers committed to underwrite an issue, they would get a bigger commission for taking a bigger risk, whereas in the MTN market, dealers would work for less because they sold MTNs on an agency basis and thus had little risk. Yet, as more and more dealers are underwriting new MTNs, the lower commissions prevailing in this market are still holding.

Increasingly, the banks are using the MTN market on a bid-wanted basis. Bankers Trust or Morgan may call three or four dealers and say, "We want to do 200MM of deposit notes. What's your bid?" Maybe the bank has an interest-rate swap on the other side and wants to lock in a price. In any case, dealers often respond to bank requests or bids by simply underwriting the paper and taking it down. At this point, more than half of the bank deposit note business is done on the basis of "What's your bid for 100MM?" There is no fee on such deals; the bank asks for an *all-in* bid or for a *bid at the net*. It is like bidding for T bills.

Two things killed the market for medium-term, fixed-rate CDs. One was the deposit note market. The other was that dealers were not making money on bank CDs. Dealers would have banks asking them to bid on 50MM of 3-year CDs. On such paper, a dealer can, if the market goes south, quickly lose lots of money. However, if the market moves in his favor, a dealer reaps no commensurate profit. The reason lies in the way CD yields respond to movements in the Treasury curve: if Treasury rates fall 20 bp, medium-term CD rates may fall only 10 bp; but if Treasury rates rise 20 bp, CD rates may rise 30 bp. Positioning medium-term bank CDs is thus a high-risk proposition, and dealers have lost lots of money doing it. For issuers, the medium-term CD market was always liquid in the sense that they could get a lot of paper out the door in a hurry by getting dealers to take it down; however, the market was never liquid in the sense that secondary trading of medium-term CDs was active.

As the deposit note market took off, dealers became less and less aggressive in their bidding for bank medium-term CDs. Now, the deposit note market is getting to look more and more like the old CD market: What is your bid for 100MM? Little by little, the banks are threatening to kill the goose that laid the golden egg.

The Secondary Market for MTNs

There has begun to be interdealer brokering of MTNs. Some of the corporate bond brokers will occasionally get involved, and there are several money market brokers who have tried to get into the business as well. The brokers list the paper by the issue offered or bid, for example, 3-year Fords carrying a 9.10 coupon, issue date was here, and they are being offered at a spread of 50 off Treasuries.

In the MTN market, there is no consistency as to whether 1MM or 5MM is a round lot. To a trader of corporate bonds, 1MM is a round lot; to a money market trader, 5MM is a round lot. Depending on the shop, MTNs may be traded by bond or money market traders.

MTNs are not actively traded like Euro CDs or Japanese BAs where there are active screens and interdealer trades going on much of the time. "In MTNs, days can pass without a trade occurring in the brokers' market," noted one bank dealer. This, however, it not to say that MTNs lack liquidity. As noted, top dealers in MTNs go out of their way to make good bids on out-standing MTNs. As one dealer noted, "We have an ongoing reason to bid aggressively, and it is called *greed*. We want to develop the market." One indicator of the liquidity of the MTN market is that, currently, Merrill's secondary volume exceeds its issuance.

With respect to the liquidity of MTNs, one top dealer observed, "The secondary market is extremely liquid. Dealers in particular feel comfortable in making bids on a quite heterogeneous mass of paper. The dealer community has proved that you can have the same liquidity for securities issued in little tranches as in securities issued in big blocks."

"There is," stated another dealer, "a huge secondary market in MTNs. The bid-offer spread depends on the size of the program, the credit of the issuer, and the frequency of issuance. In high-quality paper, the bid-offer spread is a nickel—maybe less for a Ford, but more for a weak credit. Investors view MTNs as liquid paper. In the secondary market for MTNs, there are a lot of trades for 1MM and a lot of 5s and 10s too."

One factor that adds to the homogeneity of MTNs and thus

to their liquidity is that an issuer may issue any day, but he often has two *fixed* coupon dates. (This means that new paper is likely to come with long or short first and last coupons). Currently, some issuers, especially banks, wanting to couple MTN issuance with an interest-rate swap, have moved from fixed to flexible coupon dates. If they had, say, March and September fixed coupon dates and issued in May with an interest-rate swap that settled in May, they'd have an uncomfortable gap between March and May; hence, they'd rather issue in May with a May coupon date.

In an MTN program, what is flexible is the ability of the issuer to go into the market with different coupons and different maturity dates; what is standard is the method of accruing interest and the fixed coupon dates.

Dealers in MTNs recognize that a good secondary market always enhances what they can do in the primary market: providing good liquidity in the secondary market facilitates primary sales. Thus, much of the market is swap driven: a dealer offers a customer the opportunity to swap an old piece for a new piece, maybe the opportunity to extend by swapping existing 2-year Fords for new 5-year Fords.

The success of the top dealers in trading MTNs has been that a lot of the philosophies that they used in trading money market instruments carried over well into the MTN market; in a sense, MTNs are an extension of the commercial paper market.[3] Thus, the philosophies of how dealers monitor programs, how they sponsor issuers, how they provide consistent liquidity, how they have continuous offerings—all the things that made MTNs as successful as they are—came from the commercial paper market.

Hedging Positions in MTNs

A dealer who holds a position in MTNs is subject to interest-rate risk. If he doesn't want to make a position play in MTNs, he can hold them and hedge that risk by shorting, on a duration-

---

[3]It's a measure of the success of the MTN market that MTNs are, as noted below, replacing a part of the traditional underwritten corporate bond market.

weighted basis, Treasuries, either cash or futures. The dealer's risk is then that corporate spreads may widen; if so, he loses money.

Alternatively, if a dealer shorts a swap (pays fixed and receives LIBOR), he will achieve a better correlation between the fixed rates he is long and short. At least, before event risk roiled the markets, a common definition of swap spreads was that they were synonymous with the spread of a single-A industrial to Treasuries. Because of the wide bid-offer spread in the swap market, swaps are not a cost-effective way for a dealer to hedge positions he expects to sell out shortly. However, if a dealer reasons that, as a core position, he is always going to have 100MM of 5-years, 100MM of 3-years, then for a portion of that it makes sense for him to put on a duration-weighted hedge using swaps. The dealer might put on a 5-year swap for maybe 50MM and then let that 5-year become a 4-year and then a 3-year, and then maybe get rid of it. This approach reduces not only spread (basis) risk, but transactions costs as well. Every time a dealer shorts a Treasury and then has to buy it back, he loses a 32nd. For a shop that maintains ongoing positions in MTNs, a cheaper way (from the point of view of transaction costs) to hedge that core position may be to book an interest rate: be the payer of fixed and receiver of LIBOR to hedge fixed-rate MTNs.

MTNs VERSUS CORPORATE BONDS

In the beginning and in its purest form, the MTN market dealt in unsecured, fixed-rate, medium-term paper, typically sold on a continuous basis by several dealers who acted on an agency basis. The MTN market, thus, contrasted with the corporate bond market in which issuers made discrete offerings of long-term paper that were underwritten by a syndicate of dealers.

Bells and Whistles

Over time, as the MTN market evolved, the distinction between the two markets blurred. For one thing, all sorts of bells and whistles were gradually added to MTNs. Today, an MTN could

FIGURE 24–7
Market growth comparison: Public medium-term notes versus public debt*

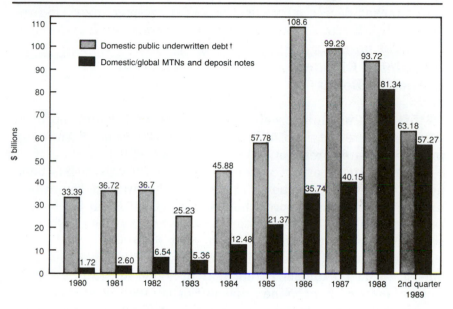

*Chart excludes programs designed exclusively for the Euromarket. Public debt excludes high-yield and collateralized mortgage obligations.

Source: IDD Information Services, Inc., June 30, 1989. Prepared by Goldman Sachs.

have a maturity at issue from nine months to 30 or even 40 years. Also, MTNs have been issued that have call and refunding provisions; utilities have been issuing MTNs as first-mortgage bonds; and thrifts, as noted, have issued collateralized MTNs. Some MTNs have been issued with floating rates. Also, MTNs denominated in foreign currencies have been issued. When an MTN is denominated in a foreign currency, the currency of denomination is likely to reflect not what currency the issuer wants to borrow, but rather conditions in the swap market. Issuers are always driven by their all-in cost of funds; they will do whatever they need to get the lowest all-in cost of funds when swap opportunities and all relevant tax considerations are taken into account.

At this point, the industry's perception of MTNs is that they are really corporate bonds. That is how they are being marketed, as corporate bonds with a lot of flexibility. The upshot of this is that the MTN market is now displacing the short end of the public-debt market. Over the years 1986 to 1988, the public-debt market decreased while the MTN market grew (Figure 24–7).

Remaining Distinctions between MTNs and Corporate Bonds

At this point, one might well ask: What remaining differences, if any, are there between MTNs and corporate bonds? And why might an issuer prefer one over the other?

Since almost every conceivable bell and whistle has been added to one MTN issue or another, the principal remaining difference between corporate bonds and MTNs is that the former are almost always underwritten deals, whereas most MTNs are sold principally by dealers on an agency basis.

Whether a big issuer, like Ford, will at a given moment choose to do an underwritten deal or MTN depends a lot on market environment. Nine times out of 10, an unwritten deal is syndicated. Such a deal guarantees Ford a fixed rate and a fixed sum. Thus, an issuer will go to the corporate bond desk when he wants to lock in a rate for a sizable amount. He uses an MTN program when he wants to dribble out his issue.

At a given point, the MTN market may be saying, "OK, Ford, today, if you just post the rate 40 over in two years, you will get some money, but you may not get a lot." At the same time the underwritten market may be saying, "For 50 over, you can get 100MM or 200MM." Ford's response might be that it does not need all of that money today, so it will go with MTNs. However, if Ford thinks that rates are going up, it will go to the corporate bond desk and say, "Guys, I want my 100MM today." How an issuer uses the two markets is really a function of size, timing, what the issuer feels he wants to accomplish, and when he wants to do so.

The same applies to thrifts. TransOhio has an MTN program and also issues mortgage-backed bonds. If they decide that today they want to do a 200MM, 5-year, callable-at-3 issue, they will ask for bids from a corporate bond desk.

Transaction cost is another factor separating the MTN from the underwritten market. Dealers estimate that it is not cost-effective for an issuer to do an underwritten deal unless he wants at least 100MM of a single maturity. If an issuer wants to do a tranche smaller than that—maybe he is doing a swap on the other side or he has an asset he wants to match fund—he can go to his MTN dealer and ask him to bid as principal on that tranche. By being willing to make such bids, the dealer adds to the issuer's flexibility.

Looking to the future, dealers anticipate that the growth of issuance of MTNs by industrial and utility companies will be explosive. Once such issuers get out of the bullet, underwritten, 30-year-maturity frame of mind and set up an MTN program to complement their underwritten issuance, they end up using MTNs to meet a lot of their ongoing funding needs; typically, such issuers do numerous *reloads:* they file to do new programs and become frequent issuers. Names now in the market include industrials such as Arco Chemical, Hilton Hotels, McDonald's, and General Mills, and utilities such as Niagara Mohawk Power, Florida Power Corporation, and Texas Utilities.

EURO MTNs

In 1986, dealers began the road work—educating potential issuers and investors—required to launch a market in Euro MTNs. Between that year and the outset of 1989, outstandings of Euro MTNs grew from 350MM to 4.4 billion. In early 1989, dealers were estimating that by 1990 Euro MTNs outstandings would hit 8 to 20 billion.

Issuers of Euro MTNs include sovereigns, bank holding companies, double-A European and U.S. corporates, as well as better-known European and U.S. single-A corporates. Naturally, GMAC began early on to borrow in this market and is now a big borrower there.

For a U.S. corporate, like an IBM, there are advantages to being able to offer both domestic and Euro MTNs and to making the choice of which to do a cost-driven decision. Because of its international name, an IBM might, on a given day, find that it could save 10 bp by issuing Euro rather than domestic MTNs. If so, it would go the Euro route. In calculating which route is cheaper, a borrower includes in his all-in cost the coupon, fees, regulatory costs—the works.

In talking to a client these days, a dealer always proposes that a suitable client set up a global MTN program and thereby have all possible borrowing avenues open to it. Most U.S. companies start with a domestic MTN program. The extra cost of then adding a Euro program is minimal. In particular, the rating agencies charge little more for rating a two-part program than for rating a one-part program. One dealer estimates that the additional cost of setting up a Euro MTN program for 100MM is 3 to 5 bp, and a company that does this will have its Euro MTN program up and running for the day it wants to use it.

By country, the principal investors in Euro MTNs are Swiss, British, West German, and offshore U.S. The three dominant types of investors in Euro MTNs are central banks, fund managers, and financial institutions; corporates buy a mere 7% of such paper.

Merrill is the dominant dealer in the Euro MTN market, just as it is in the domestic MTN market. The rest of the crowd comprises Crédit Suisse, First Boston, Sali, S. G. Warburg, Swiss Bank Corp., Morgan Stanley, and Shearson. By design, dealers, in seeking to create a market in Euro MTNs, have followed the pattern established in the highly successful U.S. MTN market.

At issuance, dealers act as agent; and for this, they collect a fee of around 5 bp for every six months of maturity. This fee structure, which is attractive relative to the 3 bp a dealer might get on a sale of Euro commercial paper, means that dealers are making money distributing Euro MTNs. For both issuers and investors, that's desirable: the secondary market in Euro MTNs, which now has good liquidity, will stay that way only if dealers, because they are making money, have an incentive to maintain ever green their commitment to provide liquidity to investors wanting to sell.

Currently, Euro MTNs are mostly fixed-rate and dollar-denominated. Maturities at issuance range from 18 to 36 months, and following the U.S. pattern, they are lengthening as investors become assured that Euro MTNs are indeed liquid. About 40% of the issuance of Euro MTNs is swap driven. The goal of such issuers is to achieve sub-LIBOR funding. Thus, any tightening of the spread between fixed and floating interest rates in the two- to five-year area, by making it more difficult for issuers to achieve that goal, threatens to slow the growth of the Euro MTN market.

In 1988 and early 1989, one complaint of dealers was that demand for Euro MTNs exceeded supply. Said one, "We have more investors than we have paper today." Demand exceeding supply in what appears to be a competitive market makes no economic sense. What seems to be the case is that investors expect a 10 to 20 bp pickup on MTNs over the yield on equivalent Eurobonds to offset the risk of investing in a new instrument lacking proven liquidity. Issuers, for their part, do not want to pay up to issue Euro MTNs. Thus, dealers are currently left trying to convince investors that Euro MTNs and Eurobonds are equivalent instruments and should trade at equivalent yields. So long as the bid-offer spread on Belgian Euro MTNs is 5 bp, whereas on seasoned Eurobonds, it may be 25 bp or more, this should be doable.

In any case, the growth of the Euro MTN market appears to be partly at the cost of slower growth of the syndicated Eurobond market. If so, Euro MTNs are following the pattern set in the U.S.: MTNs displacing underwritten debt.

THE NEXT CHAPTER

In the next chapter, we veer 180 degrees from the private-note market to the muni-note market, that is, to the market for short-term debt issued by state and local government bodies.

CHAPTER 25

MUNICIPAL NOTES

The term *municipal securities* is used in blanket fashion by the Street to denote all debt securities issued by state and local governments and their agencies. The latter includes school districts, state universities, sewer districts, municipally owned utilities, and authorities running toll roads, bridges, and other transportation facilities.

Municipal securities are issued for various purposes. Short-term notes are typically sold in anticipation of the receipt of other funds, such as taxes or proceeds from a bond issue. Their sale permits the issuer to cover seasonal and other temporary imbalances between expenditure outflows and tax inflows. In contrast, the sale of long-term bonds is the main way that state and local governments finance the construction of schools, hospitals, roads, bridges, and other capital projects. Bond issues are also used to fund long-term budget deficits arising from current operations.

Municipal securities fall into two broad categories: general obligation securities and revenue securities. On *general obligation securities* (GOs), payment of principal and interest is secured by the issuer's pledge of its full faith, credit, and taxing power. Usually, this means that the securities are backed by all of the issuer's resources plus its pledge to levy taxes without limits on rate or amount. In some states and localities, such a pledge can be made only on a qualified basis because the issuer's taxing power is limited to some maximum rate. GOs of such issuers are called *limited-tax securities*.

On *revenue securities,* payments of interest and principal are made from revenues derived from tolls, user charges, or rents paid by those who use the facilities financed with the proceeds of the security issue. An example would be bonds used to finance construction of a toll bridge and secured by toll collections.

TYPES OF MUNI SHORT-TERM PAPER

Our focus in this chapter is on short-term, tax-exempt municipal paper. It's perhaps misleading to title this chapter "Municipal Notes" because, today, municipal issuers sell to investors *two* quite distinct types of short-term paper. The first type is traditional, short-term, fixed-rate *notes,* such as TANs and BANs. The second type is what's called variable-rate demand *bonds;* the latter are long-term securities on which the rate paid is reset periodically; on each reset date, investors in such paper have the right to put it back to the issuer's marketing agent; thus, such paper is, from the investor's point of view, short term.

SHORT-TERM, FIXED-RATE NOTES

Traditional, short-term, fixed-rate muni notes typically have an initial maturity of one year or less. Such notes come in several flavors:

Tax Anticipation Notes (TANs)

TANs are issued by municipalities to finance their current operations in anticipation of future tax receipts. Usually, they are general obligation securities.

Revenue Anticipation Notes (RANs)

RANs are offered periodically for much the same purpose except that the revenues anticipated are not general tax receipts. RANs, like TANs, are usually GO securities.

Bond Anticipation Notes (BANs)

BANs are sold to get interim financing for projects that will later be funded long-term through the sale of bonds. Normally, payment on BANs is made from the proceeds of the anticipated bond issue. BANs are usually GOs.

TRANs
Issuers sometimes also sell TRANs, which are a hybrid cross of TANs and RANs. Also, the University of Missouri has even sold *FANs,* fund anticipation notes.

Going DTC (Book Entry)

Most municipal notes used to be issued as *bearer notes* (Figure 25–1). For securities of such short duration, registration wasn't worth the trouble and cost involved.

In 1982, a change in the federal tax code subjected coupon interest on municipal securities issued after 1982 to federal taxation unless those securities were issued in registered form. This provision forced the registration of new muni-bond issues. However, muni notes with an initial maturity of 14 months or less were exempted and continued for a time to be issued in bearer form.

The clearing of securities trades—buys, sells, and redemptions—as well as the payment of coupon interest (dividends in the case of stocks) is far more efficient and cheaper when a book-entry system for tracking and transferring ownership, akin to the one used for Treasuries, is used. For corporate stock and bonds, the Depository Trust Company (DTC) and its sister organization, the National Securities Clearing Corporation (NSCC), operate such a system in the U.S. By expanding and improving their operations, these organizations have in the last few years created the capability to handle at low cost commercial paper, which involves a huge number of distinct issues (distinguished both by name of issuer and by date of maturity), and muni notes as well.[1]

---

[1]For a full description of the workings of the book-entry system as well as of DTC and NSCC, see Stigum's *After the Trade* (Homewood, Ill.: Dow Jones-Irwin, 1988).

FIGURE 25-1
A municipal note

As noted in Chapter 22, some commercial paper has gone DTC. The movement of muni notes to DTC has been much more striking. When a muni-note issue *goes DTC*, the issuer issues a single *global certificate* to the depository, DTC (there are no individual certificates for investors to hold); then, against that global certificate, the DTC-NSCC organization handles in book-entry fashion the clearing of all sales and redemptions of the issue as well as maintenance of records of ownership (recall Chapter 14's discussion of the book-entry system for Treasuries).

In 1988, all of the big muni-note deals with the exception of LA country TRANs were done book entry only. In 1989, the percentage of note issues being done this way was in the 90 to 95% range.

Going DTC saves the issuer the cost of printing individual certificates. In 1986, printing costs for a bond issue ran between $2 and $4 per $1,000 of principal. That cost is probably lower today, but there's another advantage to the issuer of going DTC.

Typically, on a muni-note issue, the lag between sale of the issue to a syndicate and settlement is only five business days. Previously, the issuer had to scramble to get its certificates out of a bond printer on time, to deliver them to its agent bank, and so forth. When an issue goes DTC, issuance becomes easier and smoother.

Municipal variable-rate demand bonds (VRDBs) are also DTC eligible, provided that they meet certain technical requirements set by DTC: having a specified number of days between the record date for income distribution and the actual income payment date, and so on. Many existing VRDS are not DTC eligible, but new issues tend to be because DTC has familiarized issuers with what it requires for an issue to be DTC eligible.

Other Characteristics

The minimum denominations in which municipal notes are issued range from 5,000 to 5MM. The choice depends on whether the market for the issuer's securities is likely to comprise some individuals, only institutions, or only very large institutions. Thus, part of the dealer's job is to advise an issuer as to where the market for his securities is and what minimum denomination he should set. When New York City experienced difficulty selling its notes, dealers suggested that the city lower the minimum denomination on its notes so they would appeal to individuals. That was good advice from dealer to client, but in retrospect it looked like a conspiracy to defraud the little guy. Dealers shy away from suggesting that a borrower with a credit problem issue in small pieces.

Most municipal notes are *interest bearing,* but they may also be issued in *discount* form. At times, discount notes can be sold at a lower rate than interest-bearing notes, but usually the difference is small. One reason for the lack of popularity of discount issues is that, if a municipality, authorized to borrow 400MM, gets only 394MM by selling discount notes, the public will think that the municipality has not exhausted its borrowing authorization; that can pose problems if the municipality needs to borrow more money. A second reason why muni notes aren't sold in discount form is that the price of a muni discount note would be more volatile than that of an interest-bearing note. A third reason muni issuers have resisted issuing zero coupons is that it might create tax complications for investors; the maximum tax-exempt income an investor may earn on a muni discount note is the discount at issue.

Interest on municipal notes that bear interest is normally paid at maturity. Whereas muni bonds all accrue interest on a 30/360 day basis, issuers of muni notes use different bases: 30/360, actual/360, and actual/365.[2] Muni discount notes are redeemed at face value at maturity.

Measured in terms of participating issuers, the muni-note market is broad—something like 47,000 entities issue municipal securities. A community's access to the muni-note market depends on its credit rather than on its size or the size of its issues. Most municipalities are not a New York City that borrows tomorrow what it spent yesterday; and those that aren't have easy access to the municipal market.

The amounts and types of short-term borrowing in which a municipality may engage are controlled by state law. California sets the rules for how Los Angeles County may borrow, and New York State sets rules for how New York City may borrow. Some states' laws on local borrowing are more liberal than others.

VARIABLE-RATE DEMAND BONDS

A *variable-rate demand bond* (VRDB) is a long-term security with periodic rate-reset dates on which the investor may put the paper back to the issuer's marketing agent. VRDBs are issued to finance some sort of project: sewers, hospitals, public educational facilities, and so on. "Usually, VRDBs are issued," noted one marketing agent, "for general capital purposes. We do them for colleges, universities, hospitals—virtually any kind of issuer that has the authority to enter into a variable-rate obligation."

---

[2]Different bases for accruing interest are described in Stigum's *Money Market Calculations* (Homewood, Ill.: Dow Jones-Irwin, 1981), chap. 8. The method of accrual can significantly affect true yield on short notes carrying a high coupon.

The Mechanics

Most VRDBs are long in term, 20 or 30 years. The rate paid on them is reset at specified intervals: there are dailies, weeklies, and monthlies; also, there is a commercial paper mode in which the reset period can be anything from one day (i.e., daily) to 270 days. A VRBD with a six-month rate reset is called a *6-month put bond;* there is also an *annual put bond.*

Typically, a VRDB is backed with a credit line that ensures that there will be sufficient liquidity to meet any and all puts by investors. The cost of such a line to an issuer might range from 5 bp to ⅛.

LOC Paper

If an issuer of a VRDB isn't a top credit, it may also back its paper with a bank *line of credit* (LOC). A bank writing an LOC is writing a credit guarantee: it commits itself to pay off an issuer's bonds should the issuer default. Thus, the credit on such paper is regarded as being that of the bank writing the LOC rather than that of the issuer.

In 1981, probably 90% of the LOCs backing muni issues were written by U.S. banks, 10% by foreign banks. Today, something close to the reverse is true. Foreign banks, especially Japanese, now dominate. The reasons for this flip-flop are several. Foreign banks have an edge with respect to quality: far more foreign banks have triple-A credit ratings than do domestic banks. Also, foreign banks, especially the Japanese, have been extremely aggressive in bidding for such business—so aggressive that they have pretty much priced out domestic banks.

Pricing

For a fee, roughly ⅛, a VRDB issuer's marketing agent will price and sell its paper. The pricing of VRDBs has evolved over time into an increasingly flexible mode. Initially, such paper was priced as a percentage of prime. This created periods when the rate was unfavorable for the issuer and other periods when the rate was unfavorable for the investor. Then, for a time,

VRDB paper was priced at some percentage, 90 to 120%, of the average (based on a survey of various dealers) 30-day, tax-exempt commercial paper rate that Munifax publishes daily at 9:30 A.M. There were, however, times when that approach worked poorly from the marketer's point of view. So, most marketing agents eventually moved to a flexible approach: now, variable-rate paper pretty much sets its own rate, based on the supply of and demand for it. A complicating factor in pricing short-term muni paper is that the market for it is highly technical.

The Put

On VRDB paper, the marketing agent sets the rate daily, weekly, or whatever. The agent has a sales force that places the paper initially. Also, whenever paper is put back to the agent—there are various deadlines—its sales force tries to resell that paper the same day. If its sales force is unsuccessful, two things can happen. The marketing agent will position and finance the paper until it is sold. Or less commonly, the marketing agent will go to the issuer's backstop bank; it would generally be in the year-end pressure periods that the marketer might "drop on a backstop."

Bonding Out

Typically, in the indenture of a VRDB, there is some sort of *call notice,* maybe a 2-week or a 30-day call notice. This feature permits the issuer to notify the holders of its bonds that they will be called to be fixed out. An issuer might find it attractive to call its VRDBs and fix them out, sell them at a fixed rate to maturity, if long-term rates fell to what it viewed as an attractive level.

When a VRDB issuer calls its bonds, investors will say, "Well, I'm not going to own these notes in a month, so I'll put them back now and find something else to fill me." Consequently, an issuer's marketer will typically end up holding such paper the last week before it's bonded out. The marketer continues to reprice the paper on each reset date, which may be daily, right up until the date it becomes a long bond; at the same time, it canvasses its customer base to circle interest in the bond as a long coupon.

Advantages to the Issuer

In selling VRDBs, a principal concern of the issuer is its all-in cost of borrowing. On a VRDB, this will equal the rate paid to the investor, plus a ⅛ marketing fee, plus maybe 5 bp to ⅛ for a liquidity backstop line, plus 15 to 25 bp for an aggressively priced, Japanese-bank LOC, plus 10 to 12 bp for issuing costs. This turns out to be on average a quite attractive rate over time.

The natural and perhaps cheaper alternative for an issuer would be to simply sell tax-exempt commercial paper, and a number of tax-exempt issuers do so. The principal reason an issuer chooses VRDBs over commercial paper is *reissuance risk*. Over the muni market, the fear always hangs that Congress will diminish or eliminate the tax-exempt status of municipal securities. If an issuer is concerned about reissuance risk—fears that at some future point, securities issued by it may be deemed to be taxable—and if it consequently wants to ensure (to the extent possible) that its securities would, in that event, be grandfathered, it will want to issue a long maturity; with commercial paper, each time the paper rolls over, it is deemed to be matured, so such paper might be grandfathered but only for 30 days, not for 30 years. With a VRDB, the issuer has a 20- or 30-year maturity but, in terms of rate paid, the VRDB brings him down the yield curve and makes his rate very competitive with commercial paper rates.

Another advantage for the issuer of a VRDB is the great flexibility with which covenants are written today. Many of the newer indentures for these securities allow the issuer to flip from a daily repricing to a weekly repricing or to what's called a commercial paper mode—he can reprice different pieces of his issue to different maturities, out to 270 days. Also, he often has a conversion feature that permits him to convert the issue from floating rate to fixed rate for the remainder of its life.

A few taxable VRDBs have been done, and for certain purposes, they are useful. However, once a municipal body starts issuing paper that by law is taxable, the reissuance question becomes moot, and it generally uses commercial paper.

Advantages to the Buyer

VRDB paper has a big appeal to investors who want short-term, tax-exempt paper, the demand for which far exceeds the amount of fixed-rate, short-term notes that muni bodies sell. Tax-exempt money funds are major buyers of VRDB paper because, in calculating the average maturity of the securities in their portfolio, they can treat a VRDB as having a current maturity equal to its time to reset—as opposed to its time to maturity.

Between reset dates, the liquidity of such paper may be poor as it trades little in the secondary market. However, on every put date, a VRDB can be sold *at par*.

TAXATION

The most important advantage of municipal securities to the investor is that interest income on them is exempt from federal income taxes and usually from state and local taxes within the state in which they're issued. The federal tax exemption used to be thought to have a constitutional foundation, the courts having ruled that the constitution bars the federal government from imposing on the states without their consent any taxes that would interfere with the latter's governmental functions. Whether federal taxation of interest paid on municipal securities would in fact constitute such interference used, however, to be unclear. Then, in May 1988, the U.S. Supreme Court ruled that Congress could, at will, revoke the traditional tax exemption enjoyed by municipal issuers. This caused brief panic in the muni market, but in the end, most people concluded that Congress was unlikely to do more than whittle further at the edges of and at any new abuses of the municipal tax exemption.

The states have always reciprocated the federal exemption by exempting income on Treasury securities from state taxation. Thus, state and federal taxation of interest income on each other's securities is characterized by *reciprocal immunity*.

1986 Tax Reform Act

In a 1982 tax act, Congress required the registration of muni bonds, since the most obvious demand for bearer bonds came from people seeking to evade capital gains and inheritance taxes and from people wanting to invest, in untraceable bonds, cash they had obtained either illegally or by evading taxes.

Pressures for Change

Later, pressure built up from several sources for further limitations on the municipal tax exemption. First, the federal government was under pressure to reduce its huge budget deficit, and tax-exempt borrowings stood out, as always, as a big revenue loser for the Treasury. Second, pressure for change really heated up in 1983 when muni borrowings for nontraditional purposes began to explode. In particular, Congress took a dim view of muni bodies borrowing tax-exempt funds to provide cheap financing for *private-purpose* projects such as building factories to create local jobs; building pollution-control facilities, stadiums, and convention centers; and funding mortgage subsidies and low-cost loans to farmers and small businesses. Congress wanted to force municipalities back to issuing tax-exempt bonds strictly to finance traditional *public-purpose* activities such as road building, sewers, and fire-fighting facilities. Yet another municipal ploy that raised hackles in Washington was the issuance by muni bodies of tax-exempt bonds to earn arbitrage profits. For example, a city would issue tax-exempt bonds to finance, say, low-income housing; invest the proceeds in Treasuries paying 200 bp over its borrowing cost; and then, after receiving millions in easy profits, redeem its bonds without putting up even one unit of housing.

Provisions of the Act

The 1986 tax act imposed severe limitations on the issuance of muni bonds to finance private-purpose activities; these included shutting out America's top private universities from the tax-exempt market. The act also requires muni issuers to rebate to the Treasury any arbitrage profits they earn, except in quite restricted situations. Finally, the act ended the interest deduction that commercial banks had previously enjoyed when they borrowed to finance their holdings of tax-exempt securities.

Pain on Wall Street
The restrictions imposed by the 1986 tax act were widely anticipated. As a result, there was a bulge of muni-bond issuance in 1985 and a sharp drop-off thereafter. Thus, final enactment of the 1986 tax measure, together with high interest rates, forced city and state financings to fall, between September 1985 and November 1987, by 50%. This in turn caused a dearth in underwriting business for the Street and, at many dealers, losses in once-profitable muni departments.

To the surprise of many, Sali, the leading muni dealer, abruptly abandoned the muni business in October 1987. It was followed by L. F. Rothchild, Bank of America, Continental Illinois, and others; even those dealers who stayed the course slashed personnel in their muni departments, which nationwide had employed more than 15,000 people. Still, most key players viewed it as folly to quit dealing in munis; in their view, the ever-growing need to improve local infrastructures and looming cutbacks in federal spending were likely to sharply increase local-government dependence on the tax-exempt market by the early 1990s.

Gain on Main Street
Wall Street's pain caused a noticeable gain for Main Street borrowers. With new issuance way down, competition by dealers for municipal underwriting deals became ever fiercer. Issuers found themselves in the catbird seat; and as a result, the downtrend in underwriting fees sharpened. It's estimated that between 1984 and the fall of 1987, average underwriting fees on an issue rated A by Moody's fell from $25.57 per $1,000 to $15.03 and that, across the board for all categories of munis, underwriting fees fell by 50%.

Taxable Munis
After passage of the 1986 tax act, some municipalities began to issue taxable bonds to meet taxpayer demands for things such as low-income housing, health-care facilities, and facilities for the

disposal of hazardous wastes. It pained them, however, to have to pay high taxable rates. In response to that pain and to drum up business, dealers initially tried to come up with all sorts of gimmicky ways for muni issuers to sell taxable debt: quasi-flaky proposals such as financings linked to junk bonds and taxable munis denominated in yen. "The only thing they [the proposed new issues] had in common," noted one municipal finance officer, "was that no one had tried them before." Eventually, investment bankers toned down their proposals, since what went down best with both investors and issuers was plain-vanilla, taxable muni bonds.

Equivalent Taxable Yield

To compare yield on a municipal security with that on a taxable security, an investor must compute the *equivalent taxable yield* on the municipal security; that is, the *taxable* return that would leave him with an *after-tax* return equal to the return paid on the municipal security. For example, for a corporation taxed at a 34% marginal rate, the equivalent taxable yield on a new muni note offered at 7% would be 10.60%.[3]

The exemption from federal taxation granted on income from municipal securities applies only to interest income paid by the issuer either directly or indirectly in the case of discount notes. If, due to the rise in interest rates, a municipal security trades below its issue price, the buyer of this security will receive not only tax-free interest income, but a taxable capital gain. Consequently, a municipal security's equivalent taxable yield is lower, relative to its quoted yield to maturity, if the security is selling at a discount than if it's selling at par.

Table 25–1 shows the relationship between yield on a tax-exempt municipal and equivalent taxable yield for investors in selected federal tax brackets. The figures in the table are based on the assumption that the securities are trading at par; also, no account is taken of possible state taxes. As the figures show, the value of the tax exemption granted on income from municipal

---

[3]For the formula, see the appendix to this chapter.

TABLE 25–1
Equivalent taxable yields for selected marginal tax rates

Municipal Coupon (percent)	Investor's Federal Tax Bracket (marginal tax rate)		
	15%	28%	33%
5.0	5.88	6.94	7.46
6.0	7.06	8.33	8.97
7.0	8.24	9.72	10.45
8.0	9.41	11.11	11.94
9.0	10.59	12.50	13.43
10.0	11.76	13.89	14.92

securities is greater the higher the investor's tax bracket. For example, the equivalent taxable yield on a municipal security paying 7% is only 8.24% for an investor whose marginal tax rate is 15%, but 10.45% for an investor whose marginal tax rate is 33%. Thus, the muni market attracts highly taxed investors.

An interesting feature of the muni market is that individual issues tend to have *regional* markets in which they sell best. One reason is the state and local taxes on income. A municipal security issued by New York City offers a much higher equivalent taxable yield to an investor who lives there and must pay high city and state income taxes than it would to an out-of-state investor. A second factor creating regional markets for municipal securities is the tax on intangibles that many states levy. Normally, this tax isn't applied to local issues. Thus, to a resident of a state such as Ohio, which has a low tax on income but a high tax on wealth, ownership of local municipal securities offers a dual tax advantage.

Tax Reform
Because interest income on municipals is tax exempt, a wealthy individual can earn a huge tax-free income by investing in municipals, and many wealthy individuals do just that. Periodically, this practice leads to calls for tax reform, in particular for ending the tax exemption on municipal securities. These calls

are countered by pressure from state and local governments to maintain the present system, which permits municipal issuers to borrow more cheaply than they otherwise could.

The current system of reciprocal tax immunity amounts to an expensive, inefficient federal subsidy of state and local borrowing. It has been estimated that every $1 saved in borrowing costs by municipal issuers costs the federal government $2 to $3 in lost tax revenue. The current system also *narrows* the market for municipals because only investors taxed at high marginal rates—and that leaves out many institutional investors—have an incentive to invest in municipals. A possible alternative to the present system would be for Congress to end the federal tax exemption for municipal issues and provide a federal subsidy for such issues. Proposals of this sort have been made but never enacted.

CREDIT RISK AND RATINGS

Municipal securities, unlike governments, expose the investor to credit risk. Consequently, for a municipal issue to sell in the national market, it must, like commercial paper, be rated. The major providers of this service are Moody's and Standard & Poor's. Some smaller firms also rate issues within individual states.

In rating an issue, a rating service's main concern is whether the issuer will be able to make promised payments of interest and principal. The first thing a rating service looks at is the pledge behind the issue; it may be a general-obligation pledge, a limited-tax pledge, a revenue pledge, or a mix of these. In the case of GO issues, the relationship between the issuer's total debt burden and its tax base is crucial. In the case of municipal bonds, projections into the future necessarily play a major role in any rating; the rating service must ask how the community issuing the security is likely to fare over time: Is it growing? Does it have a diversified economy? Is local government well managed? In the case of revenue bonds, the main focus is on whether the facility being financed—be it a toll bridge or a college dorm—provides a service that the public will

TABLE 25–2
**Ratings given by Moody's and Standard & Poor's on
municipal bonds**

Rating Interpretation	Moody's*	Standard & Poor's†
Best-quality grade	Aaa	AAA
High-quality grade	Aa	AA
Upper medium grade	A	A
Medium grade	Baa	BBB
Speculative grade	Ba	BB
Low grade	B	B
Poor grade to default	Caa	CCC
Highly speculative default	Ca	CC
Lowest-rated grade	C	C

*Bonds of the highest quality within a grade are designated by A-1 and Baa-1.
†For rating categories AA to BB, a plus sign is added to show high relative standing, a minus sign to show low relative standing.

purchase in sufficient quantity to permit the issuer to service its debt.

The information and analysis that go into rating a municipal bond are summarized in a shorthand way by assigning to the issue one of several possible ratings; those given by the national rating services are listed in Table 25–2.

Municipal *notes* are rated separately by Moody in order of declining creditworthiness: MIG 1, MIG 2, MIG 3, and MIG 4. S&P rates muni notes P-1 to P-3.

Investors view the ratings assigned to municipal securities as important indicators of quality and risk, and ratings affect the yields at which notes trade. Direct comparisons are, however, difficult because the yield on a muni note depends on so many things: what type of note it is (TAN, BAN, RAN, or TRAN); how much paper the issue has in the market; and whether the paper is "double tax exempt," that is, also offers local investors exemption from high state and local taxes.

Credit Enhancements

Investors in munis tend to be risk averse; they demand quality and are willing to give up yield to get it. Consequently, a muni-note issuer, if it can't get a MIG 1 rating on its own, will buy a credit enhancement to get that rating. When the concern of the rating agency is not over the issuer's credit but over its ability to roll or refund the notes being rated, a committed facility from a bank may suffice for an issuer to get a MIG 1 rating on its paper. Such a facility takes away market risk—the bond market is terrible when the notes mature; it does not eliminate credit risk because a committed line doesn't require a line bank to bail out a borrower in default. Committed facilities have been used by many muni-note issuers in recent years because the cost of a backstop from a bank was less than the difference in yield between MIG 1 and MIG 2 paper.

When the concern of the rating agency is over the issuer's credit, an LOC is called for. Louisiana would be an example of an issuer that needs an LOC to get a MIG 1 rating for its notes.

A rating is not a once-and-for-all affair. Ratings on individual issues are constantly upgraded or downgraded in light of changes in the position of the issuer. Sometimes, instead of changing its rating of a given issue, a rating services will withdraw its rating altogether. Generally, what this means is that circumstances surrounding the issue have become so uncertain that a meaningful rating cannot be given. It may also reflect the rating service's belief that adverse factors creating the uncertainty may be temporary.

In evaluating a muni credit, investors often look, whether they're investing in notes or VRDBs, to the rating given to the issuer's long-term debt—just as investors in commercial paper consider not only the rating assigned to the issuer's commercial paper, but the rating assigned to its bonds.

Speaking of VRDBs, one dealer noted: "The way we view it out on the trading desk and the way a lot of investors view it is that if you're a double-A or a triple-A credit, you don't need any credit enhancement because Moody's and S&P are saying that they are confident you can pay off your debt. But, if you're an A1 credit, or an A−, or a Baa, an investor is going to say, 'This is getting a little risky, I need someone to step in here and provide a credit backstop—I need a credit enhancement before I'll buy.'"

Today, the credit enhancement of choice is an LOC, typically written by a Japanese bank. One problem with this is that the market can get glutted because investors have a cap on their exposure even on LOCs. An investor doesn't want 50% of his investments in muni paper to carry Japanese-bank LOCs: Today, these banks are all top credits but what if something caused all of them to be downgraded?

Credit Spreads

Poorer muni credits pay more than better muni credits, but it's difficult to generalize about credit spreads because the market for short-term muni paper is so technical; also, credit spreads rise and fall with the general level of interest rates.

"Quality spreads change," noted one muni-note trader, "throughout the year depending on technicals in the market— supply and demand—the level of rates, and investors' perception of a borrower. Right now, Massachusetts is not viewed well because they're having all these problems; their new notes are MIG 2; consequently, their old MIG 1 notes trade a little worse than other MIG 1 paper. NYS is a MIG 1, is liquid, and trades well; the same with Cal RANs. If you use Cals as a benchmark, since that is a June 30th maturity and you price things off that, a MIG 2 is probably 15 bp cheaper; but some MIG 1 names will trade 10 bp off Cals because people do not like the name. The spread, MIG 1 to MIG 2, is about 15 bp in the 1-year area; as you come in on the curve to 6- and 3-month paper, the spread might tighten to 10 bp; if you go further out than one year, where risk is greater, the spread might widen to 20 bp."

Municipal Security Insurance

To increase the marketability of their bonds, some municipal issuers have payment on new bond issues insured for a fee by one of several consortia of insurance companies: FGIC, MBIA, and AMBAC. From the issuer's point of view, such insurance is worth the premium charged if the insurance reduces the coupon interest they must pay by an even larger amount. While insurance of muni bonds has been around for years, insurance of muni notes is more recent.

Most typically, a muni issuer, needing a credit enhancement, will insure its bonds but use an LOC for its notes. Notes are shorter in maturity, and LOCs tend to be 1- to 3-year agreements.

INVESTORS

The distribution of outstanding municipal securities among investor groups differs sharply from that of federal and federal agency securities. Since the single most important advantage of municipals to the investor is the federal tax exemption, the groups holding these securities are those to whom this exemption is worth most.

Corporations

Corporations have become an important part of the tax-exempt market and probably now hold about one third of outstanding tax-exempt notes. The change in the federal tax rate on corporate profits to 34%, combined with some other 1986 changes in the tax code, made corporations big players in the muni-note market. For the first time in memory, the corporate tax rate is higher than the highest marginal rate for individuals, which is causing, at the margin, some flow of municipal securities between corporations and individuals.

How attractive municipals are to nonfinancial corporations depends partly on the amount and type of borrowing they do. The Internal Revenue Code prohibits the expensing of interest on funds borrowed for the purchase or carry of tax-exempt securities. The precise meaning of this prohibition is a gray area because the IRS has issued few definitive rulings despite many requests by investors for such rulings.

Borrowing money to directly fund holdings of municipal securities and expensing the interest paid on the borrowing is clearly a prohibited arbitrage. Many corporations take the position, however, that if they have borrowed money long term to, say, fund construction and don't spend all of the money right away, expensing the interest on the bond issue and simultaneously investing surplus funds in tax exempts is OK.

Also, some corporations with debt outstanding will invest in muni notes funds earmarked for a specific purpose such as funding dividends. The view here is that holding munis is permissible because the investment bridges a gap between an inflow of funds and a specific outflow that must be met. Despite these practices, some hard-nosed corporate lawyers advise a firm against buying munis if it has any debt outstanding.

There is one IRS guideline that states that a corporation's holdings of municipal securities should not exceed 2% of its total assets. Corporate investors are careful to comply with this ruling.

Money Funds and Other Investors

Banks used to be big investors in municipal notes, but since their ability to deduct interest expenses against tax-exempt income was taken away in 1986, their investments in munis have fallen sharply. Muni notes look attractive to a bank only when carry is positive or state tax law provides an incentive for banks to hold locally issued munis.

As banks faded out of the muni-note market, tax-exempt money funds became ever more important buyers of such paper and of VRDBs as well. At the beginning of 1989, tax-exempt money funds held over 65 billion of short-term muni paper. A number of tax-exempt muni funds are single-state funds: they hold solely securities issued in New York State, in California, in Pennsylvania, in Ohio, or in Michigan; these are high-tax states, so for investors living in them, the double tax-exemption that single-state money funds offer has great value.

In several respects, the muni-note market differs significantly from other sectors of the money market. First, it is more of an investors' market; that is, people who buy notes generally have a bona fide need for tax-free income, and they need it to the maturity date. Moreover, on the maturity date they will probably roll their old notes into new "tax frees." That is not to say that investors who expect interest rates to rise won't sell muni notes, but generally, they don't play the yield-curve game or otherwise trade these securities. In the muni-note business, most sales are to investors who hold to maturity. A second distinctive feature of the muni-note market is that individuals become a *huge* factor in this market when rates are attractive.

Institutional investors and tax-exempt money funds, some of which are limited by their prospectuses to buy MIG 1, P-1 paper, will almost without exception buy only high-quality muni notes. The principal buyers of lower-rated paper are individuals—doctors, lawyers, and Indian chiefs—to whom such paper is peddled in small blocks by Merrill and other wire houses. There are probably one or two institutional buyers who will buy MIG 2 notes. The remainder is sold to individuals. That is the difference between the MIG 1 market and the rest of the market.

On the one hand, the sharp lowering, following the 1986 tax act, of the highest marginal tax rates imposed on the incomes of individuals cut the incentive for individuals to hold municipal securities. At the same time, however, the 1986 tax-law changes worked to enhance the attractiveness of munis to individuals because these changes made holding tax-exempt securities one of the few tax shelters left to individuals.

Yield

The yield on a particular muni-note issue depends on the credit of the issuer, the maturity of the issue, the general level of interest rates, and the value of the tax exemption to investors.

Given that the tax rate on corporate profits is 34% and that the top marginal rate on individuals is 33%, it seems reasonable to assume that the average tax rate paid by buyers of muni notes is 33% or somewhat less. This suggests that, credit risk aside, 1-year munis carrying a MIG 1 rating ought to trade at a yield equal to 0.67 times the yield on the year bill (measured on a money market basis). Actually, over the last several years, MIG 1, 1-year muni notes have traded at a yield that tracks the yield on the year bill (Figure 25–2). However, the yield of 1-year muni notes having a MIG 1 rating exceeds by roughly 30 to 80 bp the yield one gets by multiplying the comparable yield on the year bill by 0.67. Presumably, these 30 to 80 bp reflect partly a difference in the credit risk that investors attach to the two

FIGURE 25–2
Over time, municipal notes trade at a spread below bills

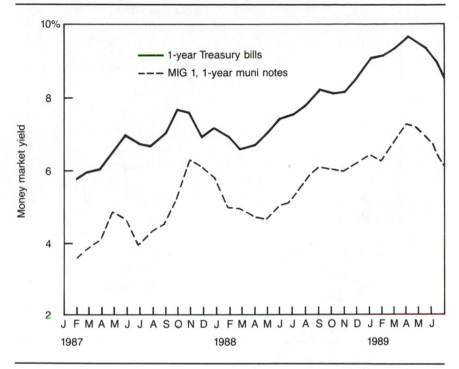

- 1-year Treasury bills
- -- MIG 1, 1-year muni notes

Source: J. P. Morgan Securities, Inc.

instruments; also, it may reflect the drawing into the note market of many investors whose marginal tax rate is less than 33%.

VOLUME OUTSTANDING

As Figure 25–3 shows, the muni-note market, which is currently a 40-billion-a-year market, grew steadily until 1975, after which it took a noticeable dip. Prior to 1974, the typical municipal officer in charge of debt issuance, usually a senior civil servant who had been around forever, operated on the principle that you don't sell long-term munis except when they yield around 3%. Also, in some states, the rate a municipality could

FIGURE 25–3
Volume of municipal notes outstanding

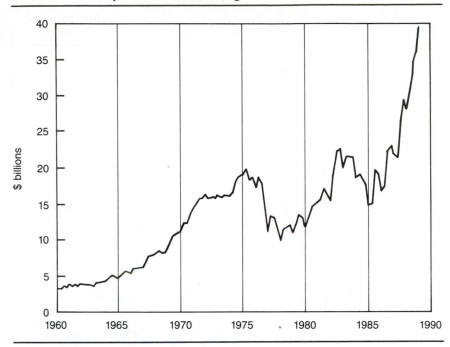

Source: J. P. Morgan Securities, Inc.

pay on bonds was limited by law. Massachusetts, for example, would not permit municipalities to pay more than 2.5% on bonds. The upshot was that, by 1974, a lot of municipal funding officers were rolling large quantities of notes, waiting for low rates that never came.

The dip that began in 1975 in municipal notes outstanding was largely the result of New York City's well-publicized difficulties. These forced the city, which had been a huge issuer of notes, and some other poorer credits out of the note market. New York City's difficulties also caused banks and dealers to take a closer look at the note issues they were underwriting. Before, no one had been concerned about or even knew if the anticipated tax revenues of a municipality selling TANs would suffice to cover these securities. After New York's problems, however, the

TABLE 25–3
Variable-rate demand bonds issued by year*

Year	Amount of New Issuance ($ billions)	Number of New Issues
1980	0.1	30
1981	1.2	80
1982	2.4	198
1983	5.1	278
1984	24.0	877
1985	57.3	2,040
1986	25.6	743
1987	14.2	688
1988	19.8	949
1989 (through July 19)	6.1	332
Cumulative:		
Jan. 1, 1980–July 19, 1989	155.8	6,215

*Includes private placements.

Source: Securities Data Co/Bond Buyer.

banks and dealers started to ask such questions and to say to municipalities, "You can't continually roll notes you can't pay off; you have to fund such accumulated debt long term." As a result some municipalities were forced to refund note issues with bonds at the worst possible moment. The dealers, having turned cautious, saddled some communities that could have borrowed at 5 or 6% in normal times with 20-year problems in the form of bonds carrying a 9 or 10% coupon; on 10MM, that works out to an extra 400,000 of interest a year.

Since passage of the 1986 tax act, issuance of municipal notes has soared. Issuance of VRDBs has followed a quite different pattern. It began in 1980, peaked at 57 billion before passage of the 1986 tax act, and by 1989, seemed to be plateauing at a much lower level (Table 25–3).

THE NEW-ISSUE MARKET

State and local governments and the authorities they create run into short-term needs for cash that are totally separate from their long-term capital needs; when they do, they borrow just

like any other spending unit. Because state and municipal borrowers differ sharply in size and character, the ways in which
they issue notes vary widely, a situation having no parallel
elsewhere in the money market.

At one extreme is the situation where a town needs 50,000
to pay for a fire engine and tax receipts are not coming in until
later. The town goes to its local bank and signs a 50,000 note,
which the bank calls a TAN and sticks in its portfolio. Deals of
this sort, which represent a big percentage of all muni-note
deals (as opposed to issuance), are not made on a competitive
basis. The rate on the note is not a market rate but often something related to prime.

At the other extreme is a situation where the amount of
money to be borrowed is huge, and the loan may not be in the
strict sense a *bridge financing*—one that tides the borrower over
until some identifiable receipt comes in. Often, state or local
governments are doing just what the federal government does:
They have gotten themselves operating on a perpetual cash-
deficit basis, and they are always in arrears because they spend
future taxes before they collect them.

At this end of the spectrum, one might, for example, find
Los Angeles County going to the Bank of America to borrow,
just as the small town in the example above went to its local
bank to get money. Only Los Angeles County needs 950MM
instead of 50,000. This is more exposure than the B of A wants to
one borrower, so—and this is where the analogy between the
little borrower paying for a fire engine and the big borrower
breaks down—the big borrower's bank says, "OK, we'll get you
the money, but we have to do a public offering."

Disclosure

Issuers of municipal bonds obtain their authority to issue such
securities from their state constitution or statutes. In some
cases, this authority is limited, and a favorable vote by the elec-
torate may be necessary before bonds can be issued.

The legality of every municipal bond issue must be approved by an attorney. Such opinions are obtained from bond
attorneys who specialize in municipal law. The legal opinion on

a bond issue is either printed on the back of the bond or attached to the security.

Municipal securities are specifically exempt from the registration requirements of the 1933 Federal Securities Act. The only exception is industrial development issues that do not qualify for tax exemption. However, every issuer of new municipal bonds—to make their issue salable—must prepare a detailed prospectus describing the issue and giving comprehensive data on which investors may judge the issuer's credit.

In the muni-note market, as opposed to the muni-bond market, disclosure on publicly issued securities used to be rather casual. The issuer would put together a one-page statement of condition, a balance sheet, and a flowchart (the municipal equivalent of a cash flow or income statement). This would be certified and possibly, but not necessarily, audited. And that was it.

In the wake of New York City's difficulties, pressure arose for change. Politicians in Washington thought investors in municipal securities deserved more information on the issuer's condition. Also, dealers became concerned over their liability if disclosure on securities they underwrote proved inadequate, so they refused to bid on note issues on which disclosure was incomplete. As a result, issuers of muni notes began to provide detailed information on their condition, often by updating their latest bond prospectus.

Before dealers bid on a muni-note issue or negotiate its sale, they often do their own research on the quality of the issue. They look at the community selling the notes: its tax collections and tax base, who lives there, and the profitability of local industry. Research of this sort protects the dealer. It also gives him a selling point when he approaches retail. Finally, it may permit a dealer to expand his business by finding borrowers with good credit who through no fault of their own find access to the public market difficult. This happened in the 1970s to some New York communities when the difficulties of New York City and New York State cast a pall over all municipal securities issued within the state.

An interesting question with respect to disclosure is why, as New York City slipped deeper and deeper into trouble, Moody's did not react faster in downgrading the city's securities and why the banks that were underwriting the city's issues did not sense trouble sooner.[4] The view of one person close to the scene is that, when the rating services and the bankers looked at the city's statement of condition, they simply couldn't believe that things were as bad as the numbers indicated. In their gut, they thought there must be a mistake somewhere, that the city must have revenues or something it wasn't disclosing. No one could believe that city officials thought that ever-increasing borrowing was a way to balance the city's budget. Unfortunately, the numbers were not lying; the unthinkable was true, and New York City was on the verge of bankruptcy.

Sale of a Public Issue

Municipal notes issued through a public offering are sold by dealers who also make a secondary market in these securities. Today, after a recent thinning of ranks, the top dealers in muni short-term paper are Goldman, Merrill, and Shearson. Erlich Bober is big, but becoming less active. So too are Citi, Morgan, Chase, and Chemical. Bankers has a lot of variable-rate product, but they tend not to trade the market as much. Unfortunately for the banks, most of the business that Sali gave up when it exited munis was captured by nonbank dealers: Goldman, Merrill, Shearson, and others. One reason was that, at the time, banks did not yet have Fed approval to underwrite municipal revenue bonds; ironically, banks got that approval several months later.

Market Technicals

The muni-note market is a technical market due to seasonal peaks in both demand and supply. With respect to the supply, a lot of states work on a fiscal year that ends on June 30; they are issuing notes basically against budgeted, working-capital needs and budgeted revenues and tax receipts. In many cases, a state

---

[4]In the spring of 1975, New York City's notes were rated MIG 1 by Moody's even after the market would no longer accept new issues of its debt securities.

can't issue notes until it gets its budget fixed, which states are often slow to do. Consequently, several billion of California notes, which are going to mature on June 30 the following year, may come to market in a lump early in August.

During certain periods of the year, one can predict with certainty that rates are going to trend upward due to withdrawals of funds from the market. April 15 and the three following weeks are one such period. Then, there are various corporate tax dates that usually cause a small blip in rates.

Year-end produces a big blip in rates due both to demand and supply factors. For certain types of muni financings, December 31 has always been a cutoff date, so there tends to be a glut of new product then; and at the same time, there's some flow of corporate funds out of the market. "During those three periods," noted one muni trader, "the marketing agents [for VRDBs] want to have the most flexibility. Basically, we can set rates where supply and demand dictate, and rates have gone, temporarily, as high as 14 in a financing environment where, three weeks before, they were 5¾. . . . We have these periods in November and December when there is a lot of issuance, and all of a sudden, we get crossover buyers."

Competitively Bid Deals

About 70% of all publicly offered muni-note issues used to be sold to dealers through competitive bidding as opposed to negotiated deals. Today, the reverse is probably true.

In the muni-note market, the overriding philosophy is that of investment banking—developing a constituency that follows the securities being bid on and getting these securities sold. Thus, a muni-note dealer, in bidding on and positioning securities, is more interested in what the muni-note market is likely to do than in market rates in general. He wants, for example, to know how many highly taxable investors are currently in the market.

Large issuers of muni notes who want bids will advertise coming issues in *The Daily Bond Buyer* or elsewhere to get as many bids as possible. Smaller issuers, in contrast, may send notices of sale to only four or five friends. Noted one dealer, "You have to hustle to find out what's there. It's not like a bill auction where the whole world is invited."

Today, big muni-note deals, those for 500MM or more, are typically done on a negotiated basis, while it is the smaller deals that are competitively bid. If a dealer is doing a competitive bid, he'll take orders against it, but he can't sell the issue short because he doesn't know if his bid will win. Instead, he goes to his retail and says, "I think to buy this deal, I'm going to have to bid a 5.80 or just behind it. I will take an order from you at a 5.80 and bid against that order." If the dealer's retail says, "OK, I'll give you an order for 25MM at a 5.80," the dealer will take that order and bid a 5.81 against it—his fulfilling the order is contingent on his buying some or all of the deal. "Most likely," noted one trader of muni notes, "the customer who gives me an order, if he really wants the notes, is also giving the order 'away' [to other dealers]."

In a competitive bid situation, various outcomes are possible. "Maybe," noted the same dealer, "my bid at a 5.81 loses, and I didn't buy it. Bankers bid a 5.80; he buys the whole thing; and now he reoffers at a 5.75. No other dealer is going to short the issue to sell to retail. Bankers controls it until he sells some. Alternatively, it might be that Bankers bought 25MM at a 5.80, I bought 25MM at a 5.81, Merrill bought 50MM at a 5.78, and Citi bought the rest at a 5.87. Now, we all own them at different levels. I can decide that I want to sell mine, thinking that Merrill or Bankers might give me a bid just to support their positions or that Citi might want to own more. Or someone else might say, 'Hum, the market does not feel good; the notes are in a bunch of different hands. I am going to short them—put them up for the bid. They won't know who's selling; and maybe, I can buy back any notes I sell later at a cheaper price.'"

Negotiated Deals

On a big negotiated deal, maybe 3.9 billion Cals, there will be a senior manager, say it's Goldman, and a number of comanagers. Goldman and each of the comanagers might have a *liability* of 200MM, which means that, if the deal is poorly received, each is responsible for taking down 200MM at the negotiated price.

Also, each comanager typically gets some *retention,* which means that no matter how well sales by Goldman go, each comanager can count on getting at least 30MM of notes to sell to its customers. Assuming that the deal isn't a complete bomb, instead it does well, orders coming into Goldman will probably be over 2 billion; those orders—maybe for 50 or 100MM each— might be from other dealers, from funds, from corporations, from insurance companies, or from other retail.

On a negotiated deal, the issuer pays a management fee which the managers split on a pro rata basis, according to their individual liabilities. Also, if there's retention, a comanager is assured of getting a certain amount of notes. And, if the deal is priced properly—it's going to do well—he'll want those notes to offer because a negotiated deal is always priced with a spread.

Also, there's a concession in takedown, just as there is in bonds. For example, suppose a New York State deal is priced (as one was) at 7% *less a dollar plus a dollar.* This means that the managers get to take down any retention due them at a price of $1,000 minus $2; this works out to a dollar price of 99.80, which, on 1-year paper carrying a 7% coupon, is equivalent to a 7.21 yield.[5] If a customer comes into Goldman presale, say it's Merrill Fund, not Merrill the dealer, and says, "I want 50MM," he gets his paper at 7% less a dollar, which works out to a dollar price of 99.90 and a yield of 7.10. The extra 10 bp offered presale is an enticement to Merrill Fund and to other customers to come in and buy notes early.

In our example, Merrill Fund gets a concession that's half the total takedown of $2. He might assign 10MM or his purchase to one of the comanagers, say, J. P. Morgan Securities, in which case Morgan would get $10,000 on the presale. If, alternatively, Merrill Fund waits to buy his 50MM until after the presale period when comanagers have gotten their retention, he will—

---

[5]The calculation: at the end of one year, the note buyer gets, for investing $99.80 today, $100 of principal *plus* $7 of interest. So, on a simple interest basis, his annual return is given by the expression:

$$1 - \$107/\$99.80 = 0.0721$$
$$= 7.21\%$$

assuming the deal is going well—have to pay a dollar price of 100, which means that he'll get a return of 7 flat, and the selling dealer or dealers will get the total takedown of $2 per $1,000, or $50,000 on Merrill Fund's purchase of 50MM notes. Or maybe the issue will take off, and dealers who get retention will be able to sell at yield below 7.

In a syndicated deal, of the sort we've described, the issuer pays the "less a dollar, plus a dollar" spread plus management fees; so the total spread might be as much as $2.50. That depends on various factors, including the size of the issue.

Big deals, such as New York State's 3.9-billion issue, are negotiated; and the dealers syndicate the liability. The alternative of competitive bidding is viewed as unattractive because, on a big issue, the bidding can get sloppy—have a big tail if the bidding is set up like an auction of T bills. However, when New York City and Texas have come, respectively, with a 1.1-billion issue and a 500MM issue for competitive bids, the dealers, in bidding, joined to form syndicates; and the bids received by these issuers seemed decent. Still, issues over 500MM are generally negotiated.

Because of market technicals, it's hard to generalize about the relationship between the size an issuer comes with and the rate he gets. Since the fiscal years of most municipalities end on June 30, a ton of notes mature then; after that, there's typically little new issuance until mid-July. The huge amount of supply that comes from mid-July through early August hurts the issuer who has a lot to do in that period: his notes have to compete with those of so many other issuers. Also, if an issuer comes with big size—New York State issues 3.9 billion notes, which is a lot for the market—he may get an attractive rate, as New York State did, because individuals come in to buy in a big way.

Wi Trading

New note issues are typically sold *settlement from dated date,* which means that they settle on the day they are dated and thus start to accure interest. However, the dated date and the settlement date don't always coincide. Sometimes notes settle later than the date that they're dated. During the period between sale and settlement, notes trade *wi*—in some cases, for weeks.

The wi period is an attractive time for a dealer to trade notes because he can do so without putting up any money and thus has no carry cost. One trader estimated, in July 1989, that, with funds at 9¾, it cost her close to 1 bp a day to hold notes. One disadvantage of delayed settlement to an issuer is that a lot of money funds won't buy such paper because they don't know what their cash flows will be on settlement day.

THE SECONDARY MARKET

Because muni investors tend to buy notes and put them away, secondary-market trading in them is a pale affair compared to that in, say, bills. Basically, the muni-note market is a placement market, not a trading market.

The Brokers

There are now three muni-note brokers: Chapdelaine, J. J. Kinney, and Cantor Fitz. They have no screens, and their volume has dropped sharply in recent years. Activity varies a lot day to day, with January, December, and June tending to be big months.

"Every morning," noted one trader, "I come in, immediately call each of the brokers, and ask, 'Do you have any opening markets today?' Or I might give the broker a market. I might ask Chapdelaine, 'Do you have a market on NYS TRANs today? What are your markets on States, Cals, Cities, Texas?' I'd also ask him about any miscellaneous names I might be following. A lot of times, the most liquid names have a two-way market: for NYSs there is always a bid and an offer. There might be only one bid out there and four offerings; the broker might say, 'I've got a 5.75 bid, good for 5MM. It's in one spot. Behind that, my next best bid is an 80. I have four people offering at a 74; and behind that, I have 70 offerings.' Then I might say, 'What's the market on LA counties?' He might reply, 'Well, on the Street, there is only 20MM, one guy's holding them [the float on LAs is only 20MM], he's offering them at 5.80. I think, if he saw a bid close to that, he might be inclined to hit it.' So right there, I know that, because one guy is holding all of the LA counties in the Street, there isn't going to be another offering—it'd be very risky to short it. Whereas with NYSs, there is a total issue size of 3.9 billion, and they are always coming in and out of the market. So there might be someone willing to offer them who doesn't own them. Also, there's typically a bid out there—people have an interest at certain levels."

Trading in the Secondary Market

Every dealer in muni notes will make a market to customers in anything they have sold him, and dealers do some secondary trading to satisfy customer needs. Investors, however, work their muni-note portfolios less hard than their taxable portfolios; they buy tax exempts for yield, taxables for trading. One deterrent to trading muni notes is taxes. An investor who, when rates decline, sells munis at a gain and replaces them with a lower coupon trades a future stream of tax-exempt income for a current taxable gain; this amounts to giving away money to the IRS. Muni dealers generate some secondary-market trading when they distribute new issues; they track their customers' holdings and might, to get a new 9-month state note sold, encourage customers to swap out of an old 8-month note for some yield pickup.

The inside or interdealer market in muni notes is active when dealers are long securities. The job of a muni-note dealer is distribution, and he is successful to the extent that he pushes out to retail one issue after another. It is when such distribution fails on one or several issues and a lot of securities are backed up on the Street that trading between dealers really comes alive, with every dealer trying to get back his bid.

Muni-note dealers quote runs to each other only occasionally in a few actively traded issues. They deal with each other more on a "can do" basis. A dealer will call another to ask for a bid on a particular issue, and the other dealer will tell him what side of the market he's on. In muni notes, dealers are not, as in governments, secretive about their positions. Usually, they advertise them in the hope that other dealers will work on them.

In the interdealer market, quotes are always good for 1MM, but an average trade is for 5MM. Spreads are narrow and may approach those in the bill market when blocks of high-quality paper trade.

A dealer in muni notes *cannot* short an outstanding issue because in doing so he would be creating new tax-free interest, something that only states and municipalities may do. A dealer can short municipal issues while they are trading on a "when, as, and if issued" basis, but that's risky. The issues are so distinctive and discrete that the substitution and swapping capabilities that are present in corporates and governments do not exist. If the dealer can't find the actual securities to cover his short, he faces a huge legal problem.

Price Volatility

Interest income on municipal securities is tax exempt, but capital gains and losses on such securities are treated for tax purposes in the same way as on taxable securities. Because of this asymmetry in tax treatment, when interest rates move, municipals are more volatile in price than are taxables.

To see why, suppose that TANs with a 6-month maturity are issued at a 5.30 and 6-month bills at 8. Later, interest rates rise, and the bills issued at 8 fall sufficiently in price to yield 9. The TANs issued at 5.30 also fall in price, and as they do, investors in them acquire short-term taxable capital gains. Assuming that investors' average marginal tax rate is 34%, this means that the TANs must rise one and a half times as fast in yield as (fall faster in price than) the bills to continue to offer investors an equivalent taxable yield. Should interest rates now reverse trend and start to fall, the muni notes would rise in price faster than the taxable bills, again for tax reasons.

GLOBALIZATION

There have been a few muni Euro issues and even offerings of yen-denominated samurai bonds, but generally globalization hasn't hit the muni market. Once a muni issuer sells abroad, he loses the value of the federal tax exemption on his paper, so foreign issues are of interest to muni issuers only if they're selling taxable paper.

THE NEXT CHAPTER

In our final chapter, we focus on money funds. Today, these funds together invest approximately 340 billion in money market instruments. While money funds may seem a touch old hat these days, their creation, 15 years ago, forced a revolution—the deregulation in the U.S. of rates paid by depository institutions; the latter, because it came inexcusably late and at a time of historically high interest rates, had impacts still with us—one being the consequent efforts by Congress to open up new areas of business to thrifts and the eventual thrift crisis.

APPENDIX TO CHAPTER 25

Calculating the *taxable* yield that's equivalent to a tax-exempt yield is trivial; still, it seems to create problems for some people. Speaking of this calculation, one fund manager quipped: "The standard answer for most people seems to be to take out their calculators and divide the [tax-exempt] yield by one minus the square root of their telephone number." Actually, nothing that difficult is required.

Let

r_{te} = the tax-exempt rate paid as a decimal

r_t = the equivalent taxable rate as a decimal

T = the taxpayer's federal marginal rate as a decimal

Then, for the ratio of the yield on a taxable security to the *equivalent* to the yield on a tax-exempt security, the following relationship must hold:

$$(1 - T)r_t = r_{te}$$

Solving this equation for r_t, we get

$$r_t = \frac{r_{te}}{(1 - T)}$$

Thus, if $r_{te} = 7\%$ and $T = 34\%$, then

$$r_t = \frac{0.07}{(1 - 0.34)}$$
$$= 0.1060$$
$$= 10.60\%$$

CHAPTER 26

MONEY MARKET FUNDS

A mutual fund is a device through which investors pool funds to invest in a diversified portfolio of securities. The investor who puts money into a mutual fund gets shares in return and becomes in effect a part owner of the fund. Professional management is provided by an outside investment company, which charges the fund a fee equal to a small percentage of the fund's assets. Mutual funds were originally developed to give people an opportunity to invest in a diversified and professionally managed portfolio of stocks or bonds—some funds invest in both. Certain equity mutual funds aggressively seek long-term growth and capital gains, others a high level of current income.

In the mid-1970s, when money market rates soared above the lids that regulators imposed on the rates that depository institutions were permitted to pay on time deposits, the stage was set for the birth of a new breed of mutual funds—funds that were able to offer investors high return plus high liquidity by investing in high-yield, short-term debt securities. Mutual funds of this sort, known as *money market funds* (or, more simply, *money funds*) first appeared in 1974; their number grew rapidly: zero in early 1974, 40 in 1978, 450 in 1982, and 572 in mid-1989.

RAISON D'ÊTRE

Money funds were initially designed to meet the needs of the small investor, for whom investing in money market securities is awkward on several counts. Minimum denominations are high. Buying securities and rolling them involves more work than some people care to do, and having a bank or broker do the job may involve high transaction costs. Also, for some instruments, yields on small denominations are lower than those on large denominations. Finally, an investor with limited funds can't reduce risk by diversifying: by buying a mix of different names or instruments.

None of these difficulties exists for a money fund, which pools the resources of many investors. Because such a fund handles large sums of money, high minimum denominations pose no problem. Transaction costs in terms of both money and time spent per dollar invested are minuscule. Finally, a money fund is able to buy a wide range of securities, thereby reducing credit risk to a negligible level.

HOW THEY WORK

Forgetting technicalities and legal niceties, a money fund resembles a special bank. This special bank accepts demand deposits only, pays daily interest on these deposits, invests all its deposits in money market instruments, holds no reserves, and keeps only a very small profit margin for itself. For the investor, the only significant differences between banking at such a special institution and putting money in a money fund are that (1) deposits in a money fund are *not* federally insured as are bank deposits, and (2) there are minimum-denomination requirements to meet on initial deposits and on certain types of withdrawals.

Investing in a Fund

Money funds do not accept deposits; they sell shares—typically $1 buys one share. All funds calculate interest daily on outstanding shares and credit interest to the investor's account periodically, usually at the end of the month. Interest credited to an investor's account buys him more shares. Money funds do not issue share certificates. Instead, they send to each investor periodic statements showing his deposits, his withdrawals, and interest credited to his account.

Initially, some money funds were load funds; that is, some of the money invested went to pay a commission to the broker who sold the fund. Today, however, no-load funds are the rule, which makes sense, since money funds are used by many investors much as a checking account—a place to hold temporary liquidity; and deposits and withdrawal are therefore frequent.

Withdrawing Funds

A depositor may withdraw funds from a money fund anytime on demand and without penalty. Typically, withdrawals can be made by requesting a fund to send the investor a check or to wire out funds from his account at the fund to an account at a commercial bank. A third method of withdrawing funds is by writing a check. Most money funds have set up an arrangement with a commercial bank under which the investor is supplied with checks and can make withdrawals and payments simply by drawing a check against that bank. Generally, the check must be for some minimum amount—$250 or $1,000. When the check is presented to the bank against which it is drawn, that bank covers it by redeeming the required number of shares in the investor's money-fund account.

Where the Money Goes

Since money invested in a money fund is available to the investor on demand, a money fund must be prepared for large and unpredictable withdrawals (redemptions of shares for cash). To do so, all funds hold a portfolio of highly liquid money market instruments. In mid-1989, the average current maturity of securities in the portfolios of all money funds was 46 days (Table 26–1).

Generally, money funds can meet the cash requirements generated by redemptions through the inflow of funds from new investors plus payments on maturing securities. However, if these sources prove inadequate, a fund can generate additional cash by selling assets in its portfolio. Since money funds hold

TABLE 26–1
Summary of money fund activity (7/19/89–7/25/89)

Number of Money Funds	Net Assets ($MM)		7-Day Yield (%)	30-Day Yield (%)	Compound 7-Day Yield (%)	12-Mo. Yield (%) (6/89)	Avg. Mat. (days)
		Taxable Money Funds					
46	14,355.0	U.S. Treasury	8.28	8.38	8.62	7.98	26
56	19,334.7	U.S. Government and Agencies	8.44	8.56	8.80	8.28	33
		Donoghue's MONEY FUND AVERAGES™/Government	**8.37**	**8.48**	**8.72**	**8.14**	**30**
90	50,644.1	Prime	8.57	8.70	8.94	8.45	41
48	53,776.8	Prime and Euro$	8.65	8.78	9.03	8.43	45
39	101,824.3	Prime and Euro$ Yankee$	8.67	8.81	9.05	8.54	47
6	1,266.0	Aggressive	8.61	8.76	8.99	8.51	60
73	72,105.6	Institutions-only	8.85	8.99	9.24	8.76	32
23	10,764.4	Special Purpose	8.66	8.80	9.04	8.55	50
381	324,070.9	Total Taxable Assets					
		Donoghue's MONEY FUND AVERAGES™/All Taxable	**8.60**	**8.73**	**8.97**	**8.44**	**41**
		Tax-Free Money Funds					
101	40,098.8	Stockbroker and General Purpose	5.56	5.68	5.72	5.66	47
24	12,840.0	Institutions-only	5.77	5.90	5.93	5.92	39
59	12,903.0	State-Specific SB & GP	5.31	5.44	5.45	5.45	55
7	2,364.8	State-Specific Inst-only	5.41	5.54	5.56	5.65	34
191	68,206.6	Total Tax-Free Assets					
		Donoghue's MONEY FUND AVERAGES™/All Tax-Free	**5.51**	**5.63**	**5.66**	**5.63**	**46**
572	392,277.5	Grand Total—All Funds					

Source: The Donoghue Organization, Inc.

large amounts of short-maturity securities, the risk of capital loss on such sales due to adverse movements in market price is small.

Money funds seek to offer the investor not only liquidity and high return, but *safety of principal*. The typical fund is restricted, as noted in its prospectus, from doing any of the following: investing in stocks, convertible securities, and real estate; buying on the margin; effecting short sales; trading in commodities; acting as an underwriter of securities; and placing more than 5% of total assets in the securities of any one issuer.

The first money funds invested only in taxable securities. Then in the 1980s, money funds that invested in tax-exempt municipal paper were created.

The bailiwick of money funds is the money market. As a group, these funds place almost all the monies invested with them in short-term governments and agencies, negotiable CDs, BAs, repos, commercial paper, and more recently, muni tax-exempt paper. There are, however, differences in practice. A few conservative funds stick to governments and agencies. The more aggressive hold a wider range of money market instruments, including Yankee and Euro CDs (Tables 26–1 and 26–2).

Accounting Procedures

When the money-fund industry was new, different people with different ideas and sometimes different objectives came to the SEC with their proposals for setting up a money market mutual fund; one would say, "We are going to account this way for capital gains and losses," and another would say, "We are going to account that way." Since every proposal looked reasonable, the upshot was that the SEC responded with an OK in each case. Thus was born a new class of institutions, with assets destined to rise from zero to $392 billion over 15 years; and each firm comprising it was using one of four different accounting methods.

Most money funds mark their portfolios to market daily, a sound practice, but one that raises the question of how capital gains and losses, realized and unrealized, should be treated—as net income, as a change in net asset value, or what. Some mark-

TABLE 26–2
Money-fund assets in the fourth quarter of 1988* ($ billions)

Demand deposits and currency	0.7
Time deposits	32.8
Repos	41.7
Foreign deposits	29.7
Credit market instruments	224.7
Treasury securities	11.6
Federal agency paper	18.4
Tax-exempt obligations	65.7
Open market paper	129.1
Miscellaneous	8.5
Total assets	338.0

*Does not precisely add due to rounding.

Source: Board of Governors of the Federal Reserve, Flow of Funds Division.

to-market funds that wanted a steady income stream choose to reflect any realized or unrealized capital gains or losses as changes in the net asset value of their shares. Other funds that wanted to maintain a constant net asset value choose to include realized and unrealized gains and losses in their daily dividends. Still other funds that wanted a constant net asset value, for example, because they sold their fund to bank trust departments, municipal bodies, and other institutions that could assume no risk of capital loss, took the straight-line-accrual approach in accounting. Such funds make it a practice to hold money market instruments in which they invest to maturity; they do not mark their portfolios to market daily; and the interest they credit each day to investors equals the average yield on all securities in the fund's portfolio.

A fourth approach is to run what's called a *penny-rounded* fund. Such a fund sets net asset value at $1 initially. It then marks its portfolio to market and reflects capital gains or losses in the net asset value of its shares. However, these funds round their net asset value to the nearest penny, that is, to the second decimal place; this means that their net asset value could deviate from $1 only if a huge change occurred in market values. On a yield basis, penny-rounded funds are almost equivalent to the amortized-cost funds.

While each of the four accounting schemes sketched above seems reasonable and can be defended as achieving some desirable objective, the existence of differences in the way money funds report net income can and does on some days distort by hundreds of basis points comparisons of current yield among different funds.

To minimize distortions caused by accounting differences, an investor comparing several funds should look at what is called in the industry a *hypothetical:* If $1,000 were put in each fund and left there for one month, what rate of return would each fund have yielded the investor? The Arthur Lipper Service quotes the yields paid by different money funds on such a basis.

Hot Money Can Burn

Most money funds mark their portfolios to market daily to reflect any appreciation or depreciation that has occurred in the value of their assets due to fluctuations in interest rates. Some funds reflect such appreciation or depreciation in the value of their assets through minor changes in their share values. Others reflect it by including changes in asset values in the interest return they credit to shareholders' accounts.

A few money funds make it a practice to hold money market instruments they have acquired to maturity. They do not mark their portfolios to market daily, and the interest credited each day to the investors in such funds equals the average yield on all securities in the fund's portfolio. A few individuals on the Street and at the SEC have voiced concern that such straight-line-accrual funds could operate like a Ponzi scheme—Ponzi, in honor of Charles Ponzi, a Boston swindler who ran a con game in which early investors were paid off with funds supplied by later investors, leaving nothing for the last investors getting out.

How does Charles Ponzi enter the picture with respect to straight-line-accrual funds? Suppose short-term interest rates were to rise sharply; then the market value of the securities in the fund's portfolio would be temporarily depressed. Suppose also that a large number of investors simultaneously redeemed their fund shares for cash. Conceivably such a fund might be forced to sell off some of its securities at a loss and the actual *market* value of the securities backing its remaining outstanding shares would fall below its fixed share value. In that case, if redemptions continued, the fund would run out of money before all shares were redeemed.

This eventuality, while theoretically possible, has a small probability of occurring. For it to happen, interest rates would have to rise sharply *and* rapidly, and *all* money invested in the fund would have to be *hot* (very sensitive to interest rates)—an improbable constellation of conditions.

Nevertheless, the SEC, after considering the question for two years, ruled that it would not allow amortized cost valuation for debt instruments with a current maturity of more than 60 days because such valuation does not reflect the "fair value of the underlying portfolio."

The SEC's ruling was challenged by a number of funds, in particular, funds serving clients such as bank trust departments and local government bodies that were unwilling or unable to invest funds in an instrument to which even a small market risk attached. In response, the SEC exempted from its ruling funds which agreed to limit their sales to institutions and to require an initial minimum investment of $50,000. The exempted funds also agreed to limit the average maturity of their portfolios to no more than 120 days, to buy no securities with a current maturity of more than one year, and to severely restrict turnover in their portfolios.

Ironically, the only money fund that ever came close to experiencing difficulties of the sort envisioned by those who feared a Ponzi-type scenario was an institutional fund administered by that most respected of dealers, Salomon Brothers, and advised by First of Chicago.

Most money coming into money funds, especially from small investors, is *hot* (interest-rate sensitive) on the way in but *cold* on the way out; when the rates money funds can pay soar, money pours in, whereas when the rates they can pay fall, money is slow to move out. Investors who put money into a money fund for rate reasons end up keeping their money there, even when money market rates fall, because they like the convenience the funds offer.

In the summer of 1980, Sali's fund, Institutional Liquid Assets (ILA), extended maturities on the incorrect view that money market rates were going to stay put or decline. Instead, rates rose so sharply that in September the fund's institutional clients started withdrawing large sums from ILA and putting that money either into other funds that had stayed short and consequently yielded a higher rate than ILA or high-yielding money market instruments. To fund these withdrawals, ILA had to sell assets. To prevent the sale at depressed prices of its relatively long-term assets from causing a decline in the net asset value of ILA shares, a rescue package was required: First of Chicago returned 1MM of previously paid advisory fees to ILA, and Sali completed the package by buying 228.5MM of governments from ILA at roughly 0.7MM above their market value.

The whole episode, which isn't likely to be repeated, has several ironic touches. First, the fund that had to be rescued had the most impeccable administrator and advisor imaginable. Second, had the fund catered to small investors, it would probably not have been penalized by large withdrawals for mistakenly extending maturities; doctors, lawyers, and Indian chiefs don't make it a daily practice to compare yields on money funds with yields on money market instruments. However, some corporate and other institutional investors do.

GROWTH OF MONEY FUNDS

Over time, money funds have grown at an astonishing pace (Figures 26–1 and 26–2). To give perspective, we note that, in July 1989, taxable funds had total assets of 324 billion; three months earlier, the total outstandings of BAs, commercial paper, and T bills were, respectively, 62 billion, 493 billion, and 414 billion. "Right now," noted one dealer, "money funds are the driving force on the investor side in the U.S. money markets."

FIGURE 26–1
Growth of taxable money fund assets (June 1979 to June 1989)

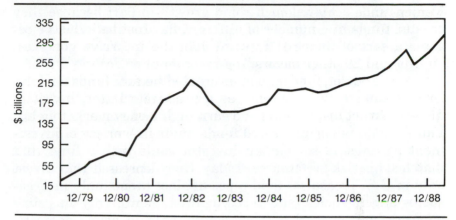

Source: The Donoghue Organization, Inc.

FIGURE 26–2
Growth of tax-free money fund assets (December 1981 to June 1989)

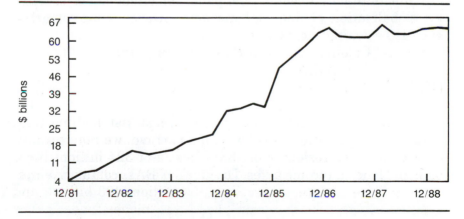

Source: The Donoghue Organization, Inc.

Pick Your Flavor

Money funds achieved such rapid growth in part because they created funds in a number of different flavors; the industry became a sort of financial Howard Johnson's: "We've got plain vanilla and 29 other flavors."

At the outset, fund managers created taxable funds for John Doe, consumer, who couldn't, as a practical matter, invest in money market instruments and earn high money market yields. Later, fund managers created funds having a variety of investment parameters so that an investor could pick a fund that matched his risk preferences. Today, there are funds that invest only in U.S. Treasuries (and repos against them), only in Treasuries and agencies (and repos against them), only in prime domestic money market instruments, only in prime domestic and Euro money market instruments, and only in domestic prime and Euro and Yankee instruments (Table 26–3).

Most recently, Dreyfus created its Worldwide Dollar Money Market Fund, which invests on a fully hedged basis in prime money market instruments worldwide; this means, for example, that the fund might buy a high-yield, Aussi-dollar, short-term asset and hedge the resulting currency risk by selling Aussi dollars forward. That's called covered *interest arbitrage,* and big corporates have long been doing it; years ago, the play was to buy Canadian-dollar commercial paper on a hedged basis. With the globalization of financial markets, covered interest arbitrage is becoming increasingly common for both investors and borrowers. Fidelity's Spartan Fund is taking the same tack as Dreyfus's Worldwide Fund.[1]

The first *tax-exempt* money funds were designed to produce income that was exempt from *federal* income taxes. Then the industry went on to create *state-specific* funds that, by investing in municipal securities issued within a particular state, produce income that, for residents of that state, is exempt from both state and federal income taxes. Dreyfus's New York Tax Exempt

---

[1]We talked about covered interest arbitrage, without calling it that in the commercial paper chapter. Also, we discussed the hedging of foreign-exchange risk in Chapter 18.

Fund gives a New York City resident a *triple* tax exemption: from federal, state, and city income taxes.

The money-fund industry also created *institutions-only* funds, both taxable and tax-free. Today, such funds hold slightly over 87 billion in assets (Table 26–1).

There are also special-purpose funds that go after a specific niche market. A good example is Federated's Liquid Cash Trust, which, besides investing in governments and bank CDs, may also sell Fed funds. Federated designed this fund specifically for depository institutions, and only such institutions may invest in it.

Central-Asset Accounts

Last but not least, there are *central-asset accounts,* of which Merrill's CMA account was the first and is today by far the largest.

Most brokers offer their clients an in-house money fund or some other money fund in which clients may park investment proceeds, funds temporarily withdrawn from the market, or new funds awaiting investment in stocks and bonds. Merrill came up with the brilliant idea that, if a broker were to add some fancy bells and whistles to such an account, it would generate a lot of large, new accounts. The name Merrill gave to its innovative account, introduced in 1979, was *Cash Management Account (CMA)*; the bells and whistles on this account, which requires a minimum deposit of $20,000 in cash or securities, are (1) a CMA checking account (with checks cleared through Bank One of Georgia) that pays interest at money market rates, (2) a weekly sweep of monies coming from a client's brokerage account into his CMA account, and (3) a free Visa card with a line of credit equal to the full amount by which any securities the client has deposited with Merrill could be margined. In lending to customers using stocks and other securities as collateral, Merrill is doing nothing banks have not and could not have done for years. Banks just never thought of making the procedure of borrowing against such collateral so easy and automatic. In July 1989, Merrill's CMA account ranked as the largest money fund; its

TABLE 26–3
Money funds with assets over $1 billion, July 25, 1989

Net Assets ($ Bl)	Taxable Funds	Annualized Yields For Period Ended 7/25/89 7-Day	30-Day	Compound 7-Day	Avg. Mat. (days)
	U.S. Treasury				
2.7	Capital Preservation	7.89	8.23	8.20	42
2.8	Merrill Lynch CMA Govt	8.49	8.76	8.85	9
1.2	Pacific Horizon Funds/Govt	8.46	8.64	8.82	51
	U.S. government and agencies				
3.0	Cash Equivalent Govt Sec	8.51	8.71	8.88	12
1.5	Fidelity U.S. Govt Reserves	8.60	8.65	8.97	45
1.4	Liberty Govt MM Trust	8.25	8.36	8.59	22
2.9	Shearson Lehman Hutton Govt & Ag	8.45	8.58	8.81	40
1.4	Vanguard MMR Federal	8.91	9.05	9.31	40
	Prime				
1.1	Alex Brown Prime	8.70	8.85	9.08	33
3.1	Dean Witter/Active Assets MT	8.88	9.03	9.28	62
10.4	Dean Witter/Sears Liq Asset	8.92	9.11	9.32	58
2.8	Fidelity Daily Income	8.62	8.68	9.00	47
1.5	Franklin Money Fund	8.33	8.49	8.68	13
1.2	Liquid Capitol Income	8.34	8.61	8.69	37
1.8	NLR Cash Portfolio	8.70	8.85	9.08	28
4.8	Paine Webber CASHFUND	8.77	8.89	9.16	43
1.5	Scudder Cash Investment Trust	8.58	8.74	8.95	51
2.6	Thomson McKinnon Natl MMF	8.64	8.80	9.02	38
1.0	Vantage Cash MMF	8.62	8.77	9.00	26
	Prime and Euro$				
1.6	Alliance Capital Reserves	8.46	8.57	8.82	53
4.3	Daily Cash Accumulation	8.63	8.76	9.01	27
7.5	Dreyfus Liquid Assets	9.00	9.11	9.41	39
2.2	Dreyfus Worldwide Dollar MMFK	9.59	9.71	10.06	34
1.4	IDS Cash Management	8.62	8.72	9.00	35
1.0	Kidder Peabody Premium	8.64	8.79	9.02	39
1.9	Kidder Peabody/Webster Cash Res	8.64	8.78	9.02	40
1.0	Pacific Horizon Funds/MMP	8.77	8.92	9.16	40
2.4	Prudential-Bache Command MF	8.85	8.94	9.25	59
1.8	Reserve Fund/Primary Port	8.37	8.58	8.72	13
15.3	Shearson Lehman Hutton Daily Div	8.81	8.98	9.20	65
	Prime and Euro$ and Yankee$				
6.7	Cash Equivalent Fund MM Port	8.47	8.63	8.83	36
1.3	Cash Management Trust	8.79	8.78	9.18	21
1.1	Delaware Group Cash Reserve	8.53	8.67	8.90	59
1.8	ED Jones Daily PassPort	8.53	8.66	8.90	42
10.6	Fidelity Cash Reserves	8.68	8.76	9.06	46
3.0	Fidelity Spartan	9.47	9.59	9.92	46
6.7	Kemper Money Market	8.87	9.01	9.27	37
25.8	Merrill Lynch CMA MF	8.64	9.03	9.02	57
10.2	Merrill Lynch Ready Assets Trust	8.54	8.99	8.91	57
2.8	Paine Webber RMA MF/MM Port	8.73	8.89	9.11	43
7.2	Prudential-Bache Money Mart Assets	8.80	8.89	9.19	52
4.3	T Rowe Price Prime Reserve	8.59	8.73	8.96	28
9.8	Vanguard MMR Prime	9.09	9.27	9.51	42
	Institutions-only				
4.6	Dreyfus Cash Management	9.23	9.43	9.66	28
1.1	Dreyfus Cash Mgt. Plus	9.25	9.44	9.68	22
1.4	Dreyfus Govt Cash Mgt.	9.02	9.18	9.43	53
2.3	Federated Master Trust	8.92	9.06	9.32	41
1.1	Federated/Auto Cash Mgt. Trust	8.80	8.93	9.19	45
2.7	Federated/Auto Govt Money Trust	8.66	8.78	9.04	22

	Portfolio Holdings (%)								12-Mo. YTD as of 6/30/89
U.S.				Bankers'	Comm'l	Euro$	Yankee$	Non-Inv.	
Treas.	Other	Repos	CDs	Accept	Paper	CDs, TDs	CDs, BAs	Grade	
100	—								7.91
6	—	94M							8.32
44	—	56M							8.23
—	25	75M							8.57
—	22	78							8.28
—	30	70M							8.13
1	48	51M							8.13
1	77	22M							8.69
—	—	1M							8.67
1	4	—	18	15	59	—	—	3	8.61
1	3	—	19	3	73	—	—	1	8.66
—	—	—	14	1	85	—	—	—	8.57
—	—	17M	—	55	28	—	—	—	8.42
—	1	5	8	—	86a	—	—	—	8.50
—	—	11M	7	8	74	—	—	—	8.53
2	2	1	—	6	89	—	—	—	8.64
—	1	1	19	7	72	—	—	—	8.49
—	—	—	2	—	98a	—	—	—	8.64
—	—	16M	5	6	73	—	—	—	8.45
—	4	—	18	1	75	2	—	—	8.19
—	21	—	14	—	64a	1	—	—	8.60
—	—	—	8	—	46	46	—	—	8.50
—	—	1	23	—	56	20	—	—	—
—	—	—	1	—	96a*	3	—	—	8.49
—	—	8M	9	12	63	8	—	—	8.51
—	—	9M	7	11	68	5	—	—	8.50
3	—	12	27	—	50	8	—	—	8.63
—	14	—	2	—	69	15	—	—	8.65
—	—	80	5	—	—	15	—	—	8.36
—	—	3	3	4	40	50	—	—	8.43
—	—	2M	16	—	68	7	7	—	8.44
—	3	4	6	3	75	1	8	—	8.69
—	—	—	14	—	37*	40	9	—	8.33
—	—	3	11	—	65	7	14	—	8.27
—	—	—	4	—	55	38	3	—	8.56
—	—	—	4	—	68	24	4	—	—
—	—	1M	18	—	66	7	8	—	8.87
4	13	—	25	1	46	8	3	—	8.64
—	1	1	31	1	49	12	6	—	8.64
—	2	—	—	—	85	2	11	—	8.68
—	—	—	2	1	73	10	14	—	8.56
—	—	—	11*	1	52a*	33	3	—	8.53
—	3	4M	14	1	69	—	9	—	8.96
1	—	—	11	—	45	43	—	—	9.04
—	—	—	16	—	33	51	—	—	9.10
9	43	48M	—	—	—	—	—	—	8.77
—	—	6	6	—	80	—	8	—	8.76
—	—	9	10	—	78	—	3	—	8.67
13	—	87M	—	—	—	—	—	—	8.41

TABLE 26–3—Concluded

Net Assets ($ Bl)	Taxable Funds	Annualized Yields			
		For Period Ended 7/25/89		Compound 7-Day	Avg. Mat. (days)
		7-Day	30-Day		
1.6	Federated/Money Market Tr	8.95	9.06	9.36	45
3.8	Federated/Trust/U.S. Govt Sec	8.76	8.86	9.15	23
5.4	Federated Trust/U.S. Treas	8.77	8.89	9.16	21
2.2	Fidelity Cash Govt	9.01	9.14	9.42	37
3.8	Fidelity Cash MM	9.21	9.33	9.64	38
1.3	Fidelity Cash Treasury	9.08	9.21	9.50	3
1.0	Fidelity Daily MF/Treas Port	8.65	8.74	9.03	5
1.3	Fidelity MMT/Domestic	8.99	9.10	9.40	35
2.2	Goldman, Sachs/ILA Govt.	8.89	9.00	9.29	30
1.2	Goldman, Sachs/ILA MMP	8.97	9.13	9.38	48
4.0	Goldman, Sachs/ILA Prime	8.96	9.09	9.37	43
1.7	Goldman, Sachs/ILA Treas.	8.85	8.95	9.25	20
1.4	Merrill Lynch Govt.	8.63	8.72	9.01	6
1.7	Merrill Lynch Institutional	8.86	9.02	9.26	45
2.1	SEI Liq Asset Tr/Prime Obligations	8.88	9.02	9.28	41
2.5	SEI Liq Asset Tr·/Treas	8.69	8.84	9.07	25
1.5	Shearson/Provident: Fed Fund	8.97	9.12	9.38	25
1.6	Shearson/Provident: T-Fund	8.87	9.03	9.27	32
5.6	Shearson/Provident: Temp. Fund	9.11	9.20	9.53	52
	Special purpose				
4.3	Merrill Lynch Retirement Reserve Money Fund	8.59	8.95	8.96	60
1.4	Paine Webber Retirement Money Fund	8.41	8.57	8.77	52

Net Assets ($ Bl)	Tax-Free Funds	Annualized Yields			
		For Period Ended 7/24/89		Compound 7-Day	Avg. Mat. (days)
		7-Day	30-Day		
	Stockbroker and general purpose				
7.4	CMA Tax-Exempt	5.76	5.92	5.93	67
2.2	CASH Equivalent Fund/T-E Port	5.59	5.79	5.75	8
1.2	Dean Witter/Active Assets T-F	5.48	5.65	5.63	19
2.2	Dreyfus Tax-Exempt MMF	5.58	5.75	5.74	33
2.9	Fidelity Tax-Exempt MM Tr.	5.68	5.84	5.84	43
3.1	Shearson Lehman Hutton Daily T-F	5.67	5.87	5.83	67
1.1	T Rowe Price T-E MF	5.40	5.63	5.55	23
1.2	The Tax Free Money Fund	5.63	5.76	5.79	59
2.0	Vanguard Muni Bond/MM	5.95	6.11	6.13	68
	Institutions-only				
2.3	Federated Tax-Free Trust	5.74	5.85	5.90	42
1.4	Federated/T-F Instruments Tr.	5.63	5.75	5.79	46
2.1	Fidelity Cash Tax-Exempt K	5.95	6.22	6.13	37
1.8	Nuveen T-E MMF	5.88	6.01	6.05	44
1.2	Shearson/Provident: Muni Fund	5.86	5.99	6.03	33
	State-specific institutions-only				
1.0	Shearson/Provident: Muni CA	5.50	5.63	5.65	27

Source: The Donoghue Organization, Inc.

Portfolio Holdings (%)

U.S. Treas.	U.S. Other	Repos	CDs	Bankers' Accept	Comm'l Paper	Euro$ CDs, TDs	Yankee$ CDs, BAs	Non-Inv. Grade	12-Mo. YTD as of 6/30/89
—	—	16	17	—	67	—	—	—	8.76
—	35	65M	—	—	—	—	—	—	8.54
13	—	87M	—	—	—	—	—	—	8.51
—	23	77	—	—	—	—	—	—	8.92
—	—	—	2	—	65	32	1	—	9.09
—	—	100M	—	—	—	—	—	—	8.91
—	—	100M	—	—	—	—	—	—	8.49
—	—	2	9	—	89	—	—	—	8.87
—	17	83	—	—	—	—	—	—	8.73
1	1	11	7	—	59	21	—	—	8.95
—	1	19	17	1	62	—	—	—	8.85
10	—	90M	—	—	—	—	—	—	8.56
14	—	86M	—	—	—	—	—	—	8.35
—	1	2M	19	1	57	4	16	—	8.66
—	—	5	32	—	63	—	—	—	8.85
22	—	78M	—	—	—	—	—	—	8.51
74	—	—	—	—	—	—	—	—	8.86
11	—	89M	—	—	—	—	—	—	8.75
—	—	28	7	—	65	—	—	—	8.99
4	4	—	43	1	37	6	5	—	8.50
—	—	—	—	—	85	2	13	—	8.38

Portfolio Holdings (%)

Demand Notes Rated	Demand Notes Unrated	General Market Notes Rated	General Market Notes Unrated	Comm'l Paper	Put Bonds 6 Mos. & Less	Put Bonds Over 6 Mos.	Other	AMT Paper	12-Mo. YTD as of 6/30/89
47	2	15	1	13	19	3	—	16	5.78
70	—	1	1	25	3	—	—	—	5.87
77	2	9	—	3	9	—	—	—	5.80
63	—	9	—	14	12	2	—	12	5.66
47	5	5	1	24	18	—	—	—	5.72
54	—	10	—	2	24	10	—	—	5.74
57	5	3	—	32p	2	1	—	—	5.78
50	—	6	—	23p	15	6	—	—	5.75
52	—	26	—	9	12	1	—	—	6.01
59	1	11	—	12	17	—	—	—	5.76
59	6	10	—	10	15	—	—	—	5.75
52	1	4	1	27	15	—	—	—	6.10
52	12	14	—	9	10	3	—	—	6.04
54	2	12	—	25	7	—	—	—	5.97
55	—	7	—	30	8	—	—	—	5.84

25.8 billion in assets were twice those of any other fund (Table 26–3).

The phenomenal success of Merrill's CMA account has led Shearson and other brokers to seek to imitate it. None did so with quite Merrill's panache and success.

In getting CMA off the ground, Merrill had to figure out how to sidestep the SEC, the Fed, and other regulators; it did this by structuring its CMA account so that it took no improper step on the securities turf where it was authorized to tread and no step at all on the banking turf where it wasn't authorized to tread.

State regulators raised more fuss than federal regulators over the CMA account. John Olin, Oregon's superintendent of banks, observed that CMA looked like a duck, walked like a duck, and quacked like a duck, and that, since his job was to regulate ducks, he was going to make rules for this new one.

Banks Fight Back

Had it not been for the lids imposed by U.S. regulators on the rates that U.S. banks and other depository institutions (DIs) were permitted to pay depositors, the money-fund business would probably never have taken off. Certainly, it has no foreign parallel because banks in major foreign countries (capitalist ones at least) have always been permitted to pay market rates on deposits. In any case, money funds compete in the U.S. with banks and other DIs for "deposits."

Since rate deregulation in the early 1980s, banks have been permitted to pay pretty much any rate they choose on consumer deposits. What level and structure of rates they in fact pay depends on the general level of interest rates, on the shape of the yield curve, on their rate outlook, and on their need for funds. Generally, banks offer higher rates on longer-term CDs, but impose a penalty on a consumer if he withdraws his funds before his CD matures. In addition, banks offer what they call *money market accounts;* these accounts, created in December 1982, pay a rate based on current short-term rates.

Money funds almost always yield a rate that's higher than the rate banks pay on their money market accounts. At times, the rate differential can be substantial. For example, *The Wall Street Journal* reported on October 4, 1988, that the yield on top-ranked money funds was over 8%; that the average 7-day yield on all money funds was 7.71%; and that the average yield on bank money market accounts was only 6.02%. That's a difference of over 100 bp. For the conservative consumer, a bank money market fund account offers the advantage, which a money fund does not, of federal deposit insurance. Also, one has to presume that many consumers are simply not rate shoppers. Depositing savings with a bank or other DI is a habit they've always had and one they haven't broken.

The central-asset accounts established by Merrill and other brokers have not gone unnoticed by banks. While Merrill was seeking with considerable success to mimic a bank, banks were making some innovative—for them—steps to mimic Merrill and other brokers. Citibank's former chairman, Walter Wriston, ruefully said at a meeting of bankers some years ago that his dream bank already existed: "It's called Merrill Lynch, Pierce, Fenner & Smith."

To compete with wide-service, one-stop-shopping brokers, banks have in recent years offered brokerage service on the terms regulators permit. In this direction, the bank that has gone the farthest is Citibank; it offers an Asset Network Account with features similar to those of Merrill's CMA account.

TAX-EXEMPT MONEY FUNDS

There are general-purpose money funds for individuals and money funds for institutions only that invest in a wide range of good-quality money market paper; and there are funds, both for individuals and for institutions only, that restrict their investments to governments or government-guaranteed paper. Like a deli that sells sandwiches, the money-fund industry has funds that meet the needs and tastes of just about every investor.

The one exception, until 1980, was the investor who wanted tax-exempt income. By 1980, rates were so high that the idea of offering a tax-exempt money fund that would limit its investments to short-term, top-quality muni paper became extremely appealing. The hitch, however, was that there was little such paper around.

To rephrase the great economist, J. B. Say: *Demand creates its own supply.* So it was with short-term, tax-exempt paper: money funds wanted it; supply was limited; so money funds literally invented the municipal VRDBs (variable-rate demand bonds) we discussed in Chapter 25. Speaking of the problem money funds faced in munis, one fund officer observed, "Traditionally, municipal notes came six months to a year—TRAs, BANs, RANs; there were no municipal demand notes or municipal commercial paper to speak of; and the floating supply of muni notes nearing maturity was very small. We said, 'If we got, as an industry, ½- to ⅔ of the total available supply, which was probably out of the question, it's difficult to see how the industry [tax-exempt money funds] could be more than 2 or 3 billion in total.' That's still true today [1989] if you run the numbers. So either we had to change our rules or we had to change the marketplace. Quickly, we thought of using variable-rate demand notes."

Taking their cue from the variable-rate master notes that commercial paper issuers had long offered to bank trust departments, money funds—Federated was the pioneer—basically said to tax-exempt issuers that they wanted paper with the following characteristics:

1. The rate paid would be 50% of prime.[2]
2. The rate would be reset at some frequent, short-term interval, for example, daily, weekly, whatever.
3. On each reset date, the paper could be put back by the investor to the issuer's backstop bank.
4. The put would be airtight, not *soft*.
5. To guarantee liquidity, the paper would be backed by a

---

[2]A money fund backed into the 50% number by saying: What's a yield that would be attractive to an issuer and that would also allow us, after paying fund expenses and earning a modest profit, to pay a rate that would be attractive to individuals in a high marginal tax bracket?

> bank line of credit, and in some cases by establishing a remarketing agent.

6. Also, if a credit enhancement were required, the paper would be backed by a bank LOC (line of credit).

The above might sound as if a money fund were asking a lot of an issuer: In particular, couldn't an issuer get money cheaper by issuing short-term, tax-exempt commercial paper? The response of a money fund was basically that, if an issuer met his terms, gave him a VRDB, that instrument would be so attractive to the fund—would permit the fund to offer, over the rate cycle, a yield so attractive to investors—that the issuer's VRDB would never, or almost never, be put back to his backstop bank. Thus, the issuer would not be paying up for short-term money, rather he'd be getting long-term money at a short-term rate, which—given that the slope of the yield curve is more often positive than negative—would be cheap long-term money.

In creating VRDBs, money funds faced a lot of resistance. First, they had to convince the issuer he was getting a good deal. Second, they had to overcome resistance from the banks: the money funds figured that they could, on average, give muni borrowers money at 50% of prime, whereas the banks had been charging muni borrowers 75% of prime and making good money doing so. Also, broker/dealers did not want to hear about VRDBs because they were trying to get municipal borrowers to do commercial paper programs on which they figured that they'd make more money.

With a VRDB, a dealer, say Goldman, might place it for a small fee, Morgan might be the remarketing agent, a Japanese bank might write the LOC, and yet another bank might give the liquidity line. Usually, the liquidity and the LOC lines are given by the same bank, but not always. Also, the initial placement may be done by a bank dealer as well as by a nonbank dealer.

Initially, 100% of VRDBs were created for money funds. Before 1986, the corporate tax rate was lower than the highest federal marginal tax rates paid by individuals. Only after the 1986 changes in the tax laws did corporations get involved in VRDBs and then only tangentially.

MANAGEMENT OF A MONEY FUND PORTFOLIO

A money fund must manage its portfolio under several constraints. The SEC puts constraints on the maturities it may buy. Second, a money fund must maintain sufficient liquidity to meet daily any demand for cash that its investors might make on it. Third, a money fund must operate in an environment in which both the general level of interest rates and the slope of the yield curve keep shifting over time.

Given these constraints, a lot of money funds end up running portfolios with an average maturity of 40 to 50 days (Table 26–3). However, there's a lot of variability fund to fund; also, some funds will stretch maturities when they anticipate a fall in rates.

Portfolio Strategies

Buying variable-rate demand notes offers a fund clear advantages with respect to portfolio management. To illustrate, consider two portfolios. One invests only in 90-day paper and ends up earning the average 90-day rate and having a 45-day average maturity (assuming it invests each day the same average amount). The second fund invests half its funds in demand notes that pay a 90-day rate and have a daily put and the other half in 180-day paper; this second fund also has about a 45-day average maturity, but if the yield curve is positive, it earns more than the 90-day rate because it picks up some extra liquidity premium.

Investing in demand notes also gives a fund a more attractive rate profile over the cycle. When rates are rising, the rate earned by a portfolio that's invested half in variable-rate demand notes having a daily reset and half in 180-day paper will lag the market but not as much as the rate on a portfolio invested in 90-day paper with a 45-day average maturity. So in a rising-rate environment, a fund with a lot of demand notes may be able to attract money from other funds. On the other hand, when rates are falling, a fund that holds half its funds in demand notes with a daily put and half in 180-day paper will find its yield falling a little faster than that of other funds; that's OK because, in a falling-rate environment, the manager of a money fund, as opposed to its marketing guy, doesn't want a lot of new money coming in: new money kills a fund's yield when rates are falling.

A final advantage to a fund of investing in demand notes is that it has, as compared to a fund that invests in 90-day paper, roughly half as much money to invest on a given day; also, it needs on average to deal with roughly half as many names per day to keep its portfolio diversified—to ensure that no one name accounts for more than 5% of its investments. The fewer investments a fund need make each day, the lower it can hold its expenses.

Taxable-Fund Portfolios

The above logic has caused some taxable funds to seek out variable-rate demand notes for their portfolios. For a governments-only fund, repo is a natural variable-rate investment; and a lot of money in such funds is invested not in governments, but in repos collateralized by governments.

Finding other taxable, variable-rate demand notes isn't easy. Some muni bodies that could once issue tax-exempt VRDBs, but which now must issue taxable paper, use the VRDB concept. That concept ought also to be attractive to certain corporate borrowers, in particular to the many firms that are too small to borrow in the commercial paper market on a cost-effective basis and who therefore borrow from their banks. One problem a money fund faces in obtaining such paper is that banks don't want to show the concept to such borrowers because, for a bank, middle-market lending is highly profitable.

Money-Fund Yields

One would expect yields on money funds, taxable and tax-exempt, to be a spread below and to lag somewhat behind yields on the open market paper in which such funds invest. Figures 26–3 and 26–4 confirm this.

FIGURE 26–3

Average yields on taxable money funds versus yields on 90-day commercial paper (yields on a money market basis)

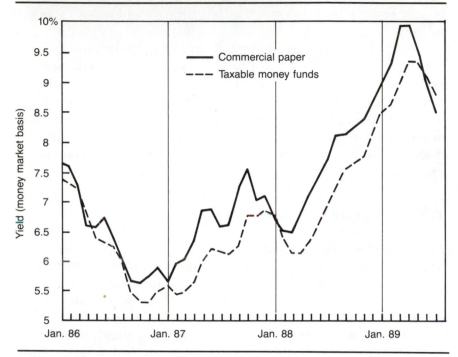

Source: J. P. Morgan Securities, Inc.

CONSUMERS' USES OF MONEY FUNDS

For consumers, money funds are a convenient, safe, and liquid investment for tucking away at a good rate temporary excess funds and a liquidity reserve. Consumers also view money funds as a safe haven for funds they normally would invest in stocks and bonds when they get nervous about the stock and/or bond markets.

In August 1987, before the stock-market crash, the allocation of assets in mutual funds was 26.2% in stock funds, 37.4% in bond funds, and 36.4% in money funds. Almost two years

FIGURE 26–4
**Average yields on tax-exempt money funds versus yields on 90-day,
tax-exempt commercial paper (MIG-1)**

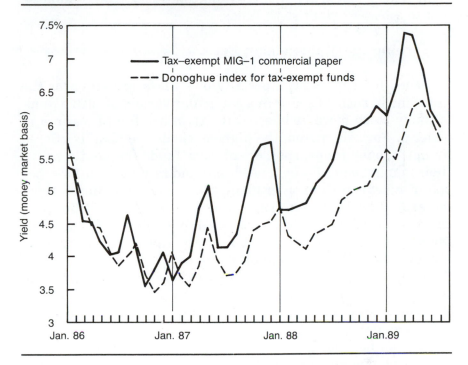

Source: J. P. Morgan Securities, Inc.

later—long after the 1987 stock-market crash—the allocation
was 23.0% in stock funds, 34.5% in bond funds, and 42.5% in
money funds. Those numbers do not bring cheer to the hearts of
the mutual fund managers, such as Dreyfus, who run a diversified family of funds: a number of stock, bond, and money funds;
they may still have as much or more money under management,
but money funds are the least profitable segment of their
business.

While some consumers aren't particularly sensitive to
yields on money funds, others are turned by high money market
rates into "high-yield junkies." As short-term rates slip, they

search out long-term investments in the hope of grabbing higher returns. In mid-1989 their choice, according to analysts, was bond funds—particularly high-yield, high-risk "junk" funds— and to a lesser extent stock funds.

Absorbing the Management Fee

A money-fund investor, especially one who's investing for the first time in such a fund or in a particular variety of such a fund, is likely to be more yield sensitive than are fund investors in general. For this reason, the highest yields are usually offered by new money funds; sponsors of such funds frequently waive their management fee on a new fund and reimburse it for other operating expenses in order to attract business. In March 1989, for example, the three money funds at the top of the yield charts—Dreyfus Worldwide Dollar Money Market Fund, Alger Money Market Portfolio, and Fidelity Investments' Spartan Money Market Fund—were all doing so.

Sometimes, established money funds will waive their fee to compensate for a bad call in running their portfolios. Still others view doing so as an attractive service to their equity-fund investors. One manager of a family of mutual funds noted that waiving the management fee on its money fund was a good use of marketing dollars, cheaper than advertising; the notion behind such reasoning is that an investor who decides to move out of a money fund into a stock or bond fund is more likely to make an intrafamily than an interfamily move.

Risk

Investors in money funds view such funds as pretty much risk free, and the track record such funds have compiled since 1974 supports this view. This is not to say that no money fund has ever made an investment that went sour. Several money funds were caught holding P-2-rated commercial paper of Integrated Resources when it defaulted in 1989. In every case, the fund managers dug into their own pockets to make the fund whole. That's presumably something that every fund manager who could afford the hit would do, since a money fund that lost money would almost certainly suffer massive withdrawals. All of which suggests that a money fund run by an entity with deep pockets, while it may not have federal insurance, certainly has something akin to private insurance. Also, thanks to the fact that funds are—by choice and by SEC requirement—well diversified, that insurance is likely to prove adequate to cover any losses sustained by the fund.

INSTITUTIONAL FUNDS

There are funds around for institutional investors, such as bank trust departments, small banks, other DIs, and small corporations.

Bank Trust Departments

In the early 1970s, many banks set up *short-term investment funds* (STIFS) in their trust departments to invest in a pool cash held short-term for one reason or another in accounts they managed. Such banks often found that they could not afford the software and hardware to do the necessary accounting: to track the earnings on and the money flows into and out of separate accounts. Also, they could not recoup these costs with a fee because they were already charging an overall fee for discretionary management of the funds held in trust.

To get around this problem, many turned to master notes. As noted in Chapter 22, these provide a stable source of funds to note issuers and provide at no cost to lenders—bank trust departments and others—subaccounting that precisely fits their needs. The withdrawal in 1977 of W. T. Grant from its master note program and its later bankruptcy focused attention on the fact that trust account funds invested in a master note—no matter how good the name of the issuer—were exposed to undue credit risk because of the resulting concentration on a single or on several names. Money funds provide trust departments, pension funds, and others running funds for numerous accounts with the convenience of subaccounting *plus* the comfort of knowing that they are satisfying the prudent man rule for diversification of risk. Thus, money funds replaced master notes in many bank trust departments; they are also widely used by other institutions having similar investment needs.

Other Institutional Investors

Although money funds were initially designed to offer individual investors a way to invest indirectly in money market securities, they can also be extremely useful to a corporation or other institution running a small short-term portfolio because the small portfolio manager labors under several disadvantages.

First, since minimum denominations are high in many sectors of the money market, it's difficult for a person managing 10MM or less to diversify: he has only limited ability to reduce credit risk by holding a mix of names and to reduce market risk by investment in different types and maturities of instruments.

Also, the net yield earned on a small portfolio is reduced far more by transactions costs than is the net yield earned on a large portfolio. If a bank imposes a $25 fee on an overnight repo, that fee will, on a $250,000 repo, reduce a gross yield of 8% to 4.35%. Moreover, if the portfolio manager must also pay a fee to wire money out of his bank account, his net yield will be still lower.

Another problem for the small portfolio manager is that he will inevitably end up buying and selling securities at rates less favorable than those big investors can obtain by buying in round-lot amounts from dealers. Also, a small portfolio typically suffers from unprofessional management: the gains to be had from actively managing a small portfolio—for example, by following the market and making the sort of maturity choices described in Chapter 11—are so small in absolute terms that hiring a skilled portfolio manager would not be cost justified.

Because it's difficult to manage small short-term balances effectively, it would make sense for many institutions holding money of this sort to invest it in an institutions-only money fund instead of investing it directly in money market instruments. A money fund typically charges about 50 bp for expenses plus a management fee that runs another 50 bp. These charges, however, are likely to be largely or fully offset by the fact that the fund, because it's professionally managing a big pool of short-term funds, can earn a significantly higher *gross* return than can a small portfolio manager.

Whether an institutional investor does or does not use a money fund, the yield it could achieve using one makes a good benchmark against which to compare the yield it achieves over time on its liquidity portfolio, provided, that is, that it adjusts that yield for the *full* investment expenses it incurs.

GLOSSARY

COMMON MONEY MARKET AND BOND MARKET TERMS

accretion (of a discount): In portfolio accounting, a straight-line accumulation of capital gains on discount bonds in anticipation of receipt of par at maturity.

accrued interest: Interest due from issue or from the last coupon date to the present on an interest-bearing security. The buyer of the security pays the quoted dollar price plus accrued interest.

active: A market in which there is much trading.

actuals: The cash commodity as opposed to the futures contract.

ACUs: *Asian currency units.* An expression for Eurodollars deposited in Far East centers.

add-on rate: A specific rate of interest to be paid. Stands in contrast to the rate on a discount security, such as a Treasury bill, that pays *no* interest.

aftertax real rate of return: Money aftertax rate of return minus the inflation rate.

agencies: Federal agency securities. See also **agency bank.**

agency bank: A form of organization commonly used by foreign banks to enter the U.S. market. An agency bank cannot accept deposits or extend loans in its own name; it acts as an agent for the parent bank. Term often used on the Street to refer to both foreign bank agencies and branches.

agent: A firm that executes orders for or otherwise acts on behalf of another (the principal) and is subject to its control and authority. The agent may receive a fee or commission.

all-in cost: Total costs, explicit and other. Example: The all-in cost to a bank of CD money is the explicit rate of interest it pays on that deposit *plus* the FDIC premium it must pay on the deposit *plus* the hidden cost it incurs because it must hold some portion of that deposit in a non–interest-bearing reserve account at the Fed.

all or none (AON):   Requirement that none of an order be executed unless all of it can be executed at the specified price.

American option: An option that may be exercised at any time during the life of the option. U.S. option exchanges, such as the CBOE, trade only American options.

amortize: In portfolio accounting, periodic charges made against interest income on premium bonds in anticipation of receipt of the call price at call or of par value at maturity.

arbitrage: Strictly defined, buying something where it is cheap and selling it where it is dear; for example, a bank buys 3-month CD money in the U.S. market and sells 3-month money at a higher rate in the Eurodollar market. In the money market, often refers: (1) to a situation in which a trader buys one security and sells a similar security in the expectation that the spread in yields between the two instruments will narrow or widen to his profit, (2) to a swap between two similar issues based on an anticipated change in yield spreads, and (3) to situations where a higher return (or lower cost) can be achieved in the money market for one currency by utilizing another currency and swapping it on a fully hedged basis through the foreign-exchange market.

asked: The price at which securities are offered.

away: A trade, quote, or market that does not originate with the dealer in question, for example, "the bid is 98–10 away (from me)."

back contracts: Futures contracts farthest from expiration.

back discount rate: Yield basis on which short-term, non–interest-bearing money market securities are quoted. A rate quoted on a discount basis understands bond equivalent yield. That must be calculated when comparing return against coupon securities.

back-to-back loan: An example of a back-to-back loan would be IBM agreeing to lend dollars to British Petroleum in exchange for the latter lending pounds to IBM. Such agreements are struck only when exchange controls in one or more countries prevent normal capital flows.

back up: (1) When yields rise and prices fall, the market is said to back up. (2) When an investor swaps out of one security into another of shorter current maturity (e.g., out of a 2-year note into an 18-month note), he is said to back up.

bank line: Line of credit granted by a bank to a customer.

bank notes: Unsecured notes issued by a bank in the form of an MTN. No FDIC premium is paid by the issuing bank.

bank wire: A computer message system linking major banks. It is used not for effecting payments, but as a mechanism to advise the receiving bank of some action that has occurred, for example, the payment by a customer of funds into that bank's account.

bankers' acceptance (BA):   A draft or bill of exchange accepted by a bank or trust company. The accepting institution guarantees payment of the bill.

BANs: Bond anticipation notes are issued by states and municipalities to obtain interim financing for projects that will eventually be funded long term through the sale of a bond issue.

basis: (1) Number of days in the coupon period. (2) In *commodities* jargon, basis is the spread between a futures price and some other price. A money market participant would talk about *spread* rather than basis.

basis point: ¹⁄₁₀₀th of 1%.

basis price: Price expressed in terms of yield to maturity or annual rate of return.

basis swap: See **interest rate swap.**

BBA.   British Bankers Association.

bear market: A declining market or a period of pessimism when declines in the market are anticipated. (A way to remember: "Bear down.")

bearer security: A security the owner of which is not registered on the books of the issuer. A bearer security is payable to the holder.

best-efforts basis: Securities dealers do not underwrite a new issue, but sell it on the basis of what can be sold. In the money market, this usually refers to a firm order to buy or sell a given amount of securities or currency at the best price that can be found over a given period of time; it can also refer to a flexible amount (up to a limit) at a given rate.

bid: The price offered for securities.

blind broker: A broker who acts as principal and does not give up names to either side of a brokered trade. Blind brokering of securities is common, whereas blind brokering of Fed funds and Euro time deposits would be infeasible.

block: A large amount of securities, normally much more than what constitutes a round lot in the market in question.

book: A banker, especially a Eurobanker, will refer to his bank's assets and liabilities as its "book." If the average maturity of the liabilities is less than that of the assets, the bank is running a **short** and **open** book.

book-entry securities: The Treasury and federal agencies are moving to a book-entry system in which securities are not represented by engraved pieces of paper but are maintained in computerized records at the Fed in the names of member banks, which, in turn, keep records of the securities they own as well as those they are holding for customers. In the case of other securities for which there is a book-entry system, engraved securities do exist somewhere in quite a few cases. These securities do not move from holder to holder but are usually kept in a central clearinghouse or by another agent.

book value: The value at which a debt security is shown on the holder's balance sheet. Book value is often acquisition cost ± amortization/accretion, which may differ markedly from market value. It can be further defined as "tax book," "accreted book," or "amortized book" value.

bp.   Market abbreviation for basis points. Thus, 1 bp means 1 basis point, 10 bp means 10 basis points.

bridge financing: Interim financing of one sort or another.

British clearers: The large clearing banks that dominate deposit taking and short-term lending in the domestic sterling market in Great Britain.

broken date: See **cock date.**

broker: A broker brings buyers and sellers together for a commission paid by the initiator of the transaction or by both sides; he does not position. In the money market, brokers are active in markets in which banks buy and sell money and in interdealer markets.

bull market: A period of optimism when increases in market prices are anticipated. (A way to remember: "Bull ahead.")

bullet loan: A bank term loan that calls for no amortization. The term is commonly used in the Euromarket.

bullet (loan or security):   All principal is due at maturity.

Bunds: German Treasuries.

buy a spread: Buy a near futures contract and sell a far one.

buy-back: Another term for a repurchase agreement.

calendar: List of new bond issues scheduled to come to market soon.

call: An option that gives the holder the right to buy the underlying security at a specified price during a fixed time period.

call money: Interest-bearing bank deposits that can be withdrawn on 24-hours' notice. Many Eurodeposits take the form of call money.

callable bond: A bond that the issuer has the right to redeem prior to maturity by paying some specified call price.

Canadian agencies: Agency banks established by Canadian banks in the U.S.

cap: A series of options in which the writer guarantees the buyer, a payor of floating, that he will pay the buyer whatever additional interest he must pay on his loan if the rate on that loan goes above an agreed rate, X.

carry: The interest cost of financing securities held. (See also **negative** and **positive carry**.)

cash commodity or security: The actual commodity or security as opposed to futures contracts for it.

cash management bill: Very-short-maturity bills that the Treasury occasionally sells because its cash balances are down and it needs money for a few days.

cash market: Traditionally, this term has been used to denote the market in which commodities were traded, for immediate delivery, against cash. Since the inception of futures markets for T bills and other debt securities, a distinction has been made between the cash markets in which these securities trade for immediate delivery and the futures markets in which they trade for future delivery.

cash price: Price quotation in the cash market.

cash settlement: In the money market, a transaction is said to be made for cash settlement if the securities purchased are delivered against payment in Fed funds on the same day the trade is made.

CBOE: Chicago Board Options Exchange.

CBT: Chicago Board of Trade, a futures exchange.

certificate of deposit (CD):   A time deposit with a specific maturity evidenced by a certificate. Large-denomination CDs are typically negotiable.

CHIPS: The New York Clearing House's computerized Clearing House Interbank Payments System. Most Euro transactions are cleared and settled through CHIPS rather than over the Fed wire.

circle: Underwriters, actual or potential as the case may be, often seek out and "circle" retail interest in a new issue before final pricing. The customer circled has basically made a commitment to purchase the note or bond *or* to purchase it if it comes at an agreed-upon price. In the latter case, if the price is other than that stipulated, the customer supposedly has first offer at the actual price.

clear: A trade carried out by the seller delivering securities and the buyer delivering funds in proper form. A trade that does not clear is said to fail.

cock date: In the Euromarket, an off-the-run period, for example, 28 days. Also referred to as a broken date. A cock date contrasts with a fixed date, which is 30, 60, 90, and so on, days hence.

collar: A cap plus a floor.

commercial paper: An unsecured promissory note with a fixed maturity of no more than 270 days. Commercial paper is normally sold at a discount from face value.

committed facility: A legal commitment undertaken by a bank to lend to a customer.

competitive bid: (1) Bid tendered in a Treasury action for a specific amount of securities at a specific yield or price. (2) Issuers, municipal and public utilities, often sell new issues by asking for competitive bids from one or more syndicates.

confirmation: A memorandum to the other side of a trade describing all relevant data.

consortium banks: A merchant banking subsidiary set up by several banks that may or may not be of the same nationality. Consortium banks are common in the Euromarket and are active in loan syndication.

convertible bond: A bond containing a provision that permits conversion to the issuer's common stock at some fixed exchange ratio.

convexity: The slope of the price-yield relationship for a fixed-income security. Convexity is normally positive but can be negative.

corporate bond equivalent: See **equivalent bond yield.**

corporate taxable equivalent: Rate of return required on a par bond to produce the same aftertax yield to maturity that the premium or discount bond quoted would.

country risk: See **sovereign risk.**

coupon: (1) The annual rate of interest on the bond's face value that a bond's issuer promises to pay the bondholder. (2) A certificate attached to a bond evidencing interest due on a payment date.

coupon swap: See **interest rate swap.**

cover: Eliminating a short position by buying the securities shorted.

covered call write: Selling calls against securities owned by the call seller.

covered interest arbitrage: Investing dollars in an instrument denominated in a foreign currency and hedging the resulting foreign-exchange risk by selling the proceeds of the investment forward for dollars.

credit enhancement: The backing of paper with collateral, a bank LOC, or some other device to achieve a higher rating for the paper.

credit risk: The risk that an issuer of debt securities or a borrower may default on his obligations, or that payment may not be made on sale of a negotiable instrument. (See **overnight delivery risk.**)

cross-currency swap: An interest-rate swap in which the interest payments due are denominated in different currencies.

cross hedge: Hedging a risk in a cash market security by buying or selling a futures contract for a similar but not identical instrument.

CRTs: Abbreviation for the cathode-ray tubes used to display market quotes.

current coupon: A bond selling at or close to par; that is, a bond with a coupon close to the yield currently offered on new bonds of similar maturity and credit risk.

current issue: In Treasury bills and notes, the most recently auctioned issue. Trading is more active in current issues than in off-the-run issues.

current maturity: Current time to maturity on an outstanding note, bond, or other money market instrument; for example, a 5-year note one year after issue has a current maturity of four years.

current yield: Coupon payments on a security as a percentage of the security's market price. In many instances the price should be *gross* of accrued interest, particularly on instruments where no coupon is left to be paid until maturity.

curve trader: A trader who does arbitrages along the yield curve.

cushion bonds: High-coupon bonds that sell at only a moderate premium because they are callable at a price below that at which a comparable noncallable bond would sell. Cushion bonds offer considerable downside protection in a falling market.

daylight overdraft: Being overdrawn (OD) in a deposit account during some of a day's business hours. Foreign banks typically run big daylight overdrafts with their U.S. correspondent bank. A daylight overdraft exposes the institution that extends it to a credit risk.

day trading: Intraday trading in securities for profit as opposed to investing for profit.

dealer: A dealer, as opposed to a broker, acts as a principal in all transactions, buying and selling for his own account.

dealer loan: Overnight, collateralized loan made to a dealer financing his position by borrowing from a money market bank.

debenture: A bond secured only by the general credit of the issuer.

debt leverage: The amplification in the return earned on equity funds when an investment is financed partly with borrowed money.

debt securities: IOUs created through loan-type transactions—commercial paper, bank CDs, bills, bonds, and other instruments.

default: Failure to make timely payment of interest or principal on a debt security or to otherwise comply with the provisions of a bond indenture.

delivery month: A month in which a futures contract expires and delivery may be taken or made.

delta of an option: The rate of change of the value of an option with respect to the price of the underlier, evaluated at the current market price of the underlier.

delta hedge of an option: A hedge of an option with a position in the underlier where the hedge ratio is based on the option's delta.

demand line of credit: A bank line of credit that enables a customer to borrow on a daily or an on-demand basis.

deposit note: An FDIC-insured, negotiable time deposit issued by a bank, in the form of an MTN, always with a maturity at issue of 18 months or longer.

direct paper: Commercial paper sold directly by the issuer to investors.

direct placement: Selling a new issue not by offering it for sale publicly, but by placing it with one or several institutional investors.

discount basis: See **bank discount rate.**

discount bond: A bond selling below par.

discount house: British institution that uses call and overnight money obtained from banks to invest in and trade money market instruments.

discount paper: See **discount securities.**

discount rate: The rate of interest charged by the Fed to member banks that borrow at the discount window. The discount rate is an add-on rate.

discount securities: Non–interest-bearing money market instruments that are issued at a discount and redeemed at maturity for full face value; for example, U.S. Treasury bills.

discount window: Facility provided by the Fed enabling member banks to borrow reserves against collateral in the form of governments or other acceptable paper.

disintermediation: The investing of funds that would normally have been placed with a bank or other financial intermediary directly into debt securities issued by ultimate borrowers; for example, into bills or bonds.

distributed: After a Treasury auction, there will be many new issues in dealers' hands. As those securities are sold to retail, the issue is said to be distributed.

diversification: Dividing investment funds among a variety of securities offering independent returns.

DM: Deutsche (German) marks.

documented discount notes: Commercial paper backed by normal bank lines plus a letter of credit from a bank stating that it will pay off the paper at maturity if the borrower does not. Such paper is also referred to as **LOC** (letter of credit) **paper.**

dollar bonds: Municipal revenue bonds for which quotes are given in dollar prices. Not to be confused with "U.S. Dollar" bonds, a common term of reference in the Eurobond market.

dollar price of a bond: Percentage of face value at which a bond is quoted.

don't know (DK, DKed): "Don't know the trade"—a Street expression used whenever one party lacks knowledge of a trade or receives conflicting instructions from the other party (for example, with respect to payment).

due bill: An instrument evidencing the obligation of a seller to delivery securities sold to the buyer. Occasionally used in the bill market.

duration: A measure of the current maturity of a fixed-income instrument as the weighted average of the time to receipt of the payments thrown off by the instrument; the weights used are the present values of the future payments to be received.

Dutch auction: Auction in which the lowest price necessary to sell the entire offering becomes the price at which all securities offered are sold. This technique has been used in Treasury auctions.

Edge Act corporation: A subsidiary of a U.S. bank set up to carry out international banking business. Most such "subs" are located within the U.S.

either/or facility: An agreement permitting a bank customer to borrow either domestic dollars from the bank's head office or Eurodollars from one of its foreign branches.

either-way market: In the interbank Eurodollar deposit market, an either-way market is one in which the bid and asked rates are identical.

elbow: The elbow in the yield curve is the maturity area considered to provide the most attractive short-term investment; for example, the maturity range in which to initiate a ride along the yield curve.

eligible bankers' acceptances: In the BA market an acceptance may be referred to as eligible because it is acceptable by the Fed as collateral at the discount window and/or because the accepting bank can sell it without incurring a reserve requirement.

equivalent bond yield: Annual yield on a short-term, non–interest-bearing security calculated so as to be comparable to yields quoted on coupon securities.

equivalent taxable yield: The yield on a taxable security that would leave the investor with the same aftertax return he would earn by holding a tax-exempt municipal; for example, for an investor taxed at a 50% marginal rate, equivalent taxable yield on a muni note issued at 3% would be 6%.

Eurobonds: Bonds issued in Europe outside the confines of any national capital market. A Eurobond may or may not be denominated in the currency of the issuer.

Euro CDs: CDs issued by a U.S. bank branch or foreign bank located outside the U.S. Almost all Euro CDs are issued in London.

Eurocurrency deposits: Deposits made in a bank or bank branch that is not located in the country in whose currency the deposit is denominated. Dollars deposited in a London bank are Eurodollars; German marks deposited there are Euromarks.

Eurodollars: U.S. dollars deposited in a U.S. bank branch or a foreign bank located outside the U.S.

Euro Feds: Eurodollars transmitted over the Fed wire instead of through CHIPS. Normally Euro Feds move from a foreign branch of one U.S. bank to a foreign branch of another U.S. bank, for example, from Citi Nassau to Morgan London. Foreign banks use CHIPS, not the Fed wire, to pay and receive Euros because they may not run daylight overdrafts at the Fed.

Euro lines: Lines of credit granted by banks (foreign or foreign branches of U.S. banks) for Eurocurrencies.

Euro MTNs: An MTN issued in the Euromarket. See **MTNs.**

European option: An option that may be exercised only at expiration of the option.

event risk: The risk that a corporate bond will be downgraded, perhaps severely, due to some unpredictable outside event, principally a leveraged buy-out.

excess reserves: Balances held by a bank at the Fed in excess of those required.

exchange rate: The price at which one currency trades for another.

exempt securities: Instruments exempt from the registration requirements of the Securities Act of 1933 or the margin requirements of the Securities and Exchange Act of 1934. Such securities include governments, agencies, municipal securities, commercial paper, and private placements.

exercise: To invoke the right to buy or sell granted under terms of a listed options contract.

exercise price: The price at which an option holder may buy or sell the underlying security. Also called the striking price.

extension swap: Extending maturity through a swap, for example, selling a 2-year note and buying one with a slightly longer current maturity.

fail: A trade is said to fail if on the settlement date either the seller fails to deliver securities in proper form or the buyer fails to deliver funds in proper form.

Fed funds: See **federal funds.**

Fedwire: A computer system linking member banks to the Fed, used for making interbank payments of Fed funds and for making deliveries of and payments for Treasury and agency securities.

federal credit agencies: Agencies of the federal government set up to supply credit to various classes of institutions and individuals; for example, S&Ls, small business firms, students, farmers, farm cooperatives, and exporters.

Federal Deposit Insurance Corporation (FDIC): A federal institution that insures bank deposits, currently up to $100,000 per deposit.

Federal Financing Bank: A federal institution that lends to a wide array of federal credit agencies funds it obtains by borrowing from the U.S. Treasury.

Federal funds: (1) Non–interest-bearing deposits held by member banks at the Federal Reserve. (2) Used to denote "immediately available" funds in the clearing sense.

Federal funds rate: The rate of interest at which Fed funds are traded. This rate is currently pegged by the Federal Reserve through open market operations.

Federal Home Loan Banks (FHLB): The institutions that regulate and lend to savings and loan associations. The Federal Home Loan Banks plays a role analogous to that played by the Federal Reserve Banks vis-à-vis member commercial banks.

figuring the tail: Calculating the yield at which a future money market instrument (one available some period hence) is purchased when that future security is created by buying an existing instrument and financing the initial portion of life with a term repo.

firm: Refers to an order to buy or sell that can be executed without confirmation for some fixed period.

fixed dates: In the Euromarket the standard periods for which Euros are traded (one month out to a year) are referred to as the fixed dates.

fixed-dollar security: A nonnegotiable debt security that can be redeemed at some fixed price or according to some schedule of fixed values (e.g., bank deposits and government savings bonds).

fixed-rate loan: A loan on which the rate paid by the borrower is fixed for the life of the loan.

flat trades: (1) A bond in default trades flat; that is, the price quoted covers both principal and unpaid, accrued interest. (2) Any security that trades without accrued interest or at a price that includes accrued interest is said to trade flat.

flex repo: A repo for a variable (usually declining) sum done for some period, often several years.

float: The difference between the credits given by the Fed to banks' reserve accounts on checks being cleared through the Fed and the debits made to banks' reserve accounts on the same checks. Float is always positive, because in the clearing of a check, the credit sometimes precedes the debit. Float adds to the money supply.

floating-rate note: A note that pays an interest rate tied to current money market rates. The holder may have the right to demand redemption at par on specified dates.

floating supply: The amount of securities believed to be available for immediate purchase, that is, in the hands of dealers and investors wanting to sell.

floor: A series of options in which the writer guarantees the buyer, a receiver of floating, that he will pay the buyer whatever interest he loses if the rate he is receiving goes below an agreed rate, Y.

flower bonds: Government bonds that are acceptable at par in payment of federal estate taxes when owned by the decedent at the time of death.

footings: A British expression for the bottom line of an institution's balance sheet; total assets equal total liabilities plus net worth.

foreign bond: A bond issued by a nondomestic borrower in the domestic capital market.

foreign-exchange rate: The price at which one currency trades for another.

foreign-exchange risk: The risk that a long or short position in a foreign currency might, due to an adverse movement in the relevant exchange rate, have to be closed out at a loss. The long or short position may arise out of a financial or commercial transaction.

forward Fed funds: Fed funds traded for future delivery.

forward forward contract: In Eurocurrencies, a contract under which a deposit of fixed maturity is agreed to at a fixed price for future delivery.

forward market: A market in which participants agree to trade some commodity, security, or foreign exchange at a fixed price at some future date.

forward rate: The rate at which forward transactions in some specific maturity are being made; for example, the dollar price at which DM can be bought for delivery three months hence.

FRABBA: The rate at which a FRA is to settle as established by the British Bankers Association.

FRAs: Under a FRA, one party agrees to pay another some fixed rate for some defined period on a Euro deposit having an agreed notional sum. If the FRA were for the 4s 5s, the agreement would concern a one-month rate to be paid four months hence. A FRA is settled at maturity via a cash payment, the amount and direction of which depends, *inter alia,* on the difference between the agreed forward rate and the prevailing market rate at the time of settlement.

free reserves: Excess reserves minus member bank borrowings at the Fed.

full-coupon bond: A bond with a coupon equal to the going market rate and consequently selling at or near par.

futures market: A market in which contracts for future delivery of a commodity or a security are bought and sold.

gamma of an option: The rate of change of the option's delta with respect to a change in the price of the underlier. Gamma measures the sensitivity of a delta-hedged position in an option to changes in the price of the underlier.

gap: Mismatch between the maturities of a bank's assets and liabilities.

gapping: Mismatching the maturities of a bank's assets and liabilities, usually by borrowing short and lending long.

gap trade: A market is said to gap trade when prices in it move discontinuously from range to range in response to announcements of economic numbers.

general obligation bonds: Municipal securities secured by the issuer's pledge of its full faith, credit, and taxing power.

Gilts: British Treasuries.

give-up: The loss in yield that occurs when a block of bonds is swapped for another block of lower-coupon bonds. Can also be referred to as "aftertax give-up" when the implications of the profit (loss) on taxes are considered.

Glass-Steagall Act: A 1933 act in which Congress forbade commercial banks to own, underwrite, or deal in corporate stock and corporate bonds.

go-around: When the Fed offers to buy securities, to sell securities, to do repo, or to do reverses, it solicits competitive bids or offers, as the case may be, from all primary dealers. This procedure is known as a go-around.

good delivery: A delivery in which everything—endorsement, any necessary attached legal papers, and so on—is in order.

good funds: A market expression for immediately available money, that is, Fed funds.

good trader: A Treasury coupon issue that can readily be bought and sold in size. If a trader can short $10 or $20 million of an issue and sleep at night, that issue is said to be a good trader.

governments: Negotiable U.S. Treasury securities.

gross spread: The difference between the price that the issuer receives for its securities and the price that investors pay for them. This spread equals the selling concession plus the management and underwriting fees.

haircut: Margin in a repo transaction; that is, the difference between the actual market value measured at the bid side of the market and the value used in a repo agreement.

handle: The whole-dollar price of a bid or offer is referred to as the *handle*. For example, if a security is quoted 101-10 bid and 101-11 offered, 101 is the handle. Traders are assumed to know the handle, so a trader would quote that market to another by saying he was at 10-11. (The 10 and 11 refer to 32nds).

hedge: To reduce risk, (1) by taking a position in futures equal and opposite to an existing or anticipated cash position, or (2) by shorting a security similar to one in which a long position has been established.

hit: A dealer who agrees to sell at the bid price quoted by another dealer is said to *hit* that bid.

IBFs (International Banking Facilities):   Shell branches that U.S. banks in a number of states may form at head office to do limited types of Eurobusiness.

IMM: International Monetary Market, a futures exchange.

the IMM swap: A swap of 1-year fixed against 3-month LIBOR, where the 3-month rate floats. The start, end, and intermediate reset dates are set to coincide with the dates on four successive IMM contracts for 3-month Eurodollars.

indenture of a bond: A legal statement spelling out the obligations of the bond issuer and the rights of the bondholder.

in the box: This means that a dealer has a wire receipt for securities indicating that effective delivery on them has been made. This jargon is a holdover from the time when Treasuries took the form of physical securities and were stored in a rack.

in-the-money option: An option selling at a price such that it has intrinsic value.

interbank: When interbank refers to a rate, as in "Japanese BAs trade at a spread to *interbank*," the rate referred to is the interbank rate on Euro time deposits.

interest-rate exposure: Risk of gain or loss to which an institution is exposed due to possible changes in interest-rate levels.

interest-rate swap: An exchange by borrowers or asset holders of interest-rate payments at two different rates (often one rate is fixed, the other floating). In a *basis swap,* both rates are floating.

investment banker: A firm that engages in the origination, underwriting, and distribution of new issues.

ISDA: International Swap Dealers Association.

JGBs: Japanese government bonds.

joint account: An agreement between two or more firms to share risk and financing responsibility in purchasing or underwriting securities.

junk bonds: High-risk bonds that have low credit ratings or are in default.

leverage: See **debt leverage.**

leveraged lease: The lessor provides only a minor portion of the cost of the leased equipment, borrowing the rest from another lender.

LIBID: The London interbank bid rate for Eurodollar time deposits of a given tenor.

LIBOR: The London Interbank Offered Rate on Eurodollar deposits traded between banks. There is a different LIBOR rate for each deposit maturity. Different banks may quote slightly different LIBOR rates because they use different reference banks.

LIFFE: London International Financial Futures Exchange.

lifting a leg: Closing out one side of a long-short arbitrage before the other is closed.

LIMEAN: The average of LIBOR and LIBID for Eurodollar deposits of a given tenor.

line of credit: An arrangement by which a bank agrees to lend to the line holder during some specified period any amount up to the full amount of the line.

liquidity: A liquid asset is one that can be converted easily and rapidly into cash without a substantial loss of value. In the money market, a security is said to be liquid if the spread between bid and asked prices is narrow and reasonable size can be done at those quotes.

liquidity diversification: Investing in a variety of maturities to reduce the price risk to which holding long bonds exposes the investor.

liquidity risk: In banking, risk that monies needed to fund assets may not be available in sufficient quantities at some future date. Implies an imbalance in committed maturities of assets and liabilities.

locked market: A market is said to be locked if the bid price equals the asked price. This can occur, for example, if the market is brokered and brokerage is paid by one side only, the initiator of the transaction.

lockup CDs: CDs that are issued with the tacit understanding that the buyer will not trade the certificate. Quite often, the issuing bank will insist that it keep the certificate to ensure that the understanding is honored by the buyer.

long: (1) Owning a debt security, stock, or other asset. (2) Owning more than one has contracted to deliver.

long bonds: Bonds with a long current maturity.

long coupons: (1) Bonds or notes with a long current maturity. (2) A bond on which one of the coupon periods, usually the first, is longer than the others or than standard.

long hedge: *Purchase* of a *futures* contract to lock in the yield at which an anticipated cash inflow can be invested.

make a market: A dealer is said to make a market when he quotes bid and offered prices at which he stands ready to buy and sell.

margin: (1) In a repo or a reverse repurchase transaction, the amount by which the market value of the securities collateralizing the transaction exceeds the amount lent. (2) In futures markets, money buyers and seller must put up to ensure performance on the contracts. (3) In options, similar meaning as in futures for sellers of put and call options.

marginal tax rate: The tax rate that would have to be paid on any additional dollars of taxable income earned.

market value: The price at which a security is trading and could presumably be purchased or sold.

marketability: A negotiable security is said to have good marketability if there is an active secondary market in which it can easily be resold.

match fund: A bank is said to match fund a loan or other asset when it does so by buying (taking) a deposit of the same maturity. The term is commonly used in the Euromarket.

matched book: If the distribution of the maturities of a bank's liabilities equals that of its assets, it is said to be running a *matched book*. The term is commonly used in the Euromarket.

medium-term notes (MTNs): Continuously offered notes, having any or all of the features of corporate bonds and ranging in maturity from nine months out to 30 years. Bank deposit notes are a form of MTN.

merchant bank: A British term for a bank that specializes not in lending out its own funds, but in providing various financial services, such as accepting bills arising out of trade, underwriting new issues, and providing advice on acquisitions, mergers, foreign exchange, portfolio management, and so on.

mismatch: A mismatch between the interest-rate maturities of a bank's assets and liabilities. See also **gap** and **unmatched book**.

MM: Market abbreviation for million. Thus, 10MM means 10 million.

MOF: Multioption facility. A type of Euro bank line.

money market: The market in which short-term debt instruments (bills, commercial paper, bankers' acceptances, etc.) are issued and traded.

money market (center) bank: A bank that is one of the nation's largest and consequently plays an active and important role in every sector of the money market.

money market certificates (MMCs): Six-month certificates of deposit with a minimum denomination of $10,000 on which banks and thrifts may pay a maximum rate tied to the rate at which the U.S. Treasury has most recently auctioned 6-month bills.

money market fund: Mutual fund that invests solely in money market instruments.

money rate of return: Annual return as a percentage of asset value.

money supply definitions used by the Fed in January 1983:
- M-1: Currency in circulation plus demand deposits plus other checkable deposits including NOW accounts.
- M-2: M-1 plus money market deposit accounts plus overnight repos and money market funds and savings and small (less than $100,000) time deposits at all depository institutions plus overnight repos at banks plus overnight Euros held by nonbank U.S. depositors in the Caribbean branches of U.S. banks plus balances at money funds (excluding institutions-only funds).
- M-3: M-2 plus large (over $100,000) time deposits at all depository institutions, term repos at banks and S&Ls plus balances at institutions-only money funds.
- L: M-3 plus other liquid assets such as term Eurodollars held by nonbank U.S. residents, bankers' acceptances, commercial paper, Treasury bills and other liquid governments, and U.S. savings bonds.

mortgage bond: Bond secured by a lien on property, equipment, or other real assets.

MTNs: See **medium-term notes.**

multicurrency clause: Such a clause on a Euro loan permits the borrower to switch from one currency to another on a rollover date.

municipal (muni) notes: Short-term notes issued by municipalities in anticipation of tax receipts, proceeds from a bond issue, or other revenues.

municipals: Securities issued by state and local governments and their agencies.

naked option position: An unhedged sale of a put or call option.

naked position: An unhedged long or short position.

nearby contract: Futures contracts nearest to expiration.

negative carry: The net cost incurred when the cost of carry exceeds the yield on the securities being financed.

negotiable certificate of deposit: A large-denomination (generally $1 million) CD that can be sold but cannot be cashed in before maturity.

negotiated sale: Situation in which the terms of an offering are determined by negotiation between the issuer and the underwriter rather than through competitive bidding by underwriting groups.

new-issues market: The market in which a new issue of securities is first sold to investors.

new money: In a Treasury refunding, the amount by which the par value of the securities offered exceeds that of those maturing.

NIF: Note issuance facility, a type of Euromarket bank line associated with the issuance of Euronotes and Euro commercial paper.

NOB: Note-bonds spread in futures contract.

noncompetitive bid: In a Treasury auction, bidding for a specific amount of securities at the price, whatever it may turn out to be, equal to the average price of the accepted competitive bids.

note: Coupon issues with a relatively short original maturity are often called *notes*. Muni notes, however, have maturities ranging from a month to a year and pay interest only at maturity. Treasury notes are coupon securities that have an original maturity of up to 10 years.

NOW (negotiable order of withdrawal) accounts: These amount to checking accounts on which depository institutions (banks and thrifts) may pay a rate of interest subject to federal rate lids.

OATs: French Treasuries.

OCC: Options Clearing Corporation, the issuer of all listed options trading on national options exchanges.

odd lot: Less than a round lot.

off-the-run issue: In Treasuries and agencies, an issue that is not included in dealer or broker runs. With bills and notes, normally only current issues are quoted.

offer: Price asked by a seller of securities.

one-man picture: The price quoted is said to be a one-man picture if both the bid and ask come from the same source.

one-sided (one-way) market: A market in which only one side, the bid or the asked, is quoted or firm.

open book: See **unmatched book.**

open repo: A repo with no definite term. The agreement is made on a day-to-day basis and either the borrower or the lender may choose to terminate. The rate paid is higher than on overnight repo and is subject to adjustment if rates move.

opportunity cost: The cost of pursuing one course of action measured in terms of the foregone return offered by the most attractive alternative.

option: (1) **Call option:** A contract sold for a price that gives the holder the right to buy from the writer of the option, over a specified period, a specified amount of securities at a specified price. (2) **Put option:** A contract sold for a price that gives the holder the right to sell to the writer of the contract, over a specified period, specified amount of securities at a specified price.

original maturity: Maturity at issue. For example, a 5-year note has an original maturity at issue of five years; one year later, it has a current maturity of four years.

out-of-the-money option: An option selling at a price such that it has no intrinsic value.

over-the-counter (OTC) market: Market created by dealer trading as opposed to the auction market prevailing on organized exchanges.

overnight delivery risk: A risk brought about because differences in time zones between settlement centers require that payment or delivery on one side of a transaction be made without knowing until the next day whether funds have been received in account on the other side. Particularly apparent where delivery takes place in Europe for payment in dollars in New York.

paper: Money market instruments, commercial paper, and other.

paper gain (loss): Unrealized capital gain (loss) on securities held in portfolio, based on a comparison of current market price and original cost.

par: (1) Price of 100%. (2) The principal amount at which the issuer of a debt security contracts to redeem that security at maturity, *face value.*

par bond: A bond selling at par.

parallel loan: An example of a parallel loan would be IBM agreeing to lend dollars to a sub of British Petroleum in exchange for the latter lending pounds to an IBM British sub. Such agreements are struck only when exchange controls in one or more countries prevent normal capital flows.

pass-through: A mortgage-backed security on which payment of interest and principal on the underlying mortgages are passed through to the security holder by an agent.

paydown: In a Treasury refunding, the amount by which the par value of the securities maturing exceeds that of those sold.

pay-up: (1) The loss of cash resulting from a swap into higher-price bonds. (2) The need (or willingness) of a bank or other borrower to pay a higher rate to get funds.

pickup: The gain in yield that occurs when a block of bonds is swapped for another block of higher-coupon bonds.

picture: The bid and asked prices quoted by a broker for a given security.

placement: A bank depositing Eurodollars with (selling Eurodollars to) another bank is often said to be making a placement.

plus: Dealers in governments normally quote bids and offers in 32nds. To quote a bid or offer in 64ths, they use pluses; for example, a dealer who bids 4+ is bidding the handle plus $4/32 + 1/64$, which equals the handle plus $9/64$.

PNs: Project notes are issued by municipalities to finance federally sponsored programs in urban renewal and housing. They are guaranteed by the U.S. Department of Housing and Urban Development.

point: (1) 100 bp = 1%. (2) One percent of the face value of a note or bond. (3) In the foreign-exchange market, the lowest level at which the currency is priced. Example: "One point" is the difference between sterling prices of $1.8080 and $1.8081.

portfolio: Collection of securities held by an investor.

position: (1) To go long or short in a security. (2) The amount of securities owned (long position) or owed (short position).

positive carry: The net gain earned when the cost of carry is less than the yield on the securities being financed.

premium: (1) The amount by which the price at which an issue is trading exceeds the issue's par value. (2) The amount that must be paid in excess of par to call or refund an issue before maturity. (3) In money market parlance, the fact that a particular bank's CDs trade at a rate higher than others of its class, or that a bank has to pay up to acquire funds.

premium bond: Bond selling above par.

prepayment: A payment made ahead of the scheduled payment date.

present value (of a future payment):   The value today of a future payment discounted at an appropriate rate of interest.

presold issue: An issue that is sold out before the coupon announcement.

price risk: The risk that a debt security's price may change due to a rise or fall in the going level of interest rates.

prime rate: The rate at which banks lend to their best (prime) customers. The all-in cost of a bank loan to a prime credit equals the prime rate plus the cost of holding compensating balances.

principal: (1) The face amount or par value of a debt security. (2) One who acts as a dealer buying and selling for his own account.

private placement: An issue that is offered to a single or a few investors as opposed to being publicly offered. Private placements do not have to be registered with the SEC.

prospectus: A detailed statement prepared by an issuer and filed with the SEC prior to the sale of a new issue. The prospectus gives detailed information on the issue and on the issuer's condition and prospects.

put: An option that gives the holder the right to sell the underlying security at a specified price during a fixed time period.

range markets: Markets with lots of sidewise motion.

RANs (revenue anticipation notes):   These are issued by states and municipalities to finance current expenditures in anticipation of the future receipt of nontax revenues.

rate risk: In banking, the risk that profits may decline or losses occur because a rise in interest rates forces up the cost of funding fixed-rate loans or other fixed-rate assets.

ratings: An evaluation given by Moody's, Standard & Poor's, Fitch, or other rating services of a security's creditworthiness.

real market: The bid and offer prices at which a dealer could do size. Quotes in the brokers market may reflect not the real market, but pictures painted by dealers playing trading games.

"red" futures contract month: A futures contract in a month more than 12 months away; for example, in November, the Dec (pronounced Dees) bond contract would mature 1 month later, the red Dec contract 13 months later.

red herring: A preliminary prospectus containing all the information required by the Securities and Exchange Commission except the offering price and coupon of a new issue.

refunding: Redemption of securities by funds raised through the sale of a new issue.

registered bond: A bond whose owner is registered with the issuer.

regular way settlement: In the money and bond markets, the regular basis on which some security trades are settled is that delivery of the securities purchased is made against payment in Fed funds on the day following the transaction.

Regulation D: Fed regulation that required member banks to hold reserves against their net borrowings from foreign offices of other banks over a seven-day averaging period. Reg D has been merged with Reg M. Reg D has also required member banks to hold reserves against Eurodollars lent by their foreign branches to domestic corporations for domestic purposes.

Regulation Q: Fed regulation imposing lids on the rates that banks may pay on savings and time deposits. Currently, time deposits with a denomination of $100,000 or more are exempt from Reg Q.

reinvestment rate: (1) The rate at which an investor assumes interest payments made on a debt security can be reinvested over the life of that security. (2) Also, the rate at which funds from a maturity or sale of a security can be reinvested. Often used in comparison to *give-up* yield.

relative value: The attractiveness—measured in terms of risk, liquidity, and return—of one instrument relative to another, or for a given instrument, of one maturity relative to another.

reopen an issue: The Treasury, when it wants to sell additional securities, will occasionally sell more of an existing issue (reopen it) rather than offer a new issue.

repo: see **repurchase agreement.**

repurchase agreement (repo or RP):   A holder of securities sells these securities to an investor with an agreement to repurchase them at a fixed price on a fixed date. The security "buyer" in effect lends the "seller" money for the period of the agreement, and the terms of the agreement are structured to compensate him for this. Dealers use repo extensively to finance their positions. Exception:

When the Fed is said to be doing repo, it is lending money, that is, increasing bank reserves.

reserve requirements: The percentages of different types of deposits that member banks are required to hold on deposit at the Fed.

retail: Individual and institutional customers as opposed to dealers and brokers.

revenue bond: A municipal bond secured by revenue from tolls, user charges, or rents derived from the facility financed.

reverse: See **reverse repurchase agreement.**

reverse repurchase agreement: Most typically, a repurchase agreement initiated by the lender of funds. Reverses are used by dealers to borrow securities they have shorted. Exception: When the Fed is said to be doing reverses, it is borrowing money, that is, absorbing reserves.

revolver: See **revolving line of credit.**

revolving line of credit: A bank line of credit on which the customer pays a commitment fee and can take down and repay funds according to his needs. Normally the line involves a firm commitment from the bank for a period of several years.

rho of an option: The rate of change of the value of an option with respect to the risk-free rate of interest.

risk: Degree of uncertainty of return on an asset.

roll over: Reinvest funds received from a maturing security in a new issue of the same or a similar security.

rollover: Most term loans in the Euromarket are made on a rollover basis, which means that the loan is periodically repriced at an agreed spread over the appropriate, currently prevailing LIBOR rate.

round lot: In the money market, round lot refers to the minimum amount for which dealers' quotes are good. This may range from $100,000 to $5 million, depending on the size and liquidity of the issue traded.

RP: See **repurchase agreement.**

RUF: A revolving underwritten facility. A type of Euro line associated with the issuance of Euro notes and of Euro commercial paper.

run: A run consists of a series of bid and asked quotes for different securities or maturities. Dealers give to and ask for runs from each other.

S&L: See **savings and loan association.**

safekeep: For a fee, banks will safekeep (i.e., hold in their vault, clip coupons on, and present for payment at maturity) bonds and money market instruments.

sale repurchase agreement: See **repurchase agreement.**

savings and loan association: Federal- or state-chartered institution that accepts savings deposits and invests the bulk of the funds thus received in mortgages.

savings deposit: Interest-bearing deposit at a savings institution that has no specific maturity.

scale: A bank that offers to pay different rates of interest on CDs of varying maturities is said to "post a scale." Commercial paper issuers also post scales.

scalper: A speculator who actively trades a futures contract in the hope of making small profits off transitory upticks and downticks in price.

seasoned issue: An issue that has been well distributed and trades well in the secondary market.

secondary market: The market in which previously issued securities are traded.

sector: Refers to a group of securities that are similar with respect to maturity, type, rating, and/or coupon.

Securities and Exchange Commission (SEC):   Agency created by Congress to protect investors in securities transactions by administering securities legislation.

sell a spread: Sell a nearby futures contract and buy a far one.

serial bonds: A bond issue in which maturities are staggered over a number of years.

settle: See **clear.**

settlement date: The date on which trade is cleared by delivery of securities against funds. The settlement data may be the trade date or a later date.

shell branch: A foreign branch—usually in a tax haven—which engages in Eurocurrency business but is run out of a head office.

shop: In street jargon, a money market or bond dealership.

shopping: Seeking to obtain the best bid or offer available by calling a number of dealers and/or brokers.

short: A market participant assumes a short position by selling as security he does not own. The seller makes delivery by borrowing the security sold or reversing it in.

short bonds: Bonds with a short current maturity.

short book: See **unmatched book.**

short coupons: Bonds or notes with a short current maturity.

short hedge: *Sale of a futures* contract to hedge, for example, a position in cash securities or an anticipated borrowing need.

short sale: The sale of securities not owned by the seller in the expectation that the price of these securities will fall or as part of an arbitrage. A short sale must eventually be covered by a purchase of the securities sold.

short the board: Sell GNMA or T-bond futures on the CBT.

sinking fund: Indentures on corporate issues often require that the issuer make annual payments to a sinking fund, the proceeds of which are used to retire randomly selected bonds in the issue.

size: Large in size, as in "size offering" or "in there for size." What constitutes size varies with the sector of the market.

skip-day settlement: The trade is settled one business day beyond what is normal.

sovereign risk: The special risks, if any, that attach to a security (or deposit or loan) because the borrower's country of residence differs from that of the investor's. Also referred to as **country risk.**

specific issues market: The market in which dealers reverse in securities they want to short.

spectail: A dealer that does business with retail but concentrates more on acquiring and financing its own speculative position.

spot market: Market for immediate as opposed to future delivery. In the spot market for foreign exchange, settlement is two business days ahead.

spot rate: The price prevailing in the spot market.

spread: (1) Difference between bid and asked prices on a security. (2) Difference between yields on or prices of two securities of differing sorts or differing maturities. (3) In underwriting, difference between price realized by the issuer and price paid by the investor.

(4) Difference between two prices or two rates. What a commodities trader would refer to as the *basis*.

spreading: In the futures market, buying one futures contract and selling a nearby one to profit from an anticipated narrowing or widening of the spread over time.

stop-out price: The lowest price (highest yield) accepted by the Treasury in an auction of a new issue.

striking price: See **exercise price.**

subject: Refers to a bid or offer than cannot be executed without confirmation from the customer.

subordinated debenture: The claims of holders of this issue rank after those of holders of various other unsecured debts incurred by the issuer.

sub right: Right of substitution—to change collateral—on a repo.

swap: (1) In securities, selling one issue and buying another. (2) In foreign exchange, buying a currency spot and simultaneously selling it forward.

swap rate: In the foreign-exchange market, the difference between the spot and forward rates at which a currency is traded.

swaption: An option on an interest-rate swap.

swing line: See **demand line of credit.**

Swissy: Market jargon for Swiss francs.

switch: British English for a swap; that is, buying a currency spot and selling it forward.

TABs (tax anticipation bills):   Special bills that the Treasury occasionally issues. They mature on corporate quarterly income tax dates and can be used at face value by corporations to pay their tax liabilities.

tail: (1) The difference between the average price in Treasury auctions and the stop-out price. (2) A *future* money market instrument (one available some period hence) created by buying an existing instrument and financing the initial portion of its life with term repo.

take: (1) A dealer or customer who agrees to buy at another dealer's offered price is said to take that offer. (2) Eurobankers speak of taking deposits rather than buying money.

take-out: (1) A cash surplus generated by the sale of one block of securities and the purchase of another, for example, selling a block of bonds at 99 and buying another block at 95. (2) A bid made to a seller of a security that is designed (and generally agreed) to take him out of the market.

taking a view: A London expression for forming an opinion as to where interest rates are going and acting on it.

TANs: Tax anticipation notes issued by states or municipalities to finance current operations in anticipation of future tax receipts.

technical condition of a market: Demand and supply factors affecting price, in particular the net position—long or short—of dealers.

technicals: (1) Supply and demand factors influencing the cash market. (2) Value or shape of technical indicators.

TED: A spread trade: T-bill futures to CD futures.

tenor: Maturity.

term bonds: A bond issue in which all bonds mature at the same time.

term Fed funds: Fed funds sold for a period of time longer than overnight.

term loan: Loan extended by a bank for more than the normal 90-day period. A term loan might run five years or more.

term repo (RP):   Repo borrowings for a period longer than overnight; may be 30, 60, or even 90 days.

theta: In options pricing, the rate at which the value of an option changes as time passes.

thin market: A market in which trading volume is low and in which consequently bid and asked quotes are wide and the liquidity of the instrument traded is low.

TIBOR: LIBOR as established in Tokyo.

tick: Minimum price movement on a futures contract.

tight market: A tight market, as opposed to a thin market, is one in which volume is large, trading is active and highly competitive, and spreads between bid and ask prices are narrow.

time deposit: Interest-bearing deposit at a savings institution that has a specific maturity.

Tom next: In the interbank market in Eurodollar deposits and the foreign-exchange market, the value (delivery) date on a Tom next transaction is the next business day. (Refers to "tomorrow next.")

trade date: The date on which a transaction is initiated. The settlement date may be the trade date or a later date.

to trade numbers: To trade securities based on the release of a new *economic statistic (number),* e.g., trading based on announcement of the latest number for the CPI, the U.S. trade deficit, etc.

trade on top of: Trade at a narrow or no spread in basis points to some other instrument.

trading paper: CDs purchased by accounts that are likely to resell them. The term is commonly used in the Euromarket.

treasurer's check: A check issued by a bank to make a payment. Treasurer's checks outstanding are counted as part of a bank's reservable deposits and as part of the money supply.

Treasury bill: A non–interest-bearing discount security issued by the U.S. Treasury to finance the national debt. Most bills are issued to mature in three months, six months, or one year.

TT&L account: Treasury tax and loan account at a bank.

turnaround: Securities bought and sold for settlement on the same day.

turnaround time: The time available or needed to effect a turnaround.

two-sided market: A market in which both bid and asked prices, good for the standard unit of trading, are quoted.

two-way market: Market in which both a bid and an asked price are quoted.

underlier: The thingamabob against which an option is written. The underlier may be a stock, a bond, a futures contract, oil, land, whatever.

underwriter: A dealer who purchases new issues from the issuer and distributes them to investors. Underwriting is one function of an investment banker.

unmatched book: If the average maturity of a bank's liabilities is less than that of its assets, it is said to be running an unmatched book. The term is commonly used in the Euromarket. Equivalent expressions are **open book** and **short book.**

value date: In the market for Eurodollar deposits and foreign exchange, value date refers to the delivery date of funds traded. Normally it is on spot transactions two days after a transaction is agreed upon and the future date in the case of a forward foreign-exchange trade.

variable-price security: A security, such as stocks and bonds, that sells at a fluctuating, market-determined price.

variable-rate CDs: Short-term CDs that pay interest periodically on *roll* dates; on each roll date the coupon on the CD is adjusted to reflect current market rates.

variable-rate loan: Loan made at an interest rate that fluctuates with the prime.

visible supply: New muni bond issues scheduled to come to market within the next 30 days.

when-issued trades: Typically there is a lag between the time a new bond is announced and sold and the time it is actually issued. During this interval, the security trades, **wi,** "when, as, and if issued."

wi: When, as, and if issued. See **when-issued trades.**

wi wi: T bills trade on a wi basis between the day they are announced and the day they are settled. Late Tuesday and on Wednesday, two bills will trade wi, the bill just auctioned and the bill just announced. The latter used to be called the wi wi bill. However, now it is common for dealers to speak of the just auctioned bill as the 3-month bill and of the newly announced bill and the wi bill. This change in jargon resulted from a change in the way interdealer brokers of bills list bills on their screens. Cantor Fitz still lists a new bill as the wi bill until it is settled.

without: If 70 were bid in the market and there was no offer, the quote would be "70 bid without." The expression *without* indicates a one-way market.

write: To sell an option.

Yankee bond: A foreign bond issued in the U.S. market, payable in dollars, and registered with the SEC.

Yankee CD: A CD issued in the domestic market (typically in New York) by a branch of a foreign bank.

yield curve: A graph showing, for securities that all expose the investor to the same credit risk, the relationship at a given point in time between yield and current maturity. Yield curves are typically drawn using yields on governments of various maturities.

yield to maturity: The rate of return yielded by a debt security held to maturity when both interest payments and the investor's capital gain or loss on the security are taken into account.

INDEX

Conversion Table
Discount Rate to Equivalent Money Market Yield (Interest on a 360-Day Basis)

Discount rate	Equivalent money market yield					
	1 mo.	2 mo.	3 mo.	6 mo.	9 mo.	1 yr.
5%	5.02	5.04	5.06	5.13	5.20	5.26
5 1/8	5.15	5.17	5.19	5.26	5.33	5.40
5 1/4	5.27	5.30	5.32	5.39	5.47	5.54
5 3/8	5.40	5.42	5.45	5.52	5.60	5.68
5 1/2	5.53	5.55	5.58	5.66	5.74	5.82
5 5/8	5.65	5.68	5.71	5.79	5.87	5.96
5 3/4	5.78	5.81	5.83	5.92	6.01	6.10
5 7/8	5.90	5.93	5.96	6.05	6.15	6.24
6	6.03	6.06	6.09	6.19	6.28	6.38
6 1/8	6.16	6.19	6.22	6.32	6.42	6.52
6 1/4	6.28	6.32	6.35	6.45	6.56	6.67
6 3/8	6.41	6.44	6.48	6.58	6.70	6.81
6 1/2	6.54	6.57	6.61	6.72	6.83	6.95
6 5/8	6.66	6.70	6.74	6.85	6.97	7.10
6 3/4	6.79	6.83	6.87	6.99	7.11	7.24
6 7/8	6.91	6.95	7.00	7.12	7.25	7.38
7	7.04	7.08	7.12	7.25	7.39	7.53
7 1/8	7.17	7.21	7.25	7.39	7.53	7.67
7 1/4	7.29	7.34	7.38	7.52	7.67	7.70
7 3/8	7.42	7.47	7.51	7.66	7.81	7.96
7 1/2	7.55	7.59	7.64	7.79	7.95	8.11
7 5/8	7.67	7.72	7.77	7.93	8.09	8.25
7 3/4	7.80	7.85	7.90	8.06	8.23	8.40
7 7/8	7.93	7.98	8.03	8.20	8.37	8.55
8	8.05	8.11	8.16	8.33	8.51	8.70
8 1/8	8.18	8.24	8.29	8.47	8.65	8.84
8 1/4	8.31	8.37	8.42	8.60	8.79	8.99
8 3/8	8.43	8.49	8.55	8.74	8.94	9.14
8 1/2	8.56	8.62	8.68	8.88	9.08	9.29
8 5/8	8.69	8.75	8.82	9.01	9.22	9.44
8 3/4	8.81	8.88	8.95	9.15	9.36	9.59
8 7/8	8.94	9.01	9.08	9.29	9.51	9.74
9	9.07	9.14	9.21	9.42	9.65	9.89
9 1/8	9.19	9.27	9.34	9.56	9.80	10.04
9 1/4	9.32	9.39	9.47	9.70	9.94	10.19
9 3/8	9.45	9.52	9.60	9.84	10.08	10.34
9 1/2	9.58	9.65	9.73	9.97	10.23	10.50
9 5/8	9.70	9.78	9.86	10.11	10.37	10.65
9 3/4	9.83	9.91	9.99	10.25	10.52	10.80
9 7/8	9.96	10.04	10.12	10.39	10.66	10.96
10	10.08	10.17	10.26	10.53	10.81	11.11
10 1/8	10.21	10.30	10.39	10.66	10.96	11.27
10 1/4	10.34	10.43	10.52	10.80	11.10	11.42
10 3/8	10.46	10.56	10.65	10.94	11.25	11.58
10 1/2	10.59	10.69	10.78	11.08	11.40	11.73
10 5/8	10.72	10.82	10.91	11.19	11.54	11.89
10 3/4	10.85	10.95	11.05	11.36	11.69	12.04
10 7/8	10.97	11.08	11.18	11.50	11.84	12.20
11	11.10	11.21	11.31	11.64	11.99	12.36
11 1/8	11.23	11.34	11.44	11.78	12.14	12.52
11 1/4	11.36	11.46	11.58	11.92	12.29	12.68
11 3/8	11.48	11.59	11.71	12.06	12.44	12.83
11 1/2	11.61	11.72	11.84	12.20	12.59	12.99
11 5/8	11.74	11.88	11.97	12.34	12.74	13.15
11 3/4	11.87	11.98	12.11	12.48	12.89	13.31
11 7/8	11.99	12.11	12.24	12.62	13.04	13.48